The Jewish Revolutionary Spirit

The Jewish Revolutionary Spirit

and its Impact on World History

E. Michael Jones

Fidelity Press
South Bend, Indiana
2008

Manufactured in the United States of America

1 2 3 4 5 6 10 09 08 07 06 05 04

Library of Congress Cataloguing in Publication Data

Jones, E. Michael
     The Jewish Revolutionary Spirit: And its Impact on
     World   History / E. Michael Jones

       p. cm.
     Includes bibliographical references and index
     ISBN 0-929891-07-4
     1. Revolution—World History. 2. Jews—World History. 3.
     Catholic Church -World History.

Yet what kind of men were they who set their hands to the task [of rebuilding the temple]? They were men who constantly resisted the Holy Spirit, revolutionists bent on stirring up sedition. After the destruction which occurred under Vespasian and Titus, these Jews rebelled during the reign of Hadrian and tried to go back to the old commonwealth and way of life. What they failed to realize was that they were fighting against the decree of God, who had ordered that Jerusalem remain forever in ruins.

St. John Chrysostom, *Adversos Judaeos*

Christianity did not bring a message of social revolution like that of the ill-fated Spartacus, whose struggle led to so much bloodshed. Jesus was not Spartacus, he was not engaged in a fight for political liberation like Barabbas or Bar-Kochba. Jesus, who himself died on the Cross, brought something totally different: an encounter with the Lord of all lords, an encounter with the living God and thus an encounter with a hope stronger than the sufferings of slavery, a hope which therefore transformed life and the world from within.

Pope Benedict XVI, *Spe Salvi*

Contents

Introduction

On September 12, 2006, Joseph Ratzinger made a triumphal return to his native Bavaria. Having chosen the name of Benedict XVI when he was elected pope, His Holiness returned not only to Germany but to the German university of Regensburg to express his gratitude for the time he spent there as a professor and to renew the Church's commitment to the university.

But more than that, Pope Benedict wanted to re-affirm the Church's position on the relationship between faith and reason. In order to do that he had to refer to a tradition where that relationship has not been so complementary, a tradition which stands outside of Europe, namely, Islam.

That's where the trouble began, specifically when Benedict quoted the Byzantine emperor Manuel II Paleologos, who felt that the Islamic world and the Christian world shared two fundamentally different views of the relationship between God and reason. The issue was religiously inspired violence: "Show me just what Mohammed brought that was new and there you will find things only evil and inhuman, such as his command to spread by the sword the faith he preached."[1]

After an initially favorable response, the world press, including the Arab press, appeared to use the quote to inflame Islamic opinion against the Church. The inflammation was a replay, at least in some ways, of the Danish cartoon crisis of a few months before. In that incident, a Danish magazine editor, with ties to American neoconservatives like Daniel Pipes, ran a series of cartoons that were calculated to outrage Muslims and provoke them to attack Denmark and, by extension, Europe. The purpose of the provocation was to drive Europe, by way of reaction to the Muslim outrage, into the arms of the Americans, who were desperately in need of support for their failing war in Iraq.[2]

In the instance of the Regensburg speech, the outrage surrounding the Manuel II Paleologos quote achieved two ends: first, it strengthened the neoconservative hold over the Catholic mind by giving the impression that Muslims were fanatics determined to wage jihad against both the pope and the Church (the Muslim/Catholic alliance against abortion, which I personally witnessed at the World Population Conference in Cairo in 1994, gave the opposite impression), and secondly, it obscured the real topic of the talk, which was Logos and the central role it plays in both Europe and the Church.

Unlike Christianity, Islam is not docile to Logos, nor for that matter is Islam's God; God's will is arbitrary, inscrutable. According to Benedict's reading of Manuel II Paleologos, "the decisive statement in this argument against violent conversion is this: not to act in accordance with reason is contrary to God's nature." This idea is not intrinsic to Islam. The "noted French Islamicist R. Arnaldez," Pope

Benedict continues, "points out that Ibn Hazm went so far as to state that God is not bound even by his own word, and that nothing would oblige him to reveal the truth to us. Were it God's will, we would even have to practice idolatry."

Christianity is different from Islam in this regard: The Christian God acts with Logos. In using the term Logos, the Pope situates Christianity and, by extension, the European culture which grew up under its influence, in the tradition of Greek philosophy. Greek philosophy is part of God's plan for humanity, something that became clear when St Paul had to change his plans and travel to Macedonia. Greek philosophy is, in other words, not just Greek; it is universal:

> Is the conviction that acting unreasonably contradicts God's nature merely a Greek idea, or is it always and intrinsically true? I believe that here we can see the profound harmony between what is Greek in the best sense of the word and the biblical understanding of faith in God. Modifying the first verse of the Book of Genesis, the first verse of the whole Bible, John began the prologue of his Gospel with the words: "In the beginning was the logos." This is the very word used by the Emperor: God acts with logos.

"In the beginning was the logos, and the logos is God," says the Evangelist. The marriage of Hebrew scripture and Greek philosophy that begat Christianity and subsequently Europe is not mere coincidence, nor is Greek philosophy some adulteration of an otherwise pure Gospel. Europe means Biblical faith plus Greek thought: Europe is based on Logos. "The encounter between the Biblical message and Greek thought," the pope continues,

> did not happen by chance....Biblical faith...encountered the best of Greek thought at a deep level, resulting in a mutual enrichment evident in the later wisdom literature....A profound encounter of faith and reason is taking place there [in the Septuagint], an encounter between genuine enlightenment and religion. From the very heart of Christian faith, and, at the same time, the heart of Greek thought now joined to faith, Manuel II was able to say: "Not to act 'with logos' is contrary to God's nature.

This means that Logos, far from being some cultural accretion, is part of the nature of God and, therefore, part of creation. The European, and by that term I include both North and South America and Australia, is traditionally born into a world that is radically reasonable, radically logical, because that world mirrors the mind of God, who behaves in ways that sometimes go beyond what human reason can comprehend but never in ways that contradict that reason.

So far so good. We agree wholeheartedly with what the Pope said about Logos, and we can see without too much effort that Islam has a radically different attitude toward the relationship between faith and reason. Europe has dealt with the threat for centuries, but from an historical perspective, the Islamic threat to Europe is only half the story.

At this point we come to the attack on Logos which is not mentioned in the Pope's speech, the Jewish attack on Logos, which manifests itself not by the threat of invasion from without, as is the case with Islam, which has sought to spread its faith by military conquest, but by the threat of subversion from within, otherwise known as revolution. If Muslims are alogos, because of Mohammed's imperfect understanding of the monotheistic traditions he absorbed from his position beyond the borders of a collapsing Greco-Roman civilization, then Jews are anti-Logos, in the sense that they reject Christ altogether. Islam did not reject Christ; Islam failed to understand Christ, as manifested in its rejection of both the Trinity and the Incarnation, and ended up trying to mask that misunderstanding by honoring Jesus as a prophet.

The situation with Jews is completely different. The Jews were God's chosen people. When Jesus arrived on earth as their long-awaited Messiah, the Jews, who, like all men, were given free will by their God, had to make a decision. They had to either accept or reject the Christ, who was, so Christians believe, the physical embodiment of Logos.

As we will see, the Jews began by wanting to have the Messiah save them on their terms, which were suffused with racial pride. When the Jews tell Jesus in John 8 that they are the "seed of Abraham," in Greek *"sperma Abraam,"* He changes the term of the argument by replying "If you were Abraham's children, you would do as Abraham did," which is to say follow God's will and accept Jesus as the son of God and Messiah. Since the Jews, or those to whom Jesus is speaking, reject Jesus, they reject their father Abraham as well, and show that "the devil is [their] father."

Once Jesus arrives in Jerusalem, the term Jew in the Gospel of St. John is no longer a purely racial term. Jew has come to mean a rejecter of Christ. Race is no longer the focus. The Jews who accept Jesus will henceforth be known as Christians. The Jews who reject him are known henceforth as "Jews." As St. John reports in the Apocalypse, "those who call themselves Jews" are really liars and members of the "synagogue of Satan" (Rev 2.9, 3.9).

By the middle of John's Gospel, the term Jew no longer has the clear racial meaning it had at the beginning when the Samaritan woman was told that "salvation is from the Jews." The other, more negative redefinition of the word Jew is also not essentially racial and becomes apparent in the story of the man born blind in John 9. That man's parents, we are told, refused to answer any questions about Jesus healing their son because they feared the "Jews." They "said this because they feared the Jews, for the Jews had already agreed that if any one should confess him to be Christ, he was to be put out of the synagogue." Clearly the split between "Jews" and followers of Christ had already begun.

The Jews rejected Christ because he was crucified. They wanted a powerful leader, not a suffering servant. Annas and Caiaphas mockingly told Christ that if he came down from the cross, they would accept him as the Messiah. When the Jews rejected Christ, they rejected Logos, and when they rejected Logos, which includes within itself the principles of social order, they became revolutionaries.

Jews may have become revolutionaries at the foot of the cross, but the full implications of their decision didn't become apparent until 30 years later, when the Jews rebelled against Rome, and Rome retaliated by destroying the Temple. At this point, the Jews had no temple, no priesthood, and no sacrifice, and as a result they had no way of fulfilling their covenant. Seeing which way the battle for Jerusalem was going, a rabbi, and deputy head of the Sanhedrin, by the name of Jochanan ben Zakkai had himself smuggled out of Jerusalem in a shroud, and, after being recognized by Roman authorities as a friend of Rome, was granted the privilege of founding a rabbinical school at Jabneh.

It is at this moment, some 30 years after the founding of the Church, that modern Judaism, Judaism as we know it, was born as essentially a debating society, because in the absence of a Temple, that was all that Jews could do. The results of these interminable debates became known as the Talmud, which got written down over the next six centuries. The debating did nothing to eradicate the spirit of revolution from the Jewish mind, but in many ways intensified it by teaching the Jews to look for a military Messiah.

The Jews got their military Messiah roughly 60 years after the destruction of the Temple, when Simon bar Kokhba rose up against Rome in 131. The rabbis in Jerusalem, with a few exceptions, recognized bar Kokhba as the Messiah, and so as if to prove that racial Judaism had become incoherent, the Christian Jews were expelled for not recognizing him as the Messiah. It didn't matter whether your mother was Jewish; the ultimate determinant of Jewishness had become rejection of Christ, and that rejection led inexorably to revolution.

II

Debate over who the Jews are never ceases. Such debate comes up against a basic philosophical issue, something akin to the nominalism of William of Ockham. The issue revolves around the use of the word "Jew." Just what does the word refer to? Does it refer to anything at all, or is it like the word "tree," a word which, according to the nominalists, has no clear meaning, since in the real world the only thing which exists are individual birches, maples, etc? According to this unwritten rule of discourse, the term "Jew" refers to no category of beings in reality. Use of the term "Jew" as a category is, as a result, ipso facto evidence of anti-Semitism.

This reasoning is not a new phenomenon. Hilaire Belloc noticed it in England in the 1920s, when he wrote that if anyone "exposed a financial swindler who happened to be a Jew, he was an anti-Semite. If he exposed a group of Parliamentarians taking money from the Jews, he was an anti-Semite. If he did no more than call a Jew a Jew, he was an anti-Semite."[3]

Things have gotten worse since Belloc's time. Now it is impossible to write about Jews without opening oneself to the charge of anti-Semitism, as Belloc's current place in the literary firmament now shows. It is impossible to refer to Belloc in polite circles without the mandatory disclaimer that he was an anti-Semite, partly because he wrote one book about the Jews. His views on Islam are much more censorious than his views on Jews, but that fact never gets mentioned. Nor is it obligatory to refer to Belloc as anti-Muslim.

If anything, what Belloc said then is *a fortiori* true today. Calling a Jew a Jew may or may not be prima facie evidence of anti-Semitism, but criticizing a group of people as Jews is regularly taken as such evidence. This is because it indicates that the group exists, that it has definable beliefs (at least in many contexts) and that it can, therefore, act in a certain way, and can even be criticized for so acting. All of this does not change the fact that the main task confronting anyone who decides to write about the Jews is precisely what he means by that term. It is precisely in the manipulation of the term "Jew" that its political benefits lie.

Since the term Jew actually gets used with some frequency, its use is determined by the political advantage of those who use it.[4] Thus, it is permissible in some circles to use the group designation when Jews are victims of some attack, but any reference to Jews as the perpetrators of some attack is, again, ipso facto evidence of anti-Semitism and also a sign of conspiracy mania as well. It's heads I win, tails you lose. So, again, according to another variation of the canons of contemporary discourse, it is permissible to say that Jews played a large role in the civil rights movement, but it would be anti-Semitic to say that they played a large role in the abortion rights movement.

Christians, however, must believe that there is a definite Jewish people who will perdure till the end of time. St Paul, addressing the Romans, says: "if the root is holy so are the branches" (Romans 11.16). St John Chrysostom, commenting on St Paul's speech, explains that the root refers to Abraham and the patriarchs, "from whom all the Jewish nation proceeded, as branches from that root: and... these *branches* are to be esteemed *holy*, not only because of the root they proceeded from, but also because they worshipped the true God. And if *some*, or a great many *of these branches*, have been *broken*, they may, as it is said (v.23) be ingrafted again. And you, Gentiles, ought to remember that, you were of yourselves *a wild-olive tree*: and it is only by the merciful call of God, that you have the happiness to *be ingrafted* upon the same root as the patriarchs; and so by imitating the faith of Abraham are become his spiritual children, and heirs of the promises, and by that means have been made partakers of *the root*.... And let me tell you, as to the Jews, if *they abide not still in unbelief*, God is able to ingraft them again into their own olive-tree: and it seems more easy, that they, who are naturally branches of the sweet olive-tree, should bring forth good fruit, when they shall be ingrafted in their own olive-tree, being of the race of Abraham, to whom the promises were made."[5]

III

The Christian then holds that the Jewish people have a perduring role and are at least in part defined by their refusal of the New Covenant and by their relationship to Abraham and his "seed". In order to discuss who counts as a Jew it might be helpful to offer a working definition. We might say that there is a disjunctive positive component: A person who is related by birth or conversion to those similarly related by birth or conversion to Abraham[6]– and a negative component: A person who has not renounced Judaism by embracing another faith (especially Christianity).

The renowned Jewish scholar Jacob Neusner, makes clear a distinction between Judaists and Jews, when he says: "The ethnic group does not define the religious system.... All Judaists—those who practice the religion, Judaism—are Jews, but not all Jews are Judaists. That is to say, all those who practice the religion, Judaism, by definition fall into the ethnic group, the Jews, but not all members of the ethnic group practice Judaism."[7]

However, Neusner adds, tellingly, that Christianity plays a special role in defining who counts as a Jew either ethnically or religiously: "the ethnic community opens its doors not by reason of outsiders' adopting the markers of ethnicity... but by reason of adopting what is not ethnic but religious.... While not all Jews practice Judaism, in the iron-clad consensus among contemporary Jews, Jews who practice Christianity cease to be part of the ethnic Jewish community, while those who practice Buddhism remain within."[8]

Without knowing it, Neusner is simply restating the thesis of this book: when Judaism rejected Christ it rejected Logos as well. In rejecting Christ, Judaism took on a negative identity, something that many Jews have realized at one time or another. The recent Jewish convert to Catholicism, Roy Schoeman, writes: "I remember praying, 'Let me know your name—I don't mind if you are Buddha, and I have to become a Buddhist; I don't mind if you are Apollo, and I have to become a Roman pagan; I don't mind if you are Krishna, and I have to become a Hindu; as long as you are not Christ and I have to become a Christian'!"[9] Schoeman presumably recognizes this perverse and deep-seated enmity to Logos as having come from a perversion of what was handed down by Moses.[10]

Such enmity to Logos as represented in the person of Jesus Christ is present in the Talmud. Princeton Jewish scholar Peter Schaefer notes that Talmudic stories mock claims of Jesus's birth from the Virgin Mary, challenge His claim to be the Messiah, and state that He was rightly executed for blasphemy and idolatry,[11] and that He resides in Hell, where His followers will go. Schaefer makes the startling claim that, rather than being ill-informed and ephemeral, parts of the Babylonian Talmud, such narratives betray a remarkably high level of familiarity with the Gospels—especially Matthew and John—and represent a deliberate and sophisticated anti-Christian polemic.[12] And while many Jews may never read such passages there can be little doubt that they arose from the defining rejection of Christ by many Jews of His time, a rejection that finds echoes in present day attitudes to Christian converts from Judaism.

Ironically, the very Talmud that vilifies Christ appears to provide some evidence that He is the Messiah. The Talmud admits the central role of Jesus in salvation history in a number of significant if indirect ways. Roy Schoeman points out that in order to ensure that the Temple sacrifice had been successful in expiating the sins of the Jews, the priests and rabbis would watch to make sure that a scarlet thread had turned white. He cites the Talmudic verse from Rosh Hashanah 31b, "For forty years before the destruction of the Temple the thread of scarlet never turned white but it remained red." According to Schoeman, the Talmud itself "unwittingly confirms" that the Temple sacrifices failed 40 years before the destruction of the Temple in 70 AD (i.e., at the time when Christ died and the veil covering the Holy of Holies was rent in two) when it "recounts that from that time on. . . the scarlet thread never again turned white." According to the Talmud, the Temple was destroyed because therein prevailed "hatred without a cause." The Talmud might be said to be referring in some mysterious way to Christ's own words in John 15:18-25: "They hated me without a cause." The Talmud, in other words, "is exhibiting a gift of prophecy, stating a profound truth that unknowingly confirms Jesus' identity as the Messiah, although unaware of that fact."[13]

While the Talmud refers to the justice of Christ's execution, the Christian must believe that Christ died for our sins. According to the Catholic Church: " 'sinners were the authors and the ministers of all the sufferings that the divine Redeemer endured.' Taking into account the fact that our sins affect Christ himself, the Church does not hesitate to impute to Christians the gravest responsibility for the torments inflicted upon Jesus, a responsibility with which they have all too often burdened the Jews alone." Moreover, the Catholic Catechism goes on to quote from an earlier Catechism: "We, however, profess to know him. And when we deny him by our deeds, we in some way seem to lay violent hands on him."[14]

It is all too easy to minimize this profound teaching, but in maximizing it we fall into another grave error by claiming that Jews were not primarily responsible *at the time and place* for bringing about the actual event in history that is known as the crucifixion. Such a position directly contradicts the Gospel accounts and makes any understanding of the nature of the Jewish split impossible. After all, that famous Jewish convert St Peter (Acts 3.14-15) refers directly to those who killed Christ in addressing and appealing to the very people he saw as having done this. This rejection of Logos, rooted in an historical event, continues to play a part in what it means to be a Jew.

IV

In dealing with such complex and highly controversial matters it is important to be clear on what is not being said as well as what is. Clearly the Christian must hold certain views regarding the Jewish people, if only regarding their existence and continuance to the Second Coming as a people. Any individual Jew, like anyone else, can choose to follow Logos. He may follow the "lower Logos" of the Natural Moral Law—i.e., the law that St Paul tells us is written in the hearts of men. That law, fully understood, leads ultimately to Christ and the Church He founded. We might call the latter the Higher Logos. Deliberate rejection of Logos is deliberate rejection of salvation. A spirit founded on rejection of Logos can only lead to disaster. True, people may be more or less ignorant—for all sorts of reasons—of Logos. But there is a special tragedy if a member of the Chosen people rejects what he or she was chosen for—as we see in the Gospels.

Anyone can choose to reject Logos—all of us do this or are tempted to reject the lower Logos every day. But to have the rejection of the Higher Logos at the unavoidable core of one's religion or even as a determining factor of who is to count as a member of one's community means that a revolutionary spirit is entwined with that community.

By revolution we mean revolution against Logos—the deepest kind of revolution.[15] This Jewish revolutionary spirit is, as we have said, an internal (understood as above) enemy of Christianity. But so too are those Christian heresies that have, in one way or another attacked Christ, His Church, or the Natural Moral Law. Part of the history to be recounted in this book is the story of the relationship between the history of the Jews and the attacks on the Universal Church by Christian heretics linked to Jews or heavily influenced by Jews.

One example of such an alliance, typical of the history this volume is concerned with, is the Arian/Jewish alliance in the 4th Century. John Henry Newman, in his work *The Arians of the Fourth Century*, makes the following observations:

> It is...a question, whether the mere performance of the rites of the Law, of which Christ came as anti-type and repealer, has not a tendency to withdraw the mind from the contemplation of the more glorious and real images of the Gospel; so that the Christians of Antioch would diminish their reverence towards the true Savior of man, in proportion as they trusted to the media of worship provided for a time by the Mosaic ritual.... In the Epistle addressed to them, the Judaizers are described as men laboring under an irrational fascination, fallen from grace, and self-excluded from the Christian privileges; when in appearance they were but using, what on the one hand might be called mere external forms, and on the other, had actually been delivered to the Jews on Divine authority.... If we turn to the history of the Church, we seem to see the evils in actual existence, which the Apostle anticipated in prophecy; that is, we see, that in the obsolete furniture of the Jewish ceremonial, there was in fact retained the pestilence of Jewish unbelief, tending (whether directly or not, at least eventually) to introduce fundamental error respecting the Person of Christ.[16]

Ultimately, the doctrinal issues are not the main issue. During the 4th century, the Jews sided with the Arians because they had become habituated to promoting revolution. In practical terms, John Henry Newman notes, "in the popular risings which took place in Antioch and Alexandria in favor of Arianism, the Jews sided with the heretical party, evincing thereby, not indeed any definite interest in the subject of dispute, but a sort of spontaneous feeling, that the side of heresy was their natural position; and further, that its spirit, and the character which it created, were congenial to their own."[17]

This book records how such a "spontaneous feeling" has played itself out in history, in a conflict between Judaism, Jewish movements, heresies and the Catholic Church.

Rabbi Louis Israel Newman[18] points out how Jews have consistently supported revolutionary movements throughout history. Jews joined forces with heretics during the Albigensian crisis, the Hussite revolution, the Reformation, and at the birth of modern England. They joined forces with revolutionaries during The Enlightenment, the Russian Revolution and the Civil Rights movement. We also see the conflict between the Church and Judaism working itself out at the birth of the Spanish Inquisition, the spread of the Polish empire and the Chmielnicki rebellion that began the break-up of that empire. Finally, we see a Jewish presence in the rise of the American Empire.

As always, movements are led by the few—a few often unrepresentative of the many. The evolutionary psychologist Kevin MacDonald, in examining Jewish movements, has suggested the following approach to the issue—that a Jewish movement is a movement dominated by Jews "with no implication that all or most Jews are involved in these movements and restrictions on what the movements are," and that one must "determine whether the Jewish participants in those movements identified as Jews *and* thought of their involvement in the movement as advancing specific Jewish interests." He adds that involvement may be unconscious or involve self-deception, but in many of the cases he examines, it is more straightforward.[19] A revolutionary movement may be led by religious or non-religious Jews and still count as a Jewish revolutionary movement.[20]

The Catholic response to the revolutionary Jewish rejection of Logos came to be known as "*Sicut Iudeis non...*," a doctrine codified by Pope Gregory the Great and reiterated by virtually every pope after him. According to "*Sicut Iudeis non...*," no one has the right to harm Jews or disrupt their worship services, but the Jews have, likewise, no right to corrupt the faith or morals of Christians or subvert Christian societies.

Since the time of Gregory the Great, the church has applied "*Sicut Iudeis non. . .*," even at the risk of appearing "anti-Semitic," a charge which has become more frequent in modern times. One of the classic instances which we are given of "modern" anti-Semitism is the pastoral letter on morals which was issued by Augustine Cardinal Hlond, the primate of Poland, on February 29, 1936. The part beginning "It is true that Jews ...have a corruptive influence on morals, and that their publishing houses are spreading pornography . . ." is invariably quoted as proof of Hlond's anti-Semitism, but no mention is made of what follows. Hlond's pastoral letter is a classic instance of the two part teaching on the Jews that goes by the name of "*Sicut Iudeis non . . .*" I will now quote the passage on the Jews in full:

So long as Jews remain Jews, a Jewish problem exists and will continue to exist. This question varies in intensity and degree from country to country. It is especially difficult in our country, and ought to be the object of serious consideration. I shall touch briefly here on its moral aspects in connection with the situation today.

It is a fact that Jews are waging war against the Catholic Church, that they are steeped in free-thinking and constitute the vanguard of atheism, the Bolshevik movement, and revolutionary activity. It is a fact that Jews have a corruptive influence on morals, and that their publishing houses are spreading pornography. It is true that Jews are perpetrating fraud, practicing usury, and dealing in prostitution. It is true that, from a religious and ethical point of view, Jewish youth are having a negative influence on the Catholic youth in our schools. But let us be fair. Not all Jews are this way. There are very many Jews who are believers, honest, just, kind, and philanthropic. There is a healthy, edifying sense of family in very many Jewish homes. We know Jews who are ethically outstanding, noble, and upright.

I warn against that moral stance, imported from abroad [he is clearly thinking of Germany] that is basically and ruthlessly anti-Jewish. It is contrary to Catholic ethics. One may love one's own nation more, but one may not hate anyone. Not even Jews. It is good to prefer your own kind when shopping, to avoid Jewish stores and Jewish stalls in the marketplace, but it is forbidden to demolish a Jewish store, damage their merchandise, break windows, or throw things at their homes. One should stay away from the harmful moral influence of Jews, keep away from their anti-Christian culture, and especially boycott the Jewish press and demoralizing Jewish publications. But it is forbidden to assault, beat up, maim, or slander Jews. One should honor Jews as human beings and neighbors, even though we do not honor the indescribable tragedy of that nation, which was the guardian of the idea of the Messiah and from which was born the Savior. When divine mercy enlightens a Jew to sincerely accept his and our Messiah, let us greet him into our Christian ranks with joy.

Beware of those who are inciting anti-Jewish violence. They are serving a bad cause. Do you know who is giving the orders? Do you know who is intent on these riots? No good comes from these rash actions. And it is Polish blood that is sometimes being shed at them.[21]

Cardinal Hlond was not expressing racial hatred here; he was warning his Polish flock about the dangers of Bolshevism, which, as all of Europe had learned during the 1920s, was an essentially Jewish movement. Cardinal Hlond was opposing Jewish revolutionary activity on the one hand, but he was also opposing the vicious reaction to Jewish revolutionary activity that was known as Nazism, which had taken over Germany at that time. The Church was consistent in its opposition to revolution on the one hand, and in defending the Jews against genuine persecution on the other. Both parts of this teaching are necessary. If either one is ignored, trouble follows.

This, of course, is precisely what happened in the wake of the Second Vatican Council. *Nostra Aetate*, the council document on other religions, was supposed to usher in a new era of interfaith dialogue, with Jews in particular. What followed can best be gleaned from a sampling of statements issued both around the time of or as part of what claimed to be a celebration of the document's 40th anniversary. In his book *A Moral Reckoning: the Role of the Catholic Church in the Holocaust and its Unfulfilled Duty of Repair*, Daniel Jonah Goldhagen wrote, "For centuries the Catholic Church...harbored anti-Semitism at its core, as an integral part of its doctrine, its theology and its liturgy."[22] As his contribution to a "celebration" of 40 years of *Nostra Aetate*, Yona Metzger, Israel's chief rabbi, wrote in the Jesuit magazine *America* that in *Nostra Aetate*, the Church rejected "the normative view of Jews that had been held throughout Christendom for many centuries" namely, that "the Jews rejected Christ and were guilty of the crime of deicide; consequently, they had been rejected by the Creator in favor of the Christians," who were "the new Israel." Rabbi Metzger went on to say that this attitude of "supercessionism," and "the teaching of contempt," "laid the groundwork for centuries of discrimination, persecution and violence against Jews, culminating in the Shoah, in which one-third of Jewry was murdered."[23]

This book then is the story of those movements that embody a spirit of rebellion (conscious or unconscious) against Logos, which more often than not meant an attack on Christ and His Church through history. This spirit is embodied not just in Judaism but in numerous Christian heresies and secular movements.

The Good Friday prayers of the Catholic Church reach out to those affected with such a spirit. The 1962 Good Friday prayer for the Jews reads:

> Let us pray also for the Jews that the Lord our God may take the veil from their hearts and that they also may acknowledge our Lord Jesus Christ. Let us pray: Almighty and everlasting God, you do not refuse your mercy even to the Jews; hear the prayers which we offer for the blindness of that people so that they may acknowledge the light of your truth, which is Christ, and be delivered from their darkness.

The Church had amended the prayer from an earlier version referring to "perfidious" or "faithless" Jews. Since that time it has been further amended, even to the point of ambiguity. However, with Pope Benedict XVI's recent *Summorum Pontificum* motu proprio, the 1962 prayer will be more commonly heard. The prayer now reads as follows: "Let us pray for the Jews. That our God and Lord may enlighten their hearts, so that they may recognize Jesus Christ, the Savior of all men. Let us pray. Let us bend our knees. Rise. Almighty and eternal God, who wants all of mankind to be saved and gain knowledge of the truth, grant that when the fullness of peoples enters your Church all of Israel may be save. Through Christ, our Lord." Far from being "anti-Semitic" it is, as the Jewish atheist Israel Shahak noted, "a prayer which asked the Lord to have mercy on Jews..."[24]

The rewriting of the 1962 prayer in a way that retains the orginal explicit call for conversion is a sign that the post-Vatican II era is drawing to a close. Nowhere is the need for closure and re-evaluation more urgent than in the Church's teaching on the Jews. *Nostra Aetate*, the council's document on non-Christian religions, was supposed to inaugurate a new era of interfaith dialogue. What it led to instead was a condemnation of the heart of the Gospel's call for conversion as "supercessionism" and confusion in the face of an increasingly imperious foreign policy under the leadership of what is now called the "Israel Lobby."

By the time Daniel Jonah Goldhagen's attack on Pius XII appeared, it had become apparent that the 40 years of interfaith dialogue inaugurated by *Nostra Aetate* had resulted in apparent heresy on the part of leading Church authorities, diatribes on the part of Jews, and political disaster for the entire world. When the Church acquiesced to the Jewish interpretation of *Nostra Aetate*, she opened the door to the rise of neoconservative foreign policy in the United States, which led to the disastrous war in Iraq. Dialogue in this context has reached a dead end on both theological and political levels. It is my hope that this book will promote a rethinking of these issues and a return to the wisdom of tradition.

No book of this size can come into existence without help. At this point I would like to acknowledge the assistance of James G. Bruen, Anthony S. McCarthy, Jeffrey J. Langan and John Beaumont for the assistance they provided in bringing this book out.

E. Michael Jones
South Bend, Indiana
December 2007

Chapter One

The Synagogue of Satan

Sensing that Hellenistic hegemony over Palestine had run its course, Pompey played off the descendants of Alexander the Great's generals against each other as a prelude to seizing power and completing the ring of Roman rule around the Mediterranean, the ocean the Romans called "ours." In 64 BC Pompey deposed Phillip II, the last Seleucid, and made Syria a Roman province. Pompey soon learned the Jews would not be incorporated into the Empire without a struggle, just as his successors found they could not keep the Jews in the Empire without bitter struggles.

One year after taking Syria without firing a shot, so to speak, Pompey was enmired in a siege of Jerusalem. He called for battering rams from Tyre and had trees felled to cross the moats surrounding the city walls, but success was uncertain. The Jews had water and food; they also had the Temple to their god, about which Pompey had heard impressive if contradictory reports. While Pompey sat outside the walls, the priests sacrificed to their god, who seemed disposed to hold the Romans at bay.

So Pompey studied the Jewish religion. The Jewish prohibition against work on the Sabbath allowed bearing arms only to defend against attack. The Roman soldiers therefore laid down their arms on the Jewish Sabbath and instead undermined the city's walls, against which Jewish religious scruple allowed no action.

In June 63 BC one Temple tower fell. Roman soldiers poured through the breach into the Temple precincts where they slaughtered the Jewish priests. Many Jews committed suicide by throwing themselves off the Temple battlements. Others immolated themselves on pyres intended for sacrificial animals. All in all, 12,000 Jews died. With victory imminent, Pompey's curiosity about the inner sanctum of the Jewish Temple replaced the concerns of war. Wading through the blood of slain priests, Pompey penetrated to the holy of holies to find that the object of Jewish worship was not an ass's head, as Alexandrian propagandists had claimed. He discovered that, in Roman terms, there was no object of worship. Perhaps Pompey found the empty shrine unsettling; perhaps he was disconcerted by a presence he felt even though no object represented it. Either way, Pompey halted before the Temple treasury with its gold and retreated empty-handed.

The Temple was left standing, but the walls of Jerusalem were razed. A tax was levied against the Jews in amounts appropriate to a conquered province. The Temple had been violated, but it remained intact. Temple sacrifices continued, but Israel ceased to exist as a nation with a state.

Pompey executed the most fanatical Jewish revolutionaries, the Zealots. He named the pliable, dim-witted Hyrcanus high-priest and ethnarch, ensuring he was only a figurehead by putting him under the authority of Antipater, whom he made governor of Judaea. The more formidable Aristobulus was sent to Rome with his son Antigonus and a horde of Jewish prisoners, whose descendants, known as *libertini,* or the emancipated, settled on the right bank of the Tiber on the slopes of the Vatican hill. The bridge across the Tiber was known as the *Pons Judaeorum,* indicating the race of the settlers, and that they had been there for a long time.

Defeat led to Jewish dispersion. From that dispersed seemingly hopeless position, the descendants of the Jews began to wage, in Graetz's words, "a new kind of warfare against long-established Roman institutions" which would ultimately "modify or partly destroy them."[1] Graetz is referring to Christianity—the most successful Jewish sect, in his view. To conquer Rome from within, Judaism had to be modified, however, and it "became estranged from and placed itself in harsh antagonism to the parent source."[2] But Graetz could have referred to other Jewish sects that were not estranged because, while they were swallowed by the Roman empire, they refused to be digested by it. As Roman oppression increased, Jewish settlements across the empire became the source of insurrection and revolutionary activity that would threaten the existence of the empire in a different way from the ultimately successful Christian threat.

The Romans were generally adept at ruling conquered nations, but Roman rule in Palestine was a story of blunders and oppression. Because the Maccabees had thrown off Greek hegemony 100 years before Pompey's triumph, a similar victory against the Romans didn't seem impossible. The defeat of the Jews by yet another foreign power, together with the arrogance and blunders of the Romans thus fueled apocalyptic fervor among the Jews.

Apocalyptic literature started under the Hellenistic hegemony due to Alexander the Great's conquests in 333 BC. Antiochus IV Epiphanes pressed assimilation in 167 BC by abolishing Jewish practices and establishing the cult of Zeus in the Temple. He ordered pagan sacrifice on the new altar of the Temple. The priest Mattathias and his five sons called upon the Jews to revolt. Three years of war followed, during which the Book of Daniel was written. Daniel is the first in a series of Apocalypses, or revelations of things hidden, that culminate in the book of Revelation, which completes the canon of Christian scripture. Apocalyptic writing enjoyed its greatest popularity from 200 BC to 100 AD, a time of distress and persecution for Jews and then for Christians. Daniel, according to the editors of New American Bible, "was composed during the bitter persecution carried on by Antiochus IV Epiphanes (167-164) and was written to strengthen and comfort the Jewish people in their ordeal" by showing "that men of faith can resist temptation and conquer adversity."[3]

In the second chapter of Daniel, King Nebuchadnezzar dreams of a statue with feet of clay, which none of his sages can interpret. Daniel explains the four parts of the statue correspond to four kingdoms which will rule the earth. The fourth kingdom "will crush and break all of the earlier kingdoms" in a sequence of events familiar to the inhabitants of Palestine. But the fourth kingdom under the dominion of the fourth beast "shall devour" as well "the whole earth, beat it down and crush it." The Book of Daniel is describing the trajectory of human history in a fallen world. One empire follows the other; the only constant: oppression, with each successive kingdom more tyrannical than the previous one.

The Book of Daniel also proposes an "end to history." "A stone broke away, untouched by any hand, and struck the statue, struck its feet of iron and earthenware and shattered them." According to Daniel's interpretation: "In the time of these kings the God of heaven will set up a kingdom which shall never be destroyed, and this kingdom will not pass into the hands of another race; it will shatter and absorb all the previous kingdoms and itself last for ever—just as you saw the stone untouched by hand break from the mountain and shatter iron, bronze, earthenware, silver and gold."

After the triumph of the worst and most oppressive fourth kingdom, Daniel has another vision in which "I saw One like a son of man coming on the clouds of heaven." The "son of man" is the messianic designation; the Messiah will establish dominion unlike any other. "His dominion is an everlasting dominion that shall not be taken away; his kingship shall not be destroyed." The divided lower part of the statue—half clay and half iron—probably refers to the failed merger of the Seleucids and the Ptolomies, Alexander the Great's successors who failed to keep his legacy of conquest unified. The fourth kingdom is traditionally taken as Rome, but that can be ascribed only to prophecy or hindsight.

Pompey did what Daniel said the fourth beast would do: he conquered Jerusalem in 63 BC. He crushed the kingdom of clay and iron, but his victory only intensified the Messianic expectation. The triumph of the fourth kingdom indicated that the Messiah's coming was imminent. The Son of Man was to deliver the Jews from foreign oppression and inaugurate an unending kingdom that would break apart all empires. Oppression fueled Messianic fervor. The Messiah "became more superhuman as the situation became more hopeless."[4] The Messiah became for the oppressed Jewish people "a mighty warrior" to destroy Israel's foes and "take captive the leader of the Romans and bring him in chains to Mount Zion, where he will put him to death" and "establish a kingdom which shall last to the end of the world." Deliverance from political oppression would occur in the only manner the Jewish people considered possible—through a mighty general who "would show himself invincible in war." As the conflict with Rome became bitterer, "messianic fantasies became with many Jews an obsessive preoccupation."[5]

From the Christian perspective, the apocalyptic age culminated in Christ. Jesus, repeatedly referring to himself as "the Son of Man," was invoking the prophecy in Daniel and pointing to himself as the inaugurator of the Messianic Kingdom. As his earthly life became more public, it became clear that Jesus was no mighty warrior of the sort the Jews admired in King David. He claimed to be of the House of David, but it was unclear how a man who was not a warrior was going to bring freedom to captives held in bondage by Roman arms.

The Jewish desire for a "superhuman" savior found fulfillment and disappointment in Jesus Christ. Christ convinced his followers He was superhuman, but he disabused them of the notion He was merely a more powerful version of David or Alexander the Great or Caesar. "Superman" is a comic book figure created in America during the Depression by Jerry Siegel and Joe Schuster, Jews of eastern European extraction who couldn't expunge the idea of a Messiah from their consciousness.[6] But it also bespeaks a perennial inability to see supernature as anything more than a comic exaggeration of the military heroes who conquered the Jews.

The Superman fantasy has plagued the Jews since the time of Christ. Was the Son of Man the same as Superman? Was the Kingdom of God a more powerful version of Rome? How would the Messiah overthrow Rome? How would the stone untouched by human hands shatter the fourth kingdom? No one had the answers because, ultimately, the ambiguity could only be cleared up by the Messiah, the Son of Man, Himself. Arrival of the kingdom is a central theme of the synoptic gospels, and Jesus, in calling himself "the Son of Man" reminds us he fulfills the destiny of this mysterious figure. Jesus identified himself as the "Son of Man," but his encounters with his fellow Jews showed their difficulty in distinguishing between the "Son of Man" and a fantasy Superman.

Graetz claims "the rapacity of the Roman rulers" intensified "the longing for the deliverer announced in the prophetical writings" so much that "any highly gifted individual ... would have readily found disciples and believers in his Messianic mission."[7] That would have come as a surprise to Jesus. The Gospel of John describes Jesus in increasingly acrimonious debate with "the lost sheep of the House of Israel," the very people he came to save, who, according to Graetz, were willing to accept "any highly gifted individual" as their Messiah. The Jews' longing for release from Roman oppression increased with each year, but it fixated on a figure who wielded military power. The Nazarean was proposing something else, and the conflict with Jewish expectations led to increasingly bitter heated discussions and recriminations until the Jews who rejected Jesus finally sought his death.

The first coming of Christ created a crisis for the Jews. In the Gospels, the Jews define themselves by their relationship to the man who claims to be the "Son of Man" or the Messiah. As a result, the discussion of Messianic expectations becomes very quickly a discussion of what it means to be a Jew. Klaus Wengst says that "the Gospel of John was written out of the situation of a hard-pressed Jewish Christian minority which found itself in the period following 70 AD confronted by the opposition of rabbinical orthodoxy."[8]

Whether the Gospel of St. John was written after the destruction of the Temple, as Wengst maintains, or before, as Markus Barth maintains, Roman hegemony created the political context for both groups of Jews, for "those who rejected Christ and for the Jews and non-Jews who believed in him as the Messiah."[9]

The conflict between these two groups of Jews pervades the Gospel of St. John. That gospel, in which the term "Jew" appears 71 times, is a protracted discussion of what it means to be a Jew. Who are "the Jews"? Well, it depends; the word has different meanings in different contexts, but the context gets increasingly specific and increasingly hostile as the Gospel narrative progresses, leading ultimately to a break between "the Jews" and Jesus that leads to His death.

One of the most interesting consequences of the Anti-Defamation League's attack on Mel Gibson's *The Passion* was the focus on whether the gospels are anti-Semitic. Abraham Foxman and Rabbi James Rudin condemned the film because it contained the passage from Matthew 27:25 when the Jewish people shout to Pilate, "His blood be on us and our children." But, if the statement is anti-Semitic, then the fault lies not with Mel Gibson but with St. Matthew. By thus framing the issue, Foxman and Rudin reveal their real position, namely, that the Gospels and by extension Christianity are intrinsically anti-Semitic; Mel Gibson needs to be censured because he makes the statement publicly, i.e., in a big budget film. Rabbi Daniel Lapin was appalled at Foxman and Rudin, "self-appointed Jewish leaders," for making a spectacle of themselves and harming the standing of all Jews in the United States, but Foxman and Rudin did frame the issue honestly from a specifically Jewish perspective by implying that the Gospels are anti-Semitic.

Philip S. Kaufman, a Christian Jew and Benedictine priest, tries to restore civility by insisting the Gospel of St. John is the least anti-Semitic (by which he means anti-Jewish) Gospel. Kaufman bases his argument on comparison of the Passion narratives, but he glosses over Chapter 8 of the Gospel of St. John, especially 8:44 where Jesus tells the "Jews" that "the devil is your father," a passage Caron calls the most anti-Semitic New Testament passage. Trying to be irenic, Kaufman argues for translation of the Johannine phrase *"hoi Ioudaioi"* as "the Jerusalem officials, leaders or authorities."[10]

Kaufman would probably find a sympathetic ear in Rabbi Lapin. Rabbi Lapin, however, is the exception that proves the rule. Jewish leaders would not be leaders if they didn't have followers, and their followers continue to be unimpressed by Catholic ecumenical outreach. The unavoidable issue is the intrinsically anti-Jewish nature of the Christian scriptures. Indeed, the disappointment is so universal since the time of *Nostra Aetate*, the Vatican II statement on non-Christian religions, that re-evaluation and course correction seems unavoidable.

At an Evangelical-Jewish dialogue at the Evangelical Academy of Arnoldshain in Germany in March 1989, Micha Brumlik, a Jewish participant, got quickly to the point. How is dialogue possible when the "irreducible Kernel" of the Gospel of St. John is "intrinsically anti-Jewish"?[11] If that Gospel is, as Brumlik claims, "an embassy of hate," then the issue is not inter-faith dialogue but the identity of Christianity itself. If the Gospel of St. John is normative for Christianity, then Christianity is a religion of hate, and there is no point in engaging in dialogue with its adherents. Brumlik engages in the dialogue, but only to denounce the foundational writings of Christianity as hate speech. In the Gospel of St. John, he writes, the message that is supposed to lead the people by way of faith and the Son to the Father, is in reality a message of marginalization, fear, anxiety and hate. There is no other scripture in the New Testament, in which Christianity more fully achieves its non-Jewish identity, and there is no other scripture in which the marginalization of the Jews, and by that I mean Judaism, is achieved in such a sharp, irreconcilable and unbridgeable manner as in the Gospel according to John.[12]

St. John achieves this by portraying Jews "both in the form of the spontaneous Mob as well as in the form of the political religious leadership" as "murderers, assassins and killers." Even the Jews who believed in Jesus, "insofar as they wanted to remain Jews," have to hear themselves denounced as "children of the Devil."[13]

The heart of the matter for Brumlik lies in Chapter 8, which he sees as "proto-racist" and manifesting "politically and socio-psychologically explainable delusions" tied together in a "consistent Satanology" demonizing the Jews and giving them "no chance."[14] According to Brumlik, St. John portrays the Jews "as a group of people, who don't recognize Jesus as the Son of God because they are ontologically and constitutionally incapable of recognizing him as such. This is part and parcel, according to this view, of the satanic nature of the Jews. They can't recognize him and so they must persecute him: "Why don't you understand what I am saying? Because you can't hear my word. The Devil is your father, and you prefer to do what your father wants. He was a murderer from the start and was never grounded in the truth; there is no truth in him at all.'"[15]

The Gospels are not and cannot be construed as anti-Semitic, because, as Caron points out in *Qui son les "Juifs" de l'evangile de Jean?* "It is clear that the expression does not include the entirety of the Jewish people. Jesus and his disciples, along with John the Baptist, are Jews."[16] The term "Jew," according to Caron, "is not used in an ethnic or racial sense."[17] The Gospels cannot be anti-Semitic because the antagonists are all Semites. The Gospels do not espouse hatred of individuals because of race; it would be impossible for them to do so because the Christians in the Gospels are all Jews. This does not preclude, however, the "anti-Jewish" nature of the Gospels, depending on how one defines the term.

How is the term "Jew" used? Brumlik is not helpful here. He's unable to clarify the issue because clarification revolves around the true identity of Christ. The Gospel of St. John, according to Brumlik, portrays "Jews, in fact all Jews, insofar as they are Jews—which is to say, insofar as they hold fast to their position as children of Abraham—as essentially damned enemies of Jesus."[18] Jesus would probably object, not because damnation was not a real possibility for his opponents (see Matthew 23:15, 23:33)—but because Brumlik portrays them as loyal children of Abraham, a contention Jesus rejects in John 8:37: "If you were Abraham's children, you would do as Abraham did."

The Gospel of St. John is not and cannot be construed as anti-Semitic, but is it, as Brumlik claims, "*judenfeindlich*"?[19] Is it anti-Jewish? Following scripture scholar Raymond Brown's lead, Kaufman avoids the issue, claiming that by "oi

Ioudaioi," St. John means "Jewish leaders." "To capture its correct meaning," Kaufman writes, *"tous Ioudaious* and *hoi Ioudaioi* could be translated in the same verse as 'the Jerusalem officials, leaders or authorities.'"[20] Kaufman says "the tendency in the past to fuel anti-Semitism by that Gospel's frequent use of the phrase 'the Jews,'" could "be eliminated by the translation of *hoi Ioudaioi* as 'hostile Jerusalem leaders,' where that translation is justified in the context."[21] Kaufman gripes that several new translations of the Bible eliminated sexist language but "did not at the same time correct 'anti-Jewish' language." Unless better translations are made, "such corrections should be made in lectionaries and all materials used for pubic reading and study."[22]

Translating *"oi Ioudaioi"* as "the Jewish leaders" creates its own problems. Nicodemus and Joseph of Arimethea were Jewish leaders, but they were also followers of Christ and thus proof there was as little unanimity among leaders as among followers. Brumlik rightly rejects translation of *oi Ioudaioi* as "leaders" because that would hide what John makes clear, namely, "that he's talking not just about the Pharisees but about all Jews ...."[23] At the beginning of the Gospel of St. John *hoi Ioudaioi* means all of the Jews; by the end of that Gospel it means all of the Jews who have rejected Christ.

The Jews aren't Judeans or Pharisees or other groups opposing the followers of Jesus; they are, in Brumlik's view, the Jewish people.[24] The fact that the "divine Word" of the Christians was a Jew doesn't change the fundamentally anti-Jewish nature of this gospel.[25] Brumlik concludes that dialogue between Christians and Jews is impossible if either takes the Gospel of St. John as its starting point.[26] There is no possible meeting point because Jesus is the essence of Christianity, according to this gospel, and that essence is "precisely what Jews, *insofar as they want to remain Jews,* must reject".[27]

Brumlik inadvertently makes the same point as St. John. To hold onto their "identity," the "Jews" had to reject Christ. The "Jews" (as opposed to the entire ethnic group, some of which accepted Christ as the Messiah) created a new identity for themselves, one that is essentially negative.

St. John brings readers to this understanding gradually as the Jews define themselves in encounters with Christ in his gospel. Jew, in the context of the Gospel of St. John, cannot mean all Jews in an ethnic or racial sense, since Jesus himself was a Jew, as were his disciples. Caron says, "this particular use of 'oi Ioudaioi' in the narrative context of the gospel denies us the possibility of using the expression in any nationalist or ethnic sense."[28] Similarly, Caron denies *"oi Ioudaioi"* can be translated as "Jewish leaders."

What does St. John mean when he refers to "the Jews"? When St. John uses the words *"oi Ioudaioi,"* he is referring to a group that has rejected Christ. The coming of Christ changed Jewish identity forever, something the Jews at His time comprehended only with difficulty. From then, the terms "Israelite" and "Jew" were no longer synonyms, because, Ferdinand Hahn points out in Caron's book, "the 'true Israelites'" from the Christian perspective "are precisely those who, like Nathaniel, recognize in Jesus the Messiah."[70]

The conflict that defines "Jew" in the fourth gospel is essentially religious.[30] Caron suggests that when St. John employs "*oi Ioudaioi*" he means "Judaism." But what does Judaism mean? Both terms are defined in John's narratives. The Jews define themselves and their religion in light of Jesus proclaiming himself the Messiah. Caron notes the dialogue with the Jews invariably occurs during a religious festival when Jesus is either in or on his way to Jerusalem. "It is not coincidence," he writes, "that the confrontation with Jesus takes place precisely on the occasion of those celebrations." Judaism celebrates the "Jews'" identity, their origins, their history and their past, and anyone who questions one of these elements, as Jesus does, is a threat to that identity.[31] The festivals celebrate and confirm Jewish identity; the encounters between Jesus and the "Jews" occur during the festivals because for John Jewish identity revolves around the person of Jesus.

Christianity is intimately connected with Christ. Judaism is just as intimately connected with Jerusalem. The "Judaism in question takes on an official character. It has its seat in Jerusalem and it is hostile to Jesus."[32] It is "*le principal accusateur*" of Jesus.[33] Its headquarters is in Jerusalem where all confrontations between Christ and "the Jews" occur; it is the center of the "systematic hostility of 'Judaism" against Jesus.

St. John mentions this systematic hostility in describing the man born blind but healed by Jesus. Word of the miracle spread, but "*the Jews* [my emphasis] would not believe that the man had been blind and had gained his sight." To confirm (or discredit) the story, the "Jews" sent for the man's parents (who, like the man, were Jewish), who were intimidated, refusing to speak "out of fear of the Jews, who had already agreed to expel from the synagogue anyone who should acknowledge Jesus as the Christ."

Brumlik claims there is no evidence of intra-Jewish dissension outside of the gospel accounts, but there is plenty within them. Some commentators claim this bespeaks a projection backward in time from the time of the writing of the gospel, which some place as late as 170 AD. The testimony of John, who says he was an eyewitness whose "testimony is true," is that the split was virtually contemporaneous with the public ministry of Jesus. It is difficult to see how it could be otherwise. The claim that Jesus was the "Son of Man" required a decision by the Jews. In John 7:11, we read that "At the festival the Jews were on the look-out for him: "Where is he?" they said. People stood in groups whispering about him. Some said, "He is a good man"; others "No, he is leading the people astray." Yet no one spoke about him openly for fear of the Jews."

The meaning of "Jew" in this context is clear: a Jew is openly hostile to Christ and willing to persecute those Jews who accept Him as the Messiah. John's mention of "fear of the Jews" indicates that Jews were then afraid of "Jews." The well-being of the Jews who accepted Christ was threatened by the Jews who rejected him. The parents of the man born blind exhibit "fear of the Jews" because the "Jews" threaten to expel followers of Jesus, also Jews, from the synagogue. The identity of both groups was essentially religious, not ethnic; both identities were a function of Christ. The Jews who acknowledged Christ were expelled from the synagogue. The Jews who rejected Him, the people John calls "the Jews," defined themselves by that rejection.

Unsatisfied by the parents' evasions, the "Jews sent for the man" to question him themselves. They ask him leading questions and tell him to "Give glory to God!" by testifying against Jesus, because "For our part, we know that this man is a sinner." The man refuses to be intimidated by "the Jews." "I only know," he responds, "that I was blind and now I can see." When "the Jews" want him to repeat his story, presumably to catch him in contradictions, the man refuses: "I have told you once and you wouldn't listen. Why do you want to hear it all again? Do you want to become his disciples too?" This outrages "the Jews," who respond indignantly "we are disciples of Moses."

At another point, Jesus rejects their claim to be disciples of Moses. In John 5:45, Jesus tells the "Jews":

> Do not imagine that I am going to accuse you before the Father:
> You place your hopes on Moses,
> and Moses will be your accuser.
> If you really believed him,
> you would believe me too,
> since it was I that he was writing about;
> but if you refuse to believe what he wrote,
> how can you believe what I say?

The arrival of Jesus, according to St. John, is the defining moment for all Jews. He brings a radical discontinuity in history too, for those who claim to be followers of Moses are not what they claim to be. They are, in fact, the opposite: in rejecting Christ they reject Moses and everything Moses stood for. The term "law," usually used in the same context as Moses, the lawgiver, is also deceptive. Jesus refuses to admit that "the Jews" are true to the law of Moses. Instead, he refers repeatedly to "the Jews" as following "their law" or "your law." As Caron says, "The term 'law' does not refer in this case to the law of Moses or to the writings of Moses, but rather to the law of the 'Jews' or that of the pharisees ... . The Jews are not faithful to the former but rather to their own law, or put another way, to a false interpretation of the law of Moses."[34] The official Judaism of Jerusalem thus is not what it pretends to be. Judaism is not Judaism at all but rather what Caron calls "un pseudo-Judaisme."[35] The "Jews" are faithful to "their law," not the law of Moses.

What is true about Moses vis a vis the "Jews" who claim him as their father is also a fortiori true about Abraham. As the discussion of spiritual parentage moves from chapter 5 to chapter 8, the terms become more intimate. Instead of talking about the law, the "Jews" talk about "*sperma*" or the biological inheritance of their status as the chosen people. In both cases there is a radical discontinuity in history. Or, to put it another way, the continuity is not what it seems. Those who accept Christ are the children of Abraham and Moses. Those who call themselves "Jews" are liars.

St. John was a Jew. More precisely, St. John was a Jew but not "a Jew." According to Overbeck: "the author of the fourth gospel" is "not a pagan Christian ... he is instead a hellenistic Jew."[36] Why, then, does St. John refer to the "Jews" as an alien "they" determined to kill Christ? The answer again revolves around how the meaning of the word evolves in the Gospel. John begins by describing Jesus' encounter with the Samaritan woman. Jesus tells the woman

> You worship what you do not know;
> we worship what we do know;

This dichotomy is simple. Jesus is a Jew; the Samaritan woman is not. The distinction is important because, as Jesus says, "Salvation comes from the Jews." His declaration seems straight-forward; the Jews are an ethnic group that is God's chosen people. From this group, salvation will come. Then, as if to complicate things, Jesus adds

> the hour will come—is in fact already here—
> when true worshippers will worship the Father in spirit and truth.

Now that Jesus has arrived, the categories "Jew" and "true worshippers" are no longer synonymous. Salvation comes from the Jews, i.e, from an ethnic group that calls itself the chosen people. Upon Christ's arrival, however, the situation changes, for the Jews have to accept Christ to remain Israel. The Jews have to accept Christ to become "true worshippers" who "will worship the Father in spirit and truth."

The full implication of his cryptic message to the Samaritan woman only becomes apparent, however, when Jesus confronts the Jews, and in this confrontation the meaning of the word "Jew" also becomes apparent. John uses the term "Jew" two ways. He begins by saying that "Salvation comes from the Jews," and ends by saying those who call themselves "Jews" are not children of Abraham or Moses and, in fact, have Satan as their father. From identifying the word Jew with "we," as he does with the Samaritan woman, Jesus goes on to refer to what John calls "Jews" as "you," which is to say, a group that does not include Jesus. Accepting or rejecting the Messiah becomes the principal way of defining what it means to be a Jew.

John makes this clear in chapter 8. The discussion becomes progressively more heated, leading to an irreparable break between Jesus and "the Jews." When Jesus says to "them," i.e., "the Jews,"

> "I am going away; you will look for me
> and you will die in your sin.
> Where I am going you cannot come."

the Jews become confused, wondering "Will he kill himself?" But Jesus indicates that a great division already exists. The "Jews" can no longer be referred to as a "we" that includes Jesus, but rather as "you," i.e., as a group that does not include Christ because it rejected him. "You," Christ continues, referring to "the Jews,"

> are from below;
> I am from above.
> You are of this world;
> I am not of this world.

The issue of what it means to be a "Jew" thus can only be resolved by resolving the issue of Christ's identity. Christ is the antithesis of sin. Those who reject Christ will die in their sins. "I have told you already," Christ tells "the Jews," "You will die in your sins." The "Jews" redefined themselves by rejecting Christ as the Messiah. They proposed false dichotomies—Moses vs. Jesus; Abraham vs. Jesus—which became nonetheless the essential defining characteristic of what it meant to be a "Jew." Thus, the term "Jew" is slowly redefined throughout the Gospel of St. John, until by the end of the Gospel it means something different from what it meant at the beginning. This new meaning necessitates the awkward use of quotation marks when the term "Jew" is used. With Christ's arrival and the annunciation of his ministry as "the Son of Man," the term "Jew" has either a completely and exclusively ethnic meaning, i.e., one shorn of any notion of chosenness, or it has a completely and exclusively theological meaning: A "Jew" is someone who rejects Christ and as a result will die in his sins. After the Jews rejected Christ, Judaism ceased being a religion and became an ideology. Or, to say the same thing another way, it went from being a true religion (in fact, the only true religion) to being a false religion, like Islam, Mormonism, Scientology, etc., in spite of the fact that it still claimed the inspired word of God as its fondationa texts. Israel simultaneously lost its biological basis. The New Israel, the true children of Moses and Abraham, was now the Church.

The Jews, aware of the redefinition of their identity, are not happy and try to return the discussion to their role as the chosen people or the ethnic group favored by God. The Jews respond to Jesus' denunciation by saying, "We are descended from Abraham." The Greek is instructive, for the Jews say to Jesus "*Sperma Abraam esmen*," that is, "we are the sperm of Abraham," or we share Abraham's DNA and are in exclusive possession, therefore, of the necessary if not sufficient condition for salvation. Jesus, however, changes the term from "*Sperma*" to "*Tekna*," which is to say from DNA, or "seed," to "children."

When the Jews repeat, "Our father is Abraham," Jesus replies: "*Ei tekna tou Abraam este, ta erga tou Abraam epoieite.*" "If you were Abraham's children (*Tekna* not *Sperma*), you would do as Abraham did."

Once Jesus denies the Jews salvation through their DNA, or through their version of keeping the law, their differences become irreconcilable, and violence becomes inescapable. The "Jews" feel Jesus is casting aspersions on their parents.

"We were not born of prostitution," they exclaim as anger builds. Jesus then pours gasoline on the fire. "If you were Abraham's children," Jesus tells them, casting their heritage in doubt,

> you would do as Abraham did.
> As it is, you want to kill me
> when I tell you the truth
> as I have learnt it from God;
> That is not what Abraham did.

The anger of the Jews and the truth of Christ collide, and out of the collision comes the new definition of what it means to be a "Jew"

"What you are doing," Christ tells the "Jews," "is what your father does."

The "Jews," sensing further insult, claim "We were not born of prostitution." But their biologism is beside the point. A child of God is known not by his DNA or *Sperma* but by what he does, as the "Jews" themselves would have to admit. The "Jews" claim to have God as their father, but their actions indicate the opposite. "If," Jesus reminds them, "God were your father, you would love me." Since the "Jews" do not love Christ, God is not their father. Either His interlocutors are Jews or Christ is a Jew, but according to St. John, both cannot be members of the same group. Indeed, they don't even speak the same language:"Do you know why you cannot take in what I say?" Christ asks the "Jews." "It is because you are unable to understand my language." Then chapter 8 reaches its crisis. The "Jews" are not children of God. Their father is Satan. "The devil," Jesus tells the "Jews," is your father and you prefer to do what your father wants."

The Jews are transformed by their encounter with Christ. Those who accept Him become the New Israel known as the Church. They are the true "children" of Abraham and Moses. Those who reject Christ become the "Jews" or followers of Satan. The "Jew," whose father is Satan, "a murderer and a liar from the beginning," defines himself by rejecting Christ and truth. At that moment, Israel ceases to be an ethnic designation. The old Israel was determined by DNA; it was the "seed" of Abraham. The new Israel, which "worships in spirit and truth," is determined entirely by behavior, most significantly acceptance of Christ and his message. The Church is the new Israel.

St. Paul's epistles are consistent with St. John's Gospel. "Not all those who descend from Israel are Israel," he writes in Romans 9:7, "not all the descendants of Abraham are his true children. Remember: it is through Israel that your name will be carried on, which means that it is not physical descent that decides who are the children of God; it is only the children of the promise who will count as the true descendants."

DNA is a chemical; children are acting individuals. The terms of election have changed. Only those "who follow this rule," Paul writes in Galatians 6:16, "form the Israel of God." Just as conscious choice and consistent behavior now form the sole basis for membership in the New Israel, the "Jews'" embrace of DNA is the basis for all subsequent ideologies of race from Nazism to Zionism. Proponents of race were always choosing more primitive formulations of community that led to intellectual bondage instead of freedom based on choice proposed by the Gospels.

The confrontation between Jesus and the "Jews" leads first to a redefinition of the word "Jew." What used to refer to the chosen people, now refers to those who reject Christ. What used to be synonymous with Israel now means its opposite. St. John's use of "*oi Ioudaioi*" indicates one of the most profound and radical discontinuities in history. Those who, according to the "Jews," seem to reject the religion of Moses and Abraham are the true children of Moses and Abraham. They are the Church, the New Israel.

What then are the "Jews"? In Revelations 2:9, John defends the nascent Christian community against the "Jews" by reporting that "the slanderous accusations" against the Christians "have been made by people who profess to be Jews but are really members of the synagogue of Satan." He revisits the theme in Revelations 3:9, referring to "the synagogue of Satan" as "those who profess to be Jews but are liars, because they are no such thing." The angel visiting the beleaguered Christian community in Philadelphia will compel the "Jews" to "fall at your feet and admit that you are the people that I love." Just as the Jews who rejected Christ have a new name, "the synagogue of Satan," so the group of Jews which accepted him, now enlarged by Gentile converts, will henceforth be known as "the new Jerusalem which comes down from my God in Heaven." Later Christian writers tried to avoid the confusion which flows from these conflicting uses of the word "Jew" by referring to the Church as the "New Israel." Unlike the word "Jew," whose meaning changes dramatically, "Israel" has only positive connotations.

Christ's coming brought about what Wengst terms "a turning point in both religious economies."[37] The Church is now the true Israel, and the "the people who profess to be Jews" are in reality liars and members of the "synagogue of Satan." Once the term "Jew" is redefined, no further dialogue or compromise is possible. Jesus tells the "Jews," "Your father is Satan," and they repay the favor by determining to kill him, a decision which, Caron says, "confirms in dramatic fashion the diabolic identity of the Jews."[38]

Pseudo-Judaism—the term Caron proposes as synonymous with "*oi Ioudaioi*"—is responsible for the death of Christ. To remain Jews, Jews must accept Christ. Those who reject him become "the Jews," *i.e.,* representatives not of the religion of Abraham and Moses, but rather adherents of a new ideology, which within the generation following Christ's death became the main source of revolutionary ferment in the Roman empire. Despite the scepticism of those like Gamaliel (Acts 5:33-40) who urged caution both in relation to Christian and to other Messianic claims, the revolutionary ideology inexorably took hold. After this revolutionary ideology failed to conquer Rome, it went into dormancy for 1000 years only to re-emerge in Christian empires when the modern era began.

Attempting to put the Church's relationship with the Jews on a new footing after the Holocaust, the fathers of Vatican II issued *Nostra Aetate*, which said

> Even though the Jewish authorities and those who followed their lead pressed for the death of Christ (cf. John 19:6), neither all Jews indiscriminately at that time nor Jews today, can be charged with the crimes committed during his passion. It is true that the Church is the new people of God, yet the Jews should not be spoken of as rejected or accursed as if this followed from Holy Scripture.[39]

One extrapolation from this passage is that the murder of Christ was a crime committed by some Jews at the time of Christ. In describing those people, *Nostra Aetate* identifies "Jewish authorities and those who followed their lead." St. John identifies them as "the chief priests and the guards," who shouted "Crucify him! Crucify him!" when Pilate presented Jesus wearing a crown of thorns and a purple robe. In the narrative leading up to the Passion, St. John identifies them as "the Jews." Jesus Himself identifies the group which is planning to kill Him in John 8:39:

> "They [i.e., the "Jews] repeated, 'Our Father is Abraham.' Jesus said to them: 'If you were Abraham's children, you would do as Abraham did. As it is, you want to kill me when I tell you the truth.'"

The group "who want to kill me" also claims "we are descended from Abraham," i.e., that they are "Jews." And so those "Jews," with the collaboration of Pilate, killed Christ. Christ was killed not by "all Jews indiscriminately" but rather by the Jews who rejected Christ. According to Caron's reading, "the trial of Jesus and his condemnation is without equivocation the doing of the Jews ... it is not the 'world' which killed Jesus, but rather the Johannine Jews."[40] "It is particularly significant that all of the references to the death of Jesus implicate the 'Jews.'"[41] The conclusion, especially in light of *Nostra Aetate*, is inescapable: the "Jews" (what Caron calls "les Juifs johanniques") killed Christ.

"How great was the woe caused by that one execution!" writes Graetz in his history of the Jews:

> How many deaths and sufferings of every description has it not caused among the children of Israel. Millions of broken hearts and tragic fates have not yet atoned for his death. He is the only mortal of whom one can say without exaggeration that his death was more effective than his life.[42]

Graetz in typically Jewish fashion is referring to the Crusades, the Inquisition, the pogroms and all other nameless tragedies when Jews died at the hands of at least nominal Christians as the fruit of Christianity. He is also being Jewish, in the sense in which St. John defined the word, in seeing Christianity as the source of Jewish woe. Graetz was right in seeing the death of Christ as the beginning of Jewish woes, but that calamity was self-inflicted, as were some, at least, of its results. However infamous the behavior of "Christian" persecutors, the original source is to be found elsewhere. The source of Jewish woe was the revolutionary spirit that proceeded inexorably from rejection of Christ. It was also the spirit of revolution which prompted Jews to reject Christ in the first place, whether those wanting a revolution or those, like Caiaphas, wanting to prevent such a revolution, with all it would entail. Jews wanted a military leader who could defeat the Roman legions. They did not want a man that the Romans could put to death on the Cross. Of the Passion, Matthew writes:

> The passers-by jeered at him; they shook their heads and said, 'So you would destroy the Temple and rebuild it in three days! Then save yourself! If you are God's son, come down from the Cross!' The chief priests with the scribes and elders mocked him in the same way. 'He saved others,' they said, 'he cannot save himself. He is the king of Israel, let him come down from the Cross now, and we will believe in him.'"

Writing 1000 years after Christ's death, Maimonides established the criteria whereby his people could identify the Messiah. "If," he wrote,

> there arises a king from the House of David, versed in Torah [who] performs the commandments like David his ancestor...and wages a war of God, it is assumed that he is the Messiah. If he successfully does this and builds the Temple in its proper place and gathers the dispersed of Israel, behold, he is certainly the Messiah.[43]

Writing 800 years after Maimonides, Graetz says the same thing. "The only stumbling block to their ["Jewish"] belief lay in the fact that the Messiah who came to deliver Israel and bring to light the glory of the kingdom of heaven, endured a shameful death. How could the Messiah be subject to pain? A suffering Messiah staggered them considerably."[44]

Once again, the "Jews" defined themselves by their rejection of Christ, a decision with incalculable consequences. Once the "Jews" defined a suffering Christ as a contradiction in terms, they made their rejection of the Logos inevitable. And once they rejected the Logos, they paved the way for the rejection of all Logos. And once they did that, they embarked upon a path of revolutionary activity that brought woe upon them almost immediately. All of the acts of self-definition revolved around Christ; since the Jewish Messiah could not be a suffering servant, he had to be a warrior king. Since the Jews did not rule their own nation, that warrior king would have to be a revolutionary who would overthrow the dominant political culture. By the time of Maimonides, the definition had become axiomatic. If the claimant did not fulfill political and revolutionary criteria, he was, ipso facto, not the Messiah. The Messiah had to be a Revolutionary Jew. This, not persecution by Christians, was the deepest source of Jewish woe, because the revolutionary stance of the Jew, redefined throughout history from political insurrection to cultural subversion, brought on persecution in reaction: persecution affecting guilty and innocent alike.

By rejecting Logos, which was simultaneously the person of Christ and the order in the universe, including the moral order, which sprang from the divine mind, the "Jew" found himself drawn inexorably to revolution. The parents of the man born blind knew "the Jews ... had already agreed to expel from the synagogue anyone who should acknowledge Jesus as the Christ." Once the Christ was crucified, the "Jews" followed through on the threat. Brumlik states "the re-constitution of Judaism as rabbinical or pharisaical Judaism" began "with the introduction of the curse of the heretics of the 18 petition prayer."[45] This curse, which was leveled at new Christians, was formulated and implemented between 80 and 120 AD, which is when scholars say the Gospel of John was written. Judaism was a 'religio licita' or permitted religion—a religion freed from offering sacrifice to the emperor. Exclusion from the synagogue must have inflicted severe hardship on Jewish followers of Jesus, because they thus also lost protection and social membership.

Brumlik denies exclusion from the synagogues took place when St. John says, i.e., at the time of Christ. He admits it affected Christians; however, he fails to see the more devastating effect on the "Jews" when it turned the synagogue into a cell of revolutionary activity. After Christ, Zealot influence over the "Jews" grew in direct proportion to the number of Jews expelled from the synagogue. That process culminated in overt revolution when the Jews rebelled against Roman hegemony in 66 AD.

The process is simple to understand. "The fanatics keep pushing the envelope," says Kevin MacDonald, "forcing other Jews to either go along with their agenda or to simply cease being part of the Jewish community."[46] MacDonald is discussing the development of Zionism, but his description applies equally to those who threatened the parents of the man born blind with expulsion. This dynamic has been at work throughout "Jewish" history from the time of Christ. (MacDonald traces it back further.) The Jews who objected to the hysteria that reigned when the Jews proclaimed Sabbetai Zevi their Messiah were expelled from the synagogue, too. Some left town to save life and limb. In both instances, "the most radical elements" in the Jewish community "end up pulling the entire community in their direction."[47]

"The radicals who determined the direction of the Jewish community" after Christ's death were known as Zealots. Jews who followed Jesus were expelled from the synagogue, just as today: "Jews living in the Diaspora who do not support the aims of the Likud Party in Israel" are "being rooted out of the Jewish community."[48] Following Christ's death, the "Jews" became progressively more committed to revolutionary activity, which is to say, military operations, to throw off the yoke of Roman hegemony. The inexorable movement of the Jewish people toward revolution began when, as Matthew puts it, "The chief priests and elders ... persuaded the crowd to demand the release of Barabbas and the execution of the Jesus." It was ratified when Annas and Caiaphas told Christ they could accept him as the Messiah if he came down from the Cross. The rejection of Christ was intimately bound up with the acceptance of Barabbas, the Zealot, i.e., choosing the revolutionary Jew over the suffering Christ. In choosing Barabbas, the "Jews" chose revolution. In rejecting Christ, the "Jews" chose revolution, setting in motion events that led to Masada and greater tragedy beyond. Graetz cites Flavius Josephus, the assimilated Jew who wrote *The Jewish Wars,* as an authority to establish the role of messianic revolutionary politics in the revolt against Rome: "According to Josephus, it was chiefly the belief in the imminent advent of a messianic king that launched the Jews upon the suicidal war which ended with the capture of Jerusalem and the destruction of the temple in AD 70. Even Simon bar-Kokhba, who led the last great struggle for national independence in AD 131, was still greeted as Messiah."[49]

The insurrection of 66 AD began when Florus, a grasping, blundering Roman ruler, used a small riot in Jerusalem as a pretext for looting the Temple. The Jews rushed to defend the Temple, hurling stones at the Roman soldiers, barring their passage through the narrow entrance, and demolishing the colonnade leading from Fort Antonia. The revolution started inadvertently, but the way had already been prepared. The combination of Roman arrogance and Jewish expectation of the coming of a military Messiah made conflict inevitable.

The Jewish population was divided between the Zealots and the peace party clustered around the rabbinical school of Hillel, among whom were King Agrippa and Princess Berenice. "[T]he party that favored revolution," clustered around the more rigorous school of Shammai.[50] When Florus' sack of the Temple was thwarted by popular resistance and the future of Jerusalem hung in the balance, Agrippa mounted the high gallery opposite the Temple, with the popular Princess Berenice at his side, and tried to persuade the people further resistance was futile and would lead to disaster. Many were moved by his arguments and felt that Roman hegemony without Florus might be workable, so Agrippa concentrated his rhetoric there. But when Agrippa tried to persuade the Jews to obey Florus until Rome replaced him, "the revolutionary party again won the upper hand, and Agrippa was obliged to flee from Jerusalem."[51]

The revolutionaries then controlled the Jewish people, who refused to pay taxes to Rome. Menahem, a descendant of Judas, the founder of the Zealots, captured the fortress of Masada, putting the Roman garrison to death. After grabbing the Roman arsenal, Menahem and his followers appeared on the field of battle to drive the Roman legions from Palestine.

Eleazar, leader of the Zealots, led his followers into the field, too. He "fanned the revolutionary spirit of the people and drove them on to complete rupture with Rome."[52] He persuaded the Jewish priests to stop offering the daily sacrifice for the emperor Nero, thus committing them to the revolution. Adherents of the school of Hillel claimed that it was unlawful to refuse the offerings of the heathen from the Temple, but their pleas fell on deaf ears. "The officiating priests ... threw themselves without reserve into the maelstrom of revolution. From that time on, the Temple obeyed its chief, Eleazar, and became the hotbed of insurrection."[53] Hoping to avert draconian measures from the Romans, Agrippa sent his cavalry to fight alongside of the remnants of the Roman garrison in Judaea, but they could not dislodge Eleazar and the Zealots from the Temple. The Zealots' counterattack drove the Romans from the city. The Sicarii, the terrorist faction under Menahem, named after their daggers, broke through the defenses of the fort where the Romans made their last stand and slaughtered them. The revolution liberated Jerusalem for a time.

Gravely underestimating the threat the Jewish revolutionaries posed, Nero dispatched his general Cestius, who left Antioch and descended on Jerusalem with 30,000 experienced soldiers. Like Nero, Cestius underestimated the revolutionary fervor of the Jews and mistakenly engaged them before the walls of Jerusalem, where they inflicted a stunning defeat on the Roman legions.

The emperor Nero, in Greece singing to the crowds and impressing them with his skill as a charioteer, trembled upon learning of Cestius' defeat, "for the revolution in Judaea might be the precursor of grave events."[54] The idea of revolution was essentially Jewish, practiced by Jews who had liberated their country from Rome, but it could be extrapolated and refined to apply to other nations. The Jewish revolutionaries posed a much greater threat to Roman hegemony than the rebellious members of other tribes, where issues never transcended the local.

The Jewish revolutionaries posed another threat because, like the Jews in Rome on Mount Vatican, there were colonies of Jews throughout the empire. Each was a potential revolutionary cell, emboldening Jews not only to revolt, but urging other subjugated ethnic groups to revolt too. The Jewish revolutionary vision was both ethnocentric and altruistic. As God's chosen people, they bore revolutionary liberation to the nations. Jewish revolutionaries saw themselves as the little stone that would shatter the Roman colossus not just for their own benefit but also for the benefit of the benighted gentiles, who would seek their own liberation under Jewish auspices.

So Nero had reason to tremble. He chose as the successor to the arrogant but unfortunate Cestius, Flavius Vespasian, who had subdued the barbaric Britons, and was one of the ablest generals of his age. Vespasian arrived in Judaea with almost twice as many soldiers as Cestius, but he arrived cautiously. Rather than meet the revolutionary Jews in open battle, where their enthusiasm could compensate for their lack of military experience, Vespasian cut the ground from under them one fortress at a time, knowing that in a landlocked nation, every hand that wielded a sword did not guide a plow. A long siege meant no planting or harvest. The Romans controlled the ocean; starvation became their most powerful weapon, as one city after another fell.

Although the Jews were losing the war, the remnant fleeing to Jerusalem, thought the city impregnable. The idea of Messianic revolution, not the size of their army, sustained the Jews. The Jews were "stimulated by their ardent belief that the Messianic period so long foretold by the prophets, was actually dawning, when every other nation of the earth would be given to the dominion of Israel."[55]

Not everyone was filled with enthusiasm. According to Graetz, "only the very young and men of no worldly position devoted themselves to the cause of the revolutionists."[56] The more sensible and the more prosperous were ready to capitulate and throw themselves on the mercy of the Romans. As the glow of the initial victories faded and the folly of rebelling against Rome became more apparent, the peace party became emboldened. Jewish adherents of the cause of Rome wrapped intelligence reports around the shafts of arrows and fired them into the Roman camp.

In February of the year 70 A.D., when Titus, son of Vespasian and heir to the imperial throne, appeared before Jerusalem, the city had maintained its independence for four years, a scandal to Rome that Titus had to resolve. Titus intended to deal leniently with the Jews, asking only that they acknowledge Rome's sovereignty and pay taxes, but the Jews refused. So Titus resolved to show no mercy. In March, Titus's army breached the outer wall of Jerusalem and seized the town of Bezetha. His offer of leniency spurned, Titus turned to cruelty to intimidate the besieged, crucifying 500 prisoners in a single day. Other prisoners he sent back with their hands cut off. Famine, more than Roman arms or cruelty, was taking a toll on the city, causing many Jews to surrender; they were then butchered. Cruelty was piled upon cruelty, but each time Titus called for negotiations he ran into the brick wall of Jewish messianism. John of Gischala was convinced that God would not abandon his people; he led the Jews into their last defensive position, the Temple itself, where they held off the Romans by setting fire to their own buildings.

When Jesus went to the Temple in Jerusalem for the last time He drew a different lesson from Daniel's messianic prophecies than the Zealots did. Discussing the Temple, Jesus told his disciples "not a single stone here will be left on another; everything will be destroyed." Jesus wept because the lost sheep of the house of Israel had chosen revolutionary politics, a decision that spelled catastrophe for the very people he came to save. "Jerusalem, Jerusalem, you that kill the prophets and stone those who are sent to you! How often have I longed to gather your children, as a hen gathers her chicks under her wings and you refused. So be it! Your house will be left to you desolate." The image of Christ as the mother hen spurned by her offspring found grim fulfillment a generation after his death when a woman who had fled to Jerusalem was driven beyond endurance by hunger and killed and devoured her own child. It was, Graetz remarked without irony, "as if not one line of the old prophecy concerning the doom of Judaea was to remain unfulfilled."[57]

Titus, sensing victory, decided to take the Temple without destroying it, but God had other plans. In August 70, one of the Roman soldiers who had beaten back a furious sally by the Jews climbed onto a comrade's back and hurled a flaming torch through the window of the Temple, where it set fire to the wooden beams of the sanctuary. Soon the whole Temple was in flames. Titus ordered his troops to extinguish the blaze, but no one heeded him. Seized by the same curiosity that had gripped Pompey a Century earlier, Titus made his way into the Holy of Holies. Titus was the last to gaze on the empty shrine at the heart of the Temple that would disappear, never to be rebuilt. Julian the Apostate tried to re-build the Temple 300 years later but the workmen were stymied by fire and brimstone explosions and work soon ceased. In the mid-1900s, Israel was restored as a nation in an act that the Jews of Middle Ages would have found astounding, but the Temple never got rebuilt. Titus had the last glimpse of the last remnant of the Jewish religion that revolved around Temple sacrifice. Judaism would be reconstituted as a religion of the book after the altar of sacrifice was destroyed.

As Titus contemplated the demise of something larger than he could understand in the Jewish Holy of Holies, the slaughter continued unabated in the Temple courtyard.

> Congregated clusters of trembling people from all the country beheld in the ascending flames the sign that the glory of their nation had departed forever. Many inhabitants of Jerusalem, unwilling to outlive their beloved Temple, cast themselves headlong into the fire. But thousands of men, women and children clung fondly to the inner court. Had they not been promised by the persuasive lips of false prophets, that God would save them by a miracle at the very moment of destruction? They fell but an easier prey to the Romans, who slew 6,000 on the spot. The Temple was burnt to the ground; only a few smoldering ruins were left, rising like gigantic ghosts from the ashes. A few priests escaped to the tops of the walls, where they remained without food for some days until they were compelled to surrender. Titus ordered their instant execution, saying "Priests must fall with their Temple." The conquering legions raised their standards in the midst of the ruins, sacrificed to their gods in the Holy Place and saluted Titus as emperor. By a strange coincidence the second Temple had fallen upon the anniversary of the destruction of the first Temple.[58]

"When you see the disastrous abomination of which the prophet Daniel spoke up in the holy place, ... then those in Judaea must escape to the mountains.... For then there will be great distress such as, until now, since the world began, there never has been nor never will be again."

Within two months, Titus leveled Jerusalem's walls and established three camps to capture and execute the escaping soldiers. More than a million lives were lost in the siege. So many Jewish women and children were put on the block that the price for slaves collapsed. The Menorah, the golden table, and the scroll of the Law were taken as booty to Rome along with the mighty Jewish warrior Simon bar Giora, who was dragged through the streets of Rome and then thrown from the Tarpeian rock in sacrifice to the gods.

While it seemed the Jewish nation had perished in the aftermath of the siege, a remnant escaped to the Diaspora communities in Arabia, Egypt, and Cyrene, whence they took both their hatred of Rome and their revolutionary messianic politics. A remnant of the peace party also escaped. Sensing the revolution was leading to catastrophe, Jochanan ben Zakkai had himself smuggled out of besieged Jerusalem as a corpse wrapped in a shroud. When Titus' Jewish spies informed him that Jochanan was a friend of Rome, the Roman general granted him one request. Jochanan asked for permission to start a school. From this school, the new religion of Judaism arose. The Jews had no Temple, no burnt offerings, no priesthood, and no Sanhedrin or ruling body. All they had was a book, and out of this book they created a new religion. The role of the rabbi was now to comment on the book. The commentary was known as Talmud, which became the basis of the new Jewish religion.

The Jewish revolutionaries lived on their fantasies of messianic omnipotence, even when messianic politics brought catastrophe to the Jewish people. The school of Jochanan and Hillel and the other friends of Rome, however, craved an opposite good, survival. The basis of their religion was the Pentateuch, upon which they built a superstructure of commentary. The Law guaranteed survival, but survival often dictated what was going to be the Law.

The political factions among the Jews became critical schools following the destruction of the Temple. The school of Shammai, having espoused the cause of the Zealots, now returned to espousing rigorism in scriptural exegesis. The School of Hillel became the school of peace with the Romans. After the Jewish religion was re-defined as a religion of the book, or of competing interpretations of the book, these two schools would define the options for generations of Jews. There would be Jews drawn to assimilation, after the model of Jochanan and Hillel, and there would be Jews drawn to political messianism, after the model of Eleazar the Zealot and the school of Shammai. Jewish life oscillated between these poles for two millennia, and the two options manifest themselves in various ways: Roy Cohn urging the death sentence for the Rosenbergs during the McCarthy era; or in contrast, Spinoza's excommunication by Rabbi Menasseh ben Israel's synagogue in Amsterdam. Jews could emulate Moses Mendelssohn on the one hand, or Theodor Herzl on the other; they could emulate David Brooks or Noam Chomsky.

Unfortunately, there was no way to adjudicate competing interpretations. The various interpretations were not organized on any scientific framework. The "Halacha" were deduced from the Pentateuch and appended randomly, handed down separately usually joined to the name of the authority from whom they were derived. They were then memorized and repeated, spawning new interpretations which were then strung together, memorized and repeated. There was no way to adjudicate between the authorities when they differed. This led to averroeism, the notion that the mind could hold two contradictory truths, both of which were right. During a contentious debate between the schools of Shammai and Hillel, a voice from heaven announced "the teachings of both schools are the words of the living God, but practically the laws of Hillel only are to carry weight."[59] At another point, the rabbis concluded: "Every man according to his choice may follow the school of Hillel or of Shammai, but the decision of the school of Hillel shall be the only accepted interpretation of the Law."[60] By becoming a religion of the book, Judaism subverted the book upon which it was based: "The contentions between the schools, which extended to various practical matters, brought about wide divergence in the view with regard to the Law and life. One teacher held some things to be permissible which another forbade. Thus, Judaism seemed to have two bodies of laws, or, according to the words of the Talmud—'The One Law had become two.'"[61]

With directives like this, the relationships between the schools became more acrimonious. By putting a premium on Jewish survival, the school of accommodation could not resolve its own disputes effectively. The Talmudic commentary was based ultimately upon the law, but the commentary often contradicted what it commented on. "The written Law (that of the Pentateuch) and the oral Law (the Sopheric) from this time ceased to be two widely sundered branches, but were brought into close relations with each other, although the new rendering *certainly did violence to the words of Scripture.*"[62] As a result, the rabbis expected to achieve unity without truth. Dissenters were expelled from the synagogue; the rabbis had to be obeyed even if they were wrong. When Joshua showed that Gamaliel's calculation for the commencement of the month of Tishri, during which the day of Atonement was celebrated, was false, Gamaliel refused to yield and threatened Joshua with expulsion from the synagogue. To preserve unity, Dossa ben Harchinas persuaded Joshua to yield, reasoning "that the arrangements of a religious chief must be uncontested even if they are erroneous."[63] With thought like this in the party of peace and accommodation, the political messianism of the Zealots soon burst into flame again.

In 115, the Jews of Babylon revolted against Rome. The revolt soon spread. In Cyrenaica, the Jews slaughtered 200,000 Greeks and Romans. In Cyprus, where 240,000 Greeks were slain, the revolutionary Jews leveled Salamis. So great was the local revulsion in Cyprus that the Jews living there were exterminated 30 years later. After that, a law decreed that no Jew would be allowed to set foot on the island, not even Jews shipwrecked off its coast.

The normally docile Jews in Egypt were also seized with revolutionary fervor, indiscriminately massacring Greeks and Romans. After plundering towns near Alexandria, the Jews boldly attacked the Roman army under the general Lupus. In their first encounter, the revolutionary spirit of the Jews triumphed over the military experience of the Romans, and Lupus fled. When terrorized Greeks and Romans took to ship on the Nile, the Jews followed them bent on revenge. The historian Appian, living then in Alexandria, wrote an account that "gives some idea of the terror excited by the Jewish populations."[64] The Jews "are said to have eaten the flesh of the captive Greeks and Romans, to have smeared themselves in the skins torn off them." Graetz finds this difficult to believe because these actions "are quite foreign to Jewish character and customs." However, he concedes, "it is probably true that the Jews made the Romans and Greeks fight with wild animals or in the arena."[65] He characterizes this as "a sad reprisal" for what Titus and Vespasian did after the rebellion of 66.[66]

In Judaea, the rebellion was led by Julianus and Pappus, Jews from Alexandria. Like his predecessor Nero, Trajan especially feared the rebellious Jews because Jewish revolution was never merely local and because there were Jewish colonies throughout the Empire since it was based on the Jewish messianic idea applicable to all oppressed ethnic groups. Then, as during the Bolshevik revolution in Russia, the Jews in the revolutionary vanguard could mobilize far greater numbers because of the message of Jewish revolution—the messianic idea they had derived from Daniel, the idea of resistance to political authority they had derived from Maccabees, and the idea of deliverance they had derived from Exodus—had universal application. Jesus' statement, "Salvation is from the Jews," would take on a political significance unintended by Jesus as Jews gravitated toward leadership in one revolutionary movement after another. The revolution against Rome was the first post-Christian attempt to put revolutionary Jewish principles into practice. The Jews—Trajan probably understood this—were motivated by an idea that was every bit as powerful as the idea of Rome. As a result, Trajan sent the cruel Moor Quietus to crush the rebellion.

Trajan died in 117; news of his death fanned the rebellion into an inferno that threatened to bring the empire down in flames. Captive nations seemed caught up in revolution, willing to test it with their lives against Rome's military might. Trajan's successor Hadrian lacked the brutal will of his predecessors. He arranged limited self-government for the provinces to the East and was even open to making concessions to the Jews. Quietus was called back to Rome and, in a gesture of reconciliation with the Jews, was executed at the command of the emperor. In peace negotiations, the Jews asked Hadrian for permission to rebuild their Temple. Hadrian, to their surprise and delight, acceded. What followed, however, were years of broken promises by Hadrian and unfulfilled expectations for the Jews. Hadrian had second thoughts. Magnanimity to subjugated peoples was unprecedented imperial behavior. The Jews became more impatient and more inclined to act on their growing revolutionary fervor.

In 130, Hadrian came to Palestine to meet the rebellious Jews. The Samaritans, who probably worshiped him as a god to curry favor, soon began to poison his mind, claiming reconstruction of the Temple was the first step the Jews planned to declare independence from Rome. As a result, Hadrian backed away from his promises. The Jews could build their Temple, but not on the original site or on a scale as large as the original. The Jews, "filled with the idea of rebellion" anyway, were not disposed to put up with Hadrian's prevarication.

Hadrian remained in Syria for a year. When he left for Egypt, he thought the issue was resolved. Jerusalem would be rebuilt as a pagan city, which would hasten the assimilation of the Jewish race into the Roman Empire. Racial and religious differences would disappear. All would be Romans, nothing more, nothing less. The Jewish revolutionaries, however, were plotting rebellion. The Romans' weapons, fashioned by Jewish armaments makers, were deliberately weak and meant to fail in battle, because the Jews knew they would have to face them soon.

Hadrian's departure was the signal for rebellion. Well planned, it broke out seemingly miraculously, taking Hadrian by surprise. Equally miraculous was the emergence from nowhere of Simon bar Kokhba, the military leader of the Jews. Virtually nothing is known about him, other than his name. Kokhba (or Cochba) means "star," as the "star which has arisen in David." Kokhba was a play on his real name, Bar-Kosiba, referring to the town of his birth. For a short time, bar Kokhba was the terror of the Roman Empire, a military figure not unlike Hannibal, another Semite whose daring and skill threatened the Roman Empire. Like Hannibal, bar Kokhba threatened Roman hegemony over the Mediterranean.

Because he personified the military leader they had longed for, the Jews proclaimed Simon bar Kokhba their Messiah. In him, the "Jews" found everything they thought lacking in Christ. Bar Kokhba was "the perfect incarnation of the nation's will and the nation's hate, spreading terror around and standing as the center-point of an eventful movement."[67] Bar Kokhba was the Messiah that the Jews wanted because he "turned the small, defeated Jewish nation into a mighty force that, for a short while, pushed back the mightiest empire the world has ever known."[68] Resnick adds without the slightest sense of irony "Bar Kokhba was a glimpse into the future, a glimpse that enabled the Jews to know that one day, the Messiah will truly come."[69]

Bar Kokhba was proclaimed Messiah by Rabbi Akiba, who also gave him the name "star." Akiba "was confirmed ... in his hopes that the Roman power would soon be overthrown, and that the splendors of Israel would once more shine forth, and he looked forward through this means to the speedy establishment of the Messianic kingdom."[70] Bar Kokhba was proclaimed Messiah largely because the "Jews," by expelling the Christian Jews from their synagogues, had become revolutionaries who defined their Messiah in exclusively political and military terms: "The outstanding quality that is attributed to [the Messiah] is that when his identity is revealed, the kings of the land will tremble when they hear of it; they will fear and shake and their kingdoms will plot how to stand against him, by sword or other means."[71] Of course, according to a counter tradition, the false Messiah "causes Israel to be slain by the sword, to scatter those who remain, and to humiliate them. He abolishes the Torah and deceives most of the world to serve a deity other than God."[72] Again, the Jews had no way to adjudicate competing claims; revolutionary fervor ended the debate by sweeping everyone into a movement headed for disaster.

As when Sabbetai Zevi was declared the Messiah in 1666, the verdict was virtually unanimous, but not completely. Rabbi Jochanan Ben Torta remained skeptical. When he heard Akiba had proclaimed Bar Kokhba the Messiah, he exclaimed, "Sooner shall grass grow from thy chin, Akiba, than that the Messiah will appear."[73] But his voice was ignored, as the Jews had ignored prophets like Jeremiah, who had warned: "do not rebel against the government; do not try to hasten the End of Days, do not reveal the mysteries of Torah and do not leave the Diaspora by force; otherwise, why should the Messiah have to come."[74] Bar Kokhba did what Jeremiah forbade, but the all but unanimous acclaim he received as Messiah increased his power and helped him unite the Jewish people.

Bar Kokhba demanded that all Christian Jews deny Jesus and make war against the Romans. Those who refused were declared traitors, punished with heavy penalties. The process that had begun when the parents of the man born blind were threatened with expulsion from the synagogue reached its completion. Now there was no longer any question. To be a Jew meant to be a revolutionary. Ethnos and religion disappeared into the political ideology of the revolutionary movement, which would henceforth masquerade, depending on the circumstances, as both ethnos and religion. The Jewish Christians were considered blasphemers and spies, because "they refused to take part in the national war."[75] Bar Kokhba was not only the alternative to Christ, he also fulfilled Christ's prophecy that others would come "saying I am Christ, and shall deceive many." Bar Kokhba's coming was accompanied by "wars and rumors of wars," at a time when the Christian Jews were going to be beaten in the synagogues, and when they were hated by all. Christ also predicted unprecedented suffering, a prediction the Jewish Christians kept alive as their co-ethnics got swept up in the hysteria and euphoria leading to war.

After Akiba proclaimed Bar Kokhba the Messiah, Jewish warriors from throughout the Roman Empire poured into Jerusalem to fight at his side. Jewish sources claim Bar Kokhba had 400,000 troops. Dio Cassius, the pagan historian, puts the number at 580,000. To test his troops' ferocity and obedience, Bar Kokhba asked them to bite off the end of a finger, and 200,000 complied. The size of the army was impressive, but when combined with the fervor of the revolutionary ideology and significant numbers of heathens who made common cause with the Jews, the "revolt became one of great dimensions," and the entire Roman empire was in jeopardy from a blow "by which the various members of its gigantic body were to be rent asunder."[76] According to Dio Cassius, "All Judaea had been stirred up. Many other nations joined them for personal gain. The whole earth, one might say, was stirred up in the matter."[77]

The rebellion of Bar Kokhba was no local matter; it was a struggle over who was going to rule the world. Jewish revolutionary thought never settled for a smaller stage. The same was true of Bolshevism and Neoconservatism; each had the same universal scope. *Aut munda aut nihil* could have been the motto of Jewish revolution. Once the Talmud became the essence of the redefinition of Judaism as anti-Christian, Judaism espoused a political view antithetical to what it perceived as Christian otherworldiness. It committed the Jews to Messianic politics. According to Resnick's reading of the Talmud, "the major distinction of the Messianic era will be political."[78] The Talmud looked forward to heaven on earth when a political Messiah would reign over a universal political system. Resnick's account of that millennial era shows its uncanny similarities to the Jewish utopias proposed by Marx, Trotsky, and the Neoconservatives:

> The Messianic Era will herald the onset of a single, universal political system, with the Messiah at its helm. There will no longer be localized concern over natural resources. The spirit of universal cooperation and brotherhood will reign supreme. There will no longer be the need to accumulate wealth.... There will no longer be diverse cultures and philosophies. Just as in the very beginning of

time, a single man was created, so, too in the end of days, all Mankind will unite as a single entity. There will no longer be the need for war.[79]

Finally, the millennial universal revolutionary political system will abolish the nations because:

> History has taught us that in a world divided into various nations, no nation can achieve eternal independence or perpetual self-reliance. But in a one-world political entity, true independence can be achieved. Man can turn his focus to the realm of the spirit and strive for moral perfection and intellectual excellence. The Messianic Era will usher in the rebirth of virtue, a renaissance of spirituality and an understanding of God's will. The world will experience a spiritual revival that will result in the perfection of the human condition. Man will achieve the same state of godliness as on the day he was created. "The wolf shall dwell with the lamb."[80]

With huge numbers of Jews pouring into Judaea and a revolutionary fervor to match their number, the "warlike Messiah" drove the Roman legions out of Palestine. The Governor of Judaea was stunned by the size and power of the military force arrayed against him. He retreated under its blows, abandoning in the first year 50 fortresses and 985 towns and villages. Like Nero who watched the impetuous Cestius go down to defeat in 66, Hadrian had to send one general after another packing before he found someone the equal of Bar Kokhba, who, in the ultimate act of defiance, had coins struck bearing his image. Known as Bar-Kokhba coins or more tellingly "coins of the revolution," they made explicit what was already obvious to the entire world. The Jews had defied Rome and created their own state. They were a model to any other ethnic group which felt oppressed by Rome, and as such they were a threat to the existence of Rome itself. The Jewish revolution had thrown off the Roman yoke. Akiba was right: Bar Kokhba had proven he was the Messiah.

In Julius Severus, who had just put down a rebellion in Britain, Hadrian eventually found the general who was Bar Kokhba's equal. Arriving in Judaea, Severus found the Jews so firmly entrenched that a quick and decisive victory was out of the question. Like the less impetuous and more effective of his predecessors, Severus took advantage of Roman control of the seas and put hunger to work as his most effective weapon. With the blockade in place, Severus reconquered Judaea one village and town at a time.

During Severus' campaign, which lasted years and extended over more than 50 battles, the tide turned against Bar Kokhba. Rabbi Akiba was captured and executed after an extended stay in prison. Deemed strategically indefensible, Jerusalem was abandoned to the Romans, and on the 9th of Ab (August), the day on which the second Temple had been destroyed in 70 AD, the Roman governor plowed up the Temple mount and offered sacrifice there to Roman gods. It was not a good omen.

The Jews retreated to the fortress of Bethar, and there, like their Messianic forebears who had perched atop Masada 70 years before, they assumed that God would protect them. The Romans settled in for a year-long siege which was to be the culmination of a three and a half years war of attrition. Eusebius states that Bethar was besieged in the 18th year of Hadrian's reign (134 AD), about two years after the revolt, and that its fall was caused by hunger and thirst.

The Jews almost outlasted the Romans. According to one account, Bar Kokhba snatched defeat from the jaws of victory by kicking the pious Eleazar, whose prayers were holding off the Romans, and whom he suspected of conniving with a Samaritan spy. When Eleazar died, a voice was heard from heaven saying, "thou hast lamed the arm of Israel and blinded his eyes; therefore shall thine arm and thine eye lose their power."[81]

Another account says the Romans were ready to call off the siege when two Samaritan brothers imprisoned by the Jews threw a detailed map of the city's subterranean passages over the city's walls to the Romans. Taking advantage of the Sabbath, Roman soldiers forced their way into the city, and a bloodbath ensued. Horses were said to wade through blood up to their nostrils. The tide of blood was said to have washed bodies to the sea. Dio Cassius claims that half a million Jews were slaughtered in addition to those who died of fire and starvation. The Romans suffered great losses too, but Bar Kokhba was captured; his head was brought to Harain. Bethar fell on the most fateful date in Jewish history, the 9th of Ab.

The Jewish population of Judaea was largely exterminated in the repression that followed Bethar's fall. Hadrian established three military stations to capture the fugitives and execute them; women and children were sold into slavery in the markets of Hebron and Gaza, as in the first revolt. Towns that offered any resistance were leveled; Judaea was "literally converted into a desert."[82] Those who could escape went to Arabia, where their descendants played a role in the rise of Islam. In place of Jerusalem, Hadrian built Aelia Capitolina, a new city slightly to the north in the Greek style. On the Temple Mount, instead of the temple promised to the Jews, Hadrian erected a column in his own honor and a temple in honor of Jupiter Capitolinus. So completely was Jerusalem eradicated that "a hundred years later a governor of Palestine asked a bishop, who said he came from Jerusalem, where that town was situated."[83]

The catastrophe following the short violent reign of the Messiah Bar Kokhba did not bring an end to the Jewish people—although it almost did just that—but it did end Jewish messianic politics for a while. For more than one thousand years, during which Christianity supplanted Rome and established its hegemony over Europe, the Jewish revolutionaries largely held their peace. The bloody suppression of the Bar Kokhba revolution brought about "the annihilation of political nationalism" which "put an end both to the apocalyptic faith and to the militancy of the Jews."[84]

Hadrian made a lasting impression on the Jews. After his governor plowed up the Temple Mount, the Jews concentrated on survival. The religion of the book took a back seat to the religion of ethnocentric survival, which would henceforth dictate the meaning of the book. Once again, the rabbis disputed one another. One group claimed "every Jew ... should be ready to die the death of a martyr."[85] The faction of Shammai, though, said, "outwardly and under compulsion, one might transgress the Law in order to preserve one's life."[86] The assembly at Lydda took a middle course, distinguishing between "important precepts and those which are less weighty." Finally a decision was reached that "all laws might be broken, with the exception of those prohibiting idolatry, adultery, and murder" in order "to avoid death by torture."[87] Graetz comments: "It was touching to note the petty tricks and pious frauds by which they endeavored to avoid death and yet to satisfy their conscience. The mental tortures which they suffered daily and hourly made them skillful in discovering loopholes of escape."[88]

The search for loopholes became a defining characteristic of the Jewish race. The law could henceforth be transgressed in the interest of survival. As one example:

> The two authorities of Tiberias, Jonah and Jose, taught that it was lawful to bake for Ursicinus on the Sabbath, and the teachers of Neve, a Gaulanite town, permitted leavened bread to be baked for the legions during Passover. In their distress the religious representatives quieted their consciences with the excuse, which they deluded themselves into believing, that the enemy did not expressly demand the transgression of the law, but simply required the regular supply of the army. But Ursicinus' intention appears really to have been to institute a religious persecution. [89]

The notion that "it is better, for a time, religious laws should be transgressed"[90] was not endorsed by Jews who became Christians. Christians died rather than offer incense to the emperor. Many died rather than violate their faith. They were known as "martyrs," which means "witnesses." And those who listened to their witness often concluded that they died believing their faith to be true, which led many to accept their faith.

The opposite conclusion applies to the Jews. If they were not willing to die for their religion, then it was probably not true. It was as if the Jews understood that with the fall of the Temple they had created a new religion, and that no one was willing to put his life on the line to attest to its authenticity. Jewish religion became a religion of ethnic survival, which became its highest good. The notion that survival somehow allowed the transgression of religious laws found no precedent in scripture. The books of Daniel and Maccabees show that a Jew must accept death rather than transgress the law of God. Christians now hold this position, but not the Jews. The fact that Christians took the position of Daniel and the Maccabees while the Jews repudiated it shows the continuity from Moses to the Church, as Christ indicated, not from Moses "to those who call themselves Jews," in St. John's words.

Graetz mocks the Jewish penchant for discovering "loopholes of escape," but he ignores the role it played in handing victory over Rome to the Christians.[91] By siding with Bar Kokhba, the rabbis made the split with their Christian co-ethnics inevitable and bitter when it finally came. The Christians conquered Rome because they had been expelled from the synagogue. Had they remained in the synagogue, they would have undoubtedly been compromised by the religion of ethnic survival, which compromised everything it came in contact with, including the Torah, its nominal basis and *raison d'etre*. "From the time of Hadrian," we are told, "all connection between Jews and Christians ceased."[92] The Bar Kokhba Revolution made the split final and irrevocable. As if to show their independence, the Christians chose an uncircumcised heathen as their bishop. Jews and Christians, henceforth, "no longer occupied the position of two hostile bodies belonging to the same house, but they became two entirely distinct bodies."[93] Paganism, a religion nourished by and in turn breeding "irrational ideas, deceit, and immorality,"[94] was replaced inevitably by ethical monotheism. Mankind cannot pretend it doesn't know certain things. Once Jewish religion and Greek philosophy were transmitted throughout the Mediterranean basin by Roman infrastructure, mankind could not return to placating irrational and petulant gods. Revulsion at Jewish revolutionary excess and contempt at the supine behavior that often followed it meant that heathens would not accept the religion of the "Jews" either. That left Christianity, the revised and renewed religion of Moses, Abraham, and Christ, alone in the field. After years of contention, Rome submitted to baptism. Following Constantine's conversion, "the last thread" connecting "Christianity with its parent stock" snapped at the Council of Nicaea when the Church decided that it would not rely on the Jewish calendar to calculate the date of Easter. "For," Constantine wrote, "it is unbecoming beyond measure that on this the holiest of festivals we should follow the custom of the Jews. Henceforward, let us have nothing in common with this odious people; our Savior has shown us another path."[95] Citing Constantine, Graetz claims "The first utterance of Christianity on the very day of its victory betrayed its hostile attitude towards the Jews and gave rise to those malignant decrees of Constantine and his successors, which laid the foundation of the bloody persecution of subsequent centuries."[96]

But history belies his claim. Persecution of the Jews was, as at the time of Masada and Bethar, a function of revolutionary activity. It was oftentimes a reaction to Jewish participation in revolutionary activity, as in Cyprus during the second Century and in Eastern Europe in the 1920s and 1930s. But the idea of revolution has a life of its own. The temptation to "judaize" has never left Christianity, and Christian writers who understood the pull of the "Jewish" idea denounced Judaizers as dogs that returned to their vomit. In the Middle Ages, as Christian cultural hegemony over Europe reached its zenith, the Jewish idea of heaven on earth would burst forth again. The dogs would return to their vomit, and Jews would be the first to feel its effects.

Chapter Two

Julian the Apostate and the Doomed Temple

It is one of the ironies of history that Flavius Claudius Julianus, the Roman emperor who was the scion of the dynasty that acknowledged Christianity as the religion religion of Rome, should come to be known to us as Julian the Apostate. Born in the year 331, Julian was raised a Christian, but watching his relatives get slaughtered by nominally Christian relatives soured him on Christianity. He never knew Basilina, his mother, who died within months of his birth. His father was a distant figure, caught up in the administration of the empire, who had Julian raised by servants until his father was murdered by Constantius II, Julian's cousin and Constantine's successor. Ricciotti says Julian "seems never to have fully recovered from this tragic shock which influenced many of his decisions in later life."[1]

When Constantine the Great died on May 22, 337, Constantius II resolved any doubts about imperial succession by brute force, murdering his rivals. In his *Life of Constantine*, Eusebius of Caesarea claims "the slaughters had their origin in a spontaneous decision of the soldiers throughout the empire,"[2] but St. Jerome, St. Athanasius, and Zosimus agreed with Julian, who held Constantius II responsible. Julian escaped death because of his age—he was six years old when Constantine died—but later gave full expression to the feeling he nurtured for throughout his life: "And what this most beneficent emperor did for us who were so closely related to him! Six of our common cousins, his uncle, my father, and another on our father's side, and my eldest brother, he put to death without a trial. My other brothers and I, whom he had intended to kill, were eventually sent into exile."[3]

Because Julian held Constantius II responsible for the murder of his relatives, his hatred gradually transformed itself into a overwhelming desire for revenge against Constantius II and his religion, Christianity. Julian also lost his inherited property, which passed to Constantius II, his Christian—albeit Arian—cousin. (Constantius II, whose reign saw a resurgence of the Arian heresy, was Christian by self-designation only. Like Constantine, he put off baptism until his death bed.) Julian hated Christianity "not by any philosophic or abstract reason but by the fact that his murderous cousin was a Christian."[4] His revulsion would grow with time.

Constantius II sent Julian to Nicomedia for education, where he was taught by Mardonius, his mother's former tutor. Julian learned the poetry of Homer and Hesiod as well as the philosophy of Plato, Socrates, Aristotle, and Theophrastus. Julian must have received instruction in Christianity there too.

Mardonius accompanied Julian to Macellum, where Julian was baptized and where he and his brother were enrolled in the Christian clergy in the minor order of lector. Julian read the Scriptures in the assemblies. At Macellum, Julian learned the habit of duplicity that remained with him for his entire life. Although baptized, in Macellum Julian also fell under the influence of Maximus of Ephesus and became convinced the ancient gods had anointed him to restore the empire to the glory it knew under paganism.

Scholars have concluded that Mardonius was an "honest pagan."[5] Julian's later pagan teachers were more dubious. Mardonius led Julian to the threshold of the sacred temple of Neoplatonic philosophy, which had become hopelessly infected with magic and the occult. If Mardonius was Julian's Vergil, Maximus of Ephesus was the temptress Beatrice who led him across the threshold into the occult. Maximus "initiated" Julian into theurgy. Under the influence of Maximus and other adepts in secret Gnosis, Julian became convinced the wisdom of the Greeks would triumph over the folly of Constantine. There was no reason why one of Constantine's relatives or successors should not come to his senses and restore Hellenism. Those in Constantinople who thought as he did soon saw in Julian their secret champion, even though Julian must have taken part in Christian services there.

At the end of 351, Constantius II ordered Julian to return to Nicomedia, but forbade him to attend the lectures of Libanius. Julian obeyed his cousin externally, but duplicitously followed them closely in secret by poring over notes taken by others. The return to Nicomedia marked "the beginning of Libanius' influence over Julian, an influence which was to increase continually until the Apostate's death."[6] Ricciotti refers to Libanius as "a rhetorician ... without depth of thought; in other words, a brilliant literary peacock."[7] Libanius, who later became teacher of St. John Chrysostom, hated Christianity as an intellectually feeble alternative to the Hellenic tradition, which boasted a pantheon of literary gods from Homer to Plato.

When Julian came under Libanius' spell, however, Plato's teaching and philosophy had fallen on hard times. Hellenism meant Neoplatonism, a compendium based on Plato's teachings as synthesized by Plotinus a Century before but split apart again by Plotinus' students Porphyry and Iamblicus.

Porphyry was a practitioner of magic and theurgy who, under the influence of Plotinus, rejected occultism in favor of reason and philosophy according to the traditional understanding of Plato's teachings. The same cannot be said of Iamblicus. As Neoplatonism's center of gravity shifted toward Asia at the beginning of the fourth Century, magic gained the upper hand over philosophy. Iamblicus was Neoplatonism's representative, leading the final decline of the Hellenism of Plato into the mumbo-jumbo of Asiatic magic. So

> The exponents of this late Neoplatonism thus gradually ceased to be philosophers, since they renounced the hope of arriving at divine contemplation by means of reason and became instead to a greater or less extent hierophants, magicians,

thaumaturges, and evokers of the gods [who] dedicated themselves to the task of bringing that divinity to light [through] "theurgy," that is, divine work.[8]

The decay of Platonic thought eventually infected Judaism. Kaballah was the Neoplatonic reading of the Talmud, and the Lurianic Kabbalah would become Talmudic Judaism infected with Iamblichus' version of Neoplatonic thaumaturgy, according to which the thaumaturge tried to rescue the scattered sparks and bring about *Tikkun Olam*, or the healing of the world. But that is to get ahead of our story.

Julian, who would live only to 32, was fully formed in his beliefs at 20. By then Julian renounced Christ in favor of Mithra, and in keeping with its dualistic nature, kept his true beliefs secret until the proper time to reveal them. In the meantime, he attended church, especially on religious feast days, while practicing his real religion in secret.

St. Gregory Nazianzen, who met Julian in Athens, felt that he was "handicapped by a number of physical and moral defects" mirrored in his appearance.[9] Julian was short, stocky and bearded. Ammanius, his pagan biographer, claims "the rabble at Antioch called him a Cercops (one of a race changed by Jupiter into apes), since being of low stature and having a beard like a billy goat's he spread his broad shoulders as he advanced with great strides through the streets."[10] Gregory felt that Julian went to Athens "to associate secretly with pagan priests and quacks, since he was no yet confirmed in his impiety."[11] His duplicitous nature was expressed in Julian's "weaving head [and] shifty feet [and] the constant changes of opinion without apparent reason"; his religious fanaticism was expressed in "the wild, wandering eyes, ... the nostrils breathing hate and scorn, the proud and contemptuous lineaments of the face, the paroxysms of uncontrolled laughter ... the breathless speech and disordered, senseless questions, interlaced with answers no more to the point." Gregory wondered, "What a monster the Roman empire is nourishing within itself."[12]

Julian visited Pergamum, then an important center for Hellenism. There Maximus of Ephesus tightened his control over Julian's mind. Iamblicus was no longer at Pergamum, but his spirit perdured through the work of his disciples, Aedisius and Maximus. Julian had the reputation of being an ascetic, but intellectually, he showed little discipline much less asceticism. Warned by Eusebius to pursue "the purification of the soul through the use of reason," Julian chose instead the meretricious thaumaturgy Eusebius condemned.[13] Maximus, "completely dedicated to the occult sciences and theurgy,"[14] invited Eusebius and Julian to a magic show at the temple of Hecate that featured the spontaneous lighting of torches and other wonders. Julian was swept away by the spectacle. "Farewell to your books, you have shown me my man," Julian said, confounding Eusebius' admonition.[15]

Julian stayed on for a course in magic, during which he was initiated into theurgic mysteries, which Gregory Nazianzen describes thus:

Julian descended into a subterranean sanctuary closed to the common people in the company of a clever conjurer, a theosophist rather than a philosopher. Such individuals practiced a kind of divination that required darkness and subterranean demons to foretell the future. As Julian advanced father and farther, he encountered terrors increasingly numerous and alarming—strange sounds, revolting exhalations, fiery apparitions, and other such prodigies. Since he was taking his first steps in the occult science, the strangeness of the apparitions terrified him. He made the sign of the Cross. The demons were subdued and all the visions disappeared. Julian regained courage and began to advance. Then the dread objects began to reappear. The sign of the Cross was repeated and they again disappeared. Julian wavered. The director of the initiation at his side explained: "We loathe but no longer fear them. The weaker cause has conquered!" Convinced by these words, Julian was led on toward the abyss of perdition. What he later heard and did only those know who have undergone such initiations. At any rate, from that day he was possessed.[16]

Like Keith Richards, the Rolling Stones' guitarist at the 1969 rock concert that returned human sacrifice to the realm of public spectacle, Julian made the sign of the Cross when demons were about to overwhelm him, until he realized at the prompting of his guide that he was there to be overwhelmed by the demons he feared. The Greek gods were real enough: the Christians called them demons or fallen angels. From then, Julian was their servant. At their behest he rose to the pinnacle of power in the Roman empire and then to doom in the deserts of what is now Iraq. Julian's career is inexplicable without consideration of his recourse to these gods. He saw them at his side during crises, and he consulted them in the entrails of animals and the flight of birds at every turn; they advised him at crucial moments.

In 355 Julian received permission to study at the School of Athens. The Athenians were described in Acts 17:21 as people who "employed themselves in nothing else but in telling or in hearing some new thing." Only the level of Athenian decadence had changed since the time of St. Paul. When Julian arrived, Athenians were living on the memories of the glorious past, but they did not measure up to that past. They talked about Plato, but they substituted theurgy for his teaching. In a stronger soul, their decadence would have inspired disgust; in Julian, it confirmed his abandonment of philosophy for magic. Julian encouraged his pagan followers by submitting to initiation into the Eleusinian mysteries in ceremonies so secret that almost nothing is known of them.

Judged by its effect, the magic seemed powerful enough. After leaving Athens, Julian was summoned to Milan, where he was crowned Caesar in November, 355. One month later, he was sent to rule Gaul. Julian was 23 years old and had spent his life immersed in books and conversing with those who possessed esoteric knowledge.

Gaul was a province in ruin. Colonia Agrippina (Cologne) the principal city of Germania Secunda had just fallen to barbarian invaders. The barbarian tribes had established a base of operations that extended 35 miles west of the Rhine from which they could pillage Roman Gaul at will. The barbarians controlled the west bank of the Rhine all the way to the North Sea, effectively cutting off ship traffic up the Rhine, preventing support from or to Britain. To make matters worse, Constantius II had made Julian a puppet Caesar answerable to generals already in Gaul, whose negligence and corruption had created the chaos.

Facing great handicaps, Julian learned to be a ruler and a general in a few months. Within a short time, he reformed the corrupt tax system of the bankrupt Gallic prefecture. Then, securing the goods to prosecute a campaign against the barbarians, he defeated Chonodomarius and 30,000 Alamanni in a battle near Strasbourg. After the victory, Julian's legions acclaimed him Augustus, or sole ruler of the empire, but he declined the honor.

By this point in his career, Julian had taken on the superhuman characteristics of the gods he worshipped. A Mars in battle, he was a Zeus in rule. He drove the barbarians across the Rhine and freed Gaul from imminent danger. His skill as an administrator won him the esteem even of his Christian enemies like Sts. Ambrose and Gregory Nazianzen. As governor of Gaul, "he succeeded in reducing the *captatio* from 25 to only seven aurei per head"[17] while providing sustenance for successful military campaigns. He was renowned for the purity of his morals. Ammanius, his pagan biographer, claims "He was so conspicuous for his undefiled chastity that after the death of his wife [Helena] it is well known that he never gave a thought to love.... Even his most confidential servants never accused him of any suspicion of lustfulness, as often happens."[18] In 359 he took the war against the Alamanni to the heart of their territory, attacking them on their side of the Rhine.

Achievement like this could not go unpunished. Constantius II stripped Julian of the better half of his troops and ordered them to the eastern front where they were to fight under Constantius II against the Persians. The fame of the Gallic troops, who it was said never turned their back on the enemy, preceded them eastward, but they refused to return the compliment. After one detachment left, the rest mutinied, refusing to leave Julian, whom they again declared Augustus. This time Julian consulted the gods before responding. "I prayed to Zeus," he wrote, "through an opening in the wall" of his quarters in Paris.[19] "I entreated the god to give me a sign, and thereupon he showed to me and ordered me to yield and not to oppose the will of the army."[20] The *genius publicus* of the empire appeared to him in his sleep and rebuked him for his timidity. "If I am not received even now," the guardian spirit of the empire told Julian, "when many men share my opinion, I shall depart sad and dejected."[21] In the morning, Julian, who "told his more intimate friends about the vision," according to Ammanius, yielded to the demands of his troops, who raised him on a military shield and proclaimed him Augustus, sole ruler of the Roman Empire.[22]

Julian, like Caesar before him, cast his die and crossed his Rubicon. He consoled himself against the reproach that he was a traitor, a usurper, and ungrateful to his cousin who had elevated him to Caesar by the "mystic conviction that he had been chosen by the gods to renew their worship."[23] Eunapius writes that Julian "after his conquest of Gaul ... summoned the heirophant from Greece, and after he had performed with his assistance certain rites known to themselves alone, he was aroused to throw off the tyranny of Constantius II."[24] His decision to rebel against his cousin was a function of his involvement in the occult and the sense of political destiny it instilled in him pushed Julian to rebel.

Summoning his troops, who had mutinied at the thought of leaving Gaul, Julian marched east and then embarked on the Danube, sailing forth to his rendezvous point in what is now Serbia. During his progress down the Danube, "the people flocked together at his passage—the Romans on the right bank to acclaim him and the barbarians on the left to gaze on him in wonder and to bend their knees in terror."[25] Cooler heads thought he was marching toward his doom. With rebellion behind him and Constantius II' army massing in front of him on the plains of Illyricum, Julian "was headed toward disaster"[26] when the gods intervened in his life once again. Constantius II suddenly died on November 3, 361 on his way to do battle. Julian took Constantius II' sudden death as proof of the gods' approval of the rebellion. Julian entered Constantinople on December 11. The court confirmed him sole Augustus because "the times required an energetic and warlike leader."[27]

Julian now found himself at the pinnacle of power and in a position to effectuate the commission for which the gods prepared him, the restoration of pagan worship throughout the empire. "I came because the gods expressly bade me, and promised me safety if I obeyed them, but they threatened me with what I pray no god may do to me if I stayed."[28]

After his accession to the imperial throne, Julian announced he had ceased being a Christian at the age of 20 and that he was anointed by Rome's ancient gods to restore her former glory. Socrates and Sozomen trace Julian's apotheosis and moral fall to the machinations of the theurgist Maximus of Ephesus, and Ricciotti writes, "considering the moral character of the theurgists, this is quite probable."[29] Socrates, Sozomen and Gregory Nazianzen, he continues, "all affirm that at this time Julian kept up the appearance of being a Christian."[30] Nevertheless, his withdrawal from Christianity in the secret of his conscience was compete and definitive. He confesses in a letter at the end of 362 that he had "walked along the road" of the Christians "till his twentieth year," but that "with the help of the gods" he had walked along another "for twelve years."[31] The chief obstacle to restoring paganism was Christianity, which had received numerous benefactions from the state since the Edict of Milan in 313.

Julian was a determined reactionary. To purify himself from baptism, which he heard left an invisible but permanent sign on those who received it, he submitted to the Mithraic sacrament known as the taurobolium. Crouching naked in a trench, the most powerful man on earth allowed the blood of a slaughtered bull to pour over his entire body, but particularly those members most in need of purification: his hands which had handled the body of Christ in the Eucharist. Gregory Nazianzen writes Julian "washed his hands, purifying them from the unbloody sacrifice through which we become partakers in the sufferings and divinity of Christ."[32]

The Petulantes and Celts, his loyal legions from Gaul, busily went from one drunken orgy to another, gorging themselves on the meat of slaughtered animals to propitiate the rehabilitated gods. Cynics began referring to Julian Augustus as "the butcher," conjuring up images of him covered with blood hacking away at sides of beef as his new priesthood of libertines and whores looked on in cynical amusement.[33]

Julian was a classic reactionary. He was determined to restore the worship of the gods, convinced they had led him through the extraordinary events of his life for that purpose. When he became Augustus, "he laid bare the secrets of his heart and with plain and final decrees ordered the temples to be opened, victims to be brought to the altars and the worship of the gods to be restored."[34]

But Julian was thoroughly modern too, which is to say, Masonic in his duplicity. He promoted the goals of his esoteric circle of thaumaturges under the exoteric guise of religious tolerance. He intended, at least he said in public, "to grant full religious liberty not only to the pagans but also to the Christians."[35] Ammanius, part of his inner circle, understood the meaning of the gesture. Julian granted universal freedom of conscience "that he might have no fear thereafter of a united populace, because such a freedom increased their dissensions, and he knew from experience that no wild beasts are so hostile to mankind as are most Christians in their savage hatred for one another."[36] Trying to "divide and conquer," Julian hoped to reduce Christianity "to extremes without appearing as an open adversary."

Julian inaugurated a thoroughly modern persecution in which the state seemed a benevolent supporter of tolerance when it was encouraging pagans to attack Christians with impunity. It was like Sargent Shriver giving $900,000 to the Blackstone Rangers in Chicago in the '60s. Certain groups had free rein to terrorize Christians because they enjoyed the favor of the emperor and would never be punished. Ricciotti calls it "disguised persecution guided by the hand in power."[37] He says "Julian shrank from the death sentence, since this would have removed the disguise from his system of veiled persecution."[38]

Julian was ahead of his times. He invented *Kulturkampf* a millenium and a half before Bismarck fired Catholic teachers from the Gymnasium in Braunsberg. Julian, like Bismarck, felt "Christians should be discredited by being deprived of their culture."[39] Julian banned Christian teachers from schools, but made it seem he was implementing a politically neutral program of educational reform. In June 362, Julian issued the constitution *Magistros studiorum* which gives the "appearance of neutrality,"[40] because the "words of the decree, taken alone, could not be interpreted as a direct plot against any individuals or groups within the empire such as the Christians."[41] But the exoteric document was interpreted in light of a circular letter to the esoteric circle of magistrates and teachers who implemented the constitution. Again

> it is necessary to keep in mind that Julian was a member of the secret society of Mithra ... and that in such associations it was the rule to reveal only the more generic and vague aspects of one's thoughts, keeping hidden what ever was more characteristic and decisive. We obviously have an example of this procedure here: Julian's generic plan was set forth in the *Magistros studiorum*, but its specific interpretation was reserved for the letter already cited.[42]

By depriving Christians of their culture, Julian rendered them powerless without the odium of bloody persecution. In this he was a typically modern ruler. He was a radical innovator who dramatically expanded the power of the state into spheres traditionally left to the family. When Rome was a republic, the state bowed to the *paterfamilias* in education. In *De republica* Cicero claimed Romans "had never wished for any system of education for free-born youths that was either definitely fixed by law or officially established or uniform for all."[43] Even in Hadrian's time, education was a private initiative. But the situation changed as the government subsidized the schools. The *quid pro quo* was to become common in other empires, too: Financial support in exchange for the schools' allegiance to the regime. "Vespasian," Ricciotti says, "was the first to assign to rhetoricians an annual salary of 100,000 sesterces from the public treasury."[44] Christian teachers had to renounce their faith or give up their careers and face poverty and social ostracism. "There was to be no bloody persecution," Ricciotti continues, "but rather a slow asphyxiation and inevitable paralysis."[45]

In one of the ironies that mark Julian's career, he articulated a position the Church would eventually take with regard to the Jews. "I do not want the Galileans to be put to death or unjustly beaten or to suffer anything else," Julian told his teachers and magistrates, "but still I emphatically maintain that those who reverence the gods must be preferred to them."[46] Under the formula "*Sicut Judaeis non*," Pope St. Gregory the Great articulated the same principle as the Church's policy toward the Jews. No one was to harm them, but they were to be given no position of cultural influence, lest they use it to engage in blasphemy and the corruption of morals.

Mesmerized by Maximus of Ephesus, whom Ricciotti compares to "a mysterious sphinx charming him from afar,"[47] Julian was drawn to ruin in the deserts of the East, but before that he succumbed to a vision of himself as the pagan messiah, a vision confected by the thaumaturges and hierophants who surrounded him. The man who studied Greek literature so avidly seemed strangely unaware of the hubris that ruled his life. Messianic politics broke out where least expected, from the very empire that crushed it among the Jews three centuries earlier:

Just as the Messianic herald had been chosen to bring back to Jahweh all the offspring of Israel and to carry the message of salvation "even to the farthest part of the earth," so Julian would bring back all the peoples of the empire who were corrupted by the Christianity of Constantine to the worship of the gods.

Ricciotti says "this pagan Messianic program" wasn't "exclusively religious in the modern sense of the word, since it also involved politics as well."[48] But it was precisely messianic politics because it mixed religion, politics, and a charismatic penchant for private revelations as the validator of preconceived policies. In this, Julian was a forerunner of George W. Bush. Both led their empires into ill-fated military campaigns against rulers of Mesopotamia; both relied more on gut feeling than rational calculation; both were influenced by the traditional source of Messianic politics, namely, the Jews—George Bush by his neoconservative advisers; Julian through the study of literature, in particular the Church fathers and their polemics against the Jews.

Julian initially espoused tolerance to all religious sects to sow dissension in the hope they would eradicate each other, saving him the trouble. His policy toward the Jews was dictated by the same principle. Julian felt the religion of the Jews was, except for its unfortunate penchant for monotheism, almost as good as the religion of the Hellenes. Julian was sympathetic to the Jews, probably because of their antipathy toward Christians, and decided to exploit it for political effect.

Although originally viewed by Rome as a sect of Judaism, Christianity became Judaism's bitterest rival after the destruction of the Temple in 70 AD and the bar Kokhba rebellion in 131. In Antioch, where Julian was despised by Christians and ridiculed by pagans, he was described as a hairy ape with the beard of a he-goat who was always buried in books. Since he was avid to refute Christianity, Julian was especially familiar with Christian texts and Christian writers. From them, he knew Jews were the main opponents of Christianity; Jews were also involved in every persecution. So he decided to use them to refute Christianity once and for all. Aware of the theological import of Matt 24:2, in which Christ prophesied the destruction of the Temple, Julian decided to reverse history by rebuilding the temple that Christ said would remain forever destroyed. "The high priest of the Hellenes would embarrass the god of the Galileans on his own terrain, making Him out to be a charlatan."

In *Against the Galileans*, now known only through writings of those who wrote to refute it, Julian accused the Christians of impiety, of atheism, of claiming that men were not divine, and of being the illegitimate offspring of Judaism. Judaism was more legitimate because it was ancient. Christianity had existed for only 300 years, and no one in his right mind could put faith in a religion that new. The dispute over the relative antiquity of the religions bespoke a deeper dispute: the issue of patrimony and lineage. The dispute between the Jews who accepted Christ as the Messiah and those who rejected him became full-blown cultural warfare within years of Christ's crucifixion. Who were the true children of Abraham and

Moses? Who was the True Israel? An astute politician, Julian would have his enemies fight each other to settle the claim. Since Christianity was the established religion, that meant promoting the cause of the Jews, the Christians' implacable enemy.

The Acts of the Apostles and the Epistles describe the founding of the Church as a life and death struggle with the Jews, who, even more than the pagan Romans, saw it as a threat precisely because it refused to see itself as new. The followers of Christ were one religion among many in the Roman empire because they lacked political power, but they could not accept the Jews as one of those many religions. The Jews, many Christian writers made clear, were different from the Hebrews. The Hebrew religion had a priesthood, a Temple, and sacrifice. After 70 AD, the Jews had none of these things, so the religion of the Jews could not be the same as that of the Hebrews. The only religion that had a priesthood, a Temple, and a sacrifice was the Catholic Church, the New Israel. The Jews did not have a separate but equal covenant; the only real basis for fulfilling their covenant had been destroyed.

Writing about 115 AD, St. Ignatius of Antioch claimed "It is absurd to have Jesus Christ on the lips, and at the same time to live like a Jew." He established the proper causal and chronological relationship between Judaism and Christianity: "Christianity did not believe in Judaism," he tells us, "but Judaism believed in Christianity, and in its bosom was assembled everyone professing faith in God."[49] The Hebrew prophets, he wrote, "lived a Christian life," because they lived "a life in union with Christ even before he came."[50] Logically then, the religion called Judaism after Christ was a spurious invention lacking continuity with Abraham and Moses.

Writing in the aftermath of the bar Kokhba rebellion, St. Justin Martyr makes the point more emphatically. Justin refers to the Old Testament as "our writings" because, though delivered to the Jews, they were destined for the Christians.[51] The Jews are incapable of understanding Scripture because they are "carnal," a word applied to them repeatedly by the Church fathers. Because they did not understand the Scriptures, the Jews rejected Christ and attacked him when he walked among them. Similarly, they also attack Christians because they do not understand the real or spiritual meaning of Scripture.

Political messianism is a manifestation of the carnal Jew. According to the Church Fathers, the Jews perennially await a Messiah who will restore their political power. Christianity is incompatible with political messianism and Jewish revolutionary activity because it recognizes another Messiah. According to Justin Martyr, who died roughly 50 years after Ignatius, Christians were persecuted during the bar Kokhba rebellion because of their loyalty to Jesus Christ. Eusebius says bar Kokhba persecuted the Christians because they would not fight the Romans because that would mean accepting bar Kokhba as their Messiah. Jewish revolutionary fervor only increased Jewish hatred of Christianity because they saw the Christians as traitors.

Justin writes "Not only do the Jews hate the Christians, but they persecute them, and treat them like the pagans do, as worthy of punishment and of death, whenever they can put their plans into execution."[52] Rejection of the true Messiah made them intolerant of those who questioned their Messianic politics, namely, the Christians, who chided them for their folly and blindness. Add the dispute over which was the True Israel, and constant friction and bloodshed resulted. When Christians claimed for themselves the antiquity of the Jews, this reproach "struck at the very roots of Jewish self-respect" because in antiquity "the proof of late origin meant that historically the people with this late origin was of little importance. Such a people received its culture from other peoples."[53] The question perdured through polemics: who had the derivative culture? The Christians or the Jews?

Justin Martyr addressed the issue in *Dialogue with Trypho*, written in the aftermath of the bar Kokhba rebellion. The dialogue was "written ... for those Jews brought up with some of the benefits of Greek training, but faithful to the Law" who were "disillusioned at the temporal collapse of Judaism in the days of their parents."[54] Justin felt that the Jewish people were held in intellectual and spiritual bondage by their rabbis, so "it was against their authority and their competence that he leveled his attack."[55] *Dialogue with Trypho* is aimed at Jews during their moment of disillusionment flowing from the ruined hope in a false Messiah. Justin could not set up a straw Judaism; his audience would see through any caricature. Harnack comments: Justin is "a reliable reporter and does not construct a Judaism that will suit his own polemical purposes."[56] The *Dialogue* is, Wilde says, "*necessarily* a substantially faithful representation of Jewish religious life in the middle of the second Century from the point of view of a Christian and with the reactions of a Christian."[57] It "shows us that the two religions are completely separated from one another." Wilde describes the *Dialogue* as "the monologue of the victor."[58]

Justin concedes to Rabbi Trypho that Christians and Jews worship the same God. But differences outweigh similarities. Trypho concedes the Messiah, according to Scripture, must suffer, but pulls back in disgust at the idea he would suffer and die in the shameful manner recounted in the Gospels. The Cross was a scandal to the Jews of St. Paul's time and to the Jews of Trypho's. Trypho, like Maimonides 1000 years later and virtually every rabbi in between, wanted a Messiah "who would be great and glorious."

Justin realized the Jewish desire for a carnal Messiah was undimmed by the disastrous bar Kokhba rebellion.[59] Because the Jews were not going to embrace Christ, Justin argued for concessions in behavior so the two groups could live in peace under Roman rule. Justin called for an end to reviling Christ in the synagogue, a common practice based on the Talmud. He also said only a Jew would claim the crucifixion was necessary so there was no guilt on their part (in contrast to what St. Paul says at Romans 3:5-8). At the end of his *Dialogue*, his Jewish interlocutors remain unconvinced and unconverted. This obdurate blindness, he suggests, will last for a long time.

The *Dialogue* is not irenic in the sense those living in the wake of Vatican II have grown accustomed to. Justin reviles Jews for "blind obedience to rabbinic control." Only in Christianity can Jews find "the fulfillment of their Messianic expectations, the explanation of the collapse of Judaism, and the freedom which their spirits craved and which their condition denied them."[60] The rejection of Christ orchestrated by the rabbis turned Judaism into anti-Christianity, distorting the Jewish personality. The Jews "are openly wicked men." They are "worse than the Ninevites who at least did penance, for they by their bad actions make the pagans calumniate God. By their merely carnal understanding of the Law, designed to be primarily spiritual; they make men calumniate the law and hence the God of the Law and are thus false to their spiritual vocation." The Jews are "wise only in doing evil" and, as a result, "unable to know the hidden plan of God."[61]

The most obvious manifestation of Jewish wickedness is the persecution of Christians, which follows logically from the Jews' responsibility for the death of Christ. Justin is not alone in ascribing to Jews the role of persecutor.

The Martyrdom of Polycarp explains the extent of Jewish participation the persecution of Christians. Polycarp was bishop of Smyrna when a persecution of Christians broke out. In Revelation 2:8 the Jews in Smyrna are described as forming the synagogue of Satan, a group habitually slandering and persecuting Christians. When the persecution commenced, Polycarp escaped. Captured later with others, they were burned alive rather than renounce their faith; the whole populace gathered wood, but "especially active in these preparations were the Jews, as was their custom, who eagerly helped people in this matter." In ascribing blame for the murder of Polycarp, the author mentions that this sort of persecution was "habitually practiced by the Jews."[62]

Origen says Jews were habitual inciters of widespread and long-standing persecution of Christians. The persecutions were too systematic to be local or personal. They were the policy of the rabbis who controlled Jewish life. Origen mentions that the Jews roused local populations to persecute Christians by repeated calumnies. The Jewish claim that Christians ate murdered infants at night meetings was a calumny that triggered one persecution, but he says the history of Jewish persecution went back to apostolic times. In 62, the apostle James was thrown to his death from the Temple. From 131-135, Simon bar Kokhba gave Christians the choice of apostasy or death. Women were whipped or stoned if they showed any intention of becoming Christians. "Opposition at all times," Wilde writes, summing up Origen, "and persecution where possible, was the policy of the Jews, once the distinction between Jews and Christians became known and understood."[63] Like other Church Fathers, Origen felt Jewish opposition to Christianity flowed from Jewish opposition to Christ; their hatred of Christ stemmed from their carnal nature and "national pride" because Christianity admitted Gentiles into the new spiritual kingdom.[64] According to Rabbi Tarphon (perhaps the model for the Rabbi in Justin's *Dialogue with Trypho*), Christians "were far worse than the pagans, for the pagans never had the truth. But the Minim [the Christians] had the truth and abandoned it. Hence we find the curse upon the Minim introduced into the Shemone Esre at the end of the first Century or the beginning of the second."[65]

The evidence for Jewish animus against Christians is not ascribable to unfortunate personal experience. It suffuses the patristic writings, just as it suffuses the canonical books of the New Testament.[66] Nor is the patristic view of the Jew based on literary stereotypes compensating for actual experience. The Jew is a personal acquaintance, unlike Shylock or the Jew of Malta, who were stereotypes based on distant memory. Origen, like Justin Martyr, was personally acquainted with Jews. Origen understood that Jewish calumny helped to cause Christian persecution, and that Jewish hatred was a fact of life for the Christians, continuing unabated after the repeated defeats of Messianic politics. As we have seen, the revolutionary Jew was born, according to Origen, when the Jews chose Barabbas in place of Christ because "it is he who holds sway over them in their unbelief."[67] Like Justin, Origen feels that rabbis are the primary source of this hatred and the force that holds the Jewish people in their thrall. The Rabbis are also responsible for the calumnies and blasphemies in the Talmud. Demonstrating familiarity with parts of the Talmud, Origen mentions the Talmudic claim that Christ was born of an adulterous union of a Jewish whore and a Roman soldier named Panthera.

Jews, according to Origen, cling to a carnal, literal interpretation of the scriptures and persecute those who have the true spiritual understanding. Jewish proselytes are "especially bitter and their hatred lasts after the peace of the church, especially against converts from Judaism."[68] Persecutions, according to Origen, flowed inexorably from the Jews' rejection of Christ. The Jews not only crucified Christ, "the hatred of the Jews for Christ extended beyond the grave, for they bribed the soldiers to deny the resurrection of Christ."[69]

Origen was not only familiar with Josephus' account of the siege of Jerusalem in 70 AD; he draws theological conclusions from it. The Church fathers saw in the destruction of the Temple a repudiation of the Jews for their rejection of Christ and the destruction of their religion too. The Jews were in darkness because they laid violent hands on the light. Jerusalem was destroyed because of the sins of the Jews; that destruction is proof of the truth of what Christ had said. The Jews, according to Origen, were abandoned because of their rejection of Christ. "Jerusalem," he says, "may now be called wretched. It has no honor, no glory. It is without Temple, without altar, without sacrifice, without prophet without priesthood, without any divine visitation whatever. The Jews are dispersed throughout the world and live as fugitives and exiles. They have been repudiated by God."[70]

Justin Martyr says the same thing. The foundation of Jewish worship was sacrifice that expiated sin and won the favor of God. With the destruction of the Temple, sacrifice became impossible. So the Jews were rendered unproductive and unfruitful, "though great and innumerable." They "drink up the doctrine of bitterness and impiety and reject the word of God."[71] Similarly, "the Jews think that because they are by the flesh the sons of Abraham and of Jacob they will be saved. In this they are completely deceived."[72] The promises to Abraham can no longer be fulfilled in the Jews. As we have seen before, if the priesthood, sacrifice, and Temple must continue, then Christians are the true Israelites, because only they, through Christ, have priesthood, sacrifice (in the Mass) and Temple (in Christ himself).

The destruction of the Temple caused a radical discontinuity in history. Origen deals with this discontinuity by refining the definition of the word Jew, a redefinition necessary because of confusion the word "*hoi Ioudaioi*" caused in the Gospel of John. Origen distinguishes between the Jew *in occulto* and the Jew *in manifesto*. The Jew *in occulto* is the spiritual Jew, the follower of Christ. The Jew *in manifesto* is the carnal Jew, the biological descendant of Israel, the Jew who claimed to be the "seed of Abraham" whom Christ repudiated. Israel, according to Origen, means one who sees God. Everyone who has obtained the vision of God through faith and a sinless soul may be called Israel. The synagogue, according to Origen, will continue to exist, but it will bear no fruit.

A number of consequences flow from this rejection. The Jews, who have abandoned the light of reason, the Logos, have no control over their passions. They will live in the darkness of unreason and, as a result, pursue their desires without restraint. They "are well represented by the figure of Barabbas," an ill-fated political insurrectionary.[73] They are also identified with Judas, "and with him go to hell."[74] The devil does not bother the Jews because "they have already fallen into his hands."[75] He now attacks the Church. The Jews are agents of the devil who accuse Christians of credulity while persecuting them and blaspheming Christ. Jews are unjustly proud of their carnal descent from Abraham and refuse to repent. The Jews practice magic, and are "foolish, hard-hearted, wise only in doing evil, unable to know the hidden plan of God," and are "useless to society."[76]

Origen, according to Wilde, "presents more clearly than any uninspired writer of the first three centuries, what was to prove to be the full traditional attitude of ecclesiastical authors toward the Jews."[77] In spite of their words, which seem harsh to modern ears, Wilde rejects the idea that the Church fathers are anti-Semitic because "there is no trace of any racial animosity on the part of Christians."[78] The fathers did not manifest "hatred of the Jews.... They were opposed to Judaism as a religion whose place is taken by Christianity and as an institution responsible for the death of Christ."[79] They also opposed the Jews because Jews were responsible for persecution of Christians. The "present wretched condition of the Jews ... is due to their rejection of Christ and is a punishment for their sin."[80] That same wretched condition, persecution of the Jews, also flowed from "the temporal character of their Messianic expectations."[81] Jewish revolutionary activity invariably created a violent reaction against all Jews. The Judaism practiced after Christ was "condemned as a religion which has been replaced, whose rites are therefore vain and useless."[82] The Judaism practiced before Christ, however, was "the precursor of Christianity, and, therefore, worthy of respect and reverence."[83] Like the Gospel of St. John, the writings of the Church fathers were anti-Jewish because they saw the Jew as a rejecter of Christ rather than someone with any real religious identity. Christian writers would often refer to Judaism as "*superstitio*," which is to say, confected by man not God, for carnal purposes. Wilde concludes "the Christian treatment of the Jews never descends to the *ad hominem* level."[84]

St. Irenaeus reiterates what Justin and Polycarp said before him and anticipates what Origen and others would say later. The Jews are rejected as Israel; their vineyard is turned over to the Gentiles; the Church is the New Israel. Irenaeus applies the parable of the wicked husbandmen to the Jews as did Jesus when he told the Jews "the kingdom of God will be taken from you and given to a people who will produce its fruit." Irenaeus makes the implication clear. The rejection of Israel as an ethnic group meant the selection of the Gentiles as the Church. After comparing the Jews to the wicked husbandmen cast out of the vineyard, Irenaeus claims that the vineyard has been expanded to include the whole world and given to other husbandmen who will render its fruits. The vineyard "is no longer hemmed in, that is, no longer limited by Jewish narrowness."[85]

Irenaeus knows his idea engenders animosity among the Jews of his time because it engendered animosity among the Jews of Jesus' time. "When they heard his parables," Matthew recounts, "the chief priest and the scribes realized he was speaking about them, but though they would have liked to arrest him they were afraid of the crowds, who looked on him as a prophet" (Matthew 21:45-46).

Irenaeus thought the choice of Barabbas over Christ had lasting political implications. "In dishonoring the Son of God they chose Barabbas, a robber and a murderer. They denied the Eternal King, and preferred to admit the temporal Emperor as their king. For this reason God delivered their inheritance to the Gentiles and does not want them to return to the Law."[86] According to Irenaeus, all Jews are responsible for the rejection of Christ, "the people by not knowing Him, and the priests for attacking Him."[87] In claiming "we have no king but Caesar," Jews committed themselves to a political program that actively manifested their rejection of Christ. Jews would henceforth implement the promise of a Messiah in a carnal fashion, which is to say, in a way opposite to the kingdom of God on earth.

St. Hippolytus of Rome takes this thought to its logical conclusion in his treatise on the Antichrist. The death of Christ at the hands of the Jews was anticipated in what they did to the Prophet Jeremiah. The desolation of Judaea and the burning of the sanctuary occurred after both events. Hippolytus says, the Jews killed Christ because "they were disappointed in Him, for they thought that he was to establish a community on earth alone."[88] The same carnal messianic political desire for heaven on earth that led the Jews to choose Barabbas will lead the Jews who perdure in the rejection deeper into the service of the devil until they finally, it is argued, bring about the reign of the Antichrist.

The Kingdom of the Antichrist, Hippolytus says, is a Jewish operation. Just as the Antichrist will bear "many apparent similarities to the true Christ," so too "the Jewish people over whom Antichrist will rule bear many apparent similarities to the people of God."[89] The Antichrist will first gather the scattered Jewish people into Jerusalem, where they will reconstruct the temple. The Antichrist, according to Hippolytus, "will resurrect the kingdom of the Jews."[90] The Antichrist thus will be the culmination of Messianic politics. He will re-establish the superseded ethnic Israel as heaven on earth, but that heaven will be a hell for Christians. The Antichrist "will kill kings in battle" and be "a harsh ruler. He will bring tribulation and persecution against his enemies,"[91] namely, the Church, the New Israel. In the meantime, each Jewish Messiah will be an avatar of the Antichrist, because the Jews, "who gave themselves over to wickedness according as their temporal prosperity grew greater" and were "a stubborn people, and full of cunning, who feared not God, and had not shame before men" were condemned to mistake "the Antichrist for the true Messias" repeatedly.[92] "The Jews had an excessive desire for the things of this world, and too great a reliance upon their own strength." As a result, "the wrath of God fell upon them because of their part in the death of Christ, and it brought with it the following punishments: eternal blindness, loss of the Way which is Christ, eternal servitude to the Gentiles and destruction of the Temple."[93] The Jews would be punished in the aftermath of each intermediary Antichrist. In fact, "in the age to come the Jews will be horror-stricken at the punishment they are to receive."[94]

Bar Kokhba's failed rebellion did not end Jewish animus against Christianity; it merely required a change in strategy. Largely eschewing armed insurrection, the Jews turned to psychological warfare and promoted heresy instead. Irenaeus' work, as its title implies, was written to combat heresy, specifically Gnosticism, but in entering that fray he had to deal with the Jews, acknowledging "from the very beginning of the Gnostic attack on Christianity," that Gnosticism was associated with judaizing.[95] Irenaeus claims Simon Magus, the proto-heretic mentioned in the Acts of the Apostles, "bears a Jewish imprint."[96] His ideas of God, of the world, of angels, of the Law and of man, according to Irenaeus, "all show Jewish influence."[97] Origen saw "Jewish influence on heresies such as Docetism and Gnosticism."[98]

Origen wrote "Heretics and Jews are grouped together as the conventicle of the wicked who build in vain"[99] over a Century before Julian became emperor, but he could not have more accurately described Julian's project to rebuild the Temple—or its outcome. "Under Julian (361-63)," we are told, "there was a revival of Jewish national ambition connected with the attempt to rebuild the temple. The Jews of Antioch were certainly involved in this revival. In fact, the Jews fitted well into Julian's plan to restore paganism."[100] Graetz says "Julian's reign ... was a period of extreme happiness for the Jews of the Roman Empire,"[101] and "Julian was greatly impressed by the God of Judaism,"[102] but the latter seems unlikely given his initiation into the Eleusinian mysteries and his desire to restore the pagan gods. Julian's attraction to the Jews was more political than theological, which historians closer to his time recognized.

Rufinus does not share Graetz's feeling that Julian was "greatly impressed by the God of Judaism." Rufinus says in *Historia ecclesiastica*, written in about 400:

So great was Julian's subtlety and shrewdness as to land even the unfortunate Jews in illusory expectations to which he himself was subject. He summoned them and confronted them with the question of why they do not perform sacrifices, although their laws obligate them to do so. But they sensing the opportunity of the moment said: 'We can do so only in the Temple of Jerusalem. For such is the command of the law.' Having obtained from him the permission to start with the work of reconstruction, they became so emboldened in their insolence as to make it appear that a prophet of theirs had come to them. From all regions and provinces there came Jews, to start with the reconstruction of the Temple which had long ago been consumed with fire. With the permission of the Emperor's representative they used public and private means to proceed in great haste. Meanwhile they started insulting our fellow Christians, as if the Jews' old kingdom were about to be reinstated. As the Jews grew in confidence and pride, they menaced Christians ever more heatedly.[103]

Socrates is more pointed in exposing Julian's political manipulation of the Jews and their messianic hopes. Julian, says Socrates,

thought to grieve the Christians by favoring the Jews, who are their most inveterate enemies. But perhaps he also calculated upon persuading the Jews to embrace paganism and sacrifices; for they were only acquainted with the mere letter of Scripture, and could not, like the Christians and a few of the wisest among the Hebrews, discern the hidden meaning.... The emperor, the other pagans, and all the Jews, regarded every other undertaking as secondary in importance to this. Although the pagans were not well-disposed towards the Jews, yet they assisted them in their enterprise, because they reckoned upon its ultimate success, and hoped by this means to falsify the prophecies of Christ.[104]

An educated man, Julian understood the thrust of Christian anti-Jewish polemic. The Christians claimed that destruction of the temple proved the superiority of Christianity and that Christianity had superseded Judaism as the New Israel. Julian's desire to rebuild the Temple fit squarely into the trajectory of anti-Jewish Christian polemic. To blunt Christian claims, he could find no more willing allies than the Jews, who hated Christians and were eager to collaborate with those who held political power. The Jews had cried that they had "no king but Caesar," and now Caesar was reaching out to them, willing to support their deepest aspirations, the restoration of Jerusalem and its Temple.

In a letter "To the Community of the Jews," Julian promised "I will use all my zeal to make the temple of the Most High God rise again."[105] His reference to "the Most High God" flattered his Jewish audience, and Graetz was still taken in by the flattery a millennium and a half later. In his letter Julian affirmed that the Temple in Jerusalem alone was recognized by the Torah, and that it would have to be rebuilt before the Jews again had "sacred precincts" and "altars for sacrifice,"[106] thereby confirming everything the Christian fathers had said about the Church as the New Israel. He also upped the ante. If he could build the Temple, he could reverse the course of history, prove that Christianity was a hoax, and prove that he himself was a god worthy of induction into the pantheon he was reconstructing. From a theological viewpoint, the decision to rebuild the Temple was the most ambitious construction project in history. "The high priest of the Hellenes would embarrass the god of the Galileans on his own terrain, making Him out to be a charlatan."[107]

St. John Chrysostom attributes more wickedness to Julian and more slyness to the Jews. Julian, according to Chrysostom (born 14 years before Julian's reign and ordained a priest 20 years after Julian's death), "surpassed all the emperors in irreligion."[108] He did not begin by enlisting the Jews in his project to repaganize the Roman Empire; rather he "invited the Jews to sacrifice to idols in an attempt to drag them to his own level of ungodliness."[109] The Jews were cleverer than the emperor. They turned his project to their advantage, saying: "If you wish to see us offer sacrifices, give us back Jerusalem, rebuild the temple, show us the holy of holies, restore the altar, and we will offer sacrifices again just as we did before."[110] But the sacrifices the Jews promised were not going to be to Roman gods.

Chrysostom, too, felt "all Jews are responsible for Christ's passion and death, that they have been repudiated and cursed by God, and that they stand condemned out of the mouths of their own prophets."[111] Like Julian, Chrysostom had "received an excellent education in the Greek paideia."[112] Like Julian, Chrysostom saw the Jew as the primary enemy of the Christian. Anyone who saw the Church as a danger to the security of state and society, as Julian did, would "favor Judaism"[113] to remove Christianity as paganism's chief rival.

The stage was set for a battle of wills in which the emperor would attempt to force God's hand. Like latter day evangelicals who show up at the Temple Mount in Jerusalem with dynamite to usher in Armageddon by blowing up the mosque built on the Temple's foundations, Julian would reverse the course of history by resurrecting the Jewish priesthood, sacrifice, and Temple.

Julian's claim was daring, but not preposterous, for as St. John Chrysostom makes clear in *Adversus Judaeos*, Christians accepted the premises of Julian's argument. If Julian could rebuild the Temple, then the Jews would be vindicated, and Christianity, the superseder, would itself be superseded. It may be difficult to imagine the construction of one building causing this, but the Temple in Jerusalem wasn't just any building. It was the *sine qua non* of the Jewish religion. If it could be rebuilt, the Jewish religion would be re-established, and if that were to happen, Christianity's claim to be the New Israel would be over. Christianity would be one sect among many, easily accommodated into Rome's pantheon.

Eusebius in *Demonstratio evangelica* claimed the Temple precincts had been completely obliterated by time and the Roman legions. The site of the Temple was "ploughed and cultivated by Roman citizens in a way not all different from other such fields."[114] Much earth and rubble, as a result, had to be removed before the foundations were laid bare and Julian's construction could begin. The Jews, "blind to all things,"[115] called on the Emperor for help, and the Emperor happily obliged. Julian turned to Alypius, distinguished prefect of Britain. Work went smoothly, at the beginning. Roman know-how combined with Jewish wealth and enthusiasm seemed unbeatable. According to Ammianus, Julian "allotted enormous (*immodicis*) sums for the enterprise," sums which "were augmented by contributions of the patriarch of all Judaism and other voluntary offerings, including costly garments and jewels handed over for the purpose by Jewish women."[116] Jewish women, according to Eusebius, even "used their garments to help carry away the earth removed by diggers busy with making room for the new foundations."[117] The lone dissenting voice was St. Cyril, bishop of Jerusalem, who according to Eusebius, predicted dire consequences for the day lime was mixed to make mortar for the foundation stones.

The Jews scorned Cyril's prediction. The enthusiastic effort went smoothly for a while. Rubble that covered the site for centuries was removed, exposing the original foundation. But when new construction was about to begin, things started to go wrong. "During the night," says Eusebius, "there arose a huge storm, the earth shook, and huge balls of fire burst forth from the ground and continued to do so through the next day. Instruments melted, workers were burnt to death, strange crosses appeared on clothes and bodies, a luminous cross shone in the sky, and the enterprise had to be abandoned. A violent tremor caused a portico to collapse killing a number of workers."[118]

According to St. John Chrysostom, Julian "overlooked nothing but worked quietly and a little at a time to bring the Jews to offer sacrifice, in this way he expected that it would be easy for them to go from sacrifice to the worship of idols."[119] The emperor's construction crew was about to start construction of the new temple, "when suddenly fire leaped forth from the foundations and completely consumed not only a great number of the workmen but even the stones piled up there to support the structure."[120]

Gregory of Nazianzen says the Jewish women "carried the dirt in their lap with no consideration for their robes and for the tenderness of their bodies, because they saw in all this a work of piety, as they carried everything downward" from the Temple foundations to a nearby valley.[121] "But," Gregory continues:

> a sudden whirlwind and the convulsion of the earth caused them to rush to a nearby church . . as they [the Jewish women] reached the door of the church which was open, suddenly those doors closed, as if by an invisible hand, which filled with fear the impious and protest the devout. It is reported unanimously and held for certain that when they tried to open the door of the church, flames that burst forth from the inside prevented them from forcing the door open. The flames then burnt some of them and destroyed others ... Still others lost various limbs of their bodies to the flames that burst from inside the church and burnt some of them to death.[122]

Gregory adds that those who refuse to admit the event's miraculous character "do not believe in any miracle of God."[123] Gregory, says Stanley Jaki, "was fully aware of the need of being credible when reporting about truly miraculous events."[124] He, therefore, scrupulously avoids embellishment in describing the second miraculous occurrence, "the appearance of a cross within a luminous circle in the sky" followed by the appearance of crosses on the clothing of the Jews:

> Anyone who was there found either on his vestments or on his body a luminous sign in the form of a cross, which exceeded the beauty of anything produced by a weaver or by a painter. On seeing this, they [the Jews] were so terrified as to invoke in one voice the God of the Christians and tried to expiate Him with many praises and supplications. Some even went so far as to seek out our priests and were after many prayers admitted into the Church, and introduced into the greater mysteries. They had their souls purified in baptism and so profited from their terror."[125]

Again, Jaki explains why Gregory could not exaggerate, much less lie: "Had he done so he would have exposed himself to immediate rebuttal by pagan admirers of Julian who were very numerous indeed and were not absent even from Cappadocia, a stronghold of Christianity. But neither Gregory, nor other erstwhile reporters of the event were challenged about the veracity of their presentation. Gregory ... was never charged of falsifying or inventing facts."[126]

St. Ambrose, a former civil servant, also could not embellish the tale because it was within the memory of those still living, and any fabrication would have undermined his credibility with the people he wanted to impress. Yet he pulls no punches in describing the incident and its meaning to the Emperor Gratian. "Have you not heard how," Ambrose asked the Emperor in reference to a synagogue he planned to build, "when Julian had ordered the Temple of Jerusalem rebuilt, those who were carrying the rubbish were burned by fire from heaven? Are you not afraid that this will happen also now? In fact, you should not have given an order such as Julian would have given."[127]

Ammianus Marcellus, Julian's pagan biographer, reports "frightful balls of flame kept bursting forth near the foundations of the temple" which "made it impossible to approach the place," even though "Alypius pushed the work forward energetically" and "was assisted by the governor of the province."[128] Alypius ordered men to their deaths by ordering them into the flames from the Temple's foundations, but he eventually conceded defeat because "the elements [i.e., fire] persistently drove them back."[129] Ammianus notes, "Julian gave up the attempt."[130]

Socrates says the Jews were driven to doom by their desire to gratify their illicit passions:

> when God caused the earthquake to cease, the workmen who survived again returned to their task, partly because such was the edict of the emperor and partly because they were themselves interested in the undertaking. Men often, in endeavouring to gratify their own passions, seek what is injurious to them, reject what would be truly advantageous, and are deluded by their ideas that nothing

is really useful except what is agreeable to them. When once led astray by this error, they are no longer able to act in a manner conducive to their own interest, or to take warning by the calamities which are visited upon them.

The Jews, I believe, were just in this state; for, instead of regarding this unexpected earthquake as a manifest indication that God was opposed to the re-erection of their temple, they proceeded to recommence the work. But all parties relate, that they had scarcely returned to the undertaking, when fire burst suddenly from the foundations of the temple, and consumed several of the workmen.[131]

Socrates concludes: the incident is "believed by all; the only discrepancy in the narrative is that some maintain that flame burst from the interior of the temple, as the workmen were striving to force an entrance, while others say that the fire proceeded directly from the earth."[132]

The explosions dumbfounded Julian and his Jewish allies. The Jews "were astonished and struck with shame."[133] Julian, formerly "madly eager" to finish the project, was suddenly filled with fear, afraid fire might fall on his own head too. So "he and the whole Jewish people withdrew in defeat." Chrysostom comments: "Even today if you go into Jerusalem, you will see the bare foundation. If you ask why this is so, you will hear no explanation other than the one I gave. We are all witnesses to this, for it happened no long ago but in our own time."[134]

Julian tried to make the best of a bad situation in "To a Priest." According to him, the Jewish prophets who scorned the worship of idols were brought low. Julian fails to note the idea to rebuild the Temple was his. Julian the idol worshipper concludes idols of all kinds are perishable. "The God of the Jews may be great," Julian says, "but He has not found worthy prophets and interpreters. The reason is that their souls have not been refined by a liberal education, and their eyes have not been purified by the light of study."[135] Julian thus tried to pin the failure on the Jews.

Some have claimed the explosions resulted from the "seepage of petroleum."[136] But there is no natural explanation. The Dead Sea, which contains asphalt, which does not explode, was 25 miles away and a thousand meters lower than the Temple. A recent *Jewish Encyclopedia* entry blithely claims no fire rose from the earth to stop work on the Temple, but Graetz is not as reckless with the truth. Graetz admits "on the occasion of the pulling down of the ruins and the excavation of the foundations, a fire broke out by which several workmen lost their lives."[137] He ascribes "this subterranean conflagration" to "gases which had long been compressed there, and which, on being suddenly released from pressure, ignited on coming into contact with the air above."[138] "[T]hese sudden explosions," Graetz says, "disheartened the workmen, so that they gradually gave up work."[139] Graetz's explanation fails twice. First, Ammianus insists "frightful balls of flame kept bursting forth near the foundations of the temple,"[140] which could not occur from pent-up gas. If construction were halted by that kind of explosion, the explosion would have solved the problem. Construction could have resumed immediately.

Ammianius states the fire "kept bursting forth,"[141] something incompatible with pent-up gas. Secondly, Graetz overlooks the implication that flows from use of Ammianus as his source. Ammanius is a pagan with a vested interest in a non-theological explanation unfavorable to the Christians. If there were evidence for a natural cause, Ammanius would have seized it.

Julian, Graetz recounts, "accused the Christians of having caused the fires to break out in the underground passages."[142] Graetz then attempts to rebut Chrysostom's account without mentioning him by name, claiming "the Christian authorities of the following generation relate the most wonderful tales of the miracles which are said to have happened during this impious rebuilding, the purpose of all of which was to warn the obdurate Jews and to glorify Christ."[143]

Graetz is playing the familiar role of the Jewish debunker, but his assessment of Chrysostom is not far off the mark. Chrysostom does assert that the attempt to rebuild the Temple was an act of impiety, and that the project's failure was a warning to obdurate Jews and a vindication of Christians. Julian did not make a second attempt. Julian and the Jews recognized the explosions as a sign the work should not continue. Julian was fatally wounded by a spear thrust in his side in his military campaign against the Persians, uttering, according to one account, "*Nenike-kas Galilaiae*," just before his death or, as Swinburne rendered the phrase, "Thou hast triumphed, O pale Galilean." Another account has him saying, "Helios, thou hast ruined me!"[144] Christian legend attributes his death to St. Mercurius, a Roman soldier martyred a Century before.[145] St. Mercurius' role in slaying Julian was memorialized in Orthodox iconography, but it appears first in the chronicle of John Malalas after 563. According to one account, Christ ordered Mercurius to slay Julian. Another says the Theotokos gave the order.

Either way, the champion of the Jews died by the rivers of Babylon, and Jewish hopes for a rebuilt Temple died with him. The Jews and the pagans were demoralized by their failure to reconstruct the Temple. Graetz says "the death of Julian in the neighborhood of the Tigris (June 363) deprived the Jews of the last ray of hope for a peaceful and unmolested existence."[146] The death of Julian for all practical purposes ended Jewish political aspiration, certainly in Europe, for roughly a millennium. Towards the end of the 14th Century, their hopes would revive briefly as they conspired with the Moors in Spain against the Reconquista, but they backed the wrong side and were expelled from Spain.

Chrysostom's explanation of Julian's efforts is straightforward; it is considerably less labored than Graetz's. The Emperor and his Jewish allies failed because they "failed to see that they were attempting the impossible" because if God destroyed their city, "no human power could ever change what God had decreed.... What God has reared up and wishes to remain, no man can tear down. In the same way, when he has destroyed and wishes to stay destroyed, no man can rebuild."[147]

The Jews' failed attempt to rebuild the Temple with help from the most powerful man on earth shows "how conspicuous our victory is" and how it could not be attributed to the efforts of Christians to halt it, because, Chrysostom says,

> This did not happen in the times of the good emperors; no one can say that the Christians came and prevented the work from being finished. It happened at a time when our religion was subject to persecution, when all our lives were in danger, when every man was afraid to speak, when paganism flourished. Some of the faithful hid in their homes, others fled he marketplaces and moved to the deserts. This is when these events occurred.[148]

The failure to rebuild the Temple happened when Christians were powerless, Chrysostom concludes, "So the Jews have no excuse left to them for their impudence."[149] Chrysostom is under no illusion that Jewish impudence will disappear, because it became part of their identity when they rejected Christ and would remain as long as they perdured in that rejection. The project of restoring the Temple was, according to Chrysostom, traceable to the Jewish character, which by resisting the Holy Spirit, has become revolutionary. What kind of men, Chrysostom asks, would rebuild the Temple? The answer is simple: the revolutionary Jew, or as he puts it:

> They were men who constantly resisted the Holy Spirit, revolutionists bent on stirring up sedition. After the destruction under Vespasian and Titus, these Jews rebelled during the reign of Hadrian and tried to go back to the old commonwealth and way of life. What they failed to realize was that they were fighting against the decree of God, who had ordered that Jerusalem remain forever in ruins.[150]

On February 27, 380, the Emperor Theodosius decreed Christianity was the official religion of the Roman Empire. In 17 years, the Jews had suffered a complete reversal of fortune. The people who cried "We have no King but Caesar" found that Caesar had suddenly become a Christian. Theodosius's decree brought many converts into the Church but it created another more complex problem for the Church, the danger of judaizing.

St. John Chrysostom was ordained to the priesthood six years after Theodosius issued his decree. The decree did not obliterate the status quo ante. Theodosius protected the Jews. The benefactions Julian had established were still in effect, and they gave the Jews a force and vitality dangerous to the local church. There were theoretical issues, too. Jewish monotheism seemed more rational than the Trinitarian formula that Christ was true God and true man; as a result, the Jews forged politically useful links with Arian heretics.

Chrysostom felt converts to the official religion of the empire often were "politically motivated to accept the Christian faith rather than committed to its way of life."[151] To meet this threat, Chrysostom gave a series of sermons known as *Adversos Judaeos*, translated as *Against the Judaizing Christians*, since that is his focus. The

Jews and their synagogues were "a risk to the faith of this Christian community" that he countered "with every weapon in his rhetorical arsenal."[152] Chrysostom, along with Augustine and Jerome, has been accused of aiding and abetting "neurotic anti-Semites in every historical crisis affecting the Jews for more than the next 1500 years."[153] Chrysostom in particular, but the Church Fathers in general, portrays the Jews as "sensual, slippery, voluptuous, avaricious and possessed by demons."[154] Additionally, Jews are "drunkards, harlots and breakers of the Law," as well as "the people who murdered the prophets, Christ and God."[155] The Jews are "pitiable" because they chose darkness over the Light. They are "pitiable and miserable" because "when so many blessings from heaven came into their hands, they thrust them aside and were at great pains to reject them. The morning Sun of Justice arose for them, but they thrust aside its rays and still sit in darkness."[156] They are also pitiable "because they rejected the blessings which were sent to them, while others seized hold of these blessings and drew them to themselves."[157]

The Church, as a result, has superseded the Jews. Christ said "it is not fair to take the children's bread and cast it to the dogs." The Jews were originally the children, and the Gentiles the dogs, but the coming of Christ and his rejection by the Jews changed that. Now, said Chrysostom, "they became the dogs, and we became the children."[158]

The animus expressed here is theological not biological. Everything depends on the Jews' rejection of Christ. Everything can be rescinded by a rejection of the rejection. That rejection is the source of Messianic Politics because, as Chrysostom points out, "the Jews rejected the rule of Christ when they said: 'We have no king but Caesar.'"[159] In rejecting Christ, Chrysostom tells the Jews "you made yourselves subject to the rule of men."[160] And when the Jews "broke the yoke," he continues, "they grew fit for slaughter."[161] Messianic Politics leads to the slaughter of the Jews who continue to reject Christ. The cycle is clear: prosperity leads to revolution and revolution leads to disaster:

> When brute animals feed from a full manger, they grow plump and become more obstinate and hard to hold in check.... Just so the Jewish people were driven by their drunkenness and plumpness to the ultimate evil; they kicked about, they failed to accept the yoke of Christ, nor did they pull the plow of his teaching.... Although such beasts are unfit for work, they are fit for killing. And this is what happened to the Jews: while they were making themselves unfit for work, they grew fit for slaughter.[162]

When Jews use their cultural influence to drag Christians after them into disaster, Chrysostom speaks out. "Dancing with bare feet in the marketplace," they lure Christians to destruction by luring them from the freedom of the Gospel back to the synagogue of Satan, where they "are gathering choruses of effeminates and a great rubbish heap of harlots."[163] In fact, "they drag into the synagogue the whole theater, actors, and all. For there is no difference between the theater and the synagogue."[164] Christians in Antioch were afflicted with the "deadly opinion" that they should "respect the Jews and think that their present way of life is a venerable one." It is Chrysostom's task is "to uproot and tear out this deadly opinion" to protect the Christians "still sick with the Judaizing disease" from seduction by the "indecency and laughter" which "fellowship with those who slew Christ" fosters.[165]

Antioch, where Chrysostom became bishop, had historical and cultural peculiarities that fostered Judaizing. Antioch had Jewish inhabitants since its founding. When Antiochus IV Epiphanes tried to Hellenize those Jews by forcing them to eat pork, the Maccabees refused, choosing martyrdom rather than compromise. The tomb of the Maccabees was in Antioch, a shrine for Christians and Jews. Christians worshipped there because they were the New Israel and the Old Testament was their history; Jews worshipped there as a sign that there was no New Israel and to show the old covenant was still in force.

The situation was bound to lead to confusion. De facto syncretism resulted among new converts so strongly that it was difficult to tell demi-Christians from demi-Jews. They were, in effect, one and the same, a group "sick with the Judaizing disease,"[166] Chrysostom said. Chrysostom felt "the Judaizing sickness raged especially among women and slaves, who should be kept at home and away from the synagogues."[167] Devotion to the seven Maccabees spawned pilgrimages. The Maccabees were properly revered as precursors to the Christian martyrs, but they were also revered because they preferred death to violation of Jewish ritual, which led many to feel the Jewish law was still valid and binding on Christians. The Church eventually took over the synagogue that housed the relics of the Maccabees, but uprooting the syncretism engendered by devotion to the relics proved more difficult.

Hence, Chrysostom's sermons, which were intended for "those who are sick with the Judaizing disease." Chrysostom had to assert the orthodox mean in the face of two heretical extremes. One the one hand, some Christians felt that going to the synagogue was the same as going to church. On the other hand, the Marcionists asserted that Jews and Christians worshipped different Gods, so great were the differences between the Old and the New Testaments.

The same golden mean applied to behavior. Jews were a pernicious threat to civil and moral order, but Jews should not be harmed. Judaizers were a constant threat to the purity of Christian doctrine, but Christians should not persecute them. If there is a curse on the Jews, it is of their own making, inflicted when they rejected Christ, and removable through acceptance of Christ. The proper place for the Jews is in the Church as Christians. The Jews can be saved. The friendly relations that existed between Justin and Trypho in the former's *Dialogue with Trypho* were both a model for future Christians and thought to be based on actual life. Christians, in other words, were opposed to Judaism on theological, not racial, grounds. The source of the animosity—rejection of Christ and persecution of Christians—could be overcome (some would later say, could only be overcome) by conversion. Conversion, however, should not be forced, nor should Jews be harmed.

But the Jews were a threat to Christian society that had to be contained. Jews were promoting syncretism in the sense that there was no difference between the Old and the New Covenant, luring unsuspecting newly-baptized but poorly catechized Christians into their synagogues, where they promised cures by Jewish doctors, who often used amulets and spells. Jews were also promoting elaborate musical productions that overshadowed the Mass. Unlike the Fathers of the Second Vatican Council, St. John Chrysostom tried to impede dialogue between Christians and Jews, especially when it entailed Christians and Jews worshipping together in the synagogue. To halt this dialogue, Chrysostom asks newly baptized Christians to consider that they are sharing their fasts "with those who shouted: "Crucify him, Crucify him," and with those who said: "His blood be upon us and our children." For those who "worship the Crucified" to "keep common festival with those who crucified him" is more than strange, it is "a sign of folly and the worst madness."[168]

Since many newly baptized Jews saw going to the synagogue as the equivalent of going to Mass, Chrysostom began his attack there: the synagogue "is no more than a theater into which the Jews drag effiminates, harlots, and actors."[169] The comparison with the theater is more invidious than it sounds to modern ears because obscene performances were often staged there. "To go to the synagogue," Chrysostom continues, "is a greater crime than going to the theater. What goes on in the theater is, to be sure, sinful; what goes on in the synagogue is godlessness."[170]

Chrysostom also hates the synagogue because of how it differs from the theater. The synagogue has the prophets; it has the law; it has the word of God; and yet it uses them to corrupt: "This is my strongest reason for hating the synagogue: it does have the Law and the prophets. And now I hate it more than if it had none of these. Why is this? Because in the Law and the Prophets they have a great allurement and many a snare to attract the more simple-minded sort of men."[171]

Chrysostom also hates Judaism because "although they possess the Law, they put it to outrageous use."[172] Because "they have heaped outrage on him whom the prophets foretold,"[173] "the man who sets a Judaizing Christian straight, wins a victory over godlessness."[174] The deceptive similarities between the Church and the synagogue are dangerous and troubling:

> this is the reason above all others *why I hate the synagogue* and abhor it. They have the prophets but do not believe them; they read the sacred writings but reject their witness—and this is a mark of men guilty of the greatest outrage. Let that be your judgment about the synagogue too. For they brought the books of Moses and the prophets along with them into the synagogue, not to honor them but to outrage them with dishonor.[175]

By luring unsuspecting Christians into synagogues, the Jews implicate the "saintly prophets" as "partners of their impiety" in rejecting Christ. So, "the harm they bring to our weaker brothers is not slight," because "when they see that you, who worship the Christ whom they crucified, are reverently following their ritual, how can they fail to think that the rites they have performed are the best and that our ceremonies are worthless"?[176]

Chrysostom finds the Jews' promotion of music especially troubling. By going to the synagogue and participating in the festivals of the trumpets, weaker brethren will "be emboldened to admire what the Jews do."[177] Blinded by spectacle and music, they will not see that what really stands "in their synagogue" is "an invisible altar of deceit on which they sacrifice not sheep and calves but the souls of men."[178] God is not worshipped in the synagogue; after the Jewish rejection of Christ, the synagogue "remains a place of idolatry."[179] Because Christ is God, "No Jew adores God!"[180] Chrysostom bases his claim on the authority of Jesus Christ, the Son of God, "For he said: 'If you were to know my Father, you would also know me. But you neither know me nor do you know my father.' Could I produce a witness more trustworthy than the Son of God?"[181]

Chrysostom cites Matthew 12:43-45 as proof "demons dwell in the synagogue" and "these demons are more dangerous than the ones of old." "When God forsakes a place," he says, "that place becomes the dwelling of demons." The synagogue "is not merely a lodging place for robbers and cheats but also for demons. This is true not only of the synagogues but also of the souls of the Jews ... who "live for their bellies; they gasp for the things of this world; their condition is no better than that of pigs or goats because of their wanton ways and excessive gluttony."[182]

Demons gained a foothold in the synagogue when the Jews "sacrificed their own sons and daughters to demons. They refuse to recognize nature, they forgot the pangs of birth, they trod underfoot the rearing of their children, they overturned from their foundations the laws of kinship, they became more savage than any wild beast."[183]

That savagery began in sexual license and culminated in rejection and crucifixion of Christ, a gratuitous act made more heinous because the Jews had their law given to them by God. "No necessity," Chrysostom continues, "forced the Jews when they slew their own children with their own hands to pay honor to the avenging demons, the foes of our life.... Because of their licentiousness, did they not show a lust beyond that of irrational animals. Hear what the prophet says of their excesses. 'They are become as amorous stallions. Every one neighed after his neighbor's wife.'"[184]

Sacrificing their children to idols paved the way for the synagogue's rejection of Christ. "Why is it," Chrysostom wonders, "that God put up with you in the old days when you sacrificed your children to idols, but turns himself away from you now when you are not so bold as to commit such a crime? Is it not clear that you dared commit a deed much worse and much greater than any sacrifice of children or transgressions of the Law when you slew Christ?"[185] As a result, the synagogue is worse than the theater, and "everything that goes on among the Jews today is a ridiculous sport, a trading in shame, filled with outrages beyond number."[186]

The Jews dedicated themselves to their lusts and sacrificing their children to idols. As a further impiety, they dedicated themselves to strict adherence to the law and rigorous fasts after rejecting Christ who abolished the law. "Now that the Law has ceased to bind," Chrysostom writes, "they obstinately strive to observe it. What could be more pitiable than those who provoke God not only by transgressing the Law but also by keeping it?"[187] The Jews offend God, "not only by transgressing the Law but also by wishing to observe it at the wrong time."[188] According to Chrysostom, Jewish legalism is as impious as Jewish lawlessness. "That is what destroyed the Jews. While they always kept looking for the old customs and life, these were stripped from them and they turned to impiety."[189]

In addition to blaspheming, Jews are "drunkards," a people in whom reason is overcome by the darkness of uncontrolled passion. Chrysostom uses the term "drunkard" because "drunkenness is nothing other than a loss of right reason, a derangement, and depriving the soul of its health."[190] For, Chrysostom continues,

> the man in love with a woman who is not his wife, the man who spends his time with prostitutes, is a drunkard. The heavy drinker cannot walk straight, his speech is rude, his eyes cannot see things as they really are. In the same way, the drunkard who is filled with the strong wine of his undisciplined passion is also unsound of speech; everything he utters is disgraceful, corrupt, crude and ridiculous; he, too, cannot see things as they really are because he is blind to what he sees. Like a deranged man or one who is out of his wits, he imagines he sees everywhere the woman he yearns to ravish. No matter how many people speak to him at gatherings or banquets, at any time or place, he seems not to hear them; he strains after her and dreams of his sin; he is suspicious of everything and afraid of everything; he is no better off than some trap-shy animal.[191]

If "the man in the grip of passion or anger is drunk" because "his reason is submerged," then "this is all the more true of the impious man who blasphemes God."[192] Just as the drunkard "has no awareness of his unseemly behavior .... So, too, the Jews are drunk but do not know they are drunk."[193] Anyone who goes to the synagogue or observes Jewish fasts, has "fallen among robbers, the Jews," who are "more savage than any highwaymen" because "they do greater harm to those who have fallen among them."[194] They did not strip a victim's clothes nor inflict wounds on his body as did robbers on the road to Jericho. The Jews have mortally hurt their victim's soul; they have "inflicted on it ten thousand wounds and left it lying in the pit of ungodliness." So Christians "must not turn to God's enemies, the Jews, for cures" because "this will only rouse his anger against them still more."[195]

Those who attend the synagogue and observe Jewish fasts destroy "the peace which comes from the harmony sent by the Spirit."[196] The Judaizers "are now tearing this peace asunder by destroying us and exalting the Jews. These men consider the Jews as more trustworthy teachers than their own Fathers; they believe the account of Christ's passion and death, which is given by those who slew Him. What could be more unreasonable than this?"[197]

Chrysostom felt the Jews would be a perennial danger to the Christian community. The Church must formulate that danger so future generations could act justly to the Jews but without prejudice to the Christian communities. "Let us," Chrysostom concludes, "not exalt our enemies' side and destroy our own."[198]

Once the Church became the established religion, it had to find a *modus vivendi* with the Jews. The Church, as a result, proposed for the first time in history a dfferent reaction to Jewish revolutionary activity, one based on Christian charity and forbearance. The normal reaction to Jewish revolutionary activity was to slaughter the Jews. That is what Vespasian, Titus, and Hadrian did, as did the Greeks on Cyprus and in Alexandria. The Church could not respond that way, but it also could not ignore the danger Jews posed in terms of cultural subversion and, ultimately, armed insurrection. It formulated its position with those dangers in mind.

Shortly after Chrysostom's death, the Church articulated what would become the constant teaching of the Church on the Jews. A law promulgated in either 412 or 418 announced: "Let no one who has done no harm be molested on the ground that he is a Jew, nor let any aspect of his religion result in his exposure to contumely; in no place are their synagogues to be set afire, or wantonly damaged." In other words, no one was to harm the Jew. The Church fathers had learned that the Jew left unmolested tended to abuse his position and act in ways subversive to the common good. So the same law "warn[ed] the Jews that, elated, it may be, by their security, they must not become insolent and admit anything which is opposed to the reverence due to Christian worship."[199]

The relationship between Christians and Jews is central to Christianity. "There is," in fact, "no moment from the beginning to the end, when Christian legislation on the Jews is silent on their providential role, especially as guardians of Scripture and as destined for final salvation. That Jews are the people first chosen by God and never abandoned, an Elect whose failure, for all its tragedy in Christian eyes, is less a fall than a 'stumbling' (Rom 9: 1-11, 32), remains Catholic teaching."[200] That same Christian doctrine absorbed Roman law, so "the Jews could expect that the rights and privileges conceded them in the decrees of past emperors would be vindicated in the imperial courts," but they should not expect to expand them.[201] Christian Roman law added theological depth to what had been Imperial law. That generally played itself out in the following fashion. Christian Roman law "declared it illegal to confiscate or to burn down existing synagogues, but, on the other hand, generally forbade the construction of new ones."[202] Jews were not permitted to ridicule the Christian faith; they were not to introduce "the sign of our worship into their buffooneries," and they must "restrain their rites, keeping them this side of contempt for the Christian Law."[203] In 1215 a decree of the Fourth Lateran Council forbade Jewish ridicule of Christian Good Friday services.

The Church dealt with Jewish subversion too. One law prohibited military careers for Jews. A decree of 439, "proclaimed as 'valid forever' a statute that declared Jews ineligible to hold any civil office that included power to judge or to pronounce sentence against Christians."[204] Similarly, if a Jew attempted to subvert the faith of a Christian with "perverse teaching" his goods and life were forfeit.[205]

The Church also forbade Jews from owning Christian slaves. This prohibition went back to the Roman empire; it was adopted by the papacy and incorporated into canon law. "In 339, Constantius II proclaimed that Jews could possess no slave 'of another sect or nation' and should he attempt to obtain one the slave was expropriated to the imperial treasury."[206] Reiterated often by popes, the prohibition became part of the teaching of the Church. "A pious Jew ought not to keep in his house a slave who refused persistently to be circumcised; after a year, he ought to be sold back to the idolaters whose convictions he refused to relinquish."[207] If a Jew knowingly bought a Christian slave, all his possessions were forfeited.

Pope Gregory the Great was especially adamant in opposition to Jews owning Christian slaves. In this, the Church added theological nuance to the practice of the Roman empire. As the epistles of St. Paul made clear, master and slave enjoyed equal stature before God. Unlike Aristotle, who felt certain men were slaves by nature, the Church considered slavery a sociological accident, even if recognized by law. The Jews were an exception because they were "willing slaves of Torah."[208] They chose the bondage of the law over the freedom of Christ and wanted to spread this bondage to anyone under their cultural influence. Pope Gregory was loath "to expose the faith of Christian slaves to the daily pressure of its Jewish denial, embodied in masters whose social superiority might seem to reinforce the plausibility of their claims to religious superiority."[209] No Christian soul was worth the risk posed by Jewish subversion. Gregory was unwilling to turn a blind eye to the risk, and so the only alternative was to forbid Jews from owning Christian slaves. When Gregory heard that Brunichilda, Queen of the Franks, permitted Jews to hold Christian slaves, he rebuked her in writing. Hearing of the circumcision of pagan slaves by Samaritan owners, Gregory declared the practice "'detestable to us, and altogether hostile to the laws'; such slaves, he directed, were to be set free immediately and far from receiving some reimbursement for them, the masters were to face the penalty of law."[210] A bishop who did not insist on enforcement of these laws was rebuked for allowing Jewish masters "less by persuasion than by virtue of their power" over Christian slaves, to bring them to subserve "Jewish superstition." Gregory felt that it was "altogether unwholesome and accursed that Christians be in servitude to Jews."[211] If a Christian slave fled his Jewish master and took refuge with the Church, he was not to be returned to his Jewish owner, nor was his owner reimbursed, whether the slave was a Christian of long standing or newly baptized. Jews who owned Christian slaves had to dispose of them to Christian masters within 40 days. If the Jew transferred the slave to another member of his family he could be prosecuted for fraud.

As in many areas of Church life—sacred music, for example—Gregory formulated the Church's position on the Jews. He is the founder of the celebrated medieval "Constitution on the Jews," which goes by the name "*Sicut Judaeis non.*" Culled from more than 850 letters, Gregory's teaching was cited by every succeeding pope when the issue arose. According to Synan, Gregory "canonized" the existing civil law. Gregory strove to balance persecution and the unjust appropriation of property on the one hand with a laxity that would allow if not encourage subversion on the other. He came up with a formula: "As the determination of law does not permit the Jews to erect new synagogues, so also does it permit them to possess their old ones without disquietude."[212]

Gregory's position was an example of theological grace perfecting Roman legal nature. From a theological perspective, the Jew was deficient in faith, "burdened with perfidia,"[213] a faith that is wrong because it is truncated, distorted, and ultimately a form of disbelief. Gregory does not refer to Judaism as a religion. Putting it on the same level as the Christian faith was unthinkable, no matter what the two shared. Judaism was a "*superstitio*," a cult outside of the official religion. "This superstition," the Pope warned, would "pollute" Christian faith and "deceive with sacrilegious seduction" simple Christian peasants.[214] Indeed, Gregory termed Judaism a disaster, *perditio*. Pope Gregory described Jews as "Stone of Darkness" and "shadow of death," "wild asses," "dragons for poisonous ideas," the "shaken reed" of Isaiah, a kingdom "gleaming without, but empty within." He describes "their hearts" as "the den of a beast."[215] Gregory got these terms from the book of Job. His appropriation of the vocabulary of the prophets was also prophetic. The split between faithful Hebrews and unfaithful Hebrews had been superseded by the split between the Jews who voluntarily chose bondage to the Law and the New Israel who embraced the freedom conferred by faith in Christ. "After the appearance of One he recognized as Messiah," Synan tells us, "Gregory could see in Judaism only a retrogression."[216]

Even though Judaism was retrogression, the Jew could not be coerced from his unbelief because the Christian faith could only be a free acceptance of a gift from God. Gregory encouraged Jewish conversion, but forbade forced baptism "with all possible firmness," according to Synan.[217] But his firmness implies that forced baptism happened nonetheless. A bishop, he wrote, ought to replace force with preaching. "Reason is so little profane that Logos, Word and thought, can serve as a divine name."[218] Reason was the only licit means to lead perfidious Jews to the Logos. Subsequent popes would interpret this by forcing Jews to listen to sermons but never forcing them to accept baptism. Gregory termed it, "A novelty, indeed a thing unheard of, is this doctrine that extorts faith through blows."[219]

The prohibition against coercion applied to overly zealous converts from Judaism as well as to bishops and heads of state. When a convert from Judaism invaded the synagogue in Caligari, Sardinia, to plant a cross and an image of Mary on the day of his baptism, he earned the rebuke of the local bishop, a rebuke Gregory would have seconded. "The unwilling," as Gregory said, "are not to be compelled."[220] He established the principle that the assent of faith cannot be the object of intimidation. "We forbid," he wrote, "that the aforesaid Hebrews be burdened or afflicted contrary to the order of reason; rather, just as they are permitted to live in accord with Roman statutes, they can, as they know, order their activities without hindrance, and to this Justice gives assent,"[221] Gregory rebuked a fellow bishop when he confiscated a synagogue and its guesthouse. "Our brother has acted unsuitably,"[222] he wrote, and what he did was not just. What has been given to sacred use cannot be withdrawn without sacrilege. The bishop responsible must pay for the buildings, thus making them the legitimate property of the Church, and guaranteeing that the Jews "should in no way appear to be oppressed, or to suffer an injustice."[223] Forbidding Jewish worship will not lead to the conversion of the Jews, Gregory continued. They are to be converted by reason; until then, "Let them enjoy their lawful liberty."[224]

The Jews, however, continued to test the limits of papal tolerance with their cultural subversion. Acting on a complaint from the Jewish community of Rome, Gregory responded with a letter of incalculable importance because it contains the formula "*Sicut Judaeis non*," a formula "destined to recur endlessly in papal documents concerning Jewish rights and disabilities throughout the Middle Ages."[225] "Just as license," Gregory writes, "ought not to be presumed for the Jews to do anything in their synagogues beyond what is permitted by law, so in those points conceded to them, they ought to suffer nothing prejudicial."[226] Jews have the right to practice their religion without harm, but they should not be granted positions of cultural influence from which they could spread error and subversion.

That would remain the papal position throughout the Middle Ages, and because of it, the Papal States often were a refuge for Jews persecuted in other Christian countries. When Jews were subjected to forced baptism, expelled from Spain, or both, many took refuge in the Papal States, much to the chagrin of Spanish princes. Poland erred in the opposite way by allowing Jews too much cultural influence, something the Poles regretted when rapacious neighbors partitioned Poland at the end of the 18th Century.

The Jews never perceived "*Sicut Judaeis non*" as a model of judicious tolerance and forbearance. Gregory's formulation occurred during unprecedented upheaval in the Roman empire, a time best described as the empire's death throes, when civil order broke down and the rule of the strong—*homo lupus homini*—seemed more likely to succeed Roman order than did the new religion. Gregory was concerned with injustices against Jews, but also about the breakdown of public order. "At this time especially," he wrote, "when there is fear of the enemy, you must not have a divided populace."[227]

The codification of the new Jewish religion occurred about the time the Church articulated its position on the Jews. The first articulation of "*Sicut Judaeis non*" appeared between 412 and 418. The Babylonian Talmud was codified during the fifth century by the Amora'im, beginning with Rabbi Ashi, who died in 427, and culminating in the work of Rabbi Abina, who died in 499. It was as if Christians and Jews needed to brace themselves against the coming barbarian invasion by putting what they believed in writing, lest it be swept away in the coming chaos. Alaric sacked Rome in 410. Augustine's *City of God* was written in response. Someone had to explain how the hand of God could be discerned in the destruction of civilization.

Those Jews not busy writing down the Talmud were preparing for another Messiah, the Cretan Moses, who announced he had come to usher in the end of the world, something predicted to occur between 440 and 470. As they would a millennium later, the Jews abandoned their property and neglected their businesses, waiting for Moses to divide the waters of the Mediterranean and lead them dry-shod back to Palestine. On the appointed day, the latter-day Moses led his followers to a cliff overlooking the ocean and commanded them to jump. Many complied. Some drowned; sailors rescued others. The false Moses disappeared never to be seen again.[228]

After one disappointment after another, the Jews' Messianic politics largely went into remission. No one, however, could predict a remission in effect lasting over a millennium. No one other than St. Hippolytus of Rome in his writings on the Antichrist would have predicted the return of revolutionary messianic politics after so long an absence. But the codification of the Talmud, the hubbub surrounding the failure of Moses of Crete and the fall of Rome (after which Genseric the Vandal carried the sacred vessels of the Temple from Rome to Carthage), and the articulation of the Church's policy toward the Jews were each a manifestation of the Zeitgeist of collapse and uncertainty. Graetz called the time of the compilation of the Babylonian Talmud "one of the most important epochs in Jewish history."[229] Thereafter, "the Babylonian rather than the Jerusalem Talmud became the fundamental possession of the Jewish race, its life's breath, its very soul."[230] The Babylonian Talmud defined Jewish life during the millennium of remission, when revolutionary politics went dormant and Catholic culture created Europe. "For more than a thousand years," Graetz says,

> nature and mankind, powers and events, were for the Jewish nation insignificant, non-essential, a mere phantom; the only true reality was the Talmud. A new truth in their eyes only received the stamp of veracity and freedom from doubt when it appeared to be foreseen and sanctioned by the Talmud. Even the knowledge of the Bible, the more ancient history of their race, the words of fire and balm of their prophets, the soul outpourings of their Psalmists were only known to them through and in the light of the Talmud.[231]

The Talmud absorbed the Torah, allowing the Jews to view the rise of Christian Europe with consolation born from disdain. Graetz claims "the Babylonian Amoraim created that dialectic, close-reasoning Jewish spirit, which in the darkest days preserved the dispersed nation from stagnation and stupidity."[232] It also ensured the Jews of Europe, unlike the Jews of Antioch, were cut off from contact with Christianity. Judaizing, as described by St. John Chrysostom, became a thing of the past, replaced by two completely separate societies even though they lived in close proximity—with contact, at least in Poland, only when usury or illicit sex was involved. The Talmud, says Graetz, "preserved and promoted the religious and moral life of Judaism," but it did so by bringing about separation and control, insuring "there could not arise that dream-life, that disdain of the world, that hatred of reality, which in the Middle Ages gave birth to and sanctified the hermit life of the monks and nuns."[233]

The Talmud may have protected the Jews from schism and sectarian divisions, but the price the Jews paid for this protection was complete rabbinic control. The Talmud took the sacred scriptures out of the hands of the Jews and made their interpretation the sole purview of the rabbis as codified in Talmudic lore. The word of God was nullified by the Talmud. The Talmud, the saying went, permitted whatever the Torah forbade. The Jew, in other words, could not appeal to sacred writ without the permission of the rabbis who controlled the Talmud. The Talmud became, as a result, control through hermeneutics. The Talmud became, according to Walsh, "the chief means employed by the Annas and Caiaphas of each age to keep the mass of the Jewish people in ignorance of the true nature of Christianity, and to fan their misunderstanding of it to hatred."[234] To fan this hatred, the Talmud contained "the most scurrilous and vindictive blasphemies against Christ."[235] The Talmud claimed that Christ was a bastard (Kallah 51A) offspring of a Jewish whore and a Roman soldier (Sanhedrin 106A) who is in hell buried in boiling excrement (Gittin 57A). During persecution, the most controversial parts of the Talmud were committed to memory and transmitted orally, but the tradition of blasphemy and subversion continued unabated. The Talmud insured blasphemy and subversion became part of Jewish culture, because, as one scholar noted, the Talmud was "the creator of the Jewish nation and the mold of the Jewish soul."

The Talmud would also be instrumental in the rise of the revolutionary spirit when it re-emerged during the Reformation. "We can boldly assert," Graetz writes, "that the war for and against the Talmud aroused German consciousness and created a public opinion without which the Reformation, like many other efforts, would have died in the hour of birth, or perhaps would never have been born at all."[236] The Talmud also became the link between the Neoplatonist thaumaturgy of Julian and later assaults on the Catholic Church from behind the mask of Freemasonry. Masonic theology, according to Rabbi Benamozegh, is "at root nothing else than ... the theology of the Kaballah."[237]

Julian the Apostate

The Jewish Revolutionary Spirit

Chapter Three

Rome Discovers the Talmud

On November 27, 1095, Pope Urban II broke precedent at the council he had convoked; he addressed not only the bishops at the cathedral but the entire population in a field outside of Clermont's eastern gate. His topic was the humiliations Christians were suffering at the hands of infidels in the Holy Land. He asked them to leave their possessions and families and march in one great Christian army marked with the sign of the Cross to Jerusalem to restore that city to its rightful owners, namely, Christians for whom Christ died there.

Urban indicated there would be other benefits too, "since this land which you inhabit, shut in on all sides by the seas and surrounded by the mountain peaks is too narrow for your large population; nor does it abound in wealth and it furnishes scarcely enough food for its cultivators."[1] Urban spoke when Europe was on the cusp of change. Prosperity and stability had increased since the collapse of the Roman empire; that prosperity led to increased population, which the feudal agricultural economy could not absorb. In subsequent centuries, the market economy would replace the agricultural subsistence economy of the feudal era.

The main vehicle for that transition was wool. Peasants and small landowners producing wool cloth for themselves already had the capital equipment—the spinning wheels, looms, etc.—to produce a surplus, which could be sold for cash, the *sine qua non* of the market economy. Because wool varied from region to region, and what was common in one was desired in another, commerce aided development of the market economy. The Danube basin became famous for Loden cloth, which was more water repellent than cloth from other areas. The German principalities became famous for black wool cloth, which the clergy demanded, and the Low Countries became famous for wool that took dye particularly well. The surplus population of northwestern Europe, a particularly rich agricultural area, drifted into the cities, taking up trades like fuller and dyer, and soon became Europe's nascent proletariat, people who owned nothing but their time, which they hired out, and who produced nothing but *proles*, or children. This uprooted, impoverished population became the mainstay of the crusading armies. With soldiers like this, trouble could be expected, and trouble followed within a year of the pope's proclamation.[2]

Within a month of Urban's call for a crusade, the Jews of France were "gripped by fear and trembling,"[3] sending letters to Jewish communities on the Rhineland warning them to fast and pray for deliverance. The French Jews were spared because of the discipline of the French crusaders, kept in line by feudal lords who responded to the pope's call. Along the Rhine, though, the rulers were weak and ineffective, and the cities were teeming with the uprooted, men who had already broken with tradition in leaving the land.

The Jews had been in France and the adjacent areas of the Rhine Valley ever since their disastrous revolutionary insurrection against Rome had been crushed and the Temple in Jerusalem destroyed. The Jews had come to the Rhein valley in the time of the Romans because they were merchants; the Rhine and the Danube rivers comprised the major commercial corridor for central Europe. In *Ashkenaz*, the Hebrew word for Germany, the *Ashkenazim* learned their new language, *Juedische Deutsch* or Yiddish.

The Jews brought their messianic politics to the Rhine Valley. Being a revolutionary was for many part of what it meant to be a Jew, even if no one had acted militarily for almost a millennium. The Jews, according to Norman Cohn, "refused to be absorbed into the populations amongst which they lived" even though "their lot in the early Middle Ages was by no means a hard one."[4] The Diaspora meant the dispersion of revolutionary politics; in the millennium following the defeat of Simon bar Kokbha, the Jews interpreted the destruction of the Temple and subsequent Diaspora as God's plan for spreading revolution. "What made the Jews remain Jews," according to Cohn, "was ... their absolute conviction that the Diaspora was ... a preparation for the coming of the Messiah and the return to a transfigured Holy Land."[5]

Around the time of the first crusade, millennialism, the Jewish Messianic philosophy of history and political liberation based on the Book of Daniel, broke out in Europe after remaining largely dormant for a millennium. Ironically, it broke out among people who were not Jews, and, more ironically, the Jews suffered at their hands. The Jews, says Cohn, "rarely inspired armed risings, and never amongst European Jews."[6] But during the rise of cities in Europe, when European Christians first came in contact with Jews in significant numbers, "the desire of the poor to improve the material conditions of their lives became transfused with phantasies of a new Paradise on earth, a world purged of suffering and sin, a Kingdom of the Saints."[7] At the close of the 11th Century, "it was no longer Jews but Christians who cherished and elaborated prophecies in the tradition of 'Daniel's dream' and who continued to be inspired by them."[8] The temptation to look for heaven on earth was known as Judaizing, which took messianic inspiration from a distorted interpretation of the Old Testament, but usually without the further distortions of the Talmud. It was a perennial temptation for Christians who failed to find solace in "a messiah who suffered and died [and] a kingdom which was purely spiritual."[9] The Book of Daniel, the Christian Scripture most likely to be corrupted by Judaizers, seemed to prophesy an earthly kingdom while also offering a key to understanding history in the parable of the colossus with the feet of clay:

> Generation after generation was seized at least intermittently by a tense expectation of some sudden, miraculous event in which the world would be utterly transformed, some prodigious final struggle between the hosts of Christ and the hosts of antichrist through which history would attain its fulfillment and justification.[10]

Heaven on earth was a Jewish idea; hence, Cohn finds it "natural enough that the earliest of these prophecies should have been produced by Jews"[11] convinced they were God's chosen people for whom things had not gone well since the destruction of the Temple. What sharply distinguished the Jews from other peoples was their attitude towards history and in particular towards their own role in history. "Precisely because they were so utterly certain of being the Chosen People," Cohn tells us, "Jews tended to react to peril, oppression and hardship by phantasies of the total triumph and boundless prosperity, which Yahweh, out of his omnipotence, would bestow upon his Elect in the fullness of time."[12] The disparity between an unbelievably happy future and a wretched present led the Jews to believe "out of an immense cosmic catastrophe, there will arise a Palestine which will be nothing less than a new Eden."[13] Throughout the Diaspora, the fantasy of a temporal heaven on earth coming about in and through history (as opposed to in eternity) captured the minds of the Jews and anyone in contact with the Jews who also considered themselves oppressed. The Diaspora created exaggeration: "for the first time the glorious future kingdom is imagined as embracing not simply Palestine but the whole world."[14] Through their suffering, the Jewish people would liberate all mankind. The Christian undertone is unmistakable. Moses Hess would take this reasoning to its logical conclusion in the 19th Century, claiming the Jewish people had become its own Messiah. In the meantime:

> The tyranny of that power will become more and more outrageous, the sufferings of its victims more and more intolerable—until suddenly the hour will strike when the Saints of God are able to rise up and overthrow it. Then the Saints themselves, the chosen, holy people who hitherto have groaned under the oppressor's heel, shall in their turn inherit dominion over the whole earth. This will be *the culmination of history.*[15]

The millennialist kingdom that will be "the culmination of history" and that "will have no successors" found numerous adherents from Karl Marx to the neoconservative Francis Fukuyama, whose *The End of History* announced the neoconservative millennium when Marx's millennium failed. The revolutionary chiliasm Marxists and anti-Marxist Neoconservatives would champion emerged in the Rhine Valley during the first crusade, and it caused problems there for four centuries, culminating in the Anabaptist uprising in Muenster in 1533. Cohn claims there is "no evidence" of revolutionary chiliasm in Europe "before the closing years of the 11th Century," i.e., before the first crusade.[16] Since revolutionary chiliasm was a Jewish idea, the necessary condition for its outbreak in the Rhine Valley seems to have been contact with Jews. Subsequent events bore this out.

Contact between Jews and Christians meant a cross-fertilization of ideas. For every Jew who became Christian, there seemed to be ten judaizing Christians eager to use Daniel as an all-encompassing theory of history that allowed them to seek heaven on earth. Judaizers repudiated Augustine's claim that the millennium arrived with the Church, the New Israel. The Judaizers wanted a more "carnal" kingdom. Millennialism broke out in the Rhine Valley among Christians because cities had replaced the monasteries as commercial entities and had contact with revolutionary ideas.

"Like so many generations of Jews before them," Cohn says, the Christians of the Rhine Valley "saw history as divided into two eras, one preceding and the other following the triumphant advent of the Messiah," who, according to Commidanus, "will be at the head not of an angelic host but of the descendants of the ten lost tribes of Israel, which have survived in hidden places, unknown to the rest of the world."[17] The idea of the Ten Lost Tribes would recur wherever Judaizing dominated, culminating in England in the 17th Century when Menassah ben Israel wrote a best-seller among the Puritans on the topic.

When Jewish revolutionary activity went dormant for almost 1000 years, the Church by and large forgot about it, until attacks on Jews after the call for the First Crusade refocused her attention. Even more confusing was the reemergence of the "error of the Jews," i.e., the desire for an earthly kingdom, among people who were not Jews and seemed to hate the Jews. Messianic revolutionary politics re-emerged among the proletariat in Christian Europe, a phenomenon as shocking and violent as it was perplexing. Millennialism inevitably resulted when the urban proletariat of the Low Countries came into contact with Jewish messianic politics. "The Church's fear of the popularity of Jewish messianism," Lea Dasberg says, "was definitely no figment of her imagination."[18] It always posed a threat to Catholic theology; now it posed a threat to the social order. St. Jerome, she continues, had condemned Millennialism as "Jewish dogma, Jewish traditions, and Jewish fables."[19] And Christians who believed this sort of thing were denounced as "judaizing Christians" and "demi-Jews." The constellation of ideas revolving around the "end of days" concept was Jewish, as much as the idea that the rise of Jerusalem would follow the decline of Rome. Add to that the notion that the Jews were again predicting the advent of the Messiah in the very year preparations were being made for the first crusade, and you get a sense of why Millennialism swept the Rhine Valley and took root among the uprooted. It did so "amongst the masses in the overpopulated, highly urbanized areas," Cohn says, because

> there were always many who lived in a state of chronic and inescapable insecurity, harassed not only by their economic helplessness and vulnerability but by the lack of the traditional social relationships on which even at the worst times, peasants had normally been able to depend. These were the people whose anxieties drove them to seek messianic leaders and they were also the people who were most prone to create demonic scapegoats.[20]

The scapegoats were the Jews; the perpetrators of violence against them, ironically, were often Judaizing priests and monks. According to Cohn's reading of John of Roquetallade's *Vademecum in tribulationibus*, "the old eschatological tradition" based on the "carnal" reading of the Book of Daniel, "had been adapted as a vehicle for the new social radicalism."[21] Rootless apostate monks assumed political leadership among the rootless proletarians of the cities; often the local and higher clergy bore the brunt of the attack after it glanced off the Jews. Just as often, the higher clergy alone could stop the violence. According to Cohn, the leadership of millennialist movements "passed into the hands of a number of *prophetae*, who seem to have consisted largely of dissident or apostate clerics." "Apostate monks in Germany" whipped the rootless masses into an apocalyptic frenzy as a way of "destroying clergy and Church." Revolutionary chiliasm was as anticlerical as it was anti-Semitic.[22]

In April, 1096, Peter the Hermit, a monk inspired by Urban II's call for a crusade against the infidel, arrived in Trier, the ancient Roman city on the Moselle River. He had letters of introduction from the French Jews, which he used to demand money and provisions from the Jews in the Rhineland. The Jews in Trier must have acceded to his demands because by the end of the month he was in Cologne making the same demands.

Peter the Hermit wasn't just interested in raising money. He was also interested in raising troops. To do that, he engaged in the motivational speaking then known as preaching. Count Emicho (or Emico or Emmerich) of Leiningen, a minor landowner from Upper Lorraine, was touched by his words. Emicho is what Liddell-Hart and Englishmen of his generation would have called a "bad hat,"[23] and typical of the bad hats who were attracted to irregular warfare. Ekkehard writes that Emicho was "count of those regions that lie about the Rhine, and long infamous in the extreme." He was a man "of very ill repute on account of his tyrannical mode of life."[24] He was also what Msgr. Knox would call an "enthusiast"; he claimed to receive private revelations from the Lord about his anointing as a charismatic leader. Emicho called himself the "Emperor of the Last Days" and claimed that he would conquer Jerusalem for Christ. Ekkehard claims he was "called to religion in this guise by divine revelations," and "like a second Saul, he usurped for himself the leadership of nearly 12,000 who had taken the Sign." Emicho then led these men "through the cities on the Rhine, the Main and the Danube." Emicho believed that, if it was meritorious to wage war on the infidel in Jerusalem, then it was doubly meritorious to wage war on the infidel at home. "Let us, therefore," he concluded, "take our revenge first on [the Jews], and extirpate them from among the nations."

One commentator described Emicho as an "accomplished charlatan," who "claimed that he had been divinely anointed for leadership in the messianic mode." As the Franciscans of Medjugorje have shown in our day, thuggery and charisma are not mutually exclusive. Indeed, they are often united by messianic politics. Emicho, according to his self-proclaimed anointing, "would defeat the forces of Islam and establish himself triumphantly in the Holy city. There he would do battle once again, this time destroying the even more powerful army of Antichrist, the satanic son of a Jewish harlot, who aspired to rule the world in the name of the devil." This would usher in the millennium—a thousand years of glory with Christ as king of the world—beginning with the military conquest of Islam, and culminating in conversion of the Jews. Because there were no Muslims along the Rhine, but there were plenty of Jews, the order of conquest was reversed. The crusaders "made it their concern, wherever the execrable Jewish people were found, either to wipe them out completely, or to force them within the bosom of the Church."

On May 3, 1096, Emicho arrived at the gates of Speyer at the head of his crusading army. He gave the Jews there the choice of baptism or death. The situation was probably similar in all towns along the Rhine, Main, and Danube when the crusading armies appeared. A large mob milled around the town square with nothing to do as negotiations took place behind the scenes. Then, growing impatient with the delay or fired up by a preacher, or both, the mob would sack homes in the Jewish quarter, motivated by a desire to punish infidelity, a desire to avenge long-standing grudges, particularly over the lending of money, or a desire to requisition material for the military campaign against the Muslims.

Unable to defend themselves, the Jews would flee to the palace (or fortress) of the local bishop and implore his protection, offering money to facilitate his altruism. The Jews of Speyer "fled for refuge to the Bishop of the city, and he undertook, not without suffering the accusation of both Jews and Christians that Jewish money assisted him in the decision, first to defend the Jews and second to punish those guilty of the outrage." Punishment meant that those implicated in the attacks on the Jews had their hands cut off by order of the bishop, who "was moved with wrath at this and bought by the Jews' money."

On May 24, three weeks after pillaging Speyer, Emicho arrived in Worms;, where similar carnage followed. The crusaders milled around the town square until a riot broke out, then the mob ran amok and killed 300 Jews. The crusaders "slaughtered young and old alike." In the Jewish quarter, they looted the Jews' homes, there trampling Torah scrolls underfoot.

Half the Jews remained in their houses in Worms. The other half fled to the bishop. A day or two after the initial attack, 500 Jews were holed up at the bishop's compound, hoping to weather the storm there. Many Jews committed suicide while waiting for the bishop to rescue them. According to one Jewish report, one "pious lady ... slew herself for the hallowing of the divine Name" rather than convert. The Jewish reports are largely hagiographic, but even so, they mention that many Jewish survivors "were rescued by the Bishop, without having to change their faith."

The sheer numbers of the crusaders overwhelmed the bishop, who had some armed men at his command. As a result, he informed the Jews he could ensure their safety only if they accepted baptism. William Thomas Walsh, though unabashedly pro-Catholic, makes no apologies for crusaders who "massacred Jews, in the summer of 1096, at Trier, Worms, Mainz, Cologne-wherever they advanced along the Main and the Danube; and when they took Jerusalem, they soiled their victory by a hideous butchery of Jews." The Second Crusade, he says, "was marred by similar atrocities in Cologne, Mainz, Speyer, Strasbourg and elsewhere."[25] Even Jewish historians, though, defend the bishops. "The Jewish chroniclers" Glick says, "speak bitterly of the bishop and the townspeople of Worms, all of whom they blame for the catastrophe, but modern historians have concluded that nothing more could have been done."[26]

The situation in Worms highlights a salient fact. The conflict with the Jews was not based on race; it was based on behavior. The segregation between Jew and Christian which existed during the previous millennium broke down when large segments of the superfluous agricultural workforce began settling in the cities and looking for jobs. The rootless proletariat that made up the crusading armies was upset with what they perceived to be Jewish behavior. If not, they would not have attacked them. All threat of violence usually ceased upon conversion, demonstrating the absence of racial animus. If the animus were racial, conversion would not have solved the problem. The Jewish issue was a religious issue, first and foremost; the mob assumed behavior would change when religion changed.

Jewish historiography, beginning with Heinrich Graetz, is a fertile source on the behavior of the Catholic Church during the Middle Ages, but it has distorting premises—some articulated, some not. The articulated premise of Jewish historiography is, in Norman Cantor's formulation, that "the Catholic Church was the most persistent fount of anti-Semitism in the world,"[27] otherwise expressed as the claim that the core of Catholicism is anti-Semitism. The unarticulated premise is that anti-Semitism has nothing to do with Jewish behavior. Both dogmas mar Jewish scholarship, but not all Jews succumb to them. Cohn, for instance, recognized explicitly that Catholic clergy divided along class and hierarchical lines when it came to treatment of the Jews. The lower clergy often encouraged the mob to attack on the Jews, but the Jews would then invariably seek protection from the bishop. The term "clergy" is itself deceptive because the clerics who joined the mob were often just as rootless as the mob. As Cohn points out, the *prophetae* who egged the mobs on to violence against the Jews were usually monks who had left their monasteries and were under obedience to no one and followed nothing but their own passions. Once mob fury was unleashed on the Jews, the next victims were the local secular clergy, who often knew the Jews and sometimes protected them. The Jews' defender was invariably the local bishop, the only one with sufficient will and power—and often a fortress and soldiers—to oppose the crusaders.

The second and unarticulated premise of Jewish historiography—that anti-Semitism has nothing to do with Jewish behavior—plays an even greater role in shaping perceptions. The rise of the cities meant more commerce; more commerce meant more contact with Jews; more contact with Jews meant more conflict. Usury was the main point of contention. The slaughter of the Jews during spring 1096 was the reaction of the uprooted to Jewish messianic politics combined with the resentment against Jewish usury. Walsh does not impugn the motives of everyone who put on the sign of the Cross in the crusades, but notes the armies attracted "some fanatics, some criminals escaping from the law, some adventurers with no more belief in Christ than the Jews themselves had," and, most importantly, "some debtors eager to escape from the crushing burden of high interest."[28]

By mid-12th Century, the time of the Second Crusade, usury was a serious social problem. "Extremely high interest rates and annual compounding," says Glick, had "led to crushing debt accumulations."[29] Glick cites a letter from Pope Innocent III complaining "bitterly that the Jews extort 'not only usury but usury upon usury'" (non solum usuras sed usuras usurarum), his term for compound interest.[30] Innocent complained about the clergy of France, "who were pawning everything from cathedral chalices to church-owned real estate."[31] Innocent could not look with indifference upon the prospect of Church possessions falling into Jewish hands. Ten years later, Innocent translated his fears into action at the Fourth Lateran Council. The problem was not new—two of the three Lateran councils convened in the 12th Century condemned usury—but it was growing alarmingly, not unlike compound interest.

The problem was systemic, not easily solved by conciliar pronouncements. High interest rates and compounding are by their nature morally problematic. The Church, following prohibitions in the Hebrew scriptures, tried to deal with it by moral condemnation. Christians were prohibited from exacting usury, so Jews had the field to themselves, with all of the social odium that went with it. Ecclesiastical prohibition, however, has only a limited effect on behavior, and in the 12th and 13th centuries, that prohibition was counterbalanced by the increasing contact between Christians and Jews made possible by the cities. Increased contact meant increased opportunity to borrow money, and that led to crushing indebtedness, and indebtedness led to the possibility of increased violence against the lender. If people deep in debt to credit card companies and paying 21 percent interest per annum knew that by burning down the house of the head of Visa they could eliminate their debts, they might understand the temptations faced by the medieval Christians in financial bondage to the Jews. Many of the financially naive borrowed from Jews to finance "immediate consumption, not productive enterprise."[32] Exorbitant interest and compounding led many to financial ruin. The Jews, Glick notes, were often guilty of "leading the least productive members of society into ruin by encouraging them to consume beyond their means."[33] The Jew could charge 40 percent interest compounded annually, insuring that his debtor would never get out of debt. In a situation like that the crusades, which promised suspension of payment on debt as a recruitment incentive, seemed like a godsend. But the crusaders would also remember the usury that compelled them to leave home when they arrived in Speyer and Mainz and saw the number of Jews living there. Again the problem was systemic:

> The connection with money was a condition of Jewish life, and money was the very substance of survival. But money was also the devil's own creation, and

handling it with such intimacy only confirmed what the Gospel of John had declared: that Jews were truly children of the devil. With this in mind, one readily understands the pervasive sense of insecurity that came to characterize so much of European Jewish life, even into the 20th Century.[34]

The Jews were often constrained to maintain high interest rates because the conditions of their survival were more political than economic. The Jews charged 40 percent interest to the average person for small sums so they could provide large sums to the lord of the land at lower interest rates. "Usury of such dimensions," Glick says,

> was inescapable if [the Jews] were to meet the lords' incessant demands for tax payments and low interest loans, but of course it meant that they soon had a reputation of greed and rapacity that confirmed everything said about them in the Gospels. Thus they were caught in a nasty trap: disliked and resented by the general populace because they did no visible work and seemed to flourish on the misfortunes of others; too weak to defend themselves, hence dependent on rapacious lords.[35]

The nobility was tempted to expel the Jews if they ceased to provide money, which could only be raised by exploiting the population at large. As a result, "Jews became pariahs."[36] Hated by the people who borrowed money that could never be paid back, the Jews were "helpless, in need of protection and obliged to please their protectors" and the natural target for any proletarian revolution.[37] Usury thus allowed Jews to buy "official protection at the price of public detestation."[38] Moneylending is "by its very nature a socially isolated and isolating activity."[39] With each loan, the Jew's position became more precarious because it engendered resentment. When the crusades seemed to suspend the laws of everyday life, moral inhibition was suspended too, especially when the crusaders came to towns where they were complete strangers, and therefore not bound by custom imposed by native places. Mob violence expressed the resentment.

The issue was moral not racial. If Jewish behavior caused the reaction, no matter how unjust, of the crusading mobs, Jewish behavior could solve the problem. The purpose of the crusade, even from the distorted perspective of Emicho, was conversion of the Jews, not their extermination. From the bishop who protected the Jews to the mob that looted their houses and killed them, all accepted the premise that Baptism solved the problem.

Coerced baptism would create a more intractable problem, though. No church authority accepted coercion as a justification for baptism. The Dominican philosopher and theologian Thomas Aquinas was very clear. "Heathen and Jews," he wrote

> are by no means to be compelled, for belief is voluntary. Nevertheless, the faithful, if they are able, should compel them not to hinder the faith whether by their blasphemies or evil persuasions or even open persecutions. It is for this reason that Christ's faithful often wage war on infidels, not indeed for the purpose of forcing them to believe, because even were they to conquer them and take them

captive, they should still leave them free to believe or not, but for the purpose of stopping them from obstructing the faith of Christ.[40]

The Church's position on coercion, as articulated by Aquinas and in *Sicut Judaeis non* never changed. Definitions of what constituted coercion, however, did change over time. A Jew who did not object when the water was poured over his head was considered a Christian, even if there were a howling mob outside the church urging him on. Church authorities also were hemmed in by the theology of baptism, according to which the sacrament left an indelible mark on the soul. The issue had been resolved by St. Augustine in the Donatist crisis. Since no Christian could be rebaptized, no Christian could be unbaptized either. If the Jew accepted baptism, he was a Christian. He would not be harmed, even by marauding mobs that would have killed him if he hadn't converted, but he would be subjected to severe penalties if he attempted to revert to what the clerics referred to as the vomit of Judaism. The Jews were never subjected to the Inquisition. But those Jews, "*qui redeunt ad vomitum Judaysmi*," to use Bernard of Clairvaux's phrase, were, and the penalties could be severe.[41]

When Emericho and his crusaders arrived in Mainz on May 25, the pattern repeated itself. After Jewish community leaders paid the archbishop and a local count large sums of money, the Jews were granted refuge in their palaces. When the bishop's guards and the local constabulary proved incapable of defending his palace, the bishop fled to his estate in nearby Rudesheim, and the Jews were on their own when the mob swarmed into the palace to murder and pillage. "The Jews," according to Glick,

> turned first (as European Jews almost invariably have done) to men at the top: local bishops.... Jews turned repeatedly to these princes of the Church, and bishops consistently did their best to defend and protect Jews, even when this meant no inconsiderable danger to themselves. We envision Jews huddling terrified in cathedral courtyards, crowded for days on end in rooms of an archbishop's' palace, racing for their lives into a cathedral sacristy filled with crucifixes and chalices."[42]

"The bishops," Glick continues, "behave[d] with commendable, even astonishing, sympathy and generosity,"[43] even when they proposed conversion, because "with hindsight that advice seems well intended and reasonable. Had more Jews gone through the motions of conversion, they would have lived to return to Judaism within a year."[44]

On June 3, the crusaders arrived in Cologne, which is not on the route between Mainz and Jerusalem. There the pattern repeated itself with happier results. The Jews fled to the bishop for protection; the bishop saved them by arranging transport to neighboring villages.

Emicho never made it to the Holy Land; instead he continued his predations along the German-speaking world's major waterways for 20 years. In 1117, he got caught up in a battle with the Hungarians, in the course of which his army was destroyed, and he barely escaped with his life. Legend had him returning to live in the mountains near Worms. Long after his life must have ended, the people of the Rhineland still recounted stories of the "Emperor of the Last Days," and many of them anticipated his return as eagerly as their forebears had joined his army. Orthodox Catholic chroniclers were less enthusiastic and not shy about drawing moral lessons from Emicho's debacle in Hungary. Albert of Aix claimed the "hand of the Lord" struck down the marauding crusaders because they "had sinned by excessive impurity and fornication," and because they "had slaughtered the exiled Jews through greed of money, rather than for the sake of God's justice, although the Jews were opposed to Christ."[45] Jews should not be coerced because "The Lord is a just judge and orders no one willingly or under compulsion, to come under the yoke of the Catholic faith."[46]

Roughly one century after Emicho arrived at Speyer, Joachim of Fiore proposed a millennialist reading of the Scriptures that applied typology to the New Testament and that broke history into three ages based on the three persons of the Trinity. The age of the Father corresponded to the Old Testament era. The Age of the Son commenced when Christ arrived on earth, but it was to be followed by the Age of the Spirit, the age then about to dawn, which would be the culmination of history. Joachim was condemned as a Judaizer, but Cohn sees him as "the inventor of the new prophetic system, which was to be the most influential one known to Europe until the appearance of Marxism."[47] Joachim's theory of history was, as Cohn notes, "wholly irreconcilable with the Augustinian view that the Kingdom of God had been realized, so far as it ever could be realized on this earth, at the moment when the church came into being and that there never would be any Millennium but this."[48] His theories were "carnal" and appealed to a population that never accepted their Messiah had died on a cross and that his kingdom was not of this world. Joachim's ideas of the three ages culminating in the "end of history" would recur in subsequent revolutionary or evolutionary philosophies: in Hegel; in Comte's ascent from the theological through the metaphysical to the scientific age; in Marx in the ascent from primitive communism through class society to the dictatorship of the proletariat, when history and class shall cease simultaneously; and in Neoconservatism, a derivative form of Trostkyism, according to which widespread acceptance of American values will bring about the "end of history." History has shown that "the route to the Millennium leads through massacre and terror,"[49] but Neoconservatism's appropriation of Joachim's paradigm shows revolutionaries are undeterred. The rise of Joachim of Fiore's philosophy of history is the strange fruit of the cross-fertilization that the medieval city brought.

The Rhineland, especially the lower Rhine and the adjacent low countries, would continue as a hotbed of revolution and Millennialism for more than four centuries following Emicho's death. Medieval millennialist messianic politics would reach its culmination in Muenster in 1533, when the Anabaptists under Johan Bokelzoon established their communist dictatorship there. After the Bishop of Cologne and his army drove out the Anabaptists, they drifted toward the Spanish Netherlands to places like Antwerp, where they linked up with Puritans from England and Jews from Spain as the seed from which the modern revolutionary movement would grow following the Iconoclast Rebellion of 1566.

On December 1, 1145, Pope Eugenius III, responding to a report that a Muslim army had overrun the principality of Edessa in what is now southeastern Turkey, called for a second crusade to protect Jerusalem from renewed attacks. As an incentive to enlistment, the pope promised crusaders remission of debts, spiritual and temporal. The pope offered a plenary indulgence and remission of all interest on debts and postponement of payment until the crusaders' return. "The King of France," according to Ephraim bar Jacob, "then allowed an order to be published to the effect that one who resolved to go to Jerusalem on the Crusade must be forgiven his debts to Jews. Most of the loans made by French Jews, however, were made on mere credit; through this they lost their fortunes."[50]

Before long it became clear that the people interested in escaping the burden of debt were no friends to the Jews. When the crusaders arrived at the Rhine, the carnage that had taken place 50 years before happened again. Just as they had done 50 years before, the Jews again turned to the local bishops, who then turned to one of the great figures of the middles ages, St. Bernard of Clairvaux. The archbishops of Mainz and Cologne wrote to Bernard asking for his assistance.

Bernard's task was not easy. Summoned in late summer 1146 from a preaching tour, he confronted open insurrection. In Mainz, he found the enormously popular renegade monk Rudolph at the head of a revolutionary mob intent on murdering the Jews. At great personal risk, Bernard confronted Rudolph, denouncing him as a renegade against the rule of monks and as a man who presumed to preach on his own authority while wandering the globe under obedience to no one in violation of his solemn vows. Bernard's courage and eloquence induced Rudolph to return to his monastery. The people of Mainz were ready to take up arms and rebel despite Rudolph's obedience; they were only restrained, says Synan, "by the consideration of [Bernard's] sanctity."[51]

Bernard thus prevented further slaughter of Jews and nipped the millennialist revolution in the bud. Nevertheless, "Bernard," Glick says, "was no friend of the Jew,"[52] because "his sermons and letters are replete with anti-Jewish invective."[53] Glick adds that Bernard "insisted always that Jews had to be dealt with humanely and permitted to live" but his accusation of anti-Semitism remains.[54] Cantor links Bernard and Anselm of Canterbury as members of a generation "who moved Catholic thought in a new direction" that was implicitly more anti-Semitic, but there was nothing new about Bernard.[55] His critique of the Jews is the same as the Church's position, reiterated since Augustine and codified by Pope Gregory the Great in *Sicut Judaeis non.* Jews, according to Catholic teaching, are carnal and blind. Not even the wonders Jesus performed could overcome their blindness. Bernard notes:

Not the flight of demons, nor the obedience of the elements, nor life restored to the dead, was able to expel from their minds that bestial stupidity, and more than bestial, which caused them, by a blindness as marvelous as it was miserable, to rush headlong into that crime, so enormous and so horrible, of laying impious hands upon the Lord of Glory.[56]

Nonetheless, "the Jews are not to be persecuted, killed or even put to flight" because "the Jews are for us the living words of Scripture, for they remind us always of what our Lord suffered. They are dispersed all over the world so that by expiating their crime they may be everywhere the living witnesses of our redemption."[57] Aware Jews might complain about being characterized as "ox-like," Bernard offers only the words of scripture, in particular Isaiah, who goes farther than Bernard because where "I put you on a par with the beasts, he puts you beneath them."[58] Jews are blind: "Jewish disbelief is a night, and a night too, is the fleshy or bestial way of life led by Catholics."[59] Catholics who engaged in usury "played the Jew" to their co-religionists.[60]

None of this rhetoric was calculated to endear Bernard to the Jews, but none of it was new either. Bernard praised those Christians who "wish to go forth against the Ishmaelites," but he warned them "whoever touches a Jew so as to lay hands on his life, does something sinful as if he laid hands on Jesus himself."[61] The Jewish chronicler Ephraim bar Jacob mentions Bernard's denunciation of "my disciple, Rudolph." In speaking against the Jews "to exterminate them," Rudolph "has preached only unrighteousness."[62] Whenever the Jews promoted violence against Christians, then Bernard held it would be right to match force with force in self-defense.

The Third Lateran Council in 1179 passed resolutions on the Jews, most of which were, as Synan notes, "already traditional policy of many years' standing."[63] Jews were not to possess Christian slaves and servants—specifically neither nurses nor midwives. Compulsion was not to be used in order to convert Jews, but sincere converts to Judaism were to be received without calumny. Jews were to suffer neither in their persons nor in their goods, apart from lawful trial and sentence; no one was to disturb their religious ceremonials. They were not to drag clerics before secular judges, and Christians could give testimony against Jews in court trials; "to give preference to Jewish witnesses fell under the penalty of excommunication.... Jews were not to obtain control over Christian churches, to the contempt of God and the loss of revenue [and] ... feudal homage could not be sworn to a Jew." The long constitution in which most of these provisions occur is the oldest extant form of the famous *Sicut Judaeis non*, already mentioned and to recur regularly in the future.[64]

The statements of the Third Lateran Council reiterate the traditional critique of the Jews, who are "clinging to a stage of faith long since rendered obsolete by the mercy of God, to which they had been blind. The kernel, in a stereotyped metaphor, remained hidden from the Jews under the shell which is the letter of the sacred text."⁶⁵ *Sicut Judaeis non* was the essence of Christian realism and Christian charity. No Christian should harm a Jew but Jews should be excluded from positions of cultural influence. Jewish converts are to be accepted "without calumny":

> No Christian is to compel an unwilling Jew by force to accept baptism, but the Jew who freely manifests a desire for baptism is to be christened "without calumny." Apart from lawful judicial sentences, no Christian is wickedly to injure their persons or violently to confiscate their possessions; no one is to change the good customs they have in any given religion. No one is to disturb their rest with clubs and stones ... and no one is to attempt to extract from Jews service unsanctioned by custom. Their cemeteries and the bodies therein, are to be respected.⁶⁶

This protection shields only those Jews innocent of plotting to subvert the Christian faith. Glick incorrectly attributes the first utterance of *Sicut Judaeis non* to 1120, but correctly states the principle behind it:

> just as Jews must not over step their bounds, so Christians must not arbitrarily mistreat them. Although Jewish faithlessness must be condemned, it begins, the Jews must not be unjustly oppressed. Although they persist in their obstinacy and refuse to understand the mysteries of their own scriptures, Christian charity demands that they be granted papal protection. Thus they are not to be forced into baptism; nor may they be injured, robbed, or persecuted in any manner. No one is to desecrate their cemeteries, or to exhume and plunder bodies. Those who violate these prohibitions are to be subject to excommunication unless they make proper amends. *But, the edict concludes, the Church extends protection only to those Jews who have not plotted to subvert the Christian faith.*⁶⁷

According to Glick, "the essential message here was forbearance. Jews were to be peacefully encouraged to see the light, but until they did so of their own free will they were to be tolerated, preserved as a form of testament to Christian truth."⁶⁸ Jews, according to his reading of *Sicut Judaeis non*, were permitted to live in their own manner until they recognized their error and entered the ranks of the redeemed.

As the italicized passage above indicates, forbearance is a two-way street. Only those Jews "who have not plotted to subvert the Christian faith" were worthy of toleration. If Jews were plotting subversion, then all bets were off. That is precisely what happened during the course of off the 13th Century with the discovery of 1) the Talmud and 2) Jewish involvement in support of heretical movements like the Albigensians in France.

Jewish historians treat Christian anti-Semitism (as opposed to anti-Judaism) as so obvious that no proof is necessary; the only question is did the Church become more anti-Semitic during the 13th Century, or did it remain as anti-Semitic as it always had been? Jewish historiography breaks down into two schools, both of which view the Church adversely. Norman Cantor maintains that nothing changed from the time of Bernard to the Second Vatican Council. The one constant of European history was the Catholic Church's anti-Semitism. Cantor claims, "in the revered Bernard's preaching on the Jewish question" one finds

> the central and authentic voice of the Catholic Church. Nothing changed funda-
> mentally in the Catholic Church's hatred for the Jews and the teaching of con-
> tempt and fury against them between the twelfth Century and the Second Vati-
> can Council of 1965. *In all that time the Catholic Church was the most persistent
> fount of anti-Semitism in the world.* Things are different now, but the truth about
> the old days, these long dark centuries of Jew hatred must not be forgotten.[69]

Cantor ignores Bernard's risking of his own life to save the lives of Jews in
Mainz. He also ignores the split between higher and lower clergy that Cohn sees
as essential to understanding the reality of revolutionary chiliasm. Not only does
the confrontation between Bernard and the renegade monk Rudolph go unmentioned, Cantor even makes Bernard accountable for Rudolph's behavior, claiming
"ecclesiastics" like Bernard "hated Jews and spewed hostility toward them that
was bound to echo through all the ranks of the hierarchy, down to the level of parish priest and simplest monk."[70] Cohn, though, shows that the mob invariably also
attacked the local clergy, and that the Jews invariably sought protection from the
local bishop. Bernard thought Jews were blind and carnal, but he defended them
against the millennialists, a group of anti-Semitic Judaizers, who were as anticlerical as they were anti-Semitic. As a result, many clergy perished at the hands of the
eschatologically inspired hordes:

> Any chiliastic movement was in fact almost compelled by the situation in which
> it found itself to see the clergy as a demonic fraternity. A group of laymen headed
> by a messianic leader and convinced that it was charged by God with the stupen-
> dous mission of preparing the way for the Millennium—such a group was bound
> to find in the institutionalized Church at best an intransigent opponent, at worst
> a ruthless persecutor.[71]

Cantor, who sees the first crusade as "the beginning of the downfall of Ashkenaz," ignores this fact to dispute the claim that Catholic anti-Semitism

> was something marginal, extraneous, disseminated by unruly and underliterate
> people. No, anti-Semitism lay at the center of medieval Christian sensibility. It
> was at the core of medieval Christian sensibility and the vanguard literary cul-
> ture of that day. Blood libel, King Arthur and the Round Table: they were jointly
> integral to the medieval ethos, inseparably bound together in the structure of
> the medieval imagination. The child-killing Jew and Sir Lancelot were equally
> fixtures of the medieval mind and embedded inextricably in the same romantic
> culture.[72]

To him, the Rhineland pogroms expressed the essential nature of Christianity, not an anti-Christian, anticlerical aberration opposed by the higher clergy.
Cantor's inability to distinguish between the Church's traditional anti-Judaism as
manifested in St. Bernard's sermons and *Sicut Judaeis non* and the revolutionary
chiliasm Bernard opposed, renders his treatment of the era increasingly and un-
necessarily opaque.

The other school of Jewish historiography isn't much better. According to Jeremy Cohen, something changed in Christian-Jewish relations during the 13th Century. Things went from bad to worse. The evidence supports Cohen more than it supports Cantor. Something did change then, but it was not the Church's teaching. Rather, the Church's image of the Jew changed. The traditional view—the Jew is a blind, carnal Israelite as at the time of Christ—was replaced by a new understanding which saw him as a social revolutionary and outlaw. This change in perception occurred for two reasons: 1) because of the conflict with the Albigensians in southern France and 2) because of the discovery of the Talmud.

This change in the Church's perception of the Jew did not call into question the principle of *Sicut Judaeis non*, but it changed how that principle would be applied. Cantor's adherence to the two pillars of Jewish historiography blinds him to the changes. According to Cantor, the "New Piety" of the 11th and 12th centuries was created by men—Pope Gregory VII and Cardinal Peter Damiani, one of his main associates; St. Anselm of Canterbury a theologian and monastic leader; and St. Bernard of Clairvaux theologian, preacher and mystic—who all "hated Jews."[73] Cantor says that "these ecclesiastics stood at the pinnacle of power in the Western church of their day and were the re-creators of medieval Christianity along the lines of a deeper and more personal sensibility. They also hated Jews and spewed hostility toward them that was bound to echo through all the ranks of the hierarchy, down to the level of parish priest and simplest monk."[74]

The situation changed dramatically when Innocent III became pope in 1198. The supreme pontiff declared war on heretics at home and infidels abroad, and one might add, the infidels at home, the Jews, after inheriting "a Church that had been sliding ominously in efficiency and esteem."[75] When Innocent III became pope, "the status of European Jews was radically altered, and the policy of the Church became imbued with an increasingly aggressive and polemical spirit. The war against the heretics of Languedoc included the Jewries of the cities involved and it was not long before 'the crusade against the Albigensians led to the crusade against the Jews.'"[76]

During his pontificate, the Orders of Dominican and Franciscan Friars came into prominence as auxiliaries of the Church. The Fourth Lateran Council of 1215 enacted measures against Jews and heretics, and the newly created mendicant orders, in particular the Dominicans, were assigned to implement them. The Dominicans were largely responsible for the attack on the Talmud; for establishment of the Inquisition; and, under the direction of Dominican General Raymond of Penaforte, for the campaign of converting the Jews over the next two centuries.

By 1200 the Albigensians and the Waldensians were firmly established in Lombardy and Languedoc. In 1204, Innocent III dispatched Diego de Acebes, the bishop of Osma, to preach among the Cathari in Languedoc. The rise of the new Mendicant orders followed as the Church employed them to fight heterodoxy. Unlike the Benedictines, bound to a place by the rule of Benedict, the Dominicans and the Franciscans moved around to fight heresy wherever it emerged. When Dominic died in 1221, his order was working throughout Europe and on the way to creating the Inquisition to combat heresy and subversion. In 1209 St. Francis of Assisi presented his rule to Innocent III for approval, also placing his order at the Church's disposal to fight heresy. When Francis died in 1226, Cohen says, "his order was already a permanent institution of the Church and like the Dominicans, an elite clerical force in the service of Rome."[77]

The rise of the mendicants responded to a growing serious threat. In 1184, Pope Lucius III told each diocese to campaign against heresy in his decretal *Ad abolendam*. Fifteen years later Innocent III labeled heresy "the worst sin possible" because it was "far more serious to attack the eternal majesty than the temporal."[78] Concerned about Albigensianism in southern France, Innocent sent special legates there to prosecute heresy. The mendicants quickly engaged European Jewry because Jews were consistently supporting heresy to subvert the social order in Christian Europe. As soon as the Dominicans entered England, they opened a priory in the heart of the Jewish quarter in Oxford.

When Saint Dominic arrived in Languedoc, he found "widespread contempt for the clergy," due, Walsh notes, to "the incessant propaganda of Jews, Saracens and heretics," and "the luxurious and easy living of some of the priests themselves, and sometimes by notorious scandals among them."[79] The Waldensians and Albigensians were "Communists of a sort," who held "unconventional views of sexual morality."[80] "The Waldenses praise continency to their believers," said Bernard Gui, "yet they grant that one ought to satisfy a burning lust by any manner of shamefulness whatsoever, their apostles explaining this by saying it is better to marry than burn (*Melius est nubere quam uri*), for it is better, they say, to satisfy lust by any act of shame whatsoever than to be tempted in the heart within; this, however, they keep very secret indeed."[81] In attacking marriage, the Cathars attacked the very foundation of the social order.

Walsh insists the Inquisition never proceeded against the Jews, "either on racial grounds as Jews, or on religious grounds as members of the synagogue."[82] The Jews came under the purview of the Inquisition for aiding heretics and for converting and then relapsing. Cohen concurs but says the Church's attitude, even as articulated by Thomas Aquinas, "facilitated attacks upon Jews":

> First, Jews were often accused of promoting heretical ideals and giving aid to heretics. Although such ties may indeed have existed in Languedoc and Lombardy, the charges of the Inquisition were undoubtedly much exaggerated; even the anti-Jewish Cathari were accused of using Judaism as a cover for spreading their own ideas. Second, both Christian converts to Judaism and Jewish converts to Christianity who "relapsed" into their former religion came under the jurisdiction of the Inquisition, as did by extension those Jews who consorted with the converts and *relapsi* in their practice of Judaism.[83]

Since Cohen admits Jews promoted heresy, how can he object to measures taken against them on these grounds? The measures he mentions were preventative, aimed not at persecuting or annihilating Jews but rather at protecting the Christian social order. The Church strove

> first to prevent Jews form aiding and associating with Christian heretics; second, to eliminate from Christian life every trace of Jewish literary influence emanating from those writings, particularly in the domain of the Talmud and Rabbinical literature, alleged to be injurious to Christian faith; third, to curtail any personal proselytizing by Jews or Jewish communities ... fourth, to prevent Jews who had accepted Christianity by baptism from reverting to Judaism, accompanied by their own families and by Christians upon whom they had provided lies with which to desert the Catholic Church.[84]

Complaints against the Jews grew throughout the 13th Century. In a letter written on June 6, 1299, Philip the Fair complained that Jews "receive fugitive heretics and conceal them."[85] Jews "received into their homes and hid from the investigation and pursuit of the Holy Office, not only Judaizing Christian Jews, namely the converts from Judaism to Christianity who had relapsed, but also Christian dissenters, whether Albigensian, Waldensian or members of any other contemporary party under the ban of the Church."[86] One Jewish historian explains "it was only natural that one group, exiled from society because of religious difference should seek the friendship and protection of another group likewise banned."[87] The Jews "carried on a continuous and effective propaganda" throughout Christendom, "which, while it persisted, was bound to make impossible the complete Christianizing of society."[88] Saying this is "freely admitted" by Jewish scholars,[89] Walsh then cites I. Abrahams, who claims that as a rule, "heresy was a reversion to Old Testament and even Jewish ideals. It is indubitable that the heretical doctrines of the southern French Albigenses in the beginning of the Thirteenth Century, as of the Hussites in the Fifteenth, were largely the result of friendly intercourse between Christians and Jews."[90] Cohen claims the newly founded mendicants used Jewish association with heretics as an excuse to harass the Jews, but the association was there nonetheless. Walsh claims "if the Jews had confined their activities to the synagogue and their allegiance to the Law of Moses, a great deal of conflict and even bloodshed might have been avoided."[91]

The prosecution of heresy in Languedoc must have been effective because in 1208 the papal legate there was murdered. Raymond of Toulouse was held responsible, and Innocent, in response, preached a crusade to liberate the area from heresy. In 1209, an army assembled at Lyon and then marched southward, engaging in indiscriminate slaughter; when a soldier asked how to tell heretics from Catholics, he was told to slaughter them all and let God sort them out. The struggle outlasted Innocent's papacy, coming to something of a conclusion in 1229 when Languedoc became part of the French royal domain. In 1244 Catholic forces stormed Montsegur, which had harbored men who murdered Dominican preachers, and burned

200 heretics at the stake without trial. After Raymond of Toulouse was flogged publicly in 1209 for employing Jews and heretics at his court, he swore to obey injunctions dictated by the papal legate, one of which ordered him "to remove the Jews from the administration of public and private affairs in all your lands" and never "to restore them to the same or to other offices, nor to take any Jews for any administrative office, nor ever to use their advice against Christians."[92]

In 1204, Moses Maimonides, champion of Jewish scholasticism, died without establishing a coherent relationship between faith and reason of the sort that Aquinas would bequeath to Christendom. "Maimonides's failure to achieve a socially approved synthesis of science and Halakic Judaism" meant the rise of irrationalism and the occult in Jewish thought. As a result, "the orthodox rabbis" never attempted another synthesis of faith and reason, turning instead "to the soft theosophy of the Cabala."[93] That turning to irrational occultism was most pronounced in southern France, known as Judaea Secunda, the area where Albigensianism took root. More than one Jewish historian traces Albigensianism to Jewish influence. "Some of the Cathari of Leon," we are told, "used to circumcise themselves, so that they might propagate heresy as 'Jews.'" "If the truth were known," says Lewis Browne, "probably it would be found that the learned Jews in Provence were in large part responsible for this free-thinking sect. The doctrines that the Jews had been spreading throughout the land for years could not but have helped to undermine the Church's power." Another modern Jewish writer goes further, considering it "indubitable" that the heretical doctrines of Southern France "were largely the result of friendly intercourse between Christians and Jews."[94]

Louis Israel Newman claimed Jews were active in "Christian Reform Movements," i.e., heresies, throughout European history beginning with the Albigensians and Waldensians, and that heresy often meant Judaizing, "the policy of imitation of Jewish ideas, practices, and customs which many Christians professed."[95] The Waldensians were, according to Newman, Judaizers, "indviduals or groups who, as in Lombardy, adopted a Jewish outlook on life, and Jewish forms of ceremony and conduct."[96] Heresies are Judaizing because, says Newman, "in almost every period of Christian Reform a return to the simple interpretation of the biblical word has played an important role in the rejection of established orthodox doctrines. The Waldensian, Hussite, Wycliffe, Lutheran, Puritan and modern Protestant movements have been accompanied by a reversion to the sources of Christian faith," i.e., the Old Testament in its chiliastic revolutionary meaning.[97] That Judaizing would reach its peak "during the Puritan Renaissance," when "the center of gravity among many scholars and believers shifted from the Gospels to the Jewish Bible."[98]

Pope Innocent III knew what his predecessors felt about those who "returned to the vomit of Judaism." Innocent III soon was upset about "Jewish insolence" as much as about Jewish usury. The Jews, he wrote to the bishop of Paris in 1205, were so insolent that they hurl unbridled insults at the Christian faith, insults which it is an abomination not only to utter but even to keep in mind. Thus, whenever it happens that on the day of the Lord's Resurrection the Christian women who are nurses for the children of Jews take in the body and blood of Jesus Christ, the Jews make these women pour their milk into the latrine for three days before they again give suck to the children. Besides, they perform other detestable and unheard of things against the Catholic faith, as a result of which the faithful should fear that they are incurring divine wrath when they permit the Jews to perpetuate unpunished such deeds as bring confusion upon our faith.[99]

Jews, he reminded the bishops of northern France, "are consigned to perpetual servitude because they crucified the Lord" and dwell among Christians only on sufferance; therefore they "ought not be ungrateful to us, and not requite Christian favor with contumely and intimacy with contempt."[100] The Jews, thus, were not simply following the Old Testament and minding their own business; they were deliberately provoking their Christian hosts. The Jews at Sens had built a synagogue "more lofty than the venerable local church."[101] Jewish cantors raised such a clamor that they disturbed the worshippers in the adjacent church. The Jews of Sens were also blasphemers, referring to Christ as "a mere rustic, gibbeted by the Jewish people."[102] The list went on: "On Good Friday, contrary to ancient law and custom, the Jews had taken to rioting through the streets and squares, ridiculing Christians for adoring One nailed to a cross, and this in the hope of diverting Christians from their religious obligations. The Jews were accused of leaving their gates unlocked until midnight for the convenience of thieves."[103] No one, Innocent concluded, "ever succeeded in recovering stolen property" from Jews.[104]

Innocent makes the traditional criticism of Jews. Jews are carnal because "the Mosaic Law promised temporal and earthly delights, a land flowing with milk and honey, the law of the talon, conjugal joy, and a numerous progeny."[105] The Christian Gospel is more spiritual because it "extols poverty, invokes a blessing in answer to a curse, venerates virginity."[106] "The carnal Jews," can only follow "what sense perceives." They differ from their own prophets, who "spoke not carnally, but spiritually." Because they have the word of God in the Torah, Jews are culpable; the Jew of Innocent's time differ from the Israelites before Christ, because some of the Israelites accepted Christ when he came, but all Jews of Innocent's time reject Him. Rejecting Christ was "blindness," which could be an involuntary fault. Even so, Innocent was unwilling to excuse Jewish disbelief on the ground of ignorance: "The Jew who denies that Messiah has come, and that he is God, lies.... Herod is the devil, the Jews demons; that one is King of the Jews this one the King of demons."[107] The Lord "condemned the Synagogue because of her disbelief, and chose the Church because of her obedience."[108] The "Synagogue has reason enough for envy: Her most precious possessions have been inherited by the church."[109] All this Hebrew wealth is now in the hands of the Church. The Jews are burdened with "perfidia" which meant bad faith rather than treachery. So the Church continued to pray for the Synagogue "that God might remove the veil from Jewish hearts, that she might acknowledge who is Truth."[110] The issue, as Innocent frames it, is behavior, not race. Innocent "never forgot that Jesus was a Jew,"[111] which meant everything bad about the Jews could be changed by conversion, which he saw as a labor of love, bringing those with darkened minds to the Truth:

> For we make the law that no Christian compel them, unwilling or refusing, by violence to come to baptism. But if any one of them should spontaneously, and for the sake of the faith, fly to the Christians, once his choice has become evident, let him be made a Christian without any calumny. Indeed, he is not considered to possess the true faith of Christianity who is recognized to have come to Christian baptism, not spontaneously, but unwillingly.[112]

Jewish historians rarely portray conversion to Christianity that way. Heinrich Graetz, founder of modern Jewish historiography, describes Innocent III as "the first pope who directed against the Jews the burning fury and inhuman severity of the Church." Graetz never mentions Innocent's reaffirmation of *Sicut Judaeis non*. If he had he could not have claimed "only a delusive hope restrained [Innocent III] from openly preaching a crusade and a war of annihilation" against the Jews.[113]

Innocent III never questioned *Sicut Judaeis non*, the Church's traditional teaching on the Jews, a doctrine then 600 years old: "Just as, therefore, there ought not to be license for the Jews to presume to go beyond what is permitted them by law in their synagogues, so in those which have been conceded to them, they ought to suffer no prejudice."[114] Innocent insisted that the papacy grant Jews "the buckler of Our protection." They were to be safe in life and limb; and, "in the celebration of their own festivities, no one ought to disturb them in any way," nor should any Christian dare "to dare mutilate or diminish a Jewish cemetery, nor, in order to get money, to exhume bodies once they have been buried." If any Christian did so, he was to "be punished by the vengeance of excommunication."[115]

This protection was, of course, conditional, applying only to Jews who did not plot to subvert the Christian faith.[116] The caveat is in Innocent's condemnation of blasphemous Jewish behavior on Good Friday, when "Jews, contrary to ancient custom, publicly run through streets and squares, congregating and everywhere deriding Christians for adoring in the customary way the Crucified on His cross, and by their improprieties strive to recall these from their duty to adore."[117] It is implicit in his condemnation of Jewish trafficking in stolen goods. "Blasphemers of the Christian Name," Innocent III said "ought not to be coddled at the price of oppressing the Lord's servants, but rather be repressed by the servitude of which they have rendered themselves deserving when they laid sacrilegious hands on Him who had come to confer true liberty upon them, calling down His blood upon themselves and on their children too [Matt 27: 25]."[118] Innocent criticizes "certain secular princes" who "receive Jews in their manors and town in order that they might set them up as their own again for the exacting of usury, and who are not ashamed to afflict the churches of God and the poor of Christ."[119] As a result, "widows and orphans are despoiled of their inheritances, and churches are defrauded of their tithes and other customary income because Jews, who disdain to respond to the prelates of those churches on parochial right, hold castles and manors."[120] Jews were coming into possession of Church property through usury, and they were using their economic power to exert pernicious cultural influence over those who owed them money. They were abusing the conditions under which they were tolerated in Christian states, and the state was well within its powers stop to the abuse.

Innocent III, however, did not preach a crusade against the Jews; he preached one against Albigensians. In confusing the two, Graetz shows that Innocent's concern about the connection between Jewish insolence and Jewish support of heresy was not unfounded. Innocent, Graetz tells us,

> was well aware why he so thoroughly abhorred Jews and Judaism. He hated those among them who indirectly agitated against the rotten form of Christianity, upon which the papacy had built its power. The aversion of the truly God-fearing and moral Christians to the arrogance, unchastity, and insatiable covetousness of the hierarchy had in some measure been prompted by the Jews. *The Albigenses in southern France, who were branded as heretics. and who were the most resolute opponents of the papacy, had imbibed their hostility from intercourse with educated Jews.* Amongst the Albigenses there was a sect which unhesitatingly declared the Jewish law preferable to that of Christians. The eye of Innocent was, therefore, directed to the Jews of the south of France as well as to the Albigenses, in order to check their influence on the minds of the Christians. Count Raymund VI of Toulouse and St. Gilles ... who was looked upon as a friend of the Albigenses, and consequently cruelly harassed, was also credited by the Pope with favoring the Jews [my emphasis].[121]

Innocent's animus toward the Jews was, as we have seen, not motivated by anti-Semitism but instead by Jewish behavior, specifically, usury, insolence, blasphemy, and support for heretical sects subverting the social, moral and political order. Innocent III and subsequent popes reevaluated their understanding of who and what the Jews were, gradually replacing the idea of them as blind and carnal with a new understanding of them as revolutionaries threatening the social and political order of Christendom. "The Cathars," one historian has noted, "were hardly as harmless as Graetz portrays them."[122] The people Graetz portrays as "the truly God-fearing and moral Christians" regarded "a pregnant woman as possessed by a devil, and, if she died in childbirth, certain to go to Hell." The Cathars were a secret society; they were, Umberto Eco points out in *Foucault's Pendulum*, the predecessors of the Freemasons, a group which "would resort to every subterfuge and hypocrisy to conceal their true beliefs." Their refusal to take oaths undermined feudal society as much as their attitude toward sexuality threatened to depopulate it. Perversion was, in their eyes, preferable to marriage. And their fast unto death, the endura, "cost more lives than the Inquisition ever did."[123]

Unlike Graetz, Cantor does not play down the threat Albigensianism posed to 13th Century Europe. Nor does he portray the life-denying Cathars as "truly

God-fearing and moral Christians." The papacy, says Cantor, "faced a real crisis in the early 13th Century" when "Catharism revived the old Manichean dualist doctrine."[124] The Inquisition's job was not to exterminate heretics, "but rather to persuade and frighten suspected deviants back into the church."[125] The defendant had to be recalcitrant or a triple recidivist to be "turned over to the secular arm,"[126] that is, the state, for burning. The Inquisition did not fish for Jews even though, as Cantor maintains, "The Jews were not entirely innocent victims within the religious structure of southern France, nor was the inquisitorial friars' attack on them idiosyncratic and fortuitous."[127]

Unlike Graetz, who turns the Jews into cynical manipulators of the Albigensians, Cantor claims the Jews succumbed to the Jewish version of the same error, namely, Cabala. "The Jewish community of Provence was the place where the Cabala started."[128] Vehemently rejecting Maimonides' attempts at rationalism, the rabbis of Provence succumbed to a "pastiche of mysticism, demonology, and astrology that came eventually to be called the Cabala."[129] The Zohar, the definitive cabalistic text, would not be written for another century, "but its origins lie in Provence in the early 13th Century, precisely at the same time as the flourishing of the Catharist heresy."[130] Citing Gershom Scholem, Cantor claims "Cabala was a late continuation or revival of ancient Jewish Gnosticism." Gnosticism was "hermetic among the Jews" as it was in Freemasonry, the English Protestant appropriation of Cabala, "but blatantly separatist among the Christians.... it surfaced at the same time and in the same place, southern France, among both Christians and Jews. In the case of the Christians it takes the form of Catharism; among the Jews, of Cabalism."[131] When Gnosticism first appeared in the ancient world, "the Gnostic community was the greatest internal threat that Christianity faced in the first two centuries of its existence."[132] It was no less a threat in the 13th Century.

Innocent convoked the Fourth Lateran Council to deal with the threat forcefully and directly. That Council was the fullest expression of Christendom, i.e., the integration of Church and State, Europe would see. Five of its edicts dealt with Jews. Two addressed the problem of "heavy and immoderate" usury, suggesting "Jews were still providing essential capital at high rates of interest and gaining ownership of valuable properties when debtors defaulted."[133] Another specified, "men are not to be charged interest while away on crusade."[134] Another repeats the injunction against appointing those "who blaspheme against Christ" to public office, "since this offers them the pretext to vent their wrath against the Christians."[135] The fifth addressed how to deal with converts who appear insincere.

According to one historian, the first paragraph of the Fourth Lateran's Canon 68 initiated "a new era in European Jewish history," by specifying that henceforth all Jews "shall be readily distinguishable from everyone else by their type of clothing"[136] to guard unsuspecting Christians against intercourse with Jews. In 1221, Innocent's successor, Pope Honorius III, informed the bishops of Bordeaux province that he had heard that some Jews in the region "scorn to wear the prescribed signs by which they are able to be distinguishable from Christians ... That Christians mingle [*commiscentur*] with Jewish women, and Jews wickedly mingle with Christian women."[137]

Cantor traces the roots of Canon 68 to the Albigensian crisis:

> The attack upon the Jews by the papal inquisitors—and Pope Innocent III's determination at the Fourth Lateran Council of 1215 to segregate the Jews from Christian society—was due not only to general cultural and social developments but also especially to the Jewish Gnostic involvement in the rise of Catharism. *The Jews were therefore not entirely passive victims.* When the inquisitorial friars went after them, there was an immediate cause [my emphasis].[138]

This is an atypical take on the Lateran Council's edicts on the Jews. More typical is the assertion that the Jews were to wear distinctive clothing because "they were to be treated as pariahs in society."[139] And they were treated as pariahs as a first step: "After this blow, it was just a matter of time before the Jews would be massacred or expelled." Louis IX, according to this view, was "the ideal monarch in the eyes of European society" and as such "a vitriolic hater of the Jews, intent on humiliating them and removing whatever shred of dignity, prosperity and protection remained from the glorious days of Charlemagne."[140] According to Cohen, the culmination of "the new Piety" otherwise known as the new anti-Semitism, "was institutionalized in the early 13th Century with the creation of two new religious orders of friars, the Dominicans and the Franciscans.... Conversion of the Jews became one of their favorite projects."[141]

Taken together, the papacy of Innocent III and the death of Maimonides constituted, according to one historian, "the very nadir of Jewish fortunes."[142] These "twin disasters" stood at the midpoint of the trajectory that began with Emicho of Leiningen and ended with the disappearance of the Ashkenazim from Western Europe. The sense of Jewish woe is heightened rather than ameliorated because this was not a campaign of extermination but of conversion. The Jews saw annihilation and conversion as essentially the same thing. That says much about their view of Christianity. Cantor maintains

> Nothing changed fundamentally in the Catholic Church's hatred for the Jews and the teaching of contempt and fury against them between the twelfth Century and the Second Vatican Council of 1965. In all that time the Catholic Church was the most persistent fount of anti-Semitism in the world. Things are different now, but the truth about the old days, these long dark centuries of Jew hatred must not be forgotten.[143]

Even after this outburst, Cantor is constrained to note that the Mendicants' desire to convert the Jews "is not the voice of the Nazi Holocaust" because "the Nazis would give the Jews no escape from their doom, but the Catholic church always left the door open to Jewish conversion and escape."[144]

No pope, however, could view conversion to Christianity as annihilation. The popes were constrained by their faith to view it otherwise: those who were blind could now see; those who were spiritually dead had come back to life. It was cause for rejoicing. In the medieval Church, one is struck by the remorselessness of their logic and their simplicity in responding to the alternatives that confronted them.

The Church seemed to be faced with two equally repugnant choices: either allow Jewish subversion of Christian culture through usury, blasphemy, and covert support of heresy, or allow the people affected most by it to resolve it violently. Doing nothing would have entailed choosing both options in dialectic fashion, which is to say, the former leading to the latter. The Church, however, applied the principle of *Sicut Judaeis non* as the only viable alternative to Jewish subversion on the one hand and mob mayhem on the other. No one should harm the Jew, the popes taught, nor should his conversion be forced. If a Jew wanted to persist willfully in his blindness, he should be allowed the opportunity to celebrate his religious rites, but a Jew should be allowed no cultural influence, because experience had shown he used it to subvert faith and morals. The Jew was an enemy of Christ and an enemy of Christendom, but Christians were always taught to love their enemies.

The simplest way to prevent this enemy from destroying the social order while also protecting him from the unruly mob was to work for the Jews' conversion. And this is precisely what the Church did. The mendicant orders studied Hebrew and Arabic and read the sacred writings of the Jews to understand them better. This approach bore fruit. Jews converted in significant numbers toward the end of the 13th Century, and when they did, they brought insider's information with them and shared it with those in authority in the Church.

In 1292 the Jewish congregation in Apulia in Italy disappeared because, as one Jewish historian puts it, "the friars succeeded in harassing the Jews sufficiently so that most accepted baptism."[145] A manuscript in the Vatican Library confirms the conversion of a great number of Apulian Jews by Bartolomeo and two colleagues in 1292. And Neapolitan documents dating from 1294 ... reveal that 1,300 Jewish families in Apulia have converted—probably a total of at least 8,000 proselytes. Other contemporary sources relate that many Jews fled from Apulia at this time, causing the Jewish community in at least some cities to vanish completely.[146] The Hebrew chronicler Solomon ibn Verga wrote "Some were forced to convert ... and the rest departed for distant lands."[147] Sincere conversion to Christianity is an oxymoron for Jewish historians, but even they concede "the inquisitorial endeavor achieved success during the last decade of the 13th Century." The historical record indicates most conversions were sincere, which is to say, not forced. When a group of Jews converted in Naples in 1290, Charles II granted their request "to have a synagogue building ... given to them for use as a church." When all of the Jews in Salerno converted, the Dominicans sold the building and "used the proceeds to aid impoverished converts."[148]

Innocent III had claimed the Church was the ruler of the Jews in the lands of Christendom. Jews perhaps felt the same way: Abraham of Montpellier wrote to

Gregory IX in 1232 and asked him to ban Maimonides. Unable to resolve their internal disputes, the Jews turned to the Church—in particular, the Dominicans—to use the Inquisition to resolve the issue of Maimonides' orthodoxy. Eventually, Abraham and his party won; the Mendicants burned Maimonides' writings at their request. Jewish historians say this shows the Inquisition was "perhaps actively looking for an excuse to strike out at the Jews."[149] But the Dominicans were caught between two groups of Jews who could not resolve their own dispute but who thought the Church could. Hence, both sides appealed to the Inquisition for a judgment. Abraham of Montpellier, according to one Jewish historian, was "imitating the example of Pope Gregory IX," when he "issued a ban against the Maimonist writings at the beginning of 1232." The orthodox Jews wanted "the Dominican Friars to proceed against Jewish heretics in the same fashion as against Christian dissenters." The avidity with which this group of Jews sought out the Dominicans belies the claim that "Christian orthodoxy now appeared willing and eager to try and equate Jews with heretics." The Jews sought the Church's aid in ridding the synagogue of heretics, not the other way around. The incident was the opening act in the great drama of the Church's discovery of and crusade against the Talmud. "Forty days did not pass from the burning of our teacher's [Maimonides] works until that of the Talmud," one chronicler wrote. His account though "can hardly be considered factual. Nonetheless, the thrust of his argument reveals the perspective of contemporary Jews." It also shows "in a certain measure Jews were responsible for the inauguration of the crusade against their writings."[150]

That crusade began in 1236 when Nicholas Donin, an apostate Jew who had become a Christian and a Dominican (some sources claim he was a Franciscan), was granted an audience with Pope Gregory IX. Donin called the pope's attention to the blasphemies in the collection of Hebrew writings known as the Talmud. Donin's outspoken opinions had caused his expulsion from the synagogue 11 years earlier, so revenge may have been a motive, but Donin took with him an acute understanding of the role the Talmud played in Jewish life. It was, as Graetz claimed, "the mainstay of Jewish civilization";[151] it was also full of blasphemies—claiming, among other things, that Christ was being cooked in boiling excrement in hell and that he was the illegitimate son of a Roman soldier and a whore named Mary.

The *Jewish Encyclopedia*, for example, discussing Celsus' debt to Judaism, remarks that "he asserts that Jesus was the illegitimate son of a certain Panthera, and again that he had been a servant in Egypt, not when a child as according to the New Testament, but when he was grown, and that there he learned the secret art. These statements are frequently identical with those of the Talmud." According to another source, the Jews "call Christ the illegitimate son of a whore, and the Blessed Virgin Mary, an abominable thing to say or even to think, a woman of heat or lust, and they curse both, and the Roman faith, and all its members and believers."

Before Donin, the Talmud was virtually unknown among Christians, who, like Pope Gregory IX, labored under the illusion that the Jews merely followed the Torah, books which Catholics also considered canonical. As a result of these discoveries, "the Talmud suddenly became a prime target of Christian anti-Judaism."[152] The campaign against the Talmud is the beginning of the change in the Church's attitude toward the Jews. Cohen's proposed dichotomy in Christian teaching on the Jews doesn't exist. *Sicut Judaeis non* never changed from the time of St. Gregory the Great to the time of the Mendicants. What changed was the Church's understanding of the Jews. They were in the eyes of the Church transformed from essentially blind followers of a perversely understood Torah to social revolutionaries largely as a result of the discovery of the Talmud and its blasphemies.

Cohen adverts to this when the writes "the Talmud and writings of medieval rabbis remained generally unknown to Christians for centuries after Augustine."[153] As a result, he repeatedly contradicts his own thesis, especially when he notes "when Jews had recourse to him for protection, Gregory showed himself benign, issuing in his turn the basic papal Constitution on the Jews, *Sicut Judaeis non*."[154] In other words, Gregory never deviated from *Sicut Judaeis non*. Cohen claims the popes were "bound to protect only those [Jews] who conformed to the classical Augustinian conception of the bearers of the Old Testament."[155] This is not true, but when he adds "that sort of Jew no longer existed,"[156] he is getting to the heart of the matter. This is another way of saying that the Church's understanding of the Jew changed. No pope ever said anyone had a right to harm the Jew or force his conversion. The popes never said papal protection extended to behavior that was *"extra legem."* How could they? That would mean Jews could engage in criminal activity with impunity. But the discovery of the Talmud indicated that that sort of behavior lay at the heart of the Jewish "religion." That caused Gregory's shocked response to Nicholas Donin.

When Gregory IX heard that the bands of crusaders were massacring Jews, he reiterated the prohibition against harming them. Gregory IX, according to Cohen, "passionately disliked Jews," but "like all medieval popes, Gregory drew the line at physical persecution."[157] Gregory also "sternly reminded Christian folk that baptism must never be imposed upon anybody,"[158] but he still got blamed for the excesses of those who ignored him. The same is true of his condemnation of the Talmud, which is said to have led directly to the disappearance of Jews from Western Europe, making conversion sound like another word for Auschwitz:

> Condemning the Talmud in 1239 as a heretical deviation from the Jews' biblical heritage, Pope Gregory IX probably did not conceive of the important effects his pronouncements would have on the course of history. He could not have foreseen that he had sanctioned the commencement of an ideological trend that would justify attempts to eliminate the Jewish presence in Christendom, a radical shift from the Augustinian position that the Jews occupied a rightful and

necessary place in Christian society. Yet Gregory's awakening to the discrepancy between the religion of contemporary Jews and that of the "biblical" Jews whom Augustine had wished to tolerate coupled with the pontiff's exclamation that the belief in the Talmud "is said to be the chief cause that holds the Jews obstinate in their perfidy," laid important groundwork for those who came after him. In the generations that followed the Paris disputation of 1240 and the initial burning of the Talmud in 1242, mendicant inquisitors throughout Europe continued to persecute rabbinic literature, compelled the Jews to submit to their inflammatory sermons, and where possible often worked toward the complete destruction of specific Jewish communities. Early in the 14th Century, Bernard Gui burned the Talmud even in the absence of Jews.[159]

Even Innocent III, unaware of the Talmud's existence, had dealt with the contingency it presented when he excluded from protection under *Sicut Judaeis non* Jews who plotted against the faith. "We wish," Innocent wrote, "to place under the protection of this decree only those who have not presumed to plot against the Christian faith."[160] Cohen concludes "such a stipulation might have excluded a large portion, if not all, of European Jewry."[161] Why? Was it because the pope had changed his mind? Or because, as the Talmud revealed, the Jews were not practitioners of just another false religion but of one that had revolutionary potential? "By the fourteenth Century," Cohen continues, "the *Sicut Iudeis* bull in particular and papal protection of the Jews in general had all but lost their practical effectiveness."[162] But, as Cohen points out, the popes never stopped ordering Christians not to harm the Jews. Why had the Jews lost their protection? The only logical answer is: they were perceived as operating *"extra legem"* as revolutionaries and outlaws and, therefore, no longer worthy of protection.

I am addressing only official protection. The mob, as we have already shown, ignored papal bulls when it sacked Jewish sections of medieval towns. It was only the higher clergy in general and the popes in particular whom the Jews could count on for protection, and the segregating legislation they passed was intended to protect the Jews as much to protect Christendom from Jewish subversion, a goal consistent with *Sicut Judaeis non*. In attempting to establish some dichotomy in Catholic teaching (as opposed to a dichotomy in Catholic perception, which did take place), Cohen makes absurd generalizations. Only "from the 13th Century onward," Cohen tells us, "were Jews portrayed as real, active agents of Satan."[163] Cohen evidently never read the Gospel of John. In chapter 8, Christ himself portrayed the Jews as "active agents of Satan." The same applies to the Revelation of John, which refers to Jews as "the synagogue of Satan."

The Church had always claimed the Jews were not children of Moses and Abraham but rather children of Satan. Nevertheless, the Church in *Sicut Judaeis non* consistently maintained that no one had the right to harm a Jew. If the Jew were engaged in criminal activity, as the state then construed it, the state could proceed against him, but that did not negate *Sicut Judaeis non*. What changed as a result of the discovery of the Talmud was the number of Jews that were perceived as engaged in subversive behavior. Accusations of blood libel, host desecration, the poisoning of wells, and holding the Jews responsible for the Black Plague, all emanated from the popular mind not the mind of the Church. The popes, as in the case of the plague, often went out of their way to refute them, insisting always that no one had the right to harm a Jew.

Cohen consistently misrepresents this point. He accuses the Church of "nativism," because "the romana ecclesia was also a society which strove to achieve functional unity and root out foreign influences."[164] What does he mean by foreign? Europe was a group of ethnic groups speaking different languages, all of which were foreign to each other. According to Cohen, the Church "attacked a religious group which detracted from that unity, charging it with the same basic crimes: heretical deviation from Scripture, blaspheming the ideals of the society, and immoral and unnatural hostility toward its citizens."[165] But, if the Jews did what the Talmud said they did, they were not just another religion, most certainly not the religion of Moses and Abraham. They were a group of outlaws. Why should they not be treated as outlaws? Wasn't that the role of the state? Cohen as much as admits this, then tries to deflect its implications by exaggeration. "The Jews of medieval Europe espoused a new system of belief," he tells us, which is true. But "they had lost the right to exist in Christendom previously accorded them because of their adherence to ancient, biblical Judaism."[166] If Cohen means innocent Jews could now be harmed with impunity, he is wrong. If he means the State could now proceed against them because they were operating "*extra legem*," then he is right, but it proceeded against them as criminals not as Jews. The Inquisition never proceeded against Jews on either racial or religious grounds. Gregory IX was the first pope to discover the Talmud. He was shocked by what he discovered, but he did not abrogate *Sicut Judaeis non* and its prohibition against harming the Jew. What changed was his understanding of what the Jews believed and how they acted on those beliefs.

On June 9, 1239, Pope Gregory responded to Donin's 35 petitions by dispatching him with a letter to William of Auvergne, bishop of Paris. His letter substantiates the changed perception of Jews after discovery of the Talmud. The Jews, Gregory wrote, "so we have heard, are not content with the Old Law which God gave to Moses in writing: they even ignore it completely and affirm that God gave another Law which is called 'Talmud,' that is 'Teaching,' handed down to Moses orally.... In this is contained matter so abusive and so unspeakable that it arouses shame in those who mention it and horror in those who hear it."[167] The offenses are so great that Gregory uses the word "crime" to describe them. He also claims the Talmud is "the chief cause that holds the Jews obstinate in their perfidy."[168] He ordered "on the first Saturday of Lent to come, in the morning which the Jews are gathered in the synagogues, you shall, by our order seize all the books of the Jews who live in your districts and have these books carefully guarded in the possession of the Dominican and Franciscan friars."[169] If those friars found the books offensive, they were to burn them.

The discovery of the Talmud changed the status of the Jews. In addition to "displaying no shame for their guilt nor reverence for the honor of the Christian faith," the Talmud's blasphemies indicated the Jews had equal contempt for "the Law of Moses and the prophets" which the Christians thought they honored.[170] Instead of following God's word in the Torah, the Jews "follow some tradition of their elders," giving it priority over the word of God.[171] The Talmud asserts rabbis are superior to the biblical prophets and that the Jews must obey them even to the absurd point of abrogating Mosaic Law. As a result the Jews prevent their children from studying the Bible, by placing the Talmud at the center of their educational curriculum.

It took a while for the Church to digest what it had learned about the Talmud, but Pope Gregory's letter to the bishop of Paris indicated "the attack on the Talmud heralded a change in the Church's basic attitude toward Judaism."[172] Three years later, Bishop Eudes's legantine commission reported that the Talmud was "full of innumerable errors, abuses, blasphemies and wickedness such as arouse shame in those that speak of them and horrify the hearer."[173] The books were so horrifying that they "cannot be tolerated in the name of God without injury to the Christian Faith."[174] In a letter to St. Louis IX, King of France, in May 1244, Innocent IV, Gregory's successor, drew certain conclusions. "The wicked perfidy of the Jews," he said, "does not properly heed the fact that Christian piety received them and patiently allows them to live in Christendom through pity only. Instead, it commits such grave sins that are stupefying to those who hear of them and horrible to those who tell of them."[175] The Talmud's blasphemies and its injunctions about defrauding the unsuspecting *goyim* threatened the conditions under which Jews were tolerated. They called for rethinking the whole social compact.

Upset by the harm that it was doing, St. Louis called a conference on the Talmud. In June 1240, Nicholas Donin had an extended debate with Rabbi Yehiel ben Joseph of Paris under royal auspices and presided over by the queen mother, Blanche of Castile. One Jewish commentator claims "the entire event epitomized the declining status of Jews in that century and their transformation in Christian minds into little more than embodiments of blasphemous doctrine."[176] The rabbi was dumbfounded that he had to defend Jewish esoteric writings in a hostile environment. Nothing like this had ever happened before. Rabbi Yehiel, lacking any precedent for conducting a disputation of this sort, didn't know how to respond. When asked whether it were true that the Talmud claimed "Jesus was condemned to an eternity in hell, immersed in 'boiling excrement'" and Mary, his mother, was a whore, the Rabbi could only respond, yes, those passages were in the Talmud, but they did not refer to "that" Jesus or "that" Mary. "Not every Louis born in France is the king of France," Yehiel maintained, giving new meaning to the term "chutzpah." "Has it not happened," he continued, "that two men were born in the same city, had the same name, and died in the same manner? There are many such cases."[177] One Jewish historian referred to Rabbi Yehiel's denial as the birth of Jewish humor. A Christian account of the debate, however, failed to see the humor in his statement. "Concerning this Jesus, he confessed that he was born out of adultery and that he is punished in hell in boiling excrement and that he lived at the time of Titus." But Rabbi Yehiel said, "this Jesus is different from our Jesus. However, he is unable to say who he was, whence it is clear that he lied."[178]

Having exploded his own credibility, Yehiel could do little to refute Donin's claim that the Talmud sanctioned criminal behavior, including "murder, theft, and religious intolerance." The Talmud also "included strictures against trusting Gentiles, honoring them or even returning a lost piece of property to them."[179] The Rabbis would have done better to emulate Maimonides, but "drugged ... into comfort with the narcotic of the Cabala, an otherworldly withdrawal into astrology and demonology, considered fit only for those who had mastered traditional Talmudic learning" they were no match for those trained by the Dominicans.[180] Many Jews took "the terrible deterioration of the status and security of the Jews" as "a sign of the coming of the Messiah," something one historian calls, "a characteristic figment of the Jewish mind.... In the Jewish context, it is the syndrome of waiting quietly for the holocaust. Thus the Orthodox rabbinate failed to exercise leadership on behalf of the Jews in the 13th Century Ashkenaz as was again the case in 20th Century Poland."[181]

With defenders like Rabbi Yehiel, the Talmud needed no enemies. The debate resulted in the public burning of the Talmud in Paris. The Jewish religion was now clearly seen not as biblical Judaism, but rather as a heretical deviation from the Old Testament. Over a 36-hour period in June 1242, over 10,000 volumes were consigned to the flames. As if determined to prove what the Christians had said was correct, a group of Jews appealed to Rome, "complaining that they could not practice their religion without the Talmud."[182] "Once more," one Jewish commentator writes, "it was the pope to whom the Jews had turned in their extremity."[183] In May 1244, Innocent IV, relented: "bound as we are by the Divine command to tolerate them in their Law, [we] thought fit to have the answer given them that we do not want to deprive them of their books if as a result we should be depriving them of their law."[184] The decision to return the Talmud to the Jews caused outrage. One bishop concluded the Jews had lied to the pope, and it would be "most disgraceful and a cause of shame for the Apostolic Throne, if books that had been so solemnly and so justly burned in the presence of all the scholars and of the clergy, and of the populace of Paris were to be given back to the masters of the Jews at the order of the pope—for such tolerance would seem to mean approval."[185] In 1254 Louis IX renewed the ordinance ordering the burning of the Talmud, as did both of his successors. When Louis X readmitted the Jews into France, he barred them from bringing the Talmud with them.

After the disputations, the Church made conversion of the Jews a high priority. In 1242, James I, King of Aragon, compelled Jews by force of law to listen to sermons of the Mendicants, "a measure which drew considerable praise from

Innocent IV and which James renewed in 1263."[186] In 1270, Pope Nicholas III "formally made preaching and missionizing among the Jews part of the apostolate of both the Dominican and Franciscan orders."[187] In his bull *Vineam Soreth*, Nicholas urged the mendicants to "overcome the obstinacy of the perverse Jews.... Summon them to sermons in the places where they live .... Inform them of evangelical doctrines with salutary warnings and discreet reasoning."[188]

Once Judaism ceased being the religion of the Old Testament in the mind of the Church, it was construed instead as a heresy that fell under the Church's jurisdiction as doctrinal watchdog. The Talmud was an offense not only against the Christians but against the religious life of Jews as well, which allowed the pope to intervene into their affairs "if they violate the law of the Gospel in moral matters and their own prelates do not check them" or "if they invent heresies against their own law."[189] "Innocent's line of thought quickly became the common opinion of 13th and 14th Century canonists."[190] The Church, according to the Dominican inquisitor Nicholas Eymeric, now had the right and duty "to defend genuine Judaism against internal heresy and thereby to bring Jews closer to an acceptance of Christianity."[191]

Raymond of Penaforte, General of the Dominicans, the man who told Gregory IX to listen to Nicholas Donin in 1236, organized another disputation in Barcelona over four sessions from July 20 to July 27, 1263, between another converted Rabbi, Saul of Montpellier, now known as Pablo Christiani (or Paul Chretien) and Rabbi Moses ben Nachman of Gerona. Christiani was no low-level convert. He had studied under the direction of Rabbis Eliezer ben Emmanuel of Tarascon and Jacob ben Elligah Alttes of Venice. Christiani must have been influenced by the Order of Preachers while still a Jew because he joined the Dominicans almost immediately after converting, and, consistent with the apostolate of the Dominicans, devoted the rest of his life to conversion of the Jews. As a result of the debate and Raymond's efforts, the focus of the Inquisition shifted from southern France to the Iberian peninsula, where it inaugurated "a second stage in the development of the new anti-Jewish polemic."[192]

Raymond of Penaforte entered the Order of Preachers in 1222, and eight years later, Gregory IX summoned him to Rome to be his confessor. Raymond remained at that post until 1238, when he became Master General of the Dominicans. If there is one man responsible for the Jews' disappearance from Western Europe by 1500, it is Raymond of Penaforte. His tool was not expulsion nor force but reason and persuasion, the most powerful weapons in the arsenal of cultural warfare but the most difficult to wield. Raymond persuaded Thomas Aquinas to write his conversion tract, the *Summa Contra Gentiles* in which Aquinas insisted conversion must be based on "recourse to the natural reason, to which all men are forced to give their assent."[193] The infidel, according to Penaforte, had to be converted "soothingly," by an appeal to reason and not to force.[194] Penaforte persuaded James I of Aragon to bring the Inquisition to Aragon. He was "the moving spirit ... of

Gregory IX in all that affected the Jews," including Gregory's sympathetic reception of Nicholas Donin.[195] In 1250 Raymond took the initial steps to establish a Dominican academy for the study of Arabic in Tunis, reasoning that conversion was impossible unless they learned the language and sacred scriptures of those they hoped to convert. So, too, "certain friars were thus instructed in the Hebrew language, so that they could overcome the malice and the errors of the Jews."[196]

The strategy of having Dominicans study the Talmud was not without danger, which became more apparent during the reformation. In 1275 the English Dominican Robert of Reading converted to Judaism after learning Hebrew, exposing in microcosmic form the perennial English attraction to things Jewish. Three hundred years later, England's enthusiasm for the Hebrew language was on the verge of leading that country into an orgy of Judaizing and revolutionary politics that culminated in the mid 17th Century when Puritans murdered the king. Pope Honorius IV warned the faithful "the Jews of England lived with, and corrupted Christians":

> Among the techniques [the Jews] used was that of inviting Christian to their synagogues where the Torah would be venerated by all present, including the Christian guests; another was to keep their Christian servants busy with servile labor on days of precept, *thus preparing the way for failures against the faith on the part of Christian women by first inducing them to moral failure*; in general, English Jews used social contacts to prepare apostasy. Finally, the Jews daily cursed Christians in their "supplications, or more precisely, imprecations." The English hierarchs, so the Pope berated them, had often been instructed to remedy the situation but their negligence required the present letter.[197]

Penaforte's most famous pupils were Pablo Christiani, with whom he worked out, in the words of Jeremy Cohen, "tactics [that] often resulted in a considerable number of conversions"[198] and Raymond Martini, author of *Pugio Fidei*, Dagger of the Faith, which was, in Cohen's words, "the most learned and best documented polemic against Judaism which the Middle Ages produced."[199] Post-Christian Jews like Rabbi Akiba, according to Martini's view,

> died at the hands of the Romans not because they kept the law of Moses but because they forsook it, by supporting two false messiahs in succession, inciting rebellion against Rome, and denying that Jesus was the messiah. By rejecting God as their savior, the Jews of the Talmud destroyed the whole system of divine prophecy in the Old Testament.[200]

The Jews were heretics to their own religion, and since the Torah was part of the canon of Christian scripture, they were heretics in the Christian sense, too. Since heresy was not a matter of indifference to the civil authorities, the Talmudic Jews lost the tolerance that the blind and carnal figures from the Old Testament enjoyed and became *personae extra legem*, i.e., outlaws.

Raymund Llull made the same point. Llull underwent conversion from a dissolute life at the court in Aragon. Like Martini and others of his generation, Llull considered the Jews not as preservers of the Old Testament but "outlaws." Forsaking the Torah, they now lived "*extra legem*." Like Martini, Llull dedicated his life to their conversion. Llull, says Cohen, "devised grandiose schemes for converting the Jewish community to Christianity, systematically and completely. As for those Jews who would ultimately persist in refusing baptism, he advocated their permanent expulsion from Christian society."[201] Cohen portrays the alternatives invidiously, but they flowed from the medieval notion of citizenship as privilege rather than right, something that pertained to localities often on the scale of city-states rather than nations in the modern sense. If citizenship in a state like Florence entailed fulfillment of certain duties, then aliens like the Jew lived there only by sufferance of Christian kings and not by any right. If resident aliens were dedicated to subversion of those states, evidence of which the newly discovered Talmud provided, then the Jew's status in those states was precarious at best. Cohen doesn't state it this way, but the wave of conversions and expulsions which swept virtually every state in Western Europe from the 13th to the 15th Century was based on the discovery of Talmud, what it revealed about the true nature of the Jews, and the conclusions statesmen drew from that evidence. The discovery of the Talmud changed the Jewish question fundamentally. What used to be a question of religious tolerance became an issue of civil order. The Christian king could tolerate outsiders who based their religion on a flawed but sincere understanding of the Old Testament; he could not tolerate outlaws and subversives using religion as a cover for social revolution. Hence, Llull's admonition to those who wielded the sword of civil authority: "You, therefore, owe it to these children of God that you protect them from criminals and from robbers and from arsonists, from Jews, from heathens, and from heretics, from perjurers and from illegal violence."[202] The Jews were categorized with criminals as people who promoted "illegal violence." They were, says Cohen, "no longer the Jews of the Bible, to whom the right of existence in Christendom had been guaranteed."[203] Even here, Cohen misstates the position of the Church. The Jews never had any rights in medieval Christendom. They were tolerated as aliens because they were economically useful and for theological reasons. When it became obvious that their usefulness was vitiated by their newly recognized penchant for subversion, they were offered the alternative of changing their behavior, via baptism, or being expelled. But even expulsion was not a violation of their rights because, as aliens, Jews had no rights.

Once the contents of the Talmud became known, interfaith dialogue—never strong in the Middle Ages—was absorbed into the hermeneutic of suspicion. According to Llull, the only reason "a Jew wants to make conversation with you" is "so that you might thereby become weaker and weaker in your belief." Simple folk should be on their guard, because the Jew "has thought out well for a long time how he will converse with you, in order that you might thereby become ever weaker in your faith. For the same reason it is decreed by Scripture and the papacy that no unlearned man should speak with a Jew."[204] Once the pernicious nature of the Talmud became known, the Church had to face the issue of Jewish subversion. It was time to administer the medicine of conversion to the Jews.

In 1267, Clement IV issued the bull *Turbato Corde*. With his heart in turmoil (hence the title) Clement implies proselytizing was a two-way street in medieval Europe by complaining, "exceedingly numerous reprobate Christians, denying the truth of the Catholic faith, have gone over, in a way worthy of damnation, to the rite of the Jews."[205] Clement's response was to treat the *relapsi* as heretics, i.e., subjecting them to the Inquisition, and to punish Jews who helped them relapse. He appealed primarily to the Mendicants, who ran the machinery of the Inquisition. They were told

> to proceed against Christians whom you shall have discovered to have committed such things in the same way as against heretics; Jews, however, whom you shall have discovered inducing Christians of either sex into their execrable rite, before this, or in the future, these you are to punish with due penalty.[206]

Clement's decree was consistent with the understanding of the Talmudic Jew as subversive. Since Jews were heretics to their own religion and induced unsuspecting Christians to embrace their heresy, they would be drawn closer to the Inquisition, the machinery constructed to combat heresy. The issue of conversion played a role too. If the Jew accepted baptism, it was presumed that he accepted it freely, and he was not permitted to relapse into his former life, like a dog returning to his vomit. If he relapsed, he was to be treated as a heretic, not an infidel tolerated because of ignorance. Because the theology of the sacrament of baptism claimed that that sacrament left an indelible mark on the soul, "it is necessary that they be forced to uphold the faith which they accepted under duress or by necessity, lest the name of the Lord be brought into disrepute, and the faith which they accepted be held vile and contemptible."[207]

Cohen faults Innocent III for acting "even though he himself had issued the traditional repetition of *Sicut Judaeis* only two years earlier."[208] But there is no contradiction here. Jews who consented "in the slightest degree" to baptism were no longer Jews; *Sicut Judaeis non* no longer applied to them. Jews who relapsed were heretics to be investigated by the Inquisition. If they persisted in apostasy, they could be turned over to the secular powers and burned at the stake. Jews who engaged in subversion were criminals, to be treated as such. The problem persisted: Clement's successor, Gregory X, complained in 1274 that the Jews continued to proselytize and "even some Christians by birth" had "wickedly transferred themselves to the rites of Judaism."[209]

The Talmudic Jew was seen increasingly as deliberately attacking Christians, urged on by the Talmud itself. As a result, they were perceived as a group "who endanger public safety." Martini identified contemporary Judaism as "a new religion which we were not commanded at Sinai":

> The attack of the mendicant Inquisition on contemporary Jewry relied on the claim that *rabbinic Judaism, embodied in the Talmud, which had just become*

known to the Church, was heretical and evil. In their belief that all heresy threatened the proper order of a universal Christian society, and especially incensed by evidence of hostility toward Gentiles in the Talmud which they assumed applied to Christians, the friars began to see no place for the Jews in Christendom.[210]

Once the Church discovered the Talmud and understood the threat the Jews posed to the social order, she had to do something, if for no other reason than to head off the mob violence that knowledge of the Talmud was sure to generate among Christians. The natural reaction to the threat of Jewish subversion is violence, a reaction that can be seen in the Chmielnicki pogroms in 1648 and when Bolshevism threatened the social order of Europe during the 1920s and 30s.

The supernatural reaction to the threat of Jewish subversion was based on charity, which is to say, bringing those in darkness to the light of truth, which is another way of describing conversion. The point of Martini's *Pugio Fidei* was the conversion of the Moors and the Jews, especially the latter, because they "constitute the worst enemy of the Church, and ... converting them outweighs even that of the Christian mission to the Muslims." As we have seen, Judaism, according to the new Catholic insight, was not a religion; it was a revolutionary ideology. In espousing the Talmud, the Jews deprived themselves of any correct understanding of the Bible; their allegiance, according to Martini, lies with the Antichrist. As a result, "the redeemer whom they now expect at the end of the Roman Empire is really the Antichrist."[211]

The Church could have turned the Jews over to the secular arm for prosecution as outlaws, but instead it concluded that the most charitable thing was to convert them. Martini explains at length why the Jews have not converted:

> First, the Jews have always been greedy people, and they fear that by abandoning the promise of temporal reward in their law they would invite financial penury upon themselves. Second, "from the cradle they have been nurtured in the hatred of Christ, and they curse Christianity and the Christians daily in their synagogues." The supposition upon which one is reared eventually becomes part of one's natural outlook, in this case perverting any rational, objective sense of judgment. Third, Christianity demands subscription to difficult beliefs.[212]

The Church could do nothing about the first and third conditions. Poverty and belief beyond the ken of reason were part of the Gospel the Church had to preach. But she could do something about Jews cursing Christians and Christianity in their synagogues by first exposing and then publicly burning the Talmud. She did that as her first step in converting the Jews, because the Talmud was the biggest hindrance to conversion. The Church's campaign against the Talmud led to "a crescendo of conversions," which by 1260 "already necessitated special orders to facilitate the new Christians' integration into local society."[213] The campaign was supplemented by the secular arm, which was determined to segregate the Jews to limit their pernicious influence. Louis IX implemented the anti-Jewish edicts of the Fourth Lateran Council by ordering all Jews within his realm to wear "a circle of felt or yellow cloth, stitched upon the outer garment in front and in back" about "the size of a palm," so the simple folk might not fall unsuspecting into intercourse with Jews of the sort Raymund Llull would warn against.[214] The combined power of Church and State was brought to bear on the Talmudic Jews, who considered the loving ministrations of the mendicants "an unmitigated disaster" and "unquestionably the nadir of Jewish fortunes" precisely because so many Jews were persuaded by their reasoning and voluntarily embraced Christianity.

After the discovery of the Talmud, the Jews became "the ultimate outsiders." The Jews, in Cohen's words, "had come to represent *a reversal or denial of the social order as it was intended* to be."[215] They became revolutionaries, outlaws, and subversives, and by the end of the 13th Century, they were universally recognized as such. The expulsions that followed were the official recognition of status that had its roots in the discovery of the Talmud.

As Cantor notes, "a remarkable number of Jewish converts"[216] became Dominicans because Dominican efforts struck at the heart of Judaism when they exposed the Talmud. Once the Talmud was exposed, it lost its validity. Giving his own take on the "crescendo of conversions," Cantor writes, "a small but significant minority of the rabbinate went over to the Christian side" because "a cultural civil war was being fought among the Jews in 13th Century France and later also in Iberia. We will probably never know what happened in detail, but it happened, that is for sure."[217]

Throughout this period, the Church never changed its position that no one had the right to harm the Jew. Nicholas IV at the end of the 13th Century expressly forbade the molesting of Jewish residents in Rome. When the Jews were assaulted by violent mobs, the popes were their first defenders. Clement VI reminded the faithful "Let no Christian compel Jews to come to baptism by violence, these same unwilling or refusing.... Too, let no Christian have the presumption to wound or to kill those same Jewish persons, not to take their money from them, *apart from the lawful sentence of the lord of the region*" who had authority to deal with criminals.[218]

The papal tradition of protecting the Jews manifested itself during the Black Death, when Jews were accused of spreading the plague and suffered accordingly. In October 1347, a fleet of Genoese ships brought the plague to Italy from the Crimea. By 1350, 25 million people had died. Many survivors blamed the Jews. Bands of flagellants roamed the countryside trying to stem the plague with penances. When a group of them arrived in Frankfurt in July 1349, "they rushed directly to the Jewish quarter and led the local population in wholesale slaughter." In September 1348, Pope Clement VI exonerated the Jews from responsibility for the plague. "If the Jews were guilty," he reasoned, "We would wish them struck by a penalty of suitable severity." But "since this pestilence, all but universal everywhere, by a mysterious judgment of God has afflicted and does now afflict through the diverse regions of the earth, both Jews and many other nations to whom life in common with Jews is unknown, that the Jews have provided the occasion or the cause for such a crime has no plausibility."[219] Clement concluded his bull "by commanding all ordinaries to announce to their people, as they gathered to celebrate the liturgy, that the Jews were not to be struck, not to be wounded, not to be killed, and that all those who did these things put themselves under the ban of the Church."[220] As a result, the papal states became a perennial place of refuge for Europe's Jews, often to the chagrin of princes who felt those states were harboring subversives, whereas "outside papal territory, the Jews continued to suffer persecution for witchcraft and poisoning."[221]

The "crescendo of conversions" did not diminish during the Black Plague, even though the number of people inhabiting Europe did. In 1390, St. Vincent Ferrer baptized the famous rabbi Selemoh ha-Levi, and a massive wave of conversions followed in Spain. In 1388 "an exceptionally large number of Jews came into Italy, announcing that they wished to enter the Church."[222] Trying to make sense of the wave of conversions that swept Spain in 1390, Cantor describes medieval Judaism succumbing to its own internal contradictions. Its great weakness was "its finite, static quality."[223] The Jews had rejected reason when they rejected Maimonides; as a result Judaism's "only innovative wing was in hazardous theosophic irrationalism,"[224] which "could not offer a durable response to persecution and discomfort or a comprehensive social theory."[225] But those "sephardic Jewish intellectuals who, after 1390, for whatever initial motive, proceeded to cross over into Christianity, found in Latin Christian culture a much more complex and vibrant culture that they eagerly embraced."[226] The sephardic elite who abandoned Maimonides and succumbed to the mumbo-jumbo of the Cabala descended into the Gnostic dualism the Church had defeated when it defeated the Albigensians. The descent into astrology, magic, and demonology would culminate when Cabala brought forth the false Messiah Shabbetai Zevi, 300 years later.

In the meantime, Jews converted *en masse*. "By the second quarter of the 15th Century," Cantor says

> more than half the Jewish elite and an unknown proportion of the Jewish masses—at least one hundred thousand people—had converted to Christianity. These included great merchants, government officials and rabbinical scholars. Some of the scholars advanced to prominent roles in the clergy. A prominent 15th Century bishop of Burgos in Castile was a former rabbi, and his son became a bishop.[27]

A wave of expulsions followed the wave of conversions. The Jews were expelled from Cologne in 1424, from Speyer in 1435, and from Mainz in 1438. In 1492, in an act that would have momentous consequences for the revolutionary movement, the Jews were expelled from Spain. "These events," Glick says, referring to the conversions and expulsions, "dealt a blow to Ashkenazic Jewry from which ... it never recovered."[228] By 1450 the medieval phase of Jewish history in Germany and France had ended. The Ashkenazim migrated to Poland, which would become the *paradisus Judeorum* until their excesses as tax farmers helped to eventually cause the Chmielnicki pogroms. The Sephardim migrated to the Spanish Netherlands, where they would link up with English Protestants and German Anabaptists to create the Iconoclast rebellion of 1566.

Forced conversion created a bitterness that would bring about the first major outburst of revolutionary activity since the failed uprisings of antiquity in Jerusalem. Excess is part of the tragedy of history, but it should not obscure the sincere conversions that were its antithesis. Nor should it obscure the truth that the Church of the Middle Ages, no matter what her excesses, recognized her fundamental purpose is evangelization, and that conversion is its necessary corollary. If the Church had not embarked on its campaign to convert the Jews, she would have conceded the field to those who felt the only way to deal with Jewish subversion was elimination , the choice the neopagan movement National Socialism pursued in the 20th Century.

The prelates of the Middle Ages may have been overzealous; that is for God to judge. At least in their zeal they were Christian, which is more than can be said for their 21st Century successors. On November 6, 2002, Walter Cardinal Kasper, president of the Vatican commission for Religious Relations with the Jews, announced at Boston College, that Jews "in order to be saved" do not "have to become Christians; if they follow their own conscience and believe in God's promises as they understand them in their religious tradition they are in line with God's plan, which *for us* comes to its historical completion in Jesus Christ."[229] Does "us" refer to Innocent III? Pablo Christiani? St. John Chrysostom? St. Paul? St. Peter? The term "us" is not broad enough to include both Walter Kasper and the people we just mentioned.

Chapter Four

False Conversion and the Inquisition

I n 1350, three years after the arrival of the Black Death in Genoa, Pedro the Cruel ascended to the throne of Castile. His coronation must have caused great rejoicing among Jews because within months he turned the administration of his kingdom over to them. The rejoicing, however, was short lived. Pope Urban V, reacting to hostile reports from the clergy in Castile, denounced Pedro as "a rebel to the Church, an enabler of Jews and Moors, a propagator of infidelity and a slayer of Christians."[1] Pedro's tolerance for the Jews quickly became a liability, exploited by his illegitimate brother, Henry of Trastamara, who articulated the old grievances against the Jews in a campaign to gain the throne for himself. The Jews had been blamed for the plague, a charge refuted by Pope Clement VI, but resentment did not subside when the plague did or when the pope refuted erroneous popular arguments.

The Jews were viewed as a subversive and exploitative fifth column in 14th Century Spain. Indeed, they had always been viewed that way there. The history of Jewish subversion in Spain could not be erased. There was too much evidence. The Jews had conspired with the Moors to overthrow the Visigoths. When their conspiracy became apparent, persecution followed. In 694, the 17th Council of Toledo proclaimed "the impious Jews dwelling within the frontiers of our Kingdom ... have entered into a plot with those other Hebrews in regions beyond the seas, in order that they might act as one against the Christian race ... through their crimes, they would not only throw the Church into confusion, but, indeed, by their attempted tyranny, have essayed to bring ruin to the Fatherland and to all the population."[2] In 852, the *Anales Bertinianos* described the loss of Barcelona because the Jews "played the traitor," allowing the Moors to capture it. As a result, "nearly all the Christians" were "killed; the city [was] devastated," and the Jews "retire[d] unpunished."[3] The Jews "defined themselves as the antithesis of Christianity" and conspired with Christendom's enemies.[4] Although they prospered under the Visigoths in Spain, they nevertheless conspired with Arabs in Africa to overthrow the Visigothic monarchy. At the beginning of the 8th Century, they used their contacts with African Jews to prepare the invasion of the Mohammedan Berbers across the straits of Gibraltar. When the Mohammedans conquered Spain, the Jews flourished, achieving one of the most sophisticated cultures in Europe. The Jews excelled in medicine and helped in bringing Aristotle to Europe. But the flower of Sephardic culture drew its economic substance from unsavory roots. The Sephardic Jews grew rich on slaves and usury.

When the Spaniards began the *reconquista*, the Jews were not persecuted despite further acts of bad faith:

> Saint Fernando, on taking Cordoba from the Saracens, turned over four mosques to the large Jewish population, to convert into synagogues, and gave them one of the most delightful parts of the city for their homes, on two conditions: that they refrain from reviling the Christian religion, and from proselytizing among Christians. The Jews made both promises, and kept neither.[5]

Even as Islam was rolled back to North Africa, the Jews continued to collaborate with the Muslims. Spanish Christians were persuaded that the Muslim invader had been welcomed by the Jews and assisted by them, with all this implied for the national and religious life of Spain. The Judaeo-Muslim symbiosis that characterizes most of the Arab occupation gives considerable plausibility to the Christian view that in these two communities, alien both in faith and at law, Christendom faced an unfriendly alliance.

Much of the civil order in Spain was enforced through canon law, but Jews, because they were not Christians, could not be touched by that law. "The laws against blasphemy, for example, could not be enforced against them. They could encourage heresy, and, in defense could claim the freedom of worship granted to the Jews."[6] Jews were therefore allowed to engage in many subversive activities with impunity, which caused resentment.

Because Jews were above or beyond the law, Christians were often tempted to apostatize to obtain "freedom." Heretics like the Cathars of Leon, according to Lucas of Tuy, writing about 1230, would circumcise themselves so that "under the guise of Jews," they could "propound heretical dogmas and dispute with Christians; what they dared not utter as heretics they could freely disseminate as Jews."[7] Because they had imbibed the best of Arab culture, becoming learned in science and medicine, Jews traveled in court circles with an air of sophisticated impiety, which again caused resentment among the more pious but less wealthy and powerful.

Jews thus became synonymous with enlightened decadence. "The governors and judges of the cities listened approvingly to heresy put forth by Jews, who were their friends and familiars, and if any one, inflamed by pious zeal, angered these Jews, he was treated as if he had touched the apple of the eye of the ruler; they also taught other Jews to blaspheme Christ and thus the Catholic faith was perverted."[8] Given their number, influence, and sophistication under Muslim rule, Spain's tolerance of the Jews and their heretical ideas exceeded that of any other European nation. Given their wealth, the Jews engaged in ostentatious display, which increased the odium against them by contrast with the poverty of the Christians. Preachers easily used Jews as material for their sermons, "powerfully aided by the odium which the Jews themselves excited through their ostentation, their usury and their functions as public officials":

The Oriental fondness for display was a grievous offense among the people. The wealth of the kingdom was, to a great extent, in Jewish hands, affording ample opportunity for the clergy to make invidious comparisons between the opulence of the Jews and the poverty of the Christian multitude, and the lavish extravagance with which they adorned themselves, their women and their retainers, was well fitted to excite envy more potent for evil because more wide-spread than enmity arising from individual wrongs.[9]

The reign of Pedro the Cruel pointed out a paradox that would recur: the more powerful the Jews grew, the more precarious their position became. Tolerance led to violence against the Jews because the Christian majority felt that Pedro the Cruel had given his Jewish retainers control of the government and carte blanche to oppress them culturally and financially. Jews, Walsh reminds us, "were disliked not for practicing the things that Moses taught, but for doing the things he had forbidden. They had profited hugely on the sale of fellow-beings as slaves, and practiced usury as a matter of course, and flagrantly."[10] They were also "much given to proselytizing, even by a sort of compulsion; thus they would force Christian servants to be circumcised, and urged their debtors, sometimes, to abjure Christ. Again, Moses had condemned blasphemers to death. Yet it was a custom of many Jews to blaspheme the Prophet for whom Moses had warned them to prepare."[11]

But the biggest problem was usury. As in the rest of Europe, Christians in Spain were forbidden to take interest on loans, thus granting a monopoly to Jews for a practice which, over a relatively short period, could concentrate all a nation's capital in their hands. As in France at the beginning of the 12th Century, Jews were hated because they were money-lenders; money lenders were hated because in a pre-capitalist economy usurious compound interest could quickly ruin anyone caught in its snares. Then Jews could use their financial leverage to exert cultural pressure on Christians to the detriment of faith, morals, and ultimately the social order. Jews were above the law, waging covert cultural warfare against the majority with impunity, a situation bound to lead to resentment. Their activies in certain areas became a reproach to Christian ideals.

Usury was the interface with Christian culture which caused the most resentment. According to Lea, the Jews of Aragon

> were allowed to charge 20 percent per annum, in Castile 33 1/3 and the constant repetition of these limitations and the provisions against all manner of ingenious devices, by fictitious sales and other frauds to obtain an illegal increase, show how little the laws were respected in the grasping avarice with which the Jews speculated on the necessities of their customers. In 1326 the aljama of Cuenca, considering the legal rate of 33 1/3 percent too low, refused absolutely to lend either money or wheat for the sowing. This caused great distress and the town council entered into negotiations, resulting in an agreement by which the Jews were authorized to charge 40 percent. In 1385 the Cortes of Valladolid described one cause of the necessity of submitting to whatever exactions the Jews saw fit

to impose, when it says that the new lords, to whom Henry of Trastamara had granted towns and villages were accustomed to impose on their vassals and starve and torture them to force payment of what they had not got, obliging them to get money from Jews to whom they gave whatever bonds were demanded.[12]

Faced with either starvation or usury, the farmers and small businessmen of 14th Century Spain chose usury and watched their prosperity drain into the hands of Jews. Lea claims Jews "recklessly" aided the clergy "in concentrating popular detestation on themselves."[13] As later in Poland, Jews were also hated because they were tax-farmers, which brought them into direct and unpleasant contact with large numbers of Christians. The Church tried to protect her flock from the predations of Jews involved in such activities by reminding rulers that canon law forbade employment of Jews in public office, but rulers, then as now, were too intent on short-term gain to consider the long-term consequences, which often swept them from their thrones.

In 1366 Henry of Trastamara mobilized political resentment against Pedro the Cruel and created regime-change in Aragon. When he marched into Spain with an army of French mercenaries, the Jews were the first to suffer. Thousands of Jews were slaughtered; many more took refuge in Paris, where the same cycle of usury leading to resentment started again. As one of his first official acts, Henry released Christians in his realm from their debts to the Jews. It was undoubtedly popular, but short-lived. Henry soon realized that if the Jews were unable to extort usurious interest, they couldn't pay taxes or lend the king money. Jews also possessed indispensable financial and administrative skills. Henry, who ascended to the throne on a tide of resentment against Jews, employed the same Jews to remain financially solvent and administer his realm. The cycle of exploitation leading to resentment continued toward social upheaval.

The resentment against usury combined with the suspicion that Jews were thwarting the reconquista, by controlling the reconquered regions with the secret help of the Moors, to cause the riots of the late 14th Century. When the monarchs did nothing to curb Jewish influence, the outraged citizens took the law into their own hands; widespread bloodshed resulted. Leniency only created more violence, as when Pedro the Cruel was perceived as giving "his Jewish friends complete control of his government; a circumstance that led his enemies to call him a Jewish changeling," and contributed to his denunciation by the pope.[14] By the end of the 14th Century, Spain's Christian population, convinced that the Jews were "planning to rule Spain, enslave the Christians, and establish a New Jerusalem in the West" took the law into their own hands.[15] Widespread bloodshed and widespread conversion (sincere and forced) were the results.

Henry's accession to the throne made the social situation more explosive because the Church was freer to denounce the Jews for their predations and to stimulate popular response. If the social situation was ready to explode into anti-Semitic violence, Ferran Martinez was the spark that set off the explosion. Giving voice to popular grievances in his sermons, he brought the situation into the open. Martinez was Archdeacon of Eeija and the judicial representative of the Archbishop of Seville. Lea calls Martinez "a man of indomitable firmness ... though without much learning."[16] He claims Martinez was "highly esteemed for his unusual devoutness, his solid virtue and his eminent charity" but then condemns him as a "fanatic" for whom the Jews were "the object of his remorseless zeal."[17]

In 1378, Martinez gave a series of sermons in Seville, claiming the city's 23 synagogues should be razed and Jews should be prevented from contact with Christians. Partly fearing loss of revenue, Henry of Trastamara ordered Martinez to stop inflaming the masses. When Martinez ignored the king's order, the aljama, the Jewish council, of Seville took their case to Rome, which was known for giving the Jews favorable hearings—for a fee, it was rumored—but Martinez ignored the pope as flagrantly as he had ignored the king.

The battle between Martinez and the aljama continued unabated for more than ten years. In 1382, Juan I, Henry's son and successor, reiterated his father's order, but Martinez ignored him too. When the aljama produced three royal letters ordering him to desist in 1388, Martinez replied it was better to obey God than man; he then told the Jews he still intended to have the synagogues razed because they had been erected illegally. The opposition of Rome was now more than pecuniary: *Sicut Judaeis non* specified synagogues were to be left intact and their worshippers unmolested. But the focus of the resentment was clearly motivated by religion. The rapacity of many Jews and their royal protection fueled resentment and threatened the legitimacy of the state. The longer the crown left the issue undecided, the greater the likelihood of insurrection. Popular resentment was also fueled by the murder of Yucaf Pichon, "who had been greatly beloved by all Seville."[18]

In order to avoid more trouble, the archbishop of Seville suspended Martinez in August, 1389. He was to be tried for heresy and removed from his juridical offices. He was denied the right to preach until his trial had been concluded. Within less than a year, however, Archbishop Baroso and King Juan I were dead, and the chapter of his order made Martinez one of the provisors of the diocese *sede vacante*, thus promoting him into a position to put his sermons against the Jews into effect. Martinez lost no time. On December 8, he ordered the clergy under pain of excommunication to tear down the synagogues in the diocese "within three hours."[19] Towns which housed synagogues were placed under interdict until they were torn down. Martinez was undoubtedly emboldened because King Juan I's successor was an 11-year-old invalid in no position to stop him.

On January 15, however, the chapter which had just promoted him deprived Martinez of his provisorship, again suspended his preaching faculties, and ordered him to rebuild the synagogues demolished at his command. Martinez remained defiant, declaring he repented of nothing. The mob in Seville grew bolder and more defiant too as a result of his continued preaching. When the authorities scourged two mob leaders, the mob was enraged and took its anger out on the Jews.

On June 9, 1391, the storm finally broke. The uprising in Seville sacked the *Juderia*, and 4,000 Jews were killed. Those who were not killed saved their lives by submitting to baptism. Two of the town's synagogues were converted into churches for Christians who settled in the quarter that before had housed the town's Jews. The rioting then spread north, first to Cordova, then to Toledo and Burgos, until all of Castile was swept into the vortex of anti-Jewish violence. Castile, nominally under the rule of the boy king Henry the Invalid, was in a state of interregnum. No one had the power to stop the rioting, and no one had the power to punish the rioters. As a result, 50,000 people died.

One month after the riots in Seville, a group of boys marched on the *Juderia* in Valencia crying, ""The Archdeacon is coming. The Jews must choose between baptism and death."[20] When some of them pushed their way inside, the gates closed behind them, and those on the outside shouted that their companions were being murdered. When the civil authorities arrived, the Jews, out of fear, refused to open the gate. By thwarting the authorities, the Jews turned events over to the mob, which entered the *Juderia* over the roofs of adjoining houses and by the old rampart below the bridge. Once inside, the mob sacked the *Juderia*, and hundreds of Jews were murdered. In the Jewish quarter, the mob demanded what the boys had proposed at the beginning of the riot: baptism or death. The Jews who accepted baptism were spared, but the plundering continued unabated. The mob then broke into the jail and freed its prisoners. They then attacked the Baylia and destroyed the royal registers as a way of evading payment of taxes. The same pattern repeated itself elsewhere as the rioting spread across Spain. In Palma, on the island of Majorca, three hundred Jews were slain, and the remaining Jews only escaped death by accepting baptism.

In 1395 Henry attained his majority and came to Seville to punish the insurrectionists. Martinez was put on trial, but there is no record of the verdict, an indication that the punishment was trivial if in fact there was any punishment. When Martinez died, he bequeathed a considerable fortune to the Hospital of Santa Maria. In the meantime, nothing was done to punish the assaults, robberies, and murders perpetrated against the Jews. The municipal authorities, who looked the other way when the rioting was in full-swing, blamed the rioting on "little people."

Forced conversion was more often an instrument of the state than the Church. On the eve of the converso crisis, forced conversion seemed the simplest way to calm an explosive social situation which was leading to anarchy and civil war. As Baer notes, "after the conversions, the disorders stopped."[21] The king of Castile was the exception to the rule. In October 1394, after hearing complaints that converted Jews were inciting the population against unconverted Jews, he stated categorically that forced conversion was a violation of civil and canon law, and "those who interfere in this matter, either by persuasion or in any other way, endanger themselves with both God and man."[22]

Once a Jew submitted to baptism, he could walk unharmed through the very mob which only minutes before was determined to kill him. Forced conversion as a political solution had increasing appeal the lower one descended in the hierarchies of Church and State, probably because those were the people most immediately affected by the violence and most immediately in need of a solution. "A pope might find it necessary to protect the human freedom of Jews against the excessive, and inauthentic, zeal of a bishop who saw in forced conversion a simple way to dissolve pluralist tensions in his jurisdictions."[23] Rome was more likely to defend the sincerity of Jewish conversion than a bishop "who was inordinately hesitant to receive converts he thought unreliable in principle."[24]

Not all of the conversions following the turmoil of 1391 were sincere, as numerous Jewish converts themselves indicated. The fear of reprisal created an unfortunate spate of forced conversions, which compounded the problem of subversion that had led to the riots and forced conversions in the first place. Forced conversion is antithetical to the Christian faith. "The unwilling," Pope Gregory the Great wrote at the beginning of a tradition that would remain unchanged throughout the papacy, "are not to be compelled."

Popes throughout the period in question walked a fine line between two extremes, as shown by Poland, which erred by allowing Jews to usurp Christian privilege, and Spain, which erred by promoting forced conversion. Popes protested both abuses, but, in the case of Spain, unscrupulous politicians, seeing in forced conversion a quick fix to a difficult problem, ignored the warnings and created a deeper, more intractable problem. Many Jews accepted baptism to retain their goods and their lives. "Given the forced nature of the mass conversions of 1391," Kamen writes, "it was obvious that many could not have been genuine Christians."[25] The king of Aragon repudiated the concept of forced conversion and made clear to the Jews there that they could return to their ancestral religion, but that was not the case in Barcelona, which then became a hotbed of subversive activity until the Spanish Civil War.

Conversion stopped insurrection, which made it dear to the ruler's heart. Royal involvement in forced conversion was a tradition as long standing in Spain as the tradition of suspicion of Jews as subversives. The most conspicuous advocates of violence to "convert" Jews were the Visigothic kings Reccared and Sisibut. Sisibut felt Jews "had corrupted the minds of the princes."[26] Referring to Sisibut's intentions, St. Isidore of Seville, said "He had zeal, but not zeal in conformity with knowledge [Rom 10: 2] for he compelled by means of power those whom he ought to have invited to the faith by reasoning."[27] Isidore of Seville rebuked Sisibut in the name of Pope Gregory the Great. The Fourth Council of Toledo added a further caveat. Once converted there was no turning back. Converts, the Council continued, "received the divine sacraments, the grace of baptism, were anointed by the chrism and partook in the body and blood of the lord"; so, "it is proper that they keep the faith, although they admitted to its truth under compulsion."[28]

The Church was caught in the middle. The popes did not condone forced baptism, but they affirmed that the sacrament of baptism left an indelible mark. The princes were the first to advocate forced baptism to end civil disorder, but they were also the first to allow the Jews to return to their former way of life once the disorder passed. For them, expediency trumped dogma. Princes and kings needed Jews to lend them money, so they were more likely to allow them to attempt what was theologically impossible, namely, undo the indelible mark of baptism on the soul. Bishops and popes were the first to resist forced baptism, but they were also the first to resist the idea that a baptized Jew could return to his former life.

Eventually, the Church took the lead in the matter and came down on the side of baptism. If force were so absolute that it overcame all capacity to resist it, the sacrament was not valid, and the man remained a Jew. If, on the other hand, there was some degree of assent, though, then the sacrament was valid, and the Jew was no longer a Jew, and he was subject "to the rigors of canonical penalties should he fail to practice his new religion." So, "although Jews cannot be forced to accept baptism, still, if they have in fact received it owing to force, they cannot now evade the penalties of heretics.... a will that is forced remains a will ... provided, however, that the force was not absolute."[29] If a Jew who converted with a howling mob outside the church during the riots failed to practice his religion, he was a Christian and subject to the penalties of canon law. Those who reverted to their former religion were heretics; the punishment for heresy could be death. The popes "were as consistent in requiring the fulfillment of these obligations on the part of validly baptized Jews as they were in condemning the intemperate zeal that would force the sacrament on an unwilling Jewish adult or his child."[30]

Judaism proscribed in the minutest detail the regulation of daily life, including many dietary laws. A Jewish woman who accepted baptism on Sunday did not wake up on Monday morning with new recipes in her head. The absence of catechesis after conversion meant that old habits were going to perdure. If Jewish prescriptions about the minutiae of daily life had any psychological validity, the perdurance of Jewish ritual would mean the perdurance of Jewish thought, which was oftentimes antithetical to Catholicism.

Moreover, the Jews who were likely to convert were oftentimes the Jews who lacked zeal when it came to what Jews interpreted as biblical law. This group tended to follow a "religion of the intellect" which quickly degenerated into Averroism, a rationalism that would eventually find expression through Jews like Spinoza in the Enlightenment.[31]

As the storm of anti-Semitism spread across Spain, small Jewish communities converted *en masse*. In October 1391, large numbers of Jews converted to Christianity. Many, like cartographer Judah Cresques, were famous. Some conversions were, again, insincere. Isaac Nifoci, the astronomer, converted, but at the first opportunity, he renounced his conversion and sailed to the Holy Land.

Resentment against the Jews had led to widespread rioting in 1391, and that in turn riveted the attention of the Church on the Jews. St. Vincent Ferrer, as a consequence, led crusades for the conversion of the Jews. In 1391 he achieved his most spectacular success when Rabbi Solomon ha-Levi converted to the Catholic faith and became Paul of Burgos or Paul de Santa Maria. Levi was thoroughly conversant with Talmudic literature and acquainted with the leading Jewish scholars of his day. He embraced Christianity after reading Aquinas. His conversion, however, increased the general animus against the Jews because it revealed the evidence of anti-Christian conspiracy from the inside. Paul of Burgos was a Jewish insider if there ever was one, and he implicated the Jews in a conspiracy to overthrow the Christian monarchs of the Iberian Peninsula. After his conversion, Levi published "two dialogues in which he categorically declared that the Jews were bent upon ruling Spain."[32]

St. Vincent Ferrer was in Valencia when the riot broke out there on July 9, 1391. Lea says his presence "may perhaps be an indication that the affair was prearranged."[33] But Lea does not mention that Ferrer was born in Valencia, which makes his presence there not unusual. Ferrer was born in 1350, the same year Pedro the Cruel ascended to the throne. Influenced by the spirit of Raymond of Penafort, Ferrer joined the Dominicans and its crusade to convert the Jews just as social unrest was turning into civil war in Spain. According to Gheon, Ferrer "hurled himself at the Jewish problem in a kind of frenzy."[34] As a result, he was held responsible for the pogroms, a point Lea raises and then denies. Ferrer was eager to convert the Jews, but he was equally adamant in opposing force to achieve that end. "The apostles," he claimed "did not carry lances or knives. It is not with knives that Christians must destroy Jews—destroy, that is, the errors that poison their souls and their lives—but by words. When they riot against the Jews they are rioting against God himself. The Jews must come of themselves to baptism."[35] Ferrer also denied the Jews any right to refuse to hear the Gospel preached, which meant any right to avoid listening to his sermons.

The sermons of St. Vincent Ferrer seem to have been miraculous events. Huge crowds assembled; the fact that they heard his words at all in the days before electronic amplification is miracle enough. But people from different parts of Europe understood his sermons even though he preached them in the Valencian dialect, the only language he knew. Lea claims "his Catalan was intelligible to Moor, Greek, German, Frenchman, Italian and Hungarian."[36] He also claims that Ferrer "healed the infirm and repeatedly restored the dead to life."[37] Ferrer tramped from one end of Spain to the other during 1391, and because of his efforts Jews converted by the thousands. "On a single day in Toledo," Lea reports, "he is said to have converted no less than four thousand."[38] Lea, however, can't let the magnitude of his efforts pass unscathed without a hint that Ferrer was responsible for the violence, if only by omission: "It is to be hoped that," he concludes, "in some cases at least, he may have restrained the murderous mob, if only by hiding its victims in the baptismal font."[39] On the eve of the riots, the Jews had regained prosperity. There was no reason to convert for venal reasons. Indeed, few Jews in Spain did convert, "until Saint Vincent, by his preaching and his miracles, began to touch their hearts with pity for the sufferings of the Crucified Jew."[40]

Baer cites the traditionally accepted date of Solomon ha-Levi's baptism as July 21, 1390, but adds "it is more likely that the baptism took place on the 21st of July 1391, in the midst of the great persecution."[41] He cites no evidence for changing the date, but the change undermines the sincerity of ha-Levi's conversion. Even according to Baer, however, Paul of Burgos was no opportunist. His conversion preceded the pogroms of 1391 and may have been prompted by a vision of them, but it went much deeper than the superficial pressure that would prompt conversos to convert for temporal gain.

Baer's account of Levi's conversion emphasizes the coercion of the mob but minimizes Jewish losses in the intellectual battle with the Catholics ever since Donin arranged the disputation over the Talmud in Paris in the mid 13th Century. Aquinas' *Summa Contra Gentiles* and Martini's *Pugio Fidei* figured in Levi's conversion, which was not one of "thousands of baptisms" hastily administered so "the frightened Jews" could "keep their goods and their lives."[42] He did not convert under duress. Even Baer says he "should not be looked upon merely as a careerist whose actions were in no wise influenced by study and religious considerations." Baer adds "There is undoubtedly a grain of truth in the Christian tradition that the works of Thomas Aquinas were the decisive factor in Solomon Halevy's decision to adopt Christianity."[43] Despite hints Levi was a rationalist, Baer claims "he had come to the conclusion that the messianic prophecies had been fulfilled in Jesus of Nazareth," based on a letter Levi wrote to his fellow Jews.[44] One of the Jews, Joshua Halorki read that letter and expressed shock and dismay at Levy's conversion, but admitted he too had religious doubts. Twenty years later Halorki converted, also as a result of reading Aquinas, Martini, and other disciples of Penaforte and listening to the sermons of Vincent Ferrer. Baer states explicitly about Halorki what he only hints about Levi. Halorki's faith, Baer claims, had "long before been undermined."[45] In the letter that expressed his doubts to Levy, Halorki

> reveals anew the character of those Averroist intellectuals who sought to enjoy all the cultural values and treasures of enlightenment, while their ties with the traditions of their own people slackened more and more. Eventually they turned to the Catholic Church, which, though its principles too, were irreconcilable with the religion of their intellect, nevertheless offered them a reasonably coherent system of dogmatics as well as a rich tradition of humanistic and secular culture.[46]

Levi, or Paul of Burgos, followed in the footsteps of his Dominican mentors. He studied at the University of Paris, then returned to Castile, where he rose rapidly in the hierarchy, eventually becoming Bishop of Burgos. In old age, he wrote a polemic, *Scrutinium Scripturarum,* and an addendum to the biblical commentary of Nicolaus de Lyra. Paul was no rationalist however. As the less educated Jews were agitated by messianic visions as the 14th Century closed, Paul wrote about predictions of "signs and wonders" which corresponded to the massacres of 1391 and the conversions which followed.

In 1412, as Chancellor of Castile, Paul of Burgos drew up The Ordenamiento de Dona Catalina, a rigorous set of regulations which levied stiff penalties on Jews and Moors and attempted to separate them from intercourse with unsuspecting Christians. Jews and Moors were required to wear badges distinguishing them from Christians. They could only dress in coarse cloth and were not allowed to shave or cut their hair so as to appear Christian. They could not change their place of residence; any nobleman from another land who received them if they did was heavily fined and obliged to return them to their previous abode. Any Jew caught trying to leave the country was enslaved. Jews were barred from the higher professions and forbidden to learn the trades of "apothecaries, grocers, furriers, blacksmiths, peddlers, carpenters, tailors, barbers and butchers."[47] They were forbidden to bear arms or to hire Christian servants or to drink, bathe, or eat with Christians or attend their weddings. In short, the Ordenamiento established strict segregation as well as powerful disincentives for living as a non-Christian minority in Spain. Conversely, it established powerful incentives for conversion.

In 1410, shortly before his death, Rabbi Hasdai Crescas wrote *Or Adonai* to deal with the conversions which had swept through the Jewish communities in Spain. According to Rabbi Crescas, the chief cause of conversion was "the Greek [i.e., Aristotle] who has dimmed the eyes of Israel in these our times."[48] The medieval confrontation with Aristotle exposed the Talmud as an unscientific list of opinions and commentaries, constantly turning in on itself in more and more convoluted fashion. Averroes opened the Jews to a Christianity that could accommodate the insights of the Greek philosophers and the Jewish prophets, as Aquinas' synthesis had done. As a result, "Men seeking salvation for their souls hoped to find their heart's desire in Christianity, which was expounded to the people by great popular orators and highly cultured humanists."[49]

One year after *Or Adonai*, St. Vincent Ferrer arrived in Castile at the head of a band of hundreds so touched by his preaching and his call to repentance that they followed him from town to town flogging themselves in a public display of penitence. The bands of flagellants terrified the Jews. Those who did not flee at the sight of the approaching penitents flogging themselves were subjected to St. Vincent's sermons when he entered their synagogues to preach the word of Christ to them, whether they wanted to hear it or not. Ferrer was adamant in opposing forced conversion, but just as adamant in forcing the Jews to listen to his sermons.

Toward the end of 1412, Ferrer turned his attention to neighboring Aragon. While visiting the castle of Caspe and playing a decisive role in raising Fernande de Antiquera to the throne, Ferrer met Joshua Halorki, the pope's physician, and engaged him in conversations about conversion. Twenty years earlier, Halorki had written that letter to Solomon Halevy, expressing dismay at the latter's conversion, but also expressing doubts about the Jewish religion. The doubts had evidently grown, and when Ferrer pressed the issue, Halorki converted. Halorki then changed his name to Hieronymus de De Sancte Fide, and like Levi, directed his attention to his former co-religionists. In August 1412 he presented the Avignonese anti-Pope Benedict XIII with a treatise on the Jews in Latin and Hebrew. The pamphlet must have impressed the pope because it became the seed from which the disputation at Tortosa grew.

In late 1412, Benedict XIII ordered the aljamas of Aragon to send representatives to San Mateo, near Tortosa, for a debate with the newly converted Geronimo de Sancte Fide on the proposition that the Messiah had already come. Attendance was not optional. The Jews tried to get out of attending through bribery and protest, but to no avail. The pope was determined to solve the Jewish question once and for all. Benedict felt the confrontation between Halorki and the rabbis would lead to the extinction of Judaism in Spain. It turns out that the hopes of the anti-pope were not exaggerated. Three thousand Jews from Aragon presented themselves for baptism during the debate, including members of the prominent de la Caballeria family. Aljamas across Aragon converted *en masse*. Baer explains the conversions by claiming "Aragon's Jewry was feeble and exhausted, and there was no king to protect it,"[50] but the disputation would show that the feebleness was intellectual and rooted in the Talmud, which Geronimo Sancte Fe, the former rabbi, knew intimately. Benedict XIII had arranged an all-out cultural offensive against the Jews. While Geronimo de Sancte Fide would engage them in debate, St. Vincent Ferrer would traverse Aragon preaching his miraculous sermons. Few Jews could resist this combination.

Led by Rabbi Vidal ben Veniste de la Cavalleria, a team of 14 rabbis met for debate at the pope's palace on February 7, 1413, under the supervision of Benedict. The following day, the pope laid down the ground rules. The disputation was not a debate between equals; it was rather a form of instruction, according to which the Jews were allowed to defend themselves against charges Geronimo de Sancte Fide would raise. De Sancte Fide, a genius in dividing his opponents, according to Baer, opened the disputation by pitting the writings of the Old Testament against the Talmud.

The Jews, Baer claims, had little time to prepare, although they had been in Tortosa for a month preceding the disputation. On the second day of the disputation, Rabbi Joseph Albo "got entangled in self contradictions ... and the Jewish multitude present laughed at him and considered him defeated."[51] The discussion involved the Messiah. Some of the rabbis brought up the Aggada of the Palestinian Talmud that suggested the Messiah had been born on the day the Temple had been destroyed and that he had remained alive since then in an earthly Paradise, and that occasionally he would appear at the gates of Rome. When the pope asked whether it was possible for the Messiah to live such a long time, Rabbi Astruc Halevi snapped back that it was no less plausible than what Christians believed about their Messiah. Rabbi Astruc then claimed the Jews didn't need a Messiah for the salvation of their souls—"because their souls would be saved even if the Messiah never came"—but rather for the restoration of their political kingdom.[52] The pope reminded the Rabbi, if that were the case the Jews needed no Messiah at all, and Rabbi Astruc "had to apologize."[53]

The disputants demonstrated very different notions of what the Messiah was supposed to do. The gentiles longed for release from the bondage of sin and for the salvation of their souls; the Jews "await[ed] a Messianic king who will build the earthly Jerusalem."[54] The Talmudic Messiah was "a lofty personage, a man born of a human being, and his act of redemption will be to bring the bodies out of slavery into freedom, to raise the Jewish people to a state of enduring prosperity, to build the Temple and to maintain it in splendor. All admit that such a Messiah has not yet arrived."[55] If nothing else, the disputation showed that the Jews were seeking a Messiah different from the one whom the Christians said had already arrived. The Christians saw the Messiah as "a God-man, while the Jewish definition is that of a superior human being. The function of the Christian Messiah is to save souls from Hell, which the Jewish Messiah is to keep the Jewish bodies out of servitude."[56]

The Jews were handicapped by the ground rules of the debate, which took place in an "irksome atmosphere of political pressure and moral coercion."[57] But the Jews faced internal difficulties too. Virtually all their fundamental difficulties revolved around the Talmud. The Talmud was an esoteric text, written by rabbis solely for rabbis, and never intended to be the object of public debate. As a result, when the Talmud's more embarrassing passages were dragged into the light by converts who were former rabbis, the Jews didn't know what to say. The Disputation of Tortosa thus followed the same pattern as Donin's attack on the Talmud a Century and a half before.

On June 15, 1414, Geronimo de Sancte Fide read "some Talmudic passages which should have been censored," and asked the Jews if they were ready to defend them.[58] The Jews, who probably decided to maintain silence beforehand, gave no reply. Geronimo took the Jews' silence as proof they were "dumbfounded and bewildered."[59] Baer does not dispute the claim, but adds as justification "it was naturally not pleasant for the Jews to have to discuss such passages before the tribunal."[60] The Jews, quite simply, could not defend their own sacred texts. In the minutes of July 7, 1414, they are recorded as saying::

> The Jews here assembled from all the communities in the kingdom ... declare that because of their ignorance and lack of enlightenment, they are unable to rebut the arguments of Hieronymus [de Sancte Fide] against the talmudic sayings cited by him, and do not know how to defend those sayings. They are, nevertheless, firmly convinced that, were the authors of those sayings now alive, they

would have known how to defend them because, as wise and good men, they could not have uttered any unseemly statements.[61]

This may be sly irony, but it was hardly convincing apologetics. The rabbis then petitioned the pope to allow them to go home "inasmuch as they did not have among them a champion competent and worthy of defending the Talmud."[62] The rabbis added "their weakness was not to be taken as a reflection upon the Talmud," but it certainly seemed that way.[63]

Jerome of the Holy Faith was aided by another rabbi convert, Andreas Betrandi, a scripture scholar in the employ of the pope. When the two former rabbis reminded the Jews that one false statement in the Talmud would disqualify the entire book, and when they reminded them that this was the criterion used to condemn the writings of Maimonides, Rabbi Astruc Halevi responded

> Taken literally, the talmudic passages quoted by Magister Andreas and Magister Hieronymus seemed to be heretical, inconsistent with good morals and fallacious. According to the traditional view taken by his teachers, however, these passages were to be interpreted in another sense. He himself admitted that he did not know the correct interpretation and did not intend to defend the passages; he therefore withdrew all his previous statements.[64]

Baer says it is "most unlikely that the Jews had nothing more to say," and they "were eager to hurry back to their communities no matter what, so as to try to save them from impending disintegration and collapse," but their eagerness could also be interpreted as discomfort at not knowing what to say.[65] Before long it became clear that the Jews had lost the battle. They were incapable of defending their most sacred writings. The Jews had written the Talmud to support their religion; they had then turned that religion into a manifestation of the Talmud by claiming that it was "more binding that the Torah itself," but for the second time in as many centuries, the most learned Jews could not defend their writings in the court of reason.[66]

Baer tries to explain this failure by saying the rabbis had been infected with "Averroism" and therefore "the Torah had lost its taste and fragrance and ceased to yield its strength," but the Torah was not at issue because the Christians accepted it as their sacred text as well (though not, of course, what the Hebrews would call the 'oral' Torah).[67] The Christians asserted exclusive rights over the Torah and cited the blasphemies of the Talmud as proof that the Jews had abandoned the religion of Abraham and Moses. Baer claims "Judaism was inconsistent with the religion of reason," but the disputation showed something slightly different.[68] It showed the Talmud was inconsistent with reason *and* inconsistent with the Torah as well. The issue was the Talmud, which had become the heart of the Jewish religion, distorting the Torah and shielding it from its true and infallibly protected interpretation by the Church in the light of the New Covenant upon which She is founded (the failing of the Jews regarding the Torah is also a failing of Messianic Christian heretics who in many ways imitate the Jews in belief and practice). The issue was also the Jewish inability to defend the Talmud. Once the rabbis could not defend the Talmud against the attacks of former rabbis, Judaism was perceived as irrational, outdated, and not worth defending. Jews as a result began to convert in large numbers even before the debate ended. "In March 1413 and the following months," Baer says,

> Jews appeared in Tortosa, singly at first and then in groups, declaring that after listening to the feeble arguments of their rabbis they had decided to become Christians. Others were baptized in their own localities. On February 2, 1414, some members of the de la Cavalleria family and their households were baptized. Within a few weeks several of these men, under Christian names, held important administrative and political posts.[69]

Solomon de Piera, the aged poet, joined Don Vidal de la Cavalleria, the rabbis' chief disputant, in converting to Christianity. Baer says, "Such faithlessness on the part of educated Jews of good family, who had been bred in the Hebrew tradition with its cultural treasures, was already quite common.... Nevertheless, each and every instance of betrayal cut the loyal Jews to the heart."[70] Baer feels "the king was inviting the two de la Cavallerias to his camp mainly for political and practical reasons," but the defection was devastating nonetheless, "to the remnant of Spanish Jewry it must indeed have seemed as if the sun had set with the apostasy of Don Vidal."[71] Rabbis like Bonafed compared the Jews who did not convert to "grain forgotten in the fields," it was "only by sheer accident were they not swept away by the tempest of apostasy."[72]

The conversions continued into 1414, when Astruc Rimoch, "a physician and poet of Fraga who had protected faithful Jews in 1391, converted to Christianity together with his son, also a physician and assumed the name of Magister Franciscus de Sant Jordi."[73] The Rabbis were perplexed; they could not explain why so many Jews converted. Baer returns again and again to "Averroism" as the most plausible explanation: "our pious men believe that philosophical contemplation," which is to say, "knowledge of the books of nature and of Aristotelian metaphysics" is "more important than the performance of the commandments."[74] There were external factors too. "There is reason to assume that Vincent Ferrer's sermons made an impression upon both humble and educated classes, and that the Church's 'victory' at Tortosa bewildered many."[75] In the aftermath of the disputation, St. Vincent Ferrer continued to march through Aragon with his band of flagellants, forcing the Jews to listen to his sermons, and many Jews converted there as well.

Two years after Vincent Ferrer's flagellants marched through Aragon, Benedict XIII was deposed. The king died a few months later, and a psychological reaction set in. The frenzy had worn out the Spanish nation psychologically. As normal life resumed, some of the old and the new Christians fell into the habits that had sustained them before the conversions. The Ordeniamento of Dona Catalina fell into desuetude. As the old habits reasserted themselves, the suspicion spread that the conversions of the new Christians were insincere. "Given the forced nature of the mass conversions of 1391," Kamen writes, "it was obvious that many could not have been genuine Christians."[76] As a result, the conversos were regarded with suspicion as a fifth column within the Church. Terms of opprobrium were applied to them, the most common being marrano, a word of obscure origin.

Chapter Five

The Revolution Arrives in Europe

It is clear that the Gospel, rendered purely natural (and, therefore, absolutely debased), becomes a revolutionary ferment of extraordinary violence. Jacques Maritain, *Three Reformers*

Whenever a party in Christendom opposes itself to the ruling church, it assumes a tinge of the Old Testament, not to say Jewish spirit. Heinrich Graetz, *History of the Jews*

In 1412, the "revolutionary storm" broke unexpectedly over Bohemia. According to Aeneas Sylvius Piccolomini, Bohemia had more beautiful churches and monasteries than any other kingdom in Europe. Aeneas Silvius's claim was no idle boast; he had traveled widely through Europe on the Church's business. He also wrote a history of Bohemia, took part in the Council of Basel, and eventually became head of the Catholic Church as Pope Pius II.

Prague's Jewish community was the most important in Bohemia. Jews in Bohemia invariably found their way to Prague, a center of European usury, and the "money business created over time a widespread network of familial and business connections that extended far beyond the borders of Bohemia."[1]

Prague had been linked directly to Spain by the slave trade since antiquity. Archbishop Agobard of Lyon reported that at the time of Louis the Pious, Jews were involved in slave traffic, importing pagan slaves from the Slavic lands east of the Holy Roman Empire. Jewish merchants trafficking in slaves, Bavarian salt, Bohemian wax, and horses, would stop regularly in Prague from the ninth Century onwards. Cosmas, the Czech chronicler, said in the 10th Century that Jews had been in Prague so long that no one knew when they had first settled there, although he speculated they lived in Prague from the time of the Roman Emperor Vespasian.[2]

The trade in German and Slavic slaves began in Berlin. The slaves were then sent to Prague and from there to Venice and then to Cordoba. Since the Jewish commercial network was also an intelligence network, whatever happened in Cordoba was discussed in Prague and vice versa. And much was happening in both places. Jews were converting in unprecedented numbers in Spain, and those who did not convert were looking nervously for a safe place to land. And Bohemia, the jewel of central European Catholic and monastic culture, was on the verge of the first full-blown revolution on European soil.

Trouble had been brewing in Prague for years. Ordained a priest in 1400, one year later John Huss became dean of the philosophy faculty at the Charles University, founded in 1348 at the pinnacle of Prague's golden age to honor St. Charles the Great. Charles University would prove less a monument than an occasion for the undoing of that Golden Age. After Anne of Bohemia married King Richard II of England, probably in 1382, the University of Prague became a conduit of subversive English thought, particularly the ideas of John Wycliffe, a professor of heretical leanings who became the pride of Oxford University when he was appointed Doctor there in 1371. Prague University's prominence increased in 1383 when the Dominicans transferred their Parisian college to Prague as a result of the Great Schism. By 1390 Bohemian students were studying at Oxford, and Wycliffe's philosophical works were being copied and discussed in Prague. John Huss was one of the scribes.

Wycliffe's ecclesiology made dangerous inroads into the mind of John Huss. Wycliffe does not distinguish between Church and State. He uses "Regnum," "ecclesia" and "respublica" interchangeably. Huss soon talked about the "regnum" or realm as a salvationary community. "The political ecclesiology of Wycliffe had defined the body politic of the realm as an ecclesia, an autonomous section of the Church Militant and had seen the secular powers of the realm as also the rulers of the church."[3] Wycliffe was an advocate of returning to the Primitive Church. An alliance of ill omen formed between those who espoused the "evangelical ideal" and those who wanted to "justify the nationalization of the English church and the secularization of her property."[4] This idea would reach fruition in England when Henry VIII put in motion the theft of the monasteries from the Church and their distribution to families—Cecil, Russell, Cromwell, et al—who would become the backbone of what William Cobbett regarded as a revolutionary movement there. John Huss would do the same thing sooner in Bohemia.

Wycliffe was both a Donatist and an Erastian. He believed a sacrament's validity was a function of the soul of the celebrant and transformed this idea into a political weapon to justify appropriation of Church property by the "realm." According to Huss, "The temporal lords can, as they judge proper, take temporal goods away from habitually delinquent ecclesiastics."[5] In Huss's ecclesiology, that meant "clerics so stubbornly habituated and hardened to evil as obviously to be in mortal sin."[6] This doctrine was music to the ears of the greedy nobility, who had long looked with envy on the Church's property in Bohemia, where 50 percent of the land was in Church hands.

One by one the ingredients that made up the stew of revolution took their place in Huss's mind where they simmered through years of public activity as a professor and a preacher. The idea of the realm as a salvationary community enabled an ethnic group to appropriate models from the Old Testament and define itself as a "holy nation," whose purpose was spreading heaven on earth by the sword, which became the essence of the revolutionary ideology. The idea of the realm as salvific community also explains "how the pietistic religious movements of the 14th Century, passing though the medium of Huss's leadership in the early 15th emerged as the mutiny of 1414-5 and the revolution of the following decade."[7]

Huss, like Wycliffe, appealed first to the example of the Primitive Church. That appeal soon went beyond the Primitive Church of the New Testament to a more appropriate object of imitation in the Old, Joshua leading his people in battle against flesh and blood foes, not against the principalities and powers the Church fought. Huss's appropriation of Wycliffe's conflation of *regnum* and *ecclesia* "encouraged others to revolt."[8] Rome became the Antichrist, and Huss's followers longed for "that blessed hour when the Whore of Revelations will be stripped bare and her flesh consumed by the fire of tribulation," as Nicholas of Dresden, one of Huss's followers put it.[9] The appeal to judaizing primitivism expressed "a general and comprehensive rejection of the Roman system, a kind of total alienation from the status quo."[10] In statements like that of Nicholas of Dresden, "we breathe the atmosphere of revolution, with evangelical love, humility and suffering displaced by the fanatical hatred that so often forms their psychological correlate."[11] We breathe, in other words, the toxic vapors of the revolutionary movement.

Huss was appointed preacher at the Bethlehem Chapel in Prague in 1402. Wealthy benefactors created the Chapel in the 1390s to promote preaching in the Czech language. The confluence of Wycliffe's heretical ideas and nascent Czech nationalism spawned a powerful political movement, which immediately became the vehicle for messianic politics. Huss's followers were soon carrying the conflation of *ecclesia* and *respublica* to its logical conclusion. Jerome of Prague, who would follow his master to the stake, called Bohemia "a holy nation" in his sermons and claimed the "Law of God" could be identified with "the national community loyal to King Wenceslas, the realm of Bohemia."[12] John of Jesenice took the idea a step further ideologically and a step backward toward its Jewish source when he claimed the Bohemians' relationship to King Wenceslas was comparable to Israel's relationship to God, a comparison that encouraged the King's appropriation of the Church's worldly goods. As later in England, the appeal to Scripture, to the example of the Primitive Church, and to Israel provided intellectual cover for revolution among the masses and justification for the greed of the princes.

Huss's idea that Bohemia was a "holy nation" led the Czechs inexorably into conflict with other ethnic groups, particularly the Germans, who constituted a significant minority in Prague and the northern and western sections of the kingdom. The conflict first surfaced at the university, where it took on philosophical trappings. Since most Germans were Okhamite nominalists, the Czechs gravitated via Wycliffe into the realist camp. Huss's German colleagues at the university orchestrated a condemnation of Wycliffe's teachings in 1403. Undeterred, Huss continued to promote Wycliffe, and in 1408 his priestly faculties were suspended. Proving himself a master of academic politics, Huss orchestrated a successful counter-attack, persuading the king to disenfranchise the German "nations" at the university. After Huss's coup, more than a thousand Germans decamped for Leipzig, where they started their own university in 1409. The University of Prague lost the esteem of the academic community throughout Europe, but it became a more effective instrument for Wyclifite propaganda, which became more revolutionary under Huss's guidance. Rome and Prague were on a collision course.

In December 1409, the disputed Pope Alexander V condemned Wycliffism and forbade most public preaching. When the bull was made public in Prague, Huss, who had repeatedly attacked the papacy in sermons at Bethlehem Chapel, was clearly the object of the pope's ire. Huss was not cowed. Huss appealed the bull to the archbishop on the day it appeared. More defiantly, he read it aloud at Bethlehem Chapel to elicit support. The Archbishop of Prague sided with the pope. At his request, Canon Zdenek burned 200 volumes of heretical material, including most probably books Huss had transcribed. The archbishop then fled from Prague to his castle at Roudnice, but not before excommunicating Huss and his followers for grave and pertinacious disobedience.

Huss responded in accord with the Wyclifite doctrine of the salvific *regnum* by upping the ante. Huss took his heretical doctrines and used them as a springboard to revolution by invoking the Old Testament. "Will you stand with me?" Huss asked the congregation at Bethlehem Chapel after his excommunication became public. When the people responded affirmatively in Bohemian, "We will and we do," Huss knew where to take them next. "The time has come for us," he said to the eager congregation, "*just as it did for Moses in the Old Testament*, to take up our swords and defend the law of God".[13]

Huss's contemporaries were shocked and outraged by his boldness. Peter of Unicov, the Dominican Master in Prague, publicly denounced Huss's sermon as "a summons to the people to take their swords and strike their fathers and mothers dead."[14] By 1410 clerical appeals to revolutionary violence in the name of Old Testament figures were commonplace. Jerome of Prague preached sermons that seethed with revolutionary violence against Rome and the Germans. Jerome not only encouraged others to take up the sword, he carried one himself, much to scandal of traditionalist clergy. Brandishing a sword, Jerome chased preachers of indulgences out of churches throughout Prague. He also used a sword to capture three monks he suspected of exhibiting false relics. Sword in hand, he took two to the civil authorities and imprisoned the third. Putting his sword aside, he beat the Franciscan preacher Benes of Boleslav with his fists. He was also a master of cultural and psychological terrorism, engaging in a propaganda campaign against Ernest of Carinthia and leading mobs in three incidents where they broke into churches and smeared excrement on crucifixes. He justified these acts of violence and impiety by appealing to the Czech nation as the New Israel. If Jerome of Prague were unable to invoke Moses, he would have been considered a common thug. With Moses and Israel on his lips, Jerome took thuggery to a new level, the level of revolutionary activity. Once Israel got invoked, Jerome was not a renegade priest or a sword-wielding cultural terrorist; he was Joshua leading the Bohemian Israelites, the "holy nation," into battle with "Edom," the heretics who were invariably German and loyal to Rome.

By now it should be clear that Huss could not have led a congregation of Catholics into rebellion against the Church of Rome without invoking the Old Testament. Huss and his followers had already described the Czechs as "a holy nation". Unlike the "New Israel," warned by Jesus that those who lived by the sword would die by it, the Bohemian zealots who conflated *"regnum"* and *"ecclesia"* could spread the gospel with the sword because Bohemia was their *"ecclesia,"* and their religion, derived from the messianic politics which revolutionaries from the time of Simon bar Kokhba had gleaned from the Old Testament. Since there was only one "holy nation," Bohemians became the "New Israel" by default.

The concept "holy nation" as a conflation of the secular *"regnum"* with the spiritual *"ecclesia"* is a Jewish idea. The Hussite revolution was, at its core, a rejection of the Roman Church and its adherence to Christ's claim that his kingdom was not of this world. The popes would term the idea that a holy nation wielding the sword could create heaven on earth a return to the vomit of Judaism. This was the essence of revolution then, and revolutionaries from Bar Kokhba to Trotsky have remained faithful to this creed. Many Jewish commentators have noticed the underlying congruity between Talmudic Judaism and revolution. Calling Huss, "a Czech priest" who had "loosened the bonds in which the church had ensnared the minds of men,"[15] Heinrich Graetz notes

> the flames ... fired a multitude in Bohemia, who entered on a life and death struggle with Catholicism. *Whenever a party in Christendom opposes itself to the ruling church, it assumes a tinge of the Old Testament, not to say Jewish spirit.* The Hussites regarded Catholicism, not unjustly as heathenism, and themselves as Israelites, which must wage holy war against Philistines, Moabites and Ammonites. Church and monasteries were to them the sanctuaries of a dissolute idolatry, temples to Baal and Moloch and groves of Ashtaroth to be consumed with fire and sword [my emphasis].[16]

Millennialism played an increasingly prominent role in the revolutionary mind. Millennialism was a derivation of two biblical texts—Daniel 7, describing the "fourth beast" or kingdom in Daniel's dream and Revelation 20, describing the reign of a thousand years. According to Daniel,

> The fourth beast
> is to be a fourth kingdom on earth,
> different from all other kingdoms.
> It will devour the whole earth,
> trample it underfoot and crush it.
> As for the ten horns: from this kingdom
> will rise ten kings, and another after them;
> this one will be different from the previous one
> and will bring down three kings;
> he is going to speak words against the Most High,
> and harass the saints of the Most High.
> He will consider changing seasons and the Law,
> and the saints will put into his power

for a time, two times and half a time.
But a court will be held and his power will be stripped from him,
consumed and utterly destroyed.
And sovereignty and kingship,
and the splendors of all the kingdoms under heaven
will be given to the people of the saints of the Most High.
His sovereignty is an eternal sovereignty
and every empire will serve and obey him.

Historically Daniel is referring to Alexander the Great as the fourth beast. His kingdom split after his death into two main divisions, the Seleucids and the Ptolomies, but its reign is only temporary. His kingdom will be succeeded by a kingdom which has "an eternal sovereignty." Revelations 20 complements Daniel's vision by describing the thousand year reign of Christ on earth that begins when "an angel" came "down from heaven with the key of the Abyss in his hand and an enormous chain." The angel then "overpowered the dragon, that primeval serpent which is the devil and Satan, and chained him up for a thousand years. He threw him into the Abyss, and shut the entrance and sealed it over him, to make sure that he would not deceive the nations again until the thousand years had passed. At the end of that time, he must be released, but only for a short while." When St. John wrote his Apocalypse, the fourth beast was associated with Rome, specifically with the persecutions of Nero, which took a terrible toll on the nascent Christian church.

Roughly four centuries later, St. Augustine would propose the definitive interpretation of these passages in *The City of God*. The book of Revelation was understood not in a literal historical sense but as a spiritual allegory. The Millennium had begun with Christ's death on the Cross and would continue until the Second Coming, when the Antichrist would reign for three and a half years before Christ returned in glory to judge the living and the dead and end time and human history. To consider the Millennium as anything other than the dispensation of the New Israel, the Catholic Church, was declared a heresy and a superstitious aberration by the Council of Ephesus in 431. In spite of this condemnation, Millennialism "persisted in the obscure underworld of popular religion."[17] And it would come to the fore whenever a movement challenged the Church's claim to be the "New Israel." Invariably, each heretical sect would identify the fourth beast with the Church of Rome, and each would avidly ascribe to itself the event that would inaugurate the Millennium on earth. The Fifth Monarchy men at the time of Cromwell are a prominent example, but by no means exceptional. Their calculations were strikingly similar to those of the Taborites, the revolutionary wing of the Hussite party that established itself as the revolutionary avant garde by force in the summer of 1420.

There is another interpretation of Revelations 20. Those who refused to succumb to the persecutions of the fourth beast, made up Rome, and reigned for literally one thousand years—the period between Alaric's sack of Rome in 410, the date conventionally given for the fall of Rome, and the first outbreak of revolution in Europe, when Huss was excommunicated and gave his revolutionary sermon at the Bethlehem Chapel in 1410.

If there were one institution associated with this thousand-year reign in Europe it was the monastery. Nothing symbolized the Roman religion better than the monasteries. The monastery, which antedated the Rule of St. Benedict, its most enduring norm, encouraged men to live like angels on earth by proposing a way to live the counsels of perfection Christ proposed to the rich young man in the Gospel. When the rich young man asks Jesus what he must do "to possess eternal life," Jesus tells him to "keep the commandments." When the young man replies by saying that "I have kept all these. What more do I need to do?" Jesus tells him "If you wish to be perfect, go and sell what you own and give the money to the poor, and you will have treasure in heaven; then come and follow me." Jesus' boldness shows the radically supernatural character of the New Covenant, which the Fathers of the Church stressed. The commandments are natural; the counsels of perfection are supernatural; they transcend a man's natural inclinations—sex, food, money, autonomy—which the commandments regulate by confining within the bounds of reason: "You must not kill. You must not commit adultery. You must not bring false witness. Honor your father and mother, and: you must love your neighbor as yourself." The new way involves a radical departure from the natural order. Sell everything you have, give the money to the poor, and you will have treasure in heaven; then come follow me. Thus the monastic vows of poverty, chastity and obedience, all flowing from the absence of money. Those who did not marry did not need money to support their families, nor did they need the autonomy necessary to use that money wisely as heads of households. They could live like angels on earth.

Monasticism preserved the culture of antiquity when the predations of the barbarian tribes threatened to destroy civilization after the collapse of the empire in the fifth century. The Rule of St. Benedict enabled establishment of stable autonomous communities and a cultural lingua franca, the Christianization of classical culture that prevented Europe from disintegrating into a patchwork of warring ethnicities. Monasticism did this according to the letter of the gospel, not by the sword but by gentle example. Like the mustard seed that became the tree in which the birds of the air found shelter, the monasteries gathered in the marauding barbarian tribes and civilized them. Like the yeast that inexorably but imperceptibly suffused the lump of dough to raise it, the monasteries raised the level of European culture by integrating Christianity, classical culture, and local ethnic identity into one powerful whole. The Benedictine Monks who sailed down the Danube from Regensburg brought the gospel and culture in its most practical and mundane forms. A Roman senator sent to administer the border provinces along the Danube said it was the unhappiest place on earth because its inhabitants had neither grapes nor olives. The Benedictines brought grapes, transforming the wilderness into a garden, a vineyard, and an orchard—all still standing today, bearing fruit over a hundred-fold over the thousand year reign of Benedict in Europe.

The monasteries became wealthy in the mundane sense by ignoring wealth. The individual monks renounced money, but their labors produced enormous wealth for the monasteries. That wealth grew over generations because the monks did not have children or the expenses they require. More importantly, their lands were not constantly divided as children inherited the land from their fathers. The monks who had turned their backs on wealth ended up living lives of wealth, and wealth led to moral decay. The enemies of the Gospel used that moral decay to justify their attack on a supernatural way of life deeply repugnant to the carnal mind.

Christ told his followers that those who live according to the Gospel will elicit hatred from the carnal; the monasteries were no exception. Jews would always symbolize those wise in the ways of the world, but blind to higher realities. Those who loathed the order the Church imposed on Europe allied themselves with Jews to vent their fury on those who lived according to laws that transcended nature. A wealthy Church will soon attract those with no taste for the counsels of perfection even if they have to take vows of poverty, chastity, and obedience to gain access to that wealth. Wealth can promote its own decline. Carnal clerics fuel resentment and oftentimes manifest the very resentment their own immoral behavior has fostered in others. John Zelivsky, the apostate monk, would be a good example of just that sort of behavior.

Cohn claims that the resentment arising from poverty created the Hussite revolution. Heymann disagrees; he says that largely because of laws designed to attract German settlers, the lot of the Bohemian peasant was significantly better than in the rest of Europe. "At no time again until the early 19th Century" were "Bohemia's peasants ... as relatively well off as in the period preceding the Hussite wars."[18] Slavery, the engine that drove wages down, "had disappeared in Bohemia in the course of the 12th Century."[19] Heymann contends the Church owned 50 percent of the land in Bohemia, and as such had an insurmountable advantage over peasants and the princes, who gradually united in resentment of monastic renunciation and the prosperity and moral laxity it engendered. The peasants, a "revolutionary class"[20] at Tabor, were unhappy because the wages the monks received, no matter what they did or did not do, were consistently higher that what the peasants and the proletariat could demand. Once the peasantry caught the millennial virus, no economic calculus was applicable, because what was then at stake not better wages but heaven on earth. To the carnal and uneducated peasant, the destruction of the monasteries took on a numinous quality. Destruction of the monasteries, perhaps more than any theory about communion under both species, united the revolutionary movement.

This strain of messianic politics made the Hussite revolution different from the great English peasant revolt of 1381 or the Pastoreux uprising in France in

1320. The Hussite revolution is "inexplicable" as "a purely socio-economic development."[21] "They," said one Hussite referring to Rome, "have introduced as necessary for the kingdom of God, Greek rules, Aristotelic justice, Platonic sanctity, and gentile rites and honor."[22] The Hussites would have none of this. Like the Muslims before them and the Puritans after them, they were willing to burn down whatever edifice contained more than their understanding of the word of God. To bring about the kingdom of God, then, the Holy Nation of the Bohemian warriors had to destroy the monasteries. Once that repository of secularized Christianity or the *"mulier fornicaria"* which the Bohemians identified with Rome had been destroyed, heaven on earth would rise phoenix-like from the ashes of the burned monasteries.

While Huss was urging his congregation to take up the sword, one Bohemian was doing just that, but not in Bohemia. In July 1410, John Zizka of Trocnov fought in the Battle of Gruenwald at which the Polish nobility decisively defeated the territorial ambitions of the Teutonic Knights in Prussia. Of the 50 divisions constituting the Polish army at Gruenwald, two were composed entirely of Czechs, and three in part.

Zizka, an impoverished squire who was blind in one eye, spent his younger years organizing hunts for the king. He also engaged in brigandage, plundering the estates of the local magnate Lord Oldrich Rosenberk, a man Zizka would plague his entire life. At the Battle of Gruenwald, Zizka witnessed medieval warfare in all its panoply but left the field unimpressed. Since the invention of the stirrup, the major offensive weapon in armed combat had been the cavalry. Zizka realized that the aristocratic army of armored knights on horseback could be neutralized by judicious use of terrain. Armed horsemen were unbeatable on an open plain, but they were not as effective charging uphill, especially if the defenders surrounded themselves with trenches and portable fortifications and made judicious use of the newly developed firearms, especially at close range. The Golden Lane at Hradcany Castle in Prague had traditionally been home to the King's alchemists, and one of their tasks was developing firearms and potent gunpowder. That tradition has continued to this day with the production of Semtex, developed in Czechoslovakia during the Communist era and the preferred explosive of terrorists during the 1970s. Zizka would use Czech expertise in explosives in unprecedented ways, changing the face of warfare.

When Zizka returned to Bohemia in 1411, he bought a house in Prague, intending to settle there as one of the king's retainers. One of his duties was to accompany Queen Sophie to chapel; since the queen was attending Bethlehem Chapel, Zizka imbibed Huss's messianic Bohemian nationalism *ex fontem*. He also ran head on into Huss's conflict with the pope and the local bishop, which was reaching its climax when Zizka returned from the Prussian wars.

On June 12, 1411, Archbishop Zbynek placed all of Prague under interdict, which meant that none of the sacraments could be confected there. King Wenccslas told Praguers to ignore the bishop, fostering Huss' agenda of creating a national church. If the king could lift an interdict, then his power exceeded that of the bishop, and even that of the pope. In meddling in spiritual affairs, Wenceslas may have been influenced by the Wyclifite doctrine of the supremacy of lords temporal in matters spiritual, which had been preached at the Bethlehem Chapel. Vindicated by the king's defiance, Huss continued to preach sermons derived from Wycliffe, and the masses who attended Bethlehem Chapel edged closer to revolution.

Wenceslas, though, was motivated by something less lofty than philosophical principles. In 1412 Pope John XXIII called for a crusade against King Ladislaus of Naples. To finance this campaign, the pope authorized the sale of indulgences. When papal representatives arrived in Prague to sell indulgences, the king did an abrupt *volte face* and sided with the pope because he stood to benefit financially from indulgences sold in his realm. Huss denounced the sale of indulgences: "The papal legate sold whole deaconries, towns and cities to unworthy clerics living in concubinage" and to other unsavory characters, who then "taxed the population as much as they wished."[23] The pope then confirmed Huss's excommunication and the interdict on Prague. The pope also denounced Bethlehem Chapel as a "nest of heretics" and demanded it be torn down, which the pope's supporters attempted while Huss was inside preaching.[24]

Since the king had sided with the pope on indulgences, he could not contravene this interdict, and a stalemate existed until Huss resolved the impasse by leaving Prague. On 15 October 1412, unwilling to deprive the city of divine services and access to the sacraments, John Huss left Prague and went into voluntary exile. For almost two years, Huss lived in the castle Kozi Hradek and worked in the countryside of Bohemia, writing books and preaching wherever and whenever opportunity allowed. In exile, Huss continued his agitation against the Church, preaching open-air sermons to peasants, whose gatherings foreshadowed the mass Taborite rallies after his death. The propaganda campaign in Prague continued in his absence under the direction of Jerome of Prague. The Manifesto of 1412, a part of that propaganda campaign, again appealed to the sword and the patriarchs of the Old Testament as a summons to revolutionary battle against the Roman Catholic Church, now identified by Jakoubek of Stribro and others as the Antichrist: "And so, dear holy community in Bohemia," the Manifesto concludes,

> let us stand in battle line with our head, Master Huss, and our leader, Master Jerome; and whoever will be a Christian, let him turn to us. Let everyone gird on his sword, let brother not spare brother, nor father spare son, nor son father, nor neighbor spare neighbor....All should kill so that we can make our hands holy in the blood of the accursed ones, as Moses shows us in his books; for what is written there is an example to us.[25]

The outcome was predictable. Demonstrations in the streets led to assaults on priests and a number of arrests. The mob talked about a radical change of governance, a revolution, based on Huss's translation of Wycliffe's ideas. In particular, Wycliffe claimed that "dominion," the right to rule, resulted from grace. So sin, which meant the loss of grace, meant the loss of political legitimacy. Sin transformed a legitimate ruler into a usurping tyrant who could be swept from office by a "holy nation", e.g., the mob in the streets of Prague.

The propaganda campaign against the Church lasted from 1412 until the revolution of 1419. The Hussites staged obscene and blasphemous processions throughout Prague, ridiculing the official church through songs, pictures, and dramaturgy. As before, the magnet for popular wrath was the monasteries. Jerome of Prague was involved in three separate attacks on monasteries in 1414, in which excrement was smeared on crucifixes, one of his favorite psychological warfare techniques.

Heymann calls Zizka "the implacable destroyer of those whom he considered as the arch sinners: the monks."[26] Zizka's hatred of the monks was notorious, so notorious, in fact, that a legend that his sister had been raped by monk was created to explain his hatred. Zizka was drawn to the Czech nationalism promoted by revolutionary priests. Both Zizka and the priests began by identifying *ecclesia* with *regnum* and then moved to the creation of a *de facto* national church. When Jerome of Prague referred to Bohemia as a "holy nation," he made no distinction between *regnum* and *ecclesia*. Similarly, the idea of pope and emperor, the lords temporal and spiritual, would merge too.

What made the merger possible was the appeal to the Old Testament. Bohemia had supplanted the Church as the "New Israel." That meant the Hussite revolution would produce generals that promoted theology, i.e., someone like Zizka, a devoted supporter of the lay chalice, the prime bone of theological contention, who used each military campaign to promote the Four Articles of the Hussite faith. But it would also produce sword wielding priests like Jerome of Prague, John Zelivsky, and, most notably, Prokop the Bald. Inspired by Israelite genocide in the Old Testament, the Hussite warriors of God earned a reputation for cruelty. Heymann claims Zizka "always insisted on sparing the lives of women and children."[27] But that didn't prevent him from exercising a "holy hatred" on those whom he considered enemies of the Law of God,[28] above all, monks. During his attack on the castle of Sedlec, Zizka told six captured prisoners that if one were prepared to decapitate the others, his life would be spared. The man who volunteered was then invited to join Zizka's army.

In October 1414, Jakoubek of Stribro and other priests in Prague began celebrating the Eucharist *sub utraque specie* with the faithful. What seemed like a minor liturgical issue had deep political consequences. The Hussites' position that Christ had celebrated the Eucharist under both species at the Last Supper was met by Catholic insistence that only priests and bishops were in attendance then, and that only they had always communed *sub utraque specie* by consuming the body and blood of Christ under the appearance of both bread and wine at Mass. The

Hussites' position, known as Utraquism, led them to affirm the priesthood of all believers, which they implemented at the communist settlement of Tabor by urging women to participate in the act of consecration. The priesthood of the laity was an oxymoron that would usher in revolutionary change throughout Christendom.

The Council of Constance immediately condemned the lay chalice, which had become the symbol of the Hussite reformation. That Council threatened all who partook of both species at Mass with the ban of heresy and excommunication. The Council then invited Huss to explain himself. Huss had ignored similar invitations before, but he accepted this time, despite his fears, after receiving a guarantee of safe conduct from Sigismund, King of the Romans. He set out for the council on October 11, 1414 under the protection of Lords Wenceslas of Duba and Henry Lacembok, as well as John of Chlum and the latter's secretary, and a representative of the University of Prague, Master John Kardinal. Huss nevertheless made out his last will and testament before he left.

Two days after arriving in Constance, Huss received the document assuring his safe conduct from the Emperor. On November 28, however, he was summoned from his lodging and, despite the protest of John of Chlum, placed under arrest. When Sigismund arrived on Christmas Eve, he lodged a protest, but by the first of the year was reconciled to ratifying whatever the council decided. Huss was then spirited off to Gottlieben castle, where he was interrogated for months about his beliefs and put under duress to recant. Antipope John XXIII, who had excommunicated Huss, was a fellow prisoner at Gottlieben, after fleeing in disguise when he realized the council intended to depose him to resolve the Great Schism. Huss told his inquisitors he had never espoused the proposition attributed to him. The inquisitors, who seemed predisposed toward his guilt, did not believe Huss's denials, nor did Sigismund. In June 1515, Huss was found guilty of espousing the heretical doctrines of John Wycliffe, including the doctrine of remanance, or denying the real presence, which he had never held. In condemning him, the council was reacting more to the movement Huss created and the dangers it posed, which continued to metastasize. Jakoubek of Stribro, taking Huss's conflation of *"regnum"* and *"ecclesia"* to its logical conclusion was now claiming that God had created the Bohemian people to lead the church out of bondage to Rome. The universal Church had gotten the administration of the chalice wrong for 1400 years; the Bohemian Church, the Holy Nation, the New Israel, the new headquarters of the true universal church would now correct it.

On June 15, 1415, the Council of Constance condemned Utraquism. Three weeks later, the council condemned Huss to the stake for espousing doctrines, "of which many are—God knows—" he claimed "falsely ascribed to me."[29] On July 6, 1415, Huss was divested of all spiritual authority. His tonsure was shaved off and replaced with a paper dunce cap bearing the figures of three demons and the words "this is a heresiarch."[30] "Oh cursed Judas," the bishop charged with carrying out the sentence said to Huss, "who breaking away from the counsels of peace, has consulted with the Jews, we commit your soul to the devil."[31] The faggots surrounding Huss were then lit; according to one account, he died singing.

The bishop's final malediction against Huss mentions accusations that dogged Huss's movement from its inception. Huss was accused of conspiring with the Jews, which discredited the movement in the eyes of the orthodox. Most of the evidence comes from Jewish sources. Rabbi Louis Israel Newman claims the Hussite revolution was "a conspiracy between Hussites, Waldensians and Jews."[32] Huss was thus stigmatized as a "Judaizer". His followers were stigmatized as "Jews or worse than Jews,"[33] and the Hussite movement was characterized as "Judaism." The charge was based on the Hussites tendency to portray their cause in Old Testament terms, but there were other reasons. Newman claims the Hussites had "personal associations with individual Jews and Jewish communities in their country."[34] He also claims "Jewish groups participate[d] actively and publicly in the rise and spread of the [Hussite] movement."[35] According to Newman, Jewish support of heretical movements, especially when they threatened to spill over into political revolutions, "run like dark threads through the history of nearly every movement of reform in European Christendom," but they "united in a special combination in the case of the Hussite Reformation."[36] Newman sees a Jewish continuity in Europe's revolutionary movements. Newman also sees the Hussite revolt as "the second important movement to challenge the authority of the Catholic Church."[37] After "the Albigensian-Waldensian heresy in Languedoc and Lombardy had been crushed, ... the impulse to revolt was transplanted to other countries, and during the 15th Century gave birth to the Bohemian Reformation."[38]

The pattern of Jews supporting Judaizers in rebellion against the Church repeated itself over the next few centuries. Before long, the trajectory was predictable. The "reformers" would urge a return to Scripture and the purity of the early Church, which would lead to a resurrection of figures from the Old Testament as models of how to use the sword to bring about heaven on earth. Vernacular editions of the bible (often falsified and published by Jews) were crucial, leading the Bohemians to think of themselves as a "chosen race." So, too, the Puritans in England and America, who, like "Christian biblicists of every period," felt "a strong and immediate sense of identity with many figures in Jewish history."[39] Their study of the Bible prompted the Hussites to challenge the ordained priesthood and to see themselves as Israelites reincarnated with a new mission from God. Huss compared Czechs who would have nothing to do with Germans to "the Jews whom Nehemiah forbade to intermarry with foreigners."[40] Citizens of Prague whose speech was "half Bohemian, half German deserve[d] a whipping." Huss closely "sought to follow the example of the Hebrew Prophet."[41]

When word of Huss's death reached Prague, fierce indignation spread, uniting the Bohemian people against Rome and the Emperor. Hundreds of Bohemian lords affixed their seals to a document protesting the Council's action against

Huss, but their protest only earned them excommunication by the same council. The Jews of Prague joined the Christians of Bohemia in their protest. They were, of course, immune to ecclesiastical sanction, but the way in which they described Huss's death is instructive. The anonymous author of a contemporary Jewish chronicle described Huss' death as "*Kiddush hashem*" or Sanctification of the Divine Name, a term Gladstein says was "applied only to the martyrdom of Jews."[42] Gladstein cites the term as "further proof that the Jews considered the Hussites were Jews."[43] The Hussites' view of themselves was no different. Heymann says the Hussites "did not think of themselves as innovators' or "as creators of a new form of religion and society," but rather "as restorers of the old ways of God, as the direct successors of the people of Israel" determined to create "little theocratic communities" in the mountains of Bohemia, which took their names from "Biblical mountains like Tabor and Oreb" and espoused a creed that was "stern, puritan, old-testamentarian, often fanatic in its determination to purge this world for all sins and sinner by fire and sword."[44] They were classic revolutionaries, in the mold of Simon bar Kokhba at Bethar and the Jews who committed suicide at Masadah.

Less than a year after Huss's death, Jerome of Prague followed him to Constance and suffered the same fate, burning at the stake on May 30, 1416. Jerome did not die singing. His death was long, slow, and painful. Their deaths, as the anonymous Jewish chronicler noted, rallied the Czech people around Huss, whom they declared their saint. From 1416 on, the anniversary of Huss's death was celebrated in Prague. Huss and the chalice became "joined from then on in a mutually reinforcing union"[45] that threatened to fall apart whenever external opposition lagged. Sigismund's brutal and stupid policies, however, ensured that that would not happen soon. Galvanized by the death of Huss, his movement became increasingly messianic. In March, 1417, the Hussite faction at the University of Prague redoubled its support of the utraquist position, saying that communion under both species was necessary for salvation. They also declared the Roman rite invalid, and made the Bohemian Hussite movement the one true church of Christ on earth. The chalice, images of which would soon be sewn on the sleeves of Taborite soldiers, became the official symbol of the Bohemian revolution, which, true to the Old Testament model, was both political and religious.

Eight months after the Hussites declared spiritual independence, the Council of Constance resolved the Great Schism by electing Oddone Cardinal Colonna pope. Pope Martin V soon met a procession of Jews in Constance, informing them while astride a white horse with silk and gold harness "You have the law, but understand it not."[46] The Jews, though, hadn't come to be lectured on the Christian faith or their blindness to its truth. Still smarting from the accusations of a Jewish-Hussite conspiracy, the Jews feared for their lives at the hands of Catholic crusaders, and so pleaded with the pope for protection. Graetz claimed the request was accompanied by large sums of money. What the Jews got for their money, although Graetz doesn't put it this way, was a reiteration of *Sicut Judaeis non*, the traditional teaching of the Church on the Jews. The Jews were blind, and they were a pernicious influence in Christian society, but they should not be harmed. Or as Martin V put it: "Whereas the Jews are made in the image of God and a remnant of them will one day be saved, and whereas they have besought our protection, following in the footsteps of our predecessors we command that they be not molested in their synagogues; that their laws, rights and customs be not assailed; that they be not baptized by force, constrained to observe Christian festivals, nor to wear new badges and that they be not hindered in their business relations with Christians."[47]

Martin V was not as lenient or as understanding with the Hussites. A few months after his election in spring 1418, Martin V in conjunction with the Council, which dissolved in April, sent King Wenceslas 24 recommendations to rid Bohemia of the Hussite heretics and to repair what they vandalized and restore what they stole. On April 22, Martin appealed to Sigismund to enforce the decrees, granting him the right to organize a crusade against the heretics. Each time the Council of Constance tried to impose order by force in Bohemia, it united a people that otherwise threatened to dissolve into warring factions, unable to resolve internal theological differences without recourse to force of arms. Martin V demanded that Huss' followers publicly approve his condemnation and execution. Coupled with the economic boycott imposed on Bohemia and the threat of a crusade, Martin V's demand united the Bohemian nation behind the most radical Hussite leaders.

In spring 1419, John Zelivsky, a violent revolutionary priest became *de facto* dictator of Prague. Zelivsky was an "apostate monk," who never missed an opportunity to attack the institution he had abandoned.[48] Zelivsky was a sword-wielding priest who aspired to be Zizka's equal as a military leader. He failed miserably as a military leader, but he was adept at agit-prop and mobilizing the mob for violence, which culminated in the defenestration that touched off the revolution. The transition from priest to revolutionary is discernable in Zelivsky's sermons, which became progressively more revolutionary and violent during 1419. Zelivsky turned Sigismund's unfortunate use of words in creating an "Order of the Dragon" into the claim that Sigismund was the Antichrist. The second coming of Christ was thus was at hand, and Prague had a special role to play. The Holy Nation of Bohemia was going to inaugurate the millennium, Christ's reign, heaven on earth. The time had come for God's holy nation to grab the sword and bring on the millennium. Intoxicated by his rhetoric, the mob in Prague began to bring on the millennium by vandalizing images, often destroying whole churches, and beating up Catholic priests or monks unfortunate enough to be caught alone on the street.

To whip the masses into a revolutionary frenzy, Zelivsky organized processions, leading the faithful to a church with a monstrance firmly grasped in both hands, and standing back as the mob vandalized the church under this blasphemous sanction. During the late spring and summer of 1419, as Wenceslas IV lost control of his capital city and his kingdom, the revolutionary priests staged blasphemous processions featuring bare breasted whores riding beasts symbolizing the Whore of Babylon from the book of Revelations. The rest of the whore's body was covered with scrolls representing papal bulls and tiny bells that tinkled, in mockery of the bells rung during the consecration of the Mass. The riotous procession eventually wound its way to the New Town Square, where a fire was kindled and the bulls, stripped from the whore's body, were burnt in defiance. Festivals and processions of this sort, replete with obscenity and blasphemy, served as "visual and dramatic propaganda" that tended toward "temporal subversion of the social order." For a time, "the world was turned upside down. The lecherous whore played the virgin or pope, the fool became bishop, the criminal donned the king's crown, the ass brayed at the altar, while everyone ran leaping though the cathedral singing uproariously the drunken liturgy."[49]

Hussite songs would play an even more crucial role in the revolution. The most famous was "Ye Warriors of God." Hussite warriors could win battles just by singing "Ye Warriors of God," because its melody would throw opposing armies into panic. Even the music had an Old Testament referent. Zizka seemed a reincarnation of Joshua, and the Hussites were bringing the walls of Jericho down with their music. But the connection was in the music too, or at least in the lyrics. In "Arise, Arise Great City of Prague," the Hussites call upon God to protect them

> against that king of
> Babylon who threatens the city of
> Jerusalem, Prague, and all faithful people.

Hussite propaganda could only subvert the medieval ecclesiastical order by appealing to models from the Old Testament. If Bohemia were now Israel, then Prague was Jerusalem, and if Prague were Jerusalem, then Rome must be Babylon, and so on. This logic of analogy was essential to the revolutionary project because it was the only way the revolutionaries could legitimize their cause. "Matej of Janov," we are told, "had earlier written in his *Narracia de Milicio* that the Jerusalem experiment founded by Jan Milic of Kromeriz was the beginning of a divine action though Christ to create from Prague, formerly a city of Babylon full of filth and shame, a city of light upon a hill—Jerusalem."[50] These appeals to the Old Testament de-legitimized a social order based on the Catholic Church and its appropriation of classical culture. The cultural agit-prop proved it possible to construe sacred realities in another compelling way.

The mass gatherings on the hills throughout summer, 1419, showed that an alternative society, where there was neither lord nor servant, nor mine or thine, was possible. The Hussites named these Woodstock-like gatherings on the hills Tabor, after the mountain in Palestine where Jesus was transfigured and appeared in glory alongside Moses and Elijah. Napoleon would stand on Tabor centuries later after defeating the Ottoman Turks in a moment of apotheosis that led many Jews to proclaim him the Messiah. Tabor, in turn, towered over the plains of Megiddo, where, it is said, the antichrist would fight his final battle. In Bohemia in 1419, Tabor symbolized the alternative to the Catholic social order, symbolized by the monasteries. Tabor was an assembly in nature, outside the city, and therefore outside of history and the sinful accretions of Roman culture. Tabor was the locus of the Transfiguration, a manifestation of glory in the here and now. In the gospel, Jesus warns his disciples not to erect permanent structures on Tabor, a warning that stresses how fleeting glory and exaltation are in this world. The judaizing Taborite priests, however, imposed the opposite meaning. Tabor was to be the basis of a new social order. During the summer of 1419, thousands of peasants abandoned their farms and cottages, wives, and families to live on top of a hill near Usti overlooking the Luznice river according to the new dispensation.

"Nothing," Norman Cohn says, "could show more clearly the extent to which these people lived in and from eschatological phantasies than the names which they gave to this town and to the river beneath it. While the latter became the Jordan, the former became Tabor—that is to say, the Mount of Olives [sic] where Christ had foretold his Parousia, where he had ascended to heaven and where, traditionally, he was expected to reappear in majesty. It was Tabor which became the spiritual center of the whole radical movement."[51]

The Taborite settlement in Bohemia was the locus of different movements: iconoclasm, communism—"Mine and thine do not exist at Tabor ... whoever owns private property commits a mortal sin"[52]—Millennialism, Adventism, and, if we include the Adamites, who were eventually expelled, nudism and sexual liberation. But they were united in their revolutionary messianic politics derived from their reading of the Old Testament. "The Taborites," Newman says, "were dominated by Old Testament influence almost to the same degree as the Puritans of England and early America."[53] Like the Puritans, they "compared themselves to the ancient Israelites, regarded themselves as God's Chosen People and denounced their foes as impious Canaanites, inhabitants of Edom, Moab and Amalek, as they designated the adjacent German provinces."[54] Newman says the Taborites "rejected the entire ecclesiastical ritual system, and held invocation of saints to be heretical and idolatrous."[55] They based their iconoclasm "on Old Testament injunctions against image worship."[56] Like the Israelites, the Hussites favored an elective king. They attempted to get first the Polish King and then his Lithuanian nephew to rule them. Like Cromwell and the founders of the American republic, they based their republicanism, not on classical models, but on their reading of the Book of Deuteronomy.

Tabor began not as a settlement but as a rally. To use a modern analogy, the settlement at Tabor was as if the people who attended Woodstock never left but instead created a community, which created an army, which conquered the country, and then went on military forays into Canada and Mexico, too. The success of the rally gave credence to "mass secession from the established order,"[57] which began when the peasants heard the Millennialism of the revolutionary priests at rallies and decided not to go home but to set up a permanent dwelling outside the existing social order. The mass rally was itself an act of revolutionary defiance in a culture where the right to "convoke a multitude" was the sole prerogative of the state. Lawrence of Brezova was dumbfounded by the novelty of large masses of people congregating on hills; he consulted astrologers for an explanation, eventually concluding Saturn had set the mob in motion and inclined their minds toward "rebelling against their superiors."[58] The uneducated peasants thought the end of the age was at hand, especially since the priests were telling them that, with citations from Daniel and Revelations to prove it.

The gatherings began during the summer of 1419 as an extension of the cultural agit-prop priests like Zelivsky were promoting in Prague. Kaminsky calls Tabor, a "conspiracy" which "had diverse heads but its tails were all tied together,"[59] meaning Zelivsky was coordinating activities that linked the revolutionaries in Prague with those in southern Bohemia. Zelivsky preached sermons about the meaning of the biblical Mt. Tabor while the revolutionaries gathered on the similarly named hill on a promontory in the Luznice River. The rhetoric of his sermons made him sound like a prophet predicting the future. When the king learned of the revolutionary activity, the pace of events increased dramatically. On July 6, 1419, the king replaced the New Town City Councilors with personally picked opponents of the Hussites, but the king had waited too long. The incessant propaganda against throne and altar had turned Prague against him.

Then Zelivsky and other revolutionary priests forced the issue. The radical wing of the Hussite movement convoked a meeting on a hill near Bechyne. On July 22, between 40,000 and 50,000 people showed up. Taborite contingents from throughout Bohemia arrived with priests marching before them holding monstrances containing the body of Christ. The local Taborites were joined by contingents from the regions around Plzen in the west, Domazlice in the northwest, Hradec Kralove in the northeast, Moravia, and, of course, Prague. After arrival, the people attended Mass and received the Eucharist *sub utraque specie*.

Royal spies at the rally reported that a conspiracy involving Zelivsky and several other Taborite priests was afoot. Kaminsky stresses the rationality of the conspirators. They may have proclaimed the end of the world to the masses, but when it came to political action in Prague, "they were not fanatics; they were at home in the world of political realities and they knew a good deal about their king and how he acted. The most reasonable way to change his policy of reaction would be to undertake limited action, to convince him that continuing the policy would cause him more trouble than reversing it, and the most reasonable kind of action would be a coup against the hated magistrates he had just installed."[60] The spies did not know when the coup would occur. One chronicler claims the spies warned the king the Taborites planned to attack the royal castle of Novy Hrad in September. If the king thought he had a month to prepare for the attack, he was ill served by their intelligence. The attack came eight days after the mass rally at Bechyne, where it must have been planned.

If Zelivsky attended the rally at Bechyne, he could not have planned the attack after he returned to Prague. There wasn't enough time, especially since Zelivsky also had to write a sermon to incite his congregants to violence as well. On Sunday morning July 30, 1419, Zelivsky's Church of St. Mary was crowded as usual. The congregation had been told to come bearing arms so when Zelivsky told them to raise the sword they could follow his exhortation in a literal manner. Zelivsky looked to the Old Testament to find models to justify insurrection. He began by citing Ezekiel 6: 3-5: "Behold I, even I, will bring a sword upon you, and I will destroy your high places. And your altars shall be desolate and your images shall be broken: and I will cast down your slain men before your idols. And I will lay the dead carcass of the children of Israel before their idols and I will scatter your bones round about your altars." Zelivsky's sermon was calculated to get his congregants to act on what he preached. The anonymous chronicler claims "he vigorously incited the people to sedition in the city against the town councilors and those who supported them."[61]

Concluding his sermon at around 8:30 a.m., Zelivsky picked up a monstrance and urged the congregation to follow him into the streets. The fired-up congregants marched in an illegal procession to St. Stephen's Church, forced open its doors, and held an impromptu service there. Zelivsky celebrated Mass and the congregants received communion *sub utraque specie.* After Mass, Zelivsky again picked up the monstrance; this time he led the mob to the New Town Hall, where, although it was Sunday morning, a number of city councilmen had gathered, probably to discuss what to do about Zelivsky.

Hearing the mob outside, the mayor and a number of the town magistrates, all wearing the chains that were the insigniae of their office, went to the window and began an ill-advised colloquy with the mob, which demanded release of Hussite prisoners. The mayor might have been stalling for time. A troop of mounted horsemen had already been dispatched from Hradcany castle across the river to disperse the mob. However, the mob, having heard sermon after sermon about sinful men being cast down to destruction from high places, was in no mood to negotiate with the Antichrist or his minions. The confrontation grew more heated until someone claimed a magistrate threw a stone at Zelivsky, who was standing off to the side holding the monstrance containing the sacred species. The mob then rushed the door to the New Hall, broke the bolts holding it shut, and swarmed upstairs, where they murdered some of the councilmen on the spot and threw the others out of the window, thereby giving the first successful revolution of its kind on European soil its name, i.e, the First Defenestration of Prague (the second took place at the outbreak of the Thirty Years War). Those who survived the fall were set upon by the mob outside the hall and slain. The golden chains of office were left on their bodies, as if to indicate the symbols of office had lost their legitimacy.

During the carnage, Zelivsky stood by holding up his monstrance and urging the mob not to be reticent about shedding the blood of the Antichrist and his minions. The anonymous chronicler says, while the slaughter was going on, "the priest called John...bearing the body of Christ ... continued to incite the people."[62] He also says "John Zizka, King Wenceslas' most personal attendant, was present at the slaying of the councilors."[63] This probably explains the coup's stunning success. Not only were the councilmen overpowered in their own bastion, the troop of horses sent to rescue them was also turned back, and the hall was quickly turned into a garrison by the Hussites. The chronicler adverts to Zizka's treachery too. As a personal attendant to the king, he broke a personal oath of allegiance when he engaged in the insurrection, a fact generally brought up only by Catholic commentators. Hoefler mentions Zizka's solemn oath and compares him in his impiety to George Washington, although not the way whiggish historians usually do, as an example of treason justified only by saying that the end justifies the means. The revolution, when it is successful, justifies the oathbreaking impiety of those who would otherwise be condemned. Even Lawrence of Brezova, the moderate Hussite who knew that Zizka committed an act of grave disobedience toward the king in whose service he was bound, characterizes Zizka as an extraordinary defender of the law of Christ.[64]

The successful attack on New Hall indicates Zizka was privy to the planning of the operation. This was not a haphazard *ad hoc* outburst of pent up emotion that would spend itself in looting and then burn itself out as quickly as it had sprung up. The Hussites installed their own government and neutralized political opposition. The defenestration meant the revolution had reached "the absolute point of no return."[65] The revolutionary regime had been established, and now it would serve, as all true revolutions claim to do, as a model for the rest of the world. On August 13, Zelivsky preached an exultant sermon claiming that Prague "now, at this time" was "the model for all the faithful—not only in Moravia, but in Hungary, Poland and Austria."[66]

Three days later, King Wenceslas suffered a second stroke more severe than his first, which happened when word of the insurrection reached him, and he died the same night "roaring like a lion" in pain, as Lawrence of Brezova put it.[67] There was now no king to oppose the revolution; a town council installed by the revolution claimed to be the rightful government of Prague. Heymann comments "important inhibitions to open revolutionary action disappeared."[68] The king died without an heir, complicating matters. The legitimate claimant to the throne was now Sigismund, who had allowed the Council of Constance to burn John Huss and Jerome of Prague at the stake.

A day after the king's death, the looting of the monasteries began. The first to go was the great chapter house of the Carthusians at Smichov. The monasteries' wealth made them an object of envy for the entire social spectrum in Bohemia from nobles to peasants. Hatred of the monasteries united priests like Zelivsky and soldiers like Zizka. The German heritage of many monks fueled the Czech nationalism inherent in the Hussite rebellion as well. One of the great monuments to medieval culture went up in flames.

The Jews were unmolested in the looting, even though they were usually the first victims of the mob in medieval towns. Heymann considers this "a remarkable fact, especially if one considers the religious fervor underlying the movement and remembers that the Jews were often considered the servants of anti-Christ."[69] The Jews were unmolested because of what they shared with the revolutionaries, namely, "their ways of life," which Heymann claims were "just as austere and puritan as those followed by the adherents of the new creed."[70]

The Taborite gatherings continued after the defenestration. On September 17, a large gathering of Hussites assembled near Pilsen. Less than two weeks later an equally large assembly took place at Na Krizkach (At the Crosses) near Benesov, not far from Prague. Zelivsky must have been busy in Prague during the rally at Na Krizkach because the star of the show there was Wenceslas Koranda. But personality was irrelevant. All Taborite priests thought of themselves as Old Testament warriors. "Brethren," Koranda told the mob at Na Krizkach, "the time has come to lay down the staff of the pilgrim and take up the sword."[71] It was at Na Krizkach, Koranda first met Zizka.

Fired up by Koranda's sermons, the Taborites moved from Na Kriskach to Prague, arriving there after dark, where they were met by John Zelivsky at the head of a torch-bearing mob. The Church bells rang in their honor; the following day the mob broke into local churches and defaced crucifixes and other works of sacred art. The radical Taborite clergy rapidly consolidated power in Prague under Zelivsky's leadership. In their manifestos, which began showing up in university towns across Europe from Leipzig to Cambridge, the Hussites denounced the pope as the Antichrist and his clergy as "the priests of Pharaoh" and "followers of Satan."[72] True to the judaizing paradigm, they called themselves "faithful fighters of God" and compared themselves to the Maccabbees.[73]

But an anti-Hussite reaction was building, one which satirized their reliance on Old Testament models to subvert the social order. "When," the anti-Hussites wrote, "our Moses—Zizka, the executioner—talks to God ... [then the Hussites] will strike their clubs against the rock ... water will come forth from the rock. And when you cross the Danube on dry ground like the Israelites at Jordan...when this happens all the land beyond the Danube will belong to you."[74] Something like the satire actually happened when Hussite armies invaded German lands to the north of Bohemia. Under the leadership of the warrior priest Prokop the Bold, Hussite armies would march undefeated all the way to the Baltic.

By late October hundreds of Taborite revolutionaries had streamed into Prague from the provinces. The first pitched military battle of the Hussite rebellion occurred when Taborites on their way to Prague ran into royalist troops near Zivohost and suffered heavy losses. Fighting soon broke out in Prague, too. On October 25, Zizka stormed Vysehrad, the royalist castle on the Old Town side of the Vltava, successfully wresting it from royalist troops. Now the city was open to Taborite movement from the South, even if movement from the west was still cut off by Hradcany castle.

When news of the defeat of the Taborites at Zivohost reached Prague, a group of radical priests under Ambrose of Hradec Kralove attacked the royalist positions across the river. After initial success, including forcing Queen Sophie to flee from Hradcany, they were unable to prevail, leaving Hradcany in the hands of the royalists.

During the winter of 1419-1420, millennialist fever increasingly took over the Hussite movement. "During this time," Lawrence of Brezova wrote, "certain Taborite priests were preaching to the people a new coming of Christ in which all evil men and enemies of the truth would perish and be exterminated, while the good would be preserved in five cities."[75] Lawrence of Brezova was not unsympathetic to the revolutionaries, yet he concluded the devil took over the movement that winter, leading many Taborite priests "to reject the doctrines of the Church Fathers and of the Church tradition and to interpret Scripture on their own. According to the new Taborite hermeneutic, everything necessary to the salvation of man here on earth is sufficiently expressed in the New Testament; however, any interpretation necessary to understand the New Testament can be drawn from the Old for the two Laws expound each other."[76] That hermeneutic would lead inexorably to the preeminence of the Old Testament over the New, and that would affect the Taborite priests, who let their hair grow long and grew beards so they would resemble more closely the priests of the Old Testament. "The priests of the Taborites," Lawrence tells us,

> fleeing human traditions, walked about with beards and unshaven heads, in gray clothing. They did not read the canonical hours, and, without chasubles, corporals, or special chalices, they performed divine rites under the heavens or in houses, not on a holy altar, but on any sort of table covered with a linen cloth. Nor did they observe the rite of the mass by saying the collects with the canon; but all at once the priests would kneel with the brethren place their heads on the ground ... and pray the Lord's Prayer; then the one who was to make the sacrament of the altar got up and said in a loud and intelligible voice, in the vernacular, no more than the words of consecration over the hosts and the wine.[77]

John Pribram also noticed a change in the movement that winter. Priests like Wenceslas Koranda were changed by the Old Testament rhetoric of their own sermons into "seducers" who

> began to preach enormous cruelty, unheard-of violence and injustice to man. They said that now was the time of vengeance, the time of destruction of all sinners and the time of God's wrath ... in which all the evil and sinful ones were to perish by sudden death, on one day.... those cruel beasts, the Taborite priests, wanting to excite and work up the people so that they would not shrink from these afflictions, preached that it was no longer the time of mercy but the time of vengeance, so that the people should strike and kill all sinners.... And they called us and others who admonished them to be merciful, damaging hypocrites.[78]

The rhetoric of the revolution was drawn from historical events described in the Old Testament, but the revolution had its own inner logic, its own formal causality, that would be repeated in subsequent revolutions. Plato had described it as *metabolia*, a "quasi-natural transformation of one form of government into another" as Hannah Arendt described the devolution from democracy to tyranny.[79] Kaminsky says "the new communities formed in the winter of 1419-1420 were not stable societies, they were essentially mass movements, with a character determined by the ... realities of the movement itself."[80]

In 1418, "Pikarti," probably Beghards or Beguines living in the area now called Belgium, migrated en masse to Prague after hearing of the revolutionary upheaval there. The Waldensians were already there; soon, according to Graetz, Jews expelled from Austria for collaborating with the Hussites joined them. All of these groups contributed ideas to the revolution, which took on a life of its own during the winter of 1419-1420.

Adventism was part of that life. In "The Story of the Priests of Tabor," John Pribram names 26 Taborite priests who "preached that Judgment Day would come in 1420."[81] As more peasants streamed into the city, preachers upped the ante, until finally they named the day, proclaiming that the second coming would occur between February 10 and 14, 1420. Citing Revelation 18:2, the radical preachers predicted the entire old order would perish. Their claims split the Hussite movement. The split widened when the world did not end on schedule. Jakoubek of Stribro argued against the Adventists that "even the worst calamities did not annul the sure path to salvation taught by Jesus, the path of virtuous and humble suffering."[82] But the appeal of Millennialism, Adventism, and the whole judaizing tendency toward messianic politics and heaven on earth through the sword lay precisely in its rejection of humble suffering. The Hussite conservatives found themselves swept up in a movement that was no longer Christian in any identifiable sense. Hussitism had become a Jewish revolutionary movement. The revolution was a parasite inside the Hussite host. It infected the movement, then it weakened it, and then it took over the host and turned it into the vehicle for revolution. Jakoubek realized the withdrawal from society happening all around him was not only unprecedented, it was also profoundly subversive:

> the peasant who gave up his land, burnt his house and in some cases left his family, in order to flee to "the mountains," was behaving in a way for which there was no precedent. And when that peasant claimed the right to wield arms, his *behavior was more than anomalous, it was revolutionary.*" [83]

"Did you not formerly preach against killing," Jakoubek asks Master John of Jicin and by extension all of Tabor's revolutionary priests, "how then has everything come to be turned into its opposite?"[84] By the "opposite" Jakoubek was referring to the revolutionary messianic politics preached by the Taborite priests urging the use of "carnal and secular arms against the enemy."[85] This led to "the danger of homicide and bloodshed" as "hatreds are thereby generated which bring about a falling away from charity and a neglect of spiritual arms."[86] Jakoubek felt the priests of Tabor "should persuade people to fight an evangelical battle in God's cause, according to the evangelical and Catholic sense, with spiritual arms on the model of the Primitive Church of Christ's apostles."[87] Instead, the preaching and "perilous interpretations of scripture," of the Taborite priests were leading the people to take up "carnal military arms, abandoning the customary labor of their hands and living in idleness from the plundering of their neighbors' substance; they kill and shed blood."[88]

Nowhere was the change in the Hussite revolution more drastic than in the area of "carnal arms." Newman and others felt the Waldensian heretics had prepared the way for the Hussites, especially in southern Bohemia where their influence had always been strong. But the Waldensians were pacifists. The revolution turned on the Waldensians, by rejecting pacifism in favor of Israelite holy war. In summer, 1420, Peter Chelcicky tried to explain the trajectory in *On Spiritual Battle*, according to which the devil took over the Hussite movement during the winter of 1419-20 and turned it into a revolutionary movement based on Old Testament models. "The Devil," says Chelcicky,

> came to them clothed in other garb, *in the prophets and the Old Testament,* and from these they sought to confect an imminent Day of Judgment, saying that they were angels who had to eliminate all scandals from Christ's Kingdom, and that they were to judge the world. And so they committed many killings and impoverished many people, but they did not judge the world according to their works for the predicted time has elapsed with which they terrified the people, telling them strange things which they collected from many prophets.[89]

"At some point during the winter of 1419-1420, the congregations degenerated morally to the point *where their reaction to persecution in the winter of 1419-20, was not the Christian suffering of the New Testament but the self-conscious violence of the Old.*"[90] The assessment is Kaminsky's, but he is clearly following Chelcicky's lead. Chelcicky portrayed the conflict as between the old law and the new:

> If power were supposed to be administered through Christ's faith by means of battles and punishments, and try to benefit Christ's faith thereby, then why would Christ have abolished the Jewish Law and established a different spiritual one? If he had wanted people to cut each other up, to hang, drown and burn each other, and otherwise pour out human blood for his Law, then that Old Law could also have stood unchanged with the same bloody deeds as before.[91]

The turn toward revolution during that winter bespoke a reversion to the vomit of Judaism and a rejection of the Cross, the symbol under which civilization had grown for a millennium in Europe. The uprooting of thousands of peasants by the preaching of the Judaizers increased the pressure to pursue the revolutionary course. Since the uprooted peasants were no longer tilling their fields, they had to pillage their non-Adventist, non-revolutionary neighbors to survive. They had to destroy to live; the revolutionary creed rationalized their violence and gave them incentive to pursue it to its bloody conclusion. Adventism, the idea that the current order was going to be destroyed, flowed inexorably from the premises of millennialism. As we have seen, from Adventism, it was only a short step to messianic politics, which decreed that the new heaven and new earth could be brought about by the sword. Theological doctrines ratified the revolutionary situation. When the peasants left their farms and moved to Tabor, they had to pillage and destroy in order to survive. That is how the revolutionary engine got created.

By 1429, the high point of Hussite incursion into neighboring countries, Peter Payne-Englis, the English Wycliffite who joined the Bohemian revolution in 1419 and followed both Zizka and Prokop into battle, would proclaim to Sigismund that "Our Lord Jesus Christ is a most invincible soldier and Prague warrior."[92] Hussites like Jakoubek and Christian of Prachatice thought the idea preposterous, so the controversy split the Hussite movement between the "conservatives" of Prague and the "radicals" of Tabor. The split between Prague and Tabor presaged a similar split in the French and the Russian revolutions. One wing wanted to reform society (or the church); the other wanted to abolish society. The same split would take place in the Taborite movement too, when the Adamites were expelled. In the winter of 1419-20, the Judaizers took over the movement and turned it into a revolution. By spring, the new movement had "nothing in common with even the most radical variety of official Hussite scholasticism" and a civil war between Prague and Tabor was inevitable.[93] By spring, the Hussite movement centered in Prague was committed to reform, while the branch in Tabor was committed to revolution.

In March 1420, John Zizka, recognizing he could not conquer Pilsen in western Bohemia against superior royalist forces, agreed to lift his siege and withdraw but only under certain conditions. Zizka had become a devoted defender of the Four Articles, the essence of the Hussite creed. As one condition of his withdrawal, he demanded Hussites in Pilsen be allowed to communicate under both species. As another, he asked for passage under safe conduct for about 400 of the most radical Hussites to Tabor, the hill-top redoubt a few days to the southeast. Zizka set out with 400 armed men and 12 gun-carrying wagons on March 22 or 23. On March 25, they crossed the Otava River at a ford near the village of Sudomer. There they encountered two columns of royalist troops, around 2000 men, most of whom were mounted and in heavy armor. According to conventional military standards, Zizka and his men were hopelessly outnumbered and doomed to defeat. But Zizka was a military genius who was not bound by the conventions of war that held at that time. His only chance lay in quickly finding terrain disadvantageous to a cavalry charge. There were no hills in the vicinity, but Zizka found an embankment which served as a dam for a fishpond. Using the dam to cover one of his flanks and the war wagons to cover the other, he concentrated his troops on a very small front, negating the superior numbers of his foe. When the first waves of cavalry failed to dislodge the Hussites, the cavalry dismounted and tried to defeat them in hand-to-hand combat. They nearly broke through the line of wagons but were eventually beaten back. Finally it grew dark and the attackers, whose position was neither so compact nor so organized as the defenders, called off the attack and retreated. To commentators, there seemed something miraculous about Zizka's defeat of a superior force. One quotes royalist soldiers: "My pike does not pierce, my sword does not cut and my crossbow does not shoot."[94] The Battle of Sudomer was the beginning of the Zizka legend. In the eyes of many Hussite warriors, God had intervened and saved them from a superior foe.

Zizka's "army" was made up of peasants, who neither had arms nor knew how to wield them effectively. Using the sword and riding a horse, or doing both simultaneously, required skill, which peasants had neither time nor opportunity to learn. In two months in 1420, before he was summoned to defend Prague, Zizka took men armed with pitchforks and flails used to separate wheat from chaff, and turned them into an army that would become invincible, defeating over the next decade, the most powerful armies the pope and emperor could send against them. No less an authority than Aeneas Sylvius Piccolomini, later Pius II, said Zizka had been sent by God to punish the Church for its sins. Piccolomini was no fan of Zizka: at another point, he said, in Bohemia a blind people followed a blind leader. But Zizka was undeniably one of the great military geniuses of European history. Zizka could be compared to Napoleon, but the man Zizka most closely resembled was Oliver Cromwell, another military genius moved by an equally revolutionary form of Old Testament-inspired messianic politics.

Zizka was also a tactical genius. Even when he was totally blind, he could deploy his troops based on his memory of the terrain and the reports he got from his subordinates. His tactical judgment was invariably correct, and it saved his troops repeatedly from hopeless situations. But Zizka was also a genius at using what was available and developing it in ways no one had thought of before. It was pointless to use the peasant flail against a cavalry charge; but once that charge was neutralized by hill, trenches, and encircled wagons armed with mortars, forcing the knights had to dismount, then those flails, studded with iron spikes, suddenly became formidable weapons.

Zizka understood medieval warfare was largely individual combat. Battles were melees of individuals fighting other individuals. Once the battle was engaged, only those along the front did the actual fighting. So if Zizka could reduce the effective size of the front with hills, trenches, battlewagons, and embankments, as at Sudomer, he could reduce the numerical advantage of his foe. Zizka's greatest innovation was his use of the war wagon as a mobile fortress, a tactic American pioneers would later use against the plains Indians. The Boers would use the same innovation still later in South Africa. But Zizka's wagons were not simply portable walls; they had heavy boards on them as rudimentary armor, and guns, which were very effective at short range in stopping a cavalry charge.

Zizka created a very effective division of labor. He did not train the inexperienced peasants to engage in individual combat with the knights. Instead, teams of peasants were assigned to perform specific tasks on the war wagons, which were armed with two or three hand pieces, a large number of crossbows, and heavier guns on gun carriages. At the battle of Kutna Hora, Zizka used wagons as offensive weapons—as 15th Century tanks—for the first time in the history of warfare, to break out of an encirclement that would have doomed any other field commander. "The Taborite army, in the way Zizka formed it, acquired a degree of national subdivision, tactical organization and actual battle cooperation far beyond anything used before in medieval warfare."[95] Zizka did all this in less than two months, between March 27, 1420, when he arrived at Tabor, and May 18, when he left to save Prague from Sigismund's army.

Many were drawn to Tabor by the Adventism and chiliasm of the priests, who predicted the world, except for the five Bohemian places of refuge, would be destroyed. Once the date came and went without noticeable change, prophecy was replaced by will. The new world would now be brought into existence by destroying the old. Communism also made its first appearance at Tabor. Adventism may have failed, but the millennial spirit was still strong. Communism flowed from Millennialism—the time when the wolf would lie down with the lamb— and the exigencies of the revolutionary situation. Tabor was an armed camp with autonomous military units which would issue forth from the hill-top redoubt and attack local villages. Often, those villages would be burnt to the ground, and their inhabitants would then migrate to Tabor, where they too became infected with the millennialist virus. Once at Tabor, the refugees learned that, as the Millennium was about to dawn in Bohemia, "men would no longer be like wolves to one another; they would be as brothers and sisters."[96] At Tabor the gospel was going to be implemented as in the early Church. So, "following the commands of Holy Scripture, it was enacted that no one was to own anything; private property was to be abolished and everything to be common property as in the days of the apostles."[97] Wooden tubs were set up in the town square in front of the community church, so the faithful could place all their worldly goods in them. The revolutionary priests appointed "clerks of the tubs" for "giving to everyone according to his needs."[98] Private property was to be abolished "not only in Bohemia but all over the world."[99] Private property was associated with Babylon, the city from which the Taborites had fled in horror. Since Tabor was the antithesis of Babylon, property was considered sinful. At Tabor, "everything should always be in common for all, and no one may have anything privately; if he does, he sins mortally."[100] The elect were assembled, uncontaminated by the corrupt Roman system, and from this ethnic enclave, the holy Bohemian nation would spread the gospel to all mankind.

Communism flowed logically from the failure of Adventism, by making the kingdom of the New Israel a matter of will. But it flowed just as obviously from a millennialist reading of the scriptures and the exigencies of the situation. Thousands of uprooted peasants poured into Tabor weekly, and all of them had to be fed. Communism satisfied theological and practical needs. Modern Communists saw Tabor as the forerunner of Marxism, but their commitment to materialism blinded them to the religious dimensions at Tabor, for Communism at Tabor was based on a reading of the Acts of the Apostles. Czech communist Josef Macek claimed "the new revolutionary fortress Tabor" was "the first time in world history that a rebellious people, dreaming of a classless society, started to work and build a new town in which from the beginning decisive power lay in the hands of the common people."[101] Macek's materialism blinded him to Tabor's revolutionary Jewish antecedents as much as it blinded him to the influence of the Acts of the Apostles. Tabor may have been the first "new revolutionary fortress" on European soil, but this hill-top redoubt bore a striking resemblance to Masada and Bethar, where the Jewish revolutionaries took their stands against another Rome.

Like Simon bar Kokhba and his followers, the Taborites were a "holy nation" of ethnic nationalists who strove to drive "Romans" from their land. The leaders of both revolutions saw themselves as following in the footsteps of figures from the Old Testament—Moses, Joshua, Gideon, David. Both revolutions defeated the Romans initially and established a "golden age" and a "paradise on earth" by recourse to the sword. Their enemies saw them as rejecters of Christ or, more specifically, rejecters of the Cross of Christ and the political consequences which the Cross entailed. Both movements created a state religion and expelled those who would not swear allegiance to the military messiah who was to lead the "holy nation" in battle. Both revolutions were to serve as an alternative to the Roman model for all mankind, and both felt that they were inaugurating a new era of history, a concept which reached its fulfillment in the French Revolution, which denominated 1792 as the year One.

Macek and, to some extent, Cohn, fails to see how these revolutionary branches are connected to theological roots. For example, the Taborites denied the existence of purgatory. "They say that there will be no more purgative fire because when a man is poor that is his purgatory."[102] There is no purging fire in the next life because "when people live in poverty, that can be seen as their purifying fire." If the Taborite theologians could declare purgatory was on earth, why couldn't they say the same about heaven? This in fact is exactly what they did, claiming

> only God's elect were to remain on the earth—those who had fled to the mountains. And they said that the elect of God would rule in the world for a thousand years with Christ, visibly and tangibly. And they preached that the elect of God who fled to the mountains would themselves possess all the goods of the destroyed evil ones and rule freely over all their estates and villages. And they say, "you will have such an abundance of everything that silver, gold, and money will only be a nuisance to you."[103]

The failed predictions of February 1420 didn't change matters. They simply substituted the human will for God as the agency which would bring about heaven on earth. To bring about heaven on earth, the Taborites had to eradicate sin. The eradication of sin became the rationale for revolutionary violence derived directly from Old Testament. Taboritism was an extreme form of Zionism, with the Bohemian people in the role of the new Israelites. "Every place that your foot strikes," the Taborite priests told the uprooted masses in Tabor to usher in the millennium, "is yours and will remain yours."[104] The passage is from Deuteronomy 11:24, which indicates once again that the Taborites were the new Israel, "an army sent by God through the whole world to remove all scandals from the kingdom of Christ, which is the Church Militant, and to expel the evil ones from the midst of the just, and to take vengeance and visit affliction on the nations of the enemies of the Law of Christ and against their cities, villages and fortified places."[105]

The Taborite priest John Capek, who wrote sermons "more full of blood than a fish pond is of water," went out of his way to incite the mob to bloodshed. Capek developed the idea of the time of vengeance. He specified the kinds of violence to be done to the enemy "according to the will of the Holy Spirit" and insisted on absolute, universal killing and destruction outside the congregations of the elect: all sinners were to be killed, all buildings were to be destroyed, every last physical entity of the old world had to be wiped from existence. Since the only way to destroy nonmaterial institutions was to kill the people in them, "all people in high ranks were to be brought down, chopped down like pieces of wood." The violence was religious, orgiastic, ritualistic, and practical; its purpose was to purge the world in preparation for the "consummation of the age," and its sanction lay in the new situation created by Christ's secret coming, which had annihilated all traditional guides to behavior.[106]

The Millennium would usher in not the fulfillment of Christianity but its abolition. The Taborite priests talked of how the Elect will rule the earth. "All kings, princes and prelates of the church will cease to be,"[107] which is logical if God's soldiers have abolished sin on earth. Without sin, there would be no need of princes to wield the sword in earthly rule. The irony was that the revolutionary priests were going to bring this about by wielding the sword themselves, but ironies were lost on them:

> "The Elect ... will be brought back to the state of innocence of Adam in Paradise, like Enoch and Elijah and they would be without any hunger or thirst, or any other spiritual or physical pain. And in holy marriage and with immaculate marriage-bed they will carnally generate sons and grandchildren here on earth and on the mountains, without pain or trouble and without any original sin. Then there will be no need for baptism by water because they will be baptized in the Holy Spirit, nor will there be the tangible sacrament of the Holy Eucharist, because they will be fed in a new angelic mode—not in the memory of Christ's passion, but of his victory.... In this renovated kingdom there well be no sin, no scandal, no abomination, no falsehood, but all will be the chosen sons of god, and all the suffering of Christ and of his lambs will cease ... Women will give birth to their children without pain and without original sin, ... and children born in the kingdom, if they are of the kingdom, will never die, because death will no longer be.[108]

The references to women giving birth without pain gave the conservative wing of the Hussite movement pause. "If women give birth without pain," John Pribram wrote in *Contra Articulous Picardorum*, taking their thought to its logical conclusion, "then also without sin, for all pain is from sin; thus original sin will cease and so will baptism, and, consequently Christianity."[109] The new system—"a peculiar system of interpreting the New Law by the Old, and vice versa, so as to generate a third body of wisdom"—was not Christian. It was decidedly anti-Christian. Martin Huska and other Taborite priests learned this system from "Wenceslas, the tavern keeper in Prague."[110]

And why not? Prague had already become a magnet for heretics and Jews from all over Europe. In 1418, according to Lawrence of Brezova, a group of forty "Picardi," with their wives and children, came to Prague saying they had been expelled by their prelates 'because of the Law of God," and "they had heard that Bohemia offered the greatest freedom for the evangelical truth."[111] By spring, 1420, the revolutionaries had taken over Tabor. Under the leadership of Martin Huska, who was eventually expelled and then hunted down and martyred for his beliefs, the Taborites morphed into the Adamites, who decided they could bring about heaven on earth by shedding their clothes and engaging in indiscriminate sexual activity, when they were not pillaging neighboring villages and murdering anyone who opposed them. Adamitism took the idea "man can attain the same perfection of beatitude in the present as he will obtain in the blessed life to come"[112] to its logical conclusion, at least according to the logic of carnal minds. Heaven on earth became a function of pure will, disconnected from reason. Zizka would deal with the Adamites militarily, but it's hard to see how he could argue with their premises. To have heaven on earth, we must first have total war; that premise stretched from Simon bar Kokhba to Trotsky and the Neoconservatives. It had nothing to do with Waldensian pacifism. That premise provided the justification for each of the Taborite sects, even when fighting among themselves over how to bring heaven on earth into being.

Fortunately for the Hussites, Sigismund would unite them in spite of themselves and their theological differences. The conservative Hussite wing in Prague was always trying to find a *modus vivendi* with the King of the Romans, and Sigismund, through his brutality and blundering, constantly drove them back into the arms of the Taborite radicals. When Zizka was working out details of the evacuation of Pilsen, John Krasa, a Prague merchant, foolishly espoused the cause of the chalice while on a business trip to Breslau, later Wroclaw, one of Sigismund's strongholds. Krasa was accused of heresy, refused to recant, and was burned at the stake in the public square. Two days after Krasa's death, a bull announcing a crusade against the Wycliffites, the Hussites, and other heretics was proclaimed in Wroclaw. Sigismund's treatment of Krasa awakened memories of how the Council of Constance had dealt with Huss and Jerome of Prague. His treatment of Krasa drove the conservative Hussites into the arms of the Taborite radicals just when the conservatives were coming to see how radical their agenda was and how incompatible it was with Christian tradition. The crusading army was to be convened in a German city and made up of troops largely from German-speaking lands; all Czechs, not just the radical Taborites, must have viewed it with horror. The bull was aimed at all Czechs, and as its first consequence, it forced them to overcome their differences. Sigismund evidently was not conversant with the tactic of divide and conquer. He could have granted liturgical concessions to the Prague conservatives and then proceeded militarily against the revolutionaries, but his mind did not make subtle distinctions. Instead, he vowed to proceed against "all of those who took communion in the two kinds," thereby uniting the Czech nation against him.

His policy also drove the uncommitted and those who had expressed reservation about the Taborite agenda into the hands of the radicals. Once reconciliation was ruled out, those who had no other place to go swelled the ranks of the radicals. About the time of Krasa's execution, John Zelivsky, the man who orchestrated the defenestration, emerged as the *de facto* ruler of Prague. Zelivsky had identified Sigismund with the Red Dragon of Revelations, and Sigismund's actions appeared to prove that Zelivsky was a prophet.

Soon a common spirit of solidarity and defiance united Prague. On April 3, Zelivsky convoked a meeting at the city hall of the Old Town in Prague; everyone in attendance swore a solemn oath to defend their religion and their country. Five days later, Praguers began digging a moat between the city and the royalist fortress of Vysehrad south of town. The whole town mobilized for digging the trench, including—and this is the first time the Hussites are mentioned in open alliance with them—the Jews. On April 8, 1420, the Jews worked side by side with the Hussites in digging the trench opposite Vysehrad Castle, and both sang hymns composed by Rabbi Avigdor ben Isaac Kara as they worked. Open ecumenical collaboration of this sort was unprecedented. Another version of the same story explains the communal singing not as an expression of solidarity but as a Jewish attempt to proselytize Hussites. Ruth Gladstein claims the Jews sang Kara's songs in Yiddish hoping that the Czechs, who were already familiar with German, might understand the lyrics and convert to Judaism.[113] "Jew, Christian, Arab! Understand!" they sang, "God has no form that can be seen." The Jews were emboldened because they felt the Hussites were on their way to becoming Jews anyway and needed only a subtle nudge to take the final step.

The Catholics quickly used this collaboration to discredit the Hussites. The Catholics had always claimed that the Hussites were involved in a conspiracy with the Jews. Now they had proof. Gladstein says "the Jews of Bavaria were accused of the same crime," i.e, of collaborating with the Hussites.[114] As a result, the crusading armies attacked them as well. In discussing "the alleged collaboration of Jews with Hussites and the so-called Judaizing elements in Hussitism," Gladstein cites Rabbi Newman, who claims Huss was on friendly terms with Jewish teachers in

Prague, that the Vienna Theological Faculty accused the Hussites of collaborating with the Jews, and that Jews of Bavaria secretly supplied the Hussites with money and arms.[115] Any attempts to portray the Jews as neutrals are dismissed out of hand by Newman as "not ... likely."[116] St. John of Capistrano, in Wroclaw at the end of the 15th Century, leveled the same accusation: the Hussites had joined with the Jews in a war against the pope and Christendom, a contention Newman supports. Newman also says the Jews influenced the Adamites. Jewish influence pervaded the Hussite movement, according to Newman. "From its inception," virtually the entire spectrum of the Hussite movement "bore marks of Jewish, and particularly Old Testament influences."[117] Graetz says the same thing: "Catholics accused Jews of secretly supplying the Hussites with money and arms; and in the Bavarian towns near the Boehmerwald, they persecuted them unmercifully as friends and allies of the heretics. The Dominicans ... included the Jews in their fiery pulpit denunciations of the Hussites."[118]

By May, 1420, as the imperial crusade marched from Wroclaw to Prague, the Jewish/Hussite collaboration had become intolerable to Catholic princes. Reacting to accusations of such collaboration, Albert, Archduke of Austria, ordered all the Jews in his realm thrown into prison on May 23. In March, 1421, Albert had some Jews burned at the stake and the rest expelled from Austria. Conversion was also an option, but, as Graetz says, "the converts proved no gain to the church. The majority seized the first opportunity of emigrating and relapsing into Judaism."[119] Those who converted to save their skins then "bent their steps to Bohemia, rendered tolerant by the Hussite schism," swelling the revolutionary movement there.[120] This came as no surprise. The Church had been alleging a Jewish/Hussite conspiracy ever since Huss had been burned at the stake. Catholic crusaders were reported as attacking Jews, "and only them," as they marched to Bohemia in 1419 as part of the anti-Hussite crusade. The attacks were so violent that "the Maharil, the leader of Central European Jewry, found it necessary to order every Jew, men and women alike, to observe a severe and long fast."[121] The illustrious rabbi of Mainz, Jacob ben Moses Moelin Halevi, known as the Maharil, renewed his call for fasting and prayer that victory might be granted to the Hussite armies in September 1421, when Zizka faced the imperial army at Saatz. Apparently God granted their prayers; Zizka triumphed, and the crusaders who threatened to wipe the Jewish people from the earth instead begged for bread at their doors.

Gladstein claims the Jews were deeply impressed by "a drastic change in the Hussites' religious behavior,"[122] implicitly corroborating the charge levelled by the Catholics that the Jews supported the insurrection. Rabbi Avigdor Kara, who grew up in Prague and authored the hymns the Jews sang with the Hussites in the trenches outside Vysehrad, felt the Hussites were on the verge of becoming Jews. It was not an idea to be taken lightly, because any Jew who held these views risked his life, but the Jews too were caught up in the millennialist fever. The idea that the Hussites were becoming Jews was so fraught with danger, that "no Jew would have imagined such a thing as the conversion of the Hussites, let alone written about it, unless he thought that the exile was ending and the footsteps of the Messiah would soon be heard. So we can assume that Avigdor Kara believed that the days of the Messiah were imminent."[123]

The Jews felt the Hussites were ripe for conversion because, according to Jewish sources, King Wenceslas and John Huss had converted secretly to Judaism under Rabbi Avigdo Kara himself. According to the anonymous Jewish chronicler, King Wenceslas liked Kara and spoke with him often. Kara exploited this by subverting the King's faith, wearing him down "until the King acknowledged that that man's [in Hebrew writing "that man" refers to Jesus Christ] faith was false. After the King's death, there appeared a priest called Huss 'who attracted all the townsfolk and taught them the true unity—Israel's faith.'"[124]

King Wenceslas died four years after Huss, not before Huss as the chronicler alleges. So the anonymous Jewish chronicler's claim may be a fantasy based on a priori assumptions, most notably the fact that Jews didn't think that the *goyim* were intelligent enough to come up with the judaizing Hussite creed on their own. Gladstein says precisely that but rescues the credibility of the anonymous Jewish chronicler by claiming that while he was inaccurate with particular dates, he did describe "two stages in the rise of the movement: 1) the King renounces his belief in Jesus: 2) Huss teaches the essential principles of Judaism to the people of Prague and they destroy images, burn statues and kill priests. After that it says: 'and most of the people in that country (Bohemia) set themselves to dissolve that man's faith.'"[125] The Viennese Hebrew MS describes the burning of Huss at the stake as *"Kiddush hashem"* or "Sanctification of the Divine name," constituting "further proof that the Jews considered the Hussites Jews; for the expression 'sanctification of the divine name' is applied only to the martyrdom of Jews."[126] In the same manuscript, Catholic countries are referred as "Edom." This epithet is traditionally applied to enemies of the Jews, but here it denotes enemies of the Hussites, another indication the Jews considered the Hussites, if not one of their own, then at least on the way. In an era of Messianic expectation for the Jews and millennialist and Adventist expectation for the Hussites, the two groups were clearly linked in what was about to happen. When the Hussites threatened to burn Nuremberg to the ground, the German natives imposed a tax on the Jews to buy off the Czech invaders. The Jewish commentator claims "When the Hussites had no leader, they dropped their ideas and most of them relapsed. [But] on one mountain called Tabor, there are still Hussites who do not believe in 'that man.'"[127]

The full extent of the collaboration between the Hussites and the Jews, and the extent to which the Hussite judaizing meant an actual conversion to Judaism, remain objects of debate. Ben Sasson, a Jerusalem historian, indicates Hussite conversion to Judaism was largely wish fulfillment fueled by millennialist expectations: "Objection to the complex of images, altars, crosses, priests was so strong in the soul of the Jews, and they longed so much to see the fulfillment of their hope that there would be a movement from Christianity toward Judaism, that they painted reality with the colors of their hearts' desires and began to discern, in what was happening, certain elements of the disappearance of that complex and the fulfillment of the messianic hope."[128] The Hussites, like the Puritans 120 year later, hoped the Jews would convert, and probably Hussites and Jews took the conversion of the other group as a sign that the millennium was about to begin. Gladstein claims that one of Kara's poems was set to the tune of the Hussite battle song, "Ye Warriors of God." The Jews probably hoped that the song would scare off the crusaders when they sang it, as it had done more than once when Hussites sang it. There was no "better sign of the Jews' sympathy for the Hussites than the apparent adoption of their most representative tune."[129] Similarly, the Hussites found encouragement for their iconoclasm from the Jews who sang

> The mystery of faith is nowhere found
> Except among the Hebrews,
> Forbidden altars shall lie upon the ground.[130]

On May 1 or 2, 1420 King Sigismund's army started slowly but inexorably toward Prague. Sigismund demanded unconditional surrender. Since the fate of Jan Krasa was fresh in their minds, the Hussites and a large number of Bohemians felt they had no choice but to unite with groups whose theology they found repugnant to keep Bohemia from being overrun by marauding German troops. And so the inhabitants of Prague, no matter what their political or religious views, prepared the town for a siege. "Wherever there had been one chain before to barricade the streets, they put two, and they locked themselves up against the King."[131]

On May 16, the Praguers sent an urgent call for assistance to Zizka, who understanding the tactical advantage of rapid troop deployment, responded without delay. Between 50 and 60 miles separated Zizka's 9,000 men from Prague when he got the call for help. According to the standards of medieval warfare, it should have taken him at least four days to march to Prague, but he left on May 18 and was in Benesov, half way to Prague, one day later. He arrived in Prague on May 20, even though he had to fight at Porici on the way.

His arrival was met by general jubilation among the inhabitants of Prague, who arranged banquets in honor of their rescuers. Their joy changed to consternation when the Taborite rustics, most of whom had never seen a city as luxurious as Prague, repaid their hosts by engaging in iconoclasm and even went so far as to attempt to cut off the beards and mustaches of the natives. The town had already undergone a Taborite purge of "public mortal sins." Notorious brothels had already been converted to more edifying use, and Zelivsky and his followers had conducted house to house searches, asking each household to make a choice between utraquism and leaving town, something that must have made the reaction of the Taborite rustics that much more painful.

Once again, ethnicity was given an ideological spin. Expelling everyone who disagreed, including the wives and children of Germans who had already left, ensured "there would be no traitors at work in the city," but, more importantly, it pushed the Hussite movement in an irrevocably revolutionary direction.[132] Revolutionaries would take over the movement, something most Praguers must have viewed with consternation, when, for example, the women who had come from Tabor burned the monastery of St. Catherine in the New Town to the ground after evicting the nuns. It also ensured a bloody reaction since it established the principle that the most radical faction got to decide policy. The Hussites established that principle as normative by deducing it from their reading of the Old Testament. The ideologically chosen ethnic group was an idea that would wreak havoc in Europe for the next 600 years and in Israel and the Middle East after that.

Zizka had more pressing concerns. First he had to neutralize Vysehrad, the royalist stronghold south of town, so he ordered the moat dug deeper and wider. Once again Jews, women, priests, and boys too young to bear arms were put too work. By the time King Sigismund's armies arrived on June 12, Zizka had been at work for three weeks, digging fortifications outside the city and stretching chains and other impediments across the streets inside the town walls. Zizka was at a major disadvantage because large royalist fortresses blocked the western and southern approaches to the city. He also suffered a major setback when Sigismund replenished Hradcany on the west bank of the Vltava. That entire bank was occupied by imperial troops, who were close enough to shout insults and provocations at the natives. "Ha, Ha! Huss, Huss! Heretic, Heretic," the imperial forces shouted across the river, and, to show it was not merely good-natured ribbing, any Czechs who fell into their hands were immediately burnt as heretics. Lawrence of Brezova claims Sigismund had 150,000 troop under arms "of many different nations, tribes, and tongues.[133] Even if Sigismund had half that number of troops, he still had a four or five to one advantage over Zizka.

Sigismund's strategy was rational. Since he already controlled the southern and western approaches to the city, all he had to do was block access to the farms of the Elbe valley to the north, and the city would starve to death in days. That meant occupying the Vitkov Hill on the old town side of the river. Zizka understood the importance of the hill too and had two wooden forts built on its summit. On July 14, 1420 Sigismund's armies crossed the Vltava and started up the gradual northeast slope of Vitkov Hill, putting heavy pressure on the badly outnumbered defenders. Once again, the Hussites were aided by their choice of terrain. The narrow ridge they had to defend magnified the power of the defenders, neutralizing both the numbers and the cavalry of the attacking army and allowing time for reinforcement.

Zizka, who was in the town when the attack started, quickly ordered a counterattack. A priest holding a monstrance led the archers, who were followed by peasant soldiers wielding flails and pikes, all singing a Hussite battle song. Lawrence of Brezova claims it was the sight of the body of Christ in the monstrance that routed the Hussites' enemies. The author of the Magdeburger Schoeppenchronik claimed that the Taborites had miraculous powers because the Bohemians worshipped the devil, whom the Germans had seen fighting alongside the Czech soldiers.[134]

Terror spread through the ranks of the numerically superior royalist army, and they fled back across the river in panic. The victory seemed doubly miraculous because the royalists had suffered relatively few casualties and yet were reluctant to renew the attack. There was no adequate military explanation for why Sigismund failed to renew his assault. Since he was still in possession of Hradcany, which towered over the town, he could have bombarded Prague, but he couldn't bring himself to destroy a city he loved.

During the siege of Prague the Four Articles were formulated in their final form. All faithful Bohemians were called to 1) communicate under both species, 2) promote free preaching, 3) force priests to give up pomp and avarice and worldly ambition and 4) bring about a cessation of all public mortal sins. The symbol of the Hussite Revolution was the chalice. Hussite soldiers wore the emblem of the chalice on their clothing, and royalist forces carried banners portraying a goose (Huss is the Czech word for goose) drinking from a chalice. The Chalice was both a liturgical issue and an eschatological symbol. "For the Hussites, to drink the blood of God was a sign of the reality of the present age passing away into a grand apocalyptic finale. The cup signaled this *fait acocmpli*.... the chalice in particular heralded the arrival of the eschaton in the midst of the present age."[135] No one, however, seems to have made the connection between the chalice which held Christ's blood during celebration of the Mass and the bloodthirsty priests who took it as their symbol. But the connection is there: "the true soldiers of Jesus Christ—'the warriors of God'—must ever and again drink the blood of God so that they can engage in the battle against Antichrist."[136]

Once Sigismund condemned his huge army to a summer of inactivity, natural forces ensured its dissolution. Rotting corpses lay around the Imperial camp unburied in the summer heat insuring the spread of disease. On July 22, 16 German prisoners captured in the failed attack on Vitkov, now renamed Zizkov in honor of the general who saved it, were burned at the stake in view of the German troops, thus lowering morale even further. The same chronicler who said the Taborites worshipped the devil called the crusade a "truly hateful campaign, for whomever was taken prisoner on either side for him there was no other outcome but the inhumanly bitter death."[137] Finally, the Bohemian Lords crowned Sigismund King of Bohemia at St. Vitus Cathedral in the Hradcany fortress on July 28 and persuaded him that, with his goal accomplished, he could send the German troops home.

On August 10, 1420, a Taborite mob led by Wenceslas Koranda celebrated the lifting of the siege by sacking the great Cistercian monastery at Zbraslav, one of the most famous and most beautiful buildings in the country, burning it to the ground. The monastery had no military significance. The siege of Prague was over. On finding the monastery deserted and undefended, the Taborite mob discovered wine the monks had left behind. After getting drunk in the wine cellar, the mob broke into the royal tomb, disinterred the corpse of King Wenceslas, put a crown of straw on his head, and, after placing him on the altar, poured wine over him, bellowing in drunken mockery that if the king were still alive he would be drinking with them.

The mob then lurched unsteadily back to Prague, where drunken Hussite priests led the mob in an attack against the royalist fortress of Vysehrad. The attack ended in disaster for the drunken Hussites, but even more disastrous was the effect on the morale of the citizens of Prague, who now looked upon the Taborites as "a band of irresponsible, unmanageable terrorists."[138]

On August 22, 1420 the Taborites abruptly left Prague. No reason was given. However, a few days earlier the Taborites had presented Prague with 12 demands, including one that specified that "under fixed penalties there not be allowed any drinking in taverns of any drink nor its sale on the street."[139] Having their taverns shut down by drunken looters must have struck Praguers as unreasonable. When they refused to go along, the Taborites left town. Zelivsky hoped the Taborites would remain, but not even packing the town council with a pro-Taborite group of councilmen could persuade them to stay. The Taborites were determined to make a total break with Rome by electing their own bishop, a schismatic act that would ensure that the Hussites could ordain their own clergy. Once they had their own bishop, the Taborites would shut the mouths of the university professors by trumping their authority. So they withdrew from Prague and declared war on the Roman church by creating their own national para-church with its own bishop.

In September, 1420, the Taborites elected Nicholas of Pelhrimov as their bishop, confirming their independence from Rome. The illicit consecration also exacerbated the theological conflict within Hussitism and took it one step closer to civil war. When Nicholas of Huss died on Christmas Eve 1420, the Hussite moderates, Lawrence of Brezova says, "thanked God that in His Grace he had delivered them from a cunning man who had used his knowledge to further not peace and love but disunity and hatred between the parties."[140] The Taborites, numbering around 4,000, plunged forward with their social experiment, abolishing private property and the distinctions between lord and servants, and providing for the inhabitants from a community chest administered by radical priests, who proclaimed there was no salvation outside of Tabor. With communism came the idea of total war. The Taborite priests acted as "ideological commissars," inciting bands of Taborite warriors to plunder and violence "by expounding [to them] the more bloody passages of the Old Testament."[141] Chiliasm and total war were indissolubly linked in the Taborite Utopia: heaven on earth was to be created by sword-wielding Taborite terrorists, guided by priests like Martin Huska. The antithesis of the sword was the Cross; those who chose the former did so by rejecting the latter. Messianic politics always exerts its greatest appeal over those in rebellion against the reign of the Cross on earth and the attitude toward passivity and suffering the Cross entails. "Martin," Peter Chelcicky says, "was not humble or at all willing to suffer for Christ.... And he declared to us his belief that there will be a new Kingdom of the Saints on earth, and that the good will no longer suffer.... And he said, 'If Christians were always to have to suffer so, I would not want to be a servant of God.' That is what he said."[142]

On July 21, 1421, the Hussite moderates at the University of Prague triumphed over the radicals in the liturgical battle that had raged since the Taborites had issued their demands a year before. John Zelivsky then left Prague and his role there as demagogue and master of agit-prop who mobilized the masses, to try his hand as general in the northern Bohemian town of Most. Most was also known as Bruex, which indicates the large German population living there. Zelivsky laid siege to the town in July, damaging its walls with his siege guns. The town was willing to surrender, but Zelivsky was unwilling to negotiate with the largely German "Edomites" who were unworthy of anything but the sword. Zelivsky's refusal to negotiate was a costly mistake; the margrave of Meissen was already marching to lift the siege. Had Zelivsky accepted Most's terms, he could have defended Most from behind fortified walls. Had Zelivsky used traditional Hussite battle tactics, he could have engaged the German army, which was roughly the same size as his, at the top of a hill surrounded by trenches and battlewagons. Zelivsky, however, moved by his vision of himself as the Old Testament warrior, did neither. Instead, he met the Meissner army in an open field north of town, where the Germans used their superior armed cavalry to rout the Hussites, who fled in panic back to Prague. In a war where the outcome of each battle was a crucial test of God's favor, Zelivsky's defeat had devastating psychological *sequelae*, calling into question the legitimacy of the cause rather than just his competence as a general.

Zelivsky could have benefited from Zizka's advice, but the Hussite Napoleon was on that day besieging the town of Rabi. That day would prove disastrous for Zizka too. Displeased by the siege's progress, Zizka decided to move closer to Rabi, within the range of the archers manning the town's walls. An archer loosed an arrow that struck Zizka in his right eye, blinding him completely. Zizka was immediately packed off to Prague for treatment, but infection set in, and Zizka's previously good eye was lost. Aeneas Sylvius, no friend of Zizka, editorialized: "*Coeco populo coecus placuit ductor*"; "A blind nation was happy to follow a blind leader,"[143] but he also says with astonishment that Zizka's total blindness did not impair his abilities as a general. Zizka won his most famous battles while blind. "Future generations," Aeneas Sylvius adds, "will be astonished by this story rather than believe it."[144]

Fresh from presiding over one of the few Hussite defeats in the war, Zelivsky returned to Prague and orchestrated a political coup that made him Prague's dictator. If Zizka was the Hussite military genius, its Napoleon, then Zelivsky was the Hussite Robespierre. Zelivsky was a genius at manipulating unruly urban masses in town meetings and popular assemblies, and using those meetings to concentrate power in his hands. Zelivsky then used this power to eliminate his enemies.

On October 20, one day after the coup, Zelivsky had Sadlo of Smilkov arrested and then executed on the following evening. Zelivsky would arrest many more before his reign of terror ended five months later with his own death.

Once Zelivsky was driven from power, the theological split in the Hussites became a geographical split too. After Zelivsky's death, the moderates controlled Prague, and the revolutionaries controlled Tabor, and the contest between them over who controlled Bohemia would become a military conflict and a civil war. The Taborites were determined to continue the revolution, "even if this meant fighting the conservative Hussites" and even if that meant "renouncing any hope of really regenerating—that is, revolutionizing—the society of Bohemia."[145]

But the Taborites soon learned that a "revolutionary society" is a contradiction in terms, for they soon had to deal with a rebellion within their own ranks. Under the leadership of the Taborite priest Peter Kanish (or Kanis), a group of Taborites convinced themselves the millennium had already arrived; all that remained was to act accordingly. Kanish told his followers that all human impulses came from God and were manifestations of God; since there was no original sin, it was wrong to curb any sexual desire; they, as a result, were as "innocent as Adam and Eve in paradise,"[146] hence their name, Adamites. Salvation was a matter of the will following unbridled appetite, an idea which would find its fulfillment in the sexual revolutionary theories of Wilhelm Reich in the 20th Century. Salvation was at hand for those bold enough to take off their clothes. Since they had achieved the state of innocence promised to Adam and Eve, the Adamites had no need of clothes or morals and shed both, which scandalized the moderate Hussite Lawrence of Brezova, who described them as "wandering through forests and hills," where "some of them fell into such insanity that men and women threw off their clothes and went nude, saying that clothes had been adopted because of the sin of the first parents, but that they were in a state of innocence. From the same madness they supposed that they were not sinning if one of the brethren had intercourse with one of the sisters, and if the woman conceived, she said she had conceived of the Holy Spirit."[147]

Eventually the Adamites settled on an island in the Nezarka River, from which they would periodically sally forth and plunder local villages and farms, stealing food and livestock and murdering the inhabitants. The Adamites were natural supernaturalists in the judaizing mode. Nicholas, a peasant who led them for a while, took the name Moses-Adam. Moses informed them they had "regained full the state of innocence which Adam and Eve had enjoyed in Paradise." As a result, they discarded all clothing, and "not minding heat or cold, went naked at all times."[148] They held that God was only in themselves, just as there was no devil except in humans. Since "all impulses were considered good, even divine. The sexual desire was not to be inhibited in the least." "[I]t was a sin for the desired partner to refuse. All men had all women in common, marriage was prohibited, and they liked to engage in group dances which would end as group orgies."[149] Of course, the license Moses-Adam conferred acted as a form of control, too. The chaste could not enter into the Kingdom of Heaven, but faithful Adamites could not have sex without his permission. In this, Moses-Adam predated the sexual liberation gurus of the 20th Century, who also attached political conditions to the permission slips they distributed. As if to prove that the concupiscible and irascible passions were closely connected, the Adamites "went out at night, surprising the villages in the neighborhood, taking food and pitilessly killed all inhabitants, men, women, children, even the babies in their cradles."[150]

The revolution reached a crisis that every subsequent revolution would also reach and from which none would recover. How was one to determine the limits of the revolutionary movement? The answer was clear. Since there was no internal principle of order in revolution—revolution being the antithesis of order—order was imposed by force from without, in this case by John Zizka and his ally Lord Ulrich Vavak, who hunted the Adamites down and destroyed them after a pitched battle in October 1421. Zizka took the surviving Adamites to Klokoty, a village in sight of Tabor, and tried to convince them of their errors. Failing, he burned 50 at the stake and sent the rest, 25 in all, to Tabor where they too were burnt at the stake. Only one Adamite was spared so an account of their depravities might be written for posterity. Zizka thus halted the leftward drift of the revolution and single-handedly took control of it through the imposition of physical force.

The Hussite conservatives in Prague felt vindicated because they saw in the Adamites the logical extension of Tabor, which is to say, "the subversion of all traditional law and order."[151] Commentators like John Pribram, trying to understand a movement that had passed so effortlessly from pacifism to revolutionary violence, began to see that revolution, although unknown previously in Europe, was a category of its own. Revolution had no stable content, but it did have a predictable trajectory. Taborite or Adamite freedom meant freedom from order. The trajectory meant that "infallibly, every sort of license will be given to every error, every path hitherto closed will be opened to all perversity, and in short order the world will resist not the worst errors and irremediable enormities ...[until] they have broken up their own unity into innumerable parts ... and it would be hard to find among them two men who agree with each other."[152] By the time of the French revolution, Saturn would become the revolution's model because, like Saturn, the revolution always devoured its own children. By the time of the Russian revolution, when the revolutionary Jew was seen as the specter haunting Europe, that saw would be modified to say that every revolution devoured its own Jews.

In the aftermath of the Elizabethan coup in England, Shakespeare would grapple with the same phenomena in the speech Agammemnon delivers in *Troilus and Cressida*. The speech begins, "Take but degree away, untune that string/ And hark what discord follows." There was a rational order to society, which got contradicted by revolution, which had no order but had a trajectory in which appetite imposed its will by force and ended up devouring itself. If the lawful order is turned upside down by revolution,

Force should be right, or rather, right and wrong
Between whose endless jar justice resides,
Should lose their names and so should justice too.
Then everything includes itself in power,
Power into will, will into appetite,
And appetite, a universal wolf,
So doubly seconded with will and power,
Must make perforce a universal prey,
And last eat up himself.

Once the Taborites embarked on revolution, force became their arbiter; John Zizka would become the revolution's undisputed leader because he was a genius in applying the most brutal force, namely, military force.

In December, Zizka started for Kutna Hora to battle the Imperial forces once more. Kutna Hora was famous for its silver mines and treasury; the Germans who worked in the mines were devoted supporters of Sigismund and equally fervent in their hatred of the Hussites. The Germans took revenge on captured Hussites by throwing them down an abandoned mineshaft, which with mordant irony they named Tabor. When Zizka arrived at Kutna Hora, the town promptly surrendered, providing access to rich silver mines and solving the Hussites' money problems. Zizka rejoiced too soon. Sigismund's Hungarian mercenaries marched on Kutna Hora, burning Czech villages along the way, raping and mutilating anyone unfortunate enough to get in their way. When they came within artillery range of Zizka's troops, the perfidious Germans seized the city and began slaughtering the Czechs Zizka had left there to guard his back and to provide refuge if need be. On the night of December 21, Zizka was completely surrounded and, from any realistic military assessment, doomed.

More accurately, any other general would have considered himself doomed. Without waiting for morning, Zizka organized one of the most daring and innovative counteroffensives in the history of warfare. Relying on the battlewagons that had saved him so often in the past, he turned them into offensive weapons—the first time that wagons were used that way in warfare. Part of his genius lay in putting mobile artillery to use offensively, before that time it had only been used as stationary siege guns. Creating the 15th Century equivalent of the tank, Zizka broke out of the pocket into which Sigismund's troops had driven him. "They marched forward," Lawrence of Brezova says, describing Zizka's daring move, "and by shooting at the enemy with their guns they drove the King with his whole army from the positions they had held."[153] By morning, Zizka had escaped certain defeat again. Zizka, under the pressure of direst necessity, had invented field artillery as an offensive weapon, an invention that would affect warfare for centuries.

A little over three months after that battle, the radical wing of the Hussite movement in Prague collapsed when Zelivsky, the Bohemian Robespierre, was lured to a meeting and assassinated by Hussite moderates on March 9, 1422. Jacobellus of Stribro presided over the execution of Zelivsky and nine of his lieutenants. Jacobellus was appalled at Zelivsky's constant demagoguery and subversion. Zelivsky's death set off a riot in Prague. The body of Taborite revolutionaries writhed in pain like a snake without a head, but the man who could control the mob and put their anger to political use was gone. For the first time in the Hussite revolution, a pogrom broke out. A mob from the New Town attacked the ghetto, causing considerable damage. Either the conservatives attacked the Jews because they collaborated with the judaizing Zelivsky faction, or, more probably, the Zelivsky faction attacked the Jews because they felt the Jews had switched sides and collaborated in his murder. Either way, the revolution died in Prague when Zelivsky died. "And from this time the Praguers and the Taborites began fighting one another."[154]

Tabor was now a theocracy led by military priests who saw themselves as the successors of Joshua, David, and other Old Testament warriors, fighting at the head of a "holy nation" for a sacred cause. By the time Tabor separated irrevocably from Prague, the clergy had taken over all functions of government, an irony the opponents of monasticism overlooked in their revolutionary fervor. John Capek, the radical priest whose writings were "filled more with blood than a pond with water,"[155] was a good example of the judaizing clergy. In his *Tractatus contra articulos errores picardorum*, John Pribram compiled 76 errors that, in his view, characterized the bloodthirsty priests who governed Tabor. Article 31 claimed the Taborite clergy "condemned all who failed to use the swords in shedding the blood ... of the enemies of Christ."[156] Article 32 said the Taborite clergy claimed "that all priests of Christ may lawfully kill sinners," a position which, Fudge notes, "went well beyond Zizka's position which forbade priests to engage in battle."[157] Priests in Zizka's army were to carry the monstrance into battle, not to wield the sword, but Tabor went far beyond that. Whereas Zelivsky had driven everyone who would not accept the four articles out of town on the eve of the battle of Vitkov Hill, the Taborites, according to Pribram's indictment, decreed "those who steadfastly refused to assist in this holy battle were deemed members of the satanic host and were to be slain."[158] Capek "called for the physical and material destruction of all persons refusing to assist in this great task."[159] Pribram and the Prague Hussites were understandably appalled by the fanaticism of the Taborites, who were now a greater threat to Bohemia than the "Romans." According to Pribram, reform in Bohemia "can only be achieved if those who are infected with errors or who defend heresies denounce them and reconcile themselves to the Church, not, however, if they oppose the Church and even rebel against their kind and natural lord, thus adding to the infamy of heresy the crime and infamy of lese majesty."[160]

Pribram's objections were based on theory and practice. The ranting of the bloodthirsty Taborite priests had practical consequences. When Ferdinand, Bishop of Lucena, arrived in Bohemia, he saw "with his own eyes what otherwise he would have hardly believed: burned monasteries, mutilated images of saints, the expulsion and even the murder of priests and monks—with the result that in many churches divine service had been restricted, in some had totally ceased."[161] Taborite iconoclasts had devastated the entire country, but Prague suffered the most because it had the most to lose. On August 6, 1423, a Taborite mob burned one of the country's most beautiful monasteries to the ground, that of the Kings of the Cross on the Zderaz in the New Town. The Taborite mob looked upon the elaborate vestments, altars, and sacred vessels of gold and silver as Babylon, but the Praguers saw them as their own cultural patrimony. Praguers didn't want that patrimony destroyed by rustic barbarians from the south. When the iconoclasm threatened to spread from the New Town to the Old, Praguers intervened. When word spread that the monastery of St. James was going to be sacked and burned by the Taborites, the butchers of Old Town formed a human wall around the building and saved it.

The papal legate astutely understood the tension between Prague and Tabor and cleverly played the conservatives off against the radicals, claiming he was "amazed" that the people of Prague, "who glory in the feeling of being the zealous followers of the Law of God and who are ready to stand with it and, if need be, die for it, have received within your defense the enemies of God, or that you can possibly expect any help from such people."[162] The legate went through the Four Articles one by one, giving them an orthodox interpretation that widened the gulf between Prague and Tabor. Commenting on the second article, which demanded "freedom of preaching," the legate said, "If it means that any person can freely preach, and preach as he pleases, then it is not in order, especially not if the preaching is directed against the doctrines of the Church."[163] The Praguers were coming to the same conclusion after seeing where unrestrained preaching led. Commenting on the Third Article, which complained about the riches of the Church, the legate said, "it seems that your desire is rather to acquire their property than to establish the example of a pure life."[164] If Sigismund and the Council of Constance had proceeded like that, much bloodshed would have been avoided. As we have seen, the Hussite revolt had a trajectory but no internal principle of order. As a result, "Hussite unity tended to weaken whenever the pressure from outside relented."[165] Eventually the Church split Prague from Tabor when it persuaded the Hussite moderates to accept the Basel Compactata: The Church was willing to grant the Hussites the Chalice if the Hussites were willing to turn away from revolution. Fudge claims "the Hussite ranks had successfully been divided by conciliar diplomacy," masterminded by Juan Palomar,[166] but the Praguers weren't tricked. They had learned in the expensive school of experience how destructive revolutions were.

By August 1423, the theological discussions between Prague and Tabor had ceased, and open warfare took their place. One month earlier, Zizka had issued his famous military rule, differentiating his position from that of the bloodthirsty Tabor Priests. He then moved his base of operations from Tabor to a town more congenial to his views. In August of 1423, Zizka led his army against the Praguers in the battle of Strachuv Dvur. Each army approached the other with a priest holding the monstrance, a practice the judaizing Hussites referred to as carrying the ark. It was the first time ark fought ark;[167] Zizka was furious at having his own psychological warfare techniques used against him. There could not be two Israelite armies carrying two separate arks, so Zizka resolved theological conflict once again by brute force. Zizka was appalled that a priest could "dare to lead his troops under the sacred symbol of the Body of Christ, against him Zizka, the selected instrument of God's will and the true Servant of His Law."[168] He was so appalled that "full of flaming indignation," he "let his battle club fall on the man's skull," showing "Zizka the man in his uninhibited fanaticism and his fierce self-righteousness, doubly blind when a sudden rage darkened his mind."[169] Zizka had worked with revolutionary priests, but he never really got along with them. He had conflicts with Wenceslas Koranda and John Zelivsky. His frustration finally found an outlet in killing one who had the effrontery to question his spiritual authority by carrying an ark into battle against him.

Once the opposing ark of Prague appeared to deprive Zizka of the last shred of theological legitimacy, there was little to distinguish his activities from mere "revolutionary banditry."[170] When Zizka died of the plague in October 1424, Aeneas Sylvius said of him "only death defeated the undefeated."[171] In the five years that he led the Hussite army, Zizka never lost a battle even though he was blind in one eye when he began his career as the general of the Hussites at 60 years old and blind in both eyes when that career ended undefeated with his death. Zizka single-handedly put an end to medieval warfare. Because of Zizka, Czech words like "pistol" and "howitzer" entered the military lexicon. Zizka was also a master fortress-builder. It was he who designed the hill-top redoubt on a peninsula formed by the Luznice River and the Tismenice Creek known as Tabor, and it was he who turned it into something that was literally impregnable. And he did all this in the midst of unprecedented political and religious turmoil.

Legend says his followers made a drum out of his skin and beat the drum whenever they went into battle. Like Cromwell, the historical figure who most closely resembled him, Zizka found no lasting resting place. In 1622, the Habsburgs dug up Zizka's remains and buried them under the gallows in Caslav, a fate Cromwell's headless corpse shared 40 years later, when the supporters of Charles II hanged his corpse at Tyburn. As with Cromwell, historians are divided in assessing Zizka's legacy. V. V. Tomek claims Zizka was "almost a conservative at heart and a revolutionary only in his rebellion against Sigismund; in short what might be called the George Washington of the Czech revolution."[172] Josef Pekar, though, calls Zizka

> A rabid revolutionary, ever driven by his religious fanaticism, rarely accessible to the voice of reason or of constructive patriotism, personally bloodthirsty and vindictive and on occasion deceitful, even treacherous .... Zizka ... is essentially a destructive force, his role in Bohemian history was predominantly damaging.[173]

For ten years after Zizka's death, the only armies that could defeat his troops, who now called themselves "orphans," were other Hussite troops who had learned the art of war from him too. His soldiers continued to fight; as the heirs of messianic politics they had no choice and as peasants who had abandoned their homes and fields, they had no other way of making a living. Soon the army attracted freebooters, who used the sanction of holy war as an excuse to live by pillaging their neighbors. The more the Orphans succeeded, the more freebooters they attracted; lust for gain replaced religious fervor as the prime motivation. But by then, their reputation as the scourge of God preceded them. By August 1431, the Hussites struck terror into their foes simply by singing battle songs and rolling wagons to the front.

Ironically, but not unsurprisingly, a priest succeeded Zizka at the head of the revolutionary Hussite army. During the last seven years of the Hussite revolution, from 1426 to 1434, Zizka's successor was the priest Prokop the Bald. Under Prokop, the Hussite revolution fulfilled its messianic destiny by taking the true gospel as espoused by the Holy Nation of Bohemia to the rest of the world. Prokop the Bold led the Hussite armies to conquer other lands, something Zizka never did. Hussite armies, using Zizka's innovations, were invincible, and they fought to the Baltic and back without a defeat. Each campaign was accompanied by psychological warfare that spread Hussite pamphlets across Europe, an amazing feat before the printing press. From Poland to Spain, from Italy to England, Hussite troops spread the idea of revolution as Napoleon's troops would 400 years later. In the minds of the vulgar, winning a battle was the best theological argument possible. Zizka's army thus gave Hussite revolutionary ideas a credibility they could not have earned on their merits.

Prokop may have led Hussite armies abroad, but he was no Zizka. Dispensing himself from the vow of celibacy, Prokop married. He also allowed himself to be lured from Zizka's military principles. At the battle of Lipany in 1434, Prokop's troops were lured out of their battlewagons, whereupon the calvary promptly slaughtered them in the open field. Aeneas Sylvius had the last word on Prokop too. Like his mentor Zizka, Prokop died at Lipany "wearied with conquering, rather than conquered himself."[174] A little over two years later, the moderate Hussites signed the Basel Compactata ending their participation in the revolution. Roman diplomacy had succeeded where Sigismund's arms had failed. On September 7, 1437, the last pocket of Taborite resistance collapsed when the castle Sion near Kutna Hora fell and John Rohac of Duba was captured. Rohac was taken to Prague, tortured, and then hanged by a gold chain from the topmost rung of a three story gallows. More than 50 of his co-conspirators were hanged from the lower rungs. The hapless Sigismund, who lived long enough to seen his enemies defeated and Prague returned to him as its king, had little time to savor his victory. Sigismund's leg soon became inflamed with the "fire of hell,"[175] in the words of one chronicler. His leg was amputated one piece at a time, but he could find no relief from the fire of hell and died shortly after Rohac.

Their deaths marked the end of the Hussite rebellion, but not the end of revolution in Europe. By the time the revolution burned itself out in Bohemia, toxins carried like smoke by its armies had contaminated large sections of central Europe. The Hussite Revolution was a watershed. It was fundamentally unlike the peasant revolts of the 14th Century, but very similar to the revolts that would follow. Heymann calls it "the first in the great chain of European revolutions which helped to shape the character of modern, Western society."[176] The Hussite Revolution, like "the Dutch Revolution, the Puritan Revolution in England, the American Revolution and the Great French Revolutions," was "successful" because it "involved the whole of society" and in its wake left "a profoundly changed society."[177] Like the English revolution of the 16th Century, the Hussite revolution took land from the church and gave it to the nobles, increasing their power at the expense of the peasants, who now started towards their destiny as an impoverished proletariat. "The Hussite wars," Heymann continues, "thus can be regarded as the beginning of the long process of the secularization of land which went on, in varying forms almost all over Europe until the French Revolution and the Napoleonic wars in the main finished this job."[178]

The term "Bohemian" took on its pejorative meaning as a result of the Hussite Revolution, because they

> now became so strong and mighty and so arrogant that they were feared on all sides and all honest folk were terrified lest the roguery and disorder should spread to other peoples and turn against all who were decent and law-abiding and against the rich. For it [the Bohemian Hussite revolution] was the very thing for the poor who did not want to work, yet were insolent and pleasure-loving. There were many such in all countries, coarse and worthless people who encouraged the Bohemians in their heresy and unbelief as much as ever they could.[179]

Before long "Bohemians" showed up in neighboring German kingdoms, preaching the gospel of revolution. Forty years after the battle of Lipany, the seer Hans Boehm (a name which indicated his Bohemian origin) arrived in the Bavarian town of Niklashausen, claiming the Blessed Mother had informed him that the Messianic Kingdom was at hand. Endorsed by the local parish priest, Boehm organized a mass movement that quickly became revolutionary. When Boehm was arrested, he was found preaching naked in a tavern, reminiscent of how the Bohemian Adamites "had represented symbolically the return of the state of nature to a corrupted world."[180] After Hans Boehm was arrested, the revolutionary sickness broke out next in Thuringia.

In February 1453, Breslau was awaiting the arrival of John Capistrano. The Franciscan preacher from Italy had a reputation as a fearless opponent of the enemies of the Church. In Italy he had taken on the Fraticelli, and the princes and bishops of southeastern Germany wanted him to take on the Hussites. Breslau (now known as Wroclaw) had staunchly defended Catholic orthodoxy in the face of repeated Hussite assault; Capistrano came to praise them for their faithfulness and to preach daily sermons during Lent. On Ash Wednesday, he began the sermons he would give, one a day, for the next 40 days. By Easter, Capistrano's health had broken under the strain, and he needed to recuperate. Once healthy enough to travel, he answered the summons of the bishop of nearby Neisse, who sought his council.

Troubling news followed Capistrano to Neisse. During Holy Week, some Jews of Breslau had bribed a Polish peasant to break into the village church and steal a ciborium full of sacred hosts. As the peasant hurried through an open field on his way to rendezvous with those Jews, a thunderstorm struck. Seized with panic, he threw the ciborium away, but not before he removed ten or eleven hosts, which were taken via the wife of a soldier to the Jews in Breslau. Twenty Jews then assembled in their synagogue and abused the hosts verbally and by assaulting them with whips and knives. When the Jews stabbed the host, blood spurted out of it a meter high. So much blood poured out of the desecrated hosts onto both perpetrator and bystander that the instruments of torture could not be cleansed and had to be disposed of in a nearby brook.

When the crime became known, the militia moved into the Jewish quarter and rounded up its inhabitants, interning them at the castle of King Ladislaus. Ladislaus ordered an investigation; during the investigation, Meyer, one of the main suspects in the case, committed suicide. According to Graetz's account, "a Jew by the name of Meyer ... who had bought a sacred host from a peasant, stabbed it, desecrated it, and distributed parts of it to Jewish communities in Schweidnitz, Liegnitz and elsewhere so that they could do likewise. It goes without saying that the wounded Host shed blood. This ridiculous fairy tale ... was of course widely believed. A number of Jews from Breslau were immediately thrown into jail."[181]

In May, Capistrano returned to Breslau. On June 14, the bishop, fearing innocent Jews might be implicated, asked Capistrano to investigate. Graetz's attitude is indicated by his use of the term "fairy tale." His sarcasm bespeaks an attempt to cover over sensational revelations that emerged during the trial but are unmentioned in his account. During the trial, a baptized Jewess, the wife of a citizen of Breslau, accused her father of engaging in a similar ritual 16 years earlier. That Jew had bought consecrated hosts from a woman and had then taken them to a cellar in Loewenberg, where he tried to burn them. Three times he threw the hosts into fire and three times they leaped out again, until an old Jewess who had come to witness the desecration exclaimed that, having witnessed this miracle, she now believed in the God of the Christians. The Jews flew into a rage and murdered her on the spot. They then burned her body and buried it in the same place. The Jews then took the host, placed it on a small table, and cut it into four parts, causing it to bleed so profusely that neither table nor knife could be washed clean, so both had to be thrown into a nearby stream. The same woman also testified that a child had been murdered for ritual purposes in the cellar.[182]

Acting on her testimony, the court sent a delegation to the house where the desecration allegedly took place 16 years earlier. There they dug up what looked like the charred remains of a fire as well as the bones of a woman and a child. Capistrano, we are told, handled these bones during the trial. Graetz holds Capistrano responsible for the outcome of the trial, which resulted, he claims, in the death of 41 Jews. Hofer disputes the number, but no one denies that Jews were executed for blasphemy and murder. In addition, 300 Jews were deported, and their children were taken from them, baptized, and put in Christian homes. "Capistrano," Graetz writes, "presided over them on the bench, as the court moved toward the verdict."[183] He concludes his attack on Capistrano by calling him a "Jew slaughterer" and a "cannibal."[184]

Johannes Hofer tells a different story. Capistrano did indeed hold the bones of the boy in his hands during the trial, but that evidence and the way in which it was found convinced everyone that the Jews were guilty. Hofer also claims Capistrano was merely an advisor and did not preside over the trial. Capistrano, according to Hofer,

> had nothing to do with the arrest of the Jews, nor was the supreme direction of the trial in his hands. During the first two weeks after the arrest, he was not in Breslau at all, but was the guest of the Bishop at Neisse.... That he acted thus in obedience to the express wish of the prudent and moderate Bishop, who insisted that the trial be ended before the departure of his guests, puts the affair in an entirely different light.[185]

How could the court have come to another verdict? Not even Capistrano's most vocal critics doubted the guilt of the Jews who were on trial. "Jewish historians mention Capistrano's name with horror," Hofer writes, but

> On the other hand, Jewish historians go decidedly too far when they band all such accusations as mere fables or psychological impossibilities. Unimpeachable evidence shows that cases of robbery and desecration of consecrated Hosts did occur in the Middle Ages, and still occur in our own days. Admitting that Jews as a class were not guilty, what reason can be given for denying that individual Jews never gave vent to their hatred of Christ by committing such crimes?[186]

Hofer concedes "Christians were guilty of grievous injustice when, instead of punishing individuals who were guilty, they punished also the innocent majority. They were also guilty of credulity in easily accepting the charges against Jews."[187] The evidence, however, indicates that at least some Jews were guilty of murder and sacrilege, both of which were capital crimes. Capistrano's presence on the tribunal made no difference because "Sacrileges were punished by death. That was the general European practice, which meted out the death penalty for much lesser crimes. Even the banishment of all Jews corresponded in such cases with the general view of the public. Jews were merely tolerated. The state believed itself justified, whenever public welfare required, in banishing Jews and confiscating their property."[188]

Given the evidence, the Jews would have been found guilty whether Capistrano was there or not. Furthermore, if the Jews were guilty of capital crimes, Capistrano cannot be termed a slaughterer of Jews. Hence, Graetz's portrayal of the charges as "a ridiculous fairy tale" ignores both the evidence and the law. His intent was to smear Capistrano. The state had the right to punish criminals. If "the Silesian Jews, in fact, commit[ed] the crimes which they were accused of," Hofer points out, "Capistran's position is unassailable. Ritual murder, sacrilegious crimes, would even today be punished. The sentences of 1453 were entirely in harmony with contemporary European ideas of justice."[189]

Some Jewish historians, including Graetz, claim that since the evidence was prima facie fantastic, the Jews were victims of a plot "set in motion," Hofer claims, "to get rid of pressing creditors."[190] It is easier, however, to accept the evidence for blasphemy and murder than to find evidence of a plot:

> The detailed account of the robberies, the precise reports on places and times, the definite description of all persons concerned, even of accused Christians, all this must incline us to believe in the trustworthiness of the charges.... If this whole procedure was owing to a plot, its extraordinary ingenuity and precaution become historically remarkable. With all allowances for the imperfect juridical procedure of those days, and for the prejudices of judges, how shall we account for the remarkable fact that even those who condemned the expulsion of the Jews as unchristian, still do not manifest the least doubt about the truth of the accusations. Take for instance, Peter Eschenloer, who came to Breslau in 1455, and in 1470 wrote of the affair in the sense just quoted. Nearly 20 years had passed when he wrote, 15 of which he had spent on the spot. Must we admit a plot so deep that none of the real facts ever came to the knowledge of the public? And if we admit such a plot, then we must also say that the judges were the victims of invincible error.[191]

Graetz also claims Capistrano was indirectly responsible for the trial because he inflamed public opinion against the Jews during his Lenten sermons. Hofer, however, points out that of the 40 sermons, only one referred to the Jews. In it Capistrano urged the citizens of Breslau not to refrain from work on Saturday, lest the Jews interpret this as participation in their Sabbath celebration. Capistrano did not preach sermons on the Jews or to the Jews in Breslau because Breslau, especially in comparison to Vienna and Nueremberg, had an insignificant Jewish population. According to Hofer, "The popular conception of Capistran thundering for forty days against the Jews is the purest fiction."[192]

What was Capistrano's position on the Jews? Hofer says his "general attitude toward the Jews stands out clearly in his sermons,"[193] which according to the custom of the day, Jews were forced to attend. In those sermons, he urged Jews to convert to Christianity. "The usual imagination," Hofer writes, "that on such occasions he aroused popular sentiments against the Jews is not true."[194] In a sermon in Vienna, which had a large Jewish population, Capistrano claimed that Jews felt they were entitled to kill Christians but would never say this publicly because of their small numbers.[195]

He preached to the Jews in "sorrow and disappointment" at their failure to re-spond to Christ's call to conversion.[196] He did not treat them with contempt. Like all medievals, Capistrano would have found the notion of racial hatred incomprehensible. The Jews were the enemies of Christians not because of their DNA, but because they had rejected Christ, and because the first consequence of that rejection was a war of subversion against Christian faith and morals and the culture based on it. "The Jewish question," for Capistrano, "is a religious one."[197] Once the Jew accepted baptism, there was no difference between him and the Christian. In one sermon, Capistrano claimed that were the Jews to hear the word of God, he would love them as he loved his nearest relatives. Faith, however, can never be compelled. The Jews can only be invited to believe.

If the Jews refuse to accept Christianity certain consequences follow. The first is that Christians must be protected from subversive and predatory activity, and this can only be accomplished by complete segregation. In this, he was stricter than St. Thomas Aquinas. Even after they have been segregated, Jews should not be allowed "privileges that would weaken or abrogate those protective measures of Christian society."[198] Capistrano never tired of preaching about the bad effects of usury on Christian society. As a result he "urges that spiritual rulers insist on the strict observance of the laws concerning Jews and on the abrogation of contrary privileges. In this effort he did not stand alone. Many other reformers condemned the arbitrariness and laxity manifested in this matter."[199]

Capistrano left Breslau after the trial and went to Poland, which had a significant Jewish population that was growing steadily, and whose privileges, especially usury and tax-farming, would cause Poland serious problems in the coming centuries. The Jews did not, however, receive Capistrano's undivided attention. When they met with King Casimir in Cracow, Capistrano and Bishop Zbigniew urged him to deal with both the Hussites and the Jews. According to Graetz's account, Capistrano "threatened him with the punishments of hell and prophesied a bad outcome in the war against the Prussian Knights if he didn't revoke the favorable privileges of the Jews and hand the Hussite heretics over to the bloodthirsty clergy."[200] When the war with the Teutonic Knights went badly, Graetz claims Capistrano attributed the defeat of the Polish army to the "privileges given to the Jews."[201]

After we peel away the invective, Graetz admits the Jews had been granted privileges by the princes across central Europe. Unlike Capistrano, Graetz undoubtedly considered this good, but that is no indictment of Capistrano. Capistrano was convinced that privilege for the Jews led inevitably to moral laxity and subversion of the faith. As Graetz well knew, Jews were granted privileges not out of humanitarian concern; they were granted privileges because they granted financial concessions to the prince, specifically loans at lower interest rates. To make money available to the prince on favorable terms, Jews were granted the privilege of lending to the burgher and peasant at usurious rates. Once Jews got the prince in his debt, they could demand other concessions too—the privilege to live among Christians, the privilege not to wear the badge which distinguished him from the Christians, etc. Each of these privileges allowed the Jew closer contact with Christians, contact which he could then exploit to his advantage. Capistrano was against privilege for the Jews because whenever there was free contact between Jews and Christians, the faith was endangered and morals suffered.

Capistrano felt that Jews, because of their rejection of Christ, and not because of their race, were a constant danger to any Christian society. His thought paralleled the thinking of popes as expressed in "*Sicut iudeis non.*" Capistrano felt that the Jew could be tolerated but certainly not privileged. According to Hofer, Capistrano's attitude was a function of his idea that the Christian state served as "the Christian empire of God here on earth."[202] According to Capistrano's idea, "Christ is King, and Christ's Church is the kingdom of God. The Jews are the descendants of those who killed this king. They have inherited hatred against Christ from their ancestors, and they give it full vent wherever they can do so with impunity. Therefore we are justified in suspecting them. They are now simply our enemies and are known as such. They have crucified our Lord Jesus Christ."[203]

Capistrano's recommendations for social policy flowed from that premise. Christians should not associate with Jews, so, *a fortiori*, they should not become dependent on Jews "in any shape or form."[204] Usury is one of the most debilitating forms of dependence; therefore, princes should not allow Jews the privilege of taking usury. According to Hofer:

> To prevent commercial and social contacts by strict enforcement of the laws concerning Jews, and to abrogate all privilege that stood against this plan, was the fundamental idea of Capistran's policy. How far did he succeed? That he deeply injured Jewish interests in many lands is the assertion of Jewish historians. Detailed proof of that assertion is lacking. In Italy he did succeed in having edicts issued to abrogate Jewish privileges.[205]

Because he saw the deleterious results of contact between Jews and Christians, Capistrano took the rigorist position. When asked if Christians were permitted to buy from Jews those parts of butchered animals which the Jews for ritual reasons discarded as unclean, Capistrano said, No, because "Christians would thus appear inferior in the eyes of Jews. The Jews consider unclean anything touched by Christians. Why should Christians take and use what is set aside by the wicked hands of unbelieving and perfidious Jews? Let the Jews buy and eat what they like. That is their own business. But let them have no occasion to think contemptuously of our immaculate faith and to consider themselves better than us."[206]

He took a similar position when asked if Christians could buy wine from Jews. Again the answer was, No, because "Our dignity forbids us to consume the dirt that falls from their hands and feet when they tread the grapes. In many cities matters are so regulated that the Jews buy grapes for their own use. Their unholy feet must never soil that wine which our priests use in the Holy Sacrifice. From their own meat let the Jews make offerings according to their custom. Or, if they will, let them feed that meat to the dogs who catch the quails and pheasants for their delicious banquets."[207] Capistrano, according to Hofer, felt "our Lord Jesus Christ" would "be grieved by association between His perfidious enemies and his faithful people."[208]

An age which thinks of every form of association as discriminatory has a difficult time viewing Capistrano's indictment of the Jews objectively. An age in which the idea of the common good has evaporated, or an age that celebrates self-ishness as a virtue, is in no position to throw stones at an age that occasionally made an entire race responsible for individual crimes. The corporate sense, so developed in the Middle Ages, had its dark side in that the innocent could be lumped with the guilty, one of the fears of the bishop of Neisse during the trials in Breslau. But the issues need to be separated to understand them. St. John Capistrano was no Jew-hater. He loved the Jews because he knew that the Jews were the enemies of the Church and that Christians were bound to love their enemies. His efforts to convert them were an expression of that love, no matter how the Jews construed them.

Capistrano also loved his fellow Christians, and his campaign against Jewish privilege expressed that love, because he saw how the average man suffered under debt when the princes granted the Jews privileges that enriched the prince and the Jews but impoverished everyone else. The privileges granted to the Jews caused concern to anyone who cared about the common good. The Jews understood this, and they feared Capistrano; they tried to bribe him without success.

To stigmatize Capistrano as a Jew-hater because he insisted laws be enforced is deliberate misrepresentation of the social facts of his era. Jewish involvement in usury caused problems—not least of all for the Jews—throughout the Middle Ages. "The question of Jewish privileges cannot be regarded as a war of medieval intolerance against the approaching dawn of noble humanitarianism."[209] Capistrano's contemporaries understood that, and the idea "That in dealing with heretics and Jews he transgressed established bounds and thereby failed against Christian charity is a thought practically unknown to contemporaries. He was at times censured as impractical, but never as uncharitable or inhuman. Even Doering, one of his severest critics, finds nothing to blame in Capistrano's behavior toward the Jews in Breslau."[210]

The Revolution Arrives in Europe

Chapter Six

The Converso Problem

Revenue to the crown dropped catastrophically as a consequence of the conversion of the Sephardic Jews. The Jews who submitted to baptism were no longer subject to the head tax. They were also, as Christians, qualified for governmental office. Race was not an issue. "[T]he Jew who became a Christian was eligible to any position in Church or State or to any matrimonial alliance for which his abilities fitted him."[1] The converted Jews flourished, leading the nation in its return to "normalcy." When the king of Aragon admitted officially that many conversions were forced, and therefore unacceptable, and allowed Jews to return to Judaism if they wished, the resulting laxity, prosperity, lack of catechesis, and general lethargy, combined to call commitment to the faith into question. Because the Jews' way of life often didn't change much after conversion, the lines between Christians and Jews blurred in doctrinally and socially dangerous ways. The Infante Don Alfonso summarized the situation when criticizing "conversions [which] resulted from overt pressure and coercion."[2] Forced conversions are not

> deeds pleasing in the sight of God, for He desires voluntary and not compulsory sacrifices. Moreover, experience has shown that, contrary to expectations, the recent converts to the holy Catholic faith still continue most meticulously and reverently—even in an exaggerated form—in their perversities and faith in the false religion in which they believed before the illumination of the Holy Ghost came upon them. I can testify that I have observed this in my own private concerns and at my court.[3]

The very openness of Spanish society, though favorable in the short run, was ultimately detrimental to the status of the converted Jews. Diego de Valera, a converso, wrote "there was great enmity and rivalry" on the Cordoba city council, because "the New Christians were very rich and kept buying public offices, which they made use of so arrogantly that the Old Christians would not put up with it."[4] The conversos often worked at the royal courts because their religion was no longer an impediment to putting their abilities to use as civil servants. In 1415 Juan II of Castile informed his converso treasurer, "Whereas I have been informed that members of your family were, when Jews, considered to be noble, it is right that you should be held in even more honor now that you are Christians. Therefore it is my decision that you be treated as nobles."[5] The status of the Jews who converted in the wake of the riots of 1391 and the campaigns of Vincent Ferrer in the early 15th Century has been disputed ever since. Cantor says

> not only were the great majority of Jewish converts sincere, but from among learned and aristocratic New Christian families came some of the greatest names in early 16th Century Spanish ecclesiastical and cultural history: Juan

Luis Vives, the Erasmian humanist, Bartolome de Las Casas, the apostle to the Naive Americans and nemesis of the reckless conquistadors; St. Teresa of Avila, reformer of the Carmelite order, the first female doctor of the Church, and the teacher of St. John of the Cross; as well as some leading bishops of the time, such as Herdnand de Talavaro, the first bishop of Granada, formerly Queen Isabella's confessor.[6]

Cantor goes on to say:

> It is not an exaggeration to see the role of scions of converted Jewish families as central to the Spanish Renaissance of the early 16th Century, as were Jews in the modernist cultural revolution of the early 20th Century. In both cases complete access to general culture induced an explosion of intellectual creativity. The Jewish New Christians and their children in the early 16th Century embraced Christian thought and learning with the same kind of creative enthusiasm as assimilated Jews contributed to modernism in literature and theory between 1900 and 1940.[7]

Cecil Roth says the opposite. Although "within a generation or two, the Marranos became assimilated enough," Roth feels appearances were deceiving. Although "their worldly success was phenomenal," and "they almost controlled the economic life of the country" and "made fabulous fortunes as bankers and merchants," and "thronged the liberal professions," even attaining high rank in the Church, "the vast majority of the Conversos "remained faithful at heart to the religion of their fathers.... *Their Christianity was merely a mask* ... They were Christians in nothing, and Jews in everything but name."[8]

Was the Christianity of the Catholic bishop Solomon Halevy merely a mask? That seems unlikely. The evidence for the sincerity of Jewish conversions comes largely from the biographies of eminent conversos. The evidence for insincerity comes largely from the documents of the Inquisition. Benzion Netanyahu resolves the dilemma by disqualifying all Inquisition documents as unreliable. "Most of the conversos," Netanyahu tells us,

> were conscious assimilationists who wished to merge with the Christian society, educate their children as fully fledged Christians and remove themselves from anything regarded as Jewish, especially in the field of religion.... the number of the Christianized Marranos was rising from generation to generation, while the number of clandestine Jews among them was rapidly dwindling to the vanishing point. In 1481, when the Inquisition was established the Judaizers formed a small minority in both relative and absolute numbers.... Surely there was no need to eliminate by force a phenomenon that was disappearing by itself.[9]

Netanyahu claims scholars felt the conversos were secret Jews only because of "the reliance of most scholars on the documents of the Inquisition."[10] To get an accurate picture of mid-15th Century Spain, evidence "must be obtained from sources that were absolutely free of the Inquisition's influence."[11] Evidence needs to be gleaned from "documents that antedated the Inquisition."[12] Those documents, Netanyahu says, show "virtually all Jewish authorities in Spain and elsewhere regarded the mass of the Marranos as renegades—that is, as apostates or gentiles. By any of these definitions, these were Christians, and in no way Judaizers or crypto-Jews.... Had the Marranos been secret Jews, the Jewish scholars and leaders who authored our sources would have been the first to confirm this fact.... The evidence of the Jewish sources, therefore, flatly contradicted the Inquisitional charges. Its lesson was that the New Christians were generally what their name suggested."[13]

Netanyahu thus begins to solve the problem of whether the converts were sincere, but raises another even more intractable problem. If the Jews were sincere, why did the turmoil the conversions were supposed to solve continue? If the conversions were sincere, why didn't peace return to Spain? Netanyahu's answer to that question is anti-Semitism. But, as of 1391, anti-Semitism did not exist. Animus against Jews was based purely on religious grounds. Baptism, as St. Vincent Ferrer pointed out, destroyed the Jew. There was no Jew left after conversion. According to principles that the popes reiterated repeatedly, converts were to be accepted without calumny. Why, then, was there a problem? Netanyahu's answer: the Spaniards hated the Jews and looked for any reason to discriminate against them, even after conversion. According to Netanyahu, the bishops were not interested in "true conversion or religious probity.... What they wanted was to have the Jews degraded and repressed."[14] Netanyahu claims the Spanish bishops "did not want to have all of Spain's Jews converted and fused with the Spaniards."[15] But this is precisely what happened in case after prominent case! The conversion of Solomon Halevy is one example of a Jewish convert who was accepted unequivocally by both the Church and State. There is no evidence of any reluctance of the Spanish hierarchy to accept him as a fellow bishop in good standing. Torquemada, the Grand Inquisitor, came from a converso family. Ignoring these and other salient facts, Netanyahu claims the bishops evaded a dilemma when "they formally recognized the forced converts as Christians, but in practice treated them all as Jews on the grounds that their conversion was forced."[16] There is no evidence to support this contention, and much to contradict it. Netanyahu notes some bishops attempted to thwart the mass conversions, but refuses to accept the theological justification for their actions. Theological considerations distinguished the bishops from the politicians in Spain, the latter always more willing to use forced conversion as the simplest solution to intractable conflicts. Forced conversion was not new to Spain, nor were its *sequelae*. In 633 the Fourth Council of Toledo decreed "Very many of the Jews who, some time ago, were promoted to the Christian faith, are now not only known to blaspheme Christ and perform Jewish rites, they are also presumed to practice the abominable circumcisions."[17]

After admitting "the Church often curbed the kings' zeal" and the bishops "at least to some extent, championed freedom of conscience,"[18] Netanyahu is forced to question their motives. The more Netanyahu develops his thesis the more he gets caught in the hermeneutic of his own suspicions. The bishops, he says, "hid their real motives when they attributed the slowness of their action to their attempts to convert the Jews by preaching."[19] How does he know this? In opposing forced conversion, the Spanish bishops were only reiterating the constant teaching of the Church. No hidden motives were necessary to justify their position. Netanyahu gives no evidence for his assessment of their motives. Instead, he makes apodictic statements: "No one knew better than the Spanish bishops that they could not count on mere preaching and persuasion to convert Spain's Jews to Christianity. Hence, their policy on the issue of conversion was rooted in different consider-ations."[20] Netanyahu thus contradicts his original premise that the conversions were sincere. The crusade of Vincent Ferrer shows that preaching and persua-sion led to the conversion of many Jews. The same is true of the Disputation of Tortosa, which even Jewish sources admit. Netanyahu, as a result, is in a bind. If the conversions were insincere, then the documents of the Inquisition are worth examining. If the conversions were sincere, then they were not brought about by force, but by "preaching and persuasion." Netanyahu seems unaware of the con-tradiction at the heart of his book, a contradiction required by the unquestioned tenet of mainstream Jewish historiography, namely, that anti-Semitism is never a function of Jewish behavior.

Conspicuous by its absence from Netanyahu's book is any consideration of rabbinic theology on the issue of conversion under duress. The rabbis played into the hands of racists when they collaborated with unscrupulous Spanish politicians to allow false conversion. The early Church was split over whether Christians who renounced the faith during the Roman persecutions should be readmitted to the Church. The less rigid debated which penances should apply, but the Church never condoned renunciation of the faith. Talmudic Judaism, however, accommodated lying (if not in all cases of apostasy) based on a distinction that would have conse-quences as serious as those that followed from the forced conversions. In the 15th Century, the Rabbis in North Africa distinguished between *anusim*, or unwilling converts, and *meshumadim*, those who converted voluntarily. The only Jew os-tracized by the synagogue was the sincere convert. The liar and dissembler were tolerated tacitly, in violation of the teaching of Moses and the scriptural principle articulated in the Book of Maccabees. As a result, the rabbis and unscrupulous anti-Semitic Christian politicians collaborated in creating an atmosphere where subversion flourished. Jews who prospered by converting could continue to pros-per as Christians while retaining the same opportunistic attitude toward Chris-tianity that had prevented them from dying for Judaism. The Christians who had been moved to violence against Jews now harbored the same animus, clouded by religious ambiguity, against the conversos, whom they called Marranos, a deroga-tory term, which some claim means swine. Race replaced religion as the source of the animosity, but now there was no instant theological cure, i.e., baptism, for being of the wrong race. There was, in fact, no cure other than extermination or expulsion.

Forced conversion strengthened the suspicions it was supposed to allay, and turned a difficult issue into an impossible one. And the rabbis were instrumental in strengthening the suspicions of the racially minded. Jews were regarded as a fifth column within the state, and conversos were regarded, because of the very conversion that was forced on them, as an even more dangerous fifth column within the Church. Fray Vicente de Rocamora, the confessor of Empress Maria, sister of Philip II, "threw off the mask of Catholicism and joined the Hebrew community at Amsterdam as Isaac of Rocamora."[21] In the 17th Century, the Jewish community at Amsterdam consisted almost exclusively of conversos who had thrown off the Catholic faith after escaping from Spain and Portugal. It was made up, in other words, of apostate Catholics who had lied about their faith.

The cynical Jews who converted insincerely exploited the system of forced conversion to retain power and wealth: consequently those whose conversions were sincere suffered under the growing anti-Semitism. Later Jewish apologists seem unaware of the complexity of the situation and the implications that flow from it.

Roth's description of the conversos as "Christians in nothing, and Jews in everything but name" probably described some but not all Jews who converted after the uprising of 1391. He fails to see that justifying false conversion lends credence to the anti-Semites. First, it ignores the many sincere conversions. Roth and the Spanish anti-Semites dismiss the possibility of sincere conversion out of hand. Second, Roth's justification of duplicity condones subversion and makes it a Jewish characteristic. In this, Roth is following weighty rabbinic opinion, which accepted outward conversion if coupled with an inward denial. The rabbinic acceptance of duplicity would have far-reaching consequences for European Jewry.

The regimen of false conversions in Spain made a bad situation worse. The cynical Jewish converts continued to exploit the situation under the protection of the Church, while the sincere Jewish converts lived under constant and intolerable suspicion. By the 1440s, it was clear that forced conversions had not solved Spain's Jewish problem. According to the Acts of the financial administration of Castile

> Jews controlled about two-thirds of the indirect taxes and customs within the country, on the frontier and at the ports. Occasionally, in conjunction with tax-farming, Jews also engaged in purveying grain, arms and clothing for the army that was then fighting with the Moslems. A whole network of Jewish tax-farmers and collectors was spread over the entire kingdom. Their chief was a Jewish tax-farmer general, who also acted as the king's treasurer.[22]

The old animosities returned more virulently. A Jewish tax-collector was killed. On Jewish festivals, conversos "visited their Jewish friends at the synagogue and in the succah."[23] The lingua franca of both groups became a rationalist "Averroism," according to which it was "common practice for both converso and Jewish intellectuals to compare the laws of the Torah to natural morality and natural law" and assert that Aristotle's *Ethics* was a "sufficient" guide for Christian conduct.[24] "The wholesale conversions," says Walsh, seemed to have given to this opportunist type of Jew a chance to eat his cake and have it too. He could enjoy all the advantages of going to Mass on Sunday, and going to the Synagogue on Saturday. His children were barred from no profitable and honorable occupations. They could marry, thanks to his money, into noble impoverished families, and succeed to the proudest titles in Castile. They could become priests, even bishops. There was Andres Gomalz, parish priest of San Martin de Talavera, who, according to his own confession, celebrated Mass from 1472 to 1486 without believing in it.[25]

Baer, writing from the Jewish perspective, concurs. The fervor of conversion from 1391 to 1414 was followed by reaction, during which the conversos returned *ad vomitum Iudayisme*. Baer sees a conscious return to Jewish roots rather than cultural inertia or opportunism: "Not only did actual converts (anusim) try with all their might to live as Jews, but even the children and the grandchildren of apostates who had forsaken Judaism of their own free will and choice were now inclined to retrace their steps. The conversos secretly visited their Jewish brethren in order to join them in celebrating the Jewish festivals."[26] Baer says the conversos "had Jewish prayer books and engaged their own Hebrew teachers and ritual slaughters."[27]

The conversos continued to earn the odium of the Christian majority because many lent money at interest and tax-farmed. The efficacy of baptism, and therefore, the sacramental system of the Church, was called into question, something that led inexorably to racism. Or fear was suppressed and then transformed into hatred of the Jews, who were seen as trifling mendaciously with the most sacred commitments, and therefore incapable of being trusted. The suspicions fell most heavily on the cultured conversos of the upper class who benefited most from conversion by gaining access to offices previously off-limits to Jews. The average Christian believed he was ruled by a class of philosophical intellectuals who were nihilists and opportunists with no religious beliefs. Baer cites the saying, "to be born and die; all the rest is a snare and a delusion," as epitomizing the beliefs of this class of convert.[28] Because of the large number of converted Jews prominent in Spain, it was reputedly more secular than renaissance Italy. "Lyric poetry from the period reveals, as it did in the 12th and 13th centuries, a type of Jewish courtier who had become either a converso or an open apostate." The Italians felt the Jews ruled Spain, "while secretly perverting the faith by their covert adherence to Judaism."[29]

During the posthumous trial of Pedro de la Cavalleria, killed in 1461 in an uprising in Catalonia against John II of Aragon, a Jewish weaver testified that de la Cavalleria had lived near his home in a small village in Aragon to escape the plague. While there, de la Cavalleria often visited the weaver and took part in the Sabbath meal, eating hamin and other foods. When the tailor noticed how well versed de la Cavalleria was in Hebrew prayers, he asked him, why, "being so learned in the Torah," he had converted to Christianity. De la Cavalleria replied:

Silence, fool! Could I, as a Jew, ever have risen higher than a rabbinical post? But now, see, I am one of the chief councilors (jurado) of the city. For the sake of the little man who was hanged (Jesus), I am accorded every honor, and I issue orders and decrees to the whole city of Saragossa. Who hinders me—if I choose—from fasting on Yom Kippur and keeping your festivals and all the rest? When I was a Jew I dared not walk as far as this (i.e., beyond the prescribed limits of a Sabbath day's walk) but now I do as I please.[30]

Baer concludes "Testimony as detailed can hardly be doubted."[31] Conversos could have the best of both worlds. They could advance in careers formerly barred to them, and they could continue to lend money and tax farm, without the heavy burden of the Jewish law or the equally heavily burden of taxation levied on the Jews. They had the freedom of the Gospels from the Jewish law, and they had the freedom of the Jews from Christian responsibility. No one was able to enforce either set of rules on them.

This triumph was short-lived. Their success shows there had been no antagonism of race but only of religion. That changed speedily. As apostate Jews, in many cases, they lavished hate and contempt on those who remained Jews. It proved impossible to stimulate popular abhorrence of the Jew without also stimulating the envy and jealousy excited by the ostentation and arrogance of the New Christians. Morals deteriorated at the court, and the peasants groaned under their predations. "This situation," Walsh says,

> could not go on indefinitely without an explosion, and unfortunately there were many explosions of the worst possible sort. The mob, seeing the government of Enrique el Impotente unwilling to do anything to curb the conversos, and virtually handing over to them the conduct of both State and Church, took matters into their own hands. In one city after another, just before Queen Isabel came to the throne, the conversos were put to the sword and their houses burned.[32]

The explosion occurred in Toledo in 1449, when Alvaro de Luna demanded the city pay for the defense of the frontiers. When the city refused, Alvaro ordered his tax-farmers, most of whom were conversos, to collect. The population rose in rebellion and burned the house of a prominent converso tax-farmer to the ground. The mob then turned on the houses of Toledo's other conversos and burned them to the ground too. It was the first racially based pogrom in the history of Christendom; it marked the entry of racism into European history: "the hatred which of old had been merely a matter of religion had become a matter of race. The one could be conjured away by baptism; the other was indelible and the change was of the most serious import, exercising for centuries its sinister influence on the fate of the Peninsula."[33]

State and church responded promptly. The old Christians held the conversos responsible for the uprising. Pedro Sarmiento had conversos tortured; they confessed they had been living as Jews. He sentenced them to burn at the stake and issued an edict accusing them of perfidy. The conversos, the edict claimed, had been behind Don Alvaro's ruinous levy, which was tantamount to an act of war. The conversos, further, had plundered the royal treasury "by stratagems and cunning," which had impoverished the ancient nobility, depriving them of their fortunes, rights and privileges. Sarmiento then "proclaimed all conversos of Jewish descent to be unfit for any public office whose occupants exercise authority over Old Christians in the city and the district."[34]

On September 24, 1449, Pope Nicholas V issued a bull declaring that the faithful were one and that racial distinctions had no standing in the Catholic Church. He ordered the king to enforce the laws of Alfonzo X to this effect. Converts to the Catholic faith were to be accepted without calumny. Alonso de Oropesa, General of the Geronimites, wrote *Lumen ad Revelationem Gentium*, supporting the pope's pronouncement that the Church was one. He also laid out a program of reform to deal with the converso issue, but the feuding between old and new Christians continued unabated.

The grievances of the old Christians can be gleaned from a satire written around this time. A parody of a royal document, it purports to confer privileges on a knight of old Christian descent to henceforth live like a Marrano. He could now advise the country's rulers

> and by his wicked counsel to lead them into the paths of licentiousness, lust and oppression of their poor subjects and to derive from all this the utmost possible advantages for himself. He was entitled ... to charge interest on loans, to keep the Jewish laws, to intermarry with members of the Jewish race, to hold their opinions, and to believe not in the Catholic faith but solely in birth and death.[35]

He was also granted permission

> to swindle old Christians and set them to murdering one another. He was also free to become a priest for the purpose of listening to the confessions of old Christians and to pry into their secrets. He and his posterity were permitted to become physicians and surgeons so as to kill old Christians, take away their wives, defile their pure blood and occupy their posts.[36]

The satire parodies the greed of the conversos, granting the old Christian the right to carry "tax-farming registers in place of prayer books" when attending Church services, "as many of the marranos were in the habit of doing." Christian knights were "to be called by Jewish names in private and Christian names in public so as to deceive the people."[37] Baer claims this satire marks the entry of racism into European life "because in it we find for the first time the favorite racial adage: that the pure blood of Spanish Christians was defiled when mixed with that of persons of the Jewish race."[38] Racism was deeply subversive of the Catholic faith thereafter throughout European history until the Nazi genocide, because it cast doubt on the efficacy of the sacraments, and, consequently, on the power of Christ and his Church. The Spaniards who had the misfortune to live under weak kings like Henry the Impotent "had learned from experience that a man's characteristics and beliefs were not changed by baptism, despite its 'ineffaceable character.'"[39] All conversos were now suspect; and Jews could use these suspicions to cast doubts on the successful efforts of Vincent Ferrer, Pablo Santa Maria, and Geronimo de Sancte Fide.

King John II of Castile responded to the crisis in Toledo by siding with the pope and punishing Sarmiento and the old Christians, whose anti-converso decrees were revoked. Sarmiento fled for his life. Two years later, Nicholas V bowed to political necessity when John II asked him for the authority to establish the Inquisition to try conversos suspected of practicing Judaism in secret. The nobles of the realm, however, continued to exert pressure from the opposite direction. They wanted repressive laws revoked so they could attract Jews into their service. When they were not revoked, the nobles ignored them and favored Jews for financial reasons. To fulfill the pecuniary expectations of the princes, the Jews reverted to grinding the Christian majority, a practice that further inflamed already white-hot resentment. The nobles and districts that followed the law were, in effect, punished financially for doing so, which led the Cortes of 1462 to ask Henry to rescind the offending laws and restore liberty of trade between Christian and Jew.

Henry the Impotent's inability to control the situation resulted in 20 years of increasing anarchy, leading eventually to civil war. Both Jew and Christian, old and new, were to learn that tolerance was another word for chaos. The Judaizers maintained the upper hand in government because the ruler was too weak to rein them in, but the inactivity of the princes only led to the increased activity of the prelates, who complained loudly because the prince handed his realm over to exploiters.

Six years into Henry's reign, Alfonso de Espina, a Franciscan monk, published one of the most virulent attacks on the Jews to date, *Fortalitium Fidei* (Fortress of Faith). Espina was the confessor to Henry IV and a Jewish convert himself, so once again the old pattern reasserted itself. His book and sermons followed in the footsteps of Martini's *Pugio Fidei*, but his ire focused on the conversos. The situation was as confusing as it was dangerous. In his diatribe, Espina "suggested that if an Inquisition were established in Castile, large numbers of them would be found to be only pretending Christians, engaged in judaizing and in undermining the Faith they professed."[40] Something had to be done to end the confusion, under whose cover "The judges of the people" were "being seduced by the bribes they receive from the cruel Jews who blaspheme God." Everyone pursued his gain at the expense of everyone else, but "No man takes up the cudgels for abject Spain."[41]

The complaints of the old Christians against "the religious misconduct of the conversos, who were never punished" were not exaggerated, according to Espina. They were "well-grounded."[42] When the crown did nothing, "the embittered populace rose up and took vengeance upon the conversos on their own initiative."[43] Oropesa, who proposed a more moderate course than Espina, concurred and "suggested that the king put an end to this state of anarchy by means of suitable regulations." The radical Espina and the moderate Oropesa, who defended the conversos, thought some judicial body was necessary to pursue the rumors of judaizing and either lay them to rest as fictions or establish them as fact and prosecute the guilty. Even Oropesa reproved the government for handing its reins to the Jews. His strategy was to divide the conversos from the Jews and to lead the converso to a stronger, deeper faith through Christian charity. Unfortunately, the opposite happened, but both voices were instrumental in forming the consensus that established the Inquisition in Spain.

In 1453, after Constantinople fell to the Turks, the Christians feared a resurgence of Muslim influence in Spain, thwarting the reconquista. The Jews were seized again with Messianic fervor, much of it described in Espina's *Fortalitium Fidei*. The arrival of the Messiah was imminent once again, even if "None could see the Messiah except circumcised Jews; if any non-Jews looked at him, he would blind them forthwith by his dazzling radiance."[44] In 1464, large numbers of conversos sailed for Constantinople, where they intended to revert to the religion of their fathers and give aid to the Turk Antichrist, who planned to march on Christian Europe and subdue it as the Moors had subdued Spain in the 8th Century.

During the 1460s, many Jews who fled persecution in Castile settled in Aragon, where lax conditions led to a fairly open practice of Judaism by the conversos. One refugee was Juan de Ciudad, who presented himself at the home of Rabbi Abraham Bivach for circumcision. After a rite which removed, according to rabbinic theory, the stain of baptism, Juan de Ciudad set off for the Holy Land, presumably to practice his religion and give whatever aid he could to the Turkish Antichrist. Baer summarizes the conditions then extant in Aragon: "Only religious laxity, toleration and the state of war then prevailing in the Kingdom of Aragon can explain the fact that such actions could take place almost publicly, and that the circumcised men could go their way unhindered."[45]

In 1465, Oropesa led a delegation of Christian nobles who petitioned the king to enforce the laws against Jews and Muslims; high on the list was a request to enforce anti-usury laws, an indication the issue of usury was still intractable. Henry, however, was in no position to enforce anything. His kingdom was in anarchy, which soon descended into civil war, even though he was no longer king. Later in 1465, his brother Alfonso deposed Henry IV. Alfonso ascended the throne of Castile in 1467. When Alfonso entered Toledo in May of that year, open warfare broke out between the old Christians and the conversos. On July 2, a battle raged in Toledo for three days, during which four streets inhabited exclusively by conversos went up in flames. "Many of the conversos who fought in these battles," says Baer, "were undoubtedly involuntary converts who practiced the Jewish rites and believed in the torah—a fact confirmed by the records of the Inquisition in the middle and late 1480s."[46]

In 1469 Dona Isabella of Castile married Don Fernando, son of John II of Aragon. Ferdinand and Isabella tried to resolve the civil war that raged throughout Spain. The Jews were initially well-disposed to the marriage. Pedro de la Cavalleria had brought the pearl collar that served as the equivalent of an engagement ring to Castile. The Jews felt that a strong regime that maintained law and order would benefit them. But, at least initially, Ferdinand and Isabella proved incapable of ending the civil war.

In March 1473, violence and racial hatred broke out again with renewed fury. During the conflicts of 1473, the Inquisition tried conversos in Cordova and Ciudad Real. On December 10, 1474, Henry IV died, bequeathing his kingdom and its problems to the young married couple, who began to accept a nation-wide introduction of the Inquisition as the only way to restore law and order to the realm. The only thing that united Spain was the demand for resolution of the crisis. Anton de Montora, a converso from Cordova, wrote a poem upon their accession which describes the plight of his co-religionists, "innocent people whose faith," he claims, was "as orthodox as the sovereigns."[47] The mendicant friars, though, continued to preach sermon after sermon against Judaism and the Judaizers, urging the faithful to take matters into their own hands.

There was also the matter of the Moors, who still occupied southern Spain, and who were suspected of being in league with the Jews. And there were also the recalcitrant nobles, who were a law unto themselves, pillaging and plundering at will. Isabella needed to reimpose law on her kingdom, but she also realized that military conquest was necessary before that could happen.

After victory at Toro over the party of the Beltraneja, Henry's putative daughter whom the Portuguese backed as claimant to the throne in 1476, the Cortes of Madrigal restored royal prerogatives. Jews were even more beyond the law than the renegade nobles. They were tried in their own courts. They could be prosecuted in royal courts for criminal offenses, but they could only be punished in accord with their own law. They could not be summoned to court on the Sabbath. Even polygamy was tolerated among the Jews, and so they became an ongoing incitement for contempt of the law and of the Christian faith. The Conversos quickly exploited the situation. The Cura de los Palacios claimed the practice of Judaism was widespread among the conversos. Lea claims that when the royal couple took the throne, the Judaizers were so powerful that "the clerks were on the point of preaching the law of Moses."[48] In addition, the Judaizing conversos "avoided baptizing their children, and, when they could not prevent it they washed off the baptism on returning from the church; they ate meat on fast days and unleavened bread at Passover."[49] They also continued to benefit from usury, claiming "they were spoiling the Egyptians."[50] As a result, they became wealthy and powerful enough to block the enforcement of the laws that would have restored order. Anarchy thwarted the attempt to impose order.

In July 1477, Isabella came to Seville. During her stay, which lasted until October 1478, she was subjected to the sermons of Fray Alfonso de Hojeda, the Dominican prior of Seville, who "devoted all his energies to making the crown aware of the reality of the danger from Jews and false converts."[51] Espina's successor,

Hojeda, convinced Isabella that her own court was infested with conversos, whose insincerity was incontestable; that, according to principles universally accepted, it was the sovereign's duty to restore the unity of faith; and, that the instrument to do this was the Inquisition, a juridical body that had proven its worth dealing with the Albigensian heretics two centuries previously.

Isabella was convinced radical measures were necessary. The report of Hojeda and the Bishop of Cadiz convinced her nearly all converts were secretly practicing Judaism. They convinced her as well that priests of Jewish descent were "on the point of preaching the Law of Moses from Catholic pulpits."[52] Logic dictated that she could not rely on her courts because they were staffed by Conversos. The only suitable instrument was the Inquisition, a legal body whose judges would be Dominican monks, "carefully chosen and beyond the reach of intimidation or bribery."[53]

In 1478 she sent a delegation to Pope Sixtus IV to procure the necessary bull. Less than two years later, Mohammed II, head of the newly vitalized Turkish forces in the former capital of the eastern Roman empire, ravaged the coast of Apulia in anger after failing to take the island of Rhodes. On August 11, 1480, Mohammed took Otranto in Naples, and immediately put half of the population to the sword. The archbishop and his clergy were slaughtered after being tortured. When the news arrived in Spain in mid-September, the threat of the resurgent Turk convinced Ferdinand and Isabella they could no longer vacillate. They put into immediate effect the powers Sixtus granted them two years earlier. The Spanish Inquisition came into existence when Ferdinand and Isabella were dealing with long-standing and seemingly intractable civil war and anarchy. Additionally, they declared war on the Muslim kingdom of Grenada in 1482. The creation of the Inquistion is an indication they saw Jews and Judaizers as central to both the Muslim problem in the territory yet to be conquered and the problem of anarchy in areas under their control.

On September 17, 1480, Juan de San Martin, bachelor of theology and friar of San Pablo in Seville, and Miguel de Morillo, master of theology, were appointed grand inquisitors, with Juan Ruiz de Medina as their advisor. Tomas Torquemada was brought in as a consulting expert; quite possibly, according to Walsh, "he had beside him, for reference, a copy of Eymeric's *Directorium*, borrowed from some Dominican convent in Aragon or Languedoc."[54] The friars were solemnly informed that any dereliction of duty would lead to their removal, with "forfeiture of all their temporalities and denaturalization in the kingdom."[55] By royal order, they received free transportation to Seville, the town where the Judaizing heretics were most flagrantly and deeply rooted. In Seville, the Inquisition began its work.

The question of the sincerity of the conversos has been debated continually. The Rabbis of North Africa were unequivocal. If the conversions were real and voluntary, converts were called *meshumadim*; unwilling converts were known as *anusim*. There was ample evidence "the conversos continued living in some measure as Jews, but with the advantage now of enjoying rights accorded to Christians."[56] In Mallorca, a rabbi commented, the authorities "are lenient with, the conversos and allow them to do as they will." Many modern writers, in no way anti-Semitic, consistently identify the conversos as Jews. An influential school in modern Jewish historiography has likewise ironically insisted the Inquisition was right, all conversos were aspiring Jews. Yitzhak Baer states uncompromisingly "the conversos and Jews were one people, united by destiny."[57]

The simplest way to resolve the conflict is to conclude that both sides were right. From the Christian perspective, many conversos were virtually practicing Jews. They remained Christians voluntarily, but "it was their voluntary Christianity which marked them in Jewish eyes as renegades, meshumadim."[58] Once the crown in collaboration with the Church enforced orthodoxy on the conversos, many regretted their conversions. A Jewish doctor in Soria in 1491 recalled an old converso who "told him, weeping how much he repented having turned Christian. Speaking of another converso, the doctor said, "he believed in neither the Christian nor the Jewish faith."[59]

There also was confusion due to cultural inertia, which may or may not have been innocent theologically. The Old Christians noticed "vestigial Jewish practices in matters of family habits and cuisine, residual Jewish culture in vocabulary, kinship links between Jews and conversos. These remnants were identifiably Jewish."[60] Many commentators maintain such cultural behavior did not constitute "evidence of judaizing." The same commentators argue the

> converso danger ... was invented to justify spoliation of conversos. The harvest of heretics reaped by the early Inquisition owed its success to deliberate falsification or to the completely indiscriminate way in which residual Jewish customs were interpreted as being heretical. Though it can certainly be identified in the period after the forced conversions of 1492, there was no systematic "converso religion" in the 1480s to justify the creation of an Inquisition. Much of the evidence for judaizing was thin, if not false.[61]

On the other hand, the reaction to the arrival of the Inquisition in Seville, indicates that more than dietary issues were at stake. Diego de Susan, a Seville rabbi who had amassed a fortune, delivered a fiery speech urging Jews and conversos to "recruit faithful men, collect a store of arms, and that the first arrest by the Inquistors should be the signal of a rising in which the inquisitors should be slain and thus an emphatic warning be given to deter others from renewing the attempt."[62] Susan's daughter, "whose loveliness had won for her the name of Fermosa Fembra,"[63] revealed the details of the intrigue to her lover, who informed the Inquisition the plot was afoot. When Susan was arrested, panic seized the conversos and many fled, some to Rome.

When the first *auto da fe* was celebrated in Seville, on February 6, 1481, Diego de Susan was one of six burned at the stake. Bernaldez, who was in Seville then, claimed the rabbi died as a Christian. Seven hundred conversos accused by the

Inquisition of heresy in Seville in 1481 abjured and were reconciled to the church. "There was no longer any doubt in the minds of the secret Jews that the Queen was as earnest about this affair as she had been about the murders and lootings she had punished."[64] As a result, panic spread through Spain and resistance to government authority ceased. The Inquisition claimed the lives of three of the wealthiest and most important citizens of Seville, including Susan. Fray Alonso de Hojeda preached the sermon at the ceremony; he too died a few days later, from the plague, which claimed 15,000 people in Seville.

The Inquisition began with an Edict of Grace, during which those suspected of Judaizing had time to come forward, confess their sins, be absolved, and then reconcile to the Church after performing suitable penance. The Inquisition insisted on capital punishment only if the heretic refused to recant or if he were caught at least three times in backsliding, an indication of bad faith and duplicity. Walsh insists "never in its entire history" did the Holy Office

> proceed against the Jews, either on racial grounds as Jews, or on religious grounds as members of the synagogue. Far from attacking the Law of Moses, it defended that revelation against certain sects of heretics, as an essential part of Catholic truth. Over the Jew as Jew it claimed no jurisdiction. It was a Christian tribunal, which concerned itself with Jews only when they were Christians, or when they went out of their way to commit offenses against Christians, either by deriding Christian beliefs or ceremonies, or by persuading Christians to give up the Faith.[65]

Walsh claims the Jews actively sought to bring conversos back to Judaism, and the fact that Jews

> scattered throughout Christendom carried on a continuous and effective propaganda which, while it persisted, was bound to make impossible the complete Christianizing of society, is freely admitted by Jewish scholars, as I have taken note elsewhere. "As a whole," says I. Abrahams, "heresy was a reversion to Old Testament and even Jewish ideals. It is indubitable that the heretical doctrines of the southern French Albigenses in the beginning of the Thirteenth Century, as of the Hussites in the Fifteenth, were largely the result of friendly intercourse between Christians and Jews."[66]

The Jews, as the disputations over the Talmud showed, were no longer following the law of Moses. The Talmud had absorbed the Torah and turned the Jews into a permanent fifth column in Christian culture, agitating for revolution when they were powerful enough or for subversion when they were not. "If the Jews had confined their activities to the synagogue and their allegiance to the Law of Moses," Walsh says, "a great deal of conflict and even bloodshed might have been avoided. Unfortunately, during their dispersion, under all the incredible sufferings and affronts they endured in country after country, they supplemented the revealed teachings of the Torah with others which, judging by their fruits, had a source quite other than the tables of Mount Sinai."[67] If Judaism could not survive without the Talmud, as the Jews maintained in France when it was taken away by Louis IX, then the Jews were involved in perpetual war against Christendom, because "the Jews included in the Talmud and Talmudic books many obscene and blasphemous anecdotes concerning Christ and His Church, together with curses and imprecations against Christians, and bits of practical advice for outwitting and exploiting them."[68] Jewish denial only made their stance seem more subversive.

Once the true nature of Judaism became clear in the 13th Century, both Church and State had a duty to make war on it, in some way. The only question was what kind of war. Saints like Vincent Ferrer, who felt that the only legitimate way to destroy an enemy was by making him into a friend, answered that question. Jews were subjected to persuasion as the prelude to conversion. Once the Jewish penchant for subversion and revolution became bound up with Spain's struggle with the Moors and its very existence as a nation, the spiritual program was politicized and physical force took the place of spiritual suasion. That paved the way for the ascendancy of another type of Jew, the opportunist, who was "compelled, at the sword's point, or under the sickening fear of social and economic ostracization, to accept baptism" and who would wreak havoc for centuries to come.[69] Wicked Christians wrongly forced Jews to the baptismal font, but it was also wrong of the Jews to convert under duress to a religion they believed false. Their acceptance of forced conversion deepened the Jewish commitment to subversion and revolution when the self-loathing became common and psychologically intolerable. Unlike the rabbis, the Catholic Church told its faithful to die as martyrs rather than accept Islam or any other false religion. The command was so absolute that when a Jew accepted the Catholic faith, he was presumed to have done so of his own free will. Any backsliding would be punished as heresy, especially since Judaizing was one of the most common and recurrent heresies. Worse was promoting backsliding in others. If it was a capital crime to deprive a man of his life, was not deprivation of a man's spiritual life equally grave? The logic was extended to justify torture in the bull *Ad Extirpanda*: just "as thieves and robbers of temporal goods are forced to accuse their accomplices and to tell what crimes they have committed; for these are truly robbers and homicides of souls, and thieves of the sacraments of God, and of the Christian Faith."[70]

The logic of force eventually turned Vincent Ferrer's conversion campaign upside down. The Inquisition, especially in its more severe later stages, forced Jews and conversos to rethink their position. If the wave of conversions under Ferrer drove the Jews apart, the Inquisition drove them back together. If laws had given too much incentive for conversion, promoting opportunism for social and economic gain, the Inquisition, which punished only conversos, and which punished them more and more severely, provided incentives for reversion, for the Inquisition had no jurisdiction over Jews. "While the object of the Inquisition was to secure the unity of faith," Lea tells us, "its founding destroyed the hope that ultimately the Jews would be gathered into the fold of Christ.... the awful spectacle of the autos de fe and the miseries attendant on wholesale confiscations led the Jew to cherish more resolutely than ever the ancestral faith which served him as a shield from the terrors of the Holy Office and the dreadful fate even impending over the Conversos."[71] Kamen comments:

> The reign of terror had an inevitable consequence. Conversos ceased to come forward to admit their errors. Instead, they were forced to take refuge in the very beliefs and practices that they and their parents had turned their backs on. Active Judaism, which existed among some conversos, seems to have been caused primarily by the awakening of their consciousness under persecution. Under pressure, they reverted to the faith of their ancestors. A Jewish lady living in Siguenza was surprised in 1488 to encounter a man whom she had known previously in Valladolid as a Christian. He now professed to be a Jew, and was begging for charity among the Jews. "What are you doing over here?" she asked him. "The Inquisition is around and will burn you." He answered: "I want to go to Portugal.'" After no doubt equivocating for many years, he had made his decision and was going to risk all for it.[72]

In May 1482, the Edict of Grace was announced in Valencia. All who wished to confess their sins would be received in private. According to the Andalusian priest-historian Andres Bernaldez, "most of those who 'repented' and were 'reconciled' with the Church did so as a means of being able to practice the Jewish rites in secret, as they had previously done." According to Bernaldez "the confessions made by the conversos of Seville show that all of them were Jews; and from their statements a similar inference can be drawn in regard to the conversos of Cordova, Toledo, Burgos, Segovia, and all the rest of Spain."[73] All, continues Bernaldez, "were Jews and clung to their hope, like the Israelites in Egypt, who suffered many blows at the hands of the Egyptians and yet believed that God would lead them out from the midst of them as He did with a mighty hand and an outstretched arm. So, too, the conversos looked upon the Christians as Egyptians or worse."[74]

As the Inquisition spread through Spain, the severity of the punishments increased, while legal safeguards fell by the wayside. When many conversos escaped to Rome, the pope heard their story first hand. Sixtus IV concluded their complaints were well-founded and that his intervention was necessary. In early 1482, the pope informed the royal couple that the Inquisition had gone "far beyond what he had authorized."[75] In August 1483, he sent letters of absolution to the accused conversos.

In May, Ferdinand rebuked Rome, warning the pope not to interfere in what had become a state operation. The outcome would be satisfactory only if the king, who understood the situation in Spain much better than the pope, appointed the inquisitors. The king reminded the pope that the Inquisition had been ineffective in eradicating heresy when under papal control. The Inquisition could only exist with power delegated from the pope, but once on Spanish soil, it became a function of the state. Ferdinand and Isabella jealously guarded their control over it, telling the pope to mind his own business.

In 1483, the conflict intensified. Despite the pope's letters of absolution, Seville expelled all Jews. "There can be no question," Baer tells us, "that the Inquisitors had the last word in deciding on the expulsion of the Jews from Andalusia."[76] At the end of that year, Tomas de Torquemada, the Dominican prior and confessor to the queen, was appointed grand inquisitor for all of Spain. The record of the Inquisition would prove erratic: "In some instances the tribunal proceeded in an orderly and moderate manner, while in others the methods employed were more like brutal assaults by soldiers than the conduct of a court of justice" with the latter approach becoming more prevalent over time. "Large commercial centers like Seville and Barcelona," Baer says, "were totally ruined by the Inquisition."[77]

Toward the end of 1483, the Inquisition arrived in Ciudad Real. Following the traditional Edict of Grace, the first *auto da fe* took place on November 16, 1483; many abjured, and no one was burned. However, in February 1484, 34 persons were burned at the stake, among them Maria Gonzales, who "at first denied that she was a Jewess at heart,"[78] but then confessed. Baer supports the judgment of the Inquisition: "Had she been allowed to live, she would certainly have been steadfast in her Jewish faith. This was true of most of the conversos of Ciudad Real."[79] In Guadalupe, a woman confessed she had eaten meat in her home on Good Friday. She also confessed "when her husband brought home a crucifix she trampled on it and threw it down the privy."[80] This woman admitted her guilt after her own daughter testified against her. Threatened with torture, she implicated others. The same Inquisition at Guadalupe revealed "conversos had been entering monasteries so as to be able to practice the Jewish Religion with greater safety."[81]

When the Inquisition arrived in Toledo in May 1485, the local conversos organized a revolt. The conspirators planned to assassinate the inquisitors "and the whole Christian population"[82] during the Corpus Christi processions, but the plot was discovered. The mayor of Toledo then had several conversos arrested and hanged. The Inquisition also brought out the worst in Jews, who used the trials to settle old scores. Many Jews were accused of bearing false witness against the conversos and sentenced to death by stoning. The first *auto da fe* in Toledo took place in February 1486, when 750 men and women from seven parishes were led through the streets and sentenced to various penances. In August, 27 conversos were burned at the stake. Between 1486 and 1490, 4,850 conversos were reconciled to the Church and 112 were burned at the stake. Baer says the number absolved far exceeded the number condemned because "the Christians of Toledo who demanded the utmost possible toleration of the conversos were very influential.... the clemency shown them can have been dictated only by political considerations. The conversos wielded very considerable influence; they were an essential element of the population, and the confiscated part of their fortunes could be used without annihilating the conversos themselves."[83] According to Baer, "The conversos of Teruel doubtless deserved their "ill repute" as Jews-in-fact. "It is obvious, that alongside the Jewish community of Teruel, there was a community of conversos who assembled for public worship, Bible readings, and the like. Most of them were descendants of Jews converted during the years 1391-1415."[84]

In 1485, the Inquisition came to Saragossa, and, as in Seville and Toledo, the Judaizers and their supporters conspired to kill the Inquisitors and terrorize their potential successors into inactivity. The plot included a plan to drown the Inquisition's assessor as he walked beside the Ebro River, but the assessor never walked alone, so the plotters focused next on Peter Arbues. The government knew something was afoot as early as January, but did nothing. Late in the evening of September 15, the conspirators attacked Arbues as he prayed in the cathedral. Arbues was aware of the threat to his life: he was wearing chain mail and a steel helmet; his spear was leaning against a nearby pillar. The mortally wounded Arbues prayed for 24 hours before dying on September 17. Miracles soon followed. The holy bell of Villela tolled of its own accord; the crowds mopped up his blood and worked wonders with it.

The consequences for the conversos were disastrous. The miracles attested to Arbues' sanctity, and the reaction to the murder broke the opposition to the Inquisition. In the revulsion to the murder, legal niceties were discarded, and the punishment and tortures knew no restraint. This murder turned the tide, which hitherto had been markedly hostile to the Inquisition. The news of the assassination spread through the city with marvelous rapidity and before dawn the streets were filled with excited crowds shouting, "Burn the Conversos who have slain the Inquisitor." It was probably in consequence of the murder that Ferdinand and Isabella succeeded in obtaining from Innocent VIII papal letters of April 3, 1487, ordering all princes and rulers and magistrates to seize and deliver to the Inquisition of Spain all fugitives who should be designated to them, thus extending its arms everywhere throughout Christendom and practically outlawing all refugees.[85]

The murder of Peter Arbues "annihilated all opposition to the Inquisition for the next hundred years"[86] so effectively that some historians speculate the murder may have been arranged by the crown, although there is no evidence of this. No matter, the murder played into Ferdinand's hand in his attempt to end the chaos and defeat the Moors. In 1488 he issued instructions reforming the procedure of the Inquisitors. "Thus," Baer concludes, "the last and most daring attempt by the conversos to resist the Inquisition by force ended in failure."[87] Most of the murder suspects were conversos and or others whose Jewish leanings were publicly known. In August 1487, the main conspirator, Jaime de Montesa, was executed after he confessed. He was a typical free-thinking Marrano skeptic, reported to have repeatedly quoted the saying, "In this world you will not see me in trouble, and in another world you will not see me in torment."[88] After Montesa's death, more and more conversos were implicated in Judaizing, including advisors to the royal couple. "In essence," Baer concludes, "the Inquisition was correct in its reading of the conversos' attitudes." Baer cites the *Coplas de Mingo Revulgo* of Diego

Arias de Avila, in which conversos are portrayed as a group which "trample the Christians underfoot, and plunge them into debt and enslave them in all manner of servitude so that the Christians groan under so much robbery and spoliation." Torture played a role in these confessions.

The inquisitors usually proceeded with some respect for rules of law and justice, demonstrating facts that were unquestionably correct and refraining from malicious libels. In the fury following the murder of Peter Arbues, legal niceties fell by the wayside and the classical slanders—the Jews caused the plague, engaged in ritual sacrifice, etc.—made their way into the Inquisition's proceedings. In December, 1490, Yuce Franco was tried for attempting to bring conversos back to Judaism and for crucifying a Christian child on Good Friday. The conspirators allegedly were going to use the child's heart and a consecrated host in a magic spell to kill Christians by infecting them with rabies. Franco denied the charges. Torquemada removed him from the jurisdiction of the Inquisition and appointed special judges, leading Baer to conclude his goal was "the complete extermination of Spanish Jewry."[89]

When the victorious Spanish army marched into Malaga after the successful campaign to drive the Moors from Spain, they found 400 Jews living there. Virtually all were Judaized Christians who had fled the Inquisition from Spain to Granada, where they had reverted to Judaism. The apostates were ordered to decide whether they wanted to live completely as Christians or leave the country. Shortly after the royal couple entered Granada, they extended that option to all of Spain's Jews. On March 31, 1492, while still in Grenada, Ferdinand and Isabella signed the edict expelling the Jews from the kingdoms of Castile and Aragon. As before, Jews could convert and remain, but the Inquisition had removed much of the incentive to convert. Large numbers chose to leave. Their experience in Granada convinced the monarchs that a total separation was the only solution to the Jewish problem they identified. By exporting a problem they could not solve, Ferdinand and Isabella saved Spain from the fate of Poland. Northern Europe, though, inherited Spain's problem, and cities like Antwerp became hotbeds of revolutionary activity.

The expulsion of the Jews and rabbinical justification for false conversion established the cultural matrix from which the revolutionary Jew emerged. If a Talmudic Jew could profess an idolatrous false religion in public and remain a Jew in good standing, then he simply could not be trusted, and the anti-Semites were right to view him as a dangerous subversive who threatened Church and State. Forced conversion was wrong, but the acceptance of it was also wrong. Worse still, acceptance of insincere conversion enshrined the principle of deception and subversion as part of Jewish life. The Jew, according to the principles of the Old Testament from Moses to the Maccabees, had a duty to resist idolatry and incorporation into idolatrous religions to the point of death. The Talmudic teaching that condoned false conversion broke radically from Moses' teaching. The insincere Jewish converts to Christianity made subversion and deceit a way of life.

Converso behavior and worldview were similar to that of other disaffected European Catholics. The German monks who violated their vows of celibacy with impunity led double lives too; living a lie created animosity toward the institution to which they had made vows they would not fulfill. The first Lutherans and the first Calvinists were virtually indistinguishable from each other and from the conversos in theology and practice. Both movements drew their leadership from the sexually corrupt lower Catholic clergy. Calvin's lieutenant, the erstwhile Catholic, Theodore Beza was, says Walsh,

> a glaring example of the too-common corruption. Though not even a priest, he enjoys the incomes of two benefices, through political influence, lavishes the Church's money on his concubine, and generally leads a vicious and dissolute life. When the Church is under attack, he hastens to join the enemy. As Calvin's lieutenant, this righteous man thunders against the [corruption of the] Old Church, of which he was partly the cause.[90]

Beza's example was not uncommon. The monasteries of Europe were full of monks leading double lives. Spain was no exception:

> There is no doubt about the laxity of the monasteries of Seville and Valladolid, whose members embraced Protestantism; nor of the degeneracy of the Augustinians in Saxony, who broke away from the Church almost en masse in 1521. In England it was the reformed Observatine Franciscans who withstood Henry VIII even to death, while the relaxed Conventuals and other badly disciplined monks and priests formed the nucleus of the Church of England. The first Protestants, as a rule, were bad Catholics.[91]

The Spanish expulsions began in May, 1492. The Jews had to sell their property for a song, even though "instructions were issued to all the localities to pay the Jews all that was owed to them, and to enable them to pay their own debts and to dispose of their possessions on fair and equitable terms."[92] Torquemada forbade Christians from aiding the departing Jews after August 9. No Christian was allowed to communicate with the Jews or give them food or shelter. The Jews were not allowed to sell their synagogues; the property that they could sell was devalued because so many were selling to meet the expulsion deadline imposed by the crown. Bernaldez chronicled the sufferings of the Jews; he also cites a converso woman from Almazan, who claimed years later "those who remained behind did so in order not to lose their property."[93]

In the fateful year 1492, Rodrigo Borgia ascended the papal throne and took the name Alexander VI. Pope Alexander contravened papal tradition by banning conversos from the Dominican order in Spain. In Rome he amended the proceedings of the Roman Carnival by extending the traditional footrace of the Roman Jews. But Jews could always expect a friendly reception in Rome and throughout the Papal States, and many Jews went there after the expulsion. Alexander did his part by hiring Jewish physicians.

The Inquisition and the explusion undid the work of St. Vincent Ferrer. Jews were convinced conversion was or would be a mistake. After the Edict of Expulsion was announced, the clergy launched a conversion campaign, but the incentives were gone. There were few conversions, and most Jews left. Most went to Portugal, from whence they were expelled a few years later. Many went to Turkey, which received them with open arms. It was out of the Ladino community in Ismir that the false Messiah Shabbetai Zevi would arise 150 years later, buoyed by the writings of the Lurianic Kabballah, whose school had been established in Gaza as a result of the expulsions.

On July 31, 1492, the last Jew left Spain. In 1494, Alexander VI granted Ferdinand and Isabella the title of Catholic Kings, listing the expulsion of the Jews as one of their accomplishments. Gian Pico della Mirandola praised them for it too. Guicciardini, the Florentine historian and statesman, praised them as well. The expulsion of the Jews along with the defeat of the Moors had united Spain and "raised it to the rank of a great power." When Spain was in the hands of Jews and heretics it had been in anarchy. Guicciardini concluded "had the situation not been corrected, Spain would in a few years have forsaken the Catholic religion."[94]

The Jewish Revolutionary Spirit

Chapter Seven

Reuchlin v. Pfefferkorn

Roughly 270 years after Nicholas Donin persuaded Pope Gregory IX to allow him to proceed against the Talmud, another Jew converted to Christianity and had the same idea. In 1504, Josef Pfefferkorn, a Moravian Jew, converted to Christianity, along with his wife and child. After changing his name to Johannes at his baptism, Pfefferkorn spent his first years as a Christian wandering through southern German-speaking lands preaching the conversion of the Jews. In 1509 he settled in Cologne, where he made contact with the Dominicans, who had promoted Donin's efforts to convert the Jews three centuries earlier. Pfefferkorn's enthusiasm for the Christian faith was undeniable, but the results of his preaching were meager. In 1516, at the height of his fame, he claimed he had converted 14 Jews after years of effort. He claimed another five would have entered the Church if the Jews hadn't blackened his name. Pfefferkorn would become famous as a publicist, not as a preacher. The printing press was transforming the movement of information in Europe, and he made good use of this new technology.

In one of his earliest writings, *Der Juden Spiegel* (Mirror of the Jews) Pfefferkorn candidly describes his conversion. "I was born in the Jewish faith and am now, by the grace of God, a Christian," he wrote.[1] He lived by usury before converting, but gave it up as a Christian because usury is immoral. "If I continued to associate with Jews," he continued, "and continued to take usury, what would you say other than that I was in serious sin and that I never really became a Christian, and everyone would condemn me by saying that the blood and suffering of Christ had been lost on me. What help would the holy sacrament of baptism have been to me?"[2]

Pfefferkorn's admission he was a usurer is significant in light of later slanders. He was accused of criminal activity (and even of being hanged for it), but Pfefferkorn denied the charges, saying "two Jews wanted to sully my reputation with charges of theft."[3] Pfefferkorn filed suit against his accusers before the imperial court, and "they were obliged to pay 30 florins to cover my expenses and had to retract the accusations in public."[4] Most charges against Pfefferkorn are traceable to a document originating from the Jews of Regensburg. Among its milder statements was the claim he was an illiterate butcher. He was neither illiterate nor was he a butcher, an occupation morally less reprehensible than that of moneylender.

In his groundbreaking *History of the Jews*, Heinrich Graetz recites the slanders faithfully and uncritically and adds a few of his own, calling Pfefferkorn "an ignorant, thoroughly vile creature," as well as "the scum of the Jewish people," and a "noisome insect"[5] who was a tool of the "ignorant and fanatical Dominicans" of Cologne, a city known to be "an owls' nest of light-shunning swaggerers, who endeavored to obscure the dawn of a bright day with the dark clouds of superstition hostile to knowledge."[6] The vehemence of Graetz's attack is not, it seems, a function of historical sources, but of the very specific damning charges Pfefferkorn leveled against the Jews about their rites and, more importantly, their covert attacks on Christians.

Graetz claims Pfefferkorn did not write the famous series of tracts that began with *Juden Spiegel* but instead "lent his name to a new anti-Jewish publication, written in Latin by Ortuinus Gratius," one of the light-shunning Dominican swaggerers.[7] The leader of the Cologne Dominicans was Jacob Hochstraten (or Hoogstraten, in honor of his native town). Graetz refers to him as "an inquisitor or heretic hunter ... who literally longed for the smell of burning heretics and in Spain would have been a useful Torquemada."[8] Graetz's slanders are simply not true. Pfefferkorn, as his inimitable style and intimate knowledge of Jewish ritual indicate, wrote his own tracts. Hans-Martin Kirn says he "can in no way be seen as 'tool' of the Cologne Dominicans."[9]

Ludwig Geiger, Graetz's contemporary, noted Pfefferkorn "was later accused of scandalous activity by his enemies," including the scurrilous charge that "his wife ... had illicit intercourse with the Dominicans," but Geiger concluded "there is no proof for this allegation or the others," and wonders "how did they come into existence?"[10] The answer is simple. Stung by Pfefferkorn's criticism, the Jews invented slanders to blacken his name and dissuade others from taking him seriously. Geiger, like Graetz, was a German Jew, but, unlike Graetz, not so enraged by Pfefferkorn's conversion as to accept unfounded slanders.

The times had changed since Nicholas Donin's conversion in the 13th Century; the odium of being Jewish stuck with Pfefferkorn in spite of his baptism. The Dominicans and the Franciscans faithfully supported him in his efforts to convert the Jews, but the mendicants no longer were the cutting edge of European thought. Something had happened to the European mind; it was Pfefferkorn's lot to discover what.

Pfefferkorn characterized himself as a wandering preacher to the Jews immediately following his conversion. *Der Juden Spiegel* was supposed to show Jews their errors and prove the truth of Christianity. His second book, *Judenbeichte*, ridiculed Jewish penitential practices. In 1513, Pfefferkorn received a permanent position in charge of the Hospital of St. Ursula and St. Revillen in Cologne, a position he held until the end of his life. While traveling through Mainz, Oppenheim, Heidelberg, Ulm and Munich he made contact with the Franciscans who suggested in the confessional that he take up the battle against Jewish books, Jewish usury, and for Jewish conversion.

Pfefferkorn, like Donin, knew Judaism from the inside. That familiarity precipitated Graetz's rage. Pfefferkorn had studied Jewish writings with his uncle, a rabbi. Countering the claim that he was illiterate, a butcher, and a thief was a document emanating from Dachau in 1504, in which Pfefferkorn portrayed the Jews as engaging in covert warfare against Christians through usury and the subversion of religious vows. The Jews, according to Pfefferkorn, subverted the monks' vow of poverty by bribery, their vow of chastity by sexual seduction, and their vow of obedience by undermining all authority. Pfefferkorn pointed to more than 40 Christians who had abandoned the faith as a result of Jewish subversion, almost three times the number of Jews he had brought to Christianity by his preaching.

Pfefferkorn "spoke with the air of a man who was giving away secrets."[11] Because of his insider's knowledge, his claims were a threat to the Jews. In his pamphlet, *Ich bin ain Buchlinn der Juden veindt ist mein namen*, or *The Enemy of the Jews* (1509), Pfefferkorn reiterated Donin's claims, documenting Jewish blasphemies against Jesus, Mary, and the apostles, and the curses against Christians the Jews incorporated into their daily prayers. The Jews, said Pfefferkorn, utter "various insults and shameless words ... every day against God, Mary, his most worthy mother, and the whole heavenly host."[12] The Jews call Jesus *mamser ben hanido*," which is to say, "one born from an unclean union."[13] Although Pfefferkorn doesn't say so, "mamser" is traditionally translated "bastard." The Jews are similarly vehement in denouncing Christ's mother, calling her a "*sono*," which Pfefferkorn translates as "a notorious sinner." Again Pfefferkorn is discrete; the word means "whore." Pfefferkorn says the Jews call Christian churches "*mosschoff*" or "*beskisse*," "that is [latrines or] shithouses."[14] Additionally, the Jews "hate the sign of the holy cross and find it quite unbearable. If they see pieces of wood or straw on the ground that are by chance arranged roughly in the shape of a cross, they push it apart with their feet that they may no longer have to look at it."[15] If a Jew "knowingly crosses a churchyard or listens to an organ," he "believes that his prayers will not be heard by God for 30 days."[16]

Pfefferkorn also claimed Jews were revolutionaries who "pray for vengeance against the whole Christian church and especially the Roman Empire, that it may be broken up and destroyed."[17] The prayer for revolution is so significant that the Jews "are not allowed to say this prayer sitting down; rather, they must stand. Nor are they permitted to talk among themselves until the prayer is ended."[18] Whenever "war or rebellion breaks out among us Christians," Pfefferkorn says, the Jews "are heartily pleased, hoping that the time is near when the Empire will be destroyed." Pfefferkorn wrote *Juden veindt* to "prevent the damage which the mangy dogs [i.e., the Jews] do to Christian power in both the spiritual and worldly sphere."[19] The humanists and the reformers, who saw Pfefferkorn as a tool of the powers of darkness, would ignore his warning. But within three years of his death, German peasants had driven more than one prince from his throne in Southern Germany, and it looked as if the revolutionary spirit was going to spread to France and the low countries too.

In part two of *Juden veindt*, "How the Jews ruin land and people," Pfefferkorn describes how Jews get money through usury; he also "explain[s] the harm and damage the Jews cause to the country and the people through usury" by explaining how debt accumulates when interest is compounded.[20] After 30 years, "the debt amounts to an unfathomable 106 tons of gold, 14,810 Gulden, 28 Wiesspfennig and 11 Heller!" "Thus the poor Christian, when he has nothing further to pawn, must run away and live out his life in poverty, which happens often and many times."[21]

In part three, Pfefferkorn explains how Jews use money to corrupt the morals of Christians. Jews use "their ill-gotten wealth" to "cause Christians to commit great sins."[22] Jews usually prevail in court because of bribery. "The only reason for this is their ill-gotten money, which Christians accept from them in exchange for helping to muddle and cover up their case and make it appear just."[23] Jews use their wealth "to lead astray not only the common people but even educated men"[24] by corrupting the morals of Christians and by undermining their faith. The Jews, Pfefferkorn writes,

> cause many Christians, learned and unlearned, to doubt their faith, as I have shown in other books of mine. Thus there is much heresy where Jews live; also one finds that Christians commit unchaste acts with Jews and have children by them. These children remain Jews, which is no doubt a great, notable, and shameful evil. Christian blood is subjected to eternal damnation, and, as I have mentioned at the beginning of my booklet, there is in the whole city no sect or nation that hates the Christians more than the Jews.[25]

The Jews also live in a world of political illusions, generated by the "central hope of the Jews" that "a Messiah ... will deliver them." This Messiah "will come as a secular ruler, a king with great power and wealth to rule and subdue the world." Pfefferkorn reveals the secrets of the Jews at great personal risk because "I know well, if I fell among Jews, they would devour me as the wolf devours sheep, for this was reported to me." Jews from several countries, he continues, "have made a pact to kill and murder" him. Pfefferkorn warns, "if I should disappear, have no other thoughts than that I was killed by the Jews as they killed others before me."[26]

Pfefferkorn concludes his pamphlet by urging Christian rulers to regulate the lives of Jews more closely. They should be forced to give up usury and to take on lowly occupations like sweeping dung in the streets. As his final point, he makes a recommendation that would generate conflict for the next decade. Indeed, if Graetz is right in seeing the battle of the books as the spark that set off the Reformation, it would generate conflict for centuries to come. Pfefferkorn recommended confiscating Jewish books, specifically the Talmud, because, deprived of their books, the Jews would abandon their false beliefs and embrace Christianity. Like Donin, Pfefferkorn felt Jewish heresy was a function of the Talmud. Deprived of the books that were blinding their minds and poisoning their souls, the Jews would embrace the Christian faith.

Instead of going to the pope, as had Donin, Pfefferkorn approached the emperor. In 1509 he applied to the imperial court for the right to confiscate Jewish books. Kunigunde von Bayern, the devout sister of Emperor Maximillian I, provided a letter of introduction to the emperor, who endorsed Pfefferkorn's proposals and authorized him to confiscate Jewish books and to "examine Hebrew writings anywhere in the German empire, and to destroy all whose contents were hostile to the Bible and the Christian faith."[27] In September, Pfefferkorn arrived in Frankfurt, home of the richest and most powerful Jewish community in the German empire. At his command, the city senate ordered the Jews to assemble in the synagogue, where they were told to hand over their books. One thousand five hundred manuscripts were taken from the Jews and deposited in the town hall. One letter from the archives of the Jewish community in Frankfurt recites

> On Friday [28 September 1509] the butcher [i.e., Pfefferkorn] came to us here in Frankfurt, together with three priests and two friends from the city council, and they seized the books in the synagogue—the Tefilot, Machzorim and Slechot— everything they could find, and forbade us in the name of the emperor to continue praying in the synagogue.[28]

The Jews did not sit idle. Humanistic studies of the sort promoted by Erasmus of Rotterdam had suggested that a new day of Enlightened tolerance was about to dawn after the long night of scholastic obscurantism, and so the Jews were emboldened to act. The Jews sent Rabbi Gumprecht Weissenan to the archbishop of Mainz, who was persuaded that Pfefferkorn's activities infringed on his Episcopal jurisdiction. It was unusual for an individual of no official rank to receive such a mandate, and the emperor's action drew immediate protests both from Jewish representatives and from the archbishop of Mainz, who informed Pfefferkorn that the mandate was legally defective. Rabbi Weissenan, notes the same archival letter, was "successful with his request, and, praise be to God, obtained help and salvation for the Jews."[29]

After warning German Jews that "should any community ... refuse to send money and participate in our efforts... they will no longer be regarded as members of the Association of the Remainder of Israel," the Jews sent another delegation, led by Jonathan Levi Zion, to the imperial court to negotiate withdrawal of Pfefferkorn's mandate.[30] Levi Zion was frank in his reports to the Jews in Frankfurt. "I shall not be able to achieve anything until you send a man who is prepared for three things—you know what I mean."[31] Levi Zion's letter referred to Raschi's commentary on Gen 32:8 which mention prayer, combat, and bribery as three ways to defeat an enemy. Levi Zion and the Jews at Frankfurt settled on the last alternative as the best course. After pleading for money, "as soon as possible so that I shall not be forced to borrow money here at 100 percent,"[32] Levi Zion announced by letter that he had bribed the Margrave of Baden, whom the emperor had assigned to handle Pfefferkorn's case. "For this," Levi Zion wrote, "I gave him [the Margrave of Baden] something, and should we obtain what we are asking for in the petition, I shall give him an additional one hundred Gulden for his efforts. And so he acted on our behalf and made a great personal effort" to annul Pfefferkorn's mandate.[33] Even so, Levi Zion still felt "Everything is upside down. The apostate and his courtiers have persuaded the emperor to write to the archbishop that [Pfefferkorn] should be the commissioner in this business, together with the apostate Viktor [von Karben] in Cologne, another doctor from Cologne, a doctor from Heidelberg and Dr. Reuchlin from Stuttgart."[34]

This is the first time Reuchlin's name appears in the controversy surrounding the confiscation of the Talmud, and the context is significant. Johannes Reuchlin is mentioned in the same letter in which Levi Zion admits bribing the Margrave of Baden. Levi Zion then asks for more money, presumably for more bribes. Since "it is very likely that the apostate [i.e., Pfefferkorn] will be commissioned to proceed," the Jews "must immediately send wise and prudent men from our communities to the emperor. They must of course be well supplied with gold and silver, and must beseech the emperor to be merciful and spare us ... for I fear things that I do not want to write down."[35]

The Jews reacted to the threat of losing their books by bribing court officials and slandering Pfefferkorn at the Imperial court during the winter of 1509-10. In the spring, their efforts paid off. Emperor Maximillian I ordered the Frankfurt senate to return the books. To play down the injury to Pfefferkorn and the Dominicans and "to avoid any complaints on the part of the Jews that his had been undertaken lightly and without diligent consideration,"[36] the emperor created a commission to examine the Jews' books. Maximillian authorized the archbishop of Mainz to solicit reports from four universities as well as from qualified individuals. Johannes Reuchlin was one of those qualified individuals.

As a result, Johannes Reuchlin was appointed to the commission. "It was fortunate for the Jews," Graetz writes, "that the honest, truthful Reuchlin, so enthusiastically prepossessed for Hebrew and Cabalistic literature, was asked to give his opinion of Jewish literature."[37] Johannes Reuchlin was, next to Erasmus of Rotterdam, the most prominent scholar of his day. Like Erasmus and the humanists, Reuchlin saw scholarship as the study of language rather than dialectic in the Scholastic mode. Unlike Erasmus, who confined himself to Latin and Greek texts, Reuchlin immersed himself in Hebrew as early as the mid-1480s. Reuchlin's interest in Hebrew blossomed while he was on an embassy to the papal court in 1490.

Reuchlin traveled to Italy as the crisis over the newly translated hermetic texts and their connection to magic reached its climax. There Reuchlin met the recently reborn Platonic academy in Florence under the direction of Lorenzo de Medici. In 1463, Lorenzo's father had commissioned Marsilio Ficino to translate "*Corpus Hereticum*," which a monk had brought from Macedonia. Ficino then steeped himself in the neoplatonic mysteries Julian the Apostate found so seductive a millennium earlier. Ficino aided in the translation of the "Hermitca" and "Orphica," which constituted the neoplatonic teachings, including the "Chaldean Oracles," ascribed to the followers of Zarathustra, as well as the teaching of Pythagoras, which included many magic spells, esoteric teachings, and customs.

At a certain point, Pope Innocent VIII began to suspect that the neoplatonic academy was involved in more than simple antiquarian pursuits. In 1490, one year before Reuchlin met Count Giovanni Pico dell Mirandola, Garsias alleged at Pope Innocent's urging that Pico, Ficino's pupil, was promoting magic. For two years, the sword of Damacles dangled over Pico's head. Then Innocent VIII died in 1492, and Alexander VI succeeded him. In his *46 Sentences*, Pico defended himself against the accusations of his opponents, and after his presentation, on June 18, 1493, Pope Alexander VI cleared him of the charges laid against him. The way was then clear for the resurgence of Christian interest in magic. In her book on Giordano Bruno, Frances Yates laid the responsibility for that resurgence at the feet of Alexander VI, whom she claims had a special relationship to the Egyptian mysteries, astrology, and magic, as evidenced in the Pintarucchio frescoes in the Borgia apartments. Zika is more pointed. He claims the attitude of the papal court changed when Alexander VI became pope because Alexander was intent on putting "occult magic to his own use."[38]

One year after Pico's acquittal, Reuchlin published *De verbo mirifico*, The Wonder-Working Word, his attempt to revive philosophy, lately fallen into the slumber of Scholasticism, by linking it to the Hebrew language, Caballah, and magic. In it, Baruchia, a Jew, Sidonius, a philosopher once an Epicurean but now knowledgeable in many different systems, and Reuchlin, under the name Capnion (the Greek word for smoke is *Kapnos* or *Rauch* in German. Reuchlin is the diminutive of *Rauch*), conduct a dialogue. The three are not divided by their religions; like the Masons at a later date, they are united by esoteric wisdom derived from the Caballah. Socrates was a wise man, but the wisest was Moses, who was wise not through his own intellectual powers but rather through the spirit of God in him. Only this spirit, transmitted from one race to another and now known as Caballah, makes one capable of penetrating the secrets of nature through the wonderworking word. The most wonderworking of all words is the unspeakable Tetragrammaton JHVH (the four consonants comprising the name Yahweh), which is similar to the Tetrakys of Pythagoras. Each letter has its own secret meaning. Ihsvh is the most secret name, because it adds the letter signifying Jesus.

Like Karl Marx three centuries later, Reuchlin claimed philosophy would "work wonders." It would change the world by unleashing the power of the magic words which God himself uttered to Moses and Adam. To begin the study of magic, the adept needed to learn Hebrew to use "practical Caballah," another word for magic. Like Messianic politics, magic was a way of bringing about heaven on earth and was intimately bound up with the rise of the new scientific worldview. Magic was associated in the popular mind with Jews. Jews knew how to cast the spells that would bring about this-worldly riches and power. Both magic and applied science involved a turning away from the Cross, which is to say, the God-ordained necessity of suffering in this life if one wants to attain salvation. In the place of the Cross, the adept of practical Caballah proposes the techniques refined by Jews that enable one to get what one wants. Four centuries after the publication of *De verbo mirifico*, C.S. Lewis noticed

There is something which unites magic and applied science while separating both from the "wisdom" of earlier ages. For the wise men of old the cardinal problem had been how to conform the soul to reality, and the solution had been knowledge, self-discipline and virtue. For magic and applied science alike the problem is how to subdue reality to the wishes of men: the solution is a technique, and both, in the practice of this technique, are ready to do things hitherto regarded as disgusting and impious—such as digging up and mutilating the dead.[39]

The seeds planted at the Platonic Academy of Florence under the patronage of the Medicis bore fruit at the turn of the century. In 1501, Giovanni Mercurio showed up in Lyon wearing flowing white robes and a chain around his neck, announcing he was omniscient and could change lead into gold and bring happiness to the depressed. The chain derived from the same Pythagorean chain of love and friendship whose symbology would exert its influence over Reuchlin.

Reuchlin's *De verbo mirifico* introduced the idea of neoplatonic magic to the lands north of the Alps. In it, Reuchlin tried to break down the barriers separating religion, philosophy, and magic through recourse to the Hebrew language in general and in particular through the rehabilitation of Caballah, which he saw as the oral esoteric tradition that had come from Adam himself. Caballah, of course, had no ancient pedigree. It apparently arose in the 12th Century in Provence; it was the Jewish equivalent of the Albigensian heresy, a resurgence of neoplatonic gnosticism. None of the proponents of Caballah, however, saw it that way. Instead they viewed it as the original theology, the *prisca thelolgia*, at least as old as Christianity and probably much older than that. Pico had already established a necessary connection between Caballah and magic in his writings. Reuchlin took his ideas one step further by claiming that natural magic was impossible without the Caballah. Reuchlin separated himself from the magic manuals of the Middle Ages. In place of these magic spells, which were either meaningless mumbo-jumbo or, worse, appeals to evil spirits, Reuchlin proposed the magic of the Hebrews found in the Caballah and intimately bound up with their language, the language of God Himself. Reuchlin claimed because God spoke in Hebrew, Hebrew words uttered in the proper way had an immediate physical effect. They could not bring about creation *ex nihilo*, but they might very well influence the angels put in charge of that creation by God. In learning Hebrew, as Reuchlin did at the feet of rabbis, the adept learned the language God Himself had used to speak to Moses. Men could now use that same language in speaking to the angels who ran the universe and create wonders by their very words. Zoroaster, the first theologian, according to their view, recognized the unique nature of Hebrew words and so forbade any alteration of their form because the divine power of the word was only effective in its original Hebrew form. During the dialogue between the three learned men in *De verbo mirifico*, Reuchlin expands his praise of Hebrew into an attack on Greek, which, in the words of Baruchias, the learned Jew, possesses "no words that have come down to us from heaven and no names which can be characterized as having divinely ordained syllables."[40] Moses, because he spoke Hebrew, had priority over the Egyptians as well because the Hebrew language is more ancient. "Divine names come to us from the Jews and not the Egyptians. Hebrew names are more ancient and holier than any other names."[41]

Taking his cue from Alexander VI's approval of Pico, Reuchlin defends the connection Pico established between Caballah and magic. In his *"Conclusiones,"* Pico claimed that immediate access to divine mysteries and powers was available through the Caballah. Part of the Cabballah was also the highest part of *magia naturalis*. Reuchlin claimed the Caballah demonstrated the validity of the Christian faith and also corresponded to the esoteric wisdom of Orpheus, Pythagoras, and Zoroaster. By locating the magical power of his system in the Hebrew language, Reuchlin hoped to evade the dichotomy the Church, following the classical tradition, had established. According to that dichotomy, a man either asked for power over nature, in which case his action was known as prayer and dependent on the permissive will of the deity; or he forced the issue by invoking evil spirits. Caballah seemed to indicate another possibility. The possibility of a middle ground between science and prayer based on the magical effects of angelic names in Hebrew seemed theologically unlikely, but that is the course Reuchlin pursued, hoping to evade the censure of those who claimed he was involved in black magic.

The Hebrew language saved Reuchlin, at least in his own mind, from becoming a proponent of black magic, which involved contact with demons and was practiced under the name of Solomon, Adam, or Enoch. Hebrew was the key to making contact with the good spirits whose silent help enabled the practice of *magia naturalis*. The true philosopher should not invoke demons, but if the philosopher is unable to perform wonders, he is no better than the garrulous Schoolmen who, like spiders, spin words but produce no effects. Sidonious says, "we would therefore be hardly distinguishable from the vulgar, if our miraculous vocation was not accompanied by miraculous actions."[42] Reuchlin's idea of a "wonder working" philosophy had much in common with Thomas Muentzer's view of scripture. To be truly alive, the word of God had to create signs and wonders. The same was true of Reuchlin's Caballistic Philosophy: Philosophy had no value if it couldn't work wonders beyond the power of man to explain. The Caballah would rehabilitate philosophy by its miracles, which were bound up not with evil spirits but with the power of Hebrew.

Reuchlin's fatal attraction to Caballah took root on his journey to Italy when he studied with Obadaiah Sforno, a Jewish physician, philosopher, and more importantly, collector of rare Hebrew manuscripts and books. Two years later, Reuchlin was back in Italy, this time on an embassy to the imperial court in Padua. On this journey he received instruction from the emperor's court physician, Iacob ben Iehiel Loans. Reuchlin and Loans remained in contact for the next decade, and Reuchlin repeatedly expressed his admiration for his Jewish teacher. Fully aware of Reuchlin's intercourse with the rabbis, Pfefferkorn exclaimed later, "if I had said these things I would have been burned" at the stake.[43]

Studying the Caballah required a sort of hermetic initiation. The Caballah, Rummel says, "was taught hermetically, that is, reserved for the elect, and was often associated with magic, a connection deplored even by Jewish teachers of stature such as Moses Maimonides."[44] It would not have been taught to someone who was either skeptical or disinterested. It would only have been taught to someone avid to receive initiation into its mysteries. The Jewish masters who taught Reuchlin, therefore, must have seen in him a potential adept. "Christians," Rummel continues,

> began to take an interest in the Caballah during the fifteenth Century. The Italian humanist Pico della Mirandola ... connected the Caballah with "natural magic," that is, the study of celestial bodies, but rejected its counterpart, black magic, "which is rightly excised by the church and has no foundation, no truth and no basis." ... Nevertheless it remained a controversial subject. It continued to attract the attention of inquisitorial courts and was therefore pursued by Reuchlin at some personal risk.[45]

After Reuchlin met Pico and learned about the Caballah, Graetz says, he "thirsted for Hebrew literature, but could not quench his thirst."[46] More accurately, Reuchlin desired to learn Hebrew to slake his thirst for esoteric and arcane knowledge. In *De verbo mirifico*, Reuchlin wrote "The language of the Hebrews is simple, uncorrupted, holy, terse and vigorous; God conversed in it direct with men, and men with angels, without interpreters face to face ... as one friend converses with another."[47]

In 1506, Reuchlin issued *De rudimentis Hebraicis*, the first Hebrew grammar ever written by a non-Jew. Four years later, when Reuchlin was at the height of his powers and reputation, Pfefferkorn approached him after he heard Reuchlin had been appointed an expert witness for the commission then deliberating Pfefferkorn's plan to seize the books of the Jews. Pfefferkorn came away from the meeting pleased, claiming Reuchlin had been cordial and had even graciously instructed him on the fine points of etiquette and protocol at the Imperial court.

Reuchlin completed his evaluation on October 6, 1510 and sent it to the emperor in a sealed envelope. He recommended that two books, *Nizzachon and Toledoth Jeschu*, should be confiscated and destroyed; the Jews should be allowed to keep their other works. This meant that Reuchlin did not include the Talmud among the "books which ridicule, slander and insult our Great Lord and God Jesus and his mother, and the apostles and saints."[48] He said "I have read only two such books: one called Nizzachon, the other Tolduth Jeschu ha nozri." Reuchlin gives the impression that these books had no standing in the Jewish community: "Even the Jews themselves regard them as apocryphal."[49] While at the court of Frederick III, Reuchlin "heard the Jews themselves saying in the frequent conversations I had with them that they have removed and destroyed such books and forbidden that people should in future write such books or speak thus."[50]

At this point in his report, Reuchlin's testimony becomes problematical if not erroneous and self-contradictory: "If the Talmud were deserving of such condemnation, our ancestors of many hundred years ago, whose zeal for Christianity was much greater than ours, would have burnt it."[51] Reuchlin says no pope ever burned the Talmud, but Geiger corrects the historical record by reminding the reader that both Gregory IX and Innocent IV had consigned copies of the Talmud to the flames. Reuchlin might have been an expert in Hebrew philology and grammar (Graetz disputes this), but he was abysmally ignorant of the history of the Talmud, which had been burned more than once by his "ancestors." Reuchlin claimed "The baptized Jews Peter Schwarz and Pfefferkorn, the only persons who insist on its being burnt, probably wish it for private reasons."[52] Yet Reuchlin made these claims after admitting that he, unlike Pfefferkorn, had neither read the Talmud nor understood it! "No one," Reuchlin continued, "can say in truth that the Talmud, in which the four higher faculties are described, is completely evil and that one cannot learn anything good from it. For it contains many good medical prescriptions and information about plants and roots as well as legal verdicts collected from all over the world by experienced Jews."[53]

Reuchlin then characterized the Talmud as "a work which is difficult to understand."[54] He also said that there were many strange ideas in the Talmud, but that did not justify its destruction. Of the Jews, Reuchlin said, "whether they are inimically disposed toward us in their hearts, only God can say."[55] Defense of the Caballah was unnecessary, because the pope had already recognized its value, and Pico had shown Christians could use its teachings to strengthen the Christian faith. Jews could not be called heretics because they had never fallen away from the Christian faith. The Jews had the right to retain their property, including the Talmud, because they were citizens—a then unusual term—of the German empire.

Despite stating that it needed no defense, Reuchlin then defended the Caballah, which he referred to as "the most secret speech and words of God."[56] Reuchlin claimed theologians who did not know Hebrew had made serious theological errors, an assertion that undermined theology, according to the Dominicans, by making it a function of scripture scholarship, which is to say, language studies, not dialectics. He concluded "No Christian should pass verdict on [the Jews], except in a secular case transacted in a secular court. For they are not members of the Christian church, and their faith is none of our business."[57] The claim "their faith is none of our business" combined with the equally daring claim Jews had rights as citizens, did not endear Reuchlin to the Dominicans, whose mission since Penaforte had been the papally mandated conversion of the Jews.

In his report, Reuchlin denounced Pfefferkorn's writings as the work of an ignorant hatemonger, thus establishing the debate's parameters: the refined man of letters vs. the ignorant *"tauf iud,"* a racist slur picked up by Reuchlin's supporters, including Erasmus of Rotterdam Pfefferkorn called Reuchlin a Judaizer, a term then in the process of losing its opprobrium among educated humanists. Reuchlin's claim that knowledge of Hebrew was necessary for the correct interpretation of the bible was guaranteed to offend theologians, no matter how much it pleased humanists. Those theologians, under the direction of the Cologne Dominicans, still wielded considerable political power, although not as much as in previous centuries. The conflict settled into the Humanist vs. Scholastic mode, even though (or perhaps, according to Rummel, because) it obscured the central contention of Pfefferkorn and the Dominicans, namely, that Reuchlin was a Judaizer. Indeed, Judaizing was a virtue to those who made theology a function of Hebrew grammar; it would soon become equally esteemed by the Reformers who believed that theology must be based on "Scripture alone." The most significant part of the report is Reuchlin's praise of the Caballah:

> I have read it myself. One could argue about the pros and cons for a long time in this report. But one may see from the book entitled Apologia by the earlier mentioned Count of Mirandola, which has been approved by Pope Alexander, that the books of the Cabala are not only harmless, but of great use to the Christian faith, and Pope Sixtus IV had them translated into Latin for the use of us Christians. There are sufficient grounds therefore to conclude that such books as the Cabala should not and cannot be legally suppressed and burned.... Jewish commentaries should not and cannot be abandoned by the Christian church, for they keep the special characteristics of the Hebrew language before our eyes. The bible cannot be interpreted without them, especially the Old Testament, just as we cannot do without the Greek language and Greek grammars and commentaries for the New Testament, as is confirmed and indicated in canon law.[58]

Since "the Jews are our archivists, librarians and antiquarians, who preserve books that can serve as witnesses to our faith," Christians should "take care of the existing books, protect and respect them, rather than burn them, for from them flows the true meaning of the language and our understanding of Sacred Scripture."[59]

One needn't be a learned theologian to see that Reuchlin was turning the Talmud into a meta-Scripture that would serve as the criterion of what was valid in the Bible. The hermetic texts had become the real Scriptures, and they were to be interpreted not by the Catholic Church, but by the nascent academic establishment, which had taken instruction at the feet of the rabbis in an atmosphere of quasi-Masonic hermeticism. Even Reuchlin's caveat against books promoting magic was qualified to the point of meaninglessness:

> If there are, however, Hebrew books that teach or instruct readers in the forbidden arts, such as sorcery, magic and witchcraft, if they may be used to harm people, they should be destroyed, torn up and burned because they are against nature. But if such books of magic are designed only to help and benefit human life and serve no harmful purpose, one should not burn or destroy them, except books about buried treasures.[60]

And who was to decide whether a particular Hebrew text was blasphemous or instead a "buried treasure"? The implication seems clear: only those who knew Hebrew were qualified to decide. The ultimate authority in the Church devolved upon those who had taken hermetic instruction from the rabbis, as had Reuchlin. Otherwise, "the Jews ought to be left in peace in their synagogues, and in the exercise of ceremonies, rites, customs, habits and devotions, especially when they do not go against what is right and do not manifestly insult our Christian church" because "the Christian church has nothing to do with them ... as long as the Jews keep the peace, they ought to be left in peace. And all this must be observed so that they cannot say that they are being forced and compelled to convert to our faith."[61] In an especially self-serving passage, Reuchlin recommended that the German universities should "hire for the next ten years two lecturers each, who would be capable and have the task of teaching students Hebrew and instructing them in this language.... If this is done, I doubt not that in a few years our students will be so well versed in the Hebrew language that they will be able to bring the Jews over to our side with reasonable and friendly words and gentle means."[62]

Pfefferkorn gained access to Reuchlin's report and was outraged. Every scholar appointed to the commission had written in favor of Pfefferkorn's proposal, except Reuchlin. Pfefferkorn gave his interpretation of what had happened in *Handt Spiegel*, published in Spring, 1511. Pfefferkorn claimed "a fat Jew sat on his book,"[63] which is to say, Reuchlin had been suborned by the Jews. "All," Pfefferkorn continued, "with the exception of Johannes Reuchlin, unanimously declared and wrote for Christ, inspired by the Holy Spirit. His report alone ... supported the perfidy of the Jews rather than the Apostolic See and the most holy cause of our faith."[64] Pfefferkorn denounced Reuchlin as a "half-Jew" and a "Judas."[65] As a result of Reuchlin's recommendation, the emperor did not renew the mandate to confiscate the Jewish books. Reuchlin had killed the project, and Pfefferkorn was furious.

Pfefferkorn correctly claimed "the Jews bribed Christians in high places ... and they filled the ears of the good Emperor with false advice, so that His imperial Majesty gave orders to restore the books to the Jews."[66] Pfefferkorn knew about the bribe Levi Zion gave the Margrave of Baden; he claimed that Reuchlin had been bribed also because the Jews had told him, "Reuchlin knows how to deal with you and oppose you.... They told me that they were in close contact with Reuchlin and very well informed about this matter." Pfefferkorn recalled the German proverb, *"Die Gelehrten, Die Verkehrten,"* which is to say, "The learned are easily corrupted."[67]

Pfefferkorn felt doubly betrayed because, on the basis of his private consultation with Reuchlin in 1510, felt he had nothing to fear from Reuchlin. "He treated me most cordially," he reported, "and expressed pleasure at my coming, and what is more he instructed me in what to do in the presence of the Emperor, of which I have proof in his own handwriting. Then when he had cleverly found out everything about the matter from me, he falsely reassured me and devoutly promised to write to me. He did no such thing, but instead traduced me in his report to His Royal Majesty, contrary to his promise and acting, most impiously .... And so he betrayed me, as Judas betrayed Christ."[68]

Reuchlin was furious when he learned Pfefferkorn was privy to what he considered a confidential evaluation, meant only for the emperor's eyes. He accused Pfefferkorn of breaking the seal on his report and gaining illicit access. Reuchlin claimed Pfefferkorn was a pawn of the Cologne Dominicans. In 1518, Ortwin Gratius, a leader of the Cologne Dominicans, denied they bore any responsibility for the publication of the *Handt Spiegel*. Pfefferkorn was in Mainz when *Handt Spiegel* appeared at the Frankfurt book convention in April 1511. Taking Reuchlin's part in the controversy, Graetz also claimed Pfefferkorn was a pawn of the Dominicans, who concocted the scheme to confiscate the Talmud so they could extort money from the Jews. Since the Jews "could not do without the Talmud," they "would pour their wealth into Dominican coffers to have the confiscation annulled."[69] Graetz also claimed Pfefferkorn lured Reuchlin into "a cunningly devised trap,"[70] but gives no evidence to support his claim.

The Dominicans accused Reuchlin of disingenuousness. The Jews' hatred for Christians was universally known; every Jew who had left Judaism could tell stories about it. Only a few Christians, "especially Johannes Reuchlin from Stuckarten" denied this hatred and would not admit that Jews prayed against Christians. Anyone who denied this knew nothing of Jewish scriptures; Reuchlin's admitted ignorance of the Talmud meant he had not written the document that appeared under his name. Reuchlin was handicapped in responding because he was caught in a contradiction. He claimed the Talmud was not pernicious, and yet he admitted he had never read it. The Dominicans pressed the issue, reminding Reuchlin that there weren't just two pernicious Jewish books, and that the Jews did not proscribe the two he mentioned. Quite to the contrary, the Jews read from *Toledoth Jeschu* every year at Christmastime in the hope that God would punish Jesus because of his false teaching.

After Pfefferkorn published *Handt Spiegel*, Reuchlin took his case to the emperor. Not content to wait for a legal verdict, Reuchlin joined battle in the realm of political publishing, newly created by the invention of the printing press. In late August or early September of 1511, Reuchlin issued his pamphlet *Augenspiegel* (Eye Mirror or Spectacles—an image of a pair of glasses was on the title page), which defended both Jewish books and his own integrity as a disinterested scholar. But, according to Graetz, Reuchlin was an avowed enemy of the circumcised. Reuchlin's writings were suffused with racism, including routine reference to Pfefferkorn as a "*taufft jud*," what the Spaniards would term a *marrano* or *converso*. Reuchlin wanted to rescue the Jewish scriptures for the cabalists. Neither he nor his colleagues were fond of Jews. Indeed, their dislike of Jews did not stop even after the Jew became baptized. In this, they were less like their forbears of the crusades and more like their descendants of the Third Reich, who felt, as Edith Stein was to learn, that baptism did not erase Jewishness, because Jewishness was a racial phenomenon, not religious. Pfefferkorn complained bitterly and often about the racist remarks of professors and preachers, who, as fellow Christians, should have accepted him as a brother, but instead made remarks like "To trust a Jew is like putting a snake to your bosom, a burning coal in your lap, and a mouse in your pocket."[71] Pfefferkorn thought that way about Jews, too, but was offended that his fellow Christians thought that way about him after his baptism.

In November 1510, the theology faculty at the university of Cologne issued two reports responding to Reuchlin's letter to the emperor. The theologians reminded Reuchlin that the Talmud contained "not only errors and false statements, but also blasphemies and heresies against their own law."[72] For this reason, Popes Gregory and Innocent had "ordered the said book to be burned." The Talmud and the Caballah were "corrupt;" they were fundamentally different from and therefore did not "convey the intention of Moses' books and those of other [Hebrew] prophets and wise men."[73] Unlike Reuchlin, who sought to preserve the books to derive esoteric knowledge from them, the faculty at Cologne decreed that Pfefferkorn and the Dominicans were acting for the common good. That meant "it would be impious and irreligious to allow them the use of such books which they, who are mockers and blasphemers of the Lord Christ, might use to teach their children."[74] Proceeding against the Talmud was "in the interest of the Christian faith as well as of the Jews' salvation,"[75] an idea that Reuchlin subverted when he said what Jews believed was none of their business. The Dominicans then reiterated the concerns articulated at the Fourth Lateran Council 300 years earlier:

> it seems expedient to prevent the Jews from practicing usury and to allow them to take up honest work for a living, but let them be distinguished from Christians by a badge, and let them be taught in their own language by experienced converts about the true law and the prophets for the glory of God, their own salvation and the increase of the Christian faith.[76]

The emperor was unmoved. He refused to order re-confiscation of the books. Reuchlin was wrong when he claimed the Talmud had never been burned, but he was right in claiming that the piety of his ancestors' generation exceeded that of his own. As we have seen, a new spirit was abroad, one which condoned blasphemy in the name of scholarship and disapproved of burning books as something that educated people did not do.

The Jews were overjoyed by the emperor's verdict. Like their ancestors at the foot of Mount Sinai, the Jews made two images, "one of Johann Reuchlin in angelic form, like a prophet; the other, of Pfefferkorn, in the shape of a devil."[77] They danced around the images like pagans around a sacrifice, genuflecting to Reuchlin's image and sticking knives into Pfefferkorn's. Pfefferkorn and Hoogstraten were outraged by Jewish effrontery. "If the Jews are permitted to retain the books that have been taken from them by imperial mandate," Hoogstraten wrote, "they will be confirmed in their perfidy; they will insult Christians and cast in their teeth that the books would not have been restored to them by imperial edict if they were not true and holy."[78]

Hoogstraten did not claim the Jews had bribed Reuchlin, but others did. Gregor Reisch, a Carthusian prior, made the claim, which is reported by Geiger.[79] Graetz said bribery was the charge that bothered Reuchlin the most, and he rejected it forcefully. Reuchlin admitted he had had dealings with Jews, but he was infuriated over the claim he had been bribed by the Jews: "I say therefore, by the highest faith, that in my entire life from the days of my childhood up to this hour that I have not received one nickel, not one penny, from the Jews, neither have I received gold or silver nor have I hope to."[80] "No Jew," he continued, "offered me rent, services or any kind of reward. And anyone who writes otherwise injures my honor and is a liar and a base villain.""[81]

Reuchlin's *Augenspiegel* caused an immediate sensation. Within a few weeks, it was read all over the Germanies. Pfefferkorn claimed the Jews rushed out to buy Reuchlin's book as soon as they heard it dealt with them favorably. But Geiger claims that once the Jews got their books back in 1510, they lost interest in the controversy. Graetz claims the Jews naturally saw Reuchlin as their champion and just as naturally promoted his book. They were pleased and dumbfounded "to find that so distinguished a man as Reuchlin would set an accuser of the Jews in the pillory as a calumniator and liar."[82] Having one of the most distinguished Christian scholars in Europe defend the Talmud left Jews rubbing their eyes in amazement. The Jews rushed out to buy Reuchlin's book, and, using their commercial connections, made it an instant bestseller, perhaps the first in history. "The Jews," according to Graetz, "greedily bought a book in which for the first time a man of honor entered the lists on their behalf.... They rejoiced at having found a champion ... Who would find fault with them for laboring in the promulgation of Reuchlin's pamphlet?"[83]

In September 1511, Peter Meyer, a pastor in Frankfurt, allowed Pfefferkorn to preach a counter-attack on Reuchlin's pamphlet, something which outraged Reuchlin even more since Pfefferkorn was a married layman. The Dominicans were furious because Reuchlin had ruined their centuries-old campaign to convert the Jews; they demanded confiscation and destruction of any remaining copies of the *Augenspiegel*. Arnold von Tungern, a leader of the Cologne faction, wrote to the emperor complaining that the *Augenspiegel* was full of assertions promoting Judaism that would strengthen the Jews in their defiance of the Christian faith. Since Reuchlin boldly refused to retract his errors and countered with threats of his own, von Tungern concluded correctly that he knew that he had many supporters ready to protect him. Virtually the entire Humanist community had united behind Reuchlin, and out of that group would come many "Reformers," including Martin Luther and Ulrich von Hutten, who later wrote to Reuchlin pledging his support.

By this point, the controversy had gone well beyond its initial impetus. Geiger says the affair began as a crusade against Jews, but the confrontation between humanists and scholastics soon eclipsed the original issue. By 1511, he said, "the business of the [Jewish] books was over," and the intellectual battle began ... its character changed for this and assumed an essentially different form. There were barely any references to the books from that point on, and none at all to the Jews. At issue was the right to express one's opinion freely, to counter the inquisitorial fixation on heresy."[84] But the focus of the debate also shifted because Reuchlin, with images of the Spanish Inquisition fresh in his mind, felt that the charges of judaizing were serious to the point of being life-threatening. As a result he wanted to guide the uproar into safer channels.

In September 1513, Jacob Hoogstraten summonsed Reuchlin to appear before the Inquisition in Mainz to defend himself against charges of heresy and Judaizing. If the issue, as Geiger claimed, was no longer the Jews, Hoogstraten was unaware of the change. "You," the Dominican wrote to Reuchlin

> appeared before Christian readers as a champion of the perfidious Jews. And you made this impression also on the Jews themselves, who are hostile toward the Cross and the blood through which we have been purified and redeemed. As we hear, they read your tract, which has been written and published in our vernacular language, and disseminated it. Thus you have given them an opportunity to deride us more than ever, for they found that among Christians and especially Christians who had a reputation for great learning, you were the only one who spoke on their behalf and maintained and defended their cause. [85]

The Dominicans got an order from the emperor allowing them to confiscate copies of the *Augenspiegel* and to burn them in public. The students at the university protested, but the confiscation continued, and all were to be burned on October 12, when an order halting the burning arrived. Pfefferkorn countered by publishing *Brandspiegel* (Burning Mirror), which Geiger calls "poisonous," demanding the Jews be expelled from Worms, Frankfurt, and Regensburg "forever."[86] Undeterred, Reuchlin appealed to the emperor, claiming that his opponents weren't theologians; they were theologists. The Cologne crowd were all slanderers. According to Geiger, Reuchlin gave as good as he got. Reuchlin's bitterness drove him to repeat the scurrilous stories about Mrs. Pfefferkorn's reputed sexual relations with the Cologne Dominicans. In June 1513 the emperor imposed silence on all parties.

In July, the theology faculty at the University of Louvain rendered its verdict. Cologne and Louvain would later become centers of the anti-Lutheran movement, and both considered themselves defenders of the faith. The theologians of Louvain concluded that Reuchlin's *Augenspiegel* had numerous errors, casting into question the orthodoxy of its author and promoting the cause of the Jews; therefore, all remaining copies should be confiscated and burned. The Cologne Theology faculty concurred in August. The theologians of Mainz followed suit shortly thereafter. The *Augenspiegel* was to be consigned to the flames. The theologians at Erfurt, a bastion of the new humanism and soon to go over to the Reformed camp, demurred. They found the pamphlet full of errors, but Reuchlin was not guilty because he never intended to publish it. The *Augenspiegel* was heretical, but its author was not a heretic, seemed to be their conclusion. In May 1514, a delegate from Cologne met with the theology faculty of the University of Paris to elicit their opinion. Louis XII, the French monarch, reminded the theologians there that St. Louis, his predecessor, had ordered the burning of the Talmud when he was king.

Recognizing the seriousness of the charges, Reuchlin employed a dual strategy to escape being burned at the stake. He engaged in a publicity campaign, enlisting the support of prominent writers like Erasmus and experienced publicists like Ulrich von Hutten, and he also waged a legal battle. He issued a public statement against "the Cologne slanderers" while pursuing a legal challenge to Mainz's jurisdiction over his case. He used the press to reformulate the issue from the dangerous charge of judaizing, redirecting it to the safer issue of academic freedom. Reuchlin portrayed himself as a learned preservationist who wanted to keep the obscurantists from consigning valuable historical documents to the flames. Reuchlin portrayed his battle with Pfefferkorn as a contest between "scholars, who respected books as cultural witnesses," against boors, who had no appreciation for them.[87] More specifically, "it pitted Reuchlin the humanist against Pfefferkorn and his supporters, the scholastic theologians of Cologne."[88] This implied that the study of ancient languages had priority over Aristotelian logic, which was a controversial assertion, but nowhere as controversial as the claim that Reuchlin was a Judaizer. Pfefferkorn and the Dominicans fought an uphill battle to portray themselves as the champions of orthodoxy fighting judaizing heretics because large segments of the intellectual establishment thought humanistic letters more palatable than scholasticism, which they disdained as moribund.

Reuchlin's strategy was apparent from the opening lines of his *Defensio Contra calumniatores suos Colonienses*: "their speech is rustic and barbarous; they are inexperienced in the Latin language and disgusted with humanistic studies."[89] Reuchlin launched an *ad hominem* attack on Pfefferkorn as someone "who is ignorant of theology and law, inexperienced in literature, and knowing no book written in the Latin language."[90] Although Pfefferkorn knew no Latin, his knowledge of Hebrew was superior to Reuchlin's, a charge Reuchlin attempted to deflect by saying Pfefferkorn, who was "equipped only with some childish, trite Jewish stuff undertook to write against me and published a slanderous book in German, full of invented charges."[91] That "trite Jewish stuff," though, was not insignificant: the discussion began as a dispute over the content of books written in Hebrew, books Reuchlin had apparently not read. Pfefferkorn then raised the bigger question, which echoed unresolved throughout the Realist vs. Nominalist debate since before Huss: "Learning," Pfefferkorn replied, "is no defense against the charge of depravity. All the heretics are proof of this, for they were always the most learned men."[92]

As an integral part of his *ad hominem* attack on Pfefferkorn, Reuchlin rolled out one racial slur after another, referring to Pfefferkorn as "that Jew sprinkled with water."[93] Reuchlin and his humanist allies routinely referred to Pfefferkorn as the "*tauf iud*," a slur that simultaneously maligned Jews and the sacrament of baptism. The frequency of this slur indicated that the rise of racism in Europe and the decline of the Catholic faith, specifically skepticism about the efficacy of the sacraments, were one and the same thing. Gone were the days when the howling mob would chase the Jew to the baptismal font and then let him walk away unharmed through the very same mob, like Moses dry-shod through the Red Sea, after becoming a Christian.

Willibald Pirckheimer came to Reuchlin's defense in 1517, about the time Luther nailed his theses to the door in Wittenberg. An initial supporter of the Reformed cause, Pirckheimer became quickly disillusioned with Luther's ruthless politics and the pillaging of the monasteries for political gain; he returned to the Catholic faith. In defending Reuchlin, Pirckheimer mounted an attack on Pfefferkorn by casting doubt on the efficacy of his baptism, and by extension the sacrament itself, which was suddenly powerless when faced with racial characteristics deeply ingrained in Jews. To strengthen his case, Pirckheimer referred to recent events in Spain, which

> will serve as a warning to us not to trust in extemporized and feigned conversions. It would have been much better for the so-called marranos to stay with their native perfidy than to simulate true religion and be Judaizers in secret. For we had several examples of what we can expect from these inveterate sinners who have been badly converted. The emperor ... wanted to indicate that converted Jews have as much in common with pious Christians as mice with cats.[94]

The humanists cheerfully joined forces to promote similar racial views. Pirckheimer is outraged that Pfefferkorn referred to Reuchlin as a "semi-Jew," but his outrage is purely racial. To Pirckheimer, the Jew is a function of his biology; and in this he agrees with the Jews who reminded Christ they were "*sperma Abraamu*." Pfefferkorn, though, innocently represented the traditional Catholic position by claiming that biology was irrelevant. The real issue, which the humanists tried to obfuscate and ignore, is that Reuchlin was a "demi-Jew" because of his judaizing positions, not because of his DNA. The humanists, prey to the racism that had just reared its ugly head, chose not to see things that way.

"Reuchlin's numerous friends," Graetz writes, referring indirectly to Pirckheimer, "were indignant at the insolence of a baptized Jew, who pretended to be more sound in faith than a born Christian in good standing."[95] Graetz's refusal to see the term "baptized Jew" as something of a contradiction in terms demonstrates that he shared the racial prejudices of the humanist establishment. Erasmus said of Pfefferkorn that "he could not have done a greater service to his fellow believers [sic, i.e., the Jews], than by making use of the hypocritical ruse of becoming a Christian in order to betray Christianity."⁹⁶ "This half Jew," Erasmus continued, "has done more damage to Christianity, than the whole pack of Jews together."⁹⁷ Pfefferkorn was theologically correct to refer to Reuchlin as a "half-Jew" because of Reuchlin's judaizing, but Erasmus was guilty of nothing but racism when he leveled the same accusation against Pfefferkorn. He too was casting aspersions on the efficacy of the sacrament of baptism. "Now that he has put on the mask of the Christian, he truly plays the Jew. Now at last he is true to his race. They have slandered Christ, but Christ [sic, not] only. He raves against many upright men of proven virtue and learning."⁹⁸ This muddled racist thinking indicated a precipitous decline in the faith of the sort that would become manifest when the Reformation broke out a few years later.

In a letter to Pirckheimer, Erasmus said Pfefferkorn's actions show he is "a Jew and a half whom no kind of misdeed could make worse than he already is."⁹⁹ Erasmus then adds rash judgment to his offenses against Pfefferkorn, intimating Pfefferkorn "chose to be baptized for no other reason than to be in a better position to destroy Christianity, and by mixing with us, infect the whole people with his Jewish poison. For what harm could he have inflicted, if he had remained a Jew? But now that he has put on the mask of the Christian, he truly plays the Jew. Now at last he is true to his race."¹⁰⁰ The irony of intellectual lights like Erasmus supporting anti-Semitic Christian Judaizers was not lost on Pfefferkorn, the orthodox Jewish convert, and it saddened him.

Reuchlin continued his racial attack on Pfefferkorn throughout *Augenspiegel*, feigning outrage at how "that Jew, baptized with water, rose up in the church, a married layman before the congregation of faithful, that is, before the assembled church and preached about the word of God and the Christian faith in an authoritative manner, he—a butcher and an ignoramus—blessed the people with the sign of the Cross."¹⁰¹ Reuchlin's reference to Pfefferkorn as a "butcher" shows his familiarity with the slanders the Regensburg Jews had promoted against Pfefferkorn. The reference also shows that he was not averse to stooping to their level.

One commentator noticed "the irony inherent in the fact that [the Cologne Dominicans] supported Pfefferkorn, an ethnic Jew, while manifesting paranoid fear of all things Jewish."¹⁰² But the irony is illusory: there is no contradiction. The Dominicans believed in the sincerity of Pfefferkorn's conversion, and as a result did not consider him a Jew. The humanists, though, had no qualms about casting aspersions on the efficacy of the sacrament of baptism, engaging in racial slurs, and throwing their lot wholeheartedly in with a Judaizer.

After Hoogstraten demanded that Reuchlin appear before the Tribunal in Mainz, Reuchlin panicked and tried to get the trial moved to the more sympathetic papal court at Speyer. He wrote in Hebrew to Bonet de Lates, the pope's Jewish physician, asking him, who "moves daily in the private chambers of the pope and whose body is in his care,"[103] to influence the pontiff to remove the case from the jurisdiction of the Dominicans at Mainz. Both Geiger and Graetz consider the letter conclusive evidence that proves Reuchlin conspired with the Jews. "Had the Cologne contingent read the letter," writes Geiger, the milder and less ideological of the two Jewish historians, "then they would have had fresh ammunition added to their charge that Reuchlin was a Judaizer, because Reuchlin was even more fawning toward Bonet de Lates than the usual Hebrew epistolary style demanded. No German Christian had ever written to a Jew in terms like this before."[104] Reuchlin added that he had defended the usefulness of the Jews' books and so had drawn the hatred of the Cologne crowd. Reuchlin ended by saying that he did not fear a papal verdict, only being dragged into a court under the influence of the Dominicans.

Graetz confirms that Reuchlin had "secret intercourse with the rabbis."[105] He cites Reuchlin's letter in Hebrew to Bonet de Lates as an attempt "to win over Leo X so that the trial might not take place in Cologne or its vicinity, where his cause would be lost."[106] Reuchlin told Bonet de Lates in great detail "how only his extraordinary efforts had saved the Talmud from destruction" in a particularly damning fashion, even to someone like Graetz, who was heavily prejudiced in his favor. "Had the Dominicans been able to get a hold of and read this letter," Graetz says, "they could have brought forward incontestable proof of Reuchlin's friendliness towards the Jews, *for in it he wrote much that he had publicly denied.*"[107] Reuchlin, in other words, used his position on the commission to advance the cause of the Jews, and now he was citing this service in his letter to the pope's Jewish physician, and asking for payment—if not in money, then certainly in services. Given this frank demand for *quid pro quo*, Graetz finds it "natural that Bonet de Lates brought all his influence to bear in favor of Reuchlin."[108]

Bonet de Lates must have been especially effective. Reuchlin's case was transferred to the Bishop of Speyer in November 1513, and there Hoogstraten lost his case the following April. All charges of heresy against Reuchlin were dismissed; Hoogstraten was found guilty of slander and ordered to pay a fine or face excommunication. The Dominicans raged when the judgment was announced. When the verdict was announced in Cologne, Pfefferkorn ripped it from the wall and tore it into pieces.

Shortly after the verdict, Pfefferkorn responded with another pamphlet, *Sturm Glock* or Storm Warning or Storm Bell. In it, Pfefferkorn referred with retrospective satisfaction to the condemnation of *Augenspiegel* issued by the theology department of the University of Paris. He also left no doubt about the magnitude of the danger for the entire church that Reuchlin represented as the head of a new heretical movement. Pfefferkorn claimed Reuchlin was a new Huss, encouraged and paid for by the Jews, whose followers could do more harm to the church than any external enemy. Reuchlin was the real demi-Jew. Reuchlin, the Judaizer, should be feared because from his movement would spill disorders that would make the Hussite wars of the 15th Century look like a picnic by comparison.[109]

In response to *Sturm Glock*, Reuchlin published a self-serving anthology of letters of support he had received entitled *Clarorum virorum epistolae, Letters of Famous Men*, in which he predicted that when the scholastic theologians were done with him, they would "gag all poets, one after another."[110] Other humanists embraced Reuchlin's interpretation and began a letter-writing campaign to mobilize public opinion against the Dominican theologians.

If the humanists had left it at that, Reuchlin would have gone down in history as one more pompous, self-serving academic, but the humanists felt the cause too important to be left in the hands of an academic plodder. In 1515, Reuchlin's supporters brought out one of the most successful satires in the history of European letters, the *Epistolae obscurorum virorum*, a 16th Century version of the *Screwtape Letters*, written in the pidgin Latin which the humanists loved to ascribe to their Scholastic opponents. Erasmus of Rotterdam, we are told, laughed so hard while reading the *Letters of Obscure Men* that an abscess of the throat that had plagued him burst, and he was cured of his ailment. The *Letters of Obscure Men* did for Reuchlin what the pompous plodder could not do for himself: the letters made him the victor in the first major publicity campaign since the invention of the printing press. The *Letters of Obscure Men* also marked the beginning of the transition from the Humanist/Scholastic controversy to the Reformation.

Some claimed "the Jewish question" was not central to the *Letters of Obscure Men* and that its main purpose was to lampoon Scholastic dialectics as an outmoded relic of the dark ages, but the book's opening shot was directed at the Church's directives against Jews, in particular the Fourth Lateran Council measures to segregate Jews from Christians. "By the love of God!" Rubeanus wrote under the name Ortwin Gratius, the Cologne Dominican who was one of Pfefferkorn's most stalwart defenders. "What are you doing? Those fellows are Jews, and you have taken off your cap to them!"[111] Pseudo-Gratius grapples with whether he sinned by greeting Jews as if they were Christians. "For if I had known that they were Jews and had nevertheless taken off my cap, then I would deserve to be burned at the stake for heresy. But, heaven knows, I had no idea from anything they said or did that they were Jews. I thought they were Doctors."[112] To calm his conscience, Gratius confesses, "But when I went to confession in the Dominican monastery, the confessor told me that the sin was mortal because we must always be on guard, and he told me he could not have absolved me, if he did not have an episcopal license, for it was a case for the bishop."[113] Gratius is finally absolved when he finds a confessor with "an episcopal license."

Pseudo-Gratius then moves on to the weightier theological issue of whether "when a Jew becomes a Christian, his foreskin, the part of his member that is cut off at birth according to the Jewish law, grows back."[114] He can't ask his fellow Dominicans because "they themselves are sometimes defective in that part," and so Gratius resolves "to establish the truth of this matter once and for all by asking Herr Pfefferkorn's wife."[115] Gratius made the mistake of responding to this fraternity house humor with a book of his own, *Lamentations of Obscure Men* (1518), but it had few readers and little impact other than to ensure that the book he attacked would remain in print for the next four centuries. A second edition of the *Letters of Obscure Men* appeared in 1516 with an appendix of seven new letters. The primary author of the additional material was Ulrich von Hutten, a talented poet and satirist. Emperor Maximillian crowned him poet laureate in 1517. An early supporter of Luther, he was prepared to use violence to assure the success of the Reformation. Hutten persuaded the equally volatile Franz von Sickingen to take part in the Pfaffenkrieg (the war against the priests), where the latter died in battle. Hutten then fled to the area around Basel and Zuerich, where he died of syphilis in 1523, just as the Peasant Revolt was getting underway. Graetz refers to Ulrich von Hutten, in spite of his syphilis, as "the most energetic and virile character of the time" because he "was most eager to bring about the downfall of ecclesiastic domination in Germany."[116]

Graetz says the humanists had become "virtually a society" united behind the cause of Reuchlin in Western Europe "which silently worked for one another and Reuchlin."[117] It was "a struggle of the dark Middle Ages with the dawn of the better time" whose goal was "to destroy the Dominicans, priests and bigots and establish the kingdom of intellect and free thought, to deliver Germany from the nightmare of ecclesiastical superstition and barbarism, raise it from its abjectness and make it the arbiter of Europe."[118] With this goal in mind, the Reuchlin faction "involuntarily ... became friends of the Jews and sought grounds on which to defend them." "Prominent Jews," likewise, "were working in Rome for Reuchlin, but, like the German Jews, they had the good sense to keep in the background so as not to imperil the cause by stamping it as Jewish."[119]

In July 1516 the majority of the commissioners confirmed the Speyer judgment acquitting Reuchlin. Formally, however, the decision was in the pope's hands. In a diplomatic move, he suspended proceedings, depriving Reuchlin of a clear victory but also frustrating Hoogstraten, who remained in Rome for another year before returning to Cologne in the spring of 1517. The situation was generally interpreted as a moral victory for Reuchlin, but by the time Hoogstraten returned from Rome, the Germanies had other things to think about. Luther had posted his 97 theses in Wittenberg and within seven years the empire's southern German speaking lands would witness a revolution so modern in form that the Communists of the 20th Century claimed it as their own.

Graetz thinks the Catholic Church was fatally undermined by the ridicule in the *Letters of Obscure Men*. The Church could not defend itself because "the whole tyranny of the hierarchy and the church" had been "laid bare. For, were not the Dominicans, with their insolent ignorance and shameless vices, the product and natural effect of the Catholic order and institution? So the satire worked like a corroding acid, entirely destroying the already rotting body of the Catholic Church."[120]

Graetz agrees with Erasmus that the legitimacy of the Church was also undermined by the rehabilitation of the Talmud. According to Graetz, "The discussion aroused by the Talmud created an intellectual medium favorable to the germination and growth of Luther's reform movement."[121] Erasmus supported the study of languages, including Hebrew, as a salutary antidote to Scholastic nit-picking, but he feared, nonetheless, that enthusiasm for language studies would create neo-pagan and Judaizing movements in the Church.

Graetz best explains Reuchlin's ambivalent attitude toward the Jews and things Jewish when he says that Reuchlin spared the Talmud because of "his foolish fondness for the secret doctrine" it contained.[122] Graetz is referring specifically to Reuchlin's "love for the secret doctrine" of the Caballah, which he derived from "the most confused source of information," what Graetz refers to as "the foolish writings of the Kabbalist, Joseph Jikatilla, of Castile, which the convert Paul Reccio had lately translated into Latin": "Out of love for this secret doctrine, supposed to offer the key to the deepest knowledge of philosophy and Christianity, Reuchlin had wished to spare the Talmud because in his opinion it contained mystical elements."[123] Graetz can't quite bring himself to say it, but Reuchlin, the forerunner of the Enlightenment, spared the Jewish books because he wanted to learn magic from them. Graetz, who usually scorns the mumbo-jumbo of the Caballah, defends it in the case of Reuchlin because of the damage that Reuchlin and his "fondness for secret doctrine" did to the Church.

Willibald Pirckheimer, who spent time among the Reformed party before returning to the faith, identified himself as a friend of both Erasmus and Reuchlin. In 1517, he wrote a letter defending Reuchlin against the charge of bribery. "They," Pirckheimer writes, referring to Reuchlin's detractors, "are saying that he extorted gold from the Jews and was not ashamed to write many perverted things to do them a favor."[124] Pirckheimer defends Reuchlin in a series of rhetorical questions:

> What would have impelled such a Christian man to commit so great a crime, deigning to prefer the friendship of the Jews to faith and truth? Love for the Jews? Then he would indeed deserve to be hated.... What could have motivated him then to prefer the friendship of the Jews to the truth? They rightly ask what advantage, what wealth might have served as inducements that he should be so blinded by cupidity. After all, he is a man of advanced years, who has already enjoyed positions of honor, who was born from Christian parents—why then would be venture on such a shameful deed?[125]

Pirckheimer dismisses the possibility of a bribe because "the Jews in their innate avarice would not part with a great deal of money, and little would do him no good."[126] Pirckheimer might have changed his argument had he known that Jonathan Levi Zion was willing to spend 100 Gulden, in addition to an unspecified down payment, to bribe the Margrave of Baden. "Innate avarice" and bribery are not mutually exclusive. Jonathan Levi Zion mentioned Reuchlin's appointment to the commission in the same letter in which he brags about bribing the Margrave of Baden, but that is as far as the documentation takes us. Even if he took money from the Jews, the real reason for Reuchlin's defense of Jewish books was not money but Gnosis. Reuchlin wanted to become a magus, and the only way to that end was through the Caballah.

Reuchlin was a Judaizer, but he was certainly not a philo-Semite, which Graetz brings out in spite of his praise for Reuchlin. Reuchlin, according to Graetz,

> looked on the Jewish people as utterly barbarous, devoid of all artistic taste, superstitious, mean and depraved. He solemnly declared that he was far from favoring the Jews. Like his patron, Jerome, he testified to his thoroughgoing hatred of them.... Reuchlin no less than Pfefferkorn, charged the Jews with blasphemy against Jesus, Mary, the apostles and Christians in general; but a time came when he regretted the indiscreet lucubrations of his youth. For his heart did not share the prejudices of his head.[127]

The source of Reuchlin's ambivalence was his infatuation with the Caballah. Reuchlin, according to Geiger, was drawn willy nilly into a relationship with the Jewish people, "because of the time he had spent studying the Hebrew language." Reuchlin was soon "beset on all sides with the accusation that the Jewish scriptures had taken root in his heart and turned him into a Judaizer."[128] Geiger feels that charge unfounded because of Reuchlin's antipathy to the Jews. But Reuchlin also respected the Jews because they had preserved the Bible. The fact that his opponent was a baptized Jew only confirmed Reuchlin in his racial animus against Pfefferkorn's heritage. He wasn't unprejudiced enough to attribute the errors of his enemy to one man; he had to ascribe them to the entire race from whence he came.

Geiger's confusion is easily resolved. Reuchlin was both a Judaizer and an anti-Semite. Rummel feels Reuchlin reshaped the conflict into the humanist vs. scholastic debate as a kind of plea bargaining because he recognized, with the Dominican inquisitor at his heels and recent Spanish history fresh in his mind, that Judaizing was a charge that needed to be taken seriously and quashed quickly by shifting the debate. Reuchlin had reason to be fearful because

> the researches that had made him a paragon in the eyes of humanists also made him vulnerable to the charges of Judaism. His *Rudiments of Hebrew* (1506), a combination of grammar and lexicon, contained criticism of the traditional Vulgate text which was bound to raise the hackles of scholastic theologians. He had noticed discrepancies between the Hebrew text and the Vulgate translation, declaring that the translation was inferior, the translator "dreaming" or "blathering." In many cases he suggested improvements that were not merely idiomatic but changed the meaning.... By engaging in scriptural studies, Reuchlin was therefore entering dangerous territory.[129]

Part of Geiger's confusion stems from his refusal to look squarely at Reuchlin's rehabilitation of magic. Geiger, like Graetz, was a German Jew and devotee of the Enlightenment. Both men wanted to portray Reuchlin as a forerunner of the Enlightenment rather than what he was, namely, an enthusiastic supporter of Jewish magic. When Geiger said Reuchlin knew nothing about magic, he meant to say that he himself apparently wanted Reuchlin to know nothing about it because it ruined his portrayal of Reuchlin as the disinterested Enlightenment scholar. Reuchlin's ideas, Zika says, "can only be adequately understood as part of the occult tradition of the Renaissance.... This system promised new sources of knowledge and power, not through reason, but rather through magic, astrology, hermetic and gnostic thought, Cabballah and Alchemy."[130]

Geiger claims Pico was interested in the writings of Plato, but what really fascinated Pico were the later neoplatonic texts, and what neoplatonism and Caballah had in common was gnosticism and magic. There is no Greek-Hebrew dichotomy. Pico was as avid to learn from the Hebrews as Reuchlin. He was not afraid to avail himself of Jewish teachers like Eliah del Medigo (a.k.a. Eliah Cretensis), Jehuda or Leo Abarbanel, and Jochanan Aleman, who taught him Hebrew and Caballah. Pico claimed he could derive from the Caballah proof for Christian teachings like the Incarnation of the Word, the arrival of the Messiah, and original sin. But his main interest was magic. Pico could start by studying the Chaldean and Pythagorean writers, but in the cases of Pythagoras and Moses, the written text wasn't sufficient. To get to the meat of the magic tradition, one needed the oral tradition through the Caballah and the Hebrew language. Pico claimed he used Caballah as an apologetic tool: "No science gives us more certainty about the divinity of Christ than Caballah and magic."[131] But this claim was most likely intended to placate the still dangerous and ever wary Inquisition. Reuchlin put the lessons he learned from Pico to good use in dealing with the Cologne Dominicans, assuring his critics that by magic he meant "the knowledge of the properties of the heavenly bodies."[132] The magic Reuchlin proposed was not the "forbidden art" found repugnant in others. It was, as Pico had indicated, a tool for Christian apologetics: "Caballah provides the weapon of choice against the Jews, who of course in their own way honor the Caballah but without having real insight into it."[133]

Pico convinced Reuchlin of the congruence between Pythagoras and the Caballah. What was the goal of each school? Nothing less than raising the human spirit to the level of God, to promote in him complete happiness.[134] "The cabalist adept can enjoy the happiness of the blessed *in this life*."[135] Unlike Zelivsky and the Hussites, who sought heaven on earth with the sword, Reuchlin sought it through esoteric knowledge or practical Caballah, *i.e.*, magic. Whatever the means, the end was the same. The attraction which caballistic judaizing exerted over Reuchlin was the desire for heaven on earth.

The best defense being a good offense, Reuchlin published a book affirming his love of the Caballah in 1517 at the height of his controversy with Pfefferkorn and the Dominicans. Reuchlin's *De arte caballistica* was dedicated to Pope Leo X. Reuchlin tried to establish the intellectual *bona fides* of caballistic studies by associating them with Lorenzo de Medici, father of Leo X and patron of Ficino and

Pico. "Your father," Reuchlin wrote in his dedication, "sowed the seeds of universal ancient philosophy which are now growing to maturity under your reign."[136] Reuchlin planned to build on the work of Lorenzo, Ficino, and Pico to "exhibit to the Germans a reborn Pythagoras, dedicated to your name."[137] However, he can only begin this monumental task by making use of Caballah, "for the Pythagorean philosophy has its origin in it, and with the memory of the roots being lost, it entered the books of the cabalists again via Greater Greece.... I have therefore written of the symbolic philosophy of the art of the Caballah to make Pythagorean teaching better known to scholars. But in all this I myself make no assertions; I merely recount the opinions of a third party. They are non-Christians; the Jew Simon, an experienced cabalist, who is on his way to Frankfurt, meets at an inn on the way a Pythagorean by the name of Philolaus the Younger and a Muslim by the name of Marranus."[138]

In his "*Teutsch missive*," Reuchlin claimed "only the learned Jew, who was practiced and experienced in the holy art known as Caballah," could understand sacred mysteries.[139] As a result of Reuchlin's book, Pope Leo X encouraged the publication of the same book that his predecessor Gregory IX had ordered burned. Times had indeed changed since Penaforte introduced the Jewish convert Donin to Pope Gregory IX. The Dominicans of Cologne remained true to their traditions and gave unwavering support to Pfefferkorn, but the Medici popes no longer held the position of Innocent III and Gregory IX.

De verbo mirifico marked Reuchlin's immersion in the depths of the Caballah, but his Hebrew studies were only the means to a greater end. When he published *De arte caballistica* in 1517, the controversy was winding down, and getting subsumed into the tumult of the Reformation. *De arte caballistica* is another dialogue between three men: a Jew, Simon, a Muslim, Marranus, and the Pythagorean Philolaus. The participants meet at the house of the Jew, who compares the discovery of the Caballah with the discovery of the magic herb Moly. Both can accomplish wonders; both are like a Jacob's ladder that unites heaven and earth, or creates a heaven on earth. "If you have found it," Simon says referring to Moly, "you seem to be freed from all misery." This magic herb is, next to the Caballah, "the Jacob's ladder, the golden chain or cord. This ladder stretches from the superheavenly world down to earth, and on it man ascends step by step from one level to another, just like the golden chain of Homer."[140] The key linking heaven and earth is the Hebrew names of the angels. Since the angels move the heavenly bodies, they can be ordered or beseeched to create wonders on earth. Magic is the word of God, but not in the sense that the Gospel is the word of God. We are talking about something more primitive. The word of God is literally the Hebrew tongue. Reuchlin quotes Pico: "each voice which has the power of magic in it, has it only insofar as it is formed by the word of God, only insofar as it has within it the power to exert original natural magical effects which come from the voice of God."[141] Simon the Jew informs his interlocutors "those who have mastered the Caballah give great honor to the 72 angels' names, and through them bring about wonderful things, more wonderful than I am permitted to describe."[142] The circular movement of the stars and planets is attributable to angels who move them, not to natural causes Unusual motions in the heavens are attributable to the angels' free will.

Reuchlin is thus trying to use the Caballah as a bridge between God and man. Once he created this system, a new concept of religion would arise concentrated on becoming one with God through attainment of divine wisdom, which resembled Gnosis, activated through incantation and ritual. With the recovery of the Pythagorean-Cabalistic tradition, man has spectacular new powers that can work wonders and create a heaven on earth. In Reuchlin's system, man is no longer the pathetic suffering creature who finds in the Cross the best symbol of his life on earth; he now has the power to order angels, through the medium of theurgic Hebrew spells, to work wonders for him. Gnosis and magic give man the coercive power God exerts over nature. In studying the Caballah, and especially by learning the names of the angels who run the universe, Reuchlin attempts to achieve that gnostic mastery without falling into the trap of trafficking in fallen spirits. His system was an early conflation of magic and science that was doomed to failure. But it was a failure he could not see because the Hebrew scripture and the judaizing promises of heaven on earth that went with it blinded him.

De arte caballistica confirmed the suspicions of Pfefferkorn and the Dominicans. Everything the *viri obscuri* had been saying about Reuchlin's judaizing was now confirmed in his own words. In 1519, Hoogstraten published "Destructio Cabalae," the counter-attack that exposed the agenda behind Reuchlin's actions. *The Destruction of the Caballah* stressed the scholastic method, which, Hoogstraten said, "was the principal tool in the search for doctrinal truth.... Aspects of the faith which were not explicit in scripture or the apostolic tradition depended on deductive reasoning, that is, on the use of the logical argumentation characteristic of scholastic theology."[143] Hoogstraten effectively rebutted Humanists like Pirckheimer, who claimed the "true theologian ... must understand Hebrew ... because all the mysteries of the Old and New Testament are hidden in it."[144]

In *De verbo mirifico*, Reuchlin's first attempt to rehabilitate Caballistic magic, Reuchlin had spoken as Capnion, the Greek form of his own name. In *De arte cabalistica* he speaks under a name that Hoogstraten finds especially telling. He calls himself Marranus, a play on the word Marrano, "the name of a man who on the surface proclaims his allegiance to one set of behavior, ceremony and teaching, but who inwardly practices something else."[145] Under the name Marranus, Reuchlin could praise Jewish perfidy and subvert Christian teaching, something hard to justify if he were a true Christian. By making Marranus his mouthpiece, Hoogstraten argued, Reuchlin was admitting publicly, albeit cryptically, his role as a judaizing subversive. By describing the Caballah as the "first revelation," which "Adam received after the Fall," Reuchlin undermined authentic scripture, and by making knowledge of the Caballah the *sine qua non* of theology, Reuchlin undermined both sacred and secular science.

Hoogstraten wasn't the only one who accused Reuchlin of using the Jewish Caballah to promote blasphemy and magic. The Jesuit Martin del Rio leveled precisely those charges, following the lead of Pedro Ciruello. Thomas Erastus condemned the book's advocacy of "repugnant magic."[146] Reuchlin lent credence to their charges by promoting a talisman, which he described in his book. On one side of the medal, Reuchlin prescribed the wonder-working Tetragrammaton IHSUH along with the seven astrological signs, and on the other side a star of David and various Hebrew signs. Reuchlin's recommendation of a standard instrument of Jewish magic was proof of his intention and his inspiration.

But by 1519, Germany had other things on its mind. Luther's actions and the rise of the Reformation destroyed whatever unity the "humanist" anti-Pfefferkorn/Dominican forces possessed. Luther was outspoken in his denunciation of caballistic foolishness. Even though he was a friend of and avid correspondent with Reuchlin, Erasmus was of the same opinion when it came to Caballah.

Although Reuchlin thwarted Pfefferkorn's plans to burn the Talmud, Pfefferkorn and the Dominicans thwarted Reuchlin's plan to spread the Caballah. Reuchlin's cover was blown when he was placed on the commission and had to defend the Jewish books he found repugnant (as well as the repugnant Jews) to prevent destruction of the newly emerging esoteric science that was mankind's new hope. As we have seen, Jakob Hoogstraten wrote *Destructio Cabalae* in 1519 as a warning to others, once he recognized the true magnitude of what Reuchlin was proposing. In his attack on the Caballah, Hoogstraten portrayed Reuchlin as a man who had acquired fame but brought forth only abuse and heresy, a man who falsified scripture, as well as Aristotle, Jerome and Dionysius, in the service of his occult theories.

Reuchlin was no philo-Semite, but he was a Judaizer. He was interested in Hebrew for the access that it gave him to occult science. Reuchlin restated Pico's thesis in the *Augenspiegel*: No art gave more certainty about divine things than Magic and Caballah.[147] Christianity enabled Reuchlin to derive from the Caballah a universal esoteric science which incorporated pagan, Jewish, and Christian elements, but once that esoteric science was derived it threatened to replace Christianity as the true religion. Reuchlin had proposed just this sort of syncretistic secret wisdom in *De verbo mirifico*.

Within a year of the appearance of Reuchlin's second book on the Caballah, Daniel Bomberg brought out the first complete edition of the Babylonian Talmud. Graetz describes a French pantomime in which a doctor with the name Capnion, Reuchlin's nickname, written on his back drops a bundle of sticks on the stage and departs. Another figure with the name Erasmus appears, tries in vain to ignite the sticks, and then departs. Luther succeeds, but after him the pope arrives and pours oil on the fire, making it bigger than ever. "Pfefferkorn and the Talmud," Graetz concludes, "should not have been missing in this dumb show, for they were the fuse that started the conflagration" that came to be known as the Reformation.[148]

Catholic writers like John Eck concurred, holding Reuchlin indirectly responsible for the *Letters of Obscure Men* as well as for Luther, thus establishing a connection between Reuchlin and the beginning of the Reformation. They also claimed that without the Jews, Martin Luther never would have come to the fore. The idea of Luther as the father of the Jews made its debut long before John Eck coined the term "Judenvater Luther."[149]

After 1519, most Reuchlinists became Lutherans. Erasmus, though, wrote to Reuchlin saying he regretted the Lutheran tragedy and had always tried to separate Reuchlin's cause from Luther's, an admission that shows how closely they were related in everyone's mind. Unlike Erasmus, who would become his opponent in a dispute over free will, Luther tried to link Reuchlin's cause to his own. Luther's supporters did likewise. Ulrich von Hutten wrote to Erasmus, pleading with him not to attack Luther in public thereby jeopardizing the cause of anti-Scholasticism. The Reformers should keep a united front in public, no matter what they thought privately. Hutten also wrote to Reuchlin reminding him "Even if your stated disapproval of Luther could rescue you from them, you cannot regard it as honest to oppose his party, when you see that men who belong to it whom you must always support in a respectable cause, unless you want to be the most ungrateful man of all."[150]

Maximillian I, who gave Pfefferkorn the mandate to seize Jewish books, died in 1519. In May 1520, the papal court rendered the final verdict in the Reuchlin case: the acquittal was overturned, and Reuchlin was obliged to pay the court costs. In June 1520 Leo X signed the bull *Exsurge Domine* threatening Luther with excommunication. Reuchlin's scholarly reputation remained unimpaired, however. He accepted a position at the University of Tuebingen, where he taught Greek and Hebrew until his death in 1522. It is unknown whether Reuchlin paid the fine before he died. Maximillian's successor was Charles V, during whose reign the flame that Reuchlin kindled and Luther fanned to grew into a raging inferno in which "the Talmud and the Reformation, were merged into each other."[151]

Pfefferkorn passed from the scene in 1521, one year before Reuchlin. In his unofficial last will and testament, *Ein mitleidliche Clag*, he held Reuchlin responsible for the revolutionary disorder sweeping Germany. Like the Jews, Reuchlin was a threat to the inner peace of the Germanies; the disorders which followed his judaizing could be construed as divine punishment, because "you have stolen God's honor and his good name, to cover up what you were doing with the Jews and the devil. Because of that you are not worthy to eat bread with dogs, much less consider yourself a member of the body of Christ. Instead you should take up your abode under the naked sky. Drawn and quartered on four stakes hammered into the ground; that would be your just deserts."[152]

Yet, even though another revolutionary movement took its place on the main stage of history, the occult tradition continued on the foundation Pico and Reuchlin had established. Cornelius Agrippa of Nettesheim published his ruminations on magic in 1533 as *De occulta philosophia*, inspired by Reuchlin's *De verbo mirifico*. Agrippa abandoned Reuchlin's professions of orthodoxy, returning instead to the medieval tradition of magic Reuchlin abhorred and repudiated. When Agrippa's book appeared, Reuchlin had been dead for 11 years. Gradually, people like Erasmus pulled back from their erstwhile allies in the fight against the *viri obscuri*, largely because they feared that magic, the occult, and its rituals threatened to "judaize" Christianity."[153] Ultimately, Reuchlin was no humanist, but by the time Erasmus recognized that fact, it was too late to stop what Erasmus had unwittingly promoted.

John Dee, Elizabeth's astrologer, helped spread the Caballah and its occult practices to England, but it was only in the 17th Century that Caballah studies were pursued with zeal. In England the enthusiasm for Caballah re-emerged on the other side of the Reformation as Freemasonry. Albert Pike traces Freemasonry to 1717. William Thomas Walsh claims it existed at the time of Elizabeth, who stumbled upon the first lodges and made a deal with the Masons: if they would initiate her into their secrets, she would allow their secret society to continue. By tracing Freemasonry to the Cecils and Elizabeth, Walsh links it with the judaizing anti-Catholic conspiracy that swept Germany in the wake of the Reuchlin/Pfefferkorn controversy.

Caballah and Freemasonry tend "toward spiritual perfection, and the fusion of the creeds and Nationalities of Mankind."[154] Freemasonry was linked with the Caballah, and Reuchlin had a place of honor in its annals. In his exoteric history of Freemasonry, *Morals and Dogma*, Albert Pike claims "All truly dogmatic religions have issued from the Kabalah and return to it; everything scientific and grand in the religious dreams of all the illuminati, Jacob Boehme, Swedenborg, Saint-Martin, and others, is borrowed from the Kabalah; all the Masonic associations owe to it their Secrets and their Symbols."[155] Pike echoes Reuchlin on the magical words of the Hebrew languages. Once the adept, presumably the higher degree Mason, penetrates "into the sanctuary of the Kabalah," he discovers

> The necessary union of ideas and signs, the consecration of the most fundamental realities by the primitive characters; the Trinity of Words, Letters, and Numbers; a philosophy simple as the alphabet, profound and infinite as the Word; theorems more complete and luminous than those of Pythagoras; a theology summed up by counting on one's fingers; an Infinite which can be held in the hollow of an infant's hand; ten ciphers, and twenty-two letters, a triangle, a square, and a circle,—these are all the elements of the Kabalah. These are the elementary principles of the written Word, reflection of that spoken Word that created the world![156]

Chapter Eight

Thomas Muentzer and the Peasant Revolt

On October 31, 1517, Martin Luther sent 95 objections to the Catholic Church's doctrine on indulgences to Archbishop Albrecht of Mainz. According to legend, he also nailed the theses to the door of the Schlosskirche in Wittenberg. If so, the act must have attracted considerable notice among students at the University of Wittenberg, one of whom was Thomas Muentzer. Muentzer, whose name was sometimes Latinized to Monetarius, probably came from a family of coin makers or mint masters. His academic career shows his family valued education and had the means to support him. Muentzer probably studied at the University of Leipzig in 1506, enrolled at the University at Frankfurt in 1512, and then arrived in Wittenberg in 1517, just as the drama known as the Reformation began to unfold.

Muentzer was ordained a priest in Halberstadt before 1514. In Wittenberg, he immediately became a member of the reformed party, made up largely of disaffected clergy who would soon rip half of Germany away from the Catholic Church. When he finally got around to condemning his former disciple in his letter to the princes of Saxony, Luther claimed that he had sat across a table from Muentzer in Luther's room in the Augustinian cloister and punched him in the nose.[1] Muentzer denied the claim,[2] but he certainly made contact with Luther, his ideas, and his followers in the tumultuous semesters of 1517-18.

In Wittenberg, Muentzer met Andreas Bodenstein, later known as Karlstadt, Luther's colleague on the theology faculty, who urged Muentzer to steep himself in the writings of St. Augustine. He also met Luther's superior, Schwarzerd, who like Erasmus, classicized his name by rendering it into Greek, Philipp Melanchthon, the name by which he became known as Luther's right-hand man. Muentzer corresponded extensively with Melanchthon on topics ranging from infant baptism to marriage for priests long after the choleric Luther refused to have anything to do with him. More importantly, Muentzer met Franz Guenther, to whom Luther had given the task of leading the attack on scholastic theology in his theological baccalaureate thesis *Contra scholasticam theologiam*. A fiery preacher, Guenther confronted Tetzel when he came to Wittenberg to sell indulgences. Soon the attack on indulgences was swept up into an attack on the Catholic faith with Guenther preaching "that we need not confess, because this is not commanded anywhere in the Scriptures ... that we do not need to fast, because Christ fasted for us ... that we should not call on the saints." The most brazen of Guenther's claims was, "the Bohemians are better Christians that we are."[3]

Guenther's praise for Hussite heretics was too much for the Franciscan Bernard Dappen, who informed the bishop of Brandenburg in his *Contra Lutheranos* that Guenther, who was "shamelessly preaching the repudiation of indulgences, advised the women who had brought these indulgences to use them to fasten flax to their distaffs—as spinners usually do—so that they had not spent the money all in vain."[4] The Franciscans claimed the focus on abuses surrounding the sale of indulgences was a pretext for rebellion against Rome and a desire to overthrow Roman Catholicism.

When Guenther tried the same sort of preaching in the neighboring town of Jueterborg, he got himself in trouble with the authorities there. After personally insulting the abbess of the Convent of St. Mary from the pulpit, Guenther was reprimanded by the bishop. Rather than defy the bishop, Guenther withdrew from the pulpit, and Muentzer took his place, probably at the recommendation of Martin Luther himself, arriving at the cloister church of St. Mary's during Easter week of 1519. Instead of toning down his rhetoric, Muentzer picked up where Guenther left off. Like Jan Zelivsky one hundred years earlier, Muentzer had an uncanny ability to rile people up and then mobilize them politically.

Muentzer's sermons soon plunged Jueterborg into even greater turmoil. Muentzer attacked the pope and said that a council should be convened every five years. Muentzer also attacked the scholastics, bragging in a way that would prove uncannily prophetic that if anyone could prove him wrong, he "deserved to have his head chopped off."[5] Scholastic arguments about the rational underpinnings of faith and grace were, according to Muentzer, "of the devil."[6] He also attacked bishops and monks, calling the latter "misleaders of the people."[7] In Jueterborg, Muentzer was known as the first officially designated Lutheran. Muentzer also preached that sacramental confession was unscriptural, that fasting and veneration of the saints were unnecessary, and that previous Church councils were meaningless. Dappen was especially alarmed because the population of Saxony and Thuringia had already been infected by the Hussite virus and were therefore especially susceptible to revolutionary incitement. "I am completely certain," Dappen wrote to his bishop, "that if a Waldensian or a teacher of the Bohemian heresy were to come to this place and promote his errors and claim that they were the gospel of Christ, that many would prick up their ears and listen eagerly."[8]

Given the reckless vehemence of his sermons, it is not surprising that Muentzer was banned from the pulpit, nor is it surprising that he was driven from Jueterborg in May 1519. Thereafter, he was driven from every town where he was assigned as a preacher until his death six years later. Because the revolutionaries had the apparatus of the Church at their disposal, Muentzer spent little time unemployed. After Jueterborg, he was appointed curate of the parsonage in Orlamuenda, a sinecure that allowed him to study in depth the mysticism of the German Johan Tauler, a 14th Century Dominican, and Heinrich Seuse. Kaspar Glatz, Muentzer's successor as pastor at Orlamuenda, would later say Muentzer was "corrupted"[9] by Tauler's teaching on the soul "which he never really understood."[10]

Muentzer had a profound understanding of the German mystical tradition because he had a profound understanding of the role suffering plays in the spiritual life. Commenting on Seuse's description of the angel with three pairs of wings in Ezekiel, Muentzer describes each as a representation of suffering that allows man to rise spiritually above his earthly condition. Suffering is to men what wings are to angels: "The three pairs of wings represent the following: "written on the first pair is 'accept suffering willingly.' On the second pair is written, 'Bear suffering patiently,' and on the third pair is written, "Learn to let suffering form you like Christ.""[11]

Unfortunately, Muentzer was never able to integrate his spirituality with his increasingly violent revolutionary politics. Muentzer's thought was a curious mixture of the Cross and the sword until spring 1525, when he abandoned the Cross for the "sword of Gideon," his term for judaizing and the Hussite penchant for armed revolution. "Bohemia," he said in a sermon on Easter Sunday 1519, "is the land in which John Huss was active."[12] Reform would come from Bohemia again because "the Bohemians are better Christians than we are."[13] According to Ebert, the link between Guenther, Muentzer, and Bohemia, was "the utopian and millennialist expectations of the Taborites, including their forms of community and production and even their military strategy."[14]

Many Reformers idolized HussWhen Luther disputed with Johannes Eck in June 1519, he was reproached for believing "John Huss and the Bohemians are genuine evangelical Christians, which the Church cannot condemn."[15] Knowing that support for Huss would get him in trouble, Luther nevertheless could only dispute the claim half-heartedly. Later, when Luther was more open about what he believed, he regularly referred to Huss as a saint. When Muentzer later made his pilgrimage to Prague, he referred to Huss as "beloved and holy fighter."[16]

Shortly after the defeat of the Hussite army at the Battle of Lipany, Friedrich Reiser returned to Germany and became the leader of the Hussite communities there. He was consecrated a Hussite bishop and created a secret society, the League of the Faithful, to get the German Hussites and Waldensians to rise in armed revolution. Reiser was burnt at the stake in Strasbourg in 1458, but the communities he founded continued their revolutionary work throughout the 15th Century. Hussite propaganda, according to one commentator was "a disturbing factor in the rather unstable political and social structure ... of southern Germany."[17] Macek claims "Hussitism struck roots in many places" in Germany[18] and "remained alive right up to the time of Luther and the German Peasant war."[19] In 1476, the shepherd and musician Hans Boheim (probably a variation on "Boehmen," which is to say, John the Bohemian) claimed the Blessed Mother appeared to him to announce that only in Niklashausen could one obtain full remission of sins. The Blessed Mother reputedly also told John the Bohemian, who was now known as the Whistler of Niklashausen, that the greed of the clergy was greater than that of the Jews and that the pope was a villain. The Blessed Mother told him all men were equal and no man should have more than any other. The message resonated with the peasants, presumably already corrupted by Taborite communism. Within months, thousands of peasants traveled to hear more of what the Blessed Mother was telling Boheim. Since no peasant could assemble without the permission of his lord, Boheim eventually was arrested. When Boheim's unarmed peasant supporters confronted the authorities over his arrest, the bishop's soldiers slaughtered them. Boheim was burned at the stake, singing Marian hymns in German until the flames suffocated him. For many historians, 1476 is considered the beginning of the Peasant Revolution.[20]

During the winter of 1519-20, Muentzer became confessor to the nuns at the convent at Beudiz, where his nominal duties again allowed ample time for study. In addition to reading the German mystics, Muentzer also purchased the Chronicles of Eusebius and the Jewish Wars by Josephus and the acts of the Council of Constance. His interest in the Council of Constance was understandable: Muentzer wanted to know more about the Church's condemnation of Huss. What he learned probably filled him with indignation. What Muentzer gleaned from reading about the Jews, in particular about their revolutionary activities in the classical world, is not as clear. Did he take the stories of Simon bar Kokhba and the Jewish revolutionaries at Masada as cautionary tales, a warning that those who lived by the sword would die by the sword? Probably not, for Muentzer lived and died by the sword. One of Muentzer's biographers says he pored over the acts of the Council of Constance to uncover the historical cause for the decline of the Church. More probably, Muentzer's promiscuous readings simply exacerbated his "existential bewilderment."[21] One biographer claims Muentzer "had not yet matured into the reformer who, in Manfred Bensing's opinion, began to see the Reformation as 'the fundamental remodeling of earthly life and hence as a revolution.'"[22]

Reading German mystics and classical accounts of Jewish revolutionaries could lead to no synthesis because they represented two poles of an irresolvable spiritual dichotomy represented by the sword on the one hand and the Cross on the other. The Cross symbolized the passive expiatory suffering of Christ that inaugurated the New Covenant and the thousand year reign of Christ on earth, whereby Christians conquered the Roman Empire by turning the other cheek, which is to say, by patient endurance in uniting their suffering with that of Christ. The sword symbolized the Jewish rejection of the suffering Christ and the choice of revolution instead. By taking up the sword, Jewish revolutionaries, and their judaizing Christian imitators, hoped to establish heaven on earth. The sword thus, one way or another, symbolized abandonment of the freedom of the gospel and return to the bondage of the law. Muentzer may have hoped to create a synthesis between German mystics and Jewish revolutionaries, but in doing this he ignored the scriptural admonition about sewing new patches on old garments. There was no way to reconcile the sword and the Cross.

After months of filling his mind with dangerous ideas, Muentzer complained to Franz Guenther about the isolation inherent in his position as confessor to a group of nuns in an out of the way convent. Muentzer longed to get back into the political disputes, and before long he got his wish. In May 1520, he became a substitute preacher at St. Mary's, the most important church in Zwickau, when its pastor, Johannes Sylvius Egranus, took a leave of absence to study with Erasmus in Rotterdam.

Astride the road connecting Leipzig with Augsburg and Nuremberg, Zwickau had grown famous for its cloth and beer, and prosperity soon followed bringing with it all the conflicts that would tear apart Christendom at the crucial divide between the late middle ages and the early modern era. The serious money in Zwickau, however, came from mining in the nearby Erzgebirge. When the Schneeberg silver mine went into production in the latter part of the 15th Century, the families who invested in it became fabulously wealthy. The metal-working artisans did well too, and the population of Zwickau doubled to 7,500, making it, behind Leipzig, the second largest town in the region. Frederick the Wise referred to Zwickau as the pearl of his realm. Having more silver than they knew what to do with—it often lay around in boxes waiting to be coined or worked into plate—brought problems. The families who grew rich through silver mining invested in the cloth business, stockpiling stores, and undermining the cloth producing guilds. Nikolaus Storch, a weaver, was one of the economic losers; he used his newfound time as an unemployed weaver to study the reformed gospel while becoming a leader of the town's disgruntled weavers. The miners were similarly unhappy. Soon both groups, falling under the influence of the nearby Bohemian Taborites, were spouting communist theories and engaging in riots and public disturbances.

There was no lack of Catholic social welfare agencies in the town, staffed by nuns, priests, brothers, and laymen who contributed to the town's vibrant social life. But the Church's social welfare apparatus could not keep up with increasing economic division between rich and poor, which fueled envy and resentment among those left behind. The increase in the money supply drove up prices. but wages did not keep pace. Once-prosperous weavers were out in the cold when the cloth industry was taken over by middle-men who warehoused the cloth and manipulated prices. The monasteries and convents that had accumulated land over the centuries remained wealthy while the weavers' fortunes declined. This caused envy and class conflict; it also induced people to join the monasteries for other than spiritual motives.

If the situation was the social equivalent of dry tinder, then Muentzer's nascent revolutionary theology and preaching was the match that set off the conflagration. He began his preaching in Zwickau with an inflammatory attack on the Franciscans. The monks, he said, had such fat mouths that you could cut a pound of meat from them and still have plenty left.[23] Egranus' return from Rotterdam did little to calm the situation; he was soon drawn into the conflict. Muentzer criticized Egranus as a humanist dilettante. Luther sided with Muentzer, calling Egranus a theological illiterate.[24]

Luther was having troubles of his own. In June 1520, Pope Leo X issued the bull *Exsurge domine* excommunicating Luther. At around the same time, Reuchlin's acquittal was overturned in Rome, handing victory to Pfefferkorn and the Dominicans. The tide was turning against the Reformers, whose leader, Luther, had grown a beard and gone into hiding under the name Junker Joerg.

Two months after his fat mouth sermon, Muentzer was still fighting with the Franciscans, which he dutifully reported in a letter to Luther. When not insulting monks, Muentzer kept insisting on a more "spiritual" Christianity, as opposed to the external rituals that were the cultural lifeblood of the town. Muentzer had the annoying habit of ascribing to God the effects of his intemperate sermons and reckless behavior: "It is not my work," he said repeatedly, "that I am doing, but that of the Lord."[25] His inflammatory words soon led to violence. The cloth-workers were emboldened by his preaching and took their demands to the town council. Local artisans attacked followers of the anti-Reformation pastor Nikolaus Hofer, pelting them with mud and animal dung, driving them from town. Evidently gratified by the results, Muentzer redoubled his attacks on "the godless clergy," *i.e.*, the mendicants and those who supported Rome and its liturgical system.

By October 1520, the situation had become intolerable. The secular and ecclesial authorities sought to remove Muentzer from the pulpit at St. Mary's. The move backfired when Muentzer took up residence at the working class parish of St. Catherine's, where he made alliance with the town's weavers, the backbone of the revolutionary movement in Zwickau. Clothmaking and dyeing was Europe's first industry, and, fittingly enough, the clothmakers' guilds constituted Europe's first revolutionary proletarian *avant garde*, beginning in the low countries in the high middle ages, through the Peasant Revolt and the Anabaptist commune in Muenster, and continuing to the essentially Puritan theocracy in England. When Muentzer made contact with the weavers, his revolutionary fervor increased. Crucial to Muentzer's formation as a revolutionary was the déclassé weaver Nicholas Storch, who led a group, the Zwickau Prophets, at the revolutionary heart of the weavers' guild. It is impossible to say who had greater influence on whom. Muentzer was never an avid proponent of Luther's *sola scriptura*, which he later derided as relying too greatly on the dead letter of the law. Unlike Luther, Storch was the prime example of the living word of God because he had direct revelations from God in dreams and visions. Some claim Muentzer was seduced by Storch's enthusiasm. If so, Muentzer was avid for seduction. Muentzer craved revelations and spiritual experiences that vindicated his position, and in Storch he found vindication in abundance. Storch, who "boasted of secret divine revelations and had caused considerable disturbance"[26] with his enthusiasm, was the antithesis of the scholastic theologians. The simple, unlettered, uneducated layman relied not on philosophy or human reason but on direct instruction from God. The minute he opened Holy Scripture, the Holy Ghost spoke through him.

Luther was unimpressed with the Zwickau Prophets. Storch had approached Melanchthon with questions about infant baptism; Melanchthon then met with Junker Joerg only to find Luther considered Storch "driven by a thoughtless spirit."[27] It was a mild rebuke given Luther's penchant for verbal aggression, but Luther was clearly troubled by the direction his "allies" were taking. The Zwickau Prophets were talking about abolishing all social differences: "Wouldn't it be a wonderful thing," they wrote, "if every man were equal and all belonged to the same class, and everything was put to common use, and no one had to be subject anymore to the Rat King? Who needs those horny, phony clerics? Those fat stallions need to be done away with."[28] The Zwickau Prophets were also talking about abolishing marriage, which "contradicts the nature of man and God's plan for nature as well."[29] It was as if the Taborites had come back to life one hundred years later in Zwickau. Luther was less than happy, no doubt partly because he needed the princes to protect himself and his Reformation from the pope and emperor. The Anabaptist theology that poked its head above ground in Zwickau would reach full bloom in 1534 when the weavers took over Muenster, but Luther saw trouble on the horizon already. After Zwickau, Muentzer saw himself no longer as a Roman Catholic priest, but, like Storch, an Old Testament prophet answerable to God alone. He would to destroy the existing corrupt Church and replace it with a purified assembly of the elect, who would wield the sword as their dreams and visions dictated, just as Joshua and Gideon had in Israel.

Muentzer again forced the hand of the town council, which expelled him from Zwickau on April 16, 1521, the same day Luther arrived in Worms to defend himself before the Imperial Diet against charges of heresy. Muentzer's contemporary Joachim Zimmerman made invidious comparisons between him and Luther, claiming that on the same day that Muentzer set off a riot in Zwickau and then slipped out of town in the middle of the night, Luther, "well-aware of Huss's death by fire," rode into Worms to be greeted reverently by a thousand-strong crowd, to defend his belief before the Emperor and the estates for "the sake of his soul's salvation."[30] The implication is that the Wittenberg Reformer was a hero and the Zwickau preacher a coward.

Zimmerman's sermon was an indication that the Reformation had already split into two factions: Muentzer whose views led to revolution, anarchy, communism, and the belief that the governed had a right to say who governed them, on the one hand, and Lutheran authoritarianism on the other. Luther needed the military might of the princes to move his program forward and was willing to buy them off with Church property to get it. If Luther had not defied the Emperor with his famous *mot*, "*Hier stehe ich, ich kann nicht anders*," the princes, who were his protectors and whom Luther represented, would have murdered him on the spot. His interpretation of Romans 13 proposed tyranny as the alternative to

Muentzer's anarchy; once the defeat of the peasants had been accomplished, that tyranny established the groveling German attitude toward authority that found its culmination in the Third Reich.

After his expulsion from Zwickau, Muentzer traveled through the secret Hussite communities of southern Germany, eventually penetrating to the dark heart of heretical and revolutionary thought when he arrived in Prague in June 1521. At the gates of the city, Muentzer was greeted by a torchlight parade; it was the custom "to escort renowned preachers and scholars with anticipation and festivity."[31] Muentzer was received with honors because he was viewed as a representative of Luther, whom the Praguers viewed as the latest avatar of the Bohemian martyr John Huss. Even though in the coming months he would become Luther's bitter enemy and must have already descried clouds on the horizon of their relationship, Muentzer did nothing to discourage the impression he was *emulus Martini*,[32] as the inscription on the back of Melanchthon's theses described him, because the Utraquists had already placed the mantle of Huss on Luther's shoulders. Luther would disappoint them, but, for the present, they put the town's pulpits at the disposal of the man they considered Luther's disciple.

Muentzer preached at the Teyn Church, the Corpus Christi chapel, and, predictably, at the Bethlehem Chapel where Huss had preached. He preached in German to the town's largest foreign language majority, in Latin at the university, and in Czech with the help of translators to the average man. Even though he issued no overt call to arms, the reaction to Muentzer's preaching in Prague was not unlike the reaction in Jueterborg, Orlamuenda, and Zwickau. Two weeks after his arrival, after a memorial service for Huss, an enraged mob stormed and looted a local monastery.

The Prague Manifesto is a summation of what Muentzer told the Hussites. Published in 1521, probably after he was expelled from Bohemia, the Manifesto explained he went to Prague because it was "the city of the precious and holy fighter Jan Hus," and because he hoped "the loud and moving trumpets [that once sounded in this city]" would sound throughout the whole church and remove the corruption, about which he "lamentingly complain[ed]."[33] Suffering is necessary to purify the elect, who are synonymous with the Church, which they will purify. But Muentzer was not promoting suffering as the surest means to sanctity; he was promoting an experiential religion that denied the necessity of faith. "The word of God," he wrote, "penetrates the heart, brain, skin, hair, bones, limbs, marrow, [and] fluids, [with] force and power," and "he who has once received the holy spirit as he should, can no longer be damned."[34] In other words, once a man has the right experiences he is saved: "an experienced faith is one that is certain of salvation."[35]

That formulation must have given Luther pause because it undermined *Sola Fide*, one of the three pillars of the Reformation. Once Luther broke with the apostolic Catholic Church and its sacraments and made faith the foundation of religion, it was a very short time before those who accepted the principle asked, "How do we know we have faith?" In Muentzer's view, the only possible answer was "because we have experienced faith." This transformed Christianity into a religion of experience. In typically judaizing fashion, Muentzer based his idea that Christians "should all have revelations"[36] on the Old Testament, but he did so while attacking "the Jewish, heretical parsons," who "say that such a strong thing is not necessary for salvation," prompting Baylor to explain, "in describing the clergy as Jews, Muentzer intended to call attention to the scriptural literalism and legalism, which he equated with the practices of Jewish scribes."[37]

Meditating on John Huss led Muentzer to additional conclusions. Muentzer pored over the Book of Daniel and concluded the papacy was the "fourth Beast." Conflating Rome and the Roman Church, Muentzer concluded the end of the old world was nigh; Muentzer, the New Daniel, as he would deem himself three years later, would bring about the thousand year reign of Christ on earth by reforming a terminally corrupt Roman Catholic Church. Only the Elect would be members of the reformed Church, and they would know they were the elect because of their experience of being saved. German mysticism now took a turn toward the eschatological; eschatological thinking, when widespread throughout the southern German speaking lands, would have revolutionary political consequences. The clergy who opposed the New Daniel's vision of the Church were dismissed as "thin-shitters" and "whore-mongers."[38]

Muentzer was preaching a different gospel than his reputed mentor Luther. Muentzer's Prague Manifesto not only undermined *Sola Fide*, it also undermined *Sola Scriptura*. "All true parsons," Muentzer wrote, "must have revelations so that they are certain of their cause."[39] Muentzer attacked the scholastic notion that reason provided a prolegomena to faith and that faith perfected reason. "It is not reason," Muentzer wrote, "which explains to man the meaning and purpose of history, but rather a theology, which orients itself on the living word of God, whose witness he discerns in the heart."[40] Even this subversive thought is not enough for the man Luther would deride as a "*Schwaermer*," or enthusiast. "The sheep," Muentzer continues, "should be led to revelations."[41] If the preacher does not have revelations, the gospel ceases to be the living word of God and becomes a dead letter. Luther, to his credit, realized breaking from the objective word of God was a recipe for social anarchy. Muentzer was leading the newly reformed faithful into a world where preachers, led by their own phantasms, would inspire each member of the flock to follow his own phantasms, creating a world where every man is his own visionary.

Luther did not understand, though, that he got this ball rolling when he broke with the Church, undermining its authority as guarantor and interpreter of Scripture. Luther's Catholic contemporaries were more clear-sighted. Johannes Cochlaeus held Luther responsible for the Peasant's Revolt, even though Luther urged the princes to crush it, because Luther prepared the way by eliminating the Church as the guarantor of the Scripture and the legitimate basis for social order.

Luther, "the seducer of the people,"[41] was horrified by Muentzer's actions because in them he saw his own principles carried to their logical conclusion. But Luther "was much more pernicious than Muentzer," because the latter only spread revolution in Thuringia, whereas Luther "spread it through every land of the German nation."[43]

Luther was a philo-Semite, who in a few years would become a violent anti-Semite, but he was also a Judaizer *malgré lui*. Luther did for Christianity what Jochanan ben Zakkai did for Judaism: he turned the evangelical Church into a debating society, in which the evangelical rabbis would offer competing interpretations of scripture with no way of adjudicating differences other than splitting off from whomever one disagreed with. Luther would ultimately solve the problem of competing interpretation and competing authority in the same way Jan Zizka did earlier in Bohemia and Oliver Cromwell and Stalin did later, which is to say, by *force majeure*. Like Zizka, Luther used military might to end the debate over doctrine. Two and a half centuries later, Friedrich Nietzsche, the son of a Lutheran pastor, would distill the lessons of Protestantism and Revolution into one distinct phrase: will to power.

But all of that was in the future, and Muentzer most certainly did not see the future clearly when he said of the Bohemians, "I do not doubt the people." He clearly hoped that revolution would once again rise up "in your land and afterward everywhere," i.e., in Bohemia and then spread to the German speaking lands to the north and west.[44] The people, if by that phrase we mean the Bohemians, soon had their doubts about Muentzer and expressed them in an unambiguous fashion when they placed him under house arrest and then deported him back to Thuringia at then end of 1521.

When he left Prague, Muentzer believed the world was coming to an end, especially the world that began with what might be called the thousand year reign of Christ inaugurated in Europe by the Rule of St. Benedict. Carlstadt led the mob in Wittenberg to an orgy of image breaking in December 1521, forcing Luther to abandon the safety of the Wartburg to confront a disciple who was taking matters into his own hands. In 1522, Reuchlin died; Erasmus wrote his "Apotheosis of Reuchlin," describing the caballist's entry into heaven and defending him against those he called "pseudoapostles plotting ... to obscure his glory."[45] By the 1520s, the term "pseudoapostles" was part of the polemical rhetoric of the Lutherans, "whose movement was now threatening the unity of the church." Erasmus thus found himself in a dispute neither to his liking nor of his own making. During the 1520s, many humanists who had defended Reuchlin became Lutherans, and Erasmus was caught in the same riptide, as the popular witticism, "Erasmus laid the egg, and Luther hatched it," made clear.[46]

Luther had supported Reuchlin early in his struggle against Pfefferkorn and the Mendicants. Luther's attitude toward Reuchlin was dictated not so much by principle as by opportunity. Luther did not share Reuchlin's enthusiasm for Jewish literature or Caballah. In fact, he passionately condemned what he referred to as caballistic foolishness, but defended Reuchlin because of similarities between Reuchlin's case and his own. In letters to Erasmus, Luther urged a common front among humanists, even though he was not one, as Luther's champion Ulrich von Hutten also urged in his letters to Erasmus. Both men knew the times had changed since Nicholas Donin. The Humanists were partially responsible for that change, and Luther allied himself with them to benefit from the change. Luther was committed neither to the humanist's promotion of Latin and Greek nor to Reuchlin's promotion of Hebrew; he was, however, a devout follower of the principle that the enemy of my enemy is my friend.

By siding with Reuchlin, Luther became a friend of the Jews. The alliance was based more on opportunism than principle. In his tract "Jesus Christ was born a Jew" (1523), Luther defended Jewish liberties to effectuate his larger goal of undermining the Catholic Church. Like the Puritans after him, Luther thought once the gospel was preached correctly, free of papist distortions, the Jews would convert in droves. "Those fools, the papists, bishops, sophists, and monks," Luther wrote, "have hitherto so dealt with the Jews. If I had been a Jew and received such treatment ... I'd rather have been a pig than a Christian."[47] When it was apparent 20 years later that the Jews were not going to convert to Luther's version of Christianity, Luther wrote "On the Jews and their Lies," in which he urged German princes to destroy their synagogues and burn their books, a far harsher regimen than Pfefferkorn had promoted and against which Luther had expressed much indignation. Luther also recommended that all young able-bodied Jews be impressed into forced labor gangs to perform menial tasks like removing manure from the streets. In his disappointment, Luther went far beyond the measures the Catholic Church proposed to deal with the Jews.

Graetz studiously ignores all this when he deals with the Reformation in his *History of the Jews*. He apparently shared Luther's view that the enemy of his enemy was his friend. Graetz supports the Reformation because he sees it as bringing Enlightenment to North Germany, Denmark, Sweden, Prussia, Poland, France and "even Spain, the country of the darkest and most bigoted ecclesiasticism and the home of persecution."[48] Walsh and Graetz mention Elias Levita, "another Jew who did valiant spade work for Luther's sowing."[49] When Luther translated the Bible into German, he, of necessity, relied on Jewish scholars. "For his purpose," Graetz writes, "Luther had to learn Hebrew, and seek information from Jews."[50] Rabbi Solomon, later known as Raschi, became the conduit for his father, Isaac of Troyes, who exerted influence on the reformers through a Franciscan monk of Jewish descent by the name of Nicholas of Lyra. Luther, Calvin, and Zwingli acknowledged Nicholas's influence. Add to that Sforno's influence on Reuchlin, and it becomes understandable how one Jewish writer would claim the Reformation "drew its life blood from rational Hebraism."[51]

In making *Sola Scriptura* a pillar of the Reformed Faith, Luther also continued what Reuchlin began, by demoting scholasticism and promoting the study of language in general and Hebrew in particular. The Jews later promoted the Reformed cause by printing Protestant Bibles based on unapproved and erroneous translations and arranging for their clandestine transport throughout Europe. The Jews became spies and propagandists for the Reformers, trafficking in corrupted translations of the Bible taken from Jewish scriptures:

> The most active intelligencers, liaison officers and propagandists of this international army were Jews. Only four years after Luther's first outburst, Cardinal Alexander, papal nuncio, reported that Jews were printing and circulating the German monk's books in Flanders. From the Netherlands they sent bibles even to Spain, concealed in double-bottomed wine-casks. In Ferrara, a great Jewish financial center, they printed heretical bibles for distribution in Italy and elsewhere. No less a person than Carranza, now languishing in the prisons of the Inquisition in Spain, said that this was the reason why the Church had to discourage the reading of the Bible in the vernacular, saving in approved versions. Even Jewish physicians and men of business were spies and propaganda agents. In the very year after Philip returned to Spain to stamp out Protestantism there, the Jewish Doctor Rodrigo Lopez, who was to find so unhappy an end in England, was passing over from Antwerp to London as a good Protestant.[52]

Although Graetz and Walsh agree on the role Jews played in the Reformation, they disagree in evaluating that role. Graetz sees the Reformation as the precursor of Enlightenment. Walsh views it as "one long retrogression toward the moribund Judaism of the Pharisees of the time of Christ."[53] The Reformation was not a movement from darkness to light but rather disaffected clerics, oftentimes practicing the very abuses they decried in others, returning like dogs to the vomit of Judaism. Calvin declared the prohibition against usury outdated, not because it was no longer a source of social pathology, but rather, to cite Graetz, because "the interest of the marketplace had driven the interest of the church into the background."[54] Walsh describes the Reformation as "the great betrayal" that allowed the moneychangers back into the Temple, after "they had been ousted by the medieval Church when she was most free and vigorous."[55] Unsurprisingly "most of the heresiarchs and heretics of this present Century," according to Cabrera, were seen as Jews. "It is beyond question," Walsh continues, citing a Jewish historian, "that the first leaders of the Protestant sects were called semi-Judaei, or half-Jews, in all parts of Europe, and that men of Jewish descent were as conspicuous among them as they had been among the Gnostics and would later be among the Communists."[56]

Luther hitched his fortunes to Reuchlin, who had promoted the Talmud. "We," Graetz writes, "can boldly assert that the war for and against the Talmud aroused German consciousness and created a public opinion without which the Reformation, like many other efforts would have died in the hour of birth, or perhaps would never have been born at all."[57] Graetz similarly portrays the Reformation as "the triumph of Judaism,"[58] a claim that many Catholics made in Luther's day. Graetz applauds Luther's early defense of the Jews, especially when Luther urges Christians to "show them a friendly spirit, permit them to live and to work, so that they may have cause and means to be with us and amongst us,"[59] describing Luther's sentiments as words

> which the Jews had not heard for a thousand years. They show unmistakable traces of Reuchlin's mild intercession in their favor. Many hot-headed Jews saw in Luther's opposition to the papacy the extinction of Christianity and the triumph of Judaism. Three learned Jews went to Luther and tried to convert him. Enthusiastic feelings were aroused among the Jews at this unexpected revulsion, especially at the blow dealt the papacy and the idolatrous worship of images and relics; the boldest hopes were entertained for the speedy downfall of Rome and the approaching redemption by the Messiah.[60]

Walsh claims the "stormiest preachers" of the Reformation were "of Jewish descent."[61] Michael Servetus, the first Unitarian, was influenced in his attack on the Trinity by Jews. Calvinism became a "convenient mask"[62] for Jews in Antwerp after their expulsion from Spain, confirming that Protestants were half-Jews and adding to the suspicions of Catholic leaders. Dr. Lucien Wolf claims

> Marranos in Antwerp had taken an active part in the Reformation movement and had given up their mask of Catholicism for a not less hollow pretense of Calvinism. The change will be readily understood. The simulation of Calvinism brought them new friends, who, like them were enemies of Rome, Spain and the Inquisition. It helped them in their fight against the Holy Office, and for that reason was very welcome to them. Moreover, it was a form of Christianity which came nearer to their own simple Judaism. The result was that they became zealous and valuable allies of the Calvinists.[63]

In March 1523, Muentzer became pastor at the Church of St. John in the New Town section of Allstedt, where he would remain until he was again forced to leave his flock in the middle of the night in August 1524. In Allstedt, Muentzer created the first vernacular German liturgy. It was in Allstedt that he developed his revolutionary theology and an organization, the League of the Elect, to carry it out. It was in Allstedt that he made contact with the miners from Mansfeld, his most ardent supporters. And it was in Allstedt that he broke his vow of celibacy.

On March 22, 1522, Muentzer wrote to Melanchthon explaining why he did not plan to take a wife. He also explained he had no objection to other priest Reformers marrying, which they were doing with increasing frequency, often with nuns liberated from convents sacked by Iconoclasts. The most prominent defector from the vow of celibacy was Luther himself, who admitted to being a "famous lover,"[64] was accused of drunkenness and whore mongering, and was treated for syphilis before he eventually married a nun, Catherina von Bora, who had been "liberated" from her convent by a group of reformers on Holy Saturday of 1523.

Muentzer's letter to Melanchthon is ambivalent. He applauds the theology Melanchthon has apparently confected to justify breaking the solemn vow of celibacy and getting married because "it has liberated many souls of the elect from the snares of the hunters."[65] He approves of "your priests taking wives, so that the Roman mask [of false piety] does not continue to oppress you,"[66] because he can find no scriptural basis for celibacy. An added benefit is that the children of the union of Reformed priests and nuns would "belong to the Elect from the moment of their birth."[67] Allowing priests to marry would thus provide the foundation of the church of the future. He bases this claim on Isaiah 65:20, which claims these children will see a new heaven and a new earth.

But after conceding all this, Muentzer does an abrupt about face and claims just as vehemently that marriage is not for him. He condemns in practice the very thing he just allowed in principle, telling Melanchthon that "with your counsel" the reformers are dragging "people to marriage, even though the marriage bed is no longer an immaculate one but a whorehouse of Satan, which damages the church as severely as the most damned oils of the priesthood."[68] Muentzer concludes that Melanchthon can't solve the celibacy problem because he can't comprehend the "living word of God." He also announced the end of the world, claiming that "the time of the third angel has already dawned."[69]

Within a year, Muentzer changed his mind abruptly. On July 29, 1523, Muentzer ended a letter to Andreas Karlstadt, another priest professor from the university at Wittenberg, by conveying greetings to Karlstadt's wife. He added, "I am oriented to God in the original rigor,"[70] meaning he was still adhering to the vow of chastity. Yet by August, Muentzer married a liberated ex-nun of noble birth, Ottilie von Gerson. The marriage certainly caused scandal in Allstedt among those who were not of the Reformed party. One biographer says Muentzer "openly married"[71] the runaway nun at the end of July. The interval between the marriage and the arrival of their first child indicates their relations began before the wedding. Like many of his priestly peers, Muentzer was caught in a web of conflicting vows. For Luther, this moral contradiction led to the doctrine of the enslaved will. For Muentzer, it led to revolution.

But not directly. During summer 1523, enough revolutionary monks and their runaway nun concubines arrived in Stolberg to generate a revolutionary situation, which Muentzer addressed in his Open Letter to the Brothers at Stolberg. Muentzer began by explaining the efficacy of patient suffering, but he concluded by giving tacit approval, couched in negative terms, to revolution. Since he warned the brothers to shun "unjustifiable" or "inappropriate" revolution,[72] the perceptive reader saw Muentzer's letter as justifying "appropriate" revolution. The question became, "Is this particular revolution justifiable?" Unlike Martin Luther, Catholic theologians like Thomas Aquinas admitted the possibility of rebellion against tyrants, but only under carefully specified conditions based on the Augustinian theory of a just war, according to which the benefit of the doubt went to the legitimate ruler. Muentzer disconnected the possibility of removing a tyrannical prince from any objective criteria, thereby opening the door for revolution. One commentator claimed Muentzer "transformed what was at first sight a warning against local rebellion into a proclamation of a universal revolution"[73] in his letter to the brothers at Stolberg.

Some claim Muentzer was naïve and unable to see that the principle he articulated would be implemented in ways that contravened his intentions. Others claim he was disingenuous and avid to promote revolution from the beginning. The suspicions are intensified by the way Muentzer ended his letter ("I also hear that when you have been drinking, you talk a lot about our case, but when you are sober, you are as fearful as sissies."[74]), warning the brothers not to talk in their cups, lest they spill the beans about what Muentzer was planning secretly. Baylor claims "it is uncertain whether in 1523 Muentzer was in contact with a secret organization in Stolberg, but there is little doubt that the 'cause' that he warned his associates against discussing when they had been drinking included more than purely personal piety."[75] Muentzer probably felt revolution was appropriate, but before he could proclaim it in public, he needed to create the organization that would bring it about.

In a letter to Luther just four days before Muentzer wrote to the brothers at Stolberg, Muentzer denied any role in the revolution in Zwickau that led to his expulsion. "Everybody," Muentzer wrote to Luther, "except for the blind city councilors, knows that at the time of the uprising [tumultus], I was taking a bath, with no knowledge of such matters. And if I had not intervened against it, the whole council would have been killed the following night."[76] Disavowing responsibility for what happened in Zwickau, Muentzer then discussed the differences between his and Luther's theological views. Muentzer placed heavy emphasis on "the living word of God," Who revealed himself "not only in the Scriptures but also in dreams and visions."[77] Muentzer still hoped for reconciliation with the Master, ending his letter by asking the Lord to "let our old love begin anew," but Luther was disgusted and broke off the relationship with his former student, whom he felt was ensnared by enthusiasm. "I can't stand this spirit, no matter what you want to call it," Luther said about Muentzer, whom he would soon call "the Satan from Allstedt."[78] "He praises my work ... and yet at the same time holds it in contempt and then goes off looking for greater things ... so that you have to conclude that he's either drunk or crazy."[79]

In revolutionary terms, the conflict between Luther and Muentzer was the conflict between radicals and moderates. The same conflict had taken place when Zizka turned on the Taborites, and it would take place in every subsequent revolution. Parallels exist in Cromwell's conflict with the Fifth Monarchy Men and in the Menshevik/Bolshevik split. Before long, Muentzer was fighting on two fronts, against both Wittenberg and Rome. Luther was doing the same, siding with the Princes against the peasants who threatened not only the social order but also the success of his rebellion against Rome.

Luther soon claimed "the person who has seen Muentzer may claim to have seen the devil incarnate in his very worst raging. Oh, Lord God, whenever such a spirit is abroad among the peasants, it is high time they were destroyed like mad dogs."[80] According to Muentzer, Allstedt was to be run, not by renegade university professors, but by the people themselves, who would create a religious community inspired by the Holy Spirit in dreams and visions. The Elect would rule, and if the princes didn't see it their way, the people would rise up and take the sword from their hands. Anything less was the "contrived faith" of political opportunists, whose chief agent was Luther.

Muentzer's road to revolution began not with a call to arms but rather with creation of the first German liturgy. Muentzer produced the first comprehensive liturgy in German when Luther was still reluctant to abandon Latin. In seeing the Latin liturgy, like infant baptism, as magic and idolatry, Muentzer was years ahead of Luther in implementing his master's own principles. By summer 1523, "foreigners" from all over southern Thuringia and Saxony were attending Muentzer's German liturgy. This movement of large populations was too dangerous to ignore, so Count Ernst of Mansfeld banned attendance at the liturgies, setting up a conflict between Church and State that would define Muentzer's revolutionary theology. Muentzer then abused the count from the pulpit, inviting him and the local bishop to Allstedt to "show before the whole world in what way my teaching or service is heretical."[81] If the count did not come, Muentzer would consider him "an evil-doer, a rascal and a knave, a Turk and a pagan."[82] When the people of Allstedt closed ranks behind him, Muentzer was emboldened to articulate his revolutionary theology. At the heart of that theology, which became the heart of his political theory too, was the sword. The sword, claimed Muentzer, must be used in the service of the gospel. If the princes hesitate in following Muentzer's instruction on how to wield the sword, the sword would be taken from them and given to "the people who burn with zeal" and then, alas, "peace will be in abeyance on earth."[83]

"Here," Goertz writes, "the idea of the people's sovereignty surfaces for the first time and combines with mystical piety and apocalyptical expectation to form a threatening prospect for anyone opposed to the Allstedt Reformation."[84] In October 1523, Muentzer wrote to Frederick the Wise, reiterating his position. "Princes," he wrote, "do not frighten the pious. And if it turns out that [the princes do make the pious fear them], then the sword will be taken from them and given to the ardent masses in order to defeat the godless, Daniel 7:18. Then that noble treasure, peace, will be removed from the earth Rev. 6:2."[85] The references to Daniel and Revelations emphasized the apocalyptic nature of Muentzer's thought and increased the likelihood of revolutionary violence. If the world was coming to an end anyway, why refrain? Unlike "the scribes [who] imagine Christ to be the fulfiller of the law, so that they do not have to suffer the action of God by pointing out his cross,"[86] Muentzer was telling his flock, at the end of 1523, that in their suffering, they "should not murmur and growl like whining dogs" because "he who does not die with Christ cannot be resurrected with him."[87] Muentzer cited St. Paul, who "clearly says [Col. 1:24], 'I fulfill that which the suffering of Christ still lacks.' The church suffers as his body."[88] But the suffering was ripped from the tradition of the Gospel and put in the service of revolution, by way of millennialist expectation. The Suffering of the Elect had become the birth pangs of a new revolutionary era.

In 1524, after years of holding his tongue in spite of growing reservations, Erasmus finally broke with the Lutherans when he wrote *De Libero Arbitrio*, his tract on free will. Despite Luther's support of Reuchlin and the humanist cause, Erasmus realized he had a fundamentally different agenda, perhaps furthered by a conspiracy. "After all, Luther is not so far advanced in the knowledge of the tongues or of elegant scholarship to provide supporters of such studies with an interest in his case."[89] Erasmus broke with his Lutheran allies because linking Reuchlin with Luther was "detrimental to the humanist cause." Erasmus needed "to disentangle the two movements." Rummel felt there was

> some evidence for Erasmus' conspiracy theory. Several leading reformers, Melanchthon, Bucer, and Zwingli among them, were all at one stage under the impression that Erasmus was one of them and were hoping that he, as the leading humanist, would deliver that party to them. In 1519, for example, Melanchthon spoke of Luther as "our foremost champion, second only to Erasmus"; similarly, Bucer wrote in 1518 that "Luther agrees in everything with Erasmus, the only difference that what Erasmus merely hints at, Luther teaches openly and freely." Both men revised their opinion in the 1520s. Bucer saw the light in 1524 when Luther and Erasmus engaged in a published controversy over free will.[90]

Luther wrote to Erasmus, begging "If you cannot or dare not be assertive in our cause, leave it alone and keep to your own business."[91] In a letter to Oecolampadius, Luther admitted "I feel Erasmus's barbs occasionally, but since he pretends in public not to be my enemy, I, in turn, pretend that I do not understand his clever words."[92] Hutten pleaded with Erasmus to maintain a united front against the Catholics, at least in public, and "was quite candid about the strategic importance of such a move."[93] In a letter to Erasmus, he noted that some regarded Erasmus as Luther's inspirational source. "You were the forerunner," Hutten wrote, "you taught us .... you are the man on whom the rest of us depend."[94] Hutten claimed that the success of the Reformation would guarantee "liberal studies too will flourish and the humanities will be held in honor."[95] But Erasmus not only doubted the intellectual foundations of the Reformation expressed in Luther's notion of the will, he also thought humanistic studies would get dragged into a fight that would harm it more than the scholastic *viri obscuri* could.

Disaffected worshippers continued to pour into Allstedt to take part in Muentzer's revolutionary services, in defiance of Count Ernst's ban. By spring 1524, Muentzer's chapel was full of hundreds of visiting worshippers, mostly peasants from the neighboring countryside and miners from Mansfeld. Muentzer capitalized on the crowds and created his own revolutionary organization. According to testimony gathered after the collapse of the Peasant Revolt, Muentzer assembled 30 followers in a dry moat outside town in March 1524, and initiated them into a secret organization known as the League of the Elect. Using his wife's experience in the convent, Muentzer had her organize and train the town's women, many of whom were runaway nuns. The organization would take up arms in defense of Allstedt, which, like Jerusalem under bar Kokhba and Prague under Huss and (ten years later) Muenster under Bokelzoon, would become the dwelling place of the Elect. All who were unwilling to go along with the Elect were driven from town. Members of the Elect declared their willingness to protect each other against persecutors of the Gospel and swore to back up their oath with force of arms. Martin Luther recognized the gravity of the situation; he immediately urged the princes of Saxony to retaliate, to "break and beat with the fist."[96]

The purpose of the League of the Elect was "brotherly love," but it was a love with revolutionary intent. The Elect swore to refuse to pay tithes to local convents and monasteries. The Elect believed in fraternity and equality, claiming everything was to be held in common[97] and that each should receive according to his needs.[98] If there were any doubts about their revolutionary nature, the Elect concluded their oath by warning "in all seriousness ... any princes, dukes or lords" who objected to the program of "*Omnia sunt communia*" that they "would cut off the heads or hang" any rulers who stood in their way.[99] By mid-summer 1524, the League of the Elect had grown to over 500 members, all of whom had sworn their willingness to engage in illegal activity for the sake of the Gospel.

Emboldened by their oath, members of the reformed party in Allstedt increased their attacks on the Church. Resentment focused on a chapel in a wood near town which because of its miraculous image of the Blessed Virgin was a place of pilgrimage. The Mallerbach Chapel belonged to the nuns of Naundorf and was under the custodial care of a hermit who was soon driven off by violence and vandalism. In his confession, Muentzer referred to the chapel as a "*spelunke*" or den. Muentzer incited mob violence by railing against what he considered the idolatrous worship of images there. Muentzer referred to the chapel as a "standing provocation"[100] of the devil that needed to be destroyed by good-hearted, pious people. To buttress his arguments, Muentzer cited the Old Testament, wherein "Pious Moses" in Exodus 23, proclaimed that "you shall not defend the godless."[101] If the civil authorities, Muentzer continued, do not follow this maxim, then they have lost their claim to legitimacy. Because of the violence that often followed Muentzer's sermons, the nuns removed whatever was valuable and placed it under lock and key; by the end of March, when events came to a head, the chapel stood empty and abandoned.

On Holy Thursday, March 24, 1524, a mob of the Elect marched from Allstedt to Mallerbach Chapel and burned it to the ground. Elliger says this was no spur of the moment "act of blind zealotry,"[102] but rather a well planned act of arson and iconoclasm intended, according to Muentzer's plan, to inaugurate the dawn of the Reformation in Allstedt. Muentzer claimed that only this act of symbolic arson could drive the devil's cult from Allstedt.

The Abbess of the convent at Naundorf complained bitterly to Hans Zeiss and the civil authorities, demanding the malefactors be brought to justice. The mayor and city council denied all responsibility and turned the tables on the nuns by claiming they had set the fire to incriminate the citizens of Allstedt. Sensing more than just a simple act of vandalism, Duke John of Saxony demanded a united front among the princes in dealing with Muentzer. Muentzer dealt directly with the issue by writing to Duke John on June 7, 1524, asserting that the League of the Elect was "without guilt" when they burned the chapel to the ground because everyone knew that "poor people"—even though their culpability was lessened "through lack of understanding"—"formerly honored and prayed to the devil at Mallerbach, under the name of Mary."[103] The Duke had no business punishing "good-hearted, pious people" who had destroyed this haunt of the devil. If Duke John ignored "what God our creator said through pious Moses"[104] in Exodus 23:1, "You shall not defend the godless," he was no better than the idolatrous monks and nuns. "But that we should continue to permit the devil at Mallerbach to be prayed to, so that our brothers are delivered up to him as a sacrifice, this we no more want that we wish to be subjects of the Turks."[105] The implication was clear. Princes who permitted idolatry in their realms were no better than Turks and deserved to be deposed.

On June 11, the local authorities arrested Ziliax Knaut, who was charged with arson and placed in stocks at the local castle. Muentzer was outraged; he wondered aloud how men who claimed to be pious Christian princes could defend monks and nuns, people "the whole world" agreed were "idolatrous people."[106] Not content to sermonize, Muentzer sounded the alarm on June 13 when the prince's men came to Allstedt to arrest Knaut's co-conspirators. The League of the Elect assembled immediately and, after showing their willingness to use force of arms, forced the prince's men to withdraw. Instead of apprehending the other arsonists, the administrator returned to Weimar and filed a report.

Luther's letter to the princes of Saxony concerning the revolutionary spirit in Saxony was published in August 1524, but it was written with the destruction of the Mallerbach Chapel in mind. Luther was in danger of losing control of his revolution to the more radical followers of Muentzer, who was willing to plunge Germany into anarchy in pursuit of his fantastic notion of the gospel. Muentzer, in Luther's view, was "full of babble about the holy spirit and revelations in visions, but incapable of producing miracles to prove himself. Above all his preaching bore no other fruit than that of inciting the rabble to violence."[107] If the reformers preached insurrection, "secular rulers had the right and duty to meet force with force."[108] To stop the "Satan of Allstedt," Luther drew a clear line between spiritual reform and political revolution by denouncing Muentzer as a Judaizer. Abandoning the philo-Semitism he adopted in the Reuchlin/Pfefferkorn controversy, Luther claimed those who strike with their fists are behaving like Jews. Luther fought fire with fire by quoting from Daniel and Isaiah of the Old Testament to bolster his case. "Preaching and suffering are our vocation," Luther writes, "not striking out with the fist and battling in self defense. After all, neither Christ nor his apostles broke into churches and destroyed images; rather they won over hearts by appealing to God's word, and after that churches [i.e., temples] and graven images fell of their own accord. We should do likewise."[109]

Although the Jews of Moses' time were commanded to destroy the altars and idols of the Canaanites, Luther continues, that doesn't mean the Reformed have received the same command. Nor would the Reformed be justified in sacrificing their children, as Abraham was commanded to do. If Christians are bound by Muentzer's cock-eyed interpretation of the Old Testament, then "we would all have to be circumcised and do the works of the Jews,"[110] i.e, follow the old law in its entirety. The logical conclusion of Muentzer's revolutionary theology is that Christians should behave like Jews. "If it is right for Christians to break into churches and engage in acts of iconoclasm," Luther reasoned, "then it follows that we should also murder anyone who isn't a Christian, just as the Jews were ordered to exterminate the Canaanites and the Amorites." The spirit of Allstedt will bring about nothing but bloodshed, and anyone who disagrees with their heavenly voices will end up being strangled by them."[111]

Muentzer responded in his "Highly Provoked Defense" in late summer 1524, calling Luther Doctor Luegner (Liar) and accusing him of misrepresentation. According to Muentzer, Luther is like Jews who "continually wanted to slander and discredit Christ, just as Luther now does me."[112] Muentzer protests that when Luther says "that I want to make a rebellion" Luther twists the sense of Muentzer's letter to the Mansfeld miners. But, Muentzer concedes Luther's point: "I proclaimed before the princes that the entire community had the power of the sword, just as it had the keys of remitting sin."[113] As a result, "The lords themselves are responsible for making the poor people their enemy. They do not want to remove the cause of insurrection, so how, in the long run, can things improve? I say this openly, so Luther asserts I must be rebellious. So be it."[114]

Muentzer then uses *ad hominem* arguments against Luther, bringing up Luther's notorious reputation as a drunk, glutton, and whoremonger, the very allegations that led him to marry the nun, Catherina von Bora. Luther, according to Muentzer, is "totally incapable of shame, like the Jews who brought to Christ the woman taken in adultery."[115] Muentzer finds it astonishing "this shameless monk can claim to be terribly persecuted, there [at Wittenberg] with this good Malvasian wine and his whore's banquets."[116] Luther uses his "new logic" of faith alone, which he "deceptively called the word of God"[117] to distract the faithful from his loose living and sinfulness.

Muentzer perceived what might be the personal issues at the heart of Luther's doctrine of the enslaved will. It was easy to extrapolate from Luther's behavior to a theological "principle," which wanted "to make God responsible for the fact that you are a poor sinner and a venomous little worm with your shitty humility. You have done this with your fantastic reasoning, which you have concocted out of your Augustine. It is truly a blasphemy to despise mankind impudently, which you do in your teaching concerning the freedom of the will."[118] Luther's false faith had political consequences; Luther was forced to "flatter the princes," and offer them "Bohemian gifts" of "cloisters and foundations, which you now promise the princes" in exchange for protection.[119] Muentzer has little good to say about Luther's appearance before the Imperial Diet at Worms, because "If you had wavered at Worms, you would have been stabbed by the nobility rather than set free."[120] Luther and his followers "preach what suits them, but what they really pursue is the belly.... The sole and only outcome of their teachings is the freedom of the flesh. Hence they poison the Bible for the Holy Spirit."[121]

Muentzer then claims Luther's views on insurrection are merely an attempt to curry favor with the princes by one who is morally compromised and without clear judgment.[122] Luther "wants to be a new Christ who had gained much good for Christendom with his blood. And what is more, he did this for the sake of a fine thing—that priests might take wives."[123] Muentzer, though, was also compromised on celibacy, having bound himself by two contradictory vows. The same sexual stimulus, however, drove the two reformers in opposite directions. It drove Luther to curry favor with princes, but it drove Muentzer to rebel against them.

In July 1524 Duke John and his nephew the elector prince John Frederick arrived in Allstedt without having read Luther's analysis of the revolutionary spirit there. Their arrival may have been a routine visit to a city of their realm, but it was more likely an attempt to find out what Muentzer was up to. On July 13, the princes attended Muentzer's modified Mass at the castle chapel, during which Muentzer gave a detailed explanation of his theology of revolution. For his text, Muentzer chose the story of Nebuchadnezzar's dream in Daniel 2, the *locus classicus* for millennialism. The sermon is known as *Die Fuerstenpredigt*, or sermon to the princes.

Daniel 2 begins with King Nebuchadnezzar's dream. When Nebuchadnezzar's seers prove incapable of interpreting it, Daniel interprets it correctly. The orthodox interpretation of the dream, as we have seen, is that the stone, untouched by any hand, which destroyed the statue, is Christ, and that the fifth kingdom is the reign of Christ on earth, the Roman Catholic Church, the New Jerusalem, the City of God, the kingdom which will have no end. Muentzer modifies the traditional orthodox interpretation of Daniel 2 to suit himself. The fifth empire is, according to Muentzer, not the kingdom which will have no end, but rather "the one which we have before our own eyes," i.e., the Holy Roman Empire, which "would like to be coercive. But as we see before our very eyes, the iron is intermixed with filth, vain schemes of flattery that slither and squirm over the face of the whole earth. For he who cannot be a cheat [in our empire] must be an idiot."[124]

The stone that shattered the colossus is "The poor laity and the peasants" who see that they are now shattering the Roman Church "much more clearly than you do."[125] To help the princes understand the signs of the times, "a new Daniel must arise and interpret your revelation for you. And this same new Daniel must go forth, as Moses teaches, Deut 20:2, at the head of the troops. He must reconcile the anger of the prices and that of the enraged people.... For Christ says, in Matthew 10:34, 'I have not come to bring peace but the sword.'"[126]

Before long it must have become obvious to the princes listening to his sermon that the "new Daniel" was Muentzer. Unlike Luther and the Scriptural literalists from Wittenberg, men Muentzer compares to Nebuchadnezzar's impotent seers, Muentzer has visions. Like Daniel, Muentzer could claim "the mystery was revealed to [him] in a night vision" (Dan. 2:19). True spiritual leaders have visions. Luther, who is neither conscious of nor receptive to this inner word, does "not know how to say anything essential about God, even though he may have devoured a hundred thousand Bibles."[127]

Before long, Muentzer uses visions as the validator of truth. Visions became Muentzer's substitute for the Church as the final arbiter of doctrine, just as the Bible became the arbiter for Luther. Muentzer even appropriated words traditionally associated with the Church in professions of faith like the Apostles Creed and applied them to visions, preaching "it is a truly apostolic, patriarchal and prophetic spirit that awaits visions and attains them in painful tribulation."[128]

Luther, whom Muentzer describes as "Brother Fatted Swine" and "Brother Soft Life,"[129] is a false prophet because he rejects the crucial role of visions. It would be impossible to safeguard the new Christianity "securely against error on all sides and to act blamelessly, if [the leaders of the new Church] did not rely on revelations from God—As Aaron heard from Moses, Exodus 4:15 and David from Nathan and Gad 2 Chron 29:25."[130]

Just as Nebuchadnezzar elevated Daniel, so the German princes should elevate Muentzer over Luther. "You rulers," Muentzer told the princes, "must act according to the conclusion of this chapter of Daniel [Dan 2:48]. That is why Nebuchanezzar elevated holy Daniel to office so that the king might carry out God's correct decision, inspired by the holy spirit.... For the godless have no right to life except that which the elect decide to grant them, as is written in the book of Exodus 23:29-33.... He to whom is given all power in heaven and on earth [Christ] wants to lead the government."[131] The princes should do this because Luther is an uninspired court prophet, whereas Muentzer is the reincarnation of Daniel.

By the time Muentzer gave his sermon to the princes, he had converted to what Cohn calls "bloodthirsty chiliasm."[132] Cohn attributes this conversion to the ideas of Nicholas Storch, who kept alive Taborite ideas spread by the Hussite armies one hundred years earlier. Once Muentzer turned from Luther's version of the reformed faith, he became, as Luther predicted, an ardent Judaizer. Muentzer "now thought and talked only of the Book of Revelation and of such incidents in the Old Testament as Elijah's slaughter of the priests of Baal, Jehu's slaying of the sons of Ahab, and Jael's assassination of the sleeping Sisera."[133] He got these ideas from Storch, who had been in Bohemia, and revived the Taborite teachings when he returned to Zwickau. Muentzer needed Storch's Hussite Judaizing to justify his path of revolution because political revolution and its justification by a heretical reading of Old Testament were two sides of the same coin. Neither could exist without the other; both were a function of the rejection of the Cross among clergy during the 16th Century. "The elect," wrote Cohn summarizing the political doctrine of all revolutionary Judaizers, "must prepare the way for the Millennium ... by force of arms."[134]

In his sermon, Muentzer told the princes they must wield the sword in service of the Gospel. Muentzer refused to listen to "hackneyed posturings about the power of God achieving everything without resort to your sword."[135] If the princes failed to use the sword as Muentzer saw fit, "it may rust in its scabbard."[136] God fought on the side of the Israelites when they conquered the Promised Land, "but the sword was the means used, just as eating and drinking is a means for us to stay alive. Hence the sword too is necessary for us to eliminate the godless."[137] Since Christ warned those who lived by the sword would die by it, Muentzer gravitated toward Old Testament passages to justify his theology of revolution, citing Deut. 13: 6, "do not permit evildoers, who turn us away from God, to live longer," as well as Exodus 22:1 where God says, "You shall not permit the evildoer to live."[138] The Old Testament was ransacked to justify iconoclasm as well, for it was God Himself who "commanded through Moses in Deut 7: 5 ... 'You shall not have pity on the idolatrous. Break up their altars. Smash their images and burn them so that I am not angry with you.'"[139] "Christ," Muentzer claimed, ignoring what Jesus said to Peter in the Garden of Gethsemane, "has not abrogated these words. Rather, he will help us to fulfill them."[140] According to Muentzer, anyone who claims the antichrist will be destroyed without a sword-bearing hand being lifted

> is already as fainthearted as the Canaanties were when the elect wanted to enter the promised land, as Joshua [5:1] writes. Joshua, nevertheless did not spare them from the sharpness of the sword. Look at Psalm 44:4 and Chronicles 14:11. There you will find the same solution: the elect did not win the promised land with the sword alone, but rather through the power of God. Nevertheless, the sword was the means, just as for us eating and drinking are the means for sustaining life. Thus the sword is also necessary as a means to destroy the godless, Romans 13 [1-4].[141]

Here, Muentzer touches on the same passage (Romans 13) that Luther used to proscribe all rebellion against princely authority, no matter how onerous or unjust. *Sola scriptura* obviously was not going to lead to unity of purpose even among committed reformers. Once an impasse was reached, naked physical power, not textual exegesis, would determine whose interpretation was correct. Muentzer and Luther were avid during the crucial summer of 1524 to get the princes on their respective sides. If Luther chose the carrot of "Bohemian gifts," i.e., bribing the princes with confiscated church property, Muentzer chose the stick of insurrection. If the princes will not wield the sword in the service of the gospel, "then the sword will be taken away from them, Daniel 7:27."[142] Muentzer, "together with pious Daniel," urged the princes "not to oppose God's revelation." If they refused to heed Muentzer's advice, then "may they be strangled without any mercy"[143] "as Hesekiah (2 Kings 18-22), Josiah, Cyrus, Daniel and Elija (1 Kings 18) destroyed the priests of Baal."[144] There was no possibility of reform unless the Church "return[ed] to its source,"[145] namely, Muentzer's apocalyptic Old Testament fantasy of heaven on earth. The time of the harvest was upon them, and "the tares must be pulled out of Gods' vineyard at the time of harvest."[146] Since he had "the instruction of the whole of divine law" on his side, Muentzer could say without hesitation that all "godless rulers, especially the priests and monks, should be killed."[147]

Before long it became clear that wielding the sword meant joining the revolution. If the princes didn't join the revolution, they would be swept away by it. Muentzer made Reformation and Revolution synonymous, but many of the reformers wanted no part of what he was proposing. Luther would soon send his letter to the Saxon princes condemning the revolutionary spirit. Karlstadt and the congregation at Orlamuenda followed Luther's lead, informing Muentzer they had no interest in armed insurrection. "We have not been commanded to act in this manner, for Christ told Peter to put down his sword.... If the time comes when we have to suffer for God's justice, let us be willing to do so, but in the meantime let's not run to take up knives and pikes."[148]

Unsurprisingly, Muentzer's sermon left the princes unpersuaded. Surprisingly, they didn't have Muentzer arrested for treason on the spot. If Muentzer's goal was to convey as unambiguously as possible his newly concocted theology of revolution, then he succeeded. The princes left in silence, probably disposed to think of Muentzer as Luther described him, as a *Schwaermer* or dangerous religious enthusiast. Hans Zeiss, the prince's administrator, was told not to allow "the preacher" to engage in fomenting public disorders or creating "special alliances." But the town was filling with refugees, many of whom were renegade monks and nuns eager to put Muentzer's revolutionary theories into practice, a situation the princes could not ignore much longer.

Carried away by his own enthusiasm, Muentzer began writing letters informing his followers that the end times had commenced. "The Play is about to begin,"[149] Muentzer wrote "To the God fearing at Sangerhausen" just two days after he had harangued the princes. In his letter, Muentzer indicated that the League in Allstedt was only one part of a network of "more than 30" revolutionary organizations God was using against tyrants "to tear them out by the roots" just as "Joshua 11:20 has prophesied this for us."[150] One week later he wrote to Zeiss explaining that because the princes "were violating not only the faith but also these people's natural rights, they should be strangled like dogs."[151] Muentzer also told Zeiss "the terrible phenomenon of civil war" would soon "be unleashed" and he "must no longer hold to the custom of obeying other officials" than Muentzer because the princes had discredited themselves in Gods' eyes: "Their power has an end, and it will soon be handed over to the common people. So act carefully."[152]

Muentzer also told Zeiss to resist with force anyone who came to Allstedt to apprehend "those responsible for Mallerbach." If the authorities attempt arrests, "they should be strangled like mad dogs." He advised Zeiss "the old guidelines no longer function at all, for they are vain mire."[153] As a result, Muentzer made up his own rules, as when "I gave my honest advice about how Christendom should conduct itself as I expounded ... about Holy Joshua, where the priest Hilkias found the book of the law, which he sent to the elders in Judah and Jerusalem. And he went with all the people into the temple and made covenant with God, to which the whole community agreed, so that each of the elect was able to preserve and study the witness of God with his whole soul and heart."[154]

The new rules thus demanded a new social order, according to which the Elect would rule themselves without prince or priest lording it over them. Instead of the medieval society of social classes, Muentzer proposed "a modest league or covenant [which] should be made in such a form that the common man unites with pious officials for the sake of the gospel alone."[155] In a curious aside to a letter written on the first anniversary of his marriage to the runaway nun Ottilie von Gerson, Muentzer admonished Zeiss "if he is inclined to unchastity, that he hurts his lust the very first time he sins by making a determined effort to observe both his lust and the thorns of this conscience. If he keeps his conscience active, then the filth of unchastity consumes itself in horror."[156]

Muentzer seemingly kept the filth of unchastity at bay by throwing himself into revolutionary activity. On July 24, after preaching on the covenant King Josiah and the Elders of Israel made with God, Muentzer called for a similar covenant among the Elect of Allstedt urging them to band together for mutual protection against tyrants. By that afternoon, the Elect of Allstedt, including women and girls trained by Muentzer's wife, were armed and ready to resist efforts to subdue the new revolutionary covenant, which had chosen the rainbow for its flag, a symbol from the Old Testament based on God's covenant with Noah after the flood.

When Duke John heard of Muentzer's sermon and the revolutionary organization he formed, he summoned Muentzer to Weimar. After two days of interrogation, the duke's officials informed Muentzer the League of the Elect must be dissolved and those responsible for the arson at the Mallerbach Chapel must be arrested and brought to trial. Muentzer must also shut down his newly purchased printing press, which would prevent him from responding to Luther's attack.

By June 18, 1524, Luther was referring to Muentzer as the "Satan of Allstedt" in a letter to the Elector. Muentzer was nonetheless surprised by the vehemence of Luther's attack on the revolutionary spirit in Allstedt. If he gave up his printing press, he was unable to rebut. On August 3, Muentzer complained bitterly to Friedrich the Wise that Luther's letter contained "not a hint of brotherly exhortation in it; he just barges his way in like some pompous tyrant, full of ferocity and hate."[157] Muentzer knew "the Christian faith which I preach is not in accord with that of Luther."[158] This, of course, came as no surprise to Luther or the princes. Luther urged the princes to put an end to Muentzer's seditious ravings and prevent the impending revolution. "It is obvious," Luther wrote later, Muentzer was "totally rebellious. If it had lasted longer and come to the point, he would have set the people on the authorities, and it would have gone hard with them. Then, so I am reliably informed, he has written a ferocious letter to the Mansfeld miners and encouraged them to be bold; he intends them to wash their hands in the blood of tyrants. The common people have been thoroughly poisoned by his teachings."[159]

Muentzer's alliance dissolved without contest, and the printing press shut down. Many people distanced themselves from their preacher. As a result, Muentzer did what he had become accustomed to doing for his entire adult ministry. During the night of August 7-8, 1524, Muentzer slipped "over the town's wall secretly,"[160] and, abandoning his wife and child, ran off with a goldsmith from Nordhausen. In an unsent open letter to the Allstedters, probably written more for his own benefit than theirs, Muentzer justified his flight by declaring "you would have abandoned me to the Cross."[161].

A week later, Muentzer arrived in Muehlhausen, his next base of operations. There, Muentzer met the runaway monk by the name of Heinrich Pfeiffer, who had been stirring up the town since his arrival with a group of his equally violent brethren in late 1522. He and his fellow runaways preached, without permission, in the homes of workers and artisans or in the public square. The court in Erfurt demanded that the city authorities end the practice, but the city council had difficulty executing the order because the monks had rallied many people to the reformed cause when they got them to vow to defend the vagabond preachers in the Church of St. Mary.

Muehlhausen was one of the largest cities in middle Germany, but it was on a downward economic slide when Muentzer arrived. The economic downturn meant the city was ripe for revolt. Riches, combined with a greedy oligarchy that controlled the city council, had created a great disparity in the distribution of wealth as well as widespread poverty. The city councilmen tried to deflect attention from their own greed by focusing unrest, with the help of Pfeiffer and other runaway monks, on the three monasteries in town. As became typical in Germany, the drunken dissolute renegade monks excoriated the monks who remained faithful to their vows for their dissolute lives and blamed the lot of the poor not on the policies of the oligarchy that ran the city council but on the exemption of the clergy from paying taxes.

When the city council tried to restrain the runaway monks in July 1523, Pfeiffer's supporters rose in armed revolt, plundered the local monasteries, divided up the spoils among themselves, and forced the council to accept their demands. By August, the council had regained control and expelled Pfeiffer from town, but agents continued to agitate behind the scenes, and Pfeiffer returned in December after Duke John of Weimar, who would soon mull over Muentzer's fate, interceded. Pfeiffer took up his preaching post at the Church of St. Nicholas, and social unrest followed in the wake of his sermons. Pfeiffer's female followers, mostly runaway nuns, drove the priest from the Church of the Holy Blasius after threatening him with drawn knives. The priest at St. Kilian's Church had the chalice ripped from his hands during Mass, whereupon Pfeiffer's followers, demonstrating their connection to the Hussites, distributed communion under both species.

In June 1524, Pfeiffer's followers broke into a church run by Dominicans and engaged in iconoclasm. Two months later, Muentzer wrote to the city council of Nordhausen, justifying iconoclasm by appealing to the Old Testament. Those who promote the veneration of images, Muentzer wrote, "should be stoned" to death "according to the punishment of Mosaic Law."[162] Those who used images to aid their devotion, "be it a cross or a circle," are guilty of "the greatest blasphemy against God." This blasphemy is like "the adultery and whoredom about which Hosea writes [Hos 4:2 and 4:10]. Just as one commits adultery outwardly against the spouse, using the sexual organs of the flesh so adultery also occurs inwardly in the spirit if a man delights in images or created things in order to mock him who is unlike all images or creatures."[163] The mob of apostate monks wrecking churches throughout Thuringia and Saxony should not be punished because "he who smashes an idol that blasphemes God does no injustice, for his zeal is the zeal of the Lord and his action praises God."[164] Muentzer concludes his letter "In God's name release the prisoners."[165]

On August 21, Luther wrote to the city council at Muehlhausen warning of "the false prophet and wolf in sheep's clothing" heading their way and urging them not to allow Muentzer into their town, describing Muentzer as a tree "which bore no other fruit than murder, insurrection and bloodshed,"[166] but the council was powerless to resist the monks and their followers. Muentzer arrived in Muehlhausen about the time Muentzer wrote his letter justifying iconoclasm to the city council at Nordhausen. So, unsurprisingly, the apostate monks and their followers welcomed him with open arms.

Muentzer lost no time mobilizing Pfeiffer's followers by founding a chapter of the League of the Elect. Renaming his revolutionary organization Eternal Alliance, Muentzer incorporated the renegade monks and their followers under the image of the rainbow, which he affixed to a white flag along with the motto: "This is the sign of God's eternal covenant, and all who intend to support the Alliance should march under it."[167] The insistence on acceptance of suffering as the surest way to implement God's will faded from Muentzer's sermons and was replaced by

Old Testament proof texts that justified taking up the sword, along with the promise that "the people will go free and God alone will be their Lord."[168]

Muentzer's opportunity to take up the sword came soon enough, when a furrier who was a follower of the renegade monks got drunk at a wedding reception and insulted two city council members. When the councilmen tried to arrest him, they set off an insurrection. Muentzer and Pfeiffer, wielding a naked sword and a red cross, led 200 followers out of town in protest. The sword symbolically pointed toward sedition and insurrection. By bearing the naked sword before him in procession Muentzer indicated he was *de facto* the legal authority in Muehlhausen and that he and his followers were willing to use military force. "The bearing of the sword has its significance," St. Paul said in his epistle to the Romans (13:4). Recognizing that significance, the city council released the furrier and then fled because they feared the Eternal Alliance would murder them in their beds. By September 27, the city council had regained the upper hand and, as their first act, they expelled Muentzer and Pfeiffer. Both men fled to Bibra, where they met with the bookseller Hans Hut, later founder of the Hutterites, and included him as a member of the Eternal Alliance, which was gaining momentum among the lower classes in Saxony and Thuringia. Hutt introduced them to other revolutionary groups and arranged publication of Muentzer's tract "Special Exposure."

Muentzer then traveled incognito to Basel, where he met Johannes Oecolampadius and Ulrich Hugwald, who encouraged him to visit the Hegau and Klettgau regions, where the looting of Church property was coalescing into the Peasant Revolt. Oecolampadius and Hugwald were followers of the Swiss reformer, Huldreich Zwingli. Muentzer did not meet Zwingli in Basel, probably because Zwingli was having troubles of his own. Catholics were attacking Zwingli as a Judaizer, as Luther had attacked Muentzer. "[S]o strong was the suspicion of his Jewish affiliations" that he responded in print, denying "he had derived his knowledge of Scriptures from a certain Jew of Winterthur, named Moses."[169] Zwingli was charged with secret association with the Jews, but his pamphlet denied what "certain monks are saying," namely, that "we have learned at Zurich all our knowledge of the Divine Word from the Jews."[170] Being stigmatized as a Half-Jew or a Judaizer acting as an agent of the Jews would have cost Zwingli his credibility as a reformer. So he denied "what has been said," namely, "that the Jew, Moses of Winterthur, has openly boasted that he comes to us and teaches us, and that we have repeatedly gone to him in secret and that I have received him through a third person."[171] Zwingli, however, admits "It is true that a short time ago in the presence of more than ten learned and pious men of Zurich, I had conversed with him concerning certain prophecies in the Old Testament; but all concerning their error, that they are in misery, since they refuse to accept the Lord Jesus Christ."[172]

Newman indicates there was good reason that "several of Zwingli's doctrines were called 'Judaic.'"[173] Like Muentzer, Zwingli felt "the history of Israel constituted the normal standard of Christian life; he also felt that the writings of Moses were the most ancient revelation and hence the highest authority."[174] Zwingli's "reliance on the Old Testament" had political consequences, just as they had had for Muentzer, because "Zwingli's model commonwealth had its roots in the Mosaic theocracy."[175] And in practicing "Old Testament theocratic and anti-monarchical principles, Zwingli," like Cromwell and Muentzer, "appealed to the examples of Joshua and Gideon, as he went forth to battle in both the first and second Cappel wars."[176] Zwingli, according to Newman, admitted he learned Hebrew from a Jew, Andrew Boeschenstein, and that he had debated "the Messianic prophecies" with Moses of Winterthur. The Catholics, according to Newman, correctly asserted Zwingli "not only inclined towards the Jewish Old Testament, but also had direct relations with local Jews."[177] The issue died when Zwingli died on the battlefield of Cappel, but the suspicion that the Protestants were demi-Jews collaborating with the Jews in their destruction of the Catholic Church never went away because there was too much evidence—iconoclasm, devotion to Hebrew scriptures, Old Testament prooftexting, and Unitarian attacks on the Trinity—to support it.

By Easter 1525 the Peasant Revolt was no longer a threat; it was a reality. The sporadic looting of Church property had become a concerted effort to topple princes from their thrones and put the sword-bearing, Bible-citing masses in their place. The peasant uprising began on the Upper Rhine and spread like a fire driven by a strong wind. One by one the castles and monasteries in the path of the marauding peasant horde went up in flames after their stores were looted to swell the revolutionaries' coffers.

Luther visited the war theater and witnessed the anarchy first hand. We can imagine him railing at the peasants he had indirectly inspired, and them laughing at his words as they marched off to plunder another monastery. If Luther had any qualms, they were repressed when he wrote his tract urging the princes to slaughter the murderous thieving peasant hordes. The man who strangles the revolutionary is doing a good deed in God's eyes:

> Because when it comes to revolutionaries, every man is both judge and executioner, just as when a fire breaks out, the first man to get there and put it out is the best man for the job. I say this because revolution is not an evil like murder, rather it is like a raging conflagration, something that burns an entire country to the ground and lays everything to waste in its path. Revolution brings in its wake a land full of murder and bloodshed, and it makes widows and orphans and destroys everything in its path like the worst evil imaginable. As a result everyone who is able should go on the attack and strangle and stab, either openly or clandestinely, with just one consideration in mind, namely, that there is nothing more poisonous, pathological or diabolical than a revolutionary. It's the same as when you have to slaughter a mad dog. If you don't kill him, he will kill you and, on top of that, will take your entire country with you when you go.[178]

Many princes were intimidated by the mob and by the fact that the old order seemed fated to change. Frederick the Wise witnessed the devastation from his deathbed and was overcome by an eerie lassitude. "May God turn his wrath from us," he prayed. But then, as if resigned to the inevitable, added, "if God wills it, it will turn out that the common man will rule."[179] Many nobles went over to the revolutionaries to preserve what they had and to augment it in the sacking of monasteries. The Count of Stolberg, birthplace of Muentzer, submitted to the rebels without a fight. The Counts of Schwarzburg and Hohnstein did the same, relinquishing their aristocratic titles and becoming "brother" revolutionaries, much as the Duc d'Orleans would do two and half centuries later when he became known as Philip Egalite. Their castles were handed over to the peasants, who graciously compensated them by giving them confiscated church property in exchange.

Thomas Muentzer expressed his euphoria in the many letters he wrote urging his followers to join in the upheaval. "The whole of Germany, France, Italy is awake," Muentzer wrote to his former congregation in Allstedt. "The master wants to set the game in motion; the evil-doers are for it. At Fulda, four abbeys were laid waste during Easter Week, the peasants in the Klettgau and the Hegau in the Black Forest have risen, three thousand strong, and the size of the peasant host is growing all the time."[180] Muentzer admonished the Allstedters to fight the Lord's battle by joining with the miners from Mansfeld and the peasants in neighboring towns and villages. "Go to it," he continued. "Go to it while the fire is hot! Don't let your sword grow cold, don't let it hang down limply! Hammer away ding-dong on the anvils of Nimrod, cast down their tower to the ground."[181] Muentzer regarded Nimrod, according to one commentator, "not only as the first builder of cities but as the originator of private property and class distinctions."[182]

When he addressed the League at Allstedt in April 1525, Muentzer, as a Catholic priest, knew that he had to go against the Catholic grain by reminding his flock "do not be merciful."[183] The only way he could make this anti-Christian injunction plausible was by invoking the Old Testament:

> Do not be merciful, even though Esau offers you good words, Genesis 33:4. Pay no heed to the lamentations of the godless. They will bid you in a friendly manner [for mercy], cry and plead like children. Do no let yourselves be merciful, as God commanded through Moses, Deuteronomy 7: 1-5. And God has revealed the same thing to us. Stir up the villages and cities, and especially the miners with other good fellows who would be good for our cause. We must sleep no longer.... The peasants of Eisfeld have taken up arms against their lords, and shortly, they will show them no mercy. May events of this kind be an example for you. You must go at them, at them. The time is here.... Pass this letter on to the miners.... At them, at them while the fire is hot! Do not let your sword get cold, do not let your arms go lame! Strike—cling, clang!—on the anvils of Nimrod. Throw their towers to the ground.... God leads you—follow, follow! The story is already written—Matthew 24, Ezekiel 34, Daniel 74, Ezra 16, Revelation 6—scriptural passages that are all interpreted by Romans 13.... When Jehosaphat heard these words he fell down. Do likewise.[184]

Ernst Bloch, the 20th Century Marxist, described Muentzer's exhortation as "the most impassioned, frenzied manifesto of revolution of all time."[185] The question is whether Muentzer was swept away by excitement of the moment or whether he had abandoned the principles of mystical suffering earlier. Manfred Bensing says Muentzer became a revolutionary when the peasants revolted; others claim he had been a revolutionary all along. Either way, Muentzer felt the revolutionary activity around him vindicated his theological views.

In February 1525, Muentzer surfaced in Fulda during revolutionary disturbances in that city. Soon, he was back in Muehlhausen, where he was welcomed with open arms. On March 17, Muentzer and Pfeiffer organized a coup that deposed the city council and put the Eternal Council, made up of the Elect, in its place. Marching under Muentzer's rainbow banner, the Eternal Council prepared to bring on the advent of the Millennium by force of arms. Eerie parallels with the Taborites continued to emerge. Like Jan Zelivsky, another master at political mobilization of the mob, Muentzer harangued the alliance members assembled outside city walls to engage in military exercises, until a captain cut him off and told him preachers belonged in the pulpit. Like Jan Zelivsky, Muentzer fancied himself a military leader, an illusion that would have devastating consequences for the German peasants, just as it had had for the Hussites under Zelivsky. The crowd for their part discharged the energy which Muentzer had infused into them by sacking the convent of St. Mary Magdalene when they returned to town. Once the Eternal Council took over governance of Muehlhausen, Muentzer seemed ready to spread the gospel of revolution to the rest of Germany.

When word reached the Elect in Muehlhausen that the administrator in Salza had arrested evangelical preachers and planned to execute them, Muentzer decided to act. On April 26, Muentzer marched out of town under the rainbow banner with several hundred men to liberate the preachers, punish the council that had imprisoned them, and drive the Franciscans from the monasteries. Muentzer's exalted state of mind can be inferred from letters he wrote while his army was on the march and the end of the world seemed imminent. "God," Muentzer wrote to the people of Eisenach, "is now moving nearly the whole world to a recognition of divine truth, and this recognition is also proved with the greatest zeal against the tyrants as Daniel 7:27 clearly says. There Daniel prophesied that power shall be given to the common people, which is also indicated in Revelation 11:15—that Christ shall have jurisdiction over the kingdom of this world."[186] The Lord was using the weak, i.e., Muentzer and his ragtag army of peasants, "to knock the mighty from their thrones," as he had used "unlearned people in order to bring about the ruination of the untrue, treacherous scribes."[187]

In a letter of May 12, Muentzer addressed Count Ernst of Mansfeld as, "You miserable, needy bag of maggots," asking him "who made you a prince of people whom God has won with his precious blood?" Then Muentzer informed the count that he would be "persecuted and annihilated" by Muentzer's avenging army of saints. To make this sedition more palatable, Muentzer cast it in the familiar terms of Old Testament drama. "God," Muentzer informed Count Ernst, "has hardened you like King Pharaoh and like the kings that God wanted to wipe out, Joshua 5 and 11.... In brief, through God's mighty power, you have been delivered up for destruction. If you do not want to humble yourself before the little people, then an eternal shame before all Christendom will fall on your neck and you will become a martyr for the devil.... So that you also know that we have a strict order about it, I say: The eternal living God has ordered us to push you from your throne with the power that has been given us." The entire Old Testament—here Muentzer listed "Ezekiel 34:1 and 39:1, Daniel 7:11, Micha 3:1-4," as well as "Obadiah the prophet says [Ob 4]" was unanimous "that your lair must be torn apart and smashed to pieces."[188]

On the same day, Muentzer wrote to Count Albrecht of Mansfeld with the same message, enlivened by invidious references to Muentzer's archrival Luther: "Have you not been able to find in your Lutheran grits and your Wittenberg soup what Ezekiel 37:26-7 prophesies? And have you not been able to taste in your Martinian manure what the same prophet says later Ezekiel 30:17-20"? Muentzer's message was simple. According to his reading of Daniel 7, "God has given power to the community." One day later, Muentzer said the same to the people of Erfurt. "Daniel 7:27" or at least Muentzer's reading of it, specified "power shall be given to the common people." People must be free of tyrants "if the pure word of God is to dawn." The people of Erfurt, therefore, should "Help us in every way that you can, with manpower and artillery, so that we fulfill what God himself has commanded, Ezekiel 34:25, where he says, 'I will release you from those who have beaten you with their tyranny. I will drive the wild animals from your land.'"[189]

Muentzer arrived in Frankenhausen on May 12, and was immediately accepted by the rebel hordes as their leader; he then acted as judge in a capital case, condemning three men to death and presiding over their execution. He also began signing his letters, "Thomas Muentzer with the sword of Gideon."[190] This form of signature indicated more than just turning from the Cross and taking up the sword in Old Testament judaizing fashion. It also indicated that Muentzer was increasingly preoccupied with military matters. The size of his army may have prompted him to associate his fate with Gideon's: Muentzer arrived at Frankenhausen at the head of only 300 men and eight mounted guns because of a split over strategy with Heinrich Pfeiffer. Muentzer wanted to attack Ernst von Mansfeld's army with the help of the peasant host already near Frankenhausen. Pfeiffer was less daring than Muentzer, opting for a more defensive strategy. Pfeiffer wanted to take advantage of the rich spoils near Eichsfeld. Three hundred years later, Friedrich Engels claimed Pfeiffer represented "the local narrow-minded class view of the petty bourgeois"[191] that betrayed the real revolution represented by Muentzer and his peasant army.

Pfeiffer had reason to be defensive. Pfeiffer knew their campaign was not going to consist of a series of easy looting sessions now that the princes had mobilized for war. By 1525, the princes saw the peasants as a serious threat. Instead of perceived orderly exploitation from Rome, they were confronted with anarchy from below. The time had come to end that threat and, with Luther's blessing, consolidate power in their own hands to the detriment of the peasants and the Roman Church. The year 1525 saw a rising crescendo of battles, at the end of which 100,000 peasants would be dead. Around the same time that Muentzer arrived in Frankenhausen, Luther's ally, Philip of Hesse, had just crushed the peasants at Fulda and advanced toward Frankenhausen, arriving on May 14 after an all night march. Fatigue may have contributed to his defeat in the first skirmish with the rebels, who numbered about 6,000. The peasants won the first battle, even though they were numerically far inferior to Philips' force. Philip, however, had time on his side; Saxon reinforcements were on their way from Leipzig. The peasants were unaware of all this; as a result, morale rose in the peasant camp. Gideon might win this one after all.

When the sun rose on May 15, the situation did not look good for the rebels. The Saxon troops had arrived, bolstering Philip of Hesse's army. The miners from Mansfeld who were supposed to join the rebels had been intercepted and defeated, depriving Muentzer of much needed reinforcements. Muentzer, the new Gideon, was both prophet and general, but unaware that the roles might conflict. As their general, he assembled the peasant horde behind a barricade of battlewagons at the foot of Kyfhausen, a 470-meter-high hill outside of Frankenhausen. The troop deployment indicates Muentzer had studied the tactics of Jan Zizka, the great Hussite general. However, like Jan Zelivsky, Muentzer had not studied diligently enough to understand the wagons had to be deployed behind trenches at the top of the hill to have military effect. And, in the 100 years since Zizka, the technology of war had changed. The army Muentzer faced had artillery.

In his confrontation with Philip of Hesse, Muentzer acted like a prophet, not a general. Muentzer spread the impression among the rebellious peasants that God was on their side and that numbers didn't matter. "Be bold," he told them, "and put your trust in God alone, and he will endow your small band with more strength than you would ever believe."[192] Muentzer told them God Himself had not only assured him of victory, they needn't fear the artillery of Philip and his Hessians because he, Thomas Muentzer, would catch their cannon balls in the sleeves of his cloak and fling them back upon them. God Himself would transform heaven and earth rather than see his people go down to defeat fighting the godless followers of Martin Luther. At the moment Muentzer finished his speech, a rainbow appeared in the sky. He took it as a sign of imminent success, filling his followers with courage and enthusiasm.

Their enthusiasm didn't last long. Philip claimed mendaciously that the peasants could all go home unharmed if they handed Muentzer over to him. Taken in by pretext, the peasants were lulled into letting the Hessians move dangerously close to their position. As soon as they were within artillery range, the Hessians opened fire on the unsuspecting peasants. Muentzer caught no cannonballs in the sleeves of his cloak. The peasants broke from behind their battlewagons and fled in panic across the open fields, where they were easy prey for Philip's heavy cavalry. In the ensuing slaughter, Philip of Hesse's troops slaughtered more than 6,000 peasants, losing only six of their own men. Blood flowed through the alleys of Frankenhausen, where the terrified peasants sought refuge, along with their leader, who was found cowering under a bed.

Muentzer was taken in chains to Count Ernst of Mansfeld's castle where he was interrogated and tortured. In a confession dated May 16, 1525, one day after he was captured, Muentzer admitted that in the Klettgau and Hegau regions, he had advanced propositions on how one should rule according to the gospel, but he insisted he was not responsible for the insurrections there because they were already in open rebellion. He preached to the people there not to incite them to rebellion, he insisted, but because Oecolampadius and Hugowaldus had asked him to. Lest they not believe him, the princes should consult the letters those two men had written to him, which could be found in a bag still in his wife's possession in Muehlhausen.

Under torture, Muentzer confessed that if he had captured the castle of Heldrungen, where he was being interrogated, he would have beheaded Count Ernst. Under torture, he claimed he began the rebellion so all Christians would be equal because he wanted to establish the fundamental principle "All property should be held in common."[193] Princes who disagreed "should be beheaded or hanged."[194]

Muentzer also justified his role in the execution of three prisoners by claiming he was carrying out "divine justice." George of Saxony urged him to repent for breaking his vow of celibacy. Perhaps in response, Muentzer asked that his wife and child not suffer and that they be allowed to keep his possessions. Philip of Hesse tried to engage Muentzer in theological disputes, and to get him to disavow the Old Testament as a suitable basis for political authority. Muentzer "refused to make the expected confession, and instead with his last strength, he urged the princes to burden the poor people no more, and to immerse themselves in the Old Testament Books of Kings in order to learn how the office of rulership could be held in a manner pleasing to God."[195] So, in political matters, Muentzer remained impenitent to the end. Some insisted the rest of his confession and retractions were ambiguous, but his last words, spoken "at Heldrungen in my prison and at the end of my life. May 17, 1525"[196] seem clear: "I wish to express this now, as my last words, with which I want to remove the burden from my soul, so that no further rebellion take place and so that no more innocent blood is shed."[197]

Heinrich Pfeiffer had left before the battle with a troop of 300 men and tried to break through the princes' lines to link up with rebel troops in Franconia, but he was captured near Eisenach and brought back to Muehlhausen, which had surrendered without a fight on May 25. On May 27, 1525, Muentzer and Pfeiffer were decapitated outside the walls of Muehlhausen. Christ, not Gideon had the last word. Those who lived by the sword died by it. Muentzer's early claim that, if anyone could prove him wrong, he "deserved to have his head chopped off,"[198] was apparently fulfilled. The heads of Muentzer and Pfeiffer were impaled on one set of poles, their bodies on another set. Muehlhausen endured draconian sanctions, from which it never recovered economically. The warning was clear. Those who took the sword into their own hands would die by the sword wielded ruthlessly by princes justified by Luther.

But other warnings were necessary too. Luther had ripped Scripture from its matrix in the Church and turned Scripture into an instrument of revolution. If there were no court of final appeal in the magisterium of the Church, who was to tell Muentzer he was wrong when he claimed scripture and private revelation justified revolution? The Lutheran insistence on the absolute power of the princes created the notion they were above the moral law and contributed directly to the rise of absolutism and, indirectly, to the rise of totalitarianism. The dialectic of revolution was sure to continue despite the use of Muentzer's impaled head as a terrible deterrent against taking up the sword.

Muentzer's death insured a tradition of political repression, which, paradoxically, kept his memory and the hope of revolution alive long after the Anabaptist communities had abandoned revolutionary activity. Muentzer's martyrdom insured, in the words of Friedrich Engels, "The German people, too, [would] have their revolutionary tradition."[199] When the communists took over Thuringia in the wake of World War II, they renamed Muehlhausen Thomas Muentzer-Stadt to prove, again in Engels' words, that "There was a time when Germany produced characters who could match the best men in the revolutions of other countries, when German people displayed an endurance and vigor, which would in a more centralized nation have yielded the most magnificent results, and when German peasants and plebeians were full of ideas and plans that often made their descendants shudder."[200] As Heinrich Heine would make clear, that revolutionary shudder began with the Reformation. "It seems to me that a methodical people like the Germans had to begin its philosophical preoccupations with the reformation and that they could only bring them to completion by going over to revolution."[201]

Less than ten years after Muentzer's death, revolution broke out again, at the opposite end of the Germanies, fueled by Muentzer's example and his judaizing Old Testament theology.

Chapter Nine

The Anabaptist Rebellion

Hermann Kerssenbroick, who witnessed the Anabaptist Rebellion in Muenster, felt the events were foretold by celestial warnings years in advance. On October 11, 1527, at four a.m., a marvelous sign appeared in the heavens. All across northern Europe men said they saw a bent arm holding in its hand a two-edged sword, on either side of which dark stars were arrayed. At the sword's point a larger and brighter star was visible. Then in the clouds on either side of the two-edged sword, men saw bloody swords mixed with decapitated heads. The vision caused great distress and consternation. Kerssenbroick said many who saw it went mad.

That madness was reflected in Germany during the 1520s. The Peasants' War followed close on the heels of Luther's break with Rome, reaching its bloody conclusion in 1525. Two years after the vision of the bloody sword, a disease known as the English Sweats swept the Germanies, presaging, in Kerssenbroick's words, "a horrible catastrophe among men."[1] Also in 1529, Holy Roman Emperor Charles V became concerned about the spread of a heresy that denied baptism to infants and so, in an age of high infant mortality, denied many children the beatific vision. Concerned that the sect of rebaptizers, known in Germany as the *Wiedertaueffer* and in England as the Anabaptists, was spreading heresy and insurrection, Charles ordered their extermination. The princes, recognizing the revolutionary consequences of Anabaptist religious beliefs, obliged. Henry VIII burned a dozen Anabaptists at the stake in England. Luther detested the Anabaptists and urged the German princes to follow Henry's example.

Luther saw the connection between his erstwhile disciple Thomas Muentzer and the Anabaptists and, because the connection was apparent to others too, distanced himself from the Anabaptists by the vehemence of his denunciation. The Anabaptists, according to Luther, had abandoned Christian doctrine, and had arrogated to themselves the power of the sword that rightly belonged to magistrates alone. They used religious enthusiasm to spread sedition and revolution wherever they gained a foothold, just as the whoring, thieving spawn of Muentzer had. Even Zwingli, a judaizing political revolutionary without qualms about taking up the sword, denounced them too. Even though many Anabaptists claimed to be pacifists, when Zwingli died in 1531 the Anabaptists were the cutting edge of the revolutionary upheaval sweeping central Europe under the banner of reformation.

By 1530, the main focus of Anabaptist activity was the low countries of the north, especially the Westphalian city of Muenster. Perhaps it was the similarity in the names Muentzer and Muenster, but Muenster became inextricably linked in the popular mind with the Peasant Rebellion that Muentzer orchestrated in

Thuringia five years before. Contemporary doggerel reinforced the connection: "The crowd from Muenster hoped for renown/By bringing the peasants into their town."[2]

Ditties like this were passed around by word of mouth and by the rudimentary broadsheets and newspapers that were the second fruits of the invention of the printing press. The first fruit was political unrest, due to publication of Luther's translation of the Bible. The anonymous author of the *"Newe Zeitung, die Wiedertaueffer zu Muenster belangend,"* emphasized the connection between Muenster and Muentzer: "Since the Muensterites abandoned God's word ... God afflicted them with grave errors and lust.... Thomas Muentzer tried to do the same with the help of his rebellious peasants and perished miserably."[3] The political stakes and dangers were much higher in the 1530s than in the 1520s. All of the wickedness of the Bohemian Taborites which Muenster had brought into southern German speaking lands burst forth much more virulently and threatened to spread through the north and to drag into chaos over a thousand years of patiently erected social order.

In 1525, the revolutionary fervor of the Peasant Revolt arrived in Muenster, whose name derived from the Latin word for monastery, and which had been a bishopric since 805, i.e., for roughly half of the life of the Catholic Church. As elsewhere, the monasteries were the focus of the ire of the reformers, who played on the resentments of the common man. The numerous churches, convents and monasteries paid no property taxes to the city. And the monasteries and convents ran their own businesses in this town of slightly more than 9,000, with monks and nuns working at looms producing cloth and tapestries that competed with the laymen in the same business who had to pay taxes and provide for their families.

Facing rebellion spreading to Muenster from the south, Prince Bishop Frederich von Wiede granted the city unprecedented independence from Church authority. After the disturbances of 1525, Muenster was ruled by a council of 24, two of whom functioned as co-mayors. In 1532, the guilds, full of resentment at the monasteries, placed their candidates on the town council and then forced them to install Lutheran preachers in the town's churches. As word spread that the unvarnished Gospel was being preached there, Muenster became a magnet for the disaffected. Unruly monks and nuns as well as "the propertyless, the uprooted and the failures"[4] converged on Muenster. Freedom was the magic word which drew "the Dutch and the Frisians and scoundrels from all parts who had never settled anywhere: they flocked to Muenster and collected there," bringing with them "fugitives, exiles, criminals" and "people who having run through the fortunes of their parents were earning nothing by their own industry ... growing weary of poverty, they thought of plundering and robbing the clergy and the higher Burghers."[5] Cohn emphasizes economic factors, claiming the collapse of the cloth industry in Flanders had sent the weavers to Holland2, "which now contained the greatest concentration of insecure and harassed proletarians.... it was amongst such people that Anabaptism flourished in its most militant and crudely chiliastic form; and it was such people who now streamed into Muenster."[6] Emphazising economic causes, Cohn ignores the leadership role which rebellious, judaizing priests played in the movement and the fact that a Catholic priest infected with messianic politics through exposure to a distorted Old Testament brought revolutionary chaos to Muenster.

By the early 1530s, Bernard Rothmann (or Rottman) was an itinerant preacher who brought political unrest wherever he preached. Like Muentzer, Rothmann began his revolutionary career as an "earnest intellectual who had studied with the great Melanchthon, Luther's disciple."[7] Rothmann began preaching in Muenster without permission of the bishop or any other ecclesial authority and soon gained a following because of his fiery sermons. The bishop, as a result, asked the town council to expel him. Rothmann's uncle evidently agreed with the bishop's assessment, giving his nephew a bag of gold coins and sending him in 1530 for instruction in Cologne, a bastion of Catholic orthodoxy. Rothmann never arrived in Cologne. When he returned to Muenster one year later, he proclaimed he was no longer a Catholic priest but rather a confirmed Lutheran who planned to put Lutheran doctrines into effect in the town's churches. He soon led a mob to St. Mauritz Church, his former parish, and goaded them into an orgy of iconoclasm. The elaborate wooden altar was toppled, smashed into splinters, and then dragged into the church courtyard, where it was set on fire along with the paintings of the Blessed Virgin that the mob had torn from the church's walls. The sacred vessels of silver were crushed or melted down for secular use. Rothmann soon expanded his ministry to other churches with similar results. He preached at the Overwater Church Convent that it would soon crumble and fall into the River Aa, which ran through town. He also told the nuns they had to abandon their vows of celibacy, as he had evidently done. "You must have men; you must marry; you must bear children," Rothmann told the nuns because "the Heavenly Father has also favored me with a direct and special revelation to the same effect."[8] When the collapse of the convent did not occur when he predicted, Rothmann's stature remained undiminished because he was preaching a gospel many nuns were avid to hear.

Unsurprisingly, the bishop continued to pressure the town council to expel Rothmann. The town council continued to ignore the bishop, primarily because Rothmann had gained the ear of one of the town's most influential businessmen, a cloth merchant by the name of Bernard Knipperdolling, who was no friend of the bishop. A few years earlier, Bishop von Wied had Knipperdolling kidnapped while on a business trip and held him prisoner for six months until he was ransomed. During his imprisonment, Knipperdolling became permanently crippled when his feet were forced into iron boots, crushing his toes.

Rothmann eventually published his "Confession" with the help of Knipperdolling, who had set up a printing press in the basement of his house on the market square in Muenster. Rothmann would become the Goebbels of Muenster, making use of the new communications technology, publishing fliers and pamphlets explaining the Anabaptist cause, leading like-minded Dutchmen to pour into Muenster to cast their lot with the revolutionary movement. According to Rothmann's Confession, "the so-called Mass" wasn't a sacrifice, but rather "a sign of the true sacrifice."[9] Similarly, Christians did not have to do penance because Christ perfected and sanctified them by his perfect sacrifice once and for all. The fires of purgatory, "about which one is told that they cleanse the departed from the remnants of sin," was nothing more than a "godless invention."[10] There is only one intermediary between God and man, and that is "the man Jesus Christ." So anyone who prays to "dead saints," or invokes them as "guardian gods," denies the Christian faith.[11]

Certain political consequences flowed from this theology, according to Rothmann, no matter how much Luther and Melanchthon denied it. Rothmann conceded "man owes secular authority respect and obedience." But "as soon as the commands" of the secular authorities "no longer coincide with the word of God, we are no longer bound to follow them."[12] Kerssenbroick claims Rothmann's Confession meant "all power on earth now rested with *Demos*."[13] Since self-empowered preachers like Rothmann were now the definitive explicators of the word of God, neither the common man nor the princes held any real power in this world, or, if they did hold power, it was only at the pleasure of ex-priests like Rothmann. As in Prague over one hundred years earlier, political power was exercised by clever preachers like Rothmann and Jan Zelivsky, who knew how to manipulate the mob to achieve political results.

As in Prague, so in Muenster. The effects were not long in coming, and they were invariably destructive. Luther had compared revolution to a fire which each Christian had the duty to extinguish. Kerssenbroick watched the fire of rebellion spread through Muenster, with Rothmann's incendiary sermons spreading destruction wherever he preached. "And so it came to pass," Kerssenbroick wrote of Rothmann, "that this evil, like a fire, grew steadily and consumed everything in its path.... Since the magistrates refused to punish the rebels in our city and put an end to their predations, they went from vice to vice, rage to rage, from outrage to outrage, forward step by step, until they finally reached the point of Revolution."[14]

By February 1532, Muenster had become a Protestant town on a political trajectory that was leading it willy nilly from Lutheranism to Anabaptism and political revolution. In that month, a group of prominent citizens met in Knipperdolling's house and signed a pact, which in Arthur's words, "seems to foreshadow the American Founding Fathers' words two centuries later."[15] In the pact, Muenster's Lutheran elite "swore to devote their personal fortunes, their reputations and even their lives to the cause of freedom from oppression that Rothmann now symbolized for them."[16]

Egged on by Rothmann's incendiary sermons, the mob, largely "foreigners" from Holland and Friesland, many of whom were renegade monks and nuns, broke into St. Lambert's church and claimed it for their charismatic leader who did not have a church of his own. Rothmann commandeered the pulpit to preach "evangelical freedom" and the abolition of idol worship which so enflamed his audience that "they broke into all of the parish churches in Muenster and destroyed the chalices and other sacred vessels used during the Mass, ripped down the curtains before the altar, destroyed paintings, and stole all of the churches' treasures, profaning all holy things and holding nothing for holy which did not correspond to Rothmann's teachings."[17] The desacralization of the Mass and the vessels associated with it led, in Kerssenbroick's eyes, to "turning the Republic upside down,"[18] his term for Revolution.

Huge fires consumed wax votive candles, priestly vestments, paintings and tapestries. A massive book burning took place in the market square: Latin bibles, devotional texts, as well as secular works from personal libraries—the philosophical works of Boethius and Thomas Aquinas, the poetry of Horace and Chaucer, and the engravings of Heinrich Aldgrever and the paintings of Ludger tom Ring ... all fed the swirling flames.[19]

When Bishop Friedrich, the Count of Wied, saw "these evils were going to spread unpunished throughout the town," he considered it "more advantageous to renounce his episcopal dignity," as Kerssenbroick puts it, "than to come to grips with the situation, quell the dangerous unrest, and to tame the authors of the already mentioned unrest."[20] So Bishop Friedrich von Wied sold the bishopric and the income which accrued from it and retired to Cologne.

Perhaps Bishop Friedrich invoked the ancient disclaimer "Caveat emptor" when he sold Muenster. If not, he should have. Muenster would be a devilish trial and monstrous expense for his successor. The buyer of the bishopric, was another Prince Bishop, Franz von Waldeck, who did not observe the vow of celibacy because he was not a priest. Nor did he practice the virtue of chastity. Von Waldeck had fathered an illegitimate son by a mistress. If he had any religious sympathies, they were those of his kinsman Philip of Hesse, who had crushed the Peasant Revolt in 1525. Philip, like Franz von Waldeck, was a strong believer in law and order, as long as it was his law and his order. As a leading Anabaptists would note, Philip differed from the Anabaptists only because the power of his armies imposed not law but the will of the sovereign over the chaos which Lutheran principles, ultimately, yet invariably, engendered.

Knipperdolling and Rothmann soon challenged the new Prince-Bishop by banning the Catholic Mass, a gesture of theological effrontery tantamount to an act of war. They also proscribed receiving communion, prayers for the dead, the use of Latin, the "worship" of Mary, "smearing oil" on the dying, and other instances of "disgusting idolatry."[21] Knipperdolling appointed an armed guard to protect Rothmann from attempts the bishop might make to arrest him. In place of the Mass, Rothmann instituted the feast of fools, a religious service with disturbing similarities to the *festus fatuorum* celebrated during Carnival, when the world was turned upside-down. Like similar services in Prague under Jan Zelivsky, renegade monks and nuns would smear excrement on sacred vessels and images, proving, Rothmann would later explain to the mob, that the Mass was a worthless empty ritual, especially compared to the drinking and singing and carousing Rothmann's service provided as its substitute. After Muenster had overthrown the bishop and installed its own "tailor king," to use Luther's term, Rothmann would conduct similar services in the town's ruined Cathedral. Mass would begin with the mob desecrating the altar by throwing things like cats' heads, dead rats, and horses hooves onto it, followed by a blasphemous play during which "monks" would lift their robes and fart in unison, followed by Rothmann's explanation: "Dear brothers and sisters, all the Masses in the world are exactly as holy and sanctified as the one you have just seen."[22] Kerssenbroick felt all the "poisonous beliefs that had been festering" in Rothmann's soul finally broke out in series of frenzied denunciations of the Catholic Church," which included "disparaging reference to infant baptism and to the holding of private property."[23]

The town council, which was Lutheran, considered Rothmann and Knipperdolling their own, but both had secretly converted to the religion of the Anabaptists. Knipperdolling had been secretly re-baptized by the Elijah from Leyden, the semi-literate baker Jan Matthias (or Matthys), who had in turn been re-baptized by Melchior Hoffmann, one of the founders of Anabaptism. Hoffmann, like many of his disciples, had first been a Lutheran. He soon became a disciple of Zwingli and then he became "the Anabaptist apostle of the north." In 1533, Hoffmann ended up in Strasbourg, where he predicted the imminent end of the world and was thrown into prison. Hoffmann spent the next (and final) ten years of his life in a cage in a tower of the town. Deprived of their leader, Hoffmann's followers changed the site of the imminent second coming from Strasbourg to Muenster.

Hoffmann's mantle as the Elijah of the last days fell to the new Elijah of the North, Jan Matthias, who re-baptized Knipperdolling and who would soon preside in Muenster over the arrival of the Millennium. During the late 1520s or early 1530s, Matthias received a new revelation from the Lord informing him that Hoffmann was wrong in advocating pacifism. The Anabaptists were no longer to turn the other cheek. Now they were to take up the sword and usher in the Millennium, with Jehovah and his Old Testament prophets and warrior kings as their model. Thousands of disaffected proletarians, weavers, and monks responded to his call to arms and streamed into Muenster.

Luther and Melanchthon thought Rothmann was mentally unstable. Melanchthon, Luther's colleague and Rothmann's erstwhile mentor, felt the Anabaptists were thieves and murderers and should be treated accordingly. "The kings of the Old Testament, not only the Jewish kings but also the converted heathen kings, judged and killed the false prophets and unbelievers. Such examples show the proper office of princes .... it is plain that the worldly government is bound to drive away blasphemy, false doctrine, and heresies, and to punish those who hold to these things. This sect of Anabaptists is from the devil."[24]

The Anabaptist willingness to take up the sword of insurrection led Melanchthon to consider them murderers because "like murderers, they intended to subdue the land with the sword."[25] The Lutherans suspected the Anabaptists were manipulating the passions of the disaffected to achieve political ends. Melanchthon accused them of carrying on all kinds of fornication, "thus revealing their true sprit."[26] Melanchthon failed to mention the similarities between what he and Rothmann preached. One of the greatest was their shared emphasis on *Sola Scriptura*. Luther had translated the Bible into German in 1522. After ten years of intensive promotion and distribution in the German speaking lands, the Bible as the text which needed no Church to interpret it was having demonstrable political effects, although not the ones anticipated by Luther and Melanchthon. According to the conventional wisdom, the Bible freed from the Church's hegemony led to independent thinking. "When Luther translated the Latin bible into everyday German," Arthur tells us, "he released millions from dependence on the priests for their instruction."[27] In reality, Luther's translation led to judaizing, even though Luther was urging the German princes to confiscate the property of the Jews and subject them to forced labor.

"The inevitable result of millions of people being encouraged to think for themselves," Arthur continues, "was resistance to arbitrary authority."[28] This was certainly not true in Muenster, where the principle of *Sola Scriptura* led very quickly to imposition of the most arbitrary and tyrannical authority imaginable, namely, the disordered passions of bakers, tailors, and renegade monks. Luther and Melanchthon were horrified by what they saw in Muenster because events there showed the inadequacy of the idea that the Bible could interpret itself. The new hermeneutic of Biblical interpretation in Muenster was an elaborate rationalization, according to which first the lust and then the power of the interpreter became synonymous with the truth. It was an idea Nietzsche proposed two and a half-centuries later when he deconstructed Protestant exegesis into the will to power.

Sola Scriptura led first to judaizing and then to revolution for reasons which become clear upon reflection. Luther used rabbis to construct his text, and that text was, therefore, skewed in favor of judaizing. Beyond that, when the average man read the Bible with the admonition that he has the power to interpret it unaided by pope, priest, or council, certain things were obvious to him. First, he did not find the word "Trinity" in it. Secondly, he realized the Old Testament stories of Hebrews taking numerous wives and exterminating their enemies far outnumber the texts of the New Testament containing the admonitions of Christ. By sheer weight alone, the unsuspecting reader was led to judaizing unless corrected by a larger more powerful tradition. And Luther had discredited that larger tradition, no matter how much he hated the interpretations of those who invoked his name as a justification for their messianic politics. Bernard Rothmann, like Muentzer before him, was a pupil of Luther who took Luther's principles to their logical conclusion, even if Luther felt they were unwarranted. The best example of the law of unintended consequences came from the Lutheran doctrine of *Sola Scriptura*. Luther went out of his way to give the princes who supported him all temporal power, but *Sola Scriptura* invariably led to judaizing, and from judaizing it invariably led to revolution.

By 1532, the Emperor Charles V was hearing troubling reports about Muenster even in far away Regensburg. As a result, he ordered von Waldeck to do something. In October 1532, von Waldeck imposed a blockade on the city. As part of that blockade, he captured local cattle merchants who were driving a herd of oxen to market, confiscating the animals and holding the men in contempt of his blockade. Von Waldeck's actions inflamed local opinion against him. In retaliation, the rebels in Muenster raided the Bishop's castle in nearby Telgte, capturing some of the bishop's men, who could then be used to ransom the cattle merchants. In February 1533, after acrimonious back and forth, a settlement was signed; the bishop agreed to lift the blockade and the citizens of Muenster agreed to stop harassing the city's Catholics, to silence Rothmann and his associates, and to proclaim the traditional oath of submission to the bishop in May.

The agreement was never implemented. Thousands of newcomers flooded the city as a result of reading Rothmann's sermons, printed as pamphlets in Knipperdolling's basement. As the radicals arrived in greater numbers, the beleaguered Catholics left, radicalizing the town still further. Rothmann railed against private property in his pamphlets and encouraged immigration by hinting Muenster was willing to share its riches with anyone who came and proclaimed himself a member of the company of Christ. Since those who left were not allowed to take their property, there was, at least at the beginning, enough material wealth to satisfy the needs, if not the desires, of the newly arrived revolutionaries, who in turn spread Muenster's fame as the New Jerusalem.

Months earlier, von Waldeck had warned the city council that "out of their own volition and without a proper Christian calling, quite a few vagabonds and wandering unknown fellows have penetrated our city of Muenster in order to incite the common man with their seductive and seditious teachings,"[29] not to mention with their increasing bold and defiant criminal activity. Shortly after von Waldeck's warning, the newly arrived radical preachers began organizing public baptisms on a large scale. One of those preachers was a tailor's apprentice from nearby Leyden, Jan Bockelson (or Beukelcz or Bokelzoon), known as Jan of Leyden. Bokelzoon had run an inn; some claimed he had been involved in prostitution. He had heard the dawning of the millennium would take place in Muenster, whence he had come to baptize the already baptized. During one week at the end of 1533, 1,400 Catholics were re-baptized into the revolutionary faith. Bokelzoon had been re-baptized by Jan Matthys, who had commissioned him to go to Muenster. Together they would take up the sword and prepare the way for the Millenium by turning Muenster into the New Jerusalem.

Overwater Church Convent was greatly affected by the migration of newcomers. Forced to take in renegade nuns from all over Holland, Abbess Ida von Merveldt noticed the newcomers were corrupting the nuns under her charge. They were, she wrote to the bishop, becoming more and more difficult, refusing to follow the rubrics of the traditional services, insisting on singing the new hymns in German, refusing to wear their habits, and making life in the convent unbearable because of their disobedience. When Bokelzoon and the itinerant preachers arrived in Muenster, many nuns of the Overwater Church Convent presented themselves for re-baptism, to Ida von Merveldt's chagrin.

In January 1534, the mob, which contained many re-baptized nuns from the Overwater Convent, stormed St. Lambert's Church and claimed it for Rothmann. When the women were rebuked by the city councilors, they drove those who rebuked them back inside the city hall under a hail of pig and cow manure. Rothmann returned to Overwater Church Convent to preach on February 6. Rothmann had previously preached there, urging the nuns to violate their vow of celibacy and claiming the convent would fall into the river if they didn't. Since the date for the doom of the convent had come and gone, Rothmann began his remarks by claiming the predicted catastrophe was averted because the nuns "had seen the errors of their ways, causing God to be merciful."[30] The Anabaptists were resolutely Adventist, predicting the day and the hour when the world would end, and then re-interpreting in a suitably spiritual manner when it did not.

On February 8, Bokelzoon received a vision from the Lord announcing that Muenster had become the New Jerusalem. He ran naked through the streets of Muenster announcing that vision to the town's inhabitants, calling them to repentance. Soon the town's population, swollen with renegade monks and nuns who had put off their habits and taken on the new baptism, began to imitate Bokelzoon. The liberated nuns had visions of the coming apocalypse so intense that they would tear off their clothes and roll around in mud and dung, frothing at the mouth, screaming the end times had finally arrived.

The Anabaptists received unwitting assistance from Charles V and his Spanish troops in the Netherlands, whose severity in dealing with the new heresy drove many from their homes. If the severity of the Spanish troops was the stick, then Rothmann's *Flugschriften*, printed in Knipperdolling's basement, was the carrot. Rothmann portrayed Muenster as the new Promised Land, whose prosperity was based on the abolition of private property; all shared equally in the town's wealth. There was food and clothing for all in Muenster, and if that weren't incentive enough to abandon the old life in Egypt, there were the warnings about the coming times of tribulation. "No one should neglect to go along and thus tempt God to punish him, because there is an insurrection all over the world. As it is written in Jeremiah 51:6, the Lord decrees that every man must flee out of Babylon and deliver his soul, for this is the time of the Lord's vengeance. I do not simply tell you this," Rothmann continued, "but command you in the name of the Lord to obey."[31] If a man's wife and family were unpersuaded by the new gospel, the man should leave them behind to perish in the coming conflagration.

Subsequent behavior indicated that Rothmann and his messengers were getting the message out. On February 10, seven men and seven women tore off their clothes and, "having put the old Adam aside"[32] as Hoffmann had instructed, ran naked through Amsterdam. Arrested and thrown into jail, they persuaded their fellow inmates to throw off their clothes too. The need for clothing resulted from Adam's sin. Those who wore no clothes were saying Original Sin had been eliminated. The 14 who shed their clothes in Amsterdam were soon executed, but their beliefs spread through Holland as a result of Rothmann's pamphlets and the *Newe Zeitungen* or *New Newspaper* that reported on the bizarre behavior in Muenster. The incident repeated itself on March 22, with the same results for the Anabaptists, who this time marched through the streets bearing swords. By the time these Anabaptists were executed, thousands of like-minded Dutchmen had responded to a secret letter Matthys had signed as Emmanuel, urging the faithful to converge on Hasselt to embark for Muenster. The 15,000 pilgrims who heeded the call and converged on Hasselt were dispersed by Spanish troops and sent home. One hundred of their leaders were executed.

Among those migrants who got through was Jan Matthys, the Anabaptist Elijah, who had arrived in Muenster in February, preceded by Bokelzoon and accompanied by his ex-Carmelite nun concubine, the beautiful Divara, a woman 20 years his junior, who invariably accompanied him as he stalked the streets of the New Jerusalem, uttering dire visions of death by the sword. At some point during the turmoil leading up the last days, Matthys had abandoned the pacifism of Melchior Hoffmann and had become an avid proponent of armed insurrection, in the typically Judaizing fashion of those, like his predecessor Thomas Muentzer, who saw themselves as Old Testament prophets wielding the sword of Gideon. Once Matthys joined forces with Bokelzoon, Rothmann, and Knipperdolling, political power effectively transferred from the city council, then negotiating a settlement with the bishop, to the charismatic preachers who could manipulate the mob to intimidate the council into doing its bidding.

On the evening of February 9 and 10, the mob, whipped into a threatening frenzy by Bokelzoon, Matthys, and Rothmann, forced the city council to support its cause, a result the mob took as divine vindication of their efforts. Matthys now was effectively in charge of the theocratic state whose advent he had predicted in his sermons. Re-baptism had replaced the civic oath as the basis for citizenship in the New Jerusalem.

In late February, the mob forced election of a new city council, forcing the Lutheran and Catholic moderates who had negotiated the agreement with the bishop out of government and eventually out of town. Knipperdolling was elected mayor and shared power with Matthys and Bokelzoon, with Rothmann acting as their minister of propaganda. Four days later Matthys fell face first into the muddy slush in front of Muenster's Cathedral. When he regained consciousness and arose from the muck, revived from his trance, it was with a new vision for the New Jerusalem. "Drive away the sons of Esau," the told his followers.[33] Matthys ordered the council to expel all unbelievers from town. Matthys' followers then went house to house, routing those who refused re-baptism from their hiding places and assembling them in the market place, exposed without proper clothing, for their imminent expulsion. Those who were about to be expelled had their possessions plundered to swell the coffers of the city, which could now use their confiscated wealth to maintain newly arrived revolutionaries. Kerssenbroick, who was among those expelled, described women who "carried their naked nursing babies and begged in vain for rags to clothe them in."[34] Other women, "driven from their maternity beds, gave birth in the streets. Miserable children, barefoot in the snow, whimpered beside their fathers."[35] Offered the choice of re-baptism or expulsion from her native town in the dead of winter, one old woman told Matthys, "You may baptize me in the name of the devil, for I have already been baptized in the name of God."[36]

Once the 'godless' were expelled, the Elect celebrated in an orgy of drunkenness and destruction. Bursting into the Cathedral, the mob of the Elect destroyed ancient manuscripts, including the Bible, and smeared paintings of the Blessed Virgin with excrement. They then broke into the tombs of deceased clergy and disinterred their bones, scattering them over the floor of the Cathedral. The brass pipes of the Cathedral's great organ were melted and made into shell casings. The stained glass windows were shattered and the high altar used as fuel for the fire that destroyed what they felt not worth defiling. Paintings were stripped from frames and consigned to the flames, the frames were then used as toilet seats in the guard houses on the city wall. Finally, the town clock in the Cathedral was destroyed. Now, as in other revolutions that followed, was the revolutionary year one.

The destruction was consistent with Jan Matthys revolutionary vision, and that of many who would come after him. For the new world to begin, the old world had to be destroyed. Iconoclasm was not only an expression of hatred for the Catholic world, it was also a way of hastening the Millennium, the real thousand year reign of Christ on earth which began with their plundering. Matthy's theology of salvation through destruction had political purposes. If the symbols of Church and State, twin pillars of the social order, could be shown as vulnerable, then those who destroyed them proved, to themselves at least, that they now wielded the power. Spontaneous street theater paraded and then hanged the newly disempowered bishop in effigy. Houses with straw crosses over their doors, symbolizing their owners' allegiance to the bishop, were looted and their inhabitants dragged into the streets and beaten. The mob marched through the town singing obscene lyrics to the tunes of ancient hymns. The old order had been destroyed and freedom—or its simulacrum, license—reigned in its place.

Because the new Anabaptist council reneged on the agreement with the bishop, the city was forced to renegotiate. The bishop made what he felt was a more than reasonable offer, but the offer never made it to the city council. Herman Tilbeck, the mayor and chief negotiator, had secretly become an Anabaptist. Acting as Knipperdolling's agent, he pocketed the bishop's peace offer and delivered instead what he claimed was the bishop's dismissive rebuke. The offended council then sided with the truculent Anabaptists, and the bishop, thinking the council had rejected an offer that bespoke good faith and generosity, now had to resolve the issue by force of arms.

When the town council sided with the Anabaptists and rebuffed the bishop's offer, wild celebrations erupted in the streets of Muenster. The mob celebrated with "shameless abandon."[37] Men hopped in the mud and slush as if they almost possessed the ability to fly. Women let down their hair and then threw off their clothes and threw themselves into the mixture of snow, mud, and pig manure, where they lay with arms outstretched as if to embrace a new revelation pouring down on them from heaven. Perhaps influenced by the manure into which they pressed their faces, the women squealed like pigs as their co-religionists ran around in circles, uttering prophecies while frothing at the mouth. The world had succumbed to revolution and had been turned upside down. The inversions of everyday life practiced once a year during carnival were now the norm. There was no sacrifice of the Mass anymore in the New Jerusalem; blasphemous parodies were now performed regularly by the revelers, dressed as priests, bishops and nuns, marching through the town singing songs with obscene lyrics parodying hymns. Reports of the revelry drew ever more like-minded people to the town. Slowly the voice of reason was extinguished, oftentimes by the brutal misguided actions of Bishop von Waldeck himself: Dr. Friedrich von Wyck, a lawyer from Bremen sent to negotiate a truce, was executed by the bishop, ending all possibility of a peaceful settlement.

When the denizens of the New Jerusalem awoke from their revelry on the morning of February 28, they beheld before their walls hundreds of laborers digging trenches and throwing up earthworks. The bishop's blockade had become a full-blown siege. The bishop had limited resources, but his kinsman, Phillip of Hesse, was as concerned about Anabaptism as he had been about the Peasants Revolt a decade earlier, and was willing to do whatever was in his power to stop it. The bishop had no artillery, so Philip supplied him two huge siege guns, known as the Devil and the Devil's mother. By May, the 8,000 soldiers in the bishop's employ had erected the rudiments of a four-mile-in-circumference wall of earthworks, moats, and blockhouses, which with increasing effectiveness would cut Muenster off from the outside world. The bishop's expenses were enormous, plunging his bishopric into debt for centuries to come. From the viewpoint of the Anabaptists, it seemed like money wasted. No one could defeat a city as impregnable as Muenster, they thought, certainly not someone with the limited resources of Franz von Waldeck, who had to spend 34,000 guilders a month just to keep his soldiers from deserting. Besides, God was on their side and would lead them to victory no matter how great the odds.

Like so many other tyrants, Matthys used the threat of war to consolidate his political power. As one of those measures, Matthys announced that those who were still in Muenster had no need of money; they should therefore deposit whatever gold and valuables they had with his agents, who would use it for the common good, as determined by the Elijah from Leyden. When a blacksmith complained, he was executed summarily, inaugurating a reign of terror that would soon reach unprecedented and legendary proportions. Rothmann obligingly wrote a pamphlet extolling the virtues of the now mandatory communism. Matthys took complete control of the flow of information in the town, burning all books save the Bible, whose interpreter he and he alone now was. The book banning and burning "deprived the inhabitants of Muenster of all access to theological speculations from the Fathers onwards and thereby assured the Anabaptist leaders of a monopoly on the interpretation of the Scriptures."[38]

Since Muenster was well-provisioned, protected by massive walls, with a river running through it that could fill moats and provide drinking water, the Anabaptists were not overly concerned about the siege. Life in Muenster quickly devolved into a routine of boredom punctuated by random death. To relieve the boredom of the siege, the bishop's soldiers snuck up to Muenster's walls under the cover of darkness and nailed torn pants to the town gates. Then in the light of the following day, they would call out, "Tailor," referring to Bokelzoon's previous occupation, "patch my old and torn pants."[39]

In symbolic retaliation, the Anabaptist soldiers made a cloth dummy, which they stuffed with hay and then decorated with mock papal bulls and indulgences. Then, tying it to an old mare, they drove the mare out of town towards the bishop's encampment. When that made little impression, they filled a large barrel with human excrement and sent it on the back of a driver-less wagon. The bishop's soldiers often competed to see who could get closest to the city's walls and expose his buttocks to the city's defenders. One boy in the bishop's service made the mistake of doing this in the same place several days running, enabling the Anabaptist soldiers to train a field piece on the spot. Watching the young lad pull down his pants for his last performance, the Anabaptists scored a direct hit on his naked buttocks, "scattering his limbs," in Kerssenbroick's words, "so far and wide over the field that it was impossible to find them and bring them together for burial."[40] Emboldened by the security of the city's walls, the Anabaptists daringly raided the bishop's camp. During one raid, the Anabaptists pounded steel nails into the firing holes of 19 of the bishops' cannons. The raid would have permanently disabled the cannons, but one of the bishop's men created "a particularly artful and easy to use drill"[41] which opened up the firing holes and rendered the cannons serviceable again.

Even an enthusiast like Matthys understood that without reinforcements from the thousands of Anabaptists and their sympathizers in nearby Holland, Muenster's Anabaptists were doomed. Matthys was waiting for good news from his Dutch supporters while attending a wedding on Good Friday, April 3, when he learned the Dutch rescue mission had been captured, causing him to fall into a swoon. After regaining consciousness, Matthys announced to the wedding guests that he had received another vision, which filled him with foreboding. God had informed the prophet from Leyden that he should put on the armor of battle and go forth by himself to defeat the bishop's army single-handedly, just as David had defeated Goliath. The day of the appointed battle was two days hence, on Easter Sunday before the city's walls at high noon. A token honor guard would accompany the prophet, who was now the New Jerusalem's warrior king as well.

Cynics who claim enthusiasm is simply a cover for self-serving appetite would do well to contemplate the actions of the Judaizing leader of the Westphalian Jerusalem. As the old man in full armor, carrying not a stone and sling, but a lance and sword, rode through the Ludger Gate and toward Miller's Hill, he was met by 500 of the bishop's elite shock troop, the Black Knights, who cut the prophet and his men into pieces. Kerssenbroick tells us that "every limb and part of 'the new Samson' was run through with countless sword thrusts until he was entirely in pieces."[42] The Black Knights then fought over the prophet's body parts as trophies. One knight took Matthys head and stuck it on the end of a pole which he displayed to the horrified Anabaptists watching from the city walls. Another took his testicles and nailed them to one of the city's gates. It was not a good day for dramatic prophetic gestures.

The demise of Elijah from Leiden posed a problem for those who aspired to succeed him as head of the New Jerusalem. Matthy's actions proved he was sincere in his beliefs, but they also proved dramatically that he was self-deluded. If the remaining triumvirate were suspected of self-delusion also, the legitimacy of charismatic leadership would be called into question. Bokelzoon stepped boldly into the political vacuum, announcing he had known all along that Matthys was going to die because God had revealed that to him in a vision. "The terrible end of Jan Matthias was revealed to me eight days ago by the Holy Ghost," Bokelzoon announced.[43] Some claimed Bokelzoon encouraged Matthys in his delusions so his rival would be killed and he could replace him as head of Muenster's government. They found vindication for their suspicions when Bokelzoon also announced the Holy Spirit told him, "When he is dead, you must marry his widow."[44] The Anabaptists' visions invariably revolved around sex and power and the gratification of the visionaries' passions. If the crowd had momentary doubts about Bokelzoon's vision, those doubts were erased when Knipperdolling jumped to his feet and announced Bokelzoon's vision was indisputably true. Relieved to hear that the New Jerusalem was still legitimate, the crowd tore off its clothing and began to dance in celebration. The dancing was appropriate: the New Jerusalem was based on the celebration of appetite, sanctified by messages which its devotees claimed as emanating from the Holy Spirit or interpretations of the Old Testament. Knipperdolling, as his well-timed endorsement of Bokelzoon's vision indicated, may well have conspired with Bokelzoon to get the older Matthys out of the way. Before long Knipperdolling was having visions of his own.

On April 1534, Knipperdolling announced in the Market Square that the Holy Spirit had told him exalted places must be made low and the lowly exalted. As the besotted mob stood slack-jawed wondering what his words meant, Knipperdolling interpreted his dream by announcing that the city's three architectural firms would tear down the steeples of the town's churches. The architectural patrimony of the city known as the Jewel of Westphalia was to be razed.

Not to be outdone, Bokelzoon soon had visions of his own. Running naked through the town, Bokelzoon bellowed to the still sleeping residents of the New Jerusalem, "You men of Israel, who live within the holy walls of Zion, fear the Lord your God and do penance for the sins of you former lives. Convert! Convert! The Glorious King of Zion is ready with thousands of angels to descend to earth at the sound of terrifying trumpets to judge you. Mend your ways! O, mend your ways!"[45]

Bokelzoon turned to Knipperdolling for confirmation, but that worthy was incommunicado because he was having visions of his own. So Bokelzoon continued. "The father has revealed to me that the New Israel is in need of a new constitution. The previous Magistrates received their commission from the law of man. Now a new divine constitution will be inaugurated. The prophet needed to find 12 men whom he knew were especially disposed toward him." God had commanded Bokelzoon to do the same; so Bokelzoon appointed 12 of his followers as the "elders" of the New Jerusalem and successors of the 12 tribes of Israel, granting to them, according to Kerssenbroick, "all official power, in matters spiritual and secular."[46]

Now it was Rothmann's turn to vouch for Bokelzoon's vision. In a speech to those assembled to hear Bokelzoon, Rothmann said "God was the source of his speech and that the citizens of the New Jerusalem should heed his words, just as God's own beloved people the Israelites had done in the past." After Rothmann's endorsement, the elders were summoned by name to kneel before Bokelzoon, who handed each of them a naked sword. Knipperdolling was given the special title of "*Schwertfuehrer*," granting to him the right to decapitate by sword anyone who questioned the ordinances of the New Zion. In conclusion, Bokelzoon led the assembly in singing the hymn, "*Allein Gott in der Hoeh sey Ehr.*"[47]

In early May, the bishops' troops began work on a dam that would drain the moat surrounding the town, opening an avenue of attack at the Judenfelder Gate.

On May 16, the Anabaptists intercepted a supply convoy intended for the bishop's troops, killing 30 soldiers, and destroying 16 cannons and a large supply of gunpowder. On May 22, the bishop's forces began their barrage, lobbing 700 cannonballs a day for several days at the city's gates and towers. On the day before the planned attack, a group of the bishop's soldiers got drunk and, mistaking sunset for sunrise, attacked the town ten hours early only to get lost in the ensuing darkness. As a result, the first assault on the town failed, and the Anabaptists were convinced the God of Israel had saved them from the assault of the numerically superior Philistine army.

It wasn't just the Anabaptist leaders who saw parallels between the Old Testament and the plight of God's people in Muenster. Because in theory the common man could interpret the Scriptures, an orgy of democratic judaizing followed quite naturally. About the time that Jan Matthys went to his death as the New David, a 15-year-old Dutch girl, Hille Feyken, heard a sermon based on the Old Testament account of Judith and Holofernes and became obsessed with the idea that she was New Judith, destined to break the siege by using her feminine charms to seduce and then dispatch Bishop von Waldeck. When young Hille ran the idea by Rothmann and Knipperdolling, they thought it unlikely to succeed. But neither felt that the teenage girl's life was worth enough to jeopardize the unlikely chance that the plan might work.

On June 16, the New Judith sallied forth from Muenster, "adorned with beautiful ornaments, whose art made her innately beautiful form that much more beautiful,"[48] bearing 12 Guilden, three rings with jewels, and a linen shirt, formerly owned by a leper, which had been soaked in poison. The bishop, according to Hille's plan, and approved by the highest levels of the Anabaptist regime, would be so enthralled by his lust for Hille that he would don the shirt in the throes of passion and die immediately, or have his head cut off by Hille when distracted by the pain, thereby ending the siege and liberating the people of God from their Philistine oppressors. How could a plan this clever fail to succeed?

Hille was captured as soon as she left the city and taken to Theodor von Merfeld, who questioned her closely after taking away her money and jewelry. Why, von Merfeld wanted to know, had she left her native town and gone over to the religious nuts who had taken over Muenster? Hille claimed she had been deceived and wanted to set things right by showing the bishop's soldiers secret passages that would enable them to capture the city with a minimum of casualties. Unfortunately for her, another citizen of the New Zion defected at the same time. Herman Ramert, who had taken in Bokelzoon when he first arrived in Muenster, was also brought before von Merfeld; he betrayed Hille's mission as the New Judith. Hille was then tortured, and under torture she admitted her role in the plot against the bishop. She was beheaded, suffering the fate of Holofernes, not Judith. Despite that minor modification, her vision was accurate.

After Hille's tragic adventure the bishop's troops refused to take prisoners. Not even women and children would be spared. Bokelzoon, according to the feminist interpretation of the Hille Feyken incident, needed to regain the initiative over the newly insurgent women. According to that interpretation, Bokelzoon introduced polygyny shortly after Feyken's failed mission because "the Muensterites' leader was concerned about keeping women under control and about preventing such independent actions in the future."[49] Bokelzoon's contemporaries claimed he introduced *Vielweiberei* because he lusted after Matthy's beautiful widow. Besides, women outnumbered men three to one in the New Zion. The men, so the claim went, would have to care for unattached women. The simplest explanation, however, has to do with the passions that fueled the revolution in the first place. Men came to Muenster to gratify their passions for women and gold. Great thinkers like Rothmann had to come up with a justification of the passions driving their revolution. Where Rothmann would find the justification for those passions was a foregone conclusion.

In mid-July 1534, Bernard Rothmann preached on the passage in Genesis 1:22 where God commanded his creatures to "be fruitful and multiply." The only way man could accomplish that while saving the unattached ex-nuns from their own lusts was to institute polygyny. One man was now to have several wives. Thereafter, polygyny was mandatory. All females 12 years of age or older had to be married. Bokelzoon would lead by example, taking 16 wives. Rothmann directed listeners to the examples of Abraham and David, both of whom had many wives.

There was some logic to polygyny in Muenster, and Rothmann did his best to make it sound as plausible as possible despite the shock to people from a culture where polygyny had disappeared a millennium earlier. Sexual relations outside of marriage were sinful, Rothmann noted. Because they had to be fruitful and multiply in a New Jerusalem where women outnumbered men three to one, the examples culled from the Old Testament made polygyny sound reasonable. None of these arguments, even in combination, would have carried the day, though, but for the heady atmosphere of revolutionary millennial expectation that abrogated all former laws and customs. Revolution was largely passion rationalized by an appeal to Old Testament models. A revolutionary leader could impose whatever regimen he chose in the name of his interpretation of God's law. So Bokelzoon and Rothmann declared all former marriages invalid.

Although Arthur tries to make Bokelzoon's decision sound plausible, in the end he to admits "the only way [Bokelzoon was able] to salvage his movement was to institutionalize his own perversity, to make adultery, bigamy and fornication the law of his strange land because he declared that it was the word of God."[50] "In the end," Gresbeck writes, Bokelzoon's male followers "took whatever women they cold find. They wanted to have women whether or not they were fertile .... Thus they slept first with one woman and thereafter with another. Such they did with an aura of saintliness since they wanted to increase the population."[51] Passion thus became the law of the land. Force was the only thing that could adjudicate conflicting passions, and the revolution meant the rule of the strong over the weak, with no moral law intervening for the weak.

Menno Simons, founder of the Mennonites, distanced himself from the excesses of fellow Anabaptists in Muenster and from Bokelzoon's "blasphemy." He urged his wing of the Anabaptist movement to "consent to no other arrangement than the one which was in vogue in the beginning with Adam and Eve, namely, one husband and one wife, as the Lord's mouth has ordained."[52] Simons, however, was not in Muenster, and his views did not prevail there. Cohn, for once, is forced to come up with a non-economic explanation of the Anabaptists' behavior. "The Patriarchs of Israel had given a good example," he writes, "the polygamy which they had practiced must be restored in the New Jerusalem."[53] Here as elsewhere, the dynamic of revolution is the same: passion rationalized by appeals to the Old Testament as the *vis movens* for messianic politics.

Bokelzoon's resurrection of Old Testament polygamy was also a powerful recruiting tool, not just with revolutionary Dutchmen, but with the bishop's soldiers outside the walls. Bombarded by Rothmann's leaflets extolling Muenster as the New Jerusalem of communism and free love, 200 of the bishop's mercenaries defected and went over to the Anabaptists.

A policy this novel and this draconian was bound to cause a reaction. As Menno Simons' response indicates, many initially drawn to Anabaptism were unaware polygyny was part of the deal. Henry Mollenheck was devoted to the new gospel but equally devoted to his wife. He organized a group of soldiers in Muenster who thought they had been punished unjustly for drunken carousing; they captured Bokelzoon, Knipperdolling, and Rothmann on the evening of July 30 and locked them up in the cellar of the Muenster city hall. When Hermann Tillbeck, the former mayor, heard about the coup, he organized a counter-coup with 600 soldiers who released the captives and put Mollenheck and his men in the cellar in their place. Bokelzoon was in no mood to show mercy "toward the enemies of the Lord." Mollenheck and his men were beaten by the mob as they were dragged out of the building to be executed. The women, evidently avid to become concubines of the Elect in the New Jerusalem, were more vicious than the men, cursing them and stripping the clothes from their backs on their way to the scaffold. "No pen," Kerssenbroick wrote, "can describe the rage with which their adversaries fell upon them, and the refinements of cruelty to which they became victims."[54]

Forty-nine counterrevolutionaries were executed on the spot, and Bokelzoon capitalized on the passions the incident unleashed by taking Matthy's widow as his wife, since "no one remained to offer opposition," as Kerssenbroick put it.[55] Bokelzoon's decisive act legitimized the passions of his followers, and they "rushed to follow his example." The former nuns, in particular, "gave themselves over to license and debauchery." The entire town witnessed "outrageous scenes of immorality" as Bokelzoon's followers outdid each other in committing one villainy after another "to satisfy their abominable lusts." Monks and nuns who formerly lived like angels on earth by following the vows of poverty, chastity, and obedience, descended to the level of "foul and furious beasts."[56]

On August 28, the bishop launched a second attack, which was thwarted this time not by his own derelict and drunken soldiers, but by the elements. Torrents of rain refilled the moats the bishop's troops had drained; many of his soldiers drowned trying to cross what they were told was going to be dry land. Once more Bokelzoon and his minions took the failure of the assault as a sign of God's favor and an indication of the righteousness of their cause. To his credit, Bokelzoon, mounted on a white horse, had fought bravely before the city's walls. Drenched by the rain, he slipped unscathed through the barrage of deadly projectiles aimed at him. Feeling vindicated, Bokelzoon had himself declared King of the New Jerusalem.

Instead of counterattacking to scatter the bishop's demoralized troops and open the way for Anabaptist reinforcements gathering in Holland, Jan the Tailor designed robes and jewelry appropriate to his new royal status. Johann Dusentschur, a goldsmith from nearby Warendof, had a vision that Bokelzoon was the reincarnation of King David, destined to rule the entire world, and the new insignia of his office made this clear. The golden globe on the golden chain around his neck was pierced by two swords, symbolizing that he had re-united the swords of temporal and spiritual power, pope and emperor, which Christendom had separated. Rothmann the propagandist quickly gave a judaizing interpretation of the king's new insignia. Bokelzoon was David, the priest and king who wielded both swords. Rothmann, according to Haude's reading, "justified the elevation of a king on the basis of the Old Testament, where the Jewish prophets proclaim that in the last days of the world God would erect a king."[57] According to Graesbeck, Dusentschur presented a sword to Bokelzoon, claiming he would rule with it until God took it from him. Dusentschur anointed Bokelzoon's head with oil, purportedly confirming Bokelzoon had inherited the throne of King David. "He will cast the mighty down and raise the lowly; he will seize the crown and the scepter and the throne of Saul. He will take in his hand the sword of justice and bring the divine word to all the peoples of the world."[58] Dusentschur also announced the "Trumpet of the Lord would sound thrice and that at the third blast all the inhabitants of the town must foregather at Mount Sion,"[59] i.e., in the square in front of the cathedral. When word of this revelation reached the bishop's camp, the soldiers there periodically blasted on trumpets and then shouted over the walls that the end times had come.

Bokelzoon, not surprisingly, agreed with the goldsmith who anointed him, announcing that as "David, a humble shepherd, [was] anointed by the Prophet, at Gods' command, as the King of Israel.... Now I am given power over all nations of the earth, and the right to use the sword to the confusion of the wicked and in defense of the righteous. So let none in this town stain himself with crime or resist the will of God, or else he shall without delay be put to death with the sword."[60] Bokelzoon was clear about the extent of his kingdom: "I will still rule, not only over this city but over the whole world, for the Heavenly Father has said it should be so. My kingdom which begins today shall never fall."[61] Jan the Tailor was the new David destined to rule the world. To impress his subjects with his new dignity, he had his tailors create a scarlet robe, which he wore on all occasions. He had coins struck to reflect his destiny. One coin proclaimed "The Word has become Flesh and dwells in us." Another coin proclaimed "One King over all. One God, One faith, One Baptism."[62] Following his coronation, King Jan had a throne erected in the Market Square with a cloth of pure gold placed upon it. From this throne he would order athletic contests, mock masses, and impromptu decapitations as the sole ruler of the New Jerusalem.

King David Bokelzoon also offered a return to a more primitive, ethnically homogeneous, nation state, the sort of aspiration that would culminate centuries later with the rise of National Socialism and Zionism. The Catholic Church, like the Roman Empire that preceded it, had relegated ethnicity to a subordinate status. Bokelzoon's New Jerusalem was what Bernard of Clairvaux would have termed the "vomit of Judaism." Muenster's New Jerusalem harkened to a more primitive period, when there was no distinction between temporal and spiritual powers. The new revolutionary, messianic, ethnic state was modeled on the tribes of Israel, God's chosen race on earth.

Bokelzoon, as Cohn notes, was premeditated and precise in the symbols he chose. From his throne in the Market Square, he dispensed Old Testament justice. On one side of his throne stood a page holding the Old Testament, "to show that the king was the successor of David and endowed with authority to interpret anew the Word of God—the other holding a naked sword."[63] The constant, repeated reference to Muenster as the New Jerusalem indicated repudiation of Christ and his Church and the political and philosophical and cultural sophistication that went with it. In its place, Bokelzoon was "the new David" who ruled by divine decree. The congruity between these decrees and the unruly passions of Bokelzoon's followers was ignored until their passions collided, as in the case of the men and women Bokelzoon and Knipperdolling beheaded.

The Judaizers in Muenster introduced a new form of government in which sovereignty was based not on tradition or law but on the covert manipulation of popular passion. Government now secured its subjects' allegiance by granting them permission to revoke the moral law based on models culled from the Old Testament, leading to a tyranny far worse than what it overthrew. All these threads become apparent in the new articles of government Bokelzoon proclaimed as king. Kerssenbroick describes *in extenso* how the "articles of the king in Muenster, were placed before the Israelites living in this city, according to which, they could live under the banner of righteousness as true Israelites in the current kingdom ...

under John, their true king, who has been placed on the Throne of David."[64] The First Article stipulates "in the new Temple, there can be only one king, who rules the people of God with the sword of righteousness."[65] From that premise, "there can be no authority who is not ordained by God Himself." Anyone who opposes this new order shall be punished by death. All this is necessary so the "Babylonian tyranny of Priests and monks,"[66] who use violence and injustice to darken the righteousness of God, should be suppressed. Bokelzoon also promised his followers deliverance from all their trials by the coming Easter, and went on to say that if what he predicted did not come to pass, that they should treat him like a false prophet and a vicious person with the proper punishments."

Bokelzoon then purported to divide up all of Germany among his followers, since he would soon rule the entire world anyway, making the local butcher the Elector Prince of Saxony, etc. In this he resembled, in Kerssenbroick's eyes, the fairy tale hunter who sold the bear's pelt before shooting the bear.

The terror began shortly after Bokelzoon consolidated his power. One evening after dinner as Bokelzoon sat brooding on his throne in the Market Square, he ordered a prisoner brought to him, whom he then personally beheaded. On September 25, Knipperdolling decapitated a woman who refused to have sexual relations with her "husband," i.e., a man who had used the new ordinances establishing polygyny to force her into his bed. Elizabeth Holshern prayed openly to her "heavenly father," beseeching him "if you are almighty," to "see to it that I never more in my life have to climb into this marriage bed."[67] Knipperdolling was so enraged that he cut her head off with his sword. One day later, Katherine Kockenbeckin was executed in similar fashion for having sex with two husbands. Evidently the right to have more than one spouse did not extend to women. Sexual liberation was defined on male terms, and the women had the choice of going along or losing their heads.

During the few months when revolutionary government held sway in Muenster, the trajectory of passion which the Marquis de Sade would sketch out centuries later based on his experience with the French Revolution ran its full course. Men who indulged in the simple passions soon found them insipid, forcing them to indulge in perverse passions, which led to the criminal passions, and they in turn led to the murderous passions. As in every revolution worthy of the name, sex liberated from the bond of matrimony led, one way or another, to murder. And in the case of Bernard Knipperdolling, murder led to madness.

Shortly after murdering Holshern, Knipperdolling reappeared in Market Square with froth on his lips bellowing: "Repent, Repent of our sins all of our sins for the Lord sees and knows your evil ways."[68] After running around Market Square on all fours like a dog, he jumped up and performed a lewd dance, saying, "I have often danced this way before my women, and now the heavenly father commands me to do the same before my king."[69] King Jan was dumbfounded by the mad behavior of his erstwhile supporter, who, judging from his words, was playing the fool giving credence to the suspicion that the two of them were living in a fool's paradise for what increasingly seemed likely to be a short time. Either the psychological pressure of living under siege had taken its toll on Knipperdolling's guilt-ridden psyche, or it was a test of the king's power. "Courage, brother!" Knipperdolling said to King Jan, "We go together, the king's fool and the fool-king, to do battle with the world."[70] King Jan was horrified; when he tried to speak he could only stutter. "By rights I should also be a king," Knipperdolling continued; "I made you king."[71] King Jan could tolerate the madness or the charade no longer, and falling from his throne, he ran from the square. Mad Knipperdolling sat on the throne, an affront which should have cost him his life. Instead, he was given three months in prison. After his release, he announced publicly that an evil spirit had taken possession of his faculties.

It was a narrow escape for King Jan. A few more performances like that and the king's authority would evaporate. Knipperdolling's recantation, however, did nothing to relieve the psychological pressure of the siege. To break the ever-narrowing circle, King Jan sent out 27 preachers in October, to spread the Anabaptist gospel to neighboring towns and, more likely, to solicit support to break the siege. All were captured; 26 were executed summarily. Heinrich Graes survived because he was willing to return to Muenster as the bishop's spy. Therafter, the bishop knew Bokelzoon's every move. Whenever Bokelzoon sent out preachers carrying Rothmann's pamphlets or emissaries with gold to buy weapons, the bishop's men were there to meet them.

The psychological pressure on the town increased as a result. Even King Jan was showing signs of the strain. In the middle of the night of October 23, the people of Muenster finally heard the trumpets that they had been waiting to hear. Instead of heralding the imminent arrival of the Lord, however, the trumpets called the groggy residents of Muenster to an impromptu banquet, as Dusentschur blew into his cow horn from his perch in the steeple of St. Lambert's church. Half-dreading they might be sent into a suicidal attack on the bishop's fortifications, the mob was relieved to learn of the banquet. The king arrived astride his white horse accompanied by his queen and their attendants. After Dusentschur announced "He has ordered that a great feast be prepared for you," the King and his Queen circulated through the banqueting crowd turning the feast into a weird parody of Holy Communion with King Jan telling the assembled, "I eat this and show forth the death of the Lord."[72]

Perhaps the constant reference to death caused the king's mood to change. He ordered a prisoner brought into the festivities and then promptly drew his sword and cut off his head. The headless corpse lay where it fell as the festivities continued unabated until dawn.

After his defeat in August, the bishop refused to authorize any more direct assaults on the town. Instead, he resolved to starve the Anabaptists into submission by tightening the ring of siege. By late 1534 he had erected six blockhouses at the crucial chokepoints in the four mile ring of fortifications around the city. One man, under cover of night and at great risk, might evade the blockade, but nothing of significance could get in or out of Muenster unless the bishop's troops permitted it.

On December 13, the bishop appeared before the Diet of Koblenz, where Catholic and Protestant supporters, fearing anarchy more than each other, pledged to depose "a certain unknown Tailor lately become king, who named himself the King of Zion and the New Jerusalem."[73] This Tailor King, as Luther called him, proposed to spread his teachings throughout the Christian world, and to bring about thereby "the overthrow of all Princes and Magistrates with fire and sword, subordinate the entire German empire to his power."[74] At the end of the diet, representatives from the states of the Lower and Upper Rhine renewed their pledges of support, promising reinforcements of infantry and cavalry as well as the gold needed to make the siege impenetrable.

King Jan had missed his opportunity following the defeat of the bishop's second assault in August. Now the Anabaptists were having increasing difficulty getting anything out of town. And when they did, the bishop's spies informed him in advance, preventing reinforcements. Shortly after the Diet of Koblenz solemnly resolved to bring Muenster to its knees, Bernard Rothmann composed a pamphlet entitled *Revenge* and planned to have copies run off on Knipperdolling's printing press and distributed to Anabaptists gathering in Holland. In *Revenge*, Rothmann harped on all the standard judaizing revolutionary themes: It was time for the Dutch to "turn their plowshares into swords" so that they and King Jan "wearing the armor of David" could avenge themselves on "all Babylonian power and extinguish all godlessness."[75]

On Christmas Eve 1534, Jan van Geelen, one of King Jan's Dutch agents, left Muenster with 1000 copies of Rothmann's pamphlet and gold to buy weapons. Van Geelen planned to rally supporters in Deventer, Groningen, Amsterdam, Delft, and Leyden. Around Easter, the time Bokelzoon had predicted for the deliverance of the city, they would attack the bishop's siege works from the rear while Bokelzoon's troops attacked from the other side. Five days later, Heinrich Graes slipped out of Muenster and reported the plot to the bishop. As a result, 1000 Anabaptists assembled in Groningen under the leadership of a prophet who called himself the Christ were defeated by the troops of the Duke of Gelderland. In March 1535, three ships full of Anabaptists were sunk along with their occupants as they sailed up the Ijssel to break the blockade and reach their beleaguered brothers in Muenster. The blockade and the bishop's spies were having their effect.

Graes's intelligence also revealed the blockade was having its effect internally. Fuel was gone, leaving most of population freezing in their homes in the dead of winter. The food situation was desperate. All of the horses in the town had been killed, but the meat was reserved for the king's court. Flour had disappeared shortly after the blockade began in earnest in January. Famine-induced lassitude was spreading. The promised deliverance on Easter Day, March 28, failed to materialize. Instead, Heinrich Graes, who had promised support from sympathizers in nearby Wesel, returned to town only to nail an open letter to the town's gate, announcing he was a spy in the employ of the bishop and that their hope for deliverance was in vain. "I know everything," Graes informed his former townsmen. "You can still save your lives if you will turn from your path and leave this godless business behind."[76]

In response to Graes's threat, King Jan resorted to more refined strategies of domination and distraction. The deliverance he had promised was a spiritual deliverance, he told his now apathetic subjects. By April, every pet, rodent, and vermin had been killed and eaten, and the famished mob began eating grass, moss, old shoes, whitewash, and the corpses found in the streets every morning. If those corpses got buried during the day, the starving Anabaptists dug them up at night to make gruesome meals out of them. Hoping to limit the number of mouths he had to feed, Jan allowed some women and children to leave the city in April. Made wary by Hille Feicken's attempt to murder the bishop, the bishop's troops refused to let the women and children through their lines, and so they continued to starve to death in the no-man's land between the camps, eating grass and the occasional crust of bread the besieging troops' camp followers would throw them: "women and children ... lingered on for five long weeks in the no-man's land before the town walls begging the mercenaries to kill them, crawling about and eating grass like animals and dying in such numbers that the ground was littered with corpses."[77]

Kerssenbroick described the famine in gruesome detail. Starving women made stews out of the bones and arteries of corpses, and those who consumed these deadly meals contracted horrible diseases, their bodies covered with horrible boils. Some, he continued,

> who drank contaminated water had their bellies swell up to such an extent that they were no longer able to carry that enormously heavy burden. Many helpless children starved to death in their cradles or in their mother's wombs, and many others (I shudder when I put pen to paper to describe such things) were murdered by their parents and eaten. Their dismembered body parts were found after the conquest of the city in several places preserved in brine for future consumption.[78]

Kerssenbroick remembered the plight of the women in Jerusalem when the Temple was destroyed. The Anabaptists' reference to Muenster as the New Jerusalem was an irony not lost on Kerssenbroick, because "this westphalian city was in every respect like the Jewish Jerusalem, except for the fact that it far exceeded that city in its misery and the sorrow of its circumstances. Of that I have not the least doubt. So it was not without significance that this city was rightly called the New Jerusalem."[79]

Invoking Christ's admonition that God could change stones into bread if he wanted to, the starving inhabitants of Muenster bit into stones hoping He would do just that. Then in the stillness that followed when the stones remained stones, the Anabaptists bewailed their immense misery and their even greater foolishness. Oh Death, the people cried out, why do you keep your distance from us? To which Kerssenbroick responds, "O you horrible spawn of Jerusalem! O you plague of the Jewish People."[80] The Anabaptists in Muenster were identical in Kerssenbroick's mind with the Jews who rejected Christ's tearful warnings about Jerusalem's impending doom. Since the Judaizing Anabaptists had turned away from the Church that Christ founded as his kingdom on earth, they suffered a similar fate in the New Jerusalem.

To distract the haggard and starving zombies of Muenster from grim reality, King Jan commanded them to participate in fantastically conceived diversions to continue his domination over them. Bokelzoon staged blasphemous and obscene parodies of the Mass. He ordered the starving population to take part in three days of dancing, footraces, and gymnastics. And then there were the public executions, which some must have envied as a quick end to their miseries. Else Drier was dragged before Knipperdolling's tribunal accused of prostitution. When she denounced him as a regular customer, he flew into a rage and decapitated her with his own sword. After Claes Northorn was caught trying to pass a letter to the bishop, he was tortured, then executed, then his corpse was cut up into 12 pieces and nailed to the city's gates. His head was placed on a pike on the cathedral as a warning to anyone who might want to write to the bishop. As if that weren't punishment enough, Gresbeck adds that his heart and liver "were eaten by a Hollander."[81]

We have no record of King Jan cutting off the heads of prostitutes with whom he consorted; instead, King Jan cut of the head of Elizabeth Wandscheer, his tenth wife. Elizabeth Hardwick, as she was then known, had been brought before Jan for judgment after she refused to have sex with the old man assigned to her as a husband. "There's not a man in this town that can tame me," she said when brought before King Jan.[82] Intrigued by her defiant spirit, Jan proposed marriage on the spot. Elizabeth was King Jan's second favorite wife, after Matthy's widow, but by May the siege and famine had taken their toll on her spirit. After experiencing his lust first hand and eating well with him while famine raged throughout town, she now viewed Bokelzoon as an inhuman monster and wanted to leave Muenster. Enraged that one of his wives could reject him, King Jan had Elizabeth dragged into the Market Square and condemned her to death, pronouncing the following verdict: "She was a whore and always inclined to rebellion. Therefore, Our Father in Heaven commanded me to get rid of her."[83] Then in the presence of his other wives, whom he urged to sing "Glory to God in the Highest," he chopped off her head with his sword, "and kicked her dead corpse with his foot."[84] A contemporary etching portrays him and his wives dancing around Elizabeth's headless corpse in the Market Place. "Those who contradict his judgments soon lose their heads," wrote the anonymous author of one of the *Newe Zeitungen* which reported on the event. "If a wife is angry with another one or quarrels with her, they have [already] lost their heads.... The king personally cut off the head of his housewife since she wanted to join other women, who were leaving the city. And he ordered his other housewives, thirteen that is, to watch."[85]

Distracted by famine and demoralized at the beheadings, no one noticed as six men slipped out of the city on the evening of Sunday, May 23. One, Heinrich Gresbeck, was a former Anabaptist now having second thoughts. Another, Johan Nagel, a diminutive but hot-tempered fellow who went by the name Jack in the Corner or Hansel Eck, had been a double agent from his entry into the city a few months earlier ostensibly as a refugee from unjust charges. They carried with them the secret of the city's demise, the location of an unguarded door near one of the city's gates. It was protected by a moat easily fordable by a portable bridge.

The setting sun was not visible on the evening on June 22, 1534. It was obscured by heavy clouds which dumped large amounts of rain and hail the size of bird eggs on the town, even though it was the summer solstice. The water in the moat must have been cold when Gresbeck plunged into it to drag the first section of a 20-foot long bridge across the moat to the secret door. Soldiers soon crossed the bridge and slit the throats of the first guards they came across. They then proceeded to the Cathedral, which the Anabaptists had turned into their arsenal, to wrest it from its famine weakened defenders and then open the city's gates to allow the main force of the bishop's troops under Ulrich von Dhaun into the city.

Before Wilhelm Steding, the leader of the *avant garde*, could secure the cathedral or send a group to open the gate, the Anabaptists sounded the alarm and launched a furious counter-attack, driving the bishop's men from the Cathedral into a precarious position in the streets. Forced to find his way through a strange city in the dead of night, Steding led his 400 men into a blind alley, where they were harassed by the arrows of King Jan's soldiers and furniture and bricks dropped on them by women in the neighboring houses. King Jan appeared and demanded their unconditional surrender. If King Jan had pressed the issue, he probably could have annihilated Steding and his cowering troops. Instead he entered into negotiations, which were still going on when the sun came up to reveal one of Steding's men waving a flag near the Jodefeld Gate. Von Dhaun's troops then poured into the city and began a fearful slaughter of the Anabaptists.

The Anabaptists had constructed 16 war wagons which they planned to use, as Zizka had at Kutna Hora, as primitive tanks to break through the bishop's siege. The city's blacksmiths had constructed armor from iron plates to shield the wagons and their wheels from attack. They had also armed each wagon with a small cannon and six to eight "*Hackenbuchse*," a primitive version of what the Soviets during World War II called the Stalin Organ, a stack of musket barrels which could be fired more or less simultaneously with devastating results at short range.

The war wagons were never used because the horses to pull them had been eaten, but they were now turned into a formidable fortress in the center of town, behind which Henry Krechting and 200 men defied von Dhaun. Feeling an assault would be too costly, von Dhaun's lieutenant Johann von Raesfeld gave Krechting and his men safe conduct to leave the city. Krechting and 25 men made good use of the opportunity. The others, who returned to their homes to retrieve wives and property, were cut down by the bishop's troops.

The bishop's mercenaries received on the average 16 Guilders or roughly $800 for their pains. Sensing that all of their combined boredom and terror would not yield its promised financial reward, the mercenaries vented their anger on the helpless population. "The murder," one contemporary wrote, "was too terrible to describe."[86] Hermann Tilbeck, the former mayor whose treachery helped cause Muenster's woes, was found cowering in an outhouse, where the bishop's troops dispatched him, running him through with their swords and then giving him, in Kerssenbroick's words, a burial fit for a donkey by dumping him in the cloaca. King Jan's "dukes" faired no better. Henry Sanctus, a coppersmith King Jan had dubbed Prince of Mainz, was captured and then beheaded in front of the City Hall. Tavernkeeper Evart Riemenschneider, host of so many momentous theological discussions, was found hiding on the roof of his establishment with the former nun he had married and two other wives. They were executed along with his son. King Jan was captured alive running toward the Agidii Gate. Bernard Rothmann, King Jan's theologian and propaganda minister, wore a white robe at the height of the siege, sword in hand, his side pierced by a sword, but he then disappeared, showing up neither among the living or the dead after the siege.

Bernard Knipperdolling escaped the initial slaughter by hiding with a number of his wives on the roof of a house, but thirst and one of the captured women's desire to avoid punishment led to his capture. When von Dhaun offered the Anabaptist women the opportunity to recant, most accepted and were allowed to return to their native villages. Divara, former nun, former wife of the Elijah from Leyden and former Queen, as well as one of King Jan's 16 wives, did not recant. She was beheaded in the square in front of the cathedral.

On June 29, 1535, Bishop Franz von Waldeck entered Muenster in triumph through the Agidii Gate where King Jan had sought escape, in a coach drawn by six white horses at the head of three companies of soldiers. Von Dhaun presented the bishop with the keys of the city and Wilhelm Steding, who led the attack on the night of June 22, presented the bishop with the insigniae of King Jan's messianic kingdom, including the globe symbolizing the world he intended to rule, pierced by the two swords, which were now back in the firm grasp of the lords spiritual and temporal.

Shortly after taking possession of the tarnished Jewel of Westphalia, von Waldeck visited Bokelzoon in prison. The interrogation had uncanny parallels with Pilate's interrogation of Jesus. "Are you a king?" von Waldeck asked. Bokelzoon, lacking the dignity of Christ, responded "And are you a bishop?"[87] When the bishop complained about all of the money the siege had cost, Bokelzoon suggested a way the bishop might recoup his losses. "Let an iron cage be built," Jan said. "Put me in it along with Knipperdolling, and send us out on the road throughout all of Germany. Charge everyone a penny to take a look at us. You'll earn more money than you spent in our war."[88] The story, which first appeared in an early *Newe Zeitungen* account of the siege, may be apocryphal. If so, it was based on the most famous artifact to survive the violent, short-lived Anabaptist commune in Muenster, namely, the three cages, which as of the summer of 2004, when this author saw them, were still hanging from the steeple of the St. Lambert's Church in Muenster.

A team of Inquisitors, led by Antonius Corvinus, a Lutheran theologian, interrogated Bokelzoon after his capture. Corvinus convinced him of the errors of Anabaptism by appealing to the example of the sun. Just as Jan's blindness would not keep the sun from shining, so it is "with the works and ordinances of God, especially the sacraments." Baptism dispensed grace *ex opere operata*. Corvinus had less success in dealing with polygyny. "Why should we be denied what was permitted to the patriarchs in the Old Testament?"[89] Bokelzoon said; "What we have always held is this: he who wanted only one wife was never to be forced to have more than one. But we felt that a man who wanted more than one wife should be free to do so because he was obeying God's command to be fruitful and multiply."[90] Bokelzoon was consoled by the certainty "we cannot be damned for doing what the fathers were permitted to do. I prefer to be with them and not you."[91] Corvinus, in typically Lutheran fashion, ended the interview by concluding, "We prefer to be obedient to the state."[92] During this interrogation, Bokelzoon said he accepted the Lutheran doctrine of justification by faith alone. However, he seems to have died a Catholic. Unlike Krechting and Knipperdolling, who remained impenitent, Bokelzoon accepted the ministrations of Johan von Siburg, the bishop's priest, who found him "greatly changed" on his last night on earth. Von Siburg later claimed Bokelzoon "greatly regretted his godlessness, his murder, his looting, his lack of discipline, and his shameful deeds. He admitted that he deserved the bitterest possible death ten times over, and he renounced all his errors."[93]

On January 22, after lengthy interrogation by theologians and princes, Jan Bokelzoon, Bernard Knipperdolling, and Henry Krechting had their flesh pulled off their bones by red hot tongs for one hour. The insurrectionists were then stabbed in the heart and beheaded. Then their bodies were placed in the three already mentioned cages and hung from the Lambertuskirche steeple, where birds ate what was left of them. Their bones were removed decades later, but the cages remained as a warning to future insurrectionists. When the church was damaged by allied bombers on November 18, 1944, the cages were damaged, but after the war they were repaired and put back. They remained there through the revolution of '68, when Anabaptism gained new cachet through its connection to student revolt and feminism. They remained there during the era of political correctness, in spite of letters to the editor that claimed they were "unbelievably tasteless"[94] reminders of a barbaric past.

Although Jan Bokelzoon played the most spectacular role in the Anabaptist drama in Muenster, the bishop considered him a less important figure than Knipperdolling, but Knipperdolling refused to answer any of the bishop's questions implicating him in a wider conspiracy. Bokelzoon evaded the same line of questioning by overwhelming his inquisitors with details from his life. No matter how interesting the effect his mother's seduction and his illegitimate birth had on King Jan's subsequent psychological development, it did little to help the bishop uncover any wider conspiracy and thereby prevent the same thing from breaking out elsewhere.

There was, however, evidence that Knipperdolling and Bokelzoon had not acted alone. As late at May 1535 an Anabaptist insurrection broke out in Amsterdam. In June 1534, Bokelzoon and Knipperdolling received an overture from Juergen Wullenwever of Luebeck, who offered to orchestrate an attack on the bishop's troops to help the Anabaptists break out of the siege. Wullenwever "later admitted that he had an understanding with various Anabaptist" groups in Holland; "if he and his followers succeeded in Luebeck, his partners in the other northern cities would introduce Anabaptism there as well and would deal with the magistrates as Wullenwever had done in Luebeck."[95] Had Muenster linked up with Luebeck, they could have united with rebels in Amsterdam, Deventer, Delft, Groningen, Leyden, Wesel and Kleve and might have placed the entire north German part of the Holy Roman Empire under Anabaptist rule.

There were even Anabaptist cells in Cologne, the Rhenish citadel of Catholic orthodoxy. During the 1520s, the Cologne Dominicans under Jacob Hoogstraten, who had championed Pfefferkorn in his battle against Reuchlin, tried with limited success to keep the "poison" of Lutheranism from infecting the principalities of the Lower Rhine. The Cologne city council, however, proved more tolerant than vigilant. The rise of Anabaptist communism in Muenster, only 100 miles away, changed that. Reacting to directives from Charles V in 1533, Cologne burned its first Anabaptist heretic at the stake in August of that year. "On 27 February 1534," Haude writes, "the day the Anabaptist leaders forced everyone in Muenster to be baptized or else leave the city, Cologne's council ordered its police officers (*Gewaltrichter*) to apprehend and imprison all Anabaptists and Lutherans."[96] Fearing a repetition of Muenster, the Cologne city council banned secret religious discussion and any gatherings for that purpose. Less than six months after issuing the ban, the Cologne city fathers learned to their consternation that their city had its own Anabaptist cell under the leadership of Professor Gerhard Westerburg, otherwise known as the notorious "Dr. Purgatory" because of pamphlets he had written against that popish doctrine. Westerburg had traveled to the Wesphalian New Jerusalem in January to receive re-baptism at the hands of Heinrich Roll. He then returned to Cologne to establish a cell which spread its message to Moers, Aachen, Frankfurt, Gladbach and as far as Strasbourg, on the upper Rhein. On 31 October 1534, when the police arrested three Anabaptists, the council learned about the congregation and Westerburg's instrumental role in it. By this time Westerburg had left Cologne.

Under the guise of religion, these networks spread revolutionary ideas far and wide. Lurid *Newe Zeitungen* accounts of what was happening in Muenster served as an inadvertent manual of revolutionary praxis. Bokelzoon became a comic book hero, not unlike Superman. He was a tailor who knew how to confer with princes. He was good looking. His clothes and accessories were impeccable, and in the summer of 1534 he seemed to be a military genius too. He set an example for the "*Poebel*," the German word of contempt for the common man. The specter of *Demos* drawing inspiration from the tailor king caused Phillip of Hesse to break out in a cold sweat, because he understood "if the common man saw how effortlessly he was able to depose councilors, take their belongings and act willfully against all honor, law and truth, he would continue to act as he did in Muenster."[97] Phillip had been personally involved in the defeat of the peasants in 1525. Now ten years later, Philip was fighting what seemed a much stronger foe, which had conquered one of the most important cities of the north German empire and which was threatening to spread that rebellion to the Netherlands, Flanders and who knew where else. A network linking the Muensterites to Anabaptists in other German lands was trying to replicate itself in other places, even in Hesse itself. These suspicions increased after the collapse of Muenster, because before then the evil had a specific location. Now it seemed to be everywhere. The devil had been loosed. Urbanus Rhegius "saw the devil's footprints all over Muenster."[98] He was not an apprentice devil, said Rhegius, but "the devil of a thousand arts" using the Anabaptists to attack "scripture, Christ, and Christianity and all faith" to "become the lord in Westphalia over body, soul and goods."[99] Corvinus called the events in Muenster "*ein Affenspiel*," largely because the devil aped God. Despite all his wives, King Jan produced no offspring, another sign that he was the devil incarnate. In Muenster, the Anabaptists had turned "everything upside down" to destroy it; they converted marriage into prostitution, a tailor into a king." Corvinus was convinced the world the Anabaptists "had created was an inversion of the real world, just as carnival season is a reversal of ordinary laws of reason and social order."[100] The more conventional word for a world turned upside down is revolution.

At the Council of Neuss in 1540, Herman, bishop of Cologne, and John, Duke of Cleves-Juelich, learned the confessions extracted from prophets captured after the fall of Muenster indicated Anabaptist agents had been sent "to make the people rebellious" and then "to destroy all existing secular and ecclesiastical authorities."[101] In 1536, the Hessians passed a law against Anabaptism, which averred "Heresy always involves insurrection and destruction of all good customs and morals (*Sitten*); it is preceded by the disruption of government, as is now the case with the Anabaptists ... as the horrible example of the miserable city of Muenster has demonstrated more than enough."[102] The Hessians had good reason to feel this way, because Anabaptists flooded into their territory following the collapse of the Muenster commune in 1535. Their new leader was Jan van Batenburg who, in 1537, arrived in Strasbourg to enlist the help of Hoffmann's followers in the Germanies of the south. With their help, Batenburg planned to conquer an as yet unnamed city in Holland and establish another New Jerusalem there.

Batenburg's plans for Holland must have confirmed Herman's and John's fears because they knew Brussels was in contact with Muenster during the height of the rebellion. After Graes turned spy, he reported to Bishop von Waldeck that the Anabaptists had allies in many cities in the low countries. Graes also reported that "six men were sent out from Muenster, one to Strasbourg, his name is Johan van Geel, from the little village Geel in the bishopric of Utrecht; one to Frisia, he is a grocer.... [those sent to] Holland Wesel were from Frisia ... They were supposed to start an uprising in the aforementioned cities and countries" by disseminating Rothmann's book *Von der Rache*. "A thousand books of three quartos have been sent from Muenster to the surrounding cities and villages to incite the common people so that Muenster may be freed."[103]

Anabaptist activity was still evident a generation after the fall of Muenster. In 1567, a cobbler, Jan Willemsen, set up another New Jerusalem in the area between Wesel and Kleve, about 60 miles west of Muenster. Willemsen declared himself the Messiah and proclaimed communality of wives and property. He and his followers claimed all property was to be held in common and was to be handed over to them whenever their marauding band showed up at a farm or convent. Over the next 12 years, Jan the Messiah accumulated 21 wives and a bad reputation among the local princes, who caught him and burned him at the stake in 1580.

Anabaptism still survives in a far less virulent form among the rural communities of the Mennonites and the Amish in the new world, in places like Indiana and Pennsylvania, but also as Schwenkfelders, Hutterites, Baptists, and Quakers.

Cohn relates the story of Willemsen to close the story of the millennial fever he described as coming into the world with the emergence of Emico of Leiningen at the time of the first crusade. If Cohn is truly describing "revolutionary [fanaticisms], aiming to shatter and renew the world," though, the story was far from over, which he makes clear when he writes that "militant revolutionary chiliasm—the tense expectation of a final, decisive struggle in which a world tyranny will be overthrown by a 'chosen people' and through which the world will be renewed and history brought to its consummation ... did not disappear with the fall of the New Jerusalem at Muenster."[104] The history of "revolutionary movements" which promised a terrestrial and collective salvation," was in fact just beginning.

The rejection of what Cohn terms "the one authority which was universal, embracing with its prescriptions and demands the lives of all individuals,"[105] namely, the Catholic Church, was to have far-reaching consequences which had yet to play out. Instead of finding their joy in heaven, the "rootless masses of the poor" were now told "the Heavenly city" was going "to appear on this earth, and its joys" were "to crown not the peregrinations of individual souls but the epic exploits of a 'chosen people.'" They were told that political movements would lead to heaven on earth. The only institution to consistently tell them otherwise was the Catholic Church: "By canalizing the emotional energies of the laity, by directing their yearnings firmly towards an after-life in another world, the church did indeed do much to impede the spread of revolutionary chiliasm."[106] Conversely, to the extent that the Church was removed from public life, revolutionary messianic political movements moved in to fill the void. Either way, the antinomies were clear and would remain the same for centuries to come: the Church which told men to treasure up their treasure in heaven and her revolutionary simulacrum, which claimed it could achieve all that the Church promised here on earth.

The Anabaptist Rebellion

Chapter Ten

John Dee and the Magical Transformation of England

I n July 1554, twenty years after the Anabaptist crisis in Muenster, Philip II, King of Spain, married Mary, daughter of Catherine of Aragon and Henry VIII, and became ruler of England too. The leaders of Church and State in Europe certainly hoped the marriage might heal the rift Henry VIII caused when he broke with Rome and alienated Church property. But those hopes were hedged with caveats. Pope Julius III and Reginald Cardinal Pole were adamant that Church lands be restored to the Church.

However, the emperor, Charles V felt the marriage would smooth all in its wake (especially after the arrival of an heir), and conveyed his opinion to his son Philip, who dutifully and, it could be argued, mistakenly followed his advice. Mary ruled a land where the main issue, the break with the Church and the subsequent theft of Church property, remained unresolved. The thieves had a significant portion of England's wealth, and they were determined to use it to prevent Catholic restoration.

The revolutionaries in England were no ragtag cohort of bakers and tailors, as in Anabaptist Muenster. Anabaptism had disappeared as a significant movement, replaced by something more systematic and insidious, the ideology of Calvin and his police state in Geneva. The revolutionaries in England were not about to take off their clothes and run naked in the streets as had the Anabaptists. The English revolutionaries were a network of families grown so powerful from confiscation of Church property that their names are still known today.

Thomas Cromwell grew enormously rich by plundering monasteries. Cromwell then turned to usury to get even more. He understood his desires were incompatible with the Catholic faith, so Cromwell dedicated his life and fortune to preventing Catholic restoration. He instilled these same beliefs in his family. His nephew married the daughter of a usurer from Genoa; together they became the grandparents of Oliver Cromwell, the Puritan general whose hatred for the Catholic faith the Irish experienced at Drogheda a century later. Thomas Cromwell was determined to "lead Henry by gradual steps to a position from which he could not retreat, to terrorize all political opposition by a reign of blood, and to set up a wall of material interest against both the Church and the ancient nobility he and his friends wished to supplant."[1]

Cromwell and his famous great-grandson, Thomas Gresham, the author of Gresham's law, were architects of the new England. Together with the Cecils and the Russells, Gresham helped make England the model for the modern nation.

England would turn finance into a weapon more powerful than Philip's armies. Revolution in Muenster meant communism; in England it meant capitalism. As Marx understood, the beginning of capitalism was the theft of Church property. The former wealth of the Church was put in the service of Mammon when the wealthy English families contested the Jewish monopoly on usury. Gresham was a financial genius who understood the possibilities for financial exploitation at the dawn of the capitalist age. As Elizabeth's finance minister, he knew how to debase the nation's currency in the interests of governmental policy and those who ran the government, to the detriment of the majority of the nation's citizens, who slipped farther into poverty. Gresham also knew how to precipitate financial crises among his enemies. Under Gresham's guidance England created the wretched proletariat for which it became infamous through Dickens' novels. Under Gresham's leadership:

> A whole class of decent Englishmen, of whom too little has been remembered in history, was swept off the church lands and doomed to poverty, vagabondage and often crime: mostly small farmers and farm laborers with their families, dispossessed because the new owners found it more profitable to raise sheep.

Finance wasn't the only new weapon Philip had to face. According to the mother of Philip's new wife, Henry VIII had been turned into the dupe of his own lusts by a cabal that knew how to manipulate his sexual passions as effectively as Gresham knew how to manipulate prices. Long before the pope refused to grant Henry a divorce from Catherine of Aragon, the same group that would profit from the plundering of the monasteries was using the King's infatuation with Anne Boleyn to bring him under their control. "My plea," Catherine wrote, "is not against the King my Lord, but against the inventors and abettors of this cause."[3]

> These are my real enemies who wage such constant war against me; some of them that the bad counsel they gave the king should not become public, though they have been already well paid for it, and others that they may rob and plunder as much as they can.... These are the people from whom spring the threats and bravado proffered against Your Holiness; they are the sole inventors of them, not the King, my Lord. It is, therefore, urgent that Your Holiness put a very strong bit in their mouths.[4]

Catherine seemed aware that the sexual spell Anne Boleyn exerted over her husband could be put to political use. Boleyn was educated in Navarre at the court of Marguerite d'Angolueme, "the most corrupt and anti-Catholic court in southern Europe."[5] Marguerite's Dominican spiritual advisor, Gerard Roussel (whom Walsh claims was of Jewish origin) hurried to Germany in 1521 to imbibe the new evangelical freedom at its source as Luther wrestled with his vow of celibacy. Out of that unsuccessful struggle, Luther's doctrine of the enslaved will would emerge, a doctrine that enabled Luther to marry; many monks and priests followed his example. Cranmer, who had his Lutheran wife smuggled into England in a crate, was part of this network, which had grown tired of living under the sexual prescriptions of the Catholic Church.

Many thought the Church's financial proscriptions equally onerous. The desire to profit from usury was a great incentive to join the revolutionary struggle against the Church's hegemony over European culture. The rudimentary alliance between capitalism and revolution first became apparent in England when the families grown rich with the spoils of the church lands adopted Calvin, not Muentzer, as their theological mentor. In economic matters they took as their mentors the Jews, who had been expelled officially from England in 1290. Expulsions usually meant that the principled Jews left, leaving behind the unprincipled majority (only 16,000 Jews left England in 1290) to pursue their former way of living unhindered under the mask of Christianity. These marranos provided a natural network and support system for other Jews who returned secretly to England over the next few centuries under the guise of Spanish, Portuguese, or Italian merchants. The Lombards, who practiced usury on Lombard Street in London, were probably crypto-Jews. As in Spain, many English Jews went underground to preserve their fortunes. When Jews expelled from Spain in 1492 joined them, the time was ripe for expansion of Jewish influence over English culture under the guise of the reformed faith.

Many have noted this change in English culture and the subsequent rise of Britain as the philosemitic nation. Barbara Tuchman noticed that "England changed" during the 16th Century even though she "cannot fix upon the exact date ... when the god of Abraham, Isaac and Jacob became the English God."[6] She believes the main reason "the heroes of the Old Testament replaced the Catholic saints"[7] was Tyndale's translation of the Bible, smuggled into England in 1526 in false bottom wine casks transported by Sephardic Jewish merchants. Tyndale's translation, says Tuchman, influenced England even until the Balfour Agreement establishing the Jewish presence in Palestine in the early twentieth Century:

> With the translation of the bible into English and its adoption as the highest authority for an autonomous English church, the history, traditions and moral law of the Hebrew nation became part of the English culture, became for a period of three centuries the most powerful single influence on that culture. It linked, to repeat Matthew Arnold's phrase, "the genius and history of us English to the genius and history of the Hebrew people."[8] This is far from saying that it made England a Judeaophile nation, but "without the background of the English bible it is doubtful that the Balfour Declaration would ever have been issued in the name of the British government or the Mandate for Palestine undertaken, even given the strategic factors that late came into play."[9]

Tuchman writes as if the Old Testament were unknown in England until the first half of the 16th Century, a patent absurdity. Jacques Maritain's comment is more perceptive. Whenever the Bible is ripped out of context, "revolutionary ferment of extraordinary violence"[10] erupts. Once the Church is removed as the arbiter of Scripture—once Scripture was no longer read according to what Augustine called "the spirit"—it gets read, as Augustine warned, according to "the flesh," the way the Jews read it, as a prescription for establishing heaven on earth and, ultimately, a front for appetite. The gospel becomes "carnal" when separated from the Church; it becomes a justification for violations of chastity or of the prohibition against usury. It becomes, as Nietzsche claimed, a front for the will to power.

This judaizing tendency reached its full flower when Thomas Cromwell's great grandson became dictator in England. As Tuchman says, "With the Puritans came an invasion of Hebraism transmitted though the Old Testament."[11] Tuchman adverts to the notion that Scripture is a front for appetite, saying the Puritans "followed the letter of the Old Testament for the very reason that they saw their own faces reflected in it."[12] But she takes the idea no further. Puritanism meant the end of Christian morality and the importation of "Jewish habits." According to Cunningham, as cited by Tuchman, "The general tendency of Puritanism was to discard Christian morality and to substitute Jewish habits in its stead."[13] The natural consequence was "retrogression to a lower type of social morality which showed itself at home and abroad."[14] The first manifestation of that moral retrogression was the widespread poverty characteristic of English life for centuries thereafter.

"By mid-16th Century," Tuchman concludes, "it was possible to talk about a revolution, an international political movement bent on overthrowing the medieval view of the world and replacing it with something new."[15] In England, that "something new" was the rationalization of greed, appetite, and *libido dominandi* later known as capitalism. Whenever that age referred to its new system of economic exploitation, it used the vocabulary of a by gone era. And so it referred to the dawn of a new age of mammon and usury, and to the rise to power of revolutionaries well off from the theft of Church property and bent on imitating the Jews in theology and economics. None of these advances in finance could have been accomplished without the willing collaboration of the Jews. Like the Jews, the thieving English families supported "the forces of heresy in religion and liberalism in politics."[16] That meant usury, a system Lord Bacon would defend explicitly in an essay on economics. England became Jewish not because it read the Bible, but because the leading families promoted widespread distribution of heretical translations, which everyone had the right to interpret, as a front for usury and their consolidation of political power. Freedom meant the right of the powerful to determine what was true. Everyone was free to interpret the Bible as he saw fit. When that interpretation did not correspond to the interests of the powerful, *force majeure* would become the ultimate explicator.

When the ecclesial bond uniting England and Rome was severed, the bond uniting Englishmen was fatally weakened too, because once England stopped being Catholic it became an ideological nation favoring aliens who supported the new regime over the natives who opposed it, but also over those who simply didn't understand what was happening. The recusant and the clueless were swept away by the same tide. The Protestant was the alien par excellence. His secret allegiance was to the shadowy conspiracy emanating from Geneva, not to his native country.

Not surprisingly, many of these aliens were Jews, either crypto-Jews like Marco Perez using the facade of Calvinism in Antwerp to cover his identity as a revolutionary, or descendants of Jews expelled from Spain.

If on the issue of the restoration of Church property, Mary found no support from her husband, who swayed by his father to oppose the pope and Cardinal Pole, had left the country immediately after the marriage anyway, she found even less support among her dubious advisors. Prominent among them was chief commissioner John Russell, progenitor of a family wealthy from looting the Churches that would equal the Cecils in influence. John Russell came from a family of wine merchants who traced their ancestry to the Roussels of Gascony, who traced their lineage to wine-trading Jews from Spain or Portugal. With a husband *in absentia* and advisers like Russell, the issue of Church property soon became moot. During the reign of Edward, Mary's predecessor from 1547 to 1553, "the loot went on at an appalling rate. When [Edward] died and Mary came to the throne, it was nearly completed. A mass of new families had arisen, wealthy out of all proportion to anything which the older England had known, and bound by a common interest to the older families which had joined in the grab."[17] Those families included "the Howards ..., the Cavendishes, the Cecils, the Russells, and fifty other new families" whose fortunes were based upon "the ruins of religion."[18] The monastic lands stolen by these families constituted one fifth of the wealth of the country. "[T]his transference had tipped the scale entirely in their favor as against the peasantry,"[19] who sank into a poverty from which they never recovered, only to emerge as an equally impoverished proletariat in the industrial revolution. By 1660, the king was a "salaried puppet"[20] in the hands of the magnates, while more than half of the population had been "dispossessed of capital and land. Not one man in two, even if you reckon the very small owners, inhabited a house of which he was the secure possessor, or tilled land from which he could not be turned off."[21]

The loot remained in the hands of the looters, who would use it to prevent re-establishment of the Church and economic policies inimical to usury, which they wanted to expand into a system of governance. Thwarted on the economic front, Mary tried to deal with the Protestant revolutionaries solely on theological grounds, an attempt doomed to fail. Unsurprisingly, Mary, the scion of the line that brought the Inquisition to Spain and saved it from internal subversion, brought the Inquisition to England to address the secret cabal that enabled Henry VIII to cast off her mother for the Lutheran sex agent Anne Boleyn. Philip, left for the continent shortly after the wedding (he was to return briefly in March 1557 and stay until July 1557) concurred with Mary's decision even though he was seldom there to implement it.

Mary began to burn heretics in 1555 in a campaign that the magnates condoned to foster popular hatred for the regime. Mary learned the hard way that times had changed. It was no longer 1480, and England was not Spain. The enemies of the Church had grown much more sophisticated in psychological warfare.

So Mary's enemies paid for ballads ridiculing her phantom pregnancy while she tried to get a handle on her evanescent foes.

In the five years of Mary's reign, 300 Englishmen died at the hands of her Inquisition. John Foxe, in exile in Switzerland, termed Mary's victims "martyrs." Protestant historians have expressed doubts about their piety. "The real truth about these 'Martyrs,'" according to Protestant historian Cobbett, "is that they were generally a set of most wicked wretches, who sought to destroy the Queen and her government, and under the pretence of conscience and superior piety, to obtain the means of again preying upon the people. No mild means could reclaim them."[22]

Bishop Edmund Bonner of London was one of Mary's lieutenants in her crusade against Protestant influence. Foxe devoted a couplet to Bonner, the bloody bishop of London:

this cannibal in three years space three hundred martyrs slew
They were his food, he loved so blood, he spared none he knew

On May 28, 1555, a warrant was issued for the arrest of a secret Protestant cell with direct links to Elizabeth, Mary's half sister, and the next in line to the throne. Elizabeth was brought to Hampton Court for questioning. One of the conspirators named was a young scholar, John Dee, on the staff of Bishop Bonner, working as his assistant in ferreting out and punishing secret Protestant heretics.

John Dee was born on July 13, 1527, the same year Kerssenbroick saw fiery signs in the sky, presaging the end of the old order. There is no information on his place of birth, whether he was baptized and where, or any details about his family. Dee would come to fame as Queen Elizabeth's conjurer and astrologer, and the time of birth, aligned with the position of the stars, was essential in casting a person's horoscope. "In those dark times," the 17th Century historian John Aubrey wrote, "astrologer, mathematician and conjurer were accounted the same things."[23]

Dee grew up in England under the shadow of Henry VIII's divorce and the country's looming break with Rome. Frances Yates called him the characteristic philosopher of his age. More than Tyndale's translation of the Bible, Dee is responsible for turning England into *the* Judaizing nation *par excellence*: Dee created the philosophy that allowed England's new rulers to integrate their lust for gain, their judaizing, their imperialism, and their penchant for magic into a more or less coherent whole. His enemies accused him of casting spells. He did a horoscope of the royal wedding between Mary and Philip, and informants later claimed that, in casting that horoscope, Dee had "endeavored by enchantments to destroy Queen Mary."[24] His role ranged from casting horoscopes to assign propitious dates for momentous occasions, for example, Elizabeth's coronation, to advising on matters geographical and political. By the time of his death in 1608, the tide of reaction was running against him, but by then he had left an indelible mark on what would become the world's premier Protestant empire and foremost promoter of revolution.

While a student at Cambridge in 1546, Dee put on a performance of Aristophanes' play *Peace*, during which a mechanical scarab beetle leapt off the stage in flight to the palace of Zeus. No one could explain how Dee accomplished this. Shortly after his *coup de theatre*, Dee left for the continent on the first of many trips to the centers of learning there. Dee went to Louvain, a center of what he called "the intertraffique of the mind"[25] in the Spanish Netherlands. The low countries were the delta of the continent's largest river, and analogously, all currents of thought, including the new revolutionary ideas, ended up there as well. The Anabaptists had gravitated toward the low countries after expulsion from Thuringia and Westfalia, and with them flowed the ideas of Radical Protestantism, along with Renaissance science from Italy, navigational discoveries from Portugal, and Cabala, in a millennialist redaction that tried to make sense of the expulsion of the Jews from Spain. Louvain was a home to all of these ideas, and Dee imbibed deeply. While there, Dee noted in his diary the arrival of the heir apparent, Philip of Spain, who would loom large in his career.

Dee's religious views at the time are unclear. Since he later was employed by Bishop Bonner, he probably was a Catholic, but Dee seemed equally at home intellectually in reformist England during the reign of the sickly child King Edward. In 1568 Dr., later Cardinal, William Allen, soon famous as the leader of England's exiled Catholics, warned students under his care at the new Catholic college at Douay in the Netherlands to keep their distance from "Ioannes Deus," whom he described as "*sacerdos uxoratus, magicis curiosisque artibus deditus.*"[26] Was Dee a married priest practicing magic and uncanny arts? A member of the Walsingham intelligence community claimed Dee was ordained while in Bonner's service. If so, his ordination did not recommend him to Cardinal Allen, who suspected him of trafficking in spirits and double-dealing. Dee was, according to Allen, a purveyor of "certain irreligious influences,"[27] more dangerous because of his cover as a Catholic priest.

Dee's biographer tries to resolve the religious issue by claiming "Throughout his life, Dee refused to commit himself to a particular religion."[28] The same cannot be said of his politics. Dee was at home under Protestant and Catholic regimes because he believed in neither Protestantism nor Catholicism. He believed in an alternative to both, what Yates called "the occult philosophy in the Elizabethan age."[29] The clearest expression of his beliefs came later with publication of his *Monas Hieroglyphica*. The Monad was his symbol for the key to understanding the universe. It was intimately related to the language God spoke when he loosed the divine force that caused the universe to come into existence and then stay in orderly motion. Magic, as Dee understood it, involved "the human ability to tap this force. The better our understanding of the way it drives the universe, the more powerful the magic becomes. In other words, magic is technology."[30] Neither Protestant nor Catholic, Dee believed in magic, and he was willing to work with whichever regime was willing to pay for his services. Since the Catholics considered him a magus who trafficked in unclean spirits, that meant that Dee would work for the new Protestant establishment in England, which, was avid to put his discoveries to political use.

Magic determined his politics, which determined his religion. In 1552 Dee returned to find England had changed in his absence. "Everywhere statues were destroyed in the churches," Dee wrote in the diary he kept to the detriment of his reputation. "The great crucifix ... on the altar of St. Paul's was a few days ago cast down by force of instruments, several men being wounded in the process and one killed.... There is not a single crucifix now remaining in the other churches."[31]

Seeking some explanation, Dee sought out John Cheke, his former colleague at Cambridge. Cheke introduced Dee to his son-in-law, William Cecil, who in collaboration with Elizabeth, who knighted him as Lord Burghley, would become an architect of the anti-Catholic revolution during the latter part of the 16th Century. Burghley presented Dee to the court of Edward in 1552 and, under his auspices, Dee joined the household of Northumberland later that year.

When Mary died in 1558, Cecil probably rescued Dee from his exposed and precarious position as Inquisitor, because it was through Cecil that Dee had become an Inquisitor. Once Mary died, anyone associated with her regime was in jeopardy, most certainly someone like John Dee, Bloody Bonner's chaplain. Foxe's account of Bonner's persecutions bears this out. In the first edition of *Acts and Monuments*, Dee's involvement in the persecution is documented in detail. His name then disappears from the 1576 edition, although his words do not. Everything Dee said as Inquisitor is still in the book but, as Woolley puts it, "every occurrence of his name (more than ten) has been deleted or substituted with the anonymous label 'a Doctor.'"[32] The reason is clear. Foxe learned Dee "was up to something," while ostensibly in Bonner's service, which made clear Dee was no "Catholic colluder."[33] Dee was a double agent. Claiming to be a Catholic in Bonner's service, Dee was really working for Cecil and Elizabeth and the cell identified in the arrest warrant of May 1555. Dee landed on his feet because he was working secretly for the new regime all along. In contemporary parlance, Dee was an "intelligencer." Dee was "a seeker of hidden knowledge, philosophical, scientific, as well as political."[34] As proof of his standing with the new regime, Dee chose the date of the Queen's coronation, which he set after consulting the stars and the time of her birth.

II

On October 25, 1555, roughly six months after Dee was arrested, Charles V abdicated as emperor. The abdication was complicated, and it lasted well into 1566. Charles was 55 but seemed much older, worn down by his vices and by shadowboxing with forces out to destroy him but which he had difficulty identifying. His advice to Philip on England was misguided and would cause his son much heartache. They did not realize the sinister nature of the changes in England; both were taken in by lies Elizabeth and her ministers spread about their intentions, deferring action until it was too late.

Charles came to the throne in 1516 when his father Ferdinand died. In 1496, the Jews were expelled from Portugal as part of a marriage agreement to unite the King of Portugal with the daughter of Ferdinand and Isabella. Those who refused to convert moved north, importantly to the Spanish Netherlands, where they soon made use of their skills at international trade. As early as 1512, large numbers of Sephardic Jews settled in Antwerp, "whose citizens," Nadler says, "perceived the financial advantage of admitting these well-connected merchants."[35]

In 1516 when Ferdinand died, Charles was living in the Spanish Netherlands as the Jews arrived in large numbers. Luther would nail his 95 theses to the church door in Wittenberg one year later. Within the next half-Century, Antwerp would become a center of international intrigue involving Sephardic Jews, English Protestants, and German Anabaptists, culminating in the Iconoclast rebellion of 1566. By then, the reformation was in full swing. As Charles was to discover, Spain solved its Jewish problem by exporting it to the north. One of the tenets of the Black Legend is that Spain went into decline following the expulsion of Jews. To the contrary, "the Spanish Empire attained its greatest limits and material and intellectual power in the Century after the Expulsion."[36] But the problem showed up elsewhere. Many Jews remained unbelievers, even if they professed the faith to save their wealth, and "their descendants were in communication with *Jews scattered all over Europe*, building up new commercial empires, especially in the Low Countries and in England."[37] These Jews functioned as a sophisticated spy network that "quietly kept the anti-Spanish and anti-Catholic forces of the world informed as to naval, military, and commercial happenings in the peninsula. Thus the Jews, in the long run, took their revenge on the country that had cast them out. In this sense only can it be said truthfully that the exodus led to the decline of Spain."[38] Kamen claims one consequence of the expulsion was the creation of "an international Jewish conspiracy":

> Several Spaniards later regretted the expulsion of Jewish financiers in 1492; in the seventeenth Century Spanish writers first claimed the growing wealth of countries like Holland was due to converso capital flowing into Amsterdam. Later, the mythical decline of Spain and the triumph of its enemies were blamed on the international Jewish conspiracy. Among the first to take this line was the poet Francisco de Quevedo, who claimed Jewish elders from all over Europe had held a meeting at Salonika, where they drew up secret plans against Christendom. Quevedo and others accused the count duke of Olivares of planning to invite the Jews back into Spain to undo all the consequences of 1492.[39]

What went underground in Spain came into the open in the German principalities and the low countries. In Spain, heresy took on a quietist tinge and became "Illuminism" of the sort practiced by the Gnostics and the Albigensians centuries earlier. "Catholic Jews of slight orthodoxy" collaborated with Protestants of the German-speaking north in their campaign against the Church. They offered Charles V 800,000 ducats if be would make certain "reforms" in the procedure of the Holy Office. "Charles," according to Walsh, "seemed unaware, most of his life, that he was surrounded by the agents of an international conspiracy to destroy everything that his heart loved and revered."[40]

By 1540 the converso issue was over in Spain. Spain had saved itself by importing the Inquisition from southern France, and then by exporting its problem to the north of Europe. For some indication of what might have happened in Spain if the situation there had gone unchecked, we need only look at Poland. Jewish influence over Polish political life increased in intensity, fueling Polish imperialism in the East while weakening Polish rule at home. Graetz brags that a Jew in Constantinople chose the successor of Sigismund Augustus in 1572. Polish laws codified Jewish hegemony over large areas of Polish cultural life. Since disobedience to the predations of the Jewish tax-farmers was a capital crime in Poland, animosity against the Jews was widespread but severely repressed. An explosion of violence was all but certain. The explosion came when the Sejm, dominated by the Polish magnates and their Jewish administrators, rebuffed Cossack aspirations for political reform in 1647. Cultural drift in Poland led to an explosion of the sort the Inquisition prevented in Spain. As a result, the Polish republic went into terminal decline, expiring 147 years later.

The Jewish settlements in the newly-Protestant regions of the North drew Marranos like a magnet. Disaffected Catholics who had lived double lives as clerics now made common cause with the Jews who had led double lives after converting to Catholicism to preserve their wealth. A coordinated attack on the cultural hegemony of the Catholic Church proceeded when these groups came together. Revolution was a binary weapon, a Protestant-Jewish alliance from its inception. The Jews, as Newman shows, promoted every "reform" movement in Europe, from the Hussites to the Anabaptists, to weaken the hegemony of the Catholic Church, reasoning that the enemy of their enemy was their friend. In places like Antwerp and Amsterdam, the Jews put their wealth and their considerable expertise in finance and publishing at the disposal of the Dutch Calvinists and their princely protectors to wage cultural warfare against the Catholic Church and Spain, its defender. Liberation from the stress of a double life was intoxicating, and the intensity of the intoxication demonstrates the stress it exerted on those troubled souls. An orgy of "gluttony, drunkenness and lasciviousness" followed this "liberation of the northern man from the trammels of Roman culture."[41] In the wake of this Reformation, a Venetian ambassador reported, "among the Germans, overeating was considered a virtue, and cupidity, among the Calvinists especially, was a synonym for superior industry; and that when a German was sober, he was thought to be ill."[42]

Lured by the promise of wealth from the conjunction of river and sea trade in Antwerp, Portuguese conversos settled there as early as 1512, when the Netherlands were still under Hapsburg control. Charles V, the Holy Roman Emperor, was under tremendous political challenges and had little time to figure out what was going on, much less how to stop it. Ratifying a *fait accompli*, in 1537 Charles V gave the expelled conversos permission to settle in the Spanish Netherlands as long as they did not revert to Judaism or Judaize.

Many of those Jews settled at Antwerp, a natural entrepot on the northern bank of the Scheldt River with easy access to the North Sea. Because of its location at the mouth of the Rhine delta, Antwerp was the link between European markets and the colonies European countries were establishing throughout the world. Antwerp soon became the richest city in Europe, "where merchants and usurers lived in palaces with regal pomp and luxury." It was

> "the center of that commercial system which was soon to be superseded by a large international life ... a stately and egotistical city" which was then the centre of the Jewish money power, driven from Spain three quarters of a century before. Along the river were massive warehouses, stuffed with treasures from the ends of the earth.[43]

Antwerp became the center for trade in East Indian spices and Brazilian sugar, and the agents for these firms were almost without exception Portuguese conversos. Indeed, the wealthy trading firms were almost exclusively Portuguese new Christians. In less than a generation, the Jews made Antwerp the center of world trade and finance. The Jewish merchant who came and went as a "Lombard," a "Genoese," and an "Italian," or more commonly a "Portuguese" had found a new earthly paradise. His new-found freedom allowed him to re-establish the Jewish commercial supremacy of the Middle Ages. Because of the expulsion of the Jews from Spain, Antwerp became the center of a large mercantile network that included Jewish communities in Lyons, Ferrara, Rome, Turin, Venice, and Ancona and extended to Ragusa, Salonika, and Constantinople, and south to Suez and Cairo, the line of the overland trade to the Indies. That mercantile network also doubled as a spy ring.[44]

The Jews who controlled the spice trade reinvested their profits in the new printing trade, which they quickly used for cultural subversion and psychological warfare by printing Protestant bibles. The printing business combined with the intelligence network gave the Jews and Protestants a significant advantage in the war with Spain. Soon the Jews were smuggling Protestant bibles into England, making a handsome profit from cultural subversion.

By the end of the 16th Century many conversos had moved to Amsterdam, then under Calvinist control, where they threw off the appearances of Christianity and formed their own Jewish communities. Beginning around 1603, the marranos in Holland emerged as Jews. The confessor of Phillip II's sister Maria, Fray Vicente de Rocamoro, disappeared suddenly only to re-emerge in the Jewish community in Amsterdam as Isaac of Rocamoro. The new Jews of Amsterdam had peculiarly Catholic devotions to figures like the Old Testament figure "Saint Esther," but

Catholicism disappeared gradually from their culture, replaced by the emerging Protestant revolutionary view.

In 1540 Charles received disconcerting news that the Marranos in Antwerp were engaged in a propaganda war against the Catholic Church. The Marranos had a disconcerting affinity for Protestantism and, unlike Luther, kept that affinity a secret in times of danger. Charles was surrounded by men, including clergy, who had secretly gone over to the other side. "[S]ecret Jews wound themselves into the confidence of Charles and his very family, and sapped the foundations of the Faith he loved under cover of some of the new fashionable opinions from the north; the new Jewish communities at various strategic points in Europe were quietly building up greater empires of economic and political strength to oppose and to plague him and his successors."[45]

Two years later, the Austrian branch of the Hapsburg family banished all Jews from Bohemia after they were discovered passing military intelligence to the Turks. The Jewish refugees then moved to Poland and Turkey. In 1545, Charles learned that Marranos from Spain and Portugal were involved in secret arms shipments to Turkey for use against Christians. Four years later, Charles expelled the Marranos from Antwerp. Many Jews remained as Catholics, while others became Protestants and migrated to England, where they continued in the ongoing insurgency against Spain and the Catholic Church. Sandoval found in Jews a perennial racially based inclination toward "ingratitude" and subversion. The racial interpretation of Judaism that arose in Spain was given new life by the Marranos of the Netherlands, whose evil tendencies were like "the inseparable accident of blackness"[46] among Negroes. "The slightest provocation," Sandoval continued, tended to "pervert the Marranos" into reverting to Judaism, making them "extremely dangerous in communities."[47]

Despite expelling the Jews from Antwerp, Charles was at a loss deciding how to deal with so subtle an enemy. Perhaps passion clouded Charles' judgment. According to Walsh, "If the Emperor had put on the strong armor of sanctity which the Church, his wife and his conscience had often urged upon him the result might have been different, but a Charles dallying with lusty Barbara Blomberg between fits of the gout and spurts of gluttony was no match for the Jews."[48]

Charles also failed to deal with the Protestants effectively. One of his greatest regrets as he lay dying was that he did not execute Luther as a heretic and traitor during the Diet of Worms. The limited damage done by the Protestant revolt during his reign was not due to his ineffectual efforts to stop it, but the internal fragmentation and dissension in the movement.

Writing in 1564, the year Calvin died, and 18 years after Luther's death, an English Catholic apologist described tongue-in-cheek, the many alternatives to Catholicism:

> Now, so ye be no papist, ye may be a Sacramentary, an Anabaptist, or a Lutheran; and then a Civil, a Zealous or a Disordered Lutheran, among all which ye may

choose of what sort in each branch ye list to be; whether ye allow two sacraments with the zealous Lutherans, three with the Leipsians or four with the Wittenbergers; whether ye will be an Osiandrin, a half-Osiandrin or an Antiosiandrin; whether a close Anabaptist or an open Anabaptist, a new Pelagian or a new Manichee. Whether ye say the body is with the bread, or the bread without the body, or pledge to assure the body, or the very value and effect of the body. All these with a number of other doctrines professed and defended freely of Protestants hath God now revealed for truths, faiths and gospels to recompense the darkness of nine hundred years.[49]

The half-humorous irony bespoke the confidence of the Catholic cause in the wake of the Council of Trent; it derived nothing from the befuddlement of an emperor grown old before his time and too worn out by his vices to carry on the task God had ordained for him. Nonetheless, the year of Charles' abdication saw a dramatic reversal of fortune for Catholicism. Philip II, his son, would never bear the title emperor, but as the King of Spain, he carried on the struggle for the Catholic faith that his father should have fought. His name became synonymous with the Counter Reformation, especially its military application. Beyond that, the papacy went through rebirth and revitalization, the likes of which had not happened before. The change in papal character from a Renaissance Epicurean like Alexander VI to an ascetic like Pius V was dramatic.

III

In August 1559, Pius IV was elected pope. He reconvened the Council of Trent, reassembling the church's bishops to answer the challenges of the reformers and provide a program of reform. Beginning with the election of Paul IV in 1555, the popes, strengthened by the doctrinal clarity and the ecclesial reform that Trent enabled, exercised their office in a way unheard of for decades if not centuries. By the time Pius IV became pope, the Peace of Augsburg, which tried to resolve the Protestant split in the Germanies with the formula, *"cujus regio ejus religio,"* was not working. Europe needed a thoroughgoing reform, better theological clarifications, and political resolution. The Protestants were determined to press their political advantage despite the doctrinal splintering that plagued them.

When the Council of Trent reconvened in January 1561, the English bishops weren't there, because Elizabeth would not allow the papal delegates announcing the council to set foot on English soil. But 113 other church fathers were, and when they finished their deliberations on December 4, 1563, the church tied up over 17 years of loose ends, providing successive church leaders with a blueprint that would be remarkably successful in reversing much of the damage wrought over the past half century. By the time the council was over, "simony, pluralities, nonresidence, ignorance, and racketeering" were no longer synonymous with church administration.[50] Pius IV took a knife to his own household, firing 400 hangers on in what O'Connell terms "radical surgery."[51] The operation was a success, largely because of the people who implemented the council's teachings. Pius V succeeded

Pius IV in 1566, and a series of equally remarkable popes followed Pius V, all united in implementing the same program. Ignatius of Loyola, one of the Church's great organizational geniuses, died in 1556, one year into Pius IV's reign. Ignatius did not found his organization to fight Protestants, but his followers like Edmund Campion in England and Peter Canisius in the Germanies adopted that role with remarkable success. Once equilibrium was reestablished in Europe, the Jesuits turned to the colonies of Spain and France in the New World, where their zeal was crowned with similar success. When the Counter Reformation had run its course, Protestantism was on the defensive, and the Church was run according to a new canon of organizational principles. Before 1555 the cardinals controlled the pope; after 1598 the pope controlled the cardinals as the church centralized its power to deal with the centralization of the newly emerging modern state.

Lutheranism, which was either blessed or rendered ineffective (depending on your point of view) by Luther's innate conservatism in matters not of burning personal concern, became, as Thomas Muentzer predicted, a docile tool of small German principalities; it was in no position to lead an international revolutionary movement, especially one that required close collaboration with the Jews. On May 5, 1527, Lutheran German mercenaries sacked Rome, and the Jews took it as a sign that the Messiah, a handsome Marrano named Solomon Molkho, was on his way to redeem them. In 1530 the Lutherans, under Philip Melanchthon, showed revulsion at this Jewish presumption and the complicity of the Judaizers, when they issued the Augsburg Confession, which condemned millennialism and the belief in the rule of the saints on this earth, a doctrine promoted by Anabaptists then and Calvinists later. Melanchthon and Luther were deeply offended by Molkho's apocalyptic tone and condemned the Christian version of his ideas as a Jewish doctrine. Molkho was burned at the stake in Italy in 1532. In 1542 Luther expanded his attack on the Jews by writing an intemperate invective that has caused Lutheran theologians intense embarrassment ever since. The defection of Luther and Melanchthon from the revolutionary cause left the field open to the Calvinists in Geneva, but before they could assume the mantle, they had internal issues to resolve.

The accusation that Protestants were Jews was not new. Calvin claimed an opponent "called me a Jew, because I maintain the rigor of the law intact."[52] Others claimed the Genevan reliance on "*jure gladii*," the law of the sword, to suppress dissent made Calvin "a Jew." Calvin was a lawyer before he became a reformer; his reliance on the law to micromanage the minutiae of everyday life reminded many of Jewish proscriptions in Deuteronomy and Numbers. His notion that idolatry should be uprooted by military force was consistent with the Anabaptist reading of the Old Testament. His approach was a more refined, more sophisticated, and more legalistic appropriation of the Old Testament than the version that had inspired the Anabaptists in Muenster and the Taborites in Bohemia. The idea Calvin was a Jew or he was working for the Jews was, therefore, not new or far-fetched.

The evidence that Protestantism was Judaizing was there for all to see. Graetz and Newman agree the Jews played an important role in the Protestant revolt. Walsh quotes Cabrera, a Spanish Marrano, who claims "most of the heresiarchs and heretics of this present Century have been of those people," i.e., the Jews. "It is beyond question," he continues, citing another Jewish historian, that "the first leaders of the Protestant sects were called semi-Judaei, or half-Jews, in all parts of Europe," and "men of Jewish descent were as conspicuous among them as they had been among the Gnostics and would later be among the Communists."[53]

Luther, Zwingli, and Calvin were all students of Nicholas of Lyra, a Franciscan monk of Jewish descent who lived in the 14th Century. Nicholas got his ideas from Raschi, who was the conduit that allowed the Talmudic scholarship of his father, Isaac of Troyes, to flow directly into Protestantism. Reuchlin was another conduit. When Pfefferkorn accused Reuchlin of being in the pay of the Jews to disseminate their propaganda, the essential truth of the charge caused Reuchlin to issue a violent denial in his pamphlet *Augenspiegel*. Reuchlin's battle with the Cologne Dominicans was the diversion that allowed Luther to issue his 95 theses with impunity. In each instance, Protestantism exhibited not an advance over Catholic thought, but "one long retrogression toward the moribund Judaism of the Pharisees of the time of Christ."[54]

Conversos waiting impatiently to throw off the pretext of Catholicism were in communion with the Jews throughout Europe and together they formed the nucleus for the coming international revolt. Their skill in finance and printing made them powerful culture warriors who could influence events in ways their opponents had difficulty understanding, and they were quick to put these skills in the service of Messianic political movements. The constant in Jewish participation in revolution from Simon bar Kokhba to Trotsky was not race but rejection of Christ. Revolution was a theological project from its inception:

> It was their great tragedy that, having failed to understand Who Christ was, [the Jews] could not get rid of the messianic consciousness for which they had been chosen and consecrated. Finding closed to them the only spiritual door to salvation, they were constantly driven to seek redemption in the here and now, in the resources of matter, in gold and power, in anything, anywhere but Christ. When all their kingdom had turned to dust in their patient hands, and the inevitable scourge of persecution came to scatter them again and again, they still followed leaders who kept them blind, and remained missionaries of what Saint John called "the spirit that dissolves Christ."[55]

Many of the Jews expelled from Spain and Portugal fled to cities in France. Many more made their way to the Spanish Netherlands, where Charles allowed them to flourish. Lucien Wolf claims large numbers of English Protestants—"and doubtless the most active in propaganda and organization"[56]—were Jews who had become Calvinists in Antwerp where they were active in the Protestant movement and "had given up their mask of Catholicism for a not less hollow pretense of Calvinism."[57] There was a natural affinity between the Calvinists and the Jews. Both were "enemies of Rome, Spain and the Inquisition."[58] And Calvinism was a form of Christianity similar to Judaism in its attitude toward idolatry and the law. As a result, the Jews "became zealous and valuable allies of the Calvinists."

There is no indication that Calvin or his lieutenant Beza were of Jewish descent, but many of their preachers were. Calvin was hardly as flamboyant as Bokelzoon in playing the Old Testament prophet, but he was as willing to have his followers use the sword as any latter day Gideon, even if he didn't wield it himself. In a letter to his English followers, he said anyone who refused to give up the Catholic faith must be put to the sword. Because of his legalism, his lack of charisma, and his willingness to create a systematic framework for his thought, Calvinism became an international movement that soon eclipsed less intellectually powerful rivals like Anabaptism as the *avant garde* of the revolutionary movement. Calvin tried to distance himself from the Jews, but he nevertheless relied on them as his intellectual inspiration and co-revolutionaries, especially as spies. Neither his police state in Geneva nor the imitation of it erected in England could have prospered without the Jewish intelligence ring in the spice trade in the Netherlands.

The embarrassment Molkho caused in Protestant circles would be palpable for quite some time. In 1530, Oecolampadius accused Michael Servetus, the Unitarian Spanish physician who discovered circulation of the blood before Harvey, of Judaizing. Michael Newman says "The career of Michael Servetus ... affords a vivid instance of the imprint of so-called 'Jewish influence' upon the Reform movements of the Christian Church.... Jewish friends and his study of Jewish literature ... served to create both the atmosphere and the special background wherefrom the revolutionary doctrinal system of Servetus emerged."[59] Newman dismisses race as an influence on Servetus' conversion to a Unitarianism indistinguishable from Judaism, but there is no evidence he was a Marrano. Judaizing was a matter of intellect and will, not some involuntary biological reaction. "The 'Judaizing' tendencies in individuals such as Servetus, and in movements such as the Puritan, the Unitarian and others, "by no means depended upon deeply hidden traces of Jewish blood-heritage."[60] Servetus was corrupted by contact with Marrano teachers from whom he learned Hebrew and medical lore, including what they knew about blood. "It is beyond all reasonable doubt," says Newman, that Servetus "derived his unusual Hebrew knowledge and perhaps also his advanced medical lore from Marranos in the Spanish Peninsula."[61] After finding the Jews right on medical matters, Servetus concluded they were right on the Trinity. "We are surely justified in assuming that his vigorous anti-Trinitarian views," Newman continues, "were also absorbed from these Jewish teachers."[62] The papal nuncio said Servetus was corrupted by unauthorized translations of the Bible distributed by the Jews in Spain "from their headquarters in Antwerp."[63] Newman suggests that in Paris, Servetus saw French translations of Luther's works "written and printed by Jews."[64]

In 1531, Servetus wrote *De Trinitatis Erroribus*, published in Strasbourg, a hotbed of Anabaptism, in which he used the writings of Rabbi David Kimchi to attack the dogma of the Trinity, a move certain to make him unpopular in Catholic and Reformed circles. The threat to the Protestants was significant, because Catholics could now cite Servetus's anti-Trinitarianism as the logical conclusion of the Reformation's Judaizing, and they could point to the numerous Hebrew citations in his writings as proof. Servetus was re-baptized at 30, but he soon turned on the Anabaptists too. By the 1550s Servetus was a wanted man, and wanted more by the Protestants than by the Catholics. In 1553 Calvin engineered his arrest at Vienne on charges of heresy. Escaping from prison, Servetus thought of returning to Spain. Perhaps fearing that he might fall into the hands of the Inquisition, Servetus went to Geneva instead, where he fell into the hands of Calvin's police state and was put on trial for heresy. The Calvinists claimed Servetus "had written, published and said that to believe there were three distinct persons: Father, Son and Holy Ghost, in the single essence of God was to forge or feign so many phantoms and to have a God partied into three, like the three-headed Cerberus of the heathen poets."[65] They found him guilty, burning him to death at the stake.

Calvin's resort to the tactics of the Inquisition caused considerable consternation among the Reformed Party. Calvin was not stupid enough to be unaware of the risks, and probably proceeded because the alternative was even more fraught with danger. What was the alternative? To acquiesce in the accusations that the reformed faith was judaizing and that Calvin and his associates were secret Jews? "The central contention of the opponents of Servetus," says Newman, "was that his entire theological system was a vindication of Jews and Judaism."[66] Servetus was to Calvin what Muentzer was to Luther. He was the disciple who carried the master's premise to its logical conclusion, and in so doing, left the new system dangerously exposed to attacks by its enemies. No revolution can succeed without a boundary on its flank, and the only way to create it is by brute physical force, since revolution has no internal order. So Zizka exterminated the Adamites; Luther urged the German princes to slay Muentzer and his peasant followers; and Calvin burned Servetus at the stake. Cromwell would have to deal with the Fifth Monarchy Men, and Stalin would have to deal with Trotsky, but the precedent was established. "When Calvin burned Michael Servetus at Geneva in 1553," Newman writes, "he was trying to burn away the influence exercised by Marrano Judaism on the dogmas of Christianity."[67] He was also trying to maintain control over a movement that naturally tended toward Judaism. Calvin's critics insisted that "by their strenuous insistence upon the effects of Adams's transgression as compromising mankind at large, and Abraham's readiness to sacrifice his only son," Calvin and his fellow Reformers had "interspersed the religion of Christ with such an amount of Judaism that their Christianity was in many respects a relapse into the bonds of the Law from which Christ had set us free."[68] It was a serious charge; Servetus paid for Calvin's answer with his life. Calvin dealt with the Jewish issue by burning Servetus at the stake, stopping the mouth of those who called him a judaizer, while incorporating Jewish principles into his system and baptizing them as Calvinism. By time of its founder's death in 1564, Calvinism had replaced Anabaptism as the cutting edge of Protestant revolutionary thought. By the time the Catholic Church aroused itself from the decadent indolence of the Renaissance, Anabaptism was gone and "the enemy it encountered everywhere wore the face of John Calvin."[69] Calvinism became the intellectual leadership of the revolutionary movement because, as Marvin O'Connell says, "In Geneva reformation went hand in had with revolution."[70] Calvin rescued the revolution "when the Protestant reform was wavering on the brink of anarchy."[71]

Calvin's lieutenant Beza tried to convert the King of France to Calvinism in 1561, and the Dutch descendants of Jan Bokelzoon turned to Calvinism when Anabaptism became the god that failed in Muenster. By the time of Charles V's abdication, Calvinism led the revolutionary movement, and the focus of its activity was the Spanish Netherlands.

IV

Once Elizabeth was crowned on January 16, 1559, Cecil lost no time in putting his plan to cut England off from Rome into effect. The first act of Parliament under the new regime abolished the spiritual jurisdiction and authority of the pope in England. The Act of Supremacy was the first in a line of increasingly draconian penal enactments "to eradicate the Catholic faith from England and to set up Protestantism in its place."[72] The same Parliament then abolished the Mass, making it a criminal offense to say or hear it. Taken together, the two acts were "tantamount to doing away with the Catholic religion in England."

The first ideological state followed. To be a good Englishman, Elizabeth's subjects had to affirm by oath that all spiritual jurisdiction was vested in the Queen, "who thus became supreme governor in all spiritual and ecclesiastical things and causes as in temporal."[73] The Good Englishman also had to attend the new worship or suffer onerous fines. Those who refused were known as recusants or refusers, and some paid the price of martyrdom. England became known as "perfidious Albion" because of the religious hypocrisy of its leaders: "They were ashamed to admit to catholic sovereigns abroad that they were cruel persecutors of Catholics at home and so they tried to rob their victims of the martyr's crown by pretending that they died as traitors."[74] Like Hamlet in Denmark, the recusants learned what it was like to live under a "rotten" regime which would not admit its intentions or its origins honestly and which punished those who did by deeming them traitors. "They were traitors to the godless state," Knox wrote, "because they would not be traitors to Almighty God .... Thus it was that the new religion was forced upon a reluctant people."[75] This time the English bishops did not go along, and they were replaced by a motley assembly of political opportunists, who then replaced the loyal Catholic clergy with hacks, pothecaries, and dawbers who outdid the most venal of their medieval predecessors in seeing religion as an avenue for financial gain.

Gradually, fanatical Calvinists like Francis Walsingham created a regime of mammon in England that was naturally philosemitic. On the theoretical level, this philosemitism found expression in the system known as capitalism. On the practical level, Walsingham collaborated with the international Jewish spy ring that complemented his domestic intelligence efforts. Together they would form a new, formidable weapon to thwart the Counterreformation on the continent.

Cecil's anti-Catholic legislation made apparent the error of Charles and Philip's policy toward the magnates. Elizabeth was a tool of Cecil, who, along with the other magnates, was determined to hold on to the loot stolen from the Church. If Mary had immediately returned the monastery lands to their rightful owners, and if she had an heir, things might have turned out differently. But Cecil and his gang of looters, emboldened by the inactivity of Charles and Philip, pressed their advantage as the powers behind the throne. By his opportunism, Philip had allowed the emergence of a regime "which would become the rallying point of the new Protestant world ... and plague him to the day of his death."[76]

Cautiously at first, the Protestant exiles returned to offer their services to Cecil. Francis Walsingham returned from exile in Switzerland and became Cecil's spymaster. In 1559, John Knox returned to Scotland and, collaborating with Cecil, turned Scotland into an English fief by buying off the nobility by bribing them with stolen Church lands. Once the lairds were assured they could appropriate the revenues accruing from monasteries and bishoprics, they "turned a movement into a revolution by solemnly proclaiming themselves Lords of the Congregation and protectors of the Protestant Kirk."[77] As a result, the Catholic Faith was banished from Scotland, attending Mass became a capital crime, and Mary, Queen of Scots, great grand-daughter of Henry VIII and next in line to the English throne, became a prisoner in her own country. In 1559 it looked as if all Europe might follow Germany's example and become Protestant. Scandinavia and Switzerland had thrown off the Catholic yoke. England had done the same. There was no reason to believe the rest of Europe would not follow. Emboldened, Cecil became less fearful of antagonizing Philip. When the King of Spain complained about English pirates preying on his Flemish subjects, Cecil refused to make restitution, thus encouraging the pirates. With Philip outwitted, the time seemed ripe for a bold initiative.

So Cecil inaugurated England's new foreign policy by proposing Elizabeth as the head of the anti-Catholic crusade. Referring to Cecil, O'Connell says, "Many of [Elizabeth's] closest advisers would have had her mount a Protestant crusade ... but the queen took a decided worldly view of the dangerous world she lived in.... The advantage to be pressed was English not Protestant."[78] With the Act of Supremacy, however, there was no difference between being English and Protestant. Elizabeth and Cecil had alienated the Church of England from Rome and intended to put the country in the service of the Protestant cause. To be a good Englishman, one had to be a Protestant. Anyone else was a second-class citizen and, if Catholic, a traitor fit to be hanged. Foreign policy would serve the Protestant cause, which would be bound up with an English nationalism unknown in the middle ages. Together, they would form the nucleus of British Imperialism for centuries. Shortly after coming to the throne, Elizabeth

> sent emissaries to the kings of Denmark and Sweden, the princes of Germany and the rulers of Switzerland "and all States alienated from the Catholic Church," proposing a league "not only for the defense of their religion but for its propagation and to so much for the security of their own affairs as to cause trouble and detriment to the Crown of France." To dispose men's minds to this effect she sent four English preachers, four Germans and one Frenchman, from England to Germany, who, feigning to be moved by religious zeal and ardor, went to visit many cities and princes, sometimes themselves preaching what they thought might most facilitate their object, and sometimes making the local preachers perform the office.[79]

According to the cardinal of Lorraine writing to the Venetian ambassador to France, the plot originated in Geneva. On July 13, the day of Henry II's death, Throckmorton wrote Cecil claiming the moment had come to move against France and take back Calais, even though France and Spain were at peace. Cecil felt the new order in England was a model for Europe; the time was right to press the advantage of the "invisible kingdom of opposition,"[80] a "link of mysterious cooperation between enemies of the Catholic Church, who raised such formidable obstacles, all over the world to King Philip II."

V

Shortly after Elizabeth's coronation in 1559, John Dee "performed a disappearing act."[81] Little is known about his activity during the next five years except that he went abroad, and while abroad, learned to read Hebrew. Woolley claims he "taught himself Hebrew"[82] to become involved in a new field of research, the Cabala, from which he would learn the secrets of the universe. But Dee probably did not teach himself Hebrew. If he possessed such formidable linguistic ability, he could have stayed home. He went abroad to learn Hebrew and begin his study of the Cabala. Like Reuchlin before him, he learned Hebrew at the feet of the rabbis. Learning Hebrew any other way is unlikely. No one studied Hebrew at the university, because no one taught it there. Dee could not learn Hebrew at the feet of rabbis in England, but as he probably learned in the Netherlands in the 1540s, he could do it there among the Jews newly emigrated from Spain and Portugal. He probably wanted to learn Hebrew because he wanted to learn Cabala so he could practice magic. "The chief practitioners of magic and astrology were Jews,"[83] and the people most likely to pay Dee for his occult knowledge were militant Protestants like "William Cecil and Lady Elizabeth" and "lukewarm and questionable Catholics [such] as Catherine de Medici and her weakling sons, all of them infected with heresy."[84]

The link between supply and demand is significant because we have to assume that Dee went not on his own to the continent but as an agent of the Cecil regime. Dee became an agent of the Cecil/Elizabeth faction at the time of Queen Mary, and the evidence indicates he remained one for the rest of his life. He was certainly an agent when he went to Prague in 1583. This is not to say he was well-remunerated. None of Walsingham's "intelligencers" was. They were paid according to performance, after the fact, and according the government's need; Walsingham was particularly stingy, keeping agents dependent on him rather than *vice versa*.

Dee was most probably sent abroad to learn Cabala because both Dee and Cecil considered Cabala the cutting edge of the new science and the new intelligence technology. Unlike Scholasticism, especially the English nominalist variety that had soured Luther, neither Cabala nor the occult science based on it wasted time learning about essences for the sake of truth. As Reuchlin had said over half a Century earlier, Cabala delivered tangible results like gold and power.

If Dee, as Yates maintained, truly was the characteristic philosopher of his age, the characteristic philosophy of that age was the *occulta philosophia* that Dee received directly from Reuchlin's student, Cornelius Agrippa. Through Cabala, Dee made a clear break with the Middle Ages. Because he had the support of the government, he was able to redefine England in a fashion that was both revolutionary and enduring. In the 1590s, Shakespeare would deal with the changes Dee had wrought, viewing them in both a positive and a negative light. According to the negative view, the occult philosopher was saturnine, which was also characteristic of the Jews; he was melancholy because of the deep insights the occult philosophy gave him. Hamlet was a dramatic representation of the occult philosopher. Durer's famous etching of Melancholy was a pictorial representation of the same thing. The positive view of the new man—the Renaissance man as the English Magus—shows up in the Midsummer Night's Dream and the Tempest, both of which are suffused with magic. Prospero was, according to Yates, modeled on Dee. His island kingdom was the new occult Protestant England, based on James Strachey's description of Bermuda, an island known on comporary maps as the "*insula daemonum*."

The Renaissance Man was a Magus, and Cabala made him one. An unfortunate result of the expulsion of the Jews from Spain was the introduction of Cabala into Christian circles. Reuchlin wrote his first book on Cabala in 1492, the year the Jews were expelled. It is obvious, however, that Jews had been in Italy for quite some time, but all of the Jews, whether recently expelled or not, had to come to grips intellectually with the expulsion, and the Lurianic Cabala was one way the Jews dealt with this calamity. Under the influence of the Cabala, Jewish thought became more apocalyptic, more millennialist, and the ferment in Jewish circles soon had an effect on Christians. Jews expelled from Spain brought the Cabala directly to England, initiating, Yates says, "the gradual integration of Jewish influences into European culture."[85] Yates tries to make sense of the anomalies in Dee's thought—Dee was a brilliant mathematician and geographer, but he was also a "conjurer" of angels who believed he was "an ardent reformed Christian"—by calling Dee a "Christian Cabalist" who supported "the 'more powerful' philosophy implicit in Neoplatonism as understood by Pico, Reuchlin, Giorgi, Agrippa and as developed in the Renaissance occult tradition."[86]

Before long it becomes clear that "Christian Cabalist" is a synonym, if not a euphemism, for Judaizer, and before long it becomes equally clear that is was through Dee's redefinition of science the Talmud made its first serious entry into English culture. Cabala, not Tyndale's translation of the bible, marked the beginning of England as the philosemitic nation. Cabala was the lens through which Dee saw all of the trends the new government was interested in, from usury to "intelligence," thus redefining what the now Protestant country would promote. What it would suppress was already clear: the Mass was gone and with it any connection between the Englishman and Catholic Rome. In its stead, Dee promoted imperialism, magic, usury, and the occult science as state of the art intelligence technology. "Dee is certainly following Agrippa's outline in the *De occulta philosophia* and that was a work founded on Renaissance Magic and Cabala. Also he hints in the Preface at higher secrets which he is not here revealing, probably the secrets of the angel-magic."[87] Dee's Christian Cabala would link the messianic politics of the Hussites and Anabaptists with the cabalistic arcana of Renaissance magic, and out of that marriage England would emerge as the messianic Protestant nation. Its main literary propagandist in the Elizabethan age would be Edmund Spenser. Following his lead, John Milton would become the literary propagandist for the Puritan age. The common denominator shared by messianic politics and renaissance magic was Talmudic Judaism, which sank its tenacious tendrils into English soil.

Yates' use of the term "Christian Cabala" is intended to cover a multitude of sins. On the one hand, Christian Cabala is the "'more powerful' philosophy that was to supersede scholasticism, as potentially a world-wide movement of reform, to be applied not only in Elizabethan England"[88] but throughout Europe. In this sense, "Christian Cabala" is a euphemism for judaizing Protestantism. On the other hand, Christian Cabala also means involvement in "good" or "white" magic. Dee insisted, and Yates accepts the claim, that he was only speaking with "good" angels during his conjurings. "A pious Christian Cabalist," Yates writes, "is safe in the knowledge that he is conjuring angels, not demons. This conviction was at the centre of Dee's belief in his angelic guidance, and it explains his pained surprise when alarmed and angry contemporaries persisted in branding him as a wicked conjurer of devils."[89] Dee could make that claim only because Catholicism had been banned from England by the time he began his conjurings. The Catholic position was clear: if a man attempts to summon angels, only fallen angels will respond, and then only if he puts his soul in jeopardy. Christopher Marlowe stated the orthodox position in *Dr. Faustus*, his attack on Dee's cultural hegemony over the new "England" Dee had created. The nuncios took the same position in Prague, when Dee showed up there.

Yates also claims "The sensational angel-summoning side of Dee's activities was intimately related to his real success as a mathematician."[90] This too is false. If Dee was successful as a mathematician, it was despite his involvement in Cabala, for Gematria is to mathematics what astrology is to the study of the universe, which is to say, a false start down a blind alley. Only when Mersenne cleared the intellectual rubbish the Reuchlin-Agrippa-Dee tradition had spread could science and mathematics emerge from the mumbo-jumbo Elizabeth and Cecil promoted as the antidote to Catholicism and Scholasticism. Dee undoubtedly produced wonders for the government agencies who wanted to use his magic "to drive the Prince of Parma from our land,"[91] as Marlowe put it later, but they led nowhere. It was not only Dee (or Giordano Bruno) whom Marlowe had in mind when he has Dr. Faustus say, "Tis Magick, Magick that hath ravish'd me."[92] It was his country as well.

The change in thought in England that Dee promised through Cabala was not unlike what Karl Marx promised 300 years later. Before men used philosophy to describe the world, but now Dee, as master of Cabala, would change the world through magic. The principle was simple: Hebrew was the language spoken by God himself. It was by the divine word that the world came into being and continued to function. So any man who knew those words could bend the universe to serve his will, just as God could. One technique was known as Gematria, which involved learning the numerical significance of Hebrew words, each letter of which had a numerical value. Cabala was related to the Pythagorean idea that reality was ultimately number. But another feature of Cabala was its preoccupation with angels. Copernicus' *De Revolutionibus* appeared in 1643, but Dee was still living in a universe in which things were in motion because an intelligent spirit was moving them. The spirits that moved the stars and planets were known as angels. One preoccupation of Cabala was learning the names of angels, as well as figuring out just how many there were (301,655,172, according to one set of calculations). If a man, through magic, could learn their names, he could, like God, command them to do his bidding. According to contemporary thought—thought which Dee accepted completely—the heavenly bodies determined the existence of minerals in the earth. The fact that Mercury was both a planet and an element was just one indication of this correspondence. The moon was silver. The sun corresponded naturally to gold, and so gold was normally found in the tropics, where the sun was strongest. By learning the names of the angels who moved planets like the sun, Dee would become the master of the elements, able to change lead into gold, as well as the master of intelligence, able to send messages (aggelos meant messenger) back and forth without cipher. Dee would actually come up with a way of using angels as a form of communication. In an age when the King of Spain, England's archenemy, owned the gold mines of the new world, all of this had political and military implications, which is most certainly why Dee went to the continent to learn Talmudic technology and most probably why he went there as Cecil's agent.

There is an obvious connection between magic and prayer: the former is a parody of the latter with supplication replaced by command. When Woolley writes, "incantations would work whether you were a Catholic or Protestant,"[93] he either misses the point of what magic is about or he is tacitly placing Protestants outside the Christian orbit. The point of magic is to do away with man's precarious position as a supplicant and place him in a god-like position of command. Man cannot order angels around, any more than fish can command men, because angels are superior beings. The adept, believed the man who learned Cabala, became superior to angels and ceased to be a mere man. Therein lay the temptation and the danger of magic: seeking superiority to the angels, the magician sank below the beasts because he abandoned what was distinctly human, namely reason, which alone could discern the true order of being.

Although most scholars trace Freemasonry's beginnings to the 17th Century, Walsh claims "something very like the odor of Freemasonry ... hung about the court of Elizabeth."[94] He traces that odor to Sir Thomas Sackville, modestly famous as the author of one of the first English plays, *Gorbaduc*, first performed 1561. Sackville, according to Walsh, was the Grand Master of the Grand Lodge at York. Suspicious of any secret society in her realm, especially one that withheld secrets from the world's most formidable police state, Elizabeth sent an armed force to break up its meeting and apprehend its members. Sackville, one step ahead of Elizabeth, placed Masons in the troop sent to break up the meeting. Either Elizabeth was taken in by their ruse, or they admitted her to membership in the lodge and shared with her their secrets and arcana. A pattern emerged: the leading Protestants were the leading Masons. When the Grand Lodge was divided into two groups upon Sackville's resignation in 1567, Francis Russell, Second Earl of Bedford, became head of the northern Lodge, and the Queen's financier, Sir Thomas Gresham, became Grand Master in the South. The Magnates in England all began as Protestants and ended up as Masons when the revolutionary spirit leapt like a spark from the Protestants to the Masons at the time of the Restoration.

Many have noted the connection between Freemasonry and Talmudic Judaism. The Talmud, with its "scurrilous and vindictive blasphemies against Christ" was "the chief means employed by the Annas and Caiaphas of each age to keep the mass of the Jewish people in ignorance of the true nature of Christianity, and to fan their misunderstanding of it to hatred."[95] The moment Christianity lost the will to contest the Talmud, that doctrine began to occupy the intellectual territory so badly defended by Scholasticism and the Humanists. Once Christians lost the will to contest it, judaizing was a natural consequence; the rise of the Talmud in Christian culture was a function of that loss of will. The inordinate craving for the magic which Cabala dangled before the eyes of credulous Christians became the chief impediment to contesting the Talmud. Why should these books be burned if they contained important information? Cabala was the Jewish version of the Albigenisian importation of Gnostic thought onto European soil. The Talmud and

Cabala became the crucial link between the heresies defeated by the first Inquisition in the Middle Ages and Freemasonry, which took up the revolutionary banner after Europe tired of sectarian strife in the wake of the 30 Years War.

The continental tradition differs from the English. A diffuse Gnosticism had, after some time, found a home amongst the Knights Templar. When the King of France suppressed the Knights Templar and brought about the death of Jacques (James) De Molay, it looked as though a tradition had ended. And in the ordinary sense it had. But, as Peter Parker in *The Murdered Magicians* notes, the tradition was to be fancifully resurrected. He points out that: "The transformation of ideas about the Templars during the eighteenth century shows how far from stern scientific rationalism the men of the Enlightenment could wander. In the very body of Church history which was the prime target for rationalisation and demystification, eighteenth-century men found the Templars, and turned them into a wild fantasy...". And there were no greater promoters of this "wild fantasy" than the Freemasons. The history of gnosticism, Cabala, Talmud, the Protestant revolt and the Masonic lodges were self-consciously (if not historically) intertwined by eighteenth-century men opposed to the Church. Freemasonry was always a messianic political movement, an explicit alternative to Catholicism bound up with the rituals of Judaism and Jewish symbolism. The adept must travel toward the east toward Jerusalem to find Enlightenment; he is going to rebuild the Temple and he is going to find a lost world. Sir Francis Bacon felt America was the New Atlantis; the English colonization of that continent was largely the work of John Dee, who felt Baffin Island contained, if not the ten lost tribes of Israel, as Menasseh ben Israel would claim about South America, then a people with Latin books who brewed beer. The earliest Jewish settlers in the new world brought Freemasonry with them. When 15 Jewish families arrived in Newport, Rhode Island from Holland, they brought with them the continent's first Masonic lodge. "Descendants of certain of these Jews," Walsh writes,

> originally from Spain and Portugal, went into the whaling industry, and founded some of the First New England families. A little later, according to a Masonic authority, "American Masonry was introduced into China by the captains of the clipper ships, who came out from new England to trade with the Chinese." ... The official coat of arms of the English Grand Lodge, even to this day, is the one made in 1675 by Rabbi Jacob Jehuda Leon, known as Templo, who went from Holland to England that year. "This coat is entirely composed of Jewish symbols," explains Dr. Lucien Wolf. "It is obviously an attempt to display heraldically the various forms of the Cherubim pictured to us in the second vision of Ezekiel— an Ox, a Man, a Lion, and an Eagle—and thus belongs to the highest and most mystical domain of Hebrew symbolism.... If one looks more carefully, it becomes apparent that they have the hindquarters of goats, with hairy haunches and legs and cloven hoofs that tread upon the motto holiness to the Lord.... The trail of Masonry always leads to, and crosses, that of the wandering Jew, whether he actually founded it or not.[96]

William of Orange was not a Freemason; he was a Calvinist, and Calvinism was the revolutionary movement in Holland in mid-16th Century. But his great grandson William III was a Freemason and a Protestant; because of that, he was brought from Holland to rule over England at the time of the Glorious Revolution. The Jews played an important role in keeping England in the hands of the Protestants. In collaboration with Protestants who brought William from Holland, Isaac Auaso, a Jewish banker from Amsterdam, contributed two million guilden to the effort that kept James II, the legitimate Catholic heir, from returning to the English throne. Occult Protestantism became formalized as Freemasonry during the 17th Century. "It is quite certain," Rabbi Benamozegh wrote, "Masonic theology is at root nothing else than Theosophy, and that it corresponds to the theology of the Kaballah."[97] What Walsh calls "nascent Freemasonry" is really Dee's "Christian" Cabalism.

VI

Within months of Dee's disappearance in September 1559, a newly ordained Catholic priest, Thomas Stapleton, set sail for the Spanish Netherlands. Like Dee, his goal was the university at Louvain. Dee traveled to the low countries to learn Cabala from the rabbis. But Stapleton left because England was no longer hospitable to men who took the Catholic faith seriously.

Stapleton would become "the most learned Roman Catholic of all his time."[98] Although his works have been little read since his death, they were read aloud when the pope sat down to his meals in the Vatican. Born at Henfield, Sussex in July 1535, days after the execution of St. Thomas More, Stapleton was probably named after More. Stapleton watched Nicholas Ridley and Hugh Latimer burned at the stake for heresy. Since he felt the punishment fit the crime, he probably correctly assumed his prospects as a Catholic priest were not good under the new regime.

So he left England. He probably left illegally, with all the risks that entailed, so firm was his decision. "Fearing the contagion of schism in my tender years," he wrote, "I came a fugitive to the learned benches of Louvain."[99] Just as the Spanish Netherlands were a magnet for Calvinist revolutionaries, so too it attracted many English Catholics because of its proximity to England, and because it was ruled by the Philip II, the Catholic King of Spain who had been the English sovereign as well. Shortly before his death, Stapleton described himself as "a true and trusty servant to his Majesty of Spain,"[100] who alone, it seemed to him, stood between Christianity and the abyss. "Louvain," Knox tells us, held a special attraction for the learned Catholics in England,

> because of the convenience which it afforded for writing against the heretics. Nor was it long before they set themselves to work. Treatise followed treatise in defense of the catholic faith and confutation of Protestant errors. They wrote

by preference in English for their object was to address not the learned but the multitudes. The books were printed in Flanders and then smuggled over in large quantities to England: an operation which was not difficult, on account of the continual communication existing between the two countries. As might have been expected, their labors soon bore fruit in confirming waverers and reclaiming many who had fallen away.[101]

In 1561, Stapleton was joined by fellow Oxonian William Allen. If Stapleton was the mind of the exiled recusants, providing intellectual ammunition to explode Protestant positions, then Allen was their will, deploying those weapons as a general and administrator. Allen was, like Stapleton, a priest, but unlike Stapleton, Allen would become a cardinal and the leader of the exiles in the low countries. Allen crossed to Flanders in 1561, and when he arrived at Louvain he found many of his countrymen had preceded him. Allen returned to England a year later and for the next three years he traveled from one beleaguered Catholic community to another "urging upon them the duty of abstaining from all communication with heretics in the Protestant worship by law established."[102] Because Cecil and Elizabeth had avoided the excesses of their continental allies, the Anglican and the Catholic services were confusingly similar. Many English Catholics were confused; even worse, they used the similarities to rationalize what Allen felt were unconscionable compromises. "Many priests," Knox tells us,

> said mass secretly and celebrated the heretical offices and supper in public, thus becoming partakers often on the same day (O horrible impiety!) of the chalice of the Lord and the chalice of devils. And this arose from the false persuasion that it was enough to hold the faith interiorly while obeying the Sovereign in externals.[103]

Allen would have nothing to do with compromises. As a result of his single-mindedness and his preaching, "it was brought about in a very short time that a vast number of our countrymen not only came to hold right views about religion, but abstained altogether from the communion, churches, sermons, books, and all spiritual communication with heretics."[104] Allen's labors bore most fruit in the northern counties, which were still largely Catholic, especially "in the county of Norfolk, in the family of the Duke of Norfolk, who, though himself a Protestant, gave protection to several learned Catholics."[105] His zeal drew the attention of Cecil and Walsingham, and so in 1565, Allen was forced to return to the Low Countries.

The political situation had deteriorated there in his absence. In August 1559, Philip II sailed from Flushing to Spain, appointing as governess in his absence his half sister Margaret, the Duchess of Parma. The great lords of the Netherlands were offended by the slight and withdrew from the government, aiding rising Dutch nationalism and resentment against Spain that the Calvinists, although they too were agents of a foreign power, successfully exploited. William of Orange eventually headed this treacherous faction. A religious opportunist who was by turns Lutheran (the religion of his birth), Catholic, Lutheran again, and finally a Calvinist, William would connive with the Jews and lead armies of foreign mercenaries on repeated fruitless attempts to drive the Spaniards from the low countries.

In January 1561 Philip withdrew Spanish troops from Dutch soil. If they had been the source of the problem, the problem would have ended. Instead, Philip's gesture, compelled by lack of money, accelerated the revolution by showing what his enemies considered weakness. In September 1562, English troops occupied Calais, and Elizabeth then used the French port closest to England as a staging area to support the Huguenots, who had embarked upon a campaign of savage iconoclasm in France. The Protestant rabble took a lesson from their Hussite forbears by their wanton destruction of the sacred and their desecration of the dead. Sacred hosts and the bones of the dead were scattered in the mud in front of desecrated churches and trampled under foot by men and horses. To this organized thuggery and desecration, Elizabeth contributed 6,000 men and 100,000 crowns; the emboldened Huguenots pillaged their way across Normandy to link up with the English forces. On February 18, 1563, Duke Francis of Guise, upon whom English Catholics placed their hopes, was shot; after a week, he died. Under torture, his assailant admitted he acted as an agent of Beza, Calvin's lieutenant, then laboring to convert the king of France, and Admiral Coligny, another Calvinist sympathizer. This was no local uprising based on legitimate complaint, but an international conspiracy involving the highest levels of religion and government attempting to overthrow the Catholic hegemony of Spain and put in its place the revolutionary police state of Geneva. Convinced by his three years in England that no half measures would suffice, Allen went on pilgrimage to Rome to interest the pope in a permanent institutional commitment to bring England back to the Catholic fold.

Called back to England by his father in the same year that Allen returned, Stapleton also was immediately caught in the trammels of the nascent Elizabethan police state when he was subpoenaed to appear before an Episcopal tribunal. "I was scarcely home," Stapleton wrote to his father, "when I was called before the mock tribunal of the heretic jester to whom fair Chichester had become subject."[106] Protracted negotiations followed, after which Stapleton professed his willingness to swear to the part of the Oath of Supremacy that testified to the Queen's rights as supreme governor in temporal matters.

By early 1563, Stapleton could see the situation in England was hopeless. The clouds of heresy were not going to blow away on their own. So Stapleton returned to Louvain with his family, never to set foot on English soil again. Instead, he settled in the low countries and set his pen to work to drive the illicit Elizabethan regime from England. "At this time," he wrote, "I began to write my first books against the heretics, but in the vernacular tongue only."[107] If the English Catholics had been left to wage their war of words in peace, they might have driven Elizabeth from the throne. The Spanish Netherlands became the headquarters of the recusant Catholic publishing industry, and during the 1560s, those printing presses caused Elizabeth increasing concern. The leaders of the ill-fated Northern Rising, were inspired to rebel by the recusant tracts from Louvain. An intellectual foe this formidable did not go unnoticed by Elizabeth's intelligencers, who would not respond with intellectual weapons. The recusant print apostolate was going to be crushed by subversion or by force of arms.

VII

In February 1563, John Dee resurfaced in Antwerp. Dee took up residence at the sign of the Golden Angel. Apparently Dee was drawn to Antwerp because of its publishing industry. The "escalating clatter of printing presses"[108] included the "Officina Plantiniana," one of the world's most important publishing firms, founded by Christopher Plantin. Plantin was famous as a publisher of heretical books, including those of Hendrick Nichlaes, founder of a secret society known as the Family of Love. The familists invited "all lovers of truth ... of what nation and religion soever, they be—Christians, Jews, Mahomites or Turks and heathen"[109] to join an organization a lot like the symposia Reuchlin described in his books or what was to become the Freemasons. Dee was most probably a fellow traveler. Dee was a bibliophile who haunted bookstores in England and on the continent, striking up conversations with other customers as a way to find rare books or gather intelligence.

Dee was especially interested in finding an extremely rare unfinished book by Johannes Trithemius known as the *Steganographia*. Trithemius' interest in Cabala drew the charge he was a magus, "trafficking in demons."[110] "I hoped," Carolus Bovillus wrote after meeting Trithemius, "that I would enjoy a pleasing visit with a philosopher, but I discovered him to be a magician."[111] Trithemius' work was unfinished at his death in 1516, but its fame spread nevertheless. Dee was more intrigued by Trithemius' reputation as a magician than repelled by it. Imagine then Dee's excitement when he heard a copy was available for inspection, if not purchase, in Antwerp.

The *Steganographia* brought together two of Dee's interests: angels and what later came to be known as encryption technology. In *Steganographia*, Trithemius proposed using angels as God did, as messengers. Trithemius's encryption system was simple. Volumes I and II of the Steganographia gave long lists of angel names, along with details on the powers of each, followed by conjurations to call them into service. Once an angel—Padiel, for example—appeared, Trithemius would hand over the message; Padiel would take it to the recipient, who would then mutter another incantation, whereupon the original message would be revealed. It was the occult version of the Western Union telegram, except the messengers were angels, and the master of this encryption technology was, if successful, indistinguishable from God. Woolley claims the *Steganographia* is "primarily a work of cryptography, not magic."[112] But neither Dee nor Trithemius distinguishes between the two disciplines. Books I and II "were full of ciphers, for which Europe's political tensions had produced a growing demand."[113] But if angels could spare the spy operations the trouble of encryption, so much the better. In the 16th Century, information traveled at the speed of a horse—unless, of course, angels carried it.

Impressed with its military and intelligence potential, Dee wrote to Cecil in February 1563 describing "the most precious jewel that I have yet of other men's travails recovered," and also "begging for some recompense to his costs which had left him virtually penniless."[114] All courts of significance on the continent had their magi and intelligence officers, but England, a small and insignificant power, lacked this edge. Dee volunteered as an "intelligencer" for Elizabeth to unlock the door to the vast wealth Cabala could provide, if only Cecil would provide a modest income that would allow him to criss-cross the continent purchasing books and making contact with other magicians. Cecil needed someone like him if England wanted to compete with the more advanced continental courts. At least this is how Dee felt.

There is no record of an answer from Cecil. One can imagine Dee waiting, excited someone might pay him to collect books on arcane topics, like the mysterious "Book of Soyga," reportedly written in the Adamic language in which God conversed with Adam. Dee, though, was plagued by financial need and other misgivings, some of which he expressed in his diary. At 36, Dee was no longer young, especially given life expectancy in the Elizabethan age. He describes a dilemma typical of men, who "having hesitated for some time at the Crossroads of their wavering judgment, they at last come to decision: some (who have fallen in love with truth and virtue) will for the rest of their lives devote their entire energy to the pursuit of philosophy, which others (ensnared by the enticements of this world or burning with a desire for riches) cannot but devote all their energies to life of pleasure and profit."[115] Woolley thinks "it is clear in which direction Dee imagined he would go,"[116] but Dee's letter to Cecil casts doubt on that clarity. Did Dee think asking for money as a spy and cryptographer was compatible with the vocation of a man "who [had] fallen in love with truth and virtue"? If Dee was willing to work for Cecil and Walsingham he was more likely to be "ensnared by the enticements of this world ... burning with a desire for riches." Isn't that what magic promised? Dee's diary entry indicates he had gone over to the dark side while still in Antwerp.

In 1563 Philip received troubling reports. Antwerp, the richest city in his empire, was a particular concern. Thirty years after its extermination in Muenster, Anabaptism was making a comeback in the Spanish Netherlands. According to reports from the Inquisition, two Anabaptists were burned at the stake at Alost, three at Louvain, and two at Antwerp. In Brugge, two Anabaptists told the inquisitors the headquarters of the Anabaptist conspiracy was in Antwerp. They also confessed they each had four wives, who called their husbands "Lord," and when the one of the elect tired of a wife, an Anabaptist minister would put her to death quietly in the forest. Following the example of their sainted founder Bokel-zoon the Tailor, the minister had killed six or seven (it was hard to keep track) of his wives. Unsurprisingly, the Anabaptists also taught it was no crime to plunder Catholics, or even to kill them.

More troubling were the reports about the Jews. In 1563, Philip learned there were now "an infinite number of Jews"[117] in Antwerp who circumcised themselves, assembled in synagogues, and publicly defied the Inquisition. Jews and heretics did what they pleased there. Many who paraded around Antwerp as Jews were Marranos from Spain, which meant they were lapsed Catholics who should have been punished by the Inquisition, whose office in Madrid shared information on them with the king. In early 1563 Philip sent Margaret a list of suspects who should be closely watched.

In less than a generation, the Jews had transformed Antwerp into the center of world trade and finance. It was like Genesis in reverse. The Jews had been ex-pelled into "a new earthly paradise" of their own making based on the lucrative trade between the Atlantic and the Mediterranean. The Jewish Spice Trust was a combination of the IRS and the CIA: the Jews collected a toll on goods sold all over Europe while engaging in extensive espionage. The Jewish spy ring stretched from London to Constantinople, and it became a "weapon of the greatest political as well as economic importance."

Spice ships from Portugal, and others laden with immigrants for the Nether-lands would first land at an English port, where Jewish messengers from London with the latest news from the continent would meet them and tell them wheth-er the coast was clear. If not, they would disembark, usually at Hampton (now Southampton), proceed to London and wait for a favorable chance to continue their journey to Antwerp. The chief link in the chain of espionage at London was a Marrano merchant named Christopher Fernandes. A money-changer named Antonio de Loriingue conducted a brisk trade selling bills on Antwerp to the voy-agers, for they were not allowed to carry Portuguese money out of England.[118]

One converso who became rich in the Spanish Netherlands was Joao Miques, later known as Joseph Nasi (to signify he was prince of the Jews), the Duke of Naxos, knighted for his service to the Turks. Miques married into the wealthy Mendes family, also Portuguese conversos, who were owed the stupendous sum of 160,000 ducats by the king of France. After growing wealthy through the spice trust and usury, Miques rose to fame as spy minister to the sublime Porte in Con-stantinople, and after ruining Sulieman the Sot by "leading the prince into all kinds of orgies and excesses,"[119] he terrorized Christian princes as the Sultan's chief negotiator. He orchestrated factions waging war on Philip in Spain. Because of his contacts, Miques, says Graetz, relieved the sultan "of the necessity of employ-ing spies,"[120] because the Marranos in Antwerp constituted a large spy ring that would "cause anxious hours to many a Christian ruler and diplomatist."[121] When the French royal family refused to repay him, Mendes sent Barbary pirates to seize

French ships and confiscate their cargoes, which Mendes sold. Mendes launched the Turkish fleet defeated by Don Juan of Austria at Lepanto, and Mendes urged William of Orange to revolt in Antwerp. Under the direction of Mendes, "All the powers of international Jewry were allied with, if not actually the motive power of, the vast conspiracy which produced the Protestant revolt."[122] If it weren't for Mendes and Jewish support, the Calvinists would have become the Dutch version of the Hussites. With Jewish support, in 1566 they became the manifestation of world revolution.

VIII

Dee returned to England in June 1564, accompanying a marchioness dying of breast cancer who promised to introduce Dee to the queen. Dee had just completed his magnum opus of occult studies, the *Monas Hieroglyphica*. He had written his distillation of the Cabala, as transmitted by Reuchlin, Agrippa, Trithemius and others, in 12 days, as if transcribing dictation. The Monas (or monad) "contained in the compressed form of a magic sign the whole of the occult philosophy."[123] He dedicated the book to Maximillian II, the Holy Roman Emperor and father of Rudolf II, who would relocate the court to Prague. The occult philosophy was no grassroots movement; it was to be implemented by princes, even if Dee didn't know which one.

When Maximillian showed no interest in Dee's "cosmopolitical theories," Dee focused his attention on the 31-year-old queen of England. Dee referred to himself as a "Cosmopolites," or a "Citizen and Member of the whole and only one Mystical City Universal,"[124] and it was on the young queen that Dee now placed on his hope for the fulfillment of his vision. She would use the Monas as her occult imperial sign and institute occult imperial reform as leader of the Protestant nations of Europe. England was to become the new Protestant world empire to replace the Holy Roman Empire of the Catholics.

In summer 1564, Dee and the queen sat together and pored over his baffling but intriguing book. The queen seemed drawn to it, even if she had difficulty understanding it; she also indicated she might put some of its ideas into effect. She may have even considered herself a magus (or maga). She felt she could cure scrofula with her "royal touch," and that the royal power that emanated from her was "magical." She also felt committed to a magical destiny beyond her power to revoke. When a comet appeared in the heavens, Elizabeth was warned not to look because of the "disasters" it might cause. Elizabeth looked anyway, telling her courtiers, "*Iacta alia est*,"[125] the die is already cast, indicating that she was intent to follow her "disastrous" career to its conclusion. Dee encouraged her, believing disaster would fall on the Catholics, not Elizabeth, who would triumph over their ruin. She would rise as the paradigm of the new world order over the ruins of the old church and the old political order whose destruction would fulfill her destiny. Dee would string her along for years. Four years after Dee introduced her to the Monas, Dee told her he was going to reveal "the great secret for my sake to be disclosed unto her Majesty by Nicolaus Grudius Nicolai, sometime one of the Secretaries to the Emperor Charles V."[126] He never disclosed the secret, but since it involved Grudius, the Belgian poet, it probably involved alchemy to increase gold bullion by transforming base metals, a topic dear to monarchs' hearts.

Ultimately, Elizabeth and Cecil's stinginess overcame Dee's imaginative vision. So Dee, with no prospects at court, moved into his mother's home at Mortlake, an obscure village on the Thames, where he compiled one of the most impressive libraries in Europe. Many of the books were written by Spanish Jews, like Johannes de Burgo's *Treatise on Magic*, which was written in Spanish but in Hebrew letters. Most of them had to do with magic, including *Liber Experimentorum* by Raymond Llull, another Spaniard. Like Freemasonry, which was made up of exoteric and esoteric doctrines, Dee's library had two levels. Behind the exoteric library, there was an esoteric library, a hidden room Dee called his "Interna Bibliotheca." It housed retorts in which he distilled potions from eggshells and horse dung, the same stills whose vapors would eventually poison him with fumes from toxic metals. The Interna Bibliotheca contained the magical mirror Sir William Pickering had given him, which would so amuse and impress the queen when she visited, and on the same table lay a copy of Cornelius Agrippa's *De Occulta Philosophia*, "which he kept open on the study desk for easy reference."[127]

IX

Three years after the Council of Trent concluded, Pius V became pope and implemented the council's decrees with a vigor the papacy had not shown for centuries. "The poor had alms given them in abundance, prostitutes were banished from Rome, Jews began hiding copies of the Talmud and of Protestant tracts, usurers trembled, easy-going prelates and priests began to reform their lives. Yes, something had happened at Rome. The candidate of St. Charles Borromeo and of King Philip II was proving to be all they had expected of him, and both rejoiced."[128] Pius V launched a three-pronged attack on the abuses that made the Catholic world vulnerable: he imposed order on the clergy, which meant increasing the level of education in seminaries, ended concubinage, and forced bishops to reside in their dioceses. He used the revitalized clergy, especially the newly created Jesuits, to convert heretics, and if the Jesuits failed to bring about their conversion, he turned to the civil arm to destroy them. And finally, he persuaded the Christian kings to unite in a Holy Crusade against the Infidel Turks. It was an ambitious program, but Pius V succeeded, and successors like Gregory XIII, an exceptional administrator, built on and complemented his efforts. Six successive extraordinary papacies contributed to the most significant *volte face* in the history of the Church, and it happened not a moment too soon. Sensing the change that came over Rome, the forces of revolution and disorder made their move too.

On the afternoon of August 19, 1566 Thomas Stapleton arrived in Antwerp, unaware he would soon have a front row seat for the revolution. Between five and six o'clock in the evening, Stapleton noticed a gang of Calvinist thugs milling around in front of the main church in Antwerp conducting a bit of revolutionary theater mocking the Assumption of the Blessed Virgin, a feast celebrated four days earlier. William of Orange had conveniently left town, and so, when the mob turned ugly, the task of restoring order fell to the town Margrave, who hastened to the church only to find the demonstrators inside, barring the door. Finding an unbarred entrance, the Margrave entered the church and demanded in the King's name that the demonstrators disperse. In spite of "Many words passing between the Margrave and them,"[129] the Calvinists refused, probably because their numbers were swelling, making hollow the Margrave's threat of force. Finally, seeing "nothing prevailing, neither by fair words or foul,"[130] the Margrave went home.

The mob then began singing Psalms, and, as if by prearrangement, an even greater mob swarmed into the Church. Since Stapleton was swept along by the human tide, he got to witness what happened inside the church first hand and to report "that which I saw with my own eyes."[131] At about six, the singing stopped, and the sacrilege began. The mob of Calvinist thugs broke images and pulled down altars, organs, and "all kind of tabernacles."[132] They stole chalices to melt for coins to pay ruthless German mercenaries, broke up the seats in the choir stalls, and robbed "the church warden's boxes, as well as for the church as for the poor."[133] When the mob finished, they moved to other Antwerp churches. At St. James Church, the mob left the furniture intact and concentrated on plundering the "diverse little scobbes and boxes of farthings for the poor."[134] Far into the night, the "the zealous brotherhood" plundered churches in Antwerp; they "so followed the chase that they left not one church in Antwerp, great or small, where they hunted up not good game and carried away flesh good store." The plunder was so extensive "To describe particularly the horrible and outrageous sacrileges of that night, an eternal document of the gospel-like zeal of this sacred brotherhood, would require a full treatise of itself."[135] Stapleton noticed the "zealous brotherhood" included "members of the same gang of desperadoes who had thrown down St. Thomas a Becket's image from London Bridge and who squatted impudently at that moment in the canons' stalls in Chichester Cathedral."[136]

The English contribution to the revolution was significant. Virtually all observers noted the destruction was carried out by a relatively small number of well prepared men, among whom a significant percentage were English criminals. Clough, Gresham's spy in Antwerp, felt the wreckers were paid vagabonds among whom he recognized English criminals. An English diplomat recognized 20 London criminals. Strada, who wondered at the magnitude of destruction achieved by so few, attributed their effectiveness to diabolic assistance.

The iconoclasts did not limit themselves to destroying images; the Calvinist believers in *Sola Scriptura* destroyed books too. "What shall I speak," Stapleton asks disconsolately, "of the very libraries spoiled and burned, namely of the Grey

Friars and the Abbey of St. Michael."[137] It wasn't just old books that were destroyed. The Iconoclast rebellion destroyed the English Catholic printing operation in the Netherlands. Stapleton never again wrote in English. "Until this violent summer of 1566," O'Connell writes, "almost all the Catholic émigré books had been printed at Antwerp."[138] A large number of controversial and devotional books, many of a remarkably high literary quality, were written by exiled Englishmen and printed on presses in Antwerp and Louvain before the Calvinist uprisings. After the riots, "the English printing operation moved *en masse* to Louvain, and two years later, when fresh and much graver troubles broke out, it ceased altogether."[139] It is difficult to assess how widely those proscribed works circulated in England or how much effect they had. One contemporary claimed 20,000 copies were smuggled into England, and a missionary, 15 years afterward, said these "books opened the way" and "did much to bring about [a] change in men's minds."[140] The Earl of Northumberland, leader of the Northern Rising admitted he read some of them. The zeal with which Elizabethan apologists answered them suggests they had some impact. And, demonstrating coordination, at the time of the riots, the Elizabethan police state stepped up surveillance of literature in England, increasing the penalties for possessing it and efforts to confiscate it. Stapleton thereafter wrote in Latin and devoted himself to answering Calvinists on the continent rather than supporting the Catholic resistance in England.

Within a year, the Calvinists murdered 4,000 priests, monks and nuns, drove 12,000 nuns from their convents, sacked 20,000 churches and destroyed 2,000 monasteries, including their libraries and collections of art. The attack on libraries shows that iconoclasm was not based on a noble Old Testament objection to graven images. It was protracted and sustained cultural warfare to destroy every aspect of Catholic culture. Just as the Mass had been banned in England, Catholic culture would be banned on the continent by the systematic destruction of every artifact associated with it. One incident gives particular insight into the intentions of the reformers: in one Antwerp church, a statue of Christ on the Cross was destroyed but the statues of the thieves on either side of Christ were left standing. The determination to desecrate the body of Christ also manifested itself in the attack on the Eucharist, which invariably was thrown into the mud outside the church and trampled underfoot by men and horses.

Philip was convinced the revolt was the work of an organized conspiracy headquartered in Antwerp. Correspondence with Margaret and others there confirmed his beliefs. In the aftermath, William of Orange's departure hours before the uprising convinced Philip that he was at the center of the conspiracy. His principal co-conspirator, according to his sister, "would be Marco Perez at Antwerp."[141] Perez was a Sephardic Jew, formerly a converso and Marrano, who now professed Calvinism. In March 1567, Gresham wrote to Cecil explaining Perez and other "Calvinists" had offered William of Orange "a great piece of money for to maintayne God's word and the promise he made to them that they should not be molested with their religion and preaching until the States had decided the matter."[142] The "Calvinists" in question were Spanish Jews who had renounced the mask of Catholicism for an equally deceptive mask of Calvinism. Once they had established their *bona fides* as "Christians," they funneled Jewish money into the Jewish controlled publishing houses which were responsible for the propaganda war against Philip, Spain, and the Catholic Church. In 1566, the propaganda war became an actual revolution. "From an early period," Dr. Lucien Wolf wrote,

> the Marranos in Antwerp had taken an active part in the Reformation movement, and had given up their mask of Catholicism for a not less hollow pretense of Calvinism. The change will be readily understood. The simulation of Calvinism brought them new friends, who, like them, were enemies of Rome, Spain and the Inquisition. It helped them in their fight against the Holy Office, and for that reason was very welcome to them. Moreover, it was a form of Christianity which came nearer to their own simple Judaism. The result was that they became zealous and valuable allies of the Calvinists.[143]

Perez also had contacts in England, through which he recruited the English thugs active in wrecking churches in Antwerp. Perez also used his influence in England to get his Jewish doctor friend, Rodrigo Lopez, appointed Queen Elizabeth's personal physician. Lopez, like Perez, was a "Calvinist," i.e., a Spanish Jew who abandoned the pretense of Catholicism after he migrated to the low countries. After his falling out with Lopez, Perez used his same connections to spread a rumor that Lopez was planning to poison the queen and got him hanged. Poisonings by Jewish physicians were common. Stephan Batory, the charismatic Transylvanian king of Poland, was poisoned by a Jewish physician; some claim the poisoning was to prevent him from launching a crusade to free the Slavs in the Balkans from the oppressive yoke of the Porte. Had Elizabeth crossed him, Perez would have been in position to work against Elizabeth through Lopez. The Lopez affair contributed significantly to the rise of English anti-Semitism in the 1590s.

The web also spread east to Constantinople. In 1566, Joseph Nasi wrote to the Protestant Council of Antwerp, whose president was Perez, promising that if they held out against Philip, the new sultan would send aid. In response, William of Orange wrote to Nasi urging him to ask the sultan to declare war on Spain to divert attention from the revolt the Dutch were planning in the Spanish Netherlands. William of Orange later rewarded Nasi by granting special concessions to Holland's Jews. The Holy Office claimed Perez "was secretly a part of the huge, invisible international conspiracy that extended from London to Constantinople."[144] Once he broke with the Church, he worked actively with Henry of Navarre, with Jewish agents in Paris and London, and with the Cecils. England, run by a clique of usurers, had become the headquarters of world revolution, just as Moscow would in the first half of the 20th Century. "The Protestants of that time," Prescott writes, "constituted a sort of federative republic, or rather a great secret association, extending through the different parts of Europe, but so closely linked together that a blow struck in one quarter instantly vibrated to every other."[145]

X

It took a year for Philip to digest the intelligence and respond to the assault. Meanwhile, the Huguenots, encouraged by the audacity of the Calvinists in the lowlands, armed themselves to attack churches in France. In the summer of 1567, the Duke of Alba, under orders from Philip, assembled an army in Milan and marched to Brussels, arriving in August. For the next five years, his army brutally suppressed the Calvinists, Jews, and Anabaptists who constituted the revolutionary movement in the Netherlands. Walsh claims the Duke "had made what he considered just enough show of force to uphold his King's authority;"[146] once the rebels were frightened into submission, he planned to grant a general pardon. Others take a dimmer view. O'Connell claims Alba implemented "his program of political repression and pursuit of heresy with a ruthlessness that has earned him universal condemnation."[147] As a result, "the tyranny of Alba breathed new life into the nationalist cause which had died in 1567 beneath the walls of Antwerp."[148] On June 5, 1568, Egmont was beheaded in Brussels, providing Beethoven with a theme for an overture, and providing a symbol for the cause of Dutch nationalism and its resistance to Spanish tyranny. The Dutch needed all the help they could get in this regard because William of Orange's German mercenary horde did not incite warm feelings among the natives as it raped and looted its way through the northern provinces. The major difference between Alba and William was leadership. Alba stayed by his men until Philip removed him from command. William of Orange deserted his own troops after leading them into France and running out of money.

Philip understood he was involved in a religious war; he did not neglect spiritual weapons, especially those wielded by the exiled English. Stapleton and Allen and their fellow English exiles withdrew to Douay, where they purchased two large houses, and, with four students (three from Oxford), founded the College des Pretres Anglais. The exiles were determined to prepare for the collapse of the Elizabethan regime when England would have an immediate need for trained priests. The college had an almost immediate effect on English life. One year after its founding, the lords of the north, among whom Allen had stayed a few years before, rose in an abortive counter-rebellion known as the Northern Rising. The brutal repression of that rising convinced Allen and his colleagues that the "holy war of religion" was going to be protracted. One year later, on June 2, 1570, Pius V's bull "*Regnans in Excelsis*" was nailed to the bishop's palace in London, excommunicating Elizabeth and declaring "her people forever released from obedience," thus encouraging insurrection, by telling the English "not to obey her commands and laws."[149] The bull arrived as Elizabeth dealt with the Northern Rising and probably contributed to her cruelty in suppressing it. Other plots followed, although it becomes difficult to distinguish between genuine plots and sting operations set up by Walsingham and his network of *agents provocateurs*.

Training priests in England was now out of the question. Since the Mass was now a criminal offense, the college at Douay could not assume priests could perform their duties under anything like normal circumstances. They had to be trained as counter-revolutionaries because only by using subterfuge could they survive in England. This fueled government propaganda that maintained Catholics were traitors simply because they practiced rites outlawed by the state.

Money was a perennial problem for the college, but Philip and the pope made generous donations. In April 1575, Pope Gregory XIII granted the seminary a monthly pension of 100 gold crowns, later increased by 50 percent. Rev. Gregory Martin, the English scholar responsible for the Catholic translation of the bible, claimed "swarms of theological students and candidates for holy orders ... were daily coming or rather flying to the college at the mere report of such magnificent liberality."[150] But the money was never enough to cover expenses, not even enough to provide decent meals, as Martin makes clear in his description of the refectory, "where in our time we sat down about six at one table, nearly sixty men and youths of the greatest promise were seated at three tables eating so pleasant a little broth, thickened merely with the commonest roots that you could have sworn that they were feasting on stewed raisins and prunes, English delicacies."[151] Dr. Thomas Bailey rented another house, but accommodation was still insufficient, given "the number of students daily flocking to the seminary from the town, besides those who were expected from England."[152]

With recruits streaming in, Allen and his colleagues decided in 1574 to send priests back to England. By 1580 there were 100 clandestine Catholic priests in England. When Elizabeth died in 1603, 450 had taken part in the English mission, and of those 110 had died the martyr's death. There were Jesuits among those who served (and among the martyrs as well, men like Edmund Campion) but the overwhelming number were secular priests who far excelled the intellectual caliber of the Anglican usurpers.

The ordination of priests for England was the second phase of the Catholic Counter-Reformation attack on Elizabeth's regime. Like the first, it preserved the faith in small enclaves but did not overthrow the rabidly anti-Catholic regime which knew it held the winning cards if it kept the machinery of the church firmly within its grasp.

Although books opened the way and priests from Douay kept the way open, neither could turn the tide. Douay burst at the seams with eager seminarians, but the 400 priests they sent to England over the last 30 years of Elizabeth's reign could not compete with the staffs of the 8,000 parishes the government had taken over. Cecil and Elizabeth nevertheless responded with bloodthirsty savagery. In fall 1577, Father Cuthbert Mayne was arrested near Exeter with a concealed papal bull on his person. He was convicted of treason and hanged and quartered. One hundred and eighty two more English Catholics would die in this battle. In 1581 the Jesuit Edmund Campion was convicted in a trial that was rigged so blatantly that Cecil had to defend the government in a pamphlet.

English historiography often speculates about when England ceased being Catholic. Belloc places the change at the time of the gunpowder plot. Eamon Duffy contests Whig historians by documenting the perduring attraction Catholicism held for the English people. O'Connell attributes the change to the ferocity of the Elizabethan police state: "What long years of passive obedience had begun the violence carried to conclusion and Catholicism after 1585 ceased to be a significant factor in English life."[53] Whatever the date, the unjust situation could only be changed by force of arms:

> The failed Catholic revival in England demonstrated how crucial was the existence and control of the ecclesiastical structure. In Germany and Poland the structure of diocese and parish, of monastery, university and school, though corrupt, was nevertheless intact, and through it the fervor of the Counter Reformation could be transmitted to the people. In the Elizabethan England, this was never the case, and so one might guess the movement never had a chance. One might also guess that long before the armada, most Englishmen had given up the thought of bringing back the pope.

The 1570s, beginning with the defeat of the Turkish armada at Lepanto, brought an almost unbroken string of Catholic victories. In August 1572 the French government launched a pre-emptive strike against the Huguenots in what is known as the St. Bartholomew's Day Massacre. Throughout the 1570s the Duke of Alba subdued one rebellious Dutch city after another. Alba's success in what is now Belgium forced the Dutch Calvinists to take refuge behind the maze of rivers and dikes in the northern provinces of Zeeland and Holland. The Spaniards were invincible in land warfare, but the territory north of the Waal, the Leck, and the Rijn rivers was *terra firma* only in some tenuous sense of the word. The Dutch adapted their tactics to the terrain, fighting defensive campaigns where they could control the territory by flooding the battlefields. They also cultivated contact with England via the North Sea, developing a force known as the Sea Beggars that moved in shallow draft boats. By developing these tactics, the Calvinists were able to hold on to Holland while at the same time maintaining contact with England. The opposite was true of the Spaniards, who could neither consolidate their control of the land nor link up with their own navy when the time came for the crucial move against England. In 1576, the Spaniards retook Antwerp, but the subsequent sacking of the city proved to be a public relations nightmare. That sacking would have far reaching consequences, especially for the Catholic exiles in Douay.

XI

In the months that spanned the transition from 1572 to 1573, John Dee and astronomers across Europe noticed something strange and disturbing. A new star had appeared in the heavens. According to the then regnant view of the universe, all stars (including those wandering stars known as planets) were embedded in concentric crystalline spheres. The outermost sphere separated the universe from the empyrean realm where God reigned in a realm of eternal light. Stars in this sphere were holes letting light through. The appearance of a new star meant the heavens had sprung a leak. The celestial spheres, which were considered eternal and unchangeable, had changed. Since everything on earth corresponded to influences from on high, that meant that the earthly order was about to change too. A revolution was imminent, and it was Dee's task as magus, scientist, and government agent to understand the significance of these changes and harness them politically.

Renaissance astronomy was very similar to the reformed reading of Scripture. In each instance, projection played a large if not the determinative role. Given that the structure of the universe had just changed, the time seemed ripe for a bold move by the Elizabethans. Of course, any sober reading of the military situation during the 1570s would not have encouraged English military adventurism. The Spaniards were proving repeatedly that they were masters of the continent. They had also been the first to colonize America, which Pope Alexander VI ratified by dividing the new world between Portugal and Spain in his bull *Inter Cetera* in 1493. That and the Treaty of the Torsedillas effectively excluded England from any role in colonizing the New World.

But who in England recognized the authority of the pope? Wasn't it illegal to do so? If it were illegal in ecclesial matters, could it be permissible in temporal matters, where he had even less authority? The revolution meant there was no longer one authoritative source or court of appeals. This became obvious when Rome reformed the calendar. The task was long overdue because of obvious discrepancies when the old calendar failed to take into account the extra quarter day that accumulated each year. Yet England would not accept the calendar reform for another 170 years because of ideology. When consulted, Dee claimed the pope had used the wrong starting date. Another manifestation of this loss of authority was the search for the *prisci theologi*, a quest related to the idea that Hebrew or Soyga or something or other was the language spoken by God. Antiquity became an authority, which led to the promotion of figures like Hermes Trismegistus, devotee of the Egyptian god Thoth, who was praised by Copernicus as older and therefore more authoritative. The Hermetic or occult philosophy was an attempt to trump religious controversies by outflanking them historically. Dee was a major proponent of this school.

Objectively, the times were not propitious to test the most powerful nation on earth and her staunch ally the pope. In addition to a series of victories on land in Holland, Spain had just pulled off one of the most significant victories in the history of naval warfare. In early October 1571, the fleet of the Holy Alliance under Don Juan of Austria crushed the Turkish fleet at Lepanto. Turkish hegemony over the eastern Mediterranean was broken, and God clearly had a hand in the victory at Lepanto. Pius V not only put the alliance together, he sat praying the rosary in Rome while the outcome was hanging in the balance. The Victory at Lepanto showed how self-confident the Tridentine Church had become and how effectively the Council of Trent had reinvigorated the Catholics.

In 1571, in the same year as Lepanto, Dee set off to the Duchy of Lorraine to buy laboratory equipment. He returned with a "great cart" laden with flasks and retorts for alchemical experiments. Dee could not have gotten his passport without explicit government approval, so it is safe to assume the government was as interested in alchemy as Dee. Dee's illness, probably from inhaling vapors of toxic metals, also indicated his involvement in alchemy, as did his pursuit of the writings of the German magus Theophrastus Philipus Auroelius Bombastus von Hohenheim, who nicknamed himself Paracelsus or the man "surpassing Celsus," the legendary ancient philosopher.

Dee, in desperate financial straits, wrote to Cecil in October 1574 with a plan for discovering buried treasure. Since metals were related to planets, Dee could locate metals by poring over the motions of the stars. Dee's proposal got pushed aside, but he was soon called to government service anyway. In 1574, the explorer and navigator Martin Frobisher approached the Privy Council with a proposal to seek a northern passage to the Indies and China. Since it was known in intelligence circles that Dee had studied at the University of Louvain with two of the world's leading geographers, the government drew him into the discussion. The time seemed right. Sir Francis Drake was planning to set off on the voyage on which he would sail around the world. The ambitious Frobisher aspired to become the English Columbus, but he was aware that the fame would go to Drake if Drake returned successfully. As a result, Frobisher tried to steal a march on Drake, with the help of the Privy Council, who felt he could not achieve his goal without first taking instruction from Dee. So Dee was called in to teach Frobisher the "rules of Geometry and Cosmography" and how to use navigational instruments. The Elizabethan establishment also invested in the venture, convinced it would bring wealth to the queen, increase English importance in foreign affairs, and spread the Protestant cause. Leicester invested 50 pounds; Francis Walsingham and his future son-in-law, the poet Philip Sidney, invested 25 pounds each.

The nascent British Empire needed theoretical justification every bit as much as Frobisher needed instruction in the use of the quadrant; Dee provided this justification in a series of books published in the mid- to late-1570s. In 1576 Dee wrote *Brytanici Imperii Limites*, which asserted that British claims to foreign lands extended well beyond the borders of the British Isles. He pursued the idea in *General and rare memorials pertayning to the Perfect art of Navigation* (1577). Dee thus laid the groundwork for British imperialism. Although he cited Mercator profusely in *Limits*, neither book was geographical. The claims upon which the British Empire was based were literary. Dee mentioned the voyages of St. Brendan as antedating those of Columbus by a millennium and therefore substantiating English claims to America's north Atlantic shores. Other English claims were derived from Geof-frey of Monmouth's history of England, including the Brut legend, which claimed England was founded by refugees from Troy. The main peg upon which Dee hung his claim, however, was King Arthur. King Arthur, he reasoned, had promoted exploration long before the upstart Spaniards landed in the Caribbean. He had also provided the DNA for the Tudors. So what could be more logical than to have Elizabeth, the head of a purified British Church, extend the sway of true religion and chivalry over the benighted lands of Greenland, Estotiland, and everything else north of "Florida"?

In November 1577, Dee met with the queen and her advisors at Windsor Castle to plead his case in person. Dee proposed that England, a relatively poor nation, should contest the pope's division of the New World as well as Spain's hegemony over the lands north of "Florida," a geographical entity with no clear boundaries. Dee's presentation was "the first authoritative statement of the idea of a British empire, and it was delivered to the queen during the period when that Empire was about to make its first appearance on the geopolitical scene."[154] The new empire should be dedicated to spreading the Protestant faith, and England's queen was its definitive expositor. But the new empire was bound up with Cabala too. Dee saw himself as the Saturnine Melancholic visionary, who after long immersion in the sciences of number, would ascend to a second, prophetic state, in which the adept arrives at prophecies concerning political and religious events. The new Imperium of the Protestant queen then created a new world order based on the deep insights that the Saturnine philosopher had achieved through contemplating the books of magic in the Cabala. From its inception in Dee's mind, the British Empire was a judaizing enterprise, based on the connection between messianic politics, finance, and magic. It was both the alternative to and the mirror image of the Holy Roman Empire, which the stars had foretold was on its last legs. So if the Spanish Hapsburgs persecuted the Jews by way of the Inquisition, England would welcome them to her shores.

Less than two decades after Dee's death, Sir Francis Bacon would take Dee's vision a step further in his utopian novel *The New Atlantis*. Bensalem is the name Bacon gives to his ideal state; Yates makes clear that Bacon was describing a "Christian Cabalist," i.e., a Judaizing, community. The inhabitants of Bensalem had the sign of the Cross and the name of Jesus, but their culture isn't Christian in any orthodox sense. Bensalem is a Christian Cabalist utopia dominated by occult philosophy, magic, and trafficking in spirits, which make it more powerful than societies dependent on traditional scholastic philosophies and orthodox theology. What Bacon doesn't mention is that all these characteristics are directly trace-able to Dee. The Cross, for instance, is a Red Cross, which Bacon derived from Spenser's reading of Dee, as put forth in the first book of the *Faerie Queene*. The Red Cross would become the symbol for Rosicrucianism, which is the crucial link between Dee's occult philosophy and Freemasonry.

The Jews of Bensalem are merchants—even in Utopia some things never change. The Jews of Bensalem are allowed to circumcise themselves and to practice their own religion. Bensalem, in this regard, has a lot in common with Holland. Because they are allowed the free practice of their religion, the Jews of Bensalem (by now recognizable as a combination of the Protestant nations of Holland, England, and North America) no longer have "a secret inbred rancour" against Christ and "the people amongst whom they live."[155] Instead, they "give unto our Saviour many high attributes and love the nation of Bensalem extremely."[156] The Jews are fulsome in their praise of Bensalem. They even believe "Moses by a secret Cabala ordained the laws of Bensalem which they now use, and that when the Messiah should come and sit on his throne at Jerusalem, the King of Bensalem should set at his feet."[157]

The Jews would eventually make their own contribution to the literature of England as the chosen nation, but by then the tradition had already been firmly established by Dee and his literary children, Spenser, Bacon, and Milton. Shakespeare would join that tradition too, especially in the *Tempest*, his tribute to an old and all but forgotten Dee.

England was going to become the magic island through Dee's explication of Cabala, and then they were going to export that vision to the rest of the world by exploration, colonization, and conquest. During his audience with the Queen, Dee elaborated on her claims to Greenland, Estotiland (i.e., Baffin Island), and Friseland. In May 1578 Frobisher was instructed to create an English settlement on Estotiland as the second step in establishing claims to North America. Dee had no fears about the survival of the settlement because, he said, the natives of Baffin Island spoke several languages, including Latin, had extensive libraries, and brewed their own beer. These fantastic claims would be echoed in the next Century when Rabbi Menasseh ben Israel would claim equally implausibly that the lost tribes of Israel had been discovered living in Ecuador. According to Dee's reading of Justinian, who said "what presently belongs to no one becomes by natural reason the property of the first taker,"[158] the English had a right to North America because it had been discovered by King Arthur, St. Brendan the Voyager (who happened to be Irish), and Madoc. All their British descendants had to do was occupy the territory "which the Spaniard occupieth not."[159]

With those instructions as well as his newly acquired navigation science firmly in mind, Frobisher set off on his voyage. Within months he arrived back in England with the hold of his ship full of smooth black rocks, which, he assured his influential backers, contained a high quantity of gold ore. By August of 1578, it had become clear that the black rocks were just that, black rocks. Once it became clear that there was no gold in them, they were all dumped unceremoniously into the Thames, and the voyage's backers, including the queen, calculated their losses and reminded themselves to be less credulous the next time the queen's conjurer proposed one of his harebrained schemes.

XII

On November 4, 1576 word of Alba's conquest of Antwerp reached Douay eliciting "sign[s] of cheerfulness" among the Englishmen which were misinterpreted by the natives as *Schadenfreude* over the calamities of Belgium. Before long it became clear to the English that whatever annoyance the Belgians felt was being fanned into something much more serious by the agents of Elizabeth and William of Orange. The Calvinists, "who formed the kernel of the Prince of Orange's faction" had received orders "to stir up the multitude" against the English "as partisans of Spain."[160] The English Queen was at the bottom of the intrigue. Her plan was to use Orange "to procure the destruction of the seminary, which she both feared and hated."[161] Once the seminary was destroyed, she hoped to apprehend Allen, Stapleton and the other exiles and bring them to trial in England, where their fate, as the hanging of Cuthbert Mayne had shown, was a foregone conclusion. Beginning in the fall of 1576, everything that the English did in Douay was minutely scrutinized and "evilly interpreted"[162] as part of a campaign to shut down the seminary. The Catholics there had received reports that assassins had been dispatched from England to murder Dr. Allen and his associates. Englishmen of sinister aspect were seen lurking in the town, "to all appearance the kind of men suited for the execution of such a crime."[163] As a result, many seminarians became intimidated. In a little over a year after the inception of the campaign enrollment in the seminary dropped from 120 to 42.

During the next two years, the revolutionary spirit seemed reborn in the Spanish Netherlands, and "many persons of all ranks, even of those who were sincerely attached to the Catholic faith and never dreamed of casting off their allegiance to their sovereign, had been more or less carried away by it."[164] Knox felt much of the blame was ascribable to the Duke of Alba, whose troops sacked Antwerp in 1576. The people felt "their national liberties and privileges ... had been largely infringed by the Duke of Alba while he was governor." So they "abandon themselves blindly to the guidance of the Prince of Orange and the revolutionary party."[165]

Don Juan continued his negotiations to restore harmony, but Orange and his followers were more interested in revolution. On January 25, 1578, Don Juan broke off negotiations and declared war. Six days later, his new general, Alexander Farnese, the Prince of Parma, crushed the revolutionary army with unpleasant consequences for the English at Douay. On March 14, the newly appointed Calvinist governor told them they had to leave. A week later, the magistrates of Douay reiterated the demand. Allen had scouted a new location for the seminary in Rheims under the protection of the French Catholic Guises. During Holy Week of 1578, the seminarians set out on foot on a four-day journey to their new home. In November the magistrates of Douay invited the seminary back, proving to Knox that the expulsion was the work of a Calvinist cabal, but Allen decided not to return. The situation in the Spanish Netherlands was too uncertain, the borders too porous, the likelihood that assassins from England might do serious harm too great. The idea of a united Netherlands had proven untenable by the end of 1578. On January

23, 1579, the Calvinist provinces of the north established the Union of Utrecht, a *de facto* independent Calvinist state, from which Dutch-speaking Calvinists could continue to exert military pressure on Catholics in the south.

In 1580, six years after the first Douay priest arrived in England, the Jesuits became involved in the English mission. In June, Edmund Campion, SJ, arrived in England amid optimism that Allen's ambitious plan for the conversion of England might be working. Earlier, toward the end of 1575, the Rev. Henry Saw wrote to Allen, "the number of Catholics increases so abundantly on all sides that he who almost alone holds the rudder of state has privately admitted to one of his friends that for one staunch catholic at the beginning of the reign there were now, he knew for certain, ten." "The heretics," he continued, "are as much troubled at the name of the Anglo-Douay priests which is now famous throughout England as all the Catholics are consoled thereby."[166]

The magnitude of the task before him—the return of England to the Catholic faith—tempered Allen's enthusiasm. The English at Douay and later Rheims, no matter how great their zeal, had very small numbers. And in England they were subjected to sophisticated surveillance and constant persecution. English Catholics had to fend for themselves, and without church governance, abuses were bound to arise. Difficulties arose because the Catholic Church in England

> hath no form of external commonwealth, no one that governeth the rest, no discipline or censures neither to drive the priests nor people into order, no man subject to his fellow, no way to call disorders to account, no common conference, no sovereignty nor subjection; but every one, living severally and secretly by himself, and often far from any fellows, is ruled only by his own skill and conscience, which even among the Apostles had bred disturbance, if by sundry meetings councils and conferences it had not been looked into, and, that notwithstanding, some of the best sort were now and then found reprehensible ... because no man dare nor well can in those terms take upon him to direct govern and call to account at certain times the rest of the inferior clergy in so great a dispersion and uncertainty of their abode.... Therefore where there can be no further jurisdiction or recount of their dealings than the rule of every man's own conscience and knowledge, no marvel if all be not at all times agreeable to reason and our desires.[167]

The mission to England could only be a holding action that kept Catholic hope and practice alive until the situation was resolved militarily, as Parma was then resolving it in Belgium. England needed bishops to run the machinery of the church. Allen was confirmed in his views when Edmund Campion was arrested on July 17, 1581, and, after prolonged torture, died a martyr's death at Tyburn on December 1.

XIII

In September 1580, Sir Francis Drake returned in triumph from his voyage around the world. His ship became an immediate tourist attraction, drawing large crowds, some of whom fell off the gangplank into the Thames mud. Impressed with Drake's loot, Elizabeth rewarded his piracy by making him a knight. Three months later, Christopher Marlowe entered Cambridge as an undergraduate. For four years, Marlowe was an impecunious student, taking frugal meals with the rest of the students. In 1585, however, Marlowe's fortunes inexplicably rose. He bought himself an expensive doublet and began dining on meat and wine at many times the cost of the bread and cheese that was formerly his fare. The cause of Marlowe's newfound prosperity came into being during 1581, his first year at Cambridge. During that year, shortly after Campion had arrived on English soil, the Jesuits had established a recruitment network at Cambridge. In September 1581, the Jesuit Person wrote to Claudius Acquaviva, the Jesuit General in Rome, that "At Cambridge I have at length insinuated a certain priest into the very university, under the guise of a scholar or gentleman common, and have procured him help not far from the town. Within a few months he has sent over to Rheims seven very fit youths."[168] John Ballard and John Fingelow, both of Caius college, were recruited and ended up at Rheims. Ballard returned under the pseudonym Captain Fortescue and was executed for his role in the Babington plot in 1586. Unwilling to let such a threat go unchallenged, Walsingham set up a counter-network of young men who would either make contact with Catholic sympathizers at Cambridge or go to Rheims to infiltrate the seminary from within. In 1585, when England declared war on Spain and sent an expeditionary force to the Netherlands, Walsingham's espionage budget increased dramatically, and one of the first beneficiaries was Christopher Marlowe, whose meteoric rise to fame never completely clarified his political or religious allegiance.

In May 1582, Allen wrote to the Jesuit Agazzari complaining about the tribulations of life in exile, and more particularly about the behavior of his students. The Catholics were fighting a losing battle even in Catholic areas because "the common people sometimes go to the churches of the heretics through fear of the iniquitous laws."[169] The hardships of exile had convinced Allen "it would be easier to guide to salvation a thousand souls in England than one hundred in this exile, which of itself breeds murmurings, complainings, contradictions and discontent. When Moses leads the people through the desert, he suffers much. Even at the very time that God rains down manna and quails and brings water from the rock they are not satisfied, but their soul is with the flesh-pots of Egypt."[170]

In the same letter Allen mentioned they had caught a spy. Richard Baines was ordained in Rheims in September 1581. He had arrived at the seminary in 1578, and for the three years did his best to foment discontent, encouraging students "to mislike the rule and discipline of subjection to their masters."[171] He would engage in "licentious" talk about flesh pies and sex to break the discipline of the seminarians struggling with the rigor of life in penurious exile. Baines liked to portray his actions as the result of a fall from grace, but he had been sent to Rheims as a spy. This is certainly the view Allen conveyed to Agazzari. Rheims had always been high on Walsingham's list of threats to the new order in England. His attempts to spread disunity there were consistent with other Walsingham operations.

It is unlikely that a seminarian would turn from grumbling about the food to plans for mass murder on the spur of the moment. In a long confession in May 1583, Baines admitted that he plotted "how the first President might be made away, and if that missed how the whole company might easily be poisoned."[172] Baines planned to murder the entire seminary by dumping poison into the college well or into the water the seminarians bathed in. Nicholl sees Baines as the model for Marlowe's *Jew of Malta*, a Catholic hater who poisons a convent of nuns. Marlowe's Jew is said to "go about to poison wells" and produces "a drench to poison a whole stable of Flanders mares."[173] Baines went about his duties, "daily celebrating Mass," Allen adds with scarcely concealed disgust, "believing himself unsuspected" until "his treachery and illicit dealings with the Privy Council had become known."[174] If Baines had been a Catholic in Protestant England, there is little doubt what his fate would have been. The Catholics instead set him free; before long he was devising new treachery for his Protestant masters, as Marlowe would discover to his chagrin, because Marlowe "was some kind of cog in the operations against Rheims" too.[175]

XIV

On the evening of March 8, 1582, the sky over Mortlake turned blood red, portending a momentous change in the sublunar sphere. Earlier that day, Dee the Magus had entertained a visitor who identified himself as Edward Talbot. Talbot was a 26-year-old cripple who wore a cowl that created a monkish appearance. The cowl concealed his ears, which had been mutilated, probably as punishment for counterfeiting or "coining." The visitor's real name was Edward Kelley, a criminal "necromancer," someone who exhumed dead bodies. He dug up a corpse at Walton le Dale near Preston in Lancashire and used it to invoke "some one of the Infernal Regiment."[176] Kelley needed "the Devil's foresight" to figure out the "manner and time of the death of a noble young Gentleman, as then in Wardship."[177] Kelley was a "skyrer," or medium, who could contact angels and summon them to appear. Kelley was not Dee's first skyrer. In fact, Kelley arrived at Mortlake to announce he was to replace Saul, a skyrer who had showed up a few months earlier. Dee's first recorded "action" or seance took place under Saul's direction on December 1581. Saul gazed into a crystal ball and announced he saw the Angel Annael, one of seven angels of Creation and, according to Dee, "the Angel of Intelligence now ruling this world."[178] Annael wrote on the crystal a message in Hebrew letters of transparent gold. A bright star appeared, first ascending and then descending, followed by "a great number of dead men's skulls" and a "white dog with a long head."[179]

Dee warned Kelley that he was uninterested in what was "vulgarly accounted magic."[180] Rather, Dee wanted to contact "the blessed angels of God,"[181] so they could assist Dee's "philosophical studies." Yates, among other scholars, was taken in by Dee's protestations that he was only interested in "white" magic, which rang increasingly hollow as Dee plunged deeper and deeper into the world of the occult.

Kelley told Dee he had been sent to warn Dee about Saul, Dee's previous skryer. Kelley was an emissary of a group that previously had sent others to Dee, including Richard Hickman (who would be implicated in the Hesketh plot ten years later) in June 1579. Hickman gained entry "with the commendations of Sir Christopher Hatton,"[182] which "shows that interest in spiritual communication went right to the top of government."[183] Although Woolley says "this aspect of Elizabethan political life remains largely undocumented and unexamined,"[184] he then gives an impressive list of high government officials under Elizabeth who were deeply involved in the occult and interested in having Dee come up with a military or intelligence application of the occult. He lists Leicester (and by implication Sydney), Pembroke, and, most significantly, Walsingham, the head of Elizabeth's spy network. The links are instructive and problematic. If Kelley was sent by Hatton to work with Dee, whom was Dee working for? Was Kelley sent to spy on Dee? If so, he was the man providing Dee with most of his material. This could mean, of course, that Kelley was a "projector," or agent provocateur sent to implicate Dee in some plot. Walsingham was famous for concocting schemes and was then deeply involved in what became known as the Throckmorton plot. Did Walsingham and Hatton suspect Dee had divided loyalties? Cardinal Allen, after all, had already claimed Dee was a Catholic priest. Even a *sacerdos uxoratus,* might have bouts of recurring Catholicism, especially if confronted by treachery and disappointment by his new masters.

Kelley's links with Hatton and Walsingham may explain the increasingly political nature of the visions he conjured. During a seance Kelley conducted with Dee in April 1582, the Archangel Michael appeared and announced he was going to reveal the governors who rule the lower world by revealing the names of 49 angels, "whose names are here, evident, excellent and glorious."[185] Additionally, Michael revealed an elaborate table of letters and numbers, which described divine government. This table indicated the revelations concerned not personal but political salvation, which would come about through creation of a "new global order run according to godly principles."[186] The new world order was also bound up with a new sexual order. After the seance, Kelley told Dee the Archangel Michael had suggested to Kelley that he was to break his vow of celibacy. As Luther and the Anabaptists had shown on the continent, the new world order involved liberation from the constraints of the old. No matter how much the Reformers played it down, sexual liberation and reformed Christianity went hand in hand. Now the very angels were commanding it. Did this mean that Michael the Archangel was, as a later age might put, the representation of suppressed sexual desires? If by that, we mean to the exclusion of an actual supernatural being, the answer is no. If by that we mean the supernatural being was aware of Kelley's unfulfilled sexual longings and determined to manipulate them, the answer is yes. Seven months later, Dee and Kelley conjured up the spirit King Camara, whose first question was "what is your desire?"[187] The question demonstrates the angels were interested in the desires of those who summoned them and willing to fulfill them in an as yet unacknowledged bargain. Two days after the appearance of King Camara, Dee had a nightmare in which he was disemboweled after Lord Cecil had entered his house and look "sourly" upon him. Like the intelligence agents that worked for Cecil and Walsingham in the sublunary world, the angels seemed to be double agents.

For his library, Dee acquired *De Orginibus* by the Frenchman Guillaume Postel, who told of meeting a priest from Ethiopia who told him about a Book of Enoch, lost for centuries to Europeans but well known to Ethiopians. The book contained Enoch's account of the language taught Adam straight from the mouth of God. The man who mastered it could control the universe as God had done through Adam, namely, by speaking or naming things. The passages in Postel's book describing the Ethiopian priest's testimony were heavily annotated by Dee. Imagine Dee's astonishment then when Anneal, conjured again by Kelley on March 26, 1583, began writing letters of the celestial alphabet, the language God had spoken to Adam, which had been lost since man built the tower of Babel, and commanded Dee to write them down.

Dee was on the verge of a momentous discovery, the fruition of 20 years work in magic through his study of the Cabala. The discovery would correspond to a momentous change in the heavens. On April 28, 1583, Saturn and Jupiter fell into "conjunction" or "copulation," signaling the end of one historical era and the beginning of another. The era which was coming to an end was the watery trigon under the sign of Pisces. The world would witness the dawn of the era of the "fiery trigon," characterized by "sudden and violent changes," or revolution. Dee immediately corresponded with astronomers in England and on the continent. Richard Harvey confirmed "the watery Trigon shall perish and be turned into fire."[188] A "new world" would come about "by some sudden, violent & wonderful strange alteration, which even heretofore hath always happened at the ending of one Trigon & beginning of an other."[189] Tycho Brahe felt the celestial conjunction of Jupiter and Saturn was "the end of the Roman Catholic Church's supremacy."[190] A Czech astrologer added the "sudden and violent changes" would occur first in Bohemia.

Six weeks later, the Polish Prince Albert Laski showed up at Mortlake. By the end of the summer, Dee, Laski, and Kelley embarked on a mission to Prague, capital of Bohemia, the new home of Rudolf II and his court. Rudolf, whom Walsh describes as "surrounded by Jews, astrologers, Rosicrucians, pseudo-mystics, and quacks,"[191] was the son of Maximillian to whom Dee had dedicated *Monas Hieroglyphica*, and head of the Austrian line of Hapsburgs, the family facing down the English, the Jews, and the Calvinists in the Netherlands. Although he was on the outs with the Polish king, Laski had received the royal treatment in England, where Cecil and Walsingham saw Laski as useful in providing them with a back channel access to the Hapsburgs, with whom England would soon be at open war. Laski came to Mortlake eager for occult insight. Dee obligingly summoned the angel Raphael, who informed Laski "Many witches and enchanters, yea many devils have arisen up against this stranger, but I will grant him his desire."[192] It was the sort of response one might expect from the local gypsy, but the mention of granted desires kept the Polish nobleman coming back for more. The suspicion Kelley and Dee were commissioned by Walsingham to bring Laski under control is strong: Walsingham's agent, Charles Sledd, the spy who had penetrated the English College in Rome, had arrived at Mortlake the day before Laski and had spent the night, presumably consulting with Dee and Kelley about the imminent arrival of the prince from Poland. Walsingham's house at Barn Elms was a short walk from Dee's at Mortlake. The fact that Sledd, who may have come to Mortlake from Barn Elms, did not spend the night at Walsingham's indicates that the three men must have conferred until late in the evening. Dee considered Sledd's appearances an ill omen. The outcome was invariably unpleasant, sometimes producing psychosomatic effects like nosebleeds.

If Sledd arrived at Mortlake with instructions from Walsingham on how to use Laski, then Dee probably proposed the trip to Prague to Laski and Kelley. The Queen quickly signaled her approval. Preparing for departure, Dee catalogued his books. While compiling his list, Dee received a visit from the Queen, who then sent him a gift of 40 angels, coins with more than monetary significance. Sir Walter Raleigh also sent a letter assuring Dee of Elizabeth's "good disposition." When Dee and his entourage set off by flyboat down the Thames on September 21, they were a government-sponsored operation. Dee repeatedly said as much, indicating he was embarking on a private mission in the service of the queen to use "his position as part of Laski's entourage to gather sensitive foreign information."[193]

When Dee left England with Laski, Elizabeth was in something approaching a state of panic, convinced that she was the object of a French-Spanish plot to remove her from the throne. Part of that plan involved orchestrating a Catholic invasion of England. Another part involved getting faithful Catholics in England to rise in rebellion as French and Spanish troops arrived on English shores. English involvement in that scheme came to be known as the Throckmorton Plot. Walsingham was weaving a web of intrigue that would bring a number of prominent Englishmen to the gallows, including Lord Henry Howard, a Catholic who attacked magic and religious enthusiasm in *A Defensative against the Poyson of supposed Prophesies,* an attack on Dee and the Earl of Leicester. Dee is not mentioned by name, but Howard attacks a hermeticist, suffering from "distemper of the brain,"[194] who trafficked in spirits, cast horoscopes, and "sought to entrap Diana in the coils of his occult knowledge."[195] Diana was an obvious reference to Queen Elizabeth; the unsubtle point was "the Earl of Leicester and his Protestant friends had been using diabolic powers to control the queen."[196]

Howard's brother had been hanged in 1572 for involvement in the Northern Rising. Howard was to follow him when he was arrested and executed on charges of treason. Meanwhile others were being implicated in the Throckmorton Plot by a spy named Fagot, a Frenchman who wrote reports in a peculiar French full of mistakes no Frenchman would make. John Bossy claims "Fagot" was Giordano Bruno, an Italian monk newly arrived in England hoping to make his fortune as the most brilliant expositor of the new *occulta philosophia*. Bruno inexplicably became a martyr to "science" when the Inquisition burned him at the stake on the Campo di Fiore in Rome in 1600. Walsingham probably lured him to become an informer by playing on his ambition. In addition to offering Bruno a salary, Walsingham offered introductions to Philip Sydney and Dee, his fellow magus and chief competitor as explicator of the occult. It was probably through Walsingham's influence that Bruno got to debate the Scholastics at Oxford, demonstrating his brilliance. By collaborating with Walsingham, Bruno could aspire to replace Dee as the Court magus when Dee left for Prague. Bruno was encouraged by Dee, the "intellectual godfather to the Oxford party," who "by his departure for Poland with the palatine" had "left a vacancy in England for the position of resident guru."[197]

With the arrest of Throckmorton and Howard, Bruno had done his job; with Dee gone, he could become magus in residence in England. Walsingham probably encouraged Bruno in this, as he had encouraged Dee to take the journey with Laski. The two men were his puppets. Both men promoted a political vision intimately connected with magic as a form of control: "Bruno envisaged a universal monarchy to achieve total moral redemption, assuring obedience by persuasive magic and exaltation of the 'vital spirits' of its subjects: complete freedom through complete servitude."[198] Dee and Bruno were working for Walsingham toward the same goal: the spread of magic as a way of undermining Catholic hegemony over Europe. Dee was to Rudolf what Bruno was to Throckmorton. What Howard said of Dee's influence over the Queen would now apply to Dee's influence over Rudolf at precisely the moment when the war between England and the Hapsburgs was escalating in the direction of open military conflict.

XV

Dee and Kelley's journey to Prague took almost a year. It was no mean feat to cross the northern European alluvial plain, especially in the dead of winter. Rivers swelled to impassability; carriages got bogged down in mud. Travelers got separated and had to wait in uncertainty at dubious accommodations until reunited. Illness was part of the journey. Another reason for the delay in reaching Prague was their intervening visit to Lask, Laski's ancestral estates in Poland.

Shortly after his arrival in Lask, Dee contacted the spirit Nalvage, which had the face of a child and hair like down. Dee, suffering from a fever for days, asked Nalvage for medical advice and got instead a terrifying vision of Mortlake in flames with his wife lying dead on the ground outside. Soon Madimi, a seductive female who would play a crucial role in the Dee and Kelley marriages, replaced Nalvage. Madimi told Dee the Queen mourned his absence, and Cecil would "come home shortly, a begging to you."[199] Then Nalvage returned and started to reveal "the Cabala of Nature," meaning "all of the universe's secrets" in the language Adam had spoken in Eden. Dee's fingers raced across the pages of his notebook as he struggled to keep up with the angelic dictation.

On July 13, 1584, Dee's 57th birthday, the Angel Gabriel announced the angelic revelation was complete. Dee now had "the keys of God's storehouses ... wherein you shall find (if you enter wisely, humble and patiently) treasures more worth than the frames of the heavens."[200] Dee could now write the Book of Enoch. In the same month, Nalvage reappeared and told Dee "Go to the emperor," meaning, go to Rudolf in Prague. Apparently Dee was more interested in the Book of Enoch, because on July 31 Nalvage appeared again, furious that his command had been ignored. "Were you not commanded to go after ten days," the angel raged, breathing fire. "I have brought madness into the house of the unjust."[201] Dee left the following day, finally arriving in Prague in August 1584 along with his skyrer Kelley, their servant Edmund Hilton, and Kelley's brother.

In the waning years of the 16th Century, Prague was a strange mixture of forces contending with each other over the fate of Europe in the wake of the Protestant revolution. Rudolf's removal of the Austrian court to Prague had attracted hoaxers, con men, occultists, charlatans, pseudo-mystics, and artisans determined to cash in on his obsession with things arcane: "a host of 'charlatans, knaves and blowhards,' ... were drawn to the city's gates by the prize of rich pickings and lax regulation."[202] A Greek, Mamugna, arrived from Famagosta, announcing he was the son of an Italian martyr. Mamugna radiated an aura of mystical power while pulled through the town in a cart drawn by two black mastiffs. The mode of conveyance apparently reflected the power of the message: Geronimo Scotta arrived to sell his potions in the town square in a train of three carriages drawn by 40 horses. According to the court in Vienna, Rudolf was "interested only in wizards, alchemists, kabbalists and the like, sparing no expense to find all kinds of treasures, learn secrets and use scandalous ways of harming his enemies.... He also has a whole library of magic books. He strives all the time to eliminate God completely so that he may in future serve a different master."[203] According to a Venetian visitor, Rudolf "delights in hearing secrets about things both natural and artificial, and whoever is able to deal in such matters will always find the ear of the Emperor ready."[204] The angels may have been impatient because they felt that the Emperor's ear was already overburdened. The presence of so many quacks and charlatans proved, if nothing else, that Rudolf's character flaws were well-known. The angels who reported to Dee and Kelley and were, in some sense of the word, part of Walsingham's intelligence network, knew that Rudolf's weakness for magic could be exploited by Dee to serve British interests. The purpose of his trip to Prague was simple enough to understand from the point of view of British intelligence. Dee and Kelley were to attack the Hapsburgs where they were most vulnerable at the time, which is to say on their exposed eastern occultic flank.

Walsingham also had other reasons to send Dee and Kelley to Prague. Prague, despite its distance from England, had become a center of Catholic resistance on a par with Rheims and Louvain. After Dee returned to England in 1589, Kelley became a "natural centre for English exiles in Prague."[205] One of those exiles was the amateur alchemist Richard Hesketh, who would go to the gallows as perpetrator of the Hesketh Plot. While Kelley was advising Hesketh on matters alchemical, Kelley was also in contact with Lord Burghley, who importuned him for cures for the gout, advice on how to turn lead into gold to finance the wars in the Netherlands, and information on Catholic exiles, which Kelley would transmit via Matthew Royden, who would figure in Marlowe's demise. Nicholl says "Roydon in Prague," and "Marlowe in Flushing" were "bit-players in the same complex and rather pointless intelligence game which is being played around the reluctant Catholic pretender, their patron, Lord Strange"[206] as well as Lancashire Catholics in exile like Hesketh. Hesketh was hanged purportedly for presenting a "forged indictment to Catholic rebellion"[207] to Lord Strange to remove him as the Catholic pretender, but Kelley most probably identified him as part of the Prague circle of English Catholics. According to Nicholl, "there is plenty to link Kelley with the Catholic cell to which Hesketh belonged."[208]

Kelley would have a much greater impact on Prague and the English Catholic exiles there than Dee. By the time Dee left Prague to return to England, their roles would be reversed: by 1589, Kelley had gone from famulus to magus, and Dee was all but forgotten. Alchemical formulae "used by Edoardus Gelleus, the English alchemist."[209] were quoted extensively during the 17th Century. Walsingham and Cecil ignored the failed Dee when he returned to England, but well into the 1590s, they were still assiduously courting Kelley by letter and envoy, hoping to persuade him to return to England and share his wizardry, or at least the wealth it was reportedly producing, with the English court.

The arrival of Rudolf and his court changed the modality of Jewish activity in Prague. The idea of revolutionary collaboration of the sort which took place during the heady days of 1421, when Hussites and Jews sang Jewish songs as together they dug the trenches that were to prevent the invasion of the King of the Romans, was no longer feasible. In 1584, Utraquism was a spent force politically. The Jews, therefore, got involved in the occult. Since the Cabala was the ultimate source of *occulta philosophia* that was the intellectual rage in Europe, the change in Jewish activity was not difficult. Indeed, the occult tradition began when Pico and Reuchlin got the idea of magic from the Jews. Now Prague seemed obsessed with the new mechanical man who was a product of magic. The image of the new man appeared in the figures of the town clock, who would parade around after a skeleton rang a bell announcing the beginning of the performance.

Giordano Bruno would follow Dee and Kelley to Prague, probably to cash in on Rudolf's generosity in patronizing those adept in magic and the occult philosophy. Bruno included a fulsome dedication to Rudolf in his *Articles against the Mathematicians*, which "rehearses the whole Brunonian philosophy of a single true universal religion rooted in the occult tradition, and the salvation of mankind through the institutions of an intellectual elite."[210] Like Antwerp, Prague received large numbers of Jewish immigrants after the Spanish expulsion in 1492. These Jews arrived with an interest in Cabala, especially as redacted by Isaac Luria, because its mystical explanation of a universe wracked with catastrophe seemed to explain their own catastrophe. Cabala brought with it the age-old Jewish inclination to millennialist politics, according to which the upheaval in Spain was the first pangs of labor signaling the birth of the Messiah. Magic was part of the program of messianic politics for Jews and Judaizers, who found common cause in their crusade against the Hapsburgs and the Catholic Church. Many Cabalists found places in Rudolf's court. Aware many of Rudolf's closest advisors were Jews, Dee suspected them of plotting against him. The Jews also were central to the system of imperial finance. The occult revival in Prague under Rudolf was a manifestation of "the blossoming of Jewish intellectual life at the end of the Century" that was "based on a renewed study of the Cabala."[211]

The most famous Jew in Prague during the Cabala revival was Rabbi Judah Loew ben Bezalel. Rabbi Loew was an expert in Gematria, but the source of his fame was that somewhere in the Jewish ghetto in Prague he had reportedly created a human automaton, known as the Golem, by his cabalistic arcane science. The Golem was a clay figure that came to life when Rabbi Loew put a tablet with the name of God inscribed on it into the Golem's mouth. To this day, tour guides in Prague claim Loew created the Frankenstein myth, which now finds its expression in the ubiquitous sale of marionettes and puppets in the Old Town. Loew met Rudolf, and the two of them "had a long secretive conversation."[212] Yates thinks Dee may have met Loew in Prague, but from what we know of their journey, Dee and Kelley spent most of their time with Catholics.

In Prague, Dee and Kelley lodged at the home of Thaddeus Hajek, Rudolf's physician. Hajek lived on Bethlehem Square, not far from Bethlehem Chapel, where Jan Huss launched the revolutionary movement in Europe 174 years before. Hajek was one of the foremost astronomers of Europe; he and Dee had probably made contact when the new star appeared in the early '70s. Dee felt the revolution surrounding the arrival of the Fiery Trigon in the heavens in 1584 would involve the Hapsburgs, and he probably shared those thoughts with his Protestant host Hajek, who could introduce him to his contacts in the scientific world and at the imperial court. Dee's thoughts were probably not new to Hajek. Much of what Dee predicted had already been pointed out by the Czech astrologer, Cyprian Leowitz, and published in a book approved by the Emperor Maximillian. Leowitz predicted sudden violent changes would occur in 1584; Dee heavily annotated that book and probably knew Leowitz personally.

Hajek was also an Utraquist, but Utraquism, like the Anabaptism it spawned in Southern Germany, had had its day in Bohemia. The revolutionary spirit had departed, leaving only an ideological corpse behind. One reason for the demise of Utraquism was the rise of the *occulta philosophia*. Another reason was the Counter Reformation. When Dee arrived in Prague in August 1584, the Counter Reformation had been hard at work there for years. In 1581, the church had restored the nunciature, which soon functioned as a significant counterforce in intelligence and diplomacy to the English/Jewish spy ring that arranged Dee's mission to Prague. Soon the pope and the emperor were in a battle with Walsingham and the Jews over the mind of the emperor and the future of Bohemia and the empire. In that battle, the occult English cabalists had to play catch-up, which might explain the impatience of the angels, because in 1584, Nuncio Giovanni Francesco Bonomi submitted to Rudolf a plan for the "systematic extirpation of heresy in Bohemia."[213] Bolstered by support of the Jesuits and Catholic magnates like the Rozmberk and Lobkovic families, Bonomi and his successors hoped to implement the Tridentine reforms and bring about a re-Catholicization of Bohemia. This involved conversions, new seminaries, festivals and ceremonials, education, and mission work. "The hope is growing," Botero wrote, "for a total conversion of Bohemia."[214]

Total cultural renovation along lines defined by Trent could not take place without the cooperation of the Emperor, whose weakness for occult knowledge was well known. And so the battle for Bohemia became a battle for Rudolf's mind. If Dee could get to him, Rudolf might inaugurate the era of the fiery Trigon. The nuncio was thinking similarly, but with the opposite goal.

According to Yates, "Dee's message appeared to be neither Catholic nor Protestant." It was instead "an appeal to a vast, undogmatic, reforming movement which drew its spiritual strength from the resources of occult philosophy."[215] Giordano Bruno, who seemed to follow Dee through Europe, was one of many "enthusiastic missionaries" of "universal Hermetic reform, in which there were some Cabalist elements."[216] Hermeticism or Cabala or Magic was, in the era of cultural exhaustion following the early victories of the Protestants, an alternative to Catholicism and Protestantism, which seemed to have reached a stalemate in their battle to control Europe. Hermetic Cabala was also the alternative to the Counter Reformation, which was exceptionally vigorous. Just how vigorous was obvious when Giordano Bruno mistakenly returned to Italy: Bruno fell into the hands of the Inquisition and was burned at the stake in Rome in 1600. The Counter Reformation was on its way to stopping the Protestant advance and pacifying Austria, Poland, France, the Spanish Netherlands, and, most significant of all, Bohemia.

Through Hajek, Dee met with Don Guillen San Clemente, the Spanish ambassador, as an important step in his quest to get an audience with the emperor. Dee showed San Clemente his crystal ball; the ambassador was favorably impressed. San Clemente was evidently familiar with the arcane writings of the Spanish Cabalist Raymund Llull and felt Dee had made significant progress in explicating them. This did not remove San Clemente's nagging suspicion Dee was an

English spy sent by Walsingham to foment trouble in Bohemia, the weakest link in the Hapsburg chain. Dee was an object of suspicion from the moment he set foot in Prague. He was viewed in Catholic circles as a magus and an English spy, if not agent provocateur. San Clemente probably shared his misgivings with the nuncio; before long, the nuncio was expressing the same fears. Even if he hadn't heard the story from San Clemente, Bonomi had heard rumors Dee trafficked in spirits "with the aid of certain magical characters."[217] Bonomi harbored no illusions about the sort of spirit that would respond to Dee and Kelley's conjuring, and he knew they would not look kindly upon the re-Catholicization of Bohemia. Bonomi identified Dee "as a threat to the ongoing mission to bring Prague back into the Catholic fold."[218]

Dee saw the Emperor within a month of his arrival in Prague. After a little chit chat about Dee's *Monas Hieroglyphica*, a book Rudolf had read but found beyond his capacity, Rudolf mentioned that the Spanish Ambassador had told him Dee had a special message for the emperor. Dee then explained, in a manner reminiscent of Dr. Faustus, that when he had given up hope of finding wisdom in books, he had made contact with the angels, and they had a message for the emperor. "The Angel of the Lord," Dee announced, "hath appeared to me, and rebuketh you for your sins."[219]

It was a bold move and bespoke psychological manipulation far ahead of its time. Eventually, the Illuminati, the psychoanalysts, and sensitivity trainers would refine techniques like this into sophisticated forms of control. Knowing Rudolf's obsessive interest in the occult, Dee probably assumed he was in the grip of an immoral compulsion or addiction. By broaching the matter so boldly, Dee hoped to elicit a confession, which he could later use to control the emperor and thereby integrate him into Dee's plan to bring revolution to Prague. Dee was not unlike C.G. Jung, who used the same sort of techniques to control Edith Rockefeller McCormick and her considerable fortune. Jung was well versed in the alchemical tradition Dee represented. Like Jung, Dee sought the philosopher's stone as something that could not only transform base metals into gold, but which could also bring about psychological transformations, which could have significant political ramifications, especially when they occurred in the powerful. Compared to the ability to dominate the mind of the emperor, changing lead into gold must have seemed insignificant. Dee claimed he had been "enjoined by the angel Uriel to tell the Emperor that he possesses the secret of transmutation"[220] to bring him under his control and bring revolutionary change. "A learned and renowned Englishman whose name was Doctor De," wrote the Lutheran Budovec, "came to Prague to see the Emperor Rudolf II and was at first well-received by him; he predicted that a miraculous reformation would presently come about in the Christian world and would prove the ruin not only of the city of Constantinople but of Rome also. *These predictions he did not cease to spread among the populace.*"[221]

Dee hoped the audience would be the first of many. While waiting for a sequel that never materialized, he and Kelley circulated in occult circles in Prague. If Kelley was having his effect on Prague, the opposite was also true: Prague was having its effect on Kelley. The Jesuits showed an interest in him; he showed an interest in them and the renewed Tridentine Catholicism they were preaching. It was a brand of Catholicism kept out of England by draconian laws for good reason: Under the influence of the Jesuits, Kelley showed signs he might return to the faith of his fathers. In Prague, Kelley showed the Jesuits the accounts of his "actions" with Dee. This was reckless, as Dee insisted, but Kelley persisted. In April 1585, Kelley sought out a Jesuit for confession and received absolution for "the crimes and grave errors of his entire antecedent life."[222] This, however, did not keep Kelley from trafficking in spirits, who soon dragged him into dubious theological territory as a prelude to moral fall. The angel Uriel appeared and praised Luther and Calvin, saying with angelic ambiguity that they had their "reward." Whatever their reward was, the political showdown between England and Spain intensified into open war when Robert Dudley, the Earl of Leicester, persuaded Elizabeth and the Privy Council, to take a hard line against Philip and allow Dudley to lead an expeditionary force to attack the Spanish Netherlands in late 1585.

XVI

It turns out that 1584 wasn't the year of the fiery Trigon after all. As Dee and Kelley dawdled with angels, Alexander Farnese at the head of the Spanish army took one city after another and paralysis gripped the leadership of the revolution. The fall of Dunkirk, Eindhoven, Nieupoort, and Audenhove in 1583 was followed by the fall of Ypres, Bruges, and Dendermond in the first half of 1584. Then the revolutionaries lost their leader too. On July 10, 1584, a disgruntled petitioner shot William of Orange to death as he left his dining room. In September, when Dee had his audience with Rudolf, the city of Ghent surrendered to the Duke of Parma. Ghent was the largest Calvinist stronghold outside of Holland. If Farnese could could then march on his enemies from the west, beginning with Nijmegen, where the absence of breakable dikes and floodable polders favored the Spanish army. The tide of battle in the Netherlands had turned.

The tide had turned in other areas too. In April 1585, around the time that Brugge fell to Farnese, Sixtus V was elected pope. Unlike Pius V, the ascetic who prayed the rosary as Don Juan battled the Turks at Lepanto, Sixtus was a former swineherd who never stopped being the crafty peasant. After amassing huge amounts of gold, which he lavished on building projects in Rome, Sixtus then turned on the College of Cardinals, transforming them within five years from a group of unruly barons into an assembly of docile civil servants that would run the Church for the next four hundred years. Sixtus also declared war on the 20,000 or so bandits who inhabited the Papal States and brought them under control. He then embarked on the moral reformation of Rome. Adultery was declared a capital crime, punishable by hanging. Sodomy was made a capital crime, but those found guilty were burned alive instead. By the end of his papacy, Rome was reborn from medieval ruin into the baroque metropolis that it is even today.

Farnese's business was destruction not construction, but his plans were just as ambitious. He wanted to destroy the revolution in the Spanish Netherlands. The key was Antwerp. Located on the Scheldt River, Antwerp's access to the waters of the Atlantic and central Europe had made it the richest city in the Hapsburg Empire. That access made Antwerp militarily significant, too. With Antwerp in Calvinist hands, the Dutch could control whatever came down river. The sea beggars could supply Antwerp from the sea and England in their shallow draft boats, making the south vulnerable to attack. Farnese could not concentrate his troops to assault Deventer or Nijmegen if he had to leave some behind to defend against possible attacks from Antwerp. But, if Antwerp were in Spanish hands, the Dutch were effectively bottled up in the North. The Spaniards would control what came down the Scheldt. The sea beggars would have no base in the South. And Farnese could concentrate on taking Holland one city at a time.

The situation did not look promising. Antwerp had 100,000 inhabitants, a number ten times the size of the Spanish army. But, perhaps most imposing of all, there was the Scheldt River. At Antwerp, the Scheldt was half a mile wide and 60 feet deep at the center of its channel. Farnese could build fortresses on the banks, but, given the range and accuracy of artillery, he could not prevent sea beggars from provisioning the city. Any blockade from the banks alone would be futile, and viewed by the inhabitants with contempt.

Farnese chose another option. Instead of putting gun emplacements on either side of the river, Farnese did what was thought impossible. In one of the great engineering feats of his day, he built a bridge across the river. Once completed, nothing could get up the Scheldt from the sea, and the city was doomed; surrender was only a matter of time.

On August 27, 1585, Farnese, wearing gold filagreed armor fashioned in Milan, entered the city as conqueror. With diplomacy and charm, Farnese overcame the bitterness that accompanied defeat, granting generous terms and defusing the Dutch nationalism that was so detrimental to the Spanish cause under Alba. Philip was overjoyed. "Antwerp is ours," he shouted, "Antwerp is ours." It was the most significant good news since Lepanto. The Jews, though, began leaving, taking their fortunes and relocating to Amsterdam farther to the north. Paradoxically, Antwerp's fall was good news for Walsingham and the hawks on the Privy Council because it enabled them to get the queen and council to commit to war. Walsingham and Dudley convinced the council Holland would fall into Spanish hands unless England intervened. And so, at the end of 1585, Leicester led an expeditionary force to Holland to "drive the Prince of Parma from their land." England was now part of the anti-Catholic crusade and Elizabeth was its leader.

By the end of 1585, the thought that all Europe might fall to revolutionary forces was no longer tenable. The fall of Antwerp and the entry of England into the war meant a further merging of Jewish and "English" interests, which is to say the interests of the magnates who controlled the country and who avidly emulated the usurers. So in some sense, Capitalism, as we now know it, was a result of the fall of Antwerp. If Farnese had re-conquered Holland, and if England had not resisted the Counter Reformation so effectively, capitalism would not have come into being. Without capitalism, there would have been no communism, and the history of revolution would have looked much different than it does today.

The tide turned in England too, but in the other direction. Deprived of the Mass and a functioning Catholic Church for over 25 years, English Catholics became what the usurpers wanted them to be, docile Erastians who probably would not have supported Philip's troops if they had landed in 1588.

XVII

When Baines returned to England in late 1584 or early 1585 after confessing his role in the plot to destroy the Catholic seminary in Rheims, his prospects were not good. He was a blown agent of no further use to Walsingham as a spy. He could look forward to a return to life in the half-criminal world of con men and scam artists from which British intelligence drew its agents. What he found instead was an intelligence network flush with money and opportunity.

After returning to England in 1559, Walsingham came to Cecil's notice as "most subtle searcher of hidden secrets"[223] and soon rose to prominence as Elizabeth's Secretary of State and, along with Cecil and Leicester, one of the three most powerful men in government. One reason Walsingham proved so useful to Cecil was his contacts from his exile abroad. In Europe Walsingham "acquired his famous skill in foreign languages, and the ring of political contacts that would later form the basis of his foreign intelligence network."[224] There Walsingham made contact with the international network of Jewish merchants who became "the backbone of the English spy system."[225]

One of Walsingham's spies was Geronimo Pardo, a Sephardic Jew who passed crucial information to Elizabeth and Walsingham during 1587 about the preparations for the Armada. Bernardino de Mendoza revealed Pardo's role in Walsingham's spy ring in a letter to Philip II from Paris, where he settled after his expulsion from England in 1584. According to Mendoza, Pardo, a member of a Marrano family from Spain that was part of a "vast network all over the world," arrived in London in 1587 with a shipload of cargo and "brought on that occasion two packets of letters in cipher, giving a full account of the warlike preparations which were being made in Spain. After translating them, he carried them back to Secretary Walsingham, and, within two months, Pardo was on his way back to Lisbon."[226] Pardo returned to London, delivering dispatches to another Jewish spy, Doctor Hector Nunez, while at dinner. After receiving the packet, Nunez "rose in great haste, and went directly to Secretary Walsingham's house."[227] Pardo was arrested when he returned to Spain, but even from prison he tried to smuggle letters to Walsingham. Most of the Jews in Walsingham's spy ring pretended to be Catholics except when in London, where they pretended to be Protestants, taking "the bread and wine in the manner and form as do the heretics."[118]

Walsingham depended on Hector Nunez for foreign intelligence. His biography is a road map of the revolutionary movement in the 16th Century. Born in Evora, Portugal, he moved to Antwerp and from Antwerp to London, where he practiced medicine. He married the sister of the spy Bernard Luis, who lived in Antwerp in 1566, when the Iconoclast Rebellion broke out there. Nunez was extensively involved in trade, which allowed him to gather and transmit intelligence. In 1568 he was listed as a member of the Corporation of Italian Merchants residing in London, although his nationality was listed as Portuguese. In 1579 Nunez, under the alias Francisco Pessoa, was listed as a member of the secret synagogue in Antwerp, and through that organization his wife sent money to another Portuguese doctor, Rodrigo Lopez.

Lopez, because of his unhappy fate (he was hanged in 1593 for attempting to poison the queen) was the most famous of the Jewish spies in England. Lopez joined a Jewish family famous for spying when he married the daughter of Gonsalvo Anes, alias Benjamin George, alias Gonsalvo George, scion of the famous Anes family of spies expelled from Spain. Gonsalvo Anes made a fortune selling groceries from India and was knighted by the queen in 1568. He also collaborated with Nunez and Pardo in smuggling operations. After marrying into the Anes family, Rodrigo Lopez spawned a family of spies. Walsingham used Rodrigo's sons as spies to prepare Drake's raid on the Azores.

When Rodrigo Lopez arrived in England in 1560 from Antwerp, he claimed to be a Calvinist. He soon became physician to the Earl of Leicester; his duties included poisoning Leicester's enemies. Dr. Lopez reputedly had "more skill in intrigue than in physic, and ... more cunning in poisoning that in healing."[229] One contemporary report "strongly" confirms "the common belief that he was willing, for a consideration, "to use his knowledge of drugs for a deadly purpose."[230] In 1586, Lopez was appointed physician to the Queen, but his greed led him to become a double agent, which led him to turn on Marco Perez, who then turned on him, implicating him in a plot to poison the queen, for which he was hanged in 1594. Lopez was the cause of much popular anti-Semitism in England.

Alvaro Mendez, another member of Walsingham's Jewish spy ring, was the brother-in-law of Dr. Lopez and also related to Joseph Nasi. After making his fortune in India by farming the diamond mines of the King of Nasinga (and cheating him out of his diamonds), Mendez lived in various European cities. By 1580, he was in Paris, where he became, in collaboration with Nasi, a proponent of a homeland for the Jews, as well as the architect of the Anglo-Turkish alliance against Spain, which tied up Spanish forces that otherwise could have been used against England. In 1585, Elizabeth's ambassador to the Porte, Barton, reminded the sultan he had promised under oath to fight the Spanish, calling them "our common foes, all of them cursed idolaters."[231] Even so, Elizabeth turned to Lopez and Nunez to plead her cause with Philip II to ward off the invasion by a Spanish fleet after

Parma took Antwerp.

Walsingham, as leader of the Puritan faction, which included Leicester, Sidney, Dee and Spenser, consistently argued for war. Walsingham, whose daughter was married to Sydney, argued England could check Spanish power in the low countries by supporting William of Orange, giving the King of Spain "such a bone to pick as would take him 20 years at least, and break his teeth at last."[232] With war just over the horizon, Walsingham's spy agency looked to profit handsomely. In 1582, Walsingham's secret service had a budget of 750 pounds. By 1585, with war looming, his spy budget soared to 2000 pounds.

Baines now made contact with Christopher Marlowe, the Cambridge undergraduate, and recruited him for intelligence work. During spring 1585, Marlowe became "suddenly mobile,"[233] attending class infrequently. Just as suddenly, he began spending much more money than before on food and drink. Marlowe went from a penurious student to a man of the world, spending well beyond the means of the average student. In *Edward II*, Spenser explains an intelligencer "must be proud, bold, pleasant, resolute/ And now and then stab as occasion deserves,"[234] a passage which is especially ironic advice in the light of how Marlowe died.

Corrupted by money and the prospect of travel, excitement, and intrigue, Marlowe soon accepted that his new job involved "much unfaithful dealing towards people with whom he consorted day by day at Cambridge, people whose violent disaffection he in some measure shared."[235] It is difficult to measure the allegiance of people who dedicate their lives to duplicity. Marlowe's job was most probably the ferreting out of Catholic sympathizers at the university. He thus had to pose as a Catholic, which he did so effectively that the university almost refused him a degree, so worried were they that he might "go to Rheims." Only when the government intervened, testifying that Marlowe was in service to the Queen, was his name cleared, and he was allowed to graduate. Nicholl tries to portray Marlowe as a skilled double agent with a foot in both camps ready to spring to whichever side looked to be the winner. In England, judging who might be winning was no easy matter. Mary had reimposed Catholicism and the Inquisition after Edward's Protestant reign. Now Elizabeth was undoing what Mary had done, but who could tell how long the wheel of fortune would hold her aloft?

The agents most likely to succeed in passing as Catholics were Catholics who had turned, but, as Dee noticed in Kelley's behavior in Prague, a Catholic who had been turned could turn back. It is tempting to view Marlowe as a character out of a novel by John le Carre or Graham Greene, which is often how Nicholl portrays him. But the stakes were different then. The battle was much more existential. The beliefs were closer to the existential core of the believer than in the Cold War contest between amoral players who believed in nothing but the will to power. "Is he a genuine conspirator or an agent provocateur? Is he a purveyor of information or disinformation? ... Often, the only workable answer is that he is both."[236] Or perhaps neither. Another possibility is that a young person lured into England's network of spies might experience revulsion and try to atone for past duplicity by saying what he really believed. Marlowe was, as his contemporaries noticed, fearless. The "wild young Catholic bound for Rheims" turned out to be a "faithful dealer for the government,"[237] but that doesn't mean he had to stay that way, especially after he became aware of what the government was doing.

Walsingham tried to get as many people as possible involved in plots to put Mary Queen of Scots on the throne so that he could entrap and destroy them, and ultimately her as well. There had been the Throckmorton and Ridolphi plots in the past, and there would be the Hesketh Plot in the future, but for 1585 there was the Babington Plot, which would prove fatal to the pretender in Scotland. During summer 1586, Walsingham lured Babington into approaching Mary, Queen of Scots, with a proposal for a rebellion when a Franco-Spanish force invaded the country.

On July 17, a letter in cipher documenting Mary's approval of the plot allegedly passed from Chartley to Babington in London. It passed into the hands of Walsingham, who deciphered it and resealed it, leading to the deaths of Babington and the Queen of Scots. The term alleged is advised here because the original letters have disappeared. Mary denied she wrote the letter. The ciphered versions were used as evidence at the trial. The Catholics never had any doubt: the affair was a plot to justify killing Mary and put an end to Catholic hopes of restoring England to the fold of the Church of Rome. The Jesuit Robert Southwell claimed the "chief plotters" were Walsingham, Leicester, and Cecil. "The matter of Babington was wholly of their plotting and forging, of purpose to make Catholics odious and to cut off the Queen of Scots."[238] Babington and his accomplices were "drawn blindfold to be the workers of their own overthrow."[239] The chief agent of the "chief plotters" was Robert Poley, who would figure in the death of Christopher Marlowe, as would Baines, in 1593. Poley, says Southwell, "was continually with Babington and Ballard. He heard mass, confessed and in all things feigned to be a Catholic."[240] Poley's *modus operandi* was one of Walsingham's favorite tactics. Poley was arrested as part of the plot and spent a few years in the tower, where he continued to work as a police informer, but none of the Catholics were fooled. While in prison Poley regularly had sex with the wife of an acquaintance and also, according to Southwell, "poisoned the Bishop of Armacan with a piece of cheese."[241] Poley was released from the tower in autumn 1588. Within a month, he was back in government service.

By the end of 1586, Leicester's expedition to the Netherlands had failed. The failure combined with the gruesome executions following the Babington Plot to cast a pall over England. England had become a nation of spies and pirates. Philip learned of Sir Francis Drake's terrorist attacks along the coast of Spain and Portugal, in which unarmed villages were burnt to the ground and their inhabitants put to the sword. A consistent picture of life in the new England was emerging. Freedom was a subterfuge to enslave the Catholic masses. Emancipation from Catholic rule brought the Elizabethan Police State to power. England was a country of professional informers, not unlike the Stasi Police State in East Germany, except Elizabeth offered her subjects capitalist incentives, conferring on them one-third of the goods of the person they denounced. Purified religion meant the growth of the monster state, Leviathan, which demanded undiluted allegiance, and repaid its subjects by reducing the majority to poverty unknown in medieval Europe. Small farmers were kicked off their lands so that magnates could make fortunes there raising sheep. The purgatory societies, the guilds, the monasteries, the hospitals, the entire achievement of the Church in providing social welfare in England, was dismantled and put to work increasing the wealth of insatiably greedy magnates. The poor were then punished by laws declaring them vagrants and debtors and by the emergence of a philosophy of greed that blamed the victims of the looting for their misery by attributing their poverty to character flaws.

XVIII

Throughout spring 1586, the evidence mounted among Catholics in Prague that Kelley and Dee were English spies. In March 1586 Dee and Kelley met with Germanicus Malaspina, the new nuncio. Kelley spoke imprudently about reforming the Catholic Church. Malaspina said nothing, but Dee found out later that Kelley's words had filled the nuncio with "inward fury."[242] Kelley just as imprudently told the nuncio's priests he and Dee had written down "copious volumes"[243] of angelic revelations. When a priest demanded to see the volumes so he could show them to the nuncio, Kelly refused, saying they were private. Fillipo Sega, Malaspina's successor, felt the same way about Dee, claiming that they were the "authors of a new superstition, if not heresy,"[244] and that they were in Prague to infiltrate the emperor's court. Meanwhile, as if to confirm the suspicions of the Catholics, Dee and Kelly moved into a grand palace, known as the Faust House, even though they had no visible mans of support with which they could pay for such a step up in housing.

On May 6, Dee left Prague for Leipzig, where he hoped to meet his servant Edmund Hilton, a courier between Dee and Walsingham. Upon learning Hilton was not expected for 16 days, Dee left the letter he intended to give to Hilton with his host instead. The letter was addressed to Walsingham; in it Dee told Elizabeth's spymaster "That which England suspected was also here."[245]

By May 24, Dee was back in Prague, where he learned the nuncio had submitted a dossier to the emperor accusing Dee of necromancy and "other prohibited arts."[246] Dee appealed to the emperor on May 28, but the damage had been done. On June 29, one of the Emperor's clerks arrived at Dee's door notifying him that he and Kelley and their families had been banished from the empire. They had six days to get out of town.

With appeal impossible, Dee and Kelley headed toward the German border, but within two weeks they were back in Bohemia, where they took shelter at the ancestral estates of Vilem Rozmberk and began work in one of his laboratories.

Rozmberk was a Catholic of long standing. His forebears had battled Zizka in vain. Vilem held the crown at Rudolf's coronation in 1575, and he was a member of the Order of the Golden Fleece, the Hapsburgs' highest chivalric honor. But Rozmberk had a problem. He had no heir, and if he didn't get one soon, his death would mark the end of one of the noblest families in Bohemia. This probably explains his direct violation of the Emperor's edict by inviting Dee and Kelley to join him at Trebon. Rozmberk was no stranger to occult philosophy and the art of transmutation, another word for alchemy. The murals on the walls of his castle were covered with astrological, alchemical, and biblical symbols, all interwoven promiscuously. Fertility, next to transmuting lead into gold and changing the dead to the living, was a main concern of transformation. The houses in the town were covered with occult symbols; the colors of the tower overlooking the town were said to have alchemical significance too. Rozmberk had six laboratories, and the one at Trebon was placed at the disposal of Dee and Kelly.

The first transformation was in the state of Dee and Kelley's finances. The men were suddenly flush with money, which they lavished on those around them. Francesco Pucci, an occult fellow traveler whom Dee and Kelley felt was a Catholic spy, was bought off with bags of gold. This liberality, more than their intelligence reports, caused their stock to soar in England. The English court buzzed with rumors Dee and Kelley had turned pewter dishes, flagons, and even bedpans into pure gold, and that they possessed a magic powder, one ounce of which could produce 272,330 ounces of gold. Intrigued, Cecil increased his efforts to lure them back to England, but the magician and his famulus had other issues to resolve.

In January 1587 Kelley returned from a trip to Prague, bearing a jewel-encrusted gold necklace worth 300 ducats that had formerly belonged to the Rozmberk family. Kelley presented the necklace to Dee's wife, with the remark "I commend me to Mrs. Dee a thousand times."[247] It wasn't the first time Kelley had shown an interest in Mrs. Dee. The sexual tension began as soon as Kelley entered Dee's service in 1582, but now it was more insistent. Soon even the angels were talking about sex. During an action on April 17, an angel told Dee: "All sins committed in me are forgiven. He who goes mad on my account, let him be wise. He who commits adultery because of me, let him be blessed for eternity and receive the heavenly prize."[248] The angel Madimi then appeared to Dee along with other angels, who soon departed. When Madimi was alone with Dee, she parted her cloak to reveal she was naked. After noting in his diary that she "showeth her shame,"[249] Dee records he ordered her to leave.

The angels wouldn't let the subject drop. They became strenuous moral antinomians determined to bring Dee and Kelley to their way of thinking, especially on matters venereal. "For all things are possible and permitted to the godly," the angels told Dee. "Nor are sexual organs more hateful to him than the faces of every mortal. Thus it will be: the illegitimate will be joined with the true son. And the east will be united with the west, and the south with the north."[250]

This sounded revolutionary, but hadn't Dee already predicted a revolution when he explicated the meaning of Jupiter's "copulation" with Saturn and the inauguration of the era of the fiery Trigon? As the Taborites had shown, political revolutions always entailed sexual liberation. Sexual liberation was an integral part of what happened at Muenster too. Why should Dee be shocked?

After a few more sessions, Dee understood what the angels were getting at. Dee and Kelley were to engage in the ultimate 1970s suburban lifestyle adventure: wifeswapping. When Dee, who hadn't entertained such thoughts before then, objected, the angel Madimi rebuked him for being insufficiently liberated. "Your own reason riseth up against my wisdom," Madimi told Dee. "Behold you are become free. Do that which most pleaseth you."[251]

Catholics assert that only fallen angels respond to conjurings, and they were only likely to respond if the conjurer put his immortal soul in jeopardy by committing a mortal sin to attract them. Eventually Dee came to the Catholic position, but not in the way the Catholics in Prague hoped he would. Like Faust, Dee "offered my soul as a pawn"[252] to gain knowledge that would lead to wealth and fame.

In her treatment of Dee, Frances Yates goes out of her way to support Dee's contention that he was a devout Reformed Christian Cabalist interested only in "white magic," which meant magic wrought only with the help of good angels. Dee, it should be remembered, was, in Yates' words, the characteristic philosopher of his age. He had created a new intellectual foundation for England, one that stood or fell on his contention that he was involved only in "white magic." The hopes that Dee and Elizabeth and her ministers shared of "some vast all-embracing reform through Hermetic Cabalist influence and particularly through the influence of Christian Cabala"[253] were based on the assumption Dee got his material from pure sources. The fact that the angels were proposing wife-swapping indicated this was not the case.

The same is true of Dee's literary progeny and their hopes for "pure imperial reform."[254] Spenser's *Faerie Queene* is "a great magical Renaissance poem, infused with the whitest of white magic ... haunted by a good magician and scientist, Merlin (a name sometimes used of Dee), and profoundly opposed to bad magicians and necromancers and bad religion."[255] Spenser got his idea of white magic for "pure imperial reform" straight from Dee, and dramatized it in his great poem, which portrays the Monas as Una and Elizabeth, the virgin queen, as Britomart, the agent who puts the white magic regime into effect. Yates rarely uses the term Counter Reformation. Any misgiving about the regime of white magic in England is dismissed as part of "the reaction against Renaissance magic," which derives from "the obsessive fear of dangerous spiritual forces, which swept over Europe, one of the manifestations of which was the witch craze."[256]

Spenser was not alone in insisting Dee was involved in white magic. In his pro-Dee *magnum opus*, *The Tempest*, Shakespeare's Prospero is a white magician, modeled on Dee. Prospero uses Agrippa's *De occulta philosophia* to "call on good spirits" (Agrippa mentions Ariel by name) to cause "a return to the magical world of the late Virgin Queen, her chastity and pure religion, now continuing and revived by the younger generation. Her philosopher, the white magician Doctor Dee, is defended in Prospero, the good and learned conjurer, who had managed to transport his valuable library to the island."[257]

Dee's involvement in white magic has political implications in *The Tempest*. Prospero is "the beneficent magus," who "uses his good magical science for utopian ends."[258] The fantasy of Prospero "firmly in control of his magical island through his white conjuring"[259] was to find its actual fulfillment in Walsingham's police state. Far from vindicating "the Dee science and the Dee conjuring" or allaying "the anxieties of the witch craze and establishes white Cabala as legitimate,"[260] Dee's involvement with the angels at Trebon confirmed the Counter Reformation's deepest suspicions.

According to Yates, Prospero is a white magician primarily because of "the emphasis on chastity in Prospero's advice to his daughter's lover."[261] Yates ignores the extremely inconvenient angelic pressure on Dee and Kelley that was the opposite of chastity. Madimi's call to wifeswapping destroys the whole edifice of "pure imperial reform" by revealing it is based on a demonic foundation.

Dee, it turns out, is much more like Dr. Faustus than Prospero. Dee's project for England was based on the fiction there was such a thing as white magic, that he was practicing it, and that the angels who responded to conjuring were good angels. The turn of events in Trebon disproved all that, and showed to anyone willing to see, that the project of a magical England, a "pure imperial reform," was diabolical. If Dee based his occult philosophy on the advice of demons, what else could it be? What other kind of spirit would propose wife-swapping? Good angels? Hardly.

One evening after dinner in spring 1587, Dee brought up the angelic invitation to "the common and indifferent using of matrimonial acts amongst any couple of us four."[262] The women were speechless. Dee retired to his study, where out of his distilling apparatus popped an 18-inch spirit named Ben, who prophesied the fall of Elizabeth and the invasion of England by "one of the houses of Austria made mighty by the King of Spain's death."[263] Later, Dee talked to his wife in private, insisting, "I see that there is no other remedy, but as hath been said of our cross-matching, so it must needs be done."[264] Jane finally agreed but only under certain conditions. After setting the modalities, she expressed the hope "though I give myself thus to be used, that God will turn me into a stone before he would suffer me, in my obedience, to receive any shame or inconvenience."[265] Two days later, Dee wrote up an agreement, presumably signed by all, which "acknowledge[d], that thy profound wisdom in this most new and strange doctrine (among Christians) propounded, commended and enjoined unto us four, is above human reason."[266]

On May 20, 1587, Madimi, the libidinous angel, appeared to Dee to learn if he was ready to consummate the agreement. Madimi told Dee "He that pawneth his soul for me loseth it not, and he that dieth for me, dieth to eternal life. For I will lead you into the way of knowledge and understanding; and judgment and wisdom shall be upon you, and shall be restored unto you, and you shall grow every day wise and mighty in me."[267] It sounded vaguely religious and vaguely reassuring as long as one didn't ponder the phrase, "he that dieth for me, dieth to eternal life" too closely. Dee must have been reassured: the entry in his diary the following day was "*Pactum Factum.*"[268] Forty weeks later, Jane Dee gave birth to a boy. He was christened Theodorus Trebonianus Dee to indicate the place of his conception, but with no indication of his paternity. In the meantime, we are told, that a "rift formed between the Kelleys and the Dees" during the intervening months.[269]

The idea that sexual transgression was the way to attain occult knowledge and mastery over nature thus entered the history of ideas. Nietzsche would express the idea in *The Birth of Tragedy.* Sigmund Freud would appropriate the idea from Nietzsche without attribution and make it the basis for the Oedipus Complex. Percy Bysshe Shelley, who may have read Meric Casaubon's edition of Dee's diaries with Mary Godwin, put the idea into practice when he, Mary, her half-sister, and Byron engaged in the "League of Incest" on the shores of Lake Geneva in Switzerland during the stormy summer of 1817. At the hands of Jung and Freud it would become part of the technology of control they developed from the alchemical tradition. Dee's pact put to rest any idea that good was going to come from his "white" magic. Although no one else knew about the pact then, a reaction against Dee and everything he and his magic stood for began to build at about the time his wife-swapping pact with the angels was fulfilled. The angels were proving more and more unreliable, and Dee's fortunes began to suffer the more he listened to them.

XIX

On January 29, 1587 the English suffered a serious setback when Sir William Stanley handed Deventer over to the Prince of Parma. The surrender was a huge blow to English hopes in the Netherlands. Stanley, whose name became synonymous in England with treachery, added insult to injury by placing one-third of his 900 men in the service of the Spaniards. The English denounced Stanley in a pamphlet entitled *A Short Admonition Upon the Detestable Treason*, but Dr. Allen and the Jesuits praised him.

When everything goes wrong, people look for a scapegoat, and the English found that scapegoat in John Dee. At the beginning the reaction was not so much against Dee as against magic, particularly as practiced by witches. In 1587 the *Faust Buch* appeared in Germany as a continental expression of the revulsion against magic and the occult. The witch burnings were another manifestation, as was the manual of the Catholic inquisitors, the *Malleus Malificarum,* or *Hammer of Witches*. In the same year, the King of Scotland attacked witches and witchcraft with publication of his *Daemonlogie*. James, England's future king, condemned those who used conjurations to raise spirits as belonging to "the Divel's school," making no distinction between white magic and black.

During summer 1587, Marlowe was denounced from the pulpit of St. Mary's by the university preacher at Cambridge for "spying on behalf of the seminaries of Rheims and Rome."[270] This denunciation elicited the government's endorsement of Marlowe as its agent. When the Privy Council issued a statement "it was not Her Majesty's pleasure that anyone employed, as he had been in matters touching the benefit of his country, should be defamed by those that are ignorant of th'affairs he went about,"[271] Marlowe was free to graduate and move on to other things. As of that moment in time, Marlowe seemed to be a Catholic but was really a government agent.

Marlowe was also involved with magic through the Northumberland circle. Through them Marlowe probably came in contact with Dee's ideas. Dee had contact with the group through Hariot, who is mentioned frequently in Dee's diaries. Through Northumberland, known as the Wizard Earl, Marlowe came in contact with Raleigh. Northumberland was suspected of being a crypto-Catholic, plotting political revenge for his father's death, and it was probably Marlowe's job to find out where his sympathies lay or, worse, involve him in a plot like that which ensnared his father. Catholic cells were an obsessive object of government surveillance and infiltration; judging from the Council's certificate, Marlowe was one of its agents in the summer of 1587.

A spy could insinuate himself into a household like Northumberland's as a poet. And it was ost certainly as a poet that Marlowe insinuated himself into the retinue of another patron with Catholic sympathies, Lord Strange, whose group of players had as their writers two of the greatest dramatic poets of the English language. Strange died later under strange circumstances, either witchcraft or poisoning, but during the late '80s and early '90s he was the vehicle for Marlowe's emergence as a playwright. Lord Strange was "wittingly or otherwise, a magnet for Catholic conspiracy."[272] Marlowe was known as "a young malcontent with fashionable papist sympathies."[273] As such, he was the ideal agent for spying on Catholics or turning them as he had been turned. But was Marlowe still a Catholic? Baines, the Catholic traitor lately returned when exposed as a spy at Rheims, quoted Marlowe as saying "all Protestants are hypocritical asses."[274] He also claims Marlowe said "That if there be any God or any good religion, then it is to be found in the Papists, because the service of God is performed with more ceremonies, as elevation of the Mass, organs, singing men, shaven crowns, etc."[275] Even if he was a turned Catholic, Marlowe was still a Catholic, and he might be expected to revert to earlier beliefs under the pressure of disillusionment or revulsion.

All this speculation would be pointless were it not for the evidence of his writings. Beginning in 1587 with *Tamburlaine*, Marlowe took the literary world by storm. Before his death six years later, he produced works of significant literary merit, but, more significant for our purposes, he produced a sustained critique of what England had become under the tutelage of John Dee. More important still, Marlowe's works were hugely popular and whipped up animosity against the failing project of "pure imperial reform" initiated by Dee and promoted by Leicester, Walsingham, Sydney, Spenser and the rest of the Puritan faction. In *Tamburlaine*, Marlowe portrayed an empire in which Christianity and morality had disappeared in favor of raw political will and expressed misgivings about a British empire of the sort proposed by Dee. The moral of the play is: power without Christianity must of necessity lead to tyranny. If the English abandoned the Church, they would end up at the mercy of some Asiatic despot, no matter where the despot was actually born.

One year later, Marlowe wrote *The Tragedy of Dr. Faustus*. The German *Faust Buch* made clear a year earlier that there was an actual historical prototype named Faust who lived in Heidelberg, but Marlowe took his model from someone closer to home. Robert Greene describes Marlowe as "Blaspheming with the priest of the sun,"[276] in other words, a follower of Giordano Bruno, when the opposite is the case. Marlowe's Dr. Faustus is a sustained attack on Bruno, as well as Paracelsus and Agrippa, his predecessors. Dr. Faustus is an even more sustained attack on John Dee, the quintessential English magus of his age. It is also a veiled attack on the legacy of Protestantism. Wagner, Faust's assistant, talks like a Puritan. Faustus studied at Wittenberg, where Luther taught Thomas Muentzer, the leader of the Peasant Revolt. Study at Wittenberg left Faustus "swoll'n with cunning of a self-conceit."[277]

> Philosophy is odious and obscure
> Both law and physic are for petty wits;
> Divinity is basest of the three,
> Unpleasant, harsh, contemptible and vile.[278]

Thinking he has mastered all the earthly sciences have to offer, Faustus turns to magic and finds "these metaphysics of magicians/And necromantic works are heavenly."[279] Marlowe is, however, of another opinion. Far from being heavenly, magic is from hell and leads inexorably to ruin: 'Tis magic, magic that hath ravished me,"[280] Faustus says, without understanding where magic is going to lead him. Faust wants to be "as cunning as Agrippa was/Whose shadows made all Europe honor him."[281] In this Faustus is like Agrippa's mentor Reuchlin and the other rejecters of late Scholasticism who were seduced by the mumbo jumbo of Cabala not for the truth it explained but for the power it dangled before their disordered appetites. The temptation is like the one that seduced Eve—to become like God—but the manifestations of that power are all mundane. Sex and power, "are those that Faustus most desires."[282]

> O, what a world of profit and delight,

Of power, of honour, of omnipotence
Is promised to the studious artisan!
All things that move between the quiet poles
Shall be at my command....
A sound magician is a mighty god
Here, Faustus, try thy brains to gain a deity.[283]

Faust's magic has a political purpose. Like Dee he can promise to put the new occult philosophy to military use by driving the Duke of Parma from the Netherlands

Shall I make spirits fetch me what I please
Resolve me of all ambiguities.
Perform what desperate enterprise I will?
I'll have them fly to India for gold,
And chase the prince of Parma from our land,
And reign sole king of all our provinces;
Yea, stranger engines for the brunt of war
Than was the fiery keel at Antwerp's bridge
I'll make my servile spirits to invent.[284]

In a note, Marlowe adds a gloss on what Faust meant: "I will have my obedient servants devise even more ingenious instruments of violent warfare than the famous fireship used in Antwerp, 1585, by the Netherlanders against a bridge built by the Duke of Parma."[285]

Dr. Faustus contains a parody of Dee's scheme to use Cabala to find buried treasure.

The spirits tell me they can dry the sea
And fetch the treasure of all foreign wrecks-
Ay, all the wealth that our forefathers hid
Within the massy entrails of the earth.[286]

Cabala or "Jehovah's name/Forward and backward anagrammatized" makes these wonders possible:

Faustus, begin thy incantations
And try if devils will obey thy hest,
Seeing thou hast prayed and sacrificed to them.
Within this circle is Jehovah's name,
Forward and backward anagrammatized
And characters of signs and erring stars,
By which the spirits are enforced to rise[287]

In mentioning the Cabala that "anagrammatized" Jehovah's name, Marlowe implicates the Jews. Mephistopheles confirms the connection, telling Faustus "the shortest cut for conjuring/Is stoutly to abjure the Trinity."[288]

I am a servant to great Lucifer
And may not follow thee without his leave.
No more than he commands must we perform.

For when we hear one rack the name of God,
Abjure the Scriptures and his Saviour Christ,
We fly in hope to get his glorious soul
Nor will we come unless he uses such means
Whereby he is in danger to be damned.
Therefore, the shortest cut for conjuring
Is stoutly to abjure the Trinity
And pray devoutly to the prince of hell.[289]

Throughout *Dr. Faustus*, the occult philosophy is consistently associated with Puritanism. There is a sense of regret at all Protestantism has brought into the world. Magic is only the latest manifestation of what began at Wittenberg, and Faustus at the end of the play wishes he had never been there:

O, would I had never seen Wittenberg, never read book! And what wonders I have done, all Germany can witness, yea, all the world, for which Faustus hath lost both Germany and the world, yea, heaven itself—heaven, the seat of God, the throne of the blessed, the kingdom of joy—and must remain in hell for ever. Hell, ah, hell forever.[290]

If we substitute Dee for Faustus and England for Germany, we get some sense of how upsetting this play must have been to Leicester and Walsingham and the rest of the Puritans. Marlowe is saying appetite is the common denominator shared by reformed religion (as manifest in *Sola Scriptura* and magic) and "pure imperial reform." Just as Tamburlaine worships power, Dee and his Puritan admirers worship appetite:

The god thou servest is thine own appetite,
Wherein is fixed the love of Beelzebub.
To him I'll build an altar and a church,
And offer lukewarm blood of new-born babes.[291]

If Walsingham was upset at Bruno for "weakening of Protestant resolve for the anti-Catholic crusade at just the time when the Queen had at last consented to the military option,"[292] imagine how he must have felt about Marlowe's plays, which were much more demoralizing for a nation at war to defend Dee's battered construct of England as the land of faeries. Nicholl concludes, "Marlowe's involvement in 'magick,' like his involvement in Catholicism, has this double edge,"[293] but the opposite was the case. Marlowe was as courageous (or as reckless) as Nashe said he was. In *Tamburlaine* and *Faustus*, he launched a public attack against very powerful enemies, and he would end up paying the ultimate price for the freedom of his speech. Frances Yates is more perceptive than Nicholl because she sees that Dee was Marlowe's target when he wrote *Dr. Faustus*. "Audiences," she writes, "would inevitably have recognized Faustus as an unfavorable reference to Dee."[294] She speculates that Marlowe, "in his capacity as a political agent," must "have known something about Dee's" trip to Prague. "Puritan Christian Cabalists might therefore have felt threatened by Doctor Faustus."[295] These "Puritan

Christian Cabalists" included some of the most powerful and ruthless men in England, but that is unmentioned by Yates, who sees no connection between their animus and Marlowe's death. That connection, however, cannot be ignored. Marlowe was proposing a political agenda "entirely opposed" to the "outlook which we associate with the Elizabethan age, the philosophy of Spenser, which looked to Queen Elizabeth I as the Protestant saviour of Europe."[296] Marlowe's *Doctor Faustus*, "with its obvious allusion to Dee as a conjurer, tended to undermine the Elizabethan Renaissance"[297] by exposing its roots in Cabala. Tamburlaine is Saturnine, the planetary influence associated with the Jews. He wears an "emperiall crowne,"[298] and his empire is the Jewish fantasy of heaven on earth:

> Until we reach the ripest fruit of all
> That perfect blisse and sole felicities,
> The sweet fruition of an earthly crowne[299]

Tamburlaine, Yates notes, was "published at about the time of John Dee's return to England." It is a sustained attack on "the imperial idea" proposed by Dee; it clearly does not belong to the world of Dee's "British Empire." "Marlowe's frenzied emphasis on imperial cruelty and tyranny," Yates concludes, "may even have been intended to be dangerously subversive."[300]

XX

When, on February 18, 1587 Mary, Queen of Scots, was beheaded as a result of the Babington plot, a wave of revulsion swept Europe. A clamor arose against the criminal regime in England demanding retribution. It wasn't quite regicide, but it was close enough, and a sign that the world had changed beyond recognition. Regicide proper would take place in England less than a century later, and it was the infallible sign that revolution had taken over a country.

Philip heard the clamor. After years of provocations, each of which taken individually was an act of war, the English showed no sign of relenting in their campaign against Spain. They had escalated the conflict to the point of open war. Elizabeth had condoned a policy of piracy against Spanish shipping. Drake's raids were the tip of the iceberg. In 1585 Elizabeth's favorite, Leicester, led an army of 6,000 men into the Spanish Netherlands, whereupon the States-General made him governor of Holland and Zeeland. Drake renewed his predations on the Spanish Main. Exasperated at English perfidy and appalled at their treatment of Mary, Philip ordered his admirals to prepare an invasion of England less than six weeks after her death. Perhaps it was the haste, or perhaps anger, that clouded his mind, but the plan was flawed from the beginning. Santa Cruz was to link up with Parma's army in the Netherlands and then convey that army across the channel to England where a Catholic uprising would meet them to sweep the heretics from power. William Allen, lobbying for the plan in Rome, assured Philip and the pope of the loyalty of English Catholics, but Farnese was skeptical and doubted English Catholics would rally to foreign invaders. Beyond that, there was the logistical problem of how to load the ships. The Spaniards lacked a deep water port, and Parma could not get his men out to the Spanish ships at anchor because the Sea Beggars still controlled the sea approaches to cities like Antwerp. Farnese wanted time to finish off the Calvinists in Holland. Then with a port like Amsterdam at its disposal, the Spanish fleet could transport Parma's army to England without difficulty.

The armada was launched without resolution of those issues. Kept well appraised of the Spanish preparations by Walsingham's Jewish spies, Drake launched weeks of preemptive strikes along the Portuguese coast, terrorizing towns and destroying irreplaceable stores, even sailing into the harbor at Cadiz and burning 18 warships intended for the armada. Drake's predations caused serious delay.

In anticipation of the invasion, Pope Sixtus V made William Allen cardinal of England so he could assume immediate administrative responsibility for the church when Philip's troops landed. On the same day, Sixtus wrote a letter in his own hand to Philip, stating in no uncertain terms that delay would be fatal. Two days after the pope wrote his letter the Dutch town of Sluis fell into Spanish hands. One month later, in September 1587, Leicester returned to England with his tail between his legs. Had the armada sailed then, the outcome might have been different. But the Armada did not sail then. Weakened by Drake's raids, it wouldn't sail for nine months. By then the situation had changed dramatically.

In addition to that, issues arose over which no one had control but which favored the English cause nonetheless. The weather was in this regard the most significant of all of those unpredictable factors. When the armada finally sailed in May 1588, it was immediately blown back into Lisbon harbor by a howling gale, and there it waited for almost three weeks for the storm to blow over. When the armada finally made contact with the English fleet, the terms of engagement had changed since Spain's last major naval battle, the Battle of Lepanto. At Lepanto, a naval battled entailed two ships closing and then grappling as soldiers boarded the enemy ship and fought other soldiers on its decks. Drake, who had been plundering Spanish galleons in the new world, understood his enemy better than it understood him. Drake's strategy was to prevent grappling and boarding. British ships were faster and lower in the water. Their cannons had longer range. Drake used their technical superiority to evade the slower Spanish ships while inflicting damage from a distance.

After the Spanish exhausted their ammunition on their elusive foe, they had no place to land to replenish their stores, much less link up with Farnese's army and convey it to England. Farnese was helplessly landlocked in Antwerp, a prisoner of the Dutch Sea Beggars when the weather intervened again; the Armada was blown north, forced to circumnavigate Scotland and Ireland, losing one half of its ships and two thirds of its men. Philip took the loss philosophically, blaming it on the weather and other forces beyond his control. Philip's imprudent adventure, however, would have serious consequences. Parma was never able to regain the initiative and reconquer Holland and Zeeland; eventually Spain reconciled itself to stalemate and the loss of the northern provinces to the Calvinists.

The victory produced a different stalemate in England. The regime of Elizabeth and Cecil had been spared, but it had nothing to show for its efforts. The great Protestant crusade to claim Europe had failed; the aging queen, with no prospect of producing an heir, had to deal with the failure and face a disillusioned population angry at the price they had to pay for it. She was increasingly alone, as the ministers she relied on died. Cecil would hang on until 1598, but her favorite Leicester died within a year of the victory over the armada. Walsingham died in 1590, and Sir Christopher Hatton two years after that. Meanwhile, Poland, most of Germany, half of the Netherlands, and all of France (after the defeat of the Huguenots) had been re-integrated into the Catholic fold, and the Turks (England's unacknowledged ally against Spain) had been thwarted in their effort to dominate the Mediterranean. The youthful vision of the Virgin Queen spreading "pure imperial reform" throughout Europe was gone.

XXI

It was at precisely this inauspicious moment that John Dee, the architect of the now failed "pure imperial reform" decided to return to England. Dee had been the victim of a strange alchemical transformation. He had become the apprentice, and Kelley had become the sorcerer. Kelley was granted Bohemian citizenship, and would be knighted (or recognized as already belonging to the Irish nobility) by the emperor, who was continually trying to lure "Eduardus" from Rozmberk to Prague to supervise a great alchemical work. Rudolf promised not to detain Kelley any longer than absolutely necessary,[301] but the experiment needed an expert who could produce "*mercurius solis*" to bring it to successful completion.[302] Kelley's rise to fame in Bohemia was so dramatic that the only suitable comparison is Dee's fall into obscurity in England.

Dee arrived at his home in Mortlake in December 1589 to discover that his library had been plundered. Over 500 volumes had been stolen, four of which were worth almost 600 pounds. Dee would have been justified to take the sacking of his library as symbolic of the wreck of his life's work. The conjunction of Jupiter and Saturn leading to the era of the fiery Trigon had not led to occult reform and political revolution in Europe. The opposite had happened, and it looked as if the same transformations were taking place in Dee's career too. The wreck of Dee's library was a fitting symbol of the wreck of his career as magus and the wreck of his hopes for occult reform under Elizabeth's inspired leadership.

On April 6, 1590, Walsingham died of what sounds like cancer of the testicles (a "fleshy growth within the membrane [tunicas] of the testicles). The "fleshy growth" evidently caused an occlusion of the urethra, which in turn caused his urine to come forth "at his mouth and nose, with so odious a stench that none could endure to come near him."[303] Dee sought favor with his successor, Robert

Cecil, son of Burleigh, who sent Dee a haunch of venison, but little else, and no money or work.

Publication of the first three books of Edmund Spenser's *Faerie Queene* was almost as inauspicious as Dee's arrival from the continent a few months before. The timing of a tribute to the Virgin Queen as leader of "pure imperial reform" in a crusade on the continent could not have been worse. Spenser had conceived his great work ten years earlier when Dee and his vision of occult British imperialism were enjoying intellectual acclaim and government patronage. Spenser was then in contact with two of Dee's pupils, Philip Sydney and Edward Dyer, and the contact with this circle and its vision of an occult Arthurian "British Israel" inspired him. Dee was "the true philosopher of the Elizabethan age," and Spenser hoped to use Elizabeth, in the "prophetic moment" after the Armada victory, "as the symbol of the new religion, transcending both Catholic and Protestant in some far-reaching revelation, and transmitting a universal Messianic message."[304] Since the Puritans were Judaizers, Spenser tried to use Cabala, via Dee, to launch a new movement of courtly Puritanism, with the English in the role of God's chosen people. Milton, a dedicated student of Spenser, would take up that vision during Cromwell's republic. Dee was a Cabalist and a British Imperialist and all of this found its way into Spenser's poem, which arrived when everyone, disillusioned by the failures of the military and religious adventures that vision had inspired, no longer believed in it. A reaction was setting in.

Two years after publication of *The Faerie Queene*, Raleigh introduced Spenser at court, but the introduction gained him nothing. With Leicester and Sydney gone, there was no one to second Spenser's efforts and so his hymn to Elizabethan imperialism fell on deaf ears. Spenser withdrew to "semi-banishment" in Ireland and, after his return to London in 1599, died in poverty. Yates attributes the *Faerie Queene*'s chilly reception to the poem's "expansionist vision" for Elizabethan England that "had become too dangerously provocative by the time it was published."[305] She could have just have said occult philosophy was the god that failed. At the very moment Spenser published his hymn of praise to Elizabeth as faerie queene, "the continental reaction," otherwise known as the Counter Reformation, "was in full swing."[306] Dee and now Spenser were dangerously exposed as "adherents of the occult philosophy, which the Catholic reaction, powerfully aided by the Jesuits, was endeavoring to stamp out."[307] If Dee and Spenser thought the antipathy of the Jesuits would help them in England, they were wrong; the reaction against occult imperialism was beginning there too as a result of Marlowe's plays.

By 1590 Marlowe had become a leader in the attack on judaizing cabalistic Puritanism. In *The Jew of Malta*, he responded to the occult judaizing imperialist philosophy of Dee that had provided the intellectual underpinning for Spenser's *Faerie Queene*. Marlowe had already expressed his misgivings about British imperialism and magic in *Tamburlaine* and *Dr. Faustus*. Now he was expressing misgivings about the group that united those two enterprises, the Jews. *The Jew of*

Maltu was also an attack on Dee, because it was Dee who had introduced Cabala into English thought.

The main character in *The Jew of Malta* is the merchant Barabas. The name is significant. Barabbas is the Zealot terrorist revolutionary the Jews chose over Jesus, when Pilate offered to set Jesus free. Barabas is, then, the Jewish revolutionary, hoping to create heaven on earth through gold, conniving, and subversion. At the beginning of *The Jew of Malta*, Barabas is surrounded by heaps of gold in his counting house, boasting about the superiority of Judaism to Christianity because of the riches that accrue from it.

> Thus trolls our fortune in by land and sea,
> And thus we are on every side enriched.
> These are the blessings promised to the Jews,
> And herein was old Abram's happiness.
> What more may heaven do for earthly man
> Than thus to pour out plenty in their laps[308]

Barabas would rather be hated for his wealth than "pitied in a Christian poverty" because, "I can see no fruits in all their faith."[309] A Christian may live by his conscience, but "his conscience lives in beggary."[310] The Jews, on the other hand, "have scambled up/More wealth by far than those that brag of faith."[311] The Jew's wealth is proof to him of the falsity of Christianity.

During the play, the governor of Malta takes Barabas's house and gives it to nuns. Barabas then persuades his daughter to become a nun to recover the money in the house, but he also plans his revenge on the nuns by plotting to poison them. Sometimes," Barabas declaims, "I go about and poison wells."[312] Sometimes he spreads disease. Sometimes he plays the Christian against the Turk to the detriment of both. His twin motivations are love of money and hatred of Christians. As Nicholl pointed out, Barabas sounds a lot like Marlowe's fellow spy Baines, who plotted to poison a Catholic seminary in Rheims. Marlowe, who may or may not have been a Catholic, sounds like a disillusioned paleoconservative who now regrets helping the Jews and the Judiaizing Puritans drag his country into an unwinnable war in the low countries, for goals unrelated to the interests of the average Englishman. Barabas's wealth is associated with the low countries, especially Holland, which was becoming fabulously wealthy because of the Jews. England had thrown in its lot with the Dutch Calvinists, and now they, in collaboration with the Jews, were profiting at England's expense.

Barabbas knows much about poisons because he is a physician: "Being young, I studied physic, and began/To practice first upon the Italian."[313] In describing Barabas as a physician, Yates feels Marlowe is describing Dr. Rodrigo Lopez, the Virgin Queen's physician. She says "The anti-Semitism of the play must surely have been somewhat uncomfortable for the queen, who had employed and encouraged Lopez, the Jew (as she had earlier encouraged Dee, the conjurer)."[314] Like Marlowe, Lopez came to an unhappy end, both victims of the queen's displeasure. The conclusion is inescapable. An attack on the Jews was construed as a veiled attack on the Queen. Marlowe was pointing to the influence Judaizers like Dee and the Puritans exercised over her to the detriment of national interest. The Dee faction had cast a Cabalistic spell on her, as Lord Howard had claimed years earlier.

Marlowe's attack on the Jews and their adverse effect on England was worlds apart from the enchanted magical island Spenser proposed in the *Faerie Queene*. "Marlowe," according to Yates, "is modern; he belongs to the contemporary mood of rigidity and reaction which was sweeping Europe."[315] As such, his "chief target was the Fairy Queen, and all that that conception implied of white magic, imperial reform and Christian Cabala."[316] The moral of Marlowe's *Dr. Faustus* and *The Jew of Malta* is that "magick" derived from the Cabala of the Jews has "ravished" England, and that the Jew has used that magic to corrupt the country. In the end, everyone loses, Christian and Turk alike. The Jew has no loyalty; he plots the destruction of Christian and Turk, playing his enemies against each other:

> Thus, loving neither, will I live with both,
> Making a profit of my policy;
> And he from whom my most advantage comes
> Shall be my friend.
> This is the life we Jews are used to lead,
> And reason, too, for Christians do the like.[317]

At the end of the play, Barabas falls into a boiling caldron and, after calling vainly for help, bares his soul, taking revenge on his victims by explaining his infamy. Again everyone—meaning both Catholic and Protestant—loses when the Jew is allowed free rein in the island kingdom:

> And had I but escaped this stratagem
> I would have brought confusion on you all
> Damned Christian dog, and Turkish infidels![318]

After Barabas' death, Ferneze, whose name sounds suspiciously like that of the Prince of Parma, tells his Turkish counterpart Selim to "note the unhallowed deeds of Jews." "Monstrous treason" is "a Jew's courtesy."[319]

Yates claims Shakespeare's *Merchant of Venice* was written in reaction to Marlowe's *Jew of Malta* to ameliorate Marlowe's portrait of the Jew by showing that the Jew's unpleasant characteristics were the result of treatment at the hands of Christians. The argument is plausible, but the tide of history (and reaction) was running with Marlowe and not with apologists for the failed regime of occult Puritanism and its defenders. Shakespeare, Yates tells us, "could live with the Spenserian magic, as Marlowe's plays could not."[320] Audiences who listened to *The Merchant of Venice* or *Midsummer Night's Dream* were charmed by Shakespeare's ability to infuse new life into a failed vision, but that is more a tribute to Shakespeare's art than to the viability of Dee's failed political system. "The audiences at the *Jew of Malta*," though, "were inclined to become anti-Semitic mobs."[321] The reaction had arrived in England, and Marlowe knew how to exploit it: "Marlowe's

Doctor Faustus is seen as belonging to the reaction to the atmosphere of the witch crazes and the attacks on Agrippa. With the assault on occult philosophy *Faustus* was associated the anti-Semitism of *The Jew of Malta*."[322]

In *King Lear*, Shakespeare again attempts to elicit sympathy for John Dee and his failed vision. Shakespeare got the story of King Lear and his ungrateful daughters from Spenser's *Faerie Queene*, where, according to Yates, "it forms part of the "British Chronicle" which is the preparation in history for the appearance of Gloriana and her messianic role."[323] Shakespeare describes "an ancient British monarch treated with base ingratitude, haunted by false accusations of demonic possession."[324] His identity is clear. "There was a living survivor of the great days of the Spenserian dream whom this description would pretty exactly fit—John Dee."[325] Dee had fallen on hard times after being at the center of the Elizabethan age. After he had returned from the continent with his failed vision of a magic empire, Dee, like Lear,

> was banished from court and society, suffered total neglect and bitter poverty, and might well have felt himself to be the victim of base ingratitude. He who had given so much received no reward. He was moreover pursued by scares against him as a black magician and sorcerer, though he himself had never admitted this charge, proclaiming himself a Christian, as no doubt he was, a Christian Cabalist.[326]

Dee's tragedy, Shakespeare seems to say, is synonymous with the tragedy of the Elizabethan age. The hopeful vision of a world ruled by magic had faded into the reality of the Elizabethan police state, although Shakespeare was not going to risk his life by saying so. Shakespeare's *Tempest* was another attempt to revive the myth. Prospero is what Dee aspired to be: the benign tyrant using magic from Agrippa to rule the island kingdom. According to Yates, "Shakespeare's great creations—Hamlet, Lear, Prospero—are seen as belonging to the last stage of Renaissance occult philosophy, struggling in the throes of the reaction."[327]

Because his magic derived from the Cabala, Dee/Prospero's kingdom was naturally philosemitic. Because these literary movements, from Spenser's *Faerie Queene* to Milton's *Paradise Lost*, were "fundamentally Hebraic in character,"[328] they prepared the return of the Jews to England. Because Jews like Joseph Nasi and Alvaro Mendes actively collaborated with Cecil in waging common war on Spain in alliance with the Turks, Yates wonders why the Jews weren't allowed to return during Elizabeth's reign.

> Why were the Jews not received in Elizabethan England, as they were in the other main power which resisted their persecutors, Holland? Why, after the defeat of the Armada, was that victory not followed up by the reception of the Jews, resulting in strengthening of trade and economic power in that curious mingling of practical affairs with religious enthusiasm which was characteristic, both of the Puritan millennial and the Jewish messianic outlook? The project of the return of the Jews to England had to wait until Cromwellian times.[329]

Even though "Elizabethan England was a power which resisted the persecutors and the Elizabethan imperial reform included Christian Cabala as an ingredient of the Elizabeth cult, perhaps making possible for a patriotic English Jew an easy transition to the religion of his adopted country,"[330] Yates is unable to explain why the Jews remained excluded by an otherwise philosemitic regime.

The short answer to that question is: Christopher Marlowe. The longer answer involves his relationship with a public that was always skeptical of Dee's cabalistic magic, and, now that they were living under the consequences, had turned against it. After years of plague and a long draining war in the Netherlands, coupled with the threat of another Spanish invasion, followed by sham plots, savage executions, widespread unemployment and government-orchestrated inflation, the mood in England was ugly. Marlowe read the mood of the mob and provided it with a compelling object of hatred by giving them a sophisticated analysis of the occult judaizing philosophy at the heart of the Elizabethan regime. Because he was so skillful in whipping up the mob, Marlowe, the quondam government agent, became an object of government scrutiny and ultimately an object of government attack.

In January 1592 Marlowe was arrested for "coining" in Flushing, and then accused of intending to join the English regiment under Sir William Stanley. His accuser was Reginald Baines, who had plotted to poison the Catholic seminary in Rheims and who had recruited Marlowe into government service seven years earlier at Cambridge. Marlowe was deported to England on January 27, and not released until May 1592. If it was intended as a warning, the arrest went unheeded. Before long, Marlowe was entangled in other plots whose purpose was clear; as Baines articulated it: "I think all men in Christianity ought to endeavor that the mouth of so dangerous a member may be stopped."[331]

XXII

On May 5, 1593, Londoners awoke to find a long doggerel poem attacking the predatory tactics of Dutch merchants nailed to their church. What became known as the "Dutch Church Libel" showed how deep opposition to the war in Holland and the regime had become. The English were financing a war for foreign interests who were then allowed to settle in London and take trade away from the English. A palpable sense of outrage and injustice suffuses the poem, as the English author denounces the Dutch merchants:

> Cutthroat-like in selling, you undo
> Us all & with our store continually you feast
> Our poor artificers do starve and die.[332]

At another point, the author refers to the Dutch as acting like Jews:

> Your usury doth leave us all for dead,
> Your artifex & craftsman works our fate
> And like the Jews you eat us up as bread.[333]

The Dutchman, the author of the poem complained, is a "machiavellian merchant," expert in "counterfeiting religion." He is "infected with gold," and a predatory usurer "like the Jews." As Nicholl notes, the charges against the Dutch "closely echo Marlowe's *Jew of Malta*."[334] The connection between Marlowe and the Dutch Church Libel is confirmed by the author's assumed name "Tamburlaine," the name of Marlowe's hit play of a few years before. Since it is unlikely that Marlowe would use a pseudonym that implicated him, the poem was most likely written by an admirer or, more likely, someone who wanted to discredit Marlowe by claiming to be his follower. Nicholl feels the latter is the case; "the Dutch Church libel can be seen as the opening move in the smear campaign against Marlowe."[335]

That campaign continued when the playwright Thomas Kyd was arrested on May 11 as the author of the libel. When his lodging was searched, government agents happened to find a manuscript by Marlowe among Kyd's papers, which came to be known as the Arian tract. In addition to proclaiming Unitarian beliefs, the manuscript affirmed Jesus was a homosexual and "St. John the Evangelist was bedfellow to Christ and used him as the sinners of Sodoma."[336] The manuscript also affirmed that "all Protestants are hypocritical asses" and that Marlowe "persuades men to atheism, willing them not to be afeard of bugbears and hobgoblins ... almost into every company he cometh."[337]

After being tortured by Elizabeth's thugs, Kyd affirmed he had received the manuscript containing "vile heretical conceits denying the deity of Jesus Christ our Saviour"[338] from Marlowe. Taking up the drumbeat of government propaganda, Robert Greene urged Marlowe to turn away from "diabolical atheism" and "pestilent Machiavellian policy."[339] By now, the purpose of the campaign was clear: to incriminate Marlowe, who had become the most visible and effective critic of the failed imperial policies of the Elizabeth and Cecil regime. Nicholl speculates the real target was Sir Walter Raleigh, who had publicly attacked the Dutch and their stranglehold on the English economy. "The nature of the Dutchman," he said, 'is to fly to no man but for his profit."[340] Raleigh favored expelling the Dutch from England, and large segments of the mercantile community in London supported him. London mobs, sick of the war in the Netherlands and its ruinous cost, marched in the streets shouting "down with the Flemings and strangers."[341] Marlowe had become a pawn in the Earl of Essex's attempt to eliminate Raleigh as a serious rival.

On 18 May, the Privy Council issued a warrant for Marlowe's arrest; two days later he appeared before the council to defend himself. Without enough evidence to proceed, the council released him. Ten days later, on the evening of Wednesday May 30, 1593, Marlowe was murdered in Deptford, not in a tavern brawl as later reported, but at the house of Eleanor Bull, a relative of Lord Burghley, still the Queen's chief political advisor. Also in the room was Robert Poley, the man who pulled off the Babington Plot a few years earlier. Marlowe, the quondam government agent turned playwright, had become a dangerous opponent of the regime, and the regime had him murdered to stop the spread of public discontent their failed foreign policy was causing in England.

In his obituary, Thomas Nashe praised Marlowe for his courage, claiming

he was "no timorous servile flatterer of the commonwealth wherein he lived....
Princes he spared not." "[342] Nor, it turns out, did they spare him. Nashe was probably referring to the government's role in Marlowe's death when he wrote: "His life
he contemned in comparison of the liberty of speech."[343] Nashe condemned "Puritans,' who "spew forth the venom of your dull inventions. A toad swells with thick
troubled poison: you swell with poisonous perturbations. Your malice hath not a
clear dram of any inspired disposition."[344] Shakespeare was more circumspect. In
As You Like It, Touchstone refers obliquely to Marlowe's death as "a great reckoning in a small room." On Thursday 28 June, Nicholl writes, "just four weeks after
Marlowe was buried, the Queen issued a formal pardon. Ingram Frizer had killed
his man in self defense, and the case was therefore closed."[345]

XXIII

The deaths of its *dramatis personae* signaled the end of the age. William Cardinal Allen, the leader of the English Catholics who was supposed to sail home on
the Spanish Armada, died in October 1594. Thomas Stapleton, the great Catholic
intellectual, died in October 1598. If anyone's death signified the end of the age, it
was Philip II, the man who embodied the Counter Reformation even more than
the six popes who implemented the decrees of Trent. Philip died in September
1598. The only other person whose death could signify the end of the age was Elizabeth, and she died five years later. Her successor, James I of Scotland, was the author of *Daemonlogie*, which explicitly condemned Agrippa as a conjurer.

John Dee would live another five years until 1608, but he would find no favor
with the new Scottish king, who felt that Christian Cabala was just another term
for witchcraft. Marlowe would have probably found favor with the new king, but
Marlowe had been ten years dead when James ascended to the throne. With the
accession of James, the reaction against the occult that had been raging in Europe found a home in England. Shakespeare, ever attuned to who was in power,
gave full expression to this view in his homage to the Scottish king's aversion
to witchcraft, *Macbeth*. Witch burnings would find a home in New England, but
not so much in England itself, because the English Puritans had more important
concerns.

In 1609 Amsterdam succeeded Antwerp as the Jerusalem of the north when
Philip III signed a truce with the northern Calvinist provinces of the Netherlands,
thus recognizing *de facto* the Dutch Republic. In 1615 the States General of the
United Provinces allowed the Jews to practice their religion publicly. In 1619 the
city council of Amsterdam allowed the Jews to live according to their own law, and
they began occupying the area around the Joodenbreestraat, where Rembrandt
later immortalized their leading citizens in etchings and paintings. By 1650, there
were 400 Jewish families in Amsterdam, virtually all Portuguese. Before long they
were casting their eyes across the channel to England, where they hoped to find
their true home when revolutionaries came to power there.

Chapter Eleven

Menasseh ben Israel and the Failed Apocalypse

I n 1632, the year of Spinoza's birth, so many impoverished Ashkenazic Jews descended on Amsterdam that the local synagogue set up poor boxes to collect alms for them "to prevent the nuisance and uproar caused by the Ashkenazim who put their hands out to beg at the gates."[1] The Jews in Amsterdam were very conscious they were strangers in a strange land. They were overwhelmingly Sephardic; they retained Portuguese as the language of their official documents. They were on good behavior lest they offend the Dutch Calvinists. Their self-consciousness stemmed partially from insecurity. The newly arrived Sephardic Jews had so recently thrown off Catholicism that they were unsure how to act in a land that allowed them to live as Jews. As a result, Sephardic Judaism in Amsterdam maintained a distinctly Catholic caste for a long time. The Jews in Amsterdam talked about eternal salvation, which they were to achieve though observance of the Law of Moses, not through faith in Jesus Christ. They also erected cults around Jewish saints, particularly "Saint Esther,"[2] whose feast was celebrated during Purim.

Until 1603 the Amsterdam Sephardic Jews practiced their religion in secret. In 1608 the Jews formed their first synagogue; in 1615 the States General of the United Provinces allowed Jews to practice their religion publicly, and in 1619 Jews were allowed to live according to their law. By then, Amsterdam had two synagogues, the second being Congregation Neveh Shalom or Holy Peace Congregation.

In 1632, a portly 28-year-old raised as an orphan at the congregation's expense, hurried down the Joodenbreestraat, past the home of Rembrandt van Rijn, who would do his portrait a few years later, toward the harbor to meet the newly arrived ships. Amsterdam lies on the Amstel River in the vast delta of the Rhine at the end of the river's journey from the Alps to the North Sea. The Rhine flows more directly to Rotterdam, but Rotterdam then lacked a secure harbor at the lower end of a magnificent and protected salt-water lake known as the Zuyder Zee. The portly man hurrying to be at the quay when the gangplank came down and the passengers descended was one of the second synagogue's rabbis.

His name was Manoel Diaz Soeiro, at least that is what he was baptized in 1604 on the Madeira Islands, where his family of fugitives from the Inquisition was living. He retained that name for business dealings, but like so many Sephardic Jews who threw off the trappings of Catholicism on Protestant soil, Manoel took another name at his circumcision, the name by which he would be known to posterity, Menasseh ben Israel.

The portly young rabbi "of middle stature and inclining to fatness"[3] used both names when approaching newcomers disembarking ships newly landed in Amsterdam. Duarte Guterres Estoque disembarked that day in 1632, and Manoel Diaz Soeiro was there to greet him in Portuguese, giving his Portuguese name. The tenor of the conversation quickly changed when Soeiro revealed his new name, for in revealing his new name Menasseh revealed as well why he was there greeting Portuguese-looking strangers. "He was known ... in the said city in Hebrew as Menasseh ben Israel," Guterres testified seven years later to the Inquisition in Lisbon, "and he was a publick Rabbi and professor of the Law of Moses."[4] Menasseh ben Israel quickly got down to business. Assuming any Portuguese traveler arriving in Amsterdam must be a secret Jew and a fugitive from Catholicism, Menasseh offered to circumcize the new arrivals and to induct them into his synagogue. That many Portuguese travelers were not Jews becomes evident from the files of the Inquisition in Lisbon, which are full of outraged reports about the ambitious and importunate rabbi from Amsterdam.

Why they were scandalized can be gleaned from another incident. In August 1639, Felician Dourade, a Brazilian, told a story similar to Duarte's. Upon arrival in Amsterdam, Douarde was approached by the same rabbi, who told him, "with much feeling and passion," that the Jews expelled from Spain were still operating clandestinely there because "whatever" the Spanish crown "might do in Spain they would not prevent them from being Jews." "All of the New Christians in Spain," Rabbi Menasseh said, "were Christians by violence."[5] The rabbis and the Spanish anti-Semites were of one mind on this topic. No Jew ever sincerely became a Christian. As a result, Menasseh continued, "every year there went certain Jews from Holland to the capital of Madrid and to many other parts of the realm of Spain to circumcize the New Christians."[6] Menasseh's Jewish companion then restrained the garrulous rabbi: "Hereat the other Jew caught hold of his hand, intimating to him that he did ill to reveal this before the deponent, because he would return to Spain and recount it, and might do harm to the persons of his Nation."[7] The warning cooled Menasseh's garrulous ardor. "After this warning," Menasseh "treated the matter jokingly, saying that he had not meant it seriously."[8]

Menasseh comes across as garrulous and imprudent in Inquisition documents. His actions, though, were purposeful because "Almost every vessel which arrived from the Peninsula brought fresh supporters ... Sometimes even there were clerics who had been prominent in the Church, or even familiars of the Holy Office itself, whose reversion to Judaism cased great scandal in Catholic circles."[9]

The most prominent defector was Fray Vincente de Rocamora, spiritual advisor to the sister of Philip II, King of Spain. Fray Vincente was a Catholic priest who had earned a reputation for holiness until he threw off what Graetz calls "the mask of Catholicism"[10] and got circumcised. He then joined the Jewish community at Amsterdam as Isaac of Rocamora. His defection caused the Inquisition to wonder about the loyalty of Spain's Christian Jews, especially the clergy:

In Spain and Portugal there are monasteries and convents full of Jews. Not a few conceal Judaism in their heart and feign Christianity on account of worldly goods. Some of these feel the stings of conscience and escape, if they are able.

Escape in this particular instance meant going to Amsterdam, because as one Jew noted, in Amsterdam, "and in several other places, we have monks, Augustinians, Franciscans, Jesuits, Dominicans who have rejected idolatry. There are bishops in Spain and grave monks, whose parents brothers or sisters dwell here [in Amsterdam] and in other cities in order to be able to profess Judaism."[11]

In addition to being "decidedly choleric and outspoken," the Inquisition reports indicate Menasseh ben Israel was "uncritical and extremely credulous," a man who "avidly accepted any traveler's tale," including "how, in China, men made their pots out of wood and their cloth out of stone."[12] Menasseh was an avid devotee of the Zohar and the rest of cabalistic writing. Beginning in 1626, he began a publishing career which included bringing out Jewish apologetics and polemics, including *Conciliador*, which appeared in the same year he was importuning Portuguese travelers on the Joodenbreestraat.

Gractz doesn't think much of Menasseh as a man or a thinker, something to be expected from the man who referred to the Zohar as "that lying book."[13] From the perspective of a German Jew of the Enlightenment, Menasseh was an embarrassing reminder of what Jews were like before "enlightenment." In 1632 Jews like Menasseh ben Israel were on the verge of one of their recurrent outbreaks of Messianic political fervor, greedily gleaning the reports of every newly arrived visitor for signs of the imminent arrival of the Messiah. Amsterdam, Andrew Marvell noted, became a magnet for the disaffected:

Hence Amsterdam, Turk-Christian-Pagan-Jew,
Staple of sects and mint of schism grew
That bank of conscience, where not one so strange
Opinion but finds credit and exchange[14]

It wasn't just Jews who went to Amsterdam looking for signs the Millennium was about to dawn. Once the Calvinists had wrested the northern provinces of the Spanish Netherlands from Philip II, Amsterdam became a haven for revolutionaries of every stripe, Christian and Jew. Indeed, during the first decades of the 17th Century, it was difficult to distinguish Jewish revolutionaries from their Judaizing imitators. The Jews sounded like Portuguese Catholics, and the English Christians who ended up there sounded like Jews.

In Holland, the Judaizers were often Puritans from England, where they were pilloried for their imitation of the Jews. Addressing his first Parliament, James I described Puritans as revolutionaries, a historically prescient description. They were "a sect rather than a religion, ever discontented with the present government and impatient to suffer any superiority, which maketh their sect unable to be suffered in any well-governed commonwealth."[15] The Puritan was "naturally covetous of his purse and liberal of his tongue" and naturally inclined, like the Jews he imitated, to "usury, sacrilege, disobedience, rebellion, etc."[16]

Unsurprisingly, beginning in 1604, many Puritans migrated to Holland, where Amsterdam had a reputation as "the Dutch Jerusalem." From the perspective of a Judaizer imbued with imagery of the Old Testament, as Daniel Neal, their first historian said, "It is better to go and dwell in Goshen, find it where we can, than tarry in the midst of such Egyptian bondages as is among us."[17] "In Holland," Tuchman says, "the Puritan settlers who walked in the footsteps of the ancient Hebrews became acquainted with modern Jews, and the Jews became acquainted with this odd new variety of Christians who advocated religious freedom for all, including Jews."[18]

Given the Puritans' affinity with the Jews, it was not surprising that many of them became Jews after they arrived in Amsterdam. "From the English point of view, Amsterdam was the most prominent city that allowed open and public Jewish life and worship and could be examined as a test case of the eulogists of Jewish toleration."[19]

One of the English Judaizers drawn to Amsterdam was John Traske, who arrived in London in 1617 and began preaching sermons that mixed Jewish and Christian traditions. Then his follower Hamlet Jackson had a vision in which he "fancy'd he saw ... a shining Light about him, which struck him with Amazement. Hereupon he concluded that the Light of the Law was more fully discover'd to him, than to any since the Apostles."[20] Like the Puritan Cutter in the play by Cowley, who "had a vision which whispered to me through a key-hole, 'Go call thyself Abednego,'" Jackson's vision convinced him "of the necessity of keeping the Saturday Sabbath according to the full Mosaic law."[21] He convinced Traske, who then convinced his followers, that "the Old Testament Mosaic laws applied to Christians as well as Jews."[22] The Traskeites gave scandal by keeping the Sabbath on Saturday and working on the Lord's Day, Sunday. Traske and Jackson muddled Jewish and Christian ideas so convincingly that many of their followers and opponents were convinced the Traskeites "think they may be Jewes, for ought they know to the contrary; and therefore conclude, that seeing they do doubt, it is safest for them to keep Sabbaths, and to live as do the Jewes."[23]

Traske and his followers were arrested in early 1618. In February, John Chamberlain wrote to Sir Dudly Carelton about "one Trash or Thrash who was first a Puritan, then a separatist, and now is become a Jewish Christian, observing the Sabbath on Saturday, abstaining from swines-flesh and all things commanded by the law. You will not thincke what a number of foolish followers he hath in this town and some other parts, and yet he hath not been long of this opinion. He and divers of them are in prison, but continue obstinate, whereby a man may see there can arise no such absurd opinion but shall find followers and disciples."[24] In June 1618, Traske was sentenced "to be burnte in the forehead with the lettre J: in token that hee broached Jewish opynions."[25] He was also sentenced to life imprisonment in the Fleet "to prevent him from infecting others."[26]

Jacobite authorities considered Judaizing dangerously subversive of the civil order. Commenting on the Traske case, Lancelot Andrewes wrote "It is a good work to make a Jew a Christian, but to make Christian men Jews, hath ever been holden a foul act and severely to be punished."[27] From Andrewes' perspective, Traske was a "very christened Jew, a Maran, the worst sort of Jews that is."[28] James I followed the case closely and mentioned Traske and the dangers of Judaizing in his *Meditation Vpon the Lords Prayer*, published in 1619. "Trust not," the king warned his subjects, "to that priuate spirite or holy ghost which our Puritanes glory in; for then a little fierie zeale will make them turnen Separatist, and then proceed still on from Brownist to some one Sect or other of Anabaptist, and from one of these to another, then to become a Iudaized Traskeite, and in the ende a profane Familist."[29]

Prison apparently brought Traske to his senses. After release, he renounced Judaizing: "as I haue been stout for Moses, and Christ together: so I may be as resolute for Christ alone."[30] Hamlet Jackson, however, persisted in his views by taking them to their logical conclusion. After release from prison, Jackson "seems to have given up Judaizing observations in favour of outright conversion to Judaism in Amsterdam."[31] After the rabbis in Amsterdam told Jackson and Christopher Sands, another Traskeite, that they would have to be circumcised, Sands had second thoughts, deciding he "was content only to be a National Saint, or Saint of the Gentiles, by observing the seven [Noachide] precepts."[32] Jackson, however, was not deterred; "he would be circumcised and so made Jewish Proselyte."[33] One Englishman reported that by 1634 some of the Traskeites had "returned to the Church, some to prophanenness, others fallen to flat Judaism."[34]

The Jews followed the story of the Judaizing Puritans with increasing interest:

> If contemporary reports are correct in their claim that a number of Traskeites did go to Amsterdam to make contact with the Jewish community there, then we may have discovered the first tentative links between religious radicals in England and the influential Jewish community in Holland, links which would become very important when Dutch rabbi Menasseh ben Israel would be invited to present his case to the Council of State.[35]

The Dutch Jews and the English Puritans had much in common. Both hated Spain and the Catholic Church, and both felt the Messiah's coming was imminent. Barbara Tuchman says, "It was widely believed in England and other Protestant countries that the year 1666 was going to be decisive in the fate of the Jews, either by their conversion or by the restoration of their temporal kingdom, which would be the signal for the downfall of the Pope."[36] This excitement passed between the Judaizers and the Jews, like two basketball players on a fast break to the Millennium. After attending a conference with hundreds of rabbis in Budapest in 1650, Samuel Bert reported that, with Puritanism in power in England, conversion of the Jews was imminent, as the fact of this congress proved. Rome was a hindrance to the conversion of the Jews because "it is an idolatrous church with woman gods and graven images."³⁷ With Rome on its last legs, the Protestants could usher in the Millennium by bringing about the conversion of the Jews.

In 1621 the Puritans forced the issue in Parliament by proposing Coke's Sabbath bill. Archbishop Laud denounced the bill as leading many to "Enclyne to Judaisme as the newe sect of the Thraskites and other opinionists concerninge the terrene Kingdome of the Jewes."³⁸ At the heart of the "errors of the Jews" lay the temptation to look for heaven on earth, an "idle conceit" Laud found in Finch's book, *The Calling of the Jews*. Laud denounced it in a sermon on June 19, 1621:

> It was an old error of the Jews, which denied Christ come, that when their Messias did come, they should have a most glorious temporal kingdom, and who but they? I cannot say the author of this vanity denies Christ come, God forbid;— but this I must say, that many places of the Old Testament, which concern the "resurrection from the dead," and which look upon Christ in his first or second coming, are impiously applied to this return of the Jews, which, saith he, "is to them as a resurrection from the dead." And this exquisite arithmetician ... hath found a "third" between "one" and "two," namely, His coming to this conversion of the Jews.³⁹

Laud was battling an early form of Dispensationalism and the carnal idea of heaven that went along with it. Unlike the Jews and their imitators, Christians believe that "this new-built Jerusalem must be heavenly and new. Yea, but it is against the received judgment of the Church, that these places should be understood of any Church upon earth only, whether Jew, or Gentile, or both."⁴⁰

Laud debunks the idea the ten lost tribes are waiting in the wings to usher in Armageddon, saying they no longer existed as a "distinct people." The ten lost tribes were, Laud continues, "degenerated and lived mixed with other nations that captived them till not only their tribes were confounded, but their name also utterly lost, for almost two thousand years since."⁴¹ The claim "now, forsooth, we shall see them abroad again" and they shall "root out both the Pope and the Turk, our two great enemies" is so absurd that Laud "cannot tell here, whether it be Balaam that prophesieth, or the beast he rode on."⁴² Anyone who claims "Christ shall be king" over a worldly kingdom "unthrones Christ again and assures us 'One shall be king, whom the Jews shall set up for themselves.'"⁴³ The "error of the Jews" is "they thought Christ's kingdom should be temporal, which is the ground of all this vanity." The Puritans have adopted this "Jewish dream"; indeed, "these men ... out-dream the Jews."⁴⁴

Despite Laud's sermon, the "error of the Jews" spread. The left-wing of the Puritan movement continued to proclaim themselves Jews in belief and practice according to Levitical law. Some determined individuals went abroad to study under Continental rabbis and acquaint themselves with Talmudic law and literature. In 1647 the Long Parliament appropriated five hundred pounds to buy books "of a very great value, late brought out of Italy and having been the Library of a learned Rabbi there."⁴⁵ By the middle of the century, they agitated for a return of the Jews to England, an event guaranteed to usher in the Millennium. A certain widow from Brentford bid "Religion quite adieu," and "Turn'd from a Nonconformist to a Jew" because "If one affirm he learned it of a Jew,/the silly people think it must be true."[46] Thomas Hobbes was concerned that the discussion of the Sabbath would undermine morals because when the common man saw "the commandments to be *jus humanum* merely (as it must be, if the church can alter it) they will hope also that the other nine may be so too, for every man hitherto did believe that the ten commandments were the moral, that is an eternal, law."[47]

According to Rabbi Newman, "Jews promoted by their scholarly and literary contributions those tendencies towards rationalism which arose from within Christian groups; Jews were perpetual opponents of the conventional orthodoxies of the day, and sought to bring current beliefs into harmony with their special outlook and views."[48] In the 17th Century, however, the opposite was true. Contact with the Jews tended to encourage Millennialist fervor, not "rationalism," among Judaizing Christians. The converse was also true. Contact with 17th Century millennialist sects like the Ranters, Diggers, Quakers, and Puritans, encouraged Millennialism among the Jews. Both movements were fueled by Luther's doctrine of *Sola Scriptura* and the corrupt translations of the Bible the Jews were churning out in collaboration with Protestants. Seventeenth Century England showed that when *Sola Scriptura* was combined with the natural bent of human passion, revolution was the invariable outcome. Give an Englishman the bible and tell him he was now empowered to interpret the Scriptures according to his own lights, and, one way or another, social anarchy followed as night from day. The English Catholics recognized this early, so they translated the Bible at Douay. In 1582, the translator, Gregory Martin, attacked "Jewes and Heretickes" as corrupters of texts and souls in his pamphlet, "Discoverie of the Manifold Corruptions of the Holy Scriptures by heretickes of our dais, especially the English sectaries." According to Martin,

> the ancient best learned Fathers and Doctours of the Church doe much complaine and testifie to us that both the Hebrew and Greeke editions are foully corrupted by Jewes and Heretikes, since the Latin was truly translated out of them, whiles they were more pure; and that the same Latin hath been farre better conserued from corruptions. So that the old Vulgate Latin Edition hath been preferred and used for most authentical about a thousand and three hundred years.[49] Calvin's Bible "contained misinterpretations, leading to a denial of the Divinity and Messiahship of Jesus, and thus favoring Arianism and Judaism."[50]

Forty years after Martin issued his warning, Englishmen as diverse as Laud and Hobbes admitted the *Sola Scriptura* chickens were coming home to roost. The Englishmen who grew up reading corrupted Bibles were now becoming Jews. "The fear," Rabbi Newman says, "even among Protestants, that vernacular Bible translations, based on the original Hebrew text would lead to Judaism, is one of the important facts in a study of the history of Bible versions."[51] When Amsterdam became the refuge of the Jews, it became the refuge of every judaizing revolutionary sect too.

Amsterdam provided a haven not only for Jews and Calvinists; it became a magnet for fugitives from the medieval world. Like the Anabaptist commune in Muenster one hundred years earlier, Amsterdam attracted disaffected nuns and priests. Anyone unhappy with celibacy or the ban on usury could move to Amsterdam. One of the ways to express discontent was to become a Jew. This was true of Catholics of Jewish descent from Spain and Portugal as well as of the Protestants from England. Becoming a Jew was not a reversion to a more ancient tradition, although it could be seen as that. Taking their cue from the Psalms, the medieval popes consistently referred to Judaizers, who preferred the bondage of the law to the freedom of the Gospels, as dogs who returned to their vomit. Becoming a Jew was the opposite of a return to tradition because as deconverted Catholics soon discovered, there was no genuine tradition to return to. Tradition had to be created. Menasseh ben Israel's printing of Talmudic literature was a tacit acknowledgment of the self-contradiction that traditions had to be created.

Menasseh's most famous book, *Conciliador*, was not a reconciliation of Christian and Jewish texts, but a demonstration that Jewish texts preceded and therefore outranked what followed. Becoming a Jew was an act of conscious rebellion against the Catholic Church and the medieval world it had created in Europe. Holland became the locus of this rebellion because it provided a new *modus vivendi* for Jews who wanted to throw off their Christianity just as it provided a similar opportunity for Christians who wanted to live like Jews. The Jewish community in Amsterdam "expressed and incarnated the Hope of Israel,"[52] i.e., membership in a community which was more tangible and had more tangible benefits, a community which "would be the fount of all material and spiritual good."[53] Amsterdam had become a manifestation of what Archbishop Laud would call "the terrene kingdom of the Jewes," one more heaven on earth.

Shortly after Menasseh's birth, his family moved from the Madeira Islands to La Rochelle in France where, Roth says, "Outwardly, they continued to conform to the rites of the Church, while observing in the secrecy of their homes, with rather more confidence than hitherto, their ancestral religious practices."[54] Menasseh ben Israel was a baptized Catholic, as were John Calvin, Martin Luther, and Johan Bokelzoon. Like them, he hated the Church. "Baptism," according to the *Catechism of the Catholic Church*, "seals the Christian with an indelible spiritual mark of his belonging to Christ. No sin can erase this mark, even if sin prevents Baptism from bearing the fruits of salvation. Given once for all, Baptism cannot be repeated."[55] Becoming a Jew was similar to becoming a pagan in the post-Christian era, a phenomenon depressingly familiar in Europe during the 20th Century. It was not a naive continuation of some ancient tradition, but rather a renunciation of Christ. The Sephardic Jew who came to Amsterdam to be circumcised was a revolutionary as much as the early reformers were revolutionaries. All had accepted baptism as entrance into the Catholic Church; all lived lives in rebellion against that Church. Both the Jews and the Protestants known as Demi-Jews were creating their own *sui generis* traditions out of what they appropriated from the Old Testament. Jew and Reformer could cooperate politically because they shared a common project, the repudiation of the Church and the order she had impressed on Europe. Both Jew and Demi-Jew had a mainly negative identity: Talmudic Judaism and the Reformed faith were anti-Catholicism, created by people who had accepted (through their parents) the indelible mark of baptism and who had been formed intellectually by Catholic faith and culture.

Menasseh lived 100 years after the first wave of "reform" in Europe. The Dutch Republic was a haven for those who hated Spain and what Spain stood for, namely, medieval Catholic Europe. The low countries had been a hotbed of revolutionary activity since the cloth industry began in Flanders. Prosperity, derived from the region's advanced agriculture, had created a surplus population which became dispossessed from the land and the rooted traditions there and found employment in the cities as weavers and dyers. By the end of the 13th Century all of what is now Belgium and northeastern France had become a single manufacturing district and "the most highly industrialized part of a predominantly agricultural continent."[56] The wealth the cloth industry created had a dual effect on the peasantry, which migrated from the land to the city. The city offered freedom from ancestral duties and restrictions. It also offered freedom from the customs under which those who valued freedom over duty chafed. It offered incentive to those with personal enterprise and imagination. But the spectacle of unheard of wealth provoked, in Cohn's words, "a bitter sense of frustration"[57] too. Freedom cut both ways in the new industrial towns. There was a sense of release from ancestral burdens, but there was no protection from exploitation.

The rootless proletariat of the cloth industry was, as a result, vulnerable to millennialist revolutionary movements and ideologies. A group of people, drawn "from the most impulsive and unstable elements in medieval society" was especially susceptible to "any kind of revolt or revolution." Messianic politics "acted on these people with peculiar sharpness and called for reactions of peculiar violence. And the way in which they attempted to deal with their common plight was to form a salvationist group under the leadership of some man whom they regarded as extraordinarily holy."[58] They or, more likely, their charismatic leader, would consult the Bible and come up with something apocalyptic based of the Book of Daniel and Revelations which promised a new heaven and a new earth that would be realized in carnal terms. Joachim of Fiore's three stages of history is one example. According to Joachim, the age of the father, the Old Testament, was to be followed by the age of the son, the New Testament, which was in turn to be followed by the age of the Holy Spirit, which became an empty vessel into which all manner of revolutionary content could be poured.

These movements were invariably Jewish in orientation. Indeed, the idea of revolution, the idea that a lowly people would be able to assert itself against the powerful, was only conceivable in light of biblical texts like Exodus. Israel's history was essentially a replay of Exodus, as the lowly Israelites triumphed after initial adversity over one empire after another. Eventually, the pattern was codified in the Book of Daniel, in the description of the four monarchies—the four beasts—the fourth being Rome. When Rome was defeated, the fifth monarchy would begin. That meant the advent of the millenium, a thousand year reign of peace on earth during which the rapacious feeding of the powerful on the lowly would cease, history would be reversed, and the lowly would reign in a kingdom of their own. "It is natural enough," Cohn says, "that the earliest of these prophecies should have been produced by Jews. What so sharply distinguished the Jews from the other peoples of the ancient world was their attitude towards history and in particular towards their own role in history."[59]

Natural or not, some questions remained. Most notably, what did Rome mean? Which Rome are we talking about? A Catholic millennialist could claim the millenium coincided with the rise of the Catholic Church, which succeeded the Roman Empire and created a millennium of Christian civilization in Europe. But, as we have seen, by the Council of Ephesus the Church had disavowed associating the Kingdom of God with any earthly historical epoch. That insured that millennialism would have an anti-Catholic animus because it could flourish only in opposition to the Church. As a result, the fourth monarchy began to be seen not as the Roman Empire but as the Roman Catholic Church. One need only ascertain the date on which the Roman Church had succeeded the Roman Empire, add 1000 years, and the result would be a date close to the time of revolutionary turmoil in the middle of the 17th Century. The more the turmoil increased, the more the people were driven to establish a precise date. The Jews settled on 1648 as the year of redemption, and when that date came and went without the advent of the Messiah, they adopted the Christian date of 1666 for the dawn of the millenium.

The Jewish tradition of Messianic politics that began when Annas and Caiaphas rejected Christ and culminated in the Simon bar Kokhba rebellion, which commenced in 131, was appropriated by 17th Century Christians with similarly disastrous results. Beginning in the 16th Century, the locus was the Low Countries, where the Jews expelled from Spain made contact with English Puritans, Dutch Calvinists, German Lutherans, and the remnant of the Anabaptists from Muenster. A political alliance arose between the revived millennialist proletarian revolutionary movement that haunted Flanders and the Rhineland during the Middle Ages and the dormant Jewish tradition of Messianic politics. Ironically, the Rhenish revolutionary tradition was rabidly anti-Semitic. But anti-Catholic, too.

Menasseh ben Israel's genius, if we can call it that, lay in recognizing the times had changed. Menasseh was not a deep thinker, but he understood the Protestant revolt had created new possibilities for the Jews in Europe, and he was determined to exploit them. The advent of Protestantism meant a new sphere of influence for the Jews and the possibility of a new political and social configuration too.

Despite his insight and zeal, Menasseh did not prosper as a rabbi in Amsterdam. In 1639 when the two Amsterdam congregations merged, Menasseh ben Israel was passed over in the search for head rabbi. "At present," he wrote in 1639 in *De Termino Vitae*, "in complete disregard of my personal dignity, I am engaged in trade ... . What else is there for me to do? I have neither the wealth of a Croesus, nor the nature of a Thersites."[60] Significantly, Menasseh dedicated this book to the Dutch West India Company. He was deeply interested in trade with Brazil and was thinking of moving there. "No doubt," Gerhard Johann Vos wrote in January 1640 to Grotius, the great jurist, "he will act there as rabbi ... his domestic affairs compel him to take this step; for he is far from affluent."[61]

Then, standing on the quay at the foot of the Joodenbreestraat contemplating moving to South America, Menasseh suddenly got more than he bargained for. Something strange happened. South America came to him.

On September 19, 1644, after years of importuning Portuguese travelers in the hope they might be secret Jews, Menasseh ben Israel met the wild-eyed Marrano Antonio de Montezinos, or Aaron Levi, who had come with a tale the credulous rabbi found irresistible. Montezinos had just arrived from South America, where he had been imprisoned by the Inquisition on a charge of Judaizing. In prison, Montezinos mulled over reports he had heard from the Indians for years concerning the religious practices of tribes near Quito. Unable to expel the rumors from his mind, Montezinos made a solemn vow to the God of Israel that if he ever regained freedom he would investigate them. Appparently God heard Montezinos' prayer because he was soon released and on his way to meet the tribe under the guidance of a local cacique. Once out of the reach of the Inquisition, the Indian chief made a startling revelation. He was a Jew of the tribe of Levi. What the rest of the world thought were benighted savages living in the jungles of South America were in reality the Ten Lost Tribes of Israel!

It was a moment worthy of the scene in *Blazing Saddles* where Mel Brooks has an Indian speak Yiddish, but the credulous rabbi believed every word of Montezinos' story. Beyond that, he feverishly deduced the theological consequences of this startling revelation. The Messiah, he knew, could only come when Jews had reached the "ends of the earth," a word rendered in Hebrew as "*Kezeh ha-Arez,*" a literal and erroneous translation of the French word for England, "*Angle-Terre.*" Since "*Kezeh*" meant both "angle" and "limit," England was known as the "ends of the earth" to medieval Jewish writers. Since the Ten Lost Tribes were in America, they were spread all over the earth, except for one land, England. If the Jews could get to England, then they would have spread to the ends of the earth, and the Messiah was bound to appear. It was hard to argue with evidence this convincing, especially since Montezinos swore a solemn oath that what he revealed was true. If true, then the theological insights the unerringly logical Menasseh derived were equally true. All Menasseh ben Israel needed to do was get the Jews readmitted to England. God would take care of the rest. So the portly rabbi embarked upon the great project of his life.

II

After years of watching his predecessor try to deal with the Puritan revolutionaries with weapons of the spirit, Charles I ran out of patience and decided to resort to weapons of a more mundane sort. On August 22, 1642, he threw down the gauntlet at Nottingham and led his army to war against the Puritans. His military opponent was a man who had no previous military experience but was a military genius nonetheless who would change the face of warfare just as Zizka had done in Bohemia two centuries before. The name of the English Zizka was Oliver Cromwell, and from the moment he took command of the Puritan cavalry at the Battle of Marston Moor in 1644, the tide of war turned against the king, eventuating in his ultimate defeat and capture one year later. Unlike Zizka, who devised an ingenious defense against the cavalry charge, Cromwell refined the cavalry charge as a weapon of exceptional offensive power, one that lasted for almost three hundred years, to be eclipsed only in the 20th Century by the deployment of the machine gun.

Cromwell was born in Huntingdon in 1599. His family name would have been Williams but his grandfather married the sister of Thomas Cromwell, one of Henry VIII's most powerful councilors, and then adopted the name of his wife's family to access that power. Like the Cecils and the Russells, the wealth and power of the Cromwells came from looting the Catholic Church. "The Cromwells," a biographer writes, "were a large and locally influential family, who had risen rapidly during the 16th Century and had acquired wealth and extensive property, much of it formerly belonging to the Catholic Church but disposed of in the wake of the Henrician Reformation."[62] Since Oliver grew up in a house once owned by a Catholic monastic order, he was daily reminded of where his family wealth came from and who his ancestral enemies were. In 1628, Oliver took a seat in Parliament, where he represented the Puritan cause. It was also in 1628 that he began a life-long battle with mental illness. Cromwell's personality was the unstable combination of melancholic and choleric humors that modern medicine calls bipolar disorder. Cromwell was a manic depressive; in 1628, his physician, Sir Theodore Mayern, treated the symptoms of *valde melancholicus*," by prescribing what Cromwell's biographer called "a wonderful cocktail of drugs."[63] Ten years after diagnosis as a manic depressive, Cromwell had a religious experience which gave religious justification to his mood swings. In the same year he was accused of judaizing by a fellow member of parliament. Then civil war broke out.

The civil war brought in its wake famine, pestilence, and, worst of all, Puritan pamphlets justifying revolution by appealing to the Old Testament. In 1642 Henry Archer brought forth an idea that would result in the spilling of barrels of ink and the slaying of thousands of trees over the next few centuries. In *The Personal Reign of Christ on Earth*, Archer used the Books of Daniel and Revelations to explain the contemporary political situation. Numerous Protestant would follow his example. Sometimes the contemporary political situation was used to explicate Daniel and Revelations. Archer's book became the intellectual justification for a political movement known as the Fifth Monarchy Men. As the name implies, the challenge at the heart of their movement involved discovering when the fourth monarchy described in the Book of Daniel had ended. If Archer had read history with an open mind, he might speculatively have concluded the thousand year reign of Christ on earth began with the Alaric's sacking of Rome in 410 and ended when the age of revolution began with the excommunication of John Huss. But that theory would have made the millennium co-terminus with the Church of Rome, something that could not be true because he had already declared the "fearfull Little Horne," which came up among them was the Papacy.[64] Since the Book of Daniel had to be twisted to justify the rebellion in England, Rome had to be construed as the Church of Rome. "The great question" then became "when the ten kingdoms and Papacy began in Europe?"[65] By adding 1260 to the year 406 (when Archer claims the papacy began), Archer got the year 1666, as both the limit of the papacy's duration and the number of the beast (actually 666) proposed by the Book of Revelations. This correspondence could not be coincidence, Archer reasoned, and so the thousand year reign of Christ on earth would begin in a mere 24 years. That meant, of course, that the conversion of the Jews was imminent, which meant the ten lost tribes were already massing on the other side of the river that flowed every day of the week but Saturday in preparation for their march on Jerusalem. One commentator describes Archer's scriptural scholarship as part of "the lengthy and laborious efforts of the sect to interpret the Bible in accordance with their preconceived ideas."[66] Those labors involved the conversion of the Jews and "resulted in many Fifth Monarchy Men developing strong Hebraic tendencies and sympathies."[67]

Any lingering doubt that Puritanism was a combination of *Sola Scriptura*-based proof texting and appetite was removed in August 1643 with publication of John Milton's tract on *The Doctrine and Discipline of Divorce*. Milton was the heir of the Puritan Occultism spawned by the magician John Dee and nourished by the Earl of Leicester and his nephew Philip Sidney, which achieved its first literary expression in the *Faerie Queene*. Milton was an admirer of Spenser, and from Milton's pen flowed the second great Protestant epic, the one with Satan as its "hero," *Paradise Lost*. "Milton's vision for England," according to Frances Yates, "was that of a nation of chosen people, chosen in the Hebraic sense, chosen to lead Protestant Europe against the power of the Papal Antichrist. Spenser had envisaged Elizabethan England and its queen as chosen for just such a religious role. The great difference was, of course, that Milton was not a monarchist, like Spenser, but a republican."[68] Spenser and Milton shared an unfortunate theology, a genuine gift at versification, and an exquisitely poor sense of timing. Spenser published the *Faerie Queene* one year after John Dee had returned in disgrace from his failed mission to Prague. Consequently, Spenser, like Dee, found no support for his imperialist propaganda at court. Similarly, Milton brought out his apologia for revolution and regicide six years after the collapse of the Puritan commonwealth, at the height of the Restoration, when the rage against Cromwell was so high that a mob dug up his corpse and hanged it.

Milton admired Spenser "whom," Yates tells us, "he held to be a better teacher than Aquinas."[69] Milton derived the Hebraic elements in *Paradise Lost* not directly from the Zohar or the Talmud but indirectly through the *Faerie Queene* and from Robert Fludd and Rosicrucianism, which would also become a source for Freemasonry. When the "Rosicrucian movement had failed on the continent," Yates says, "Refugees from that failure poured into Puritan England as the refuge from the Antichrist. And the Puritan revolution took over some of the aspects of the projected Rosicrucian revolution. That is why there was a 'Puritan Occultism,' why an English translation of the Rosicrucian manifestos was published in Cromwellian England, and why the philosophy of John Dee was cultivated by earnest Parliamentarians."[70]

Frances Yates shows how the trajectory of Judaizing which began with Dee's infatuation with magic and Cabala led to Cromwell and Milton's justification of revolution. Missing from her account, though, is the crucial role played by sexual appetite. Revolution was a binary weapon, which could be driven by appetite and the rationalization of appetite that thinkers could derive from *Sola Scriptura* and the ransacking of the Old Testament for proof texts.

In 1642 John Milton, then 34 years old, married Mary Powell, daughter of Richard Powell, a justice of peace. The Powells, adherents of the Cavalier party who had a lively social life, seem not to have thought out the consequences of having their daughter marry the Puritan *Penseroso*. Within a month, Mary tired of the "philosophic life (after having been used to a great house, and much company and joviality)"[71] and returned to her parents. Milton "sent for her by letter,"[72] but the letters went unanswered. The Powell family, "being generally addicted to the cavalier party,"[73] had second thoughts. They considered their new son-in-law and his radical opinions "a blot in their escutcheon,"[74] especially since it seemed Charles would soon dispatch the rebel armies and re-establish his court. Finally, Milton dispatched a messenger ordering his wife to return, but the messenger came back alone, "dismissed with some sort of contempt."[75]

In the meantime, the Puritan *Penseroso* fell in love with another woman, "one of Dr. Davis's daughters, a very handsome and witty gentlewoman," who was "averse" to marrying a married man.[76] With his sexual desires thwarted twice, Milton resolved the matter in typically Puritan fashion, ransacking the Bible for a justification for divorce that would enable him to marry Miss Davis. Milton "forthwith prepared to fortify himself with arguments for such a resolution, and accordingly wrote two treatises, by which he understood that it was against reason, and the enjoinment of it *not provable by Scripture*, for any married couple disagreeable in humor and temper, or having an aversion to each other, to be forced to live yoked together all their days."[77] The first result of the decision to dump his wife and replace her with Miss Davis was *The Doctrine and Discipline of Divorce*; the second was *Tetrachordon*.

Justification of divorce was a tall order for a Christian whose first principle was *Sola Scriptura* because, as anyone who has read the gospel knows, Christ specifically prohibited divorce. The project would have been impossible were it not for the Puritan tendency to Judaize, which emanated from the penumbra of *Sola Scriptura*. This worked in two ways. First, *Sola Scriptura* relativized the priority of the New Testament over the Old. The New Testament was no longer the fulfillment of the Old nor was it the only lens through which the Old could be seen and interpreted properly. *Sola Scriptura* tended to democratize the books of the Bible, which, since there were many more books in the Old Testament than in the New, tended to lead to the Old Testament's priority over the New. *Sola Scriptura* thus led to Judaizing. Secondly, Judaizing led to Talmudic exegesis, which is to say, a devaluation of the actual text in favor of the opinions of rabbis. Milton was a very learned rabbi, and without the Church to protect it, the Bible succumbed to the hammer blows of what looked like Milton's libido-driven "logic." His biographer presents the moral and psychological dynamics of his decision straightforwardly. Since Milton was "then in the full vigor of his manhood," and "could ill bear the disappointment he met with by her obstinate absenting," he justified divorce, so "that he might be free to marry another; concerning which he also was in treaty."[78]

The Doctrine and Discipline of Divorce became a classic in the canon of sophistry, and remained a beacon for sophists for centuries. (Stanley Fish began his career in literary criticism as a Milton scholar.) Milton's justification of divorce would have been unthinkable without Puritanism's prior commitment to Judaizing. "It follows now," Milton says, "that those places of scripture which have a seeming to revoke the prudence of Moses, or rather that merciful decree of God, be forthwith explained and reconciled. For what are all these reasonings worth, will some reply, whenas the words of Christ are plainly against all divorce, 'except in case of fornication' Matt 5: 32."[79] The relativization of Christ's prohibition of divorce could only proceed by placing Moses on the same level as Christ. This completely heretical notion, contradicted by the Gospel of St. John, was no hindrance to a devotee of *Sola Scriptura*, which, it appears, had become another word for appetite. In other words, "the necessity of justifying himself" now coincided with "a point of so great concern to the peace and preservation of families, and so likely to prevent temptations as well as mischiefs."[80]

There was a public aspect to Milton's personal problems. Parliament was debating the legalization of divorce during the time of Mary's absence. "Doubt not, worthy senators," Milton wrote, "to vindicate the sacred honor and judgment of Moses your predecessor, from the shallow commenting of scholastics and canonists."[81] Mary's departure was thus a chance to make a virtue of necessity. Extrapolating from his own situation, as Luther had done in *De servo arbitrio*, Milton could guide England's legislature, which then would become a beacon for the world. All Milton had to do was "show ... that our Saviour, in those four places of the Evangelists, meant not the abrogating [of divorce] but rectifying the abuses of it."[82]

The key to this alchemical transmutation of Christ's words was the false dichotomy Moses-Christ that judaizing had enabled. Moses is proposed as "an author great beyond exception."[83] Milton could not denigrate Christ, but he could nullify his teaching by claiming "our Savior's words touching divorce" had been "congealed into a stony rigor, inconsistent both with his doctrine and his office."[84] What culminated as special pleading that would give theologians a bad reputation in the latter half of the 20th Century as shills for appetite and special interest began in England with judaizing politics. The attraction of judaizing was immediately apparent. Moses could be portrayed as permitting what Christ prohibited. Since Moses was the lawgiver for the nation of Israel, England's solons should follow his example and promote "expedient liberty."[85] In doing this, they "shall restore the much wronged and over-sorrowed state of matrimony, *not only to those merciful and life-giving remedies of Moses*, but as much as may be, to that serene and blissful condition it was in at the beginning and shall deserve of all apprehensive men ... shall deserve to be reckoned among the public benefactors of civil and human life above the inventors of wine and oil; for this is far dearer, far nobler and more desirable cherishing to man's life unworthily exposed to sadness and mistake which he shall vindicate."[86] Milton again needs to contradict Christ and scripture, because Christ said "in the beginning it was not so," meaning that divorce was something added after the fall because Moses had to deal with the hardness of his people's hearts.

As if conceding the subversion of Christ's own words is a lost cause as long as the New Testament has priority over the Old, Milton appeals first to the reformers and then to the rabbis to bolster his argument:

> Yea, God himself commands in his law more than once, and by his prophet Malachi, as Calvin and the best translations read that "he who hates, let him divorce—that is, he who hates cannot love. Hence it is that the rabbins, and Maimonides, famous among the rest, in a book of his set forth by Buxtorfius, tells us that "divorce was permitted by Moses to preserve peace in marriage and quiet in the family."[87]

The English Parliament should take the Jews as their model, because

> Surely the Jews had their saving peace about them as well as we, yet care was taken that this wholesome provision for household peace should also be allowed them: and must this be denied to Christians? O perverseness! that the law should be made more provident of peacemaking than the gospel! that the gospel should be put to beg a necessary help of mercy from the law, but must not have it! and that to grind in the mill of an undelighted and servile copulation must be the only forced work of a Christian marriage, ofttimes with such a yoke-fellow, from whom both love and peace, both nature and religion, mourns to be separated.[88]

The logic is inexorable. As we have seen, if the New Testament no longer has hegemony over the Old and if the words of Christ can be relativized by the testimony of rabbis, then in what sense are Milton and the Puritans Christians? Urged on by libido to plead for divorce, Milton willingly abandons Christianity to gratify his appetites, proving Laud and the Catholics were right in their verdict against the Puritans: The Puritans were Jews, and their piety was a front for rationalized misbehavior.

Eventually politics solved Milton's marital problems. "The declining state of the King's cause" along with the very handsome and witty Miss Davis waiting in the wings, convinced the Powell family that it might not be so bad to have a Puritan son-in-law, so they "set all engines to work to restore the late married woman to the station wherein they a little before had planted her."[89] Mary "of her own accord came, and submitted to him, pleading that her mother had been the inciter of her to that forwardness."[90] The story had a happy ending. The couple reconciled, and a daughter was conceived as "the first fruits of her return to her husband."[91]

Before long Milton's marital problems were swept up in the Messianic politics at the heart of Puritan-Jewish revolutionary thought. England's legalization of divorce provided the world with a "magnanimous example" which "will easily spread far beyond the banks of Tweed and the Norman isles."[92] England as the new Israel has a mission to save the world, a mission that was later adopted by messianic American descendants of Jews and Puritans. "It would not be the first or second time," the author of *Paradise Lost* continues,

> since our ancient druids, by whom this island was the cathedral of philosophy to France, left off their pagan rites, that England hath had this honor vouchsafed from heaven, to give out reformation to the world. Who was it but our English Constantine that baptized the Roman Empire? Who but the Northumbrian Willibrorde and Winifride of Devon, with their followers were the first apostles of Germany? Who but Alcuin and Wycliffe our countrymen, opened the eyes of Europe, the one in arts, the other in religion? *Let not England forget her precedence of teaching nations how to live.*[93]

In Milton's tendentious pleading for legalization of divorce, one can almost hear the devotees of Planned Parenthood arguing the logical sequel to America's conquest of Afghanistan or Iraq should be contraception and abortion there. Messianic politics and sexual liberation have gone hand in hand from the beginning, and it seems they still do, now that America is the uncontested new Israel. Messianic politics cannot function without Old Testament models.

Puritans and Jews shared a desire to attain the spiritual goods promised in the Bible by secular means. Messianic politics was a form of magic; the attainment of wealth and power by spiritual means had always been the goal of Simon Magus and his followers. It appealed powerfully to people who, full of revulsion at the Cross of Christ and the ideal of suffering it embodied, were discovering the natural sciences. "It is better," St. Augustine wrote, summarizing the Catholic alternative to Simon Magus, "to love God and make use of money, than to love money and make use of God."[94] The Puritan rejection of the medieval worldview of the Catholic Church is ultimately traceable to the Jewish rejection of the suffering Christ as an unworthy Messiah. "The chief priests," St. Matthew tells us, "with the scribes and elders mocked him in the same way. 'He saved others,' they said, 'he cannot save himself. He is the king of Israel; let him come down from the Cross now, and we will believe in him.'"

The Jewish/Puritan alliance was born in a rejection of the Cross and all it stood for, and the substitution of King David or Simon bar Kokhba or Shabbetai Zevi or Oliver Cromwell or Napoleon Bonaparte as an alternative to the suffering Christ. Cromwell, as Graetz points out, was driven to consummate this revolutionary alliance between Jews and Puritans on the theoretical and practical levels:

> To bury oneself in the history, prophecy, and poetry of the Old Testament, to revere them as divine inspiration, to live in them with every emotion, yet not to consider the people who had originated all this glory and greatness as preferred and chosen was impossible. Among the Puritans, therefore, were many earnest admirers of "God's people" and Cromwell was one of them.[95]

The consummation of this revolutionary alliance against the Catholic Church and Catholic countries involved, in other words, not only rummaging through the Bible for images that would justify divorce or regicide, it also entailed bringing Jews into the land governed by the Puritan saints. According to Graetz:

> A desire was excited in the hearts of the Puritans to see this living wonder, the Jewish people, with their own eyes, to bring Jews to England, and, by making them part of the theocratic community about to be established, stamp it with the seal of completion. The sentiments of the Puritans towards the Jews were expressed in Oliver Cromwell's observation, "Great is my sympathy with this poor people, whom God chose and to whom He gave His law; it rejects Jesus because it does not recognize him as the Messiah." Cromwell dreamt of a reconciliation of the Old and New Testament, of an intimate connection between the Jewish people of God and the English Puritan theocracy. But other Puritans were so absorbed in the Old Testament that the New Testament was of no importance. Especially the visionaries in Cromwell's army and among the members of Parliament, who were hoping for the Fifth Monarchy, or the reign of the saints, assigned to the Jewish people a glorious position in the expected millennium. A Puritan preacher, Nathaniel Holmes ... wished ... to become the servant of Israel and serve him on bended knees. The more the tension in Israel increased ... the more public life and religious thought assumed Jewish coloring. The only thing wanting to make one thing [was the return of the Jews].[96]

Cromwell's followers felt that by readmitting the Jews to England they could bring about the second coming of Christ, the millennium, and the fifth monarchy. In short, the middle of the 17th Century was suffused with an apocalyptic vision of the establishment of Christ's kingdom in the here and now. Jewish refugees from Spain and English Ranters and Fifth Monarchy Men were of one mind: The

Kingdom of God was at hand. Something like this had been held by Christians for over a millennium and a half, probably because its advent had been pronounced by Christ himself. What had changed, though, was the kind of kingdom Christ's followers were supposed to expect.

As we saw earlier, St. Augustine gave the definitive Catholic explication of The Book of Revelation in the *City of God*, where he explained the millennium was a spiritual allegory concerning an essentially spiritual reality. The millennium had begun with the death of Christ, and the New Jerusalem was fully realized in the Catholic Church. Augustine's explanation became Church doctrine when it was adopted as definitive by the Council of Ephesus in 431. From then, belief in the millennium as a worldly kingdom was dismissed as a superstitious aberration, "the error of the Jews."

As Archbishop Laud made clear, the Puritans were bent on resurrecting this "error of the Jews." Heaven on earth was to be instituted by a government of English saints in the decade following 1650. Since one of the inaugural events was the murder of the English king, it promised to be a bloody kingdom for those with eyes capable of seeing its true lineaments, but a worldly kingdom nonetheless, in which sainthood was the first job requirement of every politician.

There had been no Jews in England since 1290, at least officially, so English philo-Semitism had a distinctly utopian cast. English Judaizers tended to idealize Jews according to their own idiosyncratic reading of the Old Testament. They did not evaluate Jews through empirical observation, at least not at the dawn of the Messianic Era in 1648. If they had been less preoccupied with their own revolution, the English could have learned something about Christian-Jewish relations by observing the apocalypse brewing in Poland as the English were debating the fate of their king. An objective study of what had happened in Spain might have been helpful too, but an objective English study of anything Spanish is the historical equivalent of an oxymoron.

In June 1645, Oliver Cromwell, in command of the revolutionary New Model Army, defeated the king's troops at Naseby, ending the civil war in England. In reviewing papers captured from the king's baggage, Cromwell discovered Charles had planned to recruit Irish Catholic troops by granting them religious concessions. That discovery did not bode well for the Irish or the king.

III

According to the Zohar, 1648 was to be the mystical year of resurrection, when the Jews could expect deliverance from their more than millennium long exile. Heinrich Graetz called the Zohar "that lying book" and used that prediction to impugn the entire Kabbalistic tradition. Since the Enlightenment was in some ways a result of the disappointment over the failure of the Messianic expectations in the second half of the 17th Century, his skepticism is understandable, as is his scorn for the Cabala, the mish-mash of what he considered Gnostic and Talmudic mumbo-jumbo that had led to the rise and fall of Messianic hope. Graetz espoused a worldview that was the antithesis of the Messianic fever of the mid-17th Century. He was convinced in his opposition to the Cabala because he had the benefit of historical hindsight and could see where its vaporous illusions had led the Jewish people. Expectation of redemption fostered by widespread dissemination of cabalistic doctrine made the Jews, in Graetz's words, "more reckless and careless than was their custom at other times."[97]

Just what Graetz meant by reckless can be seen in his analysis of Polish Jewry, a hotbed of cabalistic thought. Beginning with the Statute of Kalisz in 1251, the Jews of Poland were granted rights unlike anywhere else in Europe. They were even granted their own autonomous legal system, the Kahal, which allowed them to adjudicate intra-Jewish disputes without recourse to the Polish Christian legal system. This autonomy necessitated intensive study of the Talmud, which, according Graetz, led to the peculiar corruption of Polish Jews. The reliance on the Talmud created a culture of "hair-splitting judgment" among rabbis, says Graetz, as well as "a love of twisting, distorting, ingenious quibbling, and a foregone antipathy to what did not lie within their field of vision," which trickled down to the behavior of the vulgar, who "found pleasure and a sort of triumphant delight in deception and cheating."[98] By the end of the 18th Century, the overwhelming majority of Jews lived in Poland, so Jews earned the reputation of being "a nation of deceivers," in Immanuel Kant's formulation. "It does indeed seem strange," Kant, the quintessential Enlightenment philosopher, continued, "to conceive of a nation of deceivers, but it is also very strange to conceive of a nation of merchants, the majority of whom, bound by an ancient superstition accepted by the state they live in, do not seek any civil dignity, but prefer to make good this disadvantage with the benefits of trickery at the expense of the people who shelter them and at the expense of each other. In a nation of merchants, unproductive members of society ... it cannot be otherwise."[99] From his vantage point in Koenigsberg, the capital of East Prussia, a country that the Teutonic Knights wrested by force from the Slavic natives, all Jews were Polish Jews.

Graetz, the Enlightenment Jew and apostle of German culture and Jewish assimilation to it, echoed Kant but confined his censure to the Jews of Poland, who, according to his judgment, "acquired the quibbling method of the schools and employed it to outwit the less cunning."[100] Piety and knowledge of the hairsplitting distinctions of the Talmud became one and the same for the Polish Jew, a combination which, when added to the dogmatism of the rabbis, "undermined their moral sense" and made them prone to "sophistry and boastfulness."[101]

Largely as a result of the concessions of the Polish crown which began with the Statute of Kalisz, Poland became known throughout Europe as the "*paradisus Judeorum*," the paradise of the Jews. When persecutions would flare up in traditionally Jewish sections of Europe like the German principalities, the Jews who wished to escape persecution inevitably headed east toward Poland, taking their language, "*juedische Deutsch*," or Yiddish, with them. When Isaac Bashevis Singer won the Nobel Prize toward the end of the 20th Century, he was designated a Pole by the selection committee in spite of his candid admission that he understood Polish only with difficulty, even though he lived his entire youth in Poland. Jews did not assimilate in Poland; most did not learn the language of the Christian Poles, because, other than rudimentary commerce and illicit sexual activity, the Jews had no contact with them. The Jews established their own state within a state; they established their own legal system and courts, and, based on demographic evidence, the Polish paradise was the most successful *modus vivendi* Jews found in the West.

Between 1340 and 1772, at which point Poland was partitioned for the first time, the Jewish population of Poland increased 75-fold while the Christian population quintupled. The disparity in population increase is explainable in simple terms. Persecution in the west from the 11th to the 16th Century caused massive immigration. Jews moved to Polish territory during that period of time in unprecedented numbers. By the time Poland was partitioned for the third time in 1795, 80 percent of the world's Jews lived there.

This phenomenal expansion of the Jewish population in Poland was matched by a correspondingly rapid increase in wealth that in turn corresponded to a dramatic expansion of the territorial limits of Poland. The Golden Age of Polish Jews, according to Pogonowski, lasted from 1500 to 1648.[102] By 1634, Poland was the largest country in Europe. Its territory extended from the Baltic almost to the Black Sea and from Silesia in the west to the heart of the Ukraine. By the middle of the 17th Century, as much as 60 percent of Poland's population was not ethnically Polish, a situation bound to cause friction, depending on how wisely the Polish rulers treated their ethnic subjects.

What followed was a classical case of cultural drift in which imperial expansion covered over internal decay until the contradictions and injustices became so insupportable that the bubble burst, and an orgy of violence followed, dragging the Polish state to extinction. The story of Poland was the story of Imperial Rome writ small. Imperial expansion to the east into what is now the Ukraine, the Crimea, and Belorus resulted in creation of huge estates, some the size of Holland and Switzerland. The estates were called Latifundia, an ironic comment on the blindness of the Polish nobility, who failed to see the mischief the Latifundia system had wrought in ancient Rome. The Polish Nobles' republic was a classic oligarchy, as Plato defined the term in his *Republic*. As in ancient Greece, so in Poland: wealth concentrated in fewer and fewer hands led to rebellion among the lower classes. Wealth concentrated in fewer and fewer hands fueled imperialism in which the chief losers were the overwhelming majority of the Polish people. As in ancient Rome, the citizen soldiers were driven to the wall by the monopoly conditions the Latifundia fostered. When the rebellion came, all Poles would be held responsible for the excesses of the magnates who created the system that dispossessed the average Polish citizen.

The citizen soldiers who had been the backbone of the republic's legions became the disenfranchised rural proletariat once wealth was concentrated in the hands of the magnates. "The citizen-soldiers who owned small and medium estates," Pogonowski says, "suffered numerous bankruptcies and were becoming landless while still retaining their full civil rights and privileges." As a result, "many of them had to seek employment in the huge estates called Latifundia."[103] This meant more and more political power migrated to the land magnates, who now employed the enfranchised. As a result, "the political machines of the owners of the Latifundia enabled them to attain an oligarchic control of the politics of Poland. Their control of the national parliament was based on their grip on the provincial legislatures."[104]

In 1633, the Sejm passed a law forbidding Poland's nobility from selling liquor or engaging in commercial activities. The Polish nobility retained, as a result, political control of the country, but lost economic control. Because the Polish magnates owned the land but were unable to engage in commerce, they handed over income extraction to the Jews, who paid a set fee for a lease to raise the money the nobles needed. The system of pre-paid, short-term leases was known as "*arenda*." The connection between arenda tax-farming and the Jews was so intimate that it eventually was expressed in the Polish language. In legal contracts in the 17th and 18th Century, the Polish word "*arendarz*," or tax-farmer, and "Jew" are synonymous. According to Pogonowski, "15 percent of urban and 80 percent of rural Jewish heads of households were occupied within the arenda system."[105]

The Jewish legal system, or kahal, brokered these licenses to well-to-do Jews, who in turn often subleased them to less well-to-do relatives. In Polish private law, *arenda* was defined as "the leasing of immovable property or rights. The subject of the lease might be a whole territory, held either in ownership or in pledge [or] the subject might be a tavern, mill or the right to collect various payments such as a bridge toll or a payment connected with a jurisdiction."[106] A Jew, for example, might take out a short-term lease on a church, in defiance of Church law. This meant he was in sole possession of the key to the church door, which could only be opened for weddings or baptisms after payment of a fee, a practice that led to resentment among Christians. Since the lease was short-term, the Jew would charge as much as he could to recoup his investment and some profit, since the lease might not be renewed. Or, if it were renewed, someone might outbid him. There was no financial incentive to create good will among the local population from which the arendator made his money. The Jewish tax-farmers had the support of the state—Pogonowski estimates 20 to 70 percent of the income of the large estates was generated by tax-farming leases held by Jews—but lacked the good will of the community. Since the Jew was not a part of that community, and had developed, as Graetz indicates, a whole culture treating the *goyim* with contempt, he could exploit the system well beyond what would have been tolerable had Catholic Poles run the system:

Arenda-type short-term leases resulted in intensive exploitation of the leased estates, as the lessees tended to overwork the land, peasants and equipment without worrying about long-term effects. The peasants experienced additional hardships when Jewish arrendators obtained the right to collect and even impose taxes and fees for church services. The peasants and Cossacks in Kresy [the newly colonized lands of the east] bitterly resented having to pay Jews for the use of Eastern Orthodox and Greek-catholic churches for funerals, baptism, weddings and other similar occasions.[107]

Because of the arenda system and the prohibition against nobles distilling spirits, the Jews assumed control of the liquor business. They could manipulate the price of grain by diverting it to more profitable use as distilled spirits. They also intensely promoted alcohol consumption to maximize profits during the short-term of the lease. This led to chronic drunkenness, decreased productivity, and increased resentment against Jews, who were perceived as constantly seeking to exploit the weaknesses of the majority to enhance their own wealth and power.

Graetz talks about the Jew who was experienced in financial matters as a salutary counterbalance to the impetuous, headstrong, and ultimately child-like Polish nobleman:

The high nobility continued to be dependent on Jews, who in a measure counterbalanced the national defects. Polish flightiness, levity, unsteadiness, extravagance and recklessness were compensated for by Jewish prudence, sagacity, economy and cautiousness. The Jew was more than a financier to the Polish nobleman; he was his help in embarrassment, his prudent adviser, his all in all.[108]

There are other ways of viewing the "unique utilitarian alliance ... between the huge landowners and the Jewish financial elite."[109] Looked at one way, Jewish migration to Poland brought Jewish capital that was soon put at the disposal of the Polish crown and the landowning magnates, whose estates expanded dramatically. The Polish magnates then used the Jews and their money to expand the Polish empire into the fertile steppes of the Ukraine, Belorus, and the northern shore of the Black Sea. Looked at another way, this alliance concentrated the wealth into fewer and fewer hands, especially during the Jewish colonization in the Ukraine in the 80 years between 1569 and 1648. Since the leases involved monopoly rights, the Jewish tax-farmers could increase the political power of their wealthy patrons, and their own wealth and influence as well, by driving the smaller independent landowners to the wall. The short term increase in power, though, increased the magnitude and violence of the reaction when it came. The success of the new system contained within in it the seeds of its destruction.

The radical disjunction between political and economic power meant the enfranchised noble citizens gradually lost control of their culture. The easy-going Polish oligarchs, wedded to an economic system that seemed so successful in bringing new lands under the Polish crown, did not understand control over those territories was undermined from within by the very people that administered it. This happened gradually, of course, and it manifest itself first in religion. Flush with the short-term wealth which the arenda system created and the territorial expansion which it enabled, the Polish kings ignored the biggest cultural crisis of their day, the Protestant revolt against Catholic hegemony over Europe. Because there was no Inquisition in Poland, Poland became a model for tolerance, paving the way for its own extinction.

While the Duke of Parma was battling Calvinists and Jews in the Netherlands and setting up a barrier beyond which the Reformation would not pass, helping to save southern Europe from the rebellion which had devastated England and the North, Sigismund August II, ruler of Poland and Lithuania, surrounded himself with Jews and the Protestant revolutionaries the Poles called Demi-Jews. The "Reformers" in Poland were largely Unitarian and Socinian followers of Michael Servetus, who, in Graetz's words, "undermined the foundations of Christianity," by "rejecting the veneration of Jesus as a divine person."[110]

Flush with the money they provided, King Sigismund indulged his disordered passions and handed the country over to Jewish and Demi-Jewish administrators to rule as they wished. Peasants groaned under the predations of the Jewish tax-farmers, who in turn lent money to the king at less usurious interest rates, keeping him under their power too. Rabbi Mendel Frank of Brest, says Walsh, "was so influential that he was called the King's Officer."[111] As in England, the Polish nobles were torn between religious principle and economic interest. As in England, economic considerations won out and "the nobility in most cases held its protecting hand over the Jews to whom it was tied by the community of economic interests."[112] The Polish oligarchs "were either in debt to the Jews, or employed them to squeeze taxes for them out of the peasants, naturally at a good profit for the tax-farmers, who took their toll from dairies, mills, distilleries, farms."[113] The Jews "were indispensable to the easy-going magnate, who was wont to let his estates take care of themselves and wile away his time at the capital, at the court, in merry amusements, or at the tumultuous sessions of the national and provincial assemblies, where politics was looked upon as a form of entertainment rather than as a serious pursuit. This Polish aristocracy put a check on the anti-Semitic endeavors of the clergy."[114] The Jesuits warred with the Jews over the mind of the Polish oligarchs, but there was no Inquisition and no Counter-Reformation in Poland. As a result, Calvinism, Socinianism, and Unitarianism spread among the nobles unchecked by official Catholic resistance. So Poland became, in Graetz's words, "a second Babylon for the Jews."[115]

By the death of Sigismund II in 1572, the Jews had attained enough power to name his successor in collaboration with the Porte in Constantinople, the Huguenots in France, and the English Protestants. Solomon ben Nathan Ashkenazi, although sponsor to the Duke of Ferrara was involved in negotiations regarding a later king. Solomon Ashkenazi was a German Jew who had migrated to the paradise of the Jews, where he eventually became chief physician to King Sigismund. He eventually migrated to Constantinople, where he served the Sultan as faithfully as he had served the Polish king. Solomon Ashkenazi succeeded Joseph Nasi, also an adviser to the sultan, as "a sort of unofficial leader of world Jewry."[116] Like Nasi, Ashkenazi orchestrated events from behind the scenes. "Christian cabinets," Graetz says, "did not suspect that the course of events which compelled them to side with one party or the other was set in motion by a Jewish hand. This was especially so in the case of the election of the Polish king."[117]

Locked into such a profitable alliance with the Jews, the Polish magnates saw little reason to change a system from which they profited so effortlessly and enormously. As a result the exactions of the Jewish tax-farmers became onerous to the point of intolerable among the peasantry in general, but especially among the newly colonized Cossacks, who never felt themselves a part of the Polish nation or, as Orthodox, part of the Catholic culture of the west. The political crisis, which had been growing during the last 80 years of Polish imperial expansion, corresponded as well to the worst excesses of the arenda system. Reform of the system was urgently necessary, and a bill of reform eventually made its way to the Sejm.

In 1647, as one precondition that prepared for a Polish crusade against the Ottoman Empire, the Cossacks were promised full civil rights and enfranchisement over time as Polish citizens. That meant "the harsh exploitation by Jewish holders of short time leases was to be lessened by banning the collection of such payments as church fees for funerals, weddings, baptisms, etc."[118] It also meant disobedience to the tax-farmers would no longer be a capital crime. And Jesuits would no longer be assigned to Cossack territory in the Southern Ukraine, so they would no longer pressure Orthodox to submit to Rome's authority. Finally, the Jews were to be evicted from the southern Ukraine.

When the bill came to a vote in 1648, the Sejm, dominated by the alliance of huge landowners and their Jewish administrators, defeated it, showing how the concentration of wealth and power into a few hands can enable a group to pursue its own interests in disregard of the common good, over the brink of that self-interest into national disaster.

The situation in Poland was roughly analogous to that in Spain a Century and a half earlier. Spain was the only other country in Europe with a similarly influential Jewish population. As in Poland, many Sephardic Jews caused resentment among the lower classes. During the famine in Cuenca in 1326 Jewish usurers charged farmers 40 percent interest on the money they needed to borrow to buy grain for sowing. Blasphemy was a Jewish custom in Spain. Moses, according to Walsh, "had condemned blasphemers to death. Yet it was a custom of many Jews to blaspheme the Prophet for whom Moses had warned them to prepare."[119] The Jews in Spain "were disliked not for practicing the things that Moses taught, but for doing the things he had forbidden. They had profited hugely on the sale of fellow-beings as slaves, and practiced usury as a matter of course, and flagrantly."[120] Blasphemy went hand in hand with Jewish proselytizing, often by compulsion. Jews would force Christian servants to get circumcised as a condition of employment. They would encourage people to whom they had lent money to abjure Christ by promising to cancel their debts.

For many Jews in Amsterdam, who were former victims of the Spanish Inquisition, 1648 might have been the dawn of redemption. Instead of salvation, the Jews got Bogdan Chmielnicki, who brought them liberation from the ghetto in a way they neither foresaw nor desired. The defeat in the Sejm turned the hopeful expectation of the Cossacks into equally vehement outrage. That outrage was mobilized by a Cossack leader by the name of Bogdan Chmielnicki. Chmielnicki, who was 53 years old when the Sejm voted against enfranchising the Cossacks, had a personal stake in the matter as well. A Jew by the name of Zachariah Sabilenki, according to Graetz,

> had played him a trick, by which he was robbed of his wife and property. Another had betrayed him when he had come to an understanding with the Tartars. Besides injuries which his race had sustained from Jewish tax farmers in the Ukraine, he, therefore, had personal wrongs to avenge.[121]

Chmielnicki's claim, "The Poles have delivered us as slaves to the cursed breed of Jews,"[122] resonated among the Cossacks, bringing them into open revolt. When Chmielnicki and his Cossack and Tartar hordes defeated the Polish army in May 1648, widespread looting, pillaging, and murder ensued; 100,000 Jews perished in the mayhem. Some pretended to be Christian to escape the wrath. Some accepted baptism as the price of saving their lives. Chmielnicki's pogroms became what the riots in Spain would have become without benefit of the Inquisition. Resentment had built up for too long for this blaze to burn itself out quickly.

The Cossacks held the Poles responsible for the behavior of the Jews, even though the average Pole also suffered from the system of financial exploitation that enraged the Cossacks. Prince Vishnioviecki, whom Graetz calls "the only heroic figure amongst the Poles at that time,"[123] did what he could to protect the Jews, but that wasn't much given the magnitude of the forces that opposed him. In many towns, the Jews put aside their separatist instincts and allied themselves with local Catholics in mutual defense against the bloodthirsty Cossacks. Sometimes the pact succeeded; sometimes it didn't. When Chmielnicki's Cossack hordes arrived at the gates of Lwow, he demanded that all Jews within the city's walls be handed over to him as a condition of lifting the siege. The Poles refused, and many Jewish lives were saved. According to the Jewish historian Henryk Grynberg: "the Polish armies, who were at war with [the Cossacks], were the sole defenders of the Jews."[124] Chmielnicki's animus was directed equally against the Catholic Church and the Jews. When he was sober enough to dictate the conditions of peace after an attack, he invariably demanded expulsion of both from areas the Cossacks controlled.

Poland's neighbors exploited the situation, setting in motion events that would eventually lead to Poland's partition at the end of the 18th Century. Muscovy, Prussia, Sweden, Brandenburg, and the Ottoman Empire all nibbled at territory Poland was too weak to defend. Poland lost, as a result, 200,000 inhabitants, half of whom were Jews. The Uniates of the Ukraine were forcibly converted to Orthodoxy, diminishing the Catholic and Polish influence on the southern flank of Lithuania, which had converted to Catholicism largely through Polish influence.

The Chmielnicki pogroms, occurring in the purported Messianic year of redemption, strengthened those Jews who felt that messianic deliverance, ushered in perhaps by catastrophe, was closer than ever. The idea that the Messiah would hear and answer the prayers of his people in time of need became transmuted into a belief that dire need was a sign that the Messiah's arrival was imminent. The alembic that enabled this religious alchemy was Cabala, which had instilled the messianic expectation in the first place.

Gershom Scholem disagrees with those who see the Chmielnicki uprisings as the cause of the Messianic fever that swept European Jewry during the middle of the 17th Century. "If the massacres of 1648 were in any sense its principal cause," Scholem argues, "why did the messiah not arise within Polish Jewry?"[125] The source of messianic fervor, according to Scholem, was "none other than Lurianic kabbalism, that is that form of Kabbalah which had developed at Safed, in Galilee, during the sixteenth Century and which dominated Jewish religiosity in the seventeenth Century."[126] According to the Cabala, catastrophe and utopianism go hand in hand. A catastrophe like the Chmielnicki massacres meant that redemption was at hand.

The most immediate consequence of the Chmielnicki uprising was a massive exodus from the Jewish paradise in the east. Penniless Jewish refugees streamed west. It was at this moment that the legend of the wandering Jew was born. A race whose scriptures begin with a description of paradise and whose formative moment was escape from bondage in Egypt could not get the idea of escape into another paradise out of its head. So, having heard stories of the prospering displaced Sephardim, their impoverished Ashkenazic cousins streamed toward Hamburg and Amsterdam, the Dutch Jerusalem. Amsterdam thus became a staging area for the ongoing experimentation in revolution which is the modern world. With the two main branches of Judaism converging in a land recently ripped by force from the Spanish empire, a new *modus vivendi* was inevitable. It was the revolutionary idea, promoted by Jews, often not surprisingly full of outrage at the Inquisition and by German-speaking Catholics full of revulsion at the order the Church had imposed on Europe.

IV

On January 30, 1649, eight months after Chmielnicki had defeated the Polish army, while the slaughter of Jews was in full swing, the Puritan Demi-Jews executed the English king. His death warrant was signed by 59 "saints"; Cromwell's name was third on the list. One commentator called the execution of the king "an earth-shattering event."[127] He would have done better to call the regicide world-shattering, because it shattered a number of worlds, all medieval. The Jew and the Demi-Jew presided at the birth of a new age, an age they saw as the dawn of redemption. That new age and the Jewish/Puritan alliance at its heart is still with us, driving American foreign policy, to give a recent example, to war with Iraq. Like the wars it spawned, that new age would be as bloody as the events which inaugurated it.

The revolutionary link between Jews and Reformers was theoretical as well as practical. The "Reformers" could justify their criminal behavior only by cloaking it in the imagery of the Old Testament. Regicide was the most heinous of crimes and viewed with revulsion by all of Christian Europe, and yet Cromwell justified his role in the murder of Charles I by appealing to the story of Phineas. "Be not offended at the manner," Cromwell wrote to Lord Wharton in January 1650,

> perhaps no other way was left. What if God accepted the zeal, as He did that of Phineas, whose reason might have called for a jury? What if the Lord have witnessed this approbation and acceptance to this also, not only by signal outward acts, but to the heart also? What if I fear my friend should withdraw his shoulder from the Lord's work ... through scandals, though false, mistaken reasonings.[128]

The subjunctive mood of Cromwell's self-justification indicates that not even the models he dragooned from the Old Testament could erase the guilt of regicide, but if they could not absolve him of his sin, they certainly acted as a palliative. Cromwell, according to one commentator,

> was making a startling reference to the biblical story of Phineas, who thrust a javelin through a sinfully copulating couple, thus saving the people of Israel from the wrath of God. In the end, only brutal summary justice against the King had served to complete God's work to save the nation from His wrath and to secure his continuing love.[129]

By 1649, when Charles I went on trial, the tradition of Judaizing which had been extirpated from Spain had struck deep roots in England. Cromwell had become as versed in using Biblical figures as a rationalization for crimes as Walsingham had been in using Jewish spies from Spain and Portugal as agents in his war with the Catholic powers of Europe. The Puritans could implement the revolution precisely because they were Judaizers, because revolution was at its root a Jewish idea. Based on Moses' deliverance of Israel, the revolutionary saw a small group of chosen "saints" leading a fallen world to liberation from political oppression. Revolution was a secularization of ideas taken from the Bible, and as history progressed the secularization of the concept progressed as well. But total secularization of the idea would have made the idea totally useless to the Puritan revolutionaries. Secularization in the 17th Century was synonymous with Judaizing. It meant effectively substituting the Old Testament for the New. The concept of revolution gained legitimacy precisely because of its Jewish roots. Graetz sees the attraction Jewish ideas held for English Puritans quite clearly. The Roundheads were not inspired by the example of the suffering Christ, nor were they inspired by the medieval saints who imitated Him. They needed the example of the warriors of Israel to inspire them in their bellicose campaigns against the Irish and the Scots, who could be subjugated or exterminated because the Puritans saw them as latter day Canaanites. Similarly, if the King were an unworthy leader, he deserved to die at the hands of the righteous, who now acted, as the Puritans thought the Jews had, on direct orders from God. Judaizing solved the problem of moral and political legitimacy. It allowed the Judaizer a free hand to ransack the Old Testament for models that would justify sexual appetite, as in the case of Milton and the Ranters, or regicide and *libido dominandi* in the case of Cromwell. Trying to fathom the attraction the Old Testament held for the Puritans, Graetz concludes

> The Christian Bible with its monkish figures, its exorcists, its praying brethren, and pietistic saints, supplied no models for warriors contending with a faithless king, a false aristocracy and unholy priests. Only the great heroes of the Old Testament, with fear of God in their hearts and the sword in their hands, at once religious and national champions, could serve as models for the Puritans: the Judges, freeing the oppressed people from the yoke of foreign domination; Saul, David, and Joab routing the foes of their country; and Jehu, making an end of an idolatrous and blasphemous house—these were favorite characters with Puritan warriors.[130]

Graetz admits the Puritans were involved in rationalization and projection when he concludes that:

> In every verse of the books of Joshua, Judges, Samuel and Kings, they saw their own condition reflected; every psalm seemed composed for them, to teach them that, though surrounded on every side by ungodly foes, they need not fear while they trusted in God. Oliver Cromwell compared himself to the judge Gideon, who first obeyed the voice of God hesitatingly, but afterwards courageously scattered the attacking heathens; or to Judas Maccabaeus, who out of a handful of martyrs formed a host of victorious warriors.[131]

Graetz put his finger on the heart of the issue when he identified Puritan role models as "at once religious and national champions." Judaizing, as Bernard of Clairvaux said, was a reversion by Christians grown weary of the freedom of the gospels and longing for the bondage of the law, not unlike the Israelites when they longed for the fleshpots of Egypt after Moses led them from bondage. Messianic politics was one more way to return to, what was starkly called, the vomit of Judaism. Revolution as practiced by the Puritan Judaizers was a reversion to a more primitive, pre-Christian political model. There was no separation of the two swords of pope and emperor here—or, to use the terms of a later more secular era, no separation of Church and State. Instead, pope and emperor were fused into one charismatic revenant of King David. Israel had become ethnic again, except now the "real Jews" were Englishmen, the visible elect on earth, and England (or New England) was the New Jerusalem.

The Puritans wanted to become Jews for the same reason they wanted their visible elect on earth to replace the state Church, which they viewed as the Catholic Church with the king as pope. If they could absorb the Jews by converting them to their form of Judaizing Christianity, they would be Jews themselves, the new chosen people, and England would be the New Jerusalem. "A desire was excited in the hearts of the Puritans to see this living wonder, the Jewish people, with their own eyes, to bring Jews to England, and, by making them part of the theocratic community about to be established, stamp it with the seal of completion."[132] This was less a desire for conversion than an attempt at ethnic and spiritual cannibalism. "If we absorb the Jews," this reasoning went, "we will become Jews."

If proof were needed of the maxim that history repeats itself, first as tragedy and then as farce, it could be taken from English history of the Puritan era. The tragedy of the regicide was followed by the farcical behavior of Judaizing sects like the Ranters and the Diggers. Following the regicide, everything and anything seemed possible, as long as it was connected with the Jews. Parliament began a debate which sputtered along over the next few years on the topic of whether the Sabbath should be celebrated on Saturday, whether Parliament should adopt Hebrew as its official language, and whether the Torah should be the official law of the land.

Menasseh ben Israel followed these debates with increasing excitement. When Nathaniel Holmes, a Puritan divine, announced he wished "to become the servant of Israel and serve him on bended knee,"[133] what else could it mean but the time of the restoration of the Jews had come, and the coming of the Messiah and the redemption of Israel was not far behind. Like later collaboration between Zionists and televangelists, Jew and Puritan each tried to manage the mania that raged in England for his own advantage in the ensuing social chaos.

The murder of the king led to the collapse of morals, especially in the realm of sexual behavior. Cohn says the "excitement" was "most intense during the period of political instability and uncertainty which followed the execution of the King and lasted until the establishment of the Protectorate."[134] As Plato had predicted in the *Republic*, anarchy led to tyranny. Large numbers of "saints" went mad as they gave free rein to their sexual passions, until Cromwell had to impose martial law on the ungovernable population. In the meantime, sexual liberation was the infallible sign that the revolution had arrived. The logic of revolution was clear enough, and it would assume the same trajectory it had in Bohemia and Muenster. If the "saints" could commit an act as impious as murdering the king, then promoting the communality of wives seemed like small potatoes in comparison. In 1649-50 Gerard Winstanley was moved by supernatural illuminations to found the celebrated community of "Diggers" near Cobham in Surrey. The Ranters and Diggers were to England what the Taborites and Adamites had been to Bohemia and the Anabaptists in Muenster.

In 1649 George Fox, founder of the Quakers, was thrown into prison in Coventry, where he learned how Judaizing religion served as a cover for political and sexual revolution. "They said they were God,"[135] Fox said, describing the prisoners he met. After he reproved them "for their blasphemous expression," Fox realized that further preaching was a waste of breath, because "I perceived they were Ranters."[136] Other writers noticed the same sort of incorrigible behavior. Richard Baxter claimed that Ranters promoted

> a Cursed Doctrine of Libertinism, which brought them to all abominable filthiness of Life: They taught ... that to the Pure all things are Pure (even things forbidden). And so, as allowed by God, they spoke most hideous words of Blasphemy, and many of them committed Whoredoms commonly: Insomuch that a Matron of great Note for Godliness and Sobriety, being perverted by them, turned so shameless a Whore, that she was Carted in the streets of London.... They say that for one man to be tyed to one woman, or one woman to one man, is a fruit of the curse; but they say, we are freed from the curse; therefore it is our liberty to make use of whom we please ... this opinion they infer for these words of the Lord to Eve, Thy desire shall be to thy husband.[137]

The author of the pamphlet *The Routing of the Ranters* described a woman corrupted by their antinomian creed: "she tosseth of her glasses freely, and concludeth there is no heaven but the pleasures she enjoyeth on earth, she is very familiar at the first sight, and danceth the Canaries at the sound of a hornpipe."[138] The Ranters sang blasphemous parodies of the Psalms and engaged in blasphemous parodies of the Eucharist, *e.g.*, a man took a piece of beef in his hand and tore it apart while pronouncing the words, "This is the flesh of Christ. Take and eat." Emboldened by the apparent suspension of the moral order in the new apocalyptic age, a ropemaker from Andover, William Franklin, left his wife and had sex with a number of women. One, Mary Gadbury, was convinced the Lord had destroyed Franklin's former body, so sleeping with him did not constitute the sin of adultery. Franklin also persuaded Gadbury he was the promised Christ, and she, as a result of her intercourse with him, began to have visions. Like the Adamites in Bohemia, the Ranters were convinced they should throw off their clothes, because "Adam and Eve in innocency were naked, and were not ashamed."[139] Like the Anabaptists in Muenster, the Ranters held "our women are all in common."[140] In their attempt to justify the claim that "to the pure all things are pure," the Ranters, like Cromwell and Milton, invariably appealed to examples from the Old Testament. Those who were foolish enough to disagree with them were "yet on the borders of Aegypt" and not "with Moses on Mount Hermon."[141] Abiezer Coppe, once a "poor scholar" at Oxford who used to "entertain a wanton Housewife in his chamber," converted to Ranterism following the regicide of 1649.[142] Convinced that the best way to annihilate a troubled conscience was to sin boldly, Coppe preached "blasphemies and unheard-of villainies" while stark naked in broad daylight.[143] By night, he would "drink and lye with a Wench that had been also his hearer, stark naked."[144]

Coppe was arrested in January 1650 but released one year later after he recanted his errors. All of England would go through much the same process ten years later after Cromwell's death.

Cromwell was convinced the anointing of the Lord was on him. Much of the modest deprecation in his accounts of what were undoubtedly brilliant military campaigns results from his Judaizing conscience. If God had placed victory in his hands, then he was not morally responsible for his actions, whether the murder of the king or the slaughter of the Irish. Cromwell was merely extrapolating to the political and military realm the principles of exculpation Luther had announced in *De servo arbitrio*. His mental instability, particularly in its manic phase, may also have enhanced his feeling of being overpowered by the divine will.

On August 15, 1649, Cromwell landed with his army at Ringsend, near Dublin "for the propagating of the Gospel of Christ [and] the establishing of truth and peace."[145] Cromwell understood Catholic Ireland had posed a military threat to England ever since the defeat of the Spanish Armada. Had Philip II listened to Parma, he would have first crushed the rebellion in Holland and then used Ireland and Holland as twin bases of operation against England. Ireland had figured in the plans of Charles I, as Cromwell had learned after the Battle of Naseby in 1645. But he needed no special intelligence to fathom the intentions of the Irish. They had showed their hand in 1641, one year before the civil war in England, when they rose against their Protestant masters, confirming their view that the Irish were "vicious, bloody, and ruthless, and could not be trusted."[146] Ireland would provide Cromwell's first test case. Popery could be extirpated and then civilized Protestants and Jewish tax-farmers could run the country according to godly principles. "The rising of 1641," says Litton, "provided an ideal opportunity for the English government to assert its authority in Ireland and plans were laid for large-scale confiscations of land."[147]

After announcing to his army of 12,000 men that their task was to bring "the Gospel of Christ" to the "barbarous and bloodthirsty Irish and the rest of their adherents and confederates,"[148] Cromwell marched to the walls of Drogheda on the River Boyne and demanded the immediate surrender of the garrison there. Ironically, the walls of Drogheda were manned largely by English soldiers who were Catholics (some defenders were English Protestants) who threw their lot in with the Irish, just as English Catholics of an earlier generation had thrown their lot in with the King of Spain in the Netherlands. After putting his siege guns in place on September 10, Cromwell demanded unconditional surrender. When the garrison refused, Cromwell fell into a manic rage. No quarter was given when the New Model Army breached the walls and swarmed into the town. "[T]he order to give no quarter, largely obeyed, came directly from Cromwell," who later wrote that "our men getting up to them, were ordered by me to put them all to the sword. And indeed, being in the heat of action, I forbad them to spare any that were in arms in the town, and I think, that night they put to the sword about 2,000 men."[149] The killing of defenseless civilians continued for days. Cromwell's men seem to have been overwhelmed with their commander's passion, and pursued the defenders mostly English Royalist troops, through the narrow streets, killing all before them. Some attempt may have been made to avoid civilian deaths, but priests were another matter, and every priest seen was killed. In the church of St. Peter's to the north of Drogheda, dozens of people crowded into the steeple for shelter; a fire was set below them and they burned to death as if they were in a chimney.[150]

While his mood swings may have influenced the initial decision, the decision to continue the slaughter seems calculated. Cromwell wanted to spare himself the bother of further sieges; he thought spreading terror was the best means to that end. "The Enemy," he wrote later, "were filled with much terror. And truly I believe this bitterness will save much effusion of blood, through the goodness of God."[151] Cromwell rationalized his decision by claiming "he was doing God's work and that credit for the victory belonged to the Lord," but he also implied the slaughter was a just punishment for the rebellion of 1641, although "Drogheda had never been a strong Confederate Catholic town and it is unlikely that many of the civilians had been involved in the atrocities of 1641."[152] As in other battles, Cromwell ascribed the victory to God, who helped his army "hold forth and maintain ... the glory of English liberty in a nation where we have an undoubted right to it."[153] The Irish were cowed by the terror, or, as Andrew Marvell put it, "And now the Irish are ashamed/To see themselves in one year tamed."[154] In May 1650, Cromwell sailed to England, where he was greeted like a conquering Caesar. After savoring the adulation, Cromwell left for Scotland, where he crushed the numerically superior Scottish forces with brilliant cavalry maneuvers at the Battle of Dunbar. As before, Cromwell wrote a letter to Parliament modestly ascribing the victory to God, and thereby absolving his conscience. "We that serve you," he wrote, "beg of you not to own us, but God alone; we pray you own His people more and more, for they are the chariots and horsemen of Israel. Disown yourselves, but own your authority, and improve it to curb the proud and the insolent, such as would disturb the tranquillity of England."[155] Cromwell was elated. To one colleague he seemed full of a "divine impulse" and "did laugh so excessively as if he had been drunk and his eyes sparkled with spirits," feeling that the Scots had been rejected by the Lord and "my weak faith had been upheld."[156] Like the Muslims, Cromwell and the Puritans tended to take the fact as a sign of divine approval. Cromwell found this psychological weapon remarkably easy to wield against foes, all of whom, whether Scots, Irish, or Cavalier, were portrayed as godless. It would prove more difficult to wield the same theological and psychological weapons against the left-wing of his own party, as Cromwell discovered in dealings with Fifth Monarchy Men.

V

In 1625 a war broke out between Turkey and Venice over who was to control trade in the Levant. Unable to do business in Constantinople, English and Dutch merchants transferred their offices to Smyrna where they valued the honesty and probity of a certain Mordecai Zevi. English and Dutch merchants routinely hired Jews as go-betweens in dealings with the Turks because they knew the local languages and because of their influence with the Sublime Porte. Because Mordecai Zevi "executed his commissions with strict honesty," he "enjoyed the confidence of the principals and became a wealthy man."[157] One year after the outbreak of war, Mordecai's wife gave birth to a son on the 9th of Ab (August 1626), the date on which the Temple in Jerusalem had been destroyed. The Ninth of Ab must have fallen on Saturday that year, because Mordecai named his son Shabbetai. Shabbetai grew up the child of privilege. Like most Jews of his age, Shabbetai studied the Talmud, but he excelled in other fields, notably music. As a young man, Shabbetai Zevi was exceptionally good looking with a full beard and permanently rosy cheeks. In addition, he had an exceptionally pleasing hypnotic voice. Like the young Asiatic god Dionysos of an earlier age—a god, it should be noted, who also came from Turkey—or like the Dionysian rock stars of a later age, Shabbetai Zevi could sway crowds with his singing, changing their mood as if by magic.

In addition to musical talent, Shabbetai Zevi seems to have had a mystical bent, a trait probably magnified by his mental instability. Like Cromwell, Shabbetai Zevi was a manic-depressive. He differed from Cromwell only in the magnitude of his mood swings; where Cromwell felt he had been anointed by God, Shabbetai Zevi felt he was the Messiah. Shabbetai Zevi had heard the English merchants in his father's house describe the increasing political instability in England, leading to the Civil War, which broke out when Zevi was 16. Defeated by the Puritans, the English King was put on trial when Zevi was 21 and executed when he was 22. According to Graetz, Mordecai Zevi was not only familiar with the particulars of the millennial fervor which grew throughout the 1640s, he communicated his enthusiastic belief in "the apocalypse of the Fifth Monarchy" to the members of his family, "none of whom listened more attentively than Sabbatai," who was "already entangled in the maze of the Luryan Cabala and inclined to mistake enthusiastic hopes for prosaic facts."[158] Before long it would become clear that the tales of apocalypse which Shabbetai Zevi had heard in his youth became powerful enough to convince him that he himself was the Messiah which everyone had been expecting. The revolution in England, followed by the murder of that country's Christian king, coupled with the massacres in Poland and the mass migration of Jews which it encouraged there had convinced many older and more sober Jews that the end of the world was at hand. Someone as mentally unstable as Shabbetai Zevi, on the other hand, seems to have become unhinged by the course of events.

The Zohar didn't help matters any. A young man of privilege who was mystically inclined and mentally unstable would quite naturally find corroboration in the mumbo-jumbo of the Cabala. The expulsion of the Jews from Spain coupled with the massacre of the Jews in Poland led the Jews inexorably to the Zohar for an explanation of their plight, and the Zohar, given new plausibility by the writing of the Spanish refugee Isaac Luria, reinforced the apocalyptic sense that had driven people to the Cabala for explanation.

Lurianic Caballah noto nly prepared the way for the Chmielnicki pogroms, it was also the result of the other great catastrophe of Jewish life aat that time, the expulsion of the Jews from Spain. Isaac Luria ben Solomon (1534-72) gathered a group of disciples bent on spreading his explanation of Jewish exile, of how recent catastrophes fit into the plan of divine redemption. To do this Luria had recourse to the Gnostic mythology circulating in the Mediterranean world since the first heresies of the Christian era. God had created bowls to contain the light of his understanding. The bowls proved incapable of containing that light and broke, scattering the light throughout creation, where it remained imprisoned in matter. The realm of *qelippah*, where the sparks are held in bondage, is a distinctly political realm "represented on the terrestrial and historical plane by tyranny and oppression."[159] The purpose of man's existence on earth became *tiqqun* or healing, restoring the lights to their original place in the universe before the breaking of the vessels had released the forces of sin and evil. The Diaspora was now readily explainable. Jews were dispersed to be better able to discover the holy sparks, extract them from the matter they were enmired in, and then return them to their rightful place in the universe. When this was accomplished, the Messiah would come, and redemption would be complete. Redemption, according to Lurianic doctrine, was bound up with man's efforts and the process of history, a combination which was incorporated, via Hegel, into Karl Marx's revolutionary theory three hundred years later. The Jew's role is to bring about redemption, which does not descend suddenly, "in a moment, in the twinkling of an eye" from on high but rather

> appears as the logical and necessary fruition of Jewish history. Israel's labors of *tiqqun* are, by definition, of a messianic character. Final redemption is therefore no longer dissociated from the historical process that preceded it: "The redemption of Israel takes place by degrees, one purifying after another, one refining after another." The messianic king, far from bringing about the *tiqqun*, is himself brought about by it: he appears after the *tiqqun* has been achieved. The cosmic redemption of the raising of the sparks merges with the national redemption of Israel, and the symbol of the "ingathering of the exiles" comprises both.[160]

The political implications of the Lurianic Kaballah seem clear enough. The Messiah must wait upon man's efforts. He can only come once the process of *tiqqun* or purification and healing has been accomplished by man, i.e., by the Jews on earth, who act as the vanguard of redemption much as the communist party later would function as the vanguard of the proletariat. Without *tiqqun*, "it is impossible that the messianic king come."[161] From here it is but a short leap to the conclusion that Israel had become its own Messiah, or as Scholem says, "By transferring to Israel, the historical nation, much of the redemptive task formerly considered as the messiah's, many of his distinctive personal traits, as drawn in apocalyptic literature, were now obliterated."[162]

David Horowitz sees the same political meaning in the Lurianic revision of the meaning of exile. Once the meaning of exile had been transformed by its incorporation into the Gnostic creed of Luria's Cabala, "redemption is no longer a divine release from the punishment of exile, but a humanly inspired transformation of creation itself."[163] What is true of Israel's exile is *a fortiori* true of mankind's exile in the *qelippoth* or husks of matter. Luria's essentially Gnostic thought projects evil away from the heart of man into structures outside of himself, which is to say, political structures, which can be changed by human effort. Instead of evil emanating from the heart, evil emanates from evil things in an evil universe, which is begging to be changed by those who know its secrets, i.e., the cabalists. "Practical" Cabala, says Scholem, "is synonymous with magic."[164] Some of Luria's followers felt they could "force the end" by an act of "practical Kabbalah," which is to say by "invoking holy names and Kabbalistic formulae."[165] Since the sparks have been "tricked" into matter, it might be possible to trick them out again by the use of what Hayim Vital termed "holy fraud."[166]

Like the concept of insincere conversion, the concept of "holy fraud" would find its most immediate embodiment in the Jewish Messiah Shabbetai Zevi, but it would perdure long after Zevi's demise. The cabalists will lead the world to redemption through magic (or applied science and technology) and trickery, not by leading good lives while waiting patiently for the redeemer to come, because "in the Gnostic view, the evil that men do emanates not from their own flawed natures, but is the result of a flaw in the cosmos they inhabit, which they can repair."[167] As a result of Luria's Gnostic transformation of Jewish thought, "Man" becomes "his own redeemer."[168] Exile was, according to Luria,

> no longer a punishment, but a mission; no longer a reflection of who we are, but a mark of our destiny to become agents of salvation. In this Gnostic vision, Israel is dispersed among the nations in order that the light of the whole world may be liberated. In the words of the cabalist Hayim Vital: "This is the secret why Israel is fated to be enslaved by all the Gentiles of the world: In order that it may uplift those sparks of the Divine Light which have also fallen among them.... And therefore it was necessary that Israel should be scattered to the four winds in order to lift everything up." *The Israelites are the first revolutionary internationalists.*[169]

Lurianic Cabala was also a reaction to the Inquisition. By the time of the Chmielnicki massacres, it had spread to all parts of the Diaspora. "Wherever Lurianism came," Scholem writes, "it produced messianic tension."[170] It produced expectation of redemption. But now, Scholem points out, "redemption meant a revolution in history."[171] Since Lurianism created the Messianic fervor of the mid-17th Century, it is not an exaggeration to say it created the revolutionary mindset that characterizes the modern world. The modern world emerged when medieval Judaism, having fostered northern Europe's rebellion against Rome, cracked open and fell apart when Lurianism found its fulfillment in Shabbetai Zevi, the false Messiah. Jewish Gnostic messianism, with the help of English puritan revolutionaries, was released from the ghetto into the nascent modern world that succeeded the medieval world and was its antithesis. The Messianic age of the mid-17th Century "was an age characterized by rebellion against the Catholic Church and the order which the Church had imposed on Europe since the fall of the Roman Empire. A millenium of Catholic culture was threatened by the resurgence of an old idea."

The resurgent old idea was the notion that the millennium meant restoration of the "terrene Kingdome of the Jewes," an idea condemned, but not destroyed, by the Council of Ephesus in 431. The new name for that old idea was revolution. When the ghetto was cracked open, but not destroyed, by the Inquisition, the Chmielnicki pogroms, and the disillusionment which followed the False Messiah's conversion to Islam, the concept of revolution escaped through those cracks in the ghetto walls into European culture. As the Messianic fervor grew toward the mid-17th Century, the Cabala, as interpreted by Isaac Luria, became the only instrument which could make sense of the increasingly apocalyptic chain of events.

Inspired by reports from England and Poland, Shabbetai Zevi's behavior began to reflect the bizarre and apocalyptic nature of his age. Zevi married in 1648 but seems not to have consummated the marriage, something historians deduce from his wife's petition for a divorce, which Zevi did not contest, within the same year. There was a sexual component to his behavior as well. As a youth, Zevi "is said to have been tortured by nightmarish dreams, whose sexual character is beyond doubt."[172] During his waking hours, he was assailed by "the sons of whoredom" who are "the scourges of the children of man."[173] According to Scholem, "the latter is the Zohar's technical term for those demons born of masturbation."[174]

By the age of 20, Zevi's voice and charismatic personality had gathered around him a small circle of followers in Smyrna. Zevi heard a voice inside him which said, "thou art the savior of Israel."[175] Lured further into what Graetz calls "the labyrinth of the Zohar"[176] as the only plausible explanation for the apocalyptic events of the age, Zevi uttered the Tetragrammaton in the presence of his followers. Mentioning the name of God was strictly prohibited among devout Jews. The fact that Zevi uttered it meant the old age was at an end. Zevi—here the Christian influences are unmistakable—had come to abolish the law, and the surest way to show the Old Law was no longer in force was to engage in actions the Old Law forbade. "It was only in Christianity," Scholem writes, "that the messiah had revealed new commandments—or so at least it seemed to Jews who heard Christian arguments about the Law of Moses being superseded since the advent of the messiah by the laws and customs of the church."[177]

Soon Shabbetai Zevi began to preach the concept of "doing a good deed by sinning," an idea similar to the antinomianism the Ranters were preaching in England. In one of his frequent bouts of hair-splitting, Scholem attacks Graetz for claiming that Zevi got 1666 as the date of the apocalypse from the English revolutionaries, and in doing so loses sight of the forest for the trees. Radical thought moved back and forth between Jews and Judaizing revolutionaries. It is easier to believe that Zevi was influenced by radical thought, regardless of which date he chose as the mystical year of redemption, than to believe that, living in a house frequented by English merchants, he was unaffected by reports of what was going on in England. After uttering the Tetragrammaton, Shabbetai Zevi ate pork and engaged in prohibited sexual activity; he encouraged his followers to do likewise. Scholem says "there is no proof that anybody took him seriously at the time,"[178] but the historical record contradicts Scholem. Zevi and his followers were expelled from Smyrna in 1651 because of the disruption they were causing. After traveling first to Salonika in Greece, then the largest Jewish community in the Ottoman Empire, Zevi and his followers wandered around the eastern Mediterranean, like an itinerant rock band hoping to bring about revolution by their songs.

VI

Menasseh ben Israel eventually wrote up Montezinos' story of the Jewish Indians of Ecuador in *Spes Israelis*, which translated into English as *The Hope of Israel*. *The Hope of Israel* became an instant best-seller in England when published in 1650, and it fueled the Messianic fire raging in the camps of the Puritans and the Jews. The Jew and the Demi-Jew looked forward to the imminent coming of the Messiah, even if for the former it was the first coming and for the latter it was the second. Not deterred by details like this, both camps were swept up in the mania, and found themselves working for the goal of inaugurating the Apocalypse by allowing the Jews to return to England. Experts in Gematria added their fuel by developing calculations that confirmed the ravings of the Fifth Monarchy Men. The Zohar, true to the epithet Graetz attached to it, had predicted the arrival of the Messiah soon after the year 1300, but that date was adjusted by 17th Century cabalists to mean 1648. After 1648, the date was readjusted again. Some felt the prophecies would be fulfilled in 1655, but the overwhelming majority pinned their hopes on 1666.

Menasseh's hopes about Jewish migration to England were encouraged by the introduction of the Cartwright Petition in Parliament on Christmas day 1648 (Puritans did not celebrate Christ's birth as a holiday). The Cartwright petition recommended the toleration "of all Religions whatsoever, not excepting Turkes, nor Papists, nor Iewes."[179] This attempt at leveling elicited a storm of protest. Clement Walker described it as "the last damnable design of Cromwell and Ireton" and a case of "Hebrew Jewes" working with the "uncircumcised Jewes of the Councell of Warre."[180] This collaboration of Jews and Puritans was "no marvell," one Royalist writer opined. Why should it be surprising "that those which intend to crucifie their King, should shake hands with them that crucified their Saviour."[181]

It became increasingly difficult to distinguish the Jews from their judaizing admirers and vice versa. Several months after the Petition was introduced, William Everard, a Digger, announced he was "of the race of the Jews."[182] He was not alone in his enthusiasm. Thomas Tany, a London goldsmith, was so taken up by the talk of liberty of conscience that he circumcised himself in preparation for the coming of the Messiah. Tany felt that since the Christians came from the Jews, it was only logical to return in the dawning apocalyptic age. Then he and his followers, who had taken to living in tents in Lambeth and Greenwich, could proceed to Jerusalem, where they could join forces with the ten lost tribes, who were converging on Jerusalem from their secret hiding places in Egypt and Persia, to inaugurate the Apocalypse. Tany claimed he was "a Jew of the tribe of Ruben, begotten by the gospel, which is Massah, El, Jah, or Jehovah, Jesus or Christ, all these are but names of that one merciful thing that is God."[183] Although he circumcised himself, Tany remained a Christian who claimed to live according to the Mosaic covenant while still following Jesus Christ. Instead of using reason to resolve the contradictions in his theology, Tany resolved them by action. At around the same time that Menasseh set sail from Amsterdam to London, Thomas Tany set sail from London to the Holy Land in a "littel Bote"[184] he built. His carpentry was no better than his theology. While sailing to Amsterdam to rally the Jews to his cause, his "littel Bote" sank, and he drowned.

Angered by the market share the Dutch had garnered in the Orient while the English were slaughtering each other during their civil war, the English sent a delegation to Holland to propose a union of the two countries. Spurned by the Dutch, the English passed the Navigation Acts in October 1650, and then declared war, exhibiting the feeling, as one commentator put it, if you can't join them, beat them. Before returning to England to report on their failed mission, the delegation, headed by the Republican Judge Oliver St. John, met with Menasseh ben Israel in Amsterdam to discuss the possibility of Jewish migration to England. It was a severe case of mutual admiration. Menasseh was impressed with the zeal of the Puritan revolutionaries, especially by their execution of the Christian king as the fullest expression of their zeal. The English delegation was impressed by Menasseh's scholarship, as expressed in his best-seller, *Hope of Israel*.

Thomas Thorowgood had written *Jewes in America, or the Probability that the Indians are Jews* at about the same time Menasseh was writing *Hope of Israel*. When John Dury, "perhaps the most active millenarian theoretician in the Puritan revolution"[185] was asked to write a preface for Thorowgood's book, he remembered stories he had heard from Jews in Holland while acting as Cromwell's agent there. Writing to Menasseh, Dury requested a copy of the Montezinos report. When he made it public, millennial fever in England received a new jolt. If great minds like this had come independently to the same conclusion, could anyone seriously doubt the Indians in America were Jews from the ten lost tribes of Israel? And if that were the case, could anyone doubt the end times were at hand? Once the Montezinos document circulated among the divines in England, they came to the unanimous conclusion that the climax of world history was at hand. The Ten Lost Tribes had been found; the Jews had come to the "ends of the earth." When they were admitted to England, their conversion would follow almost automatically, given the pure Gospel the Puritans preached and the holy lives they led. Once the Jews converted, Christ could return in his glory. Given events this momentous, it was clear, to Dury at least, that one of two things could happen. "It is the expectation of some of the wisest Jews now living," Dury wrote, "that about the year 1650, either we Christians shall be Mosaick, or else that they themselves Jewes shall be Christians."[186] An objective observer would most probably have come to the conclusion the English were on their way to becoming Jews, but Puritans like Dury did not see it that way. "Those sometimes poor, now precious Indians," Dury continued, "may be as the first fruits of the glorious harvest of Israel's redemption."[187] As further corroboration of his theory, Dury mentioned the reports of John Eliot, the "Apostle to the Indians" of Massachusetts. One could also add the testimony of William Penn, the Quaker, who "found it easy to discover signs of Judaism amongst the Indians."[188] After his first winter in Pennsylvania, Penn wrote living among the Indians was "like being in Duke Street in London, surrounded by Jews."[189]

Once the Jewish Indian theory received the imprimatur of intellectual respectability from the Puritan divines, they wanted to draw out its implications by inviting the Jews to migrate to England. If the Jews could be brought to "the ends of the earth," otherwise known as *Kezeh ha-Arez*," or "*Angleterre*" or England, then the Puritan divines could usher in the Millennium. That was why St. John's delegation showed up at Menasseh's synagogue in Amsterdam.

Menasseh had his own reasons for pursuing the relationship with the English. During 1650, Menasseh had conversations with a Portuguese Jesuit, Antonio de Viera, who had tried to use the Jewish Indian theory to support a Joachim of Fiore inspired world-wide brotherhood of Jews and Christians under the rule of the King of Portugal. Menasseh, according to Fisch, "responded warmly to Viera's version of history in which a restored people of Israel would have a central role."[190] He also began wondering "how best these enthusiasms could be channeled into his own messianic agenda."[191] Viera's reading of the end times got Menasseh thinking how he could use millennial expectation among the Puritans to Jewish advantage. So Menasseh encouraged these ideas among the English Puritans as a way of "furthering the ends of Jewish Polity."[192] "Menasseh's Politieia is the same as that of Maimonides. Its worldly nature and it existence in time stand out against the general Christian concept of the 'Kingdom of the Spirit.'"[193] He was both Marxist revolutionary and Zionist rolled into one, which Fisch recognizes when he links Menasseh

> to the fathers of modern Zionism in the nineteenth Century. They exhibit the same messianic typology as Menasseh. Moses Hess (*Rome and Jerusalem*, 1862) situates himself, literally, at the gates of Rome. If Rome could gain her independence in these latter days, why not Israel he argues. The intuition was sound. Like Menasseh he responded to the revolutionary movements of his time. Marxist revolutionary theory was the 19th Century equivalent of Christian millenarianism in the 17th Century—Hess used it but with reservations. Herzl later read the

signs of his time—now was a time to speak of Jewish nationhood for the rights of small nations that were now a marketable commodity....This is the dialogue with history which is the mark of normal Jewish messianism.[194]

After St. John and his delegation assured Menasseh that his petition would be warmly welcomed, they returned to England, and parliament took up the idea of readmitting the Jews by considering the letter Menasseh submitted in support of his cause. Menasseh quickly got to the heart of what united the Jews and the Puritan Judaizers: hatred of the Catholic Church. "Today," Menasseh wrote, "the English nation is no longer our ancient enemy, but has changed the Papistical religion and become excellently affected to our nation."[195] This effusion was not reassuring to non-Judaizing Englishmen, especially the merchants in London, who feared the Jews as cut-throat competitors. Menasseh addressed these concerns too. If the Apocalypse took a while in arriving, other benefits would accrue to the English if they let the Jews into their country. Menasseh "knew that the prophecy of Daniel held a crucial place in English thought,"[196] but he also knew the financial benefits the Dutch were reaping by allowing Jewish commerce free rein there weighed heavily on the mind of the saints in England. Menasseh developed his argument in a pamphlet entitled "How Profitable the Nation of the Iews Are," using the examples of Amsterdam and Hamburg, cities prospering because of the admission of the Jews, while Spain, which had expelled them, was in decline. Menasseh even addressed the delicate subject of commercial competition which might ensue if the Jews were admitted to England, pointing out that local craftsmen had nothing to fear because Jews did not work with their hands.

Had the political situation remained stable, Menasseh probably would have traveled to England in 1652, but the war between Holland and England delayed his departure by three years, a period during which Cromwell's power was seriously eroded by the deteriorating economic situation in England and by the defection of the Fifth Monarchy Men. By the time Menasseh finally got to England, the Fifth Monarchy Men identified Cromwell, not King Charles, as the Little Horn that the Book of Daniel warned against as the precursor to the Antichrist.

VII

On July 4, 1653 Cromwell opened the Barebones Parliament, which marked the high-water mark of Judaizing in England. The Parliament derived its name from a London merchant of French extraction named Barbon. Full of enthusiasm for the new Puritan regime, Barbon changed his first name to Praise God, and his detractors changed his last name for him to the anglicized Barebones. Praise God Barebones wanted to change the law of the land to the Law of Moses. Cromwell was at the height of his power when he opened the Barebones Parliament. Named Lord Protector in April, and having an assembly of parliamentarians all of whom were saints, Cromwell felt he could deal with the issue of the admission of the Jews to England and all that would bring with it. "Indeed," he told the assembled saints, "I do think something is at the door: we are at the threshold ... you are at the edge of the promises and prophecies." It was time for God to "bring His people again from the depths of the sea,"[197] a veiled reference to the Jews. Others were less theological. The French ambassador to Holland felt Cromwell wanted to admit the Jews into England "to draw the commerce thither." Jewish trade had other benefits. As in the time of Walsingham, it was well known that Jewish commerce and espionage went hand in hand, and "Cromwell used Jewish spies in gathering intelligence even before the Whitehall conference and seems to have continued with this practice more openly afterwards."[198]

Cromwell soon discovered that dealing with a Parliament of Saints was a mixed blessing. The Judaizing left wing's attempt to turn Parliament into the English version of the Sanhedrin was just one of the headaches that the Barebones Parliament was to cause Cromwell. By January 1654, he had enough, and in an effort to silence enemies of the Protectorate, Cromwell issued an ordinance making it high treason to "to write, print teach or preach that the Protector's authority was tyrannical, usurped, or unlawful."[199] This increased the outrage of the Fifth Monarchy Men. Hannah Trapnell, who had attacked Cromwell from the moment he became Protector, now identified him with the Little Horn of the Book of Daniel, and in June 1654, she was jailed at Bridewell for her impertinence. In September 1654, Thomas Goodwin, another saint, attacked Cromwell in "A Sermon on the Fifth Monarchy, Proving by Invincible Arguments that the Saints shall have Kingdom here on Earth, which is to come, after the Fourth Monarchy is destroy'd by the Sword of the Saints, the followers of the Lamb." He was of one mind with John Rogers, another Fifth Monarchy Man, who claimed, "Cromwell was the great dragon who sat in Whitehall, and must be pulled down."[200]

Losing patience with the very saints he had called into being as a body, Cromwell dissolved the Barebones Parliament in January 1655. In March the Royalist Colonel John Penrudduck attempted an armed insurrection in Wiltshire; in response, Cromwell imposed martial law on England, dividing England and Wales into military districts each ruled by a major-general who reported directly and exclusively to Cromwell and the Council. Cromwell's dealings with the saints left him disillusioned, but one illusion he refused to relinquish was the return of the Jews to England. He still "waited for the day to see union and right understanding between the godly people," by which he meant "Scots, English, Jews, Gentiles, Presbyterians, Independents, Anabaptists and all."[201]

Menasseh continued to nourish the same hope. In September 1654, he sent David Dormido to London to plead his case for the admission of the Jews. Dormido hoped to curry favor for the Jews by pandering to prejudices against Spain and the Inquisition. His appeal to Cromwell was full of rhetoric "calculated to make Protestant blood run cold"[202] or to evoke Protestant pity by recounting the sufferings of the Marranos at the hands of people who were England's enemies. A month before Dormido could hand in his proposal in writing, three admirals of the English fleet drew up a petition urging Cromwell to admit the Jews to England. Since Cromwell had made peace with the Dutch in April 1654, the final impediment had been removed for Menasseh's great mission to the English.

Menasseh set sail for London in September 1655, just as Thomas Tany set sail in the opposite direction on his ill-fated mission to gather the Jews of Amsterdam together and take them to Jerusalem. Tany's mission "perished in the sea,"[203] but Menasseh's seemed destined for success. Millennialist expectations among the saints had primed England to receive his bizarre message with a credulity he would have never found before or afterward. Menasseh was no blind fanatic: if his story about the Jewish Indians met skepticism, he was ready to talk about the economic benefits of Jewish migration instead. But millennial expectation was his strong suit because "70 percent of the prolific ministers who published their works between 1640 and 1653 can be identified as Millenarians"[204] and the combined effect of these apocalyptic and millenarian speculations produced a sense of impending great events. Henry Wilkinson told the House of Commons in 1643 it was the "generall talk throughout the household among the domesticks ... that Christ their king is coming to take possession of his Throne, they doe not onely whisper this, and tell it in the ear, but they speak it publikly."[205] In his *Declaration to the Commonwealth of England*, Menasseh milked that sentiment, claiming an "all but total dispersion" of the Jews throughout the world "except only in this considerable and mighty island."[206] Menasseh continued, "before the Messiah come and restore our Nation, that first we must have our seat here likewise."[207] Menasseh got theological support from Nathaniel Holmes, who wrote "we can expect no more then, in the said 1655 yeer but the call of the Jewes, who from that time shall strive with the Turke, and all enemies of the Jewes conversion five and forty yeers, Dan. 12 afore their settlement, before which Call I expect the fall of the Roman Antichrist."[208] Holmes felt the Jews would convert to Christianity once exposed to its pure form in England. Menasseh passed over that part of the English millennial mania in silence, just as he had passed in silence over the more objectionable passages of Paul Felgenhauer's "half-insane" treatise,"[209] *Good News of the Messiah for Israel*, which Felgenhauer, the Bohemian mystic, in a moment of ecumenical warmth, had dedicated to Menasseh. Details like just who the Messiah was could be worked out after the Jews had established themselves in their new country.

In October 1655, Menasseh left his English lodgings in full rabbinic regalia with a number of pamphlets under his arm and marched to Whitehall, where the Council was in session. He was not allowed to address the Council, but he met with Cromwell, who seems to have fallen under his spell. For the next two months, Cromwell used all of the power at his disposal to get a hearing for the Jews and gain their admission to England. In November 1655 Cromwell produced a petition in favor of admitting the Jews to the Council. Cromwell had "resolved to force its acceptance with a minimum of delay,"[210] but the Council passed no resolution. On December 4, the Council concluded "there was no law which forbade the Jews' return to England."²¹¹ On December 12, Major General Whalley testified on behalf of the Jews, claiming "there are both politique and divine reasons: which strongly make for therye admission into a cohabitation with us. Doubtless to say no more, they will bring in much wealth into this Commonwealth; and where wee both pray for theyre conversion, and beleevie[ing] it shal be, I knowe not why we should denye the meanes."²¹²

Cromwell's zeal on behalf of the Jews got them wondering whether he might not be the Messiah himself. To find out, a delegation of Jews was dispatched to Cromwell's birthplace to examine the church records to see if there were genealogical evidence indicating that he was of the House of David. Cromwell packed the Council with his supporters to get a favorable vote, but again the Council declined to act. Instead they came up with a number of conditions that gave the Jews second thoughts. Menasseh found himself in the middle between two sides that both seemed to be getting cold feet. The Marranos, who were leading fairly comfortable lives in London already, saw Menasseh's mission as jeopardizing what they already had by making the darker side of Jewish life emerge during the discussion. The English, for their part, were beginning to realize that the Jews of 17th Century Europe were not identical to the Hebrews they had read about in the Old Testament.

Cromwell pulled out all stops, but when the council met for the last time on December 18, 1655, the tide had turned. Everyone had been in a state of millennial expectation too long, and the psychological fatigue was creating a reaction. Beyond that, council members had read one of the most effective polemics in the history of English logomachy, a tract known as A Short Demurrer, written by William Prynne, an opponent of the Jews. In his Demurrer, Prynne put together a "faithful compilation of the materials available in his day for a history of the Jews in England."²¹³ That history included the stories of the ritual murders of William of Norwich in 1144 and Little St. Hugh of Lincoln in 1255 in addition to a catalogue of many lesser evils. In his Demurrer, Prynne claimed the Jews had been expelled from England in 1290 for good reason. They "had been formerly greater clippers and Forgers of Money, and had crucified three or four children in England at least."²¹⁴ As a result of the Jews' behavior then and the parlous state of religious life in England in the wake of the revolution and regicide, Prynne concluded "now [was] a very ill time to bring in the Jews."²¹⁵ Since the people of England "were so dangerously and generally bent to Apostasy and all sorts of Novelties and Errors in Religion," it was more likely they "would sooner turn Jews, that the Jews Christians."²¹⁶

Prynne's Demurrer had an even greater effect on public opinion, which was weary of Puritan fanaticism and the civil discord it brought, than it did on the Council. Councilors on the way to their chamber met soldiers on the street who felt "We must now all turn Jews, and there will be nothing left for the poor."²¹⁷ Even philosemites like Josselin were having second thoughts. He prayed the Lord would "hasten their [the Jews'] conversion" because he feared the opposite might happen "if the Jews gained admission to England." He was "heartily afraid" the admission of the Jews would cause Englishmen to turn "aside from Christ to Moses." One wag claimed "they," meaning the Jews, "are all turned Devils already, and now we must all turn Jews."[218] Another opponent claimed

> though perhaps there may not be now in England, any great numbers of pro-fessed Iewes (some to my own knowledge there are, who have their own syna-gogues and there exercise Iudaisme). Yet, they who live here, as often as they are bound to use their office of Prayer (which is twice a day) so often are they bound to blaspheme Christ, and to curse him and all true Christians which beleeve in him.[219]

Cromwell did his best, but when the final meeting ended, hope for the Jews' readmission was gone. With unintended irony, Katz says "one of the oddest fea-tures of this debate was that the lack of Jews in England should have made pos-sible a positive view of them."[220] The simple fact is that the tenor of debate changed when the Council abandoned its romantic notions of the Old Testament Hebrews and replaced that with the picture of actual Jews as they then lived in countries with large Jewish populations. Through Prynne's *Demurrer*, English common sense triumphed over Puritan ideology. While many Englishmen felt "the Jews might be tolerated if suitable precautions could be devised," an equally large seg-ment, if not a majority, felt "if the Jews were admitted they would seduce and cheat the English."[221] James Harrington thought a compromise might be reached by sending the Jews to Ireland, where they could grind the Irish as tax-farmers, as in Poland. Under no circumstances, however, should the Jews be admitted to Eng-land, because to "receive the Jewes after any other manner into a Commonwealth, were to maim it," because Jews "never assimilate, and instead become parasites on the state."[222]

The most surprising conversion was that of John Dury. Dury was on the con-tinent during the Whitehall conference, but he made his feelings known to the council by letter of January 8, 1656, in which he argued admission of the Jews was lawful and "expedient."[223] Dury had contemplated admission of the Jews since the early 1640s. In fact, he had helped fuel the Jewish Indian mania by acting as a go-between between Thorowgood and Menasseh. Yet by January 22, even he was having second thoughts as a result of reading Menasseh's petition. Dury thought Menasseh's request excessive. He also felt England should "go warily and by de-grees" in granting Jews admission to England because Jews, Dury noted, "have ways beyond all other men to undermine a state and to insinuate into those that are in office and prejudicate the trade of others; and therefore, if they be not wisely restrained, they will in short time, be oppressive, if they be such as are here in Germany."[224] Dury was no anti-Semite. He was a philo-Semite who had promoted Jewish causes in the past and who would later raise money for Jews in Jerusalem who were reduced to poverty when the Swedish naval blockade of eastern Europe curtailed alms from reaching them.

Convinced Jews could not be trusted to keep oaths and mindful of the injuries Jews had inflicted on Englishmen "in life, chastity, goods, or good name,"[225] before the expulsion of 1290, the Council listed seven restrictions as the condition of their readmission. The purpose of the seven restrictions, which included prohibitions against "defaming Christianity, working on Sunday and employing Christian servants" was to "protect Englishmen against the economic and religious rapacity of the Jews."[226]

On January 25, three days after the arrival of the Dury letter, the Tuscan envoy noticed the change in mood among council members and the public at large. "In the matter of the Jews," he wrote, "people do not speak as much as they used to do at the outset. Everyone now believes that the Lord Protector will not make any declaration in their favor, but will tacitly connive at the private conventicles which they hold at present in their houses as long as they give no open scandal."[227] Sagredo, the Venetian ambassador, felt that Jewish conniving still had a fair chance of success, because "the Jews having powers to spend a great deal of money, are getting a hold and it is believed that they will make no mistake in winning over the divines and the ministers, and that they will be able to break down every obstacle by the power of gold."[228] A Royalist spy concurred. Even though "the generality oppose[d]" the admission of the Jews, the Jews "will be admitted by way of connivancy."[229]

By February 15, the Tuscan envoy concluded the prospect of admitting the Jews was dead. "Cromwell," says Roth, "had decided that public opinion was too strong for him. It would be impossible to readmit the Jews to the country excepting on humiliating conditions, so stringent as to be absolutely unacceptable to them and discouraging immigration rather than otherwise. Accordingly, he determined simply to maintain the state of affairs which he had found informally allowing the Jews established in London to continue the observance of their ancestral rites without disturbance."[230] The issue was over. The council refused to budge. The Jews found the restrictions demeaning, insulting, and unacceptable; they took out their anger on Menasseh ben Israel, who was passed over in 1656 when the Jews of London chose Rabbi Moses Athias of Hamburg to lead their congregation.

The right of Jews to live in England was eventually established indirectly when a Jew named Robles was recognized as a Jew and not as a Portuguese Catholic, the fiction under which he had been living in London, when he brought a successful property action against the Spanish government. The admission of the Jews, according to Tuchman, took place in typically English fashion in a decision which was "illogical but workable" and "fortunate for the Jews when Commonwealth gave way to Restoration." Because there was "no statute on the books for Charles II to cancel," the king "reasonably allowed things to go as they were."[231] The Jews of the Restoration, thus, no longer had to engage in the charade of attending Mass at the chapel of the Spanish ambassador.

In 1656, the Quaker Messiah James Nayler was greeted as the king of Israel when he entered Bristol. The Messiah had finally arrived in England, or so the Quakers thought. Most Englishmen, however, greeted his arrival with derision. Millennial fatigue was setting in. By the end of 1656, the disillusionment was so palpable, poets expressed it in verse:

Twere strange if this Prophetick
year which brought
Such Expectation, should have
nothing wrought[232]

By the end of 1656, another *annus mirabilis* had come and gone with the Messiah still a no show; Menasseh's great project had failed. Cromwell tried to assuage the pain by granting Menasseh a state pension of 100 pounds per annum, which he never paid. In September 1657, Menasseh wrote to Cromwell offering to "surrender my pension" if Cromwell will "supply me with 300 pounds"[233] up front. He never got that either, although his widow kept trying long after his death. After wandering about London "in a vain attempt to use his influence to procure some sort of official statement from Cromwell's government,"[234] Menasseh left England in poverty and disgrace to return to Amsterdam with no firm prospects. He needn't have worried about his worldly prospects. He died on the way home on November 20. Cromwell died one year later at the age of 59. The Fifth Monarchy Men, who considered Cromwell the Antichrist, made plans to stage the Apocalypse on the their own now that the Little Horn was in his grave. In August, 1659, the regicide Thomas Harrison issued a tract, *The Fifth Monarchy or Kingdom of Christ in Opposition to the Beasts*, demanding again that the Law of Moses be made the law of England, replacing the "heathenish tyrannous and popish laws"[235] still on the books. Harrison's suggestion was greeted with the same enthusiasm that met the Quaker Messiah Nayler. England had had enough Apocalypse for a while. It was suffering from a bad case of Millennium fatigue.

On May 29, 1660, crowds greeted Charles II's arrival in London in a mood of general rejoicing. The English, it seemed, longed for a legitimate ruler as the best protection against would-be messiahs. Harrison was arrested one month earlier. He was found guilty of regicide and hanged at Charing Cross on October 13, 1660, barely six months after the return of the King. As he was dragged to his execution, Harrison cried out several times, "I go to suffer upon the account of a most glorious cause that ever was in the world,"[236] evoking derision from the mob.

Harrison's death did not quench the thirst for revenge against the Puritans. Three months after Harrison was hanged, the mob dug up Oliver Cromwell's body and dragged it through the streets of London to the gallows at Tyburn where it was hanged and desecrated. Sensing this wasn't enough, the mob cut the head off of Cromwell's corpse and stuck on a pike outside Westminster Hall, where it remained for the 23 years. Cromwell's head, we are told, now rests in Sidney Sussex College, Cambridge, but the exact place is secret.

By 1670, the Fifth Monarchy movement had disappeared completely. Millennial fever had burned itself out ten years earlier in England, but the drama wasn't over yet. In fact, events in England had set the stage for the climax of that drama in Turkey, where the Jewish Messiah was waiting in the wings.

VIII

During his stay among the Jews in the Morea, Zevi attracted a number of followers, largely because of his good looks and singing voice. His cheeks, we are told, "were red all the time."[237] He was tall and stout to the point of corpulence. Music filled him with enthusiasm, and he conveyed that enthusiasm to others. Because of contacts made on a previous trip to Cairo, Zevi was chosen to lead a delegation to Cairo in 1663 to raise money to ransom captive Jews. He remained there for two years. While there he renewed contact with Raphael Joseph Chelibi, a wealthy Jew who became his financial backer.

He also found a third wife. In March 1664, Zevi married a refugee from the Chmielnicki pogroms by the name of Sarah. Rabbi Jacob Sasportas, then head of the Jewish congregation in London, knew Sarah as a girl, when she arrived in Amsterdam in 1655, at the climax of Menasseh's mission to England. He remembered her as "a girl devoid of intelligence," who claimed "she would marry the messianic king."[238] Rejected by the Jews in Amsterdam, Sarah moved to Leghorn, where she established a reputation as a beauty of legendary promiscuity. In Cairo, Zevi learned of her reputation and because of it he called her thither to become, in his phrase, "the wife of whoredoms."[239] All known sources document the licentious life Sarah had lived in Leghorn before the call to go to Cairo. Sasportas claims "he sent for her and married her" because of those rumors. Scholem likewise claims Zevi knew that his wife-to-be was a whore, and that he "married her precisely for that reason so as to imitate or fulfill the words of the prophet Hosea (1:2) 'take upon them a wife of whoredoms.'"[240]

Unsurprisingly, her promiscuity did not stop after the marriage. Indeed, Zevi seems to have put her to work using her sexual charms to seduce potential recruits and disarm potential opponents. Zevi once persuaded a doctor's son to enter his wife's room, hoping she would seduce him into becoming his follower. Like Joseph when approached by Potiphar's wife, the doctor's son fled, leading Zevi to complain "if he had done her will, he would have performed a great *tiqqun*."[241]

Sarah inaugurated the regime of sexual license that characterized Zevi's followers. In approving her "acts of *tiqqun*," Zevi was referring to the Cabalist notion of "*tiqqun olam*," or healing the world, which he hoped to bring about by a systematic violation of the Law. Unlike Christ who came to fulfill the law, not to abolish it, Zevi, the 17th Century Messiah of the Jews, came to abolish the law by urging the systematic violation of all its precepts. Zevi had already uttered the Tetragrammaton. Now he urged his followers to engage in anything the law considered "*treyf*," from eating pork to orgiastic sexuality. Zevi was far ahead of latter day sexual revolutionaries like Sigmund Freud and his disciple Wilhelm Reich. Freud, according to Bakan in *Sigmund Freud and the Jewish Mystical Tradition*, considered himself an avatar of Zevi. Like Zevi, he dangled the prospect of release from all sexual prohibition and guilt in front of wealthy Americans as a way of bringing them and (most importantly) their money under his control. Carl Gustav Jung, Freud's *goyische* heir apparent, practiced the same *tiqqun* on wealthy Americans like Edith Rockefeller McCormick and her wealthy brother-in-law Medill. Wilhelm Reich, however, took the lessons learned from the masters and forged it into the science of sexual liberation as political control (cf. my *Libido Dominandi: Sexual Liberation and Political Control*).

In playing the pimp to his beautiful wife Sarah, Zevi engaged in a rudimentary form of the sexual liberation perfected by Jews like Wilhelm Reich in the 20th Century. "Sarah's beauty and free manner of life," Graetz tells us, "attracted youths and men who had no sympathy with the mystical movement."[242] Writing a generation before Reich was born, Graetz had no way to articulate the full flowering of sexual liberation as a form of control that would take place during the the 20th Century. But he had an inkling of how it worked, noting that Sarah's "loose conduct worked on the passions of the male population."[243] Because the Jews of Poland had lived sexually repressed lives, the energy released when "the bonds of chastity ... were broken"[244] in Poland was much more explosive. Unchained *libido* made a significant contribution to the messianic fever sweeping from *shtetl* to synagogue across northern Europe.

With a retinue now increased by Sarah's seductive conquests and Chelibi's money, Zevi began to wend his way back to Smyrna. The steady regimen of wine, women, and song had intensified Zevi's bipolar mood. When he was up, Zevi soared in an exaltation that assured him that nothing less than the fulfillment of a divine mission could be the source of his emotion, but when he was down, he had nothing but doubts about himself. Zevi had one of those ecstatic experiences around the end of February or the beginning of March 1665. To resolve the doubts about his mission and visions, Zevi met with Nathan of Gaza, the noted Cabalist, in May 1665. Nathan was significantly younger than Zevi, but he had dedicated his life to study in the school of Lurianic Cabala that sprung up in Gaza after the master's death. Seeking *tiqqun* for his soul, Zevi approached Nathan with the trepidation of a man steeling himself to hear that he has been diagnosed with an incurable illness. To Zevi's surprise, Nathan prostrated himself before him and asked forgiveness for not recognizing him as the Messiah when he passed through Gaza on his way to Egypt. As in so many instances since then, the rise of the charismatic visionary or, in this case, the Messiah could only take place when he had been endorsed by another source of authority and guidance. For this reason, Scholem dates the beginning of the Sabbatian movement as May 31, 1665. The movement would not have existed without Nathan's endorsement. Once he certified Zevi as the Messiah, the other rabbis fell in line. Before long, it was dangerous to oppose Zevi.

When Zevi finally arrived in Smyrna in autumn 1665, his reputation, heightened by Nathan's endorsement, threw the Jews there into paroxysms of joy. "The madness of the Jews in Smyrna," we are told, "knew no bounds.... The delirium seized great and small. Women, girls and children fell into raptures and proclaimed Sabbatai Zevi in the language of the Zohar as the true redeemer."[245] Sensing the end of the world was at hand, Zevi's followers unroofed their houses and married off children of 12 and even 10 years of age, "so they might cause the souls not yet born to enter into life and thereby remove the last obstacle to the commencement of the time of grace."[246] The "confusion in men's brains" led them to incredible penances while at the same time "they abandoned themselves to the most extravagant delight."[247] Men and women danced with each other like maniacs in the streets, and as the mania spread, sexual excess proliferated, and the voice of reason was swept away in the tide of passion. Initially, the misgivings of skeptics were drowned out in the carnival of enthusiasm. When Rabbi Aaron de la Papa denounced the messianic mania, he was expelled from the synagogue and eventually driven out of Smyrna. When Chayim Penya, a wealthy Jew who had enjoyed the respect of his co-religionists, objected, he was physically assaulted in the synagogue and was "nearly torn to pieces by the raging multitude."[248]

Gradually, the messianic fervor spread beyond Smyrna, indeed, far beyond the boundaries of the Ottoman Empire to the Jewish Diaspora in Europe. In November, news of the tumult surrounding Zevi arrived at the Talmud Torah congregation in Amsterdam and "the great majority ... were seized by messianic enthusiasm" there too.[249] Sabbatian elements were introduced into the synagogue service of the congregation that had sent Menasseh ben Israel off to England ten years earlier. That congregation wrote to Zevi, announcing he was the Messiah promised by God. May God, they wrote, "bless, preserve, guard, help, assist, prosper, magnify, raise and highly exalt Our Lord the Great King, Sabbatai Sevi, the Anointed of the Lord, the Messiah son of David, the Messiah King, the Messiah Redeemer, the Messiah Saviour, our Messiah of Righteousness."[250]

In December 1665, Henry Oldenburg, John Dury's son-in-law, wrote to the young Dutch lens grinder Baruch Spinoza for his opinion on Zevi. Spinoza had been excommunicated from Menasseh's synagogue in 1656, while Menasseh was on his mission to England. Spinoza would become posthumously famous as the man who applied Descartes to faith and morals and came up with what is arguably the first book of the Enlightenment. "All the world here," Oldenburg wrote to Spinoza from London, "is talking of a rumor of the return of the Israelites, dispersed for more than two thousand years to their own country. Few believe it, but many wish it.... Should the news be confirmed, it may bring about *a revolution in all things*."[251] Spinoza' response, if there was one, has been lost. Since his excommunication, Spinoza had broken all contact with the Jews, so it is unlikely he could add anything to what Oldenburg already knew.

The Christians who burned to hear this news had pretty much disappeared from the stage of history when the news arrived. Major Harrison had been hanged five years before, and the Fifth Monarchy Men had dispersed. The Quakers had seen Nayler, their Messiah, arrive in Bristol nine years earlier, and there is no indication they were interested in a repeat of that performance. With Shabbetai Zevi, it seems the spirit of apocalyptic mania had been exorcised from the Judaizing Christians only to take up residence in more virulent form among the Jews themselves. The Jews perhaps felt the *goyim* had been deluded in thinking, not that the Messiah would come, but that he would come from their own ranks. The Messiah had to be a Jew, and when Cromwell proved unqualified, it was only a matter of time before a candidate would arise from the ranks of the Jews. The Jews of Hamburg flaunted their beliefs, claiming Christians would regret past persecution of the Jews under the new dispensation. Had the bemused Christians been able to enter the synagogues, they would have seen otherwise "serious respectable men ... of Spanish stateliness" hopping, jumping, and dancing around like madmen with the Torah rolls in their arms. The Jews of Germany turned insolent, warning Christian neighbors that the tables would soon be turned and Christians would be persecuted when Zevi restored the Kingdom of Israel. In Heidelberg, a Lutheran minister reported "The Jews are brimful of the hope of the messiah, running from one village to another and rushing in the streets from one house to another, in order to hear, with their ears pricked up, further news of the messiah."[252] To ridicule the folly of the Jews, German youths would blow trumpets in the middle of the night near the houses of the Jews so they could watch them come running out in their night clothes in expectation of the Messiah. During the carnival in Prague in 1666, a play was performed ridiculing the expectations of the Jews, who had shut themselves up in their ghetto waiting to show who would have the last laugh. Jews in Hungary, many of whom were refugees from the Chmielnicki pogroms, sold their houses and made plans to travel to Jerusalem, to be present when Zevi ascended his throne. Reports even reached America, where the reaction against Puritanism had been delayed. Still favorably disposed to the reports of Thorowgood and Menasseh, Increase Mather preached that the saints of Boston "lived in a time when constant reports from sundry places and lands gave out to the world, that the Israelites were upon their journey towards Jerusalem [and] that they had written to others in their Nation, in Europe and America to encourage and invite them to hasten to them, this seemed to many godly and judicious [people] to be a beginning of that Prophesie [Ezekiel 37:7]."[253] Samuel Pepys, reporting on the mood in London, said Jewish bookies were offering 10 to 1 odds in favor of anyone who wanted to put money on whether Zevi was the messiah or not. Pepys' comment indicates the Jews of London were no exception to the rule. The community there had elected Jacob Sasportas as their rabbi, and the otherwise level-headed Sasportas, despite what he said in post-dated documents, did nothing to oppose the notion the Messiah had come to restore the Kingdom of Israel. The rabbis of Jerusalem who could have pulled the plug on the movement remained silent when the rabbis of Constantinople wrote to ask them to certify Zevi's *bona fides* as the Messiah. Unable to contradict the mob, the rabbis of Constantinople joined the messianic madness.

Graetz claims Zevi mania derived additional encouragement from Christian enthusiasts who hoped to bring about the millennium, but that Millennialism had burned itself out among all but a few diehard religious fanatics when news of Zevi reached London. Zevi's cause was fostered less by sympathy among the Judaizers, most of whom had retired from the scene in disgrace, than by shrewd publicity. One hundred and fifty years after the Jews had made Reuchlin's pamphlet a best-seller and almost 300 years before Eddy Bernays, Sigmund Freud's nephew, would invent the science of public relations, the Jews had become masters in intelligence and the dissemination of information. By collaborating with the Protestants to produce Luther's and Calvin's bibles, they had mastered the technology of printing; they were now using that technology to announce the long-awaited Messiah had come to redeem the Jews.

Samuel Primo, Zevi's private secretary, "took care that reports of the fame and doings of the Messiah should reach Jews abroad,"[254] by feeding information into the intelligence network of Jewish spies, English and Dutch mercantile houses, and evangelical ministers that had evolved from Walsingham and Cromwell's spy agencies. Circulars announcing the events in Smyrna flooded London, Hamburg, Amsterdam and all other centers of Jewish influence in Europe. Most of what the Jews were reading came from the pen of Nathan of Gaza, whose letters provided the details of the coming messianic era to begin in 1666. During that year, Nathan wrote, Zevi "will take dominion from the Turkish king without war."[255] By the power of the hymns and praises he will sing, Zevi was going to establish the dominion of Israel over all the nations of the earth. "All nations shall submit to his rule."[256] The Jews of Hamburg who had been listening to impudent German youth blowing trumpets in the night must have felt especially vindicated when they read "there will be no slaughter among the uncircumcised ... except in German lands,"[257] by which Nathan probably meant Poland, or the land where the Ashkenazim, or German speaking Jews, had suffered recently.

After disarming the sultan with his songs, Zevi would proceed to Jerusalem, where he would "discover the exact site of the altar as well as the ashes of the red heifer" and "perform sacrifices" although he would not rebuild the temple.[258] Then he would travel east to the banks of the river Sambatyon, which can only be crossed on the Sabbath, when it ceases to flow. After locating the ten lost tribes on its far bank, Zevi "will return from the river Sambatyon, mounted on a celestial lion ... . At this sight all the nations and all the kings shall bow before him to the ground. On that day the ingathering of the dispersed shall take place, and he shall behold the sanctuary already built descending from above."[259] He will perform the final act of *tiqqun* by "restoring the divine sparks and essences to their rightful place." That, of course, meant "the dissolution of the kingdom of oppression and the end of the external, visible exile" would take place before "one year and some months" had passed.[260]

In a letter written at the end of 1665, Nathan announced that Zevi was the re-incarnation of Simon bar Kokhba. Zevi, though, was unable to make up his mind whether he was bar Kokhba or Christ. More than one commentator has noticed the Christian elements that crept into Nathan of Gaza's theology. Jews were asked, for example, to have faith, rather than just to fulfill the law. At a certain point, Nathan announced Zevi was going to redeem Jesus Christ from the pot of boiling excrement to which the Talmud had consigned him for all eternity. It was prob-ably then that Rabbi Sasportas began to doubt Zevi's credentials. "The notion of the salvation of Jesus," Scholem tells us, "whose soul, according to Talmudic tradi-tion, was forever condemned, was particularly offensive to R. Jacob Sasportas."[261]

During Hanukkah, Zevi slipped into manic exaltation and, buoyed by the frenzy his own publicity machine had created, announced on December 14, 1665, that he was the long-expected Messiah. The sequence of events bore an uncanny resemblance to the account in Luke 4:16ff, in which Jesus read from Isaiah, "rolled up the scroll" and announced "this text is being fulfilled even as you listen." Jesus, we are told, "was very much in Zevi's mind,"[262] causing him to imitate some of his actions. Instead of just announcing that the Messiah had arrived, as Jesus had done, Zevi tried to outdo Christ by taking the Torah scroll in his arms and sing-ing his favorite song, a Castilian love song popular among Ladino exiles in Turkey known as "Meliselda," about the lover who lay with the King's daughter after she got out of her bath tub. The man who lay with the "shining lass/ As she came up from the bath" was none other than Zevi, and his passionate singing infused in his listeners the mystical allegory with such power that "many unlettered men and women experienced all manner of convulsion" and proclaimed "Shabbetai Zevi is the King of Israel."[263] At the end of his performance, Zevi announced he was the Anointed One of God and that the Redemption of Israel would take place on the 15th of Sivan 5426, which is to say, in the following year. Zevi then dispatched one of his assistants to Constantinople to make preparations for his arrival there.

As if to show the new dispensation had abolished the old law, Zevi pro-nounced the Ineffable Name, ate forbidden foods, encouraged other Jews to do likewise, and did "other things,"[264] most probably involving sexual orgies, things not described in polite company in those days. The coming of the Messiah was less the result of a "carefully hatched plot" and more the result of "the eruption of irrational forces."[265] Those eruptions soon took place among his followers too because they were empowered to act on their forbidden desires by accepting Zevi as their Messiah. He had told them "Blessed is He Who hath permitted things forbidden." Of course, the prospect of unlimited sexual gratification also acted as a powerful stimulant to join the movement. Emmanuel Frances captured the mania in a poem:

Is he the Lord's anointed or a traitor,
A wicked sinner and a fornicator?
Forbidden women he embraces;
As first the one, and then the other he caresses.
The foolish people, gaping as spellbound,
Affirm: this is a mystery profound.[266]

The mobilization of sexual passion Zevi achieved through his marriage to the wife of whoredoms and the publicity it generated had its roots in the Zohar, which claimed the Messiah would repair the effects of Adam's sin and restore woman to her original freedom. Now that so many agreed that Zevi was the Messiah, he found himself riding a tiger of his own creation, a revolutionary movement unfolding under the watchful eyes of the Turkish authorities, who because they were either especially prudent or dumbfounded, allowed the events to unroll unhindered. Or so it seemed until a Jewish delegation dispatched from Constantinople arrived in Smyrna with orders from the Sultan to arrest Zevi. Fortunately for the Messiah, by the time they arrived Zevi was gone. On the first day of 1666, Shabbetai Zevi set sail for Constantinople. The voyage, which normally lasted 10 to 14 days, took over a month because of the contrary winds that blew down the Dardanelles. It was these winds which occasioned the founding of Troy. In this instance, they symbolized the revolutionary passions Zevi aroused but could not control.

Battered by the winds that had enriched Troy, Zevi's ship finally made land on the Dardanelles short of his destination. He was promptly arrested and dragged ashore in chains on February 8, 1666. The Jews who had come to greet him as the Messiah fled in panic. Those who didn't flee were beaten by the Turkish guards who waded into the crowd to create a path for their prisoner. Suddenly all the stories about how even the sea had obeyed Zevi on his voyage didn't seem so plausible. Of course, Zevi could have taken another page from the same book that contained the story about the obedient waves and claimed the Messiah had come to suffer and die, but there is no indication the Jews would have gone for that story since they had rejected it the first time around. Mehemed IV's vizier, the shrewd Ahmed Korprulu, had taken charge of this case and would handle it brilliantly.

When Zevi appeared before the Divan, three days after his arrest, he claimed he was nothing more than a humble Jewish Chacham who came to Constantinople to collect alms and could not be held responsible for the imprudent zeal of his followers. Persuaded by his testimony, the deputy vizier Mustapha Pasha, who had welcomed the Messiah to Constantinople with a blow to the ear, sentenced Zevi to an indeterminate term in the local prison for Jewish debtors. While in prison, Zevi wrote an open letter to his fellow Jewish prisoners urging them not to default on their debts to English merchants, even if the world was about to end. Defaulters, Zevi wrote, perhaps remembering the English merchants who had frequented his father's house, would have no share in his joy and glory when he ascended his throne in Jerusalem.

A little over two weeks after Zevi had been thrown in prison, the synagogue in Hamburg resolved to send a delegation to Constantinople "to prostrate ourselves, as is fitting, before our king, Shabbetai Sevi."[267] Their response was typical of the synagogues in Europe. The vast majority were swept away in the messianic hysteria, including the one led by Rabbi Jacob Sasportas. "If," Scholem reasoned, "a shrewd, sober and arrogant observer like Sasportas could be carried away ... then it is not surprising that the Jewish masses saw no reason to doubt the good news ... salvation was at hand."[268] Thousands of Jews converged on Constantinople to offer homage to their messiah, so many that food prices began to climb as demand outstripped supply. Hundreds of women assembled in Constantinople to prophesy and became so possessed by the spirit that the Turkish authorities had to beat them with whips and clubs to drive them away. The vizier Ahmed Korprulu was a shrewd observer of human nature and religion-inspired follies. With a following as fanatical as this, Shabbetai Zevi was dangerous even in prison. Since the Porte was planning a war with Crete, it had no desire for a simultaneous uprising among the Jews, something that most certainly would have occurred if Korprulu had ordered Zevi's immediate execution. No, the Porte would treat the suffering Messiah leniently, and his followers would be lulled into passivity until the *coup de grace* fell.

As a result, Korprulu had Zevi transferred to the fortress of Abydos, a minimum security prison for political prisoners near Gallipoli on the other side of the Dardanelles. Zevi arrived at his new home, which his followers called the Tower of Strength (or *Migdal Oz*), on the day of preparation for Passover. Zevi was allowed to slaughter and cook a Paschal lamb in his quarters. Then, as if to show once again that he was above the law of Moses, Zevi and his followers ate the lamb with its fat, which the Talmud forbids.

After Passover, Zevi and his followers settled into a way of life so bizarre and so disconnected from reality that one must have recourse to works of fantasy like Edgar Allan Poe's *Masque of the Red Death* to find something analogous. Jews from all over Europe continued to arrive in Constantinople to pay homage to the King of the Jews, so many that Zevi's jailer, the governor of the castle of Abydos, was able to double the admission charge without diminishing the stream of visitors. Zevi would receive his visitors sitting on a throne holding a Torah scroll that, like Zevi, was clad in red. The walls of his chamber were covered with carpets of gold. The floor of his cell was covered with rugs of silver and gold. Zevi sat at a table made of silver and covered with gold. He wrote his letters by dipping his pen into an inkstand of gold encrusted with jewels. Whatever he ate or drank was served on vessels of silver and gold, which, like his inkstand, were encrusted with jewels. When he wasn't singing or feasting, Zevi engaged in sexual orgies. The Jews hailed Zevi as their Messiah even in prison, because in that prison Zevi had accomplished what the Jews had always wanted their Messiah to accomplish. He had created heaven on earth.

Zevi would urge his visitors to eat at the times prescribed for fasting. According to one account, Zevi had a bowl of fruit brought to his visitors, who objected, "How can we eat?" Zevi calmed their scruples by telling them that breaking the law and the fast would "fulfill Scripture."[269] Zevi would then take a gold scarf and wrap it around the neck of the spellbound visiting rabbi and proclaim, "I make you kings in this world. You shall be kings and princes before me." The rabbis responded by proclaiming that they had died and gone to heaven, "for now it seems to us that we are in the celestial paradise."[270]

In August, Zevi celebrated his birthday on the ninth of Ab by abolishing the fast the law had imposed on Jews to commemorate the destruction of the temple. Since the Shekinah was now manifest, Jews no longer needed to fast on the 17th of Tammuz or the 9th of Ab. With his skill at singing and skillful staging, interweaving the erotic and the religious, Zevi had no problem convincing his followers he had created heaven on earth in his prison cell. The tales of those who had visited his fantastic quarters in prison increased his fame and the expectations of his followers. The tension surrounding the anticipated inauguration of his reign had become intolerable in Constantinople. Several dervishes had prophesied the fall of the Turkish Empire and its replacement by the kingdom of the Jews.

Zevi and his followers eagerly awaited the arrival of Nathan of Gaza so that together they could inaugurate the millennium. For thee months, from April to July, Zevi had been leading the life of a prince in his prison cell on the Dardanelles, intent only upon his own apotheosis, which would take place when Nathan of Gaza arrived. But another prophet arrived from another land, and he inaugurated Zevi's downfall rather than his apotheosis.

On September 3, 1666, Rabbi Nehemiah ha-Cohen arrived at Abydos after traveling from Poland. Since many rabbis had arrived in Abydos while Zevi had been imprisoned, nothing seemed amiss when the two closeted themselves in "secret converse."[271] During that conversation, Rabbi Nehemiah announced his own anointing and, failing to convince Zevi to share the messianic honors with him, left Abydos in a rage and went straight to the Pasha in Adrianople, where Rabbi Nehemiah announced Zevi was plotting insurrection. Rabbi Nehemiah was so outraged by his rebuke that he announced to the pasha Mustapha that he wanted to become a Muslim on the spot, leading some to believe he was a Turkish plant. On September 5, he converted to Islam. Shortly afterwards he returned to Poland, put off his turban and "greatly repented,"[272] but by then it was too late to save Zevi from his fate.

On September 15, four messengers from the sultan's court arrived to take Zevi prisoner. The Jewish heaven on earth suddenly burst like a fragile soap bubble. The governor of the prison was abruptly deprived of his lucrative income. The Jews who had thronged to greet their messiah were driven away with blows by the Sultan's soldiers, and Zevi, without even "an hour's space to take solemn farewell of his Followers and Adorers,"[273] was thrown unceremoniously into a closed carriage and driven to the Sultan's court in Adrianople, 150 miles to the northeast.

The idea that Zevi was the Messiah had taken such firm root in the mind of his Jewish followers that now they were convinced the moment of his triumph had arrived. The time had come when Zevi was to take the crown from the head of the sultan. After charming him into submission with song, Zevi would place that crown on his own head and inaugurate the kingdom of heaven on earth. Robert de Dreux, a chaplain at the French embassy, recounted later that crowds of Jews ran about spreading carpets over the streets of Adrianople in anticipation of his arrival. When de Dreux gave voice to his skepticism, he was told by an innkeeper's son "there is nothing to scoff at, for before long you will be our slaves by the power of the messiah."[274]

The Turks had lost none of their shrewdness during the months of Zevi's captivity. They knew that Zevi's death would almost certainly mean a rebellion by the Jews, who were already primed for the arrival of Armageddon. After consulting with the sultan's physician, the apostate Jew Mustapha Fawzi Hayati Zade, the Turks came up with a better strategy. Dragged before the divan, Zevi was given an opportunity to prove he was indeed the messiah. Zevi was to be stripped naked and tied to a post outside the gate of the seraglio, where the sultan's archers would shoot arrows at him. If he were indeed the Messiah, the arrows would not harm him. If he were unsure of whether he were the Messiah and, therefore, unwilling to undergo the test, there was a simpler alternative. Zevi could become a Muslim. It didn't take Zevi long to decide. Faced with either death or apostasy, Zevi chose apostasy. The Jewish Messiah fell to his knees and begged the sultan to accept him as a convert. For emphasis, Zevi "threw his [Jewish] hat down and spat on it and reviled the Jewish religion publicly desecrated the name of Heaven."[275] He then "slandered and denounced his faithful believers."[276] Impressed with Zevi's zeal for his new religion, the sultan changed Zevi's name to his own, calling him Mehmed Effendi and granted him a pension of 150 piatres per day as *kapici bahsi* or keeper of the palace gates. To prove his sincerity in adopting his new faith, Zevi agreed to take one of the queen's slave girls as an additional wife. Sarah didn't seem upset by this arrangement. She was, according to Scholem, "already familiar with the experience of outwardly professing another religion"[277] because of her days in Poland. Under the tutelage of the sultan's mother, Zevi's wife apostatized too, taking the name Fatima Cadin.

According to the *Jewish Encyclopedia*, the apostasy of the man the overwhelming number of synagogues in Europe had acknowledged as the Messiah was the greatest catastrophe to strike the Jewish people since the destruction of the Temple. Because of the time lag inherent in communication then, letters were still arriving from Europe offering homage to the failed Jewish messiah a month after his apostasy. On October 9, 1666, the day of Atonement, the Jews of Hamburg pronounced a five-fold blessing over his name. The rabbis of Amsterdam, afflicted by the same time lag, sent a letter of homage that arrived at the time of his apostasy. Like Cromwell, Zevi tried to shift the blame for his apostasy onto God. A few days after his conversion, Zevi explained in a letter to one of his brothers, "God has made me an Ishmaelite."[278]

Gradually, word of Zevi's apostasy trickled back to Europe during the fall of 1666. On November 10, 1666 Henry Oldenburg wrote he had just received news from Amsterdam that "the King of the Jews was turned Turk."[279] He noted that "our Jews"[280] didn't believe the news, but by December, news of the apostasy was accepted as undeniably true. Jews who not long before had warned Christians that the tables would soon be turned when Zevi ascended his throne, now had to endure the scorn of Muslims and Christians who ridiculed them mercilessly as blind and credulous fools. Now that Zevi had been marginalized, the sultan could move against the Jews of Turkey with impunity, which he did by having 50 rabbis executed:

> Repression was the most common Jewish response to Zevi's apostasy. The rabbis of Constantinople threatened to expel from the synagogue anyone who even pronounced Zevi's name, and, as if that weren't enough, threatened to hand violators of the ban over to Turkish authorities once they had been expelled. Conversion to Christianity was another response. Jakob Melammed, who taught at a school run by Ashkenazi community in Hamburg, converted with his family in 1676 when he realized "the noise which the Jews had made about their Shabbetai Zevi, for which we had waited for a whole year with fasts and mortifications was all lies." Zevi's apostasy "had aroused in him the first doubts about the Jewish religion."[281]

Docetism was another common response, especially among followers of the cabala. Zevi, according to this explanation, hadn't really converted to Islam. A phantom that resembled Zevi had converted, but the real Zevi had repaired to the vicinity of the Ten Lost Tribes and was even then preparing to lead them back to Jerusalem. Nathan of Gaza claimed Zevi's conversion presented a deep mystery whose meaning Nathan would reveal shortly. Samuel Primo, Zevi's spin doctor, claimed Zevi had undergone a "mock conversion," and that Zevi's duplicity proved he was the real Messiah, because like Moses at Pharaoh's court he was "outwardly sinful" but "inwardly pure."[282]

There was, of course, historical precedent for Zevi's actions. Zevi was a Sephardic Jew living in Turkey speaking a Spanish dialect precisely because so many of his ancestors had gone through the motions of converting to another religion, while all the while holding onto Judaism in secret, so why shouldn't he do the same? There was, however, no Biblical or theological justification for this behavior. No matter what excuses the rabbis of the post-Christian era concocted, the biblical paradigm for Jewish behavior remained the aged Eliezer in the book of Maccabbees, who chose death rather than violate the Law of Moses by eating pork. Shabbetai Zevi because of his apostasy became the paradigm of a new Jew, the subversive Jew, willing to lie to save his life and then subvert his new faith in the name of the one he ostensibly had renounced while claiming he was really subverting his old faith in the name of the new.

After his apostasy, Zevi became a double agent who was so skillful that no one could tell where his real allegiance, if he had any, lay. Many Jews, we are told, "flocked in, some from as far as from Babylon, Jerusalem and other remote places and casting their caps on the ground, in presence of the Grand Signior, voluntarily professed themselves Mahometans."[283] De la Croix reports he saw Zevi in the company of apostate Jews, "who followed him to the synagogues where he preached conversion to Islam with such success that during the five years or so that the mission of the zealot for the religion of Mahomet lasted, the number of Turks [that is, Jewish apostates to Islam] increased every day."[284] Leyb ben Ozer claims Zevi "caused more than three hundred Jews to apostatize in the course of two or three months."[285]

On the other hand, there were also stories of Zevi sitting with the Koran in one hand and the Torah scroll in the other. Tobias Rofe claims that in addition to doing "queer things," sometimes Zevi "prayed and behaved like a Jew and sometimes like a Muslim."[286] It was impossible to tell whether he was a Muslim subverting Jews or a Jew subverting Muslims; Zevi stood for subversion more than for any religious creed. Everything about him bespoke, in Rycaut's words, "disguise and dissimulation."[287] Zevi had become the quintessential subversive Jew and a paradigm for other subversive Jews for centuries to come. In Zevi the converso tradition found its apotheosis. Zevi, according to Rycaut, "passed his days in the Turkish Court as some time Moses did in that of the Egyptians."[288] According to Graetz, "he played the part of the Jew at one time, of Mussulman at another."[289] If Zevi became aware Turkish spies were listening to him preach, he would throw off his Jewish headdress and put on the turban. When speaking to Jews, Zevi would claim "he only persisted in Mahometanism in order to bring thousands and tens of thousands of non-Jews over to Israel. To the sultan and the mufti, on the other hand, he said his approximation to the Jews was intended to bring them over to Islam."[290] So in an atmosphere in which it became impossible to tell what he really believed, Zevi came to represent universal subversion. Before long his followers, schooled in duplicity, rationalized what Scholem calls their "double-faced existence."[291] Those rabbis still sympathetic to Zevi's claims allowed the Sabbatians to dissemble and "thereby to risk unnecessary persecution." While denouncing "active dissimulation and deceit," the same rabbis condoned the "'holy deceit' practiced by Shabbetai Zevi and those who apostatized at his behest. This act of deceit was part of the tactics of warfare against the demonic powers of the *qellippah*, and hence of a different order altogether."[292]

Just as the North African rabbis condoned insincere conversion, Zevi's followers condoned deceit, as long as it was holy. These rationalizations took root in the Jewish character and produced what Kant termed "a nation of deceivers." Graetz attributes that unfortunate characteristic to the influence that Talmudic studies exerted over Polish Jews. The story of Shabbetai Zevi, especially when seen as the culmination of the converso drama in Spain, indicates that the tradition goes back much farther. It was fostered by the Sabbatians who "were second to none in the art of interpreting, hairsplitting, and twisting texts, for which the Jews forever have had such an uncontested reputation."[293]

Zevi's apostasy and his subsequent career as a double agent contributed significantly to the rise of the Jew as a subversive because, as Scholem puts it, Zevi's apostasy, "unlike the passion and death of Jesus" was "essentially destructive of all values."[294] Zevi's apologists could find justification for their deceit in the Cabala, which talks about "the dialectical liquidation of evil" which "appears to strengthen the power of evil before its final defeat" and "requires not only the disguise of good in the form of evil but total identification with it."[295] Scholem says "it was along such lines that the subsequent theology of the Sabbatian radicals developed,"[296] without mentioning Marxism, but the connections are obvious. Sabbatian practice remained consistent with the theology of the Lurianic Cabala, which was "not content with the defeat and submission of gentiles but exulted in the idea of their ultimate annihilation."[297] The apostasy of Shabbetai Zevi did not change that goal, but it did give moral respectability to deceit as a way to achieve that goal. The Jews were subversives because their Messiah had become a subversive, as the following parable made clear:

> the king (that is, God) ... sends his trusted servant (that is, the messiah) as a spy into the enemy country to inquire about the captives. The servant has to act with great cunning "and to adopt the dress of the people through whose land he passes, and to behave as they do, lest they notice that he is a spy.... Keep this parable in your heart, for it is a foundation to satisfy you regarding severe doubts in the matter."[298]

No matter how hard the Sabbatians tried to justify their messiah's apostasy, Rabbinic Judaism could not survive a cataclysm of this magnitude unscathed. The shock was so great that Rabbinic Judaism split down the middle. Having failed to achieve in Maimonides the synthesis of faith and reason that Aquinas forged for Catholicism, Rabbinic Judaism tended to split along the fault lines of faith and reason because it was unable to withstand the shock of Zevi's apostasy and remain whole. From this moment forward, Jews would choose either faith or reason without being able to reconcile either to the other. The mantle of reason fell to Spinoza, who collaborated with the rejecters of religion to bring forth the Enlightenment. The mantle of faith fell to the Hasidim, who established their isolated pietistic communities in the *shtetls* of Poland and later the Pale of the Settlement in Russia.

The cataclysm that followed Zevi's apostasy also led to what Meyer Abrams calls "natural supernaturalism." Gershom Scholem provides a good example when he writes Zevi's apostasy "contained the seeds of a new Jewish consciousness."[299] The heart of this new consciousness lay in the recognition that "It was not he [Zevi] who made the messianic movement, but the faith of the masses which, in an explosive discharge of messianic energies accumulated during many generations, swept him to the heights of messiahship."[300] Since the Jewish people were the ultimate source of this energy, they, not the Messiah, held the ultimate power. Out of the wreckage of Zevi's apostasy, the Jews slowly came to understand that "the Jewish people must become its own Messiah."[301] Toward the end of the 19th Century Jews chose to worship themselves as their own Messiah under the form of Zionism or Marxism. According to Scholem's reading of the Zevi tragedy, the important thing was not Zevi and his failed promises, but that "for the first time since the destruction of the Temple," a "national revival" had "aroused the entire Jewish people."[302] Although this revival had been based on either a lie or a delusion, Scholem claims the important thing was the revival itself. "A unique chance of a mighty renewal seemed to present itself, and the well-nigh unanimous response indicated that the seed had not been sown in vain."[303] As long as the Jews "rediscovered pride and new self-consciousness," it didn't matter that the movement was based on an illusion or that "their behavior does not live up to our ideas of revolutionary leadership."[304] In other words, if everyone believes in the illusion, it stops being an illusion. This sounds like a good explanation of stock market bubbles but not religious movements. In both kinds of bubble, experience becomes more important than reality. "Who cares if Zevi was a coward, a fraud, and a subversive?," Scholem seems to say. As long as he united the Jewish people, his lies were as real as anything else, because the ultimate reality is "inward vision":

> Their faith in the messiah was nourished not on outward events but on the inward vision of their souls. Why then should the verdict of outward events undo the affirmation of their messianic experience? The signs of redemption had been clearly visible to all who had eyes to see. Should they now be written off as a nightmarish illusion?[305]

Once again, Jews were confronted with a choice because "the naive and simple oneness of the original messianic faith"[306] had been destroyed. The Jew could now choose "nightmarish illusion" or "disenchanting outer reality" because "The two notions which had hitherto been held to be aspects of one and the same reality now fell apart as each began to lead its own, independent life."[307] According to Scholem, "a considerable part of Jewry did, in fact, prefer the reality of their heart's vision above that of the disenchanting outer reality." For them, "historical reality became mere illusion, and only the incontestable inner reality was truly real."[308] For the followers of Karl Marx, the opposite was true. Spiritual reality became an illusion and the only reality was history and economic forces. No matter where he looked in the aftermath of the Zevi catastrophe, the Jew was confronted with dualism, forced to choose one of two repugnant alternatives.

Undeterred by Zevi's apostasy, Nathan of Gaza continued to follow Zevi's commands. Like many true believers, Nathan felt Zevi was still the Messiah even if "he had to disguise himself for a while for the better success at the execution of his great design."[309] And so on the explicit instructions of the Apostate Messiah,

Nathan of Gaza set out on a secret cabalistic mission to Rome, where he was to "perform a mystico-magical rite and to bring about the destruction of the city."[310] In March 1668, Nathan landed in Venice, where he told the Jews he was on a "divine errand" to Rome "on behalf of the whole congregation of Israel."[311] Wary of Nathan in the wake of the Zevi debacle, the Jews had Nathan deported before he caused more problems.

When Nathan arrived in Rome, he shaved his beard and put on a disguise. Then he and his companion Samuel Condor made their way before dawn to the Castel Sant'Angelo, where he chanted curses and then threw into the Tiber a scroll inscribed in the language of the Chaldeans which predicted the fall of Rome, *i.e.*, the Catholic Church, within the coming year. Satisfied his mission had been accomplished, Nathan and Condor then repaired to Leghorn, where he told the Jews what he had done. While in Leghorn, Nathan kept a low profile, confining his preaching to the private homes of believers because "Sabbatian preaching was going underground."[312]

Scholem says Nathan's secret mission to Rome was a symbolic imitation of Zevi's apostasy. Just as Zevi "had entered the Sultan's palace and the realm of Ishmael,"[313] so Nathan performed a magical rite around the Pope's palace to bring about its destruction. The messiah and the prophet, despite appearances to the uninitiated, were laboring at the heart of the *qelippah* to bring about the final *tiqqun*. Bakan says Sigmund Freud was influenced by Zevi's example, that Freud modeled his career of subversion on that of the apostate messiah. Both Zevi and Freud shared a fixation on Rome, which confirms Rome's role in establishing the continuity of the Jewish revolutionary project.

Rome was no stranger to catastrophe, but nothing catastrophic occurred in 1669 as the result of Nathan of Gaza's Chaldean curses. Zevi continued his subversive ways undeterred by the failure of the curse to cause the fall of Rome. In September 1672, Zevi was arrested in a synagogue for converting Muslims to Judaism. Zevi and his followers were again dragged in chains before the vizier Korprulu. And once again Zevi dissembled because there was as much evidence he was leading Jews to Islam as there was that he was leading Muslims to Judaism. Two years later, Moses Harari arrived in Leghorn. Harari had apostatized from Judaism to Islam under Zevi's tutelage. Now living in a non-Muslim country, he had returned to Judaism with a distinctly "double-faced" Sabbatian cast. "To the unbelievers he said that the Sabbatian faith was all lies and falsehoods, 'but in secret he went to the believers, exhorting them to persevere in their faith and [assuring them] that all he said to the unbelievers was untrue ... and was merely said for the sake of security.'"[314] So what was one to believe? The Sabbatians were like the man from Crete who said all Cretans were liars.

By 1674, Zevi had exhausted the patience of the Sultan, who imprisoned him in the fortress of Dulcigno on the Adriatic coast in Montenegro near the Albanian border. Sarah, whom Zevi had divorced in 1671, was allowed to rejoin her husband, and together they tried to resurrect the fool's paradise they had created in Abydos eight years earlier. There were no Jews in Dulcigno, so Zevi rode out the cycles of his manias and depressions without an audience. Zevi died there in September 1676, at age 50, one day short of the tenth anniversary of his apostasy. Baruch Spinoza died less than six months later, his death most probably hastened by glass dust he inhaled during his years as a lens grinder. Scholem said the Zevi apostasy burst the walls of the ghetto. The opposite, though, is the case. Judaism retreated once again, as in the wake of Julian's disastrous attempt to rebuild the temple, behind the *shtetl* walls into an ethnocentric reverie. Doubt, however, "regarding the accepted wisdom of rabbinic leadership crept into the edges of Jewish thought."[315] It would not take a millennium for revolutionary fervor to break out anew. The Jews would be swept into revolutionary fervor once again a little over a Century after Zevi's death.

Chapter Twelve

The Rise of Freemasonry

In 1605 Francis Bacon published *The Advancement of Learning*. To write on the new science without mentioning John Dee, who was still alive, was either a calculated insult or an attempt to stay out of trouble. There is no evidence of personal animus in Bacon's dealings with Dee, so avoiding trouble must have been Bacon's goal. Bacon must have been aware Dee had petitioned for support from the new Scottish king, and had been coldly rebuffed. King James I thought that Dee was a sorcerer and had made his feelings toward sorcerers and witches clear in *Demonology*, published in 1597. Given the vehemence of the king's feelings about those who trafficked in spirits, Dee was lucky that he wasn't burned at the stake. Instead Dee was condemned to internal banishment from the court whose interests he had served so faithfully as a magus and spy. If Shakespeare had written a play about Dee's life, it would have been a tragedy. Some feel Shakespeare wrote not one play about Dee, but two. Dee was most certainly Prospero in his mastery of potent spells and arcane gnosis gathered from ancient books, but he was also Lear raging poor and almost mad at the end of his life against a country that treated him so ungratefully. Bacon, attempting a project dangerously similar to what Dee proposed, was careful to ensure the same thing didn't happen to him.

Dee's main service to queen and country was his mission to Prague, which began in 1583. Walsingham sent Dee to Prague to exploit Emperor Rudolph II's craving for occult knowledge to bring him under the control of Cecil and Elizabeth in their cabal against Philip II, and to thwart the Jesuits and the Habsburgs, who were turning Prague into a bulwark of the Counter-Reformation and a center for English Catholic exiles who wanted to restore Philip II to the throne. After waiting impatiently for three years for results from Dee's mission, Elizabeth had herself declared head of the Protestant conspiracy at a meeting in Luneburg in July 1586. Elizabeth then sent emissaries to a secret Protestant conventical where she proposed a military league that would include her and the kings of Denmark and Navarre. Queen Elizabeth assumed primacy because of her resources. The meeting is mentioned in Simon Studion's *Naometria*, one of the standard Rosicrucian texts of the early 17th Century, mentioned by Andreae and others.

Emboldened by the meeting, Elizabeth sided with the hard-liners who wanted to take the war to the Catholics in the Netherlands, which was perceived as the weakest link in the Habsburg chain. Six months after her meeting, Leicester launched his intervention in the Netherlands, coming to the aid of the Dutch Calvinists, with the help of his young cousin, the paragon of Elizabethan Protestant chivalry, Sir Philip Sidney. The military campaign of 1586 was a disaster. Sidney died in battle, and English hopes of a Protestant military victory on the continent died with him. The English could dominate the seas, as the defeat of the Spanish Armada would show, but her armies were no match for the Duke of Parma, who would soon re-take Antwerp. As Christopher Dawson noted, if Philip had waited for Parma to take Holland before launching the Armada, European history would be very different.

By 1589, Dee knew his mission to the continent was a failure. However, he decided to take the long way home and conducted what seemed a triumphal progress through the Germanies, spreading his views among devotees of the Cabala. Dee's fame in Germany was considerable. His *Monas Hieroglyphica* had taken occult Hermetic Cabalism to a new level, and many followers of Reuchlin and Agrippa wanted to meet Dee. In June 1589, Dee was in Bremen ready to return to England when he received a visit from "that famous Hermetique Philosopher Dr. Henricus Khunrath of Hamburgh."[1] Khunrath was author of the *Amphitheatre of Eternal Wisdom*, which provides a crucial link between Dee and the Rosicrucian movement. So crucial was the link that Yates says Dee "sowed the seeds for the subsequent Rosicrucian movement on his journey back to England in 1689."[2]

Paradoxically, Dee's failure was more successful than if he had converted Rudolph: the movement outlasted Rudolph's reign and continued as a secret society when the Counter Reformation most certainly would have crushed any public organization. According to Yates, Freemasonry was one stream that flowed from Rosicrucianism, and the Royal Society another. Once again, the revolutionary movement found refuge in England, where it weathered the storm that all but destroyed it on the continent. Dee would never see the fruits of his labors. Nor would posterity recognize him for his achievement. Indeed, the Restoration that gave England the Masonic Lodge and the Royal Society buried Dee under a mountain of opprobrium in 1659 when Meric Casaubon published Dee's diaries along with a "damning preface ... accusing Dee of diabolical magic."[3] Casaubon was following in the footsteps of Francis Bacon. Both men needed to distance themselves from the source of their ideas.

If a great scientist must possess public relations acumen to be known to posterity, then Bacon was clearly a greater scientist than Dee. Bacon cleverly expressed his involvement in the Hermetic/Cabalist tradition only in allegorical writings published after his death in 1626. Among the papers he withheld from publication was an allegorical travel narrative, *The New Atlantis*, in which English sailors contact an advanced civilization on Bensalem, an island off the coast of Peru. The inhabitants of the island are Christians of a peculiar sort. The officials who greet English travelers wear white turbans "with a small red cross on the top,"[4] indicating the land of the Rosicrucian brotherhood. Like the brothers of the Rosy Cross, the inhabitants of Bensalem "wear no special habit or distinguishing mark but to conform in dress and appearance with the inhabitants of whatever country they were visiting."[5] Yates concludes it is "abundantly clear" Bacon "knew the Rose Cross fiction and was adapting it to his own parable."[6] As further proof of Bacon's link with the Rosicrucians, she cites John Heydon's *Holy Guide*, a 1662 adaptation of *The New Atlantis*, in which a man wearing the white turban announces: "I am by Office Governour of this House of Strangers and by vocation I am a Christian priest and of the Order of the Rosie Cross."[7]

Internal evidence suggests Bacon wrote *The New Atlantis* in the aftermath of Dee's failed mission to Prague. Unlike the *Faerie Queene*, which celebrates Elizabeth as the Protestant savior in the flush of first hope, *The New Atlantis* is veiled and cautious, more suited to an age when the Counter Reformation was triumphing across the continent. Bacon knew which side was winning and had no desire to immolate himself on the altar of a lost cause. Dee's Cabalistic British imperialism no longer found favor at the court, and so those who wanted to carry on the Protestant conspiracy in the absence of royal approval had to go underground to do so, through the formation of a secret society, which at this point came to be known as the Brothers of the Rosy Cross or the Rosicrucians, but which would later be known as Freemasonry.

Dodd claims Bacon founded the Lodge in England in 1579. This would make Bacon the founder of Freemasonry in England because "there was no Lodge of Freemasons in England prior to 1579."[8] Dodd says

> The Ritual is couched in Elizabethan English. The making of our modern tongue began with Spenser, one of Francis Bacon's Masks. And in the Spenser works are at last two allusions to the Square and the Compasses which appear to have a Masonic significance. This suspicion grows into a certainty when we examine some letters that were write in 1579 and published in 1580 between Professor Gabriel Harvey and his friend Francis Bacon who signed himself "*Immerito*."[9]

In a book Bacon published seven years later, the Two Pillars of Masonry are portrayed and between them the motto "*Plus Ultra*," or "More Beyond," for the first time in English literature.[10] Dodd also claims Bacon founded the Rosicrucians on the Continent as

> a reorganization of the old Kings Templar Order and took over primarily their Nine Degree Ceremonial which was associated with the new "Rosicrucian College." These Colleges were to be established later and attached as an inner Rite to the projected Masonic Brotherhood when established. That is exactly their procedure today. No one can become a member of a Rosicrucian College unless he is a Master mason.[11]

A certain segment of Europe was avid to hear what Bacon had to say because Europe had already been wracked by a century of religious strife. By 1605 it was heading into another century of even worse strife, soon to commence with the outbreak of the Thirty Years War. Freemasonry provided an alternative to sectarian strife; some felt it provided an antidote too. The Lodge proposed "ethics in place of creeds, acts of simple goodness in place of credulous belief, square conduct instead of hypocrisy and chicanery, love and brotherhood instead of the hatred that was sundering the church of Christ."[12] Dodd claims Bacon was the author of the Rosicrucian manifestoes that appeared on the continent. He also claims the real title of *The New Atlantis* was *The Land of the Rosicrucians*. He also claims the House of Salomon was the forerunner of the Invisible College, Gresham College, the Academie, and ultimately the Royal Society. All of those behind the founding of the Royal Society—Fludd, Boyle, Wren, Ashmole, Locke, and Sir Thomas Moray—were Freemasons and Rosicrucians. *The New Atlantis* is thus "the key to the modern rituals of Freemasonry."[13]

The connections all point to Jewish science, or Cabala, as the one thing these institutions had in common with the inhabitants of the New Atlantis. The inhabitants of Bensalem hold the Jews in high regard because they are the source of scientific knowledge. They call their college Salomon's house "and seek for God in nature"[14] by using the Cabala as the key that reveals the secrets of nature. Despite Bacon's reputation as the founder of empirical science, Yates sees *The New Atlantis* as "profoundly influenced by Hebraic-Christian mysticism, as in Christian Cabala. The inhabitants of New Atlantis respect the Jews; they call their college after Solomon and seek for God in nature. The Hermetic-Cabalist tradition has borne fruit in their great college devoted to scientific enquiry.... The inhabitants of New Atlantis would appear to have achieved the great instauration of learning and have therefore returned to the state of Adam in Paradise before the Fall—the objective of advancement for both Bacon and for the authors of the Rosicrucian manifestos."[15]

After quarantine in the House of Strangers, the English explorers are introduced to Salomon's House, which is a combination of the modern university and an early version of the CIA. Bensalem is "a land of magicians,"[16] which, like England when Dee and Walsingham spied on Catholics on the continent, "sent forth spirits of the air into all parts, to bring them news and intelligence of other countries."[17] The English travelers "were apt enough to think there was somewhat supernatural in this island; but yet rather as angelical than magical."[18] Again, the reference is to England, the island nation whose magus John Dee reputedly could summon angels to do his bidding.

Salomon's House, named after "the King of the Hebrews,"[19] proposes a science that is not empirical but rather distinctly Jewish or cabalistic. The residents of Bensalem "esteem [Salomon] as the lawgiver of our nation." To recognize the preeminence of this "King of the Hebrews" over Christ, Bensalem has erected Salomon's House as "the noblest foundation ... that was ever upon the earth" as well as "the lanthorn of this Kingdom." Salomon's House "is dedicated to the study of the Works and Creatures of God" as written down by Salomon. That includes:

> some parts of his works which with you are lost; namely, that Natural History which he wrote, of all plants, from the cedar of Libanus to the moss that groweth out of the wall and of all things that have life and motion. This maketh me think that our king, finding himself to symbolize in many things with that king of the Hebrews (which lived many years before him).[20]

Salomon's house is sometimes called "the College of the Six Days' Works," indicating the object of its study is creation or nature "whereby I am satisfied that our excellent kind hath learned from the Hebrews that God had created the world and all that therein is within six days; and therefore he instituted that House for the finding out of the true nature of all things."[21]

Salomon's House is also an intelligence operation. The rulers of New Atlantis, like Walsingham with his Jewish spy network on the Continent, would, every 12 years, send

> forth out of this kingdom two ships, appointed to several voyages that in either of these ships there should be a mission of three of the Fellows or Brethren of Salomon's House, whose errand was only to give us knowledge of the affairs and state of those countries to which they were designed, and especially of the science, arts, manufactures and inventions of all the world.[22]

Like England, Bensalem's people are "happy" not only because they study Jewish science but also because they give refuge to the Jews and have incorporated their "secret Cabala"[23] into their constitution. The Jews are so happy they no longer "hate the name of Christ,"[24] as in Catholic Spain. The Jews are so grateful at the tolerant treatment they have received in Bensalem that they have even given up the "secret inbred rancour" they usually feel "against the people amongst whom they live."[25] The Jews of Bensalem "love the nation of Bensalem extremely." They even believe the inhabitants of Bensalem "were of the generations of Abraham by another son, whom they call Nachoran; and that Moses by a secret Cabala ordained the laws of Bensalem which they now use; and that when the messiah should come and sit in his throne at Hierusalem the king of Bensalem should sit at his feet, whereas other kings should keep a great distance. But yet setting aside these Jewish dreams, the man was a wise man, and learned and of great policy."[26]

Bacon thus launches the myth of the British Israelites and adverts to the idea that society should be based on the Noachide Law, i.e., Jewish law applied to righteous non-Jews, an idea popular among 18th Century Masonic lodges. Bacon also felt re-admission of the Jews would be beneficial for England. A major benefit would be widespread promotion of Cabala, revealing the mysteries of nature to the Gentiles. The main benefit, however, was Jewish science's "wonderful" technology, which the inhabitants of Bensalem used to create heaven on earth. That technology is revealed when "one of the Fathers of Salomon's house" gives the travelers a tour of "large and deep caves of several depths," used for "all coagulations, indurations, refrigerations and conservations of bodies." The caves are also used "for prolongation of life."[27]

The residents of Bensalem also have "means to make diverse plants rise by mixtures of earths without seeds,"[28] as well as "harmonies which you have not, of quarter sounds, and lesser slides of sounds," and "ships and boats for going under water and brooking of seas; also swimming girdles and supporters." They have "diverse curious clocks and other like motions of return and some perpetual motions."[29] In their intelligence operation, they have "houses of deceits of the senses,"[30] probably an early version of television, which is deceptive in many senses of the word.

In addition to "Mystery Men," who "collect the experiments of all mechanical arts," the rulers of Bensalem have appointed 12 "Merchants of Light," who, fortified by knowledge of Cabala, "sail into foreign countries" and spread Enlightenment.[31] These Merchants of Light gained significance in the 18th Century when the Whigs took Baconian science and combined it with the mathematical cosmology of Newton and then promoted this mixture as the Enlightenment. Promoters of the Whig Enlightenment would travel to the continent, especially Holland, where they linked up with Huguenot exiles in an attempt to topple the Bourbon dynasty in France. The Whigs used Freemasonry and the Newtonian science of the Royal Society against the Bourbons in the same way Walsingham and Elizabeth had used Dee's angelic technology against the Habsburgs. Bacon's *New Atlantis* links both campaigns. Bacon's allegory explicates the Masonic core at the heart of British foreign policy from the accession of Queen Elizabeth to the French Revolution, when the Enlightenment spun out of control.

Walsh sees in *The New Atlantis* "an allegory of Masonry, for the benefit of a few of the elect."[32] To the unsuspecting, "with no information about secret societies," Bacon's allegory "would seem a harmless tale to pass away the time." But to those who were or aspired to be adepts, Bacon provides a wealth of information about the "possible Jewish origin of the Craft, its direction by certain of the Sephardic Jews posing as Catholics in Spain, the hierarchical organization, with wheels within wheels, inner circles almost completely unknown directing the activities of the innocent novices, the elaborate spy system, the use of great wealth to gain power under cover of philanthropic and scientific purposes, the oath of secrecy concealing matters which it would not be healthy to reveal to the general public."[33] Bacon also explains to the initiate "the far-flung system of intrigue and espionage"[34] Walsingham started and Walpole used to inject subversive ideas into France during the first half of the 18th Century. Walsh uses Bacon's allegory to link the Whig Freemasonry of the Walpole era with the anti-Catholic conspiracy confected by Elizabeth, Walsingham, and Cecil, claiming Freemasonry is "one of the instruments used by the rulers of England to undermine the powers of France."[35] The work that began with Dee's occult assault on Spain culminated two centuries later when the Whig-inspired Masonic lodges brought down the Bourbon dynasty and ushered in the French Revolution. "There is much evidence," he continues, "that something like this secret society, or at least its parent organization existed in the 16th Century, and had a great deal to do with coordinating the international conspiracy against the Catholic Church."[36] According to Bacon's allegory, America is the old Atlantis, a continent lost to the civilized nations when its inhabitants lost contact with the Judaizers from Bensalem. Bacon implies the loss is temporary. Once Cabala under the guise of Freemasonry returns to America, the old Atlantis will again thrive.

The standard history of Freemasonry as beginning with the formation of the Grand Lodge in 1717 is Whig history in every sense of the term. For political reasons, Anderson's *Constitutions* deliberately obscured the real history of the Craft, causing consternation among scholars who could not make sense of historical documents that proved the lodge existed at least a century before. One document showed that the first American lodge was created in Newport, Rhode Island, in 1658, when 15 Jewish families migrated from Holland. That and the colonization of the Massachusetts Bay Colony by English Judaizers would ensure America became the "new Jewish wonder world"[37] in the 20th Century. Protestant revolution in England would be fulfilled in socialist revolution in Russia four centuries later. That revolution found supporters in America, most of whom were Jews. And the children of disaffected Trotskeyites would forge yet another vehicle for Revolution by appropriating America as the messianic anti-Communist nation. But the trajectory set in motion by Judaizing Protestants would find its fulfillment in Cabalistic Freemasonry before it would find it in Jewish Socialism, described by an American Jew as "the most glorious page in the story of the Jewish people since the destruction of the Second Temple at the hands of Titus."[38] The Jewish socialists of the early 20th Century saw World War I as one more apocalyptic "day of deliverance" which

> finally heaves in sight, and amidst the anguish and suffering of a great world war, the harrowing effect of which no part of the globe is permitted to escape, mankind experiences a new birth, and the Jew, too, at last is about to come into his own ... A new day is at hand when the weak and the oppressed of the earth will find themselves permanently delivered .... The beginning of this complete emancipation has already been made in the wonderful change in the status of six million Jews wrought over night, as it were, by the Russian Revolution.[39]

The crucial link between Protestant and Communist revolutionary eras was Freemasonry.

In 1613, Elizabeth, daughter of James Stuart, King of England, married Frederick V, Elector of the Palatinate. The wedding had a fairy-tale quality. Shakespeare staged a performance of *The Tempest* on their betrothal night pf December 27, 1612. The choice of plays was exquisitely appropriate, for many saw in the young island princess the rebirth of the magical cabalistic crusade of her namesake against the Catholic powers of the continent. When the couple sailed from Margate for the Hague, Protestant hopes sailed with them.

After a month in Holland, the young couple set out by boat to Heidelberg, in the now Protestant Palatinate, their new home. When they sailed for Holland many hoped the Counter Reformation, which was massing its forces to extinguish the last smoldering embers of the Protestant conflagration, might not have the last word after all. A couple this attractive and well-connected might well take up Elizabeth's banner, no matter how unwilling the current occupant of the English throne seemed. James, however, had no intention of being drawn into a suicidal attack on Habsburg hegemony in central Europe or of resurrecting a black operation created by the people who had murdered his mother. James wanted an England at peace. So after marrying Elizabeth to a Protestant prince, he arranged to have one of his sons marry a Spanish Catholic princess. Elizabeth and Frederick's belief that James would continue the quixotic foreign policy of the same group of people who murdered his mother was a miscalculation of enormous proportions that would have disastrous consequences for the Protestant cause.

In June 1613, the young couple arrived at Heidelberg, which continued the festivities begun six months earlier in London. Huge festival arches were erected. English players, who travelled frequently back and forth between Protestant capitals on the Thames and the Rhein, performed plays and masques. For the next six years, Heidelberg was the capital of the reborn Anti-Catholic Conspiracy and a haven for the Cabalism Dee had spread throughout Germany in 1589. It also became a center for cabalistic technology. The Vitruvian architect and engineer Salomon de Caus turned the royal gardens at Heidelberg into a cross between Prospero's magical island and the New Atlantis. The gardens at Heidelberg castle became famous for fountains that played music and for a statue of Memnon, derived from the pneumatics of Hero of Alexander, which seemed to speak or sing when the sun shone on it. It was a striking application of the cabalistic technology Bacon praised in *The New Atlantis*. In Heidelberg the promise of heaven on earth through cabalistic technology seemed on its way to fulfillment not in allegory but in fact.

During those six years, Johan Valentin Andreae published an important Rosicrucian text, *The Chemical Wedding of Christian Rosencreutz*, which may have been based on Elizabeth and Frederick's life at Heidelberg. *The Chemical Wedding* describes a young married couple living in a marvelous castle of magical wonders. The lion, Frederick's heraldic sign as king of the Palatinate, was a main symbol of the book. Christian Rosencreutz finds that, after entering the castle and participating in ceremonies and initiations, his soul rises to mystical marriage with his creator in ways vaguely reminiscent of the promises held out by initiation into the higher degrees of Freemasonry. Andreae's *Chemical Wedding* represented Dee's Monas on its title page, which leads Yates to conclude "the Rosicrucian movement in Germany was the delayed result of Dee's mission in Bohemia over 20 years earlier."[40] The Rosicrucians, Yates continues, were going to "bring about the return to the golden age of Adam and Saturn through the ceremonies and initiations described in Andreae's *Chemical Wedding of Christian Rosencreutz*."[41] The term Rosicrucian was itself a German appropriation of the symbol of the Knight of the Red Cross from Spenser's Elizabethan epic, *The Faerie Queen*. Spenser got the symbol from the House of Tudor, whose symbol was the red rose. Rosicrucianism was the name Christian Cabala took during the second decade of the 17th Century.

If the young couple were looking to fight for the Protestant cause, events soon granted their wish. In 1617, the year in which Robert Fludd's Rosicrucian *magnum opus, Utriusque cosmi historia*, was published, Rudolph II died and was succeeded as king of Bohemia by Ferdinand of Styria. Under Rudolph, Prague had become a haven for Jewish and Christian cabalists as well as a center for the Counter Reformation. Rudolph had conferred in person with Rabbi Loew, creator of the Golem, and had actually asked him for spiritual advice. Loew was the vehicle in Prague for a more virulent form of Cabalism confected by Isaac Luria. At the same time, the Catholic Church had placed the writings of Reuchlin on the index. Since contradictory forces were allowed to grow unhindered while Rudolph closeted himself in occult studies, conflict was inevitable. Moreover, the political landscape still harbored a large Hussite contingent sympathetic with neither the Jews nor the Catholics.

The situation came to a head when Ferdinand became king. Ferdinand was a staunch Jesuit-educated Bavarian Catholic. His attempts to implement the Counter Reformation led to a Hussite revolt. During one stormy meeting with his Hussite subjects, two Catholic leaders were thrown out a window of the castle, an event known as the second defenestration of Prague. This defenestration eventually led to the Thirty Years War. Its immediate effect, however, was to drive Ferdinand from Bohemia and put that kingdom in open rebellion against the Habsburgs. During the rebellion, the Hussites approached Frederick and asked him to become their Protestant king. Frederick took a month to decide. On September 28, 1619, knowing it was a declaration of war against the Habsburgs, Frederick accepted and set off for Prague to mount the Bohemian throne. The English Protestants were convinced their hopes for a revived anti-Catholic crusade were about to be fulfilled. "It seemed," Yates says, "as though the 'only Phoenix of the world,' the old Queen Elizabeth, was returning and that some great new dispensation was at hand."[42] That was one delusion Frederick's rash move inspired. Another was that James would come to his son-in-law's aid when the Habsburgs marched on Prague to demand their kingdom back, a belief shared by the English and the Hussites. The widespread sentiment found expression in verse: "Jacobus, her lord and father dear/Through her has become/ Our mightiest patron and support;/ He will not deter us/ Otherwise we would suffer great disasters."[43] The notion was widespread but wrong.

The folly of thinking James would risk his throne by engaging in a land war in Prague, hundreds of miles from any coast and deep in enemy territory, became apparent when the Duke of Bavaria crushed Frederick's forces at the Battle of White Mountain outside Prague on November 8, 1620. The defeat was so crushing and so sudden that Elizabeth and Frederick had to flee with little more than the clothes on their backs. Before Elizabeth and Frederick could make it home, troops loyal to the Spanish Habsburgs invaded Heidelberg, destroyed their castle and gardens, and deposed Frederick. The Protestant Cabalist Crusade in the age of Christian Rosencreutz was a soap bubble caught between Habsburg steel and

Stuart indifference. Eventually the young couple ended up in Holland, Europe's safe house for Protestant revolutionaries, where they spent their lives in exile and crushing penury.

One of the soldiers at the battle of White Mountain was a young Frenchman by the name of René Descartes. Almost one year to the day before the battle which drove occultism underground in Europe, Descartes was quartered on the Danube in a house which had a German *Kachelofen*. This invention allowed the young philosopher to stay warm beyond the hustle and bustle of the kitchen hearth during the winter months. So, by himself in a comfortably heated room, Descartes dozed off and had one of the most famous dreams in the history of philosophy. When he awoke on November 11, 1619, he was convinced mathematics was the key to understanding nature. All that remained was for him to draw the philosophical conclusions.

Descartes kept hearing about a brotherhood of the Rose Cross that possessed wisdom hitherto unavailable to the scholastics, whose teachings he had imbibed from the Jesuits. In 1621 Descartes traveled through Moravia, Silesia, Northern Germany, and the Catholic Netherlands, searching in vain for the secret brotherhood that was now a faint echo of the failed Protestant regime at Heidelberg. In 1623 Descartes returned to Paris only to learn his search had made him an object of suspicion. The Rosicrucian movement had incurred the ire of forces promoting the Counter Reformation in France. In 1623, an anonymous pamphlet entitled "Horrible Pacts Made Between the Devil and the Pretended Invisible Ones" appeared in Paris. Since Descartes was rumored to have joined "the Invisibles" in Germany, he was suspected of the sort of abominations described in the pamphlet:

> The adepts prostrated themselves before [the Devil] and swore to abjure Christianity and all the rites and sacraments of the Church. In return they were promised the power to transport themselves wherever they wished, to have purses always full of money, to dwell in any country, attired in the dress of that country so that they were taken for native inhabitants, to have the gift of eloquence so that they could draw all men to them, to be admired by the learned and sought out by the curious and recognized as wiser than the ancient prophets.[44]

The "Horrible Pacts" pamphlet was a garbled account of the cabalistic technology Bacon described in *The New Atlantis*. It was the first of many garbled English texts that would cause consternation in France. Eventually, the texts were deliberately garbled, as the Whigs used Huguenot refugees to foment revolution, but in this instance, the garbling was probably unintentional. The pamphlet's fears bespoke a French Catholic reading of the intentions behind the Jewish Cabalistic fantasies inspiring the Rosicrucians and their English admirers.

Descartes was rescued by his friend and former classmate at the Jesuit college of La Fleche, Fr. Martin Mersenne, who assured Church and State authorities Descartes was most certainly not and most probably never had been "invisible."

Mersenne would become one of Descartes' greatest promoters on the continent; he launched that effort in *Quaestiones in Genesim*, a key work marking the transition from the Renaissance modes of magical thinking into those of the scientific era. Mersenne's *Quaestiones* was a direct attack on the tradition of occultism as practiced by Ficino, Pico, and Reuchlin—all of whom were accused of promoting Jewish magic. He later expanded his attack on Cabala by attacking Fludd, with whom he exchanged a famous series of letters.

By the time the dust settled, Jewish occult science was history on the continent. Numerology and Gematria were replaced by mathematics, and Descartes was enthroned as the philosopher who would determine the course of history on the continent for the next three centuries. The Aristotelian *quidnuncs* had been routed by Reuchlin and the Reformation, which acted as a vehicle for Jewish Cabalism. When Mersenne destroyed that tradition, he paved the way for the triumph of Descartes, whose philosophy would sketch out all possible philosophical options. Descartes' radical disjunction of the world into *res extensa* and *res cogitans* led to both materialism and idealism. Descartes explication of the *res extensa* led inexorably to the materialism of Spinoza, and the revolutionary ideology of his followers, Toland and Collins, which led to the Enlightenment, the French Revolution, and Karl Marx. But his explication of the *res cogitans* led just as inexorably to the idealism of Fichte, Schelling, and Hegel and other apostles of the reaction to Revolution that became Romanticism in Germany.

In the aftermath of Mersenne's demolition of Fludd, Descartes' philosophy reigned supreme on the continent, but he soon had a challenger in England. Bacon would save the Protestant cause from an intellectual rout analogous to the military rout on the continent until Newton's Principia arrived in 1687, but Bacon's science could never get beyond its Jewish roots, and so England couldn't either. Protestants were judaizers, so to remain faithful to the Protestant cause England had to espouse judaizing in one of either two forms during the 17th Century: Puritanism or Freemasonry. England's colonies in America when faced with the same choice would resolve the dilemma differently.

Baconian science never stopped being Jewish science, no matter how much Whig historians later tried to sanitize it. As Yates pointed out, "the old view of Bacon as a modern scientific observer and experimentalist emerging out of a superstitious past is no longer valid."[45] Bacon's science grew out of Magia and Cabala and the desire to restore the *prisca theologia*, which was bound up with the Hebrew language, as Reuchlin had pointed out 100 years earlier. Similarly, Bacon's "'great instauration' of science" as proposed in *Novum Organum* "was directed towards a return to Adam's state before the Fall, a state of pure and sinless contact with nature and knowledge of her powers. This was the view of scientific progress backwards towards Adam, held by Cornelius Agrippa, the author of the influential Renaissance textbook on occult philosophy. And Bacon's science is still, in part, occult science."[46] No matter how embarrassing Bacon's Jewish science became for the Newtonians, they shared the same goal: defeat of the Catholic powers on the continent. English science was always intimately connected with English foreign policy.

II

In April 1650, about the time Menasseh ben Israel dedicated *The Hope of Israel* to the English Parliament in the hope that they would readmit the Jews to England, Charles II, Cromwell's rival and the son of the man he murdered, met with a group of influential Jews in Holland and tried to borrow 50,000 pounds to finance an invasion of England. During the 1650s, the Royalist supporters of Charles II were conspiring with the Jews at the same time that Menasseh was negotiating with Cromwell. Menasseh, the credulous rabbi from Amsterdam who thought American Indians were the ten lost tribes of Israel, was an agent, but he was also a pawn in a larger game. The Jews were avid to be associated with the world's premier maritime power when colonies were starting to pay lucrative returns, so avid that they hedged their bets, backing both Cromwell and Charles II.

Although the Puritans were judaizers, some observers felt the Jews had a closer affinity to the Scots. In *The Wonderfull and Most Deplorable History of the Latter Times of the Jews*, James Howell claimed Jews and Scots shared the same DNA. Edward I, the first Christian prince to expel the Jews from his territories, also disliked the Scots. Many of the Jews expelled from England went to Scotland, "where they have propagated since in great number."[47] As further proof of the blood ties between the Scots and the Jews, Howell noted "the aversion" the Scottish nation "hath above all others to hogs-flesh."[48] The Scots also "much glory in their [i.e., the Jews'] mysterious Cabal, wherein they make the reality of things to depend upon letters and words; but they hold that the Hebrew hath sole privilege of this. This Cabal ... is, as they say, a reparation in some measure for the loss of our knowledge of Adam, and they say it was revealed four times."[49]

Howell is referring to Freemasonry, which was then strong in Scotland. The Lodge, Stephenson says, was introduced into England when the court of James I arrived in London. The origins of the lodge are surrounded in mystery. Masons on the continent invariably traced their history back to the destruction of the Knights Templar in 1326. Whether the Templars fled to Scotland, as Howell claims the Jews did, is speculation based on documentation lost in the mists of time. What is fairly certain, however, is that the lodges in Scotland were operative before they were "speculative," i.e., they were originally organizations of masons, architects, and engineers who actually built buildings and military fortifications and used mathematical traditions handed down by those familiar with their practical application. Gradually, their penchant for construction took a mystical or metaphysical bent, and Freemasonry became involved in an attempt to recover something great which had been lost. Freemasonry would achieve this through the recovery of the name of Jehovah and the reconstruction of Solomon's Temple.

Sir Robert Moray, Charles II's agent, was an important link between Jews and Freemasons. Moray was also a founding member of the Royal Society. He was also a crucial link in the evolution of Freemasonry from an operative Scottish operation into a speculative Whig operation. Moray was active among the Scottish exiles eager to see the Stuart line restored to the English throne. His letters to them indicate Freemasonry was the means whereby they were going to achieve their end both practically and theoretically. These two facets of Freemasonry were intimately linked for Moray. When Alexander Bruce fled from Scotland to Swedish-controlled Bremen in 1657, Moray encouraged him to immerse himself in studies of Jewish lore, Hermetic chemistry, Paracelsan medicine, Egyptian hieroglyphics, and Masonic symbolism as a consolation for what he had lost and the first step in regaining it. The Cabala provided Moray with "the very Alphabets of things I knew," and he was conversant in Jewish lore even if he could not yet "be saluted as Rabbi."[50] Moray profited from reading Reuchlin's *De Verbo Mirifico* as well as the writings of Drusius, from which he learned about building Solomon's Temple. From Drusius's discussion of the Temple, Moray learned "in which sense Salomon and Hiram were brothers."[51] Moray was adamant, however, in insisting on the operative nature of the lodge, telling Bruce "Before you come in cheek by jowl with me at building Castles in the air, you must first be prentice as I was, then Mr. Mason as I am, and produce a masterpiece as I did."[52] Moray felt the lodge was mystical because it was first "practical," i.e., based on what masons had learned by building actual buildings. The mystical side of the craft was based on numerological theories derived from the "Zohar, Pico, Reuchlin and Montano on the magical Tetragrammaton, the androgynous Adam Kadmon, the male and female dynamics of the Hebrew letters and numbers, and the cosmic significance of the Temple architecture."[53] Unlike the "invisible" Rosicrucian brotherhood, which Descartes sought but never found, this essentially Jewish mystical building fraternity was an actual organization.[54]

Like the Jews, the Scots were in exile. The solution, taken from the Zohar, was to rebuild the Temple. Moray felt the pious man should pray "for the reunion of the scattered," for "the reappearance of justice and restoration of the former condition," and for "the return to Jerusalem, which again is to form the seat of the Divine Influence."[55] The Zohar gave explicit instructions on how post-exilic Jews, deprived of a proper place of worship when the Temple had been destroyed, could fulfill their "obligation to build a sanctuary below on the pattern of the Temple above ... and to pray within it every day in order to serve the Holy One." For, the Zohar continues,

> the synagogue below matches the synagogue above.... The Temple that King Solomon built was a house of repose on the celestial pattern, with all its adornments so that there might be in the restored world above a house of repose and rest.... A house is essential ... to enable the upper abode to descend to the lower abode, and [in the open air] there is none. Moreover, both prayer and spirit have to ascend directly to Jerusalem from a narrow confined place.[56]

Scots like Muray took the instructions from the Zohar they had received via Christian writers like Reuchlin and incorporated them into the myths and rituals of Freemasonry, where they were seen as an alternative to and antidote against sectarian strife. The lodge was more than just a society for studying Cabala and numerology; it was a secret political organization with a specific political purpose, namely, restoration of the Stuarts to the throne of England. As such, they incurred the suspicions of the Puritans. Cromwell's spies reported on William Davidson in 1654. Davidson was an Episcopalian merchant with many Jewish partners in trading ventures on the West Indian Island of Barbados. Barbados remained stubbornly royalist throughout the Interregnum, so Cromwell attempted to punish them economically and militarily. When Parliament passed the Navigation Acts to punish the Dutch for poaching on English territories, Davidson and his Jewish backers suffered financially from the loss of trade. Provoked by their continued resistance (a resistance Cromwell unwittingly fostered by banishing many Scots and Irish loyalists to the Island), Cromwell sent the Navy to Barbados and impressed over 4000 men into the ships of the Republic. During this mission, the English navy seized several Dutch ships, including the Mary of London "owned by Sir William Davidson and taken at Barbados with five other Dutch ships."[57]

Davidson had other reasons to be upset. The English Puritans were threatening to expand their economic embargo of Holland into a full-fledged military campaign. To fulfill his role as the English Gideon, Cromwell would eventually have to meet the Catholic Amalekites in battle, and he could only do that on the Continent, since they had already been extirpated from England. In 1657 George Fox, the leader of the Quakers, rebuked Cromwell for not attacking Rome, which probably means that by 1657 the planned invasion had been called off. But it also suggests William Davidson and his network of Jewish merchants and intelligencers were rightly concerned during late 1654 and early 1655 that an invasion of Holland was afoot.

The founding of the Masonic Lodge in Newport, Rhode Island, in 1658 was a sign of this concern and evidence of growing disenchantment with Puritan and Quaker attempts to convert the Jews. The Jews had relocated to Rhode Island because of its reputation for religious tolerance at a time when Cromwell was making their lives economically difficult in Barbados, religiously difficult in England by proposing conversion instead of tolerance, and physically difficult in Holland by considering a military invasion of their only safe outpost. The first Jews in America were also Masons. The evidence for Jewish-Masonic contact in Holland in the 1650s thus provides a credible historical context for an otherwise puzzling document that recorded a meeting of Masons in Newport in 1658: "wee mett at y House of Mordecai Campunall and affter Synagog Wee gave Abm Moses the degrees of Maconrie."[58] According to Katz, "Masonic historians have instead chosen to ignore the possibility, no doubt reluctant to claim Jews as the first known Masons in America. Such early connections between Jews and Masons would hardly be surprising, given the strong cabalistic, magical, and Hermetical associations of the movement in the 17th Century, and the many later Jews who became Freemasons."[59] Jewish historians share this reluctance; they "shy away from accepting this Masonic document, no doubt because of an unwillingness to confirm that the first Jews in English America were Freemasons."[60] Katz believes the Jewish Freemasons of Newport probably came from Barbados, where they had been tolerated along with the Quakers. However, the Scottish connection of certain Jews in Barbados, as well as Amsterdam, suggests another explanation for the Masonic ceremony in 1658.

The time was ripe for Jewish-Royalist collaboration, and Charles II exploited the opportunity. In 1652 Charles ordered John Middleton, his lieutenant-general in Scotland, to travel to the Hague to obtain supplies for a Scottish rebellion. In the Hague, Middleton contacted Davidson and his network of Jewish agents and intelligencers, whose economic interests had been adversely affected by Cromwell's Navigation Acts. As a result of the contact, the Jews expressed a willingness to contribute financially to Middleton and Davidson's plan for an uprising in Scotland.

In 1654 Menasseh ben Israel had been languishing in Holland since publication of *The Hope of Israel*. The war between England and Holland prevented him from traveling to England when messianic fervor was burning red-hot. When he arrived, the ardor had cooled as the Puritans reflected more soberly upon the fact that the Ashkenazim might have different habits than the people the Puritans read about in the Old Testament. At the still point which indicates the turning of the tide, Menasseh had become interested in Queen Christina of Sweden, a philo-Semitic bibliophile who had purchased a number of Hebrew books from him. Menasseh hoped to parley his role as the agent purchasing books for her library into becoming her mentor so he could persuade her to let the Jews emigrate to Sweden.

His plans were dashed when she abdicated in June of 1654. Disillusioned with sectarian fragmentation besetting the Protestant cause, Christina went off to search for a "higher" version of Christianity that would eschew religious strife and incorporate the *prisca theologia* Reuchlin had descried in the Hebrew scriptures. Christina, who eventually founded a secret Academy for esoteric studies, was drawn to a "higher" Christianity strikingly similar to Freemasonry. Christina's public conversion to Catholicism understandably provoked a barrage of criticism. When asked if she were Lutheran or Catholic, she replied, "I myself believed in a third religion, which, having found the truth, has cast aside the beliefs of these established churches, because it has rejected these beliefs as untrue."[61]

The Jews were only too happy to oblige her in her quest. In July Christina arrived in Hamburg with her entourage, including a number of well-connected Jews, among them her physician Dr. Benedict De Castro and Abraham Texeira, the wealthy banker, at whose house she stayed. The Puritans were scandalized.

The feelings were mutual. Angered that Carl X, her successor, had allied himself with Cromwell after her abdication, thereby associating her with a regicide, Christina denounced the Protector publicly. The Puritans responded in kind. One propagandist (known only by the initials I.H.) published *A Relation in the Life of Christina*, accusing her not only of taking up residence in Hamburg with a Jew, "a man, who is by profession, a sworn enemy of Jesus Christ,"[62] but also of having sexual relations with him and of being waited on by demons which she and the Jew conjured.

Christina moved to Antwerp in August, where she lodged with another wealthy Jew, a friend of Texiera. Hoping to get reimbursed for his services as book dealer, Menasseh traveled to Antwerp to meet with Christina. When the meeting came to nothing, Menasseh turned back to England. Aware Menasseh was again working for Cromwell, Christina arranged a meeting with Charles Stuart in October and assured him of her support. More importantly, she assured him of the support of the network of Jewish bankers and merchants she had assembled since her abdication. Delighted by the prospect of significant financial support, Charles knighted William Davidson, his contact with the Jews, for his role in bringing all of this together.

Charles also enlisted the support of Sir Marmaduke Langdale, another Catholic convert with mystical inclinations who had converted after seeing a vision in a magician's glass in Italy. Langdale was "very sorry" the Jews agreed with Cromwell and did his best to convince them to change sides. "The Jews," Langdale informed Charles,

> are considerable all the world over, and be great masters of money. If his Ma'ty could have them or divert them from Cromwell, it were a very good service. I heard of this three yeares agone, but hoped the Jewes, that understand the interest of all the princes in the world, had bene too wise to adventure themselves and estates under Cromwell, where they may by his death or the other alteracion in that kingdome runn the hazared of an absolute ruine but they hate monarchy and are angry for the patent that was granted by King James to my Lord of Suffolke for the discovery of them, which made most of the ablest of them to fly out of England.[63]

Charles sent Langdale to Brussels to meet with the Jews. These meetings probably deepened Puritan suspicion of the Jews. Before long the Puritans were convinced a Catholic-Jewish conspiracy was afoot. They were, of course, correct. In September 1655, the Duke of Ormonde visited "the Jewes sinagogue" in Frankfurt, to get more financial support for Charles' planned invasion of England.[64]

One month later, in October 1655, Menasseh finally arrived in London. It was an inauspicious moment for a number of reasons. Messianic fervor had cooled considerably since 1650. Moreover, because of Christina's public attack on Cromwell and her public association with Jews, including Menasseh, the Puritans viewed Jews with increased suspicion. The Puritans who had been so effusive in emulation of Jewish mores as garnered from their reading of the Old Testament now felt the Jews could not be trusted. Even John Dury, who had been instrumental in interesting Menasseh in coming to England, was having second thoughts. Dury felt England should "go warily and by degrees," because the Jews "have ways beyond all other men, to undermine a state, and to insinuate into those that are in offices, and prejudiciate the trade of others."[65] The Puritans must have known Jewish money supported the Glencairn rising, which General Monk had just put down in Scotland, since Davidson and Moray were involved and they were Charles' contacts with the Jews. The Puritan suspicion of the Jews came out in the open when Prynne, who had justified the regicide, published his *Short Demurrer to the Jews* shortly after Menasseh's arrival in England.

This change in public opinion had its effect on Cromwell. The readmission of the Jews had become politically impossible. In response to the public outcry, Cromwell put conditions on re-entry that the Jews found unacceptable. A report circulated that "Cromwell says it is an ungodly thing to admit the Jews."[66] Cromwell also wanted more money from the Jews than they were willing to pay. The Jews wanted assurances from Parliament, "for their being there with safety," which Parliament was no longer willing to give.[67]

As a result, by February the deal had fallen through. As soon as the Jews learned of Menasseh's failure to reach an agreement with Cromwell, they arranged a meeting with the exiled Charles II in Bruges, where they assured him they had never approved of Menasseh's mission to Cromwell. Menasseh was the sacrificial lamb that sealed the covenant between the Jews and the Stuarts. As a *quid pro quo*, the Jews would abandon their support of Menasseh and the now discredited Puritans. The Masonic conspiracy, as their part of the deal, distanced themselves from the policies of the Enthusiasts, in particular their desire to convert the Jews. The assurances were most certainly oral, but they appeared in print too. In his *Themis Aurea. the Laws of the Fraternity of the Rosie Cross,* Michael Maier stated unequivocally "That the Brethren of the Rosy Cross does neither dream of, hope for, or endeavour any Reformation in the world by Religion, the conversion of the Jews, or the policies of Enthusiasts .... They who bend their thoughts to change Commonwealths, to alter Religion, to innovate the Arts, make use very often of most despicable instruments to do their business."[68]

So, during the summer 1656, "some principal persons of the Hebrew nation residing in Amsterdam"[69] abandoned Menasseh and approached John Middleton indicating they were ready to put their financial resources at the disposal of Charles Stuart to restore him to the throne of England. Charles was delighted. On September 24, 1556, while still in Brugge, Charles II told Middleton to "Assure the Jews of our gratious disposition." When he met with the Jews in Amsterdam, Middleton was also to

> behave yourself in this commission wee have given you to the Jewes in such manner as upon their behavior to you shall judge fitt, and if you find the same good disposition in them towards our service which they expressed to you heretofore, by assuring them of our gratious disposition and how willing we shall be (when

God shall restore us) to extend our protection to them, and to abate the rigour of the Lawes against them in our several dominions, and ... they shall lay a signal obligacion upon us, it will not only dispose us to be gratious to them, and to be willinge to protecte them, but be a morall assurance to them that wee shall be able to do whatsoever wee shall be willinge when we can justly publishe and declare to all men how much we have bene beholdinge to them and how farr they have contributed to our restoration.[70]

In a second letter the same day, Charles continued:

whereas you have represented to us the good affection which some principal person of the Hebrew Nacion residing in Amsterdam have expressd towards our service, and that they have assured you that the application which has been lately made to Crumwell on their behalfe by some members of that nacion hath been without ther consent, and is utterly disavowed by them, and they are desirous of all offices to express their good will to us and desyre our reestablishement.[71]

Charles then moved to the brass tacks of the deal. In exchange for "contributions of mony, Armes or Ammuncion,"[72] Charles would readmit the Jews to England, and thereafter he would exert no pressure on them to convert. This was especially attractive to the Jews because Quaker proselytizing in Amsterdam was causing increasing resentment in the synagogue.

Freemasonry made this new alliance possible. It proposed a new *modus vivendi* that avoided the pitfalls associated with the discredited enthusiasm of the Puritans and Quakers. As part of the royalist Masonic cabal in the Netherlands, Constantijn Huygens had contacts with Moray and Davidson as well as Jews like Rabbi Jacob Jehuda Leon, who took his model of the Temple to London in 1675. Rabbi Leon also designed a coat of arms for the English Grand Lodge that is "entirely full of Jewish symbols."[73] The motto for the lodge is "Holiness to the Lord," but upon closer inspection the motto is trodden upon by figures with the hooves and haunches of goats. Rabbi Leon was consulted on various architectural projects, and his model of the Temple figured in the design of the new Amsterdam synagogue. Shuchard thinks Leon may have been a mason because "when a Jew was particularly proficient in his profession," the Amsterdam guilds "were forced to admit him."[74] Davidson became friends with another Rabbi, Jacob Abendana, at around the same time. Freemasonry provided a forum for the exchange of ideas of intense interest to the Christians. It also provided protection for the Jews. Both were bound by vows of secrecy and loyalty; both were united by a desire to learn the secret knowledge of Cabala and by a desire to find practical application for that knowledge, be it in buildings or governments.

They soon had their chance. Cromwell died in September 1658. When the incompetence of Cromwell's son Richard soon became apparent, the royalists increased their activity in Scotland, where a resistance movement had been active since January 1654. One of Cromwell's lieutenants, General Monk, had been appointed military governor of Scotland. Unlike Cromwell, Monk not only did not dislike the Scots under his rule, he fraternized with them in a way that the

Protector would have found unseemly. That fraternizing led to its logical conclusion when Monk, perhaps initiated by Tessin the Swedish architect in charge of his fortifications at Leith, became a freemason. Because Monk had an intelligence network informing him of the mood of the locals, he must have been aware of the massive shift in sentiment after Cromwell's death. Scottish preachers referred to the Scots as Israelites who would been soon be led from bondage to Pharaoh out of Egypt, and before long Monk found himself wondering if he was the Moses that was supposed to lead them. When Monk joined the lodge, he gained access to their intelligence network as well, and what he learned convinced him that the time was ripe to switch sides.

In November 1659, the Army of Scotland, with Monk at its head, marched south to free England from "the Tyranny and Usurpation of the Army."[75] In January 1660 Monk joined forces with Sir Thomas Fairfax and the Duke of Buckingham, "an old Mason,"[76] at York, where they pledged the support of the northern counties. On May 1, Charles issued the Declaration of Breda, which made universalist Freemasonry the basis for religious toleration in England under the restored monarchy. When Charles landed at Dover later that month, Monk was there to greet him. To show that there were no hard feelings over the role which Monk had played in the murder of Charles' father, the restored Stuart king took the reins of governance from Monk's hands and made him Duke of Albermarle for his troubles. He also made Monk one of his closest advisors.

During one of his first consultations with the new king, Monk in collaboration with Augustin Coronel, a Portuguese Jew who had settled in England in the early 1650s "as a merchant and royalist agent...receiving and distributing funds for the exiled King,"[77] proposed that Charles II should marry the Portuguese Infanta, Catherine of Braganza. It was Coronel who came up with the idea in April, one month before Charles returned to England. Coronel had also played a major role in bringing the Jews around to abandoning Menasseh and Cromwell and supporting Charles instead. He was in close contact with David da Costa and Bento de la Coste, and may have known Solomon Franco, who would become Ashmole's Hebrew teacher, linking him to the Royal Society as well. Eventually Coronel would become a Christian after being knighted by the king, but all of the crucial services he performed leading to the restoration had been performed as a Jew in collaboration with other Jews.

The eclipse of Puritanism caused the Puritan bard John Milton to fear he would be tried for treason and regicide before finishing his masterpiece *Paradise Lost*, but it did not diminish the use of Hebrew imagery in English poetry. Cowley used it in his "Ode upon His Majesties Restoration and Return," in which he "portrayed the King, his brother James and Monk as Jewish heroes":

Me-thought I saw the three Judaen Youths
(Three unhurt Martryes for the Noblest Truths)
In the Chaldaen Furnace walk

Tis the good General [Monk], the man of Praise
Whom God at last in gracious pitty
did to the' enthrall'ed nation raise
Their great Zarubbabel to be,
To loose the Bonds of long Captivity,
And to rebuild their Temple and their city.[78]

Charles was true to his word. When London merchants asked Charles to expel the Jews who had settled in London *sub rosa* during the Protectorate, Charles instead favored the Jewish merchants. Resentment of the Jews was not going away, no matter how much the king favored the people whose money had brought him to the throne. On December 16, the goldsmith Thomas Violet issued a Petition against the Jews taking issue with the religion "Mr. Moses, their High Priest and other Jewes" practiced openly in London "to the great dishounour of Christianity and public scandal of the true Protestant religion."[79]

In a nation burnt out from the excesses of Enthusiasm, this public zeal for Christianity fell on deaf ears. Sensing this, the Jews pressed for "endenization" and found widespread acceptance among the tolerant Masons running Charles' council. Many of his advisors needed no encouragement. Davidson pressed the king for the rapid endenization of his business partners as a reward for their support of the Restoration. The king obliged, hoping wealth from their gold-mining and trading ventures would pour into the royal coffers. In his history of the Jews in England, Cecil Roth says Jewish influence increased under Charles, who was "liberal in issuing patents of endenization" and who raised "the little Jue" Coronel to knighthood in gratitude for his marriage, which brought him the colony of Tangier and a significant increase in wealth.[80] The Jewish agent La Costa brought the dowry to England, and in gratitude Charles bestowed upon La Costa's associate Isaac Israel de Piso, a gold chain as a "Mark of our Royall Favour."[81] Collaboration this intimate could not have occurred under Catholic or even Protestant auspices, as Cromwell's failure to admit the Jews made clear. Freemasonry made it possible because Jews and Freemasons shared a common goal; they both wanted to restore a great thing which had been lost. "Like Davidson, Moray, and the Scottish Masons who returned from exile, Rabbi [Jacob] Abandana and the Jewish royalists would seek a revival of the ancient sciences of Solomon, by which 'the holy Temple' could be rebuilt within the adept and restored to its place in the center of the cosmos." Jew and Christian could unite in the worship of the same god, "the Grand Architect of the Universe," whose anointed king was now on the throne.

III

Yates says, "It is obvious that the Puritan worship of Jehova would be conducive to Cabalistic studies,"[82] but the Interregnum Years were not good for Freemasonry. Once the news of the Puritan revolution spread to the continent, the Protestant remnant of the Rosicrucian era pricked up its ears and thought of migrating to England. In 1640 Samuel Hartlib published his version of *The New Atlantis*, a utopia entitled *A Description of the Famous Kingdom of Macaria*. Comenius heard the call and migrated to England, where he felt it was now possible to build the New Atlantis the Rosicrucians had longed for since the Counter Reformation dashed their hopes on the Continent. John Dury published a similarly optimistic work. And John Milton published his work on universal reform in education in 1641.

The sense a new era was about to dawn soon died amid the realities of civil war. The Invisible College proposed in *The New Atlantis* and other Rosicrucian writings did not become a real college during the Interregnum. If anything, it became even more invisible so as to stay out of trouble. Christopher Wren, who was to become England's greatest architect at the time of the Restoration, told Evelyn "there were no masons in London when he was a young man."[83]

Once the Puritans were driven from power, the king, brought back by a conspiracy of Jews and Freemasons, would be favorably disposed to the other version of Cabala, known as "science." The reason is simple. Both movements derived from John Dee's Christian Cabalism. The exoteric part of that movement became the Royal Society; the esoteric part became Freemasonry, which popularized the cabalistic elements of Dee's thought when Newton mathematicized science. The large overlap between the early members of the Royal Society and the Lodge indicate the compatibility, if not the identity, of the two groups. Elias Ashmole, the promoter of John Dee, was admitted to the Lodge in 1646; Robert Moray, Charles II's agent with the Jews, became a member in 1641; both would later become members of the Royal Society. Gradually, the Rosicrucians who gathered around Robert Boyle, Robert Hoke, John Wilkins, and Christopher Wren formed the "Invisible College" at Oxford that would be the predecessor to the Royal Society. In 1658 John Heydon published *A New Method of Rosie-Crucian Physick*, in which he stressed the Jewish origins of Rosicrucianism. Two years later, just after Charles's restoration, Heydon had dinner with the king and the Duke of Buckingham to explain how Moses was "father and founder" of the fraternity of the Rosey Cross "of the order of Elias or Ezekiel." Rosicrucians were initiated "into the Mosaicall Theory," then graduated to the "Natural Magic of Solomon."[84] To bring this ancient science to perfection as proposed by Bacon in *The New Atlantis*, Moray, Bruce, Evelyn, Ashmole and other Masons founded the Royal Society.

Forty years after Mersenne demolished Fludd, Dee's tradition was still going strong in England, even though, after the publication of Meric Casaubon's attack on Dee, it was no longer politically astute to mention his name. Even after the founding of the Royal Society, English science was still Jewish science; it was still cabalistic, symbolical, and numerological. It had not changed since Reuchlin. Rev. John Wilkins, his disciple, wrote that "important scientific and technological information was encoded in the Jewish scriptures."[85] Science was still bound up with the *prisca theologia*; it involved recovering the lost wisdom of Adam and using that knowledge to reconstruct the Temple of Solomon. "If you believe the Jews," Wilkins wrote, "the Holy Spirit hath purposely involved in the Words of Scripture, every Secret that belongs to any Art or Science, under such Cabalisms as these. And if a Man were expert in unfolding of them, it were easie for him to get as much Knowledge as Adam had in his Innocency, or Human Nature is capable of."[86]

Rosicrucian "science" existed on three levels for members of the Royal Society, just as it had for John Dee: mathematics and mechanics for the lower world, celestial mechanics for the higher world, and angelic conjuration for the realm above the celestial spheres. Technological innovations were linked to the construction of Solomon's Temple, and drew on sources as diverse as Vitruvian architecture, Dee's reading of Euclid, Fludd's mechanical tracts, and Kircher's works on magnetism.

At the time of its founding in 1662, the Royal Society was a continuation of Dee's anti-Catholic crusade on behalf of Elizabethan British Imperialism. "Science" never lost sight of its political beginnings, but it had to consider what had happened in England in the intervening years. The science that Robert Boyle and his colleagues articulated in the Royal Society was intended as an antidote to the religious enthusiasm of the 1740s and '50s. The Jehovah that ordered Cromwell into battle was replaced by a Deity whose main characteristics could be seen in the order and harmony of the universe he had created, and then left to run according to its own rules. Human society should imitate the order in nature if men wanted to live orderly and harmonious lives. Men who felt they could ignore nature and discern the mind of God directly through private revelations threatened this order. These men—the Puritans, Quakers, Ranters, Diggers, and Fifth Monarchy Men— had implemented the Protestant vision—a conflation of Muentzer and Luther that was a combination of *sola scriptura* and mystical visions—and had failed. England was tired of prophets with visions. But it also feared atheism. Boyle's antidote to those visions was threatened from the other direction by writers like Hobbes, who wrote *Leviathan* in 1651 out of his experience of chaos in the English civil war. Hobbes and his followers felt that motion was inherent in matter, and because of that fact there was no need of divine providence in a universe which ran all on its own accord. This vision of the universe would find its fulfillment in Marx, but it had devotees before the end of the 17th Century, as we shall see.

The Royal Society was drawn toward a universe that was orderly and harmonious without fussy overseers, either in the spiritual or political realms. The stars that, according to Aristotle, moved through the heavens because angels pushed them, were replaced by bodies that continued in motion until acted on by something that would slow them down. Newton called that force gravity, which meant seriousness, a characteristic he thought inherent to God but not intrinsic to matter. It was a perfect description of the new capitalist society and its latitudinarian

Episcopal underpinnings that those tired of enthusiasm and yet fearful of materialism hoped to create with Charles on the throne.

The change in English intellectual life was profound and as vehement as the rejection of enthusiasm that took place, as Christopher Dawson put it, when "men like Nicholas Barbon, the son of Praisegod Barebones," and other "children of the saints" became "promoters and financiers." God, "who would personally whisper in the ear of Praisegod Barebones, had become the architect of the universe for his son."[87]

Boyle's philosophy allowed economic activity without a meddling sovereign or atheistic chaos of the sort Hobbes feared. Bishop Edward Stillingfleet, whose worldview was the antithesis of Milton's, felt attracted to the new world. In contrast to Puritan zealots who felt God would not bless England as long as some papist was still celebrating popish rites somewhere, Stillingfleet instilled a tone of mockery into religious discourse from which the English character would never recover. Men of property who could look after their own affairs without appealing to an absolute sovereign replaced zealots like Milton. God became a constitutional monarch in England years before the king did.

If the Royal Society under Boyle was drawn to that vision was drawn to that vision when it was founded in 1662, the vision of Solomon's Temple sat inaccessible across a great chasm that could not be crossed according to the methods the society had inherited from Dee. Indeed, for its first 20 years, it looked as if this child would perish in is cradle, the victim of rude attacks from those who felt that its Jewish science was incompatible with a Christian society.

In December 1662 Samuel Butler denounced the Royal Society as practitioners of Jewish Science. Butler was a royalist who, taking up the accusation James Howell had leveled earlier, claimed judaizing had taken root in Scotland.

> For Hebrew roots, although they're found
> To flourish most in barren ground
> He had such plenty as sufficed
> To make some think him circumcised.

Sir Hudibras, the hero of the poem, combines the worst aspects of Judaic culture in Butler's eyes. He is guilty of Puritan enthusiasm.

> Such as build their faith upon
> The holy text of pike and gun
> Decide all controversies by
> Infallible artillery
> And prove their doctrine orthodox
> By apostolic blows and knocks;[88]

In referring to "Infallible artillery," Butler probably meant Cromwell, but in his dislike for things Jewish, Butler conflates two forms of Judaizing that were at odds with each other—Puritan enthusiasm and Masonic Cabala. The revolutionary movement in England had split in two, and those two factions waged war on each other. Just as Ziska would turn on the Taborites, just as Muentzer would turn on Luther, just as Robespierre would turn on Danton and Philippe Egalite, and just as Stalin would turn on Trotsky, so the Cabalists turned on the Enthusiasists, even though they were part of the same movement. But Butler correctly saw the Jewish subtext shared by Puritans and Masons in the Royal Society. The revolutionary spirit had jumped from one Judaizing movement to another, but the commitment to revolution as a prelude to heaven on earth remained constant. The end was the same, even if the means changed. In part II of *Hudibras*, which appeared in 1663, Butler has Hudibras justify the oath-breaking and sedition of the Presbyterians, whom he refers to as a "synod of rabbins," by appealing to "Jewish precedent":

> The rabbins write, when any Jew
> Did make to God or man a vow
> Which afterward he found untoward
> And stubborn to be kept, or too hard,
> And three other Jews o' th' nation
> Might free him from the obligation:
>
> And have not two saints power to use
> A greater privilege than the Jews?[89]

Like Butler, Samuel Parker conflated Puritans with Masons. "There is," he wrote, "so much affinity between Rosi-Crucianism and Enthusiasme, that who-soever entertains the one, he may upon the same Reason embrace the other."[90] What these two opposing groups had in common was their connection to the Jews and the revolutionary spirit. Parker linked Rosicrucians and Jews as brothers in sedition. He also attacked the Cabalistic tradition, whether practiced by Jews like Isaac Luria or Christians like John Dee or, in this case, Kircher:

> I know of nothing more precarious and destitute of tolerable pretenses then these Cabalistical Traditions, being only a late and silly invention of the Jewish Rabbins ... and yet Kircher ... would have everyone that does not believe in the Divine Origin of the Cabala to be convicted of Heresie as an Enemy to Divine Providence. But, for my part, I cannot understand how any Rational man can be at all concerned for so vain and frivolous an Invention of the Modern (i.e., Tri-fling) Rabbins. But he that could find all the Learning of the world in an Egyptian hieroglyphik may find all the Articles of his faith in a Rabbinical Fable.[91]

From the orthodox Christian perspective Jews were odious because of their "obstinate adherence to the Mosaick Law."[92] The Jews were also notorious for dis-torting scripture. "They who are acquainted with the Customes and Tenets of the Modern Jewes, know what petty analogies they retch from Scripture, to abet their fond and ridiculous usages, indeed their pettinesse is so odde and surprising, that were it in any other matter, they would be as delightful as impertinent."[93] Chris-tians who took them seriously were even worse, because in incorporating perverse Jewish misreadings into their books—he mentions Reuchlin's *De Arte Cabalisti-*

ca—they not only corrupt Christian dogma, they also open the door to sedition and revolution by promoting the imitation of Jewish revolutionary thought.

The attacks did not deter the devotees of Rosicrucianism and Freemasonry from their continuing appropriation of Jewish material. Heydon, who had the king's ear when he dined with him, "stressed the Jewish origins of Rosicrucian science, utilized Hebrew letters and cited the writings of Josephus on geomancy, Ibn Ezra on sun dials and spheres, and Abraham the Jew on Alchemy."[94] Freemasonry focused Cabala on a practical project, the reconstruction of the Temple. Heydon was convinced that the Holy of Holies of the new Temple could be erected "by a process of Cabalistic meditation upon the names and attributes of God."[95] Kenelm Digby agreed, "confident if men's Minds were but truly fixt upon this Temple, they wound not prove such weather Cocks, to be turned about with the Wind of every false Doctrine, of some Atheistical Astrological vaine opinions: we should then be free from those disorders which threaten destruction to the Soul and disaster to the Common-wealth."[96] Heydon invoked Reuchlin, Pico, Agrippa, Valerianus, Khunrath, and Fludd in support of his belief that "The learned Hebrews say ... certain Divine poweres, or as it wer members of God, which by then Sepheroths ... have an influence on all things created."[97]

By 1675, the Royal society was in crisis because it still had not disentangled itself from the legacy of Jewish science. Living in Holland, which was intellectually and geographically half-way between England and France, Constantijn Huygens was worried that his fellow Masons at the Royal Society were being overtaken by the French. Alarmed by the desuetude into which "Solomon's House" had fallen in England, Huygens felt the Royal Society could be revitalized by a visit from the famous Dutch Rabbi Jehudah Leon. Leon had created a model of the Temple of Solomon that had served as the model for the Jewish synagogue in Amsterdam. Huygens felt it might also be a model for English buildings, especially since fellow Mason Christopher Wren was then reconstructing St. Paul's Cathedral. Wren sent the master mason Abraham Story to Amsterdam to study Leon's design. Rabbi Leon's secret mission to rebuild the Temple was also related to the decline of Jewish science. In a letter, Huygens explained the "Solomonic purpose" of Leon's mission to Wren. "This maketh me grant him the addresses he desireth of me, his intention being to shew in England a curious model of the Temple of Solomon."[98] The purpose was to turn the new Cathedral into a Temple of Solomon, which occurred when the building was sealed off and consecrated in a secret Masonic ceremony. Huygens wrote letters of introduction for Leon, hoping to introduce him to the Masonic elite in England. It also involved introduction to the "Cabal," what Schuchard terms, "the unofficial conclave" of high level Masons "which Charles II used as a secret instrument of government." Arlington, along with Lauderdale, Buckingham, Clifford and Ashley Cooper, "maintained friendships with various London Jews, who entertained their wives and daughters at sumptuous dinners."[99]

Since the "secret circle" were involved in "myotic rites" at Ham House, Lauderdale's London residence, Leon probably partook in their rites there and at the consecration of St. Paul's. Leon also came up with the deeply ambiguous logo of the Grand Lodge in London. Since speculative masonry was based on operative masonry, Huygens and the other promoters of Leon's trip to England probably hoped a spiritual breakthrough would follow construction of Solomon's Temple according to Rabbi Leon's design and the rituals that flowed from it. But no matter how helpful the trip was in terms of Freemasonry, it did little to jolt the Royal Society out of its cabalistic lethargy. Indeed, because of the intimate connection between Cabala and the Architecture of the Temple, Leon's trip probably harmed the Royal Society by lending renewed credence to Jewish science.

Ultimately, it was the publication of *Philosophia naturalis principia mathematica* by Isaac Newton in 1687 which diverted the Royal Society from its slow decline into oblivion by putting physical science on a firm mathematical basis and thereby ending the Dee tradition of Cabala and numerology. The new mathematical philosophy of nature banished spirits from the universe; it also created a "world natural" as a model for the operation of the "world politick" in a similarly revolutionary fashion. Armed with the philosophical underpinning of Newtonian science, the newly ascendant Whigs and Masons could spread revolutionary politics through the absolutist Catholic states, undermining the need for traditional rulers and enabling a society based on *"laissez faire"* in politics and economics. Gottfried Wilhelm von Leibniz was one of the first to claim Newton had smuggled occult properties into his system to justify creation of an "English" universe, according to which God acted like a constitutional monarch. Magic was still in the system, but now it was called "gravity." The explicitly occult imagery associated with Cabala and Cabalistic science was banished to Freemasonry, which became the main vehicle for disseminating subversive English ideas in Catholic countries. Revolution was the natural consequence of these Jewish-British ideas. Revolution came to England one year after the publication of *Principia Mathematica*, but the Glorious Revolution was different from the Puritan Revolution of almost a half a Century before. The Glorious Revolution was relatively bloodless; that experience coupled with the exposition of the mathematical laws of nature, led the Whigs, now the party of Revolution in England, to believe revolutionary forces could be harnessed for political ends.

IV

On June 10, 1688, panic spread among English Protestants when Mary, Queen of England, gave birth to a male heir to the throne. The young Prince of Wales was named James, after his father, James II, of the Stuart line, now king of England. James had ascended to the English throne in 1685, after his brother, Charles II, had died. Charles had converted to Catholicism on his deathbed. James, his brother, was a Catholic when he ascended the throne, and now it looked as if James would perpetuate the hold of the Catholic Stuart dynasty on the throne by siring an heir.

The Protestants reacted by unleashing a barrage of scurrilous propaganda against the royal couple. They could do this because a momentous change had taken place in English Protestantism during the course of Charles II's reign. The Roundheads and the Cavaliers, adversaries during the civil war of the 1640s had resolved their differences and coalesced into one pan-Protestant party. If any residual animosities remained, they were swept away by the prospect of England's return to the Catholic fold. And so the Whig propaganda machine, one of the most effective in the entire history of psychological warfare, went into high gear. Bishop Gilbert Burnet, who supported the Whig cause of Pan-Protestant unity, claimed that the infant Prince of Wales was, in reality, the bastard offspring of Edward Petre, James' Jesuit spiritual advisor, and a nun. Bishop Burnet then sailed for the Hague and told the same story to James' daughters, one of whom, Mary, was married to the Dutch Protestant prince William of Orange.

Anti-popish plots were rife in England during Charles' declining years. They were even the stuff of popular drama. John Dryden, fearing England would slide into anarchy when Charles died, published "Absalom and Achitophel" in 1681 as his defense of hereditary monarchy. A year later, Charles's brother and successor James attended Thomas Otway's play *Venice Preserv'd or a Plot Discover'd*, in which a Judaized Covenanter named Spinoza plots to restore the English Judaizers to the throne. Otway, according to Schuchard, "presented a nation on the verge of disaster."[100]

After poisoning the minds of James' daughters about the newborn Prince of Wales, Burnet and other Anglican bishops and their Whig supporters approached William of Orange and urged him to come to London and take over the government. William needed little persuading. He was already embroiled in a cold war with Louis XIV of France and needed allies. Since France under the Bourbons had succeeded Spain as the premier Catholic power on the continent, William's logical allies were Europe's besieged Protestant minorities.

Louis XIV helped unify the Protestant forces when he revoked the Edict of Nantes in 1685. His action sent thousands of French exiles into Holland, much as thousands of Jews went there after expulsion of the Jews from Spain. Once in Holland, the Huguenots thirsted for revenge, and it was only a matter of time before they joined with the English. Louis XIV may have crushed Protestantism in France, but in doing so, he only assured a more virulent form of Protestantism would spring up in Holland when it made contact with the English Whigs. "Huguenot exiles ... formed centres of militant anti-Catholic opinion and carried on an organized campaign of public propaganda and secret agitation against the government of Louis XIV and the Catholic Church." The Huguenot Diaspora, according to Dawson, "instilled a common purpose into the scattered forces of Protestantism. Nowhere was this agitation stronger than in the Netherlands, where

... they entered into relations with the exiled leaders of the English opposition who had taken refuge in Holland from the victory of the monarchical reaction in England."[101]

William responded to the Whig overtures by publicly denouncing his father-in-law's misdeeds, calling into question the legitimacy of the Prince of Wales. In November 1688 William landed at the head of an army provisioned by Jewish supporters, amid widespread anti-Catholic rioting and acts of iconoclasm, fomented by anti-Catholic Whig propaganda. James's supporters came to London to offer armed resistance to the Dutch usurper, but, perhaps because of the stress, James burst a blood vessel in his brain, which led to a stroke, which slurred his speech and impaired his judgment as he faced the battles of the next few crucial months.

Eventually, the king was captured by Dutch soldiers and brought to London under armed guard. In December 1688 James escaped and rallied the Jacobite troops in Ireland, where, at the Battle of the Boyne in July 1690, his troops were defeated by William of Orange. James then fled to France, where his supporters, familiar with the secret network that had restored Charles to the throne in 1660, established the Ecossais Masonic lodges in anticipation of another return of the Stuarts to the throne of England. The grandchildren of the men who sailed into exile in France with James in 1690 returned to Scotland with James' grandson, "Bonnie Prince Charlie," for the unsuccessful Jacobite Rising of 1745. The social cohesion of the Catholic Scots in exile was due in no small measure to the Ecossais Masonic lodges. Those lodges would attract thousands of Irish refugees, known as "Wild Geese," who would preserve the "Celtic" Masonic tradition while serving in the armies of sympathetic Catholic Kings. The Ecossais lodges would also spread to America, where they played a role in the American Revolution. On the continent, they would seek to preserve their identity in the face of a much subtler enemy, the Whig subversion and takeover of the lodges in England.

After William of Orange returned victorious from the Battle of the Boyne, he was determined to take revolution to Catholic France and to make the Jews pay for it. As one of his first public acts, he revoked the patents of endenization Charles had granted to the Jews. It was an act of singular ingratitude, but if William could treat his father-in-law so poorly, why should he treat the Jews any better, even if it was their money and materiel that put him on the throne? According to Cecil Roth's history of the Jews in England, the Glorious Revolution was "inspired by Englishmen ... executed by Dutchmen" and "financed by Jews."[102] William's biggest financial backer was Francisco Lopez Suasso, a Sephardic Jew from The Hague, who was elevated to the nobility as the Baron d'Avernas le Gras, after he "advanced the prince the enormous sum of two million crowns, free of interest for his adventure."[103] Francisco de Cordova, acting for Isaac Pereira, "provided bread and forage for the troops,"[104] and Dutch synagogues prayed for the success of the English cause. Similarly, the Jewish firm of Marchado and Periera financed William's campaign in Ireland, where a number of Jews settled after William's victory. As the Protestants subdued Catholic Ireland, the Jews offered prayers of retribution in their synagogues for "our brethren, who are imprisoned in the dungeons of the Inquisition."[105] According to Roth, the English continued to use Portuguese Sephardic Jews in their campaign against Rome and the Holy Office.

It is tempting to say the Jews deserved Williams's ingratitude because they had turned on the house of the man who had so generously allowed them into England without undue financial burden, but we are talking about two different groups of Jews. The Dutch Jews, who had supplied the military materiel for William's invasion of England, followed him to Ireland, where they hoped to prosper as tax farmers. They profited from William's conquest, but the London Jews were forced to pay for his victory. The London Jews were shocked by William's lack of gratitude, causing Norman Roth to exclaim, "this is the first case of clear discrimination against the Jews simply for being Jews in a situation that applied without distinction to all subjects of the realm.... William ... was in many ways a medieval tyrant of a ruler."[106]

In 1689 a Jacobite warned that William planned to "overthrow liberty of conscience in England." As a result, "all conscientious Dissenters will, with the Jews, be again forced to take their retreat," across the English Channel to Holland.[107] The Jews waited nervously to see what the new king had in mind. The English Jews were bitterly disappointed. They were conspicuously left out of the Toleration Act of 1689, which specifically excluded from its benefits "any person that shall deny in his preaching or writing the doctrine of the blessed Trinity."[108] To remain in England and do business there, the Jews once again had to pay large indemnities. William had deliberately excluded the Jews from the royal protection of liberty of conscience they had enjoyed under the Catholic James II, probably because he wanted to use them as a source of funds for further wars. The Jews were outraged and threatened to "remove their effects into Holland" rather than pay "the imposition which Parliament has designed to lay upon them." Sixty years later the anger of the Jews at William's war tax was still fresh in the minds of Englishmen and cited by Henry Fielding, novelist and Whig propagandist, who felt Scots were natural philo-Semites and English Jews "Jacobite Rabbins."[109]

Christopher Dawson referred to the Glorious Revolution as "the greatest victory that Protestantism had won since the independence of the Netherlands themselves."[110] The Glorious Revolution gave a new life to a Protestant Revolution, which otherwise tended toward peaceful coexistence, like the *modus vivendi* the Lutherans worked out with the Catholics in Germany. The Glorious Revolution not only "united Puritans and Episcopalians in defense of their common Protestantism," by choosing William of Orange, "the foremost representative of continental Protestantism," as its leader, "it inaugurated the long struggle against Louis XIV which broke the strength of the French monarch" and eventually brought down the House of Bourbon in France.[111]

The vehicle for the Whig assault on Catholic France was Freemasonry, after it had been purged of its Scottish and Jacobite associations. The Lodge became the vehicle for Newtonian ideas too, proposing as an alternative to the Catholic Christ of the Counter Reformation, the Grand Architect of the Universe, "who had constructed the cosmic machine and left it to follow its own laws"[112] in the same way the new constitutional monarch had handed over the English economy to Whig merchants and landlords. Newton provided the metaphysical foundation for Whig foreign policy:

> In the aftermath of the Revolution of 1688-9, liberal Christianity wedded to the new science was offered to an English and eventually to a European audience as a binding social philosophy capable of reconciling diverse Protestants and of sanctioning a stable social and constitutional order, born in revolution but intent upon repudiating revolution as an instrument of change. Newton's mechanical universe ... became the natural model for the triumph of the Whig constitution.[113]

The Glorious Revolution "gave Protestant bourgeois culture a classical form which was completely lacking in the undiluted Puritan tradition, as we see it in New England at this period," but its effect would be even greater in Catholic France:

> it was in France rather than in England that the revolutionary consequences of the new ideas were most fully realized and the attack on the traditional Christian order was pressed farthest, though the French enlightenment owed much of its success to the achievements of the English revolution and to the influence of English ideas. But in France there was no room for a Whig compromise. The majestic unity of French absolutism and Catholicism stood like a fortress which must be destroyed before the city could be taken by the forces of liberalism and revolution.[114]

One of the first to understand that a new era had dawned when William of Orange became king of England was John Locke, whose *Essay Concerning Human Understanding* appeared in 1690. During the the crucial decade of the 1680s, Locke resided in Rotterdam at the home of Benjamin Furly, a Quaker expatriate whose father had supported the Commonwealth under Cromwell. Furly *pere et fils* had become *personae non gratae* during the Restoration and had repaired to the Low Countries, which had been a safe house for revolutionaries ever since Philip II allowed the Jews to migrate to Antwerp in the mid-16th Century. Furly, like Nicholas Barbon, had undergone a subtle evolution in thought in the last half of the 16th Century, moving from Enthusiasm to freethinking. He acquired a library of heretical books and attracted a salon willing to discuss the ideas therein. John Locke was one of those freethinkers; at Furly's salon in Rotterdam he met even more radical thinkers in what Jacob described as the Dutch "entrepot between English republicans, Dutch Dissenters, and French refugees"[115] expelled when Louis XIV revoked the Edict of Nantes. These groups shared a common hatred of French Catholic Absolutism. They differed on how to deal with the common enemy. For a moderate like Locke, the answer was constitutionalism. Men of good will and property should unite in free association and establish rules to live as free and equal citizens. The Masonic Lodge hovered in the background of this discussion as the model for the new Protestant polity.

At Furly's salon, Locke met Anthony Collins and John Toland, radical Whigs whose views on religion he found appalling. John Toland had been sent to Rotterdam to study for the Presbyterian ministry. While there as a seminarian in the 1690s, he became acquainted with Furly and the freethinkers in his circle. Toland would abandon Presbyterianism to become a Spinozist and a translator of Giordano Bruno, who concluded God and nature were one and the same. Toland emerged in the 1690s as the most radical of the Whigs, "a Protestant for political reasons, but ... not a Christian."[116] A Protestant for political reasons is another name for revolutionary. Toland would show his devotion to revolution in his writings and by founding one of the first Whig Masonic lodges on the continent, the Knights of Jubilation. Toland was the fulfillment of the dreams of Dee and Bruno and the early Rosicrucian brotherhood. His goal wasn't "to abolish the materiality of the world but rather to abolish the immateriality of God."[117] Toland spiritualized matter by making it God. In the process he dethroned God as the creator of matter. This transformation would have serious political consequences.

During the 1680s, before the Whigs came to power after the Glorious Revolution, they expressed their libertine and anticlerical views at places like the Calves' Head Club or the Kit-Cat Club, where they would don priest's robes and engage in blasphemous rituals, including one in which the pope was burned in effigy. Postrevolutionary London became a magnet for this sort of person until the Whigs, fearing they might be hoist on their own revolutionary petard, deported radical foreigners to Holland. Radicals like Toland and Collins went to Holland under different auspices: they were sent as agents of the Whig government, to spread ideas which were so subversive that the government would never allow their dissemination in England. Matthew Tindal was a member of the same radical group that sought to reduce Christianity to a purely natural religion. Because of the double standard at the heart of Whig cultural revolutionary politics, Tindal's works were published in Dutch but not in English.

To rebut the views of Toland and Collins, Locke would eventually write a book about the reasonableness of Christianity. But there is no indication that it influenced their thinking, which tended toward atheism and materialism. Like Furly, Collins and Toland had roots that stretched back to the English revolutionary movement of the 1640s, and like Furly they had moved from enthusiasm to freethinking. Out of these discussions was born the black operation known as the Enlightenment. The Whigs in England were intoxicated by the political implications of Newton's laws of motion. As Freemasons they knew the physical world was the basis of the political world. That meant that some application of Newtonian physics would allow them to predict and control political motion. That meant the forces that had led to revolutions in the past could now be harnessed so that they would not get out of control. The relatively painless trajectory of the Glorious Revolution seemed the proof of that proposition. Man could now unleash the forces of nature without letting them get out of control. Some variant of Newtonian science, it was hoped, would come up with the formula which would control human passion, just as Ben Franklin would could control lightning and render it not only harmless but useful by storing it in Leyden jars for later use.

This illusion would survive among the Whigs until the French Revolution, after which Mary Godwin Shelley, daughter of two Whig radicals, would offer a more pessimistic view of man's ability to tame the forces of nature in *Frankenstein*. During the 1690s, the Whigs, fresh from securing a new social order through scientifically controlled revolution, thought they could use the same forces of nature to bring down the Catholic monarchies of Europe. During the 1690s, "the driving force behind this political and religious radicalism came from England, from a political structure and constitutional order established by revolution."[118] Newton claimed his system needed a God, the Architect of the Universe, to hold it together because motion was not intrinsic to matter. But, like Luther, Newton launched ideas that would sail beyond his intentions. The Newtonian system expelled angels from the universe, and some claimed it expelled God too:

> The mechanical philosophy made it possible to conceive of the universe as matter in motion without the need to postulate a separate and eternal Creator. Republicans converted the result in philosophic pantheism into civic religion, and the dynamics of that credo gave coherence to the Radical Enlightenment throughout the 18th Century.[119]

On those terms, the Newtonian system became the vehicle for revolutionary thought on the continent, even though it was used to justify harmony and social order in Whig England.

V

In 1704, three years after the outbreak of the War of Spanish Succession, an 18-year-old Huguenot refugee, Jean Rousset de Missy, arrived in the Hague to start a new life free from the religious oppression of Louis XIV. Rousset de Missy carried with him, like a household god packed hastily for the flight, an abiding hatred for the Bourbon monarchy and the Catholic Church, whose identities Louis XIV had fused, at least in Protestant eyes, when he expelled the Huguenots. In 1705 John Toland coined the term "pantheism" to promote Spinoza's subversive ideas. The term quickly caught on in Holland among the Huguenot exiles, who were abandoning their Calvinism, or secularizing its key concepts, as the children of those who supported Cromwell's Commonwealth were doing in England.

Given his political views, it was only natural that Rousset de Missy would run into John Toland or Anthony Collins at Furly's salon in Rotterdam, but by 1705 Toland had an organization of his own that was much more than just a place to discuss radical ideas. At around the same time that Toland invented the word "pantheism," he and Anthony Collins founded a secret society known as the Knights of Jubilation in the Hague. We know about it from a paper in Toland's manuscripts entitled, "The Hague, 1710," which described the order and its ceremonies. Toland knew Sir Robert Clayton, and most probably from him he learned about Masonic practices and terminology, or he could have learned about secret societies from radical Whig libertines at the Kit-Cat Club, which called its members "Knights" and which staged a procession through London in 1711 culminating in the symbolic immolation of the pope.

By 1710 Toland and Collins had recruited many French Huguenot exiles into the Knights of Jubilation. One was Prosper Marchand, who in 1720 became editor of Bayle's *Dictionnaire*. Rousset de Missy became a member, and he, like Marchand and Levier, would achieve modest fame as a writer, translator, publicist, and propagandist. "Every one of these refugees," Jacob notes, "possessed an affiliation with the book trade, and this gave them access to the nerve centre of the European Enlightenment. Through their publishing firms and journals they disseminated heterodoxy, the new science, and republicanism to French readers within the republic of letters."[120] Eventually, publishers in the Knights of Jubilation "made contact with a new generation of publishers ... like Marc Michel Reya ... [who] became the leading publisher of the High Enlightenment, who gave to the world works by Rousseau, Diderot and d'Holbach, as well as a vast body of materialist and anti-Christian literature."[121]

What has come to be known as the Enlightenment began as the Knights of Jubilation. After attaching themselves to the court of Eugene of Savoy in the Hague, Rousset de Missy and other Huguenot exiles served as agents for the English Whig government during the War of Spanish Succession.[122] As British agents, Rousset de Missy and other Knights of Jubilation infiltrated the Belgian postal system. Beginning in 1706, Francois Jaupian, the postmaster in Brussels and director of the Belgian postal system, received payments from the British government that lasted well into the Walpole administration. Handsomely rewarded, Jaupian easily recruited other Belgian postal officials as British agents. Two, Douxfils and Felbier, were also connected with Eugene of Savoy's court, which administered Belgium for the Austrian Habsburgs, traditional allies of the English in Holland to limit the power of the Bourbons, then the most powerful house in Europe. Douxfils' brother-in-law

> eventually married a woman who was to become Voltaire's mistress. Indeed, when Voltaire went to the Netherlands in 1722, via a stop over in Brussels, it was probably Douxfils, a friend of the poet, Jean-Baptists Rousseau, who put Voltaire in touch with Levier and Picart in the Hague [who] ... tried unsuccessfully, to publish Voltaire's epic poem *La Hendriade*.[123]

Douxfils was a Spinozist, i.e., a materialist and a revolutionary subversive, who used the postal system to circulate forbidden materials. For years he received packets from Marchand, Rousset, and other Knights and then passed them to his agents in France who used them in psychological warfare to undermine the Bourbon monarchy.

After 12 years of conflict, the English had grown tired of a semingly never-ending war in the Netherlands, and the Tories rode that discontent to power in Parliament. As one of their first acts, they concluded the Treaty of Utrecht ending the War of Spanish Succession in 1713. Toland and his cabal of Huguenot publishers were suddenly agents without portfolio, but since the black operation was also a publishing venture, they did not need direct financial support to survive. What began as a spy network became a black operation whose purpose was the subversion of the Bourbon monarchy in France. During his career as publicist in Holland Rousset de Missy became an enforcer for Whig politics on the continent, whose "overriding goal, from the 1690s until well into the 1750s" was "the subversion of French absolutism."[124] "One goal," we are told, "inspired the advocates of this alliance: the defeat of France, and after the Treaty of Utrecht (1713) when military defeat was not longer possible, the gradual subversion of French absolutism."[125]

After that treaty, the shooting war against France became a propaganda war. Huguenot exiles translated the subversive ideas of radical Whigs like Toland and Collins into French, and those ideas then circulated through the French-speaking world with the cooperation of the Belgian postal officials. Rousset de Missy appropriated Toland's term "pantheism" and soon became its apostle to the French. As a result, "the literature of the Enlightenment, much of it produced in the Netherlands, served to undermine the ancien regime in France." In 1714 Toland translated Giordano Bruno's *Spaccia* into English, and Rousset shortly thereafter translated into French the book that proposed that God was infinite matter.

The books the Knights published best show the subversive nature of this enterprise. Works like Voltaire's *Urania*, Toland's Masonic liturgy *Pantheisticon*, Diderot's pornographic *Les Bijoux discret*, as well as his Dictionary, and, most importantly, *Le Traite de Trois Imposteurs*, had one common denominator: subversion, either of the faith or the morals of the French. Rousset's colleague Levier also sold pornographic works like *Les Amours pastorales de Daphnis and Chloe* from his shop in the Hague. The book turned up in Baron Hohendorf's library; he probably bought it from Levier.

Pornography would increase in importance through the 18th Century. Eventually, pornographers at the Palais Royale under the protection of the Duc d'Orleans would defame Marie Antoinette and destabilize the Bourbon dynasty. Marchand's library, which was probably a catalogue of the subversive books the Knights were channeling into France, was also a catalogue of the intellectual decay of Protestantism. The "intellectual odyssey" that began with Calvin soon made way for "libertine literature, the new science, Toland, Collins, Tindal, works on the Hermetic tradition, hieroglyphs and Freemasonry (not to forget a few mildly pornographic, yet philosophical pieces like Diderot's *Les Bijoux in-*

discrets)."[126] This use of pornography for political subversion would culminate in the works of the Marquis de Sade, who learned his trade while incarcerated in the Bastille reading works Marchand and his fellow Knights had been disseminating for decades. Rousset de Missy promoted Diderot as the "second La Mettrie," but it was the first La Mettrie, in particular his *L'homme Machine*, which de Sade read avidly in prison, and which inspired de Sade to say "woman is a machine for voluptuousness" in *Justine*.[127]

Enlightenment publishers pursued their literary projects in Holland because "Dutch law enforcement against forbidden books was from city to city almost non-existent, and book dealers who could move their wares about from place to place were particularly immune and therefore particularly free to enter the trade in forbidden books."[128] So people like Marchand could create "literary projects" that were "often infused with subversive and polemical overtones."[129] The subversives were also shrewd businessmen, allowing their black operation to continue for decades despite the vagaries of English politics. The combination of Dutch tolerance and English *laissez faire* economics left "Enlightenment publishers like Marchand, relatively free to pursue their profession and intellectual interests in the Netherlands. The link between publishing and the spread of the Enlightenment seemed self-evident and probably a source of enormous personal pride."[130]

In 1711 Rousset de Missy passed a manuscript to Levier that would have an enormous political impact on the *ancien regime*. The *Traite de Trois Imposteurs* purported to show that Moses, Jesus, and Mohammed were frauds, not even well-versed in the magic they practiced to befuddle the credulous mob. Given the similarities between the *Traite* and Bruno's *Spaccio*, and the fact that Toland would translate the *Spaccio* into English and Rousset would translate it into French, it is likely that Rousset got the ms from Toland. The ideas of the *Traite* certainly fit in with Toland's ideas. The *Traite* claimed the miracles attributed to Moses and Jesus were accomplished by magic. (Toland had written a manuscript found among his private papers claiming Jesus was a magician.) Like Jesus, Moses was the son of a magician; Moses became an Egyptian priest, becoming thereby privy to their "pretended magic" to mobilize and deceive the "credulous" Hebrews. Freud made similar claims against Moses, claiming he wasn't really a Jew in *Moses and Monotheism* two centuries later.

With the world's major religious figures discredited, the author of the *Traite* then proposed the new religion of nature as the substitute for the failed religions of Judaism, Christianity, and Islam. That new religion was based on a much more radically materialistic science than the Newtonian physics the Whigs were promoting for general consumption in England. According to the science of nature proposed in the *Traite*, God does not impart motion to matter. Motion is intrinsic to matter, obviating the need for God, because "it is certain that there is in the Universe a very subtle fluid or very thin matter, always in motion, whose source is the sun."[131] By the end of the century this "fluid or very thin matter" was known as electricity. After Galvani's experiments with frogs' legs—electric shocks would make leg muscles twitch even though the legs were severed from the frog—electricity had become the materialist substitute for the soul, the idea Mary Shelley explored, along with its revolutionary implications, in *Frankenstein*. In electricity, science discovered the source of life and movement, making God unnecessary.

The political implications of the *Traite* were clear. If the universe did not need God to govern it, then France did not need a king. This view differed from the Newtonian view, even if the Newtonians shared many of the same assumptions about the universe. This idea would have been equally subversive in England, but the Whigs kept it out of England. Toland's books and their Huguenot translations were meant strictly for foreign consumption. Marchand tacitly recognized the revolutionary nature of the *Traite* by cataloguing it with the *Vindiciae contra Tyrannos*, a Huguenot ms. published in 1579 in the wake of the St. Bartholomew's Day Massacre two years before, which "openly advocated rebellion against tyrannical authority."[32] The massacre convinced the author of the *Vindiciae* that political compromise with the French king was impossible. The only solution to Bourbon Catholic tyranny was revolution. Not surprisingly, the *Vindiciae* was translated into English in 1648, one year before the Puritan regicides murdered Charles I. Revolution used Freemasonry as its vehicle in France in the 18th Century, but the roots of that revolutionary movement went back to the Protestantism of the 16th Century, when

> Huguenot revolutionaries belonged to an internationally linked Protestant network that practiced secrecy for survival and that waged bitter war against the Spanish Crown in the Netherlands, and after the Massacre of St Bartholomew's Day, against the French church and its king. The Freemasonry to which Rousset and his friends were drawn fulfilled many of the same social needs as did the Calvinist churches, and like those churches in their time of persecution, but for very different reasons, it too was secret and international in scope.[133]

Freemasonry was secularized Calvinism. The Elect became Lodge brothers through the alembic of time. Despite changes in names, the revolutionary distillate was the same in its essence, hatred for the Catholic social order of Europe, once embodied in the Habsburgs of Spain but now embodied in the Bourbons of France. Like the *Traite*, its secularized version, "the *Vindiciae* offered a powerful critique of absolutism and one that was compatible with the beliefs held by Whig radicals."[134] The Knights of Jubilation and their publishing arm continued the work publishers like Plantin had started at the time of the Iconoclast rebellion. Christopher Plantin

> built one of the finest and largest publishing businesses of the later 16th Century. In Antwerp, he had the lucrative right to publish Bibles for the Spanish king; in secret he belonged to a radical sect, the Family of Love, and surreptitiously published works by its leaders. The liberal beliefs and secret practices of this sect have often been seen as foreshadowing those of Freemasonry.[135]

Plantin's works ended up in the library of Baron Hohendorf, advisor to Eugene of Savoy, as part of "over a Century of semi-clandestine Protestant opposition, first to Spanish and then to French absolutism."[136]

The alliance of the Knights with the radical fringe of the Whig Party was intended to serve British interests in Northern Europe. Whig policy demanded creation of an Anglophile party in the Netherlands, and in their political activities the Knights and their Dutch associates contributed to that effort. "It is hard to believe that these French refugees were unfamiliar with its doctrines or hostile to its advocacy of rebellion before their arrival in the Hague."[137] Rousset carried this hostility with him when he left France to join "the Holland Whig party" in the Hague, where he was an enforcer of the Whig party line. He did this mostly through the "enormous volume of political propaganda, most of it in support of Whig foreign policy and the northern alliance of the Maritime Powers and Austria."[138]

Rousset de Missy founded a journal in Holland that he modeled on *The Spectator*. But in acting as a conduit for Whig ideas, he often failed to recognize that ideas acceptable on the continent, where they could subvert the French monarchy, were not acceptable in England, where the Whigs did not want the monarchy subverted. Rousset must have experienced considerable embarrassment when *The Spectator* attacked his mentors Toland and Collins as dangerous subversives. Since Whig foreign policy was Masonic, it is not surprising that it could have exoteric truths as the basis of its domestic policy and more radical esoteric truths as the source of its foreign policy. The party line in England was different from that in Holland, as Rousset was to discover.

The exoteric/esoteric distinction throws light on one of the hoariest debates in Freemasonry: whether the Continental lodges were more subversive than the English lodges. Abbe Barruel defended this thesis in *Memoirs pour servir un Histoire de Jacobinisme* at the end of the 18th Century. The Masonic constitution of 1723 specifically excluded "an irreligious libertine or a stupid atheist"[139] from membership. The formulation is radically and probably deliberately ambiguous. Would the Lodge welcome religious libertines and intelligent atheists? Probably. Similarly, the Continental/English dichotomy can be resolved easily enough. Masonry could have advocated the same ideas in England and France, but those ideas, which would have been radically subversive in France, would have been a description of the status quo in England after the Glorious Revolution. Steele's denunciation of the Radical Whigs, i.e., the ideas of Toland and Collins, in *The Spectator*, indicates that what was considered toxic by the Whigs at home was also considered good for export to France.

Toland used the Masons as his vehicle to spread subversive ideas on the continent. Between 1710 and 1726, when Voltaire arrived in England, Toland's ideas were circulating through France and condemned in England. Since the ideas were condemned in Whig journals in England and since Toland had close contact with Whig ministers in government in England and "Dutch Whigs" like William and

Charles Bentinck, it is safe to assume that Whigs like Walpole used the radicals as pawns to spread revolution on the continent. The Tories always claimed the Whig party was "infested with irreligion, with libertines, atheists and deists and the charge was not without merit."[140] The Whigs, however, were playing a double game, and agents like Toland and Collins, and Huguenot allies like Rousset de Missy, could learn their trade by attaching "themselves to political patrons in England and courts on the continent not as philosophers but as polemicists, spies and official historians."[141] Rousset became a revolutionary himself in 1747 after a career of propagating revolutionary ideas.

There is an alternative reading to the claim that Whigs used the radicals as pawns to spread revolution on the continent. Perhaps the radicals used the Whigs to spread radical ideas the Whig would have found appalling. Jacob claims that, in carrying out the northern alliance against France, the radicals operating as "official pamphleteers, spies, agents and messengers" were "in fact advancing their own views as well as forging vital links in the publishing enterprise that lay at the heart of the Enlightenment and that sought to undermine both Church and State in France."[142]

One way to resolve these conflicting explanations is to see the Enlightenment as a Whig sponsored black operation that got out of control, as black operations tend to do. By 1747 when he became a leader in the Dutch Revolution, Rousset de Missy was most probably intoxicated by his own rhetoric. It is unlikely he was operating on direct orders from Whitehall. The same could be said *a fortiori* of the French Revolution, which English Whigs hoped would unfold like a Gallic version of the Glorious Revolution, but which took on its own trajectory, and certainly, by the time of Napoleon, not one that made Whigs happy.

Although he was officially *persona non grata* in England, Toland's ideas continued to circulate on the continent. He, more than anyone, was responsible for the spread of Spinoza's ideas, which were viewed with increasing alarm, especially among Germans, whose familiarity with the Jews led them to view Spinoza with suspicion. As early as 1699, Johann Georg Wachter attacked Spinoza in *Spinozisme dans le Judaisme, ou le monde deifie par le Judaisme d'aujourd'hui et sa cabale secrete.* Kant felt Spinoza was a dangerous Jewish revolutionary, a Cabalist who got his ideas from Giordano Bruno. Spinoza was familiar with Bruno's writings and had written a dialogue in his manner as a young man. Bruno taught that "*Natura est Deus in rebus etc in De immenso, spaccio, et summa terminorum,*" and so unsurprisingly this idea found its way into the writings of John Toland, who promoted Bruno and Spinoza. Voltaire cited Toland in 1734 and linked him to Spinoza.

If pressed on the issue of religion, Toland probably would have taken the position of the *Traite de Trois Imposteurs* that all religions were fraudulent. In practice, he came down harder on Christianity, claiming (if he were the author of the *Traite*) that Jesus was ignorant of even the Egyptian magic Moses knew. By 1714, Toland was praising the Jews, claiming they "honor one supreme being or First Cause and obey the law of Nature."[143] Toland was also the first 18th Century thinker to espouse "the cause of religious toleration for the Jews."[144] This newfound sympathy may have a Masonic connection. Freemasonry aspired to be a religion that could be acceptable to all. The English lodges, at least, were admitting more and more Jews. This was another instance of ideas that were considered tame in England but subversive elsewhere. The German lodges had conflicts with the Grand Lodge in London over the admission of Jews. Germans did not want Jews in their lodges, but they were forced to accept them by the English. The Amsterdam lodge, "where a pantheist and hence a follower of John Toland served for many years as Master of its lodge," followed the English lead in admitting Jews.[145]

Gottfried Wilhelm von Leibniz was a moderate Protestant who hoped to bring about reconciliation with Catholicism. Leibniz, who is credited along with Newton with the invention of calculus, was familiar with the Newtonian system but skeptical about its claims. Leibniz felt Newton's use of gravity was occult or magical. He was convinced Newton's inability to explain how gravity was the will of God operating in the universe according to mechanical principles played into the hands of materialists and atheists. Newtonian physics was, despite Newton's attempts to make it compatible with Whig conceptions of social order, deeply subversive in Leibnitz's view. He probably felt this way because he had met John Toland in 1702 when Toland arrived in the Hague as part of an English delegation to work out the Act of Succession with the Hanoverian line. Toland was attached to the republican Whig section of the delegation, but Leibniz thought he was a spy and a materialist who had adopted the atomic principle of Lucretius.

Leibniz kept the memory of the encounter alive for over a decade before writing *Monadology* in 1714 to counter the politically subversive materialism at the heart of the English ideology spreading through Europe. "Leibniz knew perfectly well that Eugene's circle at The Hague had been a center for libertines, freethinkers and radicals who saw in him their hope to defeat militarily the French search for European hegemony."[146] The *Monadology* was Leibniz's warning about Newton and his followers. For his pains, he was left behind in Hanover to write a history when George became king of England in 1717. The mood in England was changing as disillusionment with the Glorious Revolution was stifled under the spread of a new worldview that was an amalgam of Newtonian science and Masonic politics in the service of Whig ideology.

VI

In 1717, two Protestant clergymen, Dr. John Theosophilis Desaguliers and Dr. James Anderson, met at the Apple Tree Tavern in London and created a governing authority for the lodges in England known as the Grand Lodge. During the 16 years between the death of James II in 1701 and the founding of the Grand Lodge, Stuart Freemasonry was driven into exile in France with the Jacobites who fled there in 1690, and it went underground in England and Scotland, making its history almost impossible to trace. In reorganizing the lodges under one central authority, Desaguliers and Anderson redefined their identity, making them an adjunct of the Whig party.

James Anderson was a Scots Presbyterian minister who supported the Glorious Revolution that drove fellow Scot James II from the throne and handed it to the Dutch usurper. Given his political sympathies, it is not surprising that Anderson left Aberdeen in 1710 and moved to London, where he took over a congregation in Swallow Street. There he espoused Erastian views, attacking Freethinkers, Unitarians, Jacobites—the same people, with the exception of the Jacobites, the Whigs were promoting on the continent. Anderson wrote Whig propaganda for members of the Lodge and was recognized as the Author of the new Masonic Constitution in 1723. Jacob calls Anderson's Constitution "an extraordinary example of political propaganda."[147]

Many were upset when the new Constitutions, viewing them not as a codification of what Masons believed but as a distortion of those beliefs for political purposes. Given Anderson's role as a Whig propagandist, this is not surprising. Professor John Robison, whose *Proofs of a Conspiracy* introduced Barruel's writings on the French Revolution to Americans, accused Anderson of falsifying Masonic history for political purposes. He deplored Anderson's book as "the heap of rubbish with which Anderson disgraced his Constitutions of Free Masonry"[148] because it excluded the Scottish traditions Walpole thought fatally associated with the Jacobites. Robison says the Jacobites

> took Free Masonry with them to the continent, where it was immediately received by the French and was cultivated with great zeal in a manner suited to the taste and habits of that highly cultivated people. The Lodges in France naturally became the rendezvous of the adherents of their banished King, and the means of carrying on a correspondence with their friends in England.[149]

Walpole probably encouraged Anderson and Desaguliers to take over the English lodges because he understood the role the Ecossais Lodges had played in the restoration of Charles II to the throne. If those lodges "scattered across Europe" in "established clandestine Masonic networks," were left unhindered, it was only a matter of time before history repeated itself and the lodges put an offspring of James II on the throne.[150]

Walpole's best allies were Huguenot exiles. Desaguliers was a Huguenot refugee initiated into the Lodge in 1713 and inducted as a member of the Royal Society one year later. He studied under John Keill at Oxford and was considered proficient enough in Newtonian science to take over his mentor's lectures on Newton when Keill was away. After graduation, Desaguliers became a lecturer in Newtonian science. Newton was the godfather of one of Desagulier's children, so we can assume the Master approved of what he had to say.

After 1717 Desaguliers turned the lodges into vehicles for the new science and Whig politics, even putting into verse the political implications of the Newtonian system in "The Newtonian System of the World: The Best Model of Government." Masonic promotion of Newton provided an alternative to the Cartesianism triumphant on the continent. It also provided the theoretical foundation for limited monarchy as an alternative to the absolutism promoted by Bourbons on the continent. Jacob finds it unsurprising that "Whig oligarchs and their placemen flocked to Masonic lodges whose spokesmen offered so much confirmation to their self esteem and insured the cosmic significance of their activities."[151]

The 1717 re-organization of the Lodge was really a redefinition as well. Newtonians and Whig agents presided over the expulsion of the Jacobites and redefined the lodges into something which was less Christian and more attractive to revolutionary subversives and Jews. This was especially true on the continent. Anderson and Desaguliers redefined the faith of the lodge, turning it away from its Jacobite philo-Catholic Masonic base into "the Religion in which all men can agree." The Whigs and Newtonians who refined the craft put it on a trajectory toward secularism and subversion. According to its adherents, Freemasonry was not only the *prisca theologia* Reuchlin had sought in vain, it was the true religion because it was based on the foundation of all religion. "Masonry," according to Albert Pike, its most influential American spokesman, "teaches, and has preserved in their purity, the cardinal tenets of the old primitive faith, which underlie and are the foundation of all religion.... Masonry is the universal morality which is suitable to the inhabitants of every clime to the man of every creed."[152] According to Sir John Cockburn: "Creeds arise, have their day and pass, but Masonry remains. It is built on the rock of truth, not on the shifting sands of superstition."[153]

This redefinition meant Masonry would attract a different sort of person than the Ecossais Jacobite lodges of the 17th Century had attracted. The changes in philosophy and criteria of admission made it more attractive to Jews, who began joining in greater numbers. "Jews," according to Whalen, "might well feel at home in the lodge since the Hiram Abiff legend was built on the Old rather than the New Testament and the Craft borrowed most of its terminology from the Hebrew. The core of Masonry, that mankind has suffered a great loss which eventually will be recovered, could easily be understood to mean the loss of the Temple and of Jewish Nationhood."[154]

The Catholic Church abetted the change when Pope Clement VI condemned Freemasonry in 1738. The exclusions of Catholics combined with the preponderance of Jews and Freethinkers turned the lodges into agencies of subversion, especially in Catholic countries, where "only religious rebels and Jews sought admission to the lodges. This concentration of atheists, agnostics, freethinkers, Jews, and anti-clericals turned Latin Masonry into a subversive and hostile critic of Christianity and all religions."[155] This trend toward secularism also created tension with the Mother Lodge in London, where tradition and precedent were honored over the rationalism reigning on the continent. The continental lodges took the secular principles they imbibed from England to their logical conclusion. "When the Grand Orient of France in 1877 rejected the landmark of belief in God and removed the Bible from the lodges, the Anglo-Saxons severed fraternal relations which have never been resumed."[156]

Membership in the post-1717 lodges was attractive to Jews and Freethinkers for a number of reasons. In addition to being a practical vehicle for Jewish science or Cabala, the lodge also espoused the goal of Jewish revolutionaries since Simon bar Kokhba: heaven on earth. "Masonic literature ... offered the lodge as the foundation for earthly happiness. It provided an ethical system that emphasized fraternity and equality as well as the value of liberty."[157] It was also deliberately ambiguous about revolution as the means to attain heaven on earth. The Constitutions of 1723 specifically forbade expulsion as punishment for fomenting revolution. The reason for this ambiguity is not hard to discern. Masons were supposed to be loyal to the Whig Glorious Revolution, i.e., the status quo in England, and they were also to promote the same Whig philosophy in Catholic countries on the continent, where it was seditious and revolutionary.

The man chiefly responsible for this dual policy was Sir Robert Walpole, Whig statesman and prime minister during the first two decades of the 18th Century. When the Elector of Hanover arrived in England to ascend to the throne in 1714, he was greeted almost immediately by the legacy of the usurpers who invited him. The Jacobite rising of 1715 happened within a year of his coronation. Having failed to start a rebellion among the Scots, the Jacobites tried to interest the Swedes in the Jacobite-Swedish plot of 1716. After the foundation of the Grand Lodge, Walpole was determined to use it to purge active Jacobite elements from other lodges. That battle between the "antients" and "modern" freemasons continued for a Century. The Whigs won the battle in England, but lost it elsewhere, notably in America, where "ancient" anti-Whig Freemasonry played a significant role in the American Revolution.

Walpole used Masons with Whig sympathies to spy on their Jacobite brothers. Huguenot refugees proved themselves "especially loyal to the movement," and "they often also made devoted servants of the government."[158] Jacob claims David Papillon was "a member of the Royal Society's inner circle," who "acted as a personal agent for Walpole, and probably as a spy," because "his name turns up in the correspondents' list of the Grand Lodge of the Netherlands in The Hague. He also felt close enough to Walpole to recommend candidates for offices."[159] M. La Roche, a French Huguenot lodge member at Prince Eugen's Head coffee house on St. Alban's street, spied on the Jacobites in Paris. Walpole sent Martin Bladen, a Mason, on a mission to Paris in 1719. Like Bladen and La Roche, Ralph de Courteville, "loyally served Walpole as a spy on the Jacobites and as a writer of Whig propaganda for the London Journal."[160] All Whig agents on the continent eventually made contact with the Knights of Jubilation. In 1721, after receiving an assignment from Walpole, Philip von Stosch, Walpole's spy and art dealer, deposited his papers with Levier before leaving on his mission. After Levier's death, another Walpole agent, Peter August Samson, "wrote to his widow, also a publisher, to send greetings and regards for the 'maison d'Walpole.'"[161]

Walpole was, of course, a Mason himself, and he used Houghton Hall, his home, for the initiation of Francis, Duke of Lorraine, into the Lodge in 1731. As a member of the Lodge, Walpole was aware of shifting currents of internal politics in the Lodge. He was also aware that most lodges in France were founded by Jacobites and had Jacobite sympathies. After the abortive Jacobite rebellion of 1715, Walpole added offices to the king's payroll to extend Whig control over the Scots, including a royal liaison, "the king's mason," to the rebellious Scottish Masons.

During the first three decades of the 18th Century, the Scottish operative lodges were consolidated and reformed as speculative lodges in a move paralleling Whig ascendancy in parliament and administration. Before long, phrases from Anderson's Constitutions showed up in meetings of the operative lodges in Scotland. The first reference to the "secret mysteries of Masonry" occurred as power shifted to "gentleman freemasons" to the detriment of their "operative" brothers. The protective nature of the lodges as vocational guilds was abandoned in favor of free trade policies that weakened the lodges' economic standing but increased the power of the Whigs in London. The economic power of the guilds to regulate trade was destroyed and replaced by appeals to "freedom" and prosperity that would accrue from the new economic system. "By the 1720s the power of the craft guilds had been almost entirely broken by free-market economic pressures in England and Scotland."[162]

When the Jacobite Duke of Wharton tried to take control of the lodges in the 1720s, Walpole made sure that the effort was thwarted. "He should take care" Walpole warned Wharton; his "concern ... conveyed through his elaborate system of spies and agents is that an English aristocratic order, now rendered loyal to the Hanoverians, should not be sullied by Wharton's Jacobite activities."[163] French Masonic lodges were Jacobite and anti-Newtonian, as exemplified by the Chevalier Andrew Michael Ramsay. Eventually Ramsay was admitted to the Horn Lodge of London, not because he converted to Whig Newtonian views, but because he was amenable to working with the opposing group of Masons. Throughout the 1720s, Walpole continued to purge the lodge of Jacobite sympathizers and turned it into "a uniquely Hanoverian social institution, an embodiment of the Newtonian Enlightenment and officially dedicated to the ideology of court Whiggery."[164] Radical Whigs like Toland and Collins, disillusioned with the direction Whiggery took after the Glorious Revolution, were not expelled; they were simply invited to spread their revolutionary ideas on the continent where they would do the most good, most notably in the Dutch Republic. Gradually, the Masonic lodges founded in the aftermath of James II's exile in France after 1690 were eclipsed by those founded under Whig auspices during the first three decades of the 18th Century. "The freemasonry that we find throughout Europe in the period beginning in the 1730s appears to owe more to England that it does to Scotland."[165]

Under the increasing cultural influence of the Whig inspired lodges of the 1720s, radical ideas flowed from Holland south into France. The subversion leeching from Holland became a major bone of contention between the French and the Dutch. Louis XIV's agents kept close watch, even if they were unable to stop it. During the 1720s, Parisian cafes, like the Café de Procope, were centers of subversive Whig ideas, which Huguenot operatives had translated into French for consumption in France. The legend of Cromwell as a Freemason started then, an erroneous idea that circulated through France and created sympathy for regicide. By the 1720s, radicalism, directly related to subversive literature emanating from Holland, had established several intellectual beachheads in France. When the French police raided the shop of the Rouen journalist Bonnet, they found copies of *L'Esprit de Spinoza*, and an edition of *Le Traite de Trois Imposteurs*, which included a life of Spinoza. By 1721, there was an unofficial lodge in Rotterdam, where initiates could talk about the religion of Nature and other dangerous ideas emanating from England.

The French police, who had to contend with the dissemination of these tracts considered Freemasonry a subversive import from England from the beginning. Cardinal Fleury, Louis's prime minister, banned the importation of subversive and Masonic material, but to little effect. The French government could do little to stop the clandestine lodge meetings, and it could do even less to stop the clandestine spread of subversive material that provided the main topic of discussion at Lodge meetings. As early as the 1720s, police had attempted to break up lodge meetings because in them, "enemies of order seek to weaken in people's spirits the principles of religion and of subordination to the Powers, established by God."[166]

VII

In 1722 François Marie Arouet was an unknown but ambitious French writer who had written a long poem glorifying the French king he thought most resembled the constitutional monarchs who were the crowing achievement of English culture in the wake of the Glorious Revolution. The English king was a German, and the poem, known as *La Hendriade*, which sang the praises of the tolerant and enlightened King Henry IV, king of France from 1598 to 1610, was written in French, but none of this mattered to the young Arouet, who would later become famous under the name of Voltaire.

The first stop on Voltaire's road to fame was Brussels where he first heard of radical republican publishers in the Hague who might be interested in an epic poem written in French that glorified things English. *La Ligue*, as the poem was known then, glorified religious toleration. It was not a radical tract like *Traite de Trois Imposteurs*, but the publishers of the *Traite* were interested nonetheless. Lured by the prospect of a lucrative book deal, Voltaire made his way to the Hague, where he made contact with the literary circle of Marchand, Levier, and Rousset de Missy that was secretly known as the Knights of Jubilation. Voltaire also met the illustrator Bernard Picart. Together the knights expressed interest in bringing out Voltaire's poem. But the deal fell through, and Voltaire returned to Paris with his epic poem unpublished.

After his return, an anonymous poem describing Voltaire's trip to Holland circulated in Paris. In it, Voltaire was accused of attending a "pantomime *indiscret*" at an Amsterdam synagogue, part of a *"culte secret"* run by Dutch Rabbis.[167] Voltaire would never be described as a philo-Semite, so it seems unlikely he would have attended synagogue services, even though it was theoretically possible. The poem probably articulated the same inchoate suspicions that surrounded Descartes when he returned from Germany in search of the "Invisibles." Jacob speculates what the popular mind perceived as a *"pantomime indiscret"* conducted by the Dutch Rabbis was a Masonic ritual conducted by the Knights of Jubilation, the secret society the radical Whigs Toland and Collins founded to recruit angry Huguenot refugees. Jacob concludes "Almost certainly, Voltaire got his first taste of republicanism, both theoretic and practical from this early trip to the Netherlands," but if he met the Knights of Jubilation, he got more than just a "first taste of republicanism."[168] He also made contact with the continental Whig network of Masonic agents promoting subversive ideas among the French. An ambitious young Frenchman like Voltaire could be even more useful to Walpole than Huguenot exiles because Voltaire lived in Paris, the center of the empire the Whigs wanted to subvert.

In 1725, Voltaire met the Whig spy Bacon Morris. The "Honorable Governor Bacon Morris" would eventually become one of the subscribers who made publication of the English edition of Voltaire's *Hendriade* possible in 1728. In 1724 Morris was in Rome, collaborating with Walpole's spy and "art dealer" von Stosch on a mission which involved Walpole's brother Horatio, the British Ambassador to Paris. The Jacobites in Rome suspected Morris was sent by Walpole to spy on them. Morris carried a gun in Rome and he once approached the Pretender to the English throne on a street, presumably with the gun on his person. Shortly thereafter, an attempt was made on Morris's life, and the Pretender became so alarmed that he went directly to the pope, who ordered his secret service, which had Morris under surveillance, to deport him to France.

Bacon Morris returned to France desperately ill, but during 1725, he recovered his health, and he and Voltaire became acquainted and frequented the same circles. Viscount Percival would later refer to Morris as "an infamous man and a spy,"[169] in what seems the common assessment of his character among the English nobility. Even though Voltaire knew Morris was a secret agent of the British, he cultivated him as a contact, probably because Voltaire understood the deep grammar of English espionage, and how contact with the Whig network could foster his career. Foulet claims Voltaire's *"curiosite naturelle"* made him unable to resist the temptation to gather and share secrets with the English prime minister. If so, Morris was the crucial contact with power in England.

In 1726, Voltaire sailed for England carrying letters of recommendation from the British ambassador to Paris, Horatio Walpole. Voltaire almost certainly got those letters at the behest of Bacon Morris, who acted as Walpole's spy and agent in Rome. Because he arrived under these auspices, Voltaire was treated with suspicion and distrust by a certain segment of the English aristocracy. Crowley says Voltaire was "treated with distrust and reserve in England"[170] because the aristocracy knew of his connections with Morris. He also claims this is the reason behind the puzzling fact that Voltaire, "the apostle of English ideas,"[171] never returned to England even after achieving fame as a promoter of everything English.

In England, the Whigs certainly did not treat Voltaire with suspicious reserve. They received him graciously and introduced him to the leading lights of the Whig regime in government and science. They also arranged publication of his poem *La Hendriade*, enlisting even the support of George I, because "His epic ... fitted precisely with the reigning political ideology of court and ministerial government, and with the king's new political strategy of trying to render Anglo-French relations cordial and make the French pro-Hanoverian and anti-Jacobite."[172] The ease with which Voltaire found support from the Whig government led many to conclude he was on their payroll as their spy.

The poet Alexander Pope was one of those who accused Voltaire of being a Whig spy. The charge was leveled in public when Owen Ruffhead's *Life of Alexander Pope* was published. In a conversation with Warburton, Pope claimed Voltaire met with him at Twickenham, Pope's country estate. During the visit, Voltaire pumped Pope, a Catholic, for information that made its way to Walpole, causing Pope to wonder whether Voltaire was Walpole's spy. The charge was never refuted. Voltaire's meteoric rise to fame was too puzzling to explain by appealing merely to his literary merit. He had gone in a few short years from being a prisoner in the Bastille to having an audience with the King of England and being entertained by the Walpoles and the most powerful Whig magnates in the land traditionally seen as France's ancestral enemy. This was too implausible if literary merit were the explanation. The facts "throw suspicion on Voltaire."[173] He was the undoubted beneficiary of Whig patronage. "If he was not paid for his services, he should have been."[174] Jacob said that of Rousset de Missy, but it was equally applicable to Voltaire.

The Whigs certainly got their money's worth when Voltaire became their publicity agent. During his three years in England, Voltaire met with Samuel Clarke and other prominent Newtonians, and after digesting Newton's system, launched a violent attack on Descartes, the *fons et origo* of continental philosophy. He attacked everyone the Whigs thought worthy of attacking, including the radicals of the English revolution ("*ces peoples de Sectaires, Trembleurs, Indpendants, Puritans, Unitaires*"). Years later in 1768, when the salon of Baron d'Holbach brought out the old Knights of Jubilation favorite *La Traite de trois imposteurs*," Voltaire attacked his former Dutch promoters as dangerous atheists. D'Holbach's republication of the *Traite* evoked Voltaire's famous *mot*, "if God did not exist he would have to be invented."

In 1729 Voltaire returned to France, where he became the "apostle of English ideas," promoting constitutional government, *laissez faire* economics, intellectual "freedom," Freemasonry, and Newtonian Physics. Voltaire, as the dispute with Baron d'Holbach indicated, was no radical, and for that reason he was more dangerous to the *ancien regime* than more extreme visionaries. Voltaire insisted on the existence of God, who, through Newtonian physics, became the constitutional monarch of the universe, a Deity who did not interfere. The exoteric god of the Christians was also helpful in keeping shopkeepers and chambermaids in line. These ideas were commonplace in England, but they were revolutionary in France.

In 1733 Voltaire published *Lettres philosophiques*, a piece of Whig propaganda that had an immense influence in France. In it, Voltaire promoted English government and, more importantly for France, English science, as the sure foundation of a better form of government in France, free of intellectual and economic restrictions. Voltaire became the moderate foundation upon which radicals like Diderot and de la Mettrie could erect the edifice of revolution. Four years after his return to France, he praised England as heaven on earth, singling out Newton and Locke as "the greatest minds of the human race." Voltaire was one of the earliest and most famous of a long line of Whig propagandists and agents of influence that stretches from the 18th Century to the present day, including Henry Fielding, Edmund Burke, Russell Kirk, and William F. Buckley. Voltaire's ideas "became the creed of an organized party, which gained adherents wherever the influence of French culture was dominant, from Berlin to Naples."[175]

That propaganda would have a devastating effect on the monolith of Church and State that the Baroque Bourbon monarchy had become after the Counter Reformation. French absolutism was an all or nothing proposition, and when its foundation was undermined that whole world collapsed like a house of cards. Freemasonry was the crucial link between Calvin and Voltaire. Freemasonry enabled the secularization of Calvinist concepts like predestination and the rule of the Elect. And the secularization of those concepts gave them a new lease on life. Voltaire waited until the end of his life before he became a mason. When he was initiated into the Lodge of the Nine Sisters, Benjamin Franklin was there to welcome him. By then it was a work of supererogation; Voltaire had done his revolutionary work for the lodge outside of the lodge, and he was superseded by the lodge as well, just as soon the lodge would be superseded like a single candle when the revolutionary sun rose over France a few years later.

Joining the lodge had unintended consequences for Voltaire, who was in the habit of calling upon the priests of the wretch whenever he was near death. "During Voltaire's residence in Saxony," Barruel writes,

> where Mr. Dieze served him as a secretary, he fell dangerously ill. As soon as he was apprised of his situation he sent for a priest, confessed to him, and begged

to receive the sacrament, which he actually did receive, showing all the exterior signs of repentance, which lasted as long as his danger; but as soon as that was over, he affected to laugh at what he called his littleness, and turning to Mr. Dieze, "My friend (said he) you have seen the weakness of the man."[176]

Voltaire made a habit of signing his letters *"Ecrasez l'infame,"* or "Crush the Wretch," in reference to the Catholic Church. After joining the lodge, Voltaire had the unwelcome support of brothers who made sure he didn't fall into the wretch's hands before he died. Sensing the end was near, Voltaire summoned a priest in writing on February 26, 1778, but the Masons made sure the priest wasn't available in May, when death was at the door and Voltaire, "in spite of all the Sophisters flocking around him," was crying out, "Oh, Christ! Oh, Jesus Christ!" calling for aid from the wretch he had sworn to crush. Voltaire died on May 30, 1778, "worn out by his own fury ... the most unrelenting Conspirator against Christianity that had been seen since the time of the Apostles. His persecution, longer and more perfidious that those of Nero or Dioclesian, had yet only produced apostates; but they were more numerous than the martyrs made in the former persecutions."[177] Twenty-five years before he died, Voltaire predicted the French Revolution in a letter: "Every thing is preparing the way to a great revolution, which will most undoubtedly take place; and I shall not be fortunate enough to see it. The French arrive at every thing slowly, but still they do arrive. Light has so gradually diffused itself, that on the first opportunity the nation will break out, and the uproar will be glorious. Happy those who are now young, for they will behold most extraordinary things."[178]

VIII

As a result of Voltaire's work, the Masonic god found many worshippers in the Francophone world during the mid-18th Century. By the 1730s lodges were established in large cities of northern and western Europe as outposts of English culture, promoting ideas that were subversive in Catholic countries. By the mid-18th Century freemasonry had spread across Europe, but the lodges were concentrated mostly in northern and western Europe, especially in the densely populated corridor between Amsterdam and Paris. By 1750 some 50,000 men belonged to lodges in every major European city. By the end of the 1780s, there were approximately 35,000 Freemasons in France alone and 10,000 in Paris.

During the first few decades of the 18th Century, the French lodges tended to be Jacobite, and the Dutch lodges tended to be Whig, "often sponsored by official Representatives of the British government."[179] All lodges, whether Jacobite or Whig, "carried with them British political culture and mores."[180] Wherever freemasonry was established, the lodge was an outpost of British influence. The Knights of Jubilation became a model:

the lodges on the Continent ... embodied British cultural values associated with the potentially subversive: religious toleration, relaxed fraternizing among men of mixed, and widely disparate, social backgrounds, an ideology of work and merit, and, not least, government by constitutions and elections. By the 1730s all these values were the prized ideals of a cultural movement that laid claim to the secular and the modern, that came to be called the Enlightenment.[181]

When the first official Whig lodge on the continent was established in the Hague in 1731, the British ambassador was a charter member. Another was Jean Desaguliers, the Newtonian acolyte. His presence was a sure indication of the political direction that lodge was going to take—as was the presence of Jean Rousset de Missy, one of its chief organizers. If there were any doubts, they disappeared when that lodge named Vincent La Capelle, a member of the London Lodge and the chef de cuisine to William IV, as its head.

The presence of Rousset insured the lodge would be pro-Orangist and anti-French, which insured it would be viewed with suspicion by the 200 or so Calvinist families who ruled Holland and felt that peace with France best served their economic interests. The Hague lodge was seen from its inception as a subversive organization, created to promote British interests in the cold war against France. And so it probably was no surprise Holland closed the lodge as "an improper gathering ... an unseemly conventicle."[182]

Dutch freemasonry was illegal after 1735, but it nevertheless continued its rapid expansion. Those lodges remained stubbornly Orangist; they regained their legal status when they restored the Stadholder William IV during the Dutch revolution of 1747. These lodges remained true to their British roots, and their ideas, "transmitted clandestinely by the radicals and later officially by Whig politicians, provided the social milieu of the Radical Enlightenment on the Continent."[183] In analyzing the radical ideas disseminated by Dutch lodges but not the Master lodge in London, Jacob claims to see

> no small irony in the perception that these European radicals, who supported English interests on the Continent ... unwittingly helped to promote the interest of an aristocratic and commercial oligarchy in Britain that had long ceased to practice the republican creed. Yet there is also irony in the fact that while Walpole's government persecuted radicals at home, it had little choice but to rely on them abroad.[184]

Jacob sees irony where none exists. There is no irony, although there may be hypocrisy. The Whigs promoted subversives on the continent whom they would have thrown in jail in England. Subversion became a deliberate foreign policy when the Whigs sent the radicals abroad to undermine the Bourbon monarchy, a fact which Jacob recognizes elsewhere, when she describes Rousset de Missy's career as promoter of Toland's pantheism and publisher (and probably author) of the *Traite de trois imposteurs*. Even in his sixties in exile, Rousset could still write effusively about Pantheism to his friend Marchand.

By the 1730s Rousset de Missy's role in promoting subversion was clearer. In October 1737, Gaspard Fritsch, one of Rousset de Missy's former comrades, close to death and having second thoughts about leaving this life in the cold and unconsoling arms of the god of pantheism, revealed that Levier got the *Traite des trois imposteurs* from Rousset de Missy, and that he later combined it with *La Vie de Spinoza*, another subversive text Levier copied from the library of Benjamin Furly. In a letter full of remorse to Marchand, Fritsch named Rousset as the author of the infamous *Traite*.

The Whigs were subversive in other ways as well. When the authorized lodge was set up in England in 1735, the English forced the Dutch to accept Jews in the authorized lodge in Holland. Prayers at open lodge meetings were vetted for any Christian elements Jews might find offensive. Most Jews admitted to the lodge in England and Holland were Sephardim who had taken refuge in England and Holland after expulsion from Spain. New member had names like Mendez, De Medin, De Costa, and Avares. But Ashkenazic names also began appearing on the roles of petitioners. By 1759 half of the petitioners were Jewish with Ashkenazic names like Jacub Moses, Lazars Levy, and Jacub Arons. Sometimes the Jews changed their names, making the number of Jewish initiates difficult to discern. When Menachem Mendl Herz Wolff. was admitted to the Grand Lodge in London, he had changed his name to Emmanuel Harris.

Freemasonry accelerated the acceptance of Jews in England. Soon the lodge ceremonies, always based on Cabala, took a more explicitly Jewish character. Moses was referred to as "Master of the Lodge." Christianity, hopelessly divided among continually proliferating sects, was seen as best preserved in its pristine form in Judaism.

More importantly, membership in the Lodge was defined by acceptance of the "universal morality" embodied in the Noachide Law. In the 20 years following the founding of the Grand Lodge in 1717, the lodge had become more Jewish as philo-Catholic Jacobites were expelled or driven into "irregular" lodges on the Continent. This judaizing showed up in the 1738 revision of Anderson's Constitutions. According to the 1738 edition of the *Constitutions*, it is necessary that "all agree in the three great Articles of Noah, enough to preserve the Cement of the Lodge."[185] The fact that many lodge brothers in Holland were also merchants fostered development of what could be termed Jewish cosmopolitanism. This attitude would also fit in with Whig goals because it eliminated Scots loyal to the Pretender and his restoration to the throne. Masons felt that they belonged to a "universal" organization that transcended the narrow limits of creed and country. The fraternal bonding of the lodge undermined other ties, and in the place of loyalty to realities like blood and soil substituted the abstractions of the revolution—liberty, fraternity and equality, universal values applicable to any place or time. "Are we not members of the same family," the Masons asked. "Is the universe not the country to the Masonic [brotherhood]."[186]

Katz claims a new Jew emerged in the 1730s, one eager to join the lodge and willing to sacrifice adherence to the law and religious ritual to be admitted. The

Jews were often offered pork during initiation dinners as a sign they adhered to the new "universal" religion. The Lodge thus fostered subversion of religious beliefs. Or, more likely, fostered subversion indirectly by promoting membership of people who were willing to lie to get ahead. The precedent had been established at Javne and reaffirmed during the converso crisis in Spain. If it was permissible to lie and accept baptism under duress to avoid angry mobs in Spain, then it was permissible to lie by eating pork to gain access to the lodge. Between 1730 and 1750, "a new type of Jew was emerging, one who had acquired some Western education and had adjusted his behavior to conform to the standards accepted among gentiles, to the extent that he now could aspire to full membership in their society. This new Jew first made his appearance among the Sephardim of England, Holland, and France, and afterward among the Ashkenazim of all Western countries."[187]

Membership in the lodge involved displacing traditional loyalties. The lodge thus contributed to the rise of modern ideology, where a confected creed like Marxism or Neoconservatism would replace traditional allegiances that united Christians and Jews to traditional religious faiths and their communities. The Masonic lodges solved the problem of religious war by adopting the Jewish idea of the Noachide Law as the basis for the Lodge and civil society. When the Protestants rejected the Catholic faith, they rejected universal religion. The lodge became, as a result, an example of the return of the repressed. Instead of believing in the one, holy, catholic, and apostolic church, the lodge member was initiated into "the religion in which all Men agree." After over two hundred years of sectarian strife, the Lodge picked up where the now abandoned Catholic Church left off, as "the Means of conciliating true friendship among Persons that must have remain'd at a perpetual Distance."[188] The means whereby the Englishman could transcend sectarian difference and the strife that went with it was the Noachide Law. As Anderson put it in his 1738 revision of the Constitutions:

> A Mason is obliged by his Tenure to observe the Moral Law as a true Noachide. In ancient times the Christian Masons were charged to comply with the Christian Usages of each Country where they travell'd or work'd ... they are not only charged to adhere to that Religion in which all men agree ... (leaving each Brother to his own particular Opinions) ... For they all agree in the 3 great Articles of Noah, enough to preserve the Cement of the Lodge.[189]

The solution to religious division was moralism. The lodge member could hold whatever religious views he liked, but the law of Noah, which antedated Christianity and the law of Moses, was universal and binding on all. Katz claims the Masons derived the idea from John Selden's *De jure natural et gentium juxta disciplinam Ebraeorum*, "which had described the seven Noachide Laws as part of the ancient Jewish legal heritage."[190] Selden, in turn, had derived them not from Christian tradition, which "had never known of any such concept as Noachide commandments,"[191] but from the Talmud. Masonry adopted the Talmudic idea of tolerance that the Jews were supposed to show toward *goyim* "considered deserving of respect."¹⁹⁴ This entailed selective vision because the Talmud was also full of suggestions on how the Jews were to treat *goyim* not deserving of respect, and these revelations had fueled Christian outrage during the Middle Ages. By the high noon of Masonic influence in the mid-18th Century, Christians were not seen as having a revelation superior to and superseding the revelation of the Jews. If anything Freemasonry proved the opposite. The Jews had a superior revelation because it was prior to the Christian revelation and therefore pristine and uncorrupted. This logic finds clear expression in Freemasonry's espousal of the Noachide principles:

> If a prior revelation had occurred in the time of Noah and this revelation was vouchsafed to all mankind, then all who acknowledged and obeyed the commandments given at the time would attain salvation. Christianity lacked a principle of this nature and so found difficulty in according any positive religious status to those beyond its pale. The introduction of this concept, culled from ancient Jewish jurisprudence, into European thought by identifying it with the law of nature provided non-Jewish thinkers with an intellectual instrument which allowed them to justify toleration without abandoning their belief in divine revelation.¹⁹³

An attack this radical on Christian principles could not go unnoticed, even if the members swore not to reveal the lodge's secrets. A mob attacked the meeting of the lodge in the Hague in 1735, the year the Dutch authorities shut it down, indicating a reaction was setting in. Not long after a lodge was formed in Rome, word of its existence, its popularity, and its subversive judaizing principles soon reached Pope Clement XII, who issued a bull condemning it in 1738. The Catholic condemnation of Freemasonry would remain constant and consistent for the next two and half centuries. Benedict XIV reiterated Clement's condemnation, as did Pope Leo XIII in the encyclical *Humanum Genus* on April 20, 1884. One hundred years later, Joseph Cardinal Ratzinger, who would become Pope Benedict XVI, reminded Catholics the caveats the popes had ascribed to Freemasonry were still in force.

The popes saw the Masonic lodges as hotbeds of republicanism and revolution. They proposed a coherent critique of Masonic notions of freedom based on a theory of the passion applicable to individual souls and sovereign states. Aware of how revolutionaries appropriated the Masonic concept of liberty and used it to justify the crimes of the French Revolution, Leo XII said "by liberty ... we mean [being] free from slavery to Satan or to our passions, both of them most wicked masters." Freedom, as defined by the masons, was indistinguishable from license; it allowed human lusts and passions to spin out of control, which led inevitably to civil strife and revolution:

> For, the fear of God and reverence for divine laws being taken away, the authority of rulers despised, sedition permitted and approved and the popular passions urged on to lawlessness, with no restraint save that of punishment, a change and overthrow of all things will necessarily flow. Yea, this change and overthrow

is deliberately planned and put forward by many associations of Communists and socialists, and to their undertakings the sect of Freemasons is not hostile, but generally favors their designs and holds in common with them their chief opinions.[194]

Once the revolutionaries overturned the Catholic social order, they used the freedom that was indistinguishable from license to maintain their power:

> For since generally no one is accustomed to obey crafty and clever men so sub-
> missively as those whose soul is weakened and broken down by the domination
> of the passions, there have been in the sect of the Freemasons some who have
> plainly determined and proposed that, artfully and of set purpose, the multitude
> should be satiated with a boundless license of vice, as, when this had been done,
> it would easily come under their power and authority for any acts of daring.[195]

Considering that it was written in 1884, *Humanum Genus* was a remarkably prescient prediction of how sexual liberation would be used as a form of political control in Masonic countries like the United States during the 20th Century. The popes traced Freemasonry to "the ingenuity of the English nation,"[196] born out of revolutionary experiences of the 1640s and 1688. Jacob concedes the accusation "did contain a simple truth,"[197] namely that Freemasonry was a British invention, but calls the idea that Freemasonry was linked to the English revolutions of the 17th Century a "myth."[198] There were certainly some myths associated with that tradition: in France Cromwell was consistently referred to as a Freemason throughout the 18th Century. But during the 1730s, popes were not the only ones who saw Whig freemasonry as subversive and revolutionary.

In 1737, a year before the pope condemned masons, the Tories attacked them as sodomites and subversives, claiming, "no government ought to suffer such dark and clandestine Assemblies" because they may plot against the state and because they admit "Turks, Jews, Infidels, Papists, and Nonjurers." Other accounts elaborated on the charges, adding drunkenness and sodomy to the most frequently repeated charges. In addition, the lodges were seen as places where government positions might be secured. Given the large number of court Whigs in the lodges of the 1730s, the insight held substance.[199]

In the wake of the papal condemnation of 1738, police in Paris conducted raids on the lodges there. During the 1740s, Masons were under attack as English agents who wanted to subvert both state and church. The author of pamphlet *Les Francs-Macons ecrases* (1747) claimed Freemasonry was an English and republican conspiracy based on the subversive principles of liberty and equality. The charges troubled Rousset de Missy, who may have been involved in the Masonic rebuttal, which claimed the lodge was beneficial to society and authorized by nature itself. In the lodge, "everything changes, all things in the universe are renewed and re-formed, order is established, the rule and measure of things is understood, duty is followed, reason listened to, wisdom comprehended and mortals, without changing their essence, appear as new men."[200]

As part of their counterattack in response to the papal condemnation, the publishing circle around Marchand, Levier, and Rousset brought out an atheistic tract by Anthony Collins, *Le Philosophe*. Collins' tract broke new ground, claiming "the existence of God [is] the most widespread and deeply engrained of all the prejudices."[201] In its place the enlightened man, the philosophe, puts civil society, "[as] the only divinity that he will recognize on earth."[202] Soon the word "philosophe" was circulating in France. The philosophe espoused English ideas, and as a result of the translation when those ideas crossed the English channel, Newtonian physics and Freemasonry were conflated with the revolutionary enthusiasm of 1640 which was their antithesis. The link between Cromwell and Freemasonry was probably forged by Radical Whigs like Toland and Collins, who had roots back to the commonwealth period. By not denying these connections, Toland and Collins and their Huguenot promoters handed a public relations victory to their opponents, who portrayed Freemasons as dangerous communists and revolutionaries, based on the increasingly radical writings of Whig agents like Collins. In Brussels an anonymous pamphlet appeared in French accusing the masons of wanting to create "a universal and democratic republic, which would also hold in common all of the earth's wealth."[203] Anti-Masonic pamphlets in Amsterdam linked the Masons with Oliver Cromwell, and Dutch Masons were accused of promoting English revolutionary and republican ideas. Freemasons were "the Cromwellist Society," preparing to bring English revolution to Dutch soil.

When Dutch troops were unable to prevent a small scale French invasion in April 1747, rioting broke out in Dutch cities to protest the ruling oligarchy's impotence and to demand Stadholder William IV be brought back to power. In the Hague, buildings were festooned with orange banners. Mobs of rioting sailors got their ships to fire cannon in support. The spark which set off the Dutch Revolution of 1747 was the invasion of the French, but the tinder ignited by that spark had been prepared by people like Rousset de Missy through establishment of pro-Orangist Masonic lodges which were instruments of Whig foreign policy. English agents in Holland exploited the unrest caused by the French invasion to deplore the impotence of the oligarchs and to urge a restoration of the House of Orange. Foremost among those English agents were William and Charles Bentinck, sons of the advisor to William III and, as a result of being raised in England, Dutchmen who considered themselves Whigs. Together with Rousset, the Bentincks worked for the restoration of William IV as Stadholder, and the reinstitution of Whig Orangism as the best alternative to the "corrupt and self-serving rule of oligarchy."[204] Bentinck and Rousset de Missy found in Locke a justification for representative government and revolution. Two centuries later the United States government was promoting the same thing in the Ukraine, even using the color Orange to symbolize its Lockean revolution.

The Dutch Revolution succeeded initially beyond the wildest dreams of its proponents. When the rioting in the Hague in April spread to Amsterdam in May, the States proclaimed William IV Stadholder, and he appointed Rousset de Missy as his historian. Rousset then promoted the position of the radical Doelistenbeweging, which went well beyond what Whigs were advocating in England, promoting a revolutionary democratic regime. It is difficult to tell if Rousset was an Orangist agent out of control or if the goal of Whig foreign policy was radically different from what they were willing to allow for domestic consumption. The Whigs had tried to spread the Glorious Revolution to foreign soil, but the minute it got transplanted, it threatened, like an invasive species introduced into an environment with no natural predators, to spin out of control into a genuinely democratic if not communist revolution, like the one that had taken place in Muenster and would take place in France and Russia. When England refused to send troops to support its Whig agents, the revolution sputtered out and died. In June 1749 Rousset was arrested, fined 1000 guilders, and banished from the Hague, a city which he would look upon for the rest of his life as "paradise lost."

If the Whigs, who let their Dutch allies twist in the wind, had been paying close attention to the trajectory of the Dutch Revolution, they would have realized that black operations invariably spiral out of control. This was not only true of the "irregular warfare" popularized by T. E. Lawrence after World War I, it was true of psychological warfare as well. In both, "the heaviest handicap of all, and the most lasting one, was of a moral kind."[205] The Black Operation known as the Enlightenment taught the younger generation "to defy authority and break the rules of civic morality."[206] Rousset de Missy's use of Locke as a revolutionary battering ram made "a virtue of defying authority and violating rules." When the English promoted guerrilla warfare in Spain in response to Napoleon's invasion, they created an "epidemic of armed revolutions"[207] culminating in the Spanish Civil War of the 1937.

The Dutch Revolution of 1747 was a dress rehearsal for the French Revolution of 1789. Both began with unplanned incidents that might have remained insignificant, but for the fact that the Masonic lodges were in position to exploit them. In both instances, the unintended consequences of Whig Masonic political machinations far outweighed the expected benefits. The net result of English meddling in Dutch politics was the Diplomatic Revolution of 1756, when Austria pulled out of the northern alliance and signed a treaty with France.

IX

In 1754 the war between England and France over control of North America was not going well for France. Many feared the French would invade Holland, and, in the Duke of Newcastle's words to William Bentinck, "take possession of the Low Countries, as a sort of deposit, till we had done them justice in North America."[208] Since Rousset de Missy was in regular correspondence with Bentinck, the Duke of Newcastle's words probably caused his concern. To help the English cause, Rousset brought out a French edition of Locke's *Two Treatises of Civil Gov-*

ernment (written in 1690 in the wake of the Glorious Revolution), hoping it would spread revolution in France as in Holland seven years earlier.

Rousset disguised his identity as Locke's publisher by using the cryptic initials, L.C.R.D.M.A.D.P, which only the initiated understood to mean "Le Chevalier Rousset de Missy, Academie du Plessis." The French translation radicalized Locke's words. Where Locke used "commonwealth" and "community," in French they became "*republique*." The idea of a republic would have been anathema to Whigs in England, if Rousset were talking about England. He was referring to France, however, which meant the intent behind the translation was more destructive than instructive.

Rousset de Missy's translation of Locke was the most widely reprinted edition of Locke in Europe until the French Revolution. One French intellectual who read it was Jean-Jacques Rousseau. Rousseau was in the circle that met at Charles Bentinck's estate at Nyenhuis, a center for philosophic discussion as well as scientific experimentation. Hume and Diderot dined at Nyenhuis, and Rousseau became godfather to one of William Bentinck's grandchildren. Rousset would have most certainly been part of this salon and could have met Rousseau there if he hadn't been condemned to exile. Bentinck introduced worthy writers to a new generation of publishers and made sure their books were discussed in Holland's lodges, where they learned Freemasonry restored man to the natural state praised by Rousseau. Prominent among the new generation of radical publishers was Marc-Michel Rey, who became Rousseau's publisher in the 1660s. He also published the works of the Baron d'Holbach and Diderot's *Encyclopedie*. By the late 1760s, Rey had published all the major philosophes. His symbolic link to the radical publishers of the previous generation associated with the Knights of Jubilation became clear when he published Rousset de Missy's *Traite de trois imposteurs* after d'Holbach brought that classic of the subversive genre to his attention. Rey's role as a crucial link between English radicalism and the Enlightenment in France became even clearer when he published d'Holbach's *Systeme de la Nature* in 1770. D'Holbach got the idea for that book after translating Toland's *Letters to Serena* into French; whole sections of those translations of radical English ideas found their way into his book.

Rousseau differed dramatically from Voltaire, especially from his economic views. But both men were useful to the Whigs, whose agents in Holland made sure their ideas reached a wide audience in the French speaking world. Rousseau was useful because he posited a "natural" alternative to "artificial civilization," soon to become synonymous with the court at Versailles. Unlike the pope when he talked about the relationship between passion and revolution in his condemnation of Freemasonry, Rousseau attributed all human evil to social injustice perpetrated by an ossified artificial ruling class that lobbied for nothing but its own privileges. "Man is born free, and yet we see him everywhere in chains." Rousseau's *Social Contract* was the French radicalization of Locke's treatise on government. The inspired prophet from Geneva, even if he had converted to Catholicism from the Calvinism of his youth, fulminated against a corrupt priesthood that had no basis in "nature."

Abbé Augustin Barruel, author of one of the first histories of the French Revolution, would continue the classical moral critique of Freemasonry and the revolution it engendered that Clement XII had begun in 1738. The "philosophic" meditation on "liberty" and "equality" which began with Montesquieu's *Spirit of Laws* was taken to a new level when Rousseau wrote the *Social Contract* and construed "liberty" and "equality" as "supreme happiness." "If we examine," Barruel writes synthesizing Rousseau's ideas, "in what the supreme happiness of All consists, which ought to be the grand object of every legislature, it will appear to center in these two points Liberty and Equality. In Liberty, because all private dependence is so much strength subtracted from the body of the state, in Equality, because Liberty cannot subsist without it."[209] Rousseau was only "seeking to realize Montesquieu's principle; to give to each man who feels himself a free agent the means of being his own governor, and of living under no other laws that those which he had himself made."[210]

Rousseau and Montesquieu's ideas received their first application in America. By 1760, the Whigs had lost control of Masonic Lodges in America. The American lodges were Scottish and "antient," and many of the Masons there had contempt for the revisionist history that suffused Anderson's Constitutions. The split in the lodges facilitated a split between England, whose foreign policy was in the hands of Whig ideologues, and the American colonies, which deeply resented the economic exploitation those policies entailed. The conflict with America was exacerbated by the double game at the heart of Whig freemasonry. Jacob again notices it, but can't articulate the strategy fully, when she claims "on the continent" Whig Freemasonry promoted "a series of revolutions in which Masonic rhetoric and idealism, with its British and utopian associations, may have at moments made seem more plausible. In the country of their origin, however, most Masonic orators encouraged order and stability.... Indeed the lodges were an important vehicle for inculcating loyalism to king and government."[211]

There is no dichotomy. The radical version of Whig Freemasonry was not intended for domestic consumption. This simple fact also explains one of the big issues in Masonic studies, namely, the myth of the two lodges, a myth fostered by Barruel in his history of the French Revolution—a book written under Whig auspices in England.

The lodges in America were anomalous. They were not English, in the sense of being in England, but they weren't foreign either. The lodges in America were founded long before the founding of the Grand Lodge in London in 1717. Their residual loyalty to a more "antient" tradition fostered resentment against the Whig parvenus. That loyalty combined with resentment against exploitative Whig economic policies to ensure the lodge in America would favor revolution unacceptable to Whig oligarchs in England. One source claims the lodge in Boston suspended its regular meeting so members could take part in the Boston Tea Party. If Freemasonry suffered "a cultural transformation when it crossed the channel,"[212] it suffered another when it crossed the ocean.

There were other factors at work in the American Revolution. Puritanism did not die a sudden violent death in America, as in England in 1660, when English mobs, full of hatred for the failed Commonwealth, dug up Cromwell's corpse and hanged it. Puritanism was left to expire of its own self-contradictions in America during the course of the 18th Century. As a result the Enlightenment grew up there side by side with American Puritanism. Benjamin Franklin was 22 years old when Cotton Mather died. Both walked the streets of Boston in the 1720s when, in England, the rout of Enthusiasm and its replacement by Freemasonry was all but complete. American intellectual life was always a peculiar combination of religious enthusiasm and messianic politics; Newtonian Freemasonry was the antithesis of Enthusiasm in England and, a fortiori, on the continent, but Thomas Paine combined these two contradictory ideas, and his pamphlet *Common Sense* became one of the seminal documents of the American republic.

The American mind thus was formed by the confluence of contradictory forms of judaizing, *i.e.,* Puritanism and Freemasonry. American political thought would oscillate between these two poles for the next two centuries. The revolutionary creed hatched in America found immediate acceptance in France, largely because of Benjamin Franklin, "the representative figure who embodied the new democratic ideal of a humanity, liberated from the restraints of privilege and tradition and recognizing no laws but those of nature and reason,"[213] but Franklin was not operating in a vacuum. Rousseau, whose books on the social contract and the noble savage seemed to have America in mind, prepared his way. Franklin was also a Mason, representing the Scottish tradition regnant in America, and his way had been prepared there too by the Ecossais lodges founded by the Jacobite exiles in the wake of their defeat by William of Orange in 1690.

In America, it looked as if Bacon's dream of a New Atlantis had finally come true. A government had come into existence that was totally congruent with the laws of nature as formed by the Great Architect of the Universe, or as Paine put it, "The revolution of America presented in politics what was only theory in mechanics. But such is the irresistible nature of Truth that all it asks and all it wants is the liberty of appearing. The sun needs no inscription to distinguish him from darkness, and no sooner did the American governments display themselves to the world than despotism felt a shock and man began to contemplate redress."[214]

In 1787, nine years after the American Declaration of Independence, the shock was felt in the Austrian Netherlands the Protestant revolution had failed to wrest from the Habsburgs in the 16th Century. This should have been precisely what the English wanted except the revolution spread to Holland too, where the English ally the Stadholder William V was on the throne. According to Whig political theory, not unlike the Breshnev Doctrine articulated by the Soviets two centuries later, there were good revolutions and bad revolutions, and, according to this calculus, the Dutch Revolution of 1787 was a bad revolution. Prussia, England's ally, invaded Holland and crushed it. William V continued in power, prompting one cynical Dutch patriot to claim "The English endeavor to enslave everyone and keep themselves free."[215]

Since the Dutch revolution happened two years before the French, some historians have imagined the former as a "rehearsal" for the latter. The major difference was the absence of the Prussian army in France in 1791. This absence in 1791, like the presence in 1787, is consistent with the objectives of English foreign policy, which promoted revolution in Catholic countries but suppressed it at home and in countries ruled by Protestant allies.

Jacob ridicules the idea that freemasonry or its child, the Enlightenment, caused the French Revolution. Yet a close reading of her book provides evidence that supports just that conclusion. There were most certainly Frenchmen who connected the lodge with the revolution. Some were Masons. "A provincial lodge," she writes, "writing to the Paris Grand Lodge almost offhandedly remarked that 'in the civil order the deputies of a province represent the general assemblies of the nation; it is the same in the lodges.'"[216] Jacob sees "a remarkable parallelism"[217] between the National Assembly and the republican and democratic principles Frenchmen learned in the Lodge, but she stops short of endorsing a connection because she associates the link with Barruel, whom she terms "the most famous— and paranoid—historian of 18th Century freemasonry."[218] Barruel named freemasonry as "one of the great causes of the French Revolution."[219] He was not paranoid. Indeed, he could have made a much more effective case if he hadn't become caught up in the tangled web of Whig politics.

X

Christopher Dawson does not share Jacob's reticence in linking Freemasonry to the Revolution. If Revolution became "a real religion,"[220] as he claims, it was most certainly not a religion without a Church. The Religion of Revolution possessed "a definite though simple body of dogmas which aspired to take the place of Christianity as the creed of the new age," and it also "possessed its ecclesiastical hierarchy and organization in the Order of Freemasons, which attained the climax of its development in the two decades that preceded the Revolution."[221] Inspired by Benjamin Franklin and Lodge of Nine Sisters, Freemasonry was instrumental in founding numerous societies or clubs, which provided the practical and theoretical basis for the revolution. In those clubs, as in the lodge, social standing counted for little next to the overriding principles of fraternity and equality. Once the *ancien regime* showed itself incapable of commanding its armies and running its government, club members quickly stepped forward and applied the principles they learned in the lodge to the governance of the state. If Freemasonry was the link in the revolutionary chain that connected Protestantism to Socialism, the French clubs were the link between the lodge and the revolutionary government after the fall of the *ancien regime*. It was "in the clubs and the popular societies that the Revolution found its real organs."[222] The clubs were "the churches of the new religion."[223] The clubs abolished the lodges and simultaneously raised them to a higher level, just as the revolution was to do on a much wider and larger scale.

Philippe, the Duke of Orleans, later known as Philippe Egalite, played a crucial role in the move from Lodge to Revolution. Dawson claims Philip, the leading figure of French Freemasonry, "was the center of a web of subterranean agitation and intrigue which has never been unraveled."[224] The historian could start by examining the nexus of revolutionary clubs, cafes, brothels, and publishing ventures known as the Palais Royale. Philip Egalite created the matrix from which the French Revolution sprang when he built the Palais Royale. The Palais, where "reform moved through revolt to revolution," began as the Duke of Orleans' attempt to create "a sort of Hyde Park in the French Capital," where French Whigs could debate the "mild Whiggish reformism of the London coffee houses that the House of Orleans had originally sought to imitate."[225]

Furet claims the original vision of the French radicals involved creating "an English style political class" in France in which the "liberal nobility could collaborate with the Enlightened bourgeoisie."[226] When the *ancien regime* collapsed precipitously, the French radicals had the task of becoming English overnight, a project doomed to failure. Failed or not, the French got the idea of the "circle" as the small revolutionary cell was called, from the English. Billington quotes Mercier, who explained that even before the Revolution, "the taste for circles, unknown to our fathers and copied from the English, has become naturalized."[227]

The Palais Royale was supposed to imitate the English coffee house where Whigs discussed politics. The French radicals, lacking the moral restraint that characterized the bourgeoisie in England and America, turned the Palais Royale into a center of low pleasure instead, specializing in political pornography, and bringing out classics like *The National Bordello under the sponsorship of the Queen*. The Duke of Orleans hired as his personal secretary, Choderlos de Laclos, author of *Les Liaisons Dangereuses* and a pioneer, along with his friend the Marquis de Sade, of "the liberated pornography that flourished during the revolutionary era."[228]

The Palais Royale became notorious for its prostitutes, the most notorious being Madame de Genlis (later Citoyenne Brulart), the Duc d'Orleans' mistress. The prostitutes who gathered in the gardens of Palais Royale by noon, made sure "every form of sexual gratification" described in the pornography produced there was "available in the cafes and apartments of the Palais complex," including the possibility of sex with a seven-foot-two-inch Prussian prostitute, Mlle. Lapierre.[229] Providing "the intoxicating ambiance of an earthly utopia,"[230] the cafes also incited those who frequented them to act on the "politics of desire," and bring down the government that inhibited their pleasures and political fantasies. If "distinctions of rank were obliterated" in these cafes, and "men were free to exercise sexual as well as political freedom," then "The Temple of Voluptuousness" was destined to become the birthplace of revolution.[231]

This is what the classical tradition from Plato to Barruel said would happen when passion got out of control, but it came as a shock and bitter disappointment to the Newtonian Whigs who had promoted it. They thought they could control revolutionary passion in the same way that Ben Franklin had learned to harness lightning in Leyden jars. At the Palais Royale, the French radicals, clouded by sexual passion and the pleasures of drugs and alcohol, mistook fantasy for reality, and soon "the ideal of total secular happiness" began to "seem credible as well as desirable."[232]

The French Revolution began at the Palais Royale at around 3:30 PM on July 12, 1789 when Camille Desmoulins, outraged at the dismissal of finance minister Necker, jumped on a table and shouted, *"Aux Armes!"* The Palais Royale—or to be more precise, the Cafe Foy—became the "portico of the Revolution,"[233] the gate from which it issued forth. By 4:00 the mob was coursing through the streets of Paris carrying busts of Necker and the patron of their vices, the Duc d'Orleans. At 8:00 PM royal troops opened fire on the mob, killing a number of them. The mob had little to go on by way of historical precedent. The Protestant revolutions of Huss and Muentzer were so far in the distant past that they could provide little guidance. The socialist revolutions of 1830, 1848, 1870, and 1917 were hidden unborn in the womb of the future. So the French revolutionaries "echoed the Anglophlia of the Duke of Orleans in hailing the events in France as *'cette glorieuse Revolution.'*"[234] Their intentions may have been clear, but in carrying them out in a different culture and time, Anglophile intentions gave way to a Revolution with a terrible logic of its own.

On July 14, the mob broke into the Hotel des Invalides, where they liberated 32,000 muskets in the name of the French people. The mob then headed for the Bastille, where the Marquis de Sade had been haranguing them from his cell through a funnel that served as his urinal. The mob was looking for arms so they could return fire the next time they were attacked. Faced with the cannon the mob had looted from the Hotel des Invalides, the guards at the Bastille surrendered in mid-afternoon, whereupon they were savagely murdered, and their heads, stuck on the end of pikes, were paraded through the city. By the end of the day, Louis XVI was no longer king, or was king in name only. Three days later, he went to Paris and acknowledged Bailly and La Fayette as the nation's new revolutionary rulers. It turned out Louis XIV was right when he said, *"L'etat c'est moi."* Once his grandson abdicated, the state collapsed around him, and the rioting spread, filling the vacuum his abdication created. Having rehearsed the revolution during the food riots of the winter of 1788-9, the peasants armed themselves and attacked the local chateaux and abbeys and burned the administration's deeds and records, as if, in so doing, they could obliterate the hold the past had on them.

The uprising which began on July 12 was spontaneous in the same sense in which combustion is sometimes called spontaneous: the fire broke out at the Palais Royale because Philippe Egalite had assembled so much combustible material in one place that it had become an inevitability. Billington gives three reasons why the Revolution broke out there:

> It offered, first of all, a privileged sanctuary for intellectuals where they could turn from speculation to organization. Second, its owner and patron, the Duke of Orleans, represented the point through which new ideas broke into the power elite of the old regime.... finally the Palais provided a living link with the underworld of Paris and with the new social forces that had to be mobilized for any revolutionary victory.[235]

Nesta Webster, in a book that is controversial, offers another reason, "the Gold of Pitt,"[236] as part of a narrative in which she struggles with English responsibility for the revolution in France. The facts are clear: Montmorin told Gouverneur Morris that he "had indisputable evidence of the intrigues of Britain and Prussia that they gave money to the Prince de Conde and the Duc d'Orleans."[237] Marie Antoinette told Madame Campan not to go to Paris, because "the English have been distributing money there!"[238] Webster also cites Benzenval, who in "describing the riots of July 1789, speaks of the brigands employed by the Duc d'Orleans and by England."[239]

English guineas were found on the rioters, and Englishmen were seen mingling with the mobs during the first days of the revolution. Seditious pamphlets were printed in London, and there had been a heavy traffic in money, messages, and letters between England and the revolutionary leaders in France. Many of those same leaders "were constantly in England both before and during the Revolution; Marat lived for years in Soho, whilst Danton, Brissot, Petion, St. Hururge, Theroigne de Mericourt and the ruffian Rotondo were all habitués of London. These facts admit of no denial."[240]

England, according to Webster, needed to be worried, because Louis XVI was "an enthusiast for the navy,"[241] and by opening the port of Cherbourg, threatened England's domination of the seas. English diplomats heaved an almost audible sigh of relief when the revolution broke out in Paris. In September 1789, Lord Dorset wrote from Paris that the chaos from the revolution meant it would be a long time "before France returns to any state of existence which can make her a subject of uneasiness to other nations."[242] Sorel felt England was in position "to substitute herself for France" and profit from France's misfortunes "in every market" as well as "in every chancellery" where the two nations did business.[243] Pitt, according to Sorel, "would have been careful not to obstruct the development of a revolution so advantageous to his designs. He also held that a king of France deprived of his prestige, with his rights limited and his power contested, would marvelously answer the convenience of England. But he was not one of those greedy politicians blinded by jealousy, whose covetousness leads them to take a brutal advantage of fortune."[244]

After stating her case, Webster changes horses and declares that it is "illogical and absurd" to assume the English Government "took advantage of the disturbed state of the country to wreak her vengeance on the French government by encouraging and actually financing sedition."[245] George II opposed the revolution at every turn, and Pitt, his minister, "could have had no conceivable object in furthering a movement that shook all the thrones of Europe."[246] Pitt and the Jacobins were like oil and water; they were incapable of collaborating on anything. The Jacobins were "the natural enemies of England,"[247] and they were just as indignant at the thought of Pitt supporting the revolution as Webster herself. Why, she wonders, "should 'l'or de Pitt' be mentioned by Jacobin writers with the same indignation as by Royalists?"[248] The answer is simple. The Jacobins knew the English were using that money to subvert French power.

But what about the Duc d'Orleans' anglophilia and his frequent trips to England? "This apparent love of the Duc d'Orleans for the English was in the end the cause of all the calumnies against England with which the leaders of the different factions influenced public credulity, so as to throw on the policy of that nation the excesses of which they alone were guilty." The guineas found on the English and French revolutionaries came from the Duc d'Orleans; "with diabolical cunning he drew out in English coin, and had sent over to France in order to throw suspicion on the English."[249]

In the final analysis, Webster can only exonerate Pitt by implicating the Whig radicals associated with Dr. Price and the Prince of Wales in the conspiracy she dismissed as absurd and far-fetched:

> In this case English gold did play a part in the revolutionary movement, but it was provided not by the Government, but by its opponents. The Opposition party in London formed an exact counterpart to the duke's party in Paris; headed by the Prince of Wales, the roués of Carlton House formed a Fronde against George III, such as the roués of the Palais Royale formed against Louis XVI.[250]

Webster claims further:

> it was the 'democratic' party, the revolutionaries of France and Whigs of England, who supported the follies and extravagances of these two dissolute princes, whilst in both countries the cause of order and morality was represented by the sovereign whom the democrats wished to dethrone.[251]

Louis XVI knew of his cousin Philippe's connection with the Whig radicals; this is why he exiled him to Vilier-Coterets, not to a foreign country, and most certainly not to England. In London, Philippe consorted with radical Whig masons and Jewish lodge members like Samuel de Falk, as well as Whig radicals like Lord Stanhope, Price, Priestly and the "drunkard" Thomas Paine. The Whigs were "the natural allies of their country's bitterest enemies, the Jacobins of France," and they not only abetted the revolution abroad, but were "seeking to create a kindred movement at home."[252]

The mystery surrounding Pitt's Gold resolves itself once we remove the prime minister's name. Call it Walpole's gold instead, and the Whig involvement in subversion in France is too obvious to deny. Although many Englishmen, including Whigs like Edmund Burke, opposed the French Revolution, that revolution got started as a Whig black operation, and, like all black operations, the attack on France got out of control. Just one year into the revolution, one of steam engine inventor James Watt's Dutch friends wrote to him about the progress of the revolution. "The French," he wrote, "have now outrun their instructors the English."[253] The Dutch republicans thus saw the French revolution as the application of "English principles"[254] by students who went beyond their teachers' intent.

The revolution would destroy the very thing that prepared its way, namely, the Masonic lodges, when it declared all private institutions and associations illegal. French allegiance to the revolution would become widespread when Church property was looted and distributed though the *assignats* to a much wider group than the looting of England's churches had enriched in the 16th Century. The revolution then took on a life of its own, and many came to believe the Masonic lodges were no longer necessary. The Masonic lodge was only necessary "in a despotic society."[255] No one epitomized this transition better than the Duc d'Orleans, who had been the leading figure in French Freemasonry and in constant contact with the Lodge in London before 1789. He even journeyed to London in 1789, a trip that caused him problems later.

On September 15, 1792, France became a republic, and to celebrate the change (or to ingratiate himself with the winners) Philippe presented himself to the new government and asked to change his name to "Egalite." He also asked that the Palais-Royale, his revolutionary pleasure dome, be renamed the "garden of equality." Philippe was elected to the National Convention, but many in that body, including Jean Paul Marat, questioned his loyalty and sincerity, alleging he "speculated on the revolution as on his jockies"[256] and simply acted in a way "most convenient to his interests."[257] The crux of the issue was Philippe's connection to the Masons and England. The Jacobins suspected him of being a British agent working to establish a Whig-inspired constitutional monarchy in France.

The Palais was still politically significant in 1792. The Girondists, headquartered at the Cafe du Caveau at the Palais, organized the demonstrations of August 10, 1792 that overthrew the monarchy and led to the creation of the First Republic. Conflict soon arose with the Jacobins, who considered the Girondins as Royalists because of their association with the Palais and the renamed Duc d'Orleans. "The Jacobins feared not only the royalists [like Philippe D'Orleans] who controlled the cafes within the Palais, but also the foreign friends of the Revolution who enjoyed the hospitality of the Palais-Royal."[258]

The legend that Cromwell was a freemason came to fruition on January 21, 1793 when the National Assembly executed Louis XVI. It is doubtful the convention could have taken this step without the model of the English Regicide before their eyes. If the civilized English could murder their king, could not the French do likewise? Importing the lodge had already induced them to follow English models in other areas—from Newtonian physics to coffee houses. The example of Charles I haunted the trial of Louis XVI. Charles had run legal circles around his accusers, and the convention didn't want a repetition of that embarrassment at the French king's trial.

One day before the execution of the king, on January 20, 1793 a revolutionary leader was assassinated at the Palais Royale, and Philippe was considered a suspect. Jacobin mobs periodically launched assaults on the Palais as a suspected hotbed of royalism in the months following the murder. When Philippe's son defected to the counter-revolution in the spring, Philippe was arrested. Over the summer, the Jacobins slowly shut down the Palais' operations, and Philippe Egalite prepared his legal defense, knowing his life hung in the balance. The crucial issue was Philippe's involvement in Freemasonry because Freemasonry was considered an instrument of English culture, if not foreign policy, and England and France were now at war. The Revolution had taken on a life of its own, far beyond what the English Whigs intended.

Facing the guillotine for treason, Philippe Egalite wrote a short manuscript, "*Voici mon histoire maconnique,*" to explain his involvement with Freemasonry. "At a time when no one could have foreseen our revolution, I attached myself to freemasonry, which offered a kind of image of equality, just as I attached myself to the parliaments, which offered a kind of image of liberty. I have since given up the phantom for the reality."[259] At least one historian finds it astounding that Philippe "had been attacked not by antirevolutionaries but by the Revolution's supporters for having been a freemason,"[260] but the attack is unsurprising because Freemasonry was associated in the popular as well as the revolutionary mind with England. Philippe was a suspect because he was a Freemason; the revolutionary organization that created the conditions for the revolution was an object of suspicion to the leaders of the Revolution, largely because of its association with England, which declared war on France in 1793. By 1793 Freemasonry was suspect to the French left and the French right, because every Frenchman, most especially the French masons, knew "they were participating in a system of governance inherited from another revolution, dimly remembered,"[261] namely, the Glorious Revolution. The French knew "the version of civil polity they created in their private sociability [i.e., the lodge] had first taken shape in revolutionary England. In that belief, as we can now understand it, they were more right then even they could have imagined."[262]

The Jacobins thought Philippe was conspiring with the English because of his trip to London in 1789. Philippe was seen as part of the royalists' "Anglophile maneuvering" to move France closer to a constitutional monarchy like that in England after the Glorious Revolution. The replacement of the House of Bourbon with a philo-Protestant constitutional monarch had been the goal of Whig foreign policy for almost a century. On the verge of achieving their goal, the English watched victory slip from their grasp as the revolution spun out of control. The terror lasted until March 1794, when Robespierre succumbed to his own killing machine. Philippe Egalite was guillotined on November 6, 1793 along with Marie-Antoinette and 200 other enemies of the revolution.

Once the revolution occurred in France, Freemasonry was in a bind of its own making, caught between Jewish cosmopolitanism, which the Grand Lodge insisted on promoting on the continent, and the rising tide of nationalism, which revolution engendered in France. Amsterdam was caught in the middle both geographically and ideologically. The Amsterdam Lodge had always admitted Jews. After the revolution in France emancipated the Jews there, the number of Jewish applicants to La Bien Aimée increased dramatically. The Dutch had mixed feelings about Jewish emancipation and membership in the lodge. La Bien Aimée agreed to admit "nine gentlemen of the Jewish Nation and Religion ... [under the] stipulation that none of these Gentlemen of the Jewish nation and Religion ... now or consequently will ever be able or permitted to be nominated, elected and even less appointed to any administration of the lodge."[263] Like Cromwell earlier and Napoleon later, the Dutch freemasons feared that the Jews, once admitted, would take over the lodge. German lodges expressed the same misgivings, but they were consistently opposed by the Grand Lodge in London.

La Bien Aimée became revolutionized and French in January 1795 when the French Army invaded Holland and routed the Prussians, who had been defending the Stadholder and Whig placeman William V. The forces Rousset de Missy had mobilized in 1747 finally turned on their English masters and proclaimed a new Batavian republic along French, not English, lines. Like Philippe Egalite, the Dutch Masons gave up the appearance in favor of reality. Once the sun of revolution rose over Holland, the candle of Freemasonry, which had lit the way during the dark years of the ancien regime, was no longer necessary.

In January 1795, La Bien Aimée opened a lodge meeting by adopting the revolutionary principles of liberty, fraternity, and equality. "Before opening the lodge our beloved chairman congratulated the assembled fraternity on the long-hoped-for revolution in our dear country, because of which liberty, fraternity and equality had now become the motto of our days, and furthermore announced to the brothers that from now on all honorary titles were held to be abolished among us."[264] When the brothers sang their Masonic songs, "La Marseillaise" was first on the list. The lodge, however, had become unnecessary because it had become the model of a new world, the modern world, which had adopted and would go on to implement its principles in its struggle against what was left of the Catholic order in Europe. That Masonic crusade would continue as the nationalist Freemasonry of the *risorgimento* conquered the papal states in Italy, and when the Masonic powers of America and England would dismember Austria, the last bastion of the Habsburg's Catholic empire, following World War I. Both Wilson and Mazarek, the first president of Czechoslovakia, the country Wilson carved out of the heart of the Austro-Hungarian empire, were Masons. In each case, "what began on the Continent as constitutionally governed societies for gentlemen" became "a microcosm of a new secular and civic, yet quasi-religious, political order we have now come to know simply as the modern world."[265]

XI

On August 10, 1792, fearing the increasing violence of the French mob against the clergy, abbe Augustin Barruel closed the *Journal ecclesiastique*, from whose pages he had attacked the philosophes and then the revolutionaries. Sensing greater violence was in the offing, Abbe Barruel then disappeared. After going into hiding, he made his way to Normandy, and from there he escaped to asylum in England.

Barruel, whose family emigrated in the 13th Century to France from Scotland, where they were known as Barwell, entered the Jesuits at 15, eight years before Louis XV banished them from France and 17 years before Pope Clement XIV suppressed the order in the bull *Dominus ac Redemptor*.

A priest without an order, Barruel set off for Poland after hearing the Jesuit confessor to Queen Marie Lecsinska was offering positions to expelled Jesuits from the west. When Barruel arrived in Prague, the provincial of the Jesuits in Bohemia, "charmed by his virtue and talents,"[266] persuaded him to stay. He then became tutor to a noble family in France, which allowed him to return to his native land and take up the battle against the philosophes and Catholic accomodationists, which he pursued for years as editor of the Catholic and royalist *Journal ecclasiastique*. Barruel wrote a book on the Revolution, *Discours sur les vraies causes de la revolution,* which appeared in 1789. One year later he opposed the Jacobins on the issue of divorce, publishing *Lettres sur le divorce: les vraies principes sur le mariage.*

Barruel felt that the French Revolution was divine punishment meted out to France for "having acted as the breeding place of an ideology destructive of Christian society."[267] The revolution had also been caused by a conspiracy, which he hoped to document when he got to England and had the freedom to write again. The two explanations were complementary. The anti-Christian ideology that found such disfavor with God had been put into force by people who conceived of the revolution as an attack on the Catholic Church. "If you want a revolution," Mirabeau had said two months before the mob stormed the Bastille, "you need to decatholicize France."[268]

Three years after the beginning of the revolution, Mirabeau's followers de-Catholicized France in a horribly literal way. On September 2, 1792, the attack on the Catholic Church escalated into an attack on the Catholic clergy. In four days, 300 priests were massacred and the Abby of Saint Firmin was turned into a prison where priests were subjected to the anticlerical rage of the mob. Even a supporter of the revolution like Mme Roland admitted the cruelty of the mob: "Women were brutally violated before being torn to pieces by those tigers; intestines cut out and worn as turbans; bleeding human flesh devoured."[269] Some were incarcerated in ships that were then sunk in the Seine. By the time this rage burned itself out, 20,000 French clergy were living in exile.

On September 26, 1792, Barruel, "with a certain number of French priests who had found refuge in a hospitable country,"[270] arrived in London, where he took up residence "with an old Jesuit like himself,"[271] the Rev. William Strickland. Barruel was one of 8,000 to 10,000 members of the Catholic clergy who sought refuge in Protestant England. Between September 1792 and August 1, 1793, Edmund Burke raised 32,000 pounds sterling for relief of the French clergy. King George III turned the royal castle at Winchester into a residence for 600 priests. The Archbishop of Canterbury opened his residence to French bishops who escaped the terror. Barruel was deeply grateful to "the Anglican clergy, the aristocracy, the businessmen, the citizens of every class, who had already sent assistance necessary to receive, lodge, nourish and clothe this colony of unfortunate men."[272] The pope was also grateful for the unexpected help from one of the church's most long-standing and tenacious enemies. In a letter written on September 7, 1792, Pope Pius VI thanked King George III for its generous hospitality. William Pitt, the King's Prime Minister, remembered those exiles: "Few will ever forget the piety, the irreproachable conduct, the long and dolorous patience of those men, cast suddenly into the midst of foreign people different in its religion, its language, its manners and its customs. They won the respect and goodwill of all by a life of unvarying godliness and decency."[273]

Burke was a dedicated foe of the Revolution, and his *Reflections* helped turn the tide of popular opinion against it. This was no easy task in a country where Freemasonry was firmly rooted among the ruling classes, many of whom felt the events in France were the long awaited transposition of the Glorious Revolution to French soil. English radicals like Dr. Price said this explicitly. Mary Wollstonecraft launched her career as the first feminist by attacking Burke. However, her affair with William Godwin, his scandalous memoir of their relationship, and the lifestyle of the Godwin family, coupled with Burke's *Reflections,* soon turned public opinion against them, and England became the Revolution's most determined foe. Burke supported Barruel's work, but he did not see its completion. Burke died two months after the first volume appeared.

On May 1, 1797, Burke wrote to Barruel congratulating him on publication of the first volume of *Memoirs pour servir une histoire du jacobinisme*:

> I cannot easily express to you how much I am instructed and delighted by the first Volume of your History of Jacobinism. The whole of the wonderful narrative is supported by documents and proofs with most juridical regularity and exactness. I have known myself personally five of your principal conspirators,

and I can undertake to say from my own certain knowledge, that so far back as the year 1773, they were busy in the plot you have so well described, and in the manner, and on the principle you have so truly represented. To this I can speak as a witness.[274]

Volume I of Barruel's *History of Jacobinism* dealt with the Philosophes; Volume II dealt with Freemasonry. In Volume II, Barruel concluded the hard core of the French Revolutionaries, the Jacobin cult, was Freemasonic. The Freemasons had founded the Jacobin clubs, but the Jacobins turned on the Masons when they got control of the revolutionary government. Burke endorsed Barruel's indictment of the philosophes, but did not read the volumes on Freemasonry or the Illuminati that appeared after his death.

By the time he finished his book, however, Barruel had backed away from, or at least blunted the force of, his initial assertion. In volumes three and four, Barruel deals with the Illuminati, and in dealing with them Barruel introduced an element of incoherence into his book from which it never recovered. In October 1786, the Bavarian police published their dossier on the Illuminati, the conspiracy to overthrow throne and altar. Adam Weishaupt, a professor at the University of Ingolstadt, led the cabal. Barruel received a copy of the Illuminati dossier; by incorporating it into his *Memoir* he "weakened his main contention,"[275] according to Stanley Jaki.

Joseph de Maistre, the father of continental Counter Revolution, felt the same way about Barruel's *History of Jacobinism*. It was brilliant in parts but defective as a whole. Barruel often confused "the thing with the corruption of the thing"[276] in discussing Masonic practices. Both de Maistre and Barruel were Masons, so they knew Illuminism came from Germany. In making Illuminism central to the story of the French Revolution, Barruel put the cart before the horse. Illuminism, according de Maistre, was "an effect and not a cause."[277]

By making German Illuminism the "smoking gun," Barruel let Freemasonry off the hook. He also diverted attention from England, which everyone then saw as the historical and geographical source of the Lodge. Even if we eliminate the shadowy Rosicrucian brotherhood of the 1620s, Scottish Freemasonry had agents on the continent by the 1650s. Whig-controlled lodges were founded during the first three decades of the 18th Century, and their numbers increased dramatically in France up to the outbreak of the French Revolution. It is perverse to discount that activity by shifting responsibility to an organization that came into existence in 1776 and that for the first few years of its existence—until the initiation of the Prussian Baron von Knigge—was little more than a college fraternity. Barruel argues the Illuminati took over existing lodges, but this explanation is not persuasive, given the number of lodges that needed to be subverted, and the time that would take. If German Illuminism is responsible for the French Revolution, Weishaupt and von Knigge had to complete the takeover in the six years following the 1781 Masonic convention in Wilhelmsbaden.

Barruel goes out of his way to absolve English lodges of any responsibility for the French Revolution. He has nothing but good to say about English Freemasonry: "England in particular is full of those upright men, who, excellent Citizens, and of all stations, are proud of being Masons, and who may be distinguished from the others by ties which appear only to unite them more closely in the bonds of charity and fraternal affection."[278] The reader gets the impression that Barruel doth protest too much when he adds: "It is not the fear of offending a nation in which I have found an asylum that has suggested this exception."[279] His defense of English Freemasonry is important enough to quote *in extenso*:

> England in particular is full of those upright men, who, excellent Citizens, and of all stations, are proud of being Masons, and who may be distinguished from the others by ties which appear only to unite them more closely in the bonds of charity and fraternal affection. It is not the fear of offending a nation in which I have found an asylum that has suggested this exception. Gratitude on the contrary would silence every vain terror, and I should be seen exclaiming in the very streets of London that England was lost, that it could not escape the French Revolution, if its Freemason Lodges were similar to those of which I am about to treat. I would say more, that Christianity and all government would have long been at an end in England, if it could be ever supposed that her Masons were initiated into the last mysteries of the Sect. Long since have their Lodges been sufficiently numerous to execute such a design, had the English Masons adopted either the means or the plans and plots of the Occult Lodges.

> This argument alone might suffice to exempt the English Masons in general from what I have to say of the Sect. But there exist many passages in the history of Masonry which necessitate this exception. The following appears convincing. At the time when the Illuminees of Germany, the most detestable of the Jacobin crew, were seeking to strengthen their party by that of Masonry, they affected a sovereign contempt for the English Lodges. In the letters of Philo to Spartacus, we see the English adepts arriving in Germany from London dawbed all over the with ribbands and emblems of their degrees, but void of those plans and projects against the altar and the crown which tend directly to the point. When I shall have given the history of these Illuminees, the reader will easily judge what immense weight such a testimony carries with it in favor of the English lodges.[280]

Katz's analysis of German lodges tells a different story. The German Freemasons wanted to exclude Jews, but they were consistently thwarted by their high regard for the authority of the Grand Lodge in London. There may well have been upright Masons ready to "secede from Masonry as soon as they perceived it to be infected by those revolutionary principles which the Illuminees had infused among the brethren," but they did not occupy the higher degrees, which, according to Barruel's own testimony, were suffused with a hatred of Christ and his Church as virulent as the hatred in the Jacobin clubs.

According to Barruel, the English lodges were innocent of "*complot revolutionaire*." An element of incoherence enters the narrative when he gets to the Bavarian

Illuminati: in volume I, Barruel had already blamed the lodges under Philip d' Orleans for the French Revolution: "This conspiracy only existed among the numerous lodges of the Grand Orient in Paris, directed by Phillippe d'Orleans; they were one of the major causes of the French Revolution."[281] Was Barruel distracted by the Illuminati story? The Bavarian dossier is powerfully factual in the story it lays out. Or did he use that dossier to avert his eyes from the real villains because of his involvement with them? Even granting that Freemasonry is a hierarchical esoteric organization that deliberately conceals the secrets of higher degrees from masons in lower degrees, the perceptive reader senses Barruel pulled punches and deliberately portrayed English Freemasonry in a falsely positive light because he was beholden to the English, in particular Whigs like Burke, who granted him asylum and supported him financially while he wrote his book.

When Barruel introduces Bavarian Illuminism to explain the corruption of the lodges, he does so as part of a deliberate attempt to exculpate the English: "It is certain that the system of Weishaupt is not a product of the original Freemasonry which was organized in London in 1723 [because] the constitution written by Anderson expressly states that a Mason may not be 'either a stupid atheist or a libertine without religion.'"[282] Even leaving aside the ambiguity of Anderson's formulation, Barruel himself provides examples of subversion at the highest degrees of Masonry. Even the usually sympathetic Riquet seems unpersuaded by Barruel: "But it is no less certain that Weishaupt infused the libertine and anticlerical spirit of Jacobinism which Barruel denounces, into Freemasonry."[283]

In trying to straighten things out, Riquet confuses the issue further by conflating Jacobite and Whig lodges and accepting Anderson's propaganda as the true history of the lodge. Jacob, unable to see Barruel as anything but paranoid, fails to understand the real issue. By concentrating on Barruel's "subsequent embrace of the conspiracy theory as applied to the Freemasons,"[284] she ignores his attribution of the French Revolution to the wrong conspiracy. Constantly associating Barruel with "paranoia," she obviates any need to understand why he would do that.

At one point, Jacob rejects Barruel's dichotomy, claiming, "I know of no record suggesting that French freemasonry was perceived to be markedly different in its fundamental practices and ideals from Dutch, or British or Belgian, or American masonry.... When the young Jean Paul Marat visited the Amsterdam lodge in 1774 he would have discovered discourses and ceremonies comparably familiar."[285] This implicates England and the lodge as responsible for the revolution, which then lets the *ancien regime* and its "repression and excesses" off the hook, which then aligns her with the "paranoid" conspiracy school of Barruel. Jacob does not want to be associated with "the themes [Barruel] first proclaimed—among them the persecution of the innocent by the forces of revolution rather than by monarchy, army or police—recur to this day in the historiography of the French Revolution."[286]

Ultimately Jacob accepts Barruel's dichotomy between English and Continental Freemasonry, but only to turn it against him. Jacob claims, "18th Century

England provides little evidence that Freemasonry was ever perceived as a threat to established institutions of either church or state." She continues, "In some places on the Continent, Masonry was perceived as subversive of monarchy, social hierarchy, the Catholic church and indeed all forms of organized religion,"[287] thus admitting the ideas which supported the status quo in England were subversive in France.

Freemasonry was not subversive in England because the subversion had already taken place there. In France, however, the philosophes engaged in the subversion of morals. Helvetius taught passion was good and that to moderate the passions was to "ruin the state." Women were taught "Modesty is only an invention of refined voluptuousness:—that Morality has nothing to apprehend from love, for it is the passion that creates genius, and renders man virtuous."[288] He would inform children "the commandment of loving their father and mother is more that work of education than of nature."[289] He would tell the married couple "the law which condemns them to live together becomes barbarous and cruel on the day they cease to love each other."[290] This subversion of morals extended to King Louis XV, who "without morals was soon surrounded by ministers destitute of faith, who could have seldom deceived him, had his love for religion been stimulated by practice."[291] Barruel says the subversion of morals was caused by an "inundation of bad books."[292] But he doesn't say from where they came, probably because he was unaware of the role Rousset de Missy and the Dutch Huguenots played in bringing subversive English ideas into France. Barruel mentions the Whig radicals, but fails to link them with Whig policy in England when he links the conspiracy to the moment "Collins, Bolingbroke, Bayle, and other masters of Voltaire, together with that Sophister himself, had propagated their impious doctrines against the God of Christianity."[293] Barruel says Voltaire got his ideas in England, but that they weren't subversive there. "This is not the place to observe what a multitude of errors these assertions contain: the chief is that of having converted into a principle what he had observed in England, without considering that often what has conducted one nation to Liberty, may lead another into all the horrors of Anarchy, and thence to Despotism."[294] A simpler explanation is that the Whigs were using the lodges to promote revolution in France not at home. The English had already killed their king and deposed his heir. They probably wanted to put a pro-Whig, pro-English, pro-Protestant monarch on the French throne, just as they had put William of Orange on the English throne. The subversion of morality led naturally to the hegemony of passion, and when passion got out of control, revolution occurred:

> The French revolution is in its nature similar to our passions and vices: it is generally known, that misfortunes are the natural consequences of indulging them; and one would willingly avoid such consequences: but a faint-hearted resistance is made; our passions and our vices soon triumph, and man is hurried away by them.[295]

Taken on its own terms, Barruel's conspiracy theory shows the Illuminati were peripheral, not the main cause of the revolution, as he would claim in the last volume of the *History of Jacobinism*:

> In order to prove a real Conspiracy against Christianity, we must not only point out the wish to destroy, but also the secret union and correspondence in the means employed to attack, debase, or annihilate it. When, therefore, I name Voltaire and Frederic, Diderot and D'Alembert, as the chiefs of this Antichristian Conspiracy, I not only mean to shew that each individual had impiously written against Christianity, but that they had formed the wish, and had secretly concurred in that wish, to destroy the religion of Christ; that they had acted in concert, sparing no political nor impious art to effectuate that destruction; that they were the instigators and conductors of those secondary agents whom they had misled; and followed up their plans and projects with all that ardor and constancy which denotes the most accomplished Conspirators.[296]

After staking out contradictory positions to explicate Barruel's contradictory positions, Jacob can't make up her mind. British Freemasonry "was antithetical to monarchical absolutism, to the hegemony of the universities and their official teachings, and to the old clerical and aristocratic estates with their social and legal privileges."[297] After claiming Barruel was responsible for "a vast and already paranoid literature that attempted to lay blame for the revolution on the Masonic lodges," Jacob concedes "Unquestionably, the Masonic lodges and prominent Freemasons did play a political role in the revolution, but it would be naive to imagine that they conspired to bring it about. History simply does not work that way. Yet ... it would be naive to imagine that Masonic lodges ... possess no discernible political ideology and interest."[298]

To clarify the issue, the revolution was part conspiracy and part nature, and the systematic subversion of morals the philosophes carried out in the name of Enlightenment explains how one part leads to the other. The subversion of morals led the French to the point where passions would careen out of control into revolution. Ideas considered subversive in England were reserved by the Whigs for foreign consumption.

In Barruel's *Memoirs*, the whole is less than the sum of its parts. Barruel brought together hitherto unknown sources that exposed the intentions of the philosophes and their link with the Masons. He also exposed the rhetoric of Freemasonry by analyzing their rituals in detail, exposing them for the first time publicly. Barruel's analysis of Illuminism had an impact on posterity too, but probably not what he intended. It became an inspiration for cultural revolutionaries from Shelley to Freud, who used its lessons on how to control people without their knowledge as the basis of psychoanalysis, and, through Freud's nephew, Eddy Bernays, as the basis of public relations and advertising. The volumes on Illuminism, while undeniably true, nevertheless derailed the book that set out to explain the causes of the French Revolution. Other writers noticed this. Barruel may have noticed it too; his peculiar title *"Memoirs pour servir..."* instead of simply "The

History of Jacobinism" may have been a tacit admission he could not write that history himself. All he intended to do was gather the sources so someone else could analyze the material in a way he could not.

Barruel begins his book in France not in Germany. He claims Voltaire got the idea for his conspiracy in England. The book in its original inception points the finger at England not Germany. Voltaire was inspired by his visit to London to "extol the English truths. That is, the impieties of Hume; and when he thought himself authorized to write, that in London Christ was spurned."[299] The conspiracy to annihilate Christianity began in 1728 when Voltaire returned from London to France and announced "Let the real Philosophers unite in a brotherhood like the Freemasons; let them assemble and support each other, and let them be faithful to the association."[300] Barruel says Voltaire's "most faithful disciples inform us that he had his determination" to consecrate his life "to the annihilation of Christianity," "when in England" even if he spent many years "ruminating alone his hatred against Christ."[301]

The theological foundation of the French Revolution becomes clear in Barruel's exposition of Masonic ritual. The philosophes began their assault on the ancien regime by subverting morals, but the goal was always theological. Freemasonry's attack on Christ was inspired by the Talmudic literature in the Cabala. Barruel's book powerfully brought together previously unknown material in three important areas—the writings of the philosophes, the Freemasons, and the Illuminati. Its lack of a coherent explanation of how those parts fit together should not blind us to its genius: no one had published anywhere near this volume of material before Barruel. No one had gotten to the theological roots of the revolution in Talmudic Judaism either, because no one had studied the Masonic texts in such detail. Barruel witnessed the attack on Christ that began in the Lodge first hand, where it was portrayed as a necessary preliminary to the Masonic recovery of the name of Jehovah:

> In his first degree he receives the Masonic science only as descending from Solomon and Hiram, and revived by the Knights Templar.—But in the second degree he learns that it is to be traced to Adam himself, and has been handed down by Noah, Nimrod, Solomon, Hugo de Paganis, the founder of the Knights Templars, and Jacques de Molay, their last Grand Master, who each in their turns had been the favourites of Jehovah, and are styled the Masonic Sages. At length in the third degree it is revealed to him, that the celebrated word lost by the death of Hiram was the name of Jehovah. It was found, he is told, by the Knights Templars at the time when the Christians were building a Church at Jerusalem. In digging the foundations in that part on which the stones, which had formerly been parts of the foundation. The form and junction of these three stones drew the attention of the Templars; and their astonishment was extreme, when they beheld the name of Jehovah engraved on the last.

Freemasons are "High Priests of Jehovah." Freemasonry is ultimately Judaizing. Its purpose is "recovery of the Lost Name of Jehovah"[302] It proposes a return to the vomit of Judaism to create heaven on earth, the goal of all revolutionaries. As the adept proceeds up the Masonic ladder, to higher and higher degrees, he learns first who is responsible for the assassination of Adoniram and what he is expected to do about it. Christ is the "real assassin of Adoniram."[303] Barruel continues, "Christ himself in their eyes is the destroyer of the unity of God, he is the great enemy of Jehovah and to infuse that hatred of the Sect into the mind of the new adepts, constitutes the grand mystery of the new degree which they have called Rosicrucian."[304] The great thing that has been lost is the word Jehovah.

The Master asks the Senior Warden what o'clock it is. "It is the first hour of the day, the time when the veil of the temple was rent asunder, when darkness and consternation was spread over the earth, when the light was darkened when the implements of Masonry were broken, when the flaming star disappeared, when the cubic stone was broken, when the word was lost.... He thereby learns that the day on which the word Jehovah was lost is precisely that on which the Son of God dying on a cross for the salvation of mankind is consummated the grand mystery of our Religion, destroying the sign of every other, whether Judaic, natural or sophistical. The more a Mason is attached to the word, that is, to his pretended natural Religion, the more inveterate will his hatred be against the author of Revealed Religion.[305]

The deeper the adept penetrates, the more Talmudic are the mysteries revealed to him. The Rosicrucian, for example, is taught the inscription INRI which was nailed to the Cross means not *Iesus Nazarensis Rex Iudeorum*, but rather the "Iew of Nazareth Led into Iudea,"[306] a reading which deprives Christ of his divinity and reasserts the Talmudic calumny that Christ was a common criminal who deserved to be executed: "As soon as the candidate has proved that he understands the Masonic meaning of this inscription INRI, the Master exclaims, My dear Brethren, the word is found again, and all present applaud this luminous discovery, that—He whose death was the consummation and the grand mystery of the Christian Religion was no more than a common Jew crucified for his crimes."[307]

To be initiated into the higher degrees of Freemasonry, the adept must agree to become an assassin of the assassin of Adoniram. He must be willing to assassinate Christ and his representatives on earth. The revolutionary intent of Freemasonry becomes clear when the adept is informed that he must be willing to kill the king. Mystical Masonry is synonymous with Revolution. Freemasons "looked upon the Revolution as that sacred fire which was to purify the earth and these credulous adepts were seen to second the Revolution with the enthusiastic zeal of a holy cause."[308] When the adept is introduced to the degree of Knights Kadosh, "all ambiguity ceases."[309] The Freemason is the assassin of the assassin of Adoniram, which means it is his duty to kill the king, one of Christ's representatives on earth, the other being the pope.

The English lodges had already carried out their Masonic duty by killing the king and deposing his heir, but the French had not. The adept learns he must assassinate the King of France because he is the successor of Philippe le Bel, who deposed Jacques de Molay. During the initiation of the Knights Kadosh, "the candidate" is

> transformed into an assassin. Here it is no longer the founder of Masonry, Hiram, who is to be avenged, but it is Molay the Grand Master of the knights Templars and the person who is to fall by the assassin's hand is Philippe le Bel, King of France, under whose reign the order of the Templars was destroyed.... When the adept sallies forth from the cavern with the reeking head, he cries Nekom (I have killed him).... At length the veil is rent asunder. The adept is informed that till now he has only been partially admitted to the truth; that Equality and Liberty, which had constituted the first secret on his admission into Masonry, consisted in recognizing no superior on earth, and in viewing Kings and Pontiffs in another light than as men on a level with their fellow men, having no rights to sit on the throne, or to serve at the altar, but what the people had granted them.[310]

The purpose of Freemasonry is "to rid the earth of this double pest, by destroying every altar which credulity and superstition had erected and every throne on which were only to be seen despots tyrannizing over slaves."[311] But, again, this admonition is more applicable in France than in England. After admission to the last mysteries, "the brethren are declared free: the word so long sought for is, Deism; it is the worship of Jehovah, such as was known to the Philosophers of nature. The true Mason becomes the Pontiff of Jehovah; and as such is the grand mystery by which he is extricated from that darkness in which the prophane are involved."[312]

The entire thrust of Masonic activity is motivated by Jewish resentment. When admitted to the degree of Rosae Crucis, the adept learns Christ "destroyed the worship of Jehovah,"[313] and that on Christ and his representatives and on the Gospel "the adept is to avenge the brethren" who are "the Pontiffs of Jehovah." In his reception into the Knights Kadosch, the adept learns

> the assassin of Adoniram is the King, who is to be killed to avenge the Grand Master Molay, and the order of the Masons, successors of the knights Templars. The religion which is to be destroyed to recover the word, or the true doctrine, is the religion of Christ, founded on revelation. This word in its full extent is Equality and Liberty, to be established by the total overthrow of the Altar and the Throne.[314]

The adept is led from secret to secret into the judaized religion of Freemasonry, and from there he is led from secret to secret into "the whole Jacobinical code of Revolution."[315] Freemasonry is the crucial link between the ancestral Jewish hatred of Christ and Revolution. Freemasonry is cabalistic. Like Dee, Freemasonry derives its magic from Cabala. Like Julian the Apostate and John Dee, the Freemason

> looks upon the communication with, and apparitions of the Devils, whom he invokes under the appellation of Genii, as a special favour, and on them he relies for the whole success of his enchantments.... The Cabalistic Mason will be favoured by these good and evil Genii, in proportion to the confidence he has

in the power, they will appear to him and they will explain more to him in the magic table, than the human understanding can conceive. [316]

"Nor is the adept to fear the company of the evil Genii" as Julian the Apostate did when initiated into the Eleusinian mysteries because it is only from these "Genii or Devils," that the adept can learn the occult sciences that will infuse into him the spirit of prophecy. He will be informed, that Moses, the Prophets, and the three kings, had no other teachers, no other art, but that of Cabalistic Masonry, like him and Nostradamus."[317]

Ultimately, that magic is Jewish. After admission to the higher mysteries, the Masonic adept is told: "You have then the same sentiments toward the Christian which the Jews have. Like them, you insist on Jehovah, but to curse Christ and his mysteries."[318]

Taking his lead from Barruel, Poncins proposes two theories explaining the connection between Jews and Freemasonry. According to the first,

> Jews have entirely created masonry to corrupt the nations of Christian civilization and to propagate behind this veil the general revolution which is to bring about the domination of Israel. It is simply a tool and a means in the hands of the Jews. In support of this we can quote the article of Dr. Isaac M. Wise published in the Israelite of America, 3 August 1866: "Masonry is a Jewish institution, whose history, degrees, charges, passwords and explanations are Jewish from beginning to end."[319]

The other theory suggests the lodge, good at its inception, was corrupted when the Jews joined it. According to this theory, the Jews joined the lodge during the years preceding the French Revolution

> and founded secret societies themselves. There were Jews with Weishaupt and Martinez de Pasqualis, a Jew of Portuguese origin, organized numerous groups of illuminati in France and recruited many adepts whom he initiated into the dogma of reinstatement. The martinist lodges were mystic, while the other Masonic orders were rather rationalist; a fact which permits us to say that the secret societies represent the two sides of Jewish mentality: practical rationalism and pantheism, that pantheism which although it is a metaphysical reflection of belief in an only God, yet sometimes leads to kabbalistic theurgy. One could easily show the agreements of these two tendencies, the alliance of Cazotte, of Cagliostro, of Martinez, of Saint Martin, of the Comte de St. Germain, of Eckarthausen, with the Enclyclopedists and the Jacobins and the manner in which in spite of their opposition, they arrive at the same result, the weakening of Christianity. That will once again serve to prove that the Jews could be good agents of the secret societies, because the doctrines of these societies were in agreement with their own doctrines, but not that they were the originators of them.[320]

These explanations ignore the fact that every mason became an agent of Jewish revenge when and if he was initiated into the higher mysteries, when he adopted the Talmudic explanation of Christ's death on the Cross and the role he played in suppressing the name of Jehovah. This is perhaps what Disraeli had in mind when he said the Revolution: "which is at this moment preparing in Germany and which will be, in fact a second and greater Reformation, and of which so little is yet known in England is developing entirely under the auspices of the Jews."[321]

XII

Napoleon was a Mason. We know this because he was excommunicated from the lodge in 1809. Like Philippe Egalite, Napoleon saw himself as the revolutionary Sun that made the candle of Freemasonry unnecessary. Napoleon earned his reputation as a military leader by defeating the half-armed Catholic peasants of the Vendee when they tried to march on Paris to end the revolution. Napoleon proved Plato was right in the *Republic* when he said democracy invariably ends in tyranny. Napoleon learned what to do when men with a "rosary and a scapular in their hands"[322] and "armed with nothing but sticks"[323] charged his artillery. Napoleon then turned his cannon on the revolutionaries themselves and in one of the bloodiest days of the revolution wiped out the mob with grapeshot and became the *Zeitgeist* on horseback. Napoleon took the revolution under control by firing artillery into the mob. From then, he could have said, *"La Revolution, c'est moi."* Napoleon was Liberty, and Equality, and Fraternity.

If Freemasonry prepared Napoleon for his role as assassin and revolutionary, it also gave him the lens through which saw the Jews. In 1796 Napoleon marched on Italy. As was his custom, a propaganda campaign preceded the artillery barrage. "Peoples of Italy," he wrote in April 1796, "the French army comes to break your chains. "We make war as generous enemies, and we have no quarrel save with tyrants who enslave you."[324] Significantly, his subversive proclamations targeted the Jews:

> Deprived of the rights of citizens, humiliated in many places by the obligation of wearing the medieval yellow badge, confined to the secluded ghettos, the Jews of Italy offered Bonaparte the stirring sight of that persecuted minority. In every Italian city which the French army entered, the ghetto gates were removed, hacked to pieces and burned, the shameful badges thrown away, and the symbols of freedom—Trees of Liberty—planted by the delivered Jews. Their enthusiasm at the great transformation was boundless. For the first time in the history of Italian Jewry the commander of a victorious army appeared not as an oppressor but as a liberator of the Jewish people.[325]

Napoleon's proclamation had its effect on the Jews of Ancona, who plotted with the French to deliver the city. In danger of being slaughtered as traitors, the Jews were saved when the French, led by Napoleon, entered the city. The French soldiers then marched to the Ghetto to tear down its walls, tearing off yellow badges from the clothes of the Jews who greeted them as liberators and replacing those badges with the tricolor of the revolution. In like manner Jews across Europe were recruited into the revolutionary cause in the wake of Napoleon's conquest. Hebrew chroniclers described the liberation of the Italian ghettos as a miracle akin to Moses parting the Red Sea, and from then on, Napoleon was known in Jewish circles as *helek tov*, the good portion, a direct rendering of his last name into Hebrew. It was at this point that Napoleon began to take on the aura of the Messiah for the Jews, something he would attempt to manipulate to his advantage over the coming years.

Napoleon cut short his military conquest of Europe and, on May 25, 1798 set sail for Egypt in an armada of 55 warships and 250 supply ships carrying 43,000 soldiers that covered four square miles of the sea. His first conquest was Malta, which quickly incorporated the revolutionary gospel into its constitution. Slavery was abolished, and the Jews were allowed their own synagogue. Napoleon explicitly mentioned the Jews and their good fortune at the hands of the liberating French army in his proclamation on Malta.

Napoleon then sailed for Egypt, arriving on July 1. One day later French troops took Alexandria, and a few days after that Napoleon entered Cairo in triumph, taking up residence at the Ezbekyeh palace. Then the unexpected happened. England, at war with France for five years, caught up with Napoleon when Lord Nelson after searching the Mediterranean for months finally found the French fleet at anchor off the mouth of the Nile. Throwing traditional tactics to the wind, Nelson caught the French off guard by sailing between the fleet and the coast, attacking from the rear and annihilating the largest Armada to sail the Mediterranean since Lepanto.

When the Battle of the Nile ended on August 2, Napoleon found himself in charge of an army that had no way to get back to France. In addition to destroying the French fleet, Nelson imposed a tight blockade on Egypt. Necessity as the Mother of Invention caused Napoleon to revise his plans. Since Turkey had declared war on France, Napoleon would march to the north, defeat the Turkish army and liberate Jerusalem. Napoleon's natural penchant toward megalomania at this point seems to have taken a mystical turn. Aware the Jews considered him the *helek tov* and Messiah, Napoleon began to think of himself as a combination of Messiah and Antichrist who would fulfill the aspirations of the Masonic lodges by restoring the name of Jehovah, emancipating the Jews, and rebuilding the Temple. Napoleon was the new Moses, come out of Egypt to lead the Jews to the Promised Land, which their forbears lost when Christ suppressed the name of Jehovah. Napoleon was the conqueror of Alexandria and the successor to Alexander, who had also granted the Jews significant privileges. He was Herod; he was Cyrus. Were he to rebuild the Temple, he would succeed where Julian the Apostate failed. Were he to restore the Temple he would be Messiah and Antichrist, synonymous terms to the Jews, and the revolution most certainly would have succeeded in crushing the wretch, the project Voltaire had assigned to it and its Masonic acolytes.

On September 7, Napoleon appointed Sabbato Adda and Tibi di Figurea, two *"grand pretres de la nation juive"* as his advisors. The title "high priest" that Napoleon gave these Jewish advisors indicated a restoration of the old dispensation was imminent. "A company of Jews," we are told, "spoke of the [French] Commander-in-Chief as the second Messiah."[326] Or was Napoleon the second Gideon? Was Napoleon going to succeed where all other Gideons—Zizka, Muentzer, Cromwell, et al—had failed? With the exception of Julian the Apostate, who did not see himself as Gideon, none of those messianic revolutionaries got as close as Napoleon to the mystical center of judaizing revolutionary fervor.

As the French army advanced along the east coast of the Mediterranean, events seemed to confirm Napoleon's vision of himself as Antichrist/Messiah. In Jaffa, the French massacred 4,000 Ottoman soldiers and a large number of citizens. Then the army advanced to the Plain of Esdraelon, at the foot of Mount Tabor, where Napoleon routed the Syrian army of 30,000 men. Napoleon then ascended Mount Tabor, where he seems to have undergone a Transfiguration of his own. Here Gideon had defeated the Amalekites, and here Christ revealed himself as the son of God to a small group of his followers in the company of Elijah and Moses, as the fulfillment of the Law and the Prophets. It would not be surprising if Napoleon, swept up in the drama, saw himself as the avatar of a new dispensation described in Masonic rituals as the man appointed to restore what had been lost.

Flush with the victory and the vision, Napoleon conceived a Proclamation to the Jews. "I will announce to the people the abolition of servitude and of the tyrannical government of the Pashas. I shall arrive at Constantinople with large masses of soldiery. I shall overturn the Turkish empire."[327] Soon the Jews of Syria, their oppressors crushed by the *helek tov*, voiced the hope Napoleon would restore Solomon's Temple after he took Acre.

Napoleon issued his proclamation on April 20, 1799, announcing he would restore the Jews to their ancestral home. "Arise then, with gladness, ye exiled!" Napoleon exclaimed. He had come to avenge the Jews for "the almost 2000 year old ignominy put upon you":

> "Hasten! Now is the moment which may not return for thousands of years, to claim the restoration of your rights among the population of the universe which had been shamefully withheld from you for thousands of years, your political existence as a nation among the nations, and the unlimited natural right to worship Jehovah in accordance with your faith, publicly and in likelihood for ever (Joel 4:20).[328]

Napoleon was going to fulfill simultaneously the hopes of the Jews and the Freemasons. Napoleon was going to restore what had been lost—the name of Jehovah, the state of Israel, and the Temple, where the Jews could again offer their sacrifices. Napoleon intended "to rebuild the walls of the orphaned city and temple to the Lord in which His Glory shall dwell from now for evermore."[329] To help accomplish this, Napoleon, draping the mantle of Gideon over his own shoulders, summoned the Jews of the world to Jerusalem: "Let all men of Israel, capable of bearing arms gather and come up to us, let even the weak say: I am strong ... and let the whole people cry as of Gideon, son of Joash, Judges 7: 'Here the Sword of the Lord and of Bonaparte!'" Napoleon invented Zionism a century before the Jews did, referring to them as "the Rightful Heirs of Palestine."[330]

The Jews were ecstatic; their deliverance was at hand! In response to Napoleon's proclamation, a mysterious figure who called himself Aaron, son of Levi, Rabbi of Jerusalem, exclaimed to his fellow Jews:

> Brethren! The so glorious prophecies contained therein have been, as to their larger part, already fulfilled by the victorious army of the great nation, and now it depends only on us, to behave not as the children of harlots and adulteresses, but as true descendants of Israel and to desire the inheritance of the people of the Lord and the beautiful services of the Lord, Psalm of David 27:4."[331]

Later Jewish scholars saw Napoleon's statement as an attempt to manipulate the Jews, but this cynicism was missing from statements of the Jews at the time, who were caught up once again in an episode of messianic fervor. Barbara Tuchman called Napoleon's proclamation "a meaningless gesture, as artificial as any heroic strutting on the stage."[332] Simon Dubnow called it a "trick."[333] Salo Baron referred to Napoleon's "shrewd recognition of the intense interest of the Jews, whom he attempted to enlist in his expeditionary army,"[334] but Baron admits "the support the Jewish hope he had received from French and English writers" indicated how much "the European atmosphere was charged with these messianic expectations."[335]

Both views were probably accurate. The Jews of his day viewed Napoleon with "messianic expectations," and in issuing his proclamation, Napoleon sought to exploit those expectations for his own benefit. Napoleon "was aware of the prominent position which some sectors of Western and Oriental Jewry held in finance and commerce." Napoleon knew that the Jews had "immense riches," and he probably hoped to tap those riches by enlisting the Jews in restoring the Temple, just as Julian the Apostate had done.[336] In a project as grandiose as restoring the Temple, the mystical, financial, and political benefits would converge in the Masonic mind. They would not work against each other.

A Report on Napoleon's Proclamation to the Jews appeared in *Le Moniteur Unviersel*, the official government newspaper, on May 22, 1799. "Bonaparte," it said, "caused to publish a proclamation, in which he invites all the Jews of Asia and Africa to come and range themselves under his banners in order to reestablish ancient Jerusalem."[337] The report hoped Jews "will perhaps see in him [Bonaparte] the Messiah, and soon 20 prophecies will have predicted the event, the epoch, and even the circumstances of his coming. It is at least very probable that the Jewish people is about to transform itself again into a national body, that the Temple of Solomon will be rebuilt."[338]

Napoleon concluded his proclamation by announcing "the undefiled army which Providence has sent me hither, led by justice and accompanied by victory, has made Jerusalem my headquarters."[339]

Napoleon, however, never made it to Jerusalem. On April 24, Napoleon ordered an assault on Acre, but the French troops were beaten back by a combination of tenacious soldiers behind impregnable walls and English artillery from ships offshore. Napoleon tried again on April 25, May 1, 7, 8, and 10, and he failed each time. Finally, on May 20, under the cover of an artillery barrage, Napoleon abandoned the siege of Acre and began his withdrawal from Syria. Like Julian the Apostate before him, Napoleon was a Messiah who failed. He gave up the project of restoring the Temple.

Le Moniteur tried to put a positive spin on the defeat, claiming, "it is not only to give Jerusalem back to the Jews that Bonaparte has conquered Syria."[340] Once again their messiah disappointed the Jews. As in Germany and the Pale of the Settlement after Napoleon's defeat in Russia, the Jews were singled out as traitors. To exculpate themselves, the Jews sought to suppress Napoleon's proclamation to the Jews, as well as any evidence they had supported him.

In Napoleon's absence, French armies had suffered defeats in both Germany and Italy, and so, having failed to restore the Temple, Napoleon left Egypt on August 23. One year later, in an address to the State Council, Napoleon made veiled reference to his religious beliefs as well as his failed attempt to restore the temple: "It was by becoming a Catholic that I ended the Vendee war. It was by becoming a Musulman that I established myself in Egypt.... If I governed a nation of Jews I should reestablish the Temple of Solomon."[341]

His use of the subjunctive case is instructive. News of his failed attempt to restore the Jews to their homeland and to rebuild the temple spread despite his attempts to repress it. England still harbored those who carried on the tradition of Menasseh ben Israel and the Fifth Monarchy Men, who felt it was England's role to restore the Jews. In 1799 Henry Kett, in *History, the Interpreter of Prophecy,* felt that Napoleon, as the embodiment of Revolutionary Republicanism, was manipulating the Jews "to render them subservient to their designs of universal conquest."[342] The English wanted to usher in the Apocalypse on their terms, not Napoleon's. The revolutionary fervor of the 1640s was complicated by the fact that France, not England, was the bearer of the revolutionary banner. As a result, English Jews were suspected of harboring revolutionary sympathies. There were anti-Jewish riots in Ipswich, and the Alien Act of 1793 threatened Jews with deportation.

As a result the Jews in England did not respond to Napoleon's call. But Jews elsewhere did. News of the French Messiah reached Prague in 1798. By the summer of 1799 messianic expectation was running high there probably because copies of Napoleon's proclamation were circulating there. The Jews felt Napoleon was the Messiah because he had conquered Rome, imprisoned the pope, and "crushed the power of Edom." Not surprisingly, one Jewish group that responded most eagerly to the idea *Helek Tov* was the Messiah were the followers of Shabbetai Zevi known as Frankists. As one contemporary chronicler put it:

> The overturn of the papal throne has already sufficiently nourished their fancies. Publicly they declared that this is a sign of the approaching Messiah, for

this constitutes their main belief: Sabath Zebe was the Messiah and remains the Messiah, but always in another form. The conquests of the General Bonaparte gave nourishment to their superstitious doctrine. His conquests in the Orient, particularly the conquest of Palestine, of Jerusalem, his proclamation to the Israelites is oil on their flame, and it is believed that this is the very root of the connection between them and the society of Frank. However, how? and What for? Who can know this?[343]

Frankists derived their name from Jacob Frank, an eastern European Jew, born Judah ben Judah Leibowicz, a few years after but not far from where Baal Shem Tov, the founder of Hasidic Judaism was born. If the Hasid were the Jewish version of the Quietist sects that had sprung up in reaction to the Enlightenment, the Frankists were a remnant of the revolutionary and messianic sects who troubled England in the mid-17th Century. By 1666, the messianic flame had sputtered out in England, but it had become a raging blaze in the Ottoman Empire. Jacob Frank ended up in Turkey after the orthodox rabbis expelled his family from Poland. While in Turkey, he converted to the Sabbatean Doenmeh (the Turkish word for *converso*) sect and became its leader. When he returned to Podolia, he was recognized by the Sabbateans as the reincarnation of Sabbetai Zevi. Frank eventually was baptized as a Christian and received the favor of the empress of Austria—the King of Poland was his godfather—but his career was clouded by accusations of "voluntary Marranism," so no one could determine whether he and his followers were sincere Christian converts or instead implementing the principle "We must all descend into the realm of evil in order to vanquish it from within." Frank ended up living in a palatial residence surrounded by beautiful attendants and rumors of the same orgiastic sexual practices that had made Sabbetai Zevi notorious.

The Prague Frankists did not convert to Christianity but continued to practice a Judaism heavily influenced by Cabala. Jonas Beer Wehle, their leader, was a devotee not only of Isaac Luria and Sabbetai Zevi but also Moses Mendelssohn and Immanuel Kant, which made Prague Frankists strikingly similar in their intellectual beliefs to Freemasons. They were especially receptive to Napoleon's portrayal of himself as the Revolutionary Messiah. Once the Jews in Prague had heard that Napoleon had crushed Rome, they saw Napoleon as fulfilling the Sabbatean mission Nathan of Gaza had carried out at Zevi's request. "[T]he cabbalist circle around Jonah Beer Wehle could not help interpreting the event as foreboding of the coming of Sabbetai Zevi's second and last successor."[344]

Napoleon found dealing with the Jews more difficult than he had imagined when he conceived his proclamation at the summit of Mount Tabor. In 1806, after the battle of Austerliz, while making a triumphal return to Paris, Napoleon stopped in Strasbourg. Here, in a city with one of the largest Jewish populations in western Europe, the Alsatians were skeptical, because of long experience, about Jews becoming citizens, even though the revolution had granted them that privilege 15 years before. The Jews had exploited the situation through usury. In the turmoil following the revolution, they had lent money to aspiring bourgeois who wanted to buy property the revolutionary government had stolen from the Church.

When the value of the assignat collapsed, the borrowers were unable to repay their loans. So Napoleon was assailed in Strasbourg with complaints about the Jews.

Disturbed by what he learned in Strasbourg, Napoleon decided to convoke an assembly of Jews when he got back to Paris. He called that assembly the Sanhedrin, indicating he still hadn't abandoned his messianic fantasy. The ostensible purpose was to see whether Jews considered themselves loyal citizens of France. Some suspected Napoleon of ulterior motives. Prince Klemens von Metternich, the Austrian statesman who was the architect of post-Napoleonic Europe, felt Jews looked upon Napoleon as their Messiah, an idea which he encouraged so he could mobilize the vast Jewish population of Poland in his campaign against Russia. Jews, according to Metternich, were natural revolutionaries who already felt estranged from the rulers of the countries where they resided. It wouldn't take much to turn that resentment into support for Napoleonic France as the vehicle of world revolution.

Napoleon issued a decree on May 30, 1806 summoning a General Synagogue of the Jews in Paris on June 15. Napoleon scheduled the first meeting on a Saturday, causing an immediate split between orthodox and reform Jews. When they finally assembled on February 4, 1807, Napoleon put the Jews on the defensive by questioning their loyalty as Frenchmen. "The question at issue," according to one of the Jews in attendance,

> was to ascertain from the Jews themselves, if their religion was really permitted them to take up citizenship in such countries as were ready to grant it to them; whether that religion did not embody prescriptions which rendered impossible, or at least very difficult, an entire submission for the laws. Lastly, whether there were any means by which it were possible to turn to the advantage of society as a whole the talents of a population which so far had shown itself its avowed enemy.[345]

The fourth question was "do the Jews regard Frenchmen as their brethren or as aliens?"[346] Napoleon thus maneuvered the Jews into a trap. When asked if they were loyal to France, the Jews did not waste time writing down their answer but replied in one voice "Jusqu'a la mort!" If the Jews were serious about accepting Napoleon as their Messiah, he was going to make sure they accepted him on his terms, not theirs. Secretly embarrassed by his proclamation promising them a homeland in Palestine, Napoleon had learned his lesson. Taking a cue from the Catholic Church, Napoleon made France the equivalent of the New Israel. Now there was neither Jew nor Greek in France. Jews would find the fulfillment of their natural inclination to revolution in Napoleon, the embodiment of the revolutionary spirit. Napoleon promised to recognize Jews as French citizens as long as they recognized France as the Revolutionary Israel and Napoleon as the Revolutionary Messiah. He had convoked the Sanhedrin to show the Jews how to find Jerusalem in France. The position of the Jews was analogous to the position of the Freemasons. Once the revolutionary sun rose in the sky, the candle of Jewish revolutionary agitation was no longer necessary. In proclaiming their loyalty as Frenchmen, the Jews of the Sanhedrin were also to proclaim France the new Israel, which would replace the Old Israel as the object of their loyalty. Napoleon wanted the Sanhedrin to declare "Jews are obliged to defend France as they defended Jerusalem, because they are treated in France as if they were in the Holy Land. The commissars were instructed to impress upon the members of the Assembly the feeling ... to make them find Jerusalem in France."[347]

Napoleon thought that after the convocation of the Sanhedrin the Jews would recognize the French as fellow Jews and stop collecting interest on their loans. "Paris ... will inaugurate for the dispersed remnants of Abraham's posterity a period of salvation and happiness."[348] Since Napoleon embodied revolution, the revolutionary Jews were to accept him as their king. Napoleon said as much to his Irish physician and biographer, Dr. O'Meara, who felt his reasons for "for having encouraged the Jews so much" still needed clarification. The reason was simple: "as I had restored them to all their privileges, and made them equal to my other subjects, they must consider me like Solomon or Herod to be the head of their nation, and my subjects as brethren of a tribe similar to theirs."[349] That meant the Jews could not then collect interest from other Frenchmen, or conversely that all Frenchmen now had the privileges of the Jews when it came to finance. After Napoleon convoked the Sanhedrin, the Jews "were not permitted to deal usuriously with them [i.e., other Frenchmen] or me, but to treat us as if we were of the tribe of Judah.... Besides, I should have drawn great wealth to France, as the Jews were very numerous and would have flocked to a country where they enjoyed such privileges. Moreover, I wanted to establish a universal liberty of conscience and thought to make all men equal, whether Protestants, Catholics, Mohammedans, Deists or others .... I made everything independent of religion."[350] Or everything part of the judaized religion known as Revolution.

Napoleon was in the Pale of the Settlement when the Sanhedrin finally convened, but Napoleon's convocation of the Sanhedrin, which caused a sensation throughout Europe, did not move the Jews of eastern Europe to support his military campaign. They gave up neither their ethnocentrism nor their economic practices. Caught between the two colossi, Russia and France, they hedged their bets and hoped they wouldn't get caught in the reaction that inevitably followed when Jews supported a revolution that failed.

Napoleon's convocation of the Jews and his attempt to recruit them as revolutionaries had additional negative effects. By using the word Sanhedrin, Napoleon sent a shock through the counter-revolutionary movement that reverberated for another Century. When Joseph Cardinal Fesch heard that his nephew had convoked the Sanhedrin, he reportedly asked Napoleon "Do you want to bring about the end of the world?" "Do you not know," he continued, "that the Holy Scriptures predict the end of the world for the moment when the Jews will be recognized as a corporate nation?"[351] Impressed by his uncle's argument, Napoleon dissolved the Sanhedrin.

That account may be apocryphal, but conservative reaction to the word Sanhedrin was not. In August 1806, Abbe Barruel, living again in France, received a letter from an Italian military officer, Jean-Baptiste Simonini. Simonini had read Barruel's *History of Jacobinism* with gratitude for "finding an infinite of things depicted in it which I had also witnessed with my own eyes."[352] Simonini, however, wondered why Barruel did not mention the Jews who had used "their money to sustain and multiply the modern sophists, the Freemasons, the Jacobins and the Illuminati."[353] Simonini concluded the Jews joined with those groups to form "a single faction to annihilate, if that were possible, the name Christian." During the revolution in the Piedmont region, where he was born, Simonini passed for a Jew and was admitted to the lodge there, where he learned the Jews claimed that by using all means available to them, they would rule the world in less than a century, abolish all other sects to rule over them, "and reduce all of the Christians to a veritable slavery."[354]

Barruel made two copies of the letter and sent one, via Cardinal Fesch, to Napoleon. That letter eventually made its way to M. Desmarets, director of the imperial police, who had been keeping the Jews under surveillance. The other copy went to the pope along with a cover letter asking his holiness what confidence Barruel should place in Simonini's revelations. A few months later Barruel received a reply from the pope's secretary, Msgr. Testa, which confirmed what Simonini said. Barruel was no philo-Semite. He had described Talleyrand as possessing "all of the lowness and all of the vices of Judaism,"[355] but he refused to publish Simonini's letter or the pope's response because he feared innocent Jews would suffer reprisals. "I guarded the contents of the letter with a profound silence, convinced that it would lead to a massacre of the Jews."[356] In 1878, Pere Grivel said of Barruel, who died in 1820, that he wrote his *Memoirs* to convert the Jews, not to have them massacred.

Ignoring Barruel's suppression of the Simonini letter, Daniel Pipes, in his book *Conspiracy*, holds Barruel responsible for "the myth of the Jewish world conspiracy," which was unmentioned in Barruel's *Memoirs*, and also for laying "some of the intellectual foundations for the views that eventually culminated in the Soviet and Nazi regimes."[357] In demonizing Barruel as "this evil man" whose "wicked ideas"[358] led to Auschwitz and the Gulag, Pipes proves that anti-conspiracy theories are even more florid than conspiracy theories.

Eventually the Revolution, with Napoleon at its head, destroyed itself and the Enlightenment that created it and ushered in the Romantic Catholic reaction. Twenty-five years of suffering from bad ideas purged France of the facile optimism and sensuality of the Enlightenment and paved the way for a religious revival no one expected. It also brought about continental conservatism under the leadership of Joseph de Maistre, "one of the most important formative influences on French thought in the early 19th Century."[359] De Maistre had spent the revolutionary era in Russia as an impecunious diplomat representing the House of Savoy. "What we are witnessing," he wrote after the failure of revolution, "is a religious revolution; the rest, immense as it seems, is but an appendix."[360] De Maistre "regarded the Revolution as a cleansing fire in which the forces of evil were employed against their will and without their knowledge as agents of purification and regeneration."[361]

Eventually Heinrich Heine would give voice to the Jewish revulsion at the Catholic revival, and like Karl Marx at mid-Century, urge a return to revolution, but in the meantime, the revulsion at things French and revolutionary was as vehement as the attraction to things German and Catholic. The counter-revolutionary movement took the name Romanticism in Germany, and the term soon got misapplied in English speaking lands to figures like Percy Shelley. Before the term got corrupted, De Maistre was its foremost representative, and he represented Catholicism and royalism in support of the moral law and social order that would hold Europe together, in spite of recurrent revolutionary episodes, from the Congress of Vienna in 1814-15 to the outbreak of World War I, a Century later.

Like De Maistre and Metternich, the Russians saw Napoleon's Sanhedrin as a plot to use the Jews to destroy the Church of Christ. The Jews of the Pale of the Settlement did not join Napoleon because of ancestral Jewish suspicion and not for any lack of trying on Napoleon's part. But in his march on Russia, Napoleon planted the seed of modern revolution in exceptionally fertile ground, and that sowing would bear fruit throughout the 19th Century, culminating in the Bolshevik Revolution of 1917. From the assassination of the Czar in 1881, the Russian secret police suspected the Jews as the driving force behind revolutionary activity. The Holy Synod of Moscow was prescient, viewing Napoleon's convocation of the Sanhedrin in 1806 as the beginning of a larger attack on Russia and the Church of Christ:

> In order to bring about a debasement of the Church, he [Napoleon] has convened to Paris the Jewish synagogues, restored the dignity of the rabbis and founded a new Hebrew Sanhedrin, the same infamous tribunal which once dared to condemn our Lord and Saviour Jesus Christ to the Cross. And now he has the impudence to contemplate the unification of the Jews whom God in His wrath has dispersed over the surface of the earth and to organize all of them for the destruction of the Church of Christ to the purpose—oh, unspeakable audacity surpassing all the misdeeds!—that they may proclaim the Messiah in the person of Napoleon.[362]

The Messiah spread revolution and Freemasonry in every country in Europe, infecting even the countries that ultimately defeated him in battle. He inaugurated the Revolution, which would continue for another century at least in Europe and South America. Eventually, the revolution would blowback to England. Young Percy Shelley caught the revolutionary virus by reading William Godwin's book and running off with his daughter, but also by reading Barruel on the Illuminati and using what was supposed to be a warning against revolution as a manual for its implementation.

Just as the German romantic glorification of things Catholic followed as the inevitable reaction against French Enlightenment and Revolution, there was an inevitable reaction against the Jews when Napoleon was defeated. The Hep Hep riots took place in Frankfurt, stronghold of Jewish bankers. Pope Pius VII rebuilt the ghetto walls and made Jews listen to sermons and put their yellow badges back on. During the Congress of Vienna in 1814-15, the "Jewish Question" made its debut as an international issue.

The Jews, however, carried Napoleon's memory forward into other revolutions and movements. They looked back on the Napoleonic era as their "Paradise Lost" and, encouraged by what Napoleon had accomplished, were determined to resurrect that paradise in a more powerful future revolution. The German Jewish poet and contemporary of Karl Marx, Heinrich Heine created the Legend of Napoleon the Liberator, portraying him as "the Moses of the French who like the latter has led the people through the desert in order to cure them."[363] Heine proclaimed his undying faith in the Messiah that failed: "I have never swerved from my faith in the Emperor. I have never ceased to doubt his advent—My Emperor—the ruler of the people for the people."[364] Napoleon was "the secular savior" for the Jews. To make sure his readers did not confuse this Jewish savior with one who had died on the Cross 1800 years earlier, Heine continued: "We who have adopted a different symbolism see in the martyrdom of Napoleon at St. Helena no expiation in the sense here indicated, for the Emperor there did penance for his most fatal error, for his faithlessness to his mother, the Revolution."[365] By the mid-19th century, revolution had again become the religion of significant numbers of Jews. Since most Jews lived in Russia, Russia would become the focus of Revolutionary activity after France's defeat.

Theodore Herzl, founder of Zionism, was another acolyte for Napoleon, picking up the torch Heine had kept burning until the mid-19th century. Everywhere he went in Paris, Herzl felt Napoleon's presence: "There is nothing more new than Napoleon I. Truly, he is not yet dead. Every night he leaves his tomb under the dome of the Invalides and talks from all possible stages to the wonderful and variable people of France."[366] In a letter to Bismarck, Herzl said he derived "the idea to which I am devoted" from Napoleon, in particular from his "Paris Sanhedrin of the Jews of 1806," in which Herzl saw "a feeble reverberation" of the Zionism that would play an important role in world politics during the next century.[367]

The Rise of Freemasonry

Chapter Thirteen

The Revolution of 1848

The Enlightenment reached its theoretical high point in 1783 with the performance of Gotthold Ephraim Lessing's play *Nathan der Weise* in Berlin. No work of art produced by the Enlightenment epitomized its central tenets better than *Nathan der Weise*. The play was an essentially Masonic subversion of not only Christianity but Judaism and Islam as well and was in the tradition of *Le Traite des Trois Imposteurs*. After its premier in Berlin, performances of *Nathan* were banned in Frankfurt and Vienna by civic authorities who recognized its essentially subversive nature, but after the German defeat in World War II, the play became a fixture in the de-Nazified German educational system. *Oberprimaner* were forced to read it at the Gymnasium and internalize its subversive message, namely, that all religions are equally false and that only those who rise above the confessional boundaries separating Christians, Jews and Muslims are truly wise.

The model for Nathan was Lessing's friend Moses Mendelssohn, who arrived in Berlin in 1743 as a 14-year-old unable to speak the language. Up until his arrival in Berlin Mendelssohn had studied the Talmud. After his arriving and acquiring the ability to read German, which was of course related to the Yiddish he had spoken as a child, Mendelssohn immersed himself in the classics of the Enlightenment—Spinoza, Newton, Montesquieu, Rousseau, and Voltaire—and as a result of his reading made the acquaintance of the philosophes of Berlin, most notably Lessing, who wrote for the *Vossische Zeitung*, and Nicolai, in whose garden the three men would discuss literature and philosophy.

Mendelssohn soon became a writer in his own right, publishing *Philosophical Dialogues*, followed by *Letters on Sentiment* in 1755, and an adaptation of the Plato's *Phaedo* subtitled a treatise on "The Immortality of the Soul in Three Dialogues" in 1767. But it was less as a writer and more as a role model for the newly emerging Jews of Berlin and Germany that was the cause of Mendelssohn's fame. Partly through the efforts of his friend Lessing, he became the embodiment of the Age of Enlightenment.

Mendelssohn was the Jewish Ben Franklin. He arrived in Berlin in 1743 as a penniless 14-year old and by the end of his life had become one of Berlin's must illustrious citizens. Like Franklin he became a paradigm of the Enlightened Man. Mendelssohn was not the first European Jew to make a name for himself as a philosopher—that honor went to Spinoza—but he was the first European Jew to be fully assimilated into high German culture. Unlike Spinoza, who was expelled from an uncomprehending synagogue, Mendelssohn was not only honored by the Jews of his day, he became their model of the new Jew. He attained these heights by his writings but more importantly by refusing to convert to Christianity; he wanted to show that in an Enlightened culture, Jews could escape from the ghetto without converting to Christianity. A conversion was, of course still necessary, but Mendelssohn's conversion was to the culture of the German Enlightenment, which was deeply imbued with the spirit of Freemasonry at the time.

Nathan der Weise was a profoundly Masonic play for a number of reasons but primarily because it proposed for the first time in history an alternative to the Catholic and Jewish positions which had existed since the time of Christ's crucifixion. According to the tradtional Christian position, supported by both text and iconography, the Jews were blind. The symbol of the synagogue on the facade of the Cathedral in Freiburg is of a blindfolded woman. Jews are blind, according to the Christian point of view, because the Messiah came and they failed to recognize his coming. In a document issued on March 25, 1928, the Holy Office, the predecessor of the current Congregation for the Doctrine of the Faith, issued a statement "Concerning the Abolition of the Association Popularly Known as 'The Friends of Israel,'" in which they announced that the Catholic Church "has always been accustomed to pray for the Jewish people, who were the bearers of Divine Revelation up to the time of Jesus Christ: this despite, indeed on account of their subsequent blindness."

The Jewish position derived from their rejection of Christ and would perdure beyond the Enlightenment. Christians, according to this point of view, are not blind; they are credulous and self-deluded. Christians believe an impossible fairy tale about Christ rising from the dead. Because Christianity has nonetheless prospered for the past 2000 years, the Jew, religious or not, naturally tends to be a debunker, who comes up with ever new variations on a common theme: everyone thinks such and such, but the real story is this. So for Marx, everything is economic, for Freud, Moses was really an Egyptian and "all men" really want to have sex with their mothers and sisters, and for Derrida, meaning is really an illusion.

The third position is the Enlightenment position, and it received its most cogent artistic formulation in Lessing's play *Nathan der Weise*, which, as we have seen, takes an agnostic Masonic attitude toward Christianity, Judaism, and Islam. Set in the Holy Land during the 13th century, *Nathan* is essentially a dialogue between representatives of the three religions, when the dialogue threatens to reach an impasse, Nathan breaks the stalemate in which each religion insists on its own monopoly to truth by proposing the famous parable of the rings. God created the one ring, which symbolizes true religion, but there are many rings, and each man venerates his ring as from God. Lessing solves this problem by having Nathan claim that all rings are to be venerated because no one knows who has the real ring. At some time during their 13th year of schooling, German Catholics and Lutherans, the state's two established religions, learn that the real ring, symbolizing the true religion *"war nicht Erweislich." "*was nowhere to be found."¹ Just like "the true religion," Nathan the Wise adds for those who are slow in picking up the Enlightenment's solution to the religious wars of the 17th century.

Pious German Catholics and Lutherans are in for even more instruction. All three representatives of the world's major religions are "deceived deceivers":

> All three of you [Muslim, Christian, Jew] are deceived deceivers.
> None of your rings is genuine. The true ring
> Has been lost. And in order to disguise the loss
> The father has created three instead of one.[2]

With Saladin cheering him on from the sidelines—*"Herrlich! Herrlich!"*—Nathan continues to propound the doctrine of religious relativism which is to be the basis for social order in enlightened German states like Prussia:

> My advice to you is to accept the situation for what it is.
> If one of you has his ring from his father,
> then he should believe that his ring is the real ring,
> because it's just possible that the Father has had enough of the
> Tyranny of the One Ring and will no longer tolerate it in his house[3]

Over 200 years after its first performance, Jews still find the play and the vision of religious indifferentism which Nathan evokes inspiring. Amos Elon sees

> Lessing's Nathan is the antithesis of Shakespeare's Shylock. The play boldly attacks all religious and national prejudice; the idea of a "better god" is absurd, the propagating of the idea a cause for "pious rage." Not faith but moral behavior is the essence of all religion. In beautiful blank verse, Lessing restates the finest ideal of the Enlightenment—tolerance, brotherhood, and love for humanity. Set in Jerusalem, during the Crusades, the play builds to a high point with Nathan's parable of three miraculous rings given by a father to his three sons. Symbols of Christianity, Judaism and Islam, the rings assure each son the love of God and men if he but wears his in good faith.[4]

In Nathan, the Jew and the Freemason merge into one Enlightened cosmopolitan. *"Ich bin ein Mensch,"* "I am a human being," is Nathan's response to Saladin's inquiry about questions of identity that usually require ethnic or religious answers. Mendelssohn became the model for those who "sought a larger community of rational men beyond the stagnant confines of religious identity."[5] He also became a model for Jewish assimilation, at first in Germany, and then as the Enlightenment spread eastward for the overwhelming majority of Jews in the world. According to Barbara Tuchman,

> The process begins with the "Enlightenment" initiated by Moses Mendelssohn in 18th century Germany, which shattered the protective shell of orthodoxy and opened the way to acquaintance with Western culture and participation in Western affairs. The reign of the Talmud and the rabbis was broken. All over Europe the shattered windows were flying open. Jews read Voltaire and Rousseau, Goethe and Kant. The reform movement followed, shedding the old rituals, trying to adjust Judaism to the modern world. Civil Emancipation became the goal. In 1791 the French Constituent Assembly had decreed citizenship for the Jews; Napoleon confirmed it wherever he had dominions. Reaction rescinded it, and

thereafter it had to be fought for separately in each country. Civil Emancipation was won around the middle of the 19th century, and if it had been a success, Judaism would have ended there. But it was not; and in the process of discovering why not, the Jews discovered nationalism. They became aware that Judaism was dying; on the one hand petrifying into a dry husk of rabbinical mumbo jumbo, and on the other dissolving in the open air of Western "enlightenment."[6]

There is a note of violence implicit in Tuchman's description of the "shattered shell of orthodoxy," as if breaking the reign of the Talmud were akin to splitting the atom because of all the destructive energy it released. Whether intentional or not, the comparison was apt because the Enlightenment in both Germany and, more importantly, Russia opened the Jews of the shtetl to the spirit of revolution when the Mendelssohn's vision exposed the world of Kahal and the rabbis as so much "rabbinical mumbo jumbo." 2

Mendelssohn became the paradigmatic Enlightenment Jew and a model for Jews who wanted to leave the Polish shtetls of the East behind and become part of German culture. He also became the model Jew for the Germans, who were debating whether to grant the Jews the rights of citizens in the wake of Napoleon's defeat.

In 1792 Salomon Maimon, one of Kant's Jewish critics and a refuge from the Pale of the Settlement, published his autobiography. Maimon's book gave expression to Jewish hatred of the Talmud and the Kahal in a memoir about his life growing up as a Jew in the shtetls of "darkest Lithuania."[7] He abandoned that life, along with his wife and children, and, like Mendelssohn, headed to Berlin to free his mind of the chains of "Talmudic darkness,"[8] which kept the Jews of the east "bent over this mind-killing business of attempting to create meaning where none existed, expending our wits raising contradictions where none appeared, and sharpening those we could discern. We spent endless hours quibbling our way through long chains of conclusions, chasing after shadows and building castles in the air."[9]

Germany was the source of ideas for the Jews of the East. The reason for that is not hard to understand. German was easier for Jews to understand than Slavic languages like Russian or Polish because the Jews spoke Yiddish. Once the German Enlightenment arrived in Russia in the mid-19th century it caused an immediate split among the Jews there into two groups: the Halachic Jews rejected the Enlightenment in favor of the Law and the old ways, which meant of course, a continuing refusal to assimilate; the Maskilic Jews on the other hand accepted the Enlightenment, but in accepting it, they began, far more than those following the old way, to look for the Messiah in political movements, movements which invariably came from German Jews or conversos like Ferdinand Lassalle and Karl Marx. As a result, Russia's Jews were awakened from the slumber of the shtetl by Moses Mendelssohn, but they did not follow Mendelssohn's example. Instead they became progressively more radicalized during the course of the 19th century, until the German Enlightenment culminated in Bolshevism, which, according to Nora Levin, "attracted marginal Jews, poised between two worlds—the Jewish and the Gentile—who created a new homeland for themselves, a community of ideologists bent on remaking the world in their own image."[10]

Masonic convergence was in the air. At the same moment that Jews like Maimon and Mendelssohn were proclaiming their willingness to abandon the shtetl and the "darkness" of the Talmud and the Kahal, Prussians were abandoning historical Christianity in favor of something more "German." As some expression of this convergence, Enlightened Christians like Christian von Dohm wrote his treatise *On the Civic Improvement of Jews*, calling for their political emancipation. The message of the German Enlightenment was that talent was more important than religion or ethnicity. *Nathan der Weise* proposed a new paradigm for Jewish life in Germany. Jews no longer had to convert to Christianity. Caspar Lavater tried to convert Mendelssohn to Christianity but failed because he failed to gain the support of people like Goethe, who announced that he was not a Christian either. The Enlightenment led as a result to the idea of the genius as the secular alternative to the saint. It led as well to the idea of the intellectual elite as the secular clerisy, and to literary cults of personality, like the one the German Jews created around Goethe, who found that "Jewish women possess[ed] the gift of being the most sensitive audience."[11]

Conversion was still necessary for Jews, but now increasingly instead of baptism, the Enlightenment proposed a new alternative. Jews now had to convert to German *Kultur* and German *Bildung*, as defined by Goethe. In the aftermath of Lavater's attempt to convert him to Christianity, Mendelssohn wrote *Jerusalem or Upon Ecclesiastic Power and Judaism* (1783), in which, he claimed—contrary to what Maimon and everyone else knew of the Talmud and the religious establishment based on it—that Judaism, at least as Mendelssohn understood it, was compatible with the ideas of the Enlightenment. In this regard, Mendelssohn was only doing for Judaism what Immanuel Kant in his *Religion within the Bounds of Reason* was doing for Christianity.

As a result a certain Masonic convergence was inevitable. Over the course of the 19th century, the ground of that convergence would become Germany and not Freemasonry. Both Jews and Germans were in the process of defining themselves as a cultural community in which religion had ceased to be important. Heinrich Heine would go on claim that Mendelssohn had done to the Kahal and the Talmud what Luther had done to the Catholic Church, and once again it seemed that Jews and Judaizers—as the Hussites, Calvinists, and Puritans had done before them—would find common ground for a new "reformed" religion in their hatred of the Catholic Church.

The 'Church' of this new cult was the Masonic lodge, but as in France, the lodge spawned clubs which allowed not only diverse religions but both sexes to meet on common ground. The salons of Berlin allowed Jews and Christians to mix socially. Unlike the lodge, the salons admitted and were often run by women. The common denominator of the salons was Enlightened German culture. Both Jews and Christians were abandoning historical religion in favor of something that was more German and Masonic. Romance accelerated the process. Graetz was upset at the free love: "If the enemies of the Jews had designed to break the power of Israel, they could have discovered no more effectual means than infecting Jewish women with the moral depravity, a plan more efficacious than that employed by the Midianites, who weakened the men by immorality."[12] Elon claims that the salons constituted "a kind of freemasonry. . . of the heart , and a safe haven for nonconformists."[13]

Along with the daughters of Moses Mendelssohn, some of whom married Christians as a result, one of the habitués of the Berlin salons was David Friedlaender, the Jew who went on to create Reform Judaism after imbibing deeply of the sexualized Masonry that filled the air there. Elon claims that "Mendelssohn became the father, albeit inadvertently, of modern Reform Judaism" although "he himself remained traditionally devout and observant throughout his life."[14] If Mendelssohn was the Christ of reformed Judaism, David Friedlaender was its St. Paul. If Mendelssohn was the Moses of Jewish assimilationism, David Friedlaender was its Joshua.

In 1799 Friedlaender and other Jews were faced with a crisis. Largely as a result of the fact that the Enlightenment had demonstrated the "darkness" of the Talmud, the Jews in Germany were involved a massive conversion to "enlightened" Christianity. According to Graetz, half of Berlin's Jews converted to Christianity during this period. The Jews of Koenigsberg, Immanuel Kant's home town, were on the verge of disappearing completely. Four of Moses Mendelssohn's daughters converted to Christianity, as did his famous composer grandson Felix. Dorothea Mendelssohn even went so far as to convert to Catholicism, when her erstwhile Protestant husband Heinrich Schlegel did.

Faced with the greatest wave of conversions in Europe since the conversions in Spain during the first half of the 15th century, David Friedlaender decided to make an explicit proposal based on the implicit assumptions he had imbibed in Berlin's salons. Friedlaender argued for a "dry baptism"[15] in the spirit of Masonic convergence. Jews would be willing to enter the Lutheran Church if they could do so without recognizing the divinity of Christ. It seemed like a plausible solution since the Lutherans were on their way to abandoning historical Christianity as avidly as the Jews were abandoning the Talmud and Kahal. Liberal theologians had already omitted mention of the Trinity and other inconvenient Christian dogmas in their new catechisms, but Friedlaender ruined the idea by formulating it so boldly.

The Masonic convergence which the Enlightened imbibed in Berlin's salons apparently could only utter its name within the protected confines of the lodge. Under the influence of the Masonic Enlightenment, Judaism was becoming less

Jewish, and Lutheranism was becoming less Christian. Both were becoming German instead. Once the idea was broached outside the hothouse atmosphere of the Lodge or salon, however, it brought down upon Friedlaender's head a torrent of abuse and denunciations from both sides. Progressive Jews like Heinrich Graetz found the idea appalling. Even progressive theologians like Friedrich Schleiermacher, who had met Friedlaender at Henriette Herz's salon, denounced the idea as an insidious form of judaizing.

The violence of the reaction to Friedlaender's reading of what were simply the Masonic commonplaces of salon discourse showed just how out of touch the intellectual life of those salons was with the real world. The real world, in this instance, went by the name of Napoleon. Rahel Levin was a famous Jewish bluestocking who longed for a mystical convergence of Jew and Christian in the Enlightened Germany of the Berlin salons. Her dream ended in 1806 when Prussia was defeated by France and Napoleon rode into Jena under Hegel's admiring gaze like the *Zeitgeist* on horseback. Left high and dry after the tide of Enlightenment free love and Masonic syncretism flowed out of Prussia in the wake of Napoleon's arrival, all Rahel Levin could do was bemoan a world now irretrievably lost: the dream of Masonic convergence between Enlightened Christians and Jews "sank in 1806. Sank like a ship, carrying the most beautiful gifts, the most beautiful pleasures of life."[16]

Napoleon's conquest of the German principalities imposed the Enlightenment by force on the German people. When Napoleon was defeated, his defeat created the German reaction to the Enlightenment which has come to be known as Romanticism. The Germans found things dark, Catholic, and medieval an attractive alternative to the social geometry of the French Revolution.

The Jews were the first to suffer during the reaction. Beginning in August 1819 in the Bavarian city of Wuerzburg, anti-Jewish riots swept through German Cities. The rallying cry of the rioters was "*Hep, Hep, Jude verreck!*" In the word "Hep," an acronym for the Latin phrase, "*Hierlyma est perdita*," or "Jerusalem is lost," the past which the Enlightenment had repressed was back with all its former virulence. The Germans who used the phrase during the pogroms along the Rhine at the time of the crusades are said to have gotten it from the Roman soldiers who used it as their battle cry during the siege and destruction of the Temple in Jerusalem in 70 AD. The Middle Ages had returned with a vengeance. Or so it seemed to the disillusioned Jews who saw in Christianity and the Catholic Church the source of all Jewish woe. Rahel Levin blamed the Romantics and "their newfound hypocritical love for Christianity . . and the Middle Ages, with its poetry, art and atrocities, [which] incites the people to commit the only atrocity that may be still provoked to: attacking the Jews!"[17] In reality, the Hep Hep riots were only the beginning of an increasingly violent anti-revolutionary reactions which would culminate in the most violent counter-revolutionary reaction of all, the Nazi reaction to Bolshevism. It was Napoleon who, according to Chaim Potok, "invaded

Russia in June 1812 with an army of five hundred thousand men. Ecstatic eastern European Jews hailed him as the Messiah, hung his portrait on the walls of their homes, and helped provision his armies."[18] Thus it should come as no surprise that revolution was synonymous in the minds of Germans with the Jews. When Napoleon, the "Jewish" Messiah, withdrew in defeat, the Jews had to pay the price for supporting him. In Rome, the pope made Jews put on their yellow badges again. In Frankfurt the medieval laws restricting the rights of Jews were reinstated. In general the states which had passed emancipation edicts at Napoleon's command rescinded them when he was defeated.

Elon claims that "the new nationalism harkened back to the Middle Ages, its sacred union of church, people and state."[19] The Middle Ages, according to this view, was a time when Germans "worshipped homogeneity and appealed to tribal instincts."[20] Elon ignores the fact that the Middle Ages was a time completely devoid of racial thinking. Even as late as the Reuchlin/Pfefferkorn controversy, "*die Dunkelmaenner*" from Cologne, the Dominicans, took a completely antiracial line, as opposed to humanists like Erasmus, who felt that Pfefferkorn retained some ineradicable biological Jewishness. In looking for villains in all of the usual places, Elon can't bring himself to understand that the idea of race was new. It could not be a throwback to the Middle Ages because it didn't exist in the Middle Ages. After the defeat of Napoleon, the idea of race began to supplant the Masonic ideal of Lessing's *Nathan* as both its logical conclusion and its antithesis. It was an instance of Hegel's oft-cited concept of "*Aufhebung*"; race abolished the Enlightenment by exalting it to a new level. The glorification of race was the logical outcome of the simultaneous conversion to "*Kultur*" and "*Bildung*" that was taking place among progressive Lutherans and Jews under the influence of the Enlightenment. Because of the Enlightenment, German culture had replaced religion as the criterion of citizenship. The Enlightenment perdured as long a no one looked into the basis of culture, which was a combination of religion and place. The trauma of Napoleonic conquest ended that naive idyll, evoking a violent reaction that according to the cunning of history would insure a return to the symbols of the Middle Ages but not to the cult which was the inspiration of those symbols. Romanticism meant both a return to Catholicism and the exaltation of local culture, but the analytic spirit set loose by revolution eventually dissolved the Romantic synthesis into biology and race. Once that analysis began—largely as a result of the defeat of Napoleon—German *Kultur* disintegrated too and the Enlightenment synthesis which Lessing proposed in his play was over, no matter how much it would kept on artificial life support in institutions dominated by Enlightenment thought. If Romanticism had brought about a deep-rooted return to the Catholic soul of the Middle Ages, it could not have prevented an anti-Jewish reaction to the excesses of the Revolution, but it would have promoted the antithesis of racism.

The fact that racism emerged from the ruins of the Enlightenment meant paradoxically that there was still life left in that movement. Revolution did not cease to exist with the defeat of Napoleon's empire; it became nationalist in its orientation instead, culminating in what would have seemed like a contradiction in terms to Mendelssohn, namely, Jewish nationalism or Zionism, which reared its ugly head in 1862 with the publication of Moses Hess's tract *Rom und Jerusalem*. The idolatry of race in many ways only continued the abandonment of religion which the philosophes of the Enlightenment had begun. As Jews became less Jewish and Christians less Christian, their only common meeting ground was the Masonic dream of Lessing's Nathan. When Napoleon destroyed that vision of German culture, Germans could return to the universalism of Catholicism or move on to the new religion of race and nation. Residual Protestant animus insured that the latter would be the case. It also ensured that in the reaction to Napoleon, German culture began to be defined in increasingly racial terms. Johann Gottlieb Fichte in his address to the German nation urged not the conversion of the Jews but their deportation to the Middle East, an idea that Theodor Herzl, another devotee of German *Kultur*, would find congenial at the end of the century. In spite of the turn toward race, Germany would remain the center of Jewish thought for the rest of the century, and, what is more important, it would become a model for the benighted *Ostjuden* of the shtetls, who would become the cutting edge of the revolutionary movement when Mendelssohn's ideas swept through the Pale of the Settlement in the mid-nineteenth century.

II. The Partition of Poland

The Jewish longing for liberation from the Kahal and the tyranny of the rabbis became more than just a theoretical possibility for literary figures like Mendelssohn and Maimun during this same period time primarily because of the partition of Poland, which took place in three separate events beginning in 1772 and ending in 1795. When it began, 85 percent of the world's Jews lived in Poland. When it ended 50 percent of the world's Jews lived in Russia, along the porous western border in a section that came to be known as the Pale of the Settlement.

Not long after the partition of Poland, Russia became aware that it had a Jewish problem. It had inherited its new Jewish problem from the Polish nobility who had used the Jews to do what they had no desire to do themselves. With the exception of tax-farming, all of the practices which had led to the Chmielnicki pogroms and the ultimate demise of Poland were still in place, now practiced by an unassimilated minority on Russia's crucial border with the West. At around the same time that David Friedlaender made his proposal for "dry baptism" to the German Lutherans, the Czar appointed one of his most distinguished civil servants, the poet Gavriil Romanovich Dershavin to go on a fact-finding mission to the Pale of the Settlement and find out why the peasants from the greatest grain producing region in Europe were starving to death. In 1802 Dershavin issued his report. After traveling extensively in the grain producing areas of western Russia, Dershavin discovered that the Jewish vodka producers were exploiting the alcoholism of the farmers: "After I had learned that the Jews out of greed were exploiting the drinking problems of the peasants to cheat them out of their grain, in order to turn that grain into vodka, and as a result were causing famine, I ordered the distilleries in the village of Liosno shut down." "I also made enquiries among the reasonable inhabitants," as well as among the aristocracy, the merchants and the people living in the village "concerning the mores of the Jews, their business practices, their scams and all of the tricks they used to...drive the stupid and penniless inhabitants of the village to the brink of starvation. I was especially interested in how it might be possible to protect these poor devils and to enable them to live an honest and not disastrous life...to make them useful citizens."[21]

Dershavin discovered that the majority of the Jews made their living from distilling and selling vodka. Jews were no longer tax farmers, but they had a monopoly on alcohol production which when combined with usury was causing drunkenness and famine among the peasants. The Jewish vodka dealers had the bad habit of showing up with their wares at harvest time and selling alcohol to the farmers on credit. Before long the drinking habits of the peasants combined with the inexorable nature of compound interest led to a situation in which not only every bit of property was in the hands of the Jews but future harvests as well. According to a report from the Administration of Belorus, "The presence of Jews in the villages has a destructive effect on the economic and moral situation of the rural population because Jews...promoted drunkenness among locals."[22]

In other administrative reports, the same story emerged: "the Jews were the main cause of leading the peasants into drunkenness, laziness, and poverty, largely because of fact that they were willing to sell them vodka on credit (i.e., let them pawn their goods to get vodka). The production of spirits was an irresistible source of income for both the Polish magnates and the Jewish middlemen."[23] "The Jews not only cheated the peasants out of the grain they needed to live on, they also cheated them out of their seed corn, their farming implements, household items, time, health and life." "The Jews made a practice of traveling around in the fall during the harvest, getting not only the peasants but their entire families drunk, then getting them in debt, then robbing them of every last thing they needed to keep themselves alive." "By cheating the drunken peasants and plundering them of their goods, the Jews plunged the inhabitants of the villages into deepest misery."[24] The Jews became an active, irreplaceable and extremely inventive link in the chain of exploitation that plagued this group of illiterate, defenseless peasants without any rights. If it weren't for the Jews this system of exploitation would have had no foundation in the Byelorussian settlements. "Removing the Jewish link," the Byelorussian report concluded, was the only way to break the chain of exploitation that held the farming class in alcohol- and usury-induced bondage.

Dershavin felt that the heart of the problem lay with the Kahal, the autonomous Jewish legal system, as well as the rabbinic Jewish leadership, which was determined to keep the Jews themselves subservient and isolated. "The teachers of the Jewish race" according to Dershavin, "distorted the true spirit of the Faith with their 'mystic-talmudic' pseudo-exegesis of the Bible....They introduced strict laws with the goal of isolating the Jews from the other nations, and to awake in the Jews a deep hatred against other religions." The main problem was the talmudic Jewish religion, which "instead of cultivating communal virtue. . . turned worship into an empty ceremony."[25]

The solution was education, especially in modern languages, because the ability of Jews to speak to fellow Russians, would break the hold of the Kahal by ending the isolation of the Jews. Dershavin was hardly an obscurantist. In any other country—in America for instance, which would not see an educational reformer like this until the end of the same century, he would have been hailed as another Horace Mann or John Dewey. "Any Jewish reform in Russian," he continued, "must begin with the founding of public schools, in which the Russian, the German, and the Yiddish languages are taught." Dershavin was uncompromising in calling for the abolition of the Kahal, but so were many Jews. The Kahal was evil in his eyes because through it the simple Jewish people "are deceived into believing that between them and those of other faiths an impenetrable wall has come into existence." As a result, "the darkness which surrounds all Jews keeps them separated from their fellow citizens."[26] The Talmud schools were the main vehicle for the perduring and pernicious messianism which enslaved the Jewish people. In the Talmud schools, the Jewish people were kept in constant anticipation of the Messiah. They were also taught to believe that their Messiah by overthrowing all other races would "reign over them in flesh and blood, and will restore to them their fame and glory."

Dershavin concluded that the main reason for the shortage of grain in White Russia and the Ukraine was the Jews' exploitation of the peasants. As a result of writing his report, Dershavin was demonized as an anti-Semite. Because of his observations in Byelorussia, because of the conclusions he drew in his Memorandum, but especially because he praised "the sharp eye of the great Russian monarchs" which "prohibited the immigration of these clever thieves into their kingdom," Dershavin was demonized as "a fanatical foe of the Jews."[27] Far from preaching racial hatred, Dershavin, like Catherine the Great, thought he could reform the Jews by reorienting them toward productive acidity. In dealing with what he saw as the Jewish penchant to cheat people of other races, Dershavin tried to distinguish between freedom of religious conscience and "impunity for criminal behavior," and this involved a two-pronged attack on the problem. First of all, the Kahal was to be abolished along with "a ban on all previous involvement with usury."[28] At the same time, Dershavin suggested that Jews should be given access to the university, where they could become doctors and professors.

The Jews retaliated by bringing false charges against Dershavin. A Jewish woman from Liosno claimed that Dershavin beat her with a club while visiting a vodka distillery there, causing her to have a miscarriage. In response to an investigation into the charges conducted by the Russian Senate, Dershavin answered: "Since I only spent 15 minutes in this factory, I not only did not beat the Jewish lady in question, I didn't even see any Jewish women."[29] After an audience with the Czar, the Jew who had written the lying charges for his wife was sentenced to a year in prison, but ended up being released after two or three months largely because of Dershavin's efforts. Unfortunately, the Czar was murdered in May 1801 before having a chance to act on the recommendations in Derhavin's memorandum.

Gradually, Dershavin lost his influence with the new Czar, largely as a result of political intrigue. Eighteen months after the death of Czar Paul, toward the end of 1802, a "Committee for the Assimilation of the Jews" was finally created in order to consider Dershavin's Memorandum and to take corresponding steps. The big issue remained alcohol. The Jews lived in the same villages with the peasants and their prosperity was based on the exploitation their neighbors' weakness. In order to insure that the Committee's efforts came to nothing, the Jews raised a million rubles to bribe public officials. The main goal of the Jews' bribery was to discredit Dershavin as an anti-Semite and drive him from office. If that failed, the money was to ensure that at all costs the production and sale of alcohol remained in the hands of the Jews.

By the time the committee held its first meeting, it was clear that Jewish money had done its work. In spite of the warnings Dershavin had sent to the new Czar, it was clear that Count Speransky "was completely on the side of the Jews." Furthermore, "during the first meeting of the Jewish committee it became clear that all of the committee members shared the opinion that the right to sell vodka...should remain as in the past in Jewish hands." Dershavin's efforts eventually paid off in spite of the machinations of the Jews. The law which was passed in 1804 specified that "No Jew . . is allowed to sell vodka or to subcontract the sale of vodka."[30]

It might be more accurate to say that Dershavin's efforts paid off in the short run. With the money they had made from vodka production at their disposal, the Jews continued to manipulate public opinion, portraying the prohibition of the sale of vodka and the order to move out of the villages as a terrible injustice.[31] Reacting to the incessant pressure of the Jews and the bribery of public officials that went along with it, Alexander I revoked the order banning the sale of alcohol. By now the figure of Napoleon loomed large in Russian life. Napoleon had set his sights on the east and had begun a propaganda campaign, originally conceived in his campaign in Palestine against the Turks, to portray himself as the spirit of Revolution incarnate and, as a result, the Jewish Messiah. Napoleon knew that he needed Jewish support to conquer Russian, and Alexander I knew that he knew that, and so the Czar was reluctant to alienate what was already perceived as a potential fifth column on his western border by depriving the Jews of what they wanted most. In 1806 Alexander I convened another committee to decide whether the Jews should be resettled. In the end, the arrival of Napoleon convinced him to abandon both projects. Military necessity made the decision moot anyway.

Chaim Potok claims that Jews welcomed Napoleon as the Messiah. Solzhenitsyn, however, claims that the Jews remained loyal to the Czar after the war with Napoleon began. Looking back at the Napoleonic era, Nicholas I wrote in his diary "It's amazing how faithful the Jews remained to us, even risking their lives to help us."[32] During the war the Jews were the only ethnic group in Russia which didn't flee into the forests to escape from the French army. However, in the area around Vilna, the Jews who refused to be inducted into the French army could not resist the temptation to profit from the situation financially by provisioning the French army.

No matter how the Jews reacted, the threat of Napoleon coupled with the bribery of the Jews derailed Russia's first attempt to deal with its newfound Jewish problem. After 1814, the problem was compounded by the fact that central Poland became part of the Russian empire, adding another 400,000 Jews to the already large and unassimilated group living in the Pale of the Settlement. As a result, the Jewish problem in Russia became even more pressing and even more difficult to solve.

After the plan to ban Jews from the alcohol industry failed, Russian's next attempt to solve the Jewish problem involved resettling Jews on plots of land in New Russia on the steppes north of the Black Sea and training them to be farmers. The program exuded an almost American optimism about human nature along with a Jeffersonian view of the salutary nature of agriculture in an Enlightened culture. Russia, perhaps influenced by the success of the American Enlightenment, felt that it could turn saloon keeping usurers into sturdy yeomen farmers within a generation, but the program soon made contact with deeper more intractable realities, most notably, the Jewish aversion to manual labor. P. I. Pestel was convinced that this early example of social engineering was a fool's errand because, quite simply, Jews do not believe in farming. "In expectation of the Messiah," Pestel wrote, "the Jews considered themselves only temporary inhabitants of the land in which they live, and as a result want to have nothing to do with agriculture. They also hold all forms of labor in contempt and devote themselves almost exclusively to trade."[33] Farming involves lots of hard work. It is also something, as Solzhenitsyn points out, than can only be learned over the course of a number of generations and can't be forced on people against their will.

Before long, it became clear that getting Jews involved in agriculture was a hopeless cause.[34] By 1810-12, in spite of significant government promotion of the program, the Jewish colonies in the lands of the south continued to languish, because Jews were not accustomed to getting up early in the morning, nor were they accustomed to working outdoors in the cold. By the time they were ready to plant their crops, the season was so far advanced that frost would kill the plants before they were ripe enough to harvest. "The Jews waited until it was warm to sow their seed and by then it was too late." In addition to that, "Farm implements were either lost, broken or destroyed by the Jews," and the oxen which were needed to pull the plow were slaughtered, or stolen or sold. According to M. O. Gerschenson, "The spirit of the Jewish people prohibits involvement in farming because a man who tills the soil is the man most likely to put down roots in a particular place." Jews gave up the plow at the first opportunity in order to become middlemen and devote themselves to other more desirable activity. The hard work of farming was the bitter lot of the goyim;[35] the fact that Jews did not have to break their backs while engaging in hard physical labor was perhaps taken as another sign that they were the Chosen People. Jewish women soon refused to marry farmers, or they had clauses added to their marriage contracts which specified that they could not be expected to do manual farm labor.[36] Finally in 1811, in a tacit admission of failure, the government allowed the Jews of the Pale of the Settlement to get back into the vodka business and that cooled whatever interest they had in turning Jews into farmers.[37]

Before long, government officials discovered that the Jewish unwillingness to work the land did not preclude a desire to take possession of the land and have other people work it for them. Thus, the government's scheme to use agriculture to solve the Jewish problem only compounded the problem by allowing the Jews to become landlords and forcing the peasants who were exploited by them when they were saloon keepers into a new form of bondage as servants and sharecroppers. The laws of Christian countries had always specified that Jews should be prohibited from owning land and having Christian servants. That law, as many papal fulminations indicated, was flagrantly abused in Poland, but now it was Russia's turn to learn the wisdom behind these papal prohibitions. According to Count Golitsyn, Christians who live in the houses of the Jews, "not only forget the commands of the Christian religion and don't fulfill them, but also take up Jewish customs and practices."[38] The Russians viewed with increasing alarm the rise of judaizing among the Christians of western Russia following the partition. Czar Nicholas later worried that Jews would convert Christians because, beginning in the first half of the 18th century, groups of judaizers spread across Russia. In 1823 the minister for the interior reported on the "wide dissemination" of the heresy of judaizing and estimated at least 200,000 people were involved. A law was passed which forbade Jews to hire Christian servants, specifying that they should hire poor Jews instead, but the law was ignored. As in the case of alcohol production, the law was rescinded quietly after having been ignored. After 1823 Jews were allowed to hire Christian laborers legally. The "strict prohibition" against allowing Christians to work on Jewish farms "was in practice hardly enforced."[39]

Once it became apparent that Jews were not going to become farmers, the Russian government sought a solution to the Jewish problem in education (as Dershavin had suggested), which was seen as the best solution to the isolation which the shtetl imposed on the Jews. The Russian reformers concluded that, in effect, the Jewish people had to be rescued from their own leaders, who exploited the

Jews as ruthlessly as the Jews exploited the Russian peasants. The Kahal was the problem. "The Jewish priests, known as Rabbis, hold their people in an unbelievable dependence and forbid them in the name of their faith to read any book other than the Talmud....A race that does not seek Enlightenment will always remain a victim of prejudice."[40]

That was the view of a Russian official, but it was shared increasingly by many Jews, who were in many ways, the prime victims of the Polish Kahal, which functioned as the supreme judicial authority of what was in effect a state within a state. The Kahal was notorious for its corruption, creating in effect a two-tiered system which ensured that poor Jews would be punished for crimes which the rich Jews could commit with impunity. "The close relations among the Jews enable them to accumulate great sums of money for their general purposes, especially for the purpose of bribing public officials and to introduce all sorts of abuses, which are good for the Jews." Or at least good for certain Jews. The rabbis promoted early marriage because they profited from it financially. There is even evidence from Jewish historians of the Kahal authorizing murder. As their contribution to the implementation of the Czar's plan to resettle Jews to the farming lands of New Russia, the Kahal urged poor Jews to emigrate, but urged the wealthy Jews to stay where they were increasing the profit margin of those who ran the system.[41]

The Kahal was opposed to Haskalah, the Jewish Enlightenment, from the moment that rumors of Moses Mendelssohn's ideas began seeping through Russia's porous western border. The Kahal was opposed to Haskalah because they rightly saw it as a threat to their power. "The Kahal did everything within its power to extinguish the smallest spark of Enlightenment."[42] Giller Markevich wrote that the Kahal had to be abolished in order to save the Jewish people from spiritual and social ruin; the Jews had to be taught languages, which would enable access to factory work, but they also had to be granted the right to conduct commerce throughout the country and the right to have Christian workers. Before long a consensus began to emerge among progressive Russia officials and Jewish "renegades" that the tyranny of the Kahal had to be broken. The Czarist government was determined to fight against "Jewish isolation" and so promoted Haskalah without understanding that in promoting the Enlightenment that was the antithesis of talmudic obscurantism, misanthropy and ethnocentrism, they unwittingly exposed the Jews of the shtetls to the revolutionary ideas that German Jews had been formulating as their response to the French revolution. In unwittingly introducing the Maskilim to those ideas, the well-meaning Russian officials introduced them as well, to the revolution that would eventually destroy Russia.

III

On December 14, 1825, a group of young Russian aristocrats who had been infected by Freemasonry and revolution orchestrated a coup against Czar Nicholas I. There was a certain irony here, since the main exposure to these ideas came as a result of Russia's defeat of Napoleon and revolutionary France. The Decembrist

Revolt of 1825 was neither a popular revolution, nor did the Jews play a major role in its conception or execution. The only Jew (and one of the few civilians) involved in the Decembrist Revolt was Grigorii Abramovich Peretts (1788-1855). Although he joined in with the revolt of the Russian nobles, Peretts came to revolutionary conclusions by other means. He was the first of many intellectual progeny which Moses Mendelssohn would spawn among the Jews of the East.

Peretts may have been the only Jew involved in the Decembrist Revolt but he was, unlike his co-conspirators, a truly Jewish revolutionary. Left pretty much to his own devices, Peretts created a secret organization known as the "Society of Peretts" which was typically Jewish in its rules even down to secret password it had adopted, namely, *Heruth*, the Hebrew word for liberty.[43] The Society of Peretts was also quintessentially Jewish because of its attachment to Messianic politics. The political views of the society were divinely inspired and its agenda divinely ordained because, as Peretts argued, the law of Moses showed that "God favors constitutional government."[44]

On February 21, 1826, Peretts was arrested for his role in the conspiracy and imprisoned in the notorious Peter and Paul Fortress in St. Petersburg. It was during his interrogation and imprisonment and the long years of exile which followed his trial, that Peretts earned his reputation as Russia's first revolutionary Jew. He blazed the path—certainly the path into exile—which many revolutionary Jews would follow after him.

Peretts was a trail-blazer in other ways as well. In him we see the beginning of Haskalah among the Russian Jews. Peretts was the son of a wealthy merchant by the name of Abram Peretts, who had been granted residency rights in St. Petersburg by Catherine II for his service to the crown. The Perettses, along with other privileged Jews in St. Petersburg, became the nucleus of Jewish Enlightenment in Russia. Peretts, in this regard,

> stood at the beginning of a profound socio-cultural process which gave rise to a secularized Jewish intelligentsia. The process was initiated and largely characterized by the Jewish Enlightenment or Haskalah, which originated with Moses Mendelssohn in mid-eighteenth-century Berlin and then was carried to Eastern Europe by its followers—the Maskilim. Born into a family of first generation Russian Maskilim, Peretts was a child of the Haskalah and a prototype of its most radical expression: the secular educated Jewish intellectual, who, alienated from traditional Judaism and isolated from Russian society, sought salvation through revolution.[45]

The Russian Jews began to implement Mendelssohn's ideas by emphasizing culture instead of religion. This meant that Russian Jews should adopt the German concept of *Bildung* and *Kultur* as the basis for internal Jewish reform, but it also meant that, *ad extra*, the Maskilic Jews began to use their position with Russians of influence to argue for emancipation. If the internal course of *Bildung* and *Kultur* as the alternative to the obscurantist Kahal and talmudic rabbis were to succeed, the Jews had to be met half way and treated as fellow Russian citizens.[46]

Before long, the salons of Berlin began appearing in St. Petersburg. In fact, the Peretts household began to hold a salon of its own, one which became a lively meeting place where progressive Russians and Enlightened Jews could meet to discuss the new ideas trickling in from the West. As in Berlin, as David Friedlaender found out, the salon took on an air of unreality. It was a place where daring ideas could be expressed without fear, but those ideas had no real connection to either political or religious realities in Russia. To begin with, the Jews found the ideas of the Mendelssohnian *Berlinchiki* repugnant and heretical and a threat to the *modus operandi* which had proved so successful in Poland. The rabbis had no desire to allow rich, young upstarts to challenge their hegemony over the benighted Jewish people. The Kahal was determined to prevent the integration of Jews into Russian society because that system of self-government preserved the power of traditional Jewish elites, who were funded by activities—vodka and usury—from which the majority of the Jews, one way or another, earned their livelihoods, no matter how deleterious their effect on Russian fellow citizens. Beyond that, the Enlightenment never really overcame its identity as a foreign imposition among the Russians. The fact that *Aufklaerung* was a German phenomenon, which could be transplanted to Russian soil only with difficulty if at all should have been obvious to everyone involved. The convergence of Protestant and Jew which was taking place in the salons of Berlin needed German culture as its common denominator. Without German culture as the neutral ground between the confessions, no meeting of the minds was possible. Needless to say, German culture did not exist in Russia. There had been no reformation in Russia. Christendom in Russia had not been split into two branches, with all of the scandal that that split entailed. There had been no consequent intellectual dilution of the faith, and there was no need for a Masonic meta-confessional alternative among the Russian intellectual elites as there was in Germany, which had been divided between Catholic and Protestant denominations for three hundred years.

Failing to find the third way in Russian culture, Peretts exposed both the limitations of Russian Jewish Enlightenment and its origins when he converted to Lutheranism. Lutheranism was beginning a long process of dissolution under the solvent of the historical critical method in Germany, a dissolution which would find its culmination in the writings of Friedrich Nietzsche, the son of a Lutheran pastor who read the writings of Strauss. If that were the case in Germany, Lutheranism certainly had no future for a converted Jew in orthodox Russia.

As a result, Peretts quickly passed from being an Enlightened Jew to being and Enlightened Protestant. Once those steps had been taken, the distance to Peretts the Jewish revolutionary was not far. Peretts became not only a revolutionary Jew; he became the model for other revolutionary Jews to follow because of the peculiar circumstances in which the Enlightened Jews found themselves in Russia. The Enlightenment led to hopes for emancipation, but emancipation proved maddeningly elusive. As a result, those who espoused the cause of Enlightenment among the Jews and for the Jews found themselves increasingly isolated, cut off from both Jew and Christian, but still inspired by a vision of Liberty, Fraternity, and Equality that was being implemented elsewhere. Peretts became, as a result, "the archetype of nineteenth-century Russian-Jewish radical whose personality and political engagement were shaped by the modernizing ideology of the Jewish Enlightenment and its unsettling sociological consequences."[47]

The Mendelssohnian Enlightenment which turned Peretts into a revolutionary took root among Russian Jews during the period between the Decembrist uprising of 1825 and Russia's defeat in the Crimea in 1855. During this period, traditional Talmudic Judaism was largely discredited as obscurantist and obsolete in the eyes of Jewish youth, but assimilation into Russian culture did not follow. As a result, the idea of revolution began to fill the vacuum created by the former yet not filled by the latter. Jewish culture was caught in what looked like a never ending squabble between modernists and traditionalists, and young Jews, seeing no end to the bickering, took matters into their own hands by becoming revolutionaries.

Public education played a major role in this transformation. The revolutionary Jew in Russia is in large measure a product or that country's educational reforms during the course of the 19th century. Convinced that "only the re-education of Jews in Jewish schools—schools based on Haskalah principles and operated with the assistance of enlightened Jews—would lead to their 'gradual rapprochement [sblizhenie] with the Christian population and the eradication of superstitions and harmful prejudices instilled by the study of Torah,'"[48] Uvarov succeeded in getting a new law passed establishing special schools for the education of Jewish youth. By the mid-1850s, the Russian government had established a network of Haskalah based Jewish schools that rivaled the traditional talmudic Yeshivas in their influence over the rising generation of Jews in the Pale of the Settlement. What had been a persecuted minority in the days of Grigorii Peretts was now a powerful intellectual elite in search of a philosophy which would guide them out of the darkness of the Jewish past into the light of a promising but uncertain future. That elite had emancipated itself from the hegemony of the rabbis but had not as yet found a new home for itself in Russian culture. The disappointments which followed that search would lead that new generation of secularly educated Jews into the arms of the revolutionary movement which was then forming in western Europe.

IV

During the summer of 1830 Heinrich Heine was a little known poet vacationing on the island fortress of Helgoland with a soprano of the Hamburg opera who got a free summer vacation in exchange for serving as his mistress. His summer idyll was interrupted by the arrival of a newspaper announcing that revolution had broken out in France again, and immediately this Jewish convert to Protestantism felt the ancestral call of the race he had abandoned to advance his literary career. "Gone is my longing for peace and quiet," Heine wrote a few days later, "Once again I know what I want, what I ought, what I must do . . . I am a son of the revolution and will take up arms."[49] Almost before putting the newspaper down, Heine decided that he had to go to Paris to be part of the revolution there.

Heine had grown up in Duesseldorf when that German city was a French arrondissement as a result of Napoleon's conquests. Heine watched French soldiers march into his home town as a young boy and remained a devoted follower of Napoleon for his entire life. "I have never swerved from my faith in the Emperor," Heine wrote in 1852, "I have never ceased to doubt his advent—My Emperor—the ruler of the people for the people."[50] Heine's effusions about Napoleon at the end of his life indicate that it was no exaggeration to say that the Jews of Europe saw Napoleon as "the secular savior."[51] "We who have adopted a different symbolism see in the martyrdom of Napoleon at St. Helena no expiation in the sense here indicated, for the Emperor there did penance for his most fatal error, for his faithlessness to his mother, the Revolution." If Napoleon was the Messiah of the religion of revolution, Napoleon was also "the Moses of the French who like the latter has led the people through the desert in order to cure them."[52]

He was also the god that had failed. Napoleon's defeat had put an end to Jewish emancipation and plunged Jewish youth into utter disillusionment and despair, at least in 1814. In 1830, Napoleon was long dead, but it looked as if the spirit of revolution had returned. It was the converso Heine, who created the legend of Napoleon, the man who had unified Europe under the banner of revolution, to keep the idea of revolution alive, and his legend inspired generations of Jews from that time on. Heine felt that the "task of our time" was "emancipation....Not just of the Irish, the Greeks, the Frankfurt Jews, the West Indian blacks, and other oppressed people. It is the emancipation of the entire world, of Europe in particular. It has come of age and now tears itself loose from the iron reins of the privileged and the aristocracy."[53]

Heine was dismissed by many Germans as the quintessential rootless cosmopolitan Jew. Both Heine and his friend Ludwig Boerne were "born provocateurs, *ewige Ruhestoerer*, arousers, intellectual troublemakers. Both were at home first and foremost in the language. Their rootlessness provided a kind of Archimedian vantage point from which they assess the world with greater freedom wit, and acuity than others could. With Heine and Boerne, a new kind of engaged liberal intellect, soon decried as typically Jewish entered German life." According to Elon, "Both were baptized but remained Jews psychologically. Both were liberal polemicists, their recurrent theme liberty."[54] According to Heinrich von Treitschke: "With Boerne and Heine the eruption of the Jews into German literary history began, an ugly and infertile interlude."[55]

Heine, of course, wasn't a Jew, not unless race trumped religion. He was a converso, if by that term we mean a Jew who converted into an insincere Christian for apparently opportunistic reasons. Heine became famous for saying that the baptismal certificate was "the entrance ticket to European culture."[56] His cynical manipulation of the sacrament showed that religion was not something his age took as seriously as race, and his baptism of convenience ensured the rise of racial consciousness as well, a rise he knew would not bode well for Jews.

Heine converted to Christianity, but his hoped for position never materialized, and so he was forced to live off his rich uncle Salomon from Hamburg. The conversion to Christianity didn't do much for Heine's morals. He contracted syphilis in his youth and died of the malady in 1856. When he was 18, Robert Schumann met Heine in Munich in 1828 and was struck by his "bitter ironic smile."[57] Schumann, who set many of Heine's poems to music, also died of syphilis. The "bitter ironic smile" was to become Heine's trademark and a characteristic of the Jewish revolutionary manqué who turned to literature as a way of pursuing the revolution by other means.

As the revolution of 1830 continued to spread, Heine joined Boerne in Paris. Heine met Boerne in 1827. Boerne was a Jew, who had converted to Christianity in 1813. Both Boerne and Heine became disillusioned with politics after the revolution of 1830 failed to spread to Germany. Unlike Boerne, whose conversion may have been sincere, Heine found his voice as the rootless cosmopolitan. After the failure of the revolution of 1830, Heinrich briefly contemplated joining Boerne in Switzerland as co-editor of a new magazine, but before he could join Boerne there, the *Augsburger Allgemeine Zeitung* offered him its job as their Paris correspondent. Heine was only to happy to accept the offer, because by then he had fallen in love with Paris, where he felt "like a fish in water" or like, more tellingly, like "Tannhaeuser imprisoned in the Venusberg."[58]

In 1835, Heine's works were banned in Germany and his return was therefore made impossible. In order to console himself for the loss of a country, Heine went on to make the acquaintance of the leading literary and revolutionary figures in the French capital. It was there that he met Marx and Engels. It was there that he met Ferdinand Lassalle, with whom he corresponded on a number of subjects including the music of Felix Mendelssohn, a talented Jew (Heine ignored Mendelssohn's conversion almost as much as he ignored his own) who wasted his talent, at least in Heine's view, on Christian themes. "I cannot forgive this man of independent means," Heine wrote to Ferdinand Lassalle in 1846, "because he sees fit to serve the Christian pietists with his great and enormous talent. The more I admire his greatness, the more angry I am to see it so iniquitously misused. If I had the good fortune to be Moses Mendelssohn's grandson, I would not use my talents to set the piss of the Lamb to music."[59]

As a result of his friendship with Marx and Engels and Lassalle, Heine had some prophetic things to say about Communism. In 1842, he wrote:

> Though Communism is at present little talked about, vegetating in forgotten attics on miserable straw pallets, it is nevertheless the dismal hero destined to

play a great, if transitory role in the modern tragedy...[It will be] the old absolutist tradition...but in different clothes and with new slogans and catch-phrases ..
. There will then be only one shepherd with an iron crook and one identically
shorn, identically bleating human herd...Somber times loom ahead...I advise our
grandchildren to be born with a very thick skin.[60]

Heine soon made a literary name for himself in Paris, where he associated
with the leading literary figures of his day, Victor Hugo, Honore Balzac, Alexander Dumas, Alphonse de Lamartine, Alfred de Musset and George Sand. His
poetry came out in French. He was patronized by wealthy Jews like Baron James
de Rothschild, but that didn't stop him from writing poetry that appealed to the
communists. His poem on the impoverished weavers of Silesia found sympathy
among the communists. Friedrich Engels translated "The Weavers" into English,
and in the 20th century it became the name of a folk singing act in America of
communist persuasion. Treitschke, speaking from the point of view which had
banned Heine's poems in Germany, claimed that he possessed "the graceful vice
of making the mean and loathsome attractive for a moment."[61]

Even though Heine became famous in France, he never became a French
citizen, in spite of the fact that he married a French Catholic. He became instead
the alienated cosmopolitan, the German poet of *Heimweh* in exile, and a model
for European Jews who had tired of imitating Mendelssohn. Metternich admired
Heine as "the best mind among the conspirators." Indeed, that admiration led
Metternich to orchestrate the banning of his writings in Germany, an act which
simply confirmed the German Jews in their cosmopolitanism.

Paul Johnson, following Metternich's lead, saw Heine as the quintessential
subversive Jew. "It was as though," Johnson continued, "a superfine talent had
been building up in the ghetto over many secret generations, acquiring an ever
more powerful genetic coding, and then had suddenly emerged to find the German language of the early nineteenth century its perfect instrument."[62] Heine invented the literary essay, the feuilliton, as a genre and with it the *persona* of the
cosmopolitan literary man, the man with no allegiance to anything discernible,
who could deflate every pretense with his penetrating wit. Heine was in this regard "both the prototype and the archetype of a new figure in European literature:
the Jewish radical man of letters, using his skill, reputation and popularity to undermine the intellectual self-confidence of established order."[63]

Heine's uncle died in 1844 and left him a small pension, but unfortunately his
health gave out at the same time. Engels saw Heine in January 1848 and wrote that
"*Heine is am Kaputgehen*. I was with him two weeks ago when he was lying in bed
after an attack of nerves (*einen Nervenanfall*). Yesterday he was up and about but
still miserable. He can hardly take three steps on his own, creeping along the wall
supporting himself from the easy chair to the bed and back again." Elon writes
that "Heine's last several years were spent in the throes and excruciating pain of a
viral disease that paralyzed half his body and severely affected his vision."[64]

Other biographers were less evasive, claiming that "After 1844 Heine suffered financial reversals and painful physical deterioration from syphilis, the disease which also afflicted Schumann. He spent the last several years of his life in his 'mattress-grave' in a Paris apartment."[65] During his later years, his followers saw in him a Christ-like figure which had more to do with his doleful appearance than his morals. When asked about preparing his soul for the next life, Heine responded by saying "If I could walk with crutches I'd go to church, and if I could walk without I'd go to the whorehouse."[66] Heine was not a Jew, because of his baptism, but it is not clear he was a sincere Christian either. In attempting to pinpoint his real identity, Elon claims that Heine "remained loyal to his Jewish heritage only. . . out of deep antipathy to Christianity." And yet Heine saw that Europe without Christianity was going to be a much different place, which was going to be much more dangerous for Jews. Heine's prophetic verdict on the Germany of the future is never quoted because it lays the blame for Jewish suffering on neopaganism and not the Catholic Church, but it is worth citing, if as nothing else than his epitaph, and in some sense the final monument to his work as a subversive Jew:

> A drama will be enacted in Germany compared to which the French Revolution will seem like a harmless idyll. Christianity restrained the martial ardor of the Germans for a while but it did not destroy it; once the restraining talisman is shattered, savagery will rise again,...the mad fury of the berserk, of which Nordic poets sing and speak...The old stony gods will rise form the rubble and rub the thousand-year-old dust from their eyes. Thor with the giant hammer will come forth and smash the gothic domes.[67]

V

Karl Marx met Heine shortly after his arrival in Paris in 1843. Marx had been living Cologne, where he had been the youthful editor of the socialist *Rheinische Zeitung*. When the Prussian government closed the paper down, Marx emigrated to Paris, where he met up with the paper's founder, Moritz Hess, who took him on a tour of the working class districts of Paris and their revolutionary cafes. Hess, who would later change his name to Moses, was an early admirer of Marx. One year before Marx's arrival in Paris, Hess wrote to the German Jewish novelist Berthold Auerbach, praising him as the great revolutionary genius: "Imagine Rousseau, Voltaire, Holbach, Lessing, Heine, and Hegel all fused in one person... and you have Marx"[68]

Heine was, as we have noted, a converso. Marx, a generation Heine's junior, was a German Jew who had been baptized at the age of six in 1824, when Heinrich Marx, his father, led the entire family to the Lutheran baptismal font so that he could advance his career as a jurist in Trier. The conversion to Christianity caused no break in the Marx family. Even after his baptism, Heinrich would take his wife and children to regular Sabbath lunches held at the home of Karl's uncle, who also happened to be the chief rabbi of Trier. The only member of Heinrich Marx's family who seems to have taken religion seriously was Karl, who referred to it as the "opiate of the people" in *Towards a Critique of Hegel's Philosophy of Right: An Introduction*, 1848.

More than one scholar attributes that phrase to Moses Hess, who associated with both Heine and Marx in Paris but, unlike them, never converted to Christianity. The difference seems to derive from class and social aspiration. Hess was born in 1812, after Heine but before Marx, into a poor Jewish family from Cologne with virtually no prospects for upward mobility. Hess was raised by his grandfather, who taught him Talmudic lore, presumably in Yiddish because Hess had to teach himself German and then French. What Heine, Marx, and Hess had in common was neither religion, nor race, but the revolutionary spirit, which Hess and Heine saw as Jewish and Marx did not. Hess had been a utopian socialist up to his encounter with Marx, who so impressed him with his intellectual power that Hess was swept, for at least 20 years, into his intellectual orbit. It is some indication of Marx's intellectual stature (or Hess's intellectual malleability) that their collaboration was not disrupted by Marx's early writings, in particular his essay on The Jewish Question, which appeared in the same year that Hess welcomed Marx to Paris. Marx's essay has been characterized as anti-Semitic by more than one commentator, but Hess, later lionized as one of the fathers of Zionism, seems not to have noticed or been disturbed by the fact.

Marx wrote his essay in response to Bruno Bauer's claim that "If they wish to become free the Jews should not embrace Christianity, as such, but Christianity in dissolution, religion in dissolution; that its to say, the Enlightenment, criticism and its outcome, a free humanity."[69] Bauer's essentially Masonic critique of religion had been percolating through German society for 60 years, ever since the first performance of *Nathan der Weise*, by the time he got around to writing his essay. By the time Marx got ahold of the idea, it had ceased to represent the current historical options. Materialism, which had spread widely via Spinoza (and to some extent Descartes), had been nurtured by Whig subversives like Toland and Collins to the point where, now that it was finally mature, it turned around and slew its parents. Marx was the genius who made the supercession of the Enlightenment's categories perfectly clear to the remaining devotees of the Enlightenment. Communism, as the ideology of economic materialism was soon to be called, was the new sun which made the candle of the Enlightenment unnecessary. There was no point anymore, Marx makes clear, in talking about the religion of Judaism, as Lessing had done, because Judaism, according to Marx, was not a religion.

Unlike Bauer, Marx makes no attempt to "seek the secret of the Jew in his religion," but rather attempts "to seek the secret of their religion in the real Jew."[70] With that distinction in mind, Marx finds that "the proven basis of Judaism" is "practical need [and] self-interest; that "the worldly cult of the Jew" is "Huckstering," and that "his worldly god" is Money.[71] Once the Jewish religion has been deconstructed into economics, the new definition of the Jew leads to a handy resolution of the Jewish Question. The Jew will be emancipated when everyone else is emancipated from the tyranny of mammon and Jewish huckstering. It is only by destroying "practical Judaism," that "our age would emancipate itself."[72]

Beyond that,

> An organization of society which would abolish the preconditions and thus the very possibility of huckstering, would make the Jew impossible. His religious consciousness would evaporate like some insipid vapor in the real, life-giving air of society.... We discern in Judaism, therefore, a universal antisocial element of the present time, whose historical development, zealously aided in its harmful aspect by the Jews, has now attained its culminating point, a point at which it must necessarily disintegrate.... In the final analysis, the emancipation of the Jews is the emancipation of mankind from Judaism.[73]

During the course of his essay, Marx discovers that a false Jewish emancipation (which is to say one according to the Jewish, i.e., capitalist perspective) has already been taking place in the wake of the French Revolution as Jews insinuated themselves into positions of economic leadership in what claimed to be Christian countries. All of the talk about Jewish emancipation is meaningless, because the Jew has already emancipated himself in a Jewish fashion: "The Jew who is merely tolerated in Vienna, for example, determines the fate of the whole Empire by his financial power... the audacity of industry mocks the obstinacy of medieval institutions."[74] According to Marx, the main vehicle for Jewish emancipation is turning Christians into Jews through the manipulation of the power of money:

> This is not an isolated instance. The Jew has emancipated himself in a Jewish manner, not only by acquiring the power of money, but also because money has become, through him and also apart from him, a world power, which the practical Jewish spirit has become the practical spirit of the Christian nations. The Jews have emancipated themselves in so far as the Christians have become Jews.[75]

Neither Judaism nor Judaized Christianity are religions. Both are "ideologies," which is to say, rationalizations of economic exploitation, as is the Enlightened Freemasonry which claimed to transcend both. Religion, according to Marx, is nothing but a sublimated form of economic interest, and this is nowhere better expressed in religious form than in the "religion" of Judaism or in national form than in the United States of America. As Graetz was to substantiate 20 years later when he wrote about the Puritans in his history of the Jews, the American Yankees are judaizers; they worshipped the god of the Jews, which is money:

> the devout and politically free inhabitant of New England is a kind of Laocoon who makes not the least effort to escape from the serpents which are crushing him. Mammon is his idol which he adores not only with his lips but with the whole force of his body and mind. In his view the world is no more than a Stock Exchange, and he is convinced that he has no other destiny here below than to become richer than his neighbor. Trade has seized upon all his thoughts, and he has no other recreation than to exchange objects. When he travels, he carries, so to speak, his goods and his counter on his back and talks only of interest

and profit....In North America, indeed, the effective domination of the Christian world by Judaism has come to be manifested in a common and unambiguous form: they preach of the Gospel itself, Christian preaching has become an article of commerce.[76]

Marx is proposing here a dialectic according to which Christianity emerged from Judaism in the time of antiquity and was then reabsorbed by it in the period following the Protestant revolutions of the 16th century, especially those which took place in England, where Marx would do much of his research. So, "From the beginning, the Christian was the theorizing Jew; consequently, the Jew is the practical Christian. And the practical Christian has become a Jew again.... Christianity is the sublime thought of Judaism; Judaism is the vulgar practical application of Christianity."[77]

Once upon a time, Jews became Christians, but now the opposite is occurring; Christians are becoming Jews insofar as they are falling to their knees in worshipping "the god of practical need and self-interest," which happens to be money because

> Money is the jealous god of Israel, beside which no other god may exist. Money abases all the gods of mankind and changes them into commodities. Money is the universal and self-sufficient value of all things. It has, therefore, deprived the whole world, both the human world and nature, of their own proper value. Money is the alienated essence of man's work and existence; this essence dominates him and he worships it.[78]

When Marx says that "Christianity issued from Judaism. It has now been reabsorbed into Judaism,"[79] he is referring to the convergence of German and Jew brought about by the Enlightenment and German *Bildung*. Religion has ceased to be an issue. In its place, as we have seen, the German Enlightenment proposed German culture as the religiously neutral meeting ground for Enlightened Christians and Jews, but in the shock which followed Napoleon's conquest and the forced imposition of the tenets of the French Revolution, German culture lost its neutrality and became nationalistic instead. That in turn raised the question of what exactly nationalism was, and now the German principalities, deprived of the religious basis of the state had to look elsewhere for the principles which united them. The Jews were in exactly the same situation. Deprived of religious unity because Talmudic Judaism had been discredited as superstitious mumbo jumbo, the Jew could assimilate into German culture if he chose by converting or he could look for a principle of Jewish unity elsewhere. Marx proposed one alternative in class. Jews could now become the vanguard of the proletariat, and all the world could unite in the service of that class. Communism would become as a result a potent source of Jewish unity in the aftermath of the Enlightenment's attack on the Talmud.

A few years later, Moses Hess would propose race as the basis of Jewish unity. What both alternatives had in common was their common espousal of revolution, which became then a significant sign of first German and then eastern European Jews. In claiming that "the chimerical nationality of the Jew is the nationality of the trader, and above all of the financier,"[80] Marx was claiming that all nationality was chimerical, if only because "The god of the Jews has been secularized and has become the god of this world." Insofar as the modern state based its deliberations ultimately on economic considerations, it had become Jewish because "the bill of exchange is the real god of the Jew." In countries like this, the legal profession became a form of "Jewish Jesuitism, the same practical Jesuitism which Bauer discovers in the Talmud," namely, "the relationship of the world of self-interest to the laws which govern this world, laws which the world devotes its principal arts to circumventing."[81] Marx's analysis was a brilliant explanation of how capitalism was the Jewish religion; what it failed to explain was how revolution was on its way to becoming the competing new Jewish religion which would enter into a hundred year struggle with the old.

When the Revolution of 1848 broke out, Marx rushed off to supply the Belgian workers with arms, seeking in his way to bring about "the social emancipation of the Jews" through "the emancipation of society from Judaism." Others began to fear that the exact opposite was happening when they noticed that the revolutionary movement was disproportionately represented by Jews. The Jewish hegemony over Christian Europe which coincided with the rise of capitalism was now being threatened by a new form of Jewish hegemony, that of the Jewish revolutionary.

When word of the Revolution reached Heidelberg in February, Ludwig Bamberger, a native of the Jewish ghetto in Mainz and now in exile, saw in the latest revolution "a new world being born in one stroke."[82] Bamberger had attended a Catholic gymnasium in Mainz, but "like many other young intellectuals of Jewish origin, he was a free thinker by conviction, a republican and a follower of the early French utopian socialists. . . a son not of the synagogue but of the emancipation."[83] In Mainz, Bamberger, who would go on to be a representative in the new if short-lived revolutionary government, was known as "Red Ludwig," and before long, the non-revolutionary Germans began to notice that "Jews. . . nearly everywhere. . . were naturally among the rebels, and in some cities, among the leaders."[84] Jews were "natural" revolutionaries. In the widely read Jewish magazine *Der Orient*, Adolf Jellinke "urged all young Jews to join the revolution" because "Every Jew is born a soldier of Freedom .... His religion teaches him to be free, to pursue equal rights and to defend the oppressed."[85] Elon gives other examples of Jews promoting revolution:

> The leading Jewish family magazine, the *Allgemeine Zeitung des Judentums*, on March 11 called upon its readers to join this "timely movement sincerely and with all your hearts." The editors of the religiously traditional , politically conservative magazine *Der Treue Zionswaechter*, normally eager to please the authorities, found the courage to announce that their fondest dreams were coming true.[86]

After spending 6000 gold francs of his own money (inherited from his father, of course) to buy arms for the workers of Brussels. Marx traveled from Paris to Duesseldorf and then Cologne spreading copies of his recently published Communist Manifesto wherever he went, but before long it became obvious that this revolution, far from abolishing the practical Judaism of capitalism, was simply promoting the new Judaism of revolution. The proof of that fact was the predominance of Jews in the revolutionary movement. The Germans whose lives had been disrupted by the revolution began to notice that "a disproportionately high number [of the revolutionaries] were young Jews," primarily because "the prospect of equality under the law, separation of church and state, universal suffrage, and freedom from arbitrary rule generated unbridled enthusiasm and support among young men only a generation or two out of the ghetto."[87]

In Frankfurt and Breslau, according to *Der Orient*, Jews were "leaders of the freedom movements or among those who had organized them."[88] The most prominent were Ludwig Bamberger in Mainz, Ferdinand Lassalle in Duesseldorf, Gabriel Riesser in Hamburg, Johan Jacoby in Koeningsberg, Aron Bernstein in Berlin, Herman Jellinek in Vienna, Moritz Harmann in Prague, and Sigismund Asch in Breslau.

Ferdinand Lassalle, a friend of Heine, who dreamed of liberating the Jews in his youth, got his chance when the revolution arrived in Duesseldorf, Heine's home town. Lassalle's efforts would ensure that one of the "best-organized, best-disciplined uprisings...took place in Duesseldorf."[89]

As some confirmation of this general perception, reaction in the form of anti-Semitic riots followed in the wake of the revolution, especially in rural areas, where Jews were perceived as an especially alien element. Before long Christian rulers became convinced that Jews were responsible for starting the Revolution of 1848. Frederick William IV [of Prussia] subscribed to this view, claiming that the revolution was masterminded by "budding South German Robespierres and Jews." Elon dismisses the "myth" that "Jews and other foreign elements" were responsible for the Revolution of 1848, but only after telling us that "hundreds, perhaps thousands...[of Jews] participated in the clashes," including "80 percent of all Jewish journalists, doctors, and other professionals." Given evidence like this, it is not surprising then that the "myth" continued to spread in the years following 1848. Again, the evidence comes from Elon himself:

> In his memoirs Gerna Karl von Prittwitz, the officer commanding the Prussian garrison in Berlin, laid the principle blame for the uprising on Jews, rascals and vagabonds. According to the nationalist historian Heinrich Treitschke, the Jews had been the revolution's "Oriental cheerleaders." The *Neue Preussische Zeitung* of January 28, 1849, offered to pay a million Gulden to anyone who produce a "Jewish reactionary."...At year's end, even the *London Standard* claimed that "all the mischief now brooding on the continent is done by Jews."[90]

In Berlin, Leopold Zunz was a Jewish revolutionary who described what was happening in specifically biblical terms shot through with the Messianic political view which saw revolutionary politics as the fulfillment of biblical promise. Haranguing the Berlin students from the barricades, Zunz portrayed Metternich as Haman and hoped that "perhaps by Purim, Amalek will be beaten."[91] Amalek in this instance was the Prussian king Friedrich Wilhelm IV, but he symbolized (as a Protestant) "the plutocrats and bureaucrats, the black-robed papist diplomats of Metternich" who were going to perish in the bloody conflagration which would inaugurate "a new age of peace and social justice: heaven on earth seemed imminent."[92]

According to Elon, "Zunz's eschatological vision was not an isolated case. All over the country, rabbis in their sermons greeted the revolution as a truly messianic event....'The savior for whom we have prayed has appeared. The fatherland has given him to us.'" "The messiah is freedom," raved the Jewish magazine *Der Orient*: The magazine praised "the heroic Maccabean battle of our brethren on the barricades of Berlin."[93]

Berthold Auerbach, who became famous as the author of a series of sentimental German novels which glorified the salutary effects of his natal village in the Black Forest on Catholic-Jewish relations, manned the barricades in Vienna with other revolutionary Jews in September of 1848. By that time, however, it was clear that the revolution's days were numbered. Croatian troops loyal to the Austrian emperor set up artillery emplacements around Vienna and began to bombard to the city. Soon those same troops had routed the revolutionaries from their barricades and began looting the city as part of their reward. Before long, the Jewish hucksters which Marx had pilloried went into action after the revolutionaries had been routed, buying back from the Croatians what they had looted a fraction of its actual cost. In June of 1849, the revolutionary assembly offered the crown to Frederick William of Prussia, who repaid the favor by having his troops drive the assembly from its home in Stuttgart. One more revolution had failed, and Marx fulminated that the only ones who profited were the Jewish hucksters who amassed fortunes by buying back loot from the looters at a discount.

The failure of the Revolution of 1848 affected Hess every bit as deeply as Marx but in a different way. If Marx emerged from the aftermath of the revolution convinced that class warfare was the wave of the future, Hess came to the opposite conclusion, claiming that race was going to fulfill the promise of revolution. Hess broke with Marx after the failure of the Revolution of 1848, but Frankel says that "Hess never severed his links with German socialism" because "For Hess, socialism and nationalism were always integrally connected—the nation or the proletariat within the nation was the instrument and socialism was the goal."[94]

At moments like this the uncanny similarities between Hess's national socialism (which came to be known as Zionism years after his death) and Hitler's version of national socialism become too numerous to ignore. But more on that later.

Hess spent years in revolutionary poverty, years in which he considered migrating to Texas or Palestine, until 1851 when his father died and a small inheritance allowed him to marry Sybil Pritsch (or Plesch), the prostitute who had been his mistress. By 1848, he had abandoned Marx, largely because of the latter's ruthlessness and the constant political infighting which was necessary to remain abreast of the movement. Hess attached himself to the more moderate theories of Lassalle, whom Marx, in referring to Lassalle's hair and dark features, described as "the Jewish Nigger." Frankel characterizes Hess as "a man easily influenced and easily disheartened, a man of sudden enthusiasms, lonely, dependent on others for leadership" who nonetheless "remained true throughout to the broad outlines of his earliest vision—of a monistic and purposeful historical development that would culminate in the ideal egalitarian society."[95]

The discontinuities in Hess's intellectual life are, however, more apparent that the continuities because the man who joined in with Marx in denouncing Judaism as the worship of money eventually resurrected the same religion as the worship of race. After drifting intellectually like a ship without a rudder for a number of years, Hess suddenly found new inspiration when he read the first volume of Heinrich Graetz's monumental *History of the Jews*. Suddenly, the nation of money grubbing hucksters took on a hitherto unrecognized nobility in his eyes. Hess read Graetz at a time when nationalistic movements of unification were sweeping through both Italy and Germany, and so it should come as no surprise that Hess, disillusioned with Marx's ruthless engine of class warfare, should find a more palatable if equally revolutionary alternative in the Jewish nationalism that would eventually become known as Zionism. The work Hess wrote to give simultaneous expression to his conversion to racial thinking and his Jewish roots was *Rom und Jerusalem*. Hess wrote his magnum opus in 1862 while residing in Germany when a wave of racial feeling was sweeping the German principalities toward unification in 1870 under Prussian hegemony. Hess was a Freemason, and during his twenties he identified himself as a German and felt that it was the duty of every Jew to assimilate to German culture. By the 1860s, faced with the rise of German nationalism and the anti-Semitism which had increased with each subsequent revolution, Hess rejected the Masonic ideal of the merger of all religions and put the religion of race in its place. The only thing which remained constant was the Jewish penchant for revolution and the antipathy toward the Catholic Church, which was the other side of the same coin.

In returning to his roots, Hess returns to the ancestral Jewish hatred of the Catholic Church:

> Ever since Innocent III conceived of the plan to annihilate morally the Jews who brought the light of Spanish culture into Christendom by forcing them to wear the badge of shame up until the time that a Jewish child was kidnapped from its home under the regime of Cardinal Antonelli, papal Rome has been nothing less than a unconquerable swamp of poison which even our German Christian enemies have decided to drain so that it might die of starvation.[96]

The eternal antipode of the Jewish people is Rome, as in the Rome of the popes, which at that very moment was being besieged by the forces of Italian nationalism. The decline of Rome, which Hess was then witnessing with his own eyes, meant the rise of Jerusalem:

> with the liberation of the eternal city on the Tiber, the emancipation of the eternal city on Mt. Moriah begins. The rebirth of Italy signals the resurrection of Judea. Jerusalem's orphaned children will also be able to take part in the great ethnogenesis which marks the resurrection from the death-like hibernation of the Middle Ages with its evil dreams.[97]

This historic event was intimately bound up with the history of revolution. In fact, it was the culmination of that history. The springtime of race began with the French Revolution; the year 1789 was the vernal equinox of the historical peoples. The Jewish race, largely as a result of Napoleon's efforts, had been liberated by revolution, so that it could now follow its historic calling, namely uniting the world in fraternal harmony by bringing the revolutionary era to its fulfillment:

> the Jewish race is being carried on the floodtide of events; from the ends of the earth their gaze turns toward Jerusalem. With the secure racial instincts of their cultural-historical calling to unite the world and its peoples and to bring together in fraternal harmony, the Jewish race has preserved its nationality in its religion and now both are united under their eternal creator the All in One, in the ineffable land of their fathers.[98]

At this point an uncanny convergence of opinion begins to emerge. Like Marx, both Hess and the Catholic reaction were unanimous in believing that the French Revolution had brought about the hegemony of the Jews in France. Their only difference concerned the value judgments which they attached to that fact. For both Marx and the Catholic reaction, the hegemony of the Jews was known as capitalism, and the state of affairs was bad. For Hess, who also believed that the revolution led to the hegemony of the Jews, the present historical moment offered an unprecedented opportunity for the Jewish people:

> Germany blazed the path of philosophy; the French on the other hand are responsible for the great political social transformation, which goes hand in hand with the progress of the exact sciences. The French showed the rest of the world this way through their great Revolution, asking the nations to follow their example.[99]

The Jewish nation could take the lead in revolutionary activity and become in effect the Messiah for which it had waited millennia in vain. According to Barbara Tuchman, Hess got the idea from Heinrich Graetz: "The rise of Jewish nationalism became apparent in 1864 when Heinrich Graetz wrote that Jews must become their own Messiah."[100]

Suddenly Hess, as he put it in *Rom und Jerusalem*, found himself again in the midst of his people after a 20-year absence:

The one thought that I tried to suppress in my own breast is there alive in front of me: the idea that my nationality is inseparable from the DNA of my fathers, from the Holy Land and from the eternal city, which is the birthplace of the Faith in the divine unity of life and the future brotherhood of all Men.[101]

For Hess, race was the primary reality. Race is the source of the Jewish faith (and not the other way around), but more importantly it is the source of "the divine unity of life and future brotherhood of all Men," from which a powerful political movement can emerge to create heaven on earth. Race is the source of family, and it "is out of this invincible source of Jewish family love that the savior of mankind will come."[102] Hess combined Jewish Messianism with the principle of Equality he had learned from the French Revolution and came up with a new racial revolutionary ideal: "Every Jew has the makings of a Messiah in him. Every Jewess, a mater dolorosa."[103]

Hess is a racist who feels that religion derives from race. "Judaism is not a passive religion, rather it is an active recognition, which is organically indistinguishable from the Jewish race."[104] Judaism is racial, but it is also revolutionary because race is the logical conclusion of the French Revolution:

> Today's nationalism is nothing more than a journey down the road which the French Revolution opened for all mankind. Ever since their great Revolution during the century past, the French people have been calling on all the peoples of the world for help. [105]

Eight years after the publication of *Rom und Jerusalem*, Wilhelm Marr popularized the term "anti-Semitism" to convey the idea that being Jewish was racial and not religious. Faithfully mirroring the German anti-Semitism which he sensed in the ascendancy, Hess proposes the Jewish version of the same thing. According to Hess, race trumps every other consideration, including baptism. As a result there is no reason for a Jew to deny his Jewishness anymore by succumbing to conversion. Hess launches a vicious attack on assimilation, while at the same time conforming in a uncanny way to the rising tide of German racism:

> Because of the anti-Semitism which surrounds him on all sides, the German Jew is always inclined to strip himself of any Jewish characteristics and to deny his race. No reform of the Jewish religion is radical enough for these cultured Jews. Not even baptism can save him from the nightmare of German anti-Semitism. The Germans hate Jewish religion less than they hate the Jewish race, less their peculiar faith than their peculiar noses..... Black kinky Jewish hair isn't transformed into blonde hair by baptism and it isn't made straight by any comb. The Jewish race is the original race which reproduces itself in its integrity in spite of climatic influences. The Jewish type has remained unchanged over the course of the centuries.[106]

Hess's rejection of baptism would find uncanny fulfillment in the racial policies of Hitler, who felt that Jewishness was biological and therefore ineradicable.

He goes to absurd lengths to prove this, citing "Egyptian monuments from a later period [which] depict Jews whose similarities with our contemporaries is striking."[107] The only problem with racial theories in general and this one in particular is that subsequent biology, in particular the Genome project, seems to show that Ashkenazi Jews were not Semites. They have nothing in common genetically with the Semites Moses led out of Egypt.

The main point of the appeal to race is to show that baptism is pointless: "You see, my dear friend, that it is pointless for Jews to get baptized and to deny their heritage by attempting to immerse itself in the great ocean of indogermanic and Mongolian tribes. The Jewish type is ineradicable."[108] Once again, Hess supplies the rationale for Hitler's extermination campaign against the Jews. If the Jewish type is both "ineradicable," which Hess claimed, and bad, which Hitler claimed, then extermination (or at least forced exile) is the only solution to the Jewish problem. Marx's proposal to eliminate Judaism by eliminating capitalism seems humane by comparison. But Hess seems determined to put all of his eggs in the racial basket: The "modern" Jew, who denies his Jewish nationality, is not only an apostate or renegade in the religious sense of he word, he is also "a traitor to his race and his family."[109]

Hess may have started out in biology, but he quickly ended up espousing the "Messianic faith" of the Revolutionary Jew which got hatched at the foot of the cross. Indeed, the two components are closely related since race was now offering the Jews a better faith than the one they rejected at the foot of the cross. The idea first occurred to him when he was a communist:

> This, my friend, was my thinking during the time I was working for the benefit of the European proletariat. My messianic faith was then what it is today, faith in the rebirth of the world historical cultural races by raising up what had sunken so low to the level of that which has been exalted. Today, as when I first started publishing, I still believe that Christianity was a big step on the way to a noble goal, one which the prophets had called the Messianic period. Today, as then, I still believe, that this period of world history began to emerge in the mind of humanity with Spinoza. But I never believed, nor did I ever say that Christianity would have the last word in mankind's salvation history, or that Spinoza was the endpoint of that history. What is certain, and what I have never doubted, is that today we are longing for a much broader salvation than Christianity has ever, or could ever, offer. Christianity was the evening star, which rose to give consolation to the nations for the eclipse of antiquity.[110]

As proof that Israel's historical moment has arrived, Hess sites the fact that the papal states are on their last legs. "The Italian nation has risen up from the ruins of Christian Rome."[111] The Italian Freemasons are only bringing to completion what the French Revolution began, because "The soldiers of modern civilization, the French, break the hegemony of the barbarians. With their Herculean arms, they rolled back the stone from the tomb of those who have fallen asleep and the nations are waking."[112] Now the Jews are ready to succeed the Italians as the racial vanguard of revolution, just as the Italians succeeded the French. The future is being announced by Jewish Movements. Hess cites Simon bar Kokhba and Shabbetai Zevi as avatars of the current Messianic, i.e., revolutionary age:

> Once again in this age, during the vernal equinox of humanity, the great future which all of us are facing, is being announced by Jewish movements of which the world has taken little note, but which have no less meaning that those which took place during the period of transition in Jewish history from antiquity to the middle ages. Already at the beginning of the modern period we witnessed a messianic movement of the sort the world had not seen since the destruction of the Temple and the bar Kokhba rebellion, one which energized both oriental and occidental Jews, whose false prophet was Shabbetai Zevi and whose true prophet was Spinoza. Even our modern Sadducees , Pharisees and Essenes, by which I mean the Reform Jews, the Rabbinics and the Hasids, will disappear without a trace once our critical epoch, the last crisis of world history has passed, after which the Nations, who have the Jews to thank for their historical religion, and with them the Jewish people as well will be reborn to new life. Judaism rejects both spiritualistic and materialistic sects. Jewish life is unitary, just like its God, and this unitary life is what is now reacting against modern Materialism, which is just the flip side of Christian spiritualism.[113]

Life is a direct result of race, which forms its social institutions according to innate faculties and inclinations. As a result, the Jewish penchant for revolution is inbred and ineradicable. Messianic biology is the true Jewish destiny. Now that the "spring of nationalism . . approaches its fruitful summertime," the "modern society which was born out of revolution regenerates itself by itself; it reforms not by sewing new patches on old wine skins but by creating completely new situations."[114] The essence of modernity is revolution, which is also the racial heritage of the Jewish people, according to Hess. "As long as the Jews failed to recognize the essence of modernity, which was from beginning to end their own essence as well, they were simply carried along by the current of modern history."[115] All that remains at this moment of history is for the Jewish race to become conscious of its true revolutionary identity. In order to be saved, all the Jews need to do is become what they are. Since all of philosophy and morals is ultimately Jewish in Hess's view, the French were only imitating Jews when their philosophes overthrew their Catholic king:

> There is nothing in Christian morals, neither in the scholastic philosophy of the Middle Ages, neither in modern Philanthropy, and if I add to that the final manifestation of Judaism, Spinozism, nothing in modern philosophy which is not rooted in Judaism. The Jewish people was, up until the time of the French Revolution, the only race in the world which had both a national and a humanitarian cult. It is through Judaism that the history of mankind became a holy, history, and by that I mean a unitary, organic process of development which began with the love of the family and which will not be completed until all of mankind becomes one family, whose limbs are united through the Holy Spirit, which is the creative genius of history.[116]

It is clear from the terminology that he uses that Hess is still under the sway of Heine's teacher Hegel. He shares this debt with Marx. However, as we have seen, Hess, unlike Marx, felt that race, as a biological phenomenon, not class was the vehicle for the religion of history. Revolution is the soul or *spiritus movens* of world history. The Jews kept this spirit alive in secret when people like Pope Innocent III ruled over Europe. The proof that they were God's chosen people lay in the fact that they kept this spirit of rebellion and revolution alive in the face of what seemed like insurmountable odds. But ever since the French Revolution, that smoldering ember, the one preserved by the Jews in their secret shrines, has burst into flame again. It is now the sacred duty of the Jews as acolytes of what Hess calls "the religion of history" to join in with the French and spread revolution to the rest of the world.

> As long as no nation other than the Jews had this national-humanitarian religion of history, the Jews were alone God's chosen people. But ever since the great Revolution, which has spread from France, we have in the French nation, as well and in other nations which have joined the French, noble rivals and true collaborators. With the final victory of these nations over the medieval reaction, the human aspiration, which I recognize wholeheartedly, will blossom and bear fruit.

According to Hess, "every modern race. . . has a special vocation as an organ of humanity."[117] As their special vocation, the Jews "have carried around with us the faith in the messianic epoch of the world since the beginning of history."[118] That messianic epoch has finally arrived, and it is the Jews who will bring the age to its fruition by spreading revolution throughout the world. Those who don't see this don't understand history. Those "who don't understand the revelation of the religious genius of the Jews" see nothing but chaos in the events around them. Those who do, understand that the 19th century is the Messianic Age, and that that age began with the French Revolution:

> This age began according to the tenets of our religion of history with the Messianic age. It is the time in which the Jewish nation and all historical peoples are raised from the dead to new life, the age of "the resurrection of the dead," the "return of the Lord", and the new Jerusalem, and other symbolic designations....The Messianic age is the present age, which began to sprout with Spinoza and which entered world historical reality with the great French Revolution. The rebirth of the nations began with the French Revolution, thanks to the religion of history which came from the Jews.[119]

Nearly every Jewish scholar refers to Hess as a proto-Zionist, but as Frankel rightly points out, this is in many ways an anachronism. Zionism would not appear on the stage or world history for at least another 30 years. When it became a significant political movement, the Zionists appropriated his writings and deemed Hess a prophet. It would be more accurate to refer to Hess as a Jewish revolutionary, as one more avatar of the Jewish revolutionary spirit which had emerged throughout history and which had caused the Jewish people so much sorrow. Hess was a prophet; he was the man who announced two of the most significant Messianic movements of human history—Zionism and Communism—movements which would occupy the full spectrum of Jewish political alternatives for the next century and a half, but he was also a revolutionary Jew with his feet planted firmly in the vocabulary of his age. As a result, his immediate prognosis was that "right now we are witnessing the final racial and class battles which will lead to a reconciliation of all opposites, and bring about an equilibrium between production and consumption."[120]

Like Jabotinsky after him, Hess felt that the way to the promised land in Palestine led through the travails of revolution in Europe. The Jews had to emulate the French before they could have a land of their own because it was "France, dear Friend, France" who was "the hero and savior, who put our race back on the tracks of world history."[121] This is the case not only because "the way of culture in the desert [has been] made straight by the Suez canal, and by rail lines that connect Europe and Asia,"[122] but more importantly because "the idea of taking possession of our Fatherland can only be taken seriously in an age in which all rigidity has been broken. And that has happened in our day, not only among the Enlightened, but also among the pious Jews and Christians."[123]

In other words, revolution cannot succeed until the Jews have been liberated from the obscurantism of the shtetls of the East. The *conditio sine qua non* which will enable the advent of the Messianic age is "the liberation of the Jewish masses from a spirit-deadening formalism."[124] The Jews can only achieve national unity through revolution because revolution is their racial essence. "Every Jew," according to Hess, "even the baptized, is responsible for the rebirth of Israel,"[125] but the Jews can only reach this promised land by wading through the river of revolution, "by fighting for liberated national soil, by the annihilation of every race and class membership from within and without."[126]

In a way that was sure to antagonize the Germans who read his book, Hess praised the French for inaugurating the modern revolutionary era. France, under Napoleon had "extend[ed] its salvific activity to the Jewish nation, after toppling the victorious armies of the modern Nebuchadnezzar from their thrones,"[127] but it was now up to the Jews to reciprocate by making the revolutionary cause their own. Since France got the idea of revolution from the Jews in the first place, it shouldn't be difficult to convince the Jews to become the revolutionaries they were *in potentia* all along, for as Hess asks, "What race is better suited for revolution than the Jews?"[128]

> It is up to France, to see the streets to India and China full of nations, who are willing to follow France to the death in order to fulfill their historical task, which has been their lot since their great Revolution. What race is better suited to that task than the Jews, who have been called to the same mission from the beginning of history?[129]

The German nation was still smarting from the Napoleonic conquests. Eight years after the publication of Hess's book they would lose a war and Alsace Lorraine to the French, creating further animosity. If Hess wanted to antagonize the Germans, who still had memories of Jewish collaboration with Napoleon in mind, he could have found no more effective way to do it than by linking Frenchmen and Jews in some common revolutionary enterprise.

Which is precisely what Hess did: "Frenchmen and Jews!" he wrote sailing off into the empyrean on the wings of one more revolutionary fantasy, "They were made for one another. They complement each other by the differences which could not be united in one people.... The generous assistance, which France lent to the civilized peoples in their restoration of their nationhood, will never find a more grateful race that the Jews.... The Jewish people must first show themselves worthy of the rebirth of their world historical cult."[130]

As Voltaire said of God, if Hess didn't exist, the German anti-Semites would have had to invent him because in Hess they found a writer who expressed their fantasies of the revolutionary Jew better than they could themselves. "Judaism is the religion of history," and Revolution is the essence of Judaism. The Enlightenment dream of Jewish assimilation which found its first expression in *Nathan der Weise*, found in Hess its assassin and the man who wrote its epitaph as well:

> Occidental Jews are still encased in an unbreakable crust, composed of the dead remains of the first stirrings of the modern spirit, from the organic calcified shell of an extinct rationalist Enlightenment which has not been melted by the fire of Jewish patriotism but can only be broken from pressure from without, whose force will exterminate anything which has no future....race can emerge from the hearts of our modern cultured Jews only by way of a violent shattering stroke from without.[131]

The pressure from without was the revolutionary spirit which as of the 1860s was spreading through the shtetls of the Pale of the Settlement releasing destructive energy whenever it "shattered the protective shell of orthodoxy."

The Revolution of 1848

Frederick Douglass

Chapter Fourteen

Ottilie Assing and the American Civil War

During the summer of 1830 Heinrich Heine cut his vacation on the island of Helgoland short and rushed off to join what came to be known as the Revolution of 1831 in Paris. "Gone," he wrote, "is my longing for peace and quiet. Once again I know what I want, what I ought, what I must do . . .I am a son of the revolution and will take up arms."[1]

On February 12, 1831, Nat Turner, a slave who had been born in Southhampton, Virginia in 1800, took a solar eclipse as the sign that he was to begin planning for a slave rebellion on the coming July 4. When another eclipse took place on August 13, Turner, who had been receiving visions with increasing frequency, was confirmed in his belief that the Lord wanted him to lead a rebellion. One week later, on August 21, Turner freed 50 fellow slaves and urged them to "kill all whites," regardless of age or gender. By the time the Virginia militia put down the rebellion 48 hours later, 57 men, women and children had been murdered by Turner's band of revolutionaries.

Turner eluded capture for another two months, but on October 30, he was found hiding in a cave, brought to trial, and hanged on November 11. His body was then dismembered and its various parts distributed as souvenirs of the crushed rebellion. His lawyer, Thomas Ruffin Gray, interviewed him in jail before his execution, and published *The Confessions of Nat Turner* after his death. In this account, Turner recounted the visions he had had throughout his life. As one has come to expect, revolutionary fervor in America had a religious cast, descending as it did from the enthusiast millennialist sects which had proliferated in England during the 17th century, many of whom ended up emigrating to America.

Slave rebellions had occurred throughout history, probably as long as the existence of slavery itself. One could cite the rebellion of Spartacus in Rome or the story of Moses and the Exodus as examples. The history of Negro chattel slavery in the New World was no different. Slave revolts had taken place in New York City in 1712, at Stono, South Carolina in 1739, and in Southern Louisiana in 1811. Numerous conspiracies had been broken up before they could emerge as full-blown revolts. The conspiracy at Point Coupee, Louisiana in 1795 was one example. To that could be added the conspiracies of Gabriel Prosser in Richmond, Virginia in 1800 and of Denmark Vesey in Charleston, South Carolina in 1822.[2]

But there was a new and disquieting element to Nat Turner's rebellion. The Turner rebellion sent a new wave of fear throughout the South because it included "the new forces that had been building since the American and French Revolutions."[3] These new forces "had secularized the cause of national-popular liberation and proclaimed the Rights of Man."[4] The slave revolt which best epitomized those "new forces" was the rebellion led by Toussaint L'Overture in Haiti.

Toussaint's rebellion had been set off not so much by the miserable conditions of servitude as by the arrival of French troops on that island in the wake of the revolution in France. The arrival in Sant Domingue of French soldiers imbued with the principles of liberty, fraternity, and equality and determined to spread those principles throughout the world convinced Toussaint L'Overture that these revolutionary principles had a direct application to the lot of Haiti's black slaves, and he spent the rest of his career creating a new revolutionary synthesis, and playing off the factions which opposed him against each other. The slave rebellions which had occurred since time immemorial now had a new ideological foundation in the principles which leaders of the French Revolution had articulated in the wake of their successful overthrow of the *ancien regime*.

In the wake of Toussaint's rebellion in Haiti in 1798, the world was a different place. W. E. B. Du Bois argued that Toussaint changed American history, largely because

> The interlocking French and Haitian revolutions shattered the tranquility... of the slave holding regions everywhere in the hemisphere and generated rational fear among the slaveholders. They stirred the slaves and free Negroes to rebellion under a modern ideology that posed a new and more dangerous threat to the old regimes than anything previously encountered. The threat declined after the collapse of Toussaint's rapprochement with France and Napoleon's brutal attempt to re-enslave the island. During the 1790s, however, the interest of revolutionaries of Paris in breaking the counterrevolutionary power of England and Spain, not to mention of their own Girondists, resulted in efforts, often carried by French-speaking blacks, to encourage slave revolts and movements for national liberation.[5]

Just as Toussaint L'Overture could invoke the Rights of Man, Denmark Vesey could claim that he was acting on the principles articulated in the Declaration of Independence. The fact that the leaders of slave rebellions appealed to the Declaration in this manner led Edwin Clifford Holland to describe blacks in the aftermath of the Vesey plot as "Jacobins":

> "Let it never be forgotten that our Negroes are freely the Jacobins of the country; that they are the Anarchists and the Domestic Enemy: the common enemy of civilized society, and the barbarians who would if they could become the destroyers of our race."[6]

The spectre of Toussaint in Haiti evoked fears in the mind of the South which refused to go away. Playing on those fears, William Watkins told a meeting of free Negroes in Baltimore in 1825 that Toussaint's rebellion provided "an irrefutable argument to prove that the descendants of Africa were never designed by their creator to sustain an inferiority, or even a mediocrity in the chain of being."[7] Thomas Jefferson noticed the same thing when he said, "the West Indies appears to have given considerable impulse to the minds of the slaves... in the United States."[8]

The condition of servitude among American blacks and the ideology of revolution then sweeping through Europe constituted a binary weapon. As soon as the two elements of that weapon made contact, an explosion would occur. Toussaint's revolution in Haiti was the first indication that the two elements had made contact. "The Haitian revolution," writes Eugene Genovese, "in contradistinction to one more rising of slaves, would have been unthinkable without the French Revolution.... The revolutionary ideology that emerged in the 1790s was fed from both sides of the Atlantic."[9]

The revolution in Saint-Domingue propelled a revolution in black consciousness throughout the New World. Louisiana became a natural conduit for this revolutionary ideology as it spread from the islands to the mainland of North America. The French language and the fact that Louisiana was still a French colony when the revolution in Saint-Domingue took place facilitated the movement of revolutionary ideology among black slaves. Revolutionary songs were still sung in French in Louisiana as late as the mid-19th century, where revolutionary oratory of the following sort could also be heard:

> "Brothers! The hour strikes for us; a new sun, similar to that of 1789, should surely appear on our horizon. May the cry which resounded through France at the seizure of the Bastille resonate today in our ears.... Let us all be imbued with these noble sentiments which characterize all civilized people.... In sweet accord with our brothers, let us fill the air with these joyous cries: *"vive la liberte, vive l'union! Vive la justice pour tous les hommes."*[10]

In Haiti, a slave revolt had become part of the revolutionary movement sweeping Europe. The great fear of the South was that that revolutionary movement would take root in America, a place where the soil seemed to offer the ideal conditions for any seeds the wind might blow from Europe or the Caribbean. American soil was fertile ground for revolution because that nation had been born out of revolution to begin with, and, secondly, because it still denied the liberty which flowed from that revolution to the black slaves living within its borders.

The situation in America was compounded by the fact that that country was based on two documents which contradicted each other when it came to the issue of slavery. The Constitution of the United States accepted slavery as one of the conditions of union, but the Declaration of Independence repudiated it when it claimed that all men were created equal and had the right to life, liberty and the pursuit of happiness. Thus it was not surprising that slaveholders discouraged black attendance at 4th of July celebrations. Nor was it surprising that the leaders of slave rebellions used the language of rebellion found in the Declaration of Independence against their own masters. That and the fact that Puritanism had never been repudiated in America, as it had in England, led to a strain of revolutionary thought that was uniquely America because it was made up of a mixture of Puritan and Enlightenment thought that in other parts of the world was considered self-contradictory. Tom Paine perfected the rhetoric of this dual vision in pamphlets like *Common Sense*. It was part of the lingua franca of American life and so it should come as no surprise that the leaders of slave rebellions in America would make use of it as well. "Each of these outstanding rebel leaders," Genovese notes, "blended religious appeals to the slaves with the accents of the Declaration of Independence and the Rights of Man. Each projected an interpretation of Christianity that stressed the God-given right to freedom as the fundamental doctrine of obligation underlying a political vision that itself reflected the new ideologies."[11] Even Denmark Vesey, who looked to Haiti for both spiritual guidance and material support for his rebellion, "combined the language of the Age of Revolution, as manifested in the Declaration of Independence and the Constitution, with the biblical language of the God of Wrath."[12] Neither Paul's Epistles, which counsel reconciliation and moderation in relations between masters and slaves, nor the Gospels seem on first reading congruent with the revolutionary manifestoes of the 18th century. But in America, scripture had always been refracted through the lens of 17th century Puritan judaizing, and no one could read the accounts of Gideon or of Moses and the Exodus and not think of ethnic political liberation movements, certainly not in the 19th century in America.

The South was of a different theological mind on this matter, but they had not descended from the Puritans, a group which their Cavalier ancestors had always identified with regicide and revolution. This split between Cavaliers and Roundheads was present in America at the moment of that nation's birth. Intellectually the United States were an uneasy alliance, held together at best by Enlightenment premises that papered over deeper divisions, divisions which only became more apparent at time went on. The South never got over its ambivalence toward the Declaration of Independence. And the North never got over its ambivalent feelings about a constitution which accepted slavery. "The southern Federalists," according to Genovese, "...berated the Jeffersonians for spreading a French gospel of liberty, equality, and fraternity that the slaves would hear, interpret with deadly literalness, and rally around. Increasingly, during the 19th century, slaveholders lectured each other on the need to keep blacks away from Fourth of July celebrations.... Every election campaign echoed the language of the American Revolution and threatened to generate slave unrest no matter how much care was taken to control the rhetoric."[13]

The Nat Turner rebellion was a sign that those hybrid seeds were now germinating on American soil. It was also a sign of the fault lines within the revolutionary movement itself. Unlike America, which retained the rhetoric of the Bible in its own revolutionary movement, the 19th century European revolutionary was radically secular and radically anti-Christian. When the French Revolution arrived in Haiti, it was radically anti-Christian as well. The revolutionaries went out of their way to eradicate any traces of Christianity from the hearts of potential black revolutionaries. Christianity was portrayed as an alien imposition on the black soul, which needed to be extirpated if the revolution was to have any chance of success.

The atheism of the French Revolution only made matters worse. Stories circulated of how the revolutionaries in Saint-Domingue tried to get the Negro slaves to abandon Christianity. In the early stages of the revolution in Saint-Domingue, the Voodoo priest Boukman urged his followers to discard their crucifixes as the first step to waging war against their oppressors: "Throw away the Symbol of the god of the whites who has often caused us to weep and listen to the voice of liberty, which speaks in the hearts of us all."[14]

The Haitian revolutionaries' abandonment of Christianity led to revolutionary excess which exacerbated the fears of the slaveholders in the South. One of those fears was that Negro slaves in throwing off Christian morality would rise up and violate white women. Nat Turner's rebellion did nothing to allay those fears, nor did the remark of the one of the Denmark Vesey rebel leaders that "the slaves would know what to do with white women,"[15] nor did the stories of how the rebels of Saint-Domingue had raped white women over the dead and dying bodies of their husbands.

The new fear which swept the American South in the wake of Nat Turner's rebellion was that the Haitian rebellion, which the French Revolution had inspired among black slaves there, would spread to the chattel slaves in the South. The South feared that Nat Turner was an imitation of Toussaint L'Overture and that what had happened in Haiti was destined to happen across the South. The South feared further that

> the French Revolution provided the condition in which a massive revolt in Saint-Domingue could become a revolution in its own right. The brilliance with which Toussaint L'Overture claimed for his enslaved brothers and sisters the rights of liberty and equality—of universal human dignity—that the French were claiming for themselves constituted a turning point in the history of slave revolts and, indeed, of the human spirit.[16]

The result of this fear was a hardening of the lines. The South felt beleaguered, and any of the human contacts between slave and master that led to a natural amelioration of the harshness of servitude were subordinated to the fear of revolution and the necessity of self-defense. Realizing that unity was the *sine qua non* of survival, the slaveholders persuaded whites of all classes to close ranks, something which coincided with the Nat Turner rebellion. After Nat Turner, "the slaves confronted a solid and overwhelming white majority until the end of the regime."[17]

The crucial link between Nat Turner and the European revolutionary movement was William Lloyd Garrison. Turner had taught himself how to read, but there is no indication that Nat Turner had ever heard of Heinrich Heine. Whether he had heard of William Lloyd Garrison was another matter. The South was convinced that Garrison's *Liberator* was responsible for the Nat Turner rebellion. The Nat Turner rebellion of 1831 had made Garrison a household word in America. Garrison was the impoverished son of an alcoholic seaman who learned the printing trade from the bottom up and launched his own newspaper, *The Liberator*, at around the same time that Heinrich Heine was heading off to Paris. No one in the North or the South had read anything like this before. The first issue was "unbelievably inflammatory."[18] The fact that within eight months of the first issue,

Nat Turner had butchered entire white families and burned down plantations was seen as proof in the South that *The Liberator* had inspired the uprising. "The Georgia senate," Scott writes, "tried Garrison in absentia, found him guilty of inciting insurrection, fined him $500 and set a price of $5000 on his delivery. That was a higher sum than Garrison and circle combined could raise, and his continued liberty remained as much of a marvel as the speed with which he had entered the consciousness of the nation through words alone."[19]

But behind the outrage, a deeper more troubling thought began to emerge. Were the United States, which at this point were less than 50 years old, really a nation, as the US claimed in its founding documents? Or had two nations emerged over the short period of time following the American Revolution? Revolutions throughout history had invariably led to civil wars among the victors. Now for the first time in its history, citizens of the United States were forced to confront the possibility that the same thing might occur in the wake of their revolution as well. Garrison's role in the Nat Turner rebellion also called racial solidarity into question. "What shocked White southerners," Scott writes, "was the realization that men of their own race, in their own country, would consign them to death at the hands of another race."[20] The fact that the North did nothing to stop Garrison's attempt to foment slave rebellion undercut whatever national solidarity the Southerners might otherwise have felt. Garrison fueled "the suspicion that a Nat Turner might be in every family; that the same bloody deed might be acted over at any time and in any place; that the materials for it were spread through the land, and were always ready for a like explosion."[21]

The Turner rebellion and Garrison's propaganda polarized the nation less than 50 years after its inception. The question of slavery divided the North and the South, and that polarization would find its ultimate expression in a civil war which would break out 30 years in the future. The theoretical divide in the United States was based on that nation's two founding documents. The citizens of the United States were forced to choose between the Constitution, which accommodated the institution of slavery to make the union possible, and the Declaration of Independence, which opposed slavery in theory when it announced that all men were created equal and had an inalienable right to liberty. By the time of the civil war, the revolutionary party felt that the Declaration of Independence had rendered the Constitution morally inoperable.

The slave rebellions created a determination in the South to resist no matter what the cost, and that cost included union. At the same time, Nat Turner and the slave rebellions in the Caribbean became an inspiration for northern white revolutionaries like John Brown, whose Messianic politics, in true American fashion, partook equally of the Declaration of Independence, the Rights of Man and Cromwell's appropriation of selected passages of the Old Testament. Tom Paine had used the same volatile mix of Enlightenment science and Old Testament Judaizing to enflame the colonists against King George. Now the same revolutionary spirit was reborn among the abolitionists:

John Brown, who had taken inspiration and instruction from the experience of the Jamaican maroons, missed the point to his cost when he envisioned impregnable guerilla bases in the Allegheny Mountains. Long before Harper's Ferry, he planned to secure these bases with the support of dissident poor mountain whites, whose racism he seems to have underestimated and whose ideology and politics he certainly misjudged.[22]

As in England during the 1790s, so in America during the first half of the 19th century: the descendents of the Puritan revolutionaries had become admirers of the French Revolution. Like Rev. Price's congregation in England, the revolutionary party in America, before the advent of the German refugees of the failed Revolution of 1848, was overwhelmingly Unitarian. Edmund Burke, who wrote his reflections on the French Revolution in response to Rev. Price's sermons, considered the Unitarians a political party and not a religion, and wanted them shut down as inherently seditious. Similarly, "The entire abolitionist movement was essentially a revolt of young clergymen and seminarians."[23]

Chief among them was Dr. William Ellery Channing. The father of American Unitarianism, an open admirer of the French Revolution who "had been influenced early by the writings of Rousseau, Voltaire, and other 'bearers of light.'"[24] Dr. Channing, according to Scott,

> had been deeply impressed by the English Unitarian Richard Price, whose book he said, "Probably molded my philosophy into the form it has always retained, and opened my mind into the transcendental depths. And I have always found in the accounts I have read of German philosophy in Madame de Stael... that it was cognate to my own."[25]

It was precisely this influence of Unitarianism from England—with its denial of the divinity of Jesus and the literal truth of the bible, its open scorn and dislike of whatever remained of Calvinism and Puritanism and Presbyterianism—that made Dr. Channing anathema to the older, more orthodox clergymen of Boston. "It was precisely his approval of the higher criticisms of the German scholars who were shredding traditional Christianity into mountains of footnotes, denials and arguments and icy drops of water that made Channing so popular with the young."[26]

Channing's intellectual progeny were even more radical. George Ticknor and Edward Everett returned from Germany to spread the gospel according to Kant, Hegel, and Strauss at Harvard University, where they found Channing as one of their supporters. Ralph Waldo Emerson found himself in much the same situation. He imbibed German idealism indirectly via Coleridge and Carlyle, but when he considered studying for the ministry, it was to Channing that he went for advice.

Over the course of the first half of the 19th century, Unitarianism begat Transcendentalism, and Transcendentalism begat Abolitionism as its political arm. Scott sees abolitionism as ultimately the revolutionary offspring of Cromwell.

Some of these echoes were buried very deep in the American psyche, especially among the descendants of the Presbyterians and Puritans. Their movements had, after all, begun against the reigns of Mary Stuart and Charles II, when John Knox and his successors under Cromwell had argued that resistance to "ungodly" authority was a Christian duty.[27]

New England was populated with the descendants of Puritans; some of whom had emigrated before Cromwell, in the reign of James I, and others from those who fled during the Restoration. Their family traditions were that they should not obey a Parliament—or a congress—that violated God's law.

The Southerners were dumbfounded when the Bible, which nowhere prohibits slavery, got turned into an abolitionist tract at the hands of Northern revolutionaries:

> The Southerners'... ministers assured them they were not sinners in the eyes of the Lord. And what began as a political dispute took on many of the aspects of a religious one... .the call to apply the rules of Heaven on earth.[28]

The Southerners began to suspect that the version of the Christian faith being preached by the radicals in Boston was nothing more than the French Revolution recast in biblical language:

> To confuse physical slavery, as it existed in the United States in the 1850s, with slavery of the soul, as did the radical abolitionists, was to mount an unanswerable challenge and to revive heresies dormant in the Western world since the French Revolution.[29]
>
> It was then, after all, that liberty, equality, and fraternity were linked—and death threatened to all who opposed that linkage. For this and similar reasons, therefore, the eyes of European revolutionaries were irresistibly drawn to the United States and the abolitionist movement. Its combination of religious rhetoric—used even by persons unconnected with any church or creed—its calls for violence and its denial of the laws of the majority constituted a movement of great and novel potential. It marched under the banner of antislavery, but as it grew it became clear that many causes could be furthered by the tactics it developed.[30]

In addition to the Cromwellian version of revolution which Channing and his peers imbibed with their mothers' milk, Unitarianism had also been influenced by German idealism. Transcendentalism was the German Enlightenment adapted by the children of the Puritan divines. Transcendentalism was the confluence of two revolutionary traditions, epitomized by Cromwell, the Puritan, and Kant, the father of German idealism, respectively.

This same synthesis became the basis for America's revolutionary party, which focused on the abolition of slavery as its ultimate political goal. Theodore Parker was a revolutionary who "denied Protestantism, dismissed concepts of sin, denied atonement, summarized God as goodness, and 'each man as his own Christ.'"[31] "Poverty," Parker opined, "can only be eliminated when its causes are removed. The alternative is revolution."[32]

Eventually, a small cabal of the most radical figures in the Transcendentalist/Abolitionist movement coalesced into a group known as the Secret Six, and they became the men who financed John Brown, who precipitated the crisis which led to America's second revolution, otherwise known as the Civil War.

II

In 1835 two German teenagers from Hamburg, Ottilie and Ludmilla Assing, made a literary pilgrimage to Paris, where they saw Heinrich Heine. We do not know if they actually spoke with the man who had become a demigod among liberated and subversive-minded Germans, but the pilgrimage was certainly religious in a literary way. Ottilie's biographer assures us that, in addition to their encounter with Heine, the Assing sisters made "a special pilgrimage to worship the goddess of their literary and feminist dreams, George Sand."[33]

Ottilie Assing was born in Hamburg on February 11, 1819, the offspring of the salons of Berlin that had arisen during the late phase of the German Enlightenment and were swept away by Napoleon's invasion and the reaction against all things foreign and French which followed his defeat. Ottilie Assing was also in quite literal fashion, the offspring of the merger of Jewish and Protestant culture which the salons aspired to bring about. Ottilie's aunt was Rahel Levin Varnhagen, one of Berlin's most famous bluestocking salonnieres. Ottilie's grandparents had been enthusiastic disciples of the French Revolution. Ottilie's mother, Rosa Maria, was an ardent supporter of the Enlightenment in both the political and sexual arenas. As a young woman she had an affair with the poet Justinus Koerner, who introduced her to the man she would eventually marry, David Assur, a Jewish physician from Koenigsberg, the capital of East Prussia and home of Immanuel Kant, godfather of the German Enlightenment.

Though raised in an orthodox Jewish environment, David, growing up in Kant's Koenigsberg, could not avoid being exposed to Enlightenment philosophy, and to his father's chagrin he became a disciple of the Enlightenment and its Jewish counterpart, represented by leading intellectuals like Moses Mendelssohn and Gotthold Ephraim Lessing.

As a result, Ottilie referred to herself for the rest of her life as a "half Jew."[34] Ottilie "grew up in an intellectual environment in which education was regarded as a secular form of individual salvation"[35] and "defiance became a family tradition."[36]

Rosa Maria, Ottilie's mother, sublimated her sexual desires into literary channels. "We drifted in an ocean of lust"[37] was the phrase she used to describe her affair with Koerner. Unlike Aunt Rahel, who continued to have affairs after her marriage, Rosa Maria confined herself to steamy short stories in which chimney sweeps and fishermen married young women above their station, and love triumphed over considerations of race and class. All of Rosa Maria's stories had the same central theme: "love and controlled passion."[38]

> The pattern of all these texts is identical: beautiful young lovers of a sensuous innocence encounter violent opposition to their relationship from their elders,

who plan to marry them off to socially unsuitable partners, and they either overcome this opposition by faithful perseverance, defy convention by consummating their love against official morality, or escape into death.[39]

Ottilie's heroines were Rahel Levin and George Sand, and in the salons she frequented, she imbibed an intoxicating mixture of free love, champagne, cigars, and revolution. Goethe was another hero, particularly as the author of *Die Leiden des Jungen Werthers*, which sparked a craze of wearing yellow vests and committing suicide. Ever the pedagogue, Ottilie's mother taught her that suicide, "far from being a sin, a crime, an act of escapism or a sign of weakness, can express individual autonomy, personal integrity, and strength—and act of self-liberation, a sensuous embrace."[40] It was a lesson Ottilie learned well and one which ended her life many years down the road.

There were other literary models as well. There was "the German George Sand,"[41] Fanny Lewald, a converted Jew from Koenigsberg who preached free love and agonized over loss of Jewish identity. And there was Clara Mundt, the pen name of Luise Muehlback, who wrote *Aphra Behn*, the story of an English bluestocking who became sexually involved with Oroonoko, the leader of a slave revolt in the New World. It was *Aphra Behn*, perhaps more than any other book she read, which provided Assing with the template upon which she would model her life in the new world. Like Rahel Levin Varnhagen in Berlin, the Assings had their own salon in Hamburg, a salon which was always open to "violators of convention."[42] As a result of her upbringing, Ottilie Assing became a revolutionary for whom transgressing what she considered bourgeois morality became the highest form of virtue:

> Intellectually she was a daughter of the most radical segment of the German Enlightenment and of German Romanticism, and the models she chose were proud members of a small elite of exceptionally, aggressively unconventional individuals of turn-of-the-century salon culture in Berlin. Living with a lover was regarded as perfectly legitimate, even fashionable in the circles the Assing girls had been taught to idealize by their mother, provided that the lover was of an "exotic" background and had the right attitude.[43]

In this milieu, revolutionary virtue meant transgressing both moral and racial boundaries. Concretely, that meant having affairs in which Jews, Christians and freethinkers intermingled promiscuously:

> Rahel's famous salon had been a meeting place not only for intellectuals and artists, radicals, and noblemen, but for Jews, Christians, and freethinkers; parallel to sophisticated discussions of literature and politics, a young poet could make advances to a Jewish femme fatale, a nobleman flirt with an actress, a married woman could signal her interest in a would-be revolutionary.... The "business of mistresses" those violations of "race" boundaries, was central to the self-definition of these salons. Rahel Levin herself had had several passionate affairs.[44]

Jewish customs were "carefully respected"[45] in the Assing household, as long as they were congruent with the Enlightenment, something that was an on-going source of concern to David, who became more melancholy and withdrawn as time passed. David Assing believed in the Enlightenment intellectually, but was intelligent enough to see that these ideas would influence the behavior of his daughters in ways that he could not condone. The fact that the Enlightenment cut David off from his Jewish roots meant that he could not reprove either. And so he remained for the rest of his days "an outsider in his own house," frightened by the "radicalism and aggressiveness of the Young Germans," "appalled by their love affairs, their irreverence about religion [and] their challenge to marriage as an institution," and yet unable to do anything that might have saved his daughters from the destructive consequences of the ideas which got espoused in his own house.[46] Assing was worried about the effect of these radical ideas on his daughters, and history would show his fears were well-founded. The girls became atheists as a result of hearing texts like David Friedrich Strauss's *Life of Jesus* debated in the family salon. The girls also became life-long devotees of free love. Ottilie had a number of affairs and never married. Ludmilla married an Italian fortune hunter 20 years her junior when she was in her fifties, and that marriage ended in divorce less than a month after it began.

"The Assings most intimate friends," Diedrich assures us, "were Jews,"[47] but Jews of a particular sort:

> Ottilie and Ludmilla knew Jewish rituals and traditions by heart. The girls spent every Monday with Johanna and Salomon Steinheim, both strict opponents of the Jewish Enlightenment, yet intimate enough with the Assings to identify themselves as their aunt and uncle. David had moved away from Orthodox Judaism, but he wanted his children to accept it as an important segment of their past, an essential part of their composite present identity.[48]

Judaism was considered inferior to Protestant Christianity and was considered "a dying remnant of the past,"[49] destined to merge in true Hegelian fashion with the deracinated Protestantism that was the state religion of Prussia. Together both would give birth to a new synthesis, otherwise known as German culture, which was both Protestant (as the new biblical exegetes understood the term) and Jewish (as Mendelssohn understood the term) but ultimately neither. German was the only word which could adequately describe the new synthesis, as long as one excluded Catholicism as practiced on the Rhein and in Bavaria from the mix.

Tolerance was the essence of the new religion, and tolerance had been defined for the Germans by Lessing, whose play *Nathan der Weise* had been modeled on the life of Moses Mendelssohn. The Assing girls were left to figure out on their own how Judaism and the Enlightenment fit together. Diedrich gives a postmodern reading of an identity crisis that was undeniably real:

The Assing girls, ostracized by conservative Germans on the one hand, and orthodox Jews on the other, may have suffered severe "category" crises. They learned the painful lesson that identity was not a mater of choice but defined by those who held the power to define, yet they clung to the creed they had inherited from their parents. The ostracism to which they were exposed sharpened their eyes for all expressions of discrimination, but it also burdened them with a need to belong, at times overwhelming. The almost excessive pride they took in the elitist circles they moved in, the arrogance they displayed against the petty bourgeois and "philistine" people.[50]

In the absence of coherent principle as a guide to life, the Assing girls fell back on imitating members of the older generation, and that meant that, next to their mother, Aunt Rahel was their primary role model. Eventually all of the talk about free love and the stultifying effects of convention and marriage had their effect on Ottilie. During the mid-1840s she became involved in what came to be known as the "theater wars" in Hamburg, and in 1846 Ottilie moved in with Jean-Baptiste Baison, one of the great actors in the German theater of his day and star of Hamburg's Municipal Theater. Baison came from Huguenot stock in France, but in her biography of Baison, Ottilie characterized him as favored "by Nature herself" and destined for the stage where "his tall slim figure had an innate grace which was ennobled by a perfect physique, and his exquisitely and regularly formed features mirrored each emotion with lightning speed."[51]

The fact that Baison's wife did not move out when Ottilie moved into their household only underscored the unconventional nature of their relationship and their scorn for moral propriety. It was because of Baison, that Ottilie missed the Revolution of 1848. Baison died on January 13, 1849, and Ottilie had spent the Revolution of 1848 taking care of his family and nursing him through his final illness. Throughout Baison's last days, Ottilie, according to Diedrich, "refused to seek solace in religion. In fact, it appears that Baison's death consolidated her atheist commitment."[52]

Johann Steinheim blamed the Baison affair for Ottilie's political ideas: "Without this unfortunate relationship to the Baison family she would never have developed such quixotic ideas."[53] But it seems clear in retrospect that Steinheim has the moral cart before the horse here. If Ottilie had not been morally corrupted by a steady diet of toxic culture in the salons run by her mother and her aunt, she most probably would not have begun the affair with Baison in the first place.

Ottilie Assing had squandered her fortune on Baison. In addition, her affair with Baison had ruined her reputation in Hamburg. No one was willing to hire a fallen woman as a tutor to their children. That and the failed Revolution of 1848, which sent thousands of Germans into exile, got Assing thinking about America, and on August 16, 1852 Ottilie Assing put theory into practice once again when she sailed out of Hamburg bound for New York and the New World. Her sister Ludmilla saw the voyage to America as an admission that Ottilie had ruined her life. Unable to admit that fact, Ottilie chose America as an escape from the unhappiness which flowed from her own "character traits, which will always accompany her!"[54]

Ottilie, however, felt that "America spelled promise."[55] *"Amerika, du hast es besser,"* was Goethe's verdict. The land without a history proved irresistible to those who wanted to escape from history, personal and otherwise. In addition to all that, America was the home of the noble savage, and in particular it was the home of millions of Negro slaves waiting for liberation of the sort that Ottilie had imbibed from her mother's and aunt's salons. Diedrich is even more specific:

> Like all educated Germans of her day, she had read Heinrich von Kleist's "Engagement in Santo Domingo" (1811) and she shared the enthusiasm of German radicals for the Haitian revolution and its hero, Toussaint L'Ouverture.[56]

Kleist wasn't Ottilie's only source of information about the racial situation in the New World. In 1849, three years before she left for America and one year after the Revolution of 1848 had failed, Ottilie read Clara Mundt's *Aphra Behn*, a book which evoked in her "visions of a black revolution, of a militant alliance transcending established boundaries of race and gender"[57] sure to make Ottilie's broken heart beat strong again. Ottilie lived in a world of literary models, and so it is hardly far-fetched to think that she saw in Kleist and Mundt's fictions some premonition of her own future in the new world, as well as the fact that "expert radicals like her" would be able "to liberate" America "from its self-imposed bondage."[58] Diedrich finds it entirely possible that "the glorification of Toussaint L'Ouverture among German radicals roused the hope in her that another great black liberator would arise in the US."[59] It was clear that Ottilie was Aphra Benn, the bluestocking from Europe who was to liberate the Negro slaves. But who was Oronooko? Ottilie had no idea when she left Germany, but after a short time in New York City the answer to that question would become clear to her.

III

Shortly after the Assing sisters had arrrived to pay homage to their literary heroes Heinrich Heine and George Sand in Paris in the aftermath of the failed Revolution of 1831, a slave who eventually renamed himself Frederick Douglass fled North from the home of his master on Maryland's eastern shore. Douglass had been born a slave in 1818, but on September 3, 1838, with the help of Anna Murray, a woman seven years his senior, he had fled to the North, where he allied himself with the abolitionists, in particular with William Lloyd Garrison. Shortly after his arrival in New York, Douglass married Anna Murray at the church of James W. C. Pennington, one of the first blacks Ottilie Assing would idolize after her arrival in America.

Murray eventually bore Douglass four children, but before long, it became clear that liberation meant one thing for Anna Murray and something quite different for Frederick Douglass. Murray was a deeply religious woman who felt, along with his early mentor the Rev. Lawson, that God had granted Douglass extraordinary gifts so that he could preach God's word and, like a new Moses, lead his people out of bondage.

Unlike Douglass, the self-made man who taught himself to read and write, Anna Murray remained an illiterate for her entire life. As a result Douglass associated her and her religious views with Negro backwardness, the very thing his race needed to overcome if it were to gain equality with the white race. Before long Douglass began to view his wife as a burden. Anna Murray became "the woman left behind, a static, slowly dimming, and voiceless figure in the distance."[60] In Douglass's autobiography,

> the woman who paid for his heroic flight, who at times was the family's prime wage earner, who had given him four children and whose devotion empowered him to make his glorious career, is almost absent from the text—"an afterthought," as David Leverenz notes. A few years later, in his novel "The Heroic Slave" (1853), Douglass distanced himself even further from the kind of black womanhood he associated with slavery: in the story he kills off Susan, the wife of his slave protagonist, Madison Washington, whose support had enabled him to hide from slave catchers for five year before his heroic escape from the South.[61]

In Douglass's eyes, his wife had committed the unpardonable sin. She had not liberated herself from what he saw as intellectual bondage, and before long he began to treat her more like a servant than a wife, something that visitors to his house noticed. Diedrich says that Douglass and his wife "began to live separate lives less than five years into their marriage."[62]

If so, his career as the great liberator didn't help matters any. In 1845 Frederick Douglass published the first of a number of autobiographies, *The Narrative of the Life of Frederick Douglass*. He then traveled to England, where he made contact with Wilberforce and the antislavery movement there. While in England, Douglass noticed that he cast a sexual spell over the white women who came to hear him speak. The feeling was mutual. Douglass was attracted to white women because they symbolized not only forbidden fruit for the former slave from the South, but because they represented everything that his wife was not. They represented the higher culture that blacks needed to appropriate to raise themselves to the level of white culture. In a poem he wrote later in life, when contemplating marriage to another white woman, he described both white women and the culture they represented as forbidden fruit and himself as the Adam willing to seize that fruit no matter what the consequences. Modern commentators try to pick their way through this minefield without stepping on anything that might set off an explosion of political correctness. Douglass, we are told,

> was surrounded with enamored white women of his class wherever he traveled, and his interest in them and their obvious enjoyment of his presence both fascinated and shocked his contemporaries, as it continues to occupy his biographers. The observations of the "white woman phenomenon" in Douglass's life which William S. McFeely offered in his biography of 1991 is typical. "There was, and is, much prurient speculation—not always devoid of racism—about the sexual

components of Douglass's friendship with white women and lurking within are fantastic images of a not-so-noble savage turned gleaming black beast and proving fatally attractive to pale virgins anxious to yield their chastity to some imagined hugeness."[63]

Eighteen hundred and forty-seven was an *annus mirabilis* of sorts for Frederick Douglass. In 1847 Douglass broke with William Lloyd Garrison and moved to Rochester, New York, where he started his own newspaper, the *North Star*. When he returned home in triumph from his speaking tour in England in the same year, Julia Griffiths, an ardent English abolitionist and the daughter of a friend of William Wilberforce, not only followed him back to America, she moved into the Douglass household and became his constant companion for the next seven years. Griffiths helped set up his press and raise the money needed to launch his magazine. She even accompanied him on the piano when he played the violin. Worse than all of that, she accompanied Douglass on his speaking tours, appearing in public with him at a time when this sort of behavior was a huge source of public scandal for the abolitionist cause and a source of comfort to the enemies of black emancipation. Diedrich tries to put Douglass's behavior in a positive light by claiming that "Julia seemed to have everything that Anna Murray was lacking."[64] But the real message of their cohabitation was much more damaging than that. If Frederick Douglass was to be construed as a role model for his race, then it looked as if the first fruit of emancipation was going to be emancipation from sexual morality. Douglass did not abandon his black wife, but the fact that he took up with a white woman in the same house made the situation that much worse in the eyes of the public, who were treated to numerous "insinuating" accounts in the press over the course of the next few years.[65]

Since the creation of the *North Star* was tantamount to a break with Garrison anyway, Garrison lost no time in leading the attack against Douglass. It may well be that Douglass showed lack of gratitude and that Garrison was loath to have a competitor as the chief champion of abolitionism, but the political and social realities of the times made these considerations secondary anyway. The main issue was Douglass's sexual mores. "The abolitionists," Diedrich tells us, "had been alarmed at how excitedly women lionized and besieged Douglass on his tours; they feared lest these encounters through a negative light on their movement; did they not confirm the allegation that abolition of slavery would expose white women to the sexual lust of black men?"[66]

As Douglass's behavior became more brazen, the *Liberator* increased the vehemence of its attacks on him, wondering out loud how a man who cheated on his wife could be trusted with the responsibilities of leadership in the anti-slavery movement. The feminists agreed in this with Garrison. Julia Griffiths had become a source of division in the abolitionist movement because of Douglass's affair with her. In a letter to Garrison, Susan B. Anthony claimed that her friends felt that he had been right to ostracize Douglass, because, as Amy Post put it, "Julia that has made Frederic hate all his old friends. Said she, I don't care anything about her being in the office—but I won't have her in my house."[67]

Ignoring the threats of his erstwhile allies, Douglass did nothing to hide his affair with Julia Griffiths. Traveling together with her and appearing with her in public were deliberate acts of provocation which called into question the strict segregation of black men and white women which Douglas had grown up under. But it also alienated support in the North for the abolitionist cause. Douglass's behavior seemed calculated to prove the Southerners right when they claimed that emancipation was the first step toward miscegenation and black men taking up with white women. Once the affair with Julia Griffiths was made public, Garrison found himself in the position of Dr. Frankenstein. The man he had promoted as the leader of the black cause was now more useful to the propagandists for slavery than he was for the abolitionists. A break was inevitable.

In spite of the break with Douglass, Garrison continued to be a major player in the psychological warfare campaign against the South, a campaign which was predicated on the threat of black rebellion. Garrison wasn't alone in waging this campaign. *The New York Tribune* under the editorship of Horace Greeley was only slightly less strident than Garrison, and because of its high speed presses the *Tribune* reached a much wider audience in the North. The pundits from the North were careful to couch their calls for revolution in phrases that sounded as if they had come from the Bible. Those who opposed their extremism found themselves powerless to resist much less oppose the pull of the revolutionary tide. In a statement which Herman Melville would appropriate and put into the mouth of Captain Ahab in *Moby Dick*, Daniel Webster, whose main concern was preserving the Union, noted that "There are men who... if their perispicacious vision enables them to detect a spot on the face of the sun, they think it good reason why the sun should be struck down from heaven."[68] President Fillmore was getting letters from Theodore Parker, one of the Secret Six, informing him that it was his duty to break the law and engage in illegal activity:

> For the first time, the United States government was faced with a revolutionary movement that denied its authority and its power to exert that authority. The movement was a minority, but its leaders held high and respected positions. The number of clergymen in its ranks and their arguments—in Parker's words—that "antislavery is the Law of God," and "the constitution was not morally binding" made them difficult and embarrassing opponents.[69]

The South, like President Fillmore, was now aware that the existence of chattel slavery had been used to create a revolutionary situation in the North, which under the orchestration of figures public and private urged the destruction of the South and what it stood for. Slavery, in a sense, was only the tip of the iceberg. The real issue was that the South had remained unchanged, an essentially feudal society in the heart of what was becoming a revolutionary republic, ever since the colonies separated from England.

The South for its part responded by sitting back and taking a beating at the hands of the northern radicals who controlled the organs of public opinion. Otto Scott describes their retreat into sullen silence:

> The South smarted under a wave of denigration that issued from hundreds of Northern presses and hundreds more lecture platforms. The South's culture and religion were denied, its classes mocked, its heritage and accomplishments ignored. Millions of Northerners regarded the South as a region of nightmare and evil.... Southern anger rose steadily under a Northern barrage that insisted the South revolutionize itself, dislocated its economy, and change its pattern of relations between the races—all to please the consciences of men in another region who would suffer no pain, loss, or change of status from such changes.[70]

Scott claims that "The reality was far different. The South was a region... where the bible was revered as the base of Western civilization."[71] But the existence of slavery as the cornerstone of southern culture made a coherent defense of that culture an impossible task. As a result the Southerners retreated into sullen silence, and increased their vigilance over and oppression of the slaves, who seemed to be the main target of northern propaganda efforts.

> At first the South was content to seal its mailbags against Northern propaganda and to issue denials and refutations. In time, abolitionist propaganda led to a worsening of the conditions of blacks; efforts to educate slaves were halted and emancipations made more difficult. The conditions of free blacks declined remarkably. The South moved toward the condition of a garrison state in its own nation.[72]

Long after the South had lost the battle for the public mind, Richard Weaver would concede that the South had produced no one who could articulate the Southern point of view or defend the Southern way of life. Weaver called the South "the last non-materialist civilization in the Western World."[73] If so, it failed nonetheless to come up with an effective critique of the materialist revolutionaries who were determined to destroy its way of life:

> The South spoke well on a certain level, but it did not make the indispensable conquest of the imagination. From the Bible and Aristotle it might have produced its *Summa Theologia*, but none measured up to the task, and there is no evidence that the performance would have been rewarded. It needed a Burke or a Hegel; it produced lawyers and journalists. Perhaps the sin for which the South has most fully though unknowingly atoned is its failure to encourage the mind.
>
> It has had to compete against the great world with second-rate talent, and to accept the defensive where an offensive was indicated. One may understand the feeling which could boast of the South's freedom from isms, but this implies the existence of a satisfactory theology and metaphysics, which were not on hand. The lack continues....[74]

The fatal flaw was chattel slavery. Pushed to the wall by the northern propaganda offensive arrayed against it, the South was hampered by its religious roots in *sola scriptura* and the political legacy of the American Revolution. The South turned to the Bible to find a justification for its way of life, and found that it was impossible to fight against the revolution armed with revolutionary assumptions. The Christian religion tolerated slavery in ancient Rome, but it did not endorse it in the way that the South found necessary.

> Against the South was arrayed the power of the North, dominated by the spirit of Puritanism, which, with all of its virtues, has ever been characterized by the pharisaism which worships itself, and is unable to perceive any goodness apart from itself, which has ever arrogantly held its ideas, its interests, and its will higher than fundamental law and covenanted obligations, which has always "lived and moved and had its being" in rebellion against constituted authority.[75]

In his warning to the South, John Calhoun raised the specter of black insurrection leading to black hegemony. The Negro would become the pawn of northern revolutionaries, whose goal was nothing short of the destruction of the South's culture:

> A shift in power [from the balance of power which had been maintained since the Missouri compromise of 1820], said Calhoun, would be accompanied by a reinterpretation of the Constitution, the emancipation of slaves, and "the overthrow of Southern whites." He warned that "in the hours of abolitionist triumph the blacks would be raised to favor, office and power. The South would then become the abode of disorder, anarchy and wretchedness." Calhoun argued that a unified South might avert this fate, and that its appearance alone might deflect the Northern drift and direction.[76]

As a result of losing the scriptural war to the proponents of German scripture scholarship, the South sought to preserve its culture by clamping down on the Negro slave. Had the South been allowed another century to work out its problems, the balm of local affinity could have come up with a *modus vivendi* which allowed for the preservation of all that was good in Southern culture, but the whole point of the revolutionary strategy was to deny them this time and to provoke a crisis by the systematic use of propaganda, and even terrorism if necessary.

The campaign of terrorism began in rumor. There were rumors of slave uprisings on the borders of Arkansas and Louisiana. Other slave rebellions were reported along the Kentucky-Tennessee border as well as in the Cumberland Valley, Virginia, South Carolina, Alabama, Florida, and Mississippi.

When Douglass broke with Garrison in 1847 to form his own newspaper, one of his backers was Gerit Smith, the richest man in New York State because of extensive property inherited from his father. The fact that Smith was also a member of the Secret Six, the cabal which backed John Brown, makes the fact that Frederick Douglass met with John Brown in 1847 seem like something other than coincidence. After arriving in Rochester, Brown carefully explained his plan to Douglass. Ever a man who saw the hand of God in the movements of his will and appetites, Brown explained to Douglass that he planed to create an army of abolitionist liberators in the Allegheny Mountains, which, Brown claimed, had been "placed [there] by God for the emancipation of the Negro race."[77] Brown would sally forth from his mountain redoubt periodically and liberate ever-increasing numbers of slaves, who would then regroup at this mountain hideout until further raids could swell their numbers even further. "I know these mountains well," Brown told Douglass, "and could take a body of men into them and keep them there despite all the efforts of Virginia to dislodge them."[78] Brown was, of course, totally unfamiliar with the mountain range which stretched from Gerit Smith's home state into enemy territory in Virginia, but knowing that God had created the mountains for him to use in his war of liberation was knowledge enough for Brown. Brown felt that "Slavery was a state of war, and a slave had a right to anything necessary to his freedom."[79] That was an anticipation of the later sermons of Theodore Parker, who would argue that slaves had a right to kill for freedom. How Douglass reacted to Brown's proposal is anyone's guess. Years later, when he had to flee to England in the wake of Brown's disastrous attack on Harpers Ferry, Douglass made light of Brown, claiming that he wanted no part of what was sure to be a suicidal assault. But his daughter told a different story and claimed that Douglass promised to support Brown.

Four years after his initial meeting with Douglass, Brown had refined his plans for revolution based on black insurrection and the murder of whites even further. Brown's new organization was called the United States League of Gileadites, a name which gave a clear indication that Brown, like his revolutionary forebears in 17th century England, was drawing on the story of Gideon as the source of his inspiration. He also made reference to contemporary national liberation movements throughout the world. If the Greeks could rise up against the Turks, and the Poles could rise up against the Russians, and the Hungarians could rise up against the Austrians, then the Negroes of the United States, whose sufferings far exceeded those of the groups already mentioned, could certainly rise up against the white slave owners of the South. Brown concluded his new manifesto with instructions on how to spread "confusion and terror."[80]

IV

On May 19, 1856 Senator Charles Sumner took the floor of the United States Senate to give what he considered "the most philippic [speech] ever uttered in a legislative body."[81] The subject of this diatribe was "The Crime against Kansas," and it took the better part of two days for Senator Sumner to expatiate on the magnitude of this crime. Scott characterizes Sumner as "an ideologue in the Robespierre mold: austere, aloof, warm only toward those who agreed with him, cold as ice to everyone else."[82] During the course of his speech, Sumner described the citizens of the state of Missouri as "hirelings, picked from the drunken spew and vomit of an uneasy civilization,"[83] but in this was only warming up to the point where he could deliver the full force of his literary blow squarely on the head of the South in general and the state of South Carolina in particular. Stephen Douglas, who at this point was trying to lower the temperature of debate and save the union, was appalled at what he heard, "Is it his object,' Douglas wondered "to provoke some of us to kick him as we would a dog in the street, that he may get sympathy upon the just chastisement?"[84]

Equally amazed was South Carolina Representative Preston S. Brooks, who felt that Sumner had besmirched not only his state but his uncle, Senator Andrew P. Butler as well. On May 22, Brooks approached Sumner on the Senate floor and informed him that after reading over his speech twice carefully, he considered it a libel on South Carolina and Mr. Butler. Before Sumner could respond, Brooks began beating him with his gutta percha cane. The beating continued until Brooks' cane broke into slivers and he was physically restrained from continuing. Normally, Brooks would have challenged the author of such insults to a duel, but duels were reserved for resolving disputes between gentlemen, and Brooks didn't consider Sumner a gentleman.

Three days later, on May 25, John Brown and his sons made their way to a remote farm cabin near Pottawatomie, Kansas in the middle of the night and asked the farmer who lived there for hospitality. When he opened the door to admit them, Brown and his sons slew the man with swords in the sight of his wife and children and then released the man's slave, who was now free to wander off onto the prairie by himself and starve to death. The slave insurrection which the South had feared ever since the Nat Turner rebellion had begun, even though it didn't seem that way at the time. Brown had begun to "carry the war into Africa,"[85] his phrase for the slave insurrection that would usher in the second American Revolution and the American version of heaven on earth.

Fifty years after Brown's death Oswald Garrison Villard, William Lloyd Garrison's grandson, and one of the founding fathers of the NAACP, claimed that "John Brown still remains the outstanding example of a life in which man's spirit and courage in the face of certain death achieved immortality for him, where his resort to murderous violence and to armed revolt against his government failed completely."[86]

Villard went on to liken Brown "to the Hebrew prophets or to a Cromwellian roundhead,"[87] situating him squarely in the tradition of the judaizing revolutionaries who had emigrated out of England in the 17th century and went on to leave an indelible mark on the American colonies, where they sought refuge. Brown's Puritan heritage becomes clear in Villard's biographical sketch:

> John was born on May 9th, 1800 at Torrington in Litchfield County, Connecticut of poor but respectable parents: a descendant on the side of his father of one of the of the company of the Mayflower who landed at Plymouth in 1620. His mother was descended from a man who came at an early period to New England from Amsterdam in Holland. Both his Father's and his Mother's father served in the war of the revolution.[88]

On May 28, 1856, a warrant was issued against John Brown, Jr. for treason. One day later, a journalist by the name of James Redpath mysteriously appeared at Brown's camp in Kansas. Redpath, whose articles on Brown would appear in the *New York Tribune*, then embarked on a publicity campaign which created the first and subsequently indelible image of Brown in the public mind. Brown was neither a criminal, nor a terrorist, nor a revolutionary who could only function if he was supported by people wealthier and better connected than he. No, Brown was Oliver Cromwell come back from the dead: "a new Cromwell had appeared in Kansas."[89] Redpath was not alone in portraying Brown as Cromwell *redivivus*. When Julia Ward Howe, wife of Dr. Samuel Gridley Howe, another member of the Secret Six cabal, met Brown, she exclaimed, "He looked a Puritan of the Puritans, forceful, concentrated, and self-contained."[90] Her husband felt the same way, seeing Brown as Cromwell, as well as other

> parallels everywhere he looked, with the English Civil War. He mentally considered the antislavery forces... the equivalent of the Puritans and Presbyterians of that earlier conflict. These were notions derived from Sir Walter Scott rather than history; Howe did not recall what the religious principles of the Puritans might have been; in his mind antislavery had assumed the force and coherence of a religion.[91]

Rev. Thomas Wentworth Higginson, another member of the Secret Six cabal, had similar praise for the Kansas Free Soilers, who as a result of Brown's raid were "better prepared for revolution than they had been a few months previously." They were now, in fact, "ready to add their lives for revolution."[92]

Redpath's accounts of Brown's raid fired the imagination of the Secret Six. His willingness to kill unarmed farmers convinced them that he was their man. Brown's counterproposal was fairly straightforward. "He wanted $30,000 to arm a provisional force of 100 men under his leadership to 'fight for freedom' in Kansas and 'carry the war into Africa.'"[93]

On March 13, 1857, the Supreme Court of the United States handed down its infamous Dred Scott decision and transformed Brown from a criminal into a hero. Brown was "lionized in a manner later made familiar to many momentarily famous revolutionists when received by wealthy radicals."[94]

The Dred Scott decision prompted Higginson to write an article in the *Atlantic Monthly* advocating revolution as the only solution to the slavery problem. "The question of slavery is a stern and practical one. Give us the power and we can make a new Constitution...how is that power to be obtained? By politics? Never. By revolution and that alone."[95]

By the time Higginson used the term revolution in his *Atlantic* article, he was not referring to some antiquated movement of English ranters from the 17th century. Senator Charles Sumner, the same Charles Sumner who had endured a thrashing at the hands of Preston Brooks, knew many European revolutionaries. It was Sumner who introduced Higginson to an adventurer by the name of Colonel Hugh Forbes. Forbes had fought with Garibaldi during the Italian Revolution of 1848 and fancied himself an expert in mountain warfare. Since Brown had already made contact with the Secret Six, it was presumably Higginson who introduced Forbes to Brown. Anyone could see that the two men's gifts dovetailed nicely. Since Brown's base of operations for the Gileadites of the United States was to be the Allegheny Mountains, Forbes' expertise in these matters would be of benefit to him and the cause of Negro insurrection.

Eventually Brown met with Forbes in New York, where Forbes introduced Brown to his *magnum opus*, his *Compendio del Voluntario Patriotico*, which had been published in Naples in two volumes. The fact that Garibaldi had made Forbes a colonel and had endorsed his book seems to have impressed Brown, who agreed to pay Forbes $100 a month (plus $600 in advance) to translate his work into English and distil what it had to say into a form which would be accessible to the volunteers who would follow Brown in his efforts to carry the war into Africa. After the translation was completed, Forbes was to join Brown and his "army" in Tabor, Iowa. Forbes then met with Gerit Smith and tried to sell him the same book. Smith, who knew of Brown's dreams of mountain warfare, was equally delighted and gave Forbes another $150. Forbes then got $20 from Horace Greeley and an undisclosed sum from the Garibaldi-Mazzini colony in New York. Fortified with this new-found wealth, Forbes made his way to Iowa, where, on August 9, 1857, he found an "army" made up of Brown and his crippled son Owen.

At this point Forbes realized that he, and everyone else involved with the Secret Six, had been duped into believing Brown's grandiose rhetoric. Undeterred by Forbes' skepticism, Brown began to elaborate on his plan in detail. The entire black population of the South, Brown assured Forbes, was ready to rise up in rebellion as soon as a leader like Brown arrived on the scene. Basing the rest of his plan on that dubious assumption, Brown went on to assure Forbes that "between 200 and 500 slaves would swarm to his standard the first night."[96]

Forbes, however, remained skeptical of John Brown's plans to carry the war into Africa and pointed out the flaws to its author. The foremost consideration was whether, in fact, the slaves would rebel, even if Brown offered them weapons and commissions at the rank of lieutenant in his "army." Forbes felt that they wouldn't. He also felt that the military forces in the South would quickly defeat any military force which lacked experience, as the Negro slaves did. Southern whites had been trained in the use of firearms from childhood; Southern Negroes had no experience with any weapon other than a knife, and their experience with this weapon consisted in using it on each other in drunken brawls and fights over women. Brown's own military plans eventually took this fact into consideration. Brown himself had no plans to give the Negroes firearms because he knew full well that they didn't know how to use them. He planned to arm his phantom army of insurrectionists with pikes when he made his raid on Harpers Ferry. Finally, Forbes warned Brown that the New Englanders would not support his cause unless and until he achieved total victory, and so they could not be counted on to bring that victory about.

If Forbes hoped to sober Brown with the cold judgment of a man tried in battle, he was mistaken. Nothing could cool Brown's ardor to bring the war to Africa. Brown was the classic enthusiast. He felt called by God to do what he wanted to do. In Brown Luther's doctrine of *sola scriptura* and Muentzer's notion of the living word enlivened by visions, signs, and wonders merged and found their apotheosis in will, years before Nietzsche came to the same conclusion and ushered in the end of the Protestant age. With the Secret Six cabal willing to bankroll his schemes, Brown planned to bring on the racial apocalypse even if it meant shedding innocent blood.

"The slave," Brown concluded, rejecting all of Forbes' warnings, "will be delivered by the shedding of blood—and the signs are multiplying that this deliverance is at hand."[97]

V

At around the same time that Colonel Forbes conferred with John Brown in Kansas, Ottilie Assing decided to move to Hoboken, New Jersey. By the time she arrived in Hoboken, 1,500 of the town's 7,000 inhabitants were German, and many of them were German intellectuals who were exiles from their country because of their participation in the Revolution of 1848. It was in Hoboken that Assing first met Dr. Hans Kudlich from Lobenstein, liberator of Silesia's farmers during the Revolution of 1848. It was in Hoboken too that she met Friedrich Kapp, a lifelong friend of Ludwig Feuerbach, whose book *The Essence of Christianity*, which had been published in 1841, had become the Bible, if you'll pardon the expression, of Germany's atheist American Diaspora. Kapp, like Kudlich, had to flee Germany when the Revolution of 1848 collapsed. Most of the exiled '48ers viewed America as the proverbial port in the storm, and, if anything, saw themselves not so much as immigrants yearning to breathe free as apostles sent by adversity to convert the puritanical Americans to the higher religions of German atheism and free love. Few if any of them were prescient enough to see, as Assing would, that the revolutionary spark had jumped across the ocean, and that the revolutionary flame would burst forth in America before it would flame up anywhere else in the world. Their myopia was a function of their blind adherence to German culture as the highest expression of the world spirit to date. There were no Negroes in Germany, and so the average German, even one who fed on the bread of Marx and Feuerbach, had difficulty understanding race as the vehicle for revolution in America, especially when the rhetoric of revolution there got mixed so promiscuously with the language of the Bible.

Because of how she had been brought up, nurtured on the interracial fantasies of Kleist and Clara Mundt, Ottilie Assing had no difficulty in seeing race as the vehicle for the coming American revolution. In fact, from the beginning of her stay in America, Assing felt that "The New World ...was a laboratory where an abstract vision of a composite nationality could be tested and realized....The ideal

American society she envisioned was raceless."[98] Assing went out of her way to violate America's racial taboos, something that her German accent allowed her to get away with after a fashion. On her visit to a Negro religious revival, she separated herself from the rest of the white race tourists and insisted on spending the night in one of the tents set aside for the Negro pilgrims. Assing loved to shock the sensibilities of her fellow white Americans. In fact, her biographer finds it "impossible to ignore the condescension in Assing's attitude toward her black neighbor, her self-righteousness, her love of performance, her need to shock her fellow white travelers."[99]

Since no one knew of her reputation as the fallen woman from Hamburg, Ottilie Assing could have earned a living as a tutor to the children of the German Diaspora in New York, but instead she decided to earn her living as a journalist. This was hardly the most logical choice, since the competition was fierce. There were lots of German revolutionaries in America competing for a limited number of slots in an even more limited number of German journals. It was clear that Assing needed to specialize, and so at some point she decided to become Germany's Negro expert. Assing felt that her own mixed racial background as a "half Jew" rendered her uniquely qualified for this role.

It was in many ways an inspired choice in 1857, when her adopted country gagged on the Dred Scott decision and plunged headlong toward civil war. The first Negro on her agenda was the preacher James W. C. Pennington, who had penned an up-from-slavery narrative of his own. But soon thereafter, Assing, who was no stranger to literature, picked up *The Narrative of Frederick Douglass*, and it was as if in Douglass the sun rose and rendered Pennington's candle insignificant by comparison.

Within a year, which is to say, by the summer of 1858, Assing had gone from an admirer of his prose, to the woman who shared his bed. Douglass had always been fascinated by white women, probably from the time he had reached puberty, but certainly from the time of his triumphal English speaking tour in 1847. Now that Julia Griffiths, Douglass's first white mistress, had returned to England, there was a significant amount of space in Douglass's bed to share.

Perhaps Assing was drawn to Douglass because both he and she were of mixed racial descent. Ottilie's father was a Jew, and Douglass's father, although no one could be certain, was most probably the white master of the plantation he had escaped from when he fled north in 1838. Roughly ten years after her arrival in the New World, Assing reviewed a 72-page pamphlet entitled *"Miscegenation: the Theory of Blending of the Races Applied to the American white Man and Negro,"* for the January 1864 issue of the *Morgenblatt*. Assing wholeheartedly endorsed the central premise of the pamphlet, which was that if America wanted to be great, it had to promote race mixing, blending "all that is passionate and emotional in the darker races, all that is imaginative and spiritual in the Asiatic races, and all that is intellectual and perceptive in the white race."[100] The anonymous author of this pamphlet went on to argue that it was a well-established fact, "that the miscegenetic or mixed races are much superior mentally, physically, and morally, to those pure or unmixed."[101] In endorsing the pamphlet, Assing let her love affair with Douglass get the better of her political acumen. She failed to understand that the pamphlet was a political hoax perpetrated by the Democratic Party, which attempted to portray the Republican Party as promoters of interracial sex. As part of the same campaign, the Democrats had young women marching in parades carrying banners proclaiming, " Fathers, save us from nigger husbands."[102]

Yet it was more likely that it was the mutual differences that attracted Assing and Douglass to each other. Unlike Douglass's Negro wife, who had been relegated to the role of domestic servant, Assing embodied European culture in what she considered its highest and most advanced form, namely, the German Enlightenment. Assing was, quite literally, a child of that Enlightenment and well versed in all of its literature. She could lead Douglass into the company of Goethe, who had frequented her Aunt Rahel's salon in Berlin, and Kant, who was still taking his daily walks when her father was growing up in Koenigsberg. In addition to all that, she could accompany him on the piano when he played the violin, and could manage his affairs with a combination of Jewish financial acumen and Germanic efficiency.

What Douglass offered Assing was even easier to discern. Douglass, with his boxer's body and leonine head, embodied the idea of "Rousseauvian naturalness" which Ottilie had imbibed from her early education in the salons of Berlin and Hamburg.[103] Douglass was Ottilie's noble savage, or, better still, he was the embodiment of Oroonoko, the noble Negro revolutionary whom Assing had read about in the pages of Clara Mundt's novel, *Aphra Behn*. By uniting in an illicit adulterous relationship, both Assing and Douglass could live lives that testified to the intrinsic illegitimacy of bourgeois morality:

> In a society that worshipped chastity, she gloried in her role as a black and married man's lover. She ridiculed her contemporaries' notions of piety with her belligerent atheism. Her life as a professional woman appeared like a denial of woman's true destiny—wife and motherhood. Douglass was enchanted by a rebelliousness that neither apologized nor explained.[104]

The fact that the radical Hoboken German émigrés accepted Douglass on Assing's terms and that access to Douglass gave her the journalistic edge in becoming Germany's Negro expert when the racial situation was the big story in America only confirmed Assing in her belief that her life had finally settled onto its proper path. Assing was fulfilling her destiny as the child of the German Enlightenment by bringing freedom and revolution to the slaves of America.

Her first task as the bringer of high culture to the American Negro was the education of Frederick Douglass himself. It was Assing who introduced Douglass to the literature of European revolutionary thought, and Douglass, for his part, seems to have been a willing pupil. As some indication of his personal pantheon,

Douglass decorated his study with busts of Ludwig Feuerbach and David Friedrich Strauss. He also displayed portraits of the abolitionists Wendell Philips, Charles Sumner, and John Brown in his study, as well as portraits of Toussaint L'Overture and Abraham Lincoln.[105]

Under Assing's tutelage, Douglass read Marx, Mazzini, Bakunin, and Lassalle. But her crowning achievement was introducing Douglass to the thought of Ludwig Feuerbach. Assing had heard about Feuerbach for years, both before and after she had moved in with the radical émigré community in Hoboken. But then one day in the fall of 1859, she stumbled across George Eliot's translation of Feuerbach's attack on the Christian religion in a bookstore in New York City. It was an important moment in the intellectual history of their relationship, because up to that point, Assing had been unable to convert Douglass to atheism. Or as Assing put it in a letter she wrote to Feuerbach himself, 12 years later, "Personal sympathy and concordance in many central issues brought [Douglass and me] together, but there was one obstacle to a loving and lasting friendship—namely, the personal Christian God."[106] It took no less a thinker than Feuerbach, combined with the sexual wiles of the German/Jewish Delilah, to push Dark Fred over the brink into atheism.

The sexual and intellectual seduction of Frederick Douglass was a moment of historical significance because for the next century the chief obstacle which America's largely Jewish revolutionaries would find to their goal of turning the Negro into the avant garde of the revolutionary movement in America was the Negro's faith in Christ. Now, almost eight decades before Wilhelm Reich would come up with the scientific explanation of how sexuality and German revolutionary thought could be used as a potent form of discipline and control, Ottilie Assing had used the same combination in corrupting America's black Moses, the man whom both his wife and his preacher mentor considered as marked by God to deliver his people from bondage. From Feuerbach, Douglass learned that

> God is a projection of the human imagination, of human needs and desires; the substance of religious dogma is human. Man, Feuerbach declared, created God in his own image, and then God returned the favor. This analysis abolished the opposition between the divine and the human and defined religion as a first step toward self-knowledge.[107]

Besotted by Assing's sexual charms, Douglass found himself incapable of answering Feuerbach's critique and so he succumbed, as she hoped he would, to his ideas. "The book," Assing wrote to Feuerbach referring to *The Essence of Christianity*, "resulted in a total reversal of his attitudes."[108] The final result of their long evenings of reading and discussion, Assing continued, was that "Douglass became your enthusiastic admirer, and the result is a remarkable progress, an expansion of his horizon, of all his attitudes."[109] Part of that progress meant repudiating the prophesy of Charles Lawson, the slave from Baltimore whom Douglass had always considered his "spiritual father." It was Lawson who claimed that Douglass had been freed from the bondage of slavery and illiteracy because the Lord "had a great work for him,"[110] namely preaching the Gospel. Douglass's sense of mission and vocation disappeared when his lust-darkened mind, weakened by Assing's wiles, capitulated intellectually before a German cultural icon whose writing he could dimly decipher but was unable to refute.

Slavery became the occasion which both intensified and justified his rebellion. As Assing well knew, the seeds of rebellion were already there. Midway through his affair with Julia Griffiths, on the 4th of July 1852, Douglass gave a speech in which he attacked the proslavery distortion of Christianity by exclaiming, "For my part I would say, welcome infidelity! Welcome atheism! Welcome anything! In preference to the gospel as preach by the Divines!" Diederich goes on to tell us that Douglass's "belief in human perfectibility and the need for human moral action was strengthened when he encountered Theodore Parker's Transcendental Unitarianism."[111] Feuerbach finished the conversion which Theodore Parker's transcendentalism had begun, and Assing described Douglass's conversion to atheism in frankly religious terms.

> They struck him like a ray of light, and accomplished a complete revolution of his opinions. I add with great satisfaction that it was German radicalism which worked that revolution, and that to our great, venerated Feuerbach, above all others our thanks are due for having pointed out the path to intellectual liberty to the distinguished man, after he had freed himself of the fetters of slavery.[112]

Chattel slavery was only a metaphor in the mind of German radicals like Assing for the intellectual bondage which flowed from Christianity. In this regard, Assing's approach conformed precisely to the reproaches which the southerners were making against the northern radicals. Slavery was a pretext, the southerners had claimed all along; the real issue was revolution. With slavery as their cover, the Secret Six were bent on exporting revolution to the South. It was at this point in their relationship that Douglass introduced Assing to Gerit Smith, the financial power behind the Secret Six cabal. Assing was in complete agreement with the revolutionary goals of the Secret Six, but still found them, like virtually all Americans, disagreeably religious. "The freethinking German visitor," she wrote in one of her *Morgenblatt* articles, "is bothered only by a certain aura of religious orthodoxy that unfortunately infects even the best of men over here."[113]

In the early autumn of 1859, Frederick Douglass received a visit from John Brown, Jr., a fugitive from justice since he and his father had murdered three men in Pottawotomie, Kansas in May 1956. Brown's son had come to recruit Douglass into his father's guerilla army. Assing was staying at the Douglass household when the younger Brown arrived and, since she considered Brown a hero (even though she had never met him in person) she was probably favorably disposed to Brown's request. It seemed as if her Oronooko fantasy was about to become a reality. Diederich does a good job in articulating those fantasies: "There would be an insurrection, perhaps the beginning of a revolution and she and Douglass would be in the midst of it all—Douglass as the liberator and leader of the African American people, and she as his faithful companion. White America had created a wall of scorn around the Douglass home; history might someday celebrate it as the place where the second American revolution was launched!"[114]

Douglass, however, had his doubts, or at least this is how he portrayed his reaction after the attack on Harpers Ferry had failed. To be fair to Douglass, four years before Harpers Ferry, he had written that "I never see much use in fighting, unless there is a reasonable probability of whipping somebody,"[115] and the more he heard about Brown's plan from Brown's son the more he concluded that Brown was going to get whipped. And yet, the idea of taking the war to Africa still had an attraction to Douglass. Douglass had raised money for Brown in black churches, but when he mentioned John Brown to a black audience in Brooklyn, no one in the audience volunteered to join the American Cromwell. This was a bad omen, especially if one considers the fact that Brown's plan for insurrection was predicated on the fact that slaves would swarm to his banner the minute he raised it.

Unable to resolve his doubts on his own, Douglass decided to meet with Brown in person in Chambersburg, Pennsylvania, a town on the Maryland border 80 miles west of Philadelphia. There in a abandoned stone quarry, Douglass met with Brown and his "secretary of war," the Swiss revolutionary John Henry Kagi and learned that Brown had abandoned his plan to create a refuge for fugitive slaves in the mountains and was planning instead a frontal assault with fewer than two dozen men on the whole slavery system as symbolized by the federal arsenal in Harpers Ferry. The whole scheme was predicated on the assumption that the slaves would rise up and support Brown once they heard of his insurrection. Douglass, who had grown up in neighboring Maryland and had just failed to generate any interest among the free blacks of Brooklyn, knew better. The one area where a slave rebellion was most likely to succeed, namely, the predominantly black counties of Georgia, Alabama, and Mississippi was hundreds of miles removed from the arsenal which Brown had chosen as the starting point of his rebellion. It would take weeks for the news to travel to where it was likely to do the most good, if it ever got there at all. The slaves of Virginia, far removed from the onerous work of the cotton fields and often integrated into the households of their masters were the candidates least likely to rise up and follow Brown. Douglass, of course, knew all this much better than Brown did, and concluded that Brown was marching his little band of dreamers into "a perfect steel trap."[116] Like Colonel Forbes before him, Douglass tried to reason with John Brown: "I looked at him with some astonishment, that he could rest on a reed so weak and broken, and told him that Virginia would blow him and his hostages sky-high rather than that he should hold Harpers Ferry an hour."[117] When Brown explained that he also planned to take prominent citizens as hostages and, if worse came to worst, use them to negotiate his freedom, Douglass was more convinced than ever that the plan to use the arsenal "as a trumpet to rally the slaves to his defense" was totally delusional and doomed to failure.[118] That, at least, is how Douglass described the meeting years after the fact. One of Brown's daughters later claimed that Brown and John Kagi told their men that Douglass "had promised that he would follow Brown 'even into death'"[119] and would join them as soon as possible.

Douglass was, of course, correct in his assessment of Brown's plan. It was doomed from the moment of its cock-eyed inception. But Brown carried it out nonetheless. On Sunday, October 16, 1859 Brown showed up at the farm of Lewis Washington, great grandnephew of George Washington, and announced that "We have come for the purpose of liberating all of the slaves of the South."[120] He then took Washington as his hostage and appropriated a pistol which his illustrious forebear had received from Lafayette and a sword Washington had received from Frederick the Great. Armed with these symbolic weapons and Washington's slaves, who were dragooned at gun point into fighting for their own liberty, the small party moved toward Harpers Ferry, where Kagi and A. D. Stevens had already struck "the first blow for liberty"[121] by inadvertently shooting Hayward Shepherd, a free Negro watchman, in their attempt to take the train trestle over the Potomac River. Shepherd died 12 hours later, and Brown's biographer, in spite of his sympathy for Brown, was unable to ignore the irony of the situation. "This was, indeed," Villard, one of his most sympathetic biographers, writes, "an ill omen for the army of liberation. The first man to fall at their hands was neither a slave-owner, nor a defender of slavery, nor one who suffered by it, but a highly respected, well-to-do colored man, in full possession of his liberty and favored with the respect of the white community."[122]

Things went downhill from there.

According to Villard, Brown was not only "without any clear and definite plan of campaign," he also "seemed bent on violating every military principle... by placing a river between himself and the his base of supplies—the Kennedy Farm—and leaving no adequate force on the river bank to insure his being able to fall back to that base. Hardly had he entered the town when, by dispersing his men here and there, he made his defeat as easy as possible. Moreover, he had in mind no well-defined purpose in attacking Harpers Ferry, save to begin his revolution in a spectacular way, capture a few slaveholders and release some slaves."[123] In addition to that blunder, Brown failed to secure the heights above the town, which allowed sharpshooters placed there to pick off his men at will. When Brown's men attempted to flee by swimming the Potomac back into Maryland, they were picked off in this manner.

Villard feels that Brown's failure as a general made him a much more likely candidate as martyr:

> As a wielder of arms, John Brown inspires no enthusiasm; not even the flaming sword of Gideon in his hands lifts him about the ordinary run of those who battled in their day for a great cause. For all his years of dreaming that he might

become another Schamyl, or Toussaint L'Ouverture, or the Mountain Marion of a new war of liberation, he was anything but a general. In his knapsack... lay instead a humble pen to bring him glory. For when he was stripped of his liberty, of the arms in which he exulted, the great power of the spirit within was revealed to him. The letters which now daily went forth to friends and relatives, and speedily found their way into print, found their way also to the hearts of all who sympathized with him misguided as he was, here was another martyr whose blood was to be the seed, not of his church, but of his creed.[124]

By Monday morning, the headlines of the nation's newspapers were screaming that "A Slave Rebellion of Immense Size" was underway in the South. The long-awaited slave insurrection had started, and terror spread through the land. As some indication of the sympathies of the northern press, the *New York Herald* printed a speech calling for armed insurrection by Gerit Smith alongside of John Brown's "provisional constitution."

Washington lost no time in reacting to this provocation. On Monday, October 17, President Buchanan ordered Colonel Robert E. Lee and Lt. J. E. B. Stuart to Harpers Ferry to apprehend the insurrectionists. By noon the Jefferson Guards had seized the Maryland side of the bridge over the Potomac, effectively cutting Brown off from his base of operations at the Kennedy Farm and any possibility of retreat. Resistance folded quickly after that. When Lee and Stuart's men stormed the arsenal, Brown's men could hardly defend themselves. Brown would have been killed on the spot had not Israel Green's sword struck his belt buckle. As a result, Brown was captured, and from that moment until he was hanged at Charlestown Court House, he was allowed to propound his own legend to the press which gathered at his feet during his last incarceration. The great slave insurrection which was the lynchpin of his military plan never happened, but in its place Brown got something better than that. He got to goad the whole country into war.

The South was appalled at the way that the North turned Brown into a hero. Ralph Waldo Emerson, who had entertained John Brown at his home in Concord, Massachusetts, referred to Brown as a "transcendentalist saint."[125] Both Emerson and his protégé Henry David Thoreau had conversed with Brown, and it was during those conversations, according to Franklin Benjamin Sanborn, another member of the Secret Six, that they gained "that intimate knowledge of Brown's character and general purpose which qualified them... to make those addresses on his behalf which were the first response among American scholars to the heroism of the man...."[126] During those conversations, Brown had convinced both Emerson and Thoreau that he was a transcendentalist, and after his death the sage of Concord and the poet of Walden Pond both participated in Brown's canonization as a "transcendentalist saint." On the day John Brown was hanged, Thoreau told a crowd of true believers that "Some 1800 years ago Christ was crucified; this morning, perchance, Captain Brown was hung. These are two ends of a chain which is not without its links. His is not Old Brown any longer; he is an angel of light...."[127]

Not to be outdone by his protégé, Emerson called Brown, "that new saint, than whom none purer or more brave was ever led by love of men into conflict and death,—the new saint awaiting his martyrdom, and who, if he shall suffer, will make the gallows glorious like the cross."[128] America's most beloved poet, Henry Wadsworth Longfellow had similar things to say in his diary, where he claimed that the day of Brown's hanging would mark "the date of a new Revolution—quite as much needed as the old one. Even now as I write, they are leading old John Brown to execution in Virginia for attempting to rescue slaves! This is sowing the wind to reap the whirlwind, which will come soon."[129] The only member of the New England literary pantheon who disagreed with Emerson's equating of John Brown with Jesus was Nathaniel Hawthorne, now recently returned from Europe, who opined that no man was more justly hanged than John Brown.

This was not simply a question of elites talking to each other. When five men and a Boston constable attempted to arrest Franklin Benjamin Sanborn in Concord on April 3, 1860, his sisters mobilized the entire town to thwart the arrest. One day later, the Massachusetts Supreme Court nullified the arrest, and Sanborn received a hero's welcome when he returned to Concord.

Once Emerson and Thoreau had taken the plunge, comparisons equating John Brown and Jesus Christ became commonplace. Virginia, Henry Ward Beecher claimed, had made John Brown a martyr, and Brown did nothing to dissuade his transcendentalist acolytes. During his final imprisonment, his words were broadcast by sympathetic newspaper accounts across the north. Taking his cue from Emerson and Thoreau, Brown now began to refer to himself as the Christ: "You know," he stated on November 1, 1859, "that Christ once armed Peter. So also in my case, I think he put a sword into my hand, and there continued it, so long as he saw best, and then kindly took it from me....I wish you could know with what cheerfulness I am now wielding the "Sword of the Spirit" on the right hand and on the left."[130]

"I do not feel conscious of guilt in taking up arms," Brown claimed, and then he added brazenly that "Jesus of Nazareth was doomed in like manner. Why should not I be?"[131]

Needless to say, the South was appalled by this sort of rhetoric. According to Otto Scott,

> The South [was] first amazed and then driven into fury by the Northern elevation of John Brown. Revelation that his raid had been incited, financed and armed by famous persons in the North, and that other Northerners rose to praise the terror he created imbued the people of the South with fear—and with a rising realization that something new and dangerous in racial conflict was upon them.[132]

When Lincoln claimed that "John Brown's effort was peculiar," because "it was not a slave insurrection. It was an attempt by white men to get a revolt among slaves," the South for once was in full agreement with Lincoln. In fact, Scott continues,

It was that peculiarity the white Southerners found inexplicable and sinister. The idea that men of their own race would kill them on behalf of another had never really been credible to them, until Harper's Ferry. Until then they had scorned the Northern concern for black slaves as a cloak for political power. The abolitionist clergy and its attempt to paint all the people of the South as Christian pariahs had not shaken the Scotch-Irish inheritors of the faith of John Knox; they knew better. But when white men were shot dead in the streets of Harper's Ferry and their murderers held aloft as examples of a higher law, the South felt itself at bay.[133]

Before Harpers Ferry, men on both sides of the Mason-Dixon line struggled to keep the Union together. After Harpers Ferry, when the White House, Congress, and the Supreme Court proved either unwilling or unable to indict the Secret Six or deal effectively with the threat they posed, the South concluded that it would have to deal with that threat in its own way:

> The Southerners agreed that Harper's Ferry was merely a harbinger of more raids to come. Led by whites, financed and armed by the North, directed by men safe in Northern sanctuaries, these raids would strike against plantations and homes alike, to create a guerilla war unprecedented in its pattern, perilous to the safety of all white Southerners.[134]

After Harpers Ferry, the South began to treat the North as not only a separate nation, but as a hostile nation which threatened invasion from without and which allowed all of its organs of public opinion free rein in calling for a slave rebellion within its borders. The threat of armed insurrection among the South's blacks produced as a result the same effect which it had produced in the aftermath of the Nat Turner rebellion and which it would also produce in the aftermath of Reconstruction: the whites cracked down on their black slaves and barred the movement of free black in the territory they controlled.

The South was appalled at the cult of John Brown which arose as a result of the collaboration of New York newspapers and Transcendental pundits from Concord.

> To them [the South] he was a fanatic who sought not only to steal cherished property, but to establish anarchy, to reenact Nat Turner's horrors, to make the terrible scenes of the Haytian Negro revolution insignificant beside the atrocities he would set on foot.[135]

Once it became clear that they were not going to be indicted for treason or conspiracy, the Secret Six joined in the propaganda offensive against the South.

> Parker was in Europe on a futile search for health, when Harper's Ferry was attacked; but he bore his testimony manfully: "Of course, I was not astonished to hear that an attempt had been made to free the slaves in a certain part of Virginia.... Such 'insurrections' will continue as long as slavery lasts, and will increase, both in frequency and in power, just as the people become intelligent and moral...It is a good Anti-Slavery picture on the Virginia shield: a man standing on a tyrant and chopping his head off with a sword; and I would paint the

sword holder black and the tyrant white, to show the immediate application of the principle."[136]

The South felt that the North was conspiring against it and wanted to nip the revolution in the bud Brown's raid on Harpers Ferry and his apotheosis at the hands of the pundits "revived with tenfold strength the desires of a Southern Confederacy."[137]

The South's determination to hang Brown confirmed the North in its suspicions that they were dealing with a barbarous race of people who were essentially un-American, members of a different culture which was not compatible with America's foundational principles. The outrage was so great that it spawned plots to liberate Brown before his execution. Lysander Spooner plotted to kidnap Governor Wise and hold him hostage aboard a sea-going tug until Brown was released. A group of German '48ers from New York, planned with the collaboration of the Secret Six, to attack Charlestown and escape with Brown to the North. It was only with the greatest reluctance that Sanborn called off the attack. "Object abandoned." Sanborn wrote to Higginson. "So I suppose we must give up all hope of saving our old friend."[138]

John Brown's raid convinced the South that it had to arm itself in self-defense. In the view of Senator Mason of Virginian: "John Brown's invasion was condemned [in the North] only because it failed. But in view of the sympathy for him in the North and persistent efforts of the sectional party there to interfere with the rights of the South, it was not at all strange that the Southern States should deem it proper to arm themselves and prepare for any contingency that might arise."[139]

After an extensive investigation, the Joint Committee of the General Assembly of Virginia concluded on January 26, 1860 that as long as the Republican party "maintains its present sectional organization and inculcates its present doctrines, the South can expect nothing less than a succession of such traitorous attempts to subvert its institutions and to incite its slaves to rapine and murder. The crimes of John Brown were neither more nor less than practical illustrations of the doctrines of the leaders of the Republican Party. The very existence of such a party is an offence to the whole South."[140] Brown's intention to "incite insurrection" among the slaves was clear; it was only because of "the loyalty and well-affected disposition of the slaves that he did not succeed in creating a servile war, with its necessary attendants of rapine and murder of all sexes, ages, and conditions."[141]

Less than two days after Brown launched his ill-fated raid, the full scope of the catastrophe began to dawn on Ottilie Assing and Frederick Douglass. John Brown had been captured; most of his men were dead, and the slave insurrection he anticipated had produced not a single Negro willing to fight at his side. But worse than that, from Assing and Douglass's point of view, when Brown was captured, Brown's carpetbag was captured along with him, and in it were letters from Gerit Smith and Frederick Douglass implicating them in a conspiracy behind the attack. Virginia's governor, Henry Wise, requested President Buchanan's assistance in arresting the conspirators, and he left no doubt that the one he wanted above all was "Frederick Douglass, a Negro man... charged with... inciting servile insurrection."[142] Douglass was in Philadelphia at the time, hoping that a crowd of his white friends there would accompany him to the Walnut Street Ferry and shield him from possible arrest by US marshals. Luckily, Douglass made it out of town without their assistance, for none of them were willing to risk their lives or fortunes on Douglass's behalf.

Once the immediate danger of arrest passed, Douglass had other equally pressing concerns. Locked in his desk in his house in Rochester were several letters linking Douglass to Brown and the other Secret Six conspirators as well as a provisional constitution in Brown's own hand for the revolutionary regime that was supposed to have taken power after Brown's success at Harpers Ferry. Fully aware of the magnitude of the charges that could be leveled against him, Douglass fled first to Canada, and then, on November 12, from New Brunswick to England aboard the steamer Scotia. "I could but feel that I was going into exile, perhaps for life," he later wrote. "Slavery seemed to be at the very top of its power.... No one who has not himself been compelled to leave his home and country and go into permanent banishment can well imagine the state of mind and heart which such a condition brings."[143] *The Baltimore Sun* was unimpressed by Douglass's self-serving account of his role in the Harpers Ferry massacre, calling it "a curiosity, a rare specimen of craven impudence."[144]

Assing eventually published her own account of the events of October 1859, in a piece entitled "The Insurrection at Harper's Ferry." Her account showed "beyond doubt that she had knowledge of Brown's venture possessed only by members of the inner circle."[145] In her attempt to exonerate Douglass of any wrongdoing, she only implicated him further. Much of what the world knew about Brown came from Colonel Forbes, who had turned on Brown when Brown failed to come up with the money he demanded. In the course of her narrative, Assing revealed that Forbes had met with Douglass at his home in Rochester in November of 1858 and that Douglass had given Forbes money as well as contacts among, as Douglass put it, "my German friends in New York," a reference for those who knew to Assing's circle of Radical friends in Hoboken.[146] Assing eventually came to the conclusion that Forbes was a con man, but not before implicating herself and Douglass even deeper in the conspiracy behind Brown.

In the same piece, Assing referred to Brown, as "the hero of Kansas," a superhuman figure who was "Stern and implacable like death itself," but "never guilty of needless cruelty; to the contrary, he often proved his innate kindness and humanity."[147] The raid on Harpers Ferry had shown not that America was under assault by terrorists who were willing to offer human sacrifice up on the altar of their own megalomania. Rather, it showed in Assing's view that "Only a society that perverted law to justify its transgressions against humanity could persecute this man as a criminal, she charged; only a corrupt world, only a debased law could denounce him as a terrorist."[148]

Assing's defense of Douglass was, if anything, more outrageous than her defense of Brown. Assing claimed that "the famous orator Frederick Douglass" was the only man who stood up to acknowledge frankly his participation in the conspiracy, even though the consequences for him are more dangerous and pernicious than for most others."[149] She then added, seemingly unaware that she was contradicting herself, that after Douglass was identified as one of the leaders of the Harpers Ferry conspiracy, that it was "only by his hasty flight to Canada did he escape the clutches of the United States marshals, these henchmen of [the] government."[150]

Douglass was reluctant to accept the honors which Assing offered him. In his autobiography, he claimed that he himself was unsure whether it was "my discretion or cowardice"[151] that prevented him from joining Brown. But he was adamant in assuring his readers that "The taking of Harpers Ferry was a measure never encouraged by my word or by my vote."[152] In her article, Assing twists Douglass's frank admission of indecision at best and cowardice at worst, into "a magnificent, brilliant manifesto dictated by that implacable hatred for slavery and that dedication to liberating the oppressed which knows no consequences, no matter how devastating their effect on his life."[153]

In retrospect, Assing's motivation in writing this frankly biased apologia for what everyone else saw as an act of cowardice is not hard to fathom. Douglass was now out of the country living on an island a mere 30 miles from the European continent where Assing still had contacts and thousands of miles away from the Negro wife Assing had come to believe had usurped her position as Douglass's one true love. If Assing positioned Douglass in the right way in the mind of the German-speaking world, her articles in combination with the German translation of his autobiography might be the beginning of their new life together on the continent. One can only imagine how many daydreams Assing savored of Dark Fred, the noble savage from America, being paraded around by an even nobler Ottilie, the half-Jewish Delilah, who opened Dark Fred's mind (and by implication the mind of his race) to the blinding light of Feuerbachian atheism. What a triumph for German culture that would be!

And yet it never happened. Douglass's daughter died, forcing him to return home no matter what the consequences. By the time he got home, whatever role he had played in the Harpers Ferry affair had become moot. Virginia could no longer extradite him because Virginia was now at war with the United States.

In April of 1861, the Civil War broke out, and the revolutionaries rejoiced when it did. Higginson was jubilant. Assing saw the Civil War as the outbreak of her long-awaited revolution. Assing repeatedly referred to the Civil War as a revolution: "The circumstances that have led to the outbreak of this revolution at this time are accidental; however, the deeper seminal cause existed already at the inception of the republic and has grown along with the country until it assumed its present dominance: it is the eternal conflict between slavery and freedom that no power in the world can resolve."[154]

According to Assing, the Civil War was a continuation of the American Revolution. Every revolution leads to a civil war, but war, according to her view, was revolutionary progress in fast forward:

> The last ten days have made a tremendous revolution in all things pertaining to the possible future of the colored people of the United States. We shall stay here and watch the current of events, and serve the cause of freedom and humanity in any way that shall be open to us during the struggle now going on between the slave power and the government. When the Northern people have been made to experience a little more of the savage barbarism of slavery, they may be willing to make war upon it, and in that case we stand ready to lend a hand in any way we can be of service. At any rate, this is no time for us to leave the country.[155]

Even after the war, Assing never wavered in her belief that war was the best method for bringing about revolutionary change: "The regular development of nations is a slow process, so that one century in that respect changes less than five years in an individual life, but let a revolution erupt, and within the shortest period progress will be made by the people that could not be effected by fifty, even 100 years of peace. By taking this step the nation has decided its fate, and there is a great future ahead."[156]

The real contribution of the German '48ers who came to America was that they ignited the second American Revolution, otherwise known as the Civil War:

> Their reward was that they were able to participate in a revolution that resurrected the American Dream: "One great revolution will educate a nation more rapidly than a century of peace. Less than ten years have elapsed since we sheltered in our houses the fugitives from Harpers Ferry and their allies, since we helped them across the borders, and only four years later our volunteers entered the conquered Southern cities and fortresses with the sounds of the hymn: John Brown's body lies a moldering in the grave; his soul is marching on."[157]

In the lecture Assing worked up on Brown's attempted insurrection at Harpers Ferry, John Brown's true errand was not the bloody slave raid but the peaceful mountain republic he planned for fugitive slaves. "I keep still a letter from John Brown to Frederick Douglass, written a few weeks before the attack on Harpers Ferry: He warmly advocated his demand, and ever represented it as Frederick Douglass's duty to comply with it. If Frederick Douglass could have been persuaded, he would in all probability have shared the fate of the others, who were either killed or executed as high traitors."[158]

In the months leading up to the war and throughout its duration, both Assing and Douglas used their journalistic skills and contacts to call for the same black uprising which John Brown failed to provoke. "Should the dreaded Negro uprising actually erupt," Assing wrote in January 1861

> it would squelch all rebellious movements more quickly and more surely than all repressive measures of the government would do, for none of the slave states has the means to fight a superior black force. At the first news of the destruction of a few plantations and the killing of some slaveholders and overseers, these very

loudmouths and ruffians who today are only too eager to curse the North would come crawling for its protection and assistance.[159]

On July 4, 1861, Douglass denounced Union General Butler as a traitor because he offered to use United States troops to put down a slave insurrection in Maryland. Assing could not have agreed more. Both Douglass and Assing criticized Lincoln's Emancipation Proclamation because it did not include an explicit appeal for black insurrection. In a speech he delivered in Philadelphia on January 14, 1862, Douglass advocated arming the slaves in the South as insurrectionists.

Before long, Assing and Douglass's campaign to set off a slave rebellion began to bear fruit, although probably not the fruit they had hoped for:

> In December 1862 Jefferson Davis declared that the Southern slave code would be used against African American soldiers caught by the Confederates—that is, they would be treated as insurrectionists. As a result of this proclamation, black prisoners of war were executed in the South, the wounded were refused medical treatment or murdered on the spot; exchange of black prisoners was ruled out.[160]

Once again, the dialectic of the Nat Turner rebellion reasserted itself. Calls for armed insurrection from the North were met by renewed repression in the South, and the hapless Negro was caught in the middle. He resented the oppression of the slaveholder, but at the same time, as John Brown's raid had shown, he was reluctant to become the pawn of northern revolutionaries as well.

The Emancipation Proclamation seemed to put Frederick Douglass out of a job, but as the reaction to Reconstruction spread throughout the South after the war, Douglass began to have second thoughts. Ottilie continued to be the apostle of German atheism and continued to write to Feuerbach about the progress of her star pupil:

> there was one obstacle to a loving and lasting friendship—namely, the person Christian God. Early impressions, environments, and the beliefs still dominating this entire nation held sway over D. The ray of light of German atheism had never reached him, while I thanks to natural inclination, training and the whole influence of German education and literature, had overcome the belief in God at an early age.[161]

But as a half-Jew she still remembered the reaction which had swept through Germany in the wake of Napoleon's defeat. Assing feared "a tragic repetition of the fate to which the Jewish community in Germany had been forced to submit during the restoration period."[162] As a result

> she vowed that she would do everything she could to save "her" successful American revolution from falling in to the hands of the enemy. The lesson of 1848 deeply implanted in Assing's mind could never be erased. The revolution in Germany had not just been defeated by military forces but had also fallen by a process of self-deconstruction—undermined by political wavering and bickering, by lack of courage, by cheap compromises, by betrayal of radical commitments.[163]

Now it looked as if the same thing were going to happen in America in the wake of the Civil War. The excesses of the Reconstruction era had led Nathan Bedford Forest to found the Ku Klux Klan. Confronted with ever increasing resistance, the Republicans began to lose their revolutionary fervor in dealing with the South and began to cut deals that would lead to a *modus vivendi* rather than revolutionary reform. Andrew Johnson's restoration of home rule in the South began a process which led eventually to what the South would call its "redemption," which is to say the all but total disenfranchisement of the Negro and the reassertion of the hegemony which white Southerners had lost during the war and Reconstruction. This chain of events caused Frederick Douglass to rethink the retirement from the abolitionist struggle which the Emancipation Proclamation seemed to invite. Instead of retiring, Douglass re-tooled and came up with a new slogan: "Slavery is not abolished until the black man has the ballot."[164]

By 1870 Ottilie Assing had succeeded in bringing the light of atheism to Dark Fred. The result was that he lost his constituency among rankd and file Negroes, who retained their faith in Christ. Shortly after President Grant announced the ratification of the Fifteenth Amendment, on March 30, 1870, Douglass addressed a celebration of the event in Philadelphia and succeeded in scandalizing all present by talking like a German Marxist. Douglass began his speech by refusing to engage in any "hackneyed cant about thanking God for this deliverance."[165] He then proceeded to attack the churches which "led everything against the abolition of slavery, always holding us back by telling us that God would abolish slavery in his own good time."[166] The black clergy in attendance were shocked and dismayed by Douglass's atheism. Douglass's response, which Diedrich claims probably came from Assing's pen, did little to mollify them. Freedom had come about "Thanks not to faith, but to the enlightenment of the age, and the growth of rational ideas among men, to differ with the church today does not bring torture and physical death."[167] In a letter to a comrade in arms, Assing exulted in the fact that she had goaded Douglass into doing battle with what she termed with thinly veiled contempt as "the pious party."

> Finally Douglass is in open battle with the pious party, after they had long ceased to know what to make of him. On the occasion of the ratification celebration for the Fifteenth Amendment in Philadelphia he spoke up against the silly drivel about "divine providence" and the resolutions "to thank God for this miracle," saying "I deal here in no hackneyed cant about thanking God for this great deliverance; I look upon this great revolution as having been brought about by man, rather than by any special intervention of Divine Providence."[168]

Missing from Assing's account was any understanding that the "pious party" was largely made up of the black preachers who comprised the backbone of political and ethnic organization in the black community and would remain so for the foreseeable future. Assing failed to see that in alienating Douglass from the "pious party," she also alienated him from his own people.

Cut off from his own people by his German-Jewish mistress, Douglass became of necessity tied more and more closely to the Republican Party at a time when it was willing, if not eager, to abandon its revolutionary claims in favor of more stable and longer-lasting political power. Eventually as Reconstruction gave way to Redemption, Frederick Douglass abandoned revolution and allowed the Republicans to buy him off with a series of increasingly demeaning patronage jobs. After working tirelessly for the election of Rutherford B. Hayes, Douglass received his reward when the Senate confirmed Douglass as Marshal of the District of Columbia on March 17, 1877. One month before receiving this honor, Hayes had taken Douglass aside and informed him that he planned "to pursue conciliatory policy toward the South."[169]

The Redemption of the South began in 1877 when President Hayes ordered the withdrawal of federal garrisons from the former states of the Confederacy. In 1890 Senator Henry Cabot Lodge of Massachusetts introduced the "Force Bill" into the Senate, a bill which would have "authorized Federal supervision of elections in all districts where there was evidence of fraud or intimidation."[170] The bill was an attempt to guarantee the franchise to the South's Negroes, but it was soundly defeated and signaled that the cause of white supremacy was now in the ascendancy in America. The main reason for this *volta -face* was the wretched excess of the Reconstruction era, which the North imposed as punishment on the South, but which it felt it could no longer justify. When men like Governor Vance of North Carolina pointed out that during Reconstruction "the criminals sat in the law-making chamber, on the bench and in the jury-box, instead of standing in the dock,"[171] the North had no reply.

During that same year, the event which Weaver terms "the final Confederate offensive" also took place when the men who had defended the South in her hour of need assembled in Chattanooga and formed the United Confederate Veterans "to breathe defiance at Yankee civilization."[172] The South could now portray itself as "high-minded Cavaliers fighting fanatical Roundheads" or as "La Vendee, destroyed and desecrated by infidel armies,"[173] but in its hatred of Yankee culture it failed to understand that there was a difference between a Transcendentalist zealot like Thaddeus Stevens and an industrialist like Andrew Carnegie. Nor did they understand that the Civil War marked the passing of the former as the cultural icon of the North and the rise of the latter. Both men were conflated in the image of the hated Yankee, and as a result the South fought a culture war on two fronts, often battling an enemy which no longer existed.

The promoters of southern Redemption failed to understand that the Civil War had destroyed not only the South but Concord, which is to say, the high culture of the North, as well. Symbolic of that demise was the death in 1864 of Nathaniel Hawthorne, the flower of New England culture. In the aftermath of the Civil War, New York displaced Concord as the literary capital of the United States, and money became the criterion of literary merit as well as every other kind of merit. "Puritan zealots trailing clouds of Transcendentalism" had been replaced by

> the money-seeking class which, as De Bow's Review had once declared, "cared nothing for the Negroes unless to dislike them," and "nothing for the Abolitionists, unless to with that they would hold their tongues and stay their pens, or transport themselves en masse to Exeter Hall, never to return to America."[174]

Once the Republicans backed away from Reconstruction, the punishment of the South took a back seat to its financial and industrial exploitation. At this point the disenfranchisement of the Negro made perfect sense to the Yankee robber barons if, by that gesture, the peace that allowed for the financial exploitation of the South could be secured. At this point Yankee financiers arrived in their private railway cars and bought up the resources of the South at 10 cents to the dollar.

By accepting his patronage job as Federal Marshall, Douglass signaled his acquiescence to those plans. Douglass was 59 years old at the time and cut off from both his own natural constituency and the men who were willing to fund him when he was younger. As a result the temptation to trade in principle for a steady income was too great to resist.

Assing heard about Douglass's capitulation while in Europe, with the unfulfilled hope still in her heart that he would eventually join her there. That hope was given new life when news of Anna Murray's death reached Assing. Now the way was clear for the fulfillment of the fantasy she had been nurturing for over two decades as the other woman.

The fundamental flaw in this plan was Assing's failure to understand the Negro slave's attitude toward marriage. For Assing and her revolutionary friends, the issue was quite clear. Marriage was, to use the term of William Godwin which so impressed Percy Shelley, "the most odious of all monopolies." The war on the south liberating the slaves was only a prelude in Assing's mind to the greater revolution which would abolish matrimony, private property, and religion. Only after that act of cleansing destruction had taken place could a man call himself free.

Douglass having been raised as a slave in the South, however, had already been liberated by that very slavery from the burdens of matrimony and property. In fact he himself was a product of sexual liberation, and as a result never knew who his father was. In abandoning Anna Murray, the woman who had bought his freedom and by whom he had children who knew who their father was, Douglass would be handing a victory to the slave owners who felt that slaves could breed but not marry.

According to Diedrich, Assing never understood that Douglass's attitude toward marriage and family differed fundamentally from hers. For her, as for Clara Mundt's Aphra Behn, "it means profaning marriage when you turn it into indissoluble fetters which may not even be shattered when it has chained us to a hell of pain."[175] For Douglass, however, slavery had already nullified marriage and "made my brothers and sisters strangers to me; it converted the mother that bore me into a myth; it shrouded my father in mystery and left me without an intelligible beginning in the world."[176]

There were other more obvious things that Assing either didn't understand or refused to admit. The most obvious was that she was no longer as sexually attractive as she had been 22 years ago. Assing tried to disguise this fact by writing long letters about the "rejuvenation" she was experiencing in Europe, but intellectual rejuventation could only go so far in a relationship like this, especially since she had lost her teeth and was showing other signs of age. In the absence of the legal bond of marriage, which she had scorned openly for her entire adult life, what exactly was to bind her to him? Her mind? More discussions of Feuerbach? These were slim reeds indeed, especially when confronted with the power of human passion unconstrained by reason for so long. Whatever she had to offer Douglass at this time in her life, there were indications that it wasn't enough. After his demotion from Federal Marshall to recorder of deeds, Douglass hired an adoring white feminist 20 years his junior as his clerk. Before long, the old pattern reasserted itself. Douglass agonized for a while, writing poems in which he compared himself to Adam in the garden of Eden, and Helen Pitts, his clerk, to forbidden fruit: "Amazed I stood in wonder sound/Till then such fruit I'd never found,/I needed help and looked around/ For means to gain possession."[177]

All the while Assing became increasingly despondent, writing him reproachful letters from Europe, where she still hoped beyond hope that they could create a life together. Douglass continued to resist the call to Europe, nor did he invite Assing to come to America. By the summer of 1883, "the conflict between inclination and obligation had become so fierce that he was 'depressed almost to the point of a breakdown.'"[178] Then, early in 1884, Douglass resolved the conflict by marrying Pitts. As if this were not rejection enough, Douglass made the break with Assing even more dramatic by marrying his new bride in a Presbyterian Church in Washington, at a ceremony at which a minister officiated.

Assing held fire for eight months but then on August 21, 1884 she responded to Douglass's double betrayal by committing suicide in the Bois de Boulogne in Paris. When he heard the news, Douglass was quick to put his own spin on her final act of defiance and despair by claiming that she was suffering from breast cancer, thereby absolving himself for any responsibility for her death. If Douglass was hoping to forget her, Assing, who knew Douglass's weaknesses well enough, made sure that that would not happen when she willed him as her legacy the yearly interest on her $13,000 fortune. Upon Douglass's death the principle would go to the Society for the Prevention of Cruelty to Animals.

Douglass lived out the rest of his life as an accomplice both in the death of Ottilie Assing and in the redemption of the South. Instead of proposing revolution, Douglass ended his public career by giving lectures on himself as a "self-made man," urging other Negroes to follow his example. He was succeeded as America's premier Negro by Booker T. Washington, who was smart enough to understand that Douglass's new message was tailor-made for their age. In an era of reaction to the excesses of war and revolution, it was the only message the Negroes were allowed to share with each other in the public forum.

Booker T. Washington had founded the Tuskegee Institute, his school for blacks who were to be given industrial and agricultural training, in 1881 right around the time Frederick Douglass was falling in love with Helen Pitts. Four years later, Washington gave a speech entitled "Cast down your buckets where you are" at the Atlanta Exposition which catapulted him to a position of leadership among America's Negroes. In a country in which both North and South had offered up the Negro on the altar of political expedience and where the promise of emancipation had faded into the reality of segregation and disenfranchisement, Washington looked around for a ray of hope and found it in the Jews: "Ever since I can remember," he wrote,

> I have had a special and peculiar interest in the history and progress of the Jewish race. As I learned in slavery to compare the condition of the Negro with that of the Jews in bondage in Egypt, so I have frequently, since freedom, been compelled to compare the prejudice, even persecution, which the Jewish people have to face and overcome in different parts of the world with the disadvantages of the Negro in the United States and elsewhere.[179]

Negroes, in other words, could succeed in the harsh realities of post-Reconstruction America if they imitated Jews. In *The Future of the American Negro*, Washington wrote: "These people [the Jews] have clung together. They had had a certain amount of unity, pride and love of race; and, as the years go on, they will be more influential in this country—a country where they were once despised, and looked upon with scorn and derision. It is largely because the Jewish race has had faith in itself. Unless the Negro learns more and more to imitate the Jew in these matters, to have faith in himself, he cannot expect to have any high degree of success."

In the wake of this and similar utterances, affluent German Jews began to pour their money into Washington's school. "Julius Rosenwald," Murray Friedman tells us, "had been moved by Washington's autobiography, *Up from Slavery*," and "soon became one of the school's most energetic trustees."[180] As part of his duties, Rosenwald, once a year, would send Washington "a list of wealthy men, many of them Jews, whom he thought should be solicited for contributions."[181]

In 1904 Washington created a "Jewish seat" on Tuskegee's board and persuaded Paul M. Warburg to take it.[182] Among the wealthy Jews who were subsequently to contribute to Tuskegee were Jacob and Mortimer Schiff, James Loeb, and Felix Warburg (all members of Kuhn, Loeb), as well as the Seligmans, the Lehmans, Joseph Pulitzer, Jacob Billikopf and Julian Mack. Schiff continued this arrangement annually until Washington's death in 1915. Friedman sees in the relationship which Washington established with "Jewish philanthropists like Schiff, Rosenwald and Warburg who supported him with money, time, and effort... the first organized ties between the black and Jewish communities,"[183] ties that would eventuate in what came to be known as the Black-Jewish Alliance. That alliance, culminating in the rise of Martin Luther King and the Civil Rights Movement, would become the main source of revolutionary activity in the United States for the greater part of the 20th century. Friedman, however, is wrong in thinking that the Black-Jewish Alliance began with Jacob Schiff linking up with Booker T. Washington. The pattern for the Black-Jewish Alliance had already been set in Frederick Douglass's relationship with Ottilie Assing. For more than a century after John Brown's raid on Harper's Ferry, Jews (or half-Jews) like Ottilie Assing, Jacob Schiff, Norman Mailer and Robert Scheer, creator of Eldridge Cleaver, would attempt to remake the Negro in their own image and turn him into the avant garde of the revolutionary movement in America.

Support for Tuskegee was only one of Jacob Schiff's many philanthropic projects. Another one was the Russian revolution.

Chapter Fifteen

From Emancipation to Assassination

n 1861, when Moses Hess was still hard at work on his book *Rom und Jerusalem,* Czar Alexander II emancipated the serfs, anticipating by two years the Emancipation Proclamation of America's President Abraham Lincoln. Emancipation was in the air, and soon it was the turn of the Russian Jews to be liberated from the restrictions that had been placed on their race since time immemorial. The wary prudence of rulers like Pope Innocent III seemed to be nothing more than proof of the darkness of a bygone age, especially when compared to the Enlightenment which had now reached the throne of a notoriously backward country like Russia.

In November of the same year in which Alexander II emancipated the serfs, he also made Jews eligible for state employment. The law of November 1861 more importantly permitted Jews to pursue professional careers outside the Pale of the Settlement. Alexander's Jewish legislation, coming as it did on the heels of the emancipation of the serfs, gave the impression that "Jewish emancipation was in the offing and that education could make it an immediate reality."[1]

Eighteen Sixty One was the *annus mirabilis* of emancipation, but the "golden age of Russian Jewry" had begun six years before that when Alexander II ascended to the Russian throne. "On the very day of his coronation in 1855 Alexander II inaugurated what been called 'the golden age' of Russian Jewry by abolishing juvenile conscription. The conscription edict was followed by a series of decrees which, between 1856 and 1865, improved Jewish access to education and rights of residence."[2] For reasons which will become apparent later, the Czar's actions, which everyone saw as well-intentioned, would have unforeseen consequences by "initiating a process which eventually led to the political radicalization of Jews."[3]

The Russians had been working to integrate the Jews into Russian culture almost from the day that 50 percent of the world's Jews found themselves living on Russian soil after the partition of Poland. Russian reformers were not discouraged when the first faltering attempts to regulate Jewish involvement in alcohol production failed. In 1844, the Russian government abolished the Kahal, and its functions were divided up among various local governments. In order to forestall this eventuality the Russian Jews had recourse to tactics which would become increasingly significant by the end of the century. They called in outside help. In 1846, when Czar Nicholas I, the man who had abolished the Kahal, was intent on resettling Jews out of the villages of the Pale and onto the virgin land of New Russia as a way of putting an end to Jewish smuggling, he received a distinguished visitor from England. Sir Moses Montefiore, the hero of Damascus, had arrived at his door with a letter of recommendation from Queen Victoria, hoping to bring about "an improvement in the lot of the Jewish people." It came as no surprise to the Czar that Montefiore, an English Jew, recommended lifting all restrictions on Jews in Russia. Representing the views of David Ricardo, another English Jew of Sephardic extraction, Montefiore condemned the idea of resettling the Jews and insisted that at the heart of the Jewish problem consisted in the limitation of freedom of commerce imposed on the Jews.[4]

Montefiore's attitude is consistent with the conventional views of Jewish historians, who insisted that the Jews of Russia rebelled because they had been oppressed. Evidence, however, shows that the opposite was the case. The Jews rebelled because they had been emancipated. "Jews," Nora Levin writes describing the aftermath of 1917, "had little reason to lament the downfall of a regime that had confined them to a huge ghetto—the Pale of Settlement and had, with few exceptions, barred them from the normal course of Russian life."[5] The simple fact of the matter is that it was the openness of the Czar to Enlightenment ideas like education and emancipation which fueled the rise of the Jewish revolutionary in Russia during the Golden Age inaugurated by Alexander II. As Solzhenitsyn says, "When the label 'persecutor of the Jews' is put on the Russians, their intentions are falsified and their competence exaggerated."[6]

In 1866 Alexander II decided to lift all of the measures that were supposed to turn Jews into farmers because by 1866, it was clear that the Russian effort to turn Jews into farmers had failed. Those who understood the situation, knew from first hand experience that "The Jew would abandon work in the field as soon as he learned that someone in the neighborhood had a horse, an ox or anything else to buy or sell."[7] Unfortunately, Russian generosity had created other problems as well. The Jews had refused to learn farming, but had not refused the lands which the Czar had offered them to become farmers. Now "huge areas" of the best farming land, "with fertile black soil" had been transferred into "the hands of Jews, without bringing in any results...." Or if there were results they were not the ones intended at the inception of the program. "The best land was reserved for the Jews" but it was producing nothing because the Jews either could not work the land because of ignorance or refused to because it would divert them from more lucrative ways of making money. On the other hand, the Russians who lived near the Jews were outraged over the fact that they didn't' have any land or by the fact that they had to rent land at exorbitant rates from the Jews.[8] Once this realization sank into the mind of the Russian peasants it led to attacks on Jewish settlements.

After it became apparent that Jews were not going to become farmers, Czarist ministers tried to Russify them by allowing them to study at Russian universities. As a result of these liberalizations, Jews got the impression that emancipation was around the corner and flocked into the Russian schools. The Russian belief in the Enlightenment dogma that education would lead to assimilation "acted as an irresistible stimulus for Jews to enter Russian schools in the hope of claiming an academic degree or professional certificate. The first to make good on this promise were the students of the rabbinical seminaries who had been allowed to continue their education in Russian universities since 1856."[9]

By the 1860s, there was a genuine meeting of the minds in Russia. Both the enlightened Russian *Nomenklatura* and the Maskilic Jews agreed that education was the solution to Russia's Jewish problem. Haskalah had begun as a German-Jewish idea with Mendelssohn, but by the 1860s it had been succeeded by the Russian-Jewish idea of assimilation or "Russification" which was now understood as "the enlightenment of Jews through Russian language and in the Russian spirit."[10] But as Haberer points out, "The Russian spirit of the 'new enlightenment' produced more than loyal, educated, and 'useful ' Jewish subjects of the tsarist state: it also produced Jewish cadres for the Russian revolutionary movement."[11]

Solzehnitsyn agrees, feeling that the fatal flaw in Russification which led to the rise of the revolutionary was not the malevolence of the Czar; it was his benevolence coupled with a naive acceptance of the platitudes of the Enlightenment, especially those promoting the supposed benefits of education. Far from wanting to persecute the Russian Jews, Czar Alexander II "intended to bring about the assimilation of the Jews with the other Russian peoples."[12] Unfortunately, the Czar began tearing down fences without inquiring into why they had been erected in the first place. Or, as Solzehnitsyn puts it, "Alexander II began to abolish the limitations on the Jews without inquiring into the inner causes for their isolation in the hope that they would solve all of the other problems by themselves."[13] As a result, "One limitation after another was lifted,"[14] but nothing had changed in the Pale. The Jews were still selling vodka; the situation was still intolerable. In 1870, an official report proclaimed that "the production and sales of alcoholic beverages in the western regions is almost exclusively in the hands of the Jews, and the abuses which occur in these taprooms has gone far beyond the boundaries of what is tolerable."[15]

The Revolutionary strain of the "Mendelssohnian virus" hadn't made its appearance by the 1850s, but it did soon thereafter, when

> It...penetrated the high-castles of rabbinical Judaism, the yeshivas, and claimed converts to the Haskalah among its talmudic students. Even among the teachers of the Kheder, the bulwark of Jewish elementary religious education, there were some Germanophile melamdim who, in their wanderings from one shtetl to another, had become infected with the Mendelssohnian virus spread far and wide by the Maskilic intelligentsia.[16]

By the 1860s, the virus began to spread because "external conditions were propitious for creating the right environment to produce a revolutionary off-spring."[17] As Moses Hess predicted in *Rom und Jerusalem*, the Jews became revolutionaries within ten years of the arrival of the Enlightenment in Russia. "Its members," Isaiah Berlin wrote, describing the new Jewish-Russian intelligentsia, "thought of themselves as united by something more than mere interest in ideas; they conceived themselves as being a dedicated order, almost a secular priesthood, devoted to the spreading of a specific attitude to life, something like a gospel."[18] Once the ideas of the Enlightenment cracked open the orthodox shell surrounding the shtetl, Jews saw their participation in revolution as ordained by God. Revolution was the task of God's chosen people. Haberer explains how education led Russian Jews to nihilism during the 1860s and how by the late 1860s, these Jews began to assume the leadership role in the revolutionary movement:

> The historical significance of this new intelligentsia for the evolution of Jewish radicalism was enormous. Aside from the fact that the state schools—especially the rabbinical seminaries—furnished the Russian revolutionary movement of the 1860s and 1870s with its first Jewish recruits, it was the intelligentsia nourished by these schools who created the ideological and social atmosphere that enveloped a rising generation of Jews. It imbued them with an activist, Maskilic Weltanschauung.[19]

As a result of their contact with the German Enlightenment, the Jews of the younger generation converted to nihilism during the course of the 1860s. The transformation was as dramatic as it was unexpected and requires some explanation. The Talmud played a crucial role in that transformation. The Talmud, as Jacques Derrida noted 100 years after the Russian Jews turned to revolution in the 1860s and 1870s, has always been a sign of absence. When the Temple was destroyed, "everything became discourse," which is to say talmudic-like commentary on commentary. As Derrida puts it:

> The surrogate does not substitute itself for anything which has somehow pre-existed it. From then on it was probably necessary to begin to think that there was no center, that the center could not be thought of in the form of a being-present, that the center had no natural locus, that it was not a fixed locus, but a function, a sort of non-locus in which an infinite number of sign-substitutions came into play. This moment was that in which language invaded the universal problematic; that in which, in the absence of center or origin, everything became discourse—provided we can agree on this word—that is to say, when everything became a system where the central signified, the original or transcendental signified, is never absolutely present outside a system of differences. The absence of the transcendental signified extends the domain and the interplay of the signification ad infinitum.[20]

The Mendelssohnian Enlightenment had a catastrophic effect on young Russian Jews in the 1860s because it destroyed orthodoxy without putting anything in its place. The Talmud had been a source of contention among Jews since Maimun's attacks in Berlin in the 1780s. When the Talmud finally succumbed to the blows of the Maskilim, the Jews awoke to the realization that there was nothing to take its place, and nihilism, always latent in the Talmud's methodology, followed almost automatically. According to one writer,

> Some "fanatical Yeshiva students who had previously been immersed in the Talmud" abandoned the world view of the patriarchs and Jewish garb after one or two discussions with the nihilists. As soon as even a small break was made in

the orthodox world view, nihilism broke through and drove the Jews to the most extreme positions.[21]

The Talmud was an all-encompassing world unto itself. Unlike, say, Aristotelian philosophy, it could not be integrated by some Maskilic Thomas Aquinas into a Jewish-Enlightenment synthesis. Once the absurdity of its structure became apparent, no amount of fiddling could save its intellectual pretensions, and it sank into obscurity without leaving even an oil slick on the surface where it went down. The Jews who had been trained in Talmudic studies, nonetheless, could not get rid of their training or their Messianic sense of themselves as God's chosen people, and so, as Hess predicted, they took that Messianic sense and transferred it to German socialism, after they discovered that believing in nothing was humanly impossible: "These young Jews were immediately obsessed with universal ideals. All men will become brothers, and the same prosperity for everyone. What an grandiose task: liberating all of mankind from misery and servitude."[22]

Once the young Jews had become convinced that "traditional Judaism" was "a parasitic anomaly," "they assimilated rapidly and absorbed the Russian national spirit."[23] The Russian liberals, in other words, succeeded beyond their wildest dreams in Russifying the Jews, but that transformation would have unintended consequences. Those unintended consequences can be summarized best by saying that as soon as the Jews learned the Russian language they began reading Nikolai Chernyshevsky's revolutionary polemic *What Is To Be Done?* Chernyshevsky's novel appeared in 1863 and before long it was providing a blueprint for how life could be lived outside the norms of the moral order and the traditional mores of both Christians and Jews. Vera Pavlovna, the heroine of the novel, and her companion Pavel Rahkmetov stood for the values of the 1860s, especially free love and communal meaningful work. Chernyshevsky became a conduit for all of the social and political thought which had been causing revolutions in western Europe for the past three decades.

Jewish nihilism soon took root in a cultural movement composed of numerous informal study circles:

> Spear-heading this crusade were Jewish gymnasium students and rabbinical seminarians. In places like Vilna, Mogilev, Zhitomir, and Kiev, they formed 'circles of self-education' which, in turn, proliferated by attracting talmudists, pupils of Jewish crown schools, and privately educated children of wealthy Jewish merchants. Meeting more or less regularly, members would read and discuss Russian literature, articles from the Russian-Jewish periodical press, and works of the German-Jewish Haskalah. Some ventured to write their own Russian, Hebrew, and Yiddish compositions criticizing and satirizing Jewish life and its Orthodox leadership. Both orthodox rabbis and Czarist officials opposed these groups, but they could do little to stop them.... On almost every level they had to struggle against unyielding opponents who viewed their unconventional behavior and unauthorized activity as subversive to the established order of traditional Jewish and official Russian society....In attracting and socializing numer-

ous youths, the subculture of Jewish nihilism created a reservoir of prospective socialist Jews who eventually became active as propagandists, technicians, and organizers of revolution.[25]

In the meantime, as "nihilist enlightenment" conquered the Jewish youth, Russian radicalism put forth its first revolutionary tendrils with the founding of *Zemlia I Volia* (Land and Freedom) in 1861. Three years later, Nikolai Ishutin and Dmitrii Karakazov created a conspiratorial "Organization," which was the front for a deeper inner circle known as "Hell," which took Nihilism to is logical conclusion by first advocating and then engaging in acts of terrorism. On April 4, 1866, Karakazov decided to turn revolutionary dreams into political realities when he attempted to assassinate Alexander II. Karakazov was captured and promptly executed, but the wave of repression which followed his death brought new recruits to the movement, although not many Jews, who remained aloof from revolutionary violence and the movements which promoted it in the years preceding 1868.

Before long, however, seasoned revolutionaries began to notice a change, as Jews started drifting into the movement. Mikhail Bakunin, the Russian revolutionary, who had fought at the barricades of Dresden with Wagner in 1849, noticed the attraction which revolution held for Jews and fulminated against the takeover of the revolutionary movement by the "dictator-messiah Marx" and his "army of German Jews" with the "little Russian Jew Utin" in the lead.[26] If he hoped by speeches like this to keep the Jews away from the revolution, he could just have easily argued against moths being attracted to candle flames.

In 1868 Mark Natanson, the son of a well-to-do Jewish merchant from the Lithuanian province of Kovno, entered medical school in Vilna, after graduating from the gymnasium there. Natanson would go on to become "the most important revolutionary of the first half of the 1870s."[27] Natanson received a traditional Jewish education at the local Kheder until the age of 12 or 13, at which point he became exposed to the currents of Haskalah which would sweep him far out onto the sea of revolution. It wasn't so much that Haskalah replaced the traditional Judaism that he learned in the Kheder as that it entered into combination with it creating the potent binary weapon known as Jewish nihilism. Natanson read Chernyshevsky's *What Is to Be Done?* and that novel combined with his talmudic training led to "an amalgamation" which was only possible "because of his Jewishness." Natanson had also read Nechayev's *Catechism of the Revolutionary*, but without his "Jewish background" none of these elements would have coalesced into a coherent, much less, effective revolutionary program.

Before long, Natanson's example began to be replicated in the study groups of young Jews, many of whom had met at rabbinic schools, which proliferated throughout the Pale of the Settlement during the 1860s and 1870s. It was during this time that Vilna became a hotbed of Jewish revolutionary activity, much of it emanating from Vilna Rabbinical Seminary. Jewish revolutionary activity became as a result a function of Jewish participation in higher education. "Jewish revolutionary activity increased in direct proportion to the number of Jewish students"[28] and by the beginning of the 1870s, "a group of young Jews in Vilna, who had met in the rabbinic school there, began to play a significant role in the Russian revolutionary movement."[29] That group included Aron Zundelevich, who would go on to fame as the first man to import dynamite into Russia, and the first of many to use it as a technique of assassination. It also included Iankel-Abel (Arkadii) Finkelshtein, whose activity "initiated the beginning of Vilna's Jewish revolutionary tradition."[30] Finkelshtein grew up in Vilna, where he quickly earned the reputation of being a rebellious troublemaker who was constantly in trouble with school authorities. His rebelliousness gave expression to " a deep-seated animosity against the Jewish faith in particular and religious beliefs in general."[31] In sharing his dislike of religion, he came in contact with other like-minded students, and before long founded with Aron Zundelevich the First Vilna Circle, "the first exclusively Jewish revolutionary organization in the Russian Populist movement."[32] Although the First Vilna Circle was made up exclusively of Jewish students, those students had imbibed revolutionary cosmopolitan international internationalism from a number of sources, and they, like Hess and Marx, would have felt that it was provincial to talk about Jewish emancipation when all of mankind needed to be set free, especially when Jews were so skilled as revolutionary leaders. Like good students, they had correctly inferred that the goal of their education was assimilation, and so, instead of just focusing on Jewish issues, they decided in the name of assimilation to bring the Jewish salvation known as revolution to the Russian people. "Slowly but surely they realized that the 'Russian people' were as much in need of liberation as their own kin, and that until this was accomplished Russian Jewry could hope neither for emancipation nor assimilation."[33]

In 1873, the tsarist authorities recognized that the Vilna Rabbinical Seminary was a hotbed of revolutionary activity and shut it down. The Jewish students who wanted to continue their education could do so at the Teachers' Institute. If this move was intended to forestall Jewish involvement in revolutionary activity, it had the exact opposite effect. First of all, it increased the resentment of the Jewish students, and secondly, by sending them to the Teachers' Institute it gave them greater access to the Russians that they wanted to revolutionize. Those who didn't transfer were radicalized as well.

Other Jewish revolutionaries had similar experiences. Virtually all of them had Russian higher education to thank for their radicalism. Chudnovskii, another Jewish student from the other end of Russia, organized a smuggling ring in Odessa after witnessing the pogrom of 1871. Three years later, Chudnovskii was arrested and sent to Siberia but not before organizing a significant smuggling ring. Like Chudnovskii, Samuil Kliachko, the son of a Jewish merchant in Vilna, became involved in the distribution of radical books in both Moscow and St. Petersburg. Chudnovskii was even more successful in Odessa, which soon began to rival Vilna as a center of Jewish revolutionary activity, because Jews dominated the city, which was also in the process of undergoing rapid modernization and industrialization. Twenty-seven percent of Odessa's citizens were Jews in 1873; by 1892 their number had grown to 33 percent. Odessa was a stronghold of Haskalah, "so much so that the pious Hasidim used to say as early as the 1830s that 'the fires of hell began five miles outside of Odessa.'"[34]

It was this Enlightened atmosphere that allowed Chudnovskii to organize the "red mail" service from Lvov. The Jewish involvement in smuggling helped him as well; in fact without it, he could not have succeeded in the "book business." It was in fact a Jewish smuggler who destroyed the "red mail" service when he turned Chudnovskii in to the Tsarist authorities. Chudnovskii was sent off to Siberia and the red mail disappeared with him.

One of the young Jews who was radicalized by what he read in the red mail was Lev Akselrod. Akselrod was appalled at the idea of Jewish leaders making a living from Jewish misery. His revolt was predicated on specific Jewish circumstances and probably would have remained confined to their orbit were it not for the red mail and the type of subversive literature it brought into Russia from the West. In the winter of 1871, Akselrod picked up a copy of Ferdinand Lassalle's speeches, and what he imbibed from reading it elevated Akselrod's revolutionary understanding to a whole new level. In Lassalle, Akselrod discovered a German Jew whose Messianic "churches of the future" would "conquer the whole world," and attain "universal happiness, freedom and equality," as well as establishing "universal brotherhood."[35]

Before long, Akselrod began to see himself as "the Russian Lassalle," who would eschew the narrow goal of Jewish emancipation in favor of the universal quest for brotherhood and equality. The Jewish question paled in significance next to Lassalle's universal vision which encompassed all of mankind:

> I still remember how, reading the book of Lassalle, I felt a kind of shame at my concern for the interests of the Jewish people. What significance, it seemed to me, could the interests of a handful of Jews have in comparison with the "idea of the working class" and the all-embracing, universal interests of socialism. After all, strictly speaking, the Jewish question does not exist. There is only the question of the liberation of the working masses of all nations, including the Jewish. Together with the approaching triumph of socialism the so-called Jewish question will be resolved as well. Would it not be senseless and also sinful to devote one's energies to the Jewish people, which is no more than a single element in the vast population of the Russian Empire?[36]

This was Russification with a vengeance, and before long its consequences were enough to give pause to even the most ardent educational reformer. It soon became equally apparent that the revolutionary movement suddenly had a large Jewish component to it.

In 1877 M. M. Merkulov, an official with the Third Department, noticed that Jews were an important part of the Revolutionary Movement in Russia. By the mid-'70s, it had become impossible not to notice that young Jews "had become an important source of recruits for the revolutionary movement."[37] Before long, it was obvious to the most obtuse observer that, as Haberer puts it, "Jewish radicals made up a significant component of Populist circles both quantitatively and qualitatively." Jews, he continues,

> comprised a staggering 20 per cent of all Chaikovtsy (that is, 22 out of 106 persons) who were definitely members or close associates of the organization in St Petersburg, Moscow, Odessa, and Kiev. A breakdown by circles shows that they were well represented in each of these cities with 11 per cent in St Petersburg, 17 per cent in Moscow, 20 per cent in Odessa, and almost 70 per cent in Kiev. Even more striking is the fact that in the persons of Natanson, Kliachko, Chudnovskii, and Akselrod they were the founders and for some time the leading personalities of these circles. This means that 18 per cent of Jewish Chaikovtsy (four out of twenty-two) belonged to the category of leaders. Clearly, this puts in question the conventional claim that in the movement of the 1870s Jews were only of secondary importance, and that this importance was limited to their 'technical functions' in organizing the revolutionary underground.... This sort of minimalist interpretation, politically motivated by anti-Semitic fairy tales solely blaming the Jews for revolutionary subversion, seriously distorts the actual role of Jew in the Russian revolutionary movement.[38]

Like Mark Natanson, Lev Deich was young Jew from a well-to-do family which aspired to assimilate. Deich's father had come to Russia from Austria and had made a fortune selling medical supplies during the Crimean War. As the result of his father's good fortune, Deich had access to a gymnasium education which introduced him to the Mendelssohnian Enlightenment (along with Chernyshevsky), which turned him as result of the strange alchemy of German ideas interacting with Russian Jews, into a revolutionary. Once Deich became a socialist, "everything fell into its proper place." Deich himself "states unequivocally that Jews played an *ershtklasike* role in all the revolutionary groupings of the 1870s."[39]

What began when Grigorii Peretts imbibed from the stream of Mendelssohn ended when Trotsky rode Bolshevism to power in 1917. That same stream of Messianic politics would continue via Trotskyites like Irving Kristol on to the Neoconservatives, who would carry the banner of Messianic politics into the 21st century. The continuity in radical Jewish behavior was traceable to the Enlightenment in general and Mendelssohn in particular. Haberer feels that Mendelssohn is the ultimate source of Jewish Nihilism because Mendelssohn's "example proved irresistible to the younger generation of Maskilim who had been seized and cast adrift by the forces of modernity which irreparably cut them loose from the moorings of Judaism."[40]

This link between Mendelssohn, Trotsky, and Irving Kristol gives some indication that neoconservatism never really abandoned its internationalist, Trotskyite roots, for this is the same vision that informs Thomas Friedman's vision of the new globalist economy in *The Lexus and the Olive Tree* and David Brooks' vision of "heroic bourgeois states" like Israel and the United States in column after column in the *Weekly Standard*. Like Trotsky, the neoconservative apologists for globalism, free trade, and American cultural imperialism find that "national bias and national prejudices had only bewildered my sense of reason, in some cases stirring in me nothing but disdain and even a moral nausea."[41] The same vision of universal transnational brotherhood based on class—in the case of Trotsky, the proletariat; in the case of David Brooks, the bourgeoisie—was deeply appealing to Jews who grew up feeling that they were men without a country. Once the socialist revolution took place, all would henceforth be men without a country. National boundaries, tariffs, ethnic prejudice—all of this would be a thing of the past. Socialism (or global free market capitalism), in other words, was going to succeed where religion had failed in bringing about universal harmony and brotherhood. To ignore the Jewish contribution to this vision is "short-sighted," according to Haberer, because it "prevents us from comprehending the mental processes which drove alienated men and existentially troubled individuals like Vittenberg to sanctify socialism and to commit themselves to terrorism."[42]

Socialism was, in other words, a political movement with deep roots in secular Messianic Jewish thought. As a result Jews began to play a major role in socialist, and, therefore, revolutionary and terrorist activity in Russia at around the middle of the 19th century. "Jews," according to Haberer, "were indeed attracted to revolutionary activity—and terror in particular—due to specific Jewish circumstances."[43] They saw the Jewish mission in terms that were both Biblical and secular at the same time. The Jews were now the revolutionary vanguard, which resembled God's chosen people, who were called if not by God then by their own idealism, which also had biblical roots, to bring about the salvation of all mankind or, in secular terms, "the liberation of all oppressed groups." Salvation, in other words still came from the Jews, but now it was a different kind of salvation—utopian socialism—coming from a different kind of Jew, the underground revolutionary terrorist. Aron Zundelevich, according to Tscherikower, intentionally chose for himself the party name "Moishe," because he saw himself as leading not only the Jewish people but all people out of bondage. The Czar was simply the Pharaoh in his latest incarnation. The future promised a utopia not only for Jews but for all people, who would be grateful that the Jewish revolutionaries had led them out of bondage. The revolution fulfilled the deepest longings of a group of people who had stopped waiting for the Messiah and who now felt that the revolution was going to bring about the paradise on earth which the Messiah had promised but failed to deliver. Revolution was a deeply Jewish project, both in terms of its rationale and in terms of the people who filled the ranks of its organizations. The Elizavetgrad Circle of Lev I. Rozenfeld, which helped organize the assassination of suspected agent-provocateur, Nikolai E. Gorinovich "consisted almost exclusively of Jews." Jews, in fact, "were a major and very active component in virtually all radical circles which in the south of Russia acted as catalysts of political terrorism."[44]

The revolutionary movement in Russia attracted large number of Jews from predominantly Jewish areas because of the philosophical and political and religious reasons we have already mentioned, but they became prominent in the movement primarily because of their skills. Because they lived in the Pale of the Settlement on the western border of the Russian empire, Jews had close contact with Jews in the easternmost parts of both Prussia, including cities like Berlin, and the Austro-Hungarian Empire. Because of their Jewish upbringing and where it took place they became adept at smuggling and other activities useful to the revolutionary movement. "It was the Jews, with their long experience of exploiting conditions on Russia's Western frontier which adjoined the Pale for smuggling and the like, who organized the illegal transports of literature, planned escapes and illegal crossings, and generally kept the wheels of the whole organization running."[45] Jews were also adept at running printing presses and forging passports and other essential documents. Jews, in other words, were much better at running illegal "underground" operations than they were in educating and mobilizing the vast army of Russian peasants at the other end of Russia, something the early revolutionary organizations tried but failed to achieve. Soon the revolutionary movement began to take on Jewish characteristics, moving away Narodnaia Volia away from education and organization of peasants and workers and toward terrorism.

The Jews who were employed in "underground" operations as both *techniky* and *praktiky* soon learned how to put the new technologies to use as weapons of terrorism. Jews from Nikolaev were the first to produced explosives from pyroxylin. It was the Jewish business magnate Dmitrii Lizogub who set up a special fund to pay for the assassination of Czar Alexander II. And it was Aron Zundelevich who used that money to fund "the dynamite workshop," which was to provide the explosives that would mine the railroad tracks which were to explode when the Czar's special train passed over them:

> Zundelevich perhaps more than any other Narodovolets ensured the realization of its efforts to disorganize the government by striking at the Tsar himself with the most modern means available—dynamite.... The role of Zundelevich in utilizing dynamite for revolutionary purposes has been confirmed by several of his contemporaries. Gregory Gurevich states that he and his comrades in the Berlin circle "knew that Arkadii had bought dynamite from somewhere and had brought it to St. Petersburg." This, he claims, "was the first dynamite which the revolutionaries received in Russia." Lev Deich goes so far as to attribute to Zundelevich alone the idea of using the newly invented explosive for terrorist objectives. "To Zundelevich," he writes, "belongs the initiative" to replace knives and revolvers with dynamite and bombs which, due to his efforts began to be produced by home-made methods in Russia.[46]

Jews were not only more proficient with the new technologies than the average Russian revolutionary, they were also more willing to support terrorism than Gentile revolutionaries. Because of their skills and because of their quasi-religious ideological commitment, the Jews carried the revolutionary movement through its darkest days in Russia. In fact without Jewish support, it is doubtful that the revolution would have succeeded there. Before long, the police began to notice a preponderance of Jewish names among the lists of terrorists and revolutionaries. The police, according to Haberer, "had a more accurate appreciation of the role of Jews in the terrorist movement than the revolutionaries themselves or historians who joined them in downplaying the Jewish contribution."[47]

VII

In 1874 Osip Aptekman decided to leave the Pale of the Settlement and "go to the people" to bring revolution to the Russian peasant. When he returned in 1875, it was clear that the idea had backfired. Instead of converting the peasants to socialism, they converted the Jewish revolutionary Aptekman to Orthodox Christianity. When Aptekman returned to St. Petersburg in the spring of 1875, he entered the Russian Church.

Aptekman's experience was typical in some ways but not in others. Conversion to Orthodoxy was atypical, but his failure to convert the peasants was not. When the Jewish revolutionaries decided to "go to the people," "the people" more often than not saw them as alien seditionists and turned them in to the police. They most certainly did not perceive them as Russians. When it became apparent that the revolutionary Jews could not convert the Russian peasants, they turned to what they could do best—dynamite, smuggling, disinformation—and the revolutionary movement as a whole turned away from education and toward terrorism.

Mark Natanson returned to St. Petersburg around the same time that Osip Aptekman did. Natanson, however, was returning from a four-year stint in Siberia. He also did not return to St. Petersburg to convert to Orthodoxy. He came back to create a "party of struggle." Together with another Jew, Lev Ginzberg, Natanson resurrected *Zemlia I Volia* and sent it off in the direction of armed insurrection and terrorism. Eventually the contradictions between the two factions were too big to be ignored and the organization split into two organizations: Chernyi Peredel, which continued the populist direction of education and organization, and Narodnaia Volnia, which became the underground arm of terrorism. Either way, Natanson was the "veritable *deus ex machina* of Russian radicalism," and it is doubtful that the movement could have survived without him nor is it possible to understand the triumph of revolution in Russia without first understanding "the remarkable story of 'how and why' a Jew created Russia's first truly revolutionary party."[48]

No political movement can sustain itself on organizational genius alone, no matter how brilliant, and Mark Natanson's organization was no exception in this regard. And so it was more a stroke of luck than genius that Natanson founded a party and found a backer in the same year. In late 1875 Natanson met a wealthy Jew by the name of Dmitrii Lizogub, who had recently inherited an estate worth over 200,000 rubles. Lizogub was so impressed with Natanson that he agreed on the spot to finance Natanson's new party. The only condition was that the assassination of the Czar be part of the new party's program. As a result of Lizogub's largesse, Natanson now had the wherewithal to put his ideas into practice.

In November of 1875 Natanson linked up with the St. Petersburg Lavrovists led by Lev Ginzburg and formed the Union of Russian Revolutionary Groups. The Jewish background which Natanson and Ginzburg shared was not fortuitous. It brought them together in the first place and it allowed them to move their new organization beyond "the ethnocentric peasantism of their Russian comrades."[49] The de facto Jewish leadership of the Union of Russian Revolutionary Groups allowed Natanson and Ginzburg to link up with other Jewish groups, like Zundelevich's network of Jewish smugglers, which allowed the passage of money, revolutionary literature, forged documents, arms, and, most importantly, dynamite to pass through the network of illegal border crossings which connected London and Geneva, via Berlin, Koenigsberg and Vilna, with revolutionary groups in Russia. The revolutionaries in Russia could not have survived during this period of persecution at the hands of the Czarist police without the Jews, because "this line of communication and its central transfer points for goods and people was manned almost exclusively by Jews."[50] The Zalman family was responsible for the border region between Koenigsberg and Vilna. "Particularly sensitive and valuable items such as printing press accessories and, later on, dynamite were taken directly to St. Petersburg by Zalman himself and sometimes by Zundelevich."[51] The main post office for the "red mail" in the Pale was in Vilna. In Berlin the "red mail" was handled largely by Russian-Jewish students, like Grigorii, Gurevich, Pavel Akselrod, Leizer Tsukerman, Vladimir Iokhelson, Iosel Efron, Khasia Shur, Augustina and Nadezhda Kaminer, Nakhman and Leizer Levenral, and Semen Lure—all of whom had been active in Vilna, Mogilev, and Kiev—and who were now working under the supervision of Aron Zundelevich, who then forwarded their contraband to Arkadii Finkelshtein who managed the "red" post office in Koenigsberg. From there the contraband was ferried over the Russian border by a host of German, Polish and Lithuanian peasants in the pay of the Zalman family, the most famous of whom was known as the "Red Schmul."[52] When Natanson visited Zundelevich in Berlin in the fall of 1875, he found that he could devote his organizational genius to other projects because, thanks to Zundelevich and his Jewish collaborators in the Pale of the Settlement the red mail was already up and running.

In 1877 Natanson was arrested and banished to Irkutsk, but the proof of his organizational genius soon became apparent when his organization showed itself capable of functioning in his absence. Over the next few years a series of increasingly violent revolutionary Jews arrived in St. Petersburg with one goal in mind— the assassination of the Czar, which had become the Holy Grail of the revolutionary movement. The continuity of that movement was ethnic. When one Jew was caught another appeared on the scene to take his place. In Kiev, we are told, the nihilistic circle which gathered around Lev Deich "consisted exclusively of Jewish students."[53] The same was true of circles which stretched from Vilna to Odessa. Gradually, the Messianic politics of these Jewish revolutionary circles began to crystallize around one numinous act, the assassination of the Czar, which in one stroke would usher in the millennium and bring liberty to the oppressed peoples of Russia, both Jew and Gentile alike. This is not to obscure the differences between revolutionary Jews like Natanson and Ginzburg—the former the man of action and the latter the quiet organizer—but only to emphasize their ability to take two different and essentially complementary paths to the same end.

By the summer of 1876 Natanson's followers were known as "Troglodytes" to indicate that their activity was now "underground." More than anyone else, Mark Natanson was responsible for the change in revolutionary tactics. He was more interested in terrorism than populism, and his organization as the "lengthened shadow of one man," began to act on his ideas.

One of their especially clever projects was the Chigirin conspiracy which Natanson endorsed after the fact. A group of revolutionaries in Kiev conceived the idea of printing "A Secret Imperial Charter" according to which the Czar called upon Russia's peasants to rise up in rebellion against the land owners and aristocrats who were now thwarting his emancipation decree of February 1861. With the help of Anna Rozenshtein, who arranged the printing of the decree on a printing press which had been smuggled in from abroad, the Kiev revolutionary circle convinced the peasants to act. By November 1877, a large group of peasants were ready to rebel "in the name of the Czar." From the conception of the idea in the mind of Lev Deich to its execution on Anna Rozenshtein's printing press, the "Jewish input" of the Chigirin conspiracy was "obvious." The Chigirin conspiracy was not only organized by Jews, it bespoke Jewish *chutzpah* as well as a view of the *goyim* as gullible and willing to believe anything that they saw in print. It also bore the stamp of Mark Natanson, because "the realization of this scheme was made possible in the last analysis only because Mark Natanson supported the Chigirintsy whole-.heartily when they turned to him for assistance."[54]

By 1876 Mark Natanson had created in *Zemlia I Volia* a revolutionary movement that was uniquely Jewish in both its tactics and its organization. If the Russians had been running it instead of the Jews, it would have been a different organization. The Jews as a result of their effectiveness as revolutionaries began to determine the course of the movement in all of the crucial areas but most notably away from "back to the people" populism and toward revolutionary terror. In collaboration with the dynamite importer Aron Zundelevich, Natanson "ensured the development of an explicitly terrorist party with an overtly political program of action" when *Zemlia I Volia*'s "disorganization group" arranged the assassination of the informer N. F. Sharashkin in June 1877. Sharashkin's murder in St. Petersburg had been preceded by a botched assassination attempt on the life of a suspected agent-provocateur in Odessa by the name of Nikolai E. Gorinovich. On June 11, 1876, Lev Deich poured sulfuric acid on Gorinovich's face and left him for dead with a note attached to his body which read "Such will be the fate of all spies." Gorinovich survived the assassination attempt, albeit horribly mutilated, and eventually testified at the trial of his would be assassins. Of the seven men who were convicted, three, including Lev Deich, were Jews.

The death of Sharashkin and the near death and mutilation of Gorinovich seems to have propelled *Zemlia I Volia* over a threshold of inhibition into a realm where revolutionary violence became the preferred choice of revolutionary activity. Russia was now entering an era when politically motivated murder and terrorism were to become common occurrences, for which the Jews can be held accountable:

> Jews constituted an important, if not crucial, national element in turning the region into a hotbed of terrorist violence....The statistical findings of Kappeler (as they relate to Jews) show up in the presence of Jewish radicals in almost all "southern circles" which were directly or indirectly involved in acts of terrorism or physical resistance against the authorities. For instance, the Elizavetgrad circle of Lev I. Rozenfeld, which was closely linked with the Kiev Buntarists and helped them in organizing the Gorinovich assassination, consisted almost exclusively of Jews. The same was the case in Nikolaev where the "rebels" were in contact with Solomon Vinenberg, Aron Gobet, Lev and Savelii Zlaropolskii, all of whom were leading activists among the local, predominantly Jewish, radical youth." Indeed, Jews were a major and very active component in virtually all radical circles which in the south of Russia acted as catalysts of political terrorism.[55]

By the late 1870s, the Russian authorities viewed all Jews as potential revolutionaries. The attitude surfaced as early as 1872 with the arrest of Arkadii Finkelshtein, when the governor of the Vilna province upbraided an assembly of prominent Jews for doing nothing to stop the spread of terrorism among Jewish youth. "To all the other good qualities which you Jews possess," the governor noted sarcastically, "about the only thing you need is to become nihilists too."[56] When the police broke up the First Vilna Circle of revolutionaries in June of 1875, the Vilna police chief continued the indictment which the governor had leveled against the Jews three years earlier: "Until now," he said, "we considered you Jews only swindlers; now we will also consider you as rebels."[57] In 1877, an official with the Third Department concluded that Jewish youth was "highly susceptible to revolutionary fermentation." Three years later another official claimed that it was an "irrefutable fact" that Jews rather than Poles or Russians not only "adhered to social-revolutionary ideals," but were also extremely sophisticated in preparing Jewish youth for political subversion.[58]

The idea that Jews were drawn to revolution was firmly established in the mind of Russian officials by the second half of the 1870s. The increase in terrorism in the period from 1879 to 1881 only increased Russian anger against Jews as an essentially "alien people" who had a congenital propensity toward subversion. By 1880 the idea was firmly established in the Russian mind. When Isaak Gurvich was imprisoned in St. Petersburg in May 1880, he was told that his release was unlikely because "Jews were considered particularly subversive."[59] When on February 22, 1880, Ippolit Osipovich Mlodetski was publicly executed in St. Petersburg for his attempt on the life of Count Loris-Melikove, the crowd of 40,000 who watched him die suspected that he was part of a far-flung Jewish conspiracy because, as the loyalist press put it, "these Jews, being from time Immemorial the representatives of the revolutionary spirit, stand now at the head of Russian Nihilists."[60] *The London Times*, however, blamed the execution of Mlodetskii on a resurgence of Russian anti-Semitism:

> The sheer fact that the would-be assassin, Mlodecki [sic], was of Jewish descent has sufficed to renew in certain circles of the community and in some public organs, more specifically those circulating among the lower orders of the people, the old war-cry of persecution against the Jews in general...[Any] one listening to the flood of invective which is being poured forth against the Hebrews must imagine the evil days to have returned when hatred of the Jews was prevalent in respectable society.[61]

Jews were in the forefront of those who "embraced the terrorist alternative to revolutionary Populism." Solomon Vittenberg, who organized the "first armed demonstration" of the revolution in Odessa on July 24, 1878, decided to assassinate the Czar with the help of a circle of co-conspirators, who with one exception, a Ukrainian, were all Jews. Vittenberg was caught and hanged on August 10, 1879, before he could carry out his plan. His death along with his quasi-Christian justification for his actions inspired other Jewish revolutionaries to follow his example. Jacques Maritain's insight seems like the best gloss on Vittenberg's last testament: the Gospel separated from the Church had become a revolutionary document with incredibly destructive power.

Inspired by the same Messianic fervor which motivated Vittenberg, Grigorii Goldenberg murdered the governor of Charkov and then showed up in St. Petersburg asking his revolutionary comrades for the privilege of murdering the Czar. The Narodwolzen were more than a little impressed by his ruthlessness but decided nonetheless that it would be better "that Russians and not Jews pull the trigger in the most important assassinations."[62] Goldenberg was eventually arrested for transporting dynamite, and after betraying his fellow revolutionaries in a series of devastating confessions, committed suicide in prison. Goldenberg was a creation of (and victim of) Haskalah and Russification at the hands of clueless but well meaning educational bureaucrats. His father had been allowed to move to Kiev from the Jewish shtetl of Berdichev because of Alexander II's liberalization of state residency requirements hitherto imposed on the Jews. In the tortured alchemy of Jewish Enlightenment, that was turned into a reason for killing the Czar in Goldenberg's mind. The Jews of Grigorii Goldenberg's generation "were set adrift to seek for themselves a meaning in life by drinking from foreign wells which poured forth all sorts of enticing ideas."[63] Education created the Revolutionary Jew in Russia. The Whigs' black operation continued to have unintended repercussions in Russia long after it had brought about unintended repercussions in France. Haskalah created Revolutionaries. Leizer Tsukerman, who went from participating in a Maskilic study circle to running Narodnaia Volia's underground printing press in the course of a decade provides one of many examples of a generation of young Jews who found a new religion in revolutionary socialism when the old talmudic religion failed.

It was Tsukerman's Jewishness that allowed him to inspire the revolutionaries: "it was as a Jewish Jew, as a Quintessential Jewish personality, that he impressed them and won their hearts and minds. His Yiddish songs, jokes, and stories drawn from the his repertoire of Jewish life in the Pale brought humor, informality, and joy into their midst.... Tsukerman was in his element. Joining Narodnaia Volia's printing shop was like a homecoming, a home where his presence made a difference, a life among people who shared his sentiments and unquestionable dedication to socialist ideals."[64]

Tsukerman, like Goldenberg, ended up in jail when the police raided his printing operation on January 18, 1880. Goldenberg's confession was full of the names of other revolutionaries, and most of them were Jewish. Goldenberg as a result became the stereotypical Jewish terrorist, and proof, if any was needed, "that behind every terrorist plot there was a Jew."[65]

Here was a Jewish terrorist par excellence who had not only assassinated the Governor General of Kharkov, but who had advised others to kill the Tsar—a task, moreover, which he desired to execute himself. In addition, his written testimony was full of Jewish names implicating Jews like Aronchik and Zundelevich in terrorist activities. In the light of the previous arrest of Vittenberg and Jewish associates of his circle, including Gobet, all this merely confirmed the government's suspicion that Jews were principal agents of terrorism.

After the split of *Zemlia I Volia* into Nardonaia Volia and Chernyi Peredel, the Jews gravitated toward the more violent Narodnaia Volia because it supported terrorism. In November 1879 Aizik Aronchik, member of Narodnaia Volia planted a large amount of dynamite under the tracks which he thought the Czar's train was going to cross in Odessa, Alexandrovsk, and Moscow. None of the explosions succeeded in killing the Czar, and Aronchik was eventually arrested along with two other Jews directly involved in the conspiracy, Savelii Zlatopolskii and Grigorii Goldenberg. Aronchik was sentenced to life-long imprisonment in Siberia, but when that was not deemed rigorous enough he was transferred to the Fortress of St. Peter and Paul and ultimately the Schluesselberg prison where he went insane in 1885, dying shortly after that. Goldenberg went insane in prison and then committed suicide but not before betraying many of his revolutionary colleagues.

Goldenberg's confession could have devastated Narodnaia Volia if it had come sooner after his arrest. As it was, the Narodniki had time to disperse and evade arrest, and the reprisals did nothing more than strengthen their determination to kill the Czar. The culmination of those efforts occurred on March 1, 1881 when the revolutionaries, using both gun and bomb, finally made good on their promise to kill the Czar. What followed the assassination was not the hoped for reign of heaven on earth, but retaliation against the Jews, who were seen as responsible for his death.

VIII

Six weeks after the murder of the Czar, pogroms "broke out suddenly like an epidemic that spread far and wide" across the Pale of the Settlement. Barbara Tuchman claims that the reasoning behind the Pogroms "was the same as the Nazis': to use the Jews in the classic role of scapegoat, to create a diversion from oncoming disaster, to draw off mass discontent from the governing class."[66] Chaim Potok, like Tuchman, holds the Czarist government responsible for the pogroms, claiming that "a frightened regime rallied the people by blaming the Jews for the assassination."[67]

Virtually every Jewish historian says that the pogroms were orchestrated by the government, but Solzhenitsyn cites sources who claim just as vehemently that "their spontaneous character was obvious,"[68] which leads him to conclude that the assertion that "the government was held responsible for fomenting pogroms" was "completely baseless and ... absurd."[69] The fact that much of the violence centered on the saloons and taprooms of the Pale indicated that the pogroms focused on long-standing resentments, which needed no government orchestration. The Jews living in Russia were beaten and their houses looted and burned not because those Jews were held responsible for the death of the Czar but, according to Gleb Uspensky, "because they had made themselves rich off of the labor of other and did not earn their bread with their own hands."[70] Beginning in the 1870s, the Jews became involved in capitalism and manufacturing and as a result "the Jews began to make hell hot with the ruble, and the people couldn't stand it."[71]

There is no real evidence that the government promoted the pogroms, but there is a significant body of material showing that the revolutionaries did. The revolutionaries, many of whom were Jews, felt the same way about the Jews as Karl Marx did and promoted the pogroms as an attack on nascent Russian capitalism and the abuses that went along with it as a way of parleying local resentment into global revolution. The failed pogroms in Odessa and Yekaterinoslav were probably the work of Narodnaia Volia, which hoped to capitalize on the pogroms to foment a general revolution in Russia. On August 30, 1881 the Narodniki, who were, it should be remembered, significantly Jewish, circulated fliers attacking the Jews: "Who took over the land, the woods, and the bars? The Jews.... The Jew offends mankind, deceives him and drinks his blood."[72]

The Narodniki were seeking to exploit the resentment which the Jews had created among the general population. Jews were seen as both capitalist vampires and potential revolutionaries, and there was truth—the Narodniki could certainly affirm the latter proposition—in both assertions. Marx had already provided the model for Jews attacking Jews: "Thanks to a falsely generalized notion of equality, which has been used to deleterious effect against the general population, the Jews have succeeded in gaining economic control."[73] The Jewish faith enables the Jew to exploit "every weakness and every form of trust" among those of other faiths.[74] Beyond that, "the Jews will exploit the advantages of nationhood without ever becoming a member of any nation or willing to bear the burdens of citizenship." As a result of lowering the guard against exploitation erected by Christian monarchs, the Jews get to take over any country that tolerates them and their practices because "The morality of the Talmud puts no boundaries on letting Jews enrich themselves at the expense of those of other faiths."[75] This was the sort of talk that was being promoted in revolutionary circles to turn the pogroms into something bigger and wider. When the pogroms finally came in reaction to the assassination of the Czar, the revolutionaries, including many Jews, who had conspired to murder the Czar, turned around and supported the pogroms against fellow Jews because they saw in the pogroms the beginnings of the revolution in Russia. Commenting on the situation in Minsk, his hometown, Isaak Gurvich wrote:

> [Like our gentile comrades] we were also under the influence of the theory that the pogroms are a popular uprising (a *folksoyfstand*), and any *folksoyfstand* is good. It revolutionizes the masses. Certainly, the Jews suffered as a consequence—but all the same, the gentile revolutionaries of the nobility also called on the peasants to rise up against their fathers and brothers![76]

"Among the Jewish revolutionaries," Abraham Cahan wrote in his autobiography,

> were some who considered the anti-Semitic massacres to be a good omen. They theorized that the pogroms were an instinctive outpouring of the revolutionary anger of the people, driving the Russian masses against their oppressors. The uneducated Russian people knew that the Czar, the officials and the Jews sucked their blood, they argued. So the Ukrainian peasants attacked the Jews, the "percentniks." The revolutionary torch had been lit and would next be applied to the officials and the Czar himself.[77]

Revolutionaries did not denounce pogroms for fear of alienating peasants, and as a result, some Jews began to have doubts about the Revolution. The issue of Jewish loyalty—to race or to revolution—was going to cause some serious soul-searching among Russian Jews. The issue in Russia would follow lines that had already been articulated in Germany, when Hess split with Marx and proposed racial solidarity as superior to class consciousness. Hess's position, however, was still the minority opinion among Jewish revolutionaries, who like Lev Deich, speaking on behalf of the Geneva Chernoperedeltsy, claimed that "our approach to the [Jewish] problem must be based on a universal-socialist standpoint that seeks to fuse nationalities instead of isolating one nationality [the Jews] still more than is already the case."[78]

The issue which threatened the revolution more than any other was emigration. Recognizing this, Deich felt that emigration to Palestine was the worst possible option, because it would isolate the Jews in ethnocentric fantasies. As a result, Deich urged Jews to go "to America where they will merge with the local population."[79] As a result of Jewish immigration, America would play a major role in the Russian revolution, but the Narodniki had more immediate problems, problems which were essentially impossible to resolve from a Jewish perspective. If the revolutionaries supported the Jews, they would alienate the peasants, but if they didn't support the Jews, they would alienate the most significant faction of the revolutionary movement, namely the Jews. As a result, Deich concluded that "the Jewish question is now almost insoluble for the revolutionaries. What, for example, are they to do now in Balta where they beat up the Jews? To intercede for them means, as Reclus says, 'to call up the hatred of the peasants against the revolutionaries who not only killed the Tsar but also defend the Jews'.... (This] is simply a dead-end avenue for Jews and revolutionaries alike."[80]

The Tsarist police were worried for exactly the same reasons. The pogroms, they feared, might get out of hand and turn into full-scale revolution. Today, wrote one official, "they are harassing the Jews.... Tomorrow it will be the turn of the so-called kulaks ... then of merchants and landowners. In a word, if the authorities stand by passively, we can expect the development of the most devastating socialism."[81]

In many ways the tsarist official was right. The pogroms radicalized Jewish youth, who turned to the revolutionary movement as the way of expressing their outrage at the attacks on the Jews. Nora Levin noticed the same thing during the Russian civil war some 40 years later. The anti-Bolshevik armies visited reprisals on all Jews for what they saw as Jewish participation in revolutionary and terrorist activity, and that in turn radicalized Jewish youth who felt that the only way to die with a gun in their hands was to join the Red Army. So Jewish revolutionary activity led to the pogroms and the pogroms led to more Jewish revolutionary activity. Eventually, the pogroms would turn into Jewish revolutionary uprisings, when the armed Jewish defense groups which arose in the aftermath began taking the initiative in pre-emptive fashion.

By 1887, it appeared to the authorities that the revolutionary movement in Russia was kept alive, in spite of heavy losses, only because of the continuous supply of Jewish recruits, who, skillfully evading the police, constantly started up new pockets of revolutionary resistance. Venting his frustration over this phenomenon, the Moscow chief of police wrote in February 1887: "The very people who resist a transition to a peaceful program are the Jews who recently have been quietly attempting to grasp the initiative of the revolutionary movement in their hands."[82]

As a result the new alarm about revolutionary activity, especially after the assassination of the Czar, began to merge with the older, traditional anti-Semitism producing an especially virulent animus against all Jews, not just the Jews who fomented revolution. The triumph of Bolshevism in the revolution of 1917 increased the fear and the animus against the Jews once again. And once again it was the most visible Jews, which is to say the ethnic, religious Jews who bore the brunt of that animus when the reaction came. "The Trotskys make the revolution, but the Bronsteins pay for it," is how one Jew formulated the phenomenon. Hitler, far from being *sui generis*, was simply a manifestation of the same sort of anti-Semitism which followed the assassination of the Czar in Russia in the 1880s. Those who felt that Jews were in the forefront of revolutionary activity then felt confirmed by subsequent events, by the triumph of Bolshevism not only in Russia but in Germany and throughout eastern Europe in the chaotic years following the end of World War I. The fears of Bolshevism combined with traditional animus against Jews helped to create a reaction that brought Hitler to power and would have terrible consequences for Jews, especially for religious Jews, who were least responsible for the revolutionary excesses of people like Trotsky, ne "Bronstein," who in addition to changing their names didn't consider themselves Jews.

The widely publicized case of Grigorii Goldenberg only fueled the fires of anti-Semitism and confirmed the average Russian in his belief that a Jew was behind every terrorist plot. After plotting the assassination of the Czar and being convicted of actually assassinating the Governor General of Kharkov, Goldenberg turned state's evidence and revealed in writing up his terrorist connections, a list full of Jewish names, which "confirmed the government's suspicions that the Jews were the principal agents of terrorism."[83] Looking at the Jews from a position outside their group, the average Russian failed to see the ideological fissures dividing Jews. Since they saw Jews as possessing "complete unity and solidarity," they held the Jewish community responsible for the actions of Jewish terrorists claiming that its leaders "willingly if not purposefully, failed to exercise their authority over Jews who conspired against the state." As a result, the myth of a Jewish revolutionary conspiracy against 'Holy Russia' was readily available as a new weapon in the arsenal of Russian anti-Semitism.[84]

Revolution was seen as "a Jewish disease" in part as a rationalization of the government's failure to stop it, but also because there was a "modicum of truth" in the assertion. "No matter how much prejudiced fantasy entered into the making of Russian Political anti-Semitism, its ideologues were also rational human beings who relied on some sort of concrete evidence to substantiate their 'demagogic reasoning.'"[85] Salo Baron calls the idea that Jews were revolutionaries "a new powerful myth" which arose in spite of the fact that "most tsarist officials, including the successor to the throne, Alexander III, were aware that the tsaricide could not be blamed on the Jews, at least not directly."[86] Baron goes on to quote Czarist officials in support of his contention. The fact that they say the exact opposite and blame Jews for the unrest is taken as proof, not of Jewish involvement in revolutionary activity, but of their anti-Semitism. Czarist Minister of Internal Affairs, N. P. Ignatiev, we are told, felt that there was "one common denominator which explained everything—the Jews : 'Judaism was the natural breeding ground of subversion.' It propagated radical Jews who, along with Poles, were ' the basis for the nihilists' secret organization ' which incited the people to attack their Jewish tormentors in a disorderly, antigovemment fashion.'"[87]

Salo Baron dismisses Jewish participation in revolutionary activity as "officially inspired rumors"[88] and in support of his contention cites the fact that of the seven conspirators executed for the murder of the Czar, only one was Jewish and a woman at that. Baron's comment ignores the fact that Jewish revolutionaries like Aron Zundelevich deliberately discouraged Jews from playing the prominent role as trigger pullers in assassination attempts because of fear of reprisals and because it would lead the Russian peasants to conclude that revolution was an essentially Jewish affair. Baron's comment also ignores the meticulous organization necessary for a successful revolutionary movement, and the fact that it was at this sort of organization that the Jewish revolutionaries excelled. Baron tries to portray Gesia Helfman as an insignificant cog in the second tier of the revolutionary organization whose contribution "consisted merely in providing shelter for her fellow conspirators."[89]

The testimony at her trial, however, told a different story. Helfman was effectively in charge of the entire operation from September 1880 until the assassination in 1881. It was she who set up the workshop which produced the dynamite which killed the Czar. As the police chief General Shebeko noted, Helfman's involvement in "secondary, techno-organizational tasks" was "vital to the machinery of political violence—and in this sense they, in fact, contributed as much to, and thus bore as much responsibility in, the execution of terrorist acts as the assassins themselves."[90] It would be misleading to say that Jews had only "secondary functions" in Narodnaia Volia's campaign to assassinate the Czar. "As intermediaries between the party's Executive Committee and its rank and file, the Jewish Narodovoltsy occupied an important position in the propagation an organization of political terrorism."[91] The government's case in blaming "Jewish nihilists" for revolutionary violence "had a more accurate appreciation of the role of Jews in the terrorist movement than the revolutionaries themselves or historians who joined them in downplaying die Jewish contribution."[92]

In 1882, one year after the assassination of Alexander II, the Czarist committee founded ten years earlier to promote Jewish assimilation concluded that their efforts had failed. The Czar who had inaugurated the golden age of Russian Jewry by lifting restrictions on the Jews had been murdered by revolutionaries who were to a significant extent Jewish. Once the Jews had been exposed to the rage of the pogroms, the overwhelming majority of their number were inclined to agree with the Czar's committee. Russification based on the internalization of Mendelssohn's example in Germany had failed. In the aftermath of the assassination of the Czar, the Russians had concluded that the Jewish people were irredeemably afflicted with the bacillus of revolution. The Jews, on the other had, were no longer interested in assimilation, a fact which led to the intensification of both emigration and revolutionary activity. Nora Levin claims that it was oppression which led the Jews into the arms of the revolutionaries. The Czarist officials, however, laid the blame at the feet of the Enlightened Alexander II's education policies. It was education more than oppression that turned Jews into revolutionaries. The only agent of change more effective in this regard was education followed by oppression, which was the course taken by Alexander III after the assassination of his predecessor.

During the period surrounding the murder of the Czar, which is to say from 1876 to 1883, Jews poured into Russia's public schools. The number of Jews attending the gymnasium doubled, and from 1878 to 1886, the number of Jewish university students sextupled to the point where Jews, who comprised 4 percent of the population made up 14.5 percent of Russia's university students. In the 30 years which followed Alexander II's accession to the throne, Jews became a plurality and in some cases a majority at Russian universities, especially in the South. In 1886 "over 40 per cent of law and medical students at the University of Kharkov and the University of New Russia in Odessa were Jewish."[93] In the business schools, Jews made up 50 percent of the students. In Odessa, one third of whose inhabitants were Jews, 72 percent of the students at the school of business were Jews, and 19 percent of the university students.[94]

Sensing that the situation was getting out of control, the Russians instituted a *numerus clausus* for Jews, which fostered the revolutionary spirit even more than Haskalah. In 1889, Alexander III learned from his justice minister that the Jews were on the verge of taking over the legal profession, both by the large numbers of Jews who had become lawyers but also because those Jews, because of the way that they did business, had destroyed the moral standing of the legal profession and as a result, were forcing non-Jews out of the profession. The Czar expressed his concern and as a result "for the next 15 years virtually no Jew was admitted to the bar in Russia."[95]

In 1887 General N. I. Shebeko issued a comprehensive report on the revolutionary movement in Russia. The good news was that revolutionary activity had declined in the years after the assassination of Alexander II, but there was bad news too. During the same period of time, the revolutionary movement had become more Jewish. "The profession of destructive ideas," he wrote, "has generally, little by little, become the property of the Jewish element, which very often figured [prominently] in revolutionary circles." The really shocking part of the report came in a parenthetical remark following his pessimistic assessment of Jewish involvement in revolution. "Approximately 80 per cent of known socialists in the South [of Russia] in 1886-1887," he noted, "were Jews."[96]

Haberer puts Jewish participation at between 25 and 30 percent, but essentially agrees with Shebeko's assessment. By the late 19th century, "revolutionary subversion without Jews had become unthinkable." This, he continues, was particularly true with respect to the principal area of revolutionary activity—the heavily Jewish populated provinces of the South. Here, especially in 1886-87, Jews made up approximately 35 to 40 per cent of the movement's membership. While this is substantially below Shebeko's claim of 80 per cent, there can be no question that even half this figure is still an impressive indication of the degree to which Jews had become a critical mass in the Russian revolutionary movement over the course of some twenty years that witnessed on the average a five-fold increase in their share of participation.[97]

Shebeko's report not only refutes Jewish apologists like Salo Baron, who claims that Jewish participation in Russia's revolutionary movement never exceeded 4 percent, it also changes the force of the argument by moving it away from sterile statistics. As Shebeko's report indicates, the revolutionary movement suffered severe setbacks in the wake of the 1881 assassination, so severe in fact, that without Jewish support the movement could not have survived. The Jews not only played a numerical role in revolution out of all proportion to their numbers in Russia, they also saved the revolution from extinction by "the continuous supply of Jewish recruits"[98] as well as by bringing it back to the impenetrable (at least by Czarist agents) shtetls of the Pale when it could not longer survive in the capitals of Moscow and St. Petersburg.

After the government crack-down in the wake of the assassination, the revolution moved south to Odessa and west back to the Pale, where it became more Jewish. The shift was also generational. The second generation joined Narodnaia Volia after the assassination of Czar Alexander II and promptly moved south because the Czarist government was so effective in eradicating the movement in Moscow and St. Petersburg. Once it moved south, the revolutionary movement of necessity became more Jewish. With the exception of the work of Alexander Ulianov, Lenin's brother, who was executed for an attempt on the life of Czar Alexander III in 1887 and the work of Sofia Ginzburg, revolutionary activity had ceased in St. Petersburg by 1885. The fact that it didn't die out altogether can be traced to the shelter it found in the densely Jewish areas of the Pale and Odessa.

> Having undergone their revolutionary bar mitzvah while studying in St Petersburg, which usually led at least to one arrest and a term of imprisonment, they returned home to Minsk, Vilna, Kiev, Taganrog, or Odessa, often as expelled students subject to domiciliary exile. Here they resumed their subversive work together with local Jewish radicals who, like themselves, had served their revolutionary apprenticeship as gymnasium and/or university students. Working in a familiar terrain that in towns like Minsk and Taganrog was still poorly policed, these individuals were for some time relatively free to propagate socialism and organize circles which were often predominantly Jewish in composition. Their Jewishness, as well as their ability to operate in ' native surroundings, made for easy contacts with Jewish intelligenty and workers. The net effect of all this was that although the centralized party was destroyed in 1881-2, new provincial centers of revolutionary subversion were constantly and autochthonously recreated

by Jewish Narodovoltsy in 1883-87. The shifting nature of Narodnaia Volia activity, both in terms of geography and decentralization, therefore, enhanced rather than diminished the Jewish presence in the revolutionary movement.[99]

As further indication that the revolutionary movement had retreated into the Jewish areas of Russia, Shternberg and Krol set up a revolutionary student organization at the University of Odessa within weeks of enrolling there. Virtually every member of the organization was a Jew, most of whom had undergone their revolutionary apprenticeship in St. Petersburg before the police crack down. Shternberg's revolutionary worldview was quintessentially Jewish. He advocated terrorism, as opposed to populist education and organization among the Russian peasants, as a way of bringing about the final goal of the party, and his battle cry was "the God of Israel is alive!"[100] a phrase he used more than once in his pamphlet "Politcal Terror in Russia," published in 1884. "Jews," as a result, "thus completely dominated the technical and organizational work of the Odessa group."[101]

The connection with Halaskah was there, but the chain of events that Mendelssohn set in motion when he proposed the paradigm of German Reformed Jewish assimilation had been turned inside out. Instead of joining the culture that excluded them, the Enlightened Jews of Russia were now determined to destroy it. The connection with Mendelssohn had become an in joke among the children of the first generation of Russian Maskilim. When the Revolutionary Orzhikh met Natan Bogoraz the founder of the revolutionary cell in Taganrog, he gave expression to his admiration of Bogoraz's revolutionary organizational skills by referring to him as "Nathan the Wise."[102] Because they had high Jewish populations and because their local constabularies lacked the skills and resources of their counterparts in St. Petersburg and Moscow, provincial cities like Ekaterinoslav became centers for revolutionary activity. The high proportion of Jews living there made the revolutionary circles in towns like Odessa much more radical than they would have been otherwise. At one of their congresses, the split over the use of terrorism was essentially "a split between Jewish and Gentile delegates, with the latter opposing terrorism as injurious to the cause of socialist propaganda, and the former arguing for 'the systematic and uninterrupted repetition of terrorist acts' as the only means to destroy tsarism."[103] Revolutionary subversion without Jews, in other words, had become unthinkable.

Commenting on Shebeko's report, Haberer writes that "anti-Semitic generalizations insinuating a deliberate Jewish revolutionary conspiracy in Russia should not prevent us from recognizing the factual basis underlying the phobia in official and reactionary circles that the Jew was poised to destroy Holy Tsarist Russia."[104] As we have seen, Shebeko's claim that 80 percent of the revolutionaries in the South were Jews "was not a product of anti-Semitic fantasy"; "it was based on compelling impressions derived from police reports covering the fight against political subversion in 1885-7."[105] In the ensuing years the same trend continued. In

1889 the police broke up the Circle of Narodovoltsy, which as of March 1889 was run by the Jewess Sofia Mikhailovna Ginsburg and was at the moment the police raided its headquarters was plotting the assassination of Czar Alexander III. The membership of the Russian Circle of Narodovoltsy was 77 percent Jewish. The international organization had a similar number of Jews on its staff, and they in turn relied on Jewish contacts in Berlin, Grodno, Vilna and Minsk for communication and materiel. As a result,

> it was hard to escape the impression that by the end of the 1880s the revolutionary profession was dominated by socialist Jews, who surpassed numerically all other national minorities, and perhaps even the Russians, in the Principal areas of continued anti-government activities—the émigré colonies of Western Europe and provinces of the Jewish Pale of Settlement.[106]

The Pogrom Crisis drove Jews out of the ranks of the more moderate Chernyi Peredel and into the ranks of Narodnaia Volia, which advocated revolutionary terrorism. The pogrom crisis, in other words, reinforced rather than weakened their Jewish consciousness.[107] The same could be said of the May Laws of 1882 and the introduction of the *numerus clausus* at the universities in 1887; both measures increased resentment and as a result contributed to the rise of revolutionary fervor among young Jews.

Bad press contributed to the situation. Solzhenitsyn points out that European Jews, who had been meddling in Russian affairs since Moses Montefiore's visit in 1844 tried to prevent the expulsion of Jews from Moscow. The American Jewish banker Seligman, for example, traveled to the Vatican to ask the pope to try to moderate the behavior of Alexander III,[108] ignoring the fact that Russia was under a state of terrorist attack and the fact that legal limitation imposed on the Jews in Russia was never racial in nature.[109] Even the otherwise philosemitic Englishman James Parkes, who condemned these measures, had to admit "that in the period before World War I, certainly Jews had concentrated a significant amount of wealth in their hands and ... as a result created concern that if the Jews were granted full rights that they would quickly take over the entire country."[110] Parkes also admitted that there was an element of truth in portraying the Jew as the taproom owner and usurer, and that it was the Jews' involvement in vodka sales and production that created the most hatred among Eastern European peasants. The foreign Jews who became so adept at manipulating public opinion against the Czar and the Russian government promoted revolution by portraying it as a religious crusade. The Russian revolution was "the true embodiment of society's progressive strivings, [and] contains within itself all the conditions for the salvation of Jews."[111]

After the assassination of the Czar in 1881, the revolutionary movement became something that could not survive without the Jews. The pogroms were followed by a series of countermeasures which turned the situation into a vicious circle in which violence begot more violence as Russia was dragged inexorably down into the spiral of revolutionary chaos. The pogroms followed by the *numerus clausus* at the university created more revolutionary Jews, who now began to arm themselves in Jewish Defense Groups, which became more inclined to engage in revolutionary violence.

For the next four decades, the situation in the Pale was aggravated by foreign press accounts of the pogroms. The riots in the Bessarabian (or Moldavian) town of Kishinyov began on April 6, 1903 on the last day of Passover and the first day of the orthodox Easter celebration. The attack took place over 20 years after the assassination of the Czar and so could not realistically have been seen as motivated by that event. More significant were the town's demographics: out of a population of 50,000 Jews and 50,000 Moldavians, the 8,000 Russians considered themselves a beleaguered minority. By four in the afternoon the crowd of malingerers and young people included many who were drunk. At that point, the mob began to throw stones through the windows of the neighboring Jewish houses. The police, although warned in advance that something was afoot, did nothing to stop the mob, and so a number of Jewish stores and houses were destroyed, but at the end of the first day, according to the police report the Jews themselves remained unharmed.

On the morning of April 7, a crowd of Jews armed with metal bars, clubs and shotguns showed up at the New Market to confront the unarmed Russian Christians. The Jews were enraged by the inactivity of the police, and now claimed that "today we are going to defend ourselves."[112] In addition to shotguns, the Jews also carried bottles of sulfuric acid, obtained from Jewish drug stores, which they splashed on any Christians who happened to be passing by. Soon rumors of Jewish atrocities against Christians began circulating through the town, rumors which became more exaggerated the more they spread. Soon people were claiming the Jews had vandalized the Cathedral and murdered its priests. Soon groups of 15 to 20 Christians began roaming through the town led by the youths who the day before had thrown stones at the Jewish houses. More plundering of Jewish stores followed. The mob moved on to the synagogues, which were totally destroyed. Torah rolls were shredded and thrown into the streets. Then the mob broke into the liquor stores and what they didn't drink immediately got thrown into the streets. During this time the inactivity of the police, who often stood by watching, only encouraged the rioters further. Their inactivity was largely the result of inadequate training in riot control and poor leadership, but the failure of the police to intervene nourished rumors among the Jews that the government was behind the riot and supporting it by the inactivity of the police. As a result the Jews panicked and began firing revolvers into the already angry mob when it approached them. The Jews who fired their revolvers into the crowd for the most part hit no one, but their actions enraged the mob even further. At that point the mob stormed the Jews who had been firing on them and beat them unmercifully. One Jew who fired his revolver into the crowd killed a Russian boy by the name of Ostapov, and crowd reacted with especial violence in this instance. By five o'clock in the evening a number of people had been killed.

By the time the governor got the army to restore order in the town, 42 people were dead, of which 38 were Jews. All of the dead had been killed by blunt instruments. None of them had been shot. There was also no indication that the bodies had in any way been violated, according to the reports of the doctors who had conducted the autopsies of the victims. Of the 456 people who reported injuries as a result of the rioting, 62 were Christians and eight of them reported gun shot wounds. Of the 394 Jews who reported injuries, only five reported serious injuries. Two thirds of those injured were grown men. Rape charges were filed against three people. One soldier had his face mutilated by sulfuric acid. One thousand three hundred and fifty houses were destroyed, along with 500 Jewish owned stores. Eight hundred and sixteen people were arrested, and of that number 664 were brought to trial.

The facts of the case, which were bad enough, were soon lost, however, in the publicity campaign which followed. Before long fact became mixed with fiction as a host of gruesome stories got repeated in newspapers throughout the western world. The official report said that the pogrom was spontaneous, but the news reports abroad claimed that the government was behind it. The police report insisted that no evidence of rape of any other abuse was found during the course of the autopsies, but the press reported all sorts of bestiality. Realizing that they were outgunned by the reports which the Jewish Defense Office had sent to newspapers in all of the world's capitals, the government reacted by banning stories on the pogroms, but this only facilitated the spread of unfounded rumors in Europe and America and enabled even more shameless exaggerations since no one had access to police reports. One official of the Jewish Defense Office wrote: "We sent explicit reports about the terrible bestialities ... to Germany, France, England and the United States.... Our reports had an enormous effect everywhere: in Paris, in Berlin, in London, and in New York there were protest gatherings where the speakers held up pictures of the crimes committed by the Czarist government."[113] Before long, the American and European press joined in. The worst example was William Randolph Hearst, whose paper wrote, "We accuse the Russian government of being responsible for the Kishinyov massacre. We declare that it is up to its ears in guilt as a result of this holocaust."[114]

As a result, the Jews controlled the dissemination of news about the pogroms, and the Kishinyov Pogrom was used to stigmatize Russia forever after. After reading press reports like this, it became apparent to literate westerners that an enemy like this deserved nothing but extermination.[115] Russia was not adept at public relations at the turn of the century, and not capable of rebutting the charges. They simply didn't know how to deal in damage control. At the same time, Jewish control of the press was on the rise in both America and Europe. As a result, the Czarist government lost credibility at home and legitimacy abroad, and it became one of the pieties of acceptable progressive opinion to hope for revolutionary change there. "May the god of Justice," fulminated the Hearst press, "return to earth and judge Russia as he once judged Sodom and Gomorrah and sweep this incubator of pestilence from the face of the earth!"[116]

Civiltà Cattolica echoed the complaints of the Russian Orthodox:, complaining about how

> the Israelite race combines the rule of gold with that one which directly subjugates the mind: we mean the magisterium of the pubic press and academia. In 1848 at the Jewish congress held in Krakow . . it was decreed that the dispersed Israel had to take possession of Europe's most powerful newspapers.... Journalism and public education are like the two wings that carry the Israelite dragon, so that it might corrupt and plunder all over Europe. [According to] Pastor Stoecker...."The Jews buy the press, over half of the newspapers are in their power, and they use it on behalf of their ideas."[117]

Not long after the pogrom in Kishinyov, the Jewish groups which had been founded for self-defense began talking about revenge. It wasn't difficult for the Jews to smuggle weapons in from abroad and before long those weapons ended up the hands of the young men who began looking for an excuse to use them. The "pogrom" in Gomel was a good example.

On March 1, 1903 the Gomel committee of the Jewish Bund organized a celebration of the anniversary of the "execution of Alexander II." The Jews of Gomel, who made up 50 percent of the population, organized demonstrations that were designed to outrage the sensibilities of ordinary Russians, including target practice outside of town with a portrait of the Czar as their target. The Jews had begun to arm themselves years before and created armed self defense units. Before long talk about self-defense had degenerated into talk about the necessity of seeking revenge for the Kishinyov Pogrom.

According to a police report describing the events of the late summer of 1903, "The Jews of Gomel began ... acting in a particularly provocative manner. There were words with peasants and even in their dealings with the educated Russians there was a tendency to emphasize their contempt, as when for example Jews would force soldiers in uniform to get out of their way when walking down the sidewalk."[118]

On August 29, 1903 events escalated after a fist-fight broke out when a customer spat in the face of a Herringmonger by the name of Schalykow. Once the incident occurred, a previously agreed upon signal brought the city's Jewish population running to the market place. Everywhere one heard the cry, "Jews! To the market place! A Russian pogrom!" The Jewish mob divided itself in groups and then fell upon the fleeing peasants, beating them as they ran away. Eyewitnesses testified that the Jews beat unmercifully any Russian peasants who were unable to escape, including old men, women and children. The Jews dragged a young girl from a cart and dragged her by the hair over the cobblestones. The Peasant Silkow was standing off to the side eating a roll when a Jew attacked him from behind stabbing him to death. At that point the Jewish mob dispersed.

When the police chief was hit on the head by a roofing tile thrown at him by Jews, the Russian mob screamed "The Jews have just killed the police chief and then proceeded to destroy Jewish houses and stores."[119] When soldiers intervened, "the Jewish mob then threw stones at the soldiers and fired revolvers at them." The soldiers asked Rabbi Marjanz and Doctor Salkind to calm down the Jewish mob, but "their speeches had no effect and the Jews continued to riot."[120]

A legal document later described the events as a Russian pogrom, i.e., a pogrom in which Jews attacked Russians.[121] This assessment was confirmed by the local police report. Long before the riot actually broke out on August 29, 1903, "The Jewish population began to . . .arm itself with weapons and created self-defense groups in anticipation of anti-Jewish disturbances.... Many of the inhabitants of Gomel had the opportunity to see Jewish youth engage in target practice outside of town in which as many as 100 Jews participated." Once the riot broke out, the police reported that "the Jews fired on the troops which had been sent to protect their property." "Descriptions of this sort," Solzhenitsyn opines, "are nowhere to be found among Jewish authors."[122] As is always the case with armed groups of this sort, he continues, "there was no clear demarcation point between defense and attack. The first instance referred back to the Kishinyov pogrom, in the second instance it had to do with the revolutionary attitude of the organization."

Jews not only controlled the press accounts of what happened in Gomel. After the dust had settled they sent lawyers to the trial to undermine the proceedings, in a way that was becoming the typical Jewish response to high profile cases involving Jews. The Jews made use of virtually the same *modus operandi* in the Leo Frank case in America, when a Jew was accused a raping a 12-year-old girl in Atlanta a few years later and in the Mendel Beilis case, in which a Jew was accused of the ritual murder of a Russian boy. After the corpse of a 12-year-old boy by the name of Andrei Jushtshcinsky was found drained of blood during the first week of Passover and at the same time that the cornerstone of a new synagogue had just been laid, a 37-year-old factory worker by the name of Menachem Mendel Beilis was arrested and charged with the crime.[123] The first ritual murder trial in Russia (usually it was Catholic countries which held them) became an overnight sensation in America and Europe. The Duma wanted to know if there was a sect of Jews that practiced ritual murder. As in the case of the Gomel pogrom, Jews attempted to disrupt the trial, which ended with Beilis's acquittal.[124] The murder remained unsolved, but, in spite of the acquittal, the European press screamed that the Russian government had declared war on the Jews, in spite of the fact that no one ever held the American government responsible for the trial of Leo Frank, a Jew tried for raping a girl in Atlanta during the same period (1913-15). The Jews, for their part, never forgave Russia. It became a sign of virtue to long for revolution there.

The Jewish Defense Bureau sent two of its lawyers to the trial in Gomel, A. S.

Sarudnyi and N. D. Sokolow, who announced upon their arrival that they had "absolute proof" that the pogrom in Gomel had been organized by the Czar's secret police. Six more Jewish lawyers subsequently arrived in Gomel and claimed that it was an injustice that any Jew had been arrested. The fact that 36 Jews were on trial (in addition to 44 Christians), the Jewish lawyers opined, was meant to serve as a warning to Jews that they were from then on not allowed to defend themselves.[125] The Jewish lawyers ignored the fact that the Jews they were defending had lost significant amounts of property in the pogrom and concentrated instead on exposing "the political motives" of the prosecutors and as way of diverting attention from the fact that during the riots young Jews ran through the town shouting, "Down with autocracy," a fact which lent credence to the claims of those who felt that what happened in Gomel was a Jewish revolution and not a pogrom at all. In the end, when it became apparent that the trial was not going their way, the Jewish lawyers stalked out of court abandoning their Jewish clients to their fate in favor of more spectacular attempts to manipulate public opinion to discredit the entire Czarist legal system.

Once again the Czar was caught flat-footed and pilloried in the press at the hands of a public opinion he was helpless to sway. What applied to the world of the press applied a fortiori to the world of finance, as American Jews like Jacob Schiff used their considerable financial power to undermine the Czarist government. Russia came to be seen as the typical Asiatic land, where darkness and exploitation of the people reigned unchecked, and it became not only completely acceptable but honorable to hope for a revolution in Russia in the near future. That revolution, it would be claimed in what came to be routine fashion, would not only be beneficial for Russian Jews, it would benefit all of mankind.[126]

IX.

In 1894 Captain Alfred Dreyfus, the highest ranking Jewish artillery officer in the French army was convicted of treason for passing military secrets to the Germans and sent to prison on Devil's Island. One of witnesses at his public degradation was an Austrian Jewish playwright by the name of Theodor Herzl. After listening to the mob outside the Ecole Militaire shout, "Death to the Jews," Herzl took up where Moses Hess had left off 30 years before and wrote his Zionist tract, *The Jewish State*. More importantly, Herzl, who embodied the high culture of the Austro-Hungarian Empire, began to lobby Europe's most influential leaders to bring about its realization.

What has come to be known as the Dreyfus affair began years before when an increasing number of French writers began to express concern about what Father Ratisbonne, himself a convert from Judaism, called as the title of his book *La question juive*. Similar titles proliferated in the period around the 100th anniversary of the French Revolution—Eduard Drumont's *La France Juive*, appeared in two volumes at around the same time. Many of the authors, like the already mentioned Father Ratisbonne, were Catholics and part of the ongoing Catholic reaction to the Revolution which had begun with the Vendee. Abbe Chabautey wrote *Les juifs nos maitres* and Lemann wrote *Rome et les juifs*. Many of the writers during this period cited Abbe Barruel as one of their primary sources, but Barruel had never mentioned the Jews in his memoirs for the history of Jacobinism. At some point during the course of 19th century, what Barruel called *francmaconnerie* had become *judeo-maconnerie* in the writings of his admirers. It was a change of more than semantic interest.

Before long Rome took notice of all the books about Jewish influence emanating from the Church's eldest daughter. One year after the 100th anniversary celebration of the French Revolution, *Civiltà Cattolica* published a three part series on "the Jewish Question" in three successive numbers over the fall of 1890. *Civiltà Cattolica* was founded in 1849 in the aftermath of revolution in Europe and edited by Italian Jesuits. Although it is not the official organ of the Vatican, it has a uniquely authoritative status. The unsigned articles in *Civiltà Cattolica* on the Jewish Question were not only published with the recent celebrations in mind, they saw a causal connection between the ascendancy of Jews in France and the aftermath of the Revolution. The approach to the issue was primarily theological: "modern Hebrews constitute the scourge of divine justice."[127] Lured to their destruction by the "sweetness of liberalism," Catholics awake up to find themselves in "the embrace of the voracious octopus of Judaism."[128] The hegemony of the Jews in France was the punishment for the sin of apostasy, which took place on a national scale at the time of the French Revolution:

> Heaven's chosen instrument of anger for punishing the degenerate Christianity of our time is the Hebrews. Their power over Christianity is continually increasing, along with the predominance of that evil spirit in it that followed up the rights of God with the rights of man in its bosom. The justice of the Eternal makes use of the most apostate and most cursed people in order to scourge the apostasy of the nations more favored by his Mercy.[129]

The text-book case in this regard is France, the country which in 1889,

> celebrated the first centenary of that revolution which separated her from God, the Church and her kings. But how did she celebrate this solemnity? France prostrated herself in the dust of the Masonic temple of Solomon, humiliated under the feet of the talmudic synagogue, as a slave of a swarm of foreign vultures who have already drained three-fifths of her ancestors' patrimony from her. And thus, the revolution of 1789 has yielded her the glorious profit of passing from the noble submission to her most Christian kings over to the ignoble servitude of the kings of Mammon.[130]

The theological overview the Jesuits provide did not preclude a critique of recent French history in political and philosophical terms because the rise of Jews in France was in some logical but nevertheless uncanny way the logical result of the introduction of revolutionary principles a century before. Any country which abandons the Catholic Faith and turns from God's law, as France, did in 1789, will end up being ruled by Jews, because

> in effect, the modern principles, or the so-called rights of man, were invented by Jews in order to cause the people and their governments to divest themselves of their defensive arms against Judaism, and to multiply the offensive arms redounding to this latter's advantage. Once having acquired absolute civil liberty and equality in every sphere with Christians and the nations, the dam which previously had held back the Hebrews was opened for them, and in a short time, like a devastating torrent, they penetrated and cunningly took over everything; gold, trade, the stock market, the highest appointments in political administrations, in the army and in diplomacy; public education, the press, everything fell into their hands or into the hands of those who were inevitably depending on them. The result was that in our days Christian society encounters in the very laws and constitutions of the states the biggest obstacle which hinders it for shedding the yoke of Hebrew audacity, imposed under the guise of liberty.[131]

Evidence for this claim was taken from foreign sources, like the

> great synod of Israelites having come together from all over Europe, which took place in Leipzig on June 29, 1869, at which Dr. Lazarus of Berlin claimed that "The synod recognizes that the development and practice of modern principles offers the most solid security for the present and future prosperity of Judaism and its followers. These principles contain the most efficacious seeds for its thrilling vitality and its further expansion."[132]

According to the *Civiltà Cattolica* article, "This is the source of the presumption of Judaism, which, as said Prince Metternich, supplies the states with 'first class revolutionaries,' and of the arrogance by which it already predicts its definitive triumph over Christianity."[133] In Russia too, Jews were simultaneously "in the first ranks of those who created capitalism" as well as "in the avant garde of those who were active in advocating the destruction of the monarchy and the destruction of the bourgeois order."[134]

France was not alone in this regard. Virtually every country which experienced revolutionary ferment, whether home grown or imposed by Napoleon, emancipated the Jews and put laws in place which secularized social, economic and political life. In each instance, including Russia, which had yet to experience revolution, the Jews, as Karl Marx noted, flourished in those countries' newly created capitalist economies. This economy coupled with industrialization uprooted huge numbers of people who had lived on the land for generations and herded them into the cities, where they became the revolutionary proletariat. By promoting capitalism, the Jews also promoted revolution. It was a dual role that Jacob Schiff would carry to new levels in a few years.

As a result of the revolution, France awoke to find itself in bondage to the Jews and it is "just this subjugation burdening the European peoples in economic, moral and political aspects that constitutes the kernel of the Jewish question in our time."[135] The main form of modern bondage is finance:

> The accumulation of money by the Hebrews under the aegis of the rights of man—the system initiated a hundred years earlier and also in France—is ample cause for loathing.... The bloody revolution of 1793 which wasted the goods of the nobility and the clergy, attracted that swarm of rapacious vultures. A century later here in France, perhaps even more so than in the Austrian Empire and in Italy, they have become the lords of everything.... The entire so-called High Finance is in the grip of non-French Jews who possess inestimable wealth. The litany of these princes of Israel is long and all have last names which sound as French as those of Arabs or Zulus. The Dreyfuses, Bischoffheims, Oppenheims, Erlangers, Hottinguers and so on, altogether form a banking sanhedrin that represents a value of at least 10 billion, entirely extracted from the veins of France, thanks to the *rights of man*, invented by this cosmopolitan and insatiable race itself and granted to it.... So as already today one cannot negotiate a loan in Europe without the good will of the Rothschilds, likewise, before long, no one will be able to do any business at all without the consent and the interest of the international Jewish league. Hebraism, with its adoration of the golden calf, which represents its power, must necessarily degrade itself below the civilized world.... Now there is no longer any virtue on earth but industry, no religion other than profit, no priesthood other than business, no rite other than money-changing, no God but gold.[136]

Because of their ascendancy in finance, the Jews were able to extend their domination of French culture to newspapers and education:

> The Israelite race combines the rule of gold with that one which directly subjugates the mind: we mean the magisterium of the pubic press and academia. In 1848 at the Jewish congress held in Krakow... it was decreed that the dispersed Israel had to take possession of Europe's most powerful newspapers....Journalism and public education are like the two wings that carry the Israelite dragon, so that it might corrupt and plunder all over Europe.... The Jews buy the press, over half of the newspapers are in their power, and they use it on behalf of their ideas. Jews are responsible for the moral decline in France because, "entirely Jewish is the pornographic and irreligious press which sullies the country and has no equal in any civilized place.... The Jews sully France with the most obscene, most scandalous, most nauseous journalism imaginable and the Freemasons eagerly disseminate it.[137]

By the early 1900s, some people came to believe that certain fields were actually "dominated" by Jews, so great was their presence. In 1912, Moritz Goldstein, a young Jewish journalist, "delighted anti-Semites" by publishing an article in the conservative magazine *Der Kunstwart* claiming that Jews now largely controlled German culture. As he saw it, "we are administering the spiritual property of a nation that denies our right and our ability to do so."[138]

Throughout their series on the Jewish question, the Jesuits at *Civiltà Cattolica* maintained that there was causal connection between Jewish hegemony and revolution. Once the revolution broke down the barriers against evil which Christian nations had erected in self-defense, the Jews colonized that nation and turned its inhabitants into their slaves. The only cure is repentance, which is to say, a return to the Gospel. That cure will be impossible,

> as long as there are governments which continue to replace the ten command-
> ments, the faith and the Gospel of Christ with the principles glorified by the
> French Revolution. If the Christian societies, having been removed from the
> Church of Jesus Christ, won't return to her, they will wait in vain for their libera-
> tion from the iron joke of the Jews. As long as sin will endure, punishment also
> will endure and even intensify.[139]

The authors of the article on the Jewish question mentioned Russia repeatedly as the only country in Europe which, as of 1890, had not succumbed to Jewish control. Solzhenitsyn viewed the Jewish contribution to the rise of the revolutionary spirit in Russia from a spiritual perspective that was not dissimilar to the explanation which the authors of *Civiltà Cattolica* proposed, when he claimed that "It is not Christian Europe which suffers under the Jews; it is unbelieving Europe which suffers."[140] One manifestation of the suffering was the constant discussion of the Jewish question which echoed across the continent around the turn of the century. "By 1898 anti-Semitism had reached the level of a paroxysm in all of western Europe"—in Germany, France, "Great Britain and the US."[141] At around this time, in cities like Vienna and Budapest, large numbers of Jews began to dominate the press, theater, legal profession and media which did not correspond to their numbers in the general population. It was also at this time that the Jewish businessmen and bankers began to accumulate their huge fortunes. As a result, an anti-Semitic movement began to spread through Austria and Bohemia toward the end of the 19th Century, prompting Eugen Duehring, later attacked by Engels, to respond that "The Jews are not only an alien but also a real and unconvertably degenerate race."[142] As both *Civiltà Cattolica* and Solzhenitsyn indicated, the demise of religion which followed the revolutionary secularization of formerly Christian countries created a culture which no longer saw baptism as the "cure" for the Jewish problem, which was now construed in racial terms by both Jews like Moses Hess and their anti-Semitic opponents.

The power of the Jews increased over the French with each subsequent revolution during the 19th century. "The revolution of September 4, 1870 raised six Israelites to the apex of power and the terrible government of the Paris Commune numbered another nine of theirs, mainly leaders and intriguers. Prominent among these were: Gustave Dacosta, who hunted the priests; Lisbonne, who tried to open a tavern served by prostitutes in nuns' habits; and Sione Mayer, who presided at the destruction of the Vendrome column." The revolutionaries were "supported by a journalism that confuses, screens, deceives and frightens off whoever doesn't bow to the whims of Judaism," and it does it with "the help of the Masonic sects."[143]

The same thing occurred in Italy, where in September 20, 1870, "Rome was conquered with shells and the Papacy made a prisoner, the conspiracies, the uproars, the rebellions, the assassinations, the massacres, the wars, the so-called revolutionary deeds, everywhere and always had the same success of increasing the Hebrews' wealth and of humiliating and oppressing the Christian civilization."[144] *Civiltà Cattolica* was referring here to the same series of Masonic-inspired revolutions that had inspired Moses Hess. In both countries the Catholics who participated in the revolution thinking they would free themselves from oppression were later subdued by the oligarchies controlled by Jews and their Masonic allies:

> Freedom... uniquely redounded to the Hebrews' advantage. Through it, they have acquired complete power to subjugate the nations and to ordain that the few might tyrannize the many, and this under the guise of legality, with regard to material goods, to conscience, to faith, to family, yes and what is more to blood and life. Out of such a spasm of liberty, equality and fraternity has arisen the despotism of the tyrannical oligarchies to which the modern states reduce themselves and whoever glances into them will observe that they are oligarchies of Jews or of Freemasons, the Jews' base serfs. The religious right of Catholics is chained; this is the freedom of Masonic Judaism. Permission of blaspheming and committing sacrileges is converted into a public right; this is its equality. Brutal hatred against whoever possesses faithfulness to the God of his forefathers is applauded as patriotism, this is its fraternity. In the Rome of the Popes, carrying the Cross of Christ through the streets in a procession is a crime; but carrying the bust of Giordano Bruno or the horn of Satan there is a noble homage paid to the state.[145]

Six years earlier, in 1876, in his encyclical *Humanum Genus*, Pope Leo XIII had already criticized the rise of Freemasonry in formally Christian countries like France, without, of course, linking them to the Jews. Leo's critique of the Masonic subversion of education, which "allow[s] no share either of teaching or of discipline to the ministers of the Church," is extended by the Jesuits to include their Jewish allies. Again they cite France as the prime example of a country where the Masons collaborated with the Jews to take control of education. In France, they write,

> The war cry "Clericalism is the enemy" was conceived in the midst of the overflowing jewel cases of the Jews, Rothschild, and broadcast by way of Cousin,the Grand Master of Masonry to Gamteeta who wore it on his sleeve.... Among the most pitiless persecutors of Catholicism, the prize goes to the Jews Hendle, Schnerb and Levaillant.... The Jew Giedroye mutilated the masterpieces of the classical authors, purging away from them the holy name of God, so that it would never come under the eyes of young scholars. The Jew Lyon-Alemand ended a teacher's career because that teacher had praised, in a book sent to be printed, the beneficial influence of Christianity on civilization. The Jew Naquet proposed the wicked law promoting divorce and saw to it that it was approved. The Jews tear down the crucifixes from the walls of the Paris schools, breaking them and giving orders to throw them into the sewers, and they defend sword in hand, children's obligatory attendance of secular schools, that is of those without and against the Christian God.[146]

All of the revolutionaries active in Europe in general and in Italy in particular—they mention Mazzini, Cavour, and Garibaldi—have "flirted with the synagogue."[147] What begins as liberation ends as bondage, because "This ultimate purpose is universal domination, is world domination cherished as an article of faith by the degenerate cabalists of Israel. Jews always win out in a society organized according to revolutionary principles."[148] Whenever a state promotes the "absolute equality of all citizens" and "unrestricted liberty" it transforms society, as Shakespeare noted in Troilus and Cressida, "into a tumultuary struggle between opposing forces, of which the most powerful will get the upper hand. And, unfortunately, the most powerful force is always the most malicious one, that in the choice of weapons doesn't even shrink from dishonesty."[149]

X

The emigration of Russian Jews did not begin immediately after the assassination of Czar Alexander II but it did increase dramatically in the years following his death. Emigration, in fact, was negligible up until 1887, six full years after the first pogroms following the assassination. The first dramatic jump took place in the period from 1889-92. The really massive jump took place in 1897. The pogroms are listed as the usual cause of migration, but in retrospect they must be considered as one cause among many. In 1904 at the beginning of the Russo-Japanese war huge numbers of Jewish draft dodgers left Russia and emigrated to America.[150] Avoiding the draft was a significant reason to migrate, especially to America, because America was at peace at the time and there was no draft.

One of the biggest waves of emigration followed the Czarist government's nationalization of the vodka industry in 1896. In order to deal with an abuse that had plagued the Russian state since the final partition of Poland, the Czarist government made the distilling of vodka a state monopoly in 1896. Jews could no longer produce vodka, nor was it legal to sell vodka on credit anymore.[151] As the first result of the ban, the state took in 285 million in alcohol sales and 98 million rubles in taxes. The enormous revenue which accrued to the state from vodka production gave some indication of why the Jews fought so bitterly to retain control of it. When they concluded that retaining control was a lost cause, large numbers of Jews simply left Russia and emigrated to America.

The Jews accused Russia of economic oppression and used that charge to justify revolution, but the economic figures tell another story. The Jews prospered financially throughout the course of the 19th century in Russia. In addition to the huge number of Jews involved in the sale and production of alcohol, the Jewish-dominated sugar industry employed hundreds of thousands of Jewish families. The Jews owned two million desyatines of land in 1908 even though they actually farmed only 113,000. Of 1000 grain dealers in the northwest, 930 were Jews.[152] Jewish capitalists contributed to the rise of the revolutionary workers' movement by the way they treated their employees. "Jews owned mines and exploited the workers."[153] Before long the same complaints that had come to the fore in France, as recorded in the *Civiltà Cattolica* article, began to be common in Russia. "The ranks of Russian businessmen are being taken over more and more by Jews....Jews control finance and credit."[154]

One of the most ominous social indicators showed that there was an inverse ratio between Jewish prosperity and Jewish assimilation over the course of the 19th century. Jews made more and more money but at the same time became less and less interested in becoming Russians. The Mendelssohnian dream of Jewish Russification that had been imported from Germany during the heady days of the Russian Enlightenment now seemed glaringly outdated. It had been replaced in the Jewish mind by Zionism and Socialism. The halting steps toward assimilation which Russian Jews had made falteringly in the 1850s had stopped altogether. Russia's educational system had failed in its project of integrating Russian Jews into Russian culture. After over 40 years of Enlightened reform, only 67,000 out of over five million Russian Jews spoke Russian, a troubling figure when one contemplated the fact that in 1900 50 percent of the world's Jews were living in Russia. The Jews had become not only an unassimilable minority with considerable financial power in their own right, they also had inside connections to world finance in New York through Jacob Schiff and Paris through the Rothschilds. Their connections with the financial oligarchy didn't quench their thirst for revolution. In fact, during this same period of time, they had become fixated on violent revolution as the only feasible solution to their problems—both real and imagined.

Migration didn't solve the revolution problem either, as one might have expected, because the Jews migrated to colonies in places like New York which still nourished that fantasy and provided shelter for recruits like Leon Trotsky, who hurried back from New York city once the revolution broke out in earnest. After resettling in New York in 1890, Gurwich discovered a "Russian workers aid society" that was made up almost entirely of craftsmen from Minsk, and which celebrated "the Russian New Year" by putting on a "ball of the Minsker Socialists" in New York.[155] On the other hand, Jewish emigration to New York was so massive that it threatened to cripple the revolutionary movement in Russia by depleting its source of recruits. Our work, said one revolutionary, "was hindered more by the growing migration to America than by the persecution of the Police. We created the socialist workers for America."[156] The net result of that immigration would be to turn America into Russia's successor as the world's premier revolutionary power by the beginning of the 21st century.

Virtually every Jew who emigrated to America had to pass through Germany to the port cities of Bremen and Hamburg to get there, but the German Jews showed no interest in allowing the *Ostjuden* to settle in Germany. In fact, the newcomers from the East often embarrassed the assimilated German Jews by reminding them of their unenlightened forebears. Gustav Mahler wrote to his wife from Lvov (Lemberg) that Polish Jews "run about this place as dogs do elsewhere."[157]

Walter Rathenau, AEG heir and minister in the Weimar Republic, fulminated against this "Asiatic horde."[158] As Solzehnitsyn puts it, German Jews did not welcome them but contributed generously to their upkeep and the "eventual integration" of those who made it through the border into Germany. Jewish migration to cities like Berlin would provide fodder for national socialist propagandists during the '20s and '30s.

The normal method of German Jewish philanthropy meant making sure that the Ostjuden remained in the sealed trains which carried them to the ports of Bremen and Hamburg, where they were put on boats to America. Between 1882 and 1914, millions of Jews crossed Germany on their way to England and the New World. All of them were aided by the Jewish *Hilfsverein*, whose slogan was "German thoroughness and Jewish heart."[159] The refugees were not as sanguine about their treatment as the German Jews were. They complained of being confined in trains for days on end and allowed out only to pass through delousing stations. "We emigrants were herded at the stations, packed in the cars and driven from place to place like cattle...." Not even the great cholera epidemic of 1892 stopped the flow of immigrants through Germany, although it did lead to an increase of medical measures along the way."[160] Sealed trains would soon take on greater meaning as the 20th century progressed.

Before he died in 1904, Herzl learned from Police Chief V. K. Plehve that the Western Jewish financial world was supporting revolution in Russia. One of the key figures in this support was Jacob Schiff, a German Jew who had emigrated to New York.[161] Eventually two million Jews emigrated to the United States, and most of them ended up staying in New York City, which became as a result a center of anti-Russian agitation. Schiff became a player in American-Russian relations when he used his influence in the world of finance to back the Japanese and thwart Russian credit during the Russo-Japanese war. He also helped sway the mind of Theodore Roosevelt, whose sympathies were totally on the side of Japan.

Schiff came to New York from Germany and became the head of the Banking firm Kuhn, Loeb & Co. In 1912 "he was known in America as the railroad king, and was in possession of 22,000 miles of track." Schiff took to heart the plight of the Russian Jews and was hostile to Russia until 1917. According to the Jewish Encyclopedia, Schiff "belonged to the most important creditors of both his own and many foreign governments, part of which was the 200 million dollars which he lent to Japan during the Russo-Japanese war of 1904-5. Infuriated at the anti-Semitic politics of the Czarist regime in Russia, he happily supported the bellicose activities of the Japanese. Conversely he also refused to have anything to do with lending money to Russia, and he used his influence to convince other banking firms not to lend money to Russia, while at the same time financing the Jewish "self-defense" groups. Schiff, we know from conversations with his distant relative G. A. Vilenkin, an official in the Russian finance ministry, "admitted that through him money was flowing to Russian revolutionary organizations" and that the "situation was so far advanced" that the aid couldn't be halted.

Count Sergei Witte tried to borrow money from Schiff but got nowhere. He soon found that he had to deal with Schiff's influence on the president of the United States when Theodore Roosevelt warned Witte not to impose restriction of American citizens traveling in Russia. Roosevelt was referring to American "salesmen" in Russia, without adverting to the fact that the majority of these "salesmen" were in reality Russian Jews who received American citizenship only to return to Russia, often to promote revolutionary activity. As salesmen, they were expected to be allowed to sell whatever they wanted, including the Colt revolvers which ended up in the hands of the students of Odessa during the revolution of 1905. Schiff was nothing if not forthright about his support for revolution, even if he kept the details of his financial support out of the headlines: "If the Czar can't guarantee his own people their Freedoms which are their right, then this will lead to a Revolution and to the creation of a Republic, in which these rights can be attained."[162] Solzehnitsyn agrees with Haberer in the belief that "the general ardor of the Russian revolutionary movement was doubtless ignited (fanned) by the Jewish revolutionaries."[163]

Over the course of the first decade of the 20th century, the Jews' revolutionary activity became more overt and more violent. In Krynki the revolutionaries fired on the police from the shtetl plunging the town into anarchy for two full days. "According to local reports, the unrest began when Jews outraged the local Russian residents by using a picture of the Czar for target practice outside of town."[164] It was becoming increasingly obvious that the Russian revolutionaries needed the Jews as the fuse that would set off the revolution.[165] (The number of Jews increased with each decade until by the turn of the century, they made up one quarter to one third of the revolutionary movement in Czarist prisons).

Before long, the Russian police began to notice that the revolutionary movement would have been unthinkable without Jewish support. At this point, Jews who made up 5 percent of Russia's population comprised over 25 percent of all political prisoners in Russian prisons and in exile. The historian M. N. Pokrowsky estimated that... "Jews made up from one fourth to one third of the organizational cadres of all revolutionary parties." In 1903 Count Sergei Witte told Herzl that the Jews, who made up 5 percent of Russia's population, were the source of 50 percent of all the revolutionary recruits. G. P. Fedotow wrote "The Jews... were intellectually liberated during the 1880s... in a manner similar to what happened to the Russian intelligencia in the epoch of Peter the Great. They became to a large extent deracinated, international in their understanding of themselves and intellectually active.... They took a leading role in the Russian Revolution, and they also brought about the moral corruption of the Russian revolutionaries."[166]

The Jews saw revolution as a perverse form of assimilation and as the answer to the "burning deracination" which swept over them when the Kahal was abolished and talmudic Judaism was exposed as the essence of benighted superstition. M. Agursky claims that "Participation in the revolutionary movement was in a certain sense a simpler form of assimilation than the usual form, which required baptism."[167] Jewish society was saturated with revolutionary ideas. And the intoxication which these ideas fostered was transgenerational. The rich Jeweler from Kiev, Marschak gave his terrorist son complete freedom of action. The brothers Goz came from a wealthy Moscow Jewish family which also included the Wysosky family, millionaires from tea manufacture, whose grandfather gave the social revolutionary party hundreds of thousands of rubles.

Rationalism found its fulfillment in Marxism, which spread like wildfire through the Pale of the Settlement providing a bracing dose of Messianic politics, which provided immediate relief from the depression which followed deracination. Suddenly, in Marxism, Jews had a purpose in life consonant with the lofty calling they derived from the Jewish heritage of Messianic politics going all the way back to Simon bar Kohkba:

> The Jews believed... that the Revolution was a step on the way toward the realization of the kingdom of God on earth. Not to condemn the Jews but to praise them, they wrote about the role which Jews played as the leaders of the people's movement for Freedom, Equality and social justice, a leader who was not reticent to bring about the destruction of the current state and social order in order to reach this high goal.... In his book *Die Juden als Rasse und Kulturvolk,* Fritz Kahn claimed that "Moses, 1250 years before Christ, is the first proclamation of human rights in the history of mankind. . . Christ paid for proclaiming this communist manifesto in a capitalistic state with his death,... and then in 1818 the star rose over Bethlehem for the second time. Once again he rises over the roofs of Judea, Karl Marx."[168]

With weapons and subversive literature flooding into the Pale, Vilna, the "Lithuanian Jerusalem," was awash in revolutionary ideas and the wherewithal to carry them out. Weapons plus revolutionary ideas plus pogroms led to the creation of fighting units, known as self-defense groups, in the Pale, especially in Vilna, which in the 19th century became for Russian what the Hague in the 18th century had been for France. The rise in revolutionary consciousness corresponded to the rise in Zionism. In 1897 the Bund was founded in the same year as the First World Zionist Congress was held. Yet Zionism did not provide a safety valve for revolutionary Jewish fervor, as Herzl claimed it would in Germany, because revolutionary Zionists like Jabotinsky felt that revolution had to take place in Russia before the Jews could move to Palestine.

When the revolution finally arrived in 1905, the Jews, especially Jewish students in the south, played a major role in its execution. In October 1905 one of the Zionist synagogues in Odessa became not only the place where the student and worker revolutionaries assembled, it became the place where they picked up their weapons as well. Inspired by the resistance they had witness among the Jews of Gomel, thousands of Jews joined the Odessa defense leagues. Before long they were marching through the town taunting the Russians by saying , "We gave you your God and now we will also give you your Czar." At one point the Jews opened fire on a crowd of workers. On the following day, a group of patriotic Russian organized a procession carrying icons and portraits of the Czar. They were attacked by the Jews as well. Twenty years later, the revolutionary Semyon Diamantstein admitted that the "an explosive device was thrown into the Orthodox procession to provoke a reaction."[169] In the reaction that followed many Jews were killed. Foreign press reports claimed in what had become predictable fashion that "thousand and tens of thousands of Jews had been murdered and that young girls and children were raped and strangled."[170] But Diamantstein unwittingly corroborated the official reports on the incident which claimed that no women and children were among the slain when he wrote, "The overwhelming majority of the dead and injured Jews belonged to the best, willing to fight, younger element, who were in the self-defense groups. They died in battle, but they didn't give in." What got reported as a pogrom was in reality a revolutionary "battle" in which many Jewish soldiers died.

The police claimed that the Jews were responsible for the riots and the official Senate investigation backed them up in their claim, concluding that "the October riots were clearly provoked by revolutionary activity and ended exclusively as Jewish pogroms [i.e., attacks on Russian Christians], because representatives of this ethnic group were disproportionately involved in the revolutionary movement." Ignoring the evidence available in the official reports, the Encyclopedia Judaica claimed that "From their beginning these pogroms were inspired by the government."[171]

After two years of revolutionary turmoil, the Jewish leaders, who now held the upper hand, were no longer content to strive for equal rights in small increments. They saw themselves on the threshold of victory and no longer felt it was necessary to present themselves as loyal petitioners to the Czar.[172] As a result of this revolutionary activity, by 1907, "the western half of Russian from Beassarabia to Warsaw" was "boiling over with hatred for the Jews, who [were] held as chiefly responsible for all of the troubles there."[173]

As in France during the same period, the Jews in Russia inexorably took control of the national mind and culture. "The brain of the nation," wrote W. Schulgin in the 1920s, "was in Jewish hands and it became business as usual to think in Jewish categories.... In spite of all of the restrictions, the Jews... controlled the mind of the Russian people."[174]

In October of 1905, the Czar tried to mollify the Jews by granting them new rights at the beginning of the Duma monarchy under Prime Minister P. A. Stolypin. The Duma monarchy was in many ways the Russian imitation of the Glorious Revolution. As in France, the English idea of controlled revolution could not sink roots into Russian soil. The Czar's concessions were ridiculed by the press which was seen as controlled by the Jews. Witte considered the press "Jewish" or "half-Jewish," a fact which the representative Purischkevich confirmed when he referred to the press section of the Duma as "our Jewish Pale of the Settlement."[175]

D. I. Pichno, who had spent 25 years with the newspaper *Kiewljanin* felt that the press constantly belittled the efforts of Stolypin and the Czar because "The Jews... have committed themselves to the Russian revolution..... Serious Russian society understood that the press was a power in moments like this, but they had no power over it, because that power was in the hands of their enemies, who across Russia spoke in their name and had to be read. There were no other organs." Andrei Belyj had similar things to say about the press. It was controlled by Jewish writers who were "alienated from this culture.... Just take a look at the list of the employees of the newspapers and magazines in Russia. Who are the music and literature critics? You'll find only Jewish names on the list.... The overwhelming majority of the Jewish critics are completely alienated from Russian art, and write in an Esperanto jargon and terrorize every attempt to enrich or deepen the Russian language."[176]

Even an enemy of the Czar and a devoted revolutionary like Jabotinsky warned that "nothing good" would come from "the progressive magazines, which are kept going by Jewish money and run by Jewish writers...not for Russian politics or for the Jews." The government's reform measures were caught between the Jewish papers which "proposed the insufferable Talmud of democracy," and the right-wing papers, which could barely . . keep their heads above water, but which accused Stolypin of favoring the Jews. All the while, Jewish influence increased. The number of Jews living outside the Pale of the Settlement increased year by year, and the chairs at the universities were invariably held by "Jews, social revolutionaries or social democrats."[177] The best indication of Jewish prosperity under the Czars was demographic; over the course of a century, the Jewish population under the Russian crown rose from 820,000 to over five million, even though 1.5 million emigrated.[178]

In September 1911, P. A. Stolypin, the Russian prime minister who had been accused of favoring the Jews because he had worked so hard for Jewish rights was assassinated by a Jew. D. G. Bogrov, the assassin, had been raised in an atmosphere of burning hatred for the Czarist regime. The Jewish animus against the Czar became apparent when Bogrov's father said he was proud of his son. Bogrov later claimed that he really wanted to murder the Czar but was afraid that that act "would have set off a witchhunt against the Jews and would have led to a limitation of our rights." M. Menshikov, who had reproached Stolypin for conceding too much to the Jews when he was alive, mourned his passing. "Our great statesman, the best leader we have had for a century and a half—murdered! And the murderer was a Jew! Doesn't he have any shame? How could he dare to shoot the prime minister of Russia?"[179]

The murder set off panic among Kiev's Jews, but the government which had been accused of fomenting pogroms in the past made sure there were no disturbances in the wake of Stolypin's death. There was, however, widespread horror and indignation, especially against the Jews. "After Stolypin was murdered," wrote W. Rosanow in December 1912, "I ceased to have any feelings toward the Jews. Would a Russian have dared to murder Rothschild or one of their leaders?"[180] When the Duma looked into the murder they were accused of anti-Semitism. "Why didn't the Octobrists suppress the fact that Stolypin's murderer was a Jew?" Representative Nisselowich wondered. The fact that they didn't smacked of anti-Semitism. When Solzhenitsyn brought up the fact that Bogrov was a Jew 70 years later in his novel *August 1914* (part of the cycle known as *The Red Wheel*), he was accused of anti-Semitism as well. "Why did I mention the fact that Stolypin's murderer was a Jew.... The fact that I didn't suppress that fact was proof of anti-Semitism."

Stolypin was the only politician who could have kept Russia out of the war which finally broke over Europe three years later in August 1914. With him gone, Russia plunged down the path leading to defeat and revolutionary chaos, followed by the iron heel of Bolshevism and the inevitable reaction against it at the hands of Germany's National Socialists. The murder of Stolypin led to Russia's defeat in the war, which led to the rise of Bolshevism, which led to the German reaction, under which the Jews suffered terribly for Bogrov's crime and that of the other revolutionary Jews.

Emancipation

Chapter Sixteen

The Redemption of the South and the NAACP

The Jews .. have already leaped en mass upon the millions of liberated Negroes and have already taken a grip upon them in their, the Jews' own way, by means of their sempiternal "gold pursuit" and by taking advantage of the inexperience and vices of the exploited tribe....the Negroes have been liberated from the slave owners, but that will not last because Jews, of whom there are so many in the world, will jump at this new little victim.

Fyodor Dostoyevsky on Reconstruction, 1877[1]

By 1905 the Redemption of the South was complete. As a literary commemoration of that fact, Thomas Dixon wrote a novel trilogy expounding the South's position. The most famous novel of the trilogy was *The Clansman: an Historical Romance of the Ku Klux Klan*, in which Dixon portrayed in fictional form the South's rebellion against Reconstruction, and, to use the title of the film based on it which appeared 10 years later, "The Birth of a Nation." The dictum that generals always fight the last war applied to Dixon's novel as well. By focusing on a war which had been won 28 years in the past, namely the South's successful overthrow of Reconstruction, Dixon created a myth which allowed his readers to ignore the form of Yankee imperialism which the South faced in 1905, namely, financial and industrial exploitation. The key to this settlement, which allowed both mystification and accommodation, was racism, in particular the "scientific" racism that was making dramatic cultural inroads in the now Anglophile WASP North in the aftermath of the triumph of Darwinism in England.

The odium surrounding racism has become so all-pervasive that it is worth taking a moment to understand just what it is and what it is not. What it is not is religion. And so to transpose the American racial argument back to its origins in European anti-Semitism, recourse to racism meant that Christianity had been superceded and that baptism could have no real effect in changing the biological substratum which determined human behavior, or what Dixon referred to as "the Leopard's Spots." Dixon took that phrase as the title of one of the other novels in his trilogy on the South. In that "Romance of the White Man's Burden," Dixon expounded upon his belief that biology trumped religion in every instance. By choosing biological determinism over religion, Dixon ingratiated himself with the northern industrialists, who, quite rightly, saw in Darwinism a covert justification of capitalism. In doing this, Dixon all but guaranteed that the arbiters of culture in the North would do nothing to oppose his vision of the new South. Dixon was posturing defiantly in front of the corpse of an enemy that had already been defeated, namely the zealots of the transcendentalist/abolitionist stripe, while at the same time distracting the attention of his readers from the enemy currently occupying their country, namely, the northern industrialists who promoted things like child labor and enslaved lower class Southern whites in ways undreamt of by the defenders of chattel slavery. In doing this, Dixon also cut the nerve of reform and social amelioration because if behavior was a function of the immutable characteristics of race no reform was possible because, to use the terms of his argument, the leopard was unable to change his spots. Dixon's recourse to biological determinism, as manifested in race, as the ultimate explicator of human behavior destroyed any possibility of understanding revolution or its roots in the Puritan/Yankee culture of the North. In his analysis of Dixon's *Clansman*, Richard Weaver cites Dixon's claim that the Southerner is "an ultraconservative, and the last man on earth to become a revolutionist,"[2] but he fails to point out that the main character of *The Clansman*, who joins the Klan to save Southern culture annonces at the end of the novel that he has become a "revolutionist" too. Dixon's racism turns the South's victory over Reconstruction into a pyrrhic victory because in order to defeat the Yankees, the Southerners had to become revolutionaries themselves.

In order to accomplish this, Dixon has to change the terms of the debate. Lincoln is the first figure in Dixon's novel to undergo this change. Instead of portraying Lincoln as a Republican, which is to say as an American Jacobin and the heir of the European revolutionary tradition, which is how the South portrayed him before the war, Dixon portrays Lincoln is a racist, i.e., a good person. Lincoln, according to Dixon, believes "that there is a physical difference between the white and black races which will forever forbid their living together on terms of political and social equality. If such be attempted, one must go to the wall."[3] "No more insane blunder," Lincoln continues,

> could now be made than any further attempt to use these Negro troops. There can be no such thing as restoring this Union to its basis of fraternal peace with armed Negroes, wearing the uniform of this Nation, tramping over the South and rousing the basest passion of the freedmen and their former masters.[4]

America, according to Dixon's Lincoln, is a white man's country:

> there is no room for distinct races of white men in America, much less for two distinct races of whites and blacks. We can have no inferior servile class, peon or peasant. We must assimilate or expel. The American is a citizen king or nothing. I can conceive of no greater calamity than the assimilation of the Negro into our social and political life as our equal. A mulatto citizenship would be too dear a price to pay for emancipation.[5]

Race-mixing of the sort that will inevitably follow from the defeat of the South will lead to the destruction of the American character, which is based on the innate biological characteristics of the white race. Therefore, in order to save the republic, Lincoln sees it as his duty to deport the Negroes living in the United States to some American colony in the tropics:

> "If the Negro were not here would we allow him to land?" the President went on, as if talking to himself. "The duty to exclude carries the right to expel. Within 20 years we can peacefully colonize the Negro in the tropics and give him our lan-

guage, literature, religion and system of government under conditions in which he can rise to the full measure of manhood. This he can never do here. It was the fear of the black tragedy behind emancipation that led the South into the insanity of secession. We can never attain the ideal Union our fathers dreamed, with millions of an alien, inferior race among us, whose assimilation is neither possible nor desirable. The Nation cannot now exist half white and half black, any more than it could exist half slave and half free... God never meant that the Negro should leave his habitat or the white man invade his home."[6]

Had Lincoln lived, according to Dixon's reading of American history, he would have brought about reconciliation in America after the war by expelling the nation's Negroes and establishing whiteness as the basis of the nation's identity. This plan was thwarted by Lincoln's assassination, which was carried out, according to Dixon, by a revolutionary cabal led by Congressman Austin Stoneman, Dixon's disguised portrait of Thaddeus Stevens. In the introduction to his book, Dixon tells us that

> The chaos of blind passion that followed Lincoln's assassination is inconceivable today. The Revolution it produced in our Government, and the bold attempt of Thaddeus Stevens to Africanise ten great states of the American Union, read now like tales from "The Arabian Nights."[7]

Dixon leaves no doubt that "the master hand [which] has organized a conspiracy in Congress to crush the President"[8] belonged to Austin Stoneman. He also leaves no doubt in the reader's mind about the political course which Stoneman was determined to pursue. "Stoneman," Dixon writes, "is a revolutionary." He was "In temperament a fanatic, in impulse a born revolutionist; the word conservatism was to him as a red rag to a bull."[9] Stoneman admits as much to Lincoln's successor: "We, too, are revolutionists and you are our executive. The Constitution sustained and protected slavery. It was 'a league with death and a covenant with hell,' and our flag 'a polluted rag.'"[10]

Stoneman is part of a cabal that wants to enslave the South and turn it into a "second Poland." As one despairing Southerner puts it: "My son, we are now in the hands of the revolutionists, army sutlers, contractors, and adventurers. The Nation will touch the lowest tide-mud of its degradation within the next few years. No man can predict the end."[11] The revolutionary plan is to destroy the South: "Blot every Southern state from the map. Strip every rebel of property and citizenship, and send them into exile beggared and infamous outcasts."[12] In order to accomplish his plan, Stoneman needs to confiscate the property of the white southerners and redistribute it to the Negroes. "The one thing on which the success of my plan absolutely depends is the confiscation of the millions of acres of land owned by the white people of the South and its division among the Negroes and those who fought and suffered in this war."[13]

Stoneman will accomplish his plan by turning Negroes into revolutionaries. The Negro is the avant garde of Revolution which will begin in the South but will soon spread to the North. Once Stoneman "had the South where he wanted it, he would turn and ram Negro suffrage and Negro equality down the throats of the reluctant North."[14] The "ship of state" was

> in the hands of revolutionists who had boarded her in the storm stress of a civic convulsion, but among them swarmed the pirate captains of the boldest criminals who ever figured in the story of a nation.[15]

The "Black Plague of Reconstruction" was the result of a conspiracy among revolutionaries who "threw to the winds the last scruple of decency" and had "organized a conspiracy" that would solve the race problem by creating a situation in which "the Negro shall rule the land of his bondage."[16]

Stoneman's "experiment" is an early form of social engineering. "We have the printing press, railroad, and telegraph—a revolution in human affairs," Stoneman explains. "This experiment is going to be made. It is in the book of Fate."[17] At another point, Stoneman describes his plan to destroy southern culture as "a cold-blooded scientific experiment." Stoneman plans "to give the Black Man one turn at the Wheel of Life. It is an act of just retribution."[18]

In putting the words "just retribution" into Stoneman's mouth, Dixon reintroduces morality into his story, something that is always a problematic issue. The main question at this point is whether social engineering of the sort that Stoneman is proposing, i.e, the political manipulation of environment and culture, is stronger than race. Dixon thinks not, because

> The breed to which the Southern white man belongs has conquered every foot of soil on this earth their feet have pressed for a thousand years. A handful of them hold in subjection three hundred million in India. Place a dozen of them in the heart of Africa, and they will rule the continent unless you kill them.[19]

But in order to thwart Stoneman's plan the Southerners have to bestir themselves, which implies of course, moral effort on their part. In fact, the whole plot revolves around the moral outrage which is generated when a black man attempts to molest a white woman. She and her mother thwart his plan by committing suicide. "The suicide of Mrs. Lenoir and her daughter," Weaver tells us, "who leap hand-in-hand from a precipice after the latter has been violated by a Negro, was based on an actual occurrence in the vicinity."[20]

Moral outrage demands a moral response. Negroes belong to a "lower order of animals"[21] who lust after white women. The Southerner, Dixon tells us, was "the last man on earth to become a revolutionist. All his traits were against it. His genius for command, the deep sense of duty and honour, his hospitality, his deathless love of home, his supreme constancy and sense of civic duty, all combined to make him ultraconservative."[22] However, the vision of the black hand on the white woman's throat changed all that and roused the Southerner to a pitch of "righteous indignation." The only thing which can overcome the aversion which Ben Cameron's father has toward "lawlessness and disorder" and the conspiracies which bring "exile or death," is the spectre of "a black hand on a white woman's throat."[23]

Confronted with that challenge, the South joined forces under the leadership of the great Scotch-Irish leader Nathan Bedford Forrest and became a nation of "revolutionists." Ben Cameron hears the call and joins Forrest's new organization, the Ku Klux Klan, but in doing so he proclaims, "I am a revolutionist."[24] The reader's confusion is compounded further when he is forced to wade through the mixed metaphors Dixon uses to describe the rebirth of the South which the Klan brought about.

> A gale of chivalrous passion and high action, contagious and intoxicating, swept the white race. The moral, mental, and physical earthquake which followed the first assault on one of their daughters revealed the unity of the racial life of the people. Within the span of a week they had lived a century.[25]

Dixon invokes images of racial fate and moral indignation, of revolution and the middle ages, as well as images of race and the cross: "I raise the ancient symbol of an unconquered race of men... the Fiery Cross of Old Scotland's Hills!"[26] Like mixed metaphors in general, the conflation of race and cross is calculated to produce emotional affect more than careful analysis. The one thing Dixon does not explain is how all of these images fit together into some coherent understanding of man's nature and how the men of the South called upon the stores of tradition and personal courage to thwart Stoneman's attempt to destroy them.

At another point, Dixon refers to the birth of the Klan under Forrest as "the resistless movement of a race, not of any man or leader of men,"[27] which of course turns it into something like the migratory instincts of lemmings and deprives it of whatever moral significance it might have had. When Ben Cameron informs Elsie Stoneman "That I am a successful revolutionist," the reader isn't sure whether this is good news or bad, or whether it carries no moral meaning whatsoever, even if he is quick to add "—that Civilisation has been saved, and the South redeemed from shame."[28] If the South had to rouse itself under the leadership of Nathan Bedford Forrest to throw off the yoke of northern tyranny, then it would be worth praising them for their efforts. But if men like Ben Cameron were simply puppets of "the resistless movement of race," then it's not clear why we should be interested in their story, any more than we should cheer on a snake in the process of shedding an old skin, even if that biological process could be construed as a metaphor for higher moral effort.

Dixon, in other words, gives us no way to make sense of the dichotomies he proposes in his novel. Before the reader is more than a few chapters into his book, Dixon's theory runs into trouble. Dixon needs to explain how a white man can become a revolutionary. If the real issue is race, how can someone who is white be evil? If behavior is a function of biological determinism, how can a white man be a revolutionary? Or, to view the whole issue in another way, why should we care one way or the other? If Negroes can't help being bad, how can we hold them accountable for their actions? Dixon can't have it both ways. He can't have both moral indignation and biological determinism as the engine driving the same novel.

As in the above-mentioned instance, Dixon introduces sex as the *deus ex machina* which saves him from the incoherence of his own world view. Dixon saves the appearances of his racial theory by introducing the idea of sexual corruption. Austin Stoneman, the Yankee revolutionary, has been corrupted by his colored mistress, Lydia Brown, who is portrayed as "a mulatto, a woman of extraordinary animal beauty and the fiery temper of a leopardess."[29] Once again, we are back to the leopard's spots, and racism has been preserved as the universal explicator of human behavior.

This also explains how racial purity can re-assert itself in Stoneman's daughter, even though she flows from biological stock that has obviously been corrupted. Elsie Stoneman's father may have been corrupted "by a strange brown woman of sinister animal beauty and the restless eyes of a leopardess,"[30] but there is hope. Race will triumph over politics, because Elsie Stoneman has good Scotch Covenanter blood in her veins:

> The heritage of centuries of heroic blood from the martyrs of old Scotland began to flash its inspiration from the past. Her heart beat with the unconscious life of men and women who had stood in the stocks, and walked in chains to the stake with songs on their lips.[31]

This forms the basis of Elsie's appeal to President Andrew Johnson, Lincoln's successor: "Mr. President, you are a native Carolinian—you are of Scotch Covenanter blood. You are of my own people of the great past, whose tears and sufferings are our common glory and birthright."[32]

Sexuality provides the crucial link between moral indignation and the biological determinism which robs it of any meaning. Stoneman, the Puritan, was corrupted by the high-yaller vampire. Sexual contact between the races leads to contamination. The higher races are corrupted and their standards of behavior are lowered, as Stoneman ruefully admits at the end of the novel:

> My will alone forged the chains of Negro rule. Three forces moved me—party success, a vicious woman, and the quenchless desire for personal vengeance. When I first fell victim to he wiles of the yellow vampire who kept my house, I dreamed of lifting her to my level. And when I felt myself sinking into the black abyss of animalism, I, whose soul had learned the pathway of the stars and held high converse with the great spirits of the ages.[33]

At every turn in the book's plot, we find confusion of the moral and the biological. America is great because of the purity of its racial stock:

> We are great because of the genius of the race of pioneer white freemen who settled this continent, dared the might of kings, and made a wilderness the home of Freedom. Our future depends on the purity of this racial stock. The grant of the ballot to these millions of semi-savages and the riot of debauchery which has followed are crimes against human progress.[34]

Dixon tries to square this circle by implying that somehow the white race, unlike Stoneman's high yaller mistress, is genetically moral. This, of course, implies that the Negro race is genetically immoral. But if human behavior is a function of biological determinism, then there is no morality at all, and if that's the case, there is no room for moral indignation when the black hand reaches out for the white woman's throat. The more we ponder Dixon's prose, the more our confusion deepens.

> No more curious or sinister figure ever cast a shadow across the history of a great nation than did this mulatto woman in the most corrupt hour of American life. The grim old man who looked into her sleek tawny face and followed her catlike eyes was steadily gripping the nation by the throat. Did he aim to make this woman the arbiter of its social life, and her ethics the limits of its moral laws?[35]

When it comes to thwarting Stoneman's schemes, race trumps individual morality. But if this is the case, then why did Stoneman succumb to the mulatto vampire in the first place? And if race trumps morality why do we need to fear a lower race imposing its "moral laws" on a higher race? In fact, if race trumps morality why are we talking about "moral laws" at all? In the end all we are left with the incoherence of Dixon's novel. If there is a moral reason for Stoneman's downfall (even if he succumbed to the wiles of the high-yaller vampire), then this undermines Dixon's theory of racial and biological determinism. If there is a racial reason, then morals are irrelevant, and so is race for that matter.

Weaver claims that "These three novels must be remembered for their influence in molding the mind of the time.... The general reception accorded *The Leopard's Spots* was the first indication that the South might yet win the ideological battle."[36] Yet, Weaver also admitted that the South failed to produce its own Aquinas or Burke, an apologist capable of defending the South and its way of life against the Northern radicals and their revolutionary fervor.

Since the fundamental fact of Southern life was the Negro, Southern apologists were drawn first to the Bible to justify slavery. When slavery was abolished and the South lost the war, this form of apologetics was no longer necessary. Apologists for the Southern way of life then abandoned religion and embraced "scientific" racism as the next best defense of their way of life. "Scientific" racism, however, was no more intellectually respectable than prooftexting the Bible was in finding a justification for slavery.

The South's intellectual failure, however, did not mean that it could not come up with a way to overthrow the Reconstruction regime imposed upon it in the aftermath of the Civil War. Unable to come up with a coherent explantion of the relationship between biology and morality, the South attempted to resolve the issue by recourse to *force majeure*, which in this context meant lynching. Mississippi's Governor Vardaman warned that if it were necessary, every Negro in the state would be lynched to maintain white supremacy.[37] Pfeifer argues that

> Lynching in postbellum America was an aspect of a larger cultural war over the nature of criminal justice waged between rural and working-class supporters of "rough justice" and middle class due-process advocates.[38]

According to this argument,

> Lynchers failed to assimilate conceptions of an abstract, rational, detached, and antiseptic legal process that urban middle-class reformers wrote into statutes, particularly those pertaining to capital punishment, and that state appellate courts increasingly enshrined in rulings pertaining to legal procedure in capital case.... Mobs were impatient with the inevitable delays of legal process and disdainful of the alleged leniency of legal solutions and the seeming distance of a newly professionalized and bureaucratized criminal justice apparatus. They instead enforced racial and class goals through ritualized, community based punishment. Postbellum mobs did not respond to an absence of law but rather to a style of criminal justice that was careful and deliberative, ostensibly impersonal and neutral, in which the rights of the defendant, the reform of the criminal and humanitarian considerations were factored in beyond the punitive demands of communal opinion.... To rough-justice advocates, real justice was lodged in the community. It was administered face-to-face with a measure of retribution that matched the offense, and it sought to "preserve order," that is, to uphold the hierarchical prerogatives of the dominant residents of the locality.[39]

Lynching was a function of failed authority. After the South lost the war, the North went out of its way to de-legitimatize all of its institutions, all of which, including the institution of slavery, were derived from and legitimatized by the constitution of the United States. When the North imposed Reconstruction and racial equality on the South, they failed to establish the legitimacy of the new regime. As a result the South, more than any other section of the country, was prone to take the law into its own hands. The Civil War, followed by Reconstruction,

> marked a turning point in Lynching violence across the United States. The war upset prevailing economic, social, racial, legal and constitutional orders. It precipitated racial leveling, centralization of state authority, and the ascendancy of the North's dynamic industrial and agricultural capitalism.[40]

Unable to accept the legitimacy of the regime which the Union army sought to impose by force, the South resorted to lynching to restore what they considered a legitimate social order, which is to say one legitimatized by the consent of the white people of the South. As a result,

> In the late 1860s and 1870s a vast wave of homicidal violence swept the South as whites, often through paramilitary organizations such as the Ku Klux Klan and the Knights of the White Camelia, which in southern Louisiana reclaimed political power from enfranchised African American men.... After "Redemption" and the return of power of conservative white southern state governments in the 1870s, lynching remained a valuable device for sustenance of white power and the periodic crises of a continuously contested racial order. White elites in Cotton Belt areas such as the river valleys of north central and northwestern Louisiana allowed formal legal agencies to languish in favor of extralegal violence to punish black resistance and criminality.[41]

The New Orleans *Picayune* defended the lynching of 11 Sicilians in March 1890 as an example of the popular sovereignty guaranteed by the Constitution:

"Yesterday the people of this city rose in wrath and indignation at the corruption and perversion of the machinery to which was delegated the administration of justice. They did not overwhelm and sweep away the officials, but brushing them aside, they took in their own hands, the sword of justice, and they did not lay it down until they had executed vengeance upon the criminals whom the corrupt ministers had excused and set free."[42]

Just as slavery and abolitionism created the dialectic of history in the antebellum South, lynching and the anti-lynching organizations which sprang up in the North after the Redemption of the South provided the historical dialectic for the postbellum years. Lynching was one more manifestation of the vicious circle which came into being in the South in the wake of the Nat Turner rebellion. Oppression led to resistance, and resistance, egged on by northern "reformers" who were perceived as revolutionaries, led to further oppression.

In the wake of the Civil War, however, that dialectic now operated in a different way. Now northern radicals had unhindered access to the South and could use their control of the media to stir up the Negroes in a way that would have been impossible during the time of Nat Turner. The result was an increase in northern agitation, which only exacerbated the cultural climate which led to the rise of lynching as a form of social control in the first place. After the war, northern agitation led to lynching, and retaliatory lynching led to more northern agitation.

One of the prime agencies of northern agitation was the National Association for the Advancement of Colored People, a New York organization that was founded in reaction to a lynching in Springfield, Illinois in 1908. One of the founders of the NAACP was Oswald Garrison Villard, grandson of William Lloyd Garrison. Villard's father was a German revolutionary and came to the United States after the Revolution of 1848 failed. Ottilie Assing met Villard's mother and admired his grandfather as "the veteran apostle of liberty, whose country is the world and whose countrymen all mankind."[43]

The NAACP inherited the revolutionary mantle from both the abolitionists and the German '48ers. No one epitomized this legacy better than Oswald Garrison Villard, one of the founders of the NAACP. On February 12, 1909, the centenary of Lincoln's birth, Villard called "upon all believers in democracy to join in a national conference for the discussion of present evils, the voicing of protests and the renewal of the struggle for civil and political liberty."[44] In lynching, the Negro issue was joined once again. The circumstances had changed, but the dialectic, *mutatis mutandis*, remained the same. The abolitionists brought about Reconstruction, which in turn begat Redemption, which in turn begat Lynching, which in turn brought the grandchildren of the abolitionists back into the fray with the creation of the NAACP.

The NAACP got its revolutionary pedigree from other sources as well. The 1908 race riot in Springfield, Illinois angered William English Walling, a white Southerner and social worker, and his Russian-Jewish wife, Anna Strunsky, a revolutionary who had been imprisoned by the Czar. In 1908 Anna Strunsky, declared that "America's treatment of the Negro was even worse than Russia's treatment of its Jewish minority."[45]

The founding of the NAACP marked the beginning of Jewish influence on American life. It also marked the beginning of what would come to be known as the Black-Jewish Alliance. It also marked the beginning of the new form of revolutionary activity that would characterize almost the entire 20th century in America. At the beginning of that alliance, Jews, largely German Jews, joined with the descendents of America's home-grown revolutionary movement, as manifested best in the person of Oswald Garrison Villard, and together they would spend the next 60 years trying, in John Brown's words, to carry the war into "Africa," i.e., turn the Negro into a revolutionary. Anna Strunsky represented the beginning of what would become one of the main sources of revolutionary activity in America, namely, Russian Jews who fled the crackdown on revolutionary activity in Russia following the assassination of Czar Alexander II in 1881. But in 1909, when the NAACP was founded, Strunsky was the exception. The main source of funding for the NAACP came from German Jews. According to Heimrich,

> The New York-based German Jewish aristocracy played a crucial role in the early Black-Jewish Alliance. Names such as Jacob Schiff, Felix Warburg, Isaac Seligman, and James Loeb were often the financial might behind many of the seminal endeavors to address the plight of blacks in this country, including the Urban League and the NAACP. Philanthropist Julius Rosenwald would make a huge contribution toward educating Southern black children, and other German Jews, such as Louis Marshall, Jacob Schiff and Joel Spingarn also made important contributions on the legislative and legal fronts. In the next generation or two, Jews with immigrant Eastern European, and often labor-left backgrounds, would take these German Jews' place at the forefront of the black-Jewish partnership.[46]

If we're talking about the NAACP, the term partnership is misleading if by it we mean collaboration between Jews and Negroes as equals. The NAACP was a Jewish organization, run by a board with no black representatives. To disguise this fact, the most visible member of the NAACP was a Harvard educated mulatto by the name of W. E. B. Du Bois. Given the ethnic make-up of the organization, it is not surprising that before long it was accused of paternalism in dealing with the Negro. Harold Cruse would level even stronger charges in 1967 when he accused the Jewish elite of creating organizations like the NAACP as a way "to fight anti-Semitism by remote control."[47]

The NAACP was created around the same time that other Jewish organizations were coming into existence to fight anti-Semitism in Russia. The American Jewish Committee came into existence three years before the NAACP in 1906 largely as a result of the Kishinev pogrom in Russia. In 1913, B'nai B'rith created the Anti-Defamation League to fight anti-Semitism in the United States.

In many ways the term "Black-Jewish Alliance" is deceptive, especially when it is applied to the NAACP. Du Bois was a product of Harvard and the German university system of the late 19th century which idolized Hegel and had born its first political fruit in the Revolution of 1848. A covert Marxist for his entire life, Du Bois waited until he was in his nineties to join the Communist Party. In his early writings Du Bois shared Marx's suspicions of the Jews as economic exploiters. In *The Souls of Black Folk*, published in 1903, Du Bois claimed that the "defense of deception and flattery or cajoling and lying which the Jews of the Middle Ages used left its stamp on their character for centuries."[48] Du Bois's claim upset Jacob Schiff, Rabbi Stephen Wise, and other Jewish leaders, but not enough to cause them to withdraw their financial support from the NAACP, which supported Du Bois as editor of its magazine *The Crisis*. Once Du Bois became editor of *The Crisis* he no longer made statements criticizing Jews.

The Spingarn brothers, Joel and Arthur, arrived at the NAACP in 1911 in the middle of a power struggle between Du Bois and Villard. The issue was revolution. Should the Negro be told to confine his efforts within the framework of the nation's laws? The man who epitomized the conservative approach was Booker T. Washington. After his arrival at the NAACP, Joel Spingarn allied himself with Du Bois and began urging armed resistance among the nation's Negroes, a stand that appalled Villard. In 1913, Spingarn

> incurred Villard's wrath by counseling Baltimore Negroes not to confine the means of securing their rights to peaceful methods. Negroes heard Spingarn refer to the black man standing at his cabin door with shotgun in hand as a means of protecting what was rightfully his—a statement that one New Jersey Negro leader found appalling.[49]

After listening to Spingarn's rabble-rousing speech, *The Quincy (Illinois) Herald*, concluded that "he wishes to seize the US Arsenal and be a John Brown the second."[50] Spingarn, like Du Bois, considered not the southern racists but Booker T. Washington as their main enemy, and gave speech after speech in which he "asked his black audiences to abandon Washington's gradualism for the more militant program of the NAACP and to switch their allegiance to Du Bois as the symbol of blacks' ideals and ambitions."[51] Villard felt that Spingarn was an irresponsible "firebrand" who would create a reaction among Negroes, who supported Washington. The NAACP was vulnerable to counterattacks in the Negro press, which often referred to it as a "white" organization. The internal split over gradualist versus revolutionary tactics eventually led to a "public altercation after Spingarn arose with his usual unrelenting candor and 'coolly' disputed Villard's advice that Negroes use only peaceful means to secure their rights."[52]

In 1914 Spingarn succeeded in ousting Villard, replacing him as NAACP chairman. The issue was violence. Villard felt that Negro protest should remain within the law. Spingarn argued for violent insurrection. Eventually, "Spingarn and Du Bois went on to dominate the NAACP and shape the direction of the civil rights struggle for the next 20 years, giving it a decidedly more militant tone."[53] Once Spingarn became chairman of the NAACP he spent the greater part of 1914 and 1915 promoting what he termed "the new abolitionism." Preaching violent insurrection among Negroes and attacking Booker T. Washington were two sides of the same coin, and Spingarn engaged in both. Spingarn implored "black audiences to demand their rights in language that was sometimes so harsh that some thought he was advocating violence."[54] He also "openly declared that Booker T. Washington's accommodationist stance and popularity within the black community posed the single greatest threat to black advancement and the growth of the NAACP."[55] Like Lenin, Spingarn felt that things had to get worse before they would get better. Spingarn knew that, rather than end violence and lynching, these early manifestation of black power might temporarily increase it but pursued the revolutionary course nonetheless.

In pondering the collapse of what he terms the "Black-Jewish Alliance" that began with the founding of the NAACP, Murray Friedman gives the following analysis of Jewish motivation:

> Jews did not just organize for their own defense; they also rallied to the defense of blacks, who faced even greater terrors. Why did Jews do so? Possibly it was because, as a pariah people themselves, they easily identified with another group of even more oppressed outsiders. They were no doubt also encouraged by the implicit moral imperatives of Judaism.[56]

If so, the concrete expression of the "moral imperatives of Judaism" as manifested by the NAACP under Joel Spingarn's leadership was 1) spreading revolution, which led to more lynching, and 2) the destruction of any Negro leader not acceptable to the Jewish leadership of the NAACP. W. E. B. Du Bois's first job with the NAACP was the destruction of Booker T. Washington, who had emerged as America's premier Negro leader after he had articulated a philosophy of race relations known as the Atlanta Compromise, based on his famous address at the Atltanta Exposition of 1895.

At the beginning of 1911, Washington considered W. E. B. Du Bois and the NAACP his mortal enemy in the battle over control of the Negro mind in America. By the end of 1911, however, "a note of unprecedented harmony came to dominate the relations between the NAACP and Washington's forces."[57] What happened in between has come to be known as "the Ulrich Affair." On a business trip to New York City in mid-March 1911, Washington was attacked by "a big German" by the name of Henry Albert Ulrich, who accused Washington of making improper advances to his "wife," as well as "peep[ing] into the flat between the shade and the window sill."[58] When Ulrich found Washington "looking through the keyhole"[59] of another apartment in the same building, he chased him into the street and beat him so severely that Washington was treated for injuries at a local hospital.

On the following day, Washington filed charges of felonious assault against Ulrich, but by then the newspapers had picked up the story, and Washington, the leading black figure in America, was now associated with voyeurism and the fatal sin of sexual attraction to white women.

The initial reaction to the Ulrich Affair was an overwhelming outpouring of support for Washington, including letters from then President Taft and Woodrow Wilson, as well as virtually unanimous support in the black press. Washington was aided in this regard by the fact that Ulrich had abandoned his wife in New Jersey. The woman Washington had addressed in New York was Ulrich's mistress, a woman married to a Spaniard by the name of Alvarez. In mounting his defense, however, Washington gave the impression that he was more interested in avoiding bad press and preserving his image than in confronting his accuser and getting at the truth. The legal strategy backfired on Washington. Washington's lawyers continued to postpone the case hoping the bad publicity would go away, but the postponements caused even Washington's friends to become impatient. One newspaper opined

> that Negroes were entitled to know whether the man who claimed to speak for them was really innocent of "questionable intentions in being in that 'free and easy' section of New York at that time of night." This reference to the unsavory reputation of the neighborhood in which Washington was assaulted merely put into print rumors that had been widely circulated ever since the occurrence.[60]

The defenders of southern Redemption had a field day with the reports. Thomas E. Watson, who would soon come to national fame and a political career in Washington as a defender of racial segregation in the South, claimed that Washington, like all Negroes, was the slave of "his inherited appetites" when it came to white women. It was the "recrudescence of nigger" which led Washington inexorably "to the white woman's bed-room door." The fact that people like Woodrow Wilson had "SENT BOOOKER WASHITNGTON A MESSAGE OR CONDOLENCE AND CONFIDENCE WHEN THAT COON WAS CAUGHT AT A WHITE WOMAN'S BEDROOM DOOR AND WAS DESERVEDLY BEATEN FOR IT"[61] only made matters worse.

Sensing that Washington had been fatally weakened by bad publicity, Oswald Villard used the Ulrich incident to forge an *entente cordiale* between the NAACP and the Washington forces, but before the year was out, Villard was ousted by Du Bois and the Spingarns, and hostilities resumed on both sides. The fact that NAACP attempted to capitalize on the sentiments of people like Tom Watson gave further evidence that their intent was revolution not amelioration.

Matters went from bad to worse when Ulrich, as a result of these tactics, won an acquittal. At this point, Washington felt that he had been compromised by the whole affair, confessing in private that his "unfortunate experience in New York and the events which followed it had left him in rather collapsed condition." Gatewood claims that Washington "never fully recovered from the psychological and physical strain" before his death in 1915.[62]

As a result, he was willing to make peace with the NAACP, which then pressed its advantage by undermining his gradualist stance among the Negroes and using

Du Bois to promote a radicalism more in line with the thinking of the Spingarn brothers and their Jewish backers.

The idea that the NAACP was promoting a Jewish-Black Alliance becomes even less tenable when one considers that organization's attitude toward Marcus Garvey. After spending years discrediting Booker T. Washington, Du Bois moved on to his second job: the destruction of Marcus Garvey. After Washington's death, both Du Bois and Garvey saw each other as potential allies. Garvey, however, began to have second thoughts when he visited NAACP headquarters in 1917 and saw "so many white faces."[63] After the ouster of Villard, the Spingarn brothers consolidated their control over the NAACP and turned it into what their historian calls "a closed corporation."[64] The fact that the NAACP's central office exercised such tight control of the branch offices "meant essentially that a few New York administrators determined NAACP policy on a nationwide scale."[65] That in turn meant that the NAACP was vulnerable to counterattack from black organizations and grassroots black leaders like Garvey, who portrayed it as essentially a closed corporation controlled by Jews. Du Bois's job at the NAACP was to de-legitimatize any Negro leader whom the New York German Jewish elite found unacceptable. By the mid-1920s, it had become apparent to Marcus Garvey that Du Bois was, in his words, "a white man's nigger."[66]

Redemption

Chapter Seventeen

The Leo Frank Trial

On April 26, 1913, Mary Phagan was found dead in the basement of the National Pencil Factory in Atlanta, Georgia. Mary Phagan was a pretty, busty 14-year-old pencil factory employee and the object of unwanted attention from the factory manager, Leo Frank, head of the local B'nai B'rith Lodge. Eventually Frank was indicted for her murder. At the time of the Leo Frank case there was next to no anti-Semitism in the South. Jews were perceived as people of the book. Up until the time of the Leo Frank case, the most famous instance of anti-Semitism in the South was perpetrated by a Yankee. On December 17, 1862, General Ulysses S. Grant, writing from his headquarters in Holly Springs, Mississippi, announced that "the Jews, as a class violating every regulation of trade established by the Treasury Department and also departmental order, are hereby expelled from the department within 24 hours from the receipt of this order."[1] The North could hardly accuse the South of anti-Semitism because no official in the North had a rank as high as the one which Judah P. Benjamin, Jefferson Davis's right-hand man, held during the period of the Confederacy. After the war Jewish peddlers made their way down South, but, in spite of their often sharp business practices, there weren't enough of them to provoke anti-Semitism. Besides, when it came to racial issues, the South had other more pressing problems.

Racial prejudice in the South was a black and white issue. The Frank trial took place at a time when the South's redemption from reconstruction was an accomplished fact. Lynching was, if anything, on the wane in 1913, and the citizens of the state of Georgia were eager to prove their allegiance to the rule of law. In this regard, most Georgians viewed the Frank proceedings with a sense of pride, as showing how far they had come from their recent troubled past. In spite of the volatile material at the heart of the case —the rape and murder of a 14-year-old girl—no one had been lynched—not even the Negro watchman Jim Conley—before the case went to trial. If anything, the Frank trial showed lack of prejudice when it indicted Frank over the pencil company's Negro watchman, Jim Conley.

Once the trial began, Leo Frank's character, specifically his sexual morals became the central issue. Female employees testified that Frank often entered their dressing room and favored them with unwanted attention that included kissing and fondling. A newspaper boy who was a friend of Mary Phagan testified that she had been pursued by Frank and was afraid to be alone with him, as she was on the last day of her life when she went to his office to pick up her paycheck. On that Saturday in April, the city of Atlanta was preparing for a parade commemorating its Civil War veterans, and the pencil factory's office was empty except for Frank and Phagan, a fact Frank would have known when he told Phagan to come in and pick up her pay. Phagan's salary for a week's work at a machine which put erasers on pencils was $1.20.

The Leo Frank case put Atlanta's Jews on trial because they chose to close ranks around Frank even though four Jews were on the panel which indicted him. But the Frank trial also put the new south on trial. The boosters at the local chamber of commerce may have benefited financially from the new southern economy, but the average to poor man in Georgia wasn't particularly happy about the fact that the South had been turned into the cheap labor pool for northern industrialists because it was his daughters who ended up working in their factories. The fact that cheap labor in the South meant child labor made a bad situation even worse. When the sexual exploitation of child labor was added to the mix, the sullen South reached the limit of its patience and demanded an expeditious trial. The southern ruling class which was trying to ingratiate itself with the northern industrialists by offering the malnourished children of Atlanta as cheap labor knew that justice delayed in this instance was an open invitation to a return to the rule of lynch law.

Leo Frank and his lawyers, however, went to trial blithely unaware of the real dynamics that informed the case. When Leo Dorsey, the state prosecutor called a witness who claimed that he saw Frank engage in an act of sexual perversion with a local prostitute, the defense attorneys woke up to the fact that everyone, including most importantly the jury, felt that Leo Frank's character was on trial. The fact that they refused to question Frank and let him clear the air on his own character, a move which would subject him to cross-examination of the sort they tacitly admitted would harm his case, only confirmed the character issue as central in everyone's mind. When Frank finally did take the stand he talked for hours about the ins and outs of the pencil business, further alienating his southern audience by giving the impression that he was a totally callous and self-absorbed alien who viewed the girls who worked for him as nothing more than the robots who ran his machines. If the girls were robots, the Georgians reasoned, why couldn't the more attractive girls, like Mary Phagan, be seen as sexual robots as well?

II

Realizing that their strategy was in deep trouble, Frank's lawyers decided to play the race card. Luther Z. Rosser, one of Frank's attorneys, called Jim Conley to the stand and tried his best to entrap the Negro in his own testimony. When that failed, he resorted to naked race-baiting, which took two forms. In the first instance, Rosser claimed that the only reason that Frank had been indicted was because of his race, implying that the South was a hotbed of anti-Semitism. "Gentlemen," Rosser told the court, "take a look at this spectacle if you can. Here is a Jewish boy from the North. He is unacquainted with the South. He came here alone and without friends, and he stood alone. He is defenseless and helpless...."[2] Frank's other attorney Reuben R. Arnold was, if anything, even franker about the accusations the defense attorneys now leveled against the state of Georgia. "I tell everybody, all within the hearing of my voice, that if Frank hadn't been a Jew he never would have been prosecuted. I am asking my kind of people to give this man fair play. Before I'd do a Jew injustice, I'd want my throat cut from ear to ear."[3]

The defense then moved to the other prong of its race strategy, its attack on Jim Conley in particular and all Negroes in general as unreliable and incapable of being trusted. Pandering to the lowest anti-Black sentiments in the South, Luther Rosser told the jury that "Conley is a plain, beastly, drunken, filthy, lying nigger with a spreading nose through which probably tons of cocaine have been sniffed."[4]

"They got a dirty, black Negro," Rosser continued, "and in order to give impetus to his testimony they had a barber cut his hair and shave him, and they gave him a bath. They took rags from his back and he came in here like a slicked onion. They tried to make him look like a respectable negro."[5]

Rosser and Arnold's strategy was predicated upon a fundamental rule of the South. If a disputed issue comes down to the word of a white man versus the word of a Negro, the nod always goes to the white man. Neither Rosser nor Arnold, however, seemed aware that they had undermined their own case by playing up the fact that Frank was a Jew. If he were a member of an alien race from New York, a section of the United States that had been traditionally hostile to the South, it was not clear that he fulfilled the Southerner's criterion of whiteness. Beyond that, Rosser and Arnold failed to understand that in calling the citizens of Georgia anti-Semites, the defense insulted the very group they needed to persuade. Was the jury supposed to feel that they were somehow above the accusations of anti-Semitism leveled against their fellow Georgians when the jury knew full well that it was nothing more than a randomly chosen sample of that citizenry?

Dorsey, the state's attorney, jumped on an even more glaring inconsistency. If the state's case was motivated by prejudice, why would they ignore a suspect as tempting as the Negro Jim Conley and go after someone whose Jewishness had been irrelevant until the defense raised it as an issue?

"Gentlemen," the state's attorney asked the jury, "do you think that I, or that these detectives, are actuated by prejudice? Would we as sworn officers of the law have sought to hang Leo Frank on account of his race and religion and passed up Jim Conley, a Negro? Prejudice?"[6]

Dorsey reminded the jury that it was the defense which brought up the issue of prejudice in the first case. His rebuttal then "all but obliterated the defense's accusation" and exposed "the cry of anti-Semitism [as] a deliberate ploy to salvage a losing case."[7] A short peroration on Jewish leaders which included praise of Benjamin Disraeli and Judah P. Benjamin, allowed Dorsey to take the high ground and announce to a jury that was already sensitive to the idea that northern capital had unlimited rights over the south, that all men were equal when they stood before the bar of justice.

Having demolished the charge of anti-Semitism, Dorsey could then probe the inconsistencies in the defense's case. "What business did this man have going into those dressing rooms?" Dorsey wondered, resurrecting the moral issue that the defense had been so eager to dodge.[8] Oney underscores the shocking nature of the charges leveled against Frank's character and the effect they would have on a jury in Georgia in 1913:

To accuse Frank of attempted rape and murder was bad enough, but to imply that due to some unspecified physical abnormality he had tried to perform what most Atlantans would have considered an act of perversion and what Georgia law regarded as the capital offense of oral sodomy was devastating.[9]

There were other issues that argued for the truthfulness of Conley's testimony. The defense attorneys tried to discredit Conley's claim that Frank told him he would never go to jail for the crime because he had rich relatives in New York. "Why should I hang?" Frank allegedly told Conley, "I have wealthy people in Brooklyn?" How, Dorsey wondered, did an ignorant Negro like Conley know that Brooklyn existed in the first place and that Frank had wealthy relatives there, and that "they had $20,000 in cool cash out at interest" if Frank hadn't mentioned that fact to him?[10] How was it that the note which Frank claimed Conley wrote said, "the Negro did it," when Conley would have said, "the Negro done it"?[11]

As Dorsey bore down on the defense's case, his words began to have their effect on the people in the court room. Both Frank's wife and mother burst into tears. (At another point Frank's mother stood up and called Dorsey "a Christian dog," putting another nail in her son's coffin.)[12] Even Atlanta's pro-Frank newspaper, *The Georgian*, claimed that Dorsey's summation speech to the jury was a "a white hot philippic, the greatest ever heard in a criminal court in the South."[13]

Unaware of the fact that their racial strategy was alienating the very jury they needed to persuade, Frank's defense attorneys continued to invoke racial prejudice without understanding that Frank's failure to confront the Negro's attack on his character condemned him in the eyes of the jury because "never in the history of the Anglo-Saxon race, never in the history of the African race in America, did an ignorant filthy Negro accuse a white man of a crime and that man decline to face him."[14] Knowing that he couldn't deal with the issue of Frank's sexual morals directly and fearing that his race-baiting tactics had failed, Defense Attorney Arnold in desperation called for a mistrial.

The plea for a mistrial was based on Arnold's claim that "the behavior of the spectators throughout this trial has been disgraceful."[15] That claim was based on the fact that the judge, reacting to the fact that the temperature in the courtroom had reached 91 degrees at the height of the Atlanta summer in the days before air conditioning, ordered the courtroom's windows opened, exposing the proceedings to the scrutiny of the spectators who had assembled in the square in front of the courthouse. The charge of jury intimidation would gain a life of its own as it became embellished by subsequent news accounts ("Kill the Jew or we'll kill you," the most famous line, was totally apocryphal and made up by the press as part of a campaign to exonerate Frank.)[16] Eventually, those claims made their way into the deliberations of Oliver Wendell Holmes, when the Frank appeal was heard by the U.S. Supreme Court. However, no one who was at the trial substantiated the claim.

In the end, the defense strategy failed miserably, and Frank was found guilty of murder and sentenced to death. The guilty verdict made Leo Dorsey, who was carried on the shoulders of three men through the crowd of 5,000 which had assembled to hear the verdict, a local hero. Dorsey would go on to run for political office based on his conviction of Frank. The people of Georgia felt that the Frank case had vindicated the legitimacy of their state's institutions. Frank had had his day in court. No one had resorted to lynch law. Justice had been served.

The guilty verdict, however, had the exact opposite effect on Atlanta's Jews, who began to talk about Frank as the American Dreyfus and banded together to do whatever was necessary to overturn his conviction. Frank was found guilty during one of the greatest waves of Jewish migration since the flight from Egypt. Beginning with the assassination of Czar Alexander II and continuing in light of the publicity which flowed from a series of pogroms that the Jews claimed were orchestrated by the czarist government, millions of Russian Jews fled, via ports like Hamburg, to the United States and congregated in places like the lower east side of Manhattan. This huge influx of Russian Jews arrived at a time when the German Jews who had arrived during the middle of the 19th century had achieved unprecedented political power largely because of their influence over publishing, Broadway, and the fledgling motion picture industry. Taken together, all of these factors contributed to a situation in which American Jews were prone to see an anomalous American incident like the Frank case as part of a larger European pattern of anti-Semitism of the sort that had created the Dreyfus incident in France and the pogroms in Russia, and that made them determined to do something about it.

The first indication of what was to come had already happened in Atlanta during the early days of the trial. Upset by what they considered the unfair coverage of the trial in *The Georgian*, the Jews put editorial pressure on the paper by withdrawing their advertising. The other papers in Atlanta, *The Journal* and *The Constitution*, "paid no attention to the demands of the Jews,"[17] but they were locally owned. *The Georgian* was owned by William Randolph Hearst, and soon pressure was brought to bear in New York, where Jewish influence was much stronger than it was in Atlanta. Gradually, Hearst succumbed to the pressure and when he did the editorials in *The Georgian* began to take a definite pro-Frank stance. In order to placate the Jews, *The Georgian* created a columnist whose only beat was the Frank trial. That columnist, who was identified only as "the Old Police Reporter," was unfailingly sympathetic to Frank and, before long, the machinations of his Jewish backers.[18]

The Georgian would remain determinedly pro-Frank throughout the trial, something that other papers began to notice. Writing in the *American Mercury*, Herbert Asbury, who had worked for the *Georgian* during the Frank trial, admitted that "Although evidence was constantly piling up against [Frank], toward the end we worked as hard trying to prove his innocence and build up sentiment for him and against the Negro, Jim Conley."[19] Reacting to pressure from Hearst in New York, who was in turn reacting to pressure from Atlanta's Jews, *The Georgian* opined that it was "the present Grand Jury's DUTY to indict Conley without further ado!"[20] When the Grand Jury did not indict Conley, *The Georgian* ignored the fact that several Jews were on the panel, even though that fact constituted a "stunning victory" for the prosecutor.[21]

Shortly after their complaints reached his ears, Hearst arrived in Atlanta, where he met with the city's rich Jews and the newly elected governor of the state John Slaton. Slaton, in addition to having been elected to the highest office in the state, was also a member of the same law firm as Frank's lawyers, a fact which raised questions of conflict of interest which became harder to avoid as the clamor to get Slaton to pardon Frank became greater. Before long, the ramifications of the case became clear for the citizens of Georgia. At issue was the rule of law and whether the law applied to all of Georgia's citizens regardless of their race or wealth or connections. Having suffered through the manipulation of the political process as a form of covert Yankee-inspired social engineering during the Reconstruction era, the South had used the Klan and lynching to restore popular sovereignty. Now with that era safely in the past, Georgians prided themselves on their return to the judicial process, only to be denounced by the nation's press as bigots because they had convicted a Jew in a trial that everyone in attendance had considered fair and above board. To the average Georgian, the fact that the state had not railroaded Jim Conley or the fact that a mob hadn't lynched him was a sign that Georgia's legal system had conquered prejudice. Now the national press was attacking Georgia for a prejudice which it never knew it had, namely, anti-Semitism, and ignoring all of the evidence that the trial had amassed to testify for their belief in the rule of law and the fairness of the proceedings. The Georgians were in effect being called anti-Semitic bigots because they had given Leo Frank a fair trial and not succumbed to the special pleading of the northern newspapers, most of which were owned by Jews.

After Frank was found guilty and sentenced to die on October 10, 1913, Judge Roan went out of his way to assure him that "I have tried to see that you had a fair trial for the offense for which you were indicted." The people of Georgia may have agreed with Judge Roan, but the Jews were convinced that Frank was the victim of an anti-Semitic conspiracy, and it was this view which got trumpeted throughout the northern press.

Once the full fury of the northern press became apparent in the aftermath of Frank's conviction, it became clear that the Jews were going to create the very anti-Semitism they wanted to avoid as the Frank case took on a life of its own as the test case for the moral legitimacy of the New South. Who had more power, Atlantans began to wonder, the state of Georgia, and by extension the people who appointed its judges and representatives, or the *New York Times* and all of the other Jewish owned newspapers who were demanding Frank's acquittal and then his pardon?

III

Atlanta's Jews were appalled by the verdict and saw it as a personal attack on their community, even though until that time there had been no evidence of anti-Semitism in Atlanta. Rabbi David Marx, heretofore leader of Atlanta's assimilationist minded synagogue, decided to make the Frank case his personal cause. Marx headed for New York, where he planned to elicit support from the heads of organized American Jewry. In a letter to one potential supporter, Marx claimed that the Frank case was "without doubt an American 'Dreyfus' case" because "the evidence against Frank is purely prejudice and perjury. The feeling against the Damned Jew is so bitter that the jury was intimidated and feared for their lives, which undoubtedly would have been in danger had any other verdict been rendered."[22]

While in New York, Marx met with Adolph S. Ochs, publisher of the *New York Times* and that profession's most powerful Jew. Marx was not going to have an easy time selling the Frank case to Ochs, who had the reputation of being a "non-Jewish Jew" who "will have nothing to do with any Jewish movement."[23] Ochs had rejected an invitation to join the board of the newly formed American Jewish Committee and had sworn that the *New York Times* would never become "a Jewish newspaper."[24] By the end of their meeting, all the zealous rabbi could elicit from Ochs was a promise to look into the matter. In fulfilling his promise, Ochs got a report from the Atlanta stringer for the *Times*, informing him that it would be a mistake to support Frank, not just for Ochs and the *Times* but for Frank himself, who would bear the brunt of the backlash. In fact, the stringer said, "that the worst thing for him that could happen would be for Jews to rally to him as Jews."[25] Ultimately, Ochs made the mistake of ignoring this advice, and as the stringer indicated Frank paid the ultimate price for that mistake.

Marx had an easier sell before him when he met with Louis Marshall, president of the American Jewish Committee. Unlike Ochs, Marshall was an openly Jewish advocate who had spent the past ten years fighting anti-Semitism. In 1911 he had persuaded the United States to abrogate a treaty with Russia which prevented "American Jews from freely conducting business in Russia."[26] That that business involved selling revolvers to Jewish revolutionaries went unmentioned by the AJC and the American press. Marshall agreed with Marx and felt that the Frank case met the criteria for AJC involvement, but he feared open advocacy of the case might backfire, especially in Georgia, and create more anti-Semitism, which would, in turn, make overturning the verdict impossible. According to Marshall, "any action that is taken must emanate from non-Jewish sources."[27] This meant creating front groups and giving the impression that the newspapers which orchestrated the campaign were reporting on a groundswell of popular opinion. Marshall proposed working behind the scenes to change Atlantans' thinking. "There is only one way of dealing with this matter," he wrote to another AJC board member, "and that is in a quiet unobtrusive manner to bring influence to bear on the Southern press [to create] a wholesome public opinion which will free this unfortunate young man from the terrible judgment which rests against him."[28]

By the end of September, articles began appearing in papers like Cincinnati's *American Israelite*, claiming that "Frank's religion precluded a fair trial.... The

713

man was convicted at the dictates of a mob, the jury and judge fearing for their lives."[29] This, of course, was precisely what Marshall did not want to happen, and it brought about precisely the reaction which Marshall feared. Stung by claims in the press, the jury responded by saying that it had not been influenced much less intimidated by the crowd which had gathered outside the court house. The jury felt compelled to repudiate false reports which had appeared in the press. The buggy salesman Henslee denied explicitly Samuel Aron's claim that he told the Atlanta Elks Club: "I'm glad they indicted the God damned Jew."[30] The claim was preposterous, Henslee claimed, because the Elks had many Jewish members. Monroe S. Woodward, an Atlanta hardware store salesman who had served on the jury testified that "I did not at any time, while a juror, hear any applause except such as occurred in open court, and which was heard by the judge and attorneys in the case.... There was never any applause or cheering inside or outside of the court within my knowledge while the case was being considered."[31] Accounts of mob intimidation in the press followed by the vehement denials by those who were actually there as participants confirmed the idea in the mind of Georgians that the Frank case was a contest between big northern interests controlled by Jews and the common man, who still had faith in the American legal system.

States Attorney Leo Dorsey articulated these sentiments when he argued in court against the new trial that the newspapers were proposing, claiming that another trial would be an attack on the people of Georgia. "If," Dorsey argued, "the verdict of guilty against Leo Frank is set aside upon such trivial grounds as the convicted man's lawyers recite in their motion, it will justify very largely the contempt in which people are beginning to hold their courts and the administration of their laws."[32]

Dorsey went on to claim that the Jews were willing to slander the entire state of Georgia in order to overturn Frank's conviction. Dorsey maintained that race had nothing to do with Frank's conviction: "The people were not aroused against Leo M. Frank because he is a Jew but because he is a criminal of the worst type. In the name of the Gentiles of Atlanta, I declare that when the counsel for the defense charges the jury with bias and charges Atlantans with intimidating the jury with a display of mob spirit, they are slandering the citizenship of the entire community."[33] Moved by Dorsey's argument, the judge denied the motion for a new trial.

On November 8, 1913, eight days after the motion for a new trial was denied, Jacob Schiff and the board of the American Jewish Committee met at Temple Emanu-El in New York to discuss their next move. Louis Marshall again warned that any expression of Jewish solidarity which gave the impression that the Jews were determined to get Frank off the hook no matter what would only create the very anti-Semitism their organization strove to avoid. Marshall's caveat, however, was no match for Jacob Schiff, the most powerful Jew in America, who argued for the AJC's open involvement in the Frank case. In the end a compromise of sorts was reached, and the AJC agreed to support Frank's case by manipulating public opinion from behind the scenes. The AJC voted to retain Albert Lasker, head of a Chicago public relations firm who had established famous brands such as Bud weiser beer and Quaker Oats, to undermine the legitimacy of the Frank verdict and orchestrate public opinion to get it overturned.

None of the Jews involved in the compromise leading to the approval of this campaign seems to have considered the dangers it involved, especially for Leo Frank, whose life hung in the balance. Even the open publicity campaign which Marshall feared posed fewer dangers. A backlash against Jewish support for Frank had begun to manifest itself—and not just in Georgia. Even in New York, the capital of the Jewish publishing industry, there was no mystery to what was going on if the *New York Sun* could run headlines like, "Jews fight to save Leo Frank."[34] If it could be shown that the Jews were working behind the scenes to orchestrate this sort of feeling, the reaction would be that much worse, and Marshall's fears that the very anti-Semitism which they opposed would become a very ugly reality.

Ultimately all of the dire predictions of the Jews became self-fulfilling prophecies. In response to the attack on the state of Georgia, its citizens and its institutions, "Prejudice did finally develop against Frank and against the Jews. But Frank's friends were responsible for this anti-Semitic spirit.... The supposed solidarity of the Jews for Frank, even if he was guilty, caused a Gentile solidarity against him."[35]

Cruse claims that the Frank case revealed that even if Jews experienced discrimination it had no economic consequences. And that fact called the significance of the Black-Jewish Alliance into question. In his view, "It was the crucial disparity between the economic status of blacks and Jews that qualified the meaning of any alleged social significance of the Black-Jewish Alliance."[36] "Black marginality" and "Jewish marginality," far from being "two sides of the coin of racial prejudice" were totally different phenomena because they had no economic common denominator. This double standard would go on to have far-reaching consequences, but its existence emerged for the first time in the Frank case.

By late fall of 1913, Albert B. Lasker had not only agreed to orchestrate the publicity campaign to exonerate Frank, he had contributed $1000 of his own money to the cause and had raised equal amounts from his father and fellow Chicagoan Julius Rosenwald, the chairman of Sears Roebuck and Company. At around the same time Adolph Ochs had overcome his scruples about using his paper as a vehicle for Jewish advocacy and had committed the *New York Times* to Frank's cause as well. From that moment until the time of Frank's death, the *Times* devoted front-page coverage to every aspect of the story.

The conspiracy to exonerate Frank got into trouble almost immediately, which is not surprising considering the methods it had chosen to use. As one of his first acts, Lasker hired the famous detective William Burns, a celebrity of rock star stature in his day, who in turn set himself up in Atlanta's most expensive hotel and announced that he was going to get to the bottom of the case and solve a mystery which the courts of Georgia had already resolved "I am in the Frank case to the finish," Burns announced after his arrival in March 1914.[37] Instead of informing Burns that the jury had already rendered its verdict, the Hearst paper in Atlanta went along with this publicity stunt and announced in a front page headline: "Detective promises Decisive Probe."[38]

In the meantime, Albert Lasker, the man who had paid Burns his $4,500 retainer fee, had, seemingly independently, come up with the slogan which would do for Leo Frank what Lasker had done for Quaker Oats and Budweiser Beer. The phrase, "The Truth is on the March," began appearing in articles on Frank across the country and from the lips of Frank himself, who included the phrase in just about all of the interviews he granted from his jail cell.[39]

"A rallying cry had been born"[40] and it looked as if it were making inroads in Atlanta itself, when one of the locally owned papers, *The Journal* reversed its previous position and came out for a new trial. Appearances in this instance were deceptive. The publicity campaign may have caused the defection of one paper, but it mobilized the opposition further by bringing another paper into the battle on the side of the Georgians. *The Jeffersonian* had nowhere near the circulation of the *Journal* when the Frank case began, but the *Journal* didn't have an editor like Tom Watson, who turned out to be a genius in articulating the resentment which the common man in Georgia felt over the Frank case and the heavy-handed interference of the Jews which provoked it. For 11 months, Watson had ignored the Frank trial in the pages of the *Jeffersonian*, which up until that time had distinguished itself by running a series attacking the Catholic Church, in which Editor Watson referred to the pope as "a fat dago."[41] The defection of the *Journal* had brought Watson into the fight, and Watson was outraged at Yankee Jewish meddling in the Georgia legal system and determined to ask the questions which the other papers had pointedly ignored.

"Who is paying for all this?" Watson wondered when William Burns, the world's highest paid detective showed up in Atlanta. The spike in circulation that *The Jeffersonian* enjoyed in the wake of Watson's entry into the Frank case indicated that many other Georgians had similar questions on their minds. "Does a Jew expect extraordinary favors and immunities because of his race?"[42] Again Watson seemed not only capable but willing to articulate the questions on everyone's mind.

"Is it wise," Watson continued, "for the Jews to risk the good name and the popularity of the whole race in the extraordinary, extra-judicial and utterly unprecedented methods that are being worked to save this decadent offshoot of a great people."[43]

There no indication that the Jews who were bent on orchestrating Frank's pardon were aware of Tom Watson at this stage of the game, nor is there any indication that they would have heeded his warnings if they were. With the machinery of public relations firmly behind their cause and with hitherto hostile newspapers now calling for a new trial, victory seemed within the grasp of the Frank camp. In the meantime, Lasker and his associates were counting the cost for final victory. On April 20, Lasker came up with another $5,000 for the cause, and estimating that a total of $20,000 would be needed for victory, Lasker wrote what Oney calls "the cordial equivalent of a shakedown letter"[44] to Louis Wiley, the business manger of the *New York Times,* informing him that "New York ought to give at least $10,000, and much more.... Will you please get the ball in motion and raise the maximum amount you can?"[45] On April 22, Wiley complied with Lasker's demand by writing a letter—on *New York Times* stationery—to Jacob Schiff asking for the rest of the money, prompting Oney to opine that "by the date Wiley wrote Schiff, the *Times* had clearly crossed the boundary between journalism and advocacy."[46]

Tom Watson had surmised as much from his vantage point in Georgia. The state of Georgia was now on the receiving end of undeserved "Nation-Wide Abuse,"[47] as he phrase it in one *Jeffersonian* headline, and the main culprit in this campaign was the *New York Times* under the leadership of Adolph Ochs, who serves as "a most useful servant of the Wall Street interests, runs a Tory paper in New York, whose chief end in life seems to be to uphold all the atrocities of Special Privilege and all the monstrous demands of Big Money."[48]

Favorable press coverage was, however, only the tip of the iceberg when it came to the conspiracy to exonerate Frank. Most of the money in that campaign was going to Detective Burns, who was using it to bribe witnesses to recant the testimony they had given under oath. The Jewish plot to exonerate Frank blew up in the faces of the wealthy Jews who were orchestrating it when accusations of bribery began appearing in the *Jeffersonian*. "How much longer," Watson asked in the April 23 edition of *The Jeffersonian*, "will the people of Atlanta endure the lawless doings of William J. Burns? What right does this sham detective have to tamper with the witnesses that told the truth on Leo Frank, that foul degenerate who murdered little Mary Phagan?"[49] Watson concluded that "This man Burns richly deserves a coat of tar and feathers, plus a ride on a fence-rail. He has been engineering a campaign of systematic lies tending to blacken this state and tending to provoke an outbreak of popular indignation."[50]

Popular indignation did in fact break out in Marietta, Mary Phagan's hometown, when Burns and his assistant Dan Lehon showed up, ostensibly to bribe other witnesses. Recognizing Burn's face from newspaper photos, Robert E. Lee Howell attacked him on the street. A crowd quickly formed and soon cries of "Lynch Him!" filled the air, forcing "the great detective," according to Watson's account, to run "through several dark alleys as fast as his legs would carry him."[51] Even the normally hostile *New York Times* was forced to admit that "outside influence" had become the crucial issue in the Frank case. According to the report in the *Times*, "Bob Howell's hand, which slapped Burns in the face, struck fire out of all Georgia. In a dramatic way, it focused attention on a growing opinion that money and 'outside influence' were being used to save a rich man from punishment for the murder of a working girl."[52]

The issue of outside influence went from bad to worse when subsequent events showed that Tom Watson was also right when he leveled charges of bribery against Burns. Burns was using the money of Lasker and Schiff and other wealthy Jews to bribe witnesses to recant their testimony. On April 27, Rev. C. B. Ragsdale "re tracted his statement that he had overheard Jim Conley confess to Mary Phagan's murder, asserting that an unnamed Burns agent had paid him to make the claim."[53] Watson felt vindicated by the revelation, but the full extent of Burns' largesse with Jewish money was just beginning to emerge.

Eventually the state became involved in an inquiry into Burns' activity since his arrival in Atlanta. After State Attorney Dorsey put Burns on the stand, the famous detective admitted that he had "spirited Annie Maude Carter out of Atlanta, making it impossible for state's officers to question her."[54] Burns also admitted that he had promised one witness a job as a Pullman porter. Burns coupled that promise with the threat "that if he did not renounce his assertion regarding the superintendent's allegedly suspicious behavior on the day of the murder, 'the Jews' would get him."[55] Dorsey then went to work on "the half-dozen retractions the defense had secured from factory girls who at the trial had sworn to Frank's moral turpitude,"[56] discovering that one of Burns' agents posed as an author and promised to share his commission with Carrie Smith if she were willing to sign an affidavit repudiating testimony damaging to Frank's case.

Eventually Burns and his associates were convicted of suborning witnesses and Burns had to close his office when the Atlanta City Council revoked his license. Even though Dorsey was never able to trace Burns' money to Lasker and Schiff, Burn's testimony did "irretrievable damage" (Herbert Haas's words to Lasker) to Frank's cause.[57]

Even though it came close to being named as a co-conspirator in the case, the *New York Times* did not back off. It continued to find fault with Georgia and its legal system, giving further credence, if that was needed, to Tom Watson's charge of "outside interference."[58] When Judge Hill denied the extraordinary motion for a new trial, the *Times* fulminated once again that "The trial of Leo M. Frank in Atlanta for the murder of Mary Phagan was from the beginning about everything that a murder trial ought not to be. Judge Hill of the superior court denied the extraordinary motion for a new trial, yet it is impossible to feel that the first trial was fair."[59]

The Burns debacle and the fact that Rabbi Marx had also been implicated in a bribery scheme caused a new eruption of discord among the councils of New York Jewry. "I have been disgusted at the farcical methods to which Burns has resorted," the American Jewish Committee's Louis Marshall wrote the *NYT*'s Louis Wiley. "Every one of his acts has been a burlesque upon modern detective ideas. It is deplorable that a case so meritorious as that of Frank should have been brought to this point of destruction by such ridiculous methods."[60]

"I am afraid," Samuel Untermeyer, Marshall's law partner, concluded, contemplating the indictments that were sure to be handed down against Burns and Lehon, "the whole business has been terribly botched."[61]

All of these revelations, of course, meant vindication for Tom Watson, who could crow 'I told you so' and have the common man of Georgia nod in solemn agreement.

As troubling as the "outside influence" issue had been, it was not over when Burns had been exposed as the agent of as yet anonymous Jewish backers. The same forces that gave Burns the money he needed to bribe witnesses could now exert their influence on the governor of the state, a man who had always been involved in a flagrant conflict of interest. "There isn't a right-thinking man of us," Watson wrote, "who does not feel troubled because of Governor Slaton's connection with the lawyers of the defense."[62]

On October 14, 1914, the Georgia Supreme Court upheld Judge Benjamin Hill's motion denying Frank a new trial. The world of subsidized journalistic fantasy could enflame public opinion, but it was gaining no purchase on the mind of the judiciary. The Supreme Court claimed "There was no abuse of discretion on the part of the trial judge in refusing to grant a new trial, nor was there any error in overruling the motion on any of the grounds set out therein."[63] Nor did it know of any

> provision in the constitution of the United States or of this state . . .which gives an accused person the right to disregard the rules of procedure in a state and demand that he shall move in his own way and be grated absolute freedom because of an irregularity (if there is one) in receiving the verdict.[64]

Undeterred by either the Georgia Supreme Court ruling or the failure of their agent to bribe the witnesses in the Frank case, the Jewish campaign to exonerate Frank turned to what had always been their strong suit, orchestrating favorable publicity. To accomplish this end, Lasker tapped Christopher Powell Connolly, an Irish-Catholic journalist from Butte, Montana, to write Frank's story. Connolly was given unlimited access to the prisoner and his legal defense team, and Frank considered him his Zola, whose book *J'accuse* had cleared Dreyfus's name. It was Connolly who first launched the famous "Kill the Jew or we'll kill you" quote, but he introduced it in a way that was unverifiable, absolving himself of any accountability while at the same time insinuating the idea into an already inflamed public mind. "On the last day I was in Atlanta," Connolly wrote, "I went to the office of one of Frank's lawyers to say good-by. The telephone rang. 'If they don't hang that Jew, we'll hang you,' came the message."[65] From Connolly's pen the famous phrase entered the public mind as if it had been shouted by the mob at an intimidated jury, long after the jury itself had denied that this ever happened. At Connolly's hand, the man whom the prosecution had portrayed as a pervert and child molester became a "shy nervous intellectual."[66] Unlike the Burns scheme, Lasker picked a winner in Connolly. The *Collier's* article had its desired effect by introducing the Frank case to the entire nation.

"Outside the state of Georgia," Albert Lasker wrote, "the press of the United States, including the leading papers of every city in the South are editorially agitating public sentiment for the unfortunate Frank. Daily, hundreds of papers are editorially crying out that Frank's execution would amount to judicial murder."[67] The New York papers, most significantly, William Randolph Hearst's flagship, the *Journal* (following in the footsteps of his Atlanta property) took the lead in pleading the case for the condemned man. "If Frank's life is saved," wrote Arthur Brisbane, "Frank will owe [it] not least to any one of the lawyers you have paid so liberally but to W. R. Hearst, a man of real power and of a kindness of heart that is not appreciated."[68]

The *Collier's* article coupled with sympathetic treatment in the Hearst papers and the *New York Times* had the desired effect: "Outside of Georgia, the perception that the state and its citizens were involved in an anti-Semitic persecution of an innocent man became universal."[69] Inside Georgia, however, the opposite was true. Largely as a result of the work of Tom Watson, Georgians came to see the Frank case as an attack on their state and their way of life that was being orchestrated by the rich Jews who owned the northern press and were using it as a weapon against the South. "Never before in the history of this country," Watson wrote on December 4, 1914,

> has any convicted criminal been given the freedom of the daily papers that Frank has enjoyed..... Simultaneously, with the appearance of this stuff in the Georgia papers, it appears in the northern papers which are owned by rich Jews. *The Baltimore Sun*, owned by the Abells, the *New York World*, owned by the Pulitzers, the *Times* owned by Ochs seem to receive Frank's statement by telegraph at the same time that he hands out copy to the dailies in Georgia.

Watson was quick to point out the hypocrisy of the press accounts. Normally, the North criticized the South for its treatment of the Negro. However, groups like the NAACP and other racial watchdogs of the North were silent when Frank's defense team launched into racial tirades which described Jim Conley as a cocaine-sniffing nigger, whose testimony couldn't be trusted because the man giving it was black. Apparently this type of racial slur was acceptable if it was used to get an acquittal for a Jew. Watson was quick to point out other forms of hypocrisy as well:

> In the Frank case, the great point emphasized by the Jewish papers is that the main witness against Frank was a Negro!.. It seems that Negroes are good enough to hold office, sleep in our beds, eat at our tables, marry our daughters, and mongrelize the Anglo-Saxon race, but are not good enough to bear testimony against a rich Jew![70]

Watson was not alone in feeling this way. The circulation figures of *The Jeffersonian* proved that he was adept in formulating the issues in ways that articulated the frustrations which the common man felt in this case. But it wasn't just the common man who was incensed at coverage of the Frank case in the northern press. Thomas Loyless, editor of the *Augusta Chronicle* accused the *Times* and Adolph

Ochs of slandering the people of Georgia by making it appear "that Frank's race or religion had anything whatsoever to do with his conviction."[71] In mid-January, former Georgia Governor Joseph Brown wondered aloud on the pages of the *Augusta Chronicle*, "Are we to understand that anybody except a Jew can be punished for a crime?"[72] Brown's statement was a sign that the lines were hardening. It was now Georgia versus the World.

Georgians who thought that Frank deserved a new trial were seen as traitors. As the *Kansas City Star's* McDonald had observed, "The managing editor, associate editor, city editor, assistant city editor and court reporter of an Atlanta newspaper said to me they knew Frank was entitled to a new trial... [but] "We dare not; we would be accused of being bought by Jew money," they answered.[73] On the other hand, the American Jewish Committee was in no mood to back down because they "understood that Supreme Court justices read the *New York Times* and could be influenced by a national hue and cry. With the case headed back to the capital, Louis Marshall made the calculated decision that continuing coverage by crusading northern newspapers was of greater strategic value than not."[74]

However, even after the Connolly article appeared in *Collier's* and caused a stir nationwide, enkindling new hope in Frank, the news on the judicial front continued to be bad. Frank's last judicial hope now lay with the Supreme Court of the United States, and this is where Marshall and Frank's legal team directed their attention. A delegation of AJC lawyers headed by Marshall first paid a call on Supreme Court Justice Joseph R. Lamar, who found the issue unworthy of review. Then on November 26, the AJC turned to Oliver Wendell Holmes, in whom they found a more sympathetic reception.

On February 25, 1914, Frank's case was heard by the Supreme Court of the United States, with Louis Marshall leading off with his version the "Kill the Jew or we'll kill you" story of jury intimidation. "The crowd," Marshall told the court, "almost trespassed upon the jury box, hanging over the jury box, and their whispers were heard throughout the courtroom."[75] Watson attacked Marshall's testimony attacking "the outsiders who cannot or will not weigh the facts which prove Frank's terrible crime.... If Frank's rich connections keep on lying about this case, SOMETHING BAD WILL HAPPEN."[76]

In the end Marshall and the AJC got no farther with the United States Supreme Court than they had gotten with the legal system in Georgia. By a margin of seven to two, the Court upheld the denial of Frank's petition for a new trial, and denied every point Frank's lawyers made. In his dissent, Holmes claimed "Mob law does not become due process by securing the assent of a terrorized jury,"[77] but there was no basis in fact to the claim that the jury had been terrorized. It was becoming clear that anything that happened in the South which the northern press disliked could be characterized as mob law. But the seven-member majority on the court was not impressed with this sort of slur. "In our opinion," the Court concluded, "he is not shown to have been deprived of any right guaranteed to him the Fourteenth Amendment or any other provision of the Constitution or laws of the United States."[78]

Frank took the verdict calmly, claiming that "I will never suffer the death penalty" because "Truth will ultimately prevail."[79] In the end, even though, as the *New York Times* put it, "Justice to Frank Doubted by Holmes,"[80] the Supreme Court refused to overturn the decision of the Georgia Court. This meant that there was only one hope left, and that hope resided, as Tom Watson feared, with Governor Slaton, who was now approaching the end of his term as governor.

Having lost their case at the Supreme Court, Lasker, Connolly and Rosenwald focused their efforts on Governor Slaton, who was scheduled to leave office on June 22, 1915. From the time the Supreme Court handed down its decision in the Spring of 1915 until late June, Slaton was bombarded with letters and telegrams from "United States Senators representing Connecticut, Idaho, Illinois, Louisiana, Mississippi and Texas, as well as the governors of Arizona, Louisiana, Oregon, Michigan, Mississippi, Pennsylvania, Texas and Virginia."[81]

In addition to the letters from prominent figures, Slaton received more than 100,000 letters from the nonprominent and petitions containing over two million signatures. Everyone seemed convinced that Frank was innocent, everyone that is, but the people of Georgia, and the man who articulated their position best, Tom Watson, urged Governor Slaton to stand firm in the face of a publicity campaign waged by the "millionaire Jews" and their press agents.[82] On May 27, less than a month from Slaton's last day in office, Watson once again brought up the conflict of interest issue, claiming that it was "embarrassing to the majority of Georgians that John M. Slaton is a member of the law firm to which Frank's leading attorney belongs."[83] Watson then went on to deliver a warning: The Governor of Georgia should consider

> that if the Law is not allowed to take its course in the Frank case, we might as well abolish the law and save all future expense of similar mockeries of justice.
> that if the Prison commission or the Governor undertake to undo—in whole or in part—what has been legally done by the courts that were established for that purpose, there will almost inevitably be the bloodiest riot ever known in the history of the South.[84]

Both Watson and Slaton knew that Georgians were united in support of the death penalty for Frank. Georgians were offended by the meddling of outsiders. They were particularly upset about the machinations of rich Jews. Fred Morris, a lawyer and former University of Georgia football star, weighed in by claiming: "Mary Phagan was a poor factory girl. What show would she have against Jew money? When they found they couldn't fool the people of Georgia, they got people from Massachusetts, New York and California to try and raise trouble. Well, we throw the advice of these outsiders back in their teeth. To hell with what they think."[85]

A delegation from Marietta, Mary Phagan's hometown told the Prison Commission: "we believe the evidence shows Frank guilty. People outside of Georgia who have read biased, I might say subsidized, accounts of this case have been urging you to commute. But if you commute this sentence, capital punishment might as well be abolished. If the extreme penalty should be enforced, it is in this case."[86]

Outside of the building where the commutation hearings were held on Frank's fate, thousands of Georgians gathered to hear Fiddlin' John Carson sing his latest composition, "The Ballad of Mary Phagan," a performance which by the very fact that it took place underscored the widespread sentiment that Georgians had to hold the line against "outside influence" if they wanted to honor the memory of Mary Phagan and prevent the same thing from happening to their other daughters.

In the hearings themselves, Hugh Dorsey hammered away at the line of argument which had sustained Frank's guilty verdict over the course of seven separate appeals. Addressing the issue of jury intimidation, specifically the cry "Hang Frank or we'll hang you," Dorsey declared that "the record shows that at no time from the beginning to the end of the trial did anybody cry out against Frank or offer to do him harm."[87] Dorsey concluded his testimony with a warning: "I am fearful that if the verdict of juries in plain cases, as I conceive this to be, shall not be carried out against the influential as well as the friendless, it would be an incentive to lawlessness in our state, the consequences of which no man can calculate, and I am unwilling even passively to be a party to the encouragement of such a situation."[88]

On Monday morning, Georgians awoke to the news that Governor John Slaton had commuted Frank's sentence, and although some agreed with Slaton's decision, outrage quickly spread through the population and the city's normal routine ground to a halt as people digested what had happened. Before long, the outrage which the majority of people felt at the commutation found expression when at 8:30 AM a mob shouting "Pay the governor a call" started marching toward Slaton's mansion, six miles away.[89] As some indication of what they planned to do when they got to the governor's mansion, the mob broke into hardware stores along the way in search of guns. Police Chief Beavers along with 50 mounted men confronted the mob halfway to Slaton's mansion, turning back roughly half of the men. Which meant of course that 2,000 armed men were headed toward the governor's mansion. What they planned to do had become apparent after another mob hanged the governor in effigy in the town square. Around the effigy's neck hung a sign proclaiming, "John M. Slaton, King of the Jews and Traitor Governor of Georgia."[90] In the end it was only the state militia and its machine guns and the fact that Slaton declared martial law which saved him from the rage of the mob and the noose they had prepared for him.

The reaction to the commutation followed along the lines that had already been established by the publicity campaign to save Frank. Slaton received "hosannas from the national press," and the *New York Times* led the way, proclaiming that if Governor Slaton look beyond the boundaries of the State of Georgia, he can know and feel to how high a place he has raised himself in the esteem and admiration of the whole country....Governor Slaton has saved Georgia from herself. He has made his name illustrious."[91]

Needless to say, the *New York Times* did not articulate the feelings of the majority of Georgians. As in the past, that job fell to Tom Watson, who, like Hugh Dorsey, claimed that the governor's decision had undermined the rule of law. Watson once again brought up the issue of conflict of interest, claiming that "Either his firm should have withdrawn from the case, or he should have withdrawn from the firm."[92] But the big issue was the betrayal of the people of Georgia who had elected Slaton to office. Instead of representing the interests of the people who had elected him, Slaton ended up selling out to the rich Jews from New York. The real issue, as Watson framed it, was money. "Jew money has debased us, bought us and sold us—and laughs at us."[93] In Watson's eyes, Slaton's commutation of Frank's sentence abolished the rule of law in Georgia establishing in its place "One law for the rich and another for the poor."[94] According to the new law those with "Unlimited Money and Invisible Power," can prey on young Georgia girls with impunity because "they have established the precedent in Georgia that no Jew shall suffer capital punishment for a crime committed on a Gentile."[95]

Needless to say, Watson and his readers found this state of affairs intolerable, but when confronted with the question of "what are the people to do?" the only answer Watson could come up with was "Lynch law": "Hereafter, let no man reproach the South with Lynch law: let him remember the unendurable provocation; and let him say whether Lynch law is better than no law at all."[96]

As some indication that Watson was articulating the feelings of a significant percentage of the population of Georgia, a mob of 200 men opened fire on the governor's mansion at two o'clock in the morning of June 22, 1915, Slaton's last day in office. This was just the beginning of what was going to be a long day for the outgoing governor. When Governor Slaton left the capitol after giving his farewell address, a mob descended on his car shouting "Lynch him!" At this point a man in the mob tried to assassinate the governor.

Eventually the governor was able to escape from the mob, but he did not return to his mansion. Instead, he and his wife escaped by train to New York City, where upon his arrival, he checked into the Waldorf Astoria hotel and held a press conference at which he was "accorded... the sort of welcome usually reserved for war heroes."[97]

In a move that seemed calculated to confirm the citizens of the state of Georgia in their suspicion that Slaton had sold out to New York money, Slaton and his wife then celebrated a night on the town with William Randolph Hearst after a dinner party at the publisher's palatial apartment. After a summer-long vacation and cross-country train trip, the Slatons joined up with the Hearsts at San Simeon, Hearst's version of Xanadu on the California coast. From there, the Slatons sailed to Hawaii. If this was political exile, the Slatons seemed to be enjoying it.

As the stories of Slaton being feted by the rich New Yorkers filtered back to Georgia, the outrage spiked upward once again. The Georgians who were outraged at the commutation on Frank's sentence were even more outraged at the welcome their traitorous governor received in New York, and at a certain point a group of them decided to take the law into their own hands. A group of 150 Marriettans joined together on the day the commutation was announced to form the Knights of Mary Phagan and vowed revenge on both Slaton and Frank. At around the same time a smaller much more influential group of men came to the same conclusion and hatched a plan that was nothing if not audacious. They planned to abduct Frank from the state prison farm in Milledgeville, transport him halfway across the state, and then hang him in Marrietta, Mary Phagan's home town. Tom Watson was informed of the conspiracy to murder Frank and kept up the drumbeat of publicity throughout the summer of 1915. On August 12, 1915, in response to a blatantly pro-Frank documentary produced by Marcus Loew, Watson wrote: "Let the rich Jews beware!... THE NEXT JEW WHO DOES WHAT FRANK DID IS GOING TO GET EXACTLY THE SAME THING THAT WE GIVE TO NEGRO RAPISTS!"[98]

Then on August 17, the cabal carried out its threat. Frank was abducted from the state prison farm in Milledegeville, transported to Marietta and hanged. The lynching of Leo Frank set off an orgy of vituperation in the press of the sort the nation had not seen since the hanging of John Brown. Newspaper after newspaper condemned the South, in the words of the *Chicago Tribune*, as "a region of illiteracy, blatant self-righteousness, cruelty and violence. Until it is improved by the infusion of better blood and better ideas it will remain a reproach and a danger to the American Republic."[99] "If Georgia approves lynching," opined the *New York Times*, "then honors bestowed upon the lynchers would attest to the shameless courage of the Georgia public and its willingness to defy public opinion in the other States of the Union."[100] And for good measure, the *Akron Beacon Journal* added, "Georgia is a good place for every decent man and woman to stay away from."[101]

The outrage continued to grow in New York. Twenty thousand Jews showed up for a protest meeting at the Cooper Union, a crowd which overflowed the hall onto the surrounding streets. At a meeting at Faneuil Hall in Boston, Jews heard speeches whose rhetoric was "equaled in radicalism only in the days before the Civil War" and resurrected memories of the abolitionists.[102] Fired by this sort of rhetoric the crowds demanded retaliation, and suggestions ranged from boycotting peaches and coca-cola to promoting guerilla warfare. Groups of detectives were dispatched to Marietta but they uncovered nothing because, "Every stranger who comes into town is under observation the moment he arrives. The surveillance is not obtrusive, but it is unmistakable. [The town's] mood is one of determination to protect the man who, in its eyes, executed the law after it had been trampled on. It is resolved that not a hair on their heads shall be harmed."[103]

Tom Watson remained defiant in his defense of the lynching: "In putting the sodomite murderer to death, the Vigilance committee has done what the Sheriff would have done, if Slaton had not been of the same mould as Benedict Arnold. Let Jew libertines take notice. Georgia is not for sale to rich criminals."[104] Watson's defiance coupled with the fact that no one was indicted for Frank's murder caused *The Boston Post* to wonder, "Is Georgia in America?"[105]

Sobered by what had happened and now relieved of its duties as what amounted to Frank's propaganda ministry, *The New York Times* tried to make sense of Frank's killing and the role it had played in bringing it about. In an article entitled "Frank Lynching due to Suspicion and Prejudice," *Times* reporter Charles Thompson finally got to talk "honestly about the sentiment of Georgia,"[106] a verdict which implied that hitherto that had not been the case at the *Times*. Thompson gave three reasons for the lynching:

> First—the [citizens of Georgia] believed that the Jews of the country, hitherto not the object of any hostility or dislike, had banded themselves together to save a criminal because he belonged to their race and religion and thus ranged themselves in opposition to men of other races and religions. Against this belief no argument was effective, no denial was listened to.
>
> Second—The bitter resentment over what everybody in Georgia to whom this correspondent has talked calls "outside interference": and this does not mean only the "interference" of the New York newspapers by a long shot, though Tom Watson has done his level best to make it appear that the New York newspapers are attempting to govern the state of Georgia
>
> Third—And this is the thing which turned the smoldering fire into a raging flame and maddened men who were merely angered—it is believed that from one end of the State to the other that Governor Slaton was Frank's lawyer and pardoned his client after every court had upheld that client's conviction. The ignorant believed that Slaton was bribed, or that at best he received as Frank's lawyer a share of the fee paid to his firm: the more intelligent believe that he was merely influenced in his judgment by the fact that Frank was his firm's client.[107]

Thompson's article was a rebuke to Adoph Ochs, who was chagrined by what he read because it implied that Tom Watson was right and that ultimately it was the overreaction of influential Jews like Ochs which had led to Frank's hanging. Ochs had gone against his own better judgment in putting the *Times* at the service of Frank's cause and "The *Times*... had overstepped its bounds by persistently editorializing on his behalf."[108] Ochs had ignored repeated warnings, at first from his stringer in Atlanta and then from W. T. Anderson, editor of the *Macon Telegraph*, a newspaper which had consistently opposed lynching. Anderson had written to Ochs on behalf "of the decent people of Georgia," claiming that "It was the outside interference of the Jews, led by the *Times*, that had made it necessary to lynch Frank. The Jews in fact were responsible for what had happened to him.... The men responsible are the Strauses, the Ochses, the Pulitizers and other leading Jews of New York and the East generally. These men now hold the comfort, safety, peace and happiness of the Jews of Georgia in the hollow of their hands."[109]

Ochs was shaken by the rebuke. Not only had he turned the *Times* into "a Jewish newspaper" by his naked advocacy of Frank's case, he had brought about Frank's death as well. Confronted with these arguments at an editorial meeting on the Frank case, Ochs appeared "wan and subdued."[110] As one of Ochs associates put it at this meeting, the "simple facts" of the case were inescapable:

> Mr. Ochs was the prominent newspaper publisher in the country. He was a Jew. The *Times* had printed more stuff for Frank that any other newspaper and [had] a special correspondent in Georgia... a majority of the people in Georgia approved of the law having been taken into the hand of the mob because they believed that money had been used to thwart justice.[111]

Unable to counter the charges leveled against him and the *Times*, Ochs decided that the *Times* was going to drop the Frank case. Ochs then spent the next few days at home "nursing his nerves."[112]

In his own post-mortem, Tom Watson claimed that the Frank case was punishment for the sinful economic exploitation of children. "The National Pencil Factory, owned by Frank's people, fought our Child Labor bill fiercely and helped to kill it—and in God's mysterious way, it cost the Superintendent his life."[113] In closing ranks behind Frank, the nation's wealthy Jews had "blown the breath of life into the Monster of Race Hatred; and this Frankenstein, whom you created at such enormous expense, WILL HUNT YOU DOWN!"[114]

As a result of the Frank case, the Jews declared war on the South. Louis Marshall of the AJC tried to get Watson tried for obscenity, but Watson remained defiant, informing the attorney general "you cannot remove me from the Southern district of Georgia. If I have to give up my life for having incurred the savage hatred of the rich Jews, it will be given up right here in the same region where my ancestors gave up theirs."[115] Marshall's attempt not only failed, in failing it probably bolstered Watson's political career, contributing to his eventual election to the United States Senate. It backfired in other ways as well.

On page one of the September 2 edition of *The Jeffersonian*, Watson called for the resurrection of the Ku Klux Klan. "The North can rail itself hoarse, if it chooses to do so, but if [it] doesn't quit meddling with our business and getting commutations for assassins and rapists who have pull, another Ku Klux Klan may be organized to restore HOME RULE."[116] The Klan, which Nathan Bedford Forrest had disbanded in 1869, had experienced a surge of renewed interest when D. W. Griffith turned Thomas Dixon's novel *The Clansman* into *The Birth of a Nation*, which premiered in January 1915, when the clamor over the Frank case had reached its peak. The NAACP had tried to block distribution of the film, but those efforts came to naught when Griffith persuaded his college classmate Woodrow Wilson to view the film in the White House.

Less than two weeks before *The Birth of a Nation* opened in Atlanta, William Joseph Simmons and 34 other men climbed to the top of Stone Mountain, Georgia and ignited giant cross which had been soaked in pitch and kerosene, announcing the rebirth of the Klan, Simmons had already filed a petition with Georgia's secretary of state on October 16, signaling his intention to resurrect the Klan and become its imperial wizard. Leo Frank's role in all of this became apparent when it was revealed that several of the 34 men who climbed Stone Mountain that Thanksgiving evening in November 1915 were members of the Knights of Mary Phagan. The restored Klan reached the height of its power at the Democratic convention of 1924, but it too fell into decline as a result of a young woman's murder.

In 1926, David C. Stephenson, who had ousted William Simmons from the leadership of the Klan and was at that time Imperial Wizard, was convicted of second-degree murder in the death of Madge Oberholzer, whom with the help of other Klansmen, he had kidnapped, raped and abducted to Chicago from Irvington, Indiana. The case, which included some revolting perversions, created a widespread revulsion against the Ku Klux Klan. Throughout the 1930s, its influence weakened irreparably. In 1944, it was formally dissolved.[117]

The death of Mary Phagan led to the birth of other organizations as well. Leo Frank was president of the Atlanta chapter of B'nai B'rith. After his death, B'nai B'rith founded the Anti-Defamation League to combat anti-Semitism in the United States. The Anti-Defamation League would go on to work closely with the NAACP. Murray Friedman calls the Frank case "the defining moment in the partnership between blacks and Jews" even though he admits later on that the case "set Jews and blacks against each other."[118] Friedman, who spent most of his adult life working for the American Jewish Committee, does his best to play down the frankly racist statements which Frank's attorneys made during the course of his trial. He also mentions the fact that the NAACP "expressed resentment at what they saw as an organized effort to implicate Conley simply because he was black."[119] He also mentions that the AJC's Louis Marshall joined the board of the NAACP and served on its legal defense committee as a result of the Frank lynching. The aftermath of the Frank lynching brought Herbert Seligman on board the NAACP as well, as its "new Jewish director of pubicity." Together with Joel Spingarn, these men "campaigned relentlessly against lynching" and "helped to awaken the nation's conscience."[120]

Friedman's book on the Black-Jewish Alliance was written, however, because another interpretation of events had arisen calling the very existence of that alliance into question. In their book *Plural but Equal*, black revisionists like Harold Cruse and David Levering Lewis called the traditional narrative of black-Jewish cooperation into question by accusing the Jews of promoting a hidden agenda, according to which organizations like the NAACP used front men like W. E. B DuBois to destroy any black leader not acceptable to Jewish interests. Cruse accuses Louis Marshall in particular "of using the NAACP to 'salve the bitter defeat he had experienced in the Leo Frank case.'"[121]

If that were the case, then Marshall's move to the NAACP takes on a sinister hue. Suspicions of this sort first arose during the NAACP's attack on Booker T. Washington. They would deepen in the wake of the Frank case when the NAACP devoted even more of its energies to destroying Marcus Garvey. According to Cruse's reading of these events, there was no Black-Jewish Alliance. What went by that name was really covert Jewish revenge on the South for the role it played in the Frank lynching. The simplest way to visit revenge on the South was the plan first articulated by John Brown: bring the war to Africa by turning the nation's Negroes into revolutionaries. That meant destroying any black leader who wanted to steer his people in another direction. That meant destroying Booker T. Washington, because he wanted to turn the Negro into a skilled craftsman. And it meant destroying Marcus Garvey because he wanted to awaken in the American Negro a racial consciousness which was incompatible with the integration which Jewish organizations like the NAACP seemed determined to impose, as Cruse claimed, on everyone but themselves.

Tom Watson died in Washington of a cerebral hemorrhage on September 26, 1922. At his funeral in Georgia, the most impressive floral arrangement was an eight-foot-high cross of red roses sent by the Klan.

Chapter Eighteen

The Spread of Bolshevism

When A. I. Shingarov, a member of the Russian parliamentary delegation which was sent to London at the beginning of 1916 to arrange for loans for the Czarist government, he was told by the French Baron Rothschild, "A great number of influential Jewish personalities now live in America and over there they don't like you." Jacob Schiff was one of those "influential Jewish personalities." Schiff's hatred of Russia had reached such proportions that he would lend money to England and France only on the condition that none of it would end up in Russian hands. "We are willing to lend money to England and France," Schiff told the French MP Bache, "if we can received some assurance that Russia is willing to do something to resolve the Jewish question. Otherwise you'll be taking in money for Russia, and we have no desire to give Russia anything."[1]

The *Jewish Encyclopedia* claims that Schiff "exerted pressure on other banks, so that Russia didn't get any money." Schiff was not alone among the Jews in supporting revolutionary activity, nor were the recipients of that support invariably revolutionaries. According to an entry written in his diary in May of 1916, the French ambassador to Russia, Maurice Paleologue claimed that the Jews supported Rasputin as well. "A pack of Jewish financiers and dirty speculators, Rubinstein, Manuse and others," he wrote, "made a pact with him [Rasputin] and support him generously. According to their directions, he sends messages to the ministers, to the bank and to various influential persons."[2] Rasputin became, as a result, "a friend and benefactor to the Jews and supported without contradiction my attempts to improve their situation."[3]

It was at this time that the rumors about collaboration between Jewish revolutionaries and the German government began to surface. "In 1915," Salon Baron wrote, "the most shameful anti-Jewish propaganda was started in the army; all Jews in Poland and Galicia were declared the spies and enemies of Russia. A disgusting program broke out in Molodechno. It has been established that this Jew-baiting originated at headquarters, and, of course, it could not but contribute to the disintegration of the army, in which there were about half a million Jews."[4] Baron is adverting here to the fact that Jews were considered a fifth column both behind the lines and at the front. The English ambassador assumed that the wealthy Jewish Banker D. L. Rubinstein, who was later arrested for treason, was working for the German secret service.[5] According to the report issued by Police chief K.D. Kafow on January 9, 1916

Jews engaged openly in revolutionary propaganda, but also in addition to criminal agitation .. engaged in the artificial inflation of the price of daily necessities, and the withdrawal of money out of circulation [The Jews] tried to create insecurity about the stability of the Russian currency....[6]

On the western front the Jews were suspected of being German spies: "the word on the street was that Jewish soldiers were cowards and deserters and that the Jewish population was full of spies and traitors."[7] When the army attacked, the Jews always dropped back. When the army retreated, the Jews were always in the forefront. The Jews often said that they hoped Germany would win the war.[8] In evaluating the reports, Solzhenitsyn concludes that, in spite of the bravery of individual Jews, "It would be unrealistic to conclude that all of these accusations were nothing but fairy tales."[9] Unable to ignore the rumors any longer, the Czar demanded a census of the Jews fighting on the western front, a move which alienated the Jews who had been loyal. He then ordered Jews removed from the front, which increased the alienation even further, driving the Jewish soldiers into the arms of the Zionists and revolutionaries.

The Germans did whatever they could to foster treason among the Jews of the east and tried to portray the war as a crusade against the last despotic and openly anti-Semitic regime in Europe. At long last Russia would be punished for the pogroms of Kishinyev and Gomel, the philosopher Samuel Hugo Bergmann, a Zionist, noted in his diary. He thanked the Lord that as an officer serving in the Austro-Hungarian army on the Russian front he would be able personally to avenge his people.[10]

Jewish enthusiasm for the cause of Germany during World War I knew no bounds. In 1915 Lissauer wrote a poem entitled "The Hymn of Hate against England" which was quickly put to music and became an immediate success. The "Hymn" made hatred of England a popular emotion in Germany. But Lissauer soon came to regret the song when he had to leave Germany for exile when the Nazis came to power. German Jews responded enthusiastically to the war, but Russian Jews had the exact opposite reaction, prompting many Russians to view all Jews as potential traitors. A German Jew by the name of Fritz Haber, a chemist and friend of Albert Einstein, responded to the Kaiser's call by inventing poison gas to be used against allied troops. He also developed Zyklon B, the deadly gas that was used on Jews during World War II.[11]

Many Russian Jews defected and began working for the Germans. According to Elon, the "Russian-born Nahum Goldmann, a future president of the World Zionist Organization, joined the German War Ministry as a propagandist.[12] (Two years later, Goldmann had changed his mind and wrote in Martin Buber's pro-Zionist journal *Der Jude*, that Jews should have nothing to do with the war.) Max Bodenheimer became one of their most effective propagandists by repeating "his favorite argument to the effect that Jews had long been pioneers of German culture and commerce in the east. And while the mass of Russian Jews might well be primitive and lice-ridden, direct German rule would have a salutary effect on them." Bodenheimer recommended that the Germans promote "Jewish national self-determination in the East," lending credence to the Russians who claimed that Jews were a fifth column in league with the Germans. Not surprisingly, the Zionists living in the Pale of the Settlement "responded positively to this initiative drafting an appeal to Jews of the East to rise up in arms against their oppressors.[13] As a result when large parts of the Pale came under German rule, Russian Jews welcomed the Germans as "liberators."[14] The Russian authorities, in turn, responded by deporting half a million Jews to the interior.

When Fritz Haber's poison gas failed to rout the Russians on the eastern front, the Germans turned to black operations involving their Jewish fifth column. The German Jew Schiff had supported the revolutionaries for some time, and at this point the Germans turned to Lenin, who was transported across Germany in a sealed train with the collaboration of German officialdom like a "bacillus," to use Winston Churchill's phrase. Most of the 160 passengers on the famous sealed train which arrived at the Finland station were Jews. Trotsky, who was not on the train, returned to Russia bearing an American passport and a large amount of money as just one of hundreds of Jews who streamed into Russia from the United States in the wake of the Bolshevik coup of October 1917. In London alone, 10,000 Jews expressed the desire to return to Russia.[15]

Once Trotsky and his Jewish friends unpacked their bags, they quickly found their way into influential positions in the new government. Jews were represented in the new government out of all proportion to their numbers in the population at large.[16] Much has been made, pro and con, of the numbers of Jews among the Bolsheviks, but the percentage of Jews in the leadership of the Mensheviks and the Social Revolutionary Party and the Anarchists was higher than in the Bolsheviks. The most significant detail of all, however, invariably gets left out of the discussion, namely, the fact that when it became apparent that the Bolsheviks were the winners in Russia's civil war, large numbers of Jews abandoned the other revolutionary parties and streamed into the Communist Party to take the positions that formed the administrative heart of the new regime. A glaring example of this, especially in light of the notorious relationship between Jews and agriculture in Russia could be seen in the example of the newly formed Executive committee of the Farmers; three of 30 committee members were farmers but seven were Jews.[17]

Before long Bolshevism began to be seen in Russian eyes as a Jewish phenomenon. In the now ubiquitous lines outside stores, "the word Jew was on everyone's lips." When Zinoviev and Kamenev were nominated for prominent government posts, voices were heard shouting, "Tell us their real names."[18] The revolution of February 1917 was Russian not Jewish, but once the Christian bulwark against revolution fell, Jews took over, just as the Jesuits at *Civiltà Cattolica* had predicted. Solzhenitsyn agreed with the Jesuits' assessment when he claimed that the revolution succeeded because "the Orthodox faith was too weak in us."

When the Bolsheviks finally succeeded in taking power in October 1917, Jacob Schiff, "the most well known leader of the anti-Russian forces in North America," expressed his approval, saying "I always been a foe of Russian Autocracy, which had persecuted my co-religionists mercilessly. Allow me at this moment to congratulate the Russian people for the noble deed which they have brought to completion."[19]

Schiff, who had actively financed the revolutionaries for years, was not the only Jew who rejoiced. A Methodist Pastor by the name of Simon who happened to be living in St. Petersburg at the time of the revolution testified before the American Senate that "Soon after the February revolution of 1917 groups of Jews were everywhere to be seen in Petrograd, on benches, soap boxes and other stands giving speeches....The Jews had limited right to live in Petrograd, but after the Revolution they came in hordes, and the majority of the agitators were Jews."[20]

Once the communist hold on power was secure, Jews streamed into the new administration. *The Jewish Encyclopedia* said that "for the first time in Russian history Jews occupied high posts in the central and local administrations."[21] When the fledgling Bolshevik regime was threatened with a dire financial crisis, it was the Jews who raised the money which rescued Soviet communism at that crucial juncture. In April 1918, 22 million rubles were raised in the Moscow synagogue, Schiff and Rothschild contributing a million rubles each. Jewish ethnicity trumped class when it came to preserving the revolution against the hated Czar.

Some Jews claim that Bolshevism wasn't Jewish because the Bolsheviks weren't religious. According to Nora Levin,

> Having abandoned their own origins and identity, yet not finding, or sharing, or being fully admitted to Russian life (except in the world of the party), the Jewish Bolsheviks found their ideological home in revolutionary universalism. They dreamt of a classless and stateless society supported by Marxist faith and doctrine that transcended the particularities and burdens of Jewish existence. Such Jews exhibited vehement hostility toward other Jews such as Bundists, Zionists, and observant Jews who proudly proclaimed or expressed their Jewishness, and became extremely zealous officials in the new regime.[22]

Trotsky, according to this reading of Jewishness, which vacillates conveniently between religion and ethnicity, depending on the circumstances, wasn't a Jew:

> Leon Trotsky, born Lev Davidovich Bronstein, a central figure in the early years of the Bolshevik Revolution, was typical of the Russified, Bolshevik Jew. In his autobiography, he speaks about "sailing away" from his petit bourgeois environment with its "instinct of acquisition," and his brief, meaningless contact with Hebrew, the Bible, and religious tradition. He was aware of national inequalities, the restrictions on Jews and other minorities, and the violent anti-Semitism of the Black Hundreds, but these "were lost among all the other phases of social injustice" and "intense hatred of the existing order, of injustice, of tyranny." "The national question [he wrote] so important in the life of Russia, had practically no personal significance for me. Even in my early youth, the national bias and national prejudices had only bewildered my sense of reason, in some cases stirring in me nothing but disdain and even a moral nausea." In a debate with Vladimir

Medem a Bundist leader, in 1903, when Medem asked him, "You consider your-self either a Russian or a Jew?" Trotsky answered, "No, you are wrong. I am a Social Democrat and only that."[23]

By rejecting their Jewish heritage, Bolsheviks like Trotsky felt that they had become models for the Jew of the future. They felt that their fellow Jews should emulate them by becoming "Jews by family origin only" and as a result should feel "no special ties to other Jews or any interest in specific Jewish problems." According to this view, anti-Semitism was "a disease of capitalism which would disappear with the destruction of capitalism."

Solzehnitsyn, however, claims that Trotsky became an idol to the American Jews "not for no reason but precisely because he was a Jew."[24] Trotsky was "the Prometheus of October" not because he belonged "as such" but because "he was a child of this promethean people, who could have done much more for humanity if he hadn't been chained to the rock of stupid evil." Trotsky's Jewishness brings up the issue of collective responsibility. If Jews can disclaim responsibility for communism by claiming that Trotsky wasn't a "real Jew," can't the Germans do the same thing, by disowning Hitler? Hitler, after all, had been born in Austria, not Germany. Couldn't the Germans just as easily say, "these weren't real Germans, they were just the scum."[25]

Salo Baron acknowledges Jewish participation in the Communist Party but plays down its significance, claiming that it was only "anti-Semites in and outside Russia [who] glibly equated communism with the alleged Jewish world conspiracy." [26] Baron's explanation for Jewish predominance in the party is 1) oppression and 2) higher education levels: "Many Jewish intellectuals were attracted to its professed international ideals, as well as to its socialist radicalism which promised to put an end to the tsarist oppression."[27] If so, the oppression had consequences. Even in invoking Jewish suffering, Baron adverts to the dark side of Jewish participation in the new communist regime:

> Perhaps in subconscious retaliation for the many years of suffering at the hands of the Russian police, a disproportionate number of Jews joined the new Bolshevik secret service. The impression these facts made upon the ordinary Russian is rightly stressed by Leonard Shapiro: "For the most prominent and colorful figure after Lenin was Trotsky, in Petrograd the dominant and hated figure was Zinoviev, while anyone who had the misfortune to fall into the hands of the Cheka stood a very good chance of finding himself confronted with, and possibly shot by, a Jewish investigator."[28]

Solzhenitsyn claims that the Cheka, whose nominal head was the Pole Felix Derzhinsky, was run by Jews and foreigners like Latvians because Russians were reluctant to torture other Russians. After a visit to the Kremlin, one Russian exclaimed, "Everywhere I looked I saw, Latvians, Latvians, and Jews, Jews, Jews. I was never an anti-Semite, but here their number was so obvious."[29] Jews were heavily involved in food supply, and under the leadership of Lazar Kaganovich, in his campaign to starve the Ukrainian farmers into submission, "the Jews got to satisfy their sexual desires while stealing grain."[30]

Jews were also overrepresented in the party that killed the Czar and his family. After the English denied political asylum to the Czar his fate was sealed. The Bolsheviks saw him as a symbol of the possibility of counterrevolution among the Russians, who still venerated him as their ruler. Significant in this regard is not only the Jew Sverdlov's avidity to do the killing but Trotsky's off-handed remarks after the fact. Trotsky did know about the murder of the Czar and his family, but after hearing about it, he wrote that "I checked the business off in my mind and didn't ask anymore questions.... The execution of the Czar's family was not only necessary to terrorize the enemy and to take away all hope but it was also necessary to shake up our own ranks as well to show them that there was no turning back now, that we were going to have either total victory or absolute defeat."[31]

The Jews would suffer for their deeds, first at the hand of Stalin in the purges of 1937 and then at the hands of Hitler, but both events were only an indication of how eagerly the Communists had initially welcomed Jews into their ranks. "The Bolshevik ruling class had an urgent need for executive assistance, which would remain loyal without question. And the Bolsheviks found many of those people among the young, secular Jews, in concert with Slavic and international comrades."[32]

During the 1930s, it became taboo to mention Jewish participation in the Bolshevik regime, but during the 1920s, the fact was too obvious to be denied and a source of pride to the world's Jews. "If the participation of the Jews in the revolution is tabooed," the poet Naum Korshavin wrote, "it will become impossible to talk about the revolution at all. There were times when one was proud of this participation.... The Jews took part in the Revolution in numbers far out of proportion to its numbers in the population at large." The simple fact of the matter is that "Thousands of Jews joined the Bolsheviks, because they saw in them the most determined defenders of the Revolution and the most reliable internationalists." In "the lower segments of the party there was an overwhelming majority of Jews." D. S. Pamink emphasized that "The birth of Bolshevism was the result of peculiarities of Russian history, . . but the organization of Bolshevism arose in part from the activity of Jewish commissars."[33] The Socialist S. Zinjulnikow wrote, "At the beginning of the revolution the Jews...served as the basis for the new regime."[34] The best authority on the issue was Lenin himself, who according to the testimony of Semyon Diamantstein, thanked Jews for their efforts in saving the Communist regime:

The Jews, who made up the mid-intelligentsi in Russian cities came to the service of the revolution. They broke the general strike which confronted us right after the October revolution and which was very dangerous for us. The Jewish element... sabotaged this sabotage and rescued the revolution, when it was in danger.[35]

Lenin, according to Diamantstein, "didn't think it was prudent to mention this in the press, ... but he did emphasize the fact that it was thanks to this reserve of well educated and more or less sober and intelligent new civil servants that he succeeded in taking over the state apparatus and in restructuring it."[36]

Lenin, who was instrumental in making anti-Semitism illegal in the Soviet Union, recorded a speech attacking anti-Semitism, but the speech was never printed because the revolution now depended on Jews, especially in middle management, and Lenin didn't want the speech published because it would have substantiated the claims of the enemies of the revolution. It was proof that the Whites were correct in claiming that Jews and Bolsheviks were identical.[37] Many Jewish writers deny this, claiming that only Jewish "renegades" played a leading role in Bolshevism, but by now it should be obvious that the revolutionary spirit more than religious observance occupied the mainstream of Jewish consciousness throughout the ages. The most significant connection between Judaism and Bolshevism is Messianic politics, promoting the idea of social justice leading to heaven on earth.

The subsequent revolutions in Bavaria and Hungary only reinforced the connection between Jews and Bolshevism which had been established in Russia. "In Hungary Jews made up 95 percent of the leadership in the Bolshevik movement" even though "the legal situation of the Jews in Hungary was free of the limitations in Russia. The Jews already had positions in Hungarian cultural and economic life that could lead one to talk about Jewish hegemony."[38] Ethnicity trumped class even though it contradicted ideology. Accused of treason, Dmitry Rubenstein, the wealthy Jewish banker, moved to Stockholm, where he became the financial agent for the Bolsheviks.[39] Revolution spread westward in the wake of war, and as in the east Jews were, rightly or not, universally perceived as the agents of revolution. It was clear as one observer put it, "not all Jews are Bolsheviks and not all Bolsheviks are Jews, but it doesn't take long to figure out how eagerly the Jews took part in the abuse of Russia at the hands of the Bolsheviks."[40] In the end, the four years of misery and bloodshed that characterized World War I led not to peace but to decades of revolution and even bloodier counterrevolution.

As the Empires of the East collapsed during the final year of the Great War, revolution spread west. On November 5, 1918 the German navy mutinied in Kiel, refusing to fire on the British fleet. Five days later, the Kaiser fled to Holland, where he announced his abdication. As in France and Russia, the revolution was welcomed initially with optimism as the German version of the Glorious Revolution. Elon mentions German revolutionaries who "wished the uprising to emulate the English revolution, the 'model' of all true upheavals, which had abolished old idols without brutally smashing them and had respected individual rights. A mature and sensible people should now do likewise."[41]

As in France and Russia, an orderly revolution on the English model proved elusive. Anarchy spread in the wake of a lost war; the new regime panicked and lashed out at revolutionaries, invariably Jews from the east. Demobbed soldiers murdered Rosa Luxembourg because "she embodied the mythical threat of what was called 'Jewish Bolshevism.'"[42] The disproportionate participation of Jews in the German Soviets or workers' councils that sprang up after the war

> provided grist for the mills of conservatives and anti-Semites. The visibility of Jews on the soldiers' councils gave rise not only to the legend that the revolution was part of a worldwide Jewish conspiracy but also to the assertion that Germany had lost the war only because the Jews had "stabbed it in the back."[43]

Elon says German soviets "featured a disproportionate number of Jews" but contends "the reason was simple: there were relatively few Jewish army officers and, among the lower ranks, Jews were generally better educated than others. They naturally attracted attention as public speakers."[44]

As in Russia, Jews filled the vacuum after the collapse of the Reich, reaching "the highest positions of authority" in the Weimar Republic.[45] Proclaimed on November 9, 1918, the Weimar Republic quickly gained a reputation as the "*Judenrepublik.*" Twenty-four Jews were elected to the Reichstag, but more importantly, Jews became even more prominent in German culture. This would not have been a problem if the Jews had, as Mendelssohn recommended, continued the cult of Goethe, but Jewish dominance during the Weimar Republic often meant in practice redefining German culture as something most Germans found repugnant. Freud's subversion of psychology was one example; Schoenberg's subversion of tonality was another. Redefinitions of the canons of artistic expression went hand in hand with redefinitions of sexual morality. "Berlin," says Elon, "was the epicenter of Weimar culture ... vibrant with sex and intellect."[46] Magnus Hirschfeld was one of the Weimar Republic's most famous sexual revolutionaries, as was Wilhelm Reich. Elon does not mention the resentment Jewish cultural subversives like Hirschfeld and Reich created; nor does he mention the fact that Hitler was able to put this resentment to political use. Hitler used Hirschfeld as the example of the Jew bent on subverting the morals of the German nation. If the homosexual Englishman Christopher Isherwood, who went to Berlin in the '30s to have sex with German boys, felt Hirschfeld's *Institut fuer Sexualwissenschaft* was a "scientific" front for a homosexual bordello, it's not difficult to imagine that the average German thought that it was an example of what the National Socialists decried as *"Kulturbolschewismus."*

In 1918, most Germans were more concerned with ordinary Bolshevism. On November 9, three weeks after his release from jail for organizing a strike at a machinegun factory, Kurt Eisner, a Jew from Berlin, got 50,000 workers to walk off their jobs in Munich, the capital of Catholic Bavaria. By evening, the king of Bavaria had fled, and those workers controlled the Wittelsbach palace, most army barracks, and all government buildings. Eisner then declared Bavaria a Soviet republic and became its prime minister. By then, the average Russian knew that the Bolsheviks were collaborating closely with the German government. Eisner's critics soon referred to Bavaria as the "Jewish republic," a sign its days were numbered. Munich's wealthier Jews, fearing reprisals, distanced themselves from Eisner, who could not go abroad without a bodyguard. When he realized his government was destined to fall, Eisner decided to resign, but on his way to the Bavarian assembly on February 21, 1919, he was assassinated. The assailant "was a young ultranationalist aristocrat by the name of Anton Arco-Valley who had recently been thrown out of a proto-Nazi organization for having concealed the fact that his mother was Jewish."[47]

In the ensuing weeks, panic was followed by anarchy as soldiers, still armed with weapons from the lost war, roamed Munich terrorizing the local population with random shootings and systematic looting. "Nowhere," Elon writes, "were Jewish revolutionaries so visible and prominent as they were in Bavaria.... Conservatives saw them as so many Dantons and Robespierres. Anti-Semites reviled them as 'Jew pigs' and Russian agents."[48]

On April 14, another Jew came to power. Eugene Levine, the new prime minister, was Russian born, even more alien to Bavaria than the Berlin-bred Eisner. Imitating the Bolsheviks, Levine rounded up counter-revolutionaries for execution. Between Eisner's assassination and May, when the White Guards supported by troops sent by the government in Berlin began the bloody counter-revolution, Munich was gripped by lawlessness. The anarchy was blamed largely on Jewish revolutionaries who were seen as puppets of the Bolshevik regime in Russia. Levine was eventually executed, but the reign of terror he established as the hallmark of the "Jewish republic" had lasting effects. "The existential panic it left behind corrupted ethical standards, eroded manners, convulsed culture and polarized society."[49]

In April 1919, when Levine came to power, all diplomats left Munich, except the papal nuncio, Eugenio Pacelli, who then became the target of revolutionary activity. The nunciature was attacked in a drive-by shooting that pockmarked it with 55 bullet holes. Soon, revolutionaries broke into the nuncio's residence. Pacelli was at home this time and confronted the intruders, who leveled a gun at his head and demanded money and food. "I have neither money nor food," Pacelli replied, exhibiting remarkable *sang froid*, "For as you know, I have given all to the poor of the city."[50] After Pacelli reminded the revolutionaries it was never a good idea to murder a diplomat, they withdrew, but not before throwing a gun at him, denting his pectoral cross. Rychlak says many of the revolutionaries, impressed by Pacelli's courage, returned days later to apologize. They also returned the automobile they had stolen.

Shortly thereafter, Pacelli visited the Wittelsbach palace, headquarters of the Levine government. In a report to Cardinal Gasparri, the Vatican Secretary of State, Pacelli said he came across a group of women there, led by "Levine's lover, a young Russian, a Jew, and divorced."[51] The wretched excesses of the Soviet Republic in Munich, he continued, "outraged the people and caused a dramatic increase in anti-Semitism." As in Russia, all Jews were blamed for the excesses of the revolutionary few.

In a critique confected from materials gleaned from Cornwell's *Hitler's Pope*, Daniel Jonah Goldhagen claimed Pacelli, the future Pope Pius XII, was guilty of anti-Semitism because he mentioned the leaders of the revolution in Bavaria were Russian Jews. As Goldhagen puts it, "the evidence of Pius XII's anti-Semitism comes from an unimpeachable source: Pius XII himself." Cornwell quotes Pacelli's letter describing a scene of "'absolute hell' from the Communist insurrection in Munich of April 1919."[52] Goldhagen then quotes Cornwell's translation of Pacelli's letter, referring to "a gang of young women of dubious appearance, Jews like all the rest of them, hanging around in all the offices with lecherous demeanor and suggestive smiles."[53]

Goldhagen considers this damning evidence, but perhaps not damning enough, because he embellished Cornwell's translation by adding the word "all" to the phrase "Jews like all the rest of them," which in Cornwell's book was simply "Jews like the rest of them." This would seem trivial except Goldhagen repeats the word "all" in quotes throughout his work, emphasizing that Pacelli generalized from the Russian revolutionaries to "all" Jews. We know that was not Pacelli's intent because he never used the word "all." In fact, he never said, as Cornwell asserts, "Jews like the rest of them."

Cornwell's translation is itself false. In the original Italian, Pacelli described, "*una schiera di giovanni donne, dall'aspetto poco rassicurante, ebree come i primi, che stanno in tutti gli uffici, con arie provocanti e con sorrisi equivoci.*" The key phrase is not "Jews like the rest of them" as Cornwell claims, and certainly not "Jews like all the rest of them" according to Goldhagen's ideologically motivated embellishment, but rather "Jews like the first group," "*ebree come i primi.*" The only time the word "all" (tutti) appears, it refers to offices, "*tutti gli uffici,*" not Jews. Goldhagen says Pacelli referred to "Jews like all the rest of them" when what Pacelli really said was "Jews like the first group," referring to people he had already mentioned. Goldhagen amplifies his statement later, claiming Pacelli avers "the

Communist revolutionaries ... were 'all' Jews." That's not what Pacelli said. Goldhagen uses the word "all" in quotes to back up his case, but he made it up.

After deliberately amplifying what was already a falsification of Pacelli's words, Goldhagen says "this passage," upon which virtually the entire weight of his proof rests, "is Pius XII's only relatively extensive utterance about Jews that has come to light."[54] Instead of considering Pacelli's voluminous writings, none of which remotely point to anti-Semitism and much of which indicate his efforts to save Jews, Goldhagen bases his argument on one mistranslated letter which he deliberately embellished, saying "it bears the stamp of authenticity, an expression of the then-future pope's true views of Jews." Goldhagen sanctimoniously assures us "it was not a fleeting opinion, a whimsical lapse into rank anti-Semitism, but an abiding sentiment that may be reflected in other similar statements, oral or written, the evidence of which would have expired with his interlocutors or would be secured in the locked archives of the Vatican."[55] In other words, the most damning evidence Goldhagen can muster is that there is no evidence. Failing to produce any evidence, Goldhagen assures the bewildered reader that "the evidence" is "secured in the locked archives of the Vatican."

The only evidence Goldhagen musters is a statement of fact—the Bavarian Soviet Republic was run by Russian Jews—which he altered to make it sound incriminating. Pacelli, according to Goldhagen's reading of this one letter, was the author of "vicious anti-Semitic stereotypes" virtually indistinguishable from "the kind that Julius Streicher would soon offer the German public in every issue of his notorious Nazi newspaper *Der Stuermer*."[56] Frustrated by his inability to make his case, Goldhagen thus makes up in invective and innuendo what he lacks in documentation. But in doing this, he unwittingly leads the reader to truth. "Implicit in Pacelli's letter," Goldhagen continues, "is the notion of Judeo-Bolshevism—the virtually axiomatic conviction among Nazis, modern anti-Semites in general and within the Church itself that Jews were the principle bearers and even the authors of Bolshevism."[57]

Behind the equivalence between Nazism and Catholicism which Goldhagen tries to prove, another equivalence suddenly emerges, namely, the relationship between Jews and Bolshevism. In the heat of his passion to convict Pius XII, Goldhagen inadvertently introduces the issue that contextualizes Pacelli's letter in precisely the way Goldhagen does not want to contextualize it. As more than one commentator has noted, the main reason people were concerned about Jews during the 1920s is because they saw them, rightly or wrongly, as the forefront of the communist menace threatening Europe. Writing in *Outlook*, Mordecai Briemberg notes "numerous historians ... have been struck by the fact that hatred of Jews is almost always coupled with hatred of communism."[58] Hitler realized early on that attacks on Jews alone reaped him no political benefits. The Jews had to be linked to Bolshevism precisely because German Jews had been so successful in assimilating. The perception that they were assimilated Germans meant they would only be perceived as a threat if they were linked with a menacing foreign ideology and a menacing foreign power, something like Russian Communism.

By mentioning Bolshevism Goldhagen undermines his argument. Anti-Semitism during the 1920s in Europe was not directed against the existence of the Jews but rather against the behavior of Jews, who were widely seen as the force behind Bolshevism. Ignoring this, Goldhagen turns his guns on the Catholic Church, claiming, "For centuries the Catholic Church ... harbored anti-Semitism at its core, as an integral part of its doctrine, its theology and its liturgy."[59] In other words, responsibility for the Holocaust is to be laid ultimately, not at the feet of of the Bolsheviks and not even at the feet of the Nazis, but at the feet of the Catholic Church that supposedly made the Nazis possible.

Goldhagen made similar claims in *Hitler's Willing Executioners*, which he later contradicted in *A Moral Reckoning*.[60] Both subtly exculpate the Nazis as the perpetrators of Jewish genocide and propose other candidates for that role—in the first instance, "ordinary Germans," in the second, "ordinary Catholics," but Pius XII in particular. Were the Jews murdered by "ordinary Germans" because they were German or by "ordinary Catholics" because they were Catholic? He can't have it both ways. Goldhagen is trapped by the extreme nature of his thesis in *Hitler's Willing Executioners* and put into a bind whereby he must repudiate the thesis of his first book in order to propose the thesis of his second book.

There are other problems. If Germans *qua* Germans were responsible for the Holocaust, Goldhagen has no way to explain why so many non-Germans in eastern Europe joined avidly in the killing of Jews once the Germans occupied their territory. Ruth Birn mentions the Araj commandos in Latvia as one example of a local, non-German ethnic group that was more avid to kill Jews than the Nazis who ostensibly commanded them. If ordinary Catholics *qua* Catholics were responsible for the Holocaust, Goldhagen has no way to explain why Hitler persecuted Catholics, in particular Catholic clergy, from the moment he took power. The concentration camp at Dachau was full of German Catholic clergy, so much so that it evolved its own liturgical life, which, since bishops were interned there, included the ordination to the priesthood of Karl Leisner.

Goldhagen also states, "during the Weimar and Nazi period, anti-Communist diatribes and caricatures conflated Jews and Bolsheviks,"[61] without indicating that this conflation was not limited to Nazi propaganda. Most people were concerned about Communism following World War I, and many felt Jews played a crucial role in spreading it. People resented Jews in the '20s primarily because of their behavior, their perceived connection with Bolshevism, and the perception that Jews as Bolsheviks promoted revolutionary activity throughout Europe. Even Hitler couldn't make his anti-Jewish diatribes stick without associating Jews with Bolshevism. By first mentioning "Judeo-Bolshevism" and then prohibiting further inquiry into the historical record, Goldhagen undermines his argument and simultaneously attempts to save it by declaring off limits the most significant locus of Jewish behavior. Instead he asserts apodictically, as Finkelstein points out, that

> anti-Jewish animus [is] "divorced from actual Jews," "fundamentally not a response to any objective evaluation of Jewish action," "independent of the Jews' nature and actions," etc. Indeed, according to Goldhagen, anti-Semitism is strictly a Gentile mental pathology: its "host domain" is "the mind."[62]

As a result "there can be no question of Jewish guilt or innocence." But then Goldhagen says "there was nothing that Pius XII dreaded more than Bolshevism." He then wonders whether it would "be unreasonable to believe that his stance toward the Germans' persecution of the Jews was colored in some measure by his apparent identification of Communism with Jews."

Goldhagen first indicates anti-Semitism has nothing to do with Jewish behavior. Then he says Pius XII was an anti-Semite because he drew a connection between Jews and Bolshevism, which is to say he was upset by the connection between Jewish behavior and Communist behavior. But Goldhagen never says whether Jews were, in fact, involved in Bolshevism, much less whether they played "a disproportionate role" in its history.

We thus arrive at the heart of the political role the Holocaust plays in contemporary discourse. The Holocaust was a unique historical event—so unique, according to Goldhagen's *Hitler's Willing Executioners*, that it was "a radical break with everything known in human history ... completely at odds with the intellectual foundations of modern western civilization ... as well as the ... ethical and behavioral norms that had governed modern western societies."[63] Since the Holocaust had no prior history, the behavior of Jews could have no connection to the way Jews were perceived in Europe during the '20s or at any other time. So, nothing Jews do or don't do can cause people to either like or dislike them. Their behavior has no effect on other people's behavior because the fundamental fact of life is irrational anti-Semitism based on "a millennium old urge that powerfully infected and shaped European history," to give Charles Krauthammer's formulation.[64] So, Palestinian animus toward Jews has nothing to do with how the Israelis have treated them for five decades. And the pogroms in Russia in the 1880s following the assassination of the czar had nothing to do with the perception that Jews were in the forefront of revolutionary terrorism there. And the specter of Bolshevism that haunted Europe during the '20 had nothing to do with Hitler's rise to power, because nothing causes anti-Semitism. It just is.

The historical record tells a different story. The feeling that Bolshevism was a Jewish phenomenon was hardly confined to German anti-Semites. Bolshevism was a major concern in Europe, and Jews were seen, rightly or wrongly, as the driving force behind it. In the February 8, 1920 *Illustrated Sunday Herald*, Winston Churchill wrote:

> There is no need to exaggerate the part played in the creation of Bolshevism and in the actual bringing about of the Russian Revolution by these international and

for the most part atheistical Jews. It is certainly a very great one and it probably outweighs all others. With the notable exception of Lenin, the majority of the leading figures are Jews. Moreover, the principal inspiration and driving power comes from the Jewish leaders. Thus Tchitcherin, a pure Russian, is eclipsed by his nominal subordinate Litvinoff, and the influence of Russians like Bukharin or Lunacharski cannot be compared with the power of Trotsky, or of Zinovieff, the Dictator of the Red Citadel (Petrograd), or of Krassin or Radek—all Jews. In the Soviet institutions the predominance of Jews is even more astonishing. And the prominent, if not indeed the principal, part in the system of terrorism applied by the Extraordinary Commissions for Combating Counter-Revolution has been taken by Jews, and in some notable cases by Jewesses.[65]

In a letter to former Prime Minister Arthur Balfour in 1918, the Dutch diplomat Oudendyke wrote:

> Bolshevism is the greatest issue now before the world, not even excluding the war which is still raging, and unless, as above stated, Bolshevism is nipped in the bud immediately, it is bound to spread in one form or another over Europe and the whole world, as it is organized and worked by Jews, who have no nationality and whose one object is to destroy for their own ends the existing order of things.

The US ambassador in Moscow, David R. Francis, reported to Washington: "the Bolshevik leaders here, most of whom are Jews and 90 percent of whom are returned exiles, care little for Russia or any other country but are internationalists, and they are trying to start a worldwide social revolution."[66]

Even after he claimed that only "anti-Semites in and outside Russia glibly equated communism with the alleged Jewish world conspiracy,"[67] Salo Baron then substantiated the role Jews played in the Communist government, claiming that :

> They could easily point out that the first president of the Central Committee of the Party was Jacob Sverdlov, a Lithuanian Jew, that this Committee included four other Jews in its total membership of twenty-one, and that the long-time president of the Third International was Grigorii Evseevich Zinoviev (Apfelbaum). Among the leading diplomats of the period was A. A. Yoffe, Russia's chief delegate at the Brest-Litovsk Peace Conference and subsequently ambassador in Berlin. Yoffe unabashedly used his diplomatic immunity to spread communist propaganda in Germany, then in a desperate mood because of its defeat in the First World War. Later Maxim Litvinov (Wallach) helped in various capacities to reassert the position of the Soviet Union as one of the great world powers. A Galician Jew, Karl Radek (Sobelsohn), helped reorganize the Russian press and laid the foundations for communism's highly effective world-wide propaganda. From the scholarly point of view it was N. Riazanov (David Borisovich Goldenbach) who, as head of the new Marx-Engels Institute in Moscow, became the outstanding historian of the Marxist movement.[68]

And, realizing ethnic Russian communists often felt solidarity with other Russians, Lenin appointed Jews and Poles as commissars and to run the VE-CHE-KA or Cheka, the secret police responsible for revolutionary terror. Even Baron notes "a disproportionate number of Jews joined the new Bolshevik secret service.[79] This, of course, was evident to the ordinary Russian.[70]

The short-lived Hungarian Soviet Republic was even more brutal than the one that seized power in Bavaria. Richard Pipes notes, "In Hungary, they [the Jews] furnished 95 percent of the leading figures in Bela Kun's dictatorship [and were] disproportionately represented among the Communists in Germany and Austria and in the apparatus of the Communist International."[71] Tibor Szamuelly, one of Kun's Jewish henchmen, traveled through Hungary in a special train that

> rumbled through the Hungarian night and where it stopped, men hung from trees, and blood flowed in the streets. Along the railway line one often found naked and mutilated corpses. Szamuelly passed sentence of death in the train and those forced to enter it never related what they had seen. Szamuelly lived in it constantly; thirty Chinese terrorists watched over his safety; special executioners accompanied him. The train was composed of two saloon cars, two first class cars reserved for the terrorists and two third class cars reserved for the victims. In the latter the executions took place. The floors were stained with blood. The corpses were thrown from the windows while Szamuelly sat at his dainty little writing table, in the saloon car upholstered in pink silk and ornamented with mirrors. A single gesture of his hand dealt out life or death.[72]

Szamuelly, like Bela Kun, was known as a Jew and a Bolshevik. His behavior was bound to create animus against other Jews, whether Bolsheviks or not. This is the real tragedy of the period leading up to World War II. The Jewish Bolsheviks' behavior created animus against all Jews. Indeed, since religious Jews were more visible because of their clothing and the lives they led, they were more likely to bear the brunt of the anti-Semitism the Bolsheviks created; secularized Jews were often invisible as Jews because of their secularity. Like Jews in Hollywood later, the Jewish Bolsheviks tended to change their names to disguise their Jewishness, making themselves less visible and less likely to be the victims of attack when the inevitable reaction to their bloody excesses finally came.

The description of Szamuelly's brutality was published in Paris in 1919, the same year Pacelli wrote to Gasparri about the Russian Jews at the Wittelsbach Palace in Munich. The communist revolution was then a very real threat, given more urgency because the Jews who promoted it were not just in Russia. The possibility of a Soviet invasion of Europe seemed remote, but the overwhelming sympathy of Jews to the revolution created suspicion across Europe, where they were perceived as a potential fifth column.

The Frankfurt School, which would wreak havoc in America after World War II, was an offspring of the German and Hungarian revolutions. The Institute of Social Research, as it was originally called, was endowed by a Jewish grain merchant, Herman Weil, who returned to Frankfurt, the city of his birth, after making a fortune in Argentina. Rogalla von Bieberstein calls Weil a "salon bolshevist" who inherited his fortune.[73] The *Institut fuer Sozialforschung* was to politics what Hirschfeld's *Institut fuer Sexualwissenschaft* was to sex. Both were shut down when Hitler came to power; both were transposed to the United States. Hirschfeld's materials ended up at the Kinsey Institute in Bloomington, Indiana. The Frankfurt School ended up as the New School in New York. Gershom Scholem called the

Frankfurt School one of Germany's most influential "Jewish sects," but its influence went far beyond 1920s Germany. Theodore Adorno would play a leading role in introducing 12-tone music to post-World War II Germany, proving that whatever was derided as *Kulturbolschewismus* in the '30s was promoted in Germany in the '50s. Adorno also played a leading role in the American Jewish Committee's attack on Catholic ethnics in America through its "authoritarian personality" project. The Frankfurt School had its biggest effect during the cultural revolution of the '60s when Erich Fromm's books on psychology and Herbert Marcuse's books on politics became required reading on college campuses.

The Frankfurt School's impact on eastern Europe was almost as significant, largely because of Georg Lukacz. Lukacz, "the greatest Marxist intellectual of the 20th century."[74] Lukacz was born into the Lowinge family of Jewish bankers in Budapest, who, like Bela Kun (ne Kon or Kohn), later magyarized their name. After receiving his doctorate at the University of Heidelberg, Lukacz joined Bela Kun and became the Minister of Culture for the short-lived Hungarian Soviet Republic in 1918. His ruthlessness earned him the sobriquet "the Robespierre of Budapest."[75] He was condemned to death in absentia after the republic collapsed. In 1924, Lukacz was made director of the *Institut fuer Sozialforschung* in Frankfurt. For the next five years, until Lukacz was called to Moscow, where he remained until 1945, the Frankfurt School became a clearinghouse for the ideas of Jewish revolutionaries, from which "the St. Augustine of Communism" could promote "Messianic politics."[76] Ernst Bloch, who became famous for *Das Prinzip Hoffnung* and the slogan *"Ubi Lenin, Ibi Jerusalem,"* argued for the "destruction of the Austro-Hungarian Empire" with its "Christ-less Catholicism."[77] He also argued that "messianic longing for a redeemed humanity" dominated Jewish thinking. Lukacz returned to Hungary when communists took power after World War II and played the role of the reform communist there during the 1956 uprising.

The bloody excesses of Bela Kun in Hungary, of Kurt Eisner and Eugene Levine in Germany, and the Bolsheviks in Russia were bound to cause a reaction. The tragedy is that Jews were blamed *en masse* for the excesses of the Jewish Bolsheviks. "What may appear to Mr. [Chaim] Weizmann," one British diplomat wrote, "to be outrages against Jews, may be—in the eyes of the Russians—retaliation against the horrors committed by the Bolsheviks who are organized and directed by the Jews."[78] Nora Levin notes that when Jews acted as "passionately committed Bolsheviks in whatever they did, they reinforced existing anti-Jewish feeling, especially among adherents of Russian Orthodoxy."[79]

The same was true of Latvians, Ukrainians, and virtually every other ethnic group in Eastern Europe. When the Nazis arrived in the early '40s, they found many non-German "willing executioners" because of the outrages the Bolsheviks had committed after the revolutionary takeover of Russia in 1917. As we noted earlier, Ruth Birn mentions the Arajs Komando in Latvia, followers of Viktor Arajs, all of whom were Latvians active throughout the German occupation. The Arajs

Komando "did nothing but kill Jews," and were so enthusiastic that they sickened the SS assigned to command them. Birn notes "camps in the occupied Soviet Union were run with a minimum of German personnel." Some "functioned without German personnel at all and with only minimal supervision." She notes that Goldhagen ignores these facts because they undermine his thesis that Germans were "the central and only perpetrators of the Holocaust."[80] But he also ignores the excesses of Bolshevism that, more than any other single factor, fueled the animus of eastern Europeans against Jews.

Not all Bolsheviks were Jews, not all Jews were Bolsheviks. Ernest van den Haag later came up with a rule of thumb: one out of every ten Jews was a revolutionary, but five out of every ten revolutionaries were Jews. Many Jews tended to view the revolution in Russia favorably, especially when compared to other groups, like Catholics. Glazer and Moynihan compare reactions in *Beyond the Melting Pot*. In June 1919 the *Catholic World* declared: "The excesses of the Bolshevik revolution are ... not the exaggeration of otherwise worldly tendencies. They are the absolute subversion of all moral principles, the destruction of religion and the overthrow of civilization." In September 1920, the *American Hebrew* declared: "The Bolshevik Revolution eliminated the most brutal dictatorship in history. This great achievement, destined to figure in history as one of the overshadowing results of the World War, was largely the product of Jewish thinking, Jewish discontent, Jewish effort to reconstruct."[81]

If the beleaguered peoples of eastern Europe tended to conflate Jews and Bolshevism, so did the Jews, who tended to see the Russian revolution as a Jewish event, or at least an event with great significance for Jews. In October 1929, the *Jewish World* wrote

> there is much in the fact of Bolshevism itself, in the fact that so many Jews are Bolshevists, in the fact that the ideals of Bolshevism at many points are consonant with the finest teachings of Judaism, some of which went to form the basis of the last teachings of the founder of Christianity—these are things which the thoughtful Jew will examine carefully.[82]

Ten years earlier in 1919, Rabbi J. L. Magnes claimed in a speech in New York City that in Germany the Jew

> becomes a Marx and a Lassalle, a Haas and an Edward Bernstein; in Austria Victor Adler, Frederick Adler; in Russia, Trotsky. Compare for an instant the present situation in Germany and Russia: The revolution there has liberated creative forces and admires the quantity of Jews who were ready for active and immediate service. Revolutionaries, Socialists, Mensheviks, Bolsheviks, Majority or Minority Socialists, whatever name one assigns to them all are Jews, and one finds them as the chiefs or the workers in all revolutionary parties.[83]

M. Cohen wrote in the *Communist* of Kharkov of April 1919

> One can say without exaggeration that the great Russian social revolution has been made by the hand of the Jews. Would the somber, oppressed masses of

Russian workmen and peasants have been capable by themselves of throwing off the yoke of the bourgeoisie. No, it was especially the Jews who have led the Russian proletariat to the Dawn of the International and who have not only guided but still guide today the cause of the Soviets which they have preserved in their hands.[84]

Nora Levin notes the general sympathy of Jews for the revolution, saying Jews

greeted the March revolution with great joy and hope. Jews spoke of it as "the deliverance of a people," "a great tidal wave of democracy," and "a miracle ... that will be recorded as one of the greatest events in the history of Israel." A magazine for Jewish children compared it to the Passover liberation of Jews from Egypt.[85]

Levin notes "Jewish religious beliefs and practices were at variance with Bolshevism" and

the impetus for political action came chiefly from secular movements in Jewish life—Zionism and the Jewish labor and socialist movement. Both were movements of reaction against religious orthodoxy and against the intensified oppression and powerlessness of Jews in tsarist Russia, which had reached an intolerable pitch after the pogroms of 1881-82 and 1903-6. But they had worked out irreconcilably different philosophies and programs as they analyzed the Jewish predicament.[86]

The large intellectual and psychic space that the evaporation of religious belief left behind was filled with a fiery secular messianism:

These Jews were not only burdened by the exaction and strains of an illegal political life but also by the complex psychological adjustments needed to take on a new identity and dissolve out the old....Trotsky's reactions were similar to those of other Jewish Bolsheviks: Zinoviev, Sverdlov, Kamenev, Radek, Litvinov, Kaganovich, and others—all russified, cosmopolitan, hostile to the point of vindictiveness in their attitudes toward Jewish national culture, Zionism, and religious tradition. Lenin seems to have fully and wholeheartedly accepted these non-Jewish Jews for what they felt themselves to be international socialists. However, they were always identified as Jews by anti-Bolsheviks everywhere, by the masses of people in the Soviet Union, and by the Communist parties inside and outside of the Soviet Union.[87]

They have sometimes been described as "marginal men," "doubly alienated," and "self-hating," creating their own world of revolutionary agitation and formulas for a socialist utopia. These Jews had no Jewish support or following in any segment of organized Jewish life in Russia. Nor did Jews as a whole support Bolshevik ideas or the Revolution when it came. However, individual Jews loomed prominently in the Sixth Bolshevik Congress (July 26-August 3, 1917), in the Central Committee elected by the Congress, and in the top and secondary leadership of the party in the early years of the Soviet regime. It was they who stamped Bolshevism as "Jewish" in the prevailing view both of supporters and opponents of Bolshevism.[88]

What was true of the Bolsheviks was *a fortiori* true of their revolutionary predecessors. The Jewish areas of Russia were hotbeds of revolutionary activity in the second half of the nineteenth century. While not all revolutionaries were Jews, many were. The revolutionary movement could not have survived without their technical and practical skills as smugglers, printers, explosives experts, and masters of living the "underground" life. Haberer says "Jews constituted an important, if not crucial, national element in turning the region into a hotbed of terrorist violence."[89]

It would be naive, or as Haberer says, "shortsighted" to claim Jews just happened to be revolutionaries just as Abe Foxman later would claim Jews just happened to be involved in pornography. Both are forms of revolutionary activity, and Jews were drawn to them precisely because of the hold Messianic Socialism acquired over them once they abandoned traditional religious practice. Irving Kristol, in youth a follower of Trotsky and now a neoconservative, expresses the Messianic, universalist vision that neoconservatism and Trotskyism share. Jewish revolutionaries, says Kristol:

> did not forsake their Jewish heritage to replace it with another form of cultural identity or ethnic belonging. What they sought can best be described as an abstract and futuristic idealism of assimilation *qua* emancipation in a denationalized and secularized democratic society, ideally of universal scope. Leaving the world of their childhood did not necessarily imply its total abandonment in one act of irreversible forgetfulness. For many this departure under the sacred halo of socialism was the next best solution to their own existential problems—a solution that was enormously attractive since it also held out the utopian promise of the "genuine emancipation" of all Jews in a socialist republic of universal brotherhood devoid of national, religious, and social discrimination or even distinctions.[90]

After the war and the failure of the Bavarian Soviet Republic, Weimar Germany could not free itself from the downward pull of political violence. In June 1922 Walter Rathenau, Jewish heir to the AEG fortune, was assassinated four months after agreeing to become Germany's foreign minister. If there were ever a German Jew in the mold Mendelssohn had created, it was Rathenau. Yet as a completely assimilated German Jew, he had an impossible dual role, which he articulated, telling the Zionist Kurt Blumenfeld, "At night I am a Bolshevik; by day I seek an ethically regulated society." Blumenfeld and Albert Einstein urged Rathenau to resign, claiming, "a Jew should not run the foreign affairs of another people."[91] The Nazis claimed Rathenau as a Jew had sabotaged the war effort. "German Jews were caught in a vicious circle: the more they embraced the republic, the more it was discredited as a *Judenrepublik*."[92] Elon claims, "every unresolved problem and all the world's evils from the crucifixion of Christ to capitalism, Communism, syphilis and the lost war were projected onto a tiny minority representing 0.9 percent of the population."[93] To play up the irrationality of anti-Semitism, Elon ignores evidence of Jewish leadership in the revolutionary movement. Golo Mann wrote that his classmates cheered news of Rathenau's assassination. Anti-Semitism became an issue in Bavaria precisely because of the role Jews played in the revolutionary movement there.

That resentment, coupled with the devastating economic consequences of the Versailles treaty, found political expression when Hitler and Ludendorff orchestrated the Beer Hall Putsch on November 8, 1923. The authorities had no desire to revisit the anarchic days of the Bavarian Soviet Republic, so when Hitler and his supporters marched on city hall, the police opened fire. Sixteen National Socialists died, and Hitler was sentenced to a year in prison at Landsberg, where he wrote *Mein Kampf*, which proclaimed his racial theories and the idea that Jews had a genetic penchant for revolution.

Hitler rose to power by convincing a significant portion of the German people that Jews and Bolsheviks were one and the same thing. National Socialism was a reaction to communism. Goldhagen's statement that anti-Semitism has nothing to do with Jewish behavior renders an entire era incomprehensible. More comprehensible is Saul Friedlander's claim that "hatred for communism played a greater role in the rise of Hitler than anti-Jewish attitudes."[94] Hitler was stymied by Jewish assimilation and German acceptance of it; he could not have turned people against the Jews without the threat of Bolshevism and the experience of the Bavarian Soviet Republic, which he referred to as "temporary Jewish rule."[95] In *Mein Kampf*, Hitler wrote "in 1918 it was still not possible to talk about programmatic anti-Semitism. I can still remember the difficulties one encountered as soon as the word Jew was mentioned. You were either looked at as if you were crazy or you encountered the stiffest resistance."[96] In 1933 Hitler told Max Planck, "I have nothing against the Jews *qua* Jews. But the Jews are all communists, and these are my enemies, and it is against them that I am fighting."[97] As evidence that anti-Communism trumped racism, von Bieberstein quotes Hitler's saying *"Lieber sind mir 100 Neger im Saal, als ein Jude."* "Better a hundred Negroes in the room than one Jew."[98] In a diary entry for February 10, 1937, Hans Frank wrote, "I confess my belief in Germany ... which is in truth God's tool for the extermination of evil. We are fighting in God's name against the Jews and their Bolshevism. God protect us."[99] Hitler always maintained the Jew was his enemy primarily because the Jew spread revolution. In a table talk entry dated June 7, 1944, he still maintained "without Jews there would be no revolution."[100] Nazi theoretician Alfred Rosenberg said: "Bolshevism is in its essence the form of Jewish world revolution.... There is no such thing as Bolshevism without Jews."[101]

A reaction was inevitable. "The greater the successes of the communist movement," Jonathan Frankel wrote in 1988, "the greater the anti-Communist hostility to the Jews became."[102] Hilaire Belloc claimed, "the revolution in Russia was the historical starting point of a renewal of the animosity against the Jews in western Europe."

High on Hitler's list of subversive Jews responsible for the decline of Germany was Kurt Tucholsky, who "drove conservatives and Nazis downright berserk with his biting satires of every patriotic piety."[103] Franz Werfel, a Jewish writer from Prague who escaped to Hollywood where he wrote *The Song of Bernadette*, claimed Tucholsky and other Jews were responsible for the rise of the Nazis because they so savagely attacked German cultural icons. Werfel did not exclude himself from his indictment. "Applauded by the laughter of a few philistines, we stoked the inferno in which humanity is now roasting."[104] Elon disagrees with Werfel. "Had there been no Tucholsky, no Werfel, no Wolff," he writes, "Hitler would have moved to seize power anyway."[105] As before, Elon passes over the effect the revolutionary Jew had on the public, and Hitler's ability to manipulate those fears politically. Is Elon seriously suggesting Hitler would have come to power had there been no Kurt Eisner? No Eugene Levine? No Bela Kun? No Trotsky? Or no cultural bolshevists like Magnus Hirschfeld, Sigmund Freud, and Wilhelm Reich? If so, he argues against the logic of his own book.

Werfel was not alone in seeing a connection between Jewish behavior and Hitler's rise to power. Ruth Fischer claimed that Munich would never have become the birthplace of Nazism without the help of Jewish revolutionaries like Eisner and Levine.

The same was true of Austria. In *The Truth about Austria*, Guido Zernattos claimed "the most important basis for modern Austrian anti-Semitism was the part which the Jewish intellectuals played in the leadership of the social democratic party."[106] In *Juedischer Bolschewismus*, Johannes Rogalla von Bieberstein shows convincingly 1) that Bolshevism was primarily a Jewish phenomenon and 2) that it created a wave of anti-Semitism, the reaction to which swept Hitler into power in Germany.

The same was true in America: Nazism was seen as the reaction to Communism, which was seen as essentially if not predominantly Jewish. According to von Bieberstein, Father Charles Coughlin, the radio priest from Royal Oak, Michigan, criticized Nazism, but saw it nonetheless as "a defense mechanism against communism."[107] In this, he differed little from Henry Ford, who feared Jews primarily because he felt they were the leading force in spreading revolution throughout the world. Jewish writers like Philip Roth turn fear of Bolshevism into something suspicious, as if linking the two were itself proof of anti-Semitism:

> As an anti-Communist rather than a pro-Nazi organization, the Bund was as anti-Semitic as before, openly equating Bolshevism with Judaism in propaganda handouts ... holding fast to the purposes enunciated in their official declaration on first organizing in 1936: "to combat the Moscow-directed madness of the red world menace and its Jewish bacillus carriers" ... . Gone were the wall banners proclaiming "Wake up America—Smash Jewish Communists!"[108]

By stating his case this way, Roth gives the impression anyone who linked Jews and Communism was a raving Nazi anti-Semite, but this was not the case.

In May 1919, Woodrow Wilson proclaimed the Bolshevik movement was "led by Jews."[109] In 1919, Arnold Zweig, who was a Zionist and a Communist, wrote "Jewish blood" gave birth to socialism "from Moses to Lindauer."[110] Elie Wiesel wrote, "We have to make revolution, because God told us to. God wants us to become communists."[111] In 1848, Adolf Jellinek wrote, "reactionaries denounce Jews as the *perpetuum mobile* of the revolution."[112] In *Der grosse Basar*, Daniel Cohn-Bendit, a leader of the '68 Revolution, referred to Trotsky as "embodying the essence of the Talmudic Jew."[113] In 1934, in *Katholizismus und Judentum*, the Hungarian Jesuit Bela Bangha wrote, "revolutionary Marxism" corresponded "in its essence to a particular form of the Jewish soul and his intellectual posture."[114] In December 1918, the *American Literary Digest* asked "Are *Bolshewiki* mainly Jewish?"[115] In June 1920, under the title "The Jewish Peril," the *Christian Science Monitor* referred to an alleged world-wide Jewish conspiracy as demonstrated by the newly discovered and widely believed Protocols of the Elders of Zion. On the same day, the *Chicago Tribune* referred to Bolshevism as "an instrument for Jewish control of the world."[116]

Jews were no less inclined to speak this way than the *goyim*. In 1921 A. Sachs wrote, "Jewish Bolshevism has demonstrated to the entire world that the Jewish race is not suffering from degeneracy."[117] In 1990 in *Stalin's War against the Jews*, Louis Rapoport wrote "men of Jewish heritage" laid "the foundation for Communism and Socialism."[118] Franz Werfel, who wrote *The Song of Bernadette* and who participated in the 1919 communist insurrection in Vienna, wrote an article entitled "Israel's Gift to Mankind," in which he said "Moses Hess, Karl Marx and Ferdinand Lassalle" were the "church fathers of Socialism."[119] Jacob Toury claimed socialism grew out of traditional Judaism among the uprooted as substitute religion. An article entitled "The Jewish Revolutionary" in *Neue Juedischen Montsheften* in 1919 stated "no matter how the issue is exaggerated by the anti-Semitic side and no matter how anxiously it is denied by the Jewish bourgeoisie, the huge Jewish participation in the contemporary revolutionary movement is a simple fact."[120] One year later, Franz Kafka, the famous German-speaking Jew from Prague, wrote, "You don't forgive the Jewish socialist and communists. You drown them in the soup and slice them up when you're roasting them."[121]

Polish Nobel laureate Isaac B. Singer, who spoke Polish with difficulty and won the Nobel Prize in literature for writings in Yiddish, claimed "the communists in Warsaw were almost exclusively Jews, and that they brought fire and sword to all parties. They also claimed [after the October revolution] that social justice could only be found in Russia."[122] Bundespresident Friedrich Ebert claimed Jews were responsible for the revolution in Germany and that "practically every Jew was a crypto-Bolshevik."[123] In 1904, the German Zionist Franz Oppenheimer remarked, "nothing is more certain than that the contemporary Jew in eastern Europe is a born revolutionary."[124] What followed from this all but universal recognition of Jewish participation in Bolshevism was an unprecedented wave of anti-Semitism.

What made a racist organization like the Thule Society a dangerous threat was the widespread consensus "there was no such thing as Bolshevism without Jews."[125]

As Erich Haberer makes clear, Jews were the backbone of the revolutionary movement in Russia. The social dislocation that followed defeat after World War I allowed the revolutionary movement to achieve its greatest successes. The Jews could avenge themselves on the traditional Christian monarchies that had persecuted them. The Jews, according to Lerner "were enthusiastic representatives of the collapse of traditional communities because those communities discriminated against Jews."[126] Stanley Rothman and S. Robert Lichter maintain "the goal of the Jewish radicals was to alienate the Christians from their society just as the Jews had been alienated from those same cultures."[127] In 1849, in *Israels Herold*, Karl Ludwig Bernays explained "The Jews took revenge on a hostile world in a completely new way ... by liberating mankind from every religion and any kind of patriotic sentiment."[128] In the November 30, 1917 issue of *The Jewish Chronicle*, Trotsky was described "as the Avenger for Jewish suffering and humiliation" under the Czars."[129]

Von Bieberstein's survey of contemporary literature on the revolutionary movement in the period around World War I indicates Jewish involvement was bound up with the Jewish attraction to Messianic politics. Houston Stewart Chamberlain, the English racial theorist who married into the Wagner family and supported Hitler, reproached "Jewish atheists" for "planning an impossible socialistic and economic messianic kingdom without any regard for the fact that in process of doing this they would bring about the destruction of the civilization and culture which we have so laboriously erected."[130] Ernst Bloch, who described himself in 1918 as a "race conscious Jew," described the promethean project of the revolutionary Marxists as a "second incarnation."[131] Similarly, Eugen Hoeflich, the literary critic from Vienna who later changed his name to Mose Y. Ben-Gavriel, wrote "the Bolshevik Jew wants to set Europe in flames, not to fill his pockets but because he is driven by the purest idea, an idea which manifests an error which will lead to tragic consequences, which came about from a mass psychosis born of the war."

The Russian Revolution had nowhere near the psychological effect on public opinion that its daughter revolutions in Bavaria and Hungary had on the populations of eastern Europe. Bela Kun and Georg Lukacz did for the Jews in Hungary what Kurt Eisner and Eugene Levine did for the Jews of Germany; they created a huge wave of anti-Semitism. "Jew" became synonymous with "revolutionary," and soon labels like "*Umsturzjuden*," "*Revolutionsjuden*," as well as "*RevoluZion*" made the rounds. Led by Bela Kun, the Hungarian Soviet Republic spread fear and loathing among the native Hungarian population, which denounced it as the "*Judenrepublik*." According to Lichter and Rothman's *Roots of Radicalism*, 30 of the 48 commissars in the Hungarian Soviet Republic were Jews. Of 202 top officials, 161 were Jews.[132] The *London Times* described the Kun Regime as the "Jewish Mafia" in 1919. "Bolshevism in Hungary," according to Nathaniel Katzburg, was "largely a Jewish enterprise."[133] Hence, the soviet republic in Budapest was denounced as "rule of the Jews" and "*Judenrepublik.*" Unsurprisingly, a wave of pogroms swept Hungary when the soviet republic fell.

The same was true of Austria, where the dramatist Arthur Schnitzler in his diary described the revolutionaries as "a mixture of literary Jewboys, plundering rabble, and idiots."[134] The revolution in Hungary made headlines around the world. The net result was a rise in anti-Semitism, and not just in Hungary. In his book on the holocaust in Hungary, Rudolph Braham claimed the "chiliastic passions"[135] that promoted world revolution led inexorably to counter-revolution, and that the short but brutal communist regime left behind a bitter legacy which had devastating consequences for Hungarian Jews.

The Catholic Church, in particular the Jesuits, was the main opponent of the revolutionary movement. Catholics were prominent in pointing out the large Jewish participation in the revolutionary movement. An article in the October 21, 1922 *Civiltà Cattolica* entitled "*La rivoluzione mondia e gli ebrei*" (World Revolution and the Jews), described Communism as "the perversion of a Semitic fantasy" emanating "from the Jewish race."[136] In his 1926 book *Judentum und Christentum*, Father Erich Pryzwara, SJ, used quotes from Martin Buber and other Jewish thinkers to trace socialism to its roots in Jewish messianism, forcing him to the melancholy conclusion that the Jew "is driven to become the tireless revolutionary of the Christian world by an inner necessity." The Jew is "driven to his tireless activism by his deepest religious convictions. He is truly the restless Ahasver."[137]

In similar fashion, the Polish bishops traced the Bolshevik fury that had been unleashed on eastern Europe in the wake of World War I back to the "tradtional hatred" which Jews had always felt for Christendom. During Poland's war with the nascent Soviet Union in 1920, the Polish bishops released a pastoral letter in which they announced that "the true goal of Bolshevism is world conquest. The race which has the leadership of Bolshevism in its hands . .. is bent on the subjugation of the nations...especially, because those who are the leaders of Bolshevism have the tradtional hatred toward Christendom in their blood. Bolshevism is in reality the embodiment and incarnation of the Antichrist on earth." Like the Communist Parties in Germany and Hungary, the Communist Party in Poland was overwhelmingly Jewish. Sixty-five percent of the Communists in Warsaw were Jews. In the 1920s, the percentage was even higher, which again fueled anti-Semitism.

One of the classic instances which we are given of "modern" anti-Semitism is the pastoral letter on morals which was issued by Cardinal Hlond, the primate of Poland, on February 29, 1936. The part beginning "It is true that Jews...have a corruptive influence on morals, and that their publishing houses are spreading pornography . . ." is invariably quoted as proof of Hlond's anti-Semitism, but no mention is made of what follows. Far from being an anti-Semitic diatribe, Hlond's pastoral letter, as we saw in the introduction, is a classic instance of the two part teaching on the Jews that goes by the name of "*Sicut Iudeis non*," something which becomes apparent when the above-cited passage is quoted in its proper context:

> So long as Jews remain Jews, a Jewish problem exists and will continue to exist. This question varies in intensity and degree from country to country. It is especially difficult in our country, and ought to be the object of serious consideration. I shall touch briefly here on its moral aspects in connection with the situation today.

> It is a fact that Jews are waging war against the Catholic Church, that they are steeped in free-thinking and constitute the vanguard of atheism, the Bolshevik movement, and revolutionary activity. It is a fact that Jews have a corruptive influence on morals, and that their publishing houses are spreading pornography. It is true that Jews are perpetrating fraud, practicing usury, and dealing in prostitution. It is true that, from a religious and ethical point of view, Jewish youth are having a negative influence on the Catholic youth in our schools. But let us be fair. Not all Jews are this way. There are very many Jews who are believers, honest, just, kind, and philanthropic. There is a healthy, edifying sense of family in very many Jewish homes. We know Jews who are ethically outstanding, noble, and upright.

After reciting the dangers that Jews pose to a Christian society like Poland, Cardinal Hlond goes on to warn the Poles 1) that racism imported from Germany poses a danger to Polish culture and 2) that no one has the right to harm the Jews. In doing this he is simply restating *Sicut Iudais non* in its entirety:

> I warn against that moral stance, imported from abroad [he is clearly thinking of Germany] that is basically and ruthlessly anti-Jewish. It is contrary to Catholic ethics. One may love one's own nation more, but one may not hate anyone. Not even Jews. It is good to prefer your own kind when shopping, to avoid Jewish stores and Jewish stalls in the marketplace, but it is forbidden to demolish a Jewish store, damage their merchandise, break windows, or throw things at their homes. One should stay away from the harmful moral influence of Jews, keep away from their anti-Christian culture, and especially boycott the Jewish press and demoralizing Jewish publications. But it is forbidden to assault, beat up, maim, or slander Jews. One should honor Jews as human beings and neighbors, even though we do not honor the indescribable tragedy of that nation, which was the guardian of the idea of the Messiah and from which was born the Savior. When divine mercy enlightens a Jew to sincerely accept his and our Messiah, let us greet him into our Christian ranks with joy.

> Beware of those who are inciting anti-Jewish violence. They are serving a bad cause. Do you know who is giving the orders? Do you know who is intent on these riots? No good comes from these rash actions. And it is Polish blood that is sometimes being shed at them.[139]

Cardinal Hlond was not expressing racial hatred here; he was warning his Polish flock about the dangers of Bolshevism, which, as all of Europe had learned during the 1920s, was a largely Jewish movement. Cardinal Hlond was opposing Jewish revolutionary activity on the one hand, but he was also opposing the vicious reaction to Jewish revolutionary activity that was known as Nazism and had taken over Germany at that time. The Church was consistent in its oppostion to revolution on the one hand, and in defending the Jews against physical harm on the other. Both parts of this teaching are necessary. If either one is ignored, trouble follows.

Since the German bishops shared the views of their Polish confreres, they got caught up in the same apocalyptic mood. The most famous episcopal opponent of Nazism, Clemens Graf von Galen, bishop of Muenster, wrote a pastoral letter defending Hitler's incursion into the Soviet Union because it would rid the world of the "plague of Bolshevism."[140]

The Jewish inclination toward Messianic politics explains the overrepresentation of Jews in revolutionary movements throughout the 20th century. Once Poland achieved statehood in the wake of the Versailles Treaty, the Jewish population in the Soviet Union dropped to around two percent, which in turn dramatized the overrepresentation of Jews in the revolutionary parties in Russia. The Bolsheviks, with 11 percent Jews, were the least Jewish of all the revolutionary parties, even though Jewish overrepresentation was five times as high as the Jewish population in Russia. The Social Revolutionary Party by comparison was 14 percent Jewish, and the Menshevik Party was 23 percent Jewish.

If we turn to the leadership of the revolutionary movement, the overrepresentation of Jews is even more striking. Of the 21 members of the Central Committee of the Communist Party in Russia in August 1917, six, or 28.6 percent, were Jews. The percentage was even higher among the Mensheviks, where eight of the 17 members of the Central Committee were Jews. Of the list of the seven leading members of the Bolshevik leadership compiled by Culture Commissar Anatoli Lunatcharsky, four were Jews. When the Austrian foreign minister, Ottokar Graf Czernin wrote about the peace negotiations at Brest-Litovsk in early 1918, he reported the Soviets were "practically without exception Jews with crazy ideas."[141] Jews achieved this overrepresentation in the Soviet regime because Russians tended to be "patriotic" and therefore not ruthless enough in attacking fellow Russians, but also because the Jews, again unlike the Russian "peasants and workers," were highly literate. By way of illustration, the author of *Rossija I Evrei*, *Russia and the Jews*, told the following joke: "If six commissars are sitting at a table, what's under the table? The answer, the twelve knees of Israel."[142]

The percentage of Jews on the staff of the hated Cheka was even higher. As late as July 1934, eight years after Stalin's takeover, 34 percent of Cheka leadership was Jewish, a figure 17 times higher than the Jewish population of the Soviet Union. By 1939, after the purge of Jews, the percentage sank to 4 percent.

On April 20, 1920, Allen Dulles, later head of the CIA, wrote, "as a result of the leading role which Bavarian Jews played in communist groups, the tolerance of the pre-war era has changed and a new strongly anti-Semitic movement has come into being."[143] Von Bieberstein writes, "a minority of radical Jews, fighting for the dictatorship of the Proletariat, set loose an avalanche of aggressive anti-Semitism."[144] Fearing precisely this reaction, the Frankfurt lodge of the B'nai B'rith instructed Bavarian Jews to distance themselves from Kurt Eisner and his Bavarian Soviet Republic. In an article on anti-Semitism in Britain in the *Jewish Journal of Sociology* in 1989, Geoffrey Alderman wrote, "anti-Semitism flourished in the '20s as a result of the fear of Bolshevism."[145] In his 1996 book *Jews and the Russian Revolution*, Harvard historian Richard Pipes claimed one of the "most disastrous consequences" of the Russian Revolution was "the identification of Jews with Communism."[146] Reinhard Maurach, a legal observer at the Nuremberg War Crimes Trials, emphasized what he called a "combination theory," according to which "the Jewish problem merged with the Bolshevik problem" to form the basic outline of Nazi doctrine.[147]

Solzehnitsyn says that beginning in the 1930s, any mention of the role or number of Jews in the Russian revolutionary movement was avoided and people reacted with sensitivity when it was brought up: "This intentional suppression of the historical truth," he continues, "is both immoral and dangerous, because it prepares the ground for later exaggerations of the opposite sort."[148]

Jewish historians like to bring up the fact that Communists under Stalin eventually turned on the remaining Jewish Bolsheviks in the '30s. Even before that, Communists, both Jewish and Russian, tried to eradicate traditional Jewish life or bring it under party control during the '20s. Eventually Stalin purged most of the original Jewish Bolsheviks, with notable exceptions. Stalin retained Lazar Kaganovich to starve the Ukrainians into submission and to run the system of concentration camps now known as the Gulag Archipelago. In *Hitler's Willing Executioners*, Goldhagen claims the concentration camp was a uniquely German invention. But even Hitler noted that the British invented such camps during the Boer War and that the Soviet Union put them into practice before Hitler did. Goldhagen does not mention that Jews ran them for Stalin. It's worth asking whether Pius XII, whom certain people call "Hitler's pope," served Nazism the way Kaganovich served Stalin and Communism. Or whether we, unlike people who lived during the '30s and '40s, would make such a comparison solely because we have been swayed by the current campaign to defame Pius XII, Pius XI, and members of the German hierarchy like Bishop Graf von Galen of Muenster, who warned German Catholics that Hitler's racial ideology was incompatible with Catholicism. The following anecdote makes the point as effectively as extensive documentation:

> Karl Radek and Grigory Zinoviev ... had come to Germany in 1918 to stoke the fires of revolution. Like many other leading Bolsheviks (Sverdlov, Kamenev and Trotsky, for example), both Radek and Zinoviev were Jews, as was the foremost figure of the German Revolution—Rosa Luxembourg and the head of the new revolutionary government in Hungary, Bela Kun. And, of course, the inspirer of all their revolutionary exertions, Karl Marx himself, had come from a long line of famous rabbis in Trier.

Radek was addressing the crowd. "We have had the Revolution in Russia and the Revolution in Hungary, and now the Revolution is erupting in Germany," he roared, "and after that we will have the Revolution in France and the Revolution in England and the Revolution in America." As Radek worked up his passion, Zinoviev tapped him on the shoulder and whispered, "Karl, Karl, there won't be enough Jews to go around."[149]

It's also worth asking whether the preceding two paragraphs are anti-Semitic. Suppose this anecdote had been found in Pacelli's handwriting "in the locked archives of the Vatican"? Would it be evidence Pius XII was an anti-Semite? "The notion of Judeo-Bolshevism—the virtually axiomatic conviction among Nazis, modern anti-Semites in general and within the Church itself that Jews were the principle bearers and even the authors of Bolshevism"—Goldhagen's criterion of anti-Semitism—is not implicit in this statement, (as Goldhagen claims it is in Pacelli's letter); it is explicit. Does that make its author an anti-Semite? If so, then David Horowitz is an anti-Semite because he not only tells the anecdote in *The Politics of Bad Faith*, he goes on to say that although it is "apocryphal" the truth it points to is "telling," because "for nearly two hundred years, Jews have played a disproportionate role as leaders of the modern revolutionary movements in Europe and the West."[150]

No Jew of any stature ever issued a similar warning against Communism. Jewish commentators instead saw the revolution in Russia as akin to Moses leading the Israelites out of bondage. Similarly, while many Jews, most prominently Goldhagen, accuse Catholicism of complicity in the Nazi Holocaust, no Jew of any stature apologized for Jewish participation in the Communist Holocaust, which took many more lives. David Horowitz, though, comes close:

> In our time, 100 million people have been slaughtered in the revolutions of the left with no positive result, while millions more have been buried alive. Beyond the iron curtains of the socialist empires, whole cultures were desecrated, civilizations destroyed and generations deprived of the barest essentials of a tolerable life. Yet the epithet "counterrevolutionary" still strikes progressives, who supported these empires, as a term of opprobrium and moral disgrace. What this record shows, on the contrary, is that "counterrevolution" is a name for moral sanity and human decency, a term for resistance to the epic depredations of dreamers like them.[151]

The Spread of Bolshevism

Chapter Nineteen

Marcus Garvey

On March 23, 1916, a stocky Jamaican by the name of Marcus Garvey arrived in New York City. Garvey was the precocious son of a hard-headed, litigious mason, who had been inspired by reading Booker T. Washington's autobiography, *Up from Slavery*. Washington's book set Garvey's "brain... afire" with plans for redeeming the Negro race which included "uniting all the Negro peoples of the world into one great body to establish a country and Government absolutely of their own."[1] "Where is the black man's government?. . .Where is his King and his kingdom?" Garvey asked.[2] When Garvey realized that he "could not find them," he came to understand that "there was a world of thought to conquer"[3] and that he could conquer that world by applying the tenets of nationalism then reaching a fever pitch in Europe to the Black people of the world and propose Africa as the Negro equivalent of what Theodore Herzl had hoped to set up in Palestine.

Garvey's plan was Black Zionism, and he was the Black Moses who was going to set up a Negro state in Africa. Lying on his back at midnight in England during the summer of 1914, Garvey decided "that I should name the organization the Universal Negro Improvement Association and African Communities (Imperial) League. Such a name I thought would embrace the purpose of all black humanity."[4] On July 20, 1914, Garvey established his organization in Kingston, Jamaica. By 1915, Garvey concluded that he could not bring his plan to fulfillment unless he included America's former slaves in it. Garvey "unhesitatingly and unreservedly" praised people of color in the United States as the "most progressive and the foremost unit in the expansive chain of scattered Ethiopia."[5] What American Negroes had going for them, Garvey decided was white racism—what he saw as the "honest prejudices of the [white] South"[6] which forced black people to build their own segregated institutions and develop a race consciousness that could in time gain respect from their oppressors. This was to be a fundamental construct of what became Garveyism—the postulate that racial liberation and empowerment were inherent in racial opposition and alienation.

Garvey's plans to meet with Booker T. Washington were thwarted, however, by the death of the Wizard of Tuskegee. America now had no universally recognized spokesman for the Negro people. Given his vision in England in 1914, it's difficult to imagine Garvey not entertaining the thought that he was ordained to fill that vacuum.

Deprived of the opportunity to meet with Booker T. Washington, Garvey decided to meet with W. E. B. DuBois, head of the NAACP instead. On April 25, 1916 Marcus Garvey arrived at NAACP offices at 70 Fifth Ave. at what was the beginning of a speaking tour that would carry him to 38 states.

Neither Du Bois nor anyone else at the NAACP paid the visitor from Jamaica much attention. Du Bois was out of the office when Garvey arrived, and Garvey hoping for another meeting left his card.

Years later Garvey would claim that when he left Du Bois's office, he was "unable to tell whether he was in a white office or that of the NAACP."[7] When relations between the two men deteriorated, Garvey would later criticize Du Bois as "a white man's nigger."[8] The claim was partially based on the fact that DuBois was a mulatto, but it was also based on the fact that many of the NAACP's Negroes were quadroons and octoroons, men like Walter White, who looked so white that the NAACP used them as spies in the South.

Garvey was ever the race man, but his racism blinded him to the fact that white in this instance meant Jewish. The NAACP was a creation of wealthy New York Jews, whose desire to do something about lynching in the South took on new urgency in light of the death of Leo Frank. In 1915 Louis Marshall, head of the American Jewish Committee and the author of the failed motion to win him a new trial, joined the board of the NAACP. Seven years after Frank's death, Marshall was still smarting from the insult he had to bear when the Supreme Court rejected his plea for a new trial.

"There has been perhaps no crime committed in our day that can compare in lawlessness with the lynching of Leo Frank, whom I represented before the Supreme Court of the United States," Marshall wrote in 1922 during the debate on the Dyer Anti-Lynching Bill.[9]

Marshall was appalled by the lynching of Leo Frank, saying that it moved him "to form the resolution to do whatever it lay in my power to do to assist in putting an end to so monstrous an iniquity as lynching."[10] The NAACP was against lynching, so it seemed only natural that he would join the board of that organization. But that decision was to have fateful consequences for both the nation's Jews and the nation's blacks, as well as the nation as a whole. Instead of using the AJC to fight lynching, Marshall chose the NAACP as his vehicle and in doing so became involved in using the nation's Negroes as proxies in the Jews' war against anti-Semitism. Marshall, in other words, joined the board of the NAACP to get revenge on the South by turning the Negro into the nation's revolutionary *avant garde*. Harold Cruse, perhaps because he was a communist and as a result more aware of how that group of Jews tried to use the nation's Negroes as their *avant garde*, eschews revolutionary terminology in describing the NAACP's philosophy, but the accusation of duplicity is there nonetheless. Louis Marshall according to Cruse,

> was inspired to complement the program of the NAACP by virtue of the legal ax he had to grind with the Supreme Court over constitutional principles when the Court turned down his appeal arguments in favor of Leo Frank....Black civil rights and the NAACP represented the legal instrumentalities by which Marshall could salve the bitter gall of defeat he had experienced in the Leo Frank case, *Frank v. Mangum*.[11]

Cruse claims that Marshall, as head of the AJC, would never have accepted the constraints which Jews placed over black aspirations at the NAACP. But Marshall's role at the NAACP only compounded the conflict of interest that began to grate on Negro nerves. "At no time or place, on no issue or circumstance, in the duration of this alliance, were Jews of any parochial persuasion ever called upon to sacrifice Jewish interests on behalf of civil rights,"[12] but the Negroes in this alliance had to forego any form of economic ethnic solidarity (the very thing that made the Jews powerful) if they wanted continued Jewish support.

It was precisely economic ethnic solidarity which Marcus Garvey began proposing to Harlem shortly after his arrival there in 1916. And it was precisely W. E. B. Du Bois, acting as the agent of the NAACP, which opposed Garvey's vision of Black Zionism once he began to attract significant crowds. Murray Friedman claims that black and Jewish interests were identical during the '20s and the '30s, but the behavior of the NAACP belies this. The first manifestation of the so-called Black-Jewish Alliance was Du Bois's attempt to destroy Booker T. Washington. The second manifestation was Du Bois's attempt to destroy Marcus Garvey. The conclusion seems inescapable. Du Bois's job was to promote integration and destroy any black leadership in competition with the NAACP. According to Cruse, that meant an attack on anyone who proposed economics as the foundation of black ethnic solidarity. Cruse sees irony in the fact that this was precisely the basis of the ethnic solidarity which Marshall as the head of the AJC was proposing for Jews at the same time he was thwarting it for Negroes.

According to Friedman, Jews and Negroes were united in the scientific attack on racism, but as evidence for this alliance Friedman again cites Du Bois, the NAACP, and the school of anthropology which the German Jew Franz Boas founded at Columbia University. Du Bois got hired as the editor of the NAACP magazine because his book *The Philadelphia Negro*, published in 1899, linked him to Boas's school of environment based sociology. The scientific attack against racism, according to Friedman, "proved enormously significant within the academy at a time when it was still widely accepted by white Americans that blacks were genetically inferior and therefore undeserving of full citizenship rights."[13] Friedman claims that "DuBois's book broke new ground. In its emphasis on environmental factors rather than genetics as the primary cause of black poverty and crime."[14] According to Murray Friedman, "The two US leaders of this [the environmental sociological] movement early in the century were Du Bois, the black intellectual, and Franz Boas, a German-Jewish anthropologist. Du Bois attributed his own early interest in Africa to a lecture delivered by Boas at Atlanta University."[15]

The Boasian school would produce some of the most famous names in American sociology during the course of the 20th century, including Edward Sapir, Melville Herskovitz, Ruth Benedict, and Margaret Mead, whose fanatasy about adolescent free love in the South Pacific, *Coming of Age in Samoa*, was done under Boas's direction. The Boasian school also had as one of its disciples at the University of Chicago, Louis Wirth, who would go on to be extremely influential the area of social engineering in housing. Wirth would also go on to write at least eight chapters of Gunnar Myrdal's book *The American Dilemma*, which would serve as the theoretical justification of *Brown v. School Board*, the 1954 Supreme Court decision mandating school integration.

Boas saw environmental sociology as part of the revolutionary tradition which began with the French Revolution, which later found expression in the German Revolution of 1848. Boas, according to Friedman, "was born in Minden, Westphalia, and grew up in a home where notions of liberty and equality—the ideals of the 1848 revolution in Germany—were still a living force."[16] Like Ottilie Assing, Boas found American soil more congenial to revolutionary ideas than his native Germany. After landing a teaching position at Columbia University, Boas, with the backing of influential German Jews in New York, was able to launch the scientific attack on racism. In 1911 he wrote *The Mind of Primitive Man*, one of the books which helped establish the new field of anthropology, in which he wrote that

> the variations in cultural development can as well be explained by a consideration of the general course of historical events without recourse to the theory of material differences of mental faculty in different races...a similar error underlies the common assumption that the white race represents physically the highest type of man...anatomical and physiological considerations do not support these views.[17]

Boas was pure, left-wing Hegelianism, which ran parallel to Marx's version of left-wing Hegelianism, and it became the inspiration for the NAACP policies every bit as much as Marx's theories became the inspiration for the Communist Party.

Writing at around the time when Madison Grant's book on race was a bestseller, Boas felt that the concept of race was inherently ambiguous. "In an article entitled "What is Race?" published in *The Nation* in 1925, Boas rejected the idea that race consciousness and racial hatred reflected instinctual drives in human nature. Each race contained so many variations, he argued, that it was impossible to generalize about them."

One year after its founding, in 1910, Boas became active in the NAACP, writing one of its pamphlets, "The Real Race Problem from the Point of View of Anthropology." In the fall of 1933, Boas summoned a group of intellectuals to "devise ways and means for effectively counterattacking Nazi propaganda in the United States, and particularly Nazi racial theories."[18] A few years later, Boas would try to dissuade W. E. B. Du Bois from traveling to Nazi Germany on a research grant. Eventually, Gunnar Myrdal would take Boas's ideas and incorporate them into his book *An American Dilemma*. Friedman claims that Myrdal "was neither Jewish nor American," but, even after indicating that Myrdal did not in fact write *Dilemma*,[19] he fails to tell us that Louis Wirth, who wrote large sections of *Dilemma*, was both, and that Myrdal had been brought in to give credibility to what was largely a

Jewish project, because, as Friedman himself points out, "the scholarly critique of society that evolved into sociology had, like psychoanalysis, earned the reputation of being a Jewish science."[20]

Garvey arrived in Harlem before Boas's influence began to be felt; he arrived at the high tide of racial consciousness in America, on the brink of America's involvement in the Great War, and at the beginning of the greatest internal migration in American history, the movement of the former black slaves out of the agricultural regions of the south into the big cities of the North. The conditions for the emergence of racial consciousness among American Negroes were never more propitious.

The migration out of the South would last for another 40 to 50 years and would redefine the race issue in America. Like the migration during and following World War II, two factors would play a role. Negroes wanted to escape the Jim Crow system of enforced penury, otherwise known as sharecropping, which accompanied the South's redemption, and secondly, the industrial North needed cheap labor to replace the millions of soldiers who had gone to Europe to fight in the great war. Railroads and the wage differential did the rest. Between 1916 and 1918 somewhere in the neighborhood of 500,000 southern Negroes headed north. Between 1910 and 1920, the number of Negroes living in Gary, Indiana increased by more than 1,200 percent. Chicago's Negro population increased from 44,103 to 109,594 During the same decade, the Negro population rose nearly 150 percent at a time when the white population increased by only 21 percent.[21]

This was the era before the imposition of immigration restriction, which began in 1924, and so many of the new black immigrants came, as Marcus Garvey did, from the Caribbean. They came to cities like Philadelphia, Chicago, Detroit and Boston, but New York (and Harlem in particular), was unique both in what it offered its black immigrants and the Negro culture it produced.

It was in Harlem that the Negro also met revolution in its modern form. Many Negroes—Claude McKay, Langston Hughes, Richard Wright—were attracted to Communism, and it was primarily through exposure to New York's Jews that the Negro made contact with the various forms of revolutionary activity that were being promoted there. With Max Eastman, who was not Jewish, as his mentor, the Jamaican immigrant Claude McKay began working for *The Masses* where he ended up in conflict (including a fist fight on the sidewalk outside *Masses* offices) with Mike Gold, author of *Jews without Money*. Unlike the other cities we have mentioned, New York's Harlem, which began turning black around 1905 and by 1930 had 328,000 blacks living there, had a sizeable West Indian population, and this became the backbone of Garvey's UNIA movement.

Eventually, McKay was feted by Lenin in Russia in 1922 during the deliberations of the Third International as the symbol of Negro revolution in America, a role which he received because he was black and because he was there but which he abandoned shortly thereafter in favor of a literary career and ultimately conversion to Catholicism under the guidance of Bishop Sheil of Chicago.

More often than not, Jews were the Negroes' mentors in the school of revolutionary thought. A. Philip Randolph was introduced to the writings of Karl Marx by Morris R. Cohen, a young professor of philosophy at City College of New York, an institution which would become a hotbed of revolutionary thought in the 1930s. Irving Kristol, father of neoconservativism, would listen in on heated political discussions at Alcove B, the Trotskyite lunch table at CCNY, along with Daniel Bell and other Jewish thinkers, mainly sociologists, who would go on to fame in the 1950s. In 1925 when Randolph went on to organize the sleeping car porters into the nation's first black union, he got help from Jewish union leaders, as well as from Jewish politicians like Emmanuel Celler, as well as financial help from uptown Jews like Herbert Lehman, and spiritual advice from activists like Rabbi Stephen Wise.[22] Randolph's organization would go on to become one of the main pillars of the civil rights movement of the 1950s and 1960s, when Bayard Rustin took it over. Friedman refers to Randolph and Rustin as "as keystones of the black-Jewish labor alliance."[23]

The third form of revolutionary activity being proposed to Harlem's black diaspora was the liberalism of the NAACP, represented by W. E. B. Du Bois, the Harvard educated mulatto from Barrington, Massachusetts who was the editor of *The Crisis*.

Unlike all of the other destinations chosen by the Negro migrants, Harlem was unique because of the opportunities if offered. It was in Harlem as well, more than any other northern city, that the Negro met the Jew. During the 1920s, General Colin Powell's family migrated from Jamaica to Harlem, where he went to work for a Jewish shopkeeper and learned enough Yiddish to address Israel's prime minister in that language years later. Irving Louis Horowitz, who grew up in Harlem, would later say that he spoke English like a black sharecropper. He also said growing up in Harlem led him to his love of Jazz.

There was imitation on the other side of the ethnic equation as well, as Negroes started imitating Jews. During the period from 1915 to 1931, "at least eight congregations of black Jews were organized in Philadelphia, New York, Washington and other eastern cities."[24] One of those black Jews, a man by the name of Ford, went to Detroit, where he changed his name to Fard or Farrad and founded the Nation of Islam. But the main religion promoted by the Jews, and the one the Negroes found most attractive, was modernity. No one place epitomized the new era of the northern Negro better than Harlem. Harlem was where the sharecropper met the modern world, which as Yuri Slezkine has pointed out was largely a Jewish creation.[25]

Because of Jewish influence in the theater and the press, the Jews could promote their own vision of the Negro and ascribe to him a meaning that would undermine and eventually countermand the image which the South had been promoting in novels like Dixon's *Clansman*.

The so-called Harlem Renaissance was one of the better known offspring of the meeting between Jews and Negroes which took place in Harlem. If the Negro emerged as a cultural icon during the 1920s, it was largely because the Jews promoted him as such, and many thinkers—from Henry Ford to Harold Cruse—felt that the Jews never lost sight of their own ethnic self interest when they created the "New Negro Vogue."[26] Henry Ford felt that the Jews promoted Jazz to destroy America's native born musical culture. He felt the same way about the Jewish dominated New York theater. Harold Cruse, writing at the other end of the political spectrum, felt that Jews "sought to make themselves the interpreter of the Negro to American society."[27] This took the form of patronizing Negro art forms like Jazz and then colonizing them. Cruse, who spent most of the 1950s in a vain attempt to get one of his musicals produced on Broadway, felt that the Jewish take on Negro art was unmistakably clear:

> The original Negro jazz was "puerile," "shapeless and chaotic." It was left to Jewish musicians and composers to polish up this pristine black music and render it sophisticated enough for presentation to the general public.[28]

Oswald Garrison Villard, who could hardly be classified as occupying the same place in the political spectrum as Henry Ford, came remarkably close to Ford's conclusions when he as editor of *The Nation* published an article on "The Jew in the American Theater." Recently forced out of his position as chairman of the NAACP, by Joel Spingarn in collaboration with Du Bois, Villard published an article which contemplated the fact that "by 1923 American Jews had achieved domination of the theater as a corporate institution" with mixed feelings. The rise of Jewish influence meant "comparative neglect on the part of the Jew of the artistic in favor of the commercial factors of the theater."[29]

Murray Friedman viewed Jewish patronage of Black artists and writers in a positive light, but the examples he cites—Amy (wife of Joel) Spingarn's support of Langston Hughes, Joel Spingarn publishing Du Bois at his newly created Harcourt, Brace, and World publishing house—all indicate that support in the arts was achieved at a price, a price which both Cruse and David L. Lewis felt was too steep, because

> The blacks contributed the raw aesthetic ingredients of the cultural vogue in music, dance, theater and entertainment, but ended upon the short end of the material rewards, having no economic and corporate control over the vogue, which exercised an autonomously creative function that was less than negligible.[30]

To Cruse and Lewis, the Jewish patronage of Black artists that characterized the Harlem Renaissance appears ambiguous at best. Instead of being a celebration of black culture, it was "a diversionary track intended to keep blacks away from Garveyism in favor of the milder legalism of the NAACP."[31]

The end of World War I created a revolutionary situation throughout Europe and the United States. Convinced that the success of the revolution in Russia was a prelude to its spread throughout the world, Lenin promoted successful revolutions in Hungary and Bavaria. It was only his defeat at the hands of Pilsudski and the Poles that prevented him from marching into Berlin for a triumphant union with the revolutionaries waiting for him there.

That same revolutionary fervor soon spread to the United States. With Woodrow Wilson bedridden as a result of a stroke, dealing with the wave of unrest generated by the revolutions in Europe fell into the hands of Attorney General A. Mitchell Palmer, whose raids exacerbated an already tense situation. As always in America, revolution and social unrest became compounded and confounded by that country's racial situation. The sight of Negroes in uniform sparked lynchings in Mississippi and elsewhere in the South. Once again the South was haunted by fears of a Negro uprising, and the NAACP did its best to fan those fears, bringing about the lynching of a number of blacks.

From the time they began in June 26, 1919 until they sputtered out in the fall, the race riots of the Red Summer of 1919 would claim the lives of 76 Negro men and women. These riots were not limited to the South. The worst race riot began in Chicago on July 27, 1919, when a black boy strayed into the all white section of the beach at Lake Michigan and was drowned. Blacks roamed the city looking for revenge, and the whites retaliated with force of their own. In *The Crisis*, Du Bois fanned the flames of unrest by urging Negroes to prepare for white attack by arming themselves.

During the entire summer 1919, in fact, *The Crisis* under Du Bois's editorial leadership, stoked the fires of Negro rage. Before long the old vicious circle began to reassert itself in the South. Fear of uprising among the Negroes led to lynchings, which were then publicized by the NAACP, leading in turn to more fear of Negro uprisings in the South. The NAACP did nothing to break this cycle. Their inflammatory reporting if anything exacerbated the situation. "In Georgia," we are told, "a man was lynched because he was supposed to have said that the Negroes of Georgia were going to do what Negroes had done in Chicago."[32]

Lewis claims that "Du Bois and the NAACP were civil rights militants, not social revolutionaries—defenders of the Constitution, not exponents of class war—and like the association he sometimes unpredictably represented, the editor occasionally could appear exceedingly sensitive, if not squeamish, about charges of espousing political subversion and social unrest."[33] Lewis bases his claim on statements which appeared after the government cracked down: "The editor," he tells us, referring to Du Bois, "made it clear, repeatedly, that the Bolshevik Revolution was not in his eyes what it was in Asa Philip Randolph's—'the greatest achievement of the 20th century.'"[34]

Du Bois would insist in a June 1921 editorial, "The Class Struggle," that "we do not believe in revolution. We expect revolutionary changes to come mainly through reason, human sympathy and the education of children, not by murder."[35] "Curbing revolution," Du Bois continued, was being used as an excuse to deny Negroes "freedom to think."[36] The chief villain in this regard was J. Edgar Hoover, author of *Radicalism and Sedition among Negroes as Reflected in their Publications*. High on Hoover's list of subversive publications was Du Bois's *The Crisis*, especially the issues which had come out before Du Bois's turn to the right in the wake of the Palmer raids.

In fact, "Du Bois's *Crisis* provided Palmer's Department of Justice with abundant and unambiguous evidence of sedition and conspiracy...."[37] Du Bois wasn't alone in doing this at the NAACP. Joel Spingarn was, if anything, more committed to fanning the fears of Southerners and taking the war to Africa than Du Bois. His statements urging the Negroes to arm themselves led not only to "the new fighting spirit among Negroes," but efforts to shut down the NAACP as well.[38]

In August 1919, the attorney general of the state of Texas subpoened the books, papers and correspondence of the Austin branch of the NAACP on the grounds that the NAACP was not chartered to do business in the state of Texas. In order to avert a precedent which could shut down the NAACP throughout the South, John Shillady of the national office wired Governor Hobby to ask for a meeting. Hobby referred Shillady to the attorney general, but by the time he arrived in Austin all Shillady could manage was a meeting with the state's acting attorney general during which he "tried to explain that the NAACP was not engaged in organizing Negro uprisings against whites."[39]

On the morning following the meeting, Shillady was attacked and beaten by a group of six to eight men, including a judge and a constable who freely admitted their part in the attack. Both men claimed that Shillady had come to Texas to incite insurrection among Texas's Negroes. When the NAACP demanded that Shillady's assailants be brought to trial, Governor Hobby sided with his assailants, writing that Shillady deserved the beating he had "received by red-blooded white men" who did not want "Negro-loving white men" in Texas.[40] After administering the beating, Shillady's assailants informed him: "We attend to our own affairs down here, and suggest that you do the same up there."[41]

One year later, Shillady, who never really recovered from his beating, resigned from his duties as the NAACP's executive officer. James Weldon Johnson later discovered that "a prominent Negro clergyman of Austin had brought about the attack on Shillady by informing a Texas Ranger that the NAACP was banding together to excite sedition and race riots."[42] This gives some indication that the NAACP's reputation as a revolutionary organization determined to foment uprisings among the Negroes of the South was not just limited to the white population. It was almost universal in the South and shared by many Southerners who were not white.

The trouble had begun in 1918 when the Justice Department warned the NAACP about the "tone" of its journal. Ignoring the Justice Department's warning, Du Bois had written an article urging Negro soldiers "to marshal every ounce of brain and brawn to fight a sterner, longer, more unbending battle" against racism than they had fought against the Hun when they returned to the United States after the war was over.[43] This was precisely what the South and large segments of the North feared, and this fear led the Post Office to impound the May 1919 issue of *The Crisis*. Even if they gave no reason for the action, it was clear to the NAACP board that they were following up on the threat from the Justice Department.

The spectre of returning Negro soldiers, now trained in the use of modern weaponry, was scary enough for both the North and the South. When that group was incited further by Du Bois's prophecy that "we are doomed eventually to fight for our rights,"[44] the situation became intolerable for moderates on the board like Oswald Villard, who "severely criticized" Du Bois in *The Nation*, calling his opinion "dangerous and mistaken, a counsel of madness that would lead 'nowhere but to bloodshed without result.'"[45]

Villard wasn't the only one who was "horrified at the violent tone of the editorial."[46] Representative James F. Byrnes of South Carolina held *The Crisis* and other Negro publications responsible for the race riots which had occurred during the summer of 1919 and demanded that the Justice Department look further into the matter to see if they had violated the espionage act by inciting Negroes to riot and take part in mob violence. By the end of the summer, even the Negro press had joined in accusing the NAACP of promoting "Bolshevism."[47] The purpose of the NAACP, according to Joseph C. Manning, a man who had led the fight against disenfranchisement in the South, was to convert the Negro to Socialism. The situation for the NAACP worsened considerably when Dean L. B. Moore of the Negro Howard University, claimed that "a colored woman representing the national association had advised colored men to go after what they wanted with a shotgun."[48]

The NAACP tried to finesse the issue by claiming in their 1919 convention in Cleveland that Bolshevism would become more and more attractive to American Negroes if the white establishment failed to implement the reforms which the NAACP was proposing. Villard sprang to the defense of the NAACP in *The Crisis*, claiming. "What the Negro now asked was merely good Americanism, not the doctrines of Bolshevists or anarchists, but that of the founders of the American Republic,"[49] but the damage had already been done.

The NAACP had become fixed in the minds of the establishment as a revolutionary organization. Attorney General Palmer claimed that "there was a well-concerted movement" among certain Negroes to become "a determined and persistent source of radical opposition to the Government, and to established rule of law and order."[50] Palmer then made a thinly veiled reference to Du Bois, as "holding degrees conferred by Harvard University" and editor of a journal which was "always antagonistic to the white race and openly defiantly assertive of its own equality and superiority."[51] In April 1920, a *Crisis* agent was beaten and sentenced to six months in jail after the state of Mississippi banned the sale of any magazine "tending to disturb relations between the races." The situation in the North wasn't much better. The Lusk Committee of New York State denounced *The Crisis* as dangerous and trying to involve the Negro in revolutionary radicalism.

During this time of revolutionary ferment, Marcus Garvey continued to attract larger and larger crowds. Marcus Garvey, like virtually every other Negro leader in Harlem after World War I had good things to say about revolution, especially if the revolutionaries were black:

Garvey proudly recalled for his followers, though not always with complete accuracy, the stirring heroism of such leaders of American slave rebellions as Denmark Vesey, Gabriel Prosser, and Nat Turner...and the intrepid exploits of Toussaint L'Overture against the French in Haiti were not neglected in the effort to make Negroes conscious and proud of their racial heritage.[52]

Then in the summer of 1919 Garvey seized on an idea that would give symbolic but concrete form to the racial unity of the world's 400,000,000 Negroes when he incorporated the Black Star Line on July 27, 1919. When a battered Canadian ship known as the Yarmouth but soon to be rechristened as the SS Frederick Douglass docked at the 135th St. pier on September 14, 5,000 cheering Negroes greeted its arrival as "one of the greatest events in the modern history of the Negro race."[53]

Fellow Jamaican Claude McKay had hoped to bring Garvey's growing black following to Communism, but Garvey had a better grasp of political reality in America after the Palmer raids and disappointed McKay by expelling revolutionaries like W. A. Domingo from his organization. According to Lewis, "the watchword for Garveyites was now 'race first'" because "the growing number of followers certainly understood Garvey's appeal to ethnic pride better than they would have the economics of Marx and Lenin."[54]

On August 1, 1920 Garvey followed up on the triumph which the Black Star Line created among American Negroes by convoking the first International Convention of the Negro Peoples of the World. It was an expression of black nationalism, the likes of which the world had never seen. On August 3, 1920, 25,000 Negroes packed into the old Madison Square Garden after watching a parade through Harlem that afternoon that featured Garvey himself decked out to look like Toussaint L'Overture, preceded by thousands of men in uniform and thousands of women in their Black Star nurses uniforms. An entourage of 500 automobiles brought up the rear. Writing some 80 years after the fact, Lewis called the first UNIA convention "the greatest demonstration of colored solidarity in American history, before or since."[55]

Standing before this throng in Madison Square Garden, Garvey announced dramatically that he had two telegrams in his hand, one which he had received from a Jew and another which he intended to send to an Irishman:

> Reading the message from Louis Michel, a California Zionist—"there is no justice and no peace in this world until the Jew and the Negro both control side by side Palestine and Africa"—he waited for applause to die down before reading the second message, his own, to President Eamon de Valera: "We believe Ireland should be free even as Africa shall be free for the Negroes of the world. Keep up the fight for a free Ireland."[56]

If nationalism and national self-determination were good enough for Jews and Irishmen, Garvey seemed to be saying, then it was good enough for the world's 400,000,000 Negroes. "If Europe is for the Europeans," Garvey continued, "then Africa shall be for the black peoples of the world. We say it; we mean it...The other races have countries of their own, and it is time for the 400,000,000 Negroes to claim Africa for themselves....we mean to retake every square inch of the 12,000,000 square miles of African territory belonging to us by right Divine.... We are out to get what has belonged to us politically, socially, economically and in every way. And what 15,000,000 of us cannot get, we will call in 400,000,000 to help us get."[57]

Lewis goes on to add that "there is even a slight possibility that Du Bois may have been in the audience that night."[58] If so, he did not like what he heard. Confronted by a stupendous political fact like the first UNIA rally, the NAACP could no longer ignore Garvey. Less than a month after the convention ended, the September 1920 issue of *The Crisis* acknowledged Garvey's existence for the first time, in a piece entitled "The Rise of the West Indian." *The Crisis* hailed Garvey as a "new ally in the fight for black democracy,"[59] but privately Du Bois was saying other things. When contacted by a white man's business association in August 1920, Du Bois claimed that Garvey's followers "were allies of Bolsheviks and of the post-Easter Rebellion Sinn Feiners."[60] Du Bois was offended by what he called Garvey's "Pigmentocracy,"[61] by which he meant Garvey's suspicion of mullattos, quadroons, and octoroons. Du Bois also attacked Garvey for his anti-Americanism, accusing him of ingratitude for the generosity which his adopted country had shown him.

But the real issue was integration. In the wake of the Red Scare of 1919, Garvey abandoned revolution and became a race man instead. In doing so, he found a formula which would appeal to Negroes in a way that the pale abstractions of the Leftists did not. From 1918 until 1920, the numbers of new Negro migrants which came out to hear Garvey speak at Liberty Hall in Harlem increased dramatically in size. Black racism leading to black ethnic separatism was consistent with the American political system in a way that black revolution was not. It conformed not only to the conventional understanding of *Plessy v. Ferguson*, the Supreme Court decision mandating "separate but equal" educational facilities. It conformed to the ethnic separatism which was the unwritten law of the neighborhood in big cities throughout the North. It complemented as well the white racism of the newly resurgent Ku Klux Klan and resurgent nationalism in Europe in countries like Italy and Germany. Beyond that, it was completely comprehensible to the new Negro migrants of the cities of the North, who saw ethnic neighborhoods everywhere they turned and saw no reason why they shouldn't espouse the same principles in their communities.

Garvey would later say that he had no problem dealing with the Klan "and other honest white people."[62] But before long it became clear that Garvey had a major problem with the NAACP because that organization had decided that it was not interested in the ethnic pluralism which characterized the neighborhoods of cities like New York any more than it had been interested in promoting the economic gradualism of Booker T. Washington. The NAACP was interested in "integration," especially in the South, because they understood that integration would mean the end of the South as an independent culture. The same was true of all of the other "white" ethnic groups in the North. As Harold Cruse later pointed out, the Jews were interested in the integration of every ethnic group but their own, and in the Negro, people like Louis Marshall, now on the board of the NAACP and still smarting from his defeat at the hands of Southerners like Tom Watson, had found the vehicle for that subversion.

Heimreich says Garvey, who first articulated the cause of black nationalism and separatism, brought down the Black-Jewish Alliance, but the opposite was the case. The Black-Jewish Alliance brought down Marcus Garvey. Friedman accuses Garvey of "a robust antisemitism"[63] and goes on to claim that "the emergence of Marcus Garvey was a decidedly ominous development for black-Jewish relations,"[64] but that was largely because of the way the Jews had defined the terms of the alliance, which was based on an irrevocable commitment to "integration," no matter what the ultimate consequences for the Negro were. Garvey incurred the wrath of the Jewish-controlled NAACP because he had the temerity to propose the same program for blacks which Jews were proposing for Jews. Friedman notes the similarities between the Zionism of Herzl and the Black Zionism of Garvey, but fails to note the irony implicit in the fact that Jews ended up persecuting Garvey because he was too "Jewish."[65] According to Friedman,

> Garvey seemed preoccupied with Jews and Judaism. His call for an African exodus bore a striking similarity to the ideas of Jewish thinkers like Pinsker and Herzl.... In 1920, Garvey told a UNIA meeting: "A new spirit, a new courage has come to us simultaneously as it has come to other peoples of the world. It came to us at the same time as it came to the Jew. When the Jew said, 'We shall have Palestine!' the same sentiment came to us when we said, 'We shall have Africa.'"[66]

Friedman gets closer to the truth when he writes that Garvey "quarreled frequently with the NAACP, and more often than not, his grievances concerned the leadership roles of Jews in what he believed should have been an all-black organization."[67] The issue was not only the "leadership roles of Jews" at the NAACP, the issue was "integration," which Garvey saw as debilitating for any group which saw that as its highest aspiration. White racism was the best thing that could happen to America's blacks, according to Garvey, because it created racial solidarity, which was the foundation of economic solidarity, which was the basis of political power. Garvey could see that the Jews understood this fact, which is why he urged Negroes to imitate Jews. What he could not tolerate was the double standard implicit in organizations like the NAACP, which promoted integration for every group but the one which controlled the organization. Before long the feelings were mutual and the battle was joined as the NAACP, using Du Bois as its agent, set out to destroy Garvey and his movement.

From the mid-1880s until the end of open immigration in the 1920s, roughly two million Jews emigrated to the United States. No other group of immigrants would have a comparable impact on American culture. When the Jews began to arrive, America was Protestant. By the end of the twentieth century, it had become Jewish by adopting the tropes of modernity. Heinze claims the period of Jewish migration corresponded to "the rise of modern psychology as a force in American society."[1] Slezkine argues "the Modern age is the Jewish Age, and the twentieth century, in particular, is the Jewish Century," and "Modernization ... is about everyone becoming Jewish."[2] Nowhere was this truer than in America, a country founded by Christians who aspired to be Jews. Slezkine refers to the Puritans as "Max Weber's Protestants," a group of judaizers who had "discovered a humorless dignified way to be Jewish."[3] Puritans could "remain virtuous" in their own eyes "while engaging in 'usury' and deriving prestige from wealth."[4]

Given the judaizing propensities of the nation's founders and their glorification of revolution and demeaning of tradition, the Jews flourished "by becoming the model 'moderns.'"[5] Once everyone became "modern," Jews became the nation's role models and teachers, because becoming modern meant becoming Jewish.

This is not to say that the Judaization of American culture proceeded without conflict. By the 1920s, Protestants realized the Jews had brought along with them the bad habits that caused conflict in Russia. As in Russia, Jewish involvement in alchohol production was an issue. Henry Ford articulated nativist Protestant concerns in *The International Jew*, blaming Jews as the makers of "nigger gin," cheap and often toxic liquor whose "labels bore lascivious suggestions and were decorated with highly indecent portraiture of white women," which "spurred certain Negroes on to ... nameless crime."[6] "Nigger Gin," Ford wrote, was "sold by a number of companies all bearing Jewish names," and its consumption led to "Negro outbursts and subsequent lynchings."[7] The gin was never sold "in any saloon which bars the Negro," and the localities where it was served were "those where the disorders prevailed."[8]

Ford also faulted the Jews for the corruption of morals in the nascent motion picture industry. The Jews had stolen his friend Thomas Edison's invention of the movie projector and turned it to immoral purposes. The real issue was pornography, and there was precedent for claiming Jews had been major players in the obscenity trade since they arrived in America, and before that, in Poland and in the Pale of the Settlement in Russia. In *Bookleggers and Smuthounds: The Trade in Erotica, 1920-1940*, University of Pennsylvania professor Jay Gertzmann recounts coming home from school and watching on television as his uncle was arrested for trafficking in obscene material. The battle over obscenity in the 1920s was largely a Catholic-Jewish battle as Catholic prosecutors strove to keep Jews from using the mails to distribute obscenity. Gertzmann doesn't dispute this. Indeed, he substantiates "the ethnic flavor of prewar erotica distribution."[9] However, he concludes that only an anti-Semite would bring it up:

The ethnic flavor of erotica distribution still exists, although, except for extreme right-wing hate groups, critics of sexual explicitness do not exploit it. Many distributors of erotica are Jewish[10]

Von Bieberstein claims the first signs of anti-Semitic reaction in "puritanical America"[11] were a protest against the nascent Hollywood film industry, created and controlled by Jews. In *The International Jew*, Henry Ford complained about the Jewish takeover of Broadway theater. But the Jews, he continued, never had "to drive the Gentiles out of" the film industry, "because the Gentiles never had a chance to get in it."[12] Ford claimed "The motion picture influence of the United States, of the whole world, is exclusively under the control, moral and financial, of the Jewish manipulation of the public mind."[13] The Jews were able to subvert the morals of Americans because

> the stage and the cinema represent the principal cultural element of 90 percent of the people. What the average young person absorbs as to good form, proper deportment, refinement as contested with coarseness, correctness of speech or choice of words, customs and feelings of other nations, fashion of clothes, ideas of religion and law, are derived from what is seen at the cinema and theater. The masses' sole idea of home and life of the rich is derived from the stage and the movies.[14]

Any business, Ford continued, that "frankly brutalizes taste and demoralizes morals should not be permitted to be a law unto itself."[15] Echoing Ford's concerns, many legislatures in the '20s threatened to implement government censorship of movies. The threat of a boycott in 1934 prompted Harry Warner to warn MGM executive Harry Rapf, "I don't want to talk to no goddamn Communist. Don't forget you're a Jew. Jewish Communists are going to bring down the wrath of the world on the rest of the Jews."[16]

In 1929, Hollywood went deep into debt to finance its transition to talking pictures. After the stock market crash, the studios were pressured to cut costs and simultaneously increase their box office when ticket sales were dropping and normal sources of money had dried up as a result. They turned increasingly to sex and obscenity as an inexpensive way to get people into the theaters, producing films like *Diamond Lil*, featuring the suggestive Mae West, but in doing this they incurred the ire of the Catholic Church, which was to assume the role of censor that Protestant denominations no longer wanted. In August 1933, Joseph I. Breen, a public relations executive who had established contacts with American bishops during the Eucharistic Congress of 1924, invited A. H. Giannini, the Catholic banker who headed Bank of America, Hollywood's most significant source of credit, to a meeting with motion picture producers. During that meeting, Giannini informed Hollywood producers he would no longer fund films "prostituting the youth of America." One year later, Dennis Cardinal Dougherty of Philadelphia announced a Catholic boycott of that city's movie theaters, most of which were owned by Warner Brothers.

Warner Brothers was losing $175,000 a week at the height of the depression. At a meeting of Hollywood moguls to discuss the Philadelphia boycott, the normally pugnacious Harry Warner was "standing up at the top of the table, shedding tears the size of horse turds, and pleading for someone to get him off the hook. And well he should, for you could fire a cannon down the center aisle of any theater in Philadelphia, without danger of hitting anyone! And there was Barney Balaban (of Paramount Theaters), watching him in terror wondering if he was going to be next in Chicago."[17]

The man who thus described Harry Warner's plight ran the Production Code office for the next 20 years. Joe Breen was a Catholic with no illusions about the Hollywood elite:

> They are simply a rotten bunch of vile people with no respect for anything beyond the making of money.... Here [in Hollywood] we have Paganism rampant and in its most virulent form. Drunkenness and debauchery are commonplace. Sexual perversion is rampant, ... any number of our directors and stars are perverts.... These Jews seem to think of nothing but moneymaking and sexual indulgence. The vilest kind of sin is a common indulgence hereabouts and the men and women who engage in this sort of business are the men and women who decide what the film fare of the nation is to be. They and they alone make the decision. Ninety-five percent of these folks are Jews of an Eastern European lineage. They are, probably, the scum of the earth.[18]

Most historians of Breen's tenure condemn him as an anti-Semite. Virtually all only use the word "moral" in quotation marks, indicating they have internalized the standards of the victors in this cultural conflict. But Breen's work with "these folks" proves, to Mark Viera, at least, Breen was not an anti-Semite:

> Joe Breen, who had railed against the immorality of the Hollywood Jews, had learned from them, and they from him. They would not have asked him to run RKO Pictures if he had been truly anti-Semitic. They would not have flown him here and there. They would not have invited him into their homes. And they certainly would not have given him an Academy Award. He had convictions. He was a fighter, but he didn't hate.[19]

The outcry against Hollywood's subversion of morals was so great that federal, state and local legislation was proposed as an antidote. To head off legislation, Hollywood's Jews in 1934 entered into a voluntary agreement, the Production Code, with the Legion of Decency, a Catholic operation. The Catholics had forced the issue by organizing boycotts when the film industry was reeling.

Henry Ford admired Catholic resistance to Jewish Hollywood, even before imposition of the Code. Unlike Protestant clergymen who were regularly ridiculed in Hollywood films, "The Catholic clergy very soon made themselves felt in opposition to this abuse of their priestly dignity, and as a result of their vigorous resentment the Jew climbed down. You now never see a priest made light of on the screen. But the Protestant clergyman is still the elongated, sniveling, bilious hypocrite of anti-Christian caricatures."[20]

Ford felt the movies were the rehearsal for revolution in America. The Jews were using the screen in their "traditional campaign of subversion."[21] The movie screen also served "as a rehearsal stage for scenes of anti-social menace.... Successful revolution must have a rehearsal. It can be done better in the motion pictures than anywhere else: this is the 'visual education' such as even the lowest brow can understand."[22]

The Jews brought revolution with them to America. With a Jewish population half the size of that in Russia, America had a communist party with 50 percent of its members from Jewish families. Many changed their names in America, where they continued their revolutionary activity. Some Jewish revolutionaries born in America traveled back to Russia. Israel Amter was born in the United States in 1881. In 1923 he traveled to Russia. He then changed his name to John Ford and returned to New York, where he led the communist party. In 1921, Josef Pogany, former commissar under Bela Kun in the Hungarian Soviet Republic, joined the Komintern, which in 1922 shipped him to America, where he took the name John Pepper[23] and became *de facto* head of the Communist Party in America. A Ukrainian Jew, Jacob Golos, under the cover name Timmy,[24] created a spy network that included the Vassar-educated Elizabeth Bentley, who testified before the McCarthy committee in the '50s.

In an interview published in 1934 in *Class Struggle*, Trotsky claimed "Jewish workers of foreign extraction will play a decisive role in bringing about the American proletarian revolution."[25] Is it any wonder Henry Ford was upset? *Anti-Bolshevist* magazine wrote that the reaction against Russian Bolshevism was so great it was causing "a new wave of anti-Semitism," even in America.[26] Even in America, the term "Jewish Communism"[27] was making the rounds.

In the meantime, the federal government had also turned against Garvey. The NAACP may have urged the overthrow of state governments in the South, but it was docile to federal power, as evidenced by its pro-war stance. Both Spingarn and DuBois coveted commissions as officers. Two of the 25,000 Negroes listening to Garvey's speech on August 3, 1920 were FBI agents. That agency had been alerted to Garvey as a threat after the general counsel of the United Fruit Company had written to the secretary of state warning him that Garvey's activities "might repeat the French experience in Haiti."[68] Fearing the same thing, Britain's foreign office had already banned distribution of copies of Garvey's newspaper the *Negro World* throughout British Africa after the opening of UNIA branches in Cape Town and Johannesburg. Garvey wrote to Secretary of State Charles Evans Hughes disavowing any subversive intent, but the white power structure remained suspicious.

In November 1920, Du Bois who had been working behind the scenes to undermine Garvey's movement, made a significant tactical blunder when he advocated interracial marriage and race mixing as the solution to America's racial unrest. Howls of protest emanated from representatives of the entire political spectrum, and Garvey's howls were among the loudest. As a result, Du Bois and his colored aristocracy, otherwise known as the "talented tenth" begin to sense that they were losing their influence over the mind of the Negro masses. When President Warren Harding gave a speech in Birmingham, Alabama and announced "racial amalgamation there cannot be," he was greeted with cheers, and some of the loudest cheers came from Marcus Garvey, who attacked Du Bois as guilty of having committed "racial treason."[69]

As some indication that Du Bois's espousal of race mixing was more than just an isolated gaffe, Lewis cites a conversation years later between Walter White and Joel Spingarn, in which White admitted to Spingarn that "unmixed" Negroes, like Garvey and the people drawn to his cause, "were inferior—infinitely inferior now," Spingarn quoted him as saying, "whatever they might possibly become in the future."[70] Garvey had been exiled to England by the time this exchange took place in 1934. But, not surprisingly, Spingarn claimed "this is very confidential," because it lent credence to Garvey's claim that he was the victim of a quadroon/octoroon conspiracy.[71]

By the end of 1921, Garvey had successfully established himself as a viable alternative to Randolph's black socialism, McKay's black communism, and the integrationism promoted by the NAACP, whose talented tenth seemed to have slipped into irrelevance once the black masses showed themselves willing to mobilize under Garvey's banner of black nationalism. It was then that Garvey's troubles began in earnest.

After the 1920 rally, Garvey had reached the peak of his power. Things went downhill after that largely because of problems with the Black Star Line. The shipping venture had turned into a money-gobbling disaster, largely because Garvey had bought broken down ships at exorbitant prices. In late October 1919, after a rousing send-off given by 6,000 members of the UNIA who had assembled at Harlem's 135th Street pier, a battered hulk now rechristened as the SS Frederick Douglass set sail for Cuba with $4.8 million dollars of whiskey on board to avoid confiscation when the Volstead Act went into effect on January 20, 1920. The battered Douglass made it as far as 23rd St. in Midtown Manhattan when it had to turn back because it lacked the proper insurance.

Setting sail once again the Douglass was plagued by mechanical problems associated with its antiquated boilers. Because it had not been loaded properly and was listing dangerously, the Douglass had to throw much of the cargo overboard off the coast of New Jersey, where it was picked up by smugglers in boats, lending credence to the belief that the crew was involved in what was the theft of the cargo.

By the time the Douglass limped into Havana Harbor on March 3, most of the whiskey was gone, having been either stolen or drunk by the crew, exposing Garvey, who had signed a full-liability shipping contract to an enormous loss.

After three equally disastrous voyages, the rusty Frederick Douglass, which had cost the Black Star Line a total of $194,803.08 in two years of operation was sold for $2,320.90 to settle a judgement of $1,625. The financial record of the other Black Star Line ships was equally disastrous. The Shadyside, an excursion boat that the BSL hoped to use to ferry Harlemites up the Hudson during the oppressive months of the New York summer, swallowed another $31,000 of Black Star money before it ran aground and was abandoned. In less than a year and a half, the Kanawha took in $1,207.63 income after swallowing another $134,681.11 of Black Star money.

By the end of 1920, Du Bois knew enough about the Black Star Line's financial woes to publicize them in The Crisis and eventually use them to bring about Garvey's downfall. In December 1920 Du Bois published an attack on the Black Star Line in The Crisis that asked why the Black Star Line had been accepting deposits on tickets to Africa on a ship which they did not own. Desperate to get a ship that could reach Africa, the Black Star Line had fallen in with a dubious broker by the name of Anthony Rudolph Silverston (aka, Silverstone) who promptly appropriated $10,000 of Black Star money intended to be a deposit on the ship. "Silverston," according to Lewis, "later sought to claim this $10,000 as his personal property...despite the fact that the Black Star Line was repeatedly dunned for payment of the wily broker's promissory note. . . Was there any wonder that Garvey belatedly began to suspect treachery in the Black Star camp?"[72]

By bringing up the issue of the deposit on the tickets, Du Bois broached the issue of fraud in public for the first time. Garvey had fallen in with Silverstone because he needed the ship now rechristened as the Phyllis Wheatley for his plan to relocate blacks to Liberia. There is no indication that he did not intend to use the Phyllis Wheatley for this purpose, which would mean as well that his intent was not to defraud. Garvey's failure to carry out his scheme for resettlement could be laid sooner and more logically at the feet of his own business ineptitude or the machinations of Silverstone, or Du Bois's machinations with the President of Liberia.

Before long the government and the NAACP began acting in concert. During April of 1921, Du Bois was working behind the scenes to thwart Garvey's Liberian construction and resettlement scheme, communicating frequently with Liberia's President King during this period. President King, at Du Bois's urging, made his antipathy to Garvey and his schemes clear in his communications with the state department in Washington. In its June 1921 issue, The Crisis published a statement by President King, announcing that "under no circumstances will [Liberia] allow her territory to be made a center of aggression or conspiracy against other sovereign states."[73]

In August 1921, William J. Burns, the director of the FBI, wrote to the New York shipping board and asked them not to sell the Black Star Line the ship which Silverstone, who had already taken $22,500 for the sale, had promised. The shipping board, which claimed that Garvey's UNIA was "the communist party which is affiliated with the Russian Government" and that Garvey himself was "a ratical [sic] agitator" who "advocates and teaches the overthrow of the United States Government by force and violence,"[74] then took six months to issue its sale contract and when it did demanded a performance bond that amounted to twice the purchase price of the ship. The delay in the purchase of the ship lent credence to Du Bois's claims that the BSL was collecting deposits for tickets on a ship it did not own, but the fact that the BSL was unable to obtain ownership was due largely to the machinations of Silverstone and the shipping board. There was no fraudulent intent on the part of the Black Star Line.

As if Garvey didn't have enough troubles, competing Negro organizations like the dubious "Friends of Negro Freedom," began organizing "Marcus Garvey Must Go" protests, claiming among other things that Garvey was a "monkey chaser," an American Negro term of opprobrium used to refer to blacks from the Caribbean and Africa and that UNIA stood for "Ugliest Negroes in America."[75] Playing his own version of the race card, Du Bois denounced Garvey as a "West Indian Agitator,"[76] in a letter to the State Department in Washington which also solicited damaging information which Du Bois could publish in *The Crisis*. Garvey didn't help his case any by aligning himself with white racists like Senator Theodore Bilbo of Mississippi and praising groups like the Ku Klux Klan: "Between the Ku Klux Klan and the Moorfield Storey National Association for the Advancement of 'Certain' People, give me the Klan for their honesty of purpose toward the Negro."[77] Garvey made statements like this, according to Lewis, because "he was fed up with integrationist hypocrisy,"[78] especially the sort promoted by the NAACP.

When Marcus Garvey was arrested for mail fraud in January 1922 he was generous in assigning the blame for his troubles to a long list of persecutors. Before the indictments, Garvey had used the pages of *The Negro World* to claim that "Bolshevist agents"[79] had been paid to attack the Black Star Line. Equally guilty was the "white shipping industry," which had devoted a million dollar campaign to "boycott and pull [the Black Star Line] out of existence."[80] By January 1922, he was claiming that certain "Negro Advancement Associations" had "paid men to dismantle our machinery and otherwise damage it so as to bring about the downfall of the movement."[81]

When a year passed without a trial, a group of Negroes wrote an open letter on January 12, 1923 to U. S. Attorney General Harry M. Daugherty, demanding that Garvey be brought to justice. The letter demanded "that the Attorney General use his full influence completely to disband and extirpate this vicious movement, and that he vigorously and speedily push the government's case against Marcus Garvey for using the mails to defraud."[82] The fact that a number of the Negroes had ties to the NAACP only deepened Garvey's suspicions.

Once Garvey cited the NAACP as one of the conspirators determined to bring him down, it was only a matter of time before he would bring the Jews into the same picture. Garvey's suspicion that he was the victim of an NAACP/Jewish inspired conspiracy was strengthened when he learned that the presiding judge at his trial was Julian Mack, in Friedman's words, "a member of the German-Jewish aristocracy who also served on the board of the NAACP."[83] When Garvey's motion to have Judge Mack dismissed for conflict of interest was denied, he became even more convinced that he was the victim of an "international frame-up," declaring: "I am being punished for the crime of the Jew Silverstone [an agent for the line]. I was prosecuted by Maxwell Mattuck, another Jew, and I am to be sentenced by Judge Julian Mack, the eminent Jewish jurist. Truly I may say 'I was going to Jericho and fell among thieves.'"[84]

Garvey's trial finally began on May 18, 1923. Having failed to unseat Judge Mack, in spite of the fact that he "admitted having contributed to the NAACP,"[85] Garvey proceeded to fire his own lawyer and went on to represent himself, proving right the old adage about the man representing himself having a fool for a client. Garvey proved his inexperience in the law and courtroom procedure by automatically objecting to every motion of the prosecution, an action which dragged out the trial and antagonized the jury, which returned a guilty verdict four weeks after the trial began. Any doubts which Garvey might have entertained about Mack's bias in the case must have disappeared at the sentencing. Garvey was sentenced to five years in federal prison, the maximum sentence, even though

> There was nothing to indicate that the BSL had been formed for anything other than what it purported to be, a Negro improvement venture....Clearly the collapse of the corporation could be attributed chiefly to poor judgment in the purchase and maintenance of the decrepit Black Star fleet, and here the real criminals were white culprits who had unloaded rusty hulks on unsuspecting and inexperienced Negroes.[86]

Lewis calls Judge Mack, "a model of judicial patience and wise impartiality," but the fact that Mack, also in Lewis's words, was "second only to Louis Brandeis in the American Zionist movement" and "widely reputed to be both a cofounder and active member of the NAACP," causes no suspicion of bias to rise in his mind, even thought Lewis finds that "The verdict was somewhat strange in that the other three Black Star defendants were acquitted of any complicity in the crime."[87] This is, indeed, a strange outcome for a conspiracy trial.

In spite of the fact that "the feeling began to grow among Negroes that Marcus Garvey was the hapless victim of white justice and this tended to enhance his prestige both in the US and abroad,"[88] and in spite of the Jewish/NAACP connection, which the judge himself did not deny, Lewis claims that "Garvey's conviction was a self-inflicted tragedy" and goes on to accuse Garvey of anti-Semitism because

> Behind Mack's NAACP membership and presidency of the American Jewish Congress Garvey divined sinister, clandestine forces bent upon destroying black people's best hope of advancement. From this curious moment onward into the late 20th century, black Zionism would carry a distinct malodor of ideological anti-Semitism.[89]

In spite of his conviction and the concerted attack against him, Marcus Garvey's movement was stronger than ever when he spoke in Madison Square Garden on the night of March 16, 1924. The 1924 UNIA convention had if anything even more pomp and pageantry than the 1920 convention, something which caused W. E. B. Du Bois more than a little annoyance since it seemed that Garvey was on "the verge of successes that would confound his detractors."[90] Du Bois attacked the conference publicly by calling Garvey "the most dangerous enemy of the Negro race in America and in the world."[91] He was "either a lunatic or a traitor."[92] The fact that Garvey unveiled his Liberian resettlement plan at the 1924 convention allowed Du Bois to continue to work behind the scenes with the U.S. State Department as well. Cronon portrays Garvey's claim that the machinations of W. E. B. Du Bois led to the collapse of the Liberian project as paranoid fantasy:

> He blamed his old enemy Dr. W. E. B Du Bois, who was visiting Liberia at the time as the American representative to the presidential inauguration, for the collapse of the venture, charging that Du Bois had sabotaged the work of the Garvey association in order to further his won Pan African movement. Later Garvey's almost pathological hatred of DuBois, whom he called "purely and simply a white man's nigger."[93]

But Du Bois was in fact conspiring to destroy Garvey's plan. On July 10, 1924, Consul General Ernest Lyons wrote from Baltimore to inform Du Bois that "no person or persons leaving the United States under the auspices of he Garvey Movement in the United States will be allowed to land in the Republic of Liberia."[94] Two weeks after the date of Lyons' letter, a UNIA advance party arrived in Monrovia and was immediately placed under arrest and deported on a German ship. When *The Daily Worker* printed Robert Minor's suspicions about Du Bois's collusion with Liberia against Garvey, Dubois lied about his involvement, calling the story in the *Daily Worker* "an unmitigated lie."

The government continued its harassment as well. In a move that seemed designed to thwart the 1924 UNIA meeting, a grand jury indicted Garvey for perjury and income tax evasion shortly after the convention began.

As some sign that Garvey's racial appeals were having success among Negroes, a group which called itself the Negro Sanhedrin made up of three hundred black delegates from 63 organizations met in Chicago in 1924.

The Negro Sanhedrin was based on the Paris Sanhedrin of 1807, which Napoleon convoked to get the Jews on his side so that he could invade Russia. The Negro Sanhedrin was inspired by Garvey and its proceedings—as set down in "The Negro Speaks for Himself," edited by Alain Locke—were a clear rebuke of the Jewish paternalism promoted by the NAACP. In spite of the clearly Jewish inspiration for this meeting, the Jews ignored it, admitting tacitly, according to Cruse, that the "fight for the civil rights of blacks was ultimately a long-range civil rights defense of the status of Jews in American society."[95] The Jews remained adamant in their refusal to support the Negro whenever he proposed a program that was too close to the program of ethnic and economic solidarity promoted by the American Jewish Committee and other like-minded organizations.

On February 2, 1925, the US Circuit Court of Appeals rejected Garvey's appeal of his mail fraud conviction, and six days later Garvey arrived at the federal penitentiary in Atlanta to begin serving his sentence. Reacting to the growing sense that Garvey had been railroaded, President Calvin Coolidge granted Garvey a pardon in late 1927, but since Garvey was not an American citizen and had been convicted of a felony, he was immediately deported as an undesirable alien. After a triumphal progress through the Caribbean, which not even State Department harassment could deter, Garvey made his way back to Jamaica and eventually to England where he died all but forgotten in 1940.

Once he was safely out of the way, *The Crisis*, in an editorial which appeared in 1928, declared "We have today, no enmity against Marcus Garvey."[96] However, their enmity against Garvey's "fundamental issue of life"—namely, "the appeal of race to race, the appeal of clan to clan, the appeal of tribe to tribe"[97]—would continue unabated in organizations like the NAACP, even thought Zionism would continue to make the same appeal to Jews.

Chapter Twenty

The Scottsboro Boys

O n March 25, 1931, Victoria Price and her companion Ruby Bates hopped on a freight train in Chattanooga, Tennessee bound for Huntsville, Alabama. Both women were white; both were dressed in men's clothing, but Price was considerably older that Bates, who was still a minor at the time. Price and Bates were not alone on the train, nor was it unusual to find that freight trains, in the heart of the Depression, had become the poor man's passenger rail. Two hundred thousand people could be found riding the rails at any one time during the '30s, and hobo jungles had sprung up at freight yards across the country to accommodate the nation's poor and dispossessed on their way to look for work or to no place in particular.

Accommodations on freight trains in the South were not segregated, a fact which led to what might be called segregation from the ground up. When a gang of white youths met a gang of Negroes on the freight train which was traveling from Chattanooga to Huntsville, a fight ensued, and over the course of the fight, as the train was slowly picking up speed, the Negro youths who eventually triumphed threw the white boys off the train one by one, until finally there was only one left and the train was now moving at 35 mph. Rather than throw him off the train to what would have been severe injury and possibly death, the black youths let the last white boy stay on the train, and then they turned their attention to the other two youths, who, it turned out were women in men's clothing.

What happened at this point has been a matter of conjecture for the past seventy some years. When the train pulled into the small town of Paint Rock, Alabama, a posse was there to meet it. Angered by their treatment at the hands of the black youths who had thrown them off the train, the white boys had informed the station master, who telephoned the police, and when the train stopped in Paint Rock, the posse surrounded the train and apprehended nine young black men. It was then that the posse discovered the two women dressed like men. Victoria Price, the older of the two, immediately charged the Negroes with rape. The two women were taken to a local doctor to be examined; the Negroes were taken to jail, and the stage was set for what would eventually become the most famous trial of the 1930s in America, the trial of a group of Negro youths who came to be known as the Scottsboro Boys.

The Scottsboro Boys trial was a golden opportunity for the NAACP because of the very fact that it was a trial and the NAACP specialized in litigation. The NAACP had experienced one of its greatest victories in January 1923 when the U.S. Supreme Court declared that 12 sharecroppers accused of murder and insurrection in Elaine, Arkansas, had been denied a fair trial. This decision provided vindication for Louis Marshall, whose motion to overturn the conviction of Leo Frank had been denied eight years earlier. By April of 1925 all of the original defendants had been released, prompting W. E. B. Du Bois to claim that the release of the Elaine 12 was "a complete victory for the NAACP."[1]

By 1931, when the nine Negro boys were apprehended in Paint Rock, Alabama, legal victories rang hollow in a world where unemployment, hunger, and the spectre of starvation—in short, economics—had become the real issues. The NAACP itself had narrowly avoided economic extinction when contributions plummeted in the wake of the stock market crash of 1929. By 1930 their situation had become desperate, prompting William Rosenwald to offer to donate $1000 per year for the next three years if four other donors agreed to do the same. Eventually, Herbert Lehman, Mary Fels, Felix Warburg, and Harold Guinzberg, publisher of the Viking Press, came forward and matched Rosenwald's grant, and the $16,350 which the Rosenwald plan brought in allowed the NAACP to weather the financial crisis of the '30s. Murray Friedman points out that Edsel Ford was the only non-Jew to respond to Walter White's SOS, a fact which prompted Du Bois to admit that "only the strength of communal Jewish resources permitted such a degree of financial support."[2]

Not even the fact that New York Jews had to band together and save the NAACP during the Depression could move that organization away from its resolute avoidance of dealing with economic issues. The fact that the Negro in the '30s was affected by the financial crisis more than white Americans had no effect on the NAACP's philosophy of judicial activism. As a result, in the aftermath of the stock market crash of 1929, the Communist Party gained the upper hand over the NAACP because they were willing to talk about the economic dimensions of racial discrmination in a way that the NAACP was not. Thirty years later, Harold Cruse would claim that the Depression revealed the bankruptcy of the NAACP approach.

> The economic disaster of 1929 had revealed clearly that the guiding white philosophy of noneconomic liberalism was an insidiously debilitating leadership ideal to have been imposed on a nonwhite minority group seeking racial parity under American capitalism. Worse than that, noneconomic liberalism was a seductive entrapment into a fixed psychology of dependence, underdevelopment of social intelligence, and intellectual subservience. At best the free market of capitalist economic activity was free for whites only, and even then it was free only for those whites who controlled the ascending ladder of command posts in the class hierarchies of entrepeneurial advantage....At least a helot, or slave, or serf merits the right to be fed, but a freed serf without a master becomes the worst victim of the economics of scarcity. The Great Depression was an era of artificial scarcity in which the prize of civil rights was the Freedom to Starve to death without regard to race, creed color or national origin.[3]

In spite of the fact that litigation was its strong suit, the NAACP was reluctant to get involved in the Scottsboro Boys case, largely because that organization was reluctant to defend a group of Negroes who had been accused of raping two white women. Interracial sex was the third rail of political and social life in the South, and the NAACP knew that better than most organizations. Walter White, executive secretary of the NAACP, followed the Scottsboro Boys case in the newspapers. If anything, those reports convinced him that "The last thing they wanted was to identify the Association with a gang of mass rapists."[4]

The Communist Party, however, saw their opportunity and seized it. Charles Dirba, the assistant secretary of the International Labor Defense and a member of the Communist Party's Central Committee, recognized the political value of the trial immediately and sent a telegram to the Central Committee urging them to get involved in the case. As a result the Communist Party through its legal arm, the International Labor Defense, took over the case.

The Communist Party rightly saw the Scottsboro Boys trial as an opportunity to recruit members from the Black Belt. The Party had been trying to turn Negroes into revolutionaries, ever since Claude McKay had showed up in Moscow in 1922 and the Fourth Comintern Congress, meeting in Moscow discussed America's race problem for the first time. Party leaders, for the most part totally unfamiliar with the situation in the American South, had no idea how to create a program that could capitalize on the unrest there. Since Claude McKay was from Jamaica he knew only a little more about the situation in the South than Radek or Zinoviev did. But he was certainly black—blacker than W. E. B. Du Bois, who would take another 40 years before he decided to join the Communist Party, and it was as a black man that McKay made a hit in Russia. Cruse would later say that McKay was selected as a "special delegate" representing American Negroes "merely because he was the only Negro in Moscow at that moment."[5] McKay, who eventually contracted syphilis in either Moscow or Berlin and had to travel to Paris for treatment, was interested in revolution more for the sexual or artistic opportunities it offered, something that was evidently apparent to the official American Communist Party delegation, which demanded that McKay be deported back to the United States after they arrived in Moscow. McKay, like "Millions of ordinary human beings and thousands of writers," went to Russia because he was "stirred by the Russian thunder rolling around the world."[6] But when he got there Radek wanted to know if he had a plan, and McKay had to admit that he didn't.

The simple fact of the matter was that revolutionaries had been wanting to turn the Negro into a revolutionary and "take the war to Africa" ever since Toussaint L'Overture and John Brown, but no one, least of all the American blacks, knew how to do it.

As a result the Negro lost his place at the head of his own revolution, and that place was taken by the Jews, who, although they were not black, did know a lot about how to start revolutions. Since no one really understood the relationship between ethnos and class when it came to the American Negro, the Jews got to impose their position on the situation because they were in charge of the revolutionary movement. Forty-some years after the fact, Harold Cruse rails against this decision as in effect destroying whatever political power the Negro was about to gain under Marcus Garvey. What McKay should have told Radek, according to Cruse, is

> that the American Party was not a party of the American workers as such but an organization in which leftwing political power was exercised and predicated on national groups... particularly the Jewish group that later came to dominate leftwing affairs in a degree all out of proportion to its number. Jews were also able to play a three-way game inside the Communist leftwing... Leftwing Jews were able to drop their Jewishness and pick it up whenever it suited them. They were able to function as American whites without prejudice, especially in the cultural fields. They were able, as Jews to wield power through the Jewish federation. Later they were able to function as pro-Zionist nationalists within the left.[7]

Because McKay was unable to propose a plan of his own to Radek on how to turn Negroes into revolutionaries, "The Communist Left ... allowed Jewish leaders who came out of the Jewish Federation to become experts on the Negro problem in America."[8]

Unlike both Cruse and McKay, W. A. Domingo, who like McKay and Garvey also came from Jamaica, felt that if Negroes wanted to become revolutionaries "it was necessary first to go to America and learn such advanced thought from the Russian Jews" because "With the exception of the few who work in the garment industry in New York and come in contact with the wholesome radicalism of Russian Jews, the majority of Negro men and women are deprived of the stimulating influences of advanced political thought."[9] According to Cruse, the case of W. A. Domingo shows how Russian Jews diverted blacks from their natural self-interest, into supporting essentially Jewish positions, because

> This advanced political thought was, of course, Menshevik and Bolshevik Marxism. However, these Russian Jews knew exactly how to use this advanced political thought for themselves as Jews first and Marxists second. By his very act of toadying and genuflecting before the revolutionary superiority of white Socialist philosophy, Domingo revealed that he preferred to be a revolutionary Marxist first, a West Indian second, and a Negro last.[10]

Unlike Claude McKay, Domingo had become an unwitting stooge of the Jews by failing to see that the Communist Party was really a cover for Jewish ethnocentrism. McKay would learn this lesson first-hand when he clashed with Mike Gold, author of *Jews without Money*, when both men were on the board of the *Masses* and McKay had to resign. McKay was unprepared for the conflict because he had gotten along well enough with Max Eastman and his sister Crystal but never understood Jews as anything other than a subset of white folks. According to Cruse, the Jews wrecked revolution in America by their ethnocentric myopia. They failed to see the cultural revolution that was possible among American blacks, and, failing to see what was possible, imposed on America a Russia/Jewish vision that was doomed to failure: "All that the Michael Golds accomplished was to inject a foreign cultural and political ideology into a basically American cultural phenomenon, and engender confusion upon confusion."[11]

The situation led inexorably to the period of Jewish dominance in the Communist Party. It culminated in the emergence of Herbert Aptheker and other assimilated Jewish Communists, who assumed the mantle of spokesmanship on Negro Affairs thus burying the Negro radical potential deeper and deeper in the slough of white intellectual paternalism.[12]

Political life in America was irredeemably ethnic, but that situation was confused by the racial terms, black and white, which more than anything else in the years of the Black-Jewish Alliance allowed Jews to disguise their real intentions and pursue Jewish ethnic goals under the cover of pursuing racial equality. Jewish Communists were, according to Cruse, especially good at this because

These Jewish Communists were often more arrogant and paternalistic than the Anglo-Saxons, more self-righteous and intellectually supercilious about their Marxist line on America, than any other minority group striving for an ideal standard of radical Americanism.[13]

Nothing made this more apparent than the Scottsboro Boys case. In defending the Scottsboro Boys, the Communists reached the point of highest public visibility in their campaign to portray themselves as the defenders of the downtrodden Negro. But the Communists' cynical exploitation of the Scottsboro case also brought about the unraveling of the very thing they hoped to achieve by exposing the ethnic double standard at the heart of the new version of the Black-Jewish Alliance. At the beginning of the trial, Jews claimed to be ethnically invisible individuals whose patronizing behavior could be overlooked in light of their expertise as revolutionaries. By the time the trial ended, the same group was seen as ruthless political opportunists who were willing to send their clients to the electric chair if political advantage could be gained.

By the time the Scottsboro trial wound down at the end of the decade, Negro communists like Harold Cruse had come to the conclusion that the ethnic double standard was too big to ignore. That meant that the Negroes could no longer tolerate the fact that *The Communist* of September 1938 could publish an article by V. J. Jerome honoring "A Year of Jewish Life," but if a black party member were to come out with a similar piece honoring "A Year of Negro Life" he would be expelled from the party for instigating a Garveyite plot. In spite of their claim that revolutionary ideology superceded any form of ethnic idenity, Communist Jews used the party to uphold "the historical priority of Jewish cultural identity."[14] Nothing symbolized this double standard better in Cruse's mind than the fact that "As late as the 1930s, the top Communist leader... in the Harlem communist Party was Jewish."[15]

The same verdict could be applied to the ILD's handling of the Scottsboro Boys trial, which was heavy-handed and ethnocentrically Jewish and succeeded in alienating the very people—i.e., the jury—that the ILD lawyers needed to win over. Unfortunately, the position of the NAACP, while marginally better, wasn't qualitatively much different. In the end, the jurisdictional squabbles between the

NAACP and the ILD over who was going to represent the Scottsboro boys only exacerbated the situation in the eyes of Alabamians, who were reduced to calling down a pox on the houses of both groups.

The feud between the NAACP and the ILD did little to change the minds of southern observers in this regard. First there was the confusion over who was a communist and who was not. At first Walter White said that the NAACP had ""no objection to Communists... aiding the defense of the boys,"[16] but then Herbert Seligman announced that the NAACP would not associate in any way with the Communists at the trial. On June 7, William Pickens of the NAACP, accused the ILD of engaging in "communistic activity and propaganda among colored people in the South, based on the pretext of defending these boys."[17] Pickens implied that the communists' cynical attempt to turn the trial into a recruiting campaign had put the boys' lives at risk: "If the boys should be lynched, it would further play into their hands and give them material for still more sensational propaganda among the more ignorant of the colored population."[18]

The communist press reacted predictably by referring to the NAACP as "lickspittles of the capitalist class,"[19] but their reaction was overshadowed by what was becoming a generally held consensus in the South. Two groups of New York Jews were using the Scottsboro Boys as a way of gaining market share among the Negroes of the South. Both the ILD and the NAACP were seen as Yankees meddling in the affairs of the South. The NAACP/ILD squabble prompted one commentator to opine that only the "liberal, white people of the South" should handle the case, since the NAACP and the ILD seemed "engaged in a joint battle to secure the exploiting possibilities of the case rather than to defend the boys themselves."[20]

The Birmingham Age-Herald was even stronger in its condemnation of both groups. "It is now clear that these darkies do not mean a tinker's damn to the organizations which have supposedly been moving heaven and earth on their behalf."[21] The entire episode was a "nauseating struggle between the Communist group and the negro society, not so much that justice may be done as that selfish interests may be advanced though the capitalization of the episode."[22]

By the time the Scottsboro Boys went on trial, the Communist party and its front groups like the ILD had superceded the NAACP as the voice of the downtrodden Negro. In order to avert a possible lynching, the first trial began 12 days after the boys' arrest. The Defense attorneys assigned by the court were Milo Moody, a "doddering, senile" septuagenarian who hadn't tried a case in years, and Stephen R. Roddy, a Chattanooga real estate attorney who was "so stewed" on the first day of the trial "that he could hardly walk straight."[23]

The unspoken principle which provided the deep grammar for the trial had already been articulated in *The Clansman*: whenever a white woman accuses a Negro of rape, the Negro is guilty. Since race had attained a metaphysical status in the South, it challenged morality as the criterion of human action. This meant that white women, because of their racial endowment, were ipso facto virtuous. Somehow that didn't seem completely plausible, and so it was left to the successors of Thomas Dixon, to come up with the proper forumulation of the relationship between race and morals.

In their apologia for the southern point of view, Crenshaw and Miller in *Scottsboro: the Firebrand of Communism*, claimed that

> Since the first slave was brought into this country by New England traders the white race has insisted that the Negro respect the white woman, regardless of her position in society, and when he violates the person of a white woman he has committed "the unpardonable sin" in the eyes of the Southern white."[24]

Since sexual activity can be consensual, rape trials often have to deal with the character of the woman leveling the accusation. However, race at this point intervened in the issue as the South defined it and rendered such inquiry impermissible. "The character of these Huntsville girls," Crenshaw and Miller wrote, "whatever they might be, is not the concern of the authorities or of the courts."[25]

According to the racial code of the South, the character of the white woman was subordinate to her race. If she accused a member of an inferior race of rape, her word superceeded the word of the man who was accused on racial grounds alone. In 1932 the Winston-Salem, North Carolina *Journal* noted that

> in the South it has been traditional... that its white womanhood shall be held inviolate by an 'inferior race.'" And it mattered not whether the woman was a "spotless virgin or a 'nymph de pave.'" There could be no extenuating circumstances. If a white woman was willing to swear that a Negro either raped or attempted to rape her, "we see to it that the negro is executed," declared Arkansas poet John Gould Fletcher.[26]

When Victoria Price was allowed to tell her side of the story on the stand during the first trial, the defense attorneys' cross-examination was so perfunctory that the issue of her character simply did not arise. Nor did the issue of the physical evidence supporting her claim of whether she had been raped arise because the doctors who examined Price and Bates were not cross-examined. When the Scottsboro boys themselves took the stand, three of the boys said a gang rape did occur, but six denied it. In the end, no closing statement was offered by the defense attorneys.

Not surprisingly, the jury returned a verdict of guilty, which elicited "a loud roar of approval" from the crowd outside the courthouse "that was clearly heard by the second jury," which was still deliberating on the fate of the rest of the defendants.[27] In the end, eight of the nine Scottsboro Boys had been sentenced to death. The judge had to declare a mistrial in the case of ninth defendant, a 12-year-old boy by the name of Roy Wright, because 11 of the jurors held out for death despite the request of the prosecutor for life sentence in light of his tender age.

The Scottsboro trial stirred up all of the old fears, which had been circulating through the South since the time of the Toussaint L'Overture rebellion in 1798. In spite of the guilty verdict, the South, having learned that the northern press had veto power over its verdicts as a result of the Frank case, was convinced that the trial had attracted a horde of revolutionaries, who had moved into Alabama to stir up the Negroes. The fears of white Alabamians were, of course, justified because once the ILD got control of the second series of Scottsboro trials, it demanded complete subservience to the leadership of the Communist Party, USA. William L. Patterson, the National Secretary of the ILD, had lived for three years in the Soviet Union during the 1920s. When he returned to the United States he was a complete party man who felt that "The Soviet Union is the only country in the world were there is no discrimination, the only country where there is equality for all races and nationalities,"[28] and that it was his job to implement the party line in America. On May 14, 1931, the Communist Party's Central Committee issued its "Organizational Directives on the Scottsboro Case," which outlined in detail the tactics to be used. In formulating its tactics, the ILD was simply carrying out the party line which had been set during the meeting of the Sixth Comintern Congress in Moscow in 1928, when the 32-member Negro Commission:

> concluded that American negroes constituted an oppressed nation dwelling within the heart of the Deep South. Consequently, the Commission decided that the only solution to the American "race problem" was the secession of all black people from the United States. "The Communist party must stand... for the establishment of a Negro republic in the Black Belt." The architect of this resolution was Otto Kusinen, a Finnish born theoretician of Stalin, who had never met more than a handful of Negroes in his entire life. Privately, many of the American delegates regarded the program as so much nonsense.[29]

The New 1928 Party Line—"Self-determination of the Negroes in the Black Belt"—effectively cut the Negroes in the South off from their brothers in the North, many of whom had just left the South, and aligned them, because of the a priori application of class theory, with antagonistic Southern whites, who were seen as "workers." Since both the poor whites and poor blacks were "workers," there was supposed to be a natural affinity between them that overruled any racial antagonism. This was the logic of revolutionary struggle in the South, as articulated by Jews and Finns in Moscow for whom the Deep South meant Odessa. It had the sort of Russian/Jewish a priori nature that infuriated Harold Cruse, who felt that:

> By 1929 .. an unyielding, narrow-minded rigidity permeated the Party's thought on all questions. The West-Indian-American Negro braintrust could not utter a single theoretical idea about themselves unless they first invoked the precedent of the Moscow "line," so that everybody would know in advance that they had not the slightest intention of disagreeing with it.[30]

If the tactics of the ILD in racial matters inspired this sort of animosity in a left-wing Negro 30 years later, it's not difficult to imagine the effect they were having on white Southerners in the aftermath of the first Scottsboro trial. During the summer of 1931 a series of events confirmed the direst predictions of Alabamians who argued that the Scottsboro Case was a dangerous vehicle of communist agitation. Toward the end of 1930, a Communist by the name of Donald Burke opened an office for the Communist Party, USA, in Birmingham and began distributing leaflets and organizing meetings in Birmingham's black district because "The Scottsboro case renewed the Party's hopes that it could organize a significant number of Negroes in the area."[31] Burke and the three assistants who joined him during the time preceding and following the trial, distributed leaflets in Scottsboro, Huntsville, Paint Rock and other areas of Alabama, calling on white and Negro workers to "smash the Scottsboro lynch verdict."[32] On April 29, 1931, the ILD and the League of Struggle for Negro Rights called an "all-Southern Scottboro Defense Conference" to meet on May 24 in Chattanooga. Whatever gains the ILD hoped to get from organizing the "oppressed black peasantry" were offset by the hostility these efforts aroused on the part of the white Southerners, who felt that revolution was imminent. The fact that Communists were now openly advocating revolution among the area's Negroes "alarmed and disturbed conservative Southerners."[33]

When the Chattanooga conference failed to mobilize the local Negroes, the ILD sent a number of Communist organizers into Tallapoosa County, one of the rural, cotton-growing counties in central Alabama where the majority of the population was black. In early June 1931, four white men and one Negro from Chattanooga moved without announcement into the most predominantly Negro section of the county around Camp Hill. When a Negro tenant farmer informed Sheriff J. Kyle Young that Communists were meeting in the Mary Church near Camp Hill, Young approached Ralph Grey, to question him about the "radical meetings" which were reportedly being held to protest the Scottsboro case. During the course of their meeting, Grey opened fire on Young and his deputies, setting off a panic that lasted for weeks. By 2:00 AM of the day following the shooting, every white man within 20 miles had armed himself, and a posse which numbered more than 500 men began rounding up suspects in a atmosphere of panic and alarm. Files Crenshaw gives the South's view of what was happening when he states that "Thirty four Negroes were arrested in connection with the uprising."[34] Crenshaw goes on to add that a Negro church and five Negro residences had been burned down in the fall of 1931. Mayor Thomas Russell blamed the arson on "Communist sympathizers." Crenshaw also claimed that another Negro minister in Tallapoosa County received several anonymous threats that his church would be burned down if he continued his "crusade against Communism."[35]

The Alabama department of the American Legion called the attention of the state to the "horde of communists" who had descended upon Alabama "spreading a flood of propaganda opposing our form of government and social conditions, our race relationships and all the bases upon which our society rests, advocating race equality and destruction of law and authority by force and violence."[36]

Before long the panic created rumors which took on a life of their own. Reading a report announcing "Negro Reds Reported Advancing" in the Saturday morning edition of the *Birmingham Age-Herald*, 150 armed men formed a blockade at the highway bridge north of Tallapoosa only to learn that the two dozen approaching cars belonged to a funeral procession on its way to a country graveyard north of Dadeville. "Somewhat embarrassed, the men allowed the procession to go on and gradually began returning to their homes."[37] Superindendent Robert Russa Moton of Tuskegee sent several carloads of prominent Negroes to the area to prevent Tallapoosa Negroes from "going red."[38] Moton warned Alabama Negroes "against permitting themselves to be stirred up by agitators from outside... who come with plausible arguments and fair promises creating suspicion and ill will between the races."[39]

On August 4, Alabamians' fears that the Reds were stirring the Negroes up to insurrection seemed confirmed when three young women were raped by a Negro who "harangued" them about how white people had mistreated his people. One local newspaper felt the rape could be traced to the influence of communist agitators bent on stirring up insurrection.

In retelling the rape story, Crenshaw praised "Negro organizations in Birmingham [which] offered every assistance at their command in the search for the slayer ... and expressed the belief that the murderer was no product of Alabama" and "possibly came to the state for the purpose of making trouble in the furtherance of propaganda to which both races in the South were opposed."[40] Crenshaw also praised the Interracial Commission in Atlanta for issuing a "warning that Communist agitators, by pretending friendship for the Negro, were using him simply as a means to an end."[41] After claiming that the suspect in the crime had come from Chicago, Crenshaw cautioned against "condemning a whole race for the actions of a few of its criminal members" because the real issue was outside communist agitation: "The murder of the two girls and the uprising in Tallapoosa County could both be traced to the influx of the reds beginning with their defense of the Scottsboro 'Negro rapists.... As long as these 'black fiends' remained alive, they would be "used by the reds to incite our colored people to riot, rape and kill."[42]

Crenshaw recounts other rapes and claims that they resulted from ILD agitation. When three Negroes were arrested in Tuscaloosa, Alabama, on a charge of attacking and slaying Vaudine Maddos, a 20-year-old white girl, in an isolated community near the Bibb county line, the ILD got involved in the case "to inflame the public mind,"[43] and as a result the suspects—Dan Pippen, Jr., 18, A. T. Harden, 16, and Elmore Clark 28—were lynched. In his report on the incident, Tuscaloosa Sheriff R. L. Shamblin claimed that "feeling aroused by the ILD lawyers" was "directly responsible for this violence."[44] For the Left, the Scottsboro Boys trial had become a symbol of racial injustice; for the White South it became a symbol of Communist subversion.

The first victims of Communist agitation were the Scottsboro Boys themselves. One Harvard graduate from northern Alabama claimed "I might have been for aquittin' them at the first trial... but now after all this stink's been raised," we've go to hang 'em." The main group responsible for the stink was the Communists, who had been talking "about how white folks oppress the niggers and about Communism."[45]

The struggle to turn the Negro into a revolutionary would continue throughout the 1930s. Garvey, who had expelled the communists from the UNIA, could have posed an alternative to communist agitation, but Garvey was in exile in England at the time. Cruse claims that "Garvey's plans ended in fiasco because of opposition in Africa, his own egoism and financial incompetence," but he fails to add that the machinations of the NAACP played the major role in Garvey's demise. The vacuum which Garvey's expulsion left behind could not have been filled by the NAACP, which brought about Garvey's downfall, and so it unwittingly opened the door for the openly revolutionary Communist Party, which began its campaign to turn the Negro in the Black Belt of the South into the vanguard of revolution in the United States with the trial of the Scottsboro Boys.

The Scottsboro Boys trial, like the Leo Frank trial almost 20 years before, was a source of pride to liberal Southerners, who claimed it showed that the South no longer needed "Judge Lynch." Alabamians were upset when they learned that "outsiders" did not share their views about triumph of the legal system in the South over lynching. More characteristic of how those outside Alabama viewed the trial was the disgusted outcry of a New York college student. "What kind of mindless savage are you?" he asked Judge A. E. Hawkins. "Is condemning eight teenagers to death on the testimony of two white prostitutes your idea of 'enlightened' Alabama justice?"[46]

The South, above all else, feared the return of Reconstruction, a time when "Unscrupulous outsiders" used "the bayonets of Negro troops" in an effort to "put the black foot upon the white neck."[47] Reconstruction was synonymous with "outside influence," which invariably led to a return to lynch law.

The Chattanooga Daily Times claimed that the "outside interference" of "Northern organizations" into the South's legal processes "can serve no purpose other than to make it more difficult to stop lynchings in the South."[48] Oftentimes it was only the assurance of a speedy trial that quieted the mob bent on lynching the suspect. When the communist propaganda surrounding the Scottboro trial ridiculed the courts of Alabama as engaging in officially sanctioned lynching, it undermined the very thing the South was trying to uphold, namely the rule of law as an alternative to lynching.

Gradually, fear of Communism became the real issue in the case, and the nine defendants' guilt or innocence receded into the background. Judge Hawkins told Roddy that "the Communists are more of an issue than are the facts of the case."[49] The issue of Communism had made it impossible for the governor to pardon the eight young men. The Rev. Asbury Smith, pastor of one of the largest Negro churches in Baltimore, claimed "that the rapid swing of Negroes away from their traditionally conservative position was due almost entirely to the Communist campaign for the Scottsboro boys."[50]

"Alabamians were unanimous ... in their firm conviction that the Communists had seized the Scottsboro case for purely mercenary motives." The Alabama Interracial Commission charged that there was "brilliant leadership, sleepless energy and apparently unlimited money behind the malevolent [Communist] activity." These "apostles of revolution" pretended friendship for Negroes, but this was only a means to reach their selfish ends. Without a doubt, declared the commission, "Race hatred, race discord, murder rape [and] lynchings" were the Communists' "immediate object."[51]

Undeterred by the reaction they were creating, the Communists pressed on with their efforts to revolutionize the Black Belt Negroes. In order to better coordinate their activities, the ILD moved its offices into the Birmingham headquarters of the Communist Party. Aware of this and other moves by the communists, the Klan began to revive and began to distribute handbills and placards announcing how "the Klan Rides again to Stamp out Communism" and warning Negroes to be wary of Bolsheviks.[52]

During late 1931 and early 1932, when it was reviewing the first Scottsboro trials, the Alabama Supreme Court was inundated by an flood of intemperately worded invective that had the effect of hardening them in their resolve to resist "outside agitation." "These messages," said Chief Justice John C. Anderson on January 21, 1932 "are highly improper, inflammatory, and revolutionary in their nature," and were "sent with the evident intent to bulldoze this court."[53] When Joseph Brodsky quoted from Justice Oliver Wendell Holmes' dissent in the Leo Frank case, Supreme Court Justice Knight responded by saying "I have the deepest reverence for Justice Holmes, but I wonder if he had lived a little closer to the South whether he would have written these decisions, had he known how jealously we have striven to uphold our rights and protect our womanhood."[54]

Once again the communists overplayed their hand and brought about the exact opposite of what they said they wanted. On March 24, by a margin of six to one, the Alabama Supreme Court upheld the conviction of all but one of the eight defendants. Chief Justice Anderson told the NAACP's Walter White that Communist propaganda had "possibly injured the defendants."[55]

Like the Frank case, the Scottsboro Boys case went to the United States Supreme Court, but this time the Supreme Court ruled in favor of the defense, overturning the verdict of the Alabama Supreme Court.[56] The New York Times hailed *Powell v. Alabama* as a landmark in American jurisprudence. The Supreme Court decision, however, never allayed "the general suspicion ... that the ILD was perfectly willing to sacrifice the [Scottsboro] boys for whatever were deemed to be the Party's best interests."[57]

Energized by the Supreme Court decision, the Communists redoubled their efforts in the black belt, and as result there was a new outbreak of racial violence in Tallapoosa County. When word spread through Tuscaloosa in June that "the Communists had come to town,"[58] to defend three Negroes charged with raping and killing a 21-year-old white woman, an angry mob formed near the courthouse, threatening to lynch the ILD lawyers, who needed the National Guard carrying rifles with fixed bayonets to get them out of town alive. Appalled by the prospect of another Scottsboro Boys style trial in Tuscaloosa, the sheriff's deputies executed the three men in front of a firing squad in a isolated section of the county. The ILD lawyers, in other words, brought about the lynching that they claimed they were there to prevent.

The local *News* blamed the "disturbances" on the "International Labor Defense, preaching their poisoned communistic propaganda among our contented Negro population...."[59] The local press also held the ILD responsible for the suspects' deaths. The *Tuscaloosa News* claimed that "the maggoty beaks of the belled buzzards of the International Labor Defense are stained with the blood of the three Negroes."[60] As Episcopal Bishop William G. McDowell observed, the ILD's decision to defend accused Negro rapists was widely construed as an assault on the South's entire social structure. "Apparently the war is on."[61]

Crenshaw claims that in its *Norris v. Alabama* decision the U.S. Supreme Court deliberately revolutionized the jury system of the South. In doing this they paved the way for the communists, who intended to finish off the job with a violent revolution. Crenshaw cited the testimony of Borden Burr, a Birmingham attorney and former president of the Alabama Bar Association, who told an Alabama Senate Committee on May 16 that "the Communistic Party and its affiliates have between 3,000 and 4,000 members in Alabama and I have undisputed evidence showing they advocate overthrow of our good State and National governments by force."[62]

"The Communists boast," Burr told the committee, "that they have had greater success in Alabama in the last few years than in any other State, and among the evidence I have are documents proposing that Negroes rise up and establish their own government in Black Belt counties where they are in the majority."[63]

Convinced that they could now win the case, the ILD selected two attorneys to defend the Scottsboro Boys, Samuel Leibowitz, who was not a Communist, and Joseph Brodsky, who was. Less important than their politics in the minds of Alabamians was the fact that both men were Jews from New York City. By now the concepts of Communist and New York Jew had become interchangeable in the minds of the average Alabamian, which is to say the type of person most likely to be chosen to serve on a jury. The fact that both defense lawyers were Jews from New York, the fact that one of them was an agent of the ILD, and the fact that the ILD had total control over the strategy both inside and outside of the courtroom only confirmed the idea of outside interference in the minds of the men on the jury, a fact that the prosecutor would exploit.

It wasn't just Southern racists who felt that the lawyers were dangling from strings that reached back to New York City. Clarence Darrow felt the same way and said so publicly when he withdrew from the case. "If the cases were to be won," Darrow opined, "they ould have to be won in Alabama, not in Russia or New York."[64] On January 4, the NAACP National Board of Directors announced that the Association had decided to withdraw formally from the case.

The second trial

On March 13, 1933, Samuel Leibowitz arrived in Birmingham and officially assumed command of the case. Patterson of the ILD had chosen Leibowitz because of his reputation as the second Clarence Darrow. The resignation of the first Clarence Darrow over the ILD's heavy-handedness in the first trial indicates that the honor was misplaced. Darrow was smart enough to know that a Southern jury was not going to be won over by threats and moral posturing; Leibowitz, however, never figured this out.

The second trial of Haywood Patterson began on March 30, 1933, in Decatur, which was 50 miles west of Scottsboro, in the courtroom of Judge James Horton. Leibowitz moved to quash the indictments on the grounds that Negroes had been systematically excluded from the jury roles, but his motion was rejected, and the trial proceeded to cover the same ground it covered in the first trial. The difference between the first and second trial lay primarily in the fact that the defendants now had lawyers that would subject the state's witnesses to real cross-examination.

At a little after 9:00 AM on April 3, Victoria Price was called to the stand to recount her side of the story for what was now the fifth time under oath. For the first time, however, Price was subjected to grueling questioning which called her character into question. Leibowitz introduced documents from the city court of Huntsville, Alabama showing that Price had been found guilty of fornication and adultery on January 26, 1931.

If Leibowitz expected Price to crack under the strain, he was mistaken, for according to one woman in the courtroom, Price was not only "tough," she was "terrifying in her depravity"[65] and brazened out the defense attorney's accusations.

Liebowitz's cross-examination was merciless. His questions suggested his answers. There was no Callie Brochie's boardinghouse in Chattanooga, as Price claimed. She was an adulterer who had consorted with Jack Tiller in the Huntsville freight yards two days before the alleged rape, and it was his semen (or that of Orville Gilley) that was found in her vagina. She was a person of low repute, a prostitute. She was neither crying, bleeding, or seriously bruised after the alleged gang rape. She was fearful of being arrested for a Mann Act violation (crossing state lines for immoral purposes) when she met the posse in Paint Rock, so she and Bates made groundless accusations of rape to deflect attention from their own sins.

Leibowitz introduced various affidavits which cast doubt on her status as the Flower of Southern Womanhood, which is how the prosecution tried to portray her. McKinley Pitts of Chattanooga said he had seen Victoria "embracing Negro men in dances in Negro houses" and heard her talk to Negro men "in the most foul and vulgar language and ask colored men the size of his [sic] privates...."[66] Pitts went on to claim that Ruby Bates bragged to him she could "take five Negroes in one night and not hurt her . . . ." Oliver Love, who ran a Negro boardinghouse in Chattanooga, admitted that, because he needed the money, he had allowed Victoria Price to use a room in his house as a base of operation for prostitution. Asberry Clay, a friend of Love, said that a white man had approached her at the boardinghouse about paying for her services, but Price declined claiming that she was occupied that evening because it was "Negro night."[67]

The "filthy affidavits"[68] which called the character of Price and Bates into question elicited charges of bribery and witness tampering. The *Sentinel* claimed that the affidavits had been gathered by "one Chamlee, a white lawyer in Chattanooga employed by the Communist party...."[69] The *Sentinel* could not imagine that such a "filthy attack upon two white girls and supplied by Negroes of the lowest class would be given credency by anyone," especially since the Negroes who testified said that "Chamlee had paid them fifty cents for placing their marks on the affidavits."[70] In the end, the affidavits only increased the general anger against the defense attorneys.

The character issue had already flared up in May of 1931 when the ACLU published an interview which Miss Hollace Ransdell of Louisville, Kentucky had conducted with Victoria Price. During the course of the interview, Price described the rape "with zest slipping in many vivid and earthy phrases," which the local press had described as "unprintable" or "unspeakable."[71] Miss Ransdell felt that both Price and Bates routinely had sexual intercourse with both whites and Negroes, a fact which called their claim that they had been raped into question. When Ransdell met with Deputy Sheriff Walter Sanders in Huntsville, Sanders claimed that Price hadn't been arrested because she was a "quiet prostitute."[72] Quiet or well-known, Price had the reputation of being a prostitute among those who knew her in Huntsville, and this cast doubt on her testimony that she had been a "virtuous woman" up until the time of the rape.[73]

Before long doubts about whether the rape had occurred began cropping up among the prosecution's witnesses. During the course of the trial, Dr. Marvin Lynch, one of the gynecologists who examined the women, took Judge Horton aside, and, in a impromptu conference held in the court's men's room, told him that he did not believe the girls had been raped. Horton was stunned by the revelation and asked Lynch to testify under oath, but Lynch declined, claiming that it would destroy the practice he was in the process of trying to found. Thirty-four years later, Lynch denied making any statements to Horton, but it was clear that doubts were insinuating themselves into the mind of the judge and others.

Leibowitz was able to cast doubt on Victoria Price's moral character, but eventually the strategy would backfire for reasons we have already discussed. Price was seen as a symbol of white Southern womanhood because of her race and not because of her morals, which, as Files Crenshaw had claimed, were seen as irrelevant. Leibowitz, who was "not accustomed to addressing Southern juries," failed to take into account "old Southern chivalry"[74] and the corporate sense of the South which invariably closed ranks when it felt itself under attack by outsiders. Instead of casting doubt on the truth of her testimony, Leibowitz, in the words of the *Sylacuaga News*, made the average man in the jury box "feel like reaching for his gun while his blood boils to the nth degree."[75]

Instead of capitalizing on Judge Horton's doubts, Leibowitz's courtroom manner continued to antagonize the jury. Subsequent statements, made safely within the confines of New York City, would confirm Alabamians' suspicions that Leibowitz felt that he was dealing with a subhuman species of cretin when he addressed southern whites. When Leibowitz insisted that Attorney General Knight call his client "Mr. Sanford" on the stand, he antagonized the spectators who saw no slight in Knight's actions. When Leibowitz wondered why there were no Negroes on the jury roles, the jury felt that he was engaged in an attack on the jury system. The anger quickly spread to the crowd outside the courthouse, which was threatening to take the law into its own hands. That threat prompted Judge Horton to remind the court that all were equal under the law and that, like St. Paul, "we know neither native nor alien, we know neither Jew nor Gentile, we know neither black nor white."[76]

Horton's attempts to insist on the rule of law were undermined by the tactics of the Communist Party, whose organs kept referring to him as a "lyncher in sheep's clothing"[77] all the while ignoring the fact that Brodsky was paying subordinates to suborn witnesses in the case. Upon cross-examination, assistant prosecutor Wade Wright was able to elicit damaging testimony from one witness, who admitted under oath that "Joseph Brodsky had paid his room and board for almost a month and had even bought him the new $11 suit he was wearing."[78]

The prosecution knew that the two main pillars upon which their case rested was the testimony of Victoria Price and Ruby Bates. Now Price had been exposed as a prostitute, and Ruby Bates was nowhere to be found. Bates had indicated that she was having second thoughts about her testimony as early as June of 1931, when she approached defense attorneys with what she claimed was important information. Then on January 5, 1932, she had written a letter in which she claimed that "those Negroes did not touch me... I was jaze But those white Boys jazed me. I wish those Negroes are not burnt on account of me."[79]

That testimony, however, was called into question when a boxer by the name of Miron Pearlman announced that he had been paid by George W. Chamlee to "get her [Bates] drunk and have her write a letter to one of her fellows stating that the Negroes did not attack or assault her...."[80] Bates then signed an affidavit in which she claimed "I was so drunk that I did not know what I was doin" when she wrote the first letter under Pearlman's direction.[81] According to the new affadavit, the letter contained "all falsehoods, no truth being in it...." Chamlee denied the charges, but eventually The Chattanooga Bar Association was unmoved and called for Chamlee's disbarment for "conspiracy" and interference with pending criminal proceedings. Before long it was clear that Chamlee was working as an agent of the ILD, which was also instrumental, even though no one knew it at the time, in Bates' disappearance before the beginning of the second trial.

Then, in a move which caused a sensation in the courtroom, the defense and not the prosecution called Ruby Bates to the stand, and Bates waltzed down the center aisle of the courtroom decked out in a brand new outfit of New York clothes. But the jolt which Bates' theatrical arrival gave to the defense's case was soon dissipated when she was subjected to the withering cross-examination of the prosecuting attorneys, who suspected more witness tampering.

When asked about her whereabouts for the past few months, she claimed that she had hitched a ride to New York City, where she had worked for a "Jewish lady"[82] for several weeks. During her stay in New York, Ruby's conscience began to bother her, and so she sought spiritual solace from Dr. Harry Emerson Fosdick, the famous New York pastor of the Rockefeller Church. It was Fosdick, Bates claimed, who urged her to return to Alabama and testify.

By the time Bates testified on the stand that she had had sexual intercourse with Lester Carter in Chattanooga the night before her departure and that no one had raped her on the train, she had already given two contradictory versions of her story. Rather than focus on the inconsistency of her testimony, Attorney General Knight focused on her new set of clothes.

"Where did you get that coat?" Knight asked her.

"I bought it," Bates replied.

"Who gave you the money to buy it?" Knight continued.

"Dr. Fosdick of New York."[83]

Eventually, Ruby Bates got lost in the maze of her own self-contradictions. Her credibility reached such a low that at one point the spectators in the courtroom burst out laughing, something which infuriated Leibowitz and "made it clear that Ruby's testimony was not making a favorable impression on the jury,"[84] which was now coming to the conclusion that the defense had spirited her away to New York City and had bribed her to change her testimony.

When Morgan County Solicitor Wade Wright began his summation before the jury, New York City would play a large role in what he had to say. In a statement that would become the most famous line associated with the trial, Wright asked the jurors to "Show them that Alabama justice cannot be bought and sold with Jew money from New York."[85] Leibowitz immediately jumped up and demanded a mistrial, but his motion was denied. In the end, Wright was as accurate in reading the mind of the jury as Leibowitz was in misreading it, and, intentionally or otherwise, antagonizing the people who needed to be persuaded.

At 10:00 AM on Sunday April 9, 1933, the jury entered the courtroom laughing and announced that they had reached a verdict. Judge Horton then read the note in large pencil-written letters which they handed him: "We find the defendant guilty as charged and fix the punishment at death in the electric chair."[86] Leibowitz was stunned by the verdict and slumped back in his chair, showing that his ignorance of the "psychology of Southern juries" persisted until the bitter end. The defense had played right into the prosecution's hands by doing everything within its power to arouse the Alabamians' ancestral fears that the South was once again under attack by outside agitators. Mary Heaton Vorse claimed that the jury had been convinced that Ruby Bates' clothes had been "bought with Jew money from New York" and that Bates "had been contaminated" by her trip there.[87] Wade Wright's statement about "Jew money from New York" was "the most effective single statement by the counsel for the prosecution" because, as John Hammond pointed out in *The Nation*, it "registered to perfection the repressed feelings and prejudices of the twelve good men."[88]

The South, once again, was reacting to the threat of Yankee meddling—this time as carried out by New York Jews—by closing ranks, and they were willing to do this even if it meant defending two prostitutes as the Flower of Southern Womanhood and sending eight Negro boys to their deaths on the electric chair. Several southern papers entertained the idea that the verdict was not fair, but virtually all of them attributed it to outside agitation. The death of the Scottsboro Boys became a certainty once the ILD became involved in the case and began using its agents to bribe witnesses and intimidate both judge and jury. "If there has been no fair trial, outside pressure on Atlanta is chiefly responsible for it," said the Charleston, South Carolina *News and Courier*. The *Charlotte Observer* called the verdict a "natural reaction" to outside agitation:

> Unless this "Russianized northern element" was defeated there could be no peace and tranquility in Alabama. Conceivably, a local defense without the triple disadvantage of being radical, Jewish, and "Northern" could have gained a compromise such as life imprisonment, but the jury's loyalty to its white caste could only be proven unequivocally by a guilty verdict. Whether Haywood Patterson was guilty or innocent was, at most, a peripheral question.[89]

On April 10, 1933, Samuel Leibowitz returned to New York City, where he was given a hero's welcome as over 3,000 enthusiastic and cheering supporters, most of them black, jammed Pennsylvania Station to greet him. Leibowitz reacted to the adulation of the crowds in New York by insulting the entire state of Alabama. When asked by a reporter from the *New York Herald Tribune* how the jury could convict Patterson, Leibowitz responded by saying that, "If you ever saw those creatures, those bigots whose mouths are slits in their faces, whose eyes pop out at you like frogs, whose chins drip tobacco juice, bewhiskered and filthy, you would not ask how they could do it."[90] Leibowitz went on to add that he felt in need of a "moral, mental and physical bath,"[91] as a result of the two weeks he had just spent in Decatur, Alabama. Leibowitz, said this, it should be noted, when eight of his clients were still facing charges in Alabama, from whose citizens, "whose chins drip tobacco juice," their juries would have to be drawn.

When news of his remarks reached the South, Attorney General Knight denounced them as "the wail of a contemptible loser, particularly in view of the fact that in his address to the jury he lauded the people of Morgan County and the members of the jury to the skies." Knight concluded his remarks by adding that, "I, like every other Southerner, resent his despicable slurs."[92]

The Southern press agreed with Knight. "The New York Jew says there is no such thing as fair trial in Alabama," said the Athens, Alabama *Courier*. "It seems to this paper... [that] this recent recruit from Russia is a poor sort of chap to blight the good name of Alabama."[93] And the Sylacauga *News* proudly declared: "When these German communists hear of the latest echo from their New York fog horn lawyer, they will doubtless learn true blue Americans have not yet grasped the meaning of the order to retreat."[94] Judge Horton concurred: "The statement of itself of necessity must make impossible any just and impartial verdict. The accused Negro must be a victim of this statement. His leading attorney would be a millstone around his neck."

Brodsky defended his colleague, by claiming that Leibowitz had never made the statement, but, as usual, Brodsky only made matters worse, especially when he put Marxist words in Leibowitz's mouth, claiming that "Leibowitz's view is that in Decatur and the South the white workers are imbued with the idea of white supremacy and that only in union of the white and Negro workers warring against the ruling class can they gain their ends."[95]

Leibowitz refused to back down from what he had said in the *Tribune* and extended his attack to include the prosecution in the recently concluded trial in terms that were guaranteed to make a bad situation worse: "as for the rest of the braying pack, the wolves of bigotry who raised the Hilter cry of 'Jew money form New York' because we dared to demand a square deal for a poor unfortunate whose skin was black, I stand pat. They are bigots."[96]

Undeterred by the fact that he had just ruined the cases of the remaining defendants and condemned them to the electric chair, Leibowitz spent the following Thursday evening at Harlem's Salem Methodist Episcopal Church, addressing a cheering crowd of 4,000 Negroes, who hailed him as a "new Moses."

It was the beginning of many Scottsboro Boys rallies. On Friday, May 5, at a mass rally which served as the kick-off for William Davis's March on Washington, one-time prosecution, one-time defense witness, Ruby Bates told the crowd that she had lied because "I was afraid of the Southern white ruling class people...."[97]

As some indication of what "Southern white ruling class people" thought of Ruby, the *Huntsville Times* referred to Bates as "Harlem's darling."[98] If she ever tired of telling her story of oppression at the hands of "Southern white ruling class people" to the fashionable Leftists in New York, Ruby could go "on to a vaudeville engagement, where the emoluments should be more lucrative than working in a cotton mill, riding a boxcar as a hobo, or pursuing her avocation as a 'lady of leisure.'"[99] The *Huntsville Times* portrayed "being a martyr to the 'cause' of the Scottsboro boys" as "more profitable than plying the trade she once did in Huntsville."[100]

In spite of the communist invective aimed a portraying him as a mindless bigot, Judge Horton began to have doubts about the verdict shortly after the second trial ended. "The conclusion," Horton eventually wrote, "becomes clearer and clearer that this woman was not forced into intercourse with all of these Negroes upon that train, but that her condition was clearly due to the intercourse that she had had on the nights previous to this time."[101] Horton then set the judgment of the jury aside and ordered a new trial, a move which exposed him to invective from the other end of the political spectrum. The same judge who had been faulted for being a lyncher in sheep's clothing was now accused of being too lenient and "allowing that Jew lawyer who represented the defendants to say and do what he pleased."[102] By ordering a new trial, Horton was guilty of "putting wicked thoughts in the minds of lawless Negro men and greatly increasing the danger to the white women of Alabama."[103]

By ordering a new trial on June 22, 1933, Horton put an end to his own legal career. He was defeated in the May 1934 primary, but even before that happened, the third trial had been taken out his hands and transferred to the courtroom of William Washington Callahan, a befreckled septuagenarian who seemed like central casting's idea of what a hanging judge from the South ought to be.

Oblivious to the effect his tirade against the South as a bunch of frog-eyed tobacco chewing cretins would have on any possible jury, Leibowitz returned for an encore performance. Equally oblivious to how their heavy-handed interference with witnesses had convinced the jury to hand down a guilty verdict, the ILD decided to make the same mistake twice by bribing the trial's other main witness; only this time they were caught red-handed.

In June 1934, when Joseph Brodsky heard from J. T. Pearson that Victoria Price was willing to change her testimony if the price were right, he contacted a New York attorney by the name of Samuel Shriftman who was associated with the ILD and operated under the name of Daniel Swift. Schriftman/Swift spent the summer of 1934 working out a deal with Pearson, who in August offered Price $500 if she would change her testimony. When Pearson increased the figure to $1000 in September, Price told Pearson he had a deal. What she didn't tell Pearson is that she had also gone to the Huntsville police, who encouraged her to "play along with the deal."[104]

On October 1, Price and Pearson set off by car to Nashville, where they were scheduled to meet with Shriftman and Sol Kone, another associate of Brodsky, who had arrived at a downtown hotel with a briefcase containing $1,500 in one dollar bills. As soon as Pearson and Price passed the Huntsville city limits, their car was pulled over, and Pearson was arrested. At the same time, Nashville policed arrested the two New Yorkers and confiscated the "Jew money" they had brought with them to buy justice, as Wade Wright had warned, in the state of Alabama.

Shortly after the arrest of Schriftman and Kone, another lawyer by the name of Frank Scheiner arrived from New York city and posted a bond of $2,000 for each man after they were bound over to the Madison County grand jury. "After gaining their release on bond," Crenshaw/Miller write, "Shriftman and Kone left the state and have never returned. Their bonds were declared forfeited."[105]

What followed was an orgy of mutual recrimination in a relationship that was already showing severe strain. In the wake of his diatribe in the *Tribune*, the Communists had attacked Leibowitz for "condemning the Southern masses indiscriminately as morons, lantern-jawed, etc. etc."[106] Leibowitz heard about the arrests shortly after noon on October 1 and was on the phone immediately demanding an explanation from Brodsky, who explained that the ILD had been negotiating with Price for four months. Brodsky tried to calm Leibowitz down, but by the end of the day he was pouring his heart out to the NAACP, claiming that the ILD had wrecked his case from the beginning. Leibowitz blamed the Ruby Bates debacle on the ILD, claiming that "He had warned Patterson and Brodsky not to bring Ruby to New York because of the inevitable Southern reaction."[107] Leibowitz's reaction prompted many to wonder whether he was lying or whether he had no control over the case. Many Southerners felt that Leibowitz was guilty of protesting too much. Bishop William G. McDowell claimed that Leibowitz's "Public denunciation of the ILD was [a] stage play to save his face when they were caught trying to bribe Victoria Price...."[108] McDowell felt that Leibowitz "knew all along the ILD practices he denounced, and that he would like to recover his prestige by putting on another show at Decatur, no matter who pays the bills."[109]

On October 3, Leibowitz announced that he was withdrawing from the case "unless all Communists are removed from the defense."[110] One day later the ILD fired Leibowitz citing his lack of experience in appeals trials as the reason. On October 8, the *Daily Worker* escalated the conflict by claiming that Leibowitz had joined the "Alabama lynch rulers" in spreading "lying stories of attempts to bribe Victoria Price and other slanders."[111]

What followed was the judicial version of musical chairs as the NAACP and the ILD competed for the privilege of representing the Scottsboro Boys, who in turn played one set of lawyers against the other until no one knew who represented whom. On October 16 the Washington Merry-Go-Round picked up the story:

> Northern defenders of he Negro are quietly looking for a good liberal Southern democrat with an Anglo-Saxon name to take over the defense of the seven Negroes in the Scottsboro case. Their defenders, tired of supporting lawyers with Communist affiliation or foreign names, have made up their minds to get someone with the standing of John W. Davis....What has brought this decision? Is it the arrest of two defense lawyers for alleged attempted bribery of Victoria Price, a white woman who accuses the seven Negroes? The two lawyers are supposed

to be affiliated with the Communist party which unquestionably has used the Scottsboro case for its own ends.[112]

On February 15, 1935, the United States Supreme Court heard arguments in the Patterson and Norris cases. Six weeks later the Supreme Court in *Norris vs. Alabama* overturned the convictions of Norris and Patterson. Leibowitz claimed to be "thrilled beyond words"[113] by the decision, but when Haywood Patterson's fourth trial began in January, 1936, in Judge Callahan's courtroom, Leibowitz took a back seat to a local, less "Russianized" attorney by the name of Charles Watts.

In December of 1936, while Patterson's appeal was still pending and the other eight blacks awaited their trials, Thomas Knight met secretly with Samuel Leibowitz in New York to discuss a compromise. Knight told Leibowitz that the cases were draining Alabama financially and politically, and that he himself was sick of it all. He offered to drop the prosecutions of three, and give the others no more than ten years for either rape or assault.

Finally, in 1937, in a verdict that satisfied no one, four of the defendants were acquitted on the same evidence that had convicted the other four, leaving Alabama, as one wag pointed out, "in the "anomalous position of providing only 50 percent protection for the 'flower of Southern womanhood.'"[114]

In what had become a Southern ritual by now, the Scottsboro boys followed in the footsteps of Ruby Bates and traveled to New York City, where they were met by Thomas S. Harten, a Negro minister from Brooklyn who offered to become their "manager." One of their first stops in New York was the office of Samuel Leibowitz whom they attempted to shake down for money after they accused him of making millions at their expense.

Then two weeks later, the four freed Scottsboro Boys appeared on the stage of the Apollo Theater along with "a cast of Fifty Fascinating Females."[115] From 1913 until World War II, the Jews who owned the Apollo Theater had used it as a venue to promote sepia thrills to white audiences. Now Sidney S. Cohen, the man who opened the Apollo to black audiences in 1934, could add social commentary to his All-Girl Review. The Scottsboro Boys, Cohen's handbill opined, had become "the symbol of a struggle for enlightenment and human brotherhood which will go on and on until it is won!"[116] Unfortunately, neither Enlightenment and human brotherhood nor Fifty Fascinating Females could earn any money for the Scottsboro Boys, who were in debt after their first week of appearances.

In 1938, a pardon for all of the Scottsboro Boys left in Alabama seemed all but assured. Governor Bibb Graves was anxious to end the whole Scottsboro episode before he left office, and told Scottsboro Defense Committee head Allan Chalmers that the five would be released after he had his traditional pre-pardon interviews with each in his office. The interviews, however, could hardly have gone worse. First, Haywood Patterson was found to be carrying a knife when he was searched on his way to the interview. Patterson claimed he always carried a knife for protection, but authorities assumed the worst. Second, a presumably brain-damaged

Ozie Powell refused to answer Graves' questions, saying "I don't want to say nothing to you."[117] Third, according to Graves' account, Clarence Norris threatened to kill Haywood Patterson, with whom he had been feuding bitterly, after his release. Finally, none of the Scottsboro Boys admitted any knowledge or guilt concerning a rape aboard the Chattanooga to Memphis freighttrain—a rape that Graves still believed occurred. Consequently, Graves left office without issuing the pardons.

In 1948, Haywood Patterson escaped from the work gang he had been assigned to and headed north. The FBI finally caught up with Patterson on December 13, 1950 when he entered a bar in Detroit, Michigan, to sell copies of his newly released "autobiography" written with (or by) Earl Conrad with the assistance of the Communist Party. When Michigan's Governor G. Mennen Williams refused to sign extradition papers, Alabama authorities announced that they would terminate all efforts to have him returned to the state.

In criticizing the Jews' attempt to colonize the Negro mind via their control of the Communist Party, Harold Cruse cited Karl Marx's line in *Zur Judenfrage*, "What right, therefore, has he to demand of others the abdication of their religion?"[118] The line was especially applicable to the Communists' dealings with the Scottsboro Boys. Sidney Cohen's tawdry attempt at the Apollo Theater to capitalize financially on the Scottsboro Boys, paled in comparison to the Communist Party's attempt to turn Haywood Patterson into a model atheist.

According to the account he gave in his autobiography, Patterson "began to lose confidence in God" by the time of the third trial, largely because "the more talk I heard about God the more I kept seeing the freckles on the face of old Judge Callahan."[119] It was the old argument of evil. "Three times I was sentenced to die for something I never did. What was the Lord doing about it. Nothing."[120] Unlike God, the ILD lawyers brought Patterson and the other defendants "pops and candy and gave them to us boys in the visiting room." Patterson noticed that the lawyers "were Jewish," but that "was okay with me," because "I worked for Jews in Chattanooga." The Jews told Patterson and the other Scottsboro Boys that "the people were up in arms over our case in New York and if they had our say-so they would like to appeal our case."[121] Unnamed guards in the prison warned Patterson that the support of New York Jews was the main reason he had been convicted in the first place and the main reason why he could not get out of jail on appeal. "You boys would be free if you kept the New York sons-of-bitches out of the case. You'd be free,"[122] Patterson was told. But all that Patterson can conclude is "I saw how bitter they were about outsiders pressing our case."[123]

Patterson's association with Jewish Communists from New York City eventually undermined his faith in Christ, and the autobiography he wrote with their help was a calculated attempt to spread atheism among the Black Belt Negroes. The strategy was hardly new. The voodoo priests who collaborated with Toussaint L'Overture in Haiti had urged the slaves there to throw away their crucifixes. German Jews like Ottilie Assing tried the same thing with more intellectually sophisticated weapons. Her greatest achievement was introducing Frederick Douglass to the writings of Ludwig Feuerbach and turning him into an atheist. By the time that the thinking of Karl Marx began to dominate the revolutionary movement, atheism and revolution were two sides of the same coin. Haywood Patterson's autobiography simply transposed this thought into the language and culture of the Black Belt in the South:

> I read into the bible long after I began to lose confidence in it. I saw many things there, they contradicted themselves.... But the Lord never came there. Nothing but his pictures on the walls.... I saw guys pray and cry all hours of the night. What they prayed for they never got.... When you are drowning in the death row, the Bible is the straw you grab.... Just bang their backsides with a rod in one hand and flog their brains with the Bible in the other and say, "Now just you mind that white man and do like he say. You get along with him then."[124]

Christianity, while not antagonistic to ethnos, had undermined the notion of a racially based chosen people from the time of St. John's gospel, when Jesus rejected the Jews' claim that they were "the seed of Abraham." The simple fact of the matter is that both blacks and whites in the South, in spite of all of the racial antagonism that divided them, did share a culture that was fundamentally Christian and which promoted cooperation on a local level, as during the rape crisis that followed the Scottsboro trials. This localized form of Christianity always threatened to undermine the racial antagonism that the Communists wanted to turn into revolution and class warfare. Like Ruby Bates, who learned to fear the "ruling class," Patterson had learned at the hands of his Communist tutors that religion was the opiate of the Masses.

> Most of all I saw the white man wanted a black man to get down on his knees and be a pray-man. They just loved that. Then you were their "nigger." That alone taught me it couldn't be such a good thing for black folks to be so fetched up in all that Bible stuff."[125]

When his mother died in 1937, Patterson decided that he had had enough religion: "It was then I threw over religion altogether... for a couple of years now a knife had meant more to me than religion. I had faith in my knife. It saved me many times."[126]

Neither Patterson nor Conrad intended it that way, but Patterson's autobiography provided corroboration for Crenshaw and Miller, whose book, *Scottsboro: The Firebrand of Communism*, "depicted the case as a communist plot to foment revolution in Alabama."[127] The quote is from Carter, who dismisses the Crenshaw/Miller book as "intellectually dishonest" because the authors "stacked the evidence in Victoria Price's favor."[128]

As we have already indicated, Crenshaw/Miller maintained that Price's moral stature was irrelevant to the case, when it clearly was not. But the fact that they found themselves imprisoned by the South's sexual/racial code does not change the fact that Crenshaw/Miller were right in seeing the Scottboro case as "a communist plot to foment revolution in Alabama"[129] and another link in the chain of revolutionary, largely Jewish organizations that spent the better part of the 20th century trying to wean the Negro from Christ and turn him into a revolutionary.

Once it appeared in 1950, Haywood Patterson's autobiography provided independent corroboration of Crenshaw/Miller's thesis when they wrote in 1936 that "The Communist party has seized upon this case for only one reason—to stir up race antagonism in the Black Belt of the South."[130] Crenshaw/Miller cited as proof ILD literature which claimed that "With the Scottsboro case as a spearhead we have been able to penetrate broad masses of the Negro people and to extend our influence widely among them.... we have been able to organize more than 6,000 Negro share croppers and a few hundred whites."[131] Carter claims that information technology, in particular

> the pervasive sounds and images of radio and television have destroyed the physical and intellectual environment that made the Scottsboro case so chillingly representative of southern race relations. Racism and parochialism remain... but the rural and small town island community that existed in the 1930s . . has drastically shrunk.[132]

—without understanding that the "small town island community" might have solved its own problems on a local basis without the help of television or communist agitators. Crenshaw/Miller claim that the Tuskegee Institute "has remained aloof from the Scottsboro case throughout its spectacular history."[133] Whatever *modus vivendi* that had been attained was swept away by the Communists' deliberate attempt to foment racial antagonism and revolution: "With one fell swoop, Communism shattered a tranquility it had taken the black man's intellectual leadership half a century to achieve."[134]

It wasn't just the Communists who ensured that the South would be deprived of the opportunity to work out its own problems. The NAACP, the ILD's bitter antagonist in the Scottsboro Boys trials, used W.E. B Du Bois to destroy the influence of Booker T. Washington, because Washington was insufficiently revolutionary in his orientation. Anyone willing to work together over the racial barriers on a local level was dismissed as an Uncle Tom by the New York Jews, and their advocates in the sympathetic eastern press, who more and more got to determine the terms of the racial debate. Indeed, the conflict between the NAACP and the ILD was a debate between two largely Jewish organizations over the best way to spread revolution in the South. The fact that more people got lynched because of the southern perception of "outside influence" was seen by moderates like those in the NAACP as unfortunate collateral damage and by the radicals in the Communist Party as a positive benefit in radicalizing the Negro population. As Lenin once said, things have to get worse before they get better, and Crenshaw/Miller recognized that the Scottsboro Boys were the first victims of the implementation of that strategy. "Are the communists and their sympathizers even remotely interested in securing justice for the nine Negro defendants, or are they using them merely as tools to create animosity between the white and black races?"[135]

The communists succeeded as well in exacerbating the antagonism between the North and the South, widening "a breach between the North and the South that had been slowly vanishing since Reconstruction days."[136] Friedman claims that "the civil rights interests of Jews and blacks in the 1920s and 1930s were virtually identical."[137] Restating the same thesis in more modest form, Friedman adds that "That Jews [who] also benefited from Marshall's civil right litigation did not minimize its usefulness for blacks."[138] But in stating his case this way, Friedman ignores the fact that when Jewish agitators came to the South to promote revolution it was the blacks living there who got lynched as a result of their actions. Conversely, when the Jews Schriftman and Kone got caught trying to bribe Victoria Price, they did not have to hang around to face the consequences of their actions. After their arrest, they simply jumped bail and returned to New York City knowing that the North had a long history of thwarting extradition requests whenever the case involved the race question. Friedman claims that the Black-Jewish Alliance collapsed in the 1960s, but in so doing he ignores the fact that this feeling of resentment was growing around the time of the Scottsboro Boys trial, when

> Many Negroes felt—as they had in 1931- that once again the ILD was "polishing up the electric chair" for the Scottsboro boys by insisting on linking their case with the overall program of the Communist Party.[139]

The tensions which led to the collapse of the Black-Jewish Alliance were already evident in the '30s, which Friedman attempts to portray as the golden age of their mutual collaboration. As some indication of the mounting tensions, W. E. B Du Bois resigned from the board of the NAACP in 1934. Cruse claims that economics was the main reason. Du Bois felt that the NAACP leadership "recoiled from any consideration of the economic plight of the world or any change in the organization of industry."[140] But Jewish paternalism played a role as well. Du Bois, who was planning to visit Germany in 1935, reacted testily to Franz Boas's suggestion that he was going to be hornswaggled by being treated to the Nazi version of the Potemkin Village.[141]

According to Harold Cruse, the Black-Jewish Alliance ended over 30 years before Murray Friedman said it did. It ended on March 19, 1935 when a young Puerto Rican was caught stealing a ten-cent penknife from a Jewish owned store on 125th St. in Harlem. Before long, black mobs began a rampage of destruction that lasted for days. Mayor Fiorella LaGuardia, who was half-Jewish, went out of his way to deny that Jewish stores had been singled out, but, as Cruse adds, "it was clear that they had."[142] Irving Horowitz, who lived in Harlem during the riots of 1935 claims that "in public discourse this was all viewed as a black-white confrontation; but those of us who lived through the events of the Harlem riots knew better."[143] The riots were a black attack on Jews that resulted from years of pent up resentment.

The Harlem riots presented Jews and Communists with a conundrum which they could not solve. From the point of view of class warfare, the Communists should have praised the Negroes for engaging in what looked like the long-awaited black insurrection, but that would have meant turning their back on their fellow Jews. The NAACP had no qualms about condemning the riots, but they, like their counterparts in the 1960s, had no way of explaining why this insurrection took place in the North, where the Negro had comparatively more freedom. The NAACP, moreover, did not want to deal with economic issues, especially when there was a Jewish subtext to those economic issues as was the case in Harlem.

Like the situation in the South, which might have been solved on the local level if the antagonists had been left alone to work out their differences, the situation in Harlem was largely a product of the interaction between Jews and Blacks on a local level. The Negroes of Harlem were not oppressed by Jim Crow laws; they were tired of being cheated by Jewish merchants.

In his memoir about growing up as the son of a Jewish hardware store owner in Harlem, Irving Louis Horowitz described the annual ritual of cheating the *shvartzes* when they came into his father's store to get their Christmas tree bulbs tested. "Christmas," Horowitz tells us, was "a special occasion on which my father wreaked his own revenge on Christendom"[144] by cheating black Christians. "The scam," Horowitz continued,

> went like this: the unsuspecting customer would bring in all light bulbs for testing. Each bulb would be placed against the side of the bulb tester rather than against the filament that would light up the bulb. The trick was easily learned and passed on to my mother, my sister, and me. I became a master at this special bulb test. When the same bulbs were retested after the customer left, they almost always were found to be perfect, or least good enough for resale. My father placed them into inventory and sold them as new. The special bulbs were resold countless times each season. Hence, it was no accident that the volume of December bulb sales probably surpassed that of any other month. December profits also showed remarkably uncharacteristic good health. Twas, indeed, the season to be merry.[145]

Harold Cruse never mentions whether he had his Christmas bulbs tested by the Horowitz family. The prospect seems unlikely because by the 1930s, Cruse had committed himself to the Communist cause. Cruse's resentment goes deeper than the few cents here and there which the Jewish merchants gouged out of their black clientele. He felt that the Jews stole the Negro cultural heritage by promoting their form of Jazz as the authentic form and freezing Negroes like Cruse, who spent the '50s trying unsuccessfully to get his musicals produced on Broadway, out of the cultural picture. As a Jew growing up in Harlem, who attended Jazz concerts at the Apollo Theater with his sister, Horowitz was close enough to the situation to see the resentment it caused in people like Cruse:

> Jewish musicians—Goodman, Gershwin, Mezzrow, and Whiteman, among others—not only played the music, but also served as critics and interpreters. In a racially controlled pre-War America, it was the Jew who popularized black life, transforming a folk tradition into an art mode.... Although the close proximity of blacks and Jews in Harlem allowed for a rich cross-fertilization of cultures it

also engendered feelings of rivalry and resentment.... It seemed that the gain and fame of their culture went to the accursed Jewish cultural middleman, while the purity of their performance remained undersupported and undernourished.[146]

The Jews, of course, had worries of their own, seeing "this flirtation with black culture as nothing short of a desecration of Jewish life—an early warning signal that sexuality would displace marriage and undiluted individual expression would destroy family solidarity."[147]

In Harlem Jews and Negroes shared the bitter taste of poverty and little else. Horowitz describes his father as "an anti-Jewish Jew" living "in a world of pious Christian blacks."[148] His father's religion was Communism, something Horowitz described as "a religion without Christ" and "a church without crucifix" which allowed him to live "in the imaginary world of Jewish Bundism and Russian Bolshevism."[149] The irony of course is that on the practical level Horowitz *pere* had to live the life of the petty Calvinist capitalist which Marx had criticized in his essay *Zur Judenfrage*. Horowitz was a loser simply by the fact that he came from Harlem: "The Jews of Harlem, if my extended family was any barometer, were viewed as dregs—social scourges and economic failures—simply by virtue of the fact that they remained.... Harlem was the settlement village for Jews completely without money."[150]

But as the century progressed and Jews, unlike blacks, were able to move out of Harlem, the resentment began to build. Then all of the submerged tension erupted in the Harlem riots of 1935, and the Jewish-black antagonism that the Jews at organizations like the NAACP and the AJC had been trying to ignore was suddenly out in the open:

> Shopkeepers were the visible enemies. For black militants, they were the devil whites, for other blacks, Jews ascendant or ghetto profiteers. The "merchant of Venice" had come to Harlem. The chemistry was rife for rioting. World War II brought an end to depression—everywhere but in Harlem, or so it seemed.... Chain stores left the area, small shopkeepers followed, and servicepersons—who fixed window panes and repaired locks—vanished. The Harlem community was left in charge of itself. It was a self that turned out to be an empty shell, at least for the duration of the war.[151]

The riots, followed by the war, which provided Horowitz's father with a job at the Brooklyn Navy Yard as a third class mechanic's apprentice, meant that it was time to leave. "We surveyed the wreckage," Horowitz writes, "and with a few tears my father simply announced, 'It's over. We move on now.'"[152] More than anything the riots showed that the so-called Black-Jewish Alliance was largely a fiction in the collective mind of the organizations which promoted it. Those organizations were largely Jewish and they promoted the alliance as a way of securing Jewish interests, but ultimately there was no alliance because ultimately where blacks and Jews lived together there was no community. Unlike the South, Jews and blacks in the North simply lived near each other in the same neighborhood for a number of years "without community, without shared affection, without love."[153]

Cruse feels that "the gross imbalance between the comparative economic status of blacks and Jews" is what nullified the Black-Jewish Alliance:

> It was precisely over the issue of economics... that the Black-Jewish Alliance collapsed in 1935 and entered a stage of disintegration leading to the 1960 era with its rise in vocal black anti-Semitism. In 1935 the Harlem racial uprising directed at white economic exploitation, white shopkeepers, white landlords and white organized crime was also directed at Jewish shopkeepers, businessmen and landlords. From the end of World War I to 1930, the NAACP was unwilling to reorient its program to include the all-important issue of economic organization.[154]

The Jews, according to Cruse, used the civil rights movement to absolve themselves from the charges that the Jew was a "greedy clannish, miser, always out for himself."[155] The Harlem uprising, according to Cruse, was able to shatter "the flimsy premises on which the Black-Jewish Alliance had rested" because Jews had undermined by their behavior and their inability to face up to any negative criticism. No matter how much, the story of Horowitz's father repeated itself in the lives of ordinary blacks, the Jews could control the press which meant that in the final analysis they could "prove themselves generous, selfless, tolerant, and humanitarian."[156]

Marcus Garvey died in England on June 10, 1940, and with him died, at least for the time being, the idea of black nationalism. During the '40s, Harlem was awash in conflicting ideological currents. Communism went into decline after 1946 to be replaced by the ascendency of the integrationism of the NAACP, but that too led to resentment. "The fact remains," as Cruse points out, that Jews in organizations like the NAACP remained "pro-integrationist for Negroes and anti-assimilationist for Jews."[157] Since ethnicity in America, according to Cruse's reading of the theory known as the triple melting pot, is synonymous with religion, integration for the Negro meant that he would remain an ethnic anomaly cut off from any grouping which could give him real political, economic or cultural power. When he ponders the insistence of Jewish sociologists like Nathan Glazer that "Negroes be integrated as fast as possible and by any means," Cruse discerns no benevolence, not even misguided benevolence, but rather the fact that "today Negroes truly have a Jewish problem."[158] The main problem is that "As a Jew, Nathan Glazer could be said to be most magnanimously free with other people's ethnicity."[159] As Communism waned and Zionism took its place as the dominant vehicle of Jewish Messianic politics in the latter part of the 20th century, the suspicion would grow that the Jews were interested in integration for every group but itself. The corollary to that belief was that Jewish organizations could attack both "black" and "white" nationalists groups as racist, at the same time that Israel promoted the same sort of "apartheid." This double standard was covered over during the '50s and '60s by the successes of the civil rights movement, but it would reassert itself with a vengeance by the time the 20th century came to a close.

The Scottsboro Boys

Chapter Twenty-One

Revolutionary Music in the 1930s

I n 1915 Elizabeth Gurley Flynn wrote in *Solidarity* that Joe Hill, then in prison, "writes songs that sing, that lilt and laugh and sparkle, that kindle the fires of revolt in the most crushed spirit and quicken the desire for a fuller life in the most humble slave ... He has crystallized the organization's {IWW} spirit into imperishable forms, songs of the people—folk songs."[1]

Thus began the semantic permutation of the word "folk" from its original meaning into its opposite. It comes from the German word *Volk*, which means race, nation, or *ethnos*. In lectures in 1932 at Bryn Mawr, collected under the title *National Music*, Ralph Vaughan Williams claimed "conditions in America do not admit of folk-songs because there is no peasant class to make and sing them."[2] But the former peasants in Europe became workers after they arrived in America. In America in 1915, the workers were unhappy enough to form a significant social movement. Sometimes they even sang about their troubles, as their forebears had in Europe, often to the same melodies. Folk music is another word for what Vaughan Williams would call national music, but to Socialists and Communists it became the "music of the people." And since the term "worker" and "people" were synonymous for the Left, that meant music for the revolution:

> Song collections devoted to socialism and the cause of the proletariat soon made their appearance, among the earliest in English being Chants of Labour (London 1888) ... . Lenin in exile sought contact with the proletariat by occasionally venturing out to the cafes and theaters of suburban Paris to listen to revolutionary songs. As the Bolsheviks moved toward national power, *Pravda* printed "The Internationale" in its first issue. In the sixth issue, March 11, 1917, there appeared an article in bold type entitled "Revolutionary Songs" saying "we call [to] the attention of the comrades, that it is desirable to organize collective singing and rehearsals of choral performances of revolutionary songs."[3]

In the '30s, when Earl Robinson, "perhaps the most successful composer of mass music of the American Left,"[4] wrote his most famous song, "The Ballad of Joe Hill," the Left was heavily involved in the labor movement. So proletarian bards of the '30s could sing, "where workingmen defend their rights, it's there you'll find Joe Hill." When Bob Dylan started writing songs, the Left was dropping the banner of the working man and picking up the standard of sexual liberation instead. That meant that a new kind of music was necessary. Joan Baez singing "I dreamed I saw Joe Hill last night" at a Dionysian festival like Woodstock was only a little less incongruous than having the warm-up band at a Rolling Stones concert sing Palestrina.

What was revolutionary music? "The Internationale" is revolutionary even if you change the words and use it to sell Subaru. Conversely, the melody for "Wildwood Flower" is not revolutionary, even if Woody Guthrie turned it into a popular front song. Given this distinction, the first revolutionary songs weren't based on revolutionary music. Chicago, "the publishing center for revolutionary music prior to 1920," gave us *Socialist Songs with Music* in 1901, followed eight years later by IWW Songs, known as "The Little Red Songbook."[5] The Wobblies, as a result of their songbooks, were known for effective use of music as propaganda, but neither the Wobblies nor Joe Hill wrote what could be termed "revolutionary music." Both wrote revolutionary lyrics and set them to traditional tunes.

The Communists of the Third Period felt world revolution was imminent. In July 1928 Nicolai Bukharin announced "All artistic expression was to be politicized" and art was to be used "as a weapon," as agit-prop in a worldwide upheaval.[6] "Artists and bureaucrats were expected to root out any bourgeois influence in workers' cultural media."[7] At this point in time, it seemed pretty clear that America's ethnic music was not revolutionary. Henry Ford, after all, one of America's premier capitalists, was also one of America's premier promoters of traditional music. Fiddlers in the folk tradition often found employment at Henry Ford's Dearborn estate, where he put on elaborate evenings of American folk dancing. One year before Bukharin's announcement, Carl Sandburg brought out his best selling folk song collection, and John Jacob Niles gave the first formal folk song recital to a college audience at Princeton. No revolutionary upheaval followed. Indeed, the Reusses claim the IWW songbooks recruited more revolutionaries to folk music than ethnics to revolution. As a result, "the American communist movement in its first decade (1919-1928) established no firm position, favorable or otherwise, on folklore."[8]

During the Third Period, the revolutionary chorus was the preferred vehicle for communist musical propaganda. The appeal to the American worker was limited, however, because "these choruses were located entirely within the immigrant language groups, most East European, which made up the majority of the movement's early membership."[9] In other words, the Revolutionary Chorus was largely a Jewish phenomenon. The best known revolutionary chorus was the Jewish Freiheit Gesang Ferein, the "Freedom Singers' Club," founded in 1923 under Jacob Schaefer. According to the *Daily Worker* in 1934, revolutionary choruses were "one of the most popular mediums for reaching the masses" because Americans sang in church choirs, a medium the capitalist class used for "lulling the workers."[37] The revolutionary movement, though, "uses it for rousing the workers against [their] oppressors."[10]

The choral music of the Freiheit Gesang Ferein may have been genuinely revolutionary, but its appeal was limited because the music was technically difficult to perform without rehearsal, but more importantly, because the Freiheit singers sang in Yiddish. "The Freiheit Gesang Ferein does valuable work," the *Daily*

Worker informed readers, "but we have so many comrades who do not happen to be born Jews and they simply do not understand Yiddish"[11] The writer concluded it would be perhaps impossible for the workers' movement to grow "if it cannot express itself in song,"[12] meaning, of course, in English.

Beginning in 1925, the Communist Party reached beyond its Jewish base to native-born American workers. In June, 1931, members of the Communist Party established the Workers Music League, "to try to formulate a systematic theoretical approach to proletarian music."[13] In February 1932, the Composers Collective was founded to produce and perform revolutionary compositions and to formulate guidelines on what constituted proletarian music. Just about everyone in the Collective was a serious musician, including Charles Seeger, who had studied at Harvard, conducted the Cologne Symphony in his twenties and became the youngest professor (of music) in the history of the University of California at Berkeley. It also included Freiheit Gesang Ferein choral director Jacob Schaefer, George Antheil, and Aaron Copland, who had won a commission to put a May Day poem to music in the '30s. Even in its earliest days, the Composers Collective had trouble linking the music it liked to the taste and abilities of the proletarian masses. When asked by Charles Seeger whether musically untrained workers could sing Copland's prize-winning melody to Alfred Hayes's poem "Into the Streets May first," Copland admitted they probably could not.

The composers' politics were clear. "Music is propaganda—always propaganda and of the most powerful sort," wrote Charles Seeger, under his pseudonym Carl Sands. "The special task of the Workers' Music League is the development of music as a weapon in the class struggle."[14] Workers' music was to be "national in form, revolutionary in content."[15] But that was the problem. Because of their musical sophistication, the Composers Collective rightly felt that folk music wasn't revolutionary. The American "folk" never took to revolutionary music, which "still consisted of the revolutionary choral and orchestral units of the foreign-language groups."[16] Charles Seeger expressed the dilemma in personal terms: Seeger gave up composition "because I couldn't approve of the music I liked, and I couldn't like the music that I approved, and I couldn't make either one of them connect in any way with the social situation I found."[17]

The conflict between revolutionary music which was not popular and popular music which was not revolutionary is epitomized by Hanns Eisler, a communist composer who studied under Arnold Schoenberg and arrived in America in 1933. Eisler was born in Liepzig in 1898, but after World War I, he moved to Austria to learn the 12-tone method, which Schoenberg had appropriated from Josef Matthias Hauer. Eisler moved to Berlin in the '20s, where he dedicated himself with equal fervor to revolutionary music, composing left-wing cabaret hits like "Comintern" and "In praise of Learning," which the Reuses say were "indisputably successful" because "in some cases they were actually being sung by workers."[18]

Eisler hated folk music—especially when dragooned into the revolutionary struggle through affixation to revolutionary texts—calling it "a badge of servitude from pre-Revolutionary times."[19] In the 1940s, Eisler was still annoyed at Alan Lomax for creating the folk music movement and "for foisting those 'damn songs' on the working class."[20] More to Eisler's liking were the revolutionary choral pieces of Charles Seeger whose lyrics

> We are fighting with a host of foes, we do not fear guns or cannon.
> Fascist promises cannot fool us; we will fight them to a finish.
> Comrade, victory is leading you, to the battle gladly marching
> Mount the Barricades; Mount the Barricades ; for the workers' cause
> Carry on the fight for freedom.[21]

were set to a melody in what Dunaway calls the "Russian-sounding" key of F-minor, to a "darkened and dissonant piano accompaniment marked: 'relentlessly.'"[22] Eisler and Sands' compositions were undeniably revolutionary, but "had few real roots in American culture."[23] The Composers Collective understood the unrevolutionary nature of native American music, but proposed no alternative. "Not all folk tunes are suitable to the revolutionary movement," Charles Seeger wrote in 1934 in the *Daily Worker*. "Many of them are complacent, melancholy, defeatist—originally intended to make slaves endure their lot—pretty but not the stuff for a militant proletariat to feed upon."[24] Composers Collective director Henry Cowel said the same thing: "One of the great faults in the field of workers music has been that of combining revolutionary lyrics with traditional music—music which can by no means be termed revolutionary."[25] Both men grudgingly conceded a minor role for revolutionary parodies of American folk tunes: "There is still some room for occasional parodies of old songs such as 'Pie in the Sky' and 'Soup,' but not for many of them."[26]

The musicologists were right. The revolutionary lyrics of the new proletarian folk song contradicted the simple folk melodies upon which they were based. Worse still, the folk melodies subverted the revolutionary intent of the lyrics, much as the Dionysian rock and roll of Christian Rock (or Rap) would subvert the intentions of the well-meaning but musically illiterate Christian songsters of a later generation. But the Collective had no alternative that was as popular as the music they criticized or as accessible to the audience they wanted to reach.

During the 1930s, Jewish communists went to Kentucky and North Carolina to organize coal miners and textile workers, returning to New York City with Appalachian music on their minds. Often they would return with the Appalachian musicians too. In 1932 the Worker's Music League published the *Red Song Book*, featuring "Poor Miner's Farewell" by Aunt Molly Jackson, who went to New York in 1933 to attend meetings of the Composers Collective and teach them how to write her kind of song. The Composers were not impressed. The Worker Musician criticized the *Red Song Book* for "arrested development" and attributed the songs' poor quality to "the exploitation of the coal barons."[27] Seeger, embarrassed by the cold reception Aunt Molly received, told her, "Molly, they don't understand you.

But I know some young people who will want to learn your songs."[28] Seeger was referring to his son, Pete, who would take a leadership role in a new revolutionary music.

The Composers Collective may not have been impressed with Aunt Molly's music, but the communists recognized "indigenous creations were a lot more effective in recruiting and agitating the local populace than were doctrinaire slogans and pamphlets written by urban party leaders," i.e., by Jews from New York City.[29] More pragmatic CP thinkers, like Mike Gold, saw in the music of the south the proletarian music the composers had sought vainly in the 1920s. As a result, cultural symbiosis began to occur. The Jews who went to West Virginia to sing "Solidarity Forever" with the miners in 1931 returned singing "The Death of Mother Jones" at meetings in New York city; "eventually, repeated encounters with living folk cultures in the US helped reshape urban, left-wing music."[30] When Aunt Molly Jackson came north to escape being killed by the mining company goons and to testify before the Dreiser Committee in December 1931, she exposed the urban Communists to songs like "We Shall not be Moved," first sung at a 1931 West Virginia Miners' Union strike. The music, composed to a verse from the book of Jeremiah, got put into harness to pull communist propaganda, with dubious results. Whether the music was more effective in radicalizing the miners of America or Americanizing the country's radical Jews remained to be seen.

At around the same time, Mike Gold (nee Granich) author of *Jews Without Money*, wrote a complaint that might be titled "Why Communists Can't Sing." "The Wobblies knew how [to sing]," Gold wrote, "but we have still to develop a Communist Joe Hill."[31] Gold's son, Carl Granich, would become a mover in the '60s folk movement. When Bob Dylan showed up in Madison, Wisconsin in 1961 looking for a place to stay, he would mention Carl Granich as his entry into the Jewish revolutionary brotherhood's network of coffee houses.

A few years later, Mike Gold praised the singing of Ray and Lida Auvill, saying it had "the true ring of American balladry," which made it inappropriate as revolutionary music, according to Charles Seeger, who panned the collection for its low musical quality.[32] "For every step forward in the verse," Seeger opined, "one takes a step backward in the music."[33] This, of course, annoyed Gold as an irredeemably elitist attitude. "Really, Comrade Sands," Gold wrote responding to Seeger's pseudonymous article, "I think you have missed the point. It is sectarian and utopian to use Arnold Schoenberg or Stravinsky as a yardstick by which to measure class music.... What songs do the masses of America now sing? They sing 'Old Black Joe' and the sentimental things concocted by Tin Pan Alley. In the South they sing the old ballads. This is the reality, and to leap from that into Schoenberg seems to me a desertion of the masses.... I think the composers collective has something to learn from Ray and Lida Auville. They write catchy tunes than many American workers cans sing and like, and the words of their songs make the revolution as intimate and simple as 'Old Black Joe.'"[34]

The Communist Party creates folk music

Alan Lomax was born to folklorist John A. Lomax and Bess Brown Lomax in 1915 in Austin, Texas. In 1910 John Lomax's book *Cowboy Songs* garnered a favorable endorsement by Theodore Roosevelt, which appeared as a frontispiece and galvanized sales. Alan graduated from Choate at 15, and, after a year at the University of Texas, transferred to Harvard, where he studied under his father's longtime friend, the literary critic, George Lyman Kittredge. Alan, like his dad, was more interested in field work than sitting in a library, so after he read Nietzsche and "a widening variety of radical thinkers,"[35] Lomax *père et fils* went on a field trip to collect ethnic music after Alan's graduation in 1936. One year later, Alan was hired as director of the Archive of American Folk Song in the Library of Congress. The salary was modest, but the job allowed him to meet Charles Seeger. The job also lent credibility to his communist cultural offensive.

During summer 1934, Maxim Gorky and Andrei Zhdanov introduced the new doctrine of Socialist Realism. After Hitler's rise to power, world revolution took a back seat to "a united cultural front against world fascism."[36] That meant gaining popular support through art accessible to the masses, which meant "a return to familiar lyric and melodic forms more acceptable to the masses," which "led to an official communist upgrading of folklore as a positive creative force in the life of the people. In time this attitude would lead to the popularization and intellectual use of folk songs and traditional melodies of the people on a scale unimaginable in the previous decade."[37] Those who backed Aunt Molly Jackson and the Auvills were now in the ascendancy at the CPUSA as the ideological dogmatism of the Third Period gave way to the "American" pragmatism of the popular front. In January 1934, the *Daily Worker* praised folk music, even when not politically correct. Even Charles Seeger started to complain about the fact that the Freiheit Gesang Ferein insisted on singing in Yiddish. To fight the virulent threat of fascism, Communists needed new friends. Communists needed to Americanize. They needed singers who didn't have Yiddish accents. It was during the period of the Popular Front, that Earl Browder, CPUSA chairman, coined the phrase "communism is 20th-century Americanism," and that meant that "nearly all phases of radical life—including terminology, dress and social deportment—were revised to conform more closely to the routine existence of the average citizen."[38]

The Popular Front was a reality by summer 1935. Party Members forsook doctrinal purity in favor of collaboration with other anti-fascist groups, so folklore was no longer bourgeois decadence. The folk song was rehabilitated as a vehicle for revolutionary ferment:

> By the mid-1930s, though, left-wing organizations, influenced by members or supporters of the Communist Party, discovered intrinsic working-class values in folk song and other folklore genres. Without question, this radical interest initially grew out of the discovery that in certain regions the folk song idiom was a convenient musical method for spreading and reinforcing revolutionary ideas,

which was what agitation-propaganda, or agit-prop, departments of he commu-nist movement were working hard to accomplish.[39]

Alan Lomax implemented the changed party line by discovering the leading lights of the first generation of folk singers, Josh White, Burl Ives, Woody Guth-rie, Pete Seeger, and Leadbelly, fostering their careers by guiding them through the political eddies of Washington and New York society, "teaching them songs, socializing with them and serving as their intellectual guide" and ensuring their "unflagging commitment to left-wing ideology."[40] Lomax was the ideal promoter, content to work behind the scenes. By the 1940s, "the urban folk singers he had en-couraged and who shared his worldview were ready to make a substantial imprint on American musical life, on the left-wing cultural scene, as well as on the na-tional stage."[41] It is not an exaggeration to say that Alan Lomax created American folk music as we know it today. He certainly created it as it was known from 1940, when the radical choruses waned, until 1956, when the Lomax group of folksngers fell apart because of disillusionment with Krushchev's denunciation of Stalin and suppression of the Hungarian revolt.

American Folksinger

In envisioning the ideal American folksinger, Lomax was probably influenced by Will Geer, an actor who starred in *Let Freedom Ring*, a play about striking Southern textile workers. Geer, who ended his career by playing the grandfather in television's long-running series *The Waltons*, began performing folk music for radical audiences in the 1930s. In November 1935, he sang before striking textile workers in Paterson, New Jersey, and was then featured in a flattering article in the *Daily Worker*. By early 1936, "the groundwork had been laid for the American com-munist movement's subsequent ideological and social commitment to folk songs and traditional 'people's' culture. The varied work of such larger groups as the Almanac singers ... sprang from the void created by the clumsy gropings of radical musicians for a 'unique' class music for the proletariat in the early 1930s."[42]

Later that year, Charles Seeger took his son Peter to a folk music festival in Ashville, North Carolina, where he met Lomax. The two men hit it off immedi-ately, andLomax hired Pete as his assistant at the Library of Congress, allowing him to travel the country for the next ten years collecting American folk songs and to listen to recordings at the Library of Congress. Lomax suggested Pete take up the five-string banjo, an instrument unknown to urban audiences at that time. Seeger came from an old-line New England Puritan family, and his residual Pu-ritanism made him sympathetic to messianic political movements. "Resistance" Dunaway writes, "was part of the New England nature," which "viewed the world as a thing to be reformed, filled with evil forces to be abolished."[43] Dunaway could have said "Revolution," because Puritans were certainly revolutionaries, and Pete Seeger saw more clearly the potential for cultural revolution than did the Com-munist Party hacks who gave him tepid support.

Pete and the Popular Front were made for each other. As a native-born American, he was consumed by a vision of Americans taking music back from capitalist owners of radio stations and record companies. For Seeger, folk songs had a patriotic undercurrent; the music had been "carved from the rhythm of daily lives, the curves of the American land, the outline of its architecture, and its climate."[44] Seeger kept the flame burning until a generation of America's youth could be re-educated and emerge as a revolutionary movement. Seeger would eventually be run over by the movement he created, but his influence cannot be overestimated. As Dunaway says, an "industry" eventually "emerged from Seeger's enthusiasms."[45] He sold thousands of record albums and also educated an entire generation at Communist summer camps in the Catskills, teaching many of the most prominent performers of the folk revival of the early '60s. At a single concert, for instance, Seeger inspired both Joan Baez and Dave Guard of the Kingston Trio.

In many ways, the music was the simplest part of the revolution. More difficult was easing communist propaganda into it without offending listeners. That required creation of the persona of the folk singer, the man "of the people," which is to say, unpolished, forthright, but also not "ethnic," unlike America's industrial workers. The folksinger would wean them from ethnocentrism. Historians touch on this gingerly, claiming Lomax tried "to develop a similar working class cultural totality in the North based on rural folk idioms and content."[46] The working class culture in the North was different from the culture of the south from which Appalachian music sprang, and so a persona like the cowboy or the rambler, gambler a long way from home was necessary to make the music plausible, if possible, to northern workers.

The answer to the complicated question of how to make Italians from Brooklyn like hillbilly music was Woody Guthrie. Guthrie, who was named after Woodrow Wilson was born in Okemah, Oklahoma, the third of five children born to a. father who did well selling land in the oil boom of the '20s and a mother who was eventually carted off to a mental institution. When the boom went bust, the family broke up. Woody drifted to California, where he starred in a short-lived radio program with a woman with the stage name of Lefty Lou from Old Missou.

After the Paterson textile mill strike, Will Geer returned to California to find employment in the movies. There he met Woody Guthrie, California's singing Okie. When Geer returned to New York to play Jeeter Lester in the Broadway production of *Tobacco Road*, he urged Woody to follow. Guthrie arrived in New York City to participate in America's first major folk music production, the "Grapes of Wrath" concert to benefit the John Steinbeck Committee for California Farm Workers in March 1940. The concert was the public debut of the Alan Lomax school of folk music; virtually all whose performers—Aunt Molly Jackson, Leadbelly, Burl Ives, and Pete Seeger,—owed their careers to Lomax. The Steinbeck concert ensured Guthrie's induction into the Folksong Pantheon.

Guthrie's career then took off. After languishing as the singing Okie in California, Guthrie flourished as the left-wing bard from New York, largely because of Alan Lomax who arranged immediately for recording sessions at the Library of Congress. Then Lomax used his influence to get a recording contract with Victor Records, which produced his album of *Dust Bowl Ballads*. Woody got his own radio program as host for Model Tobacco's weekly program Pipe Smoking Time. His earnings allowed him to bring his wife and family to New York, but he did not change the bad habits he had acquired as the rambler and the gambler perpetually a long way from home. Eventually, Guthrie "got disgusted with the whole sissified and nervous rules of censorship on all of my songs and ballads, and drove off down the road across the southern states again."[47]

Soon it became apparent that the music that Woody sang brought life-style baggage along with it. Woody was avid to lead a life-style anathema to the listeners he was supposed to evangelize. Woody's tunes were not revolutionary music, but they fast became the music of the uprooted, just as the Negro music of the post-Civil War camps became the Blues and, eventually, Jazz. The Scotch Irish Ballads and dance tunes were the music of Okie rootlessness by the 1940s, and Woody Guthrie helped accomplish the transformation. His music was so at odds with the culturally normative Bing Crosby crooning of the time that a conflict became unavoidable. Either the culture would tame the music, and the failed attempt to do that was the main reason quit his radio job, or the music would change the culture, which is precisely what happened during the '60s, when the children raised on that music came of age..

Kristallnacht and America First

On November 20, 1938, Father Charles Coughlin, a Canadian-born Irish Catholic priest, now a pastor in Royal Oak, Michigan, devoted his radio show, *The Golden Hour of the Little Flower,* which reached 30 million people, to recent events in Germany, in particular the attack on Jewish businesses known as the night of shattered glass or "*Kristallnacht.*" The National Socialists orchestrated the attack in retaliation for the Jews' call for an international boycott of German goods, and now Father Coughlin, who received more mail in a week than Franklin D. Roosevelt, tried to give the Catholic perspective on an issue that both sides found equally repugnant.

An early supporter of the New Deal, Coughlin was now one of Roosevelt's most formidable domestic opponents. Coughlin would become known as "the father of hate radio," but he was an anomaly in American public life. He was a Canadian Catholic priest trying to articulate the Catholic position as an alternative to both capitalism and internationalist socialism. That involved seeing Kristallnacht and the rise of Hitler in their historical context as a reaction against the excesses of Bolshevism, a revolutionary movement that was seen as essentially Jewish. Coughlin was attacked not because he sympathized with the Nazis. He condemned their racial theories and their brutality. Coughlin was attacked because he brought up the taboo connection between Jews and Bolshevism. On November 20, Coughlin addressed the Jews directly, asking them to "be not indulgent with the irreligious, atheistic Jews and Gentiles who promote the cause of persecution in the land of the Communist; the same ones who promote the cause of atheism in America."[48] He said: "Gentiles must repudiate the excesses of Nazism. But Jews and Gentiles must repudiate the existence of Communism from which Nazism springs."[49]

Less than three years later, on September 11, 1941, Charles Lindbergh gave a speech to an America First rally in Des Moines, Iowa, in which he claimed that three groups--the Jews, the English, and the Roosevelt administration--were attempting to drag America into a war with Germany. "I am not attacking either the Jewish or the British people. Both races I admire. But I am saying that the leaders of both the British and the Jewish races, for reasons which are as understandable from their viewpoint as they are inadvisable from ours, for reasons which are not American, wish to involve us in the war."[50] Three months later, America was at war, and Lindbergh was transformed from an American hero to an anti-Semitic villain, who, like Coughlin, would be vilified for decades. To show the deep-seated Jewish animus against Lindbergh, in 2004 Philip Roth made him the villain of *The Plot Against America*, long after the America First movement had disappeared from popular consciousness. In one of his most bizarre flights of fantasy in *Plot*, Roth has character assassin and gossip columnist Walter Winchell run for president after he is driven off the air by Lindbergh's forces. His candidacy drives anti-Semites to rage, especially when he appears in Catholic parishes: "Winchell proceeded to draw an angry mob chanting 'Kike, go home!' in every single parish where he displayed his stigmata to the faithful," Roth writes.[51] Winchell, who "had become an out-and-out god and more important by far than Adonoy"[52] to Roth, would unleash "the worst and most widespread violence ... in Detroit," because Detroit was "the midwestern headquarters of the 'Radio Priest' Father Coughlin and his Jew-hating Christian Front."[53] The Christian Front actually was headed by a priest from Brooklyn, but facts are unimportant when writing what Roth termed a "false memoir."

Similarly, Roth links Coughlin with the Ku Klux Klan, but Coughlin began his shrine after the Klan burned a cross at his church in Royal Oak. The rioting Coughlin allegedly incited, according to Roth, "had begun at Winchell's first stop in Hamtramck (the residential section inhabited chiefly by auto workers and their families and said to contain the world's largest Polish population outside Warsaw)."[54] From Hamtramck, according to *Plot*, the rioting spread to "the city's biggest Jewish neighborhoods, shops were looted and widows broken, Jews trapped outdoors were set upon and beaten and kerosene-soaked crosses were ignited on the lawns of the fancy houses along Chicago Boulevard."[55] Roth has Coughlin defending the American version of *Kristalnacht*, which never happened in America, "as a reaction by the Germans against 'Jewish-inspired Communism.'"[56]

The real Father Coughlin did not defend *Kristalnacht*. He deplored it for what it was. We know this because his November 20, 1938 program was entitled "Persecutions: Jewish and Christian." Coughlin deplored violence against the innocent in terms Jews had been formulating for years. "The Trotskys make the revolution," said one rabbi, "but the Bronsteins are the ones who pay for it." The Jews who were visible paid for the excesses of the Jews who had changed their names. In a speech approved by his ordinary, Father Coughlin asked his audience "to oppose all persecution wherever it may originate."[57] Coughlin was unfortunately caught up in the collective amnesia of the 20th century. By the late '30s no one could mention what the Jews bragged about in the 1920s, namely, their association with Bolshevism. Leopold Trepper, the leader of Rote Kapelle, a Nazi resistance group, made the connection more succinctly than most, when he claimed, "I became a communist, because I am a Jew."[58]

February 1941: Founding of the Almanac Singers

In February 1941, buoyed by the Grapes of Wrath concert and the spate of gigs it generated, the Lomax singers formed the Almanac Singers. Woody Guthrie, just returned from touring the Northwest, joined Pete Seeger, Lee Hays, Millard Lampell, and John Peter Hawes to appropriate the American folk song as a vehicle for communist propaganda. The group took its name from one of Guthrie's lines: "if you want to know what the weather is going to be, you have to look in your Almanac,"[87] which Bob Dylan imitated 20 years later, "you don't need a weatherman to tell which way the wind blows." As some indication of how the times had changed, Dylan's line became the source of the name of a group of terrorists known as the Weathermen. Of the Almanac Singers, Millard Lampel said, "We think this is the first time there has ever been an organized attempt... to sing the folk songs of America. We are trying to give back to the people the songs of the workers."[88] That meant, of course, attaching agit-prop lyrics to standard folk tunes like "Billy Boy," "Jesse James," and "Liza Jane."

In March 1941 Almanacs released *Songs of John Doe*, their rendering of the Communist Party line in light of the non-aggression pact which the Soviet Union had signed with Hitler in 1939. The album was pacifist. Franklin Roosevelt and his wife were attacked as warmongering imperialists with such gusto that the album became a hit with America Firsters, much to the Almanacs' chagrin. "Oh Franklin Roosevelt," the Almanacs sang to the tune of the chorus of "Jesse James,"

> told the people how he felt
> We damned near believed what he said;
> He said, "I hate war—and so does Eleanor,
> But we won't be safe until everybody's dead.[89]

Then on June 22, 1941 Germany invaded Russia, and the Almanacs, ever faithful to the Party line, had to drop their peace songs and start celebrating war. As Pete Seeger said, two days after the invasion of Russia "we [stopped] singing 'Franklin D, You ain't going to send Me across the Sea.'"[90] Ron Radosh, a friend of Seeger and his student on the five-string banjo, recounts "In true Communist fashion, Peter and his comrades had to respond immediately to the change in the party line that occurred when Hitler invaded the USSR."[91] The *Songs of John Doe* were recalled, Radosh says, and "all pressings were destroyed."[92] Since Stalin and Roosevelt were now allies, the Almanacs issued an apology, and just to show that they held no grudges, the Roosevelts would, at Lomax's urging, go on to endorse their second album. In December, when Japan attacked Pearl Harbor, the Almanac Singers' musical limbo ended; they could urge all-out participation in the war against Germany as fervently as they had urged peace.

The abrupt changes in political direction which the Almanac Singers had to make, ludicrous as they were, showed that their revolutionary power resided not in politics but in lifestyle. Politically, the Almanacs spent their time preaching (or singing) to the choir. But in terms of lifestyle, they had far-reaching effects. This was a fortiori the case after the war, when the Almanacs reformed as the Weavers. Once the war against fascism had been won, geopolitics was replaced by lifestyle issues. The Weavers adopted a clothing style the Reusses term "proletarian romanticism."[93] Shucking the clothes they grew up with, they wore clothing associated with manual labor, i.e., blue jeans and denim shirts. Clothing and music would be essential to the sexual revolution of the '60s, and the Weavers pioneered virtually all the changes. The irony was great, as Seeger noted: "There I was, trying my best to shed my Harvard upbringing, scorning to waste money on clothes other than blue jeans."[94] Leadbelly, the Negro ex-con from Texas, though, "always had a clean white shirt and starched collar, well pressed suit and shined shoes. He didn't need to affect that he was a workingman."[95] Like Mick Jagger later, the Weavers often affected a southern accent while singing.

Proletarian chic styles of clothing carried sexual baggage with them as well. In this regard Pete Seeger took a back seat to Woody Guthrie, whos "uninhibited sex life," proved to be off-putting to the very audience they hoped to woo. When the "proletarian" Almanacs showed up in the early '40s for a concert for a Long Island butchers union, they were driven from the stage by well-dressed butchers who booed and threw plates. This prompted one Almanac to say it was time for "getting back and singing for real working class people again."[96]

The disparity between "bohemian" folksingers and the "bourgeois" proletariat recurred repeatedly. In 1936 Earl Robinson took Leadbelly to a progressive summer camp, where he embarrassed the left-wing but sexually middle-class audience with songs about "bad women and gun-toting Negro gamblers."[97] Leadbelly redeemed himself by singing a song about the Scottsboro Boys the next evening, saving both himself and Robinson the indignity of being kicked out of the camp by outraged Jewish mothers. Because he was a *Shvarze*, Leadbelly was probably too much of a sexual threat to pose lifestyle questions openly. In this regard he had to take a back seat to Woody Guthrie, who was even more sexually liberated, but white, and, therefore, more American. Woody Guthrie's "uninhibited sex life"⁹⁸ became the norm and the undoing of the New Left when, after World War II, sexual lifestyle issues replaced concern about workingmen's rights. Early on, Irwin Silber, a transitional figure in the generational change from Old Left to New Left, noticed changes provoked by Guthrie's "uninhibited" poor white trash lifestyle. Guthrie abandoned his wife and children and moved in with dancer Marjorie Greenblatt Mazia, who was married to someone else. Out of that union came Arlo Guthrie, who penned the folk hit "Alice's Restaurant" as the '60s folk movement ran out of steam. "The puritanical nearsighted left," Silber noted, referring to Woody,

> didn't quite know what to make of this strange bemused poet who drank and bummed and chased after women and spoke in syllables dreadful strange. They loved his songs and they sang "Union Maid" ... but they never really accepted the man ... they'd just as soon hear Pete Seeger sing the same songs.⁹⁹

Irwin Silber wrote later "We believed the world was worth saving and that we could do it with songs," which the Reusses call "the best single statement characterizing the Lomax tradition."¹⁰⁰ They are even more on target when they say "the Almanac Singers ... provided a central focal point around which to create a new personal lifestyle. Folk songs thus were at the center of ideology for the Lomax performers, who promoted them with all the missionary zeal *of a new religious sect.*"¹⁰¹

1945 The Morgenthau Plan

In September 1942 Franklin D. Roosevelt's Treasury Secretary Henry Morgenthau, Jr. met with Rabbi Stephen Wise and learned about Hitler's genocidal plans for the Jews of Europe. Morgenthau was the only Jew in Roosevelt's cabinet, and Rabbi Wise had officiated at his wedding in 1916. Morgenthau's grandfather Lazarus had immigrated to New York from Mannheim in 1866, but coming from Germany and liking Germany were two different things, especially when Morgenthau's Jewish heritage got factored into the equation.

While Secretary of the Treasury, Morgenthau imposed onerous tariffs on German goods and supported the Soviet Union. When defeat of the Axis powers seemed imminent, he turned to his aide Harry Dexter White, a Jewish economist from Eastern Europe and a communist agent, for a plan to punish Germany. The paper, whose formal title was "Program to Prevent Germany from Starting a World War III," came to be known as the Morgenthau Plan, and as a result of that plan, Morgenthau became the most hated Jew in post-war Germany and posthumous proof that everything Hitler said about Jewish bankers was true.

The Morgenthau Plan foresaw the demilitarization and de-industrialization of a partitioned Germany. Germany, which vied with England for the title of Europe's chief industrial power during the early 20th century, was to be transformed into "a country primarily agricultural and pastoral in its character."¹⁰² According to White's draft, the heart of Germany's industry and coal and steel production was to be stripped of all industrial equipment. The Allies were to "retain control over foreign trade and capital imports ... and guarantee the breakup of all large estates and their distribution among the peasants."[103] The fact that there were no peasants in Germany at the time must have set off alarm bells in some quarters. White's reference to German "peasants" and the breakup of all large estates indicated that Morgenthau was using the allies to impose not only pastoral conditions on Germany but a Marxist regime as well. In 1949, the man who was to become West Germany's Catholic prime minister, Konrad Adenauer, called the "Morgenthau Plan" a "crime against humanity" that would lead to more deaths than the Hitler regime.[104]

The WASP foreign policy establishment shared Adenauer's misgivings. Secretary of War Henry Stimson opposed the Morgenthau Plan as "Jewish vengeance."[105] Stimson used his assistant secretary of war John J. McCloy, who eventually became high commissioner over conquered Germany, to thwart it. As the alternative to Morgenthau's planned summary executions of Nazi leadership, Stimson and McCloy proposed the Nuremberg War Crimes tribunals.

General George Patton shared Stimson's views, claiming "the Red Army was the real threat and the Germans the real friends" in the changing political situation.[106] In a letter to Secretary Stimson, Patton "protested against the pro-Jewish clout in the military government. In his opinion, the early American postwar policies were the result of a conspiracy of international bankers, labor leaders, Jews and Communists, whereas he regarded the Germans as potential allies against the adversary in the East."[107] Shlomo Shafir suggests anti-Semitism caused Patton's removal as head of the third army. The story, though, is more complicated. Patton was not removed because he regarded Jewish displaced persons as "lower than animals,"[108] but because he objected to food, clothing, and medical supplies "diverted for the maintenance of the underground railway to Palestine. There is evidence that the terrorist elements among the Jews have been reinforced from the ranks of illegal immigrants."[109] The British General Morgan suffered the same fate as Patton when he claimed Jewish migration was artificially manipulated as part of a Zionist plot to populate Palestine. When Patton's replacement, General Mark Clark, became head of the US Occupation Zone in Austria "Jews from Marxist indoctrinated Eastern Europe, [began] pouring through the Clark Command into our Displaced Persons camps, throwing themselves on the American government and taxpayer."[110]

The perfidy of the Allies and their double standard became more apparent when details of Operation Keelhaul were made public after the war. Thousands of refugees were sent to death Stalin's Gulag when the allies repatriated them to Soviet Union or its eastern European satellites. At the same time that they were feeding Jewish refugees destined for Palestine, Britain handed over Croatians to Tito at Bleiberg, where they were subjected to the death march and show trials at the hands of the Communists. Unlike the Croatians, the Jews who found refuge in

Austria were in no danger. General Clark, as a result, "rendered a great service to the Marxist world power cult in letting—and abiding—the Jews to come into the US camps. At the same, time General Clark turned back to certain death or slave labour camps, the untold thousands of Genitles... running for their lives from the Red secret police"[111]

Patton died in an automobile accident in December 1945. He, not Morgenthau and White, was the prophet of the dramatic change in American policy inaugurated by Churchill's "iron curtain" speech and George Kennan's "long telegram." In February 1946, Kennan warned the state department the alliance between the Soviet Union and America was over. America's former ally was now its most dangerous opponent. As part of the new strategy required by that new conflict, President Harry S Truman issued Executive Order 9835 to root communists from influential government positions. One of the first to go was Harry Dexter White. Truman then demanded and got the resignation of Secretary Morgenthau. Harry Dexter White died in 1948, long before establishment of commissions investigating communist influence in the government. Morgenthau "was never able to resolve the question of White's Communist affiliations."[112]

The main reason for the defeat of the Morgenthau Plan was the Soviet threat in Europe. The Morgenthau Plan would have enabled a Soviet takeover by eliminating Germany as the "Bulwark against Bolshevism."[113] Although the WASPs were in charge of America's foreign policy, the Jewish-Catholic conflict was always close to the surface. The American occupation sector included Bavaria with Germany's largest Catholic population. Catholics were suspected of fraternization with Catholic Bavarians. When Robert Murphy, a Catholic diplomat who had antagonized American Jewish groups, was appointed as a political adviser to occupation forces, Morgenthau demanded his removal. Catholics were suspected of fraternization with the Catholic Bavarians, but Murphy's appointment was not revoked. The Jewish desire for vengeance was thwarted by Washington's desire to use West Germany as the showcase for the liberal values of the West.

This meant thwarting Jewish cultural politics in West Germany. One of the main Jewish goals after World War II, shutting down the Oberammergau Passion Play, seemed within their grasp, but on May 18, 1950, both John J. McCloy, the US High Commissioner, and Sir Brian Robertson, the British High Commissioner showed up at the first performance of the Passion Play since the war. The American occupation forces had just conducted a draconian program of de-nazification. Race had been replaced by environment as the key to understanding (and manipulating) man and his behavior, and every aspect of German culture was subjected to microscopic scrutiny and heavy-handed social engineering. And yet in spite of all this, no one but the Jews seems to have noticed any anti-Semitism in the Oberammergau passion play, in spite of Shapiro's assertion that "it was pretty much the same old play" which Hitler had praised.[114] Michael Cardinal Faulhaber, archbishop of Munich, found nothing theologically objectionable in the play, granting it his approval on August 20, 1949. Ten years later, his successor Joseph Cardinal Wendel gave his approval as well. The presence of both McCloy and Robertson at the play was an indication that the Jews did not run American foreign policy and that America, or the WASP foreign policy establishment, wanted Germany as an ally in the Cold War. According to James Shapiro, "Oberammergau's old argument about opposing Bolshevism held a certain appeal.... The villagers and the Americans were on the same side after all."[115]

December 31, 1945: Pete Seeger and People's Songs

After the war, lifestyle became the major concern of the Left. On the last day of 1945, more than 30 folksingers met in Pete Seeger's Greenwich Village apartment to create "People's Songs," a clearinghouse for "disseminating the songs of the people [which] truly express their lives, struggles, and their highest aspirations."[116] Once again, they were to hijack traditional melodies and yoke them with texts like "Stalin wasn't Stallin' Any More."[117]

If the rise of folk music as the cutting edge of the lifestyle revolution depended on musical sophistication or poetic skill, the movement would have never made it out of Greenwich Village. But Alan Lomax and his sister had worked for the Office of War Information, insuring that the movement would gain a favorable hearing in the mainstream press as OWI alumni fanned out into jobs publishing and broadcasting after the war. The OWI, at Lomax's urging, also recorded over a hundred hours featuring the antifascist folksinging of Burl Ives, Pete Seeger, Woody Guthrie and other Lomax musicians. In 1946, People's Songs issued its first bulletin, which morphed into the folk music magazine *Sing Out!* in the 1950s.

The Communist Party in America, however, failed to see the significance of the folk song movement, and the fact that within 15 years the People's Songs membership would create an underground network of coffee houses, which would provide the ideal medium for injecting left-wing propaganda into previously inaccessible middle America. Typical was party hack V. J. Jerome, who, according to Radosh, was "one of the Communist Party's [most] feared leaders."[118] Betty Sanders felt Jerome was "fond of folksongs and intimately familiar with the culture and traditions of East European Jews," but when it came to American folk music, Jerome was "inflexible and rigidly dogmatic."[119] When Betty Sanders showed him the People's Songs folk music anthology "his only comment was to inquire why the book contained two Israeli songs but only one Soviet song."[120] Jerome insisted on including another forgettable Soviet tune, which meant Woody Guthrie's "Roll On, Columbia" got left out.

Jerome was typical of his generation of Eastern European Jew. He was a communist who liked Jewish music, and that was end of the story. He failed to see the influence American music would have on his children.

In 1937, most Jews listened to Yiddish music, which was entering popular culture via the *Shvartze* musicians in Harlem. The first crossover hit was "Bey mir bistu Sheyn," which appeared in a Yiddish musical in 1934 and was then picked up by the Negroes of Harlem and played in their jazz clubs. G minor was in many ways the blues variation of G, and so Yiddish/Russian tunes lent themselves to blues-inspired interpretations. Jewish Jazz was first known as the "oriental fox trot," and it soon appeared in the repertoire of Duke Ellington and Fats Waller.[121] In the mid-'30s, Eddie Cantor had a hit called "Lena from Palestine," based on a popular Romanian bulgar, "Nokh a Bisl" (A Little Bit More). The clarinet was a natural crossover instrument. In 1939 Artie Shaw released "The Chant," based on "the close and presumably incidental relationship" between the "St James Infirmary Blues" and "Khosn Kale, Mazeltov" (Congratulations Bride and Groom)."[122]

The Jews who came of age immediately after World War II were in a cultural conflict that would often manifest itself at weddings when the bride and her parents and their parents would battle over whether the band should play a *freylekh* or pop standards like "Where or When." To be commercially viable, Jewish musicians had to be able perform both.

In 1947 Mickey Katz left Spike Jones's novelty orchestra and created his own band, Mickey Katz and the Kosher Jammers. Their first album had a picture of Mickey in a baby carriage, smoking a cigar and presumably still in pain from his own bris. The music for that album was straight, but having cut his teeth with Spike Jones, it wasn't long before he got into Jewish parodies, which pointed up the awkward fit between Jewish content and American forms. Mickey had touched a nerve. The Jews who found assimilation a necessity, often found it inescapably comical as well. Hence the success of his records. "I had given the Jewish record-buying public something they evidently wanted and up to now hadn't had," Katz said later.[123] What followed was a series of revues and albums like "The Borscht Capades" he produced with this son Joel Grey and a stint as a "kosher disc jockey" in Southern California from 1951 to 1956.[124] Many Jews found the idea of setting Yiddish lyrics to hit parade tunes offensive, but Katz's success indicates that many more Jews found it hilarious. As I have indicated elsewhere, the humor was also subversive, and few American institutions would survive the subversion of Jewish humor in the coming decades.

1946: The Cold War Begins

The Cold War began in 1946. Instead of Morgenthau's "Jewish vindictiveness,"[125] the Germans got the Marshall Plan. In an address to Jewish leaders, General Lucius Clay advised them "to forget what happened."[126] The American Jewish Committee, one of the most assimilationist-minded Jewish organizations, took his advice because

> Any organized opposition of American Jews against the new foreign policy and strategic approach could isolate them in the eyes of the non-Jewish majority and endanger their postwar achievements on the domestic scene. In this context the AJC also found it necessary to take issue with communist attempts to use Jewish anti-German sentiments against Washington's new course....[127]

Sensing the anti-Communist train might leave without them, the AJC ignored as Soviet propaganda what later came to be known as the Holocaust. The AJC concentrated on re-educating Germany instead of punishing it. With America tied down in Korea, Jewish vengeance took a back seat to German participation in the defense of Western Europe.

The AJC was heavily involved in social engineering. When John Slawson, a social psychologist, became its executive director in 1943, the AJC had already sponsored research on race relations by Franz Boas, the Columbia University anthropologist who was Margaret Mead's mentor. Under Boas, Mead wrote *Coming of Age in Samoa*, a piece of bogus anthropology which became popular in the mid-1920s. Boas used Mead as his *goyische* cat's paw to attack the "Christian" psychology of G. Stanley Hall. In his history of the Jewish takeover of American psychology, Andrew Heinze refers to Hall's "classic work, *Adolescence*" as "saturated in Christian reference."[128] As its alternative, Mead proposed blue lagoon anthropology, a fictitious portrait of Samoa as a paradise of uninhibited teen-age sexual liberation from Christian-inspired "*Sturm und Drang*."

During the 1930s, the AJC brought two British agents (or social scientists)— Sir Solly Zuckerman and Sir Eric Rowle—to the country to help create their own domestic intelligence agency. The ADL set up its domestic political intelligence operation, which worked with the part of the FBI responsible for "secret meetings, sedition and betrayal," at around that time.[129] In 1944, the ADL in collaboration with the FBI had 30 America First sympathizers arrested for sedition for weakening America's resolve in the fight against fascism. The ADL also hoped to bring Charles Lindbergh to trial but their efforts came to naught when the judge in charge of the case died. Claiming to be an ethnic fraternal organization, the AJC was in fact an ethnic assimilationist organizaton which "did not shrink from sacrificing fellow Jews on the altar of anti-Communism" by "offering their files on alleged Jewish subversives to government agencies."[130]

As executive director of the AJC, Slawson convened a meeting of the German émigrés who constituted the exiled Institute of Social Research, later known as the Frankfurt School. Slawson was worried about fascism and anti-Semitism, which he thought firmly rooted in America's "ethnics," largely Catholic recent immigrants. To combat them and work toward their "re-education," Slawson created the Department of Scientific Research at the AJC, headed by Max Horkheimer who became the director, along with fellow Frankfurt School alumnus Theodor Adorno, of the AJC's five volume Studies in Prejudice series. Adorno was the author of *The Authoritarian Personality*, the most important volume.

Links between AJC, the Frankfurt School, and government-sponsored social engineering existed from the beginning. During the war, Herbert Marcuse worked for the OSS. After the war, those links became increasingly important as the government got involved in more intrusive social engineering. Friedman claims the AJC was responsible for the Supreme Court's approval of race-based social engineering in education because Slawson hired the black psychologist Kenneth B. Clark. The Supreme Court declared segregated schools unconstitutional in *Brown v. Board of Education* "in no small part based upon the psychological data of Gunnar Myrdal, Clark, and other social scientists in studies introduced by the [American Jewish] Committee, the [American Jewish] Congress, and various individuals and groups."[131]

Kurt Lewin, who invented the concept of the "self-hating Jew," created sensitivity training for the AJC with a grant from the Office of Naval Research. Lewin ran experiments in group dynamics to orchestrate peer pressure to engineer consent among individuals so groups like the AJC could "change American customs and laws that separated people from each other, so as to reduce prejudice against Jews and other stigmatized minorities."[132]

The new largely Jewish field of American psychology was a main arena of Jewish/Catholic *Kulturkampf*. Bishop Fulton Sheen and Clare Boothe Luce spoke disparagingly of Freudianism, forcing Heinze to conclude "Catholics did not rush as massively as their Jewish counterparts into psychology, partly, no doubt, because of the more tentative attitude of the Church toward that precocious social science."[133]

B'nai B'rith was also involved in social engineering. The ADL persuaded Hollywood to join in "attitude modification."[134] After Bess Meyerson was crowned as the first Jewish Miss America, the ADL ensured she would travel around the country explaining to high school students that, "You can't be beautiful and hate."[135] The AJC and the ADL no longer saw themselves "simply as Jewish 'defense" agencies, [they] ... broadened their agendas to support social welfare programs of all kinds as a part of the effort to strengthen democracy. Increasingly, they employed social science research to combat bigotry against all outsiders in the society.... They came to play a central role in shaping the newly developing field of intergroup relations as an integral part of the liberal agenda."[136] The Jewish defense agencies launched "an all-out assault on prejudice and discrimination," carefully avoiding the image of being narrow or parochial as they collaborated with the WASP psychological warfare establishment to create "a particular kind of social vision built around internationalism, liberalism and modernism."[137]

The ADL was more heavily involved in psychological warfare than the AJC. University of Chicago sociologist Louis Wirth was an employee of OWI and on the board of directors of the ADL after the war. Wirth was born in in Germany in 1897 to a family of Jewish cattle merchants who had lived in in the same house for four centuries. Wirth's attitude toward Catholic ethnics and social engineering was formed early when he was involved with Marxist student organizations at the University of Chicago. He was then a dedicated admirer of Josef Stalin, whom, he felt, had solved the Soviet Union's "nationalities problem." Wirth was instrumental in bringing Gunnar Myrdal to the United States and wrote eight chapters of *The American Dilemma*, the Carnegie foundation-sponsored book cited as justification for de-segregation in *Brown*.

After the war, Wirth collaborated with Philip Klutznick to impose housing based social engineering on Chicago's Catholic ethnics. Wirth was elected to the ADL's board of directors in 1947, the same year the first Levittown was build in Hempstead, Long Island. One year later, Klutznick became the administrator for Park Forest, Chicago's version of Levittown, the new suburb that was to assimilate Chicago's Catholic ethnics when their neighborhoods succumbed to Negro migration. Wirth and Klutznick were on the Board of Governors of the Metropolitan Housing and Planning Council of Chicago during its stormiest years between 1944 when they started to engineer Chicago's ethnic neighborhoods and 1954 when the ethnic counter-attack got Elizabeth Wood fired as the head of the Chicago Housing Authority. When B'nai B'rith co-sponsored the Chicago Housing Rally in February, 1950, Wirth was a speaker, along with Wood and Samuel Freifeld, director of the Discriminations Department of the Chicago Branch of the ADL. Philip Klutznick became head of B'nai B'rith in 1953, a position he held until 1959.

1947: The ADA breaks with the Communist left

In 1947, Eleanor Roosevelt joined Arthur Schlesinger and other disillusioned Leftists to form Americans for Democratic Action. America's Left thus broke with Soviet-led communists over the new ideology of liberalism. Many former Communist front organizations followed suit. *The New Republic*, created by Herbert Croly and Walter Lippman then taken over by Michael Straight, a Soviet agent recruited by Anthony Blunt, one of the Cambridge traitors, reverted to liberalism before becoming a Zionist organ when Martin Peretz purchased it in the '70s. Similarly, the *Partisan Review*, founded by two Jews in a communist cell in Greenwich Village in 1934, supported Trotsky briefly before evolving into a liberal journal in the 1950s. *The New Leader*, a magazine with Menshevik tendencies initially, became firmly liberal under the leadership of disillusioned Jewish communists like Ralph de Toledano and Daniel Bell.

The mind of the newly emerging anti-Communist liberal also found expression in *The Nation*, where Unitarian minister Homer Jack complained about Catholic ethnic resistance to race-based social engineering. It was also in the pages of *The Nation* that Paul Blanshard first mounted the attack on Catholic sexual morals that became the bestseller *American Freedom and Catholic Power*. In the sequel, Blanshard formulated the new liberal creed as anti-Communist and anti-Catholic. In both books, Blanshard opined that Catholics had a congenital weakness for fascism, precisely the conclusion Adorno and Horkheimer reached in their work on the authoritarian personality at the AJC. The dim outline of a far-reaching alliance between WASP and Jew in America's new-found ideology of liberalism was now evident. In a sense, though there was nothing new about this alliance at all. It had already been created in England, where it was known as Freemasonry. Since the United States was a country created by Freemasons, it was no coincidence that it would flourish there.

The foundation of the edifice of liberalism which housed the ADA WASP/ Jewish Alliance was the separation of church and state, a legal fiction created from one phrase in a letter by Thomas Jefferson. The immediate cause of WASP/Jewish concern was the *Everson* decision, which permitted Catholic school children to ride government-funded school buses. The specter of those children taking over the United States and turning it into a "Catholic country" like fascist Spain gave new urgency to WASP/Jewish collaboration. The AJC and the ADL pursued the separation of church and state as the surest prophylaxis against the fascist take-over of America.

Elliott Abrams, later influential in the Reagan and Bush II administrations and a member of the first family of neoconservatism through marriage to the daughter of Norman Podhoretz and Midge Decter, articulated the attraction of the separation of church and state for Jews in *Commentary*. Rather than "stand apart as a visibly distinct group," American Jews decided it "would be wiser to Americanize and assimilate as quickly as possible and insist that government must not support religion at all."[138] The Jews came to this conclusion because many Catholic immigrants arrived when the Jews did:

> this conclusion was further reinforced by the arrival, just as the German Jews were reaching America, of large numbers of Catholics from Ireland and Germany. Given the historic link between the Catholic Church and anti-Semitism in Europe, it was predictable that Jews would fear to see Catholicism strengthened in America. Far better, again to ensure that government would do nothing to assist the Church.[139]

Instead of insisting that Judaism have an equal place with Christianity, the AJC and ADL decided to "seek a more secular America where religion's role was diminished."[140] Abrams says "Jewish immigrants became American Jews by re-defining Judaism and submerging it in Americanism, itself newly defined by the Jewish lawyers who came to lead the community."[141] What he fails to say is that promotion of separation of church and state was tantamount to submerging America in Judaism. Gradually, America was redefined in Jewish terms, and the courts capitulated to the Talmudic redefinitions of American law during the high noon of American judicial activism. Abrams claims that through Justices Marshall and Brandeis, "the rule of law that governed American Jewish life came to depend upon the Constitution, not the Torah,"[142] but it is more accurate to say the Talmud replaced the Constitution as the center of American life.

The man most responsible for de-Christianization of American culture was the AJC's Leo Pfeffer, who, says the AJC's Murray Friedman, "advised, planned and argued more church-state cases before the U.S. Supreme Court than anyone else in American history."[143] Pfeffer's "social revolution"[144] began with *Everson* in 1947 and culminated in *Lemon v. Kurtzman* in 1974. The one constant was Pfeffer's animus toward the Catholic Church. Conceding "The promotion of religion and morality along with education was seen by the founding fathers as a primary purpose of government," Friedman portrays Pfeffer's cases as a clear victory for the Jewish viewpoint.[145] "*Everson* and *McCullum*," he writes, "in which the committee, the ADL and Pfeffer's Congress were joined together, were crucial victories" because they "vindicated Pfeffer's belief that litigation could be a primary tool to achieve the Jewish agencies' objectives."[146] In reports to its members, the AJC put a less ethnocentric spin on Pfeffer's achievement, declaring "it had achieved a 'social revolution' for religious equality," but the word "revolution" let the cat out of the bag.[147] "Joined now with the ascendant Jewish intellectual and cultural elite and with liberal Protestant and civil liberties bodies, Jewish groups had come to play a critical role in the 'de-Christianizaton' of American culture."[148] Only the Catholics complained, especially the Jesuits in their journal *America*. Friedman denounced "such criticism" as "carrying with it a whiff of anti-Semitism," a phrase he uses to discredit views he finds repugnant.[149]

Friedman does not mention Pfeffer's animus against Catholics. In 1975, when Jewish victory in the culture wars of the '60s was all but complete, Pfeffer explained in the liberal Catholic journal *Commonweal* why he did not like the Catholic Church: "I did not like it because it was monolithic and authoritarian and big and frighteningly powerful. I was repelled by the idea that any human being could claim infallibility in any area, much less in the universe of faith and morals, and repelled even more by the arrogance of condemning to eternal damnation those who did not believe it."[150] Pfeffer said his feelings were formed when "Pius XI and Pius XII reigned over the Catholic world and Cardinal Spellman ruled in the United States."[151] The Jewish Apostle of the Separation of Church and State was appalled when he "saw [Catholic] children lined up in separate classes as they marched in [to Catholic schools]. All the children were white; each group was monosexual; all the boys wore dark blue trousers and white shirts, all the girls dark blue jumpers and white blouses; all the teachers were white and wore the same nuns' habits."[152] After "the triumph of secular humanism," Pfeffer's term for the defeat of Catholics in the cultural warfare, Pfeffer still disliked the Church, "but I do not like it less than I did not like it during that period, and the reason is that, while it is still what it was before, it is considerably less so, if you can make out what I mean."[153]

1948: Seeger resurrects the Almanac Singers as the Weavers

In November 1948, Pete Seeger resurrected the Almanac Singers as the Weavers, a name derived from the eponymous Gerhart Hauptmann play about the English peasant revolt of 1381. One year later, the Weavers secured a two-week gig at Max Gordon's nightclub, the Village Vanguard, which was so successful it was extended indefinitely. In spring 1950, the Weavers signed with Decca, and shortly thereafter had a string of Top 40 hits beginning with Leadbelly's "Goodnight, Irene." The Weavers were enjoying the best of both worlds—commercial success while promoting revolution, when they were suddenly cut down by the anti-Communist crusade and the Catholic senator from Wisconsin, Joe McCarthy. When the war in Korea broke out in June 1950, Alan Lomax, who didn't need a weatherman to tell which way the wind was blowing, left America for England, where he remained beyond subpoena for eight years.

In May 1950, *Sing Out!*, under Communist Party member Irwin Silber, published what was arguably the Left's greatest hit, "If I had a Hammer," by Lee Hays and Pete Seeger. It would become the anthem of the '60s folk revival when Peter, Paul and Mary did a Top 40 version in 1963. The left-wing Lomax singers got called one by one to testify before the anti-Communist committees in Washington. Burl Ives testified before the Senate McCarran Committee in 1952 as a friendly witness to clear his name; as proof of his friendliness, he named fellow-travelers and party members. Ives' testimony incensed *Sing Out!*: "We've never seen anyone sing while crawling on his belly before. But maybe Burl Ives will be able to figure it out.... Nothing's too hard for a stoolpigeon—except keeping his integrity."[154] Tex Ritter stopped calling himself a folksinger because "for a few years ... it was very difficult to tell where folk music ended and Communism began."[155] Ramblin' Jack Elliott, reminiscing about Woody Guthrie in Washington Square, said Guthrie would charge a nickel a song for his own material, but if anyone requested a Burl Ives song, the price jumped to 15 cents.

1950: Disillusionment with Communism

Wartime Jewish collaboration with the psychological warfare establishment led to collaboration with the newly created CIA. The main reason for the collaboration was Jewish disillusionment with communism, which by the late '40s had become "the god that failed," to use the title of an influential anthology published in 1949 by former communists. Arthur Koestler, a Hungarian Jew, a contributor to that anthology and one of the most disillusioned Jewish former communists, described his defection and disillusionment in *Darkness at Noon*, one of the great political novels of the 20th century.

Koestler, who committed suicide after questioning the Semitic origins of the Ashkenazi in *The Thirteenth Tribe*, had significant impact on American Jews, who moved from the Communist Party. Additionally, the attitude of the WASP elite toward the Soviet Union had changed. The Soviet Union went from America's ally to its prime enemy. Assimiliationists were painfully aware their loyalty as Americans was questioned.

The situation in the Soviet Union had changed too. Stalin's anti-Semitism, which surfaced in the show trials of 1937 when he purged the Jewish first generation Bolsheviks from the party apparatus, took a turn for the worse after the war when he imagined himself the victim of a cabal of Jewish doctors.

At around the same time, Zionism began to exert its pull on Soviet Jews. Stalin had assisted in the creation of Israel by orchestrating pogroms in Poland, specifically the Kielce pogrom, to drive Jews out of Poland to Israel. In doing this he sought to kill two birds with one stone. He would get rid of what he considered a subversive fifth column in the Soviet Empire, and he would also establish a Soviet beachhead in the middle East by supplying the largely eastern European Jews who made up the Zionist establishment with Soviet weapons as a way of thwarting US access to Arab oil.

The fact that the United States was orchestrating its own purge of Jews at the same time didn't make the situation any easier for American Jews. As Slezkine points out, "in the Soviet Union they were persecuted as Jews, and in the United States as Communists.... Senator McCarthy ... knew perfectly well that many communists, hostile witnesses and Soviet spies were Jews, but chose not to transform this fact into a political 'issue'"[156] Either way, in the United States and the Soviet Union, "the Jewish association with communism was coming to an end."[157]

But it was far from over. In fact, in espionage, it was reaching its climax. In May 1950, David Greenglass was arrested for espionage. He implicated his brother-in-law Julius Rosenberg in a spy ring that had shipped plans on how to build an atomic bomb to the Soviet Union. One month later, Greenglass's wife implicated Rosenberg's wife Ethel. The Rosenberg espionage trial caused major embarrassment to American Jews, who were suspected of being communists simply because they were Jews. With Communism America's number one enemy, Jews were tainted; the major Jewish organizations were determined to do something about it.

Sensing the allure of communism was waning among American Jews, and that those among whom it was not waning were a serious liability, the AJC rushed to collaborate with the government. The Rosenbergs' trial was an entirely Jewish affair; the Jewish defendants were prosecuted by a Jewish lawyer before a Jewish judge. In the McCarthy hearings, the Catholic senator from Wisconsin often seemed a pawn of his Jewish assistant, Roy Cohn.

Sensing the Rosenberg trial could be a disaster for American Jews, the AJC collaborated with the anti-Communist crusade and handed over its files on Jews to the US Government. Willingness to take part in the anti-Communist crusade required temporary amnesia: The AJC portrayed as Communist dupes those who referred to the Nazi holocaust. Once the United States recognized West Germany in 1949 and it became the United States' "bulwark against Bolshevism" in Western Europe, American Jewish elites let bygones be bygones and "forgot" the Nazi Holocaust to facilitate their "traditional goals of assimilation and access to power."[158] Finkelstein claims the Jewish organizations fearfed "any organized opposition of American Jews against the new foreign policy and strategic approach could isolate them in the eyes of the non-Jewish majority and endanger their postwar achievements on the domestic scene."[159] As a result,

> American Jewish elites did not shrink from sacrificing fellow Jews on the altar of anti-Communism. Offering their files on alleged Jewish subversives to government agencies, the AJC and the ADL actively collaborated in the McCarthy-

era witch-hunt. The AJC endorsed the death penalty for the Rosenbergs, while its monthly publication, *Commentary*, editorialized that they weren't really Jews.[160]

The shock waves in the Jewish community in the aftermath of the Alger Hiss trial and the execution of the Rosenbergs caused what Slezkine calls "the great alliance between the Jewish Revolution and Communism" to fall apart.[161] The Jews were also motivated by Stalin's Doctors' Plot. Once Stalin turned on the Jews, a number of Jews turned on Stalin and joined the anti-Communist Crusade. One of the first was Sidney Hook, a co-founder of the Committee for Cultural Freedom in 1939, with John Dewey as its head. Hook's operation morphed in the 1940s from an attempt to invigorate communism by marrying it to Dewey's pragmatism into liberalism, and then into conservatism in the 1950s.

In March 1949, the Soviet Union used front groups to put on the Cultural and Scientific Conference for World Peace at New York's Waldorf Astoria Hotel. Many prominent "New York Intellectuals" attended, including Leonard Bernstein, Lillian Hellman, Norman Mailer, and Arthur Miller, as well as Negro fellow travelers Langston Hughes and Paul Robeson. Russia's most famous fireman (as portrayed on the cover of *Time* in 1942), Composer Dimitri Shostakovich gave a speech denouncing America's fascism and "hatemongering."[162]

The CIA responded by holding a Congress for Cultural Freedom in Berlin in June 1950, with Arthur Koestler as a main speaker. Sidney Hook also attended. When Hook returned to the United States he affiliated his ACCF with the International Congress of Cultural Freedom. Composed in large part of former Communists, the CCF, a CIA front, was largely Jewish. Hook took the hard line against the Soviet Union. Against the establishment's policies of containment and détente, Hook urged all out destruction of the Soviet Empire.

During its heyday from 1950 through 1958, the CCF used CIA largesse to open offices in 35 countries. It also funded magazines that were CIA fronts, among them the English magazine *Encounter*, co-edited by Irving Kristol and the poet Stephen Spender in London. After he was outed as a CIA agent in the liberal *New York Review of Books* in 1968, Kristol claimed he didn't know *Encounter* was a CIA front. Murray Rothbard thought Kristol disingenuous if not downright dishonest. As Rothbard points out, Tom Braden, then head of the CIA's International Organizations division, "wrote in a *Saturday Evening Post* article, a CIA agent always served as editor of *Encounter*."[163] Later Kristol changed his story. According to Murray Friedman,

> Kristol summed up this sentiment later in an article in the *New York Times* magazine in 1968, following the pubic exposure of secret CIA financial assistance to the CCF and *Encounter* magazine. He argued that he had no objection to CIA funding or certain projects and under certain circumstances. He had no more reason to despise the CIA than he did the post office, he wrote. Both were exasperatingly inept.[164]

Kristol's explanation was disingenuous and implausible. He was an alumnus of Alcove One at the City College of New York and a protégé of Hook. When CCNY Trotskeyite Jews weren't attending class, they would hang out in Alcove One at the college cafeteria. Alcove Two was the Stalinist enclave, where Julius Rosenberg could be found. There were also alcoves for Catholics, Zionists, and Orthodox Jews, but none of their alumni attained the prominence of the Jews from Alcoves One and Two. Alcove One also produced Sejmour Martin Lipset, Melvin Lasky, and Irving Howe, who could "remember getting into an argument at ten in the morning [in Alcove One], going off to classes, and then returning at two in the afternoon to find the argument still going on but with an entirely fresh cast of characters."[165]

In 1947, years before he edited *Encounter*, Kristol was appointed junior editor at *Commentary*, the mouthpiece of the AJC, and a close collaborator in the government anti-Communist crusade. His association with *Commentary*, not the CIA front *Encounter*, gave the true coordinates of a career that became "a virtual road map of the path taken by some liberals on their way to becoming Neoconservatives."[166]

1953: Julius and Ethel Rosenberg executed

Just about one year after Ives' testimony, Julius and Ethel Rosenberg were executed for espionage. Ron Radosh stood in Union Square on June 19, 1953, listening to "Negro ballads sung by Communist Party folk singers" as tears streamed down his face.[167] Radosh considered the Rosenbergs as Jewish martyrs to fascist America, then in the throes of a witchhunt ably described by another Jew, Arthur Miller, in *The Crucible*. Miller would later marry Marilyn Monroe, the world's most famous *shiksa*, after he dumped his social worker wife. Art and life conspired in the Rosenberg case to convince Jews they were at the center of an apocalyptic drama, in which good Jews, i.e., Communist Jews, were preparing for another holocaust. Radosh had a personal stake in the case because two of his fellow campers at Camp Woodland were Michael and Robert Meerpol, the Rosenbergs soon-to-be adopted children. As Communist Party historian Herbert Aptheker would say, anti-Semitism "played and plays a part" in the Rosenberg case.[168] It was up to young Jewish Communists like Radosh,

> to convince New York's Jewish population ... that America was now "fascist" and was trying to execute two Jews for their "progressive" political beliefs. And for second and third-generation Jews like my friends and myself, the Rosenbergs' fate could just as well been that of our own parents. My mother and father, after all, were also progressive activists steeped in the secular *Yiddishkayt* culture, people who cared for the Russians, who favored civil rights for Negroes, and who had fought in or supported the valiant fight of the Abraham Lincoln Brigade against fascism in Spain.[169]

When the sun set that June evening, Radosh knew, in keeping with Jewish ritual, the Rosenbergs had been executed. The weeping turned into "a wail of heavy crying and moaning, and the singers started chanting the old hymn of slavery in Egypt land, 'Let my People Go.'"[170] When mounted police appeared, Radosh saw them as "a reprise of the Russian Cossacks attacking the Jewish poor of the *shtetl.*"[171] When Radosh attended the funeral of the spies who had given atomic bomb secrets to Stalin, the "moment would remain etched in my memory forever to be the symbol of what awaited good, progressive Jews who dared to stand up for their beliefs."[172]

Thirty years later, learning that the Rosenbergs were indeed spies, Radosh wrote an article with Sol Stern ("a colleague from my University of Iowa graduate school days and a former *Ramparts* editor and New Left Activist. Stern was a smart writer and shrewd political observer, and we shared a common background and perspective. We were both left-wing Jews from New York, for whom the Rosenberg case had been a central concern")[173] to that effect for the *New York Times*, only to learn that Abe Rosenthal spiked it because he didn't want to offend a Jewish judge deliberating in a case affecting the *Times.* The Rosenberg myth—David Rieff would claim "the Rosenbergs are the American Left's only true martyrs"—was evidently still important to "our crowd."[174]

Radosh was a high school student at Elizabeth Irwin School in Greenwich Village when the Rosenbergs were executed. "Was there anyone of note," Radosh asks, "who was part of the Old Left or the New Left who did not attend Elizabeth Irwin?"[175] The only people who didn't fit in there were the children of Trotskyites and Reichians. EI was known as "the little Red Schoolhouse for little Reds," and the faculty were every bit as Left-wing as the students, arranging a class trip to coal mines in Pennsylvania so the budding young communists could experience the proletariat and imbibe its wisdom.[176] The ethnic reality, however, was dramatically different from the Marxist fantasy. In their introduction to the working class, the EI students were taken to a working-class Catholic Church, where the priest talked about "the Miracle of the Lady of Fatima, who appeared to local Polish [sic] peasants to warn them about the coming threat of communism."

Elisabeth Irwin counted among its graduates an equal number of famous folkies and famous Reds. Among the latter were Victor Navasky, editor and publisher of *The Nation* and Angela Davis. Among the former, Eric Weissberg, the banjo picker, Joady and Nora Guthrie, and, most famous of all, Mary Travers, of Peter, Paul and Mary, who never graduated. Radosh traveled to Washington with classmate Travers as part of the Youth Committee for the Rosenbergs to picket the White House. Radosh remembers Travers most for her precocious devotion to sexual liberation, which continually got her in trouble, leading to her expulsion from the school. Mary Travers caused a scandal by posing in a sex photo tabloid, which she boldly passed around to her classmates. Travers came from a radical family that lived across the street from EI, which enabled her to harangue and insult her former classmates after her expulsion.

Jewishness, communism, and folksinging combined to form a seamless cultural garment for Radosh and his peers in New York in the '50s. During high school, Radosh hung out at Washington Square in the Village on Sundays where he met "the luminaries of the early folk scene."[177] Radosh was there when Ramblin' Jack Elliott showed up with Woody Guthrie. In fact, he's visible in one of the famous pictures of those two seminal folk musicians. Mingling with the folk legends were Radosh's radical peers—Carl Granich, the son of Mike Gold, and Bob Starobin, son of Joe Starobin, the foreign affairs editor of the *Daily Worker*. Between the Sunday afternoon sessions in Washington Square and the parties in the Village and its environs, Radosh met "the first generation of city-bred country pickers and folk singers whose names would later become household words."[178]

It was Pete Seeger, however, who continued to exert the most influence on him. Seeger taught Radosh to play the five-string banjo. Seeger entertained Radosh and his peers at Camp Woodland, and Seeger's legendary 1948 folkways album inspired them to adopt his take on America's traditional melodies. Pete Seeger is the reason so many Jews played the five-string banjo, an instrument virtually unknown before Pete Seeger started playing it. Seeger was the Elvis Presley of the Jewish Left, and Radosh knew him intimately enough to call him his hero. When Seeger needed a place to spend the night, he was always welcome at the Radosh apartment. He would reciprocate by inviting Ron to spend weekends at his Beacon, New York, refuge. Mike Gold would often spend weekends at Seeger's mountaintop retreat; he was struck how the New York teenagers "worshipped" Seeger, whom Gold called "the Karl Marx of the teenagers."[179]

Seeger was extremely popular at Elisabeth Irwin. Like the Blues Brothers, who played both kinds of music, "Country and Western," the music department at EI ran the socialist gamut from Third Period chorales to Popular Front folk tunes. The school's music director Bob DeCormier, later became director of the New York Choral Society, the Harry Belafonte Singers, and, under the name Robert Corman, musical arranger for Peter, Paul and Mary. During Radosh's years, Cormier also directed the Jewish Young Folk-Singers, which was affiliated with the Communist Party's International Workers Order. Radosh was a member of the JYF.

In 1954, an Israeli actor by the name of Theodor Bikel arrived in New York to perform in a Broadway play called *Tonight in Samarkand*. Within days, Bikel, "a gifted impersonator,"[180] introduced himself to Pete Seeger. Israeli folk songs soon joined the repertoire of the Left. Nine years later, Bikel was at Newport singing "We Shall Overcome." Bikel added a new note, Zionism, to the American folk repertoire. It was an act of supererogation, because by 1954, folk music was a Jewish phenomenon. "Jewish repertoire may not have been central to the folk song revival," Kirshenblatt-Gimblett writes, but

Jews certainly were. They owned and managed clubs and record companies. They were composers, performers, agents, and managers. They were writers and critics. Moses Asch, son of Sholem Asch, established Folkways. Jac Holzman and Leonard Ripley ran Elektra. Kenneth S. Goldstein issued innumerable recordings of songs from the field. Israel Young ran the Folklore Center on MacDougal Street. Aliza Greenblatt, the mother of Woody Guthrie's former wife Marjorie, was a published Yiddish poet; she wrote "Der fisher," which has become a favorite in the Yiddish song repertoire. Jean Richie's husband, George Pickow, a Jew from New York, made her an improved mountain dulcimer. The list goes on.[181]

The Weavers didn't remain blacklisted for long. In December 1955, the Weavers celebrated their return to respectability with a successful concert at Carnegie Hall. Ron Radosh was not there. In September, Ron, unlike most of his Jewish Communist Comrades from the LYL who "more or less automatically"[182] enrolled in City College of New York, had left for Madison, Wisconsin, where he enrolled in the history program. His purpose was not learning, but subversion. The Communist Youth League gave him "a ready-made community"[183] in Madison, and Radosh began "burrowing from within."[184] In his memoir *Commies*, Radosh describes his purpose as "classically Leninist":

> to gain influence in, and if possible take over, other existing student groups. One of our 'secret" members was a paunchy New Yorker named Jeff Kapow, who admitted in Paul Buhle's book: "There was no other choice but to work within the framework of other organizations whose aims were in some way compatible with our own. The words used to describe this activity—"infiltration" and "burrowing from within"—have an essentially negative connotation and are, as such, unjust. For we were not so much using those organizations for our own ends as we were helping them fulfill their stated aims."[185]

Radosh and his communist friends infiltrated "the NAACP, the Young Democrats, the Students for Democratic Action (youth arm of the fiercely anti-Communist ADA), the Film Society, the Student council, the Student League for Industrial Democracy (a social-democratic group)" and tuned them into organizations "to overthrow our capitalist democracy and replace it with a socialist revolution modeled on the USSR."[186] Radosh and his friends were evidently successful in subverting these organizations, assuring us that "The old Commie tactic of 'burrowing from within' really did work."[187]

Once again, Radosh, even thought he was hundreds of miles away from home, was ensconced in a seamlessly Jewish community, Communist in its politics, and involved in folk music. Radosh met his first girlfriend at the campus branch of Hillel, a Zionist who danced Israeli folk dances and criticized Radosh's politics as "adolescent rebellion against parental authorities,"[188] even though Radosh's parents were as radically communist as he. Soon Marshall Brickman and Eric Weissberg, folkies Radosh knew from Washington Square, arrived in Madison. The Jewish Communist folk scene replicated itself in one of the many coffee houses that would spread Greenwich Village across the country. Although Brickman "came from a bona fide Red-diaper-baby family,"[189] he and Weissberg, Radosh's bunkmate at Camp Woodland, were relatively apolitical, spending their time listening to Earl Scruggs' records, trying to imitate his banjo licks. Radosh looked down on Brickman and Weissberg because of their indifference to politics; they looked down on Radosh because of his lack of skill on the banjo. They performed together on Theodore Bikel's radio program, broadcast live from the Gate of Horn in Chicago, which was part of

> a network of tiny clubs [which] stretched form coast to coast, establishing a kind of alternative entertainment circuit. Folksingers with talent could develop quite a reputation as they worked their way across the country, playing popular clubs. Coincidentally, a handful of coffeehouses emerged as the "important rooms" one had to play on the way up. There was Folk City in New York, the Gate of Horn in Chicago, and in San Francisco, the hungry i and Ash Grove became essential links to the big time. Each major city had a coffeehouse or two where enthusiasts came to see folksingers on the brink of success.[190]

At this point, it's worth asking whether subversion, "burrowing from within" was essentially Communist or Jewish. The answer, of course, is that it is impossible to distinguish the two qualities. Subversion is something that Jews did because they were Communists, but it is also something that communists did because they were Jews. Just as Radosh and his LYL buddies subverted the campus branch of the ADA, so Weissberg and Brickman subverted Earl Scruggs in their way, first by slavishly imitating his technique and then appropriating his music just as Pete Seeger had subverted other American music during the '30s. Earl Scruggs was now part of the Jewish revolutionary coffee house folk-music scene, whether he wanted to be or not, and that music would be transformed into the revolutionary Dionysian anthems of the '60s willy nilly.

During summers, Radosh returned to New York to work as a counselor at another camp for Jewish communists, this time for adults. He became the folk music leader at Wingdale on the Lake, previously known as Camp Unity, "an adult resort for party members."[191] Radosh's duties "involved little more than leading songs at the campfire once a week and being MC at the Saturday night shows." As a result, he had plenty of time to socialize.[192] He took a liking to a high school student four year his junior, Alice Schweig, the daughter of a wealthy dentist from Pelham, "the only area" in New York, Radosh says, "that would vote for Barry Goldwater" in 1964.[193] There, "Alice had felt something of an alien."[194] Radosh was worried about how her parents might react to their daughter marrying a communist. But, rummaging in their attic, he discovered they too had been communists in their youth. "Although no longer open about it," Alice's parents were in "the communist orbit," and "would not look askance at a partner for Alice who was committed to the dreams and hopes of their own left-wing youth."[195]

Radosh's in-laws did have reason to worry, but not about Communism. The Left was turning from the concerns of the working class and becoming involved in the sexual revolution instead. The Jews took a leading role in this subversion, unaware that in succumbing to the siren song of Dionysos, they would destroy their own little world. Wingdale on the Lake, Radosh says,

> had a well-earned reputation as a den of free love, a place where uptight apparatchiks abandoned all pretenses and let their libidos loose. In particular, the adult female campers seemed to indulge in behavior that was never openly acknowledged or condoned, but appeared to be the favored sexual activity of the camp: sex with black male staff and campers, which could not be condemned because of the party's ongoing campaign against "white chauvinism." It was also the first I had ever heard of group sex and wife-swapping, with the highly prized black lifeguard and his white roommate regularly switching partners as part of their camp routine.[196]

1953-54: Ramblin Jack Elliott and Woody Guthrie

The cowboy—in particular, the singing cowboy—was one of the most significant cultural casualties in the communist campaign of burrowing within the traditions of American folk music. Mel Brooks presided over his funeral in his mid-70s film *Blazing Saddles*. But the singing cowboy was also one of the first roles New York Jews appropriated to become American. The best example was Elliott Charles Adnopoz, a Jewish cowboy from Brooklyn. Adnopoz ran away as a teenager and joined the Colonel Jim Eskew traveling rodeo. Adnopoz was embarrassed about his New York origin and his Jewish name, so he told rodeo folks to call him Buck. After meeting Woody Guthrie, Adnopoz changed his name to Ramblin' Jack Elliott and became the model for a generation of singing Jewish cowboys, including Bob Dylan. Elliott moved in with Guthrie and, over a few intense months, adopted his guitar and singing styles and every other aspect of his life, including his penchant for rambling.

As the documentary directed by his daughter demonstrates, the prime attraction the singing cowboy persona had for Elliott was its absolution from family responsibility. The rambler protested agaomst monogamy. No longer was the cowboy an awkwardly chivalrous John Wayne or a defender of the rights of the workingman. Instead he was a proponent of sexual liberation. Ramblin' sexuality became the prime attraction of Lifestyle Leftism during the '50s. During the warmer months of 1953 and 1954, Elliott and Guthrie would serenade teenagers in Washington Square in Greenwich Village. Elliott sported his trademark cowboy hat, and Guthrie looked like an escapee from a flophouse. Guthrie was having increasing difficulty physically, suffering from the early stages of Huntington's chorea, the nerve disorder that killed his mother and eventually killed him. His drinking didn't help. Nor did his ramblin' womanizing. Guthrie abandoned his second wife and took up with Anneke Van Kirk Marshall, a 20-year-old he met near Geer's farm in California. Ramblin' Jack would emulate his mentor, going through four wives by the time his daughter made her documentary.

Chapter Twenty-Two

Lorraine Hansberry

On October 25, 1940, the Supreme Court heard arguments in the case of *Hansberry v. Lee*, a case which challenged restrictive covenants, a real estate ploy which prevented blacks from moving into all-white neighborhoods. Carl Hansberry, a black Chicago businessman, was looking for property to buy on the south side of Chicago. In 1937 he found James Joseph Burke, a disgruntled former member of Woodlawn Property Owners Association, who had vowed revenge on the organization that had done him wrong. Burke made good on his threat to "get even with the Woodlawn Property Owners' Asociation by putting niggers in every block"[1] of the Washington Park subdivision, beginning with Carl Hansberry, who conspired with Burke to buy a three-flat brick building at 6140 South Rhodes Avenue, which he knew the law barred him from buying. Historians have concluded that "Indeed, a conspiracy existed," but they have also concluded that Hansberry was involved "a necessary conspiracy," because the "intrigue" was "aimed at righting a wrong."[2]

Necessary or not, this conspiracy to deprive a Negro of his rights did not include the usual suspects. This time there were no frog-eyed southern bigots with tobacco juice dripping from their chins. This time the enemies of racial equality were the Supreme Life Insurance Company, which "pumped more than a hundred thousand dollars...into fighting this case" and Robert Maynard Hutchins, president of the Rockefeller-endowed University of Chicago, who told Hansberry's lawyers, "It's a matter of economics.... The university has a huge investment in the South Side, and I've got to protect it.... Why don't you people stay where you belong?"[3]

The language of the covenant was frankly racial, defining a Negro as "every person having one-eighth part or more of Negro blood, or having any appreciable mixture of Negro blood and every person who is what is commonly known as a 'colored person.'"[4] But the situation in Chicago was different than the situation in the South. Chicago was a city of ethnic neighborhoods. The race riot of 1919 convinced the city fathers that the best way to keep the peace in an ethnically diverse city was ethnic pluralism, with each neighborhood its own quasi-independent fiefdom. In the wake of the first wave of black migration up from the South during World War I, southern blacks were treated like one of the many immigrant ethnic groups which had already come to Chicago by being assigned their own ethnic territory in the same way that the Germans, Poles and Irish had in the past.

The Catholic Church in Chicago, which would later be blamed for promoting segregation, simply adopted the ethnic neighborhood pattern when it set up its parishes. According to the official history of the Archdiocese of Chicago, a local parish was far more than a place of worship; it was also a community center, where immigrants could congregate and inter-marry with people of the same language and customs. Throughout the 19th century, therefore, each Catholic ethnic group built a separate community in Chicago.[5]

The instruction in parochial schools was in the language of the immigrant group which settled in that particular neighborhood, something that highlighted the fact that "Not just education, but every aspect of Catholic life and worship was subdivided along ethnic lines," with the Irish, Germans and Poles forming the "major leagues" of ethnic Chicago.[6] Black Catholics were no exception to this rule and "were considered an ethnic group like any other. If they could raise the money, they could have their own church and ethnic parish."[7] Segregation is a word that emerged during the time of redemption in the South, but it got applied to the situation in the North nonetheless, often by people who knew that the two situations were different, as when Kantorowicz writes that Black parishes were "segregated," because "most ethnic groups at the time were segregated, at least in part of their own volition."[8] Segregation in the South, needless to say, was not voluntary.

In Chicago immigrant groups banded together in particular neighborhoods for mutual support. Ethnicity and not laws created to bring about separation of the races determined the make of up of Chicago's neighborhoods and therefore its parishes:

> In 1916 the Catholic Church in the city of Chicago consisted of 93 territorial (mainly Irish) parishes with 235,600 members; 35 German parishes with 62,700 parishioners; and 34 Polish parishes, counting 208,700 parish members. The minor leagues accounted for an additional 53 parishes and 139,200 parishioners. The 646,200 active members of the Catholic Church in Chicago formed about 30 percent of the city's population.... Ethnic divisions were all-pervasive, wherever one looked throughout the archdiocese.[9]

Cardinal Mundelein, "a third-generation German-American and a confirmed Americanizer," tried to revoke "the ethnic peace treaty" that was the model for the Chicago Archdiocese, but the neighborhood was such an integral part of the warp and woof of Chicago that no one man could change it.[10] Mundelein declared a moratorium on the establishment of new ethnic parishes, insisted that the language of instruction in all subjects (except catechism and reading) in parochial schools had to be in English, and steadfastly refused to name any Polish auxiliary bishops, but Chicago remained stubbornly ethnic in spite of his efforts. Mundelein's Americanizing may well have exacerbated the racial situation, because in refusing to allow new ethnic groups to found their own parishes, he denied black Catholics from the South the same rights that every other ethnic group had enjoyed, when the black migrants needed them the most, namely, during the great period of migration up from Mississippi which stretched from 1919 to 1960.

In Americanizing Chicago Catholics, the Catholic bishops adopted racial categories that were alien to their European immigrant flock. Mundelein, like his contemporary Cardinal Dougherty in Philadelphia, refused to see black Catholics as just another ethnic group and insisted upon their integration into existing parishes. This was not only disruptive, it also brought about Americanization in a way that neither man intended by introducing recently arrived European Catholics to the racial system of the American South and convincing them that they were "white." This, in turn, thwarted the very integration that Mundelein's integrative Americanizing wanted to foster. It was a problem that would grow with time as both black migration and covert government sponsored social engineering grew during the war years.

Knowing that he was in for a hard legal fight, Hansberry and his attorney, C. Francis Stradford, approached Earl Dickerson, the star legal counsel for the NAACP. By the time Hansberry and his lawyer contacted them, the NAACP, as well as the AJC, had decided to move beyond fighting discrimination on a case-by-case basis. The change in strategy was largely the result of a report written in 1931, the same year that the Scottsboro Boys went on trial for the first time, by Nathan Margold, a Romanian-Jewish immigrant who had studied law at Harvard. Margold's report proposed "an unprecedented all-out attack on segregation itself,"[11] including attacks on restrictive covenants and housing discrimination in the North, where segregation was not *de jure*. By the time Hansberry and his lawyers contacted Earl Dickerson, Nathan Margold's report had become "the bible of the NAACP."[12]

During the 1930s and 1940s, Jews at organizations like the American Jewish Committee began to apply the principles of Boasian environmental sociology and anthropology to the burning questions of the day, the most burning of which were the rise of Nazism in Germany and the continuing hegemony of white racism in the American South. American Jews continued to be haunted by the spectre of Leo Frank, and the emerging world situation during the 1930s did little to calm their fears. The other side was just as anxious. As the circumstances surrounding the Scottsboro Boys trials became better known, the South began to fear that once again they were the victims of outside agitation. "The Niggers and Jews of New York are working hand in hand," Senator Theodore Bilbo was quoted as saying in the *Jewish Exponent*.[13]

Whether he actually said that or not, the Jews of New York were hard at work turning Boasian social science into weapons they could use against their enemies. The weapons were largely legal and would be put in the service of what later came to be known as social engineering. War, as John B. Watson had said when his book *Behaviorism* appeared in 1915, was itself a form of social engineering that would provide the perfect cover for what they had in mind. The Second World War also corresponded to a changing of the guard in which the previous generation of German-Jewish patricians—Jacob Schiff, Louis Marshall, Julius Rosenwald and Joel Spingarn—were replaced by a younger generation drawn almost exclusively from the ranks of the *Ostjuden* who had arrived during the period of upheaval in Russia following the assassination of Czar Alexander II in 1881 and before immigration quotas were imposed in 1924.

In 1943 John Slawson, who had been born in the Ukraine, became head of the American Jewish Committee and one of the leaders in what Murray Friedman calls "the Jewish phase of the civil rights revolution."[14] The Jewish phase was heavily involved in the promotion of Jewish social science as the main weapon in the fight against fascism. Under Slawson's leadership, the AJC "was the primary organizer of the social science-based attack on religious and racial discrimination."[15] In his capacity as head of the AJC, Slawson began promoting the work of the Frankfurt School refugees who had found their way to America during the 1930s. In addition to the work of Erich Fromm, Theodor W. Adorno, and Max Horkheimer, the AJC also sponsored the work of noted psychological warfare expert Kurt Lewin, who under the auspices of the AJC organized the Commission on Community Inter-relations, whose principles would get put into practice in places like Chicago after the war by people like Louis Wirth and Philip Klutznick, who went from being manager of Park Forest, one of the first experiments in using the car suburb as a form of social engineering, to being head of B'nai B'rith. Lewin was also instrumental in creating the form of social coercion known as the T-group or sensitivity group, which he hammered out with the help of a grant from the Office of Naval Research at his National Training Laboratory in Bethel, Maine. In promoting the work of the Frankfurt School refugees in America, Slawson saw himself as following in the footsteps of Cyrus Adler, the AJC's third president, who

> thought it was essential to mobilize public opinion in the United States against Hitler and his party without any reference to Jews at all. His views were shared by the group's other German-Jewish leaders, who had helped to subsidize the work of Boas and related social scientists in the interest of demolishing the Nazis' master-race mythology.[16]

The main difference between Slawson's and Adler's approach lay chiefly in the group which got targeted. After the war, the attack on fascism and racism that came to be known as social engineering was broadened to include not just Nazis but a whole group of unwitting American citizens who would have been outraged if they had known that their own government was collaborating with groups like the AJC to change their behavior.

In May 1944 Slawson convened a conference on anti-Semitism at the Biltmore Hotel in New York. At that conference members of the AJC's psychological warfare team—including Adorno, Horkheimer and Lewin—joined up with prominent members of the American social science establishment like Gordon Allport, John Dollard, Paul Lazarsfeld, Talcott Partons, and Lloyd Warner to identify "anti-Semitism as a central element in the antidemocratic personality."[17] The culmination of Slawson's efforts came in 1949-50 with the publication of the Studies in Prejudice series. "These enormously influential books," Friedman tells us, "were sponsored and paid for by the American Jewish Committee. The series central volume, *The Authoritarian Personality*, extended and strengthened Fromm's ideas."[18]

What followed was a barrage of covert social engineering unleashed on unsuspecting Americans, who were now accused of turning their children into little fascists if they ignored the Frankfurt School version of how to raise them. When Bess Myerson became the first Jewish Miss America, she joined the ADL's roster of speakers and went from school to school spreading the message, "you can't be beautiful and hate."

The Studies in Prejudice series never really got around to naming the domestic enemy who was now the successor of Nazism, but before long it became clear that the AJC was promoting an attack on two groups in particular. Southern whites and Catholic ethnics in the big cities of the north had become the prime candidates for the authoritarian personality award. As some indication of the groups that the AJC and their social science arm did not like, Leo Pfeffer, lawyer for the AJC and other Jewish organizations in the school prayer decisions of the '60s, once said that whenever his daughter wanted to get back at him, she threatened to marry a Catholic army officer from Alabama.[19]

As if on cue, Joe McCarthy, the German/Irish Catholic senator from Wisconsin emerged as the "dangerous demagogue, who perfectly epitomized the authoritarian personality described in the classic study,"[20] proving if nothing else that the psychological warfare techniques which got developed during the war were now going to be used against the opponents of the Black Jewish Alliance under the guise of social therapy.

Soon Frankfurt School messages began cropping up all over the place. The readers of *Collier's* magazine (which later published "The Body Snatchers," which got made into the film *The Invasion of the Body-Snatchers*, an early protest against social engineering) got to read "The Outcasts" by B. J. Chute, which presented in fictional form "an indictment of anti-Semitic covenants in real estate."[21] Not even Broadway musicals were exempt from doing duty as covert social engineering. Theatergoers who went to see *South Pacific* were treated to "Carefully Taught," which Friedman describes as a "show stopping song... stating that children had to be taught to hate," which "made the point in a way that Theodore Adorno and his colleagues at the AJC could never have dreamed possible."[22] It was during the postwar period, when Boasian anthropology began to be applied, via the Frankfurt School, as part of the mechanism which used social engineering to combat "prejudice," that the modern civil rights movement began to take shape.

Lorraine Hansberry was ten years old when her father won his Supreme Court case. Carl Hansberry, who would later claim that he had made a killing on the Rhoades Avenue building, would go on to make an even greater killing exploiting his new-found leverage in the Chicago real estate market. Now each time his or any other black family moved into a previously white neighborhood, panic ensued, and as white families dumped their houses on the market, black entrepeneurs like Hansberry could buy them up for a song and then sell them at the premium prices the housing market could then command to the new migrants from the South. "Black real estate speculators made a killing," wrote Truman K. Gibson, whose other client, Claude Barnett, director of the Associated Negro Press, "bought three buildings and confided to me that they were the best investments he ever made because they came at so little cost."[23]

Hansberry was a Republican who ran unsuccessfully for Congress in the November 1940 election. He was also the black version of the American Calvinist Jew Marx described in *Zur Judenfrage*. Hansberry was a member of what W. E. B. Du Bois would have called the "talented tenth," and the nation's "colored aristocracy," including Du Bois, felt welcome in his home. But Hansberry was also a slum landlord who had no qualms about exploiting his own people. Biographies of his more famous daughter sometimes list him as the inventor of the "kitchenette" apartment, which is another way of describing how he destroyed the large homes on the south side of by putting sinks and toilets in what used to be bedrooms and living rooms and then renting them at exhorbitant prices to the newly arrived sharecroppers from Mississippi. Carl's sons, under the name of Hansberry Enterprises, would carry on the same tradition in the 1950s after Carl, Sr.'s death, demanding large deposits from Mississippi sharecroppers and then evicting them so that Hansberry Enterprises could cash in on the next wave of unfortunate Negroes.

Lorraine Hansberry's biographer suggests that Carl, Sr.'s death at age 51 "was arguably caused by the strains of racism."[24] She also speculates that racism led to Lorraine's death of duodenal cancer at the age of 34. But in the case of Carl, Sr. bad business deals and extramarital affairs probably caused as much stress in his life as racism did. In the case of his daughter, class conflict was a bigger issue than racial conflict, because the Hansberrys were well off by anyone's definition of the term in the 1930s and 1940s. If anything, the Hansberry family profited handsomely from their exploitation of the racial situation in America. Carl, Sr. made a killing in real estate after the Supreme Court allowed him to cause panic in white neighborhoods with impunity. Lorraine's sister Mamie claims that her father "made quite a fortune during the depression because the white landlord simply couldn't collect the rent and he could."[25] And Lorraine Hansberry went on to became America's foremost black playwright in her day.

The Hansberrys were so well off in fact that they could afford to buy Lorraine an ermine coat for her fifth birthday. Lorraine wore her fur coat, not to church on Sunday, but to school during the week, with unfortunate consequences. Hansberry's fellow students, who considered themselves lucky if they had shoes on their feet and a bologna sandwich for lunch during the depths of the Depression, were so outraged by the Hansberrys' ostentatious display of wealth that they threw ink on Lorraine's fur coat and beat her up. If, as her biographer contends,

Lorraine Hansbery was "an outsider,"[26] it was her wealth and not her race which made her one.

If anything contributed to Lorraine's sense of herself as an outsider, it was the stigma of coming from a family of slum landlords. Consciousness of this fact made both generations of Hansberrys uncomfortable in Chicago and eager to leave. When he died suddenly at the age of 51, Carl, Sr. was planning to move to Mexico. Lorraine left Chicago at the age of 18 and never returned. In *A Raisin in the Sun*, the play which made her famous, Hansberry could allow Beneatha to distance herself from Chicago by fantasizing about an imaginary African past in which she conflated all of that continent's black ethnic groups into one proto-revolutionary mass, but her knowledge of Africa was limited at best and not first hand. Panafricanism may have been a fact of life in Chicago, but it never really caught on in Africa, as the numerous ethnic wars and genocides there indicate. At one point, Hansberry claimed that "Muzungu" was the Kikuyu name for Europeans and that it derived from "he who is dizzy." Mzungu, the word for white person, however, is Swahili not Kikuyu, and it is etymologically related to the verb to wander.

In 1950 Hansberry dropped out of the University of Wisconsin at Madison, and moved to New York, where she took writing classes at the New School for Social Research and worked as an assistant editor at Paul Robeson's new magazine, *Freedom*. It was at this point that she became the "intellectual revolutionary"[27] that she would be for the rest of her short life. Cheney sees a duality in Hansberry's life, claiming that she "never fully resolved the duality of her life and works—upper middle class affluence and black heritage and revolution,"[28] but she leaves out the main source of dichotomy.

Like Claude McKay, W. A. Domingo, Richard Wright, and many other black writers, Lorraine Hansberry learned about revolution from the Jews she met in New York. The dichotomy is evident in her major works. Hansberrry's first play, *A Raisin in the Sun*, is suffused with a Chicago that is both black and Christian, and as a result suffused with moral indignation against abortion and atheism. *The Window in Sidney Brustein's Window*, her second play, is suffused with bohemian Jewish New York but also with Hansberry's attempt to come to grips with this alien culture.

On June 20, 1953 Hansberry married Robert Nemiroff, a Jewish literature student and songwriter, whom she had met on a picket line protesting discrimination at New York University. Together they worked at odd jobs in the publishing industry and lived *la vie boheme* in Greenwich Village. Then in 1956, Nemiroff wrote a hit song, "Cindy, Oh Cindy," which earned him $100,000. Financially secure with the money from her husband's song, Hansberry quit her day job, devoted herself to writing full time, and completed a play about her experience growing up in Chicago, which she tentatively titled "The Crystal Stair," after a line in a Langston Hughes poem.

It wasn't an auspicious moment for the Black-Jewish Alliance. Friedman claims that "there was nothing phony or contrived about the commitment of most Jewish Communists to black civil rights."[29] To counter that claim, Cruse mentions that around the same time that Hansberry arrived in New York, the Jewish communists in charge of the Harlem branch of the party had ordered Harlem's Negro party members to protest *Ninotchka* at the Apollo Theater even though it was obvious that the Negroes had nothing to gain from the protest. Who but a Russian Jew would have been offended by Ernst Lubitsch casting Greta Garbo as a commissar who falls in love with her counterpart from the west in Paris? Cruse makes it clear that the Negroes had no dog in that fight.

Harold Cruse provides an interesting counterpoint to the career of Lorraine Hansberry. Like Hansberry, Cruse was a black migrant to New York. Cruse was born in Petersburg, Virginia on March 8, 1916 and moved to Harlem as a teenager. Like Hansberry, Cruse was an "intellectual revolutionary" who spent a number of years in the Communist Party learning revolution at the feet of Russian Jews. In this particular instance, Cruse was a member of the Communist Party from 1945 until 1952. When he left the party at the age of 36, Cruse had gained "a position of considerable respect among Harlem communists."[30] Like Hansberry, Cruse was interested in the theater and spent the 1950s, like Hansberry, trying to get a musical produced on Broadway. Like Hansberry, Cruse lived among the Bohemians of Greewich Village.

At this point the profiles begin to diverge. Le Roi Jones remembers Cruse as a "writer," not a political activist, who would frequent the Café Figaro in the Village and "was always complaining about how Broadway producers were turning down the musicals he was writing."[31] Unlike Hansberry, Cruse never made contact with anyone who wanted to back his plays, confirming his belief that Jews controlled Broadway for their own interests.

By the early '50s it had become clear to people like Cruse that the only reason the Jews who controlled the party were interested in Harlem was to turn Negroes into revolutionaries and use them to fight their battles. Cruse mentions the headline in the *Amsterdam News* of September 29, 1951—"Communists Woo Harlem—Open big drive in local area"—as a clear indication "that the Communists had retreated to Harlem because 'this belabored, belittled community is considered to be American's weakest link of resistance against the movement.'"[32] Friedman, who wrote his book on the Black-Jewish Alliance to refute Cruse, admits the same thing when he writes: "During the period of he Cold War, the tendency was to describe American communists as tools of Moscow utilizing the grievances of blacks for party interests alone."[33] Friedman gives even more evidence to support the thesis that Jews were using Negroes as revolutionary cannon fodder from the life of Richard Wright, even though he seems unaware that he is undermining his own thesis that "there was nothing phony or contrived about the commitment of most Jewish Communists to black civil rights"[34] in the act of presenting it:

In *The God that Failed*, Wright describes the presence of so many Jewish artists and writers in the movement as exhilarating. A Jewish writer invited him to a meeting of the John Reed club on Chicago's south side, where he was introduced to a group of young men and women who were to become leading painters, composers, novelists, and filmmakers. These men and women—all Jewish—formed with him the first sustained relationships of his life, and although he looked hard, he found no condescension in them. Wright, who twice married Jewish women, has a Jewish Communist, Boris Max, defend his black protagonist in *Native Son*. When the protagonist refuses to cooperate in a police investigation because police "hate black folks," Wright has Max reply, "They hate others too. They hate me because I'm trying to help you. They're writing me letters calling me a 'dirty Jew.'"[35]

Shortly after Hansberry and Nemiroff moved into their apartment in on Bleecker Street in Greenwich Village, the Supreme Court handed down *Brown v. Board of Education*, and what has come to be known as "the civil rights movement" came into existence. *Brown* struck down *Plessy v. Ferguson's* concept of "separate but equal," which was the cornerstone of the South's redemption and the North's withdrawal from Reconstruction. Brown, in turn, found its theoretical basis in Gunnar Myrdal's book *An American Dilemma*, which was a creation of the psychological warfare establishment under the direction of Samuel Stouffer and Louis Wirth, the University of Chicago sociologist who worked for the Office of War Information during the War.

As Murray Friedman hints, Myrdal did not and could not have written *An American Dilemma*. Nor did he need to since it was going to be based on the Boasian school of environmental sociology and anthropology anyway, and there were plenty of Boasians in the United States. The Boasians needed Myrdal as their front man because otherwise the Brown decision ran the danger of being derided as based on "Jewish science."[36] The Jews, particularly those at the NAACP were, of course, intimately involved with the *Brown* decision. Felix Frankfurter, Chief Justice on the Court which handed down *Brown*, was a German-speaking Jew from Vienna who had served on the NAACP's legal committee. Jack Greenberg of the NAACP, Friedman tells us, "drew the assignment to find experts in the Midwest for the landmark case *Brown V. Board of Education of Topeka, Kansas.*"[37] Kenneth B. Clark, the black psychologist whose study of black and white dolls indicated that students were harmed by segregated classrooms was cited in *Brown*, had been funded by the AJC. Clark's study led the court to conclude that "the average black American had been scarred by self-hatred," and that "segregation...inflicted vast psychic damage on both white and black children."[38] AJC-sponsored psychological studies festoon the decision from one footnote to another. Friedman concludes after the fact that "Clark's research... was flawed,"[39] but 50 years after the fact the point was moot. Flawed or not, the Jewish-sponsored research that made up the theoretical underpinning for the Brown decision had gotten the job done. *Brown* created both an atmosphere conducive to revolution and a weapon that could be used against the South for what it had done to Leo Frank. "The Court's May 17, 1954 decision," as Friedman put it, "would spur the civil rights revolution that followed."[40] Friedman claims that "the Black-Jewish Alliance did not exist in Dixie for good reasons."[41] First of all, the South lacked Jewish revolutionaries ("There were no Joel Spingarns there," is how Friedman put it.)[42] Secondly, southern Jews had been intimidated by the lynching of Leo Frank, who remained a "ghostly idol" into the '50s.[43] Northern Jews, who like their Southern counterparts, "grew up with the thought of Franks' lynching never far from their minds,"[44] had no qualms about antagonizing Southerners because they didn't have to live with them, and soon began to harass the South in an increasingly overt manner, one which culminated in the Freedom Summer of 1964, immortalized by the line from the Alan Sherman song, "How's your sister Ida?/She's a freedom rida."[45]

When 19 rabbis from the North arrived in Birmingham in 1963 to take part in protests against segregation and teach the local Negroes how to sing "Hava Nagila,"[46] a delegation of southern Jews met the "19 Messiahs" (as they were called by local Jews) and asked them to go home.[47] Ironically or not, Friedman concludes that "it was not racists but rather the Jewish civil rights protesters from the North and West whom southern Jews feared the most."[48]

This sort of revolutionary meddling soon created the reaction in the South which southern Jews feared. Before long "Jew" and "Communist" had become synonyms in the South. Unlike the good southern Jews, the New York Jews had come south with one purpose in mind, to stir up the Negroes and turn them into communist revolutionaries. Rep. John E. Rankin, who introduced legislation in Congress to outlaw the ADL, claimed that

> the "better element" of Jews throughout the South and West was not only ashamed but also alarmed by the activities of Jewish Communists, who were responsible for the rapes and murders of white girls by "vicious Negroes."[49]

In addition to that, Friedman notes that

> In 1948 a prominent member of the Daughters of the Confederacy's North Carolina chapter circulated a letter charging that most of the Communists in the United States were Jews and that most agitators stirring up southern Negroes were of Jewish origin. Jews also supplied most of the money for such activities.[50]

The suspicions of the Southerners were justified, but they were demonized for having them nonetheless. In *Travels with Charley*, a book which John Steinbeck dedicated to New York publisher and NAACP supporter Harold Guinzberg, Steinbeck runs into a cab driver in Louisiana, who tells him that "them goddamn New York Jews come in and stir the niggers up."[51] When Steinbeck picks up a cracker hitchhiker, who tells him he sounds like a "Commie nigger lover,"[52] Steinbeck loses no time in expelling this man from the RV which has come to symbolize deracinated America for saying the same thing that Murray Friedman would note with pride 30 some years later. By the time Friedman got around to writing his book in

1995, the civil rights movement was not only a good or necessary conspiracy; it was the Black-Jewish Alliance's finest hour.

Up until the Montgomery bus boycott of 1955, the Jews dominated the civil rights movement. Indeed, the NAACP, which was founded in 1909, did not have one black lawyer on its staff until 1933. After Montgomery, however, "The black masses now became the shock troops and the central force in the civil rights revolution."[53]

As if to prove that Steinbeck's cab driver was right all along, Friedman cites the case of Bayard Rustin, a Negro Quaker homosexual, who attended City College of New York, with its Stalinist and Trotskyite alcoves in the lunch room, and "joined the young communist league" after he arrived in New York.[54] In the summer of 1956 Bayard Rustin introduced Martin Luther King, Jr. to Stanley Levison, a "political radical who had worked on behalf of the convicted atom spies Ethel and Julius Rosenberg" who was also "a financial pillar of the Communist Party and other radical causes."[55] Levison would go on to become "enormously influential behind the scenes and throughout King's career."[56] Friedman claims that Levison became "King's closest white friend and most reliable colleague for the remainder of his life" and "would epitomize the Black-Jewish Alliance's new look."[57]

Levison got his start in politics shortly after the war when he became a financial contributor to the Communist Party. By 1953 he was assisting in the management of party finances, a job which included creating business fronts which would earn or launder money for the party. J. Edgar Hoover believed that Levison was under party discipline when he entered the King movement.

When Martin Luther King announced the creation of the Southern Christian Leadership Conference in 1957, it was Levison and Rustin who "labored behind the scenes in New York" to provide the $200,000 a year the SCLC needed for its operations in the South.[58] Eventually, Rustin and Levison were joined by two more members of the Black-Jewish Alliance—Jack O'Dell, a black communist, and Harry Wachtel. Together they came up with a list of 9,000 donors who were willing to make semiannual contributions to the SCLC to fund its operations. In 1963, the Kennedy brothers, Jack and Bobby, persuaded King to cut his ties with Bayard Rustin, but King never broke with Levison, and in fact spoke with him on the phone until King's death in 1968. Friedman gives conflicting accounts of the amount of Jewish money that ended up in the coffers of the SCLC. After citing Levison's claim "that only some 10 percent of SCLC's money came from Jews," Friedman goes on to say that "Jewish support" was "so important... that King's advisers considered dropping the word 'Christian' from the organization's title" and that Bayard Rustin "never failed to remind King to mention the Judeo-Christian tradition in his speeches."[59]

On March 11, 1959, the play Lorraine Hansberry had been working on since 1956 opened in New York at the Ethel Barrymore theater as *A Raisin in the Sun* and became an instant success. In addition to winning that year's New York Critics Circle Award as best drama of the year, Hansberry received congratulations by telegram from Tennessee Williams, was named "most promising playwright of the year" by *Variety* in June 1959, and sold the movie rights to the play to Columbia Pictures.

Hansberry's new-found fame allowed her to become a spokesman for the civil rights movement, which had reached a new phase of revolutionary development. Now instead of simply waiting for incidents to develop which could lead to litigation, the civil rights movement had taken to provoking incidents, which would invariably get televised and generate more revolutionary fervor by creating a violent backlash. In February 1960, four black students created the sit-in movement when they sat down at a whites-only lunch counter in Greensboro, North Carolina and demanded service. The students were then beaten when they refused to leave, and the sit-in movement was born as a form of passive-aggressive behavior, and the movement took another step toward violent revolution.

The sit-in movement soon found wide support among the nation's Jews, a fact that James Farmer of the Congress for Racial Equality exploited in his fundraising speeches. On the advice of his fundraiser Marvin Rich, Farmer never gave a speech without reciting what Rich called "the quote," Hillel's admonition: "If I am not for myself, who will be for me? But if I am only for myself, what am I? And if not now, when?"[60] Farmer relied on another Jew, Morris Milgram, for organizational assistance, and together Milgram and Farmer recruited Jews from the Workers' Defense League and the Young People's Socialist Alliance to fill the top administrative posts at CORE.

Once the success of the sit-in movement became apparent, Stokely Carmichael, another black Jamaican from New York City, broke with the SCLC and created the Student Nonviolent Coordinating Committee in 1960 to escalate the movement. Marion Barry, who became famous later as the first Mayor of Washington, DC to be arrested on a charge of cocaine possession, was elected first chairman of SNCC.

In the spring of 1961, Farmer and CORE called for a series of interracial "freedom rides" on public buses throughout the South, and the Jewish Freedom Riders headed South to spread revolution. Friedman estimates that "Jews probably made up two thirds of the white Freedom Riders into the South in the summer of 1961 and about one third to one half of the Mississippi Summer volunteers three years later."[61] Even Arthur Spingarn, then in his eighties, got into the act. Unlike the SCLC, SNCC did not bar Communists from membership, a fact which enabled still more New York Jews to pour into the movement. The massive numbers of arrests that the sit-movement and the freedom riders generated required an army of lawyers, and "More than half of them," including Edward I. Koch, future mayor of New York City, "were Jews."[62] Of the three civil rights workers murdered in Mississippi—Goodman, Schwerner, and Chaney—two were Jews and one was black. Schwerner, who "was the primary target of the killers, because of his longer involvement with civil rights workers in Mississippi,"[63] was an atheist who saw the civil rights movement as cutting edge of Messianic politics, which had always sought to create heaven on earth by wielding the sword, even if the revolutionary sword was disguised by the tactics of nonviolence:

> It was because Schwerner had no hope of heaven that he held such extravagant hopes here on earth. And for many the pursuit or racial justice became a kind of secular religion..... Rabbi Philip Bernstein made the point that the Jewish radical who ignored his Jewishness was still the product of messianic fervor: Though he might not be aware of it, he was spiritually wearing his yarmulke as he headed South.[64]

"Eventually," Friedman concludes, "virtually every segment of the Jewish community enlisted in the civil rights struggle.... Nothing would be the same again in the South, but a *true revolution* was under way"[65] (my emphasis).

As in Harlem in the '20s, many of the black leaders of the movement had learned their tactics from revolutionary Jews. Robert Moses, the charismatic black leader of the SNCC's Mississippi Summer Project, "was a product of the black-Jewish radical culture, having attended a Jewish socialist camp as a child and become friends with Jewish young people from similar radical backgrounds."[66]

The Black-Jewish Alliance reached its moment of triumph during the famous 1963 March on Washington when Bob Dylan, the world's most famous Jewish folksinger, sang and Martin Luther King gave his famous "I have a dream speech." Three months earlier, however, when King met with John and Robert Kennedy in the White House on June 22, he was told in no uncertain terms that his organization had ties to, and was possibly controlled by, the Communist Party. Robert Kennedy claimed that SCLC's fundraiser Stanley Levison "was acting on Soviet orders to weaken the United States by manipulating the civil rights movement."[67] John Kennedy, who was under pressure from Southern Democrats to rein in the civil rights movement, named O'Dell as "the number five Communist in the United States"[68] and claimed that Levison was his handler. Acting under pressure from the Kennedys, King fired O'Dell on July 3 but maintained covert contact with the less dispensable Levison, whom Friedman refers to as King's "closest white advisor."[69] Deprived of the Jews and Communists that provided the backbone of its financial and administrative support, the SCLC, which was now staffed by southern Negroes who sat around the office talking to each other, started to fall apart.

Chapter Twenty-Three

The Birth of Conservatism

In 1947, Henry Regnery, scion of a wealthy Chicago industrialist who had a been a pillar and major funder of the America First movement, founded a publishing house for a new "conservatism" espoused by Russell Kirk and William F. Buckley. Kirk's *The Conservative Mind* and Buckley's *God and Man at Yale* appeared under the Regnery imprint in 1951. Of the two, Kirk was more original. Kirk created modern, post-World War II conservatism by resurrecting the conservative Whiggery of Edmund Burke, emphasizing Burke's emphasis on local autonomy and the moral underpinnings of the social order, and omitting, as had Burke, mention of the Whigs setting the wheels in motion for the French Revolution.

Like the Whigs of theearly and mid-18th century, the American conservatives of the mid-20th century had a penchant for black operations. In 1955, two years after Irving Kristol became co-editor of *Encounter*, Buckley launched *National Review*, "which soon became a rallying point for the new conservatism."[1] Years later, Revilo Oliver, who was an early contributor to *NR*, would claim that it, like *Encounter*, was a CIA front. Murray Rothbard, an irrepressible libertarian who grew up among the Messianic Jewish sects of New York City, also felt *NR* was a CIA front.

As Rothbard and others have made clear, the CIA was always in the business of media manipulation. "Not long after the Central Intelligence Agency was founded in 1947," Rothbard writes, "the American public and the world were subjected to an unprecedented level of propaganda in the service of US foreign policy objectives in the Cold War.... At its peak the CIA allocated 29 percent of its budget to 'media and propaganda.'"[2]

Because of intense internecine communist hatred, the Trotskyites were willing, if not positively eager, to grasp the levers of the anti-Stalinist propaganda machine. According to Rothbard, the Neoconservatives "moved from cafeteria Trotskyites to apologists for the US warfare state without missing a beat."[3] The CIA established the Congress for Cultural Freedom as its premiere anti-Stalinist organization, but that organizaton's credibility was destroyed when it became known it was a CIA front. James Burnham, a former Trotskyite and CIA agent who co-founded *National Review*, worked for the Congress. He was also a former Trotskyite and a CIA agent. When Peter Colemant Exposed *Enconter* as a CIA front operation in his largely sympathetic book *The Liberal Conspriacy*, Irving Kristol , the father of neoconservatism, at first denied knowing that Encounter was a CIA front. Later , in his autobiorgrpahy, he admitted knowing that the CIA was involved but tried to play down the scale of his involvement. Rothbard, however felt that Kristol was being disingenuous if not downright dishonest. As Rothbard points out, Tom Braden, then head of the CIA's International Organizations Division, "wrote in a *Saturday Evening Post* article, a CIA agent always served as editor of *Encounter*."

If *National Review*, like *Encounter*, was a CIA front, what purpose did it serve? *National Review* existed to destroy competing conservatisms, especially those incompatible with the internationalist foreign policy establishment. *National Review* used conservatism to mobilize certain ethnic groups, e.g., Catholics, behind government policies. It existed to colonize certain groups, to divide and conquer, and then get them to act against their own interests. *NR* was created to destroy isolationist conservatism. Conservatives who criticized America's march to empire were demonized and decertified. *National Review* has shown undeviating consistency in this regard, the most recent example being David Frum's diatribe against the paleoconservatives, "Unpatriotic Conservatives," in the March 19, 2003 issue. According to Rothbard, "the idea for *National Review* originated with Willi Schlamm, a hard-line interventionist and feature editor with the Old Right *Freeman*," who was "at odds with the isolationism of the right."[4] Friend of the Buckley family Revilo Oliver said *NR* "was conceived as a way to put the isolationist *Freeman* out of business. A surreptitious deal was cut with one of the *Freeman* editors (presumably Schlamm) to turn the magazine over to Buckley."[5]

By 1955, when *National Review* was launched, Buckley had long been a CIA agent. In his biography of Buckley, Judis claims Buckley served under E. Howard Hunt in Mexico City in 1951. Rothbard claims Buckley was directed to the CIA by Yale Professor Wilmoore Kendall, who introduced him to James Burnham, then a consultant to the Office of Policy Coordination, the CIA's covert-action wing. While at Yale, Buckley had served as a campus informant for the FBI, "feeding," Rothbard says, "God only knows what to Hoover's political police."[6]

Buckley's sister Priscilla also worked for the CIA, as did almost everyone associated with founding *National Review*, including William Casey, who would later head the CIA. Casey drew up its legal documents. Of the $500,000 needed to launch *NR*, $100,000 came from Buckley's father. The source of the rest of the funding is unknown. Frank Meyer, author of the "fusionist" ideology that informed *NR*, confided privately to Rothbard that he believed *National Review* was a CIA front.

In his history of neoconservatism, *The Neoconservative Revolution: Jewish Intellectuals and the Shaping of Public Policy*, Murray Friedman claims even more convincingly that *National Review* was run by Jews. As the career of Irving Kristol demonstrates, we are not talking about mutually exclusive alternatives here. Following the lead of Jewish organizations like the AJC and the ADL and their avid support of America's anti-Communist crusade, many American Jews went to work just as avidly for the CIA as their parents and grandparents had worked for the CHEKA.

National Review could grow out of and absorb *The Freeman* because that magazine had already been absorbed by "conservative Jewish activists"[7] like Frank Meyer, Frank Chodorov, Morrie Raskin, and Willi Schlamm. In this regard, young Yale graduates Buckley and L. Brent Bozell, his brother-in-law to be, were both junior partners and *goyische* front men in the venture. Friedman calls Willi Schlamm one of "the forgotten Jewish godfathers"[8] of *NR*. Schlamm worked at *Time*, but hearing that Buckley had access to funding, suggested that he bring out an opinion magazine. With a promise of $100,000 from Buckley's father, Schlamm co-wrote the business plan that drew in other investors. Buckley later described Schlamm, who possessed "all the patronizing charm of the Viennese cafe intellectual along with the cultural solemnity of the Jew brought up under German culture," as one of "his two closest partners" in founding *NR*.[9] The other was Sidney Hook's protégé James Burnham, also a CIA agent. Friedman notes "Although *National Review* has often been characterized as militantly Catholic and Irish-Catholic, five Jews served on the original editorial board including Meyer and Schlamm."[10] "Buckley's circle of Jews"[11] included Frank Chodorov, who appointed Buckley president of the Intercollegiate Society of Individualists (later changed to the Intercollegiate Studies Institute) only to remove him because it was "Easier to raise money if a Jew is president."[12] ISI would produce neoconservative activists like Edwin J. Feulner, Jr., later president of the Heritage Foundation, and Irving Kristol's son, William, who would become Vice President Quayle's chief of staff and editor of the neocon flagship *The Weekly Standard*.

Another of "Buckley's circle of Jews" was Frank Meyer, whose fusionism was the philosophical underpinning for *National Review*. Meyer was a student of Louis Wirth at the University of Chicago. Like Wirth, he was a Stalinist who had second thoughts. The result was "fusionism," an eclectic ideology that sought to combine the best (or least incompatible) elements of the conservative movement. As senior editor at *National Review*, Meyer tried to combine the libertarianism of the Randians and the Austrian school with the traditionalism of Russell Kirk in his column "Principles and Heresies." The only thing that kept this radically incoherent mixture together was anti-Communism, and, when Communism fell apart in 1989, conservatism fell apart too.

What conservatism lacked in philosophical coherence, it made up for in organizing techniques its "founding Jewish fathers"[13] remembered from their days in the Communist Party or in Zionist terrorist organizations. The most influential organizer in Buckley's "circle of Jews" was Marvin Liebman, a former communist who came to conservatism *via* Zionism, in particular *via* the terrorist organization Irgun Zvai Leumi. In 1946, Liebman was captured smuggling Jews into Palestine and held in a British detention camp on Cyprus for 15 days. When the Korean War killed his enthusiasm for Communism, Liebman discovered conservatism. Liebman created a public relations firm that fronted for anti-Communist crusades, and it was in this capacity that he became the moving force behind the publishing of *National Review*. It was Liebman who mobilized the young Republicans who were disillusioned in the aftermath of Nixon's defeat in 1960 into Young Americans for Freedom, and it was Liebman, with the help of YAF, who mobilized New York for Barry Goldwater in 1964. It was Liebman who invited those activists to his farm in Sharon, Connecticut, for a meeting that issued the Sharon Statement, which was more influential than the more well-known Port Huron Statement of the SDS. Liebman's Sharon Statement was a philosophically incoherent blend of traditionalism and libertarianism, held together by anticommunism and political organizing. "Liebman," according to Friedman, "was the key figure in the creation of what one historian has called 'the most important organizational initiative undertaken by conservatives in the last 30 years.'"[14] Buckley, often credited with founding YAF, credited Liebman, saying, "my midwifery ... was purely ceremonial."[15]

Much of what is attributed to William F. Buckley was the work of Jewish thinkers and financiers who, working behind the scenes, created a foil to the socialism that held the allegiance of the majority of American Jews. Buckley was the *goyische* front man for Trotskyite conservatism in the same way Gus Hall was the *goyische* front man for American Communism. Hall reportedly was chosen to head the Communist Party in America because he was the only member who didn't have a Brooklyn accent. Buckley's role, however, was more specific and more related to his Catholic identity. Buckley was the ideological enforcer who would pronounce the political *cherem* on competing conservative sects and expel them from the synagogue. He was also the model for the Catholics he was to control by transforming them from recalcitrant ethnics into docile movement conservatives. "Buckley's most important contribution to the conservative movement," Friedman says, was "his purge of its most extreme and bigoted elements. 'Conservatism,' he wrote, 'must be wiped of the parasitic cant that defaces it.'"[16] Never a deep thinker, Buckley relied on Jews for the heavy lifting, whether getting him subscribers (Liebman) or coming up with a conservative philosophy (Meyer). Buckley's job was to serve as a model for the Catholic students from Villanova and Fordham who flocked to the YAF. His other job was to destroy any conservative movement not toeing the line of the internationalist establishment. All forms of "isolationism" were anathema. It also meant an all out attack on anything "anti-Semitic."

In October 1965, *National Review* attacked the John Birch Society, using Barry Goldwater and Frank Meyer to claim "the Birch's Society's 'psychosis of conspiracy' threatened American interests."[17] The attack, according to Friedman, "proved to be a critical moment in the development of a more responsible conservative movement."[18] Shortly after dispatching the Birchers, Buckely received his own TV show, *Firing Line*, which he used to attack George Wallace, then a significant threat to the two-party monopoly. Buckley also attacked Ayn Rand and Objectivism, which Whittaker Chambers portrayed as a competing sect that was the mirror image of Soviet Communism. Chambers, in a *NR* piece, "Big Sister Is Watching You," likened "Randian man" to "Marxian man,"—each was the center of a godless world.[19] "From almost any page of *Atlas Shrugged*, a voice can be heard commanding: 'To a gas chamber—go!'"[20] Rand fired back, denouncing *NR* as "the worst and most dangerous magazine in America."[21] In 2003 Alan Greenspan, a Randian, was still critical of Buckley. "Someone has finally defined the rational morality underlying capitalism," the economic savant wrote, "and you treat it in such a vulgar manner."[22]

Some of the Jews associated with Buckley at *National Review* eventually converted to Catholicism. Friedman claims that all of the Jews associated with *NR* were philo-Catholic without stating what was equally obvious, namely, that Buckley undermined the Catholic positions on of the crucial issues of the age, from contraception to economics, under the motto "Mater si Magistra no!" He was also the agent of choice when it came to blacklisting and/or publicly denouncing Catholics who dared to stray from the conservative reservation.

National Review's purpose was to purge "bad" conservatives by running the conservative blacklist. The first to go were isolationists and anyone with residual sympathies for the America First movement, including followers of Father Coughlin. Then the John Birch Society was purged. Then the Ayn Rand cult. Then Joe Sobran and Pat Buchanan after Buckley denounced them as anti-Semites. Most recently, David Frum excommunicated paleoconservatives as traitors during the run-up to the war in Iraq. Paleocon columnist Sam Francis was purged as a columnist at the *Washington Times* largely because of Buckley's efforts. Before his death, Francis claimed Buckley was responding to a memo from the ADL.

Before long it became clear that conservatism became whatever certain Jews defined as conservatism, and any conservative who disagreed was expelled from the synagogue of organizations like the Philadelphia Society by being labeled an anti-Semite. Russell Kirk, founder of the conservative movement, experienced Midge Decter's ire when he bemoaned Jewish influence in the movement. Even the philo-Catholic Jews at *National Review* were unable to get beyond the rhetoric of Messianic, revolutionary politics, and unable to tolerate anyone who disagreed with their essentially Talmudic understanding of conservatism. After Richard Nixon's presidential nomination, Frank Meyer lectured a group of students on the difference between real and false conservatism. Real conservatism was Jewish. Real conservatism was Talmudic. Real conservatism was revolutionary. Or, as Friedman puts it:

> Meyer declared, in a manner Jewish Neoconservatives would adopt later, "a revolutionary force" had shattered "the unity and balance of civilization." Conservatism should not be limited to an uncomplicated reverence for the past, which is the essence of natural conservatism. The conscious conservative, he proclaimed, was required to become, in a nonpejorative sense, an ideologue, with a clear understanding of how principles and institutions and men affect each other to form a culture and a society.[23]

1955: Ramblin' Jack Elliot heads for England

In 1955, Ramblin' Jack left for England, which was going through the Skiffle Craze, and became a sensation overnight. Wizz Jones remembers him, strutting around Piccadilly Circus in his cowboy outfit. "He was larger than life. With his cowboy boots and hat, he would stop traffic. But one day we realized that he really wasn't what he claimed to be. He was Elliott Adnopoz. And one day his mother and father came to the gig. That's amazing."²⁴ Instead of being disillusioned, Jones was filled with admiration for Adnopoz posturing as a cowboy, because it proved to a generation of Englishmen, including Mick Jagger, Keith Richards, Donovan, John Lennon, and Rod Stewart, "You can choose to be whatever you want to be. You can turn your back on your roots. You don't have to be what your parents wanted you to be."²⁵

The generation born to the Communist New York Jews during the 1930s and '40s came to be known as "red diaper babies." Their parents didn't want them to grow up to be cowboys. They wanted them to grow up to be decent upstanding Jewish Communists like Julius and Ethel Rosenberg, and to insure that this would happen, the Communists and their fellow travelers created a group of summer camps in the Catskills where they would be sheltered from the red-baiting of the Irish Catholics who taught them in New York's public school system. These summer camps were the laboratory in which the new personal lifestyle was created. In the late 1940s, Ron Radosh attended Camp Woodland for Children, "one of the myriad alternative institutions founded by the Communist Party in its effort to construct an alternative to America."²⁶ Woodland was technically independent although," Radosh notes, "it drew its staff from the Communist world."²⁷

The most radical of all of the Catskill red-diaper baby camps was Camp Wo-Chi-Ca, a name derived from the first syllables of the words, Workers' Children's Camp. Campers recited a pledge "to combat the influence of jokes, comic books, newspapers, radio programs that make fun of any people."²⁸ As the anti-comic book pledge makes clear, the Jewish communists of the 1940s seemingly had more in common with the Legion of Decency than with, say, the Fugs, a Reichian sex-pol rock band formed in the '60s by Tuli Kupferberg, which is to say, by their own children. Camp Kinderland was more Jewish in its orientation; it tried to hand on "to the children of Eastern European Jewish immigrants the legacy of the secular Jewish radical culture developed in the Old Country."²⁹ Camp Kinderland featured an appearance by the widow of the Yiddish writer Sholom Aleichem, "whose portraits of *shtetl* life in Poland became the basis for the musical hit *Fiddler on the Roof*," as well as "modern dance classes led by Martha Graham protégé Edith Segal, a hard-core Communist who tried to blend modern dance with Marxism."³⁰ Soviet holidays were Jewish holidays for the Jewish communists who lived in this milieu. Radosh recounts a joke: "What Jewish holidays do you celebrate?" The answer: "Paul Robeson's birthday and May Day."³¹

When Radosh joined the Communist Party, "the reasons had little to do with politics and a great deal to do with the need to find an identity."[32] He could just as easily have said that Communism was part of his ethnic identity as a New York Jew. Communism was a way of being a Jew. The Labor Youth League offered "the camaraderie of a tight-knit group of ready-made friends along with a sense of moral superiority" because it was ethnically homogeneous, something he takes up at another point in the same narrative when he says, "most of the members of ... the Upper West Side LYL, were all Jewish."[33] A salient aspect of the Communist organization was "a purely cultural *Yiddishkeit* that emphasized Yiddish literature and theater, the folk writing of Sholom Aleichem, the parables of freedom that abounded throughout Jewish culture, and most important a complete rejection of anything to do with religion."[34]

More important than Jewish religion were Jewish morals, which were in flux during Radosh's teen years. The LYL, says Radosh, "offered the possibility of what every teenage boy seeks: a girlfriend. God bless the Communist movement for giving me my very first sexual experiences from among a group of 'liberated' girls whom I found time to romance."[35] Radosh makes light of his generation's sexual experiences, but they would have far-reaching consequences for the Left. The subverters were unwittingly subverted by their own penchant for subversion. At the Upper West Side Chapter of the LYL, Radosh met David Horowitz, who would become his lifelong friend, introducing him late in life to the Jewish subversion known as neoconservatism.

Freed from the constraints imposed on them by the then largely anti-Communist public schools, counsellors at Camp Woodland could promote "progressive education," which, Radosh says, "meant the creation of a new personality to fit the new kind of culture which we saw developing in America."[36] At Camp Woodland the Jews learned they were in America but not of it. The counselors were "to liberate children not from their parents but from America;"[37] because if the camp liberated campers from their parents, they would have no longer been communists. The Jews sent their children to Camp Woodland to internalize what the camp director called the "new emerging culture of democracy," which meant "the ethos of the Popular Front, the Communist Party's attempt to domesticate itself after the disastrous, revolutionary Third Period, when it had demanded a break with liberals and social democrats."[38] Camp Woodland was creating "the new socialist man," a "new democratic personality," that was "molded to fit the socialist paradise to come."[39]

Since its educational philosophy was based on the Popular Front, folk music played a major role at Camp Woodland. There Radosh met Pete Seeger, who also had lasting effect on his life, determining what instrument he played and the politics that went along with it. According to Radosh,

The highlight of many Sunday meetings was to have Seeger gather before the camp at the outdoor amphitheater, where he first sang what much later would become hits for the Weavers, including his version of Leadbelly's "Goodnight, Irene" and "Kisses Sweeter Than Wine." The camaraderie one felt in sitting with friends and singing the beautiful words and melodies produced a belief that all would be good in the world and that the lovely music we were creating would help us build that better world.[40]

Largely because of the Catskill commie summer camps, folk music became the revolutionary *lingua franca* for a generation of Jewish revolutionaries:

I am convinced that much of the radicalism that Woodlanders would carry with them in later years came from the illusions they developed as a result of the weekly sing-alongs with Seeger. Songs are weapons, he often said. And during the years of the commercial top 40 "Hit Parade," before rock and roll, songs were helping us to build an alternative culture mirroring the alternative politics that Seeger was trying to create during the 1948 presidential campaign, when he accompanied Henry A. Wallace throughout the country and sang wherever Wallace appeared for his new Progressive Party.[41]

Seeger also educated a generation of predominantly Jewish five-string banjo pickers like John Cohen, of the New Lost City Ramblers and Eric Weissberg, whose "Dueling Banjos" became a hit from the movie *Deliverance*.

Summer 1959

Alice and Ron Radosh got married in summer of 1959. Before heading off to one more Left-wing, Jewish, folk music enclave at the University of Iowa, they spent an extended honeymoon at Wingdale on the Lake. It was not a good omen for their marriage.

Arriving in Iowa, the Radoshes found a ready-made community, namely, "the bohemian and political fringe" at "the university's first off-campus, Greenwich Village-style coffee shop." There Radosh met poet Bob Mezey, "a master guitar picker and folk singer" and Sol Stern, later editor at the '60s icon, *Ramparts*.[42] Stern, Radosh says, "was another New York Jew who had attended the City College of New York and had been active in its left-wing milieu."[43] By now, the Jewish left-wing milieu had outposts in almost every university town in the country, a network that promoted folk music, proletarian-chic clothing, sexual liberation, and radical politics *ad libidem*. Radosh could differ with Stern, who "ridiculed my orthodoxy," but they shared the same "basic socialist assumptions."[44] Even that misstates the case. They shared cultural and ethnic assumptions that would make the revolution of the '60s as inevitable as it made the politics of their fathers irrelevant. Radosh and Stern were revolutionary Jews, and they had a nationwide network of folkmusic coffee houses from which to promote revolution. The other details were irrelevant. More importantly, the music at those coffeehouses would soon be promoted by the mainstream media, magnifying the revolutionary effect, bringing revolution to the children of the *goyim*, who thought they were listening to an authentic alternative to Nelson Riddle arrangements of Frank Sinatra.

The situation in Philadelphia was no different from that in Madison, Wisconsin or Ames, Iowa. The Philadelphia folksong society was formed in 1957 by a group who mirrored the Philadelphia ADA, i.e., Left-wing Jews and WASPs united to keep the city from falling into the hands of Catholic ethnics. The Jews ran the folk music clubs, the Gilded Cage, run by Ed and Esther Halpern, and The Second Fret, run by Manny "Money" Rubin, and the premier radio show in town, hosted by Gene Shay, whose real name was Ivan Shaner. They quickly took over the movement and redefined it to suit their tastes as a vehicle for cultural revolution.

Shaner was born into a Russian Jewish family in the Nicetown section of Philadelphia, where his father owned a women's lingerie store. Shaner was drawn to Jazz after World War II, but then he met Ken Goldstein, who in 1959 became professor of anthropology at the University of Pennsylvania. Goldstein had the most impressive folk record collection in town and exerted enormous influence. Goldstein was instrumental in creating the Philadelphia Folk Festival in 1962. He also arranged recording contracts, and from his position at the University of Pennsylvania he had a major say over how things ethnic got defined in Philadelphia. "Ken," according to one folk devotee, "put Philadelphia on the map as a folk city."[45] Goldstein determined "one doesn't find traditional musicians in Philadelphia,"[46] so he imported acts from the network of clubs across the country but largely from New York. Ironically, Philadelphia, because of its traditionalism, was a bastion of traditional Jewish music. Klezmer didn't mutate in Philadelphia as it had in New York, but in the late '50s Klezmer didn't count as "traditional," which, paradoxically, had become a synonym for revolutionary.

When he met Ken Goldstein, Ivan Shaner switched from promoting Jazz to promoting folk. He changed his name too. "In those days," Shaner explained later, "ethnic names had to be changed."[47] Since Shaner "found myself getting into Anglo-American folk music, Scottish ballads, etc.,"[48] he adopted the Scotch-Irish sounding Shay, which also referred crypticly to the first syllable of Shaner. "I ... found I liked traditions,"[49] explained Shay ironically.

Through Goldstein, Shaner met Tossi Aaron and ended up managing her career. Her albums *Jewish Folk Songs for the Second Generation* and *Tossi Sings American Folk Songs and Ballads*, evince, we are told, "an original Philadelphia folk sound."[50] It was Ivan Shaner who brought Bob Dylan to Philadelphia for his first performance there. While in town, Dylan and his girlfriend stayed at Tossi Aaron's house.

1961: Bob Dylan arrives in New York

After Bob Dylan signed his first contract with Columbia Records, someone from the publicity department, whom Dylan identifies as Bill, "dressed Ivy League like he could have come out of Yale"[51] interviewed Dylan for material to promote the album. To get Dylan "to cough up some facts," Bill asked Dylan about his family, "where they were," etc., only to find that the 19-year-old folksinger had "no idea," telling Bill that they were "long gone."[52]

This was untrue. Mr. and Mrs. Zimmerman, Bob's parents, were alive and well in Hibbing, Minnesota. He had spoken with them recently on the phone. Dylan said he had just arrived in New York City via boxcar, which was also not true. He had driven there with students from Minneapolis, where he had been a student and part of the folk scene. The reference to the boxcar set up the best question:

> "What kind of music do you play?" Bill asked, and without batting an eye, Dylan responded "Folk music."[53]

When Bob Dylan uttered the term, folk music was another word for Jewish cosmopolitanism or deracination. Bob Dylan, according to Bob Spitz, one of his many biographers, "was haunted by his lack of roots."[54] Dylan "claimed little connection to an ancestral bloodline"[55] and changed his name, settling on the first name of a Welsh poet who died of alcohol poisoning. Dylan says the one thing he "didn't have too much of" was "a concrete identity."[56] So he made one up from snatches of folk songs: "'I'm a rambler—I'm a gambler. I'm a long way from home.' That pretty much summed it up"[57] is how Dylan described his "concrete identity" or lack thereof in his autobiography. Dylan would claim he was an orphan, and he would deny being Jewish. (At another point, he accused the disapproving mother of a girlfriend of being an "anti-Semite" because she didn't view him as the ideal son-in-law.) There was, of course, a certain amount of irony in this because by the time he arrived in New York City in January of 1961, folk music had become pretty much a Jewish enterprise, certainly in New York City. Bob Dylan was a genius at creating and projecting an image. He was also the quintessential Jewish folk-singer, but that image involved a certain amount of crypsis, lest the idea become a source of mirth rather than mystery. Myth was Dylan's only reality.

Fabrication of image, mythic or not, was in some sense a necessity because Dylan was a third-generation Jew, i.e., a Jew on whom the triple melting pot had done its work. Bob's grandparents came from Odessa, but his grandmother, his only surviving link to that past, was living in Duluth, a predominantly Polish patchwork of ethnic neighborhoods typical of cities across the northern tier of the United States. Bob Dylan's ethnic identity was now dependent on religion not country of origin, and since he had no religion to speak of, he had to create an identity out of the materials at hand. That meant music because he aspired to be a musician, and, in particular, it meant constructing an identity out of snatches from the folk songs of the '60s. Bob offhandedly indicates his musical heritage was Polish, most certainly not Appalachian Scotch- Irish, whose deracinated derivative passed as folk music when he arrived in New York. "Polka dances," Dylan says, "always got my blood pumping. That was the first type of loud, live music I'd ever heard. On Saturday nights the taverns were filled with polka bands."[58]

Dylan would say this after he was famous. It was not hip to be pro-polka in New York City in 1961, especially among those Dylan wanted to impress. Israel Young ran the Folklore Center, "the citadel of Americana [sic] folk music."[59] Young, "an old-line folk enthusiast," was "very sardonic and wore heavy horn-rimmed glasses, spoke in a thick Brooklyn dialect."[60] His Center was "a crossroads junction for all the folk activity you could name and you might at any time see real hard-line folksingers in there."[61] Bob Dylan wanted to become a "real hard-line" folksinger, like the lapsed Catholic from Brooklyn, Dave Van Ronk, who showed up at the Folklore Center during Dylan's conversation with Izzy Young.

Dylan would not be satisfied being a second-rate Dave Van Ronk. He wanted to become a second-rate Elvis Presley; or better, he wanted to become the Elvis Presley of folksingers. To do that, he had to impress Izzy Young, and to do that he had to keep his mouth shut about the Polka joints in Duluth and Hibbing. Dylan wasn't going to become as famous as Elvis by playing polkas. After Dylan scandalized the folk world in 1965 by playing amplified instruments at the Newport Folk Festival, Young, the folk music maven, said in *Sing Out!*: "Next year he'll be writing rhythm & blues songs when they get high on the charts; the following year, the Polish polka will make it, and then he'll write them too."[62] By 2004, Dylan was so hip he was beyond hip; he could even say he liked polkas. It was clear that he could not say this in 1961, not if he wanted to make it in New York City.

But that doesn't mean ethnic connections weren't helpful. Bob Dylan told his first New York girlfriend, Suze Rotolo, that he was an orphan who "had run away from his foster parents in Fargo, North Dakota."[63] It might have been a good line for picking up chicks, but he had something more sophisticated for Young, as he "thumbed through a lot of his antediluvian folk scrolls"[64] at the Folklore Center. When "Izzy ... asked me about my family," Dylan talked about his grandmother from Odessa: "I told him about my grandma on my mom's side who lived with us."[65] It was easy to string along a dumb *goy* like Bill from Yale, but Jewish identity had its perks when played right. Dylan's identity had to appeal to those who controlled the media and the folk-song establishment. This meant coming up with something Jewish, but cryptically so. Dylan was the consummate artist of identity. Dylan was in the "long tradition in show business that permits a performer to adopt an ethnic identity not necessarily his own."[66] As Al Jolson put on black face, so Bob Dylan put on white face, literally, during his days with the Rolling Thunder Revue. Figuratively, the scion of Odessa Jews put on both black face and white face in his search for a compelling, marketable identity. First, black face, as, according to Spitz, "he embodied Little Richard's black gospel performance,"[67] and then "white face," as he imitated Okie Woody Guthrie. It soon became impossible to distinguish the mask from the face behind it.

The most obvious identity for Bob Dylan in the early '60s, the singing Jewish cowboy, had already become a standing joke that got Lenny Bruce lots of laughs. Dylan had to come up with something more subtle without disguising himself so thoroughly that he would lose the benefit of knowing Izzy Young and Irwin Silber and all of the other singing Jewish cowboys. So Bob Dylan went to work assembling an identity from the sources available. There was, of course, Woody Guthrie but there was also, at least according to the autobiography, Bertold Brecht, Albertus Magnus (who "seemed like a guy who couldn't sleep, writing this stuff late at night, clothes stuck to his clammy body")[68], Sophocles, who wrote the Oedipus trilogy, but who, according to Dylan, was the author of a "book on the nature and function of the gods" which also explained "why there were only two sexes," and, of course, Thucydides.[69] How could we leave out Thucydides? Albertus Magnus, Dylan the polymath tells us, "was a lightweight compared to Thucydides."[70]

Dylan never explains the link binding Albertus Magnus and Thucydides, except that translations of their books sat next to each other on some bookshelf in some apartment in Greenwich Village. However, when Dylan expounds on the influence of other seminal figures, a pattern emerges. "Picasso," he says, "had fractured the art world and cracked it wide open. *He was a revolutionary*. I wanted to be like that."[71] Dylan projected as much into this disparate group of thinkers as he drew from them. He drew from them what he thought would play well with Izzy Young. That meant, in short, a penchant for revolution.

Dylan says he spent long hours hanging out with Liam Clancy of the Clancy brothers at the White Horse Tavern on Hudson Street (Jack Kerouac's hangout ten years earlier), which by the '60s had become "mainly an Irish bar frequented mostly by guys from the old country."[72] Bob was thus exposed to another form of ethnic music as genuine as the polkas. Dylan says "All through the night," he and the Clancys and their Irish buddies "would sing drinking songs, country ballads, and rousing rebel songs that would lift the roof."[73] Ever the chameleon, Dylan "was beginning to think I might want to change over," i.e., become Irish, but he restrained himself because "The Irish landscape wasn't too much like the American landscape."[74] Before he could appropriate ethnic Irish music, he would "have to find some cuneiform tablets, some archaic grail to lighten [sic] the way."[75] Dylan discovered in the Irish music at the White Horse what he had already discovered in Picasso, namely, revolution. "The rebellion songs," Dylan says, "were a really serious thing. The language was flashy and provocative—a lot of action in the words, all sung with great gusto.... They weren't protest songs, though, they were rebel ballads ... even in a simply melodic wooing ballad there'd be rebellion waiting around the corner. You couldn't escape it.... Rebellion spoke to me louder. The rebel was alive and well, romantic and honorable."[76]

Like Captain Ahab who stared at the coin he nailed to the mast and saw in it only himself, Bob Dylan sailed to New York, and everywhere he looked he saw the revolutionary Jew staring back at him. Dylan was the '60s version of Jay Gatsby, another Jew who reinvented himself according to American myths and expectations. If you take America and place the Clancy Brothers on top of it, and place Woody Guthrie on top of that, and place Picasso over him, what you come up with is revolution. The only persona—what Dylan calls the "Archaic Grail"—that could unite these disparate personae was the revolutionary Jew. Suddenly the singing Jewish cowboy had become plausible in a way Lenny Bruce could not understand. Bob Dylan took the popular front persona Woody Guthrie had created and updated it to meet the exigencies of college students plunging toward the sexual revolution. But the persona of the revolutionary folksinger didn't begin with Woody Guthrie. It began with Joe Hill, the Swedish immigrant who fought in Mexico and later wrote songs for the Wobblies. "Joe," Dylan says, "wrote the song 'Pie in the Sky' and was the forerunner of Woody Guthrie. That was all I needed to know."[75]

New York 1961

As we have seen, when Bob Dylan arrived in New York City in 1961, he found a world as avid to publish his fantasies as he was to spin them. *New York Times* folk music critic Robert Shelton was Dylan's most avid acolyte. Spitz says, "Shelton played the indulgent straight man as Bob shoveled it on thick."[76] Dylan recounted the "I'm a rambler; I'm a gambler; I'm a long way from home" line with every cliched variation imaginable. Shelton dutifully regurgitated what he heard to credulous *Times* readers. Shelton was to Dylan what the Bosnian Franciscans were to the seers of Medjugorje. He was the authority that gave an air of plausibility to the secular equivalent of the phony apparition—the urban Jew as the avatar of the '30s Okie. The important thing was not what Dylan said but that someone with the credibility of the secular clergy believed it. Once the secular clergy accepted his myth, his myth became a reality. That happened on September 28, 1961 when Shelton's article appeared in *The New York Times*. According to Spitz, Dylan read and "reread the words in a state of shock."[77] The first article ever written about him appeared in no less august a forum than the *New York Times* "and it was a goddamn rave."[78]

A day later, Dylan went to the Columbia recording studios to play harmonica for Carolyn Hester, knowing producer John Hammond would be there to offer him a recording contract on the strength of Shelton's review. Hammond "liked what he saw—the whole Dylan package, the angry young folksinger. It hit the right chord."[79] Dylan got the contract.

Dylan knew who were the players in the folk music scene and how to appeal to them. There was something artful about his deceptions and something methodically calculating about them too. Within weeks, Dylan was sleeping with a 17-year-old Italian girl, Suze Rotolo. He was also sleeping on the couch at her sister's apartment, and her sister, Carla Rotolo, was secretary to Alan Lomax.

1961: Rambling Jack Elliot returns

In 1961, Ramblin' Jack Elliott returned to America after a six-year sojourn in England and Europe. The folk music movement was a cultural craze "sweeping the nation." Elliott's timing was exquisite. A new generation born after the war and bred in prosperity was looking for a leader on whom they could shower money and adulation. Elliott, 15 years their senior, looked the logical candidate. "It was like the Messiah coming down from heaven,"[80] said Izzy Young, broker of folk music and messianic politics, describing Elliott's return to Greenwich Village.

When Ramblin' Jack traveled to New Jersey to visit Woody in the hospital, he found considerable competition for Woody's mantle as the uncontested leader of the folk music movement. While attending the gathering that the Gleasons arranged every Sunday so Woody's army of fans could serenade him, Elliott met Bob Dylan. Dylan ingratiated himself with the returned idol. He told Elliott he had all of Jack's records. He then began to hang around with Elliott as obsequiously as Elliott ten years before had hung around with Guthrie. Dylan couldn't move in with Elliott's family because Elliott didn't have one. So he moved in next door to him at the Earle Hotel. When Dylan played his first gig at Gerde's Folk City, he was billed as "The Son of Jack Elliott,"[81] which wasn't particularly flattering to Dylan or to Elliott either. When Dylan's career took off and Elliott's stalled, Elliott bore his young imitator no ill will because he was simply following in Elliott's footsteps. Sounding like Woody Guthrie had become a Jewish tradition by 1962.

What distinguished the two men was not their musical styles as much as their attitudes toward their careers. Elliott seems to have taken to heart the essential message of deracinated folk music—"I'm a rambler, I'm a gambler, I'm a long way from home" by living that life himself. Elliott had rambled all over Europe and lost his first wife when she put down roots in a Kibbutz in Israel. Ramblin' Jack just kept on rambling, which meant he didn't stay put even when he got back to Greenwich Village, which was not a smart career move at the time. He stayed only long enough to be greeted like a god at a series of sold out concerts. He was anointed by the secular clergy, praised by *Newsweek* as "authentic." He was anointed by the high priest of the folk movement, Robert Shelton, who claimed this son of a Jewish doctor from Brooklyn had "a remarkable ear for the speech and sounds of the American plains," and that he had "thoroughly mastered the idiom of genuine American folk music."[82] "Mr. Elliott," Shelton concluded, "doesn't know where the road of the future will take him. Some observers think that with stern direction he could channel his drifting and parlay his colorful demeanor and rich musical talents into a stage personality of great popular appeal."[83] "Stern direction," however, was the last thing on Ramblin' Jack's mind.

Unlike Ramblin' Jack, Bob Dylan was smart enough not to believe his own lyrics or take the persona he was cultivating for public consumption too seriously. Dylan's obsession with persona and image made him inscrutable, which further enhanced his image. "I never knew when he was playing a role or being himself," said folk singer Mark Spoelstra.[84] Dylan read the lifestyle needs of his audience and tailored his music to them. The folk music of the popular front did not fit the lifestyle of the babyboomers. When Henry Ford died in 1947, his grandson broke with the family tradition of hiring goons to beat up union organizers. With the autoworkers as a model, the nation enjoyed cooperation between labor and management, which brought unparalleled prosperity. The workers' children raised during the Dylan era would have a hard time relating to the "Ballad Of Joe Hill" and "Solidarity Forever." They needed new music or at least new lyrics to address the big issues of the day, and, as Ron Radosh indicated, the avant garde of the cultural proletariat had decided to get involved in sexual liberation.

In September 1961, Rod Radosh and his wife returned to Madison, where he hoped to earn a Ph.D. in history under William Appleton Williams, whom he describes as "an authentic American radical,"[85] i.e., not Jewish. Soon, a "very thin ... young kid ... with traces of baby fat on him" showed up looking for a place to stay.[86] The young kid, Bob Dylan, got Radosh's name and address from Carl Granich, "a friend and awesome guitar picker from the young Communist circle in New York City."[87] Dylan and Radosh shared a desire to subvert what they saw as the inhuman institutions of an incipiently "fascist" America. Dylan did not stay with Radosh—he was sent down the road to the apartment of Danny Kalb, who later formed the late '60s variation on the Jewish folksinger, the Jewish blues band.

Where Bob Dylan spent the night was irrelevant. In Madison, he lived in the Wisconsin equivalent of Jewish Bohemia. He fit in by playing the guitar at the regular impromptu Hootenanny sessions at "a small new cafe on State Street ... modeled on Greenwich Village hangouts."[88] Dylan wasn't yet a star. Indeed, he took a back seat to Radosh, who performed an agit prop ballad by Irwin Silber, "Talkin' Un-American Blues," which attacked the House Un-American Activities Committee in the style of Woody Guthrie. The song delighted Dylan, who added it to his repertoire. Dylan then sang a few Guthrie songs, including "New York Town," which must have resonated with Radosh, the New Yorker in exile. Radosh says Dylan was actually too ready to pick up his guitar. At one party, he was told "Bob, would you put that damn guitar away already? Nobody wants to hear you anymore!"[89] Dylan meekly put his guitar away and left Madison for New York.

Dylan claimed he was a rambler and a gambler and a long way from home, but only when it fostered his career. Radosh was understandably skeptical when Dylan told him "with a tone of complete assurance," that he was "going to be as big a star as Elvis Presley."[90] Dylan insisted, "No, you'll see. I'll play the same and even bigger arenas. I know it."[91] "Destiny," Dylan said of his life in 1961, "was about to manifest itself."[92] It "was looking right at me and nobody else."[93] Often, as in the *60 Minutes* interview following the release of the first volume of his autobiography, Dylan spoke as if he had been singled out by the "powers of this world"[94] to fulfill some cosmic design.

The *Zeitgeist* needed someone bright enough to put two and two together, or at the very least, to write new lyrics to the old melodies. The sexual revolutionaries would soon run into the same problem that their parents encountered. "Wildwood Flower" still wasn't a revolutionary melody. And it was even less appropriate for sexual revolution than it had been for the popular front. To update the music of the popular front, Bob Dylan had to tap into the cultural aquifer that produced the tourists that inundated the Village every weekend. The Kingston Trio was popular but culturally irrelevant. Pete Seeger had been relevant, but the Popular Front was long dead and gone. Because he was a Jew working in the Jewish folk music subset

of the Jewish popular music industry, Dylan could count on a sympathetic hearing when he articulated his deepest feelings of rebellion or revolution. "Nothing
seemed to delight Bob more than undermining the power of an authority figure,"
one biographer says.[95] In this regard, Dylan was only doing what other Jews had
done before him—Marx and Freud and Reich—and what they were going to do
with more gusto as he redefined folk music in places like Manny Roth's (uncle of
rocker David Lee Roth) club The Wha? as the vehicle for the cultural revolution,
with a little help from his friends.

Dylan's biggest friend in this regard was a self-described "Jewish businessman"[96] from Chicago by the name of Albert Grossman. Grossman, according to
Spitz, was "neither a gentleman nor political," but rather a "Jewish businessman,"
who was "a cagey operator who lived by the Teutonic [sic] theory that those who
struck first and fastest usually eat best."[97] Grossman claimed to have graduated
from the University of Chicago, which was not true, and to have walked away
from a career in Chicago city government, which was also not true. He did, however, manage a folk club there and was astute enough to understand that the future of that musical movement lay in Greenwich Village, where he arrived shortly
after Ramblin' Jack Elliott and Bob Dylan. Dave Van Ronk, approached early on
by Grossman, called him "an astute but very cruel man—extraordinarily cruel in
a very cold and calculated way," who went out of his way to corrupt the performers
he represented.[98] Grossman played "a kind of Mephistophelian role"[99] with young
village folksingers. He guaranteed them stardom "in return for their integrity."[100]

Grossman approached Van Ronk to see if he were interested in becoming
part of a folk supergroup trio which he planned to manage. Grossman saw a large
gap between commercially successful but insipid groups like The Kingston Trio
and the "authentic" but commercially unappealing imitators of Woody Guthrie.
Grossman's solution was a trio, Peter, Paul, and Mary. PP&M combined the talents of a stand-up comic, Noel Stookey (who changed his name to the vaguely
religious sounding Paul), a singer, Peter Yarrow, and Mary Travers, the sexually
liberated, platinum blonde bombshell from the Elisabeth Irwin School. Van Ronk
was Grossman's' first choice as Mary's foil, but to get into the act, Van Ronk had
to "change my name to Olaf the Blues Singer ... wear a helmet with horns growing
out of it, and pretend to be blind."[101] Van Ronk had to be willing to make a fool of
himself on stage because "Integrity bothered Albert," who "used to say that there
was no such thing as an honest man, and it was merely a question of finding out
what my price was, even if it cost him $300,000 of his own money. That was the
kind of guy Albert really was."[102]

Dave Van Ronk, five years older than Dylan, was an established figure in the
Village when Dylan arrived. In his autobiography, Dylan describes meeting Van
Ronk under the watchful eye of Izzy Young. Dylan describes Van Ronk as singing
songs "originally sung by singers who seemed to be groping for words, almost in
an alien tongue."[103] Van Ronk had recorded his first album in 1959 for Folkways

Records, a company founded by Moses Asch, and one of the critical links between the Popular Front and the folksong revival of the '60s. From a broken family in Brooklyn, Van Ronk was taught by "vicious Irish nuns"[104] in Queens. Originally a merchant seaman who sang songs and played the guitar, the blossoming folk music craze changed that. Odetta listened to him and suggested he "make a demo tape" and "send it to Albert Grossman."[105] Van Ronk hitchhiked to Chicago to present the tape and perform for Grossman, but their personalities never meshed, prossibly because of ethnic differences, although the suggestion that he change his name to Olaf the Blues Singer didn't help. The persona of the urban folksinger had already been set, and it was cryptically Jewish, not Dutch/Irish Catholic. Van Ronk abandoned the religion of his youth for socialism, but abandoning his ethnic identity proved more difficult. Paradoxically, the compatibility between Grossman and Dylan lay in the shared ethnic identity they had abandoned, or, perhaps, reworked with the *Zeitgeist* in mind. Spitz says Grossman, "much like his protégé Bobby Dylan," developed a new persona by concocting "an apocryphal autobiography."[106] And he helped Dylan do the same thing.

Bob Gibson, a successful folksinger managed by Grossman, didn't come up with the proper image either. The *goyim* were finding it difficult to compete as cultural revolutionaries. The revolutionary Jews had an advantage, especially since music promoters shared their views. According to Gibson, Grossman gave "highest priority" to "class," which meant that "you had to ... embody Albert's elitist tendencies, which also meant taking regular instruction and criticism from him and assuming aspects of his personality."[107] That meant combining the "Jewish businessman" with messianic cultural politics, because, as Gibson notes, "Albert envisioned himself as a cultural messiah."[108] Grossman wanted to get rich off his singers, but in order to do so he first had to "create a legend,"[109] to elevate the enthusiasm of the folk music fans flooding into college campuses to "a level that separated his new client from every other performer, so that no comparisons could be drawn."[110] "The cultural revolution had officially begun, and God help the folk singer who couldn't conceptualize his own myth."[111] Bob Dylan "was in a class all by himself," and Albert Grossman was "going to make damned sure that he remained there," by promoting "'the Dylan mystique,' as he refered to it."[112]

Bob Dylan's first album was released in March 1962, earning a glowing pseudonymous endorsement by the fawning Robert Shelton. He wrote under the name Stacy Williams because "it would have been regarded as un-ethical for a *New York Times* critics to objectively review an album that carried his byline on the back cover,"[113] especially in light of payola scandals. The album consisted of covers of folk tunes popular in Greenwich Village, including a version of "House of the Rising Sun," appropriated without permission from Dave Van Ronk. His only original piece, a tribute to Woody Guthrie, lifted Woody's melody from a song written about a 1913 mining disaster that Ramblin' Jack Elliott popularized.

Dylan's original music first appeared in spring 1963 when *The Freewheelin'*

Bob Dylan album was released with a picture on its cover of him and Suze Rotolo walking down Great Jones Street together. "Don't Think Twice It's All Right" was the album's biggest hit, and, like the cover photo of the two, it involved Suze Rotolo, who had gone to Europe at the urging of her mother. Dylan was desolate; the song has a clear emotional and musical focus that disappeared from his music when Dylan later joined the sexual revolution. He would then sing indistinguishable songs about indistinguishable women. But in 1963, the revolution hadn't taken place yet. He could still focus one song on one woman.

When Dylan's third album, *The Times they are a Changin'*, was released in February 1964, the revolutionary cat was out of the bag. Even though written in the folk mode, the title song had clear revolutionary intent, tailored specifically to the generation that was then coming of age and buying lots of records in their search for a new lifestyle identity. The music was different enough (a weird G chord to an insistent strum and forthright harmonica which disguised the standard G, C, D progression) to add urgency to the lyrics, which were undeniably powerful. No more Popular Front working men, but rather a denunciation of parents! "Your sons and your daughters are beyond your command/Your old road is rapidly agin'/Come get out of the new one if you can't lend a hand/ For the times they are a changin."

It wasn't the Fugs. It wasn't Dionysian excess, but it didn't throw cold water on the disordered passions either. It ennobled those passions by associating them with the civil rights movement, messianic politics, and a host of equally revolutionary themes. Everyone was blown away by the bard who made Jewish revolution plausible in a peculiarly American way. Dylan's next four albums established him as "the spokesman of his generation."[114] To explain how Dylan revolutionized folk and popular music, Spitz mixes metaphors: "Natural selection," he writes, "had chosen Bob Dylan to be the high priest of protest singers."[115] Then he calls Dylan "an enlightened prophet."[116] Finally he settles on business metaphors, saying "beneath his scruffy folk exterior beat the heart of a Jewish businessman from Minnesota" who "knew the value of self-promotion," and "in an offbeat way he courted the establishment crowd when he thought that could help his career."[117] In a plutocratic society, it's unnecessary to distinguish between businessmen, political messiahs, and revolutionaries; one person can be all three. Or, to put it succinctly, to succeed with your cultural revolution, you have to be all three rolled up in one. In America, it was all three rolled up in two—Bob Dylan and Albert Grossman.

Once Peter, Paul and Mary proved folk music could pull in mainstream money, recording contracts began to pour into Greenwich Village. Dave Van Ronk noticed that "all of a sudden there was money all over the place."[118] From 1960 to 1965, recording company executives began:

> handing out major label recording contracts like they were coming in Cracker Jack boxes. People who had been sleeping on floors and eating in cafeterias a year

or two before, all of a sudden had enough money to buy a suit, if they wanted to.[119]

Mark Spoelstra pinpoints the change in folk music from something practiced by sincere amateurs to something controled by the music "industry" to a specific week in 1962. He went to visit friends in Canada, and when he got back, Bob Dylan and his friends "were sitting around talking Big Bucks.... You'd have thought I'd walked in on a dinner party of wealthy industrialists.... What the hell happened while I was in Toronto? ... The object of our closely knit folk community had always been to sing and have fun. And suddenly it seemed as if everything had changed."[120] Spitz claimed that the point "at which folk music merged with show business ... could actually be seen by the human eye."[121] The notion that folksingers and money were incompatible became "obsolete."[122] Bob Dylan was to become the well-paid "poet-philosopher of his generation,"[123] someone who could satisfy "Young middle-class Jewish intellectuals' ... hunger for someone to put ideas into their heads."[124]

Bob Dylan's revolutionary music arrived not a moment too soon, because the other side of the collective Jewish personality in America, the Jewish comedian, had been subverting the folk scene by making it look ridiculous. In 1962, Allan Sherman released his album *My Son the Folksinger*. Dylan was no stranger to parodies of Jewish folksingers (his "Talkin' Hava Nagila Blues" is a case in point) but Sherman took the tradition established by Mickey Katz and his Kosher Jammers to a new level precisely when the folk bubble was threatening to burst. Jewish involvement in the resurrection of Popular Front Appalachian or Negro Music was a satirical target too big to ignore, and many scored direct hits, including Shel Silverstein in his parody, "Folk Singer's Blues," which talked about what to do when

And the only levee you know is the Levy who lives on the block, Yes
The only levee you know is the Levy who lives on the block[125]

The disparity was too big to ignore. Young middle class Jews singing about picking cotton in Mississippi was prime comedy material. If folk music was to survive the assaults of Alan Sherman singing "Catskill ladies sing your song, doo dah doo dah," it needed different lyrics, and a more Dionysian music to fit the mores of the new generation of Jews who went to camp not to sing folksongs around a campfire but to have sex with the Negro lifeguard.

Bob Dylan provided that music. More importantly, Dylan provided the new persona of the folksinging revolutionary that enabled others to make the music too. "What folk music needed," according to Spitz, "were performers who were willing to invest in it something unique and intensely personal," rather than simply recycling labor movement songs in the style of Woody Guthrie.[126] That music was "no longer vital to the younger generation."[127] Bob Dylan was the *Zeitgeist* on a motorcycle. "By writing new folk songs, Bob had a chance to say something compelling about the current scene and comment on his own life and times."[128]

Chapter Twenty-Four

The Second Vatican Council Begins

I n 1960, shortly before Boby Dylan arrived in New York City, a French Jew by the name of Jules Isaac went to Rome to discuss what he saw as the Catholic Church's 2000-year-old "teaching of contempt"[1] against his people. Isaac was the former inspector general of France's public schools and a historian who had written two books on Catholic attitudes toward the Jews after losing a number of family members during the war. In *Jesus et Israel* (1946) and *Genese de l'Antisemitisme* (1948), Isaac made two points that would dominate Catholic Jewish dialogue for the rest of the century. Isaac claimed 1) the Catholic Church had preached an anti-Semitism for 2000 years which 2) found its ultimate expression in the mass murder of Jews during World War II.

Father Paul De Mann from Paris and Father Gregory Baum, a Jewish convert from Canada, spread his thesis in Catholic circles. Baum called *Jesus et Israel*, "a moving account of the love which Jesus had for his people, the Jews, and of the contempt which the Christians, later, harbored for them."[2] In 1947 Isaac participated in a conference in Seelisberg, Switzerland, that issued a memo on "The rectification of Christian teaching concerning Israel."[3]

In 1949, Isaac met with Pope Pius XII. Isaac wanted the pope to write an encyclical condemning anti-Semitism, but nothing came of the meeting. It's not difficult to understand why. Despite the openly pagan ideology of National Socialism and the havoc it wrought, Isaac felt the most dangerous form of anti-Semitism was the oxymoron known as Christian anti-Semitism. Because it was theological and not racial, it perdured much longer than Hitler's racial views. Its roots went back to Christianity's fundamental texts, in particular, the Gospels of Matthew and John and the writings of Church Fathers, St. John Chrysostom, St. Ambrose, St. Augustine, and Pope St. Gregory the Great.

When Isaac arrived at the Vatican in 1960 for his second visit, the times had changed dramatically since 1949. The genial Giuseppi Roncalli had succeeded the austere Eugenio Pacelli, but the changed atmosphere was traceable to more than just a difference of personality.

Roncalli had lived through the war, but Pacelli had been nuncio to Germany during the rise of National Socialism. He had been in Munich during the First and Second Bavarian Soviet Republics. He had seen the Levine administration and their slutty hangers on when he visited the Wittelsbach Palace in 1919, and he knew the rise of Hitler in Bavaria in 1923 was predicated on the excesses of Jewish Bolshevism there and not on readings of the sermons of St. John Chrysostom or the Gospel of St. John.

Pacelli had emerged from World War II as a hero, a status the world's Jews confirmed at his death in 1958. But now a new spirit was blowing through the Vatican, and Isaac saw a window of opportunity for his ideas. Aside from its position in Communist countries, the Catholic Church was an object of universal esteem in 1960, and it wanted to use that esteem to promote unity among Christians and reconciliation with the Jews. The Vatican Secretariat for promoting Christian Unity had been set up months before Isaac's visit under the leadership of Augustin Cardinal Bea. Bea had known Jews from his days as a student and teacher in Berlin. From the Jewish perspective, the time was ripe to press for a condemnation of all it disliked about Catholic teaching on the Jews.

The French Embassy, knowing the people behind Isaac, arranged a meeting with Cardinal Tisserant, who gave Isaac the run around. Isaac wanted to meet with Pope John XXIII, but he was sent instead to the prefect of the Holy Office, Alfredo Cardinal Ottaviani, who then sent him to 83-year-old Andrea Cardinal Jullien, hoping that a meeting between two old men, both hard of hearing, would lead nowhere. Ottaviani was wrong. After pleading his case, Isaac sat in silence, waiting. Jullien finally said the word that provided the key for the door Isaac wanted unlocked: "Bea." Augustin Cardinal Bea, the German Jesuit and Biblical scholar who had authored Pius XII's encyclical on biblical scholarship, *Divini Afflante Spiritu.*

On June 13, 1960, Isaac got his meeting with Pope John XXIII. The only account comes from Isaac, who introduced himself to the pope "as a non- Christian, the promoter of *l'Amities Judeo-Chretiennes,* and a very deaf old man."[4] The pope took the initiative by discoursing on his devotion to the Old Testament. Sensing an opening, Isaac told the pope this "kindled great hopes in the people of the Old Testament."[5] It was time to fulfill those expectations by issuing a condemnation of anti-Semitism. Pope John had been thinking along those lines, but he could not do this unilaterally because the Church was not a *"monarchie absolue."*[6]

Not long thereafter, Isaac "learned with joy"[7] that the pope had conveyed his suggestions to Cardinal Bea who had been commissioned to work toward "a firm condemnation of Catholic anti-Semitism."[6] Bea would draft a text about Jewish-Christian relationships for the Council's consideration. Thus was born what came to be known as the Jewish Declaration.

The pope's desire soon was transformed into something radically different when it made contact with the realities of 20th century Jewish interest groups and publicity organs. Before long "the people of the Old Testament" were represented by international Jewish organizations like the American Jewish Committee and the Anti-Defamation League. Rather than formulating the Catholic position on the Jews in light of Catholic tradition, Cardinal Bea became a go-between between the Jewish organizations and the Council Fathers, who initially were also under the impression they were dealing with the "people of the Old Testament." Because the Council Fathers were favorably impressed by Jules Isaac's petition (as opposed to his books, which they had not read), Isaac was allowed to determine the terms of the debate, becoming the principal theorist for the Vatican's statement on the Jews. Isaac's friend Bishop Provencheres tried spin this positively by claiming it was the first time a layman and a Jew had initiated a council document, without bringing up the nagging question of who benefited from this break with tradition. Viscount Leon de Poncins was less reticent, claiming Isaac was "the principal theorist and promoter of the campaign being waged against the traditional teaching of the Church."[8] *Nostra Aetate* was destined to become "a weapon designed to overthrow traditional Catholicism, which they consider the chief enemy."[9]

Such thoughts were far from the minds of the participants in the early dialogue between Catholics and Jews. The goal of condemning anti-Semitism seemed noble enough, but the spirit of the times precluded close theological examination of the terms of the discussion. Just who was going to determine the precise meaning of "Anti-Semitism"? Popuarized in Germany in 1870 by the racial thinker Wilhelm Marr, the word had a racial meaning. This was not problematic for German racists, but it was problematic for the Catholic Church, especially if she were to incorporate uncritically an essentially a-theological and ideologically racial term into a conciliar document. It would contradict a crucial assertion of the Catholic faith, the age-old admonition *Sicut Iudeis non*: Jewish converts were to be accepted "without prejudice." If Jewish identity was based on race or blood or DNA and not on rejection of Christ, then baptism lost its efficacy.

By the time Jules Isaac finally got his meeting with the pope in June 1960, Alfredo Cardinal Ottaviani had already commissioned the preliminary documents for the Second Vatican Council. The conventional explanation of the council is summarized in one word: *aggiornamento*; which was taken to mean bringing the church up to date. From Ottaviani's point of view, the Church referred to the Curia, which had reached a state of near paralysis during the last days of Pius XII and was seen as inadequate to the challenges facing it. In the hands of the revisionists, *aggiornamento* has taken on another meaning, namely, getting the Church to accept the tenets of the Enlightenment Pius IX condemned in his syllabus of errors. According to this view, *aggiornamento* meant "reversing the craziness that had compelled Pope Pius IX to produce his famous Syllabus of Errors, which condemned a number of almost self evident propositions—including this one: 'The pope can and must try to achieve a reconciliation and a settlement with progress, liberalism and modern civilization.'"[10] From an American point of view, the term meant support for the theories of John Courtney Murray, who wanted "to baptize America's religious freedom and make it a part of Pope John's aggiornamento."[11]

According to the Americanist reading, "there was that rumor that Giuseppe Roncalli, Pope John XXIII, had been a covert sympathizer with the Modernists."[12] Ottaviani's involvement in the preparatory stages of the council tells another story, supported by a close reading of the preliminary documents. Judging from them, the point of the Council was not to baptize the Enlightenment, but to reform the

Curia and make Catholics aware of a threat to faith and morals coming from the West, in particular, the United States, more particularly, Hollywood.

In January 1962, the preparatory document on "The Moral Order" was submitted to the Council for deliberation. In it, Cardinal Ottaviani sketched out the moral challenges facing the Church. The Church needed to challenge

> The attempt ... to substitute the useful, the agreeable, the good of the race, the interests of a class, or the power of the state, as the criterion of morality. Thus, philosophical systems, literary fashions, and political doctrines have been created and propagated. These try to substitute for the Christian moral order the so-called morality of situation or individualistic morality, often condemned by Pius XII and finally condemned by a decree of the Holy Office in February of 1956. These also try to substitute the morality of independence (i.e., divorced from the Christian morality) for the idea of God, sanction and obligation.[13]

The reference to moralities of race and class referred to Nazism and Communism. But they were conjoined in condemnation with "the so-called morality of situation or individualistic morality,"[14] which could only refer to errors emanating from America. There was risk involved here, since American Catholics were overwhelmingly pious church-goers at the time (in comparison to their brothers in Europe) and contributed significantly to the Vatican's finances.

As the Council progressed, the condemnation of the American threat to Catholic morality became more and more overt. To "defend ... the immutable principles of Christian modesty and chastity,"[15] the Council warned of the energies spent by the world of fashion, movies, and the press to shake the foundations of Christian morality, as if the Sixth Commandment was outmoded and free rein should be given to all passions, even those against nature. The council was to clarify and eventually condemn attempts to revive paganism and the abuse of psychoanalysis to justify even things directly contrary to the moral order.[16]

In May 1962, Ottaviani issued The Esteem of Virginity and Chastity, which he said, "reflects the most acute and discussed moral problems of our day."[17] As Italian director Federico Fellini was saying in films like *La Dolce Vita*, American films as the vehicle for American mores were undermining the traditional way of life in Catholic Europe and in Italy in particular. If the Church lost its hold on sexual morals, it would lose control of "the ordinary way of sanctification for the majority of the human race."[18] Far from baptizing modernity, the preparatory documents condemned it as one long, drawn-out occasion of sin:

> Modern life, without doubt, multiplies invitations to evil by such distractions as beauty contests, spectacles, billboards, songs, illustrated magazines, beaches, places of vacation, promiscuity, and certain forms of sport. This is why the Church never ceases to recall to each one the principles of prudence, conscience, and responsibility, the rights and duties of liberty, and the obligation of vigilance and precaution on the part of parents, educators and civil authorities. This is also why the church points out as dangerous and condemns as erroneous all theories that are then translated into practice concerning the cult of movie stars, natural-

ism, the so-called sexual education, pansexualism, and certain injurious aspects of psychoanalysis.[19]

It didn't take a genius to know who in America was prominent in supporting "the cult of movie stars, pansexualism, and psychoanalysis." It was the Jews. So the Council became a battleground over whose interpretation of the Jews was going to be normative. Were the Jews the "people of the Old Testament" as Jules Isaac portrayed them? Or were they, in practice, the avant-garde of modernity and the promoters of sexual deviance as a covert form of control, as Ottaviani implicitly portrayed them?

The American hierarchy was plagued with its own Jewish problem ever since they began censoring Hollywood in 1934 with the creation of the production code and the Legion of Decency. Psychoanalysis had also come in for condemnation at the hands of the famous TV priest, Fulton J. Sheen. In March 1947, Sheen gave a sermon on "psychoanalysis and confession"[20] in St. Patrick's Cathedral in New York City. In it, Sheen derided Freudianism as a philosophy based on "materialism, hedonism, infantilism, and eroticism."[21] In the February/March 1947 issue of *McCall's*, Clare Booth Luce told of her conversion to Catholicism. Luce had undergone psychoanalysis by a Jewish psychiatrist shortly after divorcing her first husband. After exposure to confession, Luce resented her treatment at the hands of Jews. "We Christian innocents," she wrote, "have been duped into our present godless condition by the unholy triumvirate of communism, psychoanalysis and relativity. These three symbolized by Marx, Freud and Einstein, are the result of the messianic impulse of the religiously frustrated Jewish ego."[22]

It didn't take long for the Jews to react to this shot across their bow. Both Sheen and Luce were accused of anti-Semitism in 1948 in the *American Scholar* because they "leave the careful reader an impression that responsibility for our present spiritual inadequacy rests not only on Freud but as well on the other outstanding thinkers of Jewish origin."[23] *Time,* run by Mrs. Luce's husband, tried to patch things up by contrasting Sheen with Father Coughlin, but the cultural battle lines had been drawn; as in the Hollywood obscenity battle of the '30s, the Jews were on one side and the Catholics on the other.

By the time the Vatican Council convened, the American bishops were showing signs of battle fatigue in their culture war with the Jews, and the council looked like a way of declaring a separate peace. Or like a battle between Americans who wanted an accommodation with the Jews versus traditionalists like Ottaviani who saw Hollywood Jews, Reichian pansexualists, and Freudian psychiatrists as the main threat to Catholic morals in a Europe weakened by two catastrophic wars. Given Jewish dominance in the media, it was easy to see who was going to be portrayed as the villain in this scenario.

If someone had pointed out that the preparatory reports had used Hollywood, pansexualism, and psychoanalysis as code words for Jewish subversion of morals it would have exposed the ethnic dimensions of a struggle generally perceived as an intra-Catholic struggle between liberals and conservatives. So no one portrayed it in those terms, not in the major media anyway. As in most ethnic battles, political surrogates replaced the real players. The Vatican Council was portrayed as a battle between the forces of darkness and reaction, symbolized by Cardinal Ottaviani, and the forces of light and progress, symbolized, in American journals, by the Jesuit John Courtney Murray, who appeared on the cover of *Time* when contestation over the Council began.

If there was one man responsible for this Manichean scenario it was Robert Blair Kaiser. If there was one organ responsible for the dissemination of those views it was *Time Magazine*. Kaiser entered the Jesuits in the late '40s and was out by the mid-'50s, convinced by modernism and the evolutionary thought of Teilhard de Chardin that he could better achieve the goals of the Jesuits by leaving the order. Given what became of the Jesuits, this was at least an arguable proposition, but not as Kaiser wanted to argue it. He soon became a bachelor reporter in California, driving from one sexual encounter to another in his '56 Thunderbird. Then he married and landed a job at *Time*.

When the Second Vatican Council opened in October 1962, Kaiser was there to cover it. Kaiser takes credit for converting *Time* to the "global vision"[24] he learned as a young Jesuit scholastic by reading de Chardin and Cardinal Suhard. "By making information available to an international community of men and women who had an uncommon say in running the planet, *Time* was contributing to a better world, by opening up channels of communication that had long been clogged. That was a worthy cause."[25] Kaiser's reporting bespoke a meeting of the minds, mostly of Jesuits, who had committed themselves to "Church reform"[26] through the media. Kaiser was so zealous in "coming down in favor of the liberals,"[27] that he was reprimanded by his bureau chief, who sketched *Time*'s editorial policy in a memo to Kaiser: "We have clearly opted in print for the reformation of the Catholic church undertaken by Pope John, and now presumably being carried forward by Pope Paul. My caution is this: we should not make our stories and our reporting so one-sided that we become naked partisans in this rather than skeptical spectators."[28] *Time*'s "reformation of the Catholic church"[29] involved leveraging the pope's genial personality into sympathy for everything the modern world hated about the Catholic Church. So Kaiser portrayed the pope as "a secret Modernist all along, and then, when he became pope, an open one."[30]

The one area in which the Church was most glaringly out of sync with the modern world was its attitude toward the Jews. To remedy that, John XXIII, according to Kaiser, "asked Cardinal Bea to prepare a schema for the Council that would revise the old Catholic story about the Jews killing Christ, and thus bringing eternal damnation on them and on their children too. It was a myth that had nurtured anti-Semitism for centuries."[31] One of the tenets of Roncalli's modernism, according to Kaiser, was the belief that Jews did not need to convert in order to be saved. Kaiser related an anecdote he got from Msgr. Loris Capovilla, the pope's personal secretary. When a young Jew came to Roncalli and asked to become a Catholic, the future pope put him off, saying, "Be a good Jew" because "becoming a Catholic would kill your parents."[30] Roncalli eventually relented and had the man baptized in secret. After Roncalli became pope and the man asked the pope to confirm him, the pope allegedly replied: "All right, all right, but you've got to continue being a good Jew in your own synagogue, support the Jewish schul, because by being a Catholic, you do not become any less a Jew."[33]

If true, the anecdote reveals a fatal ambiguity at the heart of the Jewish question as discussed at Vatican Council II. The question was simple: Did a Jew remain a Jew after he was baptized? The traditional Catholic answer was no. The Jew, a rejecter of Christ, ceased being a rejecter of Christ upon baptism. Jews should be admitted to the Church "without prejudice" because through baptism they ceased being Jews. If, on the other hand, becoming a Catholic meant "you do not become any less a Jew," then Jewish identity was bound up with blood, race, and DNA, the very view which Christ rejected in the Gospel of St. John, At this point it wasn't clear which view the Church was going to espouse in its schema on the Jews.

In August 1962, Cardinal Bea granted an interview to the *Jewish Chronicle*, in which he stated unequivocally that the Church intended to use the Council to issue an official and radical condemnation of anti-Semitism. After the first session of the Council, Bea used the hiatus before the second session to consult with Jewish groups. The major Jewish organizations used the opportunity to lobby for concessions from the Church. Rabbi Abraham J. Heschel, who met Bea when both were students in Berlin 30 years earlier, collaborated with the American Jewish Committee, which had issued "The Image of the Jews in Catholic Teaching," which Bea had read in preparation for dialogue with the Jews which began in earnest in January 1963. Heschel wanted the Vatican to ban what he termed proselytizing, which meant a revocation of the belief that Jews had to accept Christ as their Savior to enter the Kingdom of Heaven. He also wanted the Council to ban any reference to the Jews as an accursed race. The "cursed race"[34] claim was a Jewish extrapolation from Matthew 27:26 in which the Jewish people "to a man shouted back [to Pilate, after he offered to release Jesus], 'His blood be on us and on our children.'"

The real issue, the issue the Jews did not want to face, was the Jewish rejection of Christ, which was on-going not by occult force but because of Jewish will. By portraying this rejection as a curse, the Jews trivialized it and placed the onus not on their rejection of Christ but on the Church as the perpetrator of some occult voodoo spell, which, while harmless of itself, had caused prejudice, which led to persecution, culminating in the Holocaust. B'nai B'rith wanted the Church to delete any language it deemed anti-Semitic from the Catholic liturgy. This was a tall order because the liturgy was based on Scripture that was, if not anti-Semitic, then certainly anti-Jewish. Virtually the entire Gospel of St. John and the Acts of the Apostles revolved around the conflict between the Jews who accepted Christ as their savior and the Jews who rejected him. Since those texts were central to any

Catholic liturgy and full of invidious comparisons between the New Israel, the Catholic Church, and the Old, repudiated by Christ for its blindness and obstinacy, it was hard to see how dialogue could succeed. Unless, of course, the purpose of dialogue was something other than what it claimed to be.

Those who came to oppose the schema on the Jews claimed that ulterior motives had been driving the discussion from the beginning. Their fears were confirmed (three years after the fact) in March 1963, when a limousine picked Cardinal Bea up at the Plaza Hotel in New York and deposited him at the offices of the American Jewish Committee six blocks away. When Bea arrived, "a latter-day Sanhedrin"[35] was waiting to greet him. The meeting, of course, was "kept secret from the press."[36] It was also kept secret from the Vatican Council fathers. "I am not authorized to speak officially," Bea told the Jews. "I can, therefore, speak only of what, in my opinion could be effected, indeed, should be effected, by the Council."[37] The Jews, Bea continued, were accused of deicide and "on them is supposed to lie a curse."[38] According to the only account of the meeting, Bea repudiated both charges. "Because even in the accounts of the Evangelists, only the leaders of the Jews then in Jerusalem and a very small group of followers shouted for the death sentence on Jesus, all those absent and the generations of Jews unborn were not implicated in deicide in any way," Bea said.[39] As to the curse, it could not condemn the crucifiers, the Cardinal reasoned, because Christ's dying words were a prayer for their pardon.

Bea concluded by claiming it was "wrong to seek the chief cause of anti-Semitism in purely religious sources—in the Gospel accounts, for example. These religious causes, in so far as they are adduced (often they are not), are often merely an excuse and a veil to cover over other more operative reasons for enmity."[40] Bea did not identify the more operative reasons for enmity, or if he did, his explanation went unreported.

As a result of the meeting, the Jewish organizations assigned two lobbyists to monitor the progress of the "Jewish schema" at the council, Joseph Lichten of B'nai B'rith's Anti-Defamation League and Zachariah Schuster of the American Jewish Committee. Both men had lost relatives to the Nazis during World War II. Both were determined to bring "the strongest possible Jewish declaration"[41] back from Rome so their respective organizations could claim credit for it.

In addition to lobbying the Church Fathers in Rome, the Jews sought to change the climate of public opinion by other means. In February 1963, Rolf Hochhuth's play, *Der Stellvertreter* (*The Deputy*), opened in Berlin. Hochhuth portrayed Pope Pius XII as criminally negligent because of his silence on the deportation of the Jews during World War II. After it opened in London, Giovanni Battista Montini, archbishop of Milan and soon to be Pope Paul VI, attacked it as a defamation of Pius XII, whose secretary he had been. The pope was probably aware that Erwin Piscator, a Jewish communist, along with the already mentioned Jewish organizations, provided financial backing for the play. Msgr. John Oesterreicher, the Jewish convert responsible for the Jewish schema under Bea, accused the AJC and the ADL of poisoning the waters by promoting the play. "Jewish human-relations agencies," he wrote in *America*, "will have to speak out against *The Deputy* in unmistakable terms. Otherwise they will defeat their own purpose."[42] The press ignored Oesterreicher's warning, playing up Hochhuth's accusations instead. Hochhuth's message was clear. If the incoming pope (John XXIII was dying; who would succeed him was unknown) didn't want to go down in history as another Pius XII, guilty because silent, he better pass the schema on the Jews.

As Oesterreicher warned, the Jewish media campaign caused a reaction. Amleto Cardinal Cicognani, a powerful conservative in the Curia and former delegate to the United States, expressed fear that issuing a statement on the Jews might not be in the Church's best interest. Bea countered that he had already assured the Jews that a statement was forthcoming, so failure to produce one would be construed as mendacity. As resistance grew among the conservatives grew, Bea kept claiming he had created a growing tide of expectation in Jewish circles and in the pluralistic society of America and Germany, and that now he had to meet that expectation. The Jewish lobby was not going to take no for an answer.

Hochhuth's play did not begin the campaign against Pius XII. In France, Francois Mauriac had attacked him in 1951, for which he received a Nobel Prize. Mauriac would later be instrumental in cleaning up Elie Wiesel's violently anti-Christian Yiddish memoir *Un di Velt hat geschwigen* and turning in into *La Nuit*, which earned Wiesel a Nobel prize as well. In 1958 the Jewish Communist Francoise Cousteix-Drohocki elaborated on Mauriac's charges. "Why," she asked, "call Pius XII 'the Pope of peace' rather than of war? He no more stopped the latter than he imposed the former.... Pius XII's pontificate was totally bankrupt: war, torture, the annihilation of the individual, and cruelty in all its forms, reached a level never before attained. It's a shame that Pius XII never got around to excommunicating Nazis with the same level of indignation that he had for excommunicating Communists. If he was not aware of what was going on in Germany, then all the Vatican's listening posts are useless. If he was aware ... ."

In June 1963, Pope John XXIII died, and Montini, who had already attacked The Deputy in his defense of Pius XII, was elected his successor, taking the name Paul VI. Paul VI was aware of the expectations Bea had aroused, but he was also aware of the growing conservative resentment, especially over the slander of Pius XII and equally aware that he had to reconcile increasingly hostile camps.

The second session of the Council opened on September 20, 1963. Its main concern was the schema *De Ecclesiae*. Hearing the schema on the Jews had been incorporated into a larger document on ecumenism, the Israeli ambassador to Italy, Maurice Fischer, called on Pope Paul VI to find out whether the document dealt with the Jewish question. Sensing he must do something to ease the disappointment of the Jews, Paul VI and his advisers came up with the idea of visiting Israel during a trip he was planning to the Middle East. In recognizing the existence of the Jewish state, Paul VI hoped that the disappointment would be lessened. The Jewish lobby, however, was not going to take no for an answer, and resistance to the document was growing among the bishops for precisely that reason. The trip to the Holy Land suggested that the tensions had become more than mere mortals could resolve. From the Jewish perspective, the second session, which ended on December 4, 1963, was a distinct disappointment. The media barrage, however, continued unabated. Schuster and Lichten were experts at getting their views into the *New York Times*. Fritz Becker, lobbyist for the World Jewish Congress, specialized in quiet diplomacy. "We don't have the American outlook," he said, referring to Lichten and Schuster, "on the importance of getting into print."[43]

The Deputy opened in Paris on December 9. Four days later it opened in Basel in Switzerland. The Jewish Lobby kept up the pressure with three more openings: in Vienna on January 22, 1964, in New York on February 28, and in Tel Aviv, on June 20. Outraged that the second session ended without passage of the Jewish schema, the Jewish Lobby demanded that the American cardinals pressure the pontiff for a declaration on the Jews, but at no stage did a delegation of American cardinals go to him and insist on the discussion of religious liberty and the Jewish document.

By this point the Jewish lobbying was beginning to cause a reaction. Pamphlets on the Jews began to appear at the council. *The Jews and the Council in the Light of Holy Scripture* by Bernardus offered the most rational presentation from the official Church standpoint. Its message: Scripture states clearly that the Jews were voluntary deicides; the Fathers of the Church supported this doctrine. St. Thomas Aquinas wrote that the attitude of the Roman Pontiffs can only be interpreted as an affirmation that the Jews partake of a world-wide plot to destroy the Church. Hence, all should be wary of the Jew and not destroy a fundamental dogma of the Church. The tract of Bernardus was followed by *Complotto contro la Chiesa,* four thousand copies of which were distributed to the Council Fathers.

Fortified with a heavy-duty expense account by *Time*, Robert Blair Kaiser turned his spacious Roman apartment into "a gathering place for conciliar progressives ... those who were pushing hardest for updating everything, and doing so with a high hilarity."[44] In addition to regular Sunday night soirees of progressives, Kaiser held intimate dinner parties where Church leaders could talk about their hopes with people they would otherwise never meet. Bishop Mendez of Cuernavaca in Mexico, for example, found himself opposite the Hollywood director Otto Preminger over dinner one evening. Joining them were Kaiser and Gregoire LeMercier, prior of the Benedictine monastery in Cuernavaca, who explained to Kaiser's dinner guests how he had profited from psychoanalysis. He explained to Preminger how Freudian psychoanalysis had transformed his monks into better Benedictines. Preminger, who like Cardinal Ottaviani and Bishop Sheen, felt that Catholicism and Freudianism were like oil and water, asked LeMercier where he had found a Catholic psychiatrist. It turns out that LeMercier couldn't find a Catholic psychiatrist, and so he brought in one who was an atheist and Jew instead. That psychiatrist brought along a woman assistant who convinced many of the monks that the only reason they had joined the monastery was their fear of sexuality. Once they understood that, many of the monks then abandoned the order. LeMercier's claim that Freudian psychoanalysis had strengthened the monastery left Preminger shaking his head in wonder. At this point, Kaiser turned to Bishop Mendez and asked his opinion on the abbot's use of Freud to empty out one of the monasteries under his jurisdiction. "With Gregorio's help," Mendez replied "I am preparing an intervention for the Council. I think it's time we baptized Freud."[45]

One wonders how Cardinal Ottaviani would have replied to Kaiser's question, but Ottaviani was not invited to his apartment. One Council father who showed up regularly was the Irish Jesuit Malachi Martin. Martin, like Bea, was connected to the Biblicum, the Jesuit-run university for scripture scholars in Rome. Like Bea, he was working behind the scenes on the Jewish schema. Kaiser felt Martin was "one of the good guys," who "cut a fine figure of a priest" in his tailored suit.[46] Martin, Kaiser heard, had been sent to Rome "to save the Biblicum from the conservatives who wanted to shut it down."[47] The admiration was mutual, or so it seemed. After one Sunday evening, Martin "whispered conspiratorially" in Kaiser's ear "how important these Sunday nights have become to the progress of the Council.... Every cleric I've met is talking about these parties. They're saying this is where ideas are incubated, friendships struck, new national alliances formed, strategies laid, plans formed for each coming week."[48] Kaiser appreciated the flattery because he believed he had been sent to Rome to influence the events he was supposedly reporting on. Martin's access to key *personae* made him a valuable source of inside information; it also allowed Kaiser to feel he was influencing the outcome of the council.

Before long Kaiser would come to doubt both propositions. The first to go was his reliance on Martin. Martin was forever feeding him inside information, but when Kaiser's reporting was challenged Martin couldn't or wouldn't back it up. Other people were learning the same lesson. After Father Gus Weigel was quoted in the *New York Times* saying the Jewish schema was in trouble, he was reprimanded by Cardinal Bea for spreading lies and blacklisted. Kaiser knew Martin was Weigel's source: Martin had tried to peddle the same story to him for *Time*. Martin maintained the story was true in spite of the denials of Willebrands and Bea, much to Weigel's perplexity, since he lost his credibility due to Martin's false report. Kaiser by this time had stopped using Martin as a source, but was still unable to figure out the agenda behind his actions.

As Bea's assistant, Martin's main concern was the "Jewish schema." Martin supplied Kaiser with a steady diet of stories to show he was thwarting reactionaries in the Curia who allied with prelates from Arab nations to "sabotage Catholic-Jewish relations by scuttling the 'schema on the Jews.'"[49] To do this, they were not above sending phony telegrams from Bea's office to the AJC in New York or forged letters on Bea's stationery to the Council Central Commission.

After the Weigel incident, Kaiser was convinced that Martin was circulating false stories about the "Jewish Schema." Once burned by using Martin's information in stories he had filed for *Time*, Kaiser soon began to feel that Martin was manipulating him for his own ends. What those ends were became apparent one Sunday evening when Martin showed up at Kaiser's apartment "with a pair of important American Jews, representatives of the American Jewish Committee" in tow.[50] Suddenly, Martin's reason for circulating the stories that had ruined Weigel's reputation became clear. "Martin," Kaiser now realized, "was their lobbyist. These Jews were using him and paying him well for his help, which they thought they needed because they were reading those stories in the *New York Times*."[51] Martin had planted the stories to give the Jews the impression his efforts were indispensable in saving a document that wasn't in trouble. The Jews had been taken in by Martin's ruse, and they rewarded him handsomely for his duplicity. During the summer between the second and third session, Kaiser "noted that Malachi had always had a wallet stuffed with hundred-dollar bills."[50] Now Kaiser knew "where he was getting them."[52]

Kaiser told his wife, but he was taken aback by her response. "What's the matter with that?" she asked.[52] "Well," Kaiser stammered, "if he's a paid lobbyist, at least he ought to register, so people know where he's coming from."[53] Regaining his composure, Kaiser went on the offensive. "Have you ever wondered why he is always with Zachariah Schuster? He used to get spending money from me. He doesn't get it from me anymore. I think he's getting it from the American Jewish Committee.... I think he's keeping the pot boiling just to make himself more indispensable to the Jews."[54]

Kaiser found his wife's response unsettling. Martin had given Mary Kaiser a copy of Betty Friedan's *The Feminine Mystique*, underlining portions denigrating husbands and writing comments in the margins. Seeing Friedan's book as a seduction device, Kaiser suspected that Martin had designs on his wife. Michael Novak, another American correspondent at the Council, aggravated Kaiser's fears by claiming Martin and Mary were having an affair. During one of his wife's increasingly frequent absences, Kaiser, consumed with suspicion, discovered birth control pills while rooting through his wife's lingerie. Kaiser had been researching a birth control story he hoped would help overturn Church teaching. In his misguided way, Kaiser thought his "reporting might help overturn the tyranny of an authority with a very limited view of marriage, one that I believed was having a damaging effect on millions of Catholic marriages."[55] Instead, it looked as if it had facilitated his wife's adultery.

The pill, however, wasn't the only facilitator that Kaiser had to worry about. It turned out that Jewish activists, in exchange for Martin's contribution toward a Jewish schema favorable to their interests, were willing to facilitate the Irish Jesuit's adultery with Mary Kaiser. While hoping for a reconciliation for his wife, Kaiser noted that instead of coming to the hotel where he had arranged to meet her in Paris, his wife, "stopped off to see Zachariah Schuster and two other friends of Malachi Martin's in the Paris offices of the American Jewish Committee."[56] The American Jewish Committee had agreed to (or led Mary to believe) give her a job when she ran off with Malachi Martin. Mary, Kaiser writes at another point, "planned a European rendezvous with Malachi in Paris, where she thought she would be given a job by the American Jewish Committee."[57] Zachariah Schuster was not only paying Martin to subvert the Jewish schema, he was also helping him commit adultery.

Blinded by his commitment to views he considered progressive, Kaiser failed to see that the Council was providing an opening for all of the Church's traditional enemies. At around the same time that Kaiser's wife began taking birth control pills to conceal any possible effects of her affair with Malachi Martin, Kaiser discovered that the Church was thinking of changing its teaching on birth control. Predictably, he considered it a good thing "if frozen Catholic attitudes on birth control would start melting under the great reforming heat of this Council," because "then the Council would start meaning more to American Catholics"[58] in the same way that it was having more meaning for Kaiser's wife.

Kaiser also came into possession of a memo written by Planned Parenthood Federation of America Chairman, Donald B. Straus, describing his visit to Rome in February 1963. Straus met with Msgr. Cardinale, who told him "that the church had no quarrel with Planned Parenthood over its goals, only wanted its assurance that the organization was not pushing 'all kinds of contraceptives without regard for moral considerations.'"[59] Straus was taken aback by the "liberal views expressed by Msgr. Cardinale" and "wondered if the word could be passed along that discussion with Planned Parenthood representatives did not amount to consorting with the devil."[60] Two years later, in the summer of '65, Rev. Theodore Hesburgh, CSC, president of the University of Notre Dame, arranged a meeting between John D. Rockefeller, 3rd, and Pope Paul VI, during which Mr. Rockefeller offered to write the pope's birth control encyclical for him. This "openness to the modern world"[61] also led to the Commission on Birth Control which Paul VI rejected when he issued *Humanae Vitae* in 1968.

Kaiser soon discovered that Martin was writing his own book on the Council under the pseudonym of Michael Serafian. Kaiser was taken aback by the news but hardly in a position to object since much of his own book on the Council had been written by Martin as well. Martin would later become a prolific author of books of dubious accuracy. His book on the Jesuits purportedly was based on inside sources but was riddled with obvious factual errors. By the end of his career, Martin confined himself to *romans à clef*, like *Windswept House*, a purported expose of corruption in the Church from a conservative viewpoint.

During the Vatican Council, Roger Straus, "one of the most distinguished guys in the New York publishing world,"[62] took on Martin as an author and established publishing connections for Martin that lasted for the rest of his life. No matter how savagely his books were panned, Martin never lost access to big name publishing houses. When Jack Shea showed Kaiser the manuscript of Martin's *The Pilgrim*, Kaiser "turned quickly to a passage concerning the schema on the Jews," and concluded, "It's Malachi all right, and it looks like a fabrication."[63] From the Jewish perspective, however, *The Pilgrim* was far from a fabrication. It was a faithful rendition of the Jewish indictment of the Catholic Church launched by Jules Isaac. "From the tolerance of an Innocent III to the attitude of most Catholics toward Jews today," Martin wrote, "there is a direct line of filiation. Between the burning and plundering of all Jewish synagogues in Mesopotamia in 388 AD on the order of the Bishop of Callinicum and the destruction or desecration of all synagogues under the recent Nazi regime, we cannot but see a relationship of origin."[64] Martin continued:

> no one conscious of what has made modern Europe can deny that the pyres and the crematoria, the mephitic smoke and stench of the extermination camps in Nazi Germany, were, if not the logical conclusion, at least one extremist consequence of the normal Christian attitude to the Jews.[65]

In June 1964, *The New York Times* reported that the denial of Jewish responsibility for deicide had been cut from the latest draft of the schema. Bea's office quickly denied the charge; the source of the rumor was most likely Malachi Martin. The Jews, however, were upset. Richard Cardinal Cushing of Boston arranged a personal meeting between Rabbi Heschel and Pope Paul VI. Heschel, who attended the meeting with Zachariah Schuster, wanted the pope and the council to ban proselytizing Jews. Sensing in mid-interview that Heschel's *chutzpah* offended the Pope, Schuster switched to French, freezing Heschel out of the conversation.

The conservatives at the Council were even more offended by Jewish effrontery. The AJC tried to distance itself from Heschel's remarks, but the conservatives used the incident to discredit their opponents, especially the American bishops, who were seen as Jewish lackeys. As if to prove the conservatives were right, Cushing demanded that the deicide denial be put back in the document, and Bishop Steven Leven of San Antonio called for a ban on converting Jews.

In the end, the heavy-handed Jewish lobbying tactics backfired. Heschel maintained that his chutzpah did some good, but the consensus began to emerge that Jewish effrontery had harmed the Jewish cause. Even a devoted supporter of the Jews like Cardinal Cushing was forced to conclude that "the only people who could beat the Jewish declaration were the Jewish lobbyists."[66]

Vatican II and Malachi Martin

Chapter Twenty-Five

Folk Music Meets the Civil Rights Movement

I n 1963 the personal became political, or politics became personal. In February of that year, Ron Radosh's wife gave birth to their first child, but the arrival of that child did not help their marriage, which in distinction to his "exciting" intellecutal life, "involved constant bickering and fighting."[1] Raddosh repressed the recurring thought they should have never married by throwing himself "into what we were beginning to call 'the Movement' and into folk music."[2] By this point in time, that "movement" was defined more by Freud than by Marx. When Radosh's wife insisted they undergo therapy, Radosh didn't know how to say no, because "besides Marxism, our other chosen -ism was Freudianism, which we thought could do for the individual psyche what Marx could do for society."[3] So Radosh and his wife made a weekly pilgrimage to Chicago where a cut-rate shrink named Alan Robertson initiated them into the mysteries of "sleep therapy," something "that allowed the patient to reach the deepest levels of the unconscious."[4] This particular form of therapy involved Robertson charging Radosh and his friends for the naps they took in his office, during which Robertson also napped. Needless to say, the therapy didn't help Radosh's marriage. When his wife developed a "serious medical problem,"[5] she moved back to New York to her family.

The personal became political for Bob Dylan too. On May 2, 1963 Gene Shay picked up Dylan and his girlfriend Suze Rotolo at the 30th Street Station in Philadelphia and drove them to Tossi Aaron's home in Cheltenham, where they rested in anticipation of Dylan's concert the following day at the Ethical Society building on Rittenhouse Square. The release of *Freewheelin' Bob Dylan* with Suze on the cover was a month away, but Dylan and Suze were already having problems. Dylan had met Joan Baez and they had fallen in love—she with his music and he with her career. An affair ensued, and a concert tour followed. On tour, Joan Baez would sing a few songs and then invite Dylan on stage, where he stole the show. The culmination of the affair and the tour was the 1963 Newport Folk Festival where Dylan was inducted into the folk music pantheon. A picture shows Dylan linking arms with Peter Paul and Mary, Baez, Odetta, Pete Seeger, and Theodore Bikel—all singing "We Shall Overcome" with unidentified Negro representatives of the Civil Right Movement.

Bob's legendary mystique took a major hit shortly after that festival when an article entitled "I am MY Words," appeared in *Newsweek*. The article exposed Dylan's roots as a Jew named Zimmerman from the Midwest. He could no longer deny the existence of his parents because they had been seen at his recent concert at Carnegie Hall. People with middle-class Jewish parents from the Midwest didn't arrive in New York City in boxcars, certainly not in 1963. According to Spitz, Dylan "flew into a rage" because "he had been unmasked as a fraud."[5] The unmasking, however, would have little effect, because by this time Robert Shelton had become a member of Dylan's entourage, hanging out, drinking, and partying with Dylan and Grossman. Shelton still had the *New York Times* at his disposal to repair Dylan's myth whenever it go threatened by impious outsiders. Shelton accused *Newsweek* of "a hatchet job on Dylan,"[6] and that laid the roots issue and the issue of Dylan's truthfulness about those roots to rest.

Actually, what the *New York Times* defense of Dylan did was simply repress the truth so that the protest which it fueled would appear in another form. The success of Peter, Paul and Mary ensured that a reaction would occur, especially when one of the biggest hits of 1963 was their cover of "If I Had a Hammer," a song which HUAC condemned as "communist inspired"[7] in 1955. In 1963, millions of high school students "from San Diego up to Maine, in every town and mill" were singing it. Pete Seeger had been sentenced to prison for writing the song, and now Albert Grossman and his protégés were making millions off it. Some people interpreted the situation as a sign of how far the country had fallen.

In summer 1963, Pete Seeger showed up to perform in Los Angeles, only to be denounced by "The Fire and Police Research Association of Los Angeles, Inc.," for using folk songs as "an unidentified tool of Communist psychological or cybernetic warfare to ensnare and capture youthful minds."[8] Perhaps sensing folk music had become a leading tourist attraction, New York's Senator Kenneth Keating denounced the California cops and fire fighters, announcing he was "stunned by the revelation that folk music is part of the Communist arsenal of weapons."[9] Keating labored under "the impression ... it was thoroughly American in sprit, it was American folk music,"[10] indicating that he was either naive or pandering for the Jewish vote in Manhattan. Jere Real, writing for the John Birch Society periodical *American Opinion*, disabused Keating of any naiveté. Folk music, according to Real, was "a very subtle but highly effective presentation of standard Communist Party propaganda" in spite of, or perhaps because of, "the handclapping, the guitar strumming, the banjo-picking the shouting and the howling" accompanying it.[11] As a result, "Not since the 1930s have so many people of the United States been so directly, so cleverly, deceived into a widespread parroting of the Communist line."[12]

The Birch Society was right about the subversion, but, as usual, they were wrong about who was subverting whom. Even Party hacks like Irwin Silber, still editor of *Sing Out!* in 1963, had resigned from the Communist Party in 1958. The Birchers failed to understand that people like Silber were revolutionaries not because they were Communists, but because they were Jewish folksingers. The Right always had a difficult time distinguishing between form and content and the part and the whole. The form in this instance was the revolutionary Jew. The revolutionary content was no longer communism; it was folk music. What the communists construed as a vehicle for Popular Front era propaganda had taken on a life of its own. The party no longer directed the revolution, nor did it define its content. People like Dylan did that based not on any party line but on the lives they were leading, as seen through the lens of the ancestral Jewish penchant for revolutionary activity. Bob Dylan was not a communist, but he was a revolutionary Jew, and as such he could redefine the revolution to meet the needs of the *Zeitgeist*, which, as Norman Mailer, another revolutionary Jew, announced in his essay "The White Negro," were increasingly sexual.

Right-Wing Critics

Other right-wing critics were equally obtuse. Rather than risk accusations of anti-Semitism, they beat the dead horse of Communism. In *The Marxist Minstrels: A Handbook on Communist Subversion of Music*, David Noebel wrote "The Communist infiltration into the subversion of American music has been nothing short of phenomenal and in some areas, e.g., folk music, their control is fast approaching the saturation point under the able leadership of Pete Seeger, *Sing Out!*, Folkways Records and Oak Publications, Inc."[13] Three years earlier, Serge Denisoff, in his book *Great Day Coming*, had documented "the Old Left's discovery and use of folksong materials."[14] Irwin Silber could resign from the Communist Party, but he never stopped being a revolutionary Jewish folksinger, and that was precisely the persona which the Revolutionary Jew adopted when it got tired of defending the largely irrelevant dogma emanating from Moscow in the years after Krushschev denounced Stalin. Music may very well have continued to be a vehicle for revolution, but the revolution was not Communism, nor was it run by commissars from Moscow. It was run by the children of the commissars from Moscow, who now considered themselves Americans, largely because of all the folk music they had played at summer camp. The Reusses explain the fate of the revolutionary Jew when he made contact with American folk music but only obliquely when the say that "to the extent that participants in the communist movement came from recent immigrant stock, absorbing American folk song and folk lore is one way to assimilate into American society."[15] So Communism didn't, in the final analysis, subvert folk music; folk music subverted Communism. The real continuity was ethnic, not political. The Revolutionary Jew would redefine the revolution to suit his needs, even if he destroyed himself in the process.

The Summer of '63 was folk music's "moment of glory,"[16] and nothing epitomized that moment more than the duets of Joan Baez and Bob Dylan. Those duets also unfortunately signaled the end of Dylan's relationship with Suze Rotolo. The lady who had marched down Great Jones Street adoringly hanging on Dylan's arm was now history, in more than once sense of the word. After Dylan left on his concert tour with Baez, Rotolo moved out of their apartment and got a job working as a waitress at a luncheonette on 12th Street. Rotolo was now finished with Dylan, or so she thought, until she discovered that she was pregnant. Bob Dylan dealt with his paternity by having Albert Grossman arrange for an illegal abortion at a doctor's office on the Upper East Side. It was a defining moment both for Dylan and for the movement he would lead. The emotional clarity of ballads like "Don't think twice" would now become muddied by a torrent of surrealistic imagery. The imagery of songs like "Mr. Tambourine Man," are usually and correctly traced to drugs, but the increased use of drugs is rarely traced back to one of its most common functions, namely, anesthesia, specifically anesthesia of conscience. Bob Dylan was notoriously cruel with anyone around him. His favorite targets were folk singers who admired him, people like Eric Anderson and Phil Ochs, who idolized Dylan in spite of the abuse he took at his hands. Eventually, Dylan turned on Joan Baez as well during their tour of England. Dylan and his buddy Bobby Neuwirth ridiculed Baez so mercilessly—some of which is caught on the Pannebaker film *Don't Look Back*—that she eventually dropped out of the tour. This is the way that Dylan repaid her kindness in fostering his career a few years earlier.

As a result, Dylan's music began to take on the characteristics of his deformed soul. The music became harsh and electronically amplified and the lyrics became increasingly opaque, as Dylan fell more and more under the influence of degenerates like the Beat poet Alan Ginsburg, whose poetry mirrored an equally depraved soul. Since the people who bought his records were undergoing the same sort of moral degeneration, each innovation in his music was greeted as an artistic breakthrough.

Chapter Twenty-six

The Sign in Sidney Brustein's Window

As if in recognition of her new-found fame, Hansberry and Nemiroff left Greenwich Village in 1962 and moved to a country estate in Croton on Hudson. At this point in her life, Hansberry, because of her marriage to Nemiroff, had become a living embodiment of the Black-Jewish alliance. She had also become increasingly involved with SNCC, which began to attract significant amounts of Jewish money because "a small coterie of radical northern Jews... were attracted by SNCC's militancy and by its willingness to take help from sources viewed with suspicion by more moderate civil rights groups."[1] Because of her Jewish husband and her new-found fame as a playwright and politically engaged intellectual, Hansberry was poised to become a spokesman for the black-Jewish alliance at the moment of its greatest success; it was at precisely this point, however, that the theoretical issues which would eventually lead to its demise began to emerge.

In February 1963, Norman Podhoretz published "My Negro Problem, and Ours" in Commentary, the official organ of the American Jewish Committee, disputing the official view of the nonviolent Negro based on his own experience with Negro gangs in New York. Podhoretz, like Irving Louis Horowitz, who had grown up in Harlem under similar circumstances, grew up in a world where Negro violence was a daily fact of life. Hansberry, whom Friedman describes as "one of the most convinced exponents of Negro-Jewish unity,"[2] was blindsided by the Jewish attack and could only retort lamely that Podhoretz had "to hold his nose"[3] in dealing with Negroes because of some personal aversion. Podhoretz's piece prompted Harold Cruse to write "My Jewish Problem and Theirs," in which "Cruse described his mistreatment by Jewish teachers as he grew up in Harlem and the subordination later of black intellectuals to Jewish control."[4]

But Norman Podhoretz wasn't the only Jew who was calling the terms of the Black-Jewish alliance into question. Hansberry had had a similar run in with Norman Mailer, whose essay "The White Negro" had effectively defined the Negro as a Jewish fantasy of liberation from sexual morals. Hansberry suddenly found herself caught in the middle. She believed in sexual liberation because she was a revolutionary, but she didn't like the way that Jews like Norman Mailer defined the Negro as a paradigm of sexual liberation. Setting a precedent which she would follow in her second play, Hansberry saw Mailer as "symbolic of all who fashion their particular fantasies and "Take the 'A' Train" to Harlem to find them... and go back downtown and write essays not on the prostitutes they met, but on—'Harlem,'"[5] but she did not bring up the Jewish issue. Instead she faulted a phantom group known as "The New Paternalists." Even though she mentioned the fact that "the most lowly of the barflies in Harlem" would start talking about the Jews the moment a writer like Sejmour Krim or Norman Mailer "left the room," she ended her essay on a consciously irenic note urging Mailer "not to write of the greatness of our peoples—yours or mine—in the past tense," because better days for the Black-Jewish alliance were just around the corner.[6] In a move that must have set Harold Cruse's teeth on edge, Hansberry ended her essay with a quote in Yiddish, "Vail kumen et noch undzer oysgebenkte sho," which Hansberry rendered in English as "Because the hour we have hungered for is near" after lifting it from "Song of the Warsaw Ghetto" by Hersch Glick.[7]

Hansberry was learning the hard way that if she aspired to be an official spokesman for the Negroes she was going to have to do it on Jewish terms. It was a lesson that James Baldwin had already learned. James Baldwin was

> another black writer whose talent was first recognized and nurtured by Jewish editors of small but influential magazines: Elliot Cohen and Robert Warshaw at *Commentary*, Saul Levitas at the *New Leader*, and Philip Rahv at the *Partisan Review*. In 1946 Levitas gave Baldwin his first book review assignment, an act the grateful author never forgot; indeed, in 1961 he told his biographer that these editors had helped save his life.[8]

Baldwin repaid the favor to the Jews who launched his literary career by misconstruing the conflict in Harlem as Black vs. White. "The Negro facing a Jew," Baldwin wrote in Commentary in 1948, 13 years after the Harlem riots had caused a mass exodus of Jewish merchants, "hates at bottom, not his Jewishness but the color of his skin. It is not the Jewish tradition by which he has been betrayed by the tradition of his native land. But just as society must have a scapegoat, so hatred must have a symbol. Georgia has the Negro and Harlem has the Jew."[9] Baldwin, who apparently never had his Christmas bulbs tested in the Horowitz hardware store in Harlem, claimed that "The Negro identifies himself almost wholly with the Jew. The image of the suffering Christ and the suffering Jew are wedded with the image of the suffering slave."[10]

Cruse claimed that Baldwin was being disingenuous when he referred to the conflict in Harlem as Black v. White. Even when he admits that the Jews in Harlem are guilty of exploiting the blacks there economically, Baldwin attempts to exonerate the Jews by claiming that they are only operating "in accordance with the American business tradition."[11] Baldwin's essay on Harlem in Commentary forces Cruse to conclude that he wants "to avoid dealing with the facts of Harlem as they exist." This means "bending over backward to avoid criticism of Jews while pretending to be angry with whites," as well as overlooking the fact that he overlooks "American Jews... are very much in control of their situation and have their enemies well 'cased' from all directions."[12]

In concluding that the battle in America is ethnic not racial, Cruse has discovered the triple melting pot, which claims that there never has been nor never will be one homogeneous mass of Americans. The same theory goes on to state that, after three generations, religion replaces country of origin as the source of ethnicity in America. By claiming that the Negro was in effect a separate ethnic group, and by denying (or ignoring) the role which religion plays in defining ethnicity in America, Cruse effectively cut the Negro off from their most important allies in America's *Kulturkampf,* namely, their co-religionists, and it is precisely this issue which Hansberry explored in her second and final play, *The Sign in Sidney Brustein's Window.*

It was after public brawls with Jews like Norman Mailer and Norman Podhoretz, when a younger generation of Jews was spreading revolution in Mississippi during the Freedom Summer of 1964 that Lorraine Hansberry decided it was her turn to speak out on the Black-Jewish alliance. Her vehicle was the play The Sign in Sidney Brustein's Window, which opened on Broadway in the fall of 1964. As an omen that this exploration of the black-Jewish alliance was not going to go well, Hansberry and Nemiroff divorced in 1964. Cruse claimed that Hansberry was "making... noisy, but superficial integrationist propaganda"[13] when she wrote Raisin. His criticism of Brustein is even more biting. Harold Cruse claimed that Hansberry had in effect become a Jew when she married Nemiroff:

> Witness the jesting "ethnic" idea behind the bit of dialogue in *Brustein's Window* to the effect that Brustein was an "assimilationist Jew." But this line has serious "folksy" intent as far as the playwright's ethnic sentiments went. Lorraine Hansberry had not simply married a man who "just happened to be of Jewish antecedents" as the liberal-humanist-moralists would have it: she had "assimilated" into white Jewish cultural life.[14]

If so, Hansberry was not a happy Jew. Lorraines's sister Mamie tried to minimize the Jewish/Black antagonism that comes out in the play by claiming that Nemiroff's family, "in their ethnic way, was very similar to our family."[15] Ossie Davis tried to pour oil on the troubled waters of the black-Jewish alliance after Brustein riled them up by claiming that "all subcultures share the common bond of being outsiders."[16] Cruse's analysis of the play is better than the generally clueless interpretation of Brustein as reflecting "harmony and acceptance between blacks and whites, Jews and Christians, and people of varied backgrounds" that has succeeded it, but even a cursory reading of Brustein indicates that the situation, as the divorce indicates, isn't as simple as he portrays it either.

Fourteen years after arriving there, Hansberry had discovered that she didn't like Bohemia or its American incarnation, Greenwich Village, which she describes as "the preferred habitat of many who fancy revolt or at least detachment from the social order that surrounds us."[17] Sidney Brustein, the main character in the play, is an unhappy Jew, and he is unhappy because he has turned his back on the only identity a Jew has, namely, being a revolutionary. Brustein longs to "smite evil" with "the sword of the Maccabees," but instead he says L'chaim and "takes a pill" for the pain in his "oozing intestine."[18]

The oozing intestine image is especially interesting in light of the fact that it was Hansberry and not Nemiroff who was dying of duodenal cancer at the time the play was being written, in rehearsal, and being performed on stage. By conflating her own very real cancer with Brustein's fictional "oozing intestine," Hansberry identifies herself as having internalized the Jewish revolutionary spirit, but not leaving it at that goes to hint symbolically that it is precisely the internalization of the principles of Jewish revolution that ends up killing her.

Hansberry claims to be grateful for what she has learned from the Jews. Speaking through the persona of Iris she tells Sidney, "I have learned a lot after five years of life with you, Sidney. When I met you I thought Kant was a stilted way of saying cannot; I thought Puccini was a kind of spaghetti....Thanks to you, I now know something that I wouldn't have learned if it hadn't been for you."[19]

In spite of her gratitude, Iris, speaking for Hansberry, feels that she has lost more than she has gained. The Jews have exacted a price for their participation in the black-Jewish alliance that was far higher than the one which Harold Cruse complained about. The price the Negro has to pay for marriage (both literal and figurative) with the Jews is 1) loss of faith in God and 2) moral corruption. At the end of her life, clutching her "oozing intestine" Hansberry suddenly realizes that the price she paid was too high but is unclear what to do about the fact.

Hansberry could invoke the name of John Brown, but her diary entries toward the end of her life indicate that she was an ambivalent revolutionary at best. "Do I remain a revolutionary?" Hansberry wrote in her journal seven months before her death. "Intellectually—without a doubt. But am I prepared to give my body to the struggle or even my comforts? This is what I puzzle about."[20] One month later she seemed determined to resolve the issue by throwing herself "back into the movement," but no sooner are the words out of her mouth (or pen) and the native hue of resolution is once again sicklier o'er with the pale cast of thought and

> that very impulse is immediately flushed with a thousand vacillations and forbidding images.... Comfort has come to be its own corruption....Comfort. Apparently I have sold my soul for it. I think when I get my health back I shall go into the South to find out what kind of revolutionary I am....[21]

Rather than allowing her to find out what kind of revolutionary she was, *Brustein* allowed her to find out what kind of revolutionary she was not. As W. A. Domingo pointed out 40 years earlier, any Negro who aspired to be a revolutionary had to sit at the feet of Russian Jews. But Hansberry soon discovered that the revolutionary spirit was spiritually destructive, to Jews and Negroes both. In becoming a Jewish revolutionary, Hansberry alienated herself from her own people, who were for the most part devout Christians. As in the past when Ottilie Assing introduced Frederick Douglass to the writings of Feuerbach and the Communists collaborated with Haywood Patterson in the writing of *Scottsboro Boy*, the Jews in Hansberry's day were still busy trying to turn Negroes into atheists as a way of completing their revolutionary education.

The conflict had already appeared in *Raisin* which was written four years after Hansberry married Nemiroff. When Mama says, "God willing," Beneatha launches into an atheist tirade:

> "God hasn't got a thing to do with it.... God is just one idea I don't accept... I get tired of Him getting credit for all the things the human race achieves through

its own stubborn effort. There simply is no God—there is only man and it is he who makes miracles."[22]

At this point, Mama slaps Beneatha violently in the face and instructs her, "Now you say after me, in my mother's house there is still God." The stage directions for *Raisin* indicate that Beneatha has been "defeated," when she repeats, "In my mother's house there is still God." In *Brustein*, Hansberry indicates that the Negro revolutionary has been defeated for the exact opposite reason. Iris and Mavis have been defeated by revolutionary Jews like Brustein, who "have all so busily got rid of God for us."[23]

Hansberry would later tell Mike Wallace "Beneatha is me, eight years ago," because, as her biographer puts it:

> At twenty, Beneatha is very much the new woman: she is planning to become a doctor, she will delay marriage until she completes her training, she doubts God, and various institutions and she toys with diverse forms of self-expression—playing the guitar, acting and horseback riding.[24]

But by now it should be obvious that every character was Hansberry, especially by the time she got around to writing *Brustein*. So perhaps Hansberry is also Ruth, who "considers having an abortion in order to prevent adding another financial burden to the family." The issue is formulated in a way that bespeaks rationalization, for no one in the Hansberry family was ever in financial straits, dire or otherwise. And yet, in spite of all of the talk about race, *Raisin* revolves around the abortion issue. Mama has her plant, which is associated with life; it is she who is determined that Ruth not have an abortion; it is she who decides that a move is necessary, no matter what the cost, because, as she puts it, "We was going backwards 'stead of forwards—talking 'bout killing babies and wishing each other was dead... When it gets like that in life—you got to do something bigger...."[25]

The conflict of ideas in *Raisin* is between Lena and Beneatha, not between Lena and Ruth. Lena believes in God and is against abortion, reflecting the Christian roots of America's blacks; Hansberry once described herself "as not being "hostile" to religion "unless it happened to be Catholic,"[26] but Beneatha is hostile to religion. Beneatha is an atheist who believes in free love and as a result would be more likely than Ruth to get pregnant and feel that abortion was a way out of that dilemma. So the question the play brings up is whether Ruth is standing in for Beneatha, who is standing in for Hansberry, who wants to talk about the sexual issues troubling her conscience in disguised form. We know from her biographer that Hansberry made a conscious decision not to have children. "Lorraine's decision not to have children," she writes, "evolved from her nurturance of her art.... Lorraine the artist triumphed over Lorraine the Mother."[27] Again the very formulation of the issue smacks of rationalization.

In fact, in trying to explain her atheism, Hansberry tells one interviewer, "We only revert back to mystical ideas—which includes most contemporary orthodox religious views, in my opinion—because we simply are confronted with some things we don't understand yet."[28] When the interviewer counters by saying that Mama "gets so much sustenance from this... kind of faith," Hansberry goes on the defensive, claiming that she doesn't "attack people who are religious at all, as you can tell from the play." Man, however, no longer needs religious crutches because now "Man exalts himself by his achievements... and this power to rationalize—or excuse me—his power to reason!"[29]

At this point, either Hansberry or her interlocutor burst out laughing after Hansberry committed what the folks in Greenwich Village in the 1950s referred to as a "Freudian slip." Then as if to cover over what this gaffe revealed about her state of mind, Hansberry added after the laughter died down, "Well, now, of course, his rationalization has its benefits too. I don't know if he could get along without either."[30]

At this point we'll never know whether Hansberry got pregnant as a result of the affairs she fantasized at the University of Wisconsin or whether the trip to Mexico was to procure an abortion, or whether an abortion had anything to do with the cancer that eventually killed her. An "oozing intestine" was a common complication arising from abortion, all of which were illegal at the time. Sometimes it led to death by septicemia within days of the abortion, sometimes the damage was repaired in time. Whatever the case, the link between a possible abortion and cancer is no more far-fetched than Mamie Hansberry's post mortem, which claims that "The black experience creates a lot of stress, and...a form of cancer can evolve from the emotional stress of racism."[31]

All of that gets covered over by the announcement that Hansberry was a lesbian. The New York critics attacked Hansberry for *Brustein's* homophobia after Hansberry had Alton say, "After a while, hanging out with queers gets on my nerves." Hansberry, according to her biographer, wrote anonymous letters to various gay and lesbian publications, but the main evidence comes from Nemiroff, who claims that Hansberry's homosexuality "was not a peripheral or casual part of her life but contributed significantly on many levels to the sensitivity and complexity of her view of human beings in the world."[32]

A husband attesting to his late wife's lesbianism has an odd sort of ring to it. But when it comes to the posthumous Lorraine Hansberry we are dealing almost exclusively with the mind of Robert Nemiroff. This meant, of course, that whatever misgivings she had about the influence of Jewish revolutionaries on her life got expunged from the public record after she died, which is when Nemiroff took over her literary estate.

When *Brustein* opened at the Longacre Theater on October 15, 1964, the play was met with mixed reviews, which meant financial problems. By November the play was already in financial trouble. To counter the possibility that the play might fold, a number of writers, artists, actors and actresses took out an ad in the *New York Times* telling New Yorkers that "Miss Hansberry's new play is a work of distinction.... We the undersigned... urge you to see it now."[33] Many of those who signed the ad were Jewish; many were black; one, Sammy Davis, Jr. was Jewish and black. In November 1964, comedian Mel Brooks and his wife, actress Anne Bancroft, opened their home for a midnight strategy meeting to keep *Brustein* alive.

The fact that prominent Jews like Mel Brooks tried to save the play could not disguise the fact that most Jews did not like it. *The New York Times* did not like sitting through two hours of listening to, as Hansberry put it "the tortures of the engage," her way of describing "the generation which grew up in the swirl and dash of the Sartre-Camus despair of the postwar years" as they "crossed each other leaping in and out of the Communist Party."[34] Norman Nadel claimed that "this play sinks under its own sordid substance."[35] The worst news of all, however, was that "Hadassah hasn't bought a single theater party."[36] Before long it was pretty clear that Hadassah stayed away in droves, because it did not like what Hansberry had to say about Jews. In the end all efforts to keep the play on life support failed, and *Brustein* died on the same day that Lorraine Hansberry did, on January 12, 1965.

After Hansberry died, Robert Nemiroff, now her ex-husband, chose as the epigraph for her black marble tombstone *Brustein*'s hosanna to the Jewish revolutionary spirit: "I care. I care about it all. It takes too much energy not to care...The why of why we are here is an intrigue for adolescents; the how is what must command the living. Which is why I have lately become an insurgent again."[37]

After Hansberry's death, Nemiroff took over the promotion of her writing. When he did, all the ambivalence toward Jewish revolutionaries disappeared. In a letter to Lisbeth Vuorijaervi, a Swedish scholar, Robert Nemiroff wrote that "Jews have played an extraordinary role, out of all proportion to their numbers... in all democratic, liberal and radical, humanizing and liberating movements" and that "other oppressed peoples—especially in the Hitler years and their aftermath— have recognized this tacitly and often explicitly, and have tended to look to Jews for greater understanding. As allies or potential allies or, at least, as the least hostile ethnic group in the society at large."[38] This may or may not be true. The question, however, is, if Hansberry felt this way, why did she write *Brustein*? *Young Gifted and Black*, Nemiroff's redaction of her writings, won a Golden Globe award in 1973.

Unlike *Young, Gifted and Black*, which was the Jewish reading of Hansberry, *Brustein* was a prophetic play because it foreshadowed the collapse of the Black-Jewish Alliance. Friedman sees the first signs of the collapse at the 1964 Democratic convention in Atlantic City, which was soon followed by a riot in Harlem, which was followed by riots in the ghettoes of cities across the country. As in Harlem, so also in Philadelphia, which had its own riot, blacks targeted small shopkeepers, almost all of whom were Jews. Friedman who was head of the Philadelphia branch of the AJC, claims that 22 Jewish merchants were killed and 27 were shot or beaten in Philadelphia alone over the course of the four years from 1968 to 1972. From 1964 until 1968 there were 329 riots in 257 cities across the country, and in just about every instance it was blacks attacking Jews and accusing them of price and rent gouging.[39] It was the riots and the black attack on Jewish merchants which prompted many Jews to pull out of the civil rights movement. When Israel went to war in 1967, many Jews pulled out for good and devoted their energies and their money to supporting Israel.

Malcolm X was murdered on February 21, 1965, but by the time he died there were many who were willing to take up the tattered banner of black nationalism and return to a more virulent version of the vision which everyone had pronounced dead when the NAACP succeeded in silencing Marcus Garvey. It was Harold Cruse, however, and not Lorraine Hansberry who wrote the definitive book on the Black-Jewish Alliance, so definitive in fact that it caused the collapse of the alliance. When *The Crisis of the Negro Intellectual* arrived in bookstores in 1967, "the civil rights movement was quagmired in a crisis of purpose from which it would never emerge."[40] Of course, one of the reasons it never emerged from its crisis lies in how well Cruse documented Jewish involvement in Negro affairs. Cheryl Greenberg argues that Cruse's claim that Jews "deliberately manipulated the movement for their own ends" is "not simple anti-Semitism" because "a look at the historical record suggests that Jews did have a great deal of self-interest in promoting a civil rights movement based on integration, and they did indeed turn away from the movement in the 1960s as their self-interest increasingly conflicted with it."[41] Greenberg concludes by saying that "The 'golden age of a black-Jewish alliance never existed."[42] Rather than try to refute what Cruse said, the Jews just lost interest in the plight of black folk. When Israel warred with Egypt in the same year, that loss of interest became permanent.

When Lorraine Hansberry died on January 12, 1965, her family received a letter of condolence from Martin Luther King which praised "Her creative ability and her profound grasp of the deep social issues confronting the world today" and claimed that it would "remain an inspiration to generations yet unborn."[43] Martin Luther King had just rented an apartment in Chicago's black belt and was planning an assault on what he saw as segregation in housing in that city. One of the great mysteries of the civil rights movement was why Martin Luther King got involved in the housing situation in Chicago, a decision that would bring about the biggest debacle of his career. His letter gives some indication that *A Raisin in the Sun* was on his mind when he made the decision.

After months of preliminary work, Martin Luther King arrived in Chicago to kick off his housing drive in June 1966. As one of his first acts, King, drawing on the symbolism of his namesake, attempt to nail the housing equivalent of 95 theses to the door of Chicago's city hall, but had to settle for taping his theses after he discovered that the door was made of steel.

Chicago had been a racial battlefield since the Chicago Housing Authority, the Quakers, B'nai B'rith/ADL and Louis Wirth redoubled their efforts to complete the social engineering of Chicago's ethnic neighborhoods that had begun during World War II. Beginning in 1946 at Airport Park and spreading across the South Side, racial war raged throughout the 1950s and 60s. The local politicians reached a *modus vivendi* in 1954 when the mayor fired the head of the Chicago Housing Authority, but the issue was not local. The federal government was promoting racial migration and the ethnic cleansing of Catholic neighborhoods in all of the major cities of the North and East. The Catholic Church, which had a huge financial stake in the outcome of this battle, was, if anything, divided on the issue, with rank and file Catholics throwing rocks through the windows of newly arrived Negroes while at the same time the hierarchy and much of the clergy welcomed the civil rights movement with open arms.

In 1963 Chicago's branch of the Catholic Interracial Council organized a centennial celebration of the Emancipation Proclamation which featured speeches by Martin Luther King and Chicago's ordinary, Albert Cardinal Meyer, who told the assembly, "Our whole future as a nation and as a religious people may be determined by what we do about the race problem in the next few years."[44]

Meyer's successor, John Cardinal Cody, continued this rhetorical and symbolic support for civil rights, and many priests, nuns and lay people played an active role in the growing civil rights movement. Cody met privately with King on February 2, 1966 and gave his tacit support to King's housing campaign. When King held his mass rally at Soldier Field that summer, tacit support became open support when Auxiliary Bishop Aloysius Wycislo, representing the Archdiocese of Chicago read a statement from Cody affirming that "your struggle and sufferings will be mine until the last vestige of discrimination and injustice is blotted out here in Chicago and throughout America."[45] Since Chicago had acquired a reputation as "a Catholic town,"[46] King's success there seemed assured.

But things started to go wrong from the beginning, and they never ended up going right. When King stepped out of his car to lead a march through "segregated" Marquette Park, he was greeted by a hail of rocks and bottles, one of which hit him on the head and made him stagger to his knees. The Lithuanians who would later set fire to the marchers' cars and chase Jesse Jackson down 63rd St. were outraged by the fact that people from another part of the country would come into their neighborhood and tell them to sell their homes. That wasn't precisely King's message, but the simple fact of the matter was that no one, not even the *Chicago Tribune*, knew exactly what King's message was. According to an editorial in the *Chicago Tribune*, the message of the "paid professional agitators" who made up the march was "give up your homes and get out so that we can take over."[47]

King was befuddled, as Mayor Daley indicated, because he didn't understand Chicago. One of King's lieutenants only strengthened this suspicion when she said, in effect, Chicago was different that what they had expected. "Down South," the SCLC's Dorothy Tillman opined, "you were black or white. You wasn't Irish or Polish or all of this."[48]

Mayor Daley was quick to capitalize on SCLC ignorance of Chicago. When King announced that he intended to end slums in Chicago, Daley announced that Chicago already had a slum clearance program staffed by people who knew more about the city than he did. "What the hell is [King] doing here anyway?" Daley's staff wanted to know. "Does he think we don't care about slums? Why Chicago, instead of Atlanta or Harlem? King has no knowledge of Chicago."[49] When King announced that the SCLC planned to march in Gage Park, Daley countered by saying that King was "very sincere" but lacked "all the facts on the local situation" because "after all, he is a resident of another city."[50] When Daley suggested in April 1966 that King go home to Georgia, seven Negro committeemen seconded his suggestion.

King's Jewish backers had a sense of foreboding about Chicago as well. Both Bayard Rustin and Stanley Levison "sensed disaster."[51] Friedman claims that "Levison sought to restrain his friend but failed to do so."[52] The main problem was King's unfamiliarity with the situation in Chicago. King's knowledge of the housing situation in Chicago was based largely on *A Raisin in the Sun*. When King vowed that "he would lead a rent strike unless the city's landlords improved their properties immediately"[53] he failed to understand that many of the landlords were black, and that Hansberry Enterprises was one of the biggest slum landlords in Chicago. King was caught up in a world he did not understand, and his ill-fated Chicago campaign soon turned into the disaster that Levison and Rustin feared it would become.

Friedman claims that Levison was "the voice of moderation in King's circle," claiming that Levison had told King, "You don't call for insurrection in a place where you're outnumbered, outgunned,"[54] but it was equally obvious that Levison wanted King to succeed for ethnocentric reasons. King "was the last major black leader to promote the legitimacy of Zionism within the black community."[124] If King were to be discredited in Chicago, his defeat would open the door for King's black nationalist competitors, who were no friends of Zionism. Like Marcus Garvey before them, and like Malcolm X and Harold Cruse, the black power advocates of the mid-'60s realized that integrationism and black nationalism were incompatible. They also realized that Zionism and Black Zionism were incompatible according to the terms of the Black-Jewish Alliance. After his failure in Chicago, King's assassination was merely anticlimactic. The "beloved community" that King and others in the Black-Jewish Alliance had tried to create during the '50s and early '60s had died two years before he did.

Chapter Twenty-Seven

The Third Session of the Council

The third session of the Second Vatican Council began in fall 1964. On November 19, the Council passed a document on the Jews so heavily influenced by Jewish lobbying that many thought it repudiated traditional Catholic teaching. The Jews rejoiced, but their rejoicing was short-lived. Paul VI refused to promulgate the schema. The approval of a flawed document by many bishops awoke conservatives to the dangers of Jewish lobbying. As a result, the conservatives now launched their own campaign. The salient issue concerned the Council Fathers' misunderstanding of who they were dealing with. Were the Jews "the people of the Old Testament" or the source of Hollywood star cults, pansexualism and Freudian psychoanalysis, and as a result a danger to Catholic morals? According to Poncins, "The majority of the Council Fathers" were "under a serious misapprehension as to what constitutes the very essence of Judaism" because they "only applied themselves to the humanitarian aspect of the problem, skillfully submitted by the spokesmen of World Jewry and by a Press largely favorable to Jewish interests."[1]

Once the November 1964 document was withdrawn from consideration, Pope Paul VI returned it to the "conciliar commission in charge of the preparation of the schema," where it was "profoundly reshaped" once again.[2] According to Poncins, "The new text submitted for the approval of the council was distinctly less favorable to Jewish demands and more acceptable to conservative consciences; however, it still contained a few ambiguities which could be interpreted as promising a prudent revision but a revision, nevertheless, of the traditional Catholic attitude toward Judaism, which has remained unaltered for 15 centuries."[3] Poncins claimed "the conservative majority had been taken entirely by surprise"[4] by the November 1964 document. If so, they were regaining their composure, now that they "had time to take stock of the situation."[5] With a better understanding of "the extreme gravity of this vote" the conservatives were able to "energetically combat ... the Jewish-Catholic coalition, which was able to dispose of a press almost entirely at its service."[6] Led by Mgr. de Proenca Sigaud, archbishop of Dimantina, Brazil, Mgr. Lefebvre, Superior General of the Holy Ghost Fathers, and Mgr. Carli, Bishop of Segni, Italy, the conservatives began to influence the mind of the council Fathers. In February 1965, Bishop Carli wrote an article for his diocesan newspaper claiming that the Jews of Christ's time and their descendants down to the present were responsible for Christ's death.

The most devastating blow came on Passion Sunday, 1965, when the pope preached a homily that held the Jews responsible for the crucifixion. "It is an extremely solemn and sad page which recalls for us the meeting between Jesus and the Jewish people," the pope said. "This people was predestined to receive the Messiah and has long been waiting for him for thousands of years and was completely absorbed in this hope and certitude, but at the very moment, that is to say, when Christ came and spoke and showed himself, not only did they not recognize him, but fought him, slandered him, abused him and finally put him to death."[7]

The Jews were dumbfounded, then furious. The Chief Rabbi of Rome, Elio Toaff, and Dr. Sergio Piperno, President of the Union of Italian Jewish communities, immediately sent a telegram to the Vatican, published in *Il Messagero de Roma*:

> Italian Jews express their sorrowful amazement at charge Hebrew people in death of Jesus contained in Sovereign Pontiff's homily, delivered shortly before Easter Roman parish Our Lady of Guadeloupe and reported official Vatican press, thus renewing deicide accusation, secular source tragic injustices towards Jews, to which solemn affirmations Vatican Council seemed to terminate for ever.[8]

The Jewish schema was causing unprecedented division at the Council. The more the Church dealt with the Jewish issue, the more contentious it became. The Jews accused the pope of reneging on their agreement with Cardinal Bea. Conservatives accused Bea of "simony,"[9] trafficking in sacred things. Bea was accused "of having accepted Jewish capital for the functions of his secretariat for unity."[10] Bea was "accused of having imprudently promised, per contra, a declaration which would, as far as it concerns the Church, be the epilogue to the Nuremberg trial: that she should demand pardon from the Jews for all the persecutions which Christian doctrine has caused them throughout the centuries (deicide Jews, the people accursed by God, etc.)."[11]

The conservatives were "ready to take the necessary steps to save the church from such an ignominy" by "appeal[ing] to the Council Fathers who have not yielded to Jewish pressure, or who have not sold themselves in simony to Jewish gold ... to repeal the perfidious declaration."[12] Paul VI was faced with the unenviable prospect of fighting both the Jews and their conservative opponents. To rescue the schema, he now had to rescue Cardinal Bea from "the grave insinuations"[13] raised against him, largely, one suspects, because of the machinations of Father Martin.

In April 1965, a *New York Times* report claimed the Jewish schema was in trouble. Robert C. Doty cited "an authorized leak from the Vatican."[14] By now this had become a code word for Malachi Martin. Nine months later, Martin was identified in *Look* as the "double agent" responsible for "Similar stories in the *Times* [that] foretold Council failings before they happened."[15] *Look* identified the priest under another pseudonym, "Timothy Fitzharris O'Boyle, S.J.,"[16] an Irish Jesuit, who wrote books under the name Michael Serafian, articles in "The American Jewish Committee's intellectual monthly, *Commentary*,"[17] under the name F. E. Cartus, and confidential memos leaking inside information to the press under the name Pushkin. Pushkin was the "inside tipster"[18] for *Time* and the *New York Times*, as well as the author of much of Kaiser's book on Vatican II.

Martin, in other words, was Pushkin, who was "Michael Serafian in book length, F.E. Cartus for the magazines, and a translator in the Secretariat for Christian Unity, while maintaining a warm friendship with the AJC. At the time, Pushkin-Serafian-Cartus was living in the Biblical Institute, where he had been known well since his ordination in 1954."[19] Martin was a ladies' man "known to be working on a book at a young married couple's flat," a living arrangement that "finished ... half of the friendship."[20] Joseph Roddy pinpointed his identification of Martin as a "double agent," by telling his readers whom Martin worked for. In his job at Bea's Secretariat, Martin was "valuable to the AJC and is still thought of by many around Rome as a kind of genuine savior in the diaspora. Without him, the Jewish declaration might well have gone under early."[21]

So Martin was considered "a genuine savior" among New York Jews. He was quoted in the *Times*, discrediting Bishop Segni as an anti-Semite and also the pope, who had said Jews were responsible for the death of Christ because he "was speaking to ordinary and simple faithful people—not before a learned body."[22] Reading Martin's self-serving anonymous account of the council's proceedings in the *Times*, Morris Abram of the AJC professed to be reassured. If so, he was deceived too. The Jewish schema was, indeed, in trouble. Martin had cried "Wolf" so many times that no one recognized the truth of what he was now saying.

1964: Fiddler on the Roof

Germany and America became more Jewish after the world wars because they became more modern. Modernity, as Yuri Slezkine argued, was Jewish. Modernity was "about ... dismantling social estates for the benefit of individuals, nuclear families and book-reading tribes (nations). Modernization, in other words, is about everyone becoming Jewish."[23] Friedman says much the same thing. The Jews transformed American society after World War II, remaking it in their image. The older generation of Protestant novelists and poets, many of whom—e.g., T.S. Eliot and Ezra Pound—had serious reservations about modernity even though their writing was "modern" in form, were replaced by almost exclusively Jewish writers. Ernest Hemingway, F. Scott Fitzgerald, Ezra Pound, and T.S. Eliot, who came to prominence in the '20s, were replaced in the '50s by Saul Bellow, Aaron Copland, Leonard Bernstein, Philip Roth, J.D. Salinger, Norman Mailer, Arthur Miller, Herman Wouk, Bernard Malamud, and Alan Ginsberg. Leslie Fiedler called it "the great takeover by Jewish American writers."[24] Friedman says the Jews not only wrote books, they also

> taught Americans how to dance (Arthur Murray) how to behave (Dear Abby and Ann Landers) how to dress (Ralph Lauren), what to read (Irving Howe, Alfred Kazin and Lionel Trilling) and what to sing (Irving Berlin, Barry Manilow, Barbara Streisand).[25]

Lionel Trilling embodied the ambivalence of American Jews toward American culture. Trilling, through *The Liberal Imagination*, created Liberalism as a way of being Jewish in America. Trilling began his literary career writing for the

Menorah Journal in the '20s. Once his career took off, Trilling distanced himself from his "provincial and parochial"[26] Jewish roots. Cynthia Ozick recalled being made to feel shame for noting in one of Trilling's classes at Columbia that Marx, Freud, and Einstein were significantly Jewish in their thought. According to Norman Podhoretz, also Trilling's student at Columbia, Trilling was unable to defend the traditional culture "because on some level he himself secretly resented or despised it, or at least he resented and despised that muted form of it that he himself embodied in his own writing and persona."[27]

Hollywood was a Jewish creation. There were always Jewish actors, like John Garfield, né Garfinkel, but they invariably changed their names. Beginning in the '60s, stars like Barbra Streisand portrayed overtly Jewish characters like Fanny Brice. On the eve of breaking the Hollywood Production Code, Hollywood introduced the showpiece of Jewish triumphalism, *Fiddler on the Roof.* Tevye the Milkman of the Sholem Aleichem tales, was proudly Jewish but also open-minded and American, except on the issue of intermarriage: "Tevye stood for tradition, of course, but he also understood the value of progress, freedom of choice, individual rights, and the nuclear family."[28] Tevye brought about a curious change in American culture and Jewish identity. As Jews became more overtly Jewish, Judaism became more American, and America became more Jewish. *Fiddler on the Roof* gave a lot of attention to pogroms but made no mention of the fact that they were connected with the assassination of two Czars and the rise of the revolutionary Jew in Russia. There is no mention of Jews like Sverdlov murdering the Czar and his family in the aftermath of the revolution that never got mentioned either, because by then Tevye was living on the lower East Side of New York.

During the 1950s, Jews taught Americans to become "specialists in alienation."[29] In promoting alienation, Jews projected their image onto American culture and weakened the mores of the Christian majority. It was only years after their works had become American icons, that Arthur Miller and Joseph Heller admitted that Willy Loman and Yossarian were essentially Jewish characters. Jews had a difficult time dealing with American culture. They began by subverting it and then began to transform it in their image and finally imposed their own draconian speech codes on it in the age of political correctness. In each instance the relationship was instrumental and manipulative.

During the '50s, New York Intellectuals imposed their image of themselves—the lonely, alienated outsider—onto the culture. The Jews imposed their image on American culture not by making Americans Jewish by religion, but Jewish by way of alienation. The new Jewish elite was "judaizing"[30] America by turning it into a nation of alienated strangers. They imposed "their own condition—their loss of religious faith and a sense of estrangement—upon the society."[31]

If the modern age was Jewish, then it was only logical that Jews should become the experts on how to live in that age successfully. "Jews acquired a mystique after World War II" because their experience of dislocation and persecution seemed to confer upon them a special sagacity about the human condition. An older myth of Jewish "genius" gave way to the new concept of the Jew as the prototypical "marginal man" who achieved insight into the social order from standing outside it.[32]

Like the European Jew before him, the modern American was "someone who had to live in two worlds at the same time."[33] As a result of dislocations due to two wars, Americans were "cosmopolitans and strangers"[34] in their own country. Before long, many would feel it was not their country.

Freudianism became a "salvation religion,"[35] with a priesthood and sacred texts, shortly after Protestantism handed the policing of Jewish Hollywood to the Catholics in the 1930s. Ministers became therapists, and therapists became ministers, and America became what Philip Reiff called the therapeutic state. "Freudianism, which was predominantly Jewish, proclaimed the beleaguered loneliness of the newly 'emancipated' to be a universal human condition."[36]

Psychology also became a locus of the struggle between Catholics and Jews over who would control American culture, because it

> provided a perfect focal point for a culture clash between Jews and Catholics as they moved from the periphery toward the center of a society traditionally dominated by Protestants. For many Jews, psychology and Freud represented a path toward a more sophisticated, cosmopolitan America; for many Catholics, Freud signified a heretical departure from fundamental religious values.[37]

The rise of psychology as a substitute for religion was linked to the de-ethnicization at the heart of the psychological warfare campaign. In ethnic America, religion "dictated what people knew about human nature."[38] "Christian followed Christian and Jew followed Jew."[39] Once psychology replaced religion, ethnic compartmentalization was no longer valid, and the Jew, who was a "genius," became the guide to how everyone should live in the "modern" world.

The redefinition of psychology was a revolution in the truest sense of the word. What was up went down, and what was down went up. Before that revolution, reason sat on instinct like a rider on a horse. After reading in the *After School Library*: "It is the untrained horse that balks or that shies; but the thoroughbred horse stands still the moment his master speaks, and he turns to the right or left at the lightest touch of the bridle," the student of pre-Jewish American psychology was admonished, "Keep your hand firmly upon the helm of thought."[40] Jewish psychologists tended to see passages like this as Christian, even though they derived from Greek sources, such as Plato and Euripedes' *Hippolytus*. Jewish psychology was either covertly, as with Freud, or overtly, as with Wilhelm Reich, instinctual. As a result, the definition of mental illness changed from passion out of control to passion repressed. This unleashing of sexual passion from the bonds of reason corresponded with Jewish involvement in pornography and the constant chafing at prohibitions against nudity in Hollywood films. The Jewish takeover of psychology put instinct in the saddle, where it was used as cultural control, as explicated by Reich in *The Mass Psychology of Fascism*.

Under Jewish influence, American psychology became Talmudic as well. University of Wisconsin psychologist Joseph Jastrow, whose father "was a distinguished rabbi and scholar whose lexicon of the Talmud, completed in 1903, remains a standard tool for English speaking students" saw psychology as the modern equivalent to the rabbinic *responsa*, in which the rabbi answered questions "about the many rituals and actions governing the daily life of Jews."[41] Modern psychology would become Talmudic in other senses too. It was seen as a weapon against Christian culture. Willi Muensterberg, an early Jewish psychologist in America, found his psyche expressed this impulse in a dream in which "a young Jew rises to an awesome height in society"[42] and then "crushes buildings" including "a church steeple—the symbol of Christian dominance above which no synagogue roof was allowed to rise."[43]

Jastrow's attitude toward the overwhelmingly Christian student body he taught at the University of Wisconsin was similarly aggressive. Jastrow

> targeted Christianity ... as the prime example of the forcible imposition of thought on a community of people. In his course at Wisconsin on the "Psychology of Belief" and in his popular writings, he spoke of the "sad page of history" that records the Church's techniques of censorship and suppression of thought. He also used the biblical and rabbinic phraseology of "the remnant" of Israel when he referred to the dissident few who fight in all times and places for freedom of thought: "There will always be a saving remnant," he wrote, "who are willing to give up dogma."[44]

If Freudianism was Jewish, behaviorism was the refuge of divinity students who abandoned religion. The third way of Erich Fromm, Carl Rogers, and Abraham Maslow was less aggressively atheistic but still retained Jewish animosity toward the unthinking *goyim*, who needed to be liberated from repression. In *The Art of Loving*, Erich Fromm "married Mamonides to Freud in order to criticize the infantile conception of God to which, in his view, most people adhered."[45] Fromm

> wanted to reconnect secular Jewish idealists with the "revolutionary" principles of their ancestors. He believed that 'the universalism and humanism of the prophets blossomed in the figures of thousands of Jewish philosophers, socialists and internationalists, many of whom had no personal connection with Judaism.[46]

Abraham Maslow debated changing his name to something less identifiably Jewish, but decided not to because "Jewishness encouraged intellectual independence and even rebelliousness."[47] Like Carl Rogers, Maslow took Kurt Lewin's research into group dynamics and turned it into a weapon against unsuspecting *goyim*. In April 1962, Maslow lectured to nuns at Sacred Heart, a Catholic women's college in Massachusetts. Maslow noted in his diary that the talk had been very "successful,"[48] which he found troubling. "They shouldn't applaud me," he wrote, "they should attack. If they were fully aware of what I was doing, they would [attack]."[49]

Once the theories of Jewish psychologists like Freud, Reich, and Maslow gained respectability in academe, they were advanced by a hoarde of female Jewish advice columnists, who popularized and spread the tenets of Jewish psychology in the mass media, contributing to the decline in sexual morals and the rise of feminism: Joyce Brothers rose to fame in the '50s after winning The $64,000 Question as an expert on boxing. Brothers introduced "millions of homemakers to the new feminism of the 1960s"[50] by popularizing the ideas of Betty Friedan (née Goldstein), a Communist who transmuted class warfare into gender warfare in *The Feminine Mystique*. Heinze claims Brothers' *In Defense of Selfishness* was "a homemaker's version of Adam Smith's philosophy of economics,"[51] but it derived more directly from the Objectivism of another Jewish guide to modern life, Ayn Rand (nee Alissa Rosenbaum), a Russian Jew who created another largely Jewish sect known as Objectivism in the '50s through best-selling novels like *The Fountainhead* and *Atlas Shrugged*.

Brothers' advice was invariably Talmudic. She favored "contracts between spouses" and "psychological techniques of manipulation" to teach women *How to Get Whatever You Want out Of Life* (the title of her 1978 book).[52] Brothers turned to Judaism for solace after her husband's death, but that did not prevent her from appearing in a comedy skit on a TV show during the traditional Jewish mourning period. Brothers, in fact, agreed to appear on Pat Sajak's TV show the day after her husband's funeral.

Joyce Brothers was the first of a long line of female Jewish advisors who told American how to negotiate the shoals of an increasingly Jewish and Talmudic culture. By the 1970s, "If a woman were going to end up as a psychological adviser to Americans, the odds were very good that she would be Jewish."[53] The Jewish twins from St. Paul, Minnesota, Esther Pauline Lederer and Pauline Esther Phillips, became advice columnists Ann Landers and Abigail Van Buren. They invariably advised "seek counseling" whenever a troubled reader brought up a problem involving sexual morality. They and Joyce Brothers contributed to the decline in American morals by psychologizing behavior that had previously been considered under the purview of faith and morals. America's largely Jewish advice columnists had become experts in persuading *goyische* America to ignore what their consciences and their ministers were telling them and to engage in Talmudic rationalization, abetted by the psychologists, instead.

When advice and attitude formation shifted to AM talk radio, Jews moved there too. The most famous radio advice show host was Dr. Laura Schlessinger. Unlike Joyce Brothers and Ann Landers, Dr. Laura was an anomaly in the American Culture Wars of the late 20th century. Dr. Laura identified herself as an Orthodox Jew, but she invariably ended up taking Catholic positions on controversial issues like abortion and homosexuality. The split mirrored her family heritage. Born in Brooklyn to a Jewish father, her mother was Catholic. As a result, her positions frequently offended the Jews whose views she claimed to promote. According to Heinze, Schlessinger's sense of "mission" and accusatory style were not characteristic of Modern Orthodox Jews, with whom she identified until her sudden break with Judaism in August 2003. She spoke of homosexuality, in particular, with a strident tone that most modern Orthodox rabbis would have found objectionable. Her pronouncements against abortion also obscured the complexity of traditional Jewish thought ... . Because she tied her views so closely to Judaism, Schlessinger became an anomalous figure: the only Orthodox Jew ever to gain such an immense audience, yet one whose success in the "shock jock" style of 1990s radio distanced her from rabbinic standards of propriety.[54]

1965 Newport Folk Festival

The best proof of Plato's statement "No change can be made in styles of music without affecting the most important conventions of society" (*Republic*, 242c), was the 1965 Newport Folk Festival, the locus of the artistic "breakthrough" that ushered in the cultural revolution of the '60s. In typically subversive fashion, Dylan had named his album of revolutionary music (as opposed to the albums of revolutionary lyrics set to traditional folk music) "Bringing it All Back Home." It was supposed to be a return to his roots, and in a sense it was—not to his roots in Hibbing but rather his psychic roots as the quintessential revolutionary Jew, only at home in some form of subversion.

If the audience in 1965 was expecting a replay of the 1963 "We Shall Overcome" sing along, there were signs early on that they were going to be disappointed. Instead of Fannie Lou Hamer, fresh from a voter registration drive in Mississippi, the crowd was treated early on to a white guy by the name of Paul Butterfield, playing the blues of the post-War black migration to Chicago, which is to say, with loud amplified instruments.

Bob Dylan exploited the behind the scenes chaos to set up his own band on stage. By now he was a man who needed no introduction at Newport. As Peter Yarrow, the MC, scurried from the mike after performing that act of supererogation, Dylan unleashed a wave of sonic assault on the audience. Technically the song was known as "Maggie's Farm," but since Dylan had instructed his road manager to crank up the amps, no one could hear anything but wave upon wave of electronic distortion over a pounding Dionysian beat. Scandalized by what he heard, Pete Seeger rushed backstage and demanded that the power to their amplifiers be cut. When no one complied, Pete grabbed a fire ax from off the wall and threatened to cut the cable himself. What ensued was the classic revolutionary moment in which the subverters were subverted by their own revolutionary ideology. The confrontation boiled down to a dispute between the old guard and the new, in this instance, a dispute between the WASP Pete Seeger—the Old Left Commie with Puritan American roots, the man who turned folk music into a lifestyle that circumvented American materialism—and Albert Grossman, the "Jewish Businessman," who felt that Messianic politics and making money were two sides of the same coin. Alan Lomax, also backstage, sided with Seeger ideologically, but he also wanted him to put down the fireaxe, even if, some people feel, it was so that he could chop the cable himself. When George Wein, another festival director, suggested that they turn the power off and have a discussion, Grossman threatened in typical fashion, "You do that, and I'll sue you."[55] Finally, it was Theodore Bikel who got Seeger to put down the ax, and he did it by appealing to the "tradition"[56] of revolution. "This band these rebels" he stammered, "they are us. They are what we were twenty years ago. Remember?"[57] Peter Yarrow threatened to have Seeger arrested for assault, but in the end the musical din prevailed.

The musical modes had changed, and, as Plato predicted, political revolution followed. At the post-festival party in 1965, rather than the traditional hootenanny, festival attendees experienced the Negro Dionysian music of The Chambers Brothers. Dionysos is the god of music, intoxication, and sexual excess, and by the early hours of the next day, he was in charge. The revelers were drunk or stoned, sweatily pounding out Dionysian rhythms not on guitars, which seemed suddenly inappropriate, but on chairs, trash cans, and whatever else was available, and those rhythms, new to the folk music crowd, "had a wild effect on the group's already steamy passions."[58] The party, Spitz says, was "unusually loose and informal ... as if someone had given them a tremendous shove, turned their heads in another direction. A new world awaited them. As such, *the party was marked by the kind of wanton promiscuity that one experiences after a revolution*, a sense of 'anything goes.' ... There were no rules anymore.... The whole place was drunk on cheap booze and excitement."[59]

The 1965 Newport Folk Festival was a metaphor for what happened to the country over the next ten years. As in the Dionysian festivals described by Euripedes, after passions got out of control, Agave would dismember her child; and, as Plato indicated, the ruling class imposed subtle but inhumanly draconian political control on the revolutionary nation blinded by its passions. Maria Muldaur, Spitz says, "remembers dancing like it was the first time she'd been set free."[60] But being set free also meant destroying the community that had nurtured her, the folk music network, especially Greenwich Village, which had been "a wonderful place to come of age in ... full of music and foolishness and camaraderie."[61] That ended in the waning hours of the 1965 Festival. Everyone was now looking for a recording contract. Everyone was in it for himself. "Even the music had changed."[62] Once the music changed, morals followed, and once morals were subverted, the state was ripe for revolution, and once the revolution succeeded, tyranny would follow. "That night everything seemed up for grabs," Muldaur said later. "Life as we had known it, was out of control."[63]

Folk music was replaced by Rock 'n Roll, now fitted with revolutionary political lyrics as opposed to Negro complaints about V-8 Fords and untrustworthy women. Rock 'n Roll itself was Negro slang for sexual intercourse. "Rock 'n roll," according to Spitz, "was meant to shake foundations; it was musical terrorism, a *revolutionary*, attention-grabbing sound."[64] Everybody was determined to imitate

Bob Dylan's political amalgamation of revolutionary lyrics and Dionysian Negro music. Known as "folk rock," one of its first hits was the Byrds' cover of Dylan's "Mr. Tambourine Man," a song, appropriately enough, about intoxication. Dave Van Ronk called it "the hippie nightmare."[65] To show he was amenable to the corrupting influences of Albert Grossman, in 1965 Dave Van Ronk formed the Hudson Dusters, a band which went nowhere. The advent of folk rock meant the folk revival was officially over, so, as Van Ronk put it, "business got very bad."[66] In the early 1970s, "the rooms were closing down, record labels weren't signing acoustic acts any more."[67]

The demise of folk music also meant the final demise of the old left. Woody Guthrie died in October 1967 at 55. Pete Seeger outlived him by decades, but he became increasingly irrelevant. "Everywhere he looked," Seeger's biographer says,

> a new culture spread among young people, one he barely understood. Why should anyone want to take LSD? Why had Abbie Hoffman left civil rights for Revolution for the Hell of It? When people handed him flowers and beads at concerts, Pete didn't know what to say. Pete kept his distance from marijuana, long hair, and free sex. In the middle of one concert, the audience filed out one by one to smoke grass on a darkened balcony. Pete didn't even realize they had gone.[68]

Soon Seeger's politics became as irrelevant as his music. Seeger promoted peace by inviting Jews and Palestinians to a hootenanny at the Tel Aviv Hilton. He dedicated a verse of "Guantanamera" "to exiles of two thousand years and exiles of nineteen years,"[69] a gesture that went over like a lead balloon. Seeger, Dunaway says, "was out of his depth;" he broke off in the middle of the song "close to tears."[70] Three days later the Arab-Israeli Six-Day War began. The Six-Day War signaled the moment the Jews pulled out of the Left and devoted themselves to Zionist causes. It also marked the moment the Left began attacking Zionism as racism. It also signaled the demise of the Jewish folksinger. Ethnicity began to reassert itself in politics and music, but the revolution was still in progress.

Fall 1965: Poncins shows up at the Council

In October 1965, Poncins showed up at the Council with thousands of copies of his pamphlet *Le Problème Juif face au Concile*, which "contained a brief history of the role of Jules Isaac in the preparation of the conciliar schema on the Jewish question and a summary of the theses."[71] In an article in *Le Figaro* in October 1965, Rene Laurentin, later the foremost promoter of the phony Medjugorje apparitions, cited Poncins' tract as a "vigorously anti-Semitic document" which "had been liberally distributed to the [Council] Fathers."[72] The message of Laurentin's attack was obvious: as Poncins put it, "these 'anti-Semites,' who use a formidable weapon, the texts of Jewish authors themselves, must at all costs be silenced."[73] Poncins was indignant. Isaac could call the Evangelists liars, but "because I simply quote Jules Isaac, Joshua Jehouda and others, I am described as a despicable anti-Semite."[74]

Convinced the Council Fathers who passed the schema had not read their writings, Poincins had the novel idea of reprinting what Jews like Isaac, Jehouda, and Memmi wrote about the Catholic Faith. Poncins was equally certain

> when Jules Isaac and his associates went to Rome, they were careful not to mention these passages in their books; they spoke of Christian charity, of ecumenical unity, of common biblical filiations, of Judeo-Christian friendship, of the struggle against racism, of the martyrdom of the Jewish people, and their efforts met with success since 1651 bishops, cardinals, archbishops and Council Fathers voted to reform Catholic teaching according to the desires of Jules Isaac, the B'nai B'rith, and the World Jewish Congress.[75]

Missing from the discussion were passages like Memmi's diatribe against Catholicism: "Your religion is a blasphemy and a subversion in the eyes of the Jews. Your God is to us the Devil, that is to say, the symbol and essence of all evil on earth."[76]

Jules Isaac is only slightly less intemperate. After making unsupported claims—"No, Pilate did not wash his hands according to the Jewish custom.... No, Pilate did not protest his innocence.... No, the Jewish crowd did not cry out: 'His blood be upon us and upon our children.'"—Isaac has the temerity to call the Gospel of St. Matthew "obviously tendentious."[77] After claims based on nothing more than his *ipse dixit*, Isaac appends a "therefore" to his non-conclusion:

> Therefore the total responsibility of the Jewish people, of the Jewish nation and of Israel for condemning Jesus to death is a matter of legendary belief and not based on solid historical foundation.... To maintain the opposite viewpoint, one would have to be intractably and fanatically prejudiced, or have a blind belief in a tradition which, as we know, is not 'normal' and thus ought not to be laid down as a rule of thought for even the most docile sons of the Church—a tradition which, moreover, is infinitely noxious and murderous, and which, as I have said and shall repeat, leads to Auschwitz—Auschwitz and other places. Some six million Jews were liquidated solely because they were Jews and thus brought shame not only upon the German people but upon the whole of Christianity, because without centuries of Christian teaching, preaching and vituperation, Hitler's teaching, propaganda and vituperation would have been impossible."[78]

Forty years later, rabbis were repeating Isaac's charge almost verbatim at *Nostra Aetate* celebrations. In fall 2005, Israel's Chief Rabbi Yona Metzger wrote in *America*

> Not only ignorant peasants or monks but also eminent theologians and spiritual teachers had attacked the Jews as the "killers of Christ," as a people now abandoned by God, a race deserving not its envied wealth but revenge for plots and acts against innocent Christians.... Not only had the Jews of Rome been forced to live in a ghetto until the pope no longer governed that city ... but almost everywhere in Europe, Jews had been made to seem strange, sinister and repulsive. A long road of disgraceful preaching was one of the paths across the centuries which led to the Nazis' death camps and in the end, not Judaism but Christianity was discredited.[79]

Isaac dealt with the Church Fathers *in simili modo*. They were "all persecutors filled with anti-Jewish hatred, the inevitable forerunners of Streicher and others, morally responsible for Auschwitz and 'six million innocent Jewish victims.'"[79]

Poncins maintained in his tract that the Schema of November 1964 passed because the bishops were ignorant of Isaac's true feelings toward Christianity, but, more broadly, they were ignorant of the difference between the Torah and the Talmud. The former is the Word of God; the latter is its antithesis. The Talmud, Poncins pointed out, was a post-Christian confection designed to keep Jews from converting to Christianity. After the destruction of the Temple, "The Talmud ... replaced the Torah as the foundation of all wisdom and the guide in every detail of daily life."[80] The point of the Talmud was "to consummate the definite break from triumphant Christianity."[494] So "The imposition of the ideals of the Talmud on the new branch of Judaism has been the calamity of the Jewish people even to this day."[81]

The Council Fathers did not understand the Jews had a fundamentally different understanding of what was going on at the Council than they did. What the bishops saw as a gesture of reconciliation, the Jews saw as "a weapon designed to overthrow traditional Catholicism, which they consider the chief enemy."[82]

The schema was dangerous because "it put the Church in the position of the accused, guilty of the permanent, unjustifiable and unatonable crime of anti-Semitism for two thousand years."[83] Beyond that, it questioned "the good faith and truthfulness of the Evangelists, of St. John and St. Matthew in particular; it discredited the teaching of the Fathers of the Church and of the great doctrinarians of the papacy by depicting them in distasteful colors; in short, it threatened to demolish the very bastions of Catholic doctrine."[85]

Given the gravity of the charges Poncins laid at the feet of the Jews, it was not surprising that the pope withdrew the 1964 text. The 1964 text was Jewish, not Catholic. Poncins cites Malachi Martin's hapless Jesuit confidante, Gus Weigel, as claiming "the declaration condemning anti-Semitism which was accepted by Cardinal Bea in 1964, was suggested by Zachariah Schuster, President of the American Jewish Committee."[86]

Poncins demolished the idea the Jews are "the people of the Old Testament" by showing they want, not a Messiah, but "a terrestrial reign in which they will control the social, economic and political life of the nations.... Judaism seeks to impose itself as the sole standard and to reduce the world to Jewish values."[87] According to George Batault, the Jews

> are instinctively sympathetic to everything which tends to disintegrate and dissolve traditional societies, nations and countries....The Jews have a feeling and love for Humanity, taken as an aggregate of individuals as abstract and similar to each other as possible, released from "the routine" of tradition and liberated from the "chains" of the past, to be handed over, naked and uprooted, as human material for the undertakings of the great architect of the Future, who will at

last construct on principles of Reason and Justice the messianic City over which Israel will reign.[88]

The Council Fathers forgot the role of the Jews in the revolutionary upheavals after World War I—until Poncins jogged their memory by resurrecting the French literature on that topic. During the 1920s Jews and Catholics knew Bolshevism was a Jewish phenomenon. The Catholics deplored that fact; the Jews applauded it, but no one disputed it. Poncins brought this to the attention of the Council Fathers to contextualize their thinking.

Poncins cited the Jewish writer Bernard Lazare, who praised Karl Marx's "clear Talmudic mind which does not falter at the petty difficulties of fact."[89] Ignoring what Marx said about Jews in his tract on the Jewish Question, Lazare claimed Marx "inspired by that ancient Hebraic materialism which, rejecting as too distant and doubtful the hope of an Eden after death, never ceased to dream of Paradise realized on earth.... With Marx, socialism became a secular version of Jewish messianism. The idea was born in Palestine and has now taken root in Moscow and Peking."[90]

Poncins also cited Charles Sarolea, who claimed:

> That the Jews have played a leading part in the Bolshevist upheaval and are still playing a leading part in the Bolshevist Government is a proposition which no one will deny who has taken the trouble to study Russian affairs.... Their dictatorship fell not only upon Russia but upon every country in Central Europe when Bolshevism attempted to implant itself by a bloody reign of terror; under Bela Kuhn and Szamuelly at Budapest, Liebknecht and Rosa Luxembourg at Berlin, and Kurt Eisner and Max Lieven at Munich.... Unfortunately, not only have men belonging to the Jewish race played a very large part both in the beginning and in the development of the Bolshevist Revolution, but they have also been the chief participators in some of the worst crimes of that Revolution.[91]

Having established the connection between Jews and revolution in the Council Fathers' mind, Poncins went on to assert that ecumenism was the latest battlefront in the war against the Church. He cited passages from the writings of Joshua Jehouda, who along with Jules Isaac, B'nai B'rith, and the World Jewish Congress, has "been carrying out a carefully prepared and concerted campaign which resulted in the recent vote at the Council ... under the guise of ecumenical unity, religious reconciliation and other plausible pretexts."[92] In spite of public statements of Jewish lobbyists, the object of the Jewish schema was "the demolition of the bastion of traditional Catholicism, which is described by Joshua Jehouda as 'the decrepit fortress of Christian obscurantism.'"[93]

From the Jewish perspective, the Vatican Council was simply one more revolutionary moment of opportunity to "rectify Christianity,"[94] which included, according to Jehouda, "The Renaissance, the Reformation, [and] the Revolution of 1789."[95] Like Rabbi Louis Israel Newman, Jehouda supported all of history's revolutionary movements from the Reformation onward. The upheaval began with

Reuchlin, who "shook the Christian conscience by suggesting as early as 1494, that there was nothing higher than Hebraic wisdom."[96] In promoting the Cabala, "Reuchlin advocated returning to Jewish sources," which unleashed "the new spirit which was to revolutionize the whole of Europe" and to find expression in the revolutions of France and Russia.[97] The French Revolution, according to Jehouda, "continues through the influence of Russian Communism, to make a powerful contribution to the de-Christianisation of the Christian world."[98] For Jews like Jehouda, history is synonymous with revolution: "the profound meaning of history, which remains unaltered in every epoch, is that of a veiled or open struggle between the forces working for the advancement of humanity [i.e., the Jews] and those that cling to coagulated interests, obstinately determined to keep them in existence to the detriment of what is to come [i.e., the Catholic Church]."[99]

Poncins concluded the Jewish schema was a covert attack on the Church "under the banner of ecumenism."[100] By allowing Jews unprecedented access in the formulation of the schema, the Church had allowed them to carry their revolutionary "war ... into the very interior of the Church itself."[101]

In their attack, the Jewish lobbyists used the carrot and the stick. To induce concessions, they promised financial support. In *Le Monde* in November 1963, Label Katz, President of the International council of the B'nai B'rith, was quoted as saying "if this declaration is accepted by the Council, Jewish communities will explore ways and means of cooperating with the authorities of the (Catholic) Church to ensure the realization of its purpose and projects."[102] But the Jews also slipped into martial imagery. One Jewish writer referred to Jules Isaac's *Jesus et Israel* as "the most specific weapon of war against a particularly harmful Christian doctrine."[103]

Eventually the Council Fathers got the message, and Poncins' pamphlet turned the tide against the November 64 schema. "There is no doubt," Poncins wrote later, "that the disclosure of these deadly texts was exceedingly embarrassing to the success of the Jewish progressive maneuver, and if they could have been published earlier they would have been even more effective."[104]

October, 1965: Final Vote on the Jewish Schema

A flurry of lobbying preceded the final vote on the Jewish schema. According to the post-mortem which got published in *Look* in January 1966, Malachi Martin had always been "around Rome when the declaration needed help."[105] But "at Vatican II's fourth and last session there was no help in sight."[106] Everywhere there were speeches on the rise and fall of the Jewish declaration, many preparing for a final letdown. Lichten's executive vice-president, Rabbi Jay Kaufman, told of his puzzlement "as the fate of the section on Jews ... shuttled between momentary declaration and certain confutation, like a sparrow caught in a clerical badminton game."[107] The Jewish hard-liners wanted total victory or no declaration, but Msgr. George Higgins persuaded them half a loaf was better than none. Lichten and

Schuster, who had access to the modifications the bishops proposed, knew the tide had turned against them. So did Msgr. Higgins. Lichten contemplated sending telegrams to 25 sympathetic, mostly American, bishops, but Higgins advised against it.

"Look, Joe," Higgins said to Lichten, "I understand your disappointment. I'm disappointed too."[108] When Higgins had Schuster and Lichten together in his room, he expanded on what he had told Lichten alone. "If you two give New York the impression you can get a better text, you are crazy," he said. "It's just insane to think by some pressures here or newspaper articles back in New York, you can work a miracle in the Council. You are not going to work it, and they will think you fell down on the job."[109] Lichten found Higgins persuasive, even though "I had to break my head and heart to think what should be done. I went through a crisis, but I was convinced by Higgins."[110]

Rene Laurentin made a last minute appeal by hinting darkly that the Church would be responsible if another Holocaust were to reoccur—but to no avail. The schema on the Jews was incorporated into a "Declaration on the Relation of the Church to Non-Christian Religions," known as *Nostra Aetate*, promulgated by the Council on October 28, 1965. Pope Paul VI then flew to New York to give his "*jamais plus la guerre*" speech. In the wake of his departure, the Jews tried to put as good a face on the document as possible.

On the whole, the conservatives were jubilant, and the Jews were disappointed, but the results in light of the actual document were mixed. Jews were disappointed that the charge of deicide was not rebuked. But conservatives were disappointed the text did not implicate all Jews in deicide. In one of the cleverest lines in the document, the Council Fathers wrote, "Even though the Jewish authorities and those who followed their lead pressed for the death of Christ (cf. John 19:6), neither all Jews indiscriminately at that time, nor Jews today, can be charged with the crimes committed during his passion."[111] According to the principles of logic, that statement could be taken to assert that some Jews were responsible for Christ's death. If we exclude from that group the Blessed Mother, the Beloved Disciple, and all of the other Jews who accepted Christ as the Messiah, we come up with a statement that is largely faithful to the gospels texts.

Even though the document finally came out in favor of the truth of gospels, the Church was left divided in its wake. The Jewish schema, according to Bishop Carli of Segni, subjected the Church to "an indignant Press campaign"[112] of unprecedented magnitude. It provoked "political and diplomatic complications and, unfortunately, in the East it has provided an excuse for some to abandon Catholicism in favor of Orthodoxy."[113] More importantly, the Church was now under suspicion. The court of public opinion had decided that there must have been merit to the charges the Jews had leveled. Both Catholic sides in the battle over the Jewish schema ended up losing: "The Fathers who support it are slandered with having sold themselves to international Jewry, whereas those who, for various reasons, consider the declaration inopportune or a least want to see it modified, are labeled anti-Zionists and practically held co-responsible for the Nazi camps."[114]

The document was testimony to the Jewish lobbyists' skill in getting their enemies to quarrel with each other. Jewish groups profited from the division. They also profited by shifting discussion from Jews' participation in revolutionary movements like Bolshevism and Freudianism. While *Nostra Aetate* retained the charge of deicide and specified who was and was not responsible, the acquittal of contemporary Jews created problems by questioning the continuity and identity of the Jewish people. The disjunction between the Jews of Christ's time and the Jews of their own emphasized the double standard the Jews espoused on collective responsibility. Jews could hold the German people accountable for Hitler's crimes, forcing generations of German taxpayers to pay billions in reparation to Jewish organizations and the state of Israel. But Jews vehemently denied collective responsibility for the death of Christ. The Council's schema tried to have it both ways, repudiating the claim the Romans alone were responsible for Christ's death but limiting Jewish guilt to Jewish leaders and their followers. As Poncins points out, in the case of Germany in the 20th century, "The whole people is considered responsible and subsequently punished for faults officials committed by its leaders, even when [those faults] are unknown to a great part of the people."[115] On the other hand, the Gospel accounts make clear that many Jewish people in Jerusalem were aware of what their leaders were doing and supported them in their efforts.

All of the Jews who had lobbied for their version of the Jewish schema were disappointed by *Nostra Aetate*, but Rabbi Heschel responded most vehemently, calling the failure to condemn the charge of Jewish deicide "an act of paying homage to Satan,"[116] without considering that his intemperate remarks to Paul VI may have contributed to that outcome.

By the end of the council, the feeling of good will toward the Jews that marked Pope John XXIII's meeting with Jules Isaac had evaporated, replaced by a feeling of resentment. The bishops "felt Jewish pressure in Rome and resented it."[117] It wasn't the first time in history that the Jews had overplayed their hand. In fact, pressing an issue beyond what prudence dictates had come to be known as the Jewish virtue of *chutzpah*. At the council's beginning, anyone who asserted Cardinal Bea "wants to turn the Church over to the Jews"[118] would have been dismissed as a crank. By its end, that charge was taken seriously, even in the philo-Semitic account of the Council which appeared in *Look*. Nahum Goldman of the WJC had warned Jews early "not to raise the issue with too much intensity."[532] After it was apparent that Jewish lobbying had backfired, Fritz Becker of the WJC met with Cardinal Bea and both of them discussed, with the now useless benefit of hindsight, "the advantages of not talking."[119]

Despite Poncins' generally sanguine interpretation of the final document, it would have deleterious effects. As Father Brian Harrison pointed out, the November 1964 document, flawed as it was, called for the conversion of the Jews: "It is important to recall that the integration of the Jewish people into the Church is part of Christian hope. For, according to the Apostle's teaching (cf. Rom. 11: 25), the Church awaits with unshakable faith and deep longing the entry of this people into the fullness of the People of God, which has been restored by Christ."[120] In this verse, the Holy Spirit, through Saint Paul, speaks of the "blindness" of the unbelieving Jews as temporary, and prophesies in the next verse the salvation of Israel as a nation, after the "fullness of the Gentiles" has come into the Church. The final version omitted that passage because, Bea explained, "Very many Fathers have requested that in talking about this 'hope', since it has to do with a mystery, we should avoid every appearance of proselytism. Others have asked that the same Christian hope, applying to all peoples, should also be expressed somehow. In the present version of this paragraph we have sought to satisfy all these requests."[121] By removing reference to conversion of the Jews (and by referring to conversion pejoratively as "proselytism"), Cardinal Bea

> 'elevate[d]' the future conversion of the Jews to the ethereal status of a "mystery," thereby insinuating that it will somehow 'just happen' spontaneously one day without the necessity of any human missionary activity on the part of Catholics. Bea himself, of course, was at that time the Church's main representative in relations with Judaism. And it seems more than likely, even though he didn't say so on the Council floor, that in proposing this amendment he had "sought to satisfy" his Jewish dialogue-partners as well as those "very many" (but unnamed) Catholic bishops who, he said, had requested the amendment.[122]

After forty years, that omission translated into a repudiation of the Gospel by prelates like Cardinal Keeler and Walter Cardinal Kasper, who told an audience at Boston College not only that Jews do not have to accept Christ to be saved, but that in taking this stance, they are "in line with God's plan." "This does not mean that Jews in order to be saved have to become Christians," Cardinal Kasper told the Center for Christian Jewish Learning in November 2002, "if they follow their own conscience and believe in God's promises as they understand them in their religious tradition, they are in line with God's plan, which *for us* comes to its historical completion in Jesus Christ."[123]

As anyone who understands Jewish hermeneutics could have predicted, the Torah of *Nostra Aetate* was irrelevant to the Talmudic interpretations which followed its promulgation. Dr. William Wexler of the World Conference of Jewish Organizations, one of the most prescient commentators on the Jewish schema, said, "The true significance of the Ecumenical Council's statement will be determined by the practical effects it has on those to whom it is addressed."[124] In terms of its practical effects, *Nostra Aetate* became a weapon against the Church, something which Poncins had claimed was its purpose from its inception. The Catholic Church lost control of the document because she lost control of its interpretation, which was forged in the media which the Jewish interest groups controlled. But there were passages that aided the hijacking of its meaning. The most glaring was, "the Church ... deplores all hatreds, persecutions, displays of anti-Semitism leveled at any time or from any source against the Jews."[125] Zachariah Schuster deplored use of the word "deplores," thinking it too weak, but from a semantic viewpoint, the significant word was "anti-Semitism." The Church had condemned anti-Semitism without defining what it meant by that term, an omission of truly catastrophic proportions because, as Poncins pointed out at the time,

> In Jewish eyes, every measure of defense and protection against the penetration of Jewish ideas and conceptions, against anti-Christian Jewish heresies, against Jewish control of the national economy, and in general every measure of defense of national Christian traditions is a manifestation of anti-Semitism. Furthermore, many Jews consider that the very fact of the recognition of the existence of a Jewish question constitutes a declaration of anti-Semitism.[126]

Poncins reminded Catholics

> Jules Isaac accuses all the Fathers of the Church of anti-Semitism ... He accuses them of having unleashed the savagery of the beast and of being the real people responsible for German anti-Semitism and the gas chambers at Auschwitz. He finds them even worse than Hitler and Streicher and others for their system resulted in the Jews being tortured slowly and being left to live and suffer interminably.... Does the Church admit Jules Issac's thesis and plead guilty?[127]

The answer came 30 years later when Pope John Paul II issued an apology to the Jews. Benedict XVI later explained the Church was not apologizing for the Holocaust because Nazism was a "neopagan ideology" for which the Church took no responsibility. But, as the behavior of Rabbi Paul Spiegel at the synagogue in Cologne during Benedict XVI's visit there in August 2005 indicated, Jews weren't listening. If the Catholic Church was unabatedly wicked, then the only reparation would be self-annihilation. Again, Bishop Carli pointed out the logic and the self-contradictions of the Jewish accusation against the Church. If what Isaac said was true, then the Catholic Church must be "the cruelest and vastest association of evil-doers that has ever existed on the face of the earth."[128] Then comes the contradiction bound up with the double standard on collective responsibility: "The Jews today no longer want to be considered responsible for everything which was done to Jesus Christ by their ancestors, to whom even now they grant the benefit of good faith; but they demand that the Catholic Church of today should feel responsible and guilty for every thing which, according to them, the Jews have suffered for the past 2000 years."[129]

Poncins and the conspiracy theorists were proven right when, on January 25, 1966, *Look* magazine published an article explaining "How the Jews changed Catholic Teaching." *Look* not only made use of the Poncins material on Isaac, it substantiated his central claim that Jewish lobbying behind the scenes was distorting Catholic teaching.

For the next 40 years, *Nostra Aetate* was used as "a weapon designed to overthrow traditional Catholicism." Within a year of its passage, *Nostra Aetate* would be used as a weapon against the Oberammergau Passion Play.

November 1966: AJC threatens a boycott of the Oberammergau Passion Play

In November 1966, Phil Baum, director of the American Jewish Congress' Commission on International Affairs, demanded the Oberammergau Passion Play purge its script of anti-Semitism or face a boycott. With a supporting cast including Arthur Miller, Lionel Trilling, Stanley Kunitz, Leonard Bernstein, Leslie Fiedler, Theodore Bikel, Irving Howe, Alfred Kazin, and German writers George Steiner, Guenter Grass, Heinrich Boell and Paul Celan, Holocaust industrialist Elie Wiesel called a news conference in New York City to announce the boycott. Wiesel said "the artist cannot be silent when the arts are used to exalt hatred. If the people of Oberammergau feel that they cannot faithfully represent their vision except though an explicitly anti-Semitic text, then others have no choice but to denounce that vision and urge that all who share our view join with us in condemning the performance."[130]

James Shapiro makes clear no group of literary and artistic luminaries would have gotten anywhere if the Catholic Church had not provided an opening in *Nostra Aetate*, not in what it said but in what the philo-Semitic media represented it as saying. The thinly-veiled aggression behind Jewish enthusiasm for conciliar documents is apparent in Shapiro's claim "it was only after Oberammergau was caught between the anvil of Vatican II and the hammering criticism of Jewish groups that serious changes were grudgingly made."[131] The Bavarians were being hammered because of *Nostra Aetate*. Without it, they could have deflected the blows. With it, the Jews played the bishop against his flock to eviscerate anything the Jews found repugnant, leading one observer to conclude "*Nostra Aetate* was the cornerstone of the abusive relationship that has hamstrung the Catholics for the last 40 years."[132] The villagers in Oberammergau blamed the Jews for the assault on their passion play. "But the truth" Shapiro says, "is that without a dramatic turn in the teachings of the Catholic Church, Jewish protesters would not have had much success in changing the play, boycotts notwithstanding."[133]

Because of *Nostra Aetate*, the Oberammergau Passion play was portrayed "as disturbingly out of step with official [Catholic] dogma."[134] The Jews would have gotten nowhere "without the liberalization of official Catholic policy following Vatican II and the intense pressure subsequently brought to bear on this conservative village."[135] The Jews considered *Nostra Aetate* as their most important weapon in their arsenal of cultural warfare. "It was," says Shapiro,

> a rude awakening for Oberammergau. The ensuing boycott of the 1970 production was the first time in this century when there were blocks of empty seats in the Passion playhouse. Until 1970, the Oberammergau play had been given a *missio canonica*, an official Church blessing signaling that Church doctrine was being taught. In that year, the first production following Vatican II and its

revolutionary "Declaration of the Relationship of the Church to Non-Christian Religions," this blessing was withheld ... [because the play] was now, according to the archbishop of Munich's pronouncement a play that "contained anti-Semitic elements and needed revision." The play hadn't changed, but the Church's message had. [136]

Shapiro is right in saying that the play hadn't changed. He is wrong in saying that the Church's teachings had changed. *Nostra Aetate*, however, did change the tactics Jews used to undermine those teachings. The Jews coopted Catholic scholars into accepting their interpretation. Shapiro claims the ADL and the AJC "quickly enlisted" Catholic theologians "in their struggle to change the play."[137] The AJC and the ADL, actively involved in interfaith dialogue, stepped up pressure on their Church contacts. "From the perspective of these Jewish organizations," Shapiro says, "Oberammergau was an important test of the commitment of the Church: if it couldn't change what was taking place on stage at Oberammergau, it could at least condemn it."[138] Cardinal Doepfner of Munich quickly asked the mayor of Oberammergau to submit the script for review. The Jews had succeeded, in the initial stage at least, in dividing the shepherd from his flock.

That this was their intention becomes clear when Shapiro discusses the play's use of typology, the fact that events in the Old Testament prefigured events in the New. All typology, he says, is triumphalist and repugnant to Jews. As a rabbi "who rejected typology categorically" put it, "all configurations in the Hebrew Bible are the mental property of Judaism" and therefore "off limits to Christians."[139] The Jews, according to Shapiro, could exploit "the sensitive issue of collective Jewish guilt ... in a post-Holocaust world," but "there is little wiggle room when it come to typology, nor can there be, insofar as Christianity is built upon its foundations."[140] "Oberammergau and the Vatican took one and the same position" on typology "leaving Jewish critics with little leverage."[141]

Leverage is precisely what the Jews got with *Nostra Aetate*—not so much because of what the document said but because the Church could never make its interpretation of its own document prevail over the interpretation which the Jews wanted to impose on it. With the help of Catholic scholars they were able to use their interpretation to drive a wedge between the hierarchy and the peasants. One of the scholars most willing to help in this regard was Leonard Swidler of Villanova University. Swidler had a long history of saying whatever the ADL wanted to say whenever it would have been considered impolitic for the ADL to say it themselves. In the early '80s, Swidler wrote that "Jesus was himself not a Christian. He was a Jew."[142] Swidler left the term Jew deliberately ambiguous as a way of undermining the Church's reading of its own historical roots. This meant that the Gospels could no longer be considered historically accurate. They were, instead, part of the "faith facts" school, which means that they "are records of the way specific communities remembered Jesus the risen Christ, rather than careful accountings of historical accuracy."[143] Swidler then collaborated with Gerard Sloyan, another Catholic, in exploiting "the gap" which "existed between the new historical research and the traditional representation of the characters of the Passion story"[148] as a way of subverting the 1984 Oberammergau production. By supporting the "new historical research" of "Catholic scholars"[149] like Swidler and Sloyan, the Jews were forcing the Bavarians into a bind. Since, according to Shapiro, "the villagers had long insisted that what they were staging was historically true,"[150] they could either capitulate to scholars like Swidler and Sloyan and eviscerate the Gospel or they could accept the Gospel in its entirety but admit that it had no historical foundation.

As a result of their inability to see through the Jewish lobby's strategy of cultural warfare, the Bavarians began to give ground and make concessions. "One by one," Shapiro tells us, "the details of their play were shown to be ahistorical."[151] Since the Jews wanted to eviscerate the play as a prelude to eviscerating the gospels, no amount of concessions would satisfy them. "Even as changes were adopted in 1970, 1980, and 1984," Shapiro writes, "more and more changes were suggested."[152] The more the Jews gained concessions, the less interested they were in historical accuracy. During the seemingly never ending negotiations someone suggested, "Some of the Jews ought to wear prayer shawls and cover their heads with kippot," *even if Jews in the first-century didn't!*" The purpose of the revisions, according to Shapiro, "was not only to make the play less offensive, *but also to change the story line.*"[153] That meant downplaying the "opposition between Jews and Christians" and rewriting it as "an intra-Jewish squabble that turns deadly only when the occupying Roman forces get involved."[154] The Jews promoted this reading because "arguing for Jesus' Jewishness also has the effect of delegitimizing Christianity itself."[155]

1967: Six-Day War and Ocean Hill-Brownsville

In 1960 Norman Podhoretz became editor of *Commentary*. Podhoretz was the son of a Brooklyn milkman and spoke Yiddish as his first language. In spite of those potential handicaps, he moved through the New York educational system, ending up as a student of Lionel Trilling at Columbia University, which he entered as a precocious 16 year old. As such, Podhoretz came by his liberalism naturally. But it had never been a particularly comfortable fit. Writing for *Commentary* in the '50s, Podhoretz had harsh things to say about the Beatniks and the novels of Jack Kerouac. He also became the Jewish white racist after the publication of his memoirs about getting into fights with black youths in Brooklyn in "My Race Problem—and Ours."

Shortly after assuming the helm of *Commentary*, Podhoretz noticed how prescient he had been about the race problem. The Jewish-Negro collaboration had begun when the Spingarn brothers created the NAACP. That same collaboration, which created the civil rights movement of the '60s, soon ran into inter-ethnic difficulties. Two-thirds of the white Freedom Riders fighting segregation in Mississippi in 1961 were Jews. Up to one-half of the volunteers during the Mississippi summer of 1964 were Jews, as were two of the three men who died there on that summer's voter registration march. The Waveland conference that year marked the beginning of feminism when Stokely Carmichael announced women's position in the movement was "prone."[156] Sexual liberation created ethnic tensions, which led to pressures for racial purity in Negro movements, which offended the Jews who had hoped the oppressed Negro would lead the revolution in America. Instead, ethnicity subverted the class conflict, leaving the Jewish supporters of the Negro civil rights movement dumbfounded. Imbued with Freudian and Reichian notions of the Negro as the embodiment of id-like passions that could bring the oppressive racist regime tumbling down, Jewish revolutionaries unleashed passions that soon led to disillusionment and, in the case of Allard Lowenstein, death.

In 1967, as part of its desire to wrest school boards from benighted local control, the Ford Foundation, under the leadership of WASP scion and social engineer McGeorge Bundy, funded the racial takeover of the Ocean Hill-Brownsville school district in metropolitan New York. The newly-empowered Negroes expressed their newly discovered ethnic solidarity by firing 19 tenured teachers, most of whom were Jewish. This enraged Albert Shanker, the Jewish head of the teachers union, who called a strike, bringing New York's multi-billion dollar budget school system to a grinding halt. When the strike ended, the Jewish liberalism Norman Podhoretz imbibed at the feet of Lionel Trilling was in ruins, and the phoenix of neoconservativism was extending its wings, ready to rise from the ashes.

The Ocean Hill-Brownsville debacle "signaled the collapse of the liberal coalition in which [Jews and blacks] had been joined together since the early days of the New Deal."[157] It inaugurated a change in Jewish political alignment as significant as the switch from communism to liberalism in the late '40s. It marked the beginning of neoconservatism, which, according to Friedman, "was a reaction to the liberal meltdown and the loss of confidence of many Americans. A group of primarily liberal Jewish intellectuals now came forward to challenge the despairing spirit of the times, the counterculture, and most especially what they believed to be aggressive Soviet designs in the world."[158]

Neoconservatism also marked a further stage in the Jewish takeover of the American political landscape. Jews had gone from being communists and socialists to liberals, and in doing so had increased both their market share and their respectability. With the rise of neoconservatism, Jews could now dominate both ends of the political spectrum in America. "Ironically," writes Friedman, "the neocons share one characteristic of the New Left: Jewish leadership. Leftists Abbie Hoffman, Jerry Rubin and Sidney Blumenthal stood on one side; Kristol, Podhoretz and Glazer on the other. The leading publications on both sides of the divide were edited by Jews as well: *Commentary* (Norman Podhoretz), *The Public Interest* (Irving Kristol), and the *New York Review of Books* (Robert Silvers, Barbara Epstein, and Jason Epstein). In some respects the coming struggle between liberals and conservatives was a struggle *within the Jewish community*."[159]

The situation is better interpreted as bespeaking an increasing Jewish dominance in American culture. The liberal/conservative battle between internationalist Protestants from the East Coast and isolationist Protestants from the mid-West in the '30s evolved by the '60s into a struggle between two groups of Jews: the party of peace, corresponding to the party around Rabbi Hillel, and the party of revolution, around Rabbi Shammai. Together the schools of Hillel and Shammai created a dialectic in which assimilation led to revolution and revolution led to assimilation. The neocons were the party of Hillel; the leftists the party of Shammai, a split that went back to the time Simon bar Kokhba. The conflict between Jerry Rubin on the one hand and Norman Podhoretz on the other corresponded to the split at the time of the destruction of the Temple between the Jews who wanted revolution and those willing to bake bread on the Sabbath or do anything else the Roman conquerors wanted.

The Ocean Hill-Brownsville debacle occurred at the time of the Six-Day War of 1967, "the most important episode in the history of Soviet (and American) Zionism."[160] That war propelled American Jews from liberalism and toward Zionism just as the Doctor's Plot and the Rosenberg trial had propelled them from Communism toward Liberalism. That war reinforced the ethnocentrism of Jewish liberals at a time when their commitment to increasingly surly and ethnocentric Negroes was diminishing. "If one thing ties Neoconservatives, Likudniks, and post-Cold War hawks together," Ian Burman concludes, "it is the conviction that liberalism is strictly for sissies."[161] In 1967 Norman Podhoretz stopped being a liberal sissy.

Once the Jews recognized that the liberal/conservative conflict was an intra-Jewish debate, they stopped being subversives and instead of working to overthrow the old regime of Protestant culture, they began to demand unconditional allegiance to the new American regime, which was now Jewish and cosmopolitan. *Commentary* was one of the first magazines to recognize the de facto Jewish takeover of American culture. Under these circumstances, it no longer made sense to be adversarial. The Jews were now the ruling elite. So now patriotism was the appropriate emotion.

By the mid-'70s, it was clear that the Jews were the new establishment. In 1982, *Forbes* reported 40 percent of the wealthiest 40 people in America were Jews. Jews made up less than 3 percent of the American population, and yet 15 of the 20 most influential intellectuals were Jews. Jews dominated the "media elite" constituting "more than one-third of the most 'influential' critics of film, literature, radio and television" as well as "almost half of the Hollywood producers of prime-time television shows and about two-thirds of the directors, writers, and producers of the 50 top grossing movies between 1965 and 1982."[162] When *Vanity Fair* did an article on "the new establishment" in October 1994, eleven of the 23 media moguls they profiled were Jews.

Chapter Twenty-Eight

Jews and Abortion

n 1967, Jewish gynecologist Bernard Nathanson was invited to a dinner party at which the ostensible topic was James Joyce. During that dinner party, Nathanson met another revolutionary Jew by the name of Lawrence Lader. Lader had been a protégé and, some hinted, lover of Margaret Sanger, the recently deceased diva of the American eugenics movement. Lader talked about Joyce, but Nathanson was soon fascinated to learn Lader had just written a book on abortion, a topic even more fascinating to Nathanson than novels by Irish apostates.

Nathanson defines Lader politically rather than ethnically. Lader became involved in radical politics in New York when he went to work for Representative Vito Marcantonio, a man who was rumored to have ties with the communist party, which was largely made up of New York Jews. Lader divorced his wife and became a freelance writer (a vocation financed by the money he inherited from his father) and became an agitator for the sexual politics of Margaret Sanger shortly after his return from World War II. From the moment he met Lader, Nathanson saw him as "brewing up a revolution" and as a result he felt "a growing sense of excitement."[1]

Nathanson felt that he came by his own revolutionary fervor naturally—he hints at some "Mendelian mechanism"[2]—because he was a Jew. Revolution, according to Nathanson, was another word for "*chutzpah*": "I come by my rebelliousness honestly. As a physician, I doubt that this is a quality passed on by any recognized Mendelian mechanism. But my father had it in abundance, except that in his generation and in the community in which he was brought up they called it *chutzpah*."[3]

Because Nathanson feels "any author on abortion must submit to religious dissection,"[4] he tells of his schooling in New York City. He went to a "fine private school with virtually 100 percent Jewish students"[5] and he attended Hebrew School, where he developed an aversion to the Talmud.

Religious instruction in that era meant endless slogging through turgid passages of Hebrew Scripture, mindless memorization of Hebrew prayers for numerous occasions and sanctimonious lectures about the chosenness of the Jewish race. Preoccupation with Zionism and fundraising left little energy for instruction in Hebrew or any demeaning excursions into the arcane regions of faith.[6]

Nathanson's experience in Hebrew School confirmed him in his aversion to the Talmud as a compendium of meaningless opinions which the rabbis enforced on Jews to maintain their control over them. In this he was not unlike the revolutionary Jews in Russia during its Maskilic period from 1860-1880, when the German Enlightenment destroyed the Jews' allegiance to the Talmud and created the vacuum which was filled by Jewish conversion to messianic revolutionary politics.

Once religion had been discredited in Nathanson's eyes, he had no guide in life other than his own passions. While in medical school, Nathanson had an affair, which led to a pregnancy, which he paid to have aborted. The mother of his child informed Nathanson afterward that "she had haggled down his price to $350 before the procedure." She handed him "the remaining $150"[7] and disappeared from his life. The experience of procuring the abortion of his own child coarsened Nathanson, causing him to become cynical about what other people considered sacred—"Marriage seemed ludicrous now,"[8]—propelling him further along the road to revolutionary politics.

Nathanson arrived at the revolution *via* sexuality, but also *via* the gynecological profession, which he felt predestined to adopt because of the influence of his gynecologist father. Gynecology plus revolutionary fervor in New York in the '60s meant abortion. After having murdered his own child, Nathanson was more disposed to act on his own "natural" Jewish inclination to revolution. He was also more likely to act on the promptings of other Jewish revolutionaries. Nathanson became a crusader for abortion at the time Wilhelm Reich's face and ideas made the cover of the *New York Times* magazine. Before long any ob/gyn who refused to admit involement in abortion was part of a "loathsome little charade."[9] Anger begat a desire to change the laws to conform to his behavior:

> I suppose that in fury at my own impotence to aid my patients and particularly in anger at the egregious inequity in the availability of abortions, the germination of an idea began: the need to change the laws. There seemed no time for the luxury of contemplating the theoretical morality of abortion or the soundness of freedom of choice. Something simply had to be done.[10]

Because Nathanson considered abortion a revolutionary act and because he considered himself a revolutionary because of the fact that he was Jewish, he became, in his own words, "an enlistee in the Revolution."[11] In this, Nathanson was influenced by the Jew from Hibbing, Minnesota, Bob Dylan, who had procured an abortion a few years earlier. He even makes use of lyrics from a Bob Dylan song at one point—"the times they were a changin"—in describing 1967 as the revolutionary *annus mirabilis* in which he joined with Lader to work for the "total abolition of abortion restrictions."[12]

> I was as enthusiastic and as cooperative a confederate as one could wish for in a revolutionary movement as profound as this one. Larry and I and others were to devote hundreds of hours of our free time to the cause in the coming years. I was almost yearning to be radicalized in a cause. This was 1967. The country was being racked by the Vietnam convulsion and challenges to authority seemed the order of the day, particularly in the intellectual breeding-grounds of the Northeast. Though I was forty, I believe that I secretly longed to be a part of the youth movement that was sweeping the country, demanding justice, pledging change, exalting "love." So my indignation, my rebellious nature, and an undeniable urge to "join the kids," combined to move me into the public arena.[13]

The abortion movement was part of the sexual revolution. The abortion revolution was, nonetheless, unique. It coincided with the rise to cultural prominence of American Jewry in the wake of their breaking of the Hollywood production code and the Arab-Israeli Six-Day War, when it became the opinion of the WASP state department elite that Israel was a strategic asset in America's quest to secure oil in the Mid-East. The abortion movement took on the same configuration as the revolution in Europe when Philip II contested Elizabeth over religious hegemony during the counter-reformation. Like Elizabeth's campaign to drive the Spaniards from Holland, the campaign to overturn abortion laws in New York State was largely an alliance of Protestants and Jews at war with the Catholics.

The list of groups attending a June 1970 meeting of the National Association for the Repeal of Abortion Laws (later, the National Abortion Rights Actions League) bears this out. NARAL always worked toward "enlisting the Protestant and Jewish clergy"[14] to provide a moral counterforce to Catholics.[15]

Karl Marx claimed the revolution would be run by the vanguard of the Proletariat, which he associated with the Communist Party. But former communists like David Horowitz felt Marx's real "vanguard"[16] was the Jews, who had been involved in every revolutionary movement since the fall of the Temple. Although Protestants were involved, Jews were the vanguard in the abortion movement as they were the vanguard of Bolshevism in Russia and of pornography in the United States. The movement to overturn abortion laws in New York was an essentially Jewish movement that saw itself as a revolutionary force against the darkness of Christianity in general and the Catholic Church in particular. The movement was certainly not exclusively Jewish, but it could not have survived or succeeded without Jewish leadership. The abortion rights movement was a quintessentially Jewish revolutionary movement that mobilized the coalition of Jews and Judaizing Protestants that America inherited from the English anti-Catholic wars of the 16th century.

The ethnic configuration of the abortion movement wasn't coincidental. The ethnically ambiguous Lader was to Lenin what Nathanson was to Trotsky. Together they carried out a crusade against Catholics. Shortly after meeting Nathanson, Lader explained his strategy of legalizing abortion by attacking Catholics. The proabortion forces had to "bring the Catholic hierarchy out where we can fight them. That's the real enemy. The biggest single obstacle to peace and decency throughout all of history."[17] Nathanson, then no friend of the Church, was taken aback by the vehemence and cosmic scope of Lader's attack. Lader

> held forth on that theme through most of the drive home. It was a comprehensive and chilling indictment of the poisonous influence of Catholicism in secular affairs from its inception until the day before yesterday. I was far from an admirer of the church's role in the world chronicle, but his insistent, uncompromising recitation brought to mind the Protocols of the Elders of Zion. It passed through my mind that if one had substituted "Jewish" for "Catholic," it would have been the most vicious anti-Semitic tirade imaginable.[18]

Lader knew "every revolution has to have its villain."[19] Historically, those villains were Catholic, except in Russia, where the Czar was orthodox, the head of an officially Christian country. "It doesn't really matter whether it's a king, a dictator, or a tsar, but it has to be someone, a person, to rebel against. It's easier for the people we want to persuade to perceive it this way."[20] In America, Lader told Nathanson, the villain would not be Catholics, who could be divided along liberal and conservative lines, but the Catholic hierarchy, which was a "small enough group to come down on and anonymous enough so that no names ever have to be mentioned, but everybody will have a fairly good idea whom we are talking about."[21] The strategy shocked Nathanson initially, but it soon made good sense when Nathanson remembered, "That was how Trotsky and his followers habitually referred to the Stalinists."[22] When Lader brought Betty Friedan into NARAL, she brought with her the communist tactics she had learned from her youthful work with the party. Making it seem that women, irrespective of ethnicity, supported abortion was a "brilliant tactic"[23] that corresponded to the "Popular Front" three decades earlier and showed the abortion movement's revolutionary pedigree.

The new popular front included Protestants and Jews, with women as props in televised demonstrations, attacking doctors and hospitals targeted because they were Catholic. One early victim was the Catholic ob/gyn Hugh Barber. Nathanson chose him to target because he "was a practicing Catholic who had stood adamantly against the widening psychiatric indications for action in his department."[24] According to Nathanson, "there has been ... no social change in American history as sweeping, as potent in American family life, or as heavily dependent upon an anti-religious bias for its success as the abortion movement."[25]

By the late '70s, when Nathanson wrote *Aborting America*, he was "heartily ashamed of the use of the anti-Catholic ploy."[26] Nathanson implicated the Jews in this "anti-Catholic ploy" by calling it a "*Shandeh fah yidden*" ("scandal for the Jews").[27] As if admitting the ethnic nature of the struggle, Nathanson converted to Catholicism a few years after converting to the prolife position. The use of anti-Catholic bigotry to promote abortion was more than "a reincarnation of McCarthyism at its worst," it was "a keenly focused weapon, full of purpose and design."[28]

Lader divided Catholics into liberal and conservative factions and then used the former to control and discredit the latter. The "'modern' Kennedy Catholics," who "were already using contraception," could be browbeaten into a public "pro-choice" position without much effort.[29] Then "The stage was set ... for the use of anti-Catholicism as a political instrument and for the manipulation of Catholics themselves by splitting them and setting them against each other."[30] NARAL would supply the press with "fictitious polls and surveys designed to make it appear as if American Catholics were deserting the teachings of the Church and the dictates of their consciences in droves."[31]

The main public relations weapon, however, was "identifying every anti-abortion figure according to his or her religious affiliation (usually Catholic)" while "studiously" refraining from any ethnic or religious identification of those who were pro-abortion.[32] "Lader's own religious beliefs" were "never discussed or mentioned," but he identified Malcolm Wilson, the lieutenant governor of New York State in 1970 as "a Catholic strongly opposed to abortion."[33] "Neither I nor Assemblyman Albert Blumenthal," Nathanson continued, "was ever identified as a Jew, nor was Governor Nelson Rockefeller ever recognized as a Protestant," even though the abortion movement was disproportionately Jewish and "from the very beginning of the abortion revolution the Catholic Church and its spokesmen took a considerable role in the opposition."[34]

Given the media's liberal bias, "it was easy to portray the church as an insensitive, authoritarian war-monger, and association with it or any of its causes as unendurably reactionary, fascistic, and ignorant."[35] Nathanson thinks Catholics should have pointed out the religious bigotry at the heart of this double standard; they also should have explained that the proabortion side was overwhelmingly Jewish, and, therefore, un-American because:

> In the public mind Protestant America is America, and had Protestant opposition been organized and vociferous early on, permissive abortion might have been perceived as somehow anti-American, the spawn of a cadre of wild-eyed Jewish radicals in New York City.[36]

Instead, there was no Catholic response to the "blatantly anti-Catholic campaign."[37] Catholics concentrated on explaining how the fetus was a human being, as if the other side were ignorant of this fact. "There was no Catholic equivalent of the Anti-Defamation League of the B'nai B'rith or the NAACP."[38] The Catholic Church "confined itself decently (though as it turned out, disastrously) to the issue of abortion."[39] By not identifying their ethnic opponents, Catholics lost the war.

The media had no qualms in this regard and were willing to engage in a flagrant violation of the rules identifying crime by race which they had just established. The "mega-press" (Nathanson's term) collaborated because they were controlled by proabortion Jews and Protestants, who encouraged liberal Catholics like the *New York Times*' Anna Quindlen, eager to make it in a competitive profession. "The media," says Nathanson,

> discreetly ignored the carefully crafted bigotry we were peddling. Many media people were young college-educated liberal Catholics, just the kind we had succeeded in splitting off from the faithful flock, and they were not about to disgrace their newly-won spurs as intelligentsia by embarrassing the liberals with anything as crass as an accusation of prejudice. Prejudice was something evil directed at Jews and blacks, not Catholics. But had our fulminations been anti-Semitic or anti-black there would have been the most powerful keening in the media—strong enough to have destroyed NARAL.[40]

The NARAL strategy was based on chutzpah. "For sheer chutzpah it had no modern parallel."[41] Nathanson calls the "Robert Byrn affair" the "most nakedly bigoted, fecklessly anti-Catholic campaign NARAL ever mounted."[42] Byrn, a Fordham University law professor characterized by the *New York Times* as "a forty-year-old Roman Catholic bachelor," went before Justice Lester Holtzman to have himself declared the legal guardian of unborn children threatened with abortion. True to the ethnic double standard, the *New York Times* "did not characterize Justice Holtzman as a married Jew."[43] When Byrn sued for an injunction against abortions in New York's municipal hospitals, Attorney General Louis Lefkowitz vowed to fight Byrn, but nothing was said about Lefkowitz's ethnic/religious status. When Nancy Stearns, a lawyer for the Center for Constitutional Rights tried to have Byrn put up $40,000 bond for each woman forced to have a child, *New York Times* correspondent Jane Brody, whose ethnic identity remained shrouded in mystery, "failed to describe Stearns as a single Jewess."[44] Because the *Times* is the national paper of record, this double standard got repeated across the country. In Philadelphia, the *Philadelphia Inquirer* repeatedly referred to anti-abortion crusader Martin Mullen as an "arch-conservative"[45] Roman Catholic, but never referred to Governor Milton Shapp, Mullen's opponent in Pennsylvania's abortion wars, as a pro-abortion Jew. Nathanson notes that Canada's Henry Morgenthaler used his stay in one of Hitler's concentration camps to justify his role as Canada's leading abortion provider. Morgenthaler's clinics violated Canadian law and yet "Morgenthaler ... is adored by the Canadian mega-press" even though he "is quite as devoted to malignant anti-Catholicism as our American exorcist, Lawrence Lader."[46]

In 1967, at around the same time that Bernard Nathanson met Lawrence Lader and NARAL was born, abortion became legal in California. Governor Ronald Reagan signed the nation's first abortion bill into law, but the law was written by Anthony Beilenson, the Jewish representative from Beverly Hills. The ethnic dimensions of the abortion battle were, if anything, even more extreme in California than they were in New York. As in New York, the battle over abortion broke down clearly along ethnic lines. As in New York, Jews generally promoted abortion, and Catholics generally opposed it. From the moment that abortion was legalized in 1967, the abortion battle in California was largely a battle between Catholics and Jews, in much the same way that Catholics and Jews had battled each other over obscenity in the California movie industry 30 years earlier.

Jews and Abortion

Chapter Twenty-Nine

The Black Panthers

On October 15, 1966, when Martin Luther King's failure to reform the housing situation in Chicago had become painfully apparent, three Negroes who were on the payroll of an antipoverty program in Oakland, California sat down and created a new revolutionary organization known as the Black Panther Party. As one of their first acts, Huey Newton and Bobby Seale, two of the three co-founders, persuaded a Japanese American by the name of Richard Aoki to give them his M-1 rifle and his 9-mm pistol, because, they reasoned, real revolutionaries need guns.

Huey Newton, one of the three founding members of the Black Panthers, was born in Louisiana and named after that state's most famous governor. His parents came to Oakland during the job boom of World War II, when that city was a major entrepot for the Pacific Theater. Newton may have gotten his first guns from a Japanese-American revolutionary, but he got the idea to turn his shakedown operation into a revolutionary organization from the Jews he met at Merritt College.

"Nothing made the idea of revolution more vivid to the white left," as Todd Gitlin put it in his history of the '60s, "than the Black Panther Party."[1] Unlike the Black Nationalists, David Horowitz tells us, "the Panthers quoted Marx and actively sought alliances with the white left."[2] Horowitz doesn't say so explicitly, at this point at least, but the so-called "white left" in the bay area and elsewhere was overwhelmingly Jewish. The saga of the rise and fall of the Black Panthers was the same old Black-Jewish Alliance story in a new more violent, overtly revolutionary key. The Black Panthers were attracted to the Jews for all of the usual reasons. The Jews were experienced revolutionaries who knew how to run organizations and raise money, or in the case of Bert Schneider, the Hollywood producer who bankrolled the Panthers, give it in large quantities as well. The Jews were attracted to the Panthers, although "no one would publicly say so," because of their willingness to use violence to bring about revolution. Horowitz claims that "it was the Panthers' violent image that provided their real attraction to the new Left."[3]

The Panthers had been inspired by Jews in other ways as well. As part of their 10 point program, the Panthers, demanded reparations payments for American blacks because the Jews had been so successful in shaking down money from the Germans after World War II:

> The Germans are now aiding the Jews in Israel for the genocide of the Jewish people. The Germans murdered six million Jews. The American racist has taken part in the slaughter of over 50 million black people; therefore, we feel that this is a modest demand that we make.[4]

In May 1966, Stokely Carmichael became chairman of SNCC. As one of his first acts, he expelled the Jews from the Civil Rights movement. David Horowitz remembers being stunned by the magnitude of the betrayal:

Jews had funded the movement, devised its legal strategies, and provided support for its efforts in the media and in the universities—and wherever else they had power. More than half the freedom riders who had gone to the southern states were Jews, although Jews constituted only 3 percent of the population. It was an unprecedented show of solidarity from one people to another. Jews had put their resources and lives on the line to support the black struggle for civil rights, and indeed, two of their sons—Schwerner and Goodman—had been murdered for their efforts. But even while these tragic events were still fresh, the black leaders of the movement had unceremoniously expelled the Jews from their ranks.[5]

Horowitz could not understand how blacks could treat Jews like this, especially "since Jews were a near majority of the whites in these organizations, and had played a strategic role in organizing and funding the struggle."[6] The Jews who had spent roughly 60 years trying to turn the Negro masses into the *avant garde* of revolutionary change in America woke up in the mid-'60s to discover that Tom Watson had been right all along; like Frankenstein, they had created a monster that was no longer under their control. Now that the revolution was actually breaking out in black ghettoes across the country, the revolution looked as if it were going to devour its own Jews.

As a result, the Jews who had poured hundreds of thousands of dollars into the civil rights movement tried to use moderates like Martin Luther King to get back at ungrateful *shvarztes* like Stokeley Carmichael. On July 25, 1966, Martin Luther King attacked black power in a paid ad in the *New York Times*. King's statement had been written by Stanley Levison. Friedman is quick to add that "Levison, of course, was only putting into words what King himself felt"[7] without understanding how this admission lent credence to the SNCC's claim that Martin Luther King had become a Jewish puppet.

SNCC, which John Lewis described as "part domestic Peace Corps and part guerilla warfare,"[8] was the cutting edge Negro revolutionary organization at the time, but since the SNCC was not interested in talking to white people anymore, Jewish alumnae of the Freedom Summer in Mississippi like Bay Area Lawyer Faye Stender gravitated into the orbit of the Black Panthers.

Faye Stender was one of the many Jewish lawyers who were involved in "interracial" romances with their black clients. The big impetus for the sexual phase of the Black-Jewish Alliance was the Freedom Summer of 1964 in Mississippi, an experience which some participants say led to 1) feminism among the Jewish women and 2) the expulsion of whites from the movement because black women had become outraged at the seduction of what they considered their men. Asked for his thoughts on the position of women in the movement in 1964, SNCC chairman Stokely Carmichael replied, "prone."

Eldridge Cleaver had been released from prison in December 1966 largely because of the efforts of Beverly Axelrod, his mistress cum attorney, and because of the articles he had written in *Ramparts Magazine*. After his release from prison, when Cleaver set himself up in a large Victorian house on Pine Street in San

Francisco's predominantly black Fillmore district, it was Axelrod who raised the money from various communist organizations to pay Cleaver's bills.

Using Black House as his base of operations, Cleaver planned to launch a new black political movement which would take up the banner that Malcolm X had let drop when he was assassinated. That meant collaborating with Betty Shabazz, Malcolm X's widow, who was invited to the Bay Area for a memorial service and negotiations.

When Malcolm X's widow, Betty Shabazz, arrived at the *Ramparts* offices for an interview, a confrontation with the police ensued. When the police ordered the Panthers to put away their weapons, Huey Newton leveled his shotgun at the officer in charge, who promptly backed down. Eldridge Cleaver was impressed. "Goddam," Cleaver said of Newton, "that nigger is c-r-a-z-y."[9] Newton's bravado so impressed Cleaver that he dropped the idea of forming his own organization and joined the Black Panthers, which promptly appointed him their "Minister of Information."

Eldridge Cleaver later wrote an article for *Ramparts* called "How I fell in Love with the Black Panther Party," describing the confrontation as the moment of truth that won his allegiance. In an introduction for a planned Newton biography, he characterized Huey as "the baddest motherfucker ever to set foot inside of history." The line, however, was not written by Eldridge, but by a white *Ramparts* editor named Peter Collier.[10]

It was the first of many instances when a white revolutionary would put words in Cleaver's mouth. One of the things Newton and Cleaver had in common was their acquaintance with a revolutionary Jew by the name of Robert Scheer. Huey Newton had already met Scheer at Merritt College. By the time Newton faced down the Oakland Police at *Ramparts'* offices, Scheer had already made contact with Eldridge Cleaver, who was serving time in Soledad Prison, and had published an article by him in *Ramparts* in June 1966.

Robert Scheer was a writer who had a small political following at his disposal as the result of an unsuccessful campaign to unseat congressman Jeffrey Cohelan. Scheer would go on to write a column for the *Los Angeles Times* and conduct the famous Jimmy Carter interview which appeared in *Playboy* in the late '70s, but he began his journalistic career as editor of *Root and Branch*, the journal that created the New Left at Berkeley. By the second issue of *Root and Branch*, Scheer had defined the style of the New Left. It was going to be a fusion of "Marxist agendas with the anarchic spirit of American mischief."[11] Once they defined the style of both the "counterculture" and "youth rebellion," revolutionary Jews like Scheer and Horowitz could once again assume their positions at the forefront of the movement and become "the self-conscious vanguard of a social revolution."[12]

Ironically, Horowitz submitted a critique of contraception as part of one of his *Root and Branch* articles, but the idea was shot down by Scheer who dismissed any misgivings about contraception as "a point of view so perverse" that "only a reactionary" and "probably only a Catholic" could hold it.[13]In addition to their work at *Root and Branch*, both Horowitz and Scheer wrote seminal books that also helped created the New Left of the '60s. Horowitz dedicated his book *Student* to Justice Hugo Black, half of the radical Black/Douglas faction on the Supreme Court that was busy ratifying the New Left's turn away from economics and toward sexual issues as the cutting edge of revolution. Scheer's book was on Vietnam. In fact, Scheer joined the staff of *Ramparts* magazine after the publication of *How the United States Got Involved in Vietnam*, a book *The Nation* called the most important analysis of the war up to that time. Once he joined the staff of *Ramparts*, Scheer took the erstwhile Catholic magazine in an increasingly revolutionary direction, largely because he brought a whole cadre of revolutionary Jews on board with him.

In the fall of 1967, David Horowitz joined Scheer on the staff of *Ramparts* to run its book publishing division. Horowitz had been a member of the NAACP at Columbia, where "like other radicals," he "followed the progress of the Montgomery bus boycott and the early sit-ins."[14] Horowitz "was pleased when my mother indicated in a conspiratorial tone that Rosa Parks was 'one of us'"[15] but doesn't explain whether "us" meant being Jewish or being a revolutionary. That's because the two terms were synonymous for Horowitz when he was growing up. Real ethnicity was bad. Revolution was Horowitz's ethnicity:

> It was Cuddihy's thesis that the revolutionary ideas of Marx and Freud were attempts to deconstruct these civil orders and replace them with a universal one in which they would finally be granted the acceptance they craved. Thus Freud claimed to show that bourgeois civility was a mask for sexual repression, while Marx argued that it mystified economic exploitation. Each had a vision of liberation ... that would provide a universal solvent in which the significance of ethnic identities disappeared.[16]

Horowitz agonized over the issue of Jewish ethnic identity in his later years. After he had become a conservative, Horowitz decided to force the ethnicity issue when he was invited to take part in a symposium organized by those who still held on to the revolutionary faith. "Just out of curiosity," Horowitz asked his former colleagues on the Left, "I'd like to hear how the other Marxists in the room identify themselves ethnically."[17]

Horowitz goes on to add, "I knew, of course, that they were all Jews, and that not one would demean himself to acknowledge that fact."[18] Rather than admit there was, in fact, a connection between being a Jew and being a revolutionary, Horowitz's colleagues dismissed "his interrogations" as an "attempt... to obstruct this seminar with questions that didn't interest anyone else."[19]

By the time he arrived at Berkeley, Horowitz, taking his cue from Marx's analysis of Jews as economic exploiters in "On the Jewish Question," had concluded that ethnicity in general and Jewish ethnicity in particular was a problem which only socialism could solve. "Socialism," Horowitz concluded, "would 'solve' the Jewish question by eliminating Judaism, along with all other ethnic and national identities."[20] As a result, Horowitz wrote,

I did not identify myself as a Jew. I was a revolutionary and an internationalist. To see myself as a Jew, a member of a real community in all its human limits, with all its human faults, to identify with the claims of such a community, would have been a betrayal of the revolutionary Idea.[21]

Even if that were the case, Horowitz was still forced to grapple with the connection between Jews and revolution and the fact that "For nearly two hundred years, Jews have played a disproportionate role as leaders of the modern revolutionary movements in Europe and the West."[22]

In dealing with the Jewish inclination toward revolution, Horowitz is forced to deal with Jewish religion, but here as before revolution becomes the central event around which everything else revolves. The central religious paradigm for "Jews of the radical Left" is exile. As the Jews' exile from the Land of Israel "became more and more permanent," an apocalyptic strain of Jewish messianism developed "which no longer conceives the event as a restoration of the good of a previous time."[23] Instead Jewish messianism presents the longing for return in a metaphysical or theological light, according to which Jews have been sent into exile so that they can redeem the world or bring about "*tikkun olam.*"

This strain can be most easily seen in the Lurianic Caballah where it appeared in explicit form for the first time in Jewish history in the aftermath of the Jews' expulsion from Spain in 1492. Jewish exile, according to this new view, was neither an unfortunate accident nor a punishment for having rejected the Messiah, but instead "a mark of our destiny to become agents of salvation."[24] As the Kabbalist Hayim Vital put it, the Jews had to "be scattered to the four winds in order to lift everything up."[25] In their attempt to bring about *tikkun olam*, the Jews became "the first revolutionary internationalists."[26]

Socialism and Communism accepted these deeply internalized Jewish principles and secularized them to make them more congruent with the intellectual standards of the 19th century, but Messianic politics retained its religious roots nonetheless:

> By carrying the revolution to its conclusion, socialists would usher in a millennium and fulfill the messianic prophecies of the pre-Enlightenment religions that modern ideas had discredited. Through this revolution, the lost unity of mankind would be restored, social harmony would be reestablished, paradise regained. It would be a *tikkun olam*, a repair of the world.[27]

It is this paradigm, according to Horowitz, which "forges the false bonds between Jewish faith and revolutionary fervor."[28]

By the time he wrote those words, Horowitz had concluded that "the Marxist idea, to which I had devoted my entire intellectual life and work, was false."[29] As a result, he concluded, "I am nothing."[30] When Horowitz lost his faith in socialism, that event precipitated an identity crisis similar to the one Lorraine Hansberry described in *The Sign in Sidney Brustein's Window*. If Jews stop being revolutionaries, both Hansberry and Horowitz began to wonder in their separate ways, do they have any identity?

Horowitz grew up in Sunnyside, a section of New York in which being a Jew meant being a revolutionary and vice versa. In Sunnyside, the rules of normal ethnicity prevailed, but they did not apply to Jews in the way they applied to other ethnic groups. The Jews never referred to themselves as Communists. The common euphemism when Horowitz was growing up was progressive, which was a bland political category and not unlike a Jew taking a WASP name. Even if communists didn't believe in ethnicity, before long young Horowitz began to notice, however, that all of the "progressives had names like Abramson, Adler, Heller, and Wolfman"[31] and that they

> were like a tiny scouting party that had infiltrated the camp of an alien tribe, vastly superior in number who were neither intellectuals, nor communists, nor Jews. They were Irish and Italian, their church was a pillar of the anti-Communist cause. Their names were Bradshaw, Canorazzi and O'Brien, and the institutions of their Catholic life were visible along Skillman Avenue, where the shops of the neighborhood were also arrayed. There were the stations of sin and redemption that marked their moral progress—the Shamrock Bar & Grill, the Amodeo family grocery, the storefront offices of the Veterans of Foreign Wars, St. Teresa's and the Shea funeral home.[32]

Catholics were an especially virulent form of *goyim*, a prejudice which Horowitz's parents had confirmed in their minds when they read the books of Paul Blanshard:

> Many of the existing governments in Eastern Europe were Catholic. Another book on my parents' shelf—*The Vatican* by Paul Blanshard—explained how the Catholic Church was in league with corrupt privilege and was the world's biggest landowner. The Catholic Church had rallied the reactionary forces in the Spanish Civil War, and now was playing a similar role in Eastern Europe. When the Communists seized the government of Hungary, Cardinal Josef Mindzenty took refuge in the US embassy and made himself a symbol of the anti-Communist resistance. In America, Catholic politicians and clerics like Cardinal Francis Joseph Spellman and Bishop Fulton J. Sheen, became leading spokesmen of the anti-Communist cause. The inflammatory currents of the international civil war simmered in the Sunnyside air.[33]

In Sunnyside, ethnic animosity flowed, not from anti-Semitism, but from the fact that Horowitz's parents felt "hostility toward the *goyim*, and indeed everything the *goyim* held dear," and "that incited the hostility back."[34]

In spite of his efforts, however, Horowitz cannot solve the ethnic problem on its own terms. In order to answer the ethnic question, Horowitz has to probe deeper into areas that are personal, familial, and psychological. Horowitz claims "I do not really have an answer to the mystery of origins—to what in particular had set my father and eventually, therefore, myself on the radical path,"[35] but in mentioning his father, he proposes a psychological starting point for his quest into why so many Jews become revolutionaries.

"My father," Horowitz wrote, "thought of himself as a revolutionary."[36] Horowitz goes on to confirm the suspicions Lorraine Hansberry mooted in *Brustein*— once the Jew ceases to be a revolutionary he has no identity—when he writes, "The [Communist] Party has become so much my father's personal salvation that without it the possibilities of life itself vanish."[37] By this point Horowitz has reached the heart of the matter, which is religious and moral. His father is lost because he has rejected the light, and as a result "He had become enclosed in his own darkness, where the only ray of light was his revolutionary fantasy, now reduced to a desperate personal quest."[38]

Irving Louis Horowitz has an equally grim assessement of his own father, whom he describes as "the perfect Sombartian man—the Calvinist Jew, convinced that the road to heaven involved good work and no nonsense."[39] Horowitz's father was a bundle of contradictions right out of Marx's essay *Zur Judenfrage*. He was a petty capitalist who would beat his son unmercifully for lifting a dime from his cash register, but he was an ardent socialist, and he identified socialism as "the religion of the future."[40] In the present, which is to say in Harlem in the 1930s, Horowitz *pere* was in the wrong place at the wrong time because as his son puts it, "Harlem was the wrong place for a Jewish Calvinist."[41]

Irving Horowitz got the impression from his father that he and his sister were an "unwanted intrusion, mouths to feed, obligations, limitations on his movements—impediments."[42] If that is the impression Horowitz got from his father, it is not surprising that he sums up life at home by saying that "the central aspect of the Horowitz family was the absence of love."[43]

Family finished a distant third behind petty everyday capitalism, which involved cheating the *shvartzes* when they brought in their Christmas bulbs for testing, and the revolutionary fantasies which made this sort of life tolerable. Like David Horowitz's father, Irving Horowitz's father lived "in the imaginary world of Jewish Bundism and Russian Bolshevism,"[44] a world which he characterizes as "a religion without Christ, a church without crucifix."[45]

Revolution, in other words, was the fantasy which Jews conjured in their own minds to make a world without light or love tolerable. The Jews David Horowitz knew as a child were "helpless to control the circumstances of their lives."[46] As a result, they turned to the opium of revolutionary fantasy for solace.

By the time he wrote those words, Horowitz had become a devout American patriot of the neoconservative persuasion, as Kristol *pere et fils* would joke. As a neoconservative, Horowitz was confronted, however, with his parents' hostility toward America. When they arrived at Ellis Island, the Jews had brought with them an ancestral hatred of Russia and the Czar, but America was not Russia. If it ever seemed appropriate, revolution was a wildly inappropriate response to the welcome America had extended to European Jews. David Horowitz feels that it is entirely possible that "Jews were more accepted, and felt more at home in America at that time than they had in the 2000 years since the destruction of the Second Temple."[47] If that is the case, then "Why had they chosen to become Bolsheviks in America?"[48] Why had Horowitz's family become "permanent conspirators in a revolutionary drama"[49] in a land where the response was totally inappropriate? "Instead of being grateful to a nation that had provided them with economic opportunity and refuge, they wanted to overthrow its governing institutions and replace them with a Soviet state."[50] Why had the Horowitz family proclaimed its allegiance to an ideology "so alien to everything around them"?[51]

The answer to these questions is: because they were Jews. They had been trained to think about the *goyim* in a particular way by their parents, who in turn had been instructed in the same way by their parents, all the way back, to the rejection of light and love that took place at the foot of the cross and sent the wandering Jew off on his revolutionary journey. In a sense, Horowitz feels that he had no choice in the matter. He became a revolutionary Jew because he was raised to be a revolutionary Jew:

> What was my own choice? In the beginning I hardly had one. I understood early that my parents' political religion was really the center of their moral life. This meant—without their necessarily intending it—that the condition of their parental love was that I embrace their political faith.[52]

When David Horowitz arrived in Berkeley it struck him as being "a larger Sunnyside where the aliens were fewer in number and our tribe greater. On arrival, I immediately became part of a group of 'red diaper babies'—the designation we used to identify ourselves as children of the Communist left."[53]

Scheer was another New York Jew who was part of the tribe at Berkeley. Scheer, according to Horowitz, "had grown up in the 'Coops' a cooperative apartment complex in the Bronx which, like Sunnyside, had been colonized by the Communist Party."[54] Unlike Comrade Jerome and his generation, Scheer was a "beatnik" and had the style of a "political hipster" whose "speech was salted with allusions to Charlie Mingus and Allen Ginsberg, along with Marx and Lenin."[55]

Ron Radosh, another Jewish revolutionary from the same era, describes Scheer in his book *Commies* as a sexual revolutionary who felt the Kim Il Sung regime in North Korea had created heaven on earth. Scheer felt this way about North Korea, according to Radosh, because it eventually offered political sanctuary to Eldridge Cleaver, whom Radosh refers to as Scheer's "protégé."[56]

Scheer and Horowitz came from a new generation of revolutionary Jews, who were more American and less Russian, as well as more cultural and less economic in their orientation. Speaking for himself and the Jews of his generation in America, Horowitz claims that

> It was exciting to hear the Marxist categories revived by someone who affected the style of the Beats and was at home in the popular culture. The Old Left had a snobbish disdain for mainstream entertainments, which it viewed as corrupt expressions of "commodity capitalism." Scheer connected the political failure of

the Old Left to its ghetto mentality. To hear him speak of a coming revolution in images that were not those of a marginalized subculture was exciting.[57]

America and communism were made for each other in a way, because both taught contempt for ethnicity and roots. Given this fact, the Jew was the ideal cultural intermediary, because he had internalized the principles of what Stalin referred to as "rootless cosmopolitanism" for centuries:

> The revolutionary belongs to a community of faith that extends beyond the classes and the nations and reaches across the boundaries that divide and oppress. Within every nation group it forms the basis of a new human community and a new human identity. Today the revolutionary is isolated, obstructed by the divisions that form the cultural and political legacy of the past; the revolutionary is of the nations, but not in them. For the revolutionary's eye is on the future. Today there is Black and Jew, American and Russian, Israeli and Arab. But within each nation—Russia, American, Israel, Egypt—there were the aliens, the persecuted, the unassimilated, the "Jews" who know the heart of the stranger and who struggle for human freedom. Today they are separate; tomorrow they will be joined.[58]

Horowitz says that *Ramparts'* "promotion of the Black Panther Party as the new vanguard of the black struggle" was "another source of Ramparts' growing influence."[59] The opposite, was of course, just as true. Even if the Panthers increased *Ramparts'* circulation and influence, it was *Ramparts* which created the Black Panthers, because it was Scheer who, in Horowitz's words, "became perhaps the key person to launch the career of Eldridge Cleaver."[60]

Eldridge Cleaver spent the civil rights revolution in Soledad Prison, where he was serving one to 14 years for assault with intent to murder. With his left-wing lawyer/mistress Beverly Axelrod as his intermediary, Cleaver made contact with *Ramparts*, which then began to receive letters from him on a regular basis. It was out of these letters that Scheer would fashion first *Ramparts* articles and then the book *Soul on Ice*.

In his first *Ramparts* piece, "Notes on a Native Son,' which appeared in the magazine's June 1966 issue, Cleaver denounced, James Baldwin and just about every other black writer as "buckdancers who were worse than Uncle Toms."[61] Baldwin had become "a white man in a black body. A self-willed automated slave, he becomes the white man's most valuable tool in oppressing other blacks."[62] Conspicuous by its absence from Cleaver's critique of Baldwin was any mention of *Commentary* or any of the other Jewish magazines and organizations which had promoted Baldwin to the position of spokesman for his race in the first place. The absence is not surprising because the Jews at *Ramparts* were doing the same thing for the career of Eldridge Cleaver.

Eventually, *Soul on Ice* would become one of Ramparts Books' biggest selling titles. In Cleaver, America had discovered a "true black," which is to say, an amoral criminal and rapist who could rationalize his crimes by appealing to the writings of French existentialists. In spite of the adulation which the literary establishment heaped on Cleaver, it didn't take a genius to see that in *Soul on Ice*, the old pattern which Harold Cruse and Lorraine Hansberry had complained about in figures as diverse as George Gershwin and Norman Mailer had reasserted itself. Once again the Jews got to define the Negro as a criminal and a sexual deviant. In the case of *Soul on Ice*, the "true black" expressed his true identity by raping white women. It was as if Scheer and the staff at *Ramparts* were determined to prove that the South's interpretation of the Scottsboro Boys trial had been right all along. The New York Jews, now transplanted to Berkeley, California, were stirring up the Negroes again. How else was one to interpret passages like the following.

> I became a rapist. To refine my technique and *modus operandi*, I started out practicing on black girls in the ghetto where dark and vicious deed appear not as aberrations or deviations from the norm, but as part of the efficiency of the evil of the day—and when I considered myself smooth enough, I crossed the tracks and sought out white prey.... There are of course many young blacks out there right now who are slitting white throats and raping the white girl "

The prose could have been lifted directly from *Scottsboro: The Firebrand of Communism*. The only difference was that Haywood Patterson never used words like "*modus operandi*." The fact that a Negro who had spent the last few years of his life in Soledad Prison did use phrases like that made Cleaver sound a lot like Ruby Bates, when she told the crowd in Washington that she had lied under oath because "I was afraid of the Southern white ruling class people...."[63] Suspicions about just who had written this book deepened when Cleaver continued in the same vein, decrying "the Slaughter of Jews by Germans" and "the dropping of atomic bombs on the Japanese people" as "deeds [which] weigh heavily on the prostrate souls and tumultuous consciences of the white youth."[64]

Skepticism about whether Cleaver had actually written *Soul on Ice* surfaced shortly after the book was published, when a black student in Tom Wolfe's book *Radical Chic and Mau-Mauing the Flak Catchers* announced:

> That book wasn't written for the ghettos. It was written for the white middle class. They published it and they read it. What is this "having previously dabbled in the themes and writings of Rousseau, Thomas Paine, and Voltaire" that he's laying down there? You try coming down in the Fillmore doing some previously dabbled in talking about Albert Camus and James Baldwin. They'd laugh you off the block. That book was written to give a thrill to white women in Palo Alto and Marin County. That book is the best suburban jive I ever heard. I don't think he even wrote it. Eldridge Cleaver wouldn't write something like that. I think his wife wrote it... don't preevy-dabble the people with no split-level Palo Alto white bourgeois housewife Buick Estate Wagon backseat rape fantasies."[65]

In discussing how *Soul on Ice* became one of *Ramparts'* best-sellers, Horowitz admits that "The nihilistic view of himself that Cleaver promoted in his book fit snugly into the radical outlook" of the magazine."[66] Horowitz also admits that he was the author of at least one article which appeared in *Ramparts* under Cleaver's name. Horowitz says that Scheer asked him to "take charge" of an article Eldridge Cleaver had written on "the Land Question" when he was arrested for shooting an Oakland policeman.[67] Horowitz also adverts to something that other readers had noticed as well, namely, that Cleaver's rape fantasies sounded a lot like Norman Mailer's essay, "The White Negro." This similarity in outlook came about either because great minds always moved in the same circles or because

> In a seminal article titled "The White Negro," Norman Mailer had cast America's blacks as Rousseau's "noble savages," representatives of humanity in its pristine state. These were the "oppressed" of the radical imagination. The Panther's roots in the ghetto were the primal symbol of social injustice. Their will to violence was the mark of their revolutionary spirit.[68]

It is entirely possible that Cleaver read Norman Mailer's essay "The White Negro" while in prison. Since David Horowitz admits to writing at least one of the articles which appeared under Cleaver's name in *Ramparts*, it is just as likely that Mailer's "White Negro" made it into Cleaver's writings via the editorial ministrations of Horowitz or Scheer. Either way, Cleaver's image of the Negro rapist came from the mind of Norman Mailer. Whatever the source of the rape material, Eldridge Cleaver was a Jewish creation, and the Black Panthers were a Jewish fantasy of revolutionary Negro sexual deviance in the tradition of Haywood Patterson and *Porgy and Bess*.

As the movement continued on its revolutionary trajectory the fantasy continued, but its imagery became more violent. Robert Scheer, who also volunteered to edit (or ghostwrite) Cleaver's second book, changed the title from Cleaver's original "How I fell in Love with the Black Panther Party" to "Courage to Kill" as if to show that the Panthers were the vanguard which would bring about the eruption, through violence, of Messianic redemption into history. It was an old story by 1968, but it had never lost its attraction to Jewish revolutionaries.

Like Scheer, Sol Stern was another Jewish editor at *Ramparts*. As if to lend further credence to the idea that the Panthers were a Jewish creation, Stern wrote an article on the Panthers which appeared in the Sunday Magazine section of the *New York Times* in August 1967, and it was that article which turned the Black Panthers "into a household name."[69] Because it appeared in the *Times*, Stern's article lent "an authority that Ramparts could not have provided"[70] to the Messianic Jewish fantasy that the Black Panthers would bring about *tikkun olam* by murdering white policemen. Stern lent credibility to Newton by cloaking his ranting in the language of the holocaust. "Every time you go to execute a white racist Gestapo cop," Stern has Newton saying, "you are defending yourself."[71] If *Times* readers missed the point, Stern was ready to give the neo-Black-Jewish Alliance interpretation of Newton's words by writing: "To these young men, the execution of a police officer would be as natural and justifiable as the execution of a German soldier by a member of the French Resistance."[72] So, according to Stern's redaction of Newton, all cops were Germans, which is to say, Nazis, which is to say expendable in the cause of revolutionary violence, which the Negroes would carry out per the instructions of their Jewish handlers, flacks, and ghost writers.

Horowitz not only agreed with Stern's take on Newton and the Panthers, he was offended when Joan Didion disagreed in her article on the Panthers in *Look Magazine* and denigrated Newton "as little more than a young hood who had added Marx to his hustler's bag of tricks."[73] When Horowitz laid the responsibility for the coming race war at Didion's feet, she shot back "I thought radicals wanted a race war."[74]

During the Summer of 1967 riots in Detroit and elsewhere gave the impression that the race war had finally arrived. H. Rap Brown, new head of SNCC, was arrested in Alexandria, Virginia and charged with inciting a riot and arson. Brown's arrest, however, could not disguise the fact that by the summer of 1967, the Black Panthers had succeeded SNCC as the cutting edge of black revolutionary politics in the United States.

Two months after Stern's article appeared in the *New York Times*, Newton was arrested for shooting an Oakland Police officer in the back at close range. The officer's name, John Frey (the Anglicized version of Frei) indicated that he was of German extraction.

The same media machinery which orchestrated the killing now went into high gear to exonerate the killer. Pictures of Huey Newton wearing a black beret and seated in his rattan chair with a spear in one hand and a rifle in the other began to appear on the walls of the counterculture's apartments across the nation, and Eldridge Cleaver, with financing from wealthy Jewish backers like Bert Schneider, mounted the "Free Huey" campaign. Cleaver turned to lawyer Charles Garry and his team of Jewish lawyers, who in turn launched a disinformation campaign among an all-too compliant press, claiming that Newton was the victim of frame-up at the hands of a government that was determined to destroy the Black Panther Party by killing off its members in a series of ambushes.

Before long Newton had become a "national icon,"[75] and a new overtly revolutionary Black-Jewish Alliance was pressing forward with its plans for race war and violent revolution. In the Bay Area, that meant a merger of the Peace and Freedom Party (people like Scheer, Michael Lerner, later editor of *Tikkun*, Tom Hayden, who had been raised a Catholic in Michigan, Jerry Rubin, and Joe Blum, who had attended Merritt College with Newton). In February 1968, both sides closed the deal. The PFP accepted the Panthers' ten point program, and Cleaver accepted their nomination as PFP's presidential candidate with Jerry Rubin as his running mate. As part of his platform, Cleaver endorsed "pussy power"[76] and any group willing to assassinate policemen. When 6,000 people gathered at Oakland Auditorium to celebrate Newton's birthday and protest his arrest for the murder of Officery Frey, H. Rap Brown brought the crowd to its feet by announcing that "Huey Newton is our only living revolutionary in this country today."[77]

Not to be outdone by Brown, former SNCC chairman James Foreman told the crowd: "We must serve notice on our oppressors that we as a people are not going to be frightened by the attempted assassination of our leaders. For my assassination—and I am low man on the totem pole—I want 30 police stations blown up, one southern governor, two mayors, and 500 cops dead.... And if Huey Newton is not set free and dies, the sky is the limit."[78] The crowd responded by chanting: "The revolution has come! Off the pig! Time to pick up the gun! Off the pig!"[79]

Martin Luther King was assassinated on April 4, 1968. The long-awaited revolution arrived two days later when Cleaver ordered an armed attack on the Oakland police force. Four car-loads of armed Black Panthers set out to ambush a police car on April 6. When the police found them instead and attempted to pull them over, a gun battle ensued. As a result of the attack, Bobby Hutton, co-founder of the Panthers, ended up dead, and Eldridge Cleaver ended up back in jail. As it had in the case with Newton, the neo-Black-Jewish Alliance quickly came to Cleaver's defense, claiming that he was the victim of an assassination attempt followed by a frame-up. In an open letter published in the *New York Times*, James Baldwin, Ossie Davis, Elizabeth Hardwick, Le Roi Jones, Oscar Lewis, Norman Mailer, Floyd McKissick and Susan Sontag opined that "We find little fundamental difference between the assassin's bullet which killed Dr. King on April 4, and the police barrage which killed Bobby James Hutton two days later. Both were acts of racism ...."[80]

In May Cleaver's wife and Bobby Seale set out for New York City to raise money for Cleaver's legal defense fund, where they were greeted as "real revolutionaries."[81] As Tom Wolfe said after witnessing the Panthers' attempt to raise money in Leonard Bernstein's posh apartment: "The very idea of them, these real revolutionaries, who actually put their lives on the line, runs through Lenny's duplex like a rogue hormone."[82] Eventually all of the money that got raised at Lenny's duplex was forfeited when Cleaver jumped bail and left the country. For the next few years, reports of Cleaver in Korea (Scheer's heaven on earth), Algeria, and France filtered back to America as the movement he inspired turned to more and more suicidal forms of violence and eventually burned itself out by the mid-'70s. But in 1968, "Eldridge's words resonated throughout the community of the Left and inspired white radicals further along the road to revolutionary authenticity and violence."[83]

In the summer of 1970 Faye Stender, the radical Jewish lawyer who had spent Freedom Summer of 1964 in Mississippi and was now a member of Charles Garry's legal staff, succeeded in persuading the appellate court to overturn Newton's conviction for manslaughter. When Newton emerged from prison on August 5, 1970, thousands of his admirers were there to greet him, "as if he were God."[84] As if to show that he agreed with the crowd that he was at least a god of the sort that the Greeks admired, Newton took off his shirt and flexed his muscles, and the crowd went wild.

Stender's brief cited the racial polarization in the Bay Area and claimed that that polarized atmosphere along with the heavy publicity surrounding the Newton's case had made a fair trial impossible. No one mentioned it at the time, but Stender's argument was one more version of Louis Marshall's Supreme Court appeal in the Leo Frank case. The euphoria surrounding the release of Huey Newton obscured the fact that the Jewish legal tradition which extended from Louis Marshall to Faye Stender had created a legal argument that would return to haunt the Jews who invented it. In setting Panthers like Newton free, Stender had created a monster that would quite literally return to destroy her. Johnny Cochran would use a variation of the same argument in the trial of fellow Panther Geronimo Pratt and, more famously, in the trial of O. J. Simpson, in which Cochran turned the tables on the prosecution, and focused the nation's attention on whether Officer Mark Fuhrman was a racist and not whether O. J. Simpson, like a latter day Eldridge Cleaver, slit the throat of the white woman who happened to be his wife. Oblivious to his own role in promoting black men slitting the throats of white women, Horowitz accused Cochran of "playing the race card."[85]

"Why hasn't justice prevailed in this matter?" Horowitz fumed. "Why is a clearly guilty individual free? The answer lies in the climate of the times, in which the testimonies of officers of the law have become more readily impeachable than the testimony of criminals."[86] If Cochran's brief "was an attack on law enforcement as a racist conspiracy to get his client,"[87] Horowitz failed to see in that strategy the legacy of the Leo Frank case and *Soul on Ice*. The chickens, as Malcolm X had said when John F. Kennedy was assassinated, had come home to roost. Horowitz criticized "The radical Left and the left-liberal media" for "elevating the rudest, most outlaw element of black America as the true keepers of the flame in all it means to be black,"[88] forgetting for the moment his own role in promoting *Soul on Ice*. Horowitz then brought up the publicity campaign surrounding the release of *Monster*, the autobiography of LA gangbanger Cody Scott. *Monster*, according to Horowitz, "was promoted in a way frighteningly similar to the way Eldridge Cleaver was introduced to the public in the late 1960s."[89] The cultural DNA which enabled Jews in the publishing industry to promote sexually liberated criminals as the "true black" had begun with the Harlem Renaissance in the 1920s, and it was still alive in the '90s:

> White journalist William Broyles, who facilitated the publication of Scott's book, is analogous to journalist Bob Scheer, who in 1966 was a facilitator of Eldridge Cleaver's career. Atlantic Monthly Press, publisher of Scott's book, is analogous to Ramparts Books, publisher of Cleaver's *Soul on Ice*. Just as Cleaver's book was touted by Maxwell Geismar of *Ramparts*, as "a document of prime importance for an understanding of the outcast black American soul today,' Morgan Entrekin of the Atlantic Monthly Press has said that Scott, as a result of his memoir, is a "primary voice of the black experience.... Scott was also written about by Leon Bing, a white former fashion model who in 1991 wrote a book about black gangs called *Do or Die*. Bing, a woman, could be analogous to that other facilitator of Cleaver's career, Beverly Axelrod.

All of this was true, of course, but missing from all of the indignation surrounding Horowitz's account was an admission that he had anything to do with promoting "the rape fantasies [which] were given direct voice in Cleaver's *Soul on Ice*."[90] Shortly before he died, Eldridge Cleaver was interviewed on *60 Minutes*. The author of *Soul on Ice*, had passed through a number of incarnations since returning to the United States to face trial for his role in the uprising of 1968. He had been a Mormon, a born-again Christian, and author of a revisionist, born-again autobiography titled *Soul on Fire*, and even a Republican, but now the chastened revolutionary could only say that the United States had treated him and his fellow blacks decently even if he didn't feel that way when the media was promoting him or because the media was promoting him. Cleaver was now glad that more people hadn't taken him seriously back then, because "If people had listened to Huey Newton and me in the 1960s, there would have been a holocaust in this country."[91]

Horowitz cites the interview but again maintains his innocence. There is no recognition of his responsibility for promoting Cleaver as the black rapist revolutionary. Nor is there any recognition of the fact that Cleaver talked the way he did because he had been coached by Jewish revolutionaries like Norman Mailer, David Horowitz and Robert Scheer.

After his release from prison Newton embarked upon a life of wretched excess, involving "tumblers of cognac, taking assorted pills, and, most of all, snorting cocaine,"[92] which eventually led to his death. The "beautiful people" from New York and Hollywood, "offered him drugs, alcohol and women to fulfill his wildest dreams and heavy appetites."[93] One of the "beautiful people" who picked up the tab was Bert Schneider, who had become the Jacob Schiff of the black revolutionary movement of the 1960s. Schneider, who was the son of Abraham Schneider, a top executive with Columbia Pictures, had made name for himself as the producer of *Easy Rider*, the 1969 countercultural biker epic, and creator of the *Monkees*, a television series about a rock band. Schneider had put up $300,000 just to finance two conferences. He wore one of the gold rings Newton gave to his inner circle and was so free with his money "because he genuinely loved Huey P. Newton."[94] Newton returned Schneider's love by subjecting him and his girlfriend of the time, Candice Bergen, to cocaine-fueled diatribes that lasted into the wee small hours of the morning.

In 1971 Horowitz and Collier succeeded in ousting Hinckle and Scheer from the board and took over *Ramparts* magazine. In retrospect it was a bit like staging a mutiny on the Titanic. By the early '70s, it had become clear to Horowitz that the "Movement" had "flamed out."[95] It had been killed by President Richard Nixon, who killed it by ending the draft. Once that happened "the 'anti-war' demonstrations stopped and the protestors disappeared"[96] and hardcore revolutionaries like David Horowitz were left high and dry. "I felt," Horowitz said later, "a need to do something to fill the void."[97]

Ramparts in the meantime had become a void that needed to be filled. Now that the movement had flamed out, *Ramparts* was chronically short of funds. That meant person-to-person fundraising, and one of the donors high on the list of every revolutionary organization in California was Bert Schneider. When Collier and Horowitz met with Bert Schneider to ask for money, Schneider, who had sided with Newton in the Cleaver/Newton power struggle over who was going to control the Black Panthers, suggested that they meet with Newton. He accompanied his suggestion with a $5,000 contribution and a request that *Ramparts* do an article on the Panthers' new school and survival programs. Following Schneider up on his suggestion, Collier and Horowitz met with Newton at his Lake Merritt penthouse, also provided by Schneider's contributions. Expecting a confrontation, Horowitz was taken aback when Newton asked to come work for the Panther's new school.

Horowitz later remembered Newton making "a dramatic announcement" to the effect that "the time had come to 'put away the gun'" It was now time to "serve the people," instead, a suggestion which Horowitz, who was looking for something else to do now that the anti-war movement had flamed out, found "sensible."[98] And so after the meeting, Horowitz "offered to help Huey with the Party's community projects and to raise money for the Panther school." Before long Horowitz had raised more than $100,000 to buy a building for the Learning Center, which was instructing more than one hundred children under the guidance of Herbert Kohl.

With respectability and the money that went with it, Horowitz soon realized that the Panthers were in need of a bookkeeper. At this point Horowitz asked a woman by the name of Betty Van Patter to serve as the Panthers' accountant. Van Patter, like Stender and Axelrod, was part of the revolutionary ladies' auxiliary in the Bay Area. She was good at numbers and enjoyed sleeping with black men. In December of 1974 she was hanging out at a local bar when she received a note asking her to meet someone and left the bar. Van Patter never came back. One month later, her body washed up on the eastern shore of San Francisco bay and an autopsy showed that she had died when a blunt instrument had caved in her head.

By the time she died, Horowitz had already abandoned the Panthers after one of their young members had been shot at a school dance. Horowitz had left the Panthers because

> Underneath all the political rhetoric and social uplift, I suddenly realized was the stark reality of the gang. I remember a voice silently beating my head, as I sat there during the service, tears streaming down my face: "What are you doing here, David?" it screamed at me. It was my turn to flee.[99]

When he fled, Horowitz forgot to tell Van Patter about the "stark reality of the gang," and now Van Patter was dead and David was feeling guilty. Instead of dealing with the guilt directly and assessing his own responsibility, Horowitz once again took refuge in the claim that he was an American Innocent and didn't really know what was going on. Horowitz, for example, didn't know that Newton was a drug addict, in spite of he fact that Newton had a perennially runny nose and Herbert Kohl "was telling people that Huey was using cocaine."[100] In another account, this time of Newton's all-night harangues at Bert Schneider's, Horowitz says that it was only years later when he "realized that it was cocaine that fueled these marathons, but at the time, I was innocent of the drug and marveled at his stamina."[101]

The same refrain gets repeated over and over in his memoirs. Horowitz portrays himself as a latter day Daisy Miller. He was an American Innocent. Horowitz claimed that he bridled when Scheer referred to him as "Little Davey Horowitz," but goes on to add, "Scheer's ascription of innocence to me was not wholly off the mark."[102] At another point, Horowitz claims that his "guilelessness made me impervious to many of the undercurrents in the office, and caused me to misinterpret others."[103]

One of the undercurrents Horowitz missed was the fact that the Panthers were stockpiling weapons and planned to use those weapons. Horowitz missed this even though by the time he joined the Black Panthers, both Huey Newton and Eldridge Cleaver had been arrested for murdering policemen. After describing Captain Franco's "revolutionary philosophy"[104] Horowitz adds:

> In time, I began to see the dark reality of the revolution according to Franco, the revolution that was not some mystical battle of glory in some distant land or time. At the deepest level there was blood, nothing but blood, unsanitized by political polemic. That was where Franco worked, in the vanguard of the vanguard.... The Panthers were... a criminal army at war with society and with its thin blue line of civic protectors.[105]

That is certainly a movingly accurate account, but the careful reader is forced to wonder why Horowitz didn't come to this understanding before 1974, when he could have warned Betty Van Patter. When one of his colleagues held Horowitz responsible for her death, Horowitz flew into a rage, but the questions about his innocence and responsibility remain, even if he didn't set her up. Like Claude Rains in *Casablanca*, Horowitz was shocked when he found out that the Panthers had stockpiled "literally thousands of weapons."[106] Is Horowitz the only one who didn't know that the Panthers were violent? Hadn't he seen all of those photos of them carrying guns? Everyone else in America had. Horowitz gets closer to the heart of the issue when he writes that the Left "in creating a protective shield around the Panthers," was merely following the example of Trotsky, who "had described the Communist parties of the world as frontier guards for the Soviet Union."[107] A more apt example could have been taken from the Black-Jewish Alliance. The Jews had tried for decades to turn Negroes into revolutionaries because 1) they could then use them to fight the revolution by remote control and 2) because the white reactionaries focused all of their attention on blacks, when, in terms of revolution, they were the symptom and not the cause.

By the time Betty Van Patter's body washed up on the shore of San Francisco Bay, the revolution had degenerated into the random acts of violence and criminality that characterize the black ghetto today. The Jews had half-succeeded in turning the Negroes into revolutionaries, which meant that they destroyed their faith, corrupted their morals, and turned them into the half-way house to revolution which Marx described as the *Lumpenproletariat*, which is another word for criminal. Or pimp. The one thing Huey Newton and Eldridge Cleaver shared with their epigoni of the '90s and beyond was a desire to live off of women.

After Cleaver left the country, his faction of the Black Pathers became known as the Black Liberation Army and their efforts at revolution ended in "total disaster,"[108] but not before a number of people, mostly from warring factions of the Black Panthers, died. One of those victims was Sandra Pratt, wife of Geronimo Pratt, who "was tortured, shot and killed by Newton faction Panthers,"[109] a fact which caused Newton to apologize eventually to her husband. Newton himself ended up being killed by a drug-dealer, after having spent his final years in Oakland high on crack ranting about how he was "the leader of the coming revolution." When one of his former colleagues claimed that Horowitz was responsible for Betty's death, he reacted with rage.

"No radical leader," Horowitz writes, "proposed any second thoughts about a gang they had annointed as their revolutionary vanguard. Nor did any radical critics. This silence of the Left would endure throughout the life of the generation." The deflection of responsibility here is not just personal, although it is certainly that. By constantly referring to the Left, the left-wing media, etc.—"how it is that my former comrades on the left can remain so stubbornly devoted to 'experiments' that have failed, to doctrines that are false, and to causes that are demonstrably wrong-headed and even evil"[110]—Horowitz deflects attention from the role that the revolutionary Jew played in the racial catastrophe which followed the '60s revolutions in America. In this Horowitz is a lot like James Baldwin, who could never quite bring himself to admit that the white people he wrote about in Harlem were in reality Jews. Harold Cruse is still the only writer to face up to this fact unflinchingly.

In May 1980 Fay Stender committed suicide in Hong Kong. Stender had also defended Black Panther George Jackson and had edited his prison papers into a book and had fallen in love with him and become his mistress as well. The Jackson story, however, didn't end as happily (at least in the short run) as the Newton story did. On August 7, 1970, two days after Newton's triumphal emergence from prison as a result of Stender's brief overturning his sentence, Jonathan Jackson, George's brother, took a number of people hostage including Judge Harold Haley, all of whom were killed when they tried to drive away from the courthouse. George Jackson was gunned down on August 21, 1971, during an escape attempt three days before he was to go on trial. Seven years later a member of Jackson's prison gang broke into Stender's apartment and in attempting to kill her succeeded only in paralyzing her from the waist down. Disillusioned with the course of black revolution which she helped orchestrate, Stender had become a feminist over the course of the '70s and at the time of the attack was living with her lesbian lover. Fay Stender, like Horowitz, had been "a missionary to the black revolutionary cause."[111] Unlike Horowitz, she "hid Jackson's dark side from the public by excising from the pages of his manuscript the passages that revealed it."[112] For her pains, the monster she created had returned to destroy her. When the Black Frankenstein she had created failed in his mission, Stender finished the job off herself by committing suicide. In a line that could have come from feminist-inspired horror film like *Alien*, Horowitz writes that Stender fled to Hong Kong because "The far end of the world was the only place she could feel safe from further retribution."[113] But like Dr. Moebius in *Forbidden Planet*, Stender learned that there was no geographical escape from Monsters from the Id. Stender was killed by the revolutionary spirit which she had nurtured within herself through all of its various incarnations—Freedom Summer in 1964, the Black Panthers in the late '60s, feminism and lesbianism in the '70s, and a Masadah like suicide in 1980. Fay Stender had to learn that the revolution devours its own Jews the hard way. The Jews created Black Frankenstein, who returned to destroy them.

Fay Stender's death by her own hand brings us back to the question of Jewish identity. Stender's identification of her Jewishness with revolution was so complete that when it became apparent that all of her revolutionary options had failed she had no identity left and had to kill herself. David Horowitz, another "missionary to the black revolutionary cause,"[114] came to a similar conclusion. After concluding that Marxism was an illusion, David Horowitz embarked upon a life of promiscuity and nihilism that almost led to his own death as well in a half-intentional automobile accident. After an affair with one of the Rockefeller siblings wrecked his marriage, Horowitz concluded that

> There was no "revolution" of attitudes or institutions that could overcome the forces of this nature. Through the deaths of Betty and Ellen, through the pain of my divorce, I had acquired a certain philosophical fatalism.[115]

Taking his cue from what he had said about his father, Horowitz indicates that a Jew without revolution is a Jew without an identity. Craving absolution but unable to find it among his former colleagues on the Left, Horowitz concludes in the wake of Betty Van Patten's death that there is no Messiah because the revolution failed to materialize: "Betty's death killed this fantasy in me. There was no revolutionary community. There would be no redemptive future. There is no one to save us from who we are."[116]

This moment was short-lived, however, because Horowitz soon converted to yet another version of Jewish Messianic politics, this time Neoconservatism. Unable to stifle the desire to be a commissar, Horowitz began a new career by attacking professors who criticized Israel or contested the details of the attack on the World Trade Towers, urging students to inform on their professors in a gesture that recalled all of the worst aspects of the Soviet regime. During the fall of 2007 Horowitz traveled from one campus to another trying to drum up support for an attack—with nuclear weapons if necessary—on Iran.

The Black Panthers

Chapter Thirty

The Messiah Arrives Again

"American Jewish funniness is a form of cultural aggression." James Bloom, *Gravity Fails*[1]

February 1969 was a lot like September 1665; the Messiah's arrival was announced among the Jews; mass hysteria followed; the hysteria was, in turn, followed by mass disillusionment. In both instances, the Messianic era was characterized by the breaking of sexual taboos. Sabbetai Zevi liberated the Jews from the law in 1665 by telling them, among other things, they could give free rein to their sexual passions. Everything that was previously forbidden was now allowed. The Jewish Messiah did much the same thing in 1969. His name was Alex Portnoy. "The publication of a book is not often a major event in American culture," Albert Goldman wrote in the February 7, 1969 issue of *Life* magazine, however, now

> every shepherd of public opinion, every magus of criticism is wending his way toward its site. Gathered at an old New York City inn called Random House, at the stroke of midnight on the 21st of February in this 5729th year since the creation of the world, they will hail the birth of a new American hero, Alexander Portnoy. A savior and scapegoat of the '60s, Portnoy is destined at the Christological age of 33 to take upon himself all the sins of sexually obsessed modern man and expiate them in a tragi-comic crucifixion. The gospel that records the passion of this mock messiah is a slender, psychotic novel by Philip Roth called *Portnoy's Complaint* ... it is being hailed as the book of the present decade and as an American masterwork in the tradition of *Huckleberry Finn*. *Portnoy's Complaint* was also portrayed as something more sinister than *Huckleberry Finn*. One reviewer compared the binding and cutting of the books pages to "the secret cutting of heroin for injection into the national veins."[2]

But why was Portnoy hailed as the Messiah? Because, like Shabbetai Zevi, he had come to liberate Jews from the moral law. Then Jews could act as missionaries to the Gentiles, as the chosen people, as the revolutionary avant garde, etc. *Portnoy's Complaint* is a 270-page monologue on a psychiatrist's couch. Portnoy's first task is to liberate himself from the curse of guilt inflicted by his Jewish mother. In the pseudo-psychiatric definition that serves as the book's frontispiece, *Portnoy's Complaint* is described as "a disorder in which strongly-felt ethical and altruistic impulses are perpetually warring with extreme sexual longings, often of a perverse nature."[3] The problem is the patient's inability to achieve personal integrity by aligning passion with reason: "as a consequence of the patient's 'morality,' however, neither fantasy nor act issues in genuine sexual gratification."[4]

The premise--that morality is a kind of fascism that is imposed by the strong on the weak to control them--is the only possible premise that makes Portnoy's role as savior plausible. The Jew is going to save the *goyim* from their worst fascist impulses. Portnoy will start his salvific ministry with the shikses, the gentile women. "It's the Eddie Fisher in me coming out, that's all," Portnoy confides, alluding to the man who dumped Debbie Reynolds, a Hollywood *shiksa* of the '50s, for Elizabeth Taylor, "the longing in all us swarthy Jewboys for those bland blond exotics called shikses."[5] Elizabeth Taylor was another *shiksa*, a "stupendous purple-eyed girl who had the supreme *goyische* gift of all, the courage and know-how to get up and ride around on a horse."[6] Taylor's interest in Fisher proved *shikses* were secretly dying for liberation from moral constraint. The shiksa "was lusting for our kind no less than we for hers."[7] Mike Todd was "a cheap facsimile of my Uncle Hymie upstairs!"[8] Rather than "doing some pathetic little Jewish imitation of one of these half-dead, ice-cold *shaygets* pricks," i.e., act like a "some hook-nosed variety of *goy*," the Jew should aspire "to be what one's uncle was, to be what one's father was, to be whatever one was oneself," which is "a brainy, balding, beaky Jew, with a strong social conscience and black hair on his balls, who neither drinks nor gambles nor keeps show girls on the side; a man guaranteed to give them kiddies to rear and Kafka to read—a regular domestic *Messiah*!"[9] As if to ensure the reader that this use of the term Messiah is no slip of the tongue, Portnoy goes on to ask, "what was I supposed to be but her Jewish savior?"[10]

Portnoy's Complaint caused Jews severe discomfort because it asked what it meant to be a Jew, an unresolved question raised with monotonous regularity. Gershom Scholem, author of a *magnum opus* on *Sabbetai Sevi*, said *Portnoy's Complaint* was "the book for which all anti-Semites have been praying."[11] *Portnoy* was, he said, "worse than the Protocols of the Elders of Zion"[12] because it was the testimony of a Jew.

An unspoken part of the animus against Roth on the part of the Jews who disliked his book was the accusation that he was, in some sense of the word, a bad Jew because he had brought disrepute on the Jewish people. Trude Weiss-Rosmarin claimed Roth spoke "for a certain segment of alienated Jewishly ignorant Jews who write and teach."[13] To claim Roth was a bad Jew, his accusers needed to define what a good Jew was, and that got them in trouble. Gershom Scholem was hoist on his own petard when he claimed there was nothing normative—i.e., no religious litmus test—to define a Jew. If Scholem defined a Jew as someone sincerely believing he was a Jew, he could hardly accuse Roth of being a bad Jew. According to Scholem's definition, Portnoy was as much a Jew as Moses Maimonides or Sabbetai Zevi.

As a result of reluctance or inability to define a Jew, the rabbis turned the Jews into a congregation of competing Messiahs excommunicating each other for deviations from a code no one propery defined. So Jewish Messiahs were raised and deposed with increasing rapidity. Marx was supplanted by Freud; the gentile Stalin was supplanted by Trotsky, who was murdered by Stalin. Marx and Freud were supplanted by Wilhelm Reich. Trotsky got supplanted by Leo Strauss. And so on. Roth was simply proposing his own version of the Jewish savior as the redeemer for the sexually liberated '60s.

And what did the Jewish savior look like in 1969? A lot like a *shvartze*, the sexually liberated Negro promoted as the paradigm of sexual liberation. Portnoy's praise of shikses sounds like Eldridge Cleaver's effusions about white women and their dirty underwear in *Soul on Ice*. Sexual attraction was inextricably fused with aggression. Cleaver's aggression was expressed in rape. "Rape," said Cleaver, "was an insurrectionary act."[14] By raping white women, Cleaver "was defying and trampling upon the white man's law, upon his system of values, and ... defiling his woman."[15]

Whether Jews like Roth got the idea of defiling *shikses* from blacks like Cleaver or vice versa is difficult to say. *Soul on Ice* appeared in 1968 one year before *Portnoy's Complaint*, so maybe Roth got the idea of Portnoy, or at least the idea of defiling shikses from Cleaver, or maybe both were the product of the influence of Wilhelm Reich on Manhattan and, therefore, on the publishing industry at the time. In keeping with the rebirth of Reichian thought in 1969, both the Jewish revolutionary and the Negro revolutionary were above all else, sexual revolutionaries. But whereas Cleaver specialized in rape, Portnoy specialized in seduction. The difference is essentially ethnic. The former relies on brute force, the latter on manipulation. In order to truly corrupt the *goyim*, their "morality," and their women, the *shiksa* has to collaborate in her own defilement, something that doesn't happen in the case of rape. The best way to accomplish this is repeated incantation of the word "liberation." Like Sabbetai Zevi, the paradigm of every Jewish Messiah since the time of Christ, Portnoy was going to liberate the *shikses* by seducing them. He was their Jewish savior, come to save dumb *goyim* from the inanities of their culture. Cleaver discovered in white folk "an irresistible urge—to just stand up and shake the ice and cancer out of their alienated white asses," and discovered in that desire the reason for the popularity of the "Hula Hoop and the Twist," which "offered socially acceptable ways to do it."[16]

Portnoy's Complaint offered the Jewish version of the same thing. The stupid *shikses* have to be saved in spite of themselves, and Portnoy is going to save them by unleashing libido from the bonds of icy Christian morality. Or "morality," as Portnoy/Roth would put it. Portnoy will be the Jewish Messiah for the new post-Christian dispensation. The new Jewish savior came "To save the stupid *shikse*; to rid her of her race's ignorance; to make this daughter of the heartless oppressor a student of suffering and oppression; to teach her to be compassionate, to bleed a little for the world's sorrows."[17] And if the Jewish messiah could get laid liberating shikses, all the better. The defilement was more complete and more pleasurable. Together, Portnoy and his girlfriend, the miner's daughter from West Virginia whom he calls The Monkey, make "the perfect couple: she puts the id back in Yid, I put the oy back in goy."[18]

To define the *shiksa*, Roth must first define the Jew, this immediately gets him in trouble. Since the *goyim*, in Roth's view, are Christian, the Jew must be the antithesis of Christianity. Roth defines the Jew as the Semitic Negro, the paradigm of sexual liberation, he turns the Jew into the champion of Dionysian appetite. At this point, Portnoy begins to resembles the Jewish stereotype of Nazi propaganda, something which other Jews, for some reason, found offensive. "Portnoy's lusts for shikses" was, says Alan Cooper, "precisely what the traditional anti-Semite said all Jews felt, what the Aryan accused the would-be-defiling Jew of trying to perpetrate."[19] Maric Syrkin says something similar

> Like Julius Streicher's satanic Jewboy lusting after Aryan maidens, Portnoy seeks blonde shikses.... the dark Jew seeking to defile the fair Nordic is standard stuff ... . There is little to choose between [Goebbels'] and Roth's interpretation of what animates Portnoy. In both views the Jewish male is not drawn to a particular girl who is gentile, but by a gentile "background" which he must violate sexually.[20]

Syrkin is, of course, right. In portraying Portnoy's attraction to the *shiksa* as he does, Roth seems to take his cue from Hitler. Portnoy is a Jew right out of *Mein Kampf*, but once that fact is established, the reader is left to decipher Roth's motives. "Streicher's and Goebbel's motives," Cooper says, "were clear. But Roth's purpose in giving these thoughts to Portnoy is the bone of all the critical contention that was emerging."[21] The key to understanding Portnoy as savior is to first understand him as the Jewish debunker of Christian myths.

Portnoy is, as James Bloom would say, "a funny Jew;"[22] and the butt of his humor is the stupid *goy* who believes in illusions like Christianity. The dumb *goyim* really believe Christ rose from the dead and Charles van Doren knew the answers to the questions on the '50s quiz show, The $64,000 Question. Portnoy's happiness consists in debunking the beliefs of the *goyim* while defiling their women, something he did while on a congressional committee in Washington: "Yes," he tells his analyst,

> I was one happy yiddel down there in Washington, a little Stern gang of my own, busily exploding Charlie's honor and integrity, while simultaneously becoming lover to that aristocratic Yankee beauty whose forbears arrived on these shores in the seventeenth century. Phenomenon known as hating your Goy and Eating One Too.[23]

The passage was especially painful for Jews who aspired to go to Washington. Unsurprisingly, *Commentary* did not like the book, not even in 1969 before the neoconservatives got their invitation. *Commentary* evaluated Philip Roth and *Portnoy's Complaint* in December 1972. Irving Howe did not like what he saw but found it difficult to say why. The review has the vagueness of the non-ethnic stories Roth wrote as an undergraduate or the literary criticism he read as a grad student in English at the University of Chicago. Howe sees "vindictive bleakness" and "a swelling nausea before the ordinariness of human existence."[24] Almost as an afterthought, Howe mentions that *Portnoy's Complaint* deals with Jews and their relationship to America. Portnoy "contains plenty of contempt for Jewish life," yearning "to be released from the claims of distinctiveness," i.e., being a Jew with all it entails in terms of ethnocentrism.[25]

Even writing to other Jews in a Jewish magazine, Howe is unwilling to tackle the Jewish issue as Roth proposes it—i.e., the Jew as corrupter of morals, the Jew as despoiler of *shiksa* morals and *goyische* culture. All he can see is Portnoy's bad influence on younger Jews, who "have taken the book as a signal for 'letting go' of both their past and perhaps themselves, a guide to swinging in good conscience or better yet, without troubling about conscience."[26] Howe concedes the book has an equally deleterious impact on the morals of *goy* readers, but his foremost concern is the book might have ended "the wave of philo-Semitism" that "swept through our culture" in the decades after World War II, when "books by Jewish writers were often praised (in truth, overpraised) and a fuss made about Jewish intellectuals, critics, etc."[27] *Portnoy's Complaint,* said Howe,

> signaled an end to philo-Semitism in American culture, one no longer had to listen to all that talk about Jewish morality, Jewish endurance, Jewish wisdom, Jewish families. Here was Philip Roth himself ... confirming what had always been suspected about those immigrant Jews but had recently not been tactful to say.[28]

Of course, the exact opposite was the case. *Portnoy's Complaint* was the high water mark of philo-Semitism in America because Jews were associated in the public mind with sexual deviance at the high water mark of the sexual revolution. *Portnoy's Complaint* inaugurated the era of the Jewish cultural sexual revolutionary hero—Bob Dylan, Abbie Hoffman, Ira Einhorn, Jerzy Kozinski, Erica Jong, Jules Feiffer, Saul Steinberg, Woody Allen—whose heroics were manifest as ribald, mocking subversion of culture, faith, and morals. If Portnoy was the Messiah, then Lenny Bruce was John the Baptist.

As we have seen, Roth's frankness about Jewish hatred of the *goyim* was deeply embarrassing to Jews who aspired to assimilate. Hence, the attack in *Commentary,* published by the American Jewish Committee. If Howe's essay was full of reticence, Norman Podhoretz's essay in the same issue was obfuscatory, attempting to direct the reader away from what Podhoretz found most embarrassing and offensive in *Portnoy,* namely, its Jewishness. Podhoretz calls Roth the "Laureate of the New Class"[29] even though cursory and superficial reading of the book indicates it is about ethnicity, not class. Roth, according to Podhoretz, "is the New Class writer par excellence," pandering to "the snobbery and self-righteousness" that is "one of the distinctive marks of those members of the professional and technical intelligentsia in America who make up what has come to be known as the New Class."[30] Roth, Podhoretz says, "so perfectly embodies the ethos of a group which began coming to consciousness of itself as a distinctive social class around the time Roth first appeared on the scene."[31] Does Podhoretz mean class or ethnic group? Is Philip Roth the spokesman for a class or for the culturally emergent third generation Jews that *Commentary* aspired to speak for? Roth's writings, according to Wisse, were

> the first literary voice that seemed to speak for our bunch, our group, our set, the particular gang of adolescents with whom I shared a mutual affection and an idea of what we stood against ... a sensibility so familiar that it seemed to have come from our own midst, and in a spark of language ... attractive to us.... Our affection for Philip Roth was part of the tenderness we felt for ourselves.[32]

Portnoy has, as Roth would say, "J-E-W written across the middle of his face"[33] but Podhoretz chooses to ignore this fact because he wanted to ignore the ethnic issues which Roth raises. According to Alan Cooper, "the *Commentary* mentality seemed to suggest" Jews could only "get into office, administrative posts, and presidencies of formerly exclusive Ivy League universities and multinational corporations" by an "unholy alliance with WASP America."[34] The Jew could succeed "only by a sellout of one's immigrant-rooted integrity."[35] *Commentary* was embarrassed not by Roth's association with a class, but by his presumption to speak for Jews, endangering what *Commentary* felt were unprecedented opportunities for influence through assimilation. *Commentary* was embarrassed by Roth's frank expression of Jewish hatred of the *goyim*. It refused to see the humor, because the humor is a function of that hatred. Roth uses humor to ridicule what the *goyim* hold sacred; doing in public what the Jew does in private made *Commentary* uncomfortable. "To have Portnoy admit to these vindictive feelings," Cooper writes, "and to sharing his father's exhortations about the absurdity of the whole Christian premise—*feelings shared by a huge proportion of his Jewish readers!*—is from Syrkin's point of view dangerous to Jewish life in a pluralistic society."[36] The issue, in other words, isn't whether what Roth says is true, but whether it's good for Jews to say it so aggressively.

Roth attempted to avoid the issue, claiming unconvincingly that he is not Portnoy. (He dedicated the rest of his literary career to proving his novels were not autobiographical.) Portnoy is a Jew who talks like Hitler, and in that ethnic reversal lies much of the book's humor because Roth is writing about a time when ethnic reversal occurred on a large scale among America's Jews. The sons and daughters of second generation Jews who had made money in the garment industry had enough money to send the third generation to college, where they learned to imitate Bloomsbury and acquired the New Jersey equivalent of the sensibility of Virginia Woolf.

Roth was the paradigmatic third-generation Jew, caught between Newark and Bloomsbury. Roth's father worked for the *goyische* insurance firm, Metropolitan Life. He sent Roth to Bucknell, which Cooper calls "a small Protestant school,"[37] in Lewisburg, Pennsylvania. "Lewisburg emanated an unpretentious civility that we could trust,"[38] says Roth. But he could never make up his mind whether to assimilate or to remain the ethnic Jew. After discharge from the army, Roth wrote *Goodbye Columbus*, for which he received The Jewish Book Council's Daroff Award and the National Book Award in fiction. Roth was 26 years old at the time. He was also a graduate student at the University of Chicago, where he met Margaret Martinson Williams, a divorced mother of two, five years his senior, who would become the archetypal *shiksa* in his next few books.

Roth never lost his sense he was sleeping with the enemy, not even when he married the *shiksa* of his dreams. Lydia, the Margaret character in *My Life as a Man*, shared a room with her mother at the home of two spinster aunts in Skokie, "whose heroes were the aviator Lindbergh, the Senator Bilbo, the cleric Coughlin, and the patriot Gerald L. K. Smith. It had been a life of little but punishment, humiliation, betrayal, and defeat, an it was to this that I was drawn, against all misgivings."[39] In marrying a *shiksa*, the Roth character "was waging a kind of guerrilla war against the army of slobs, philistines, and barbarians who seemed to me to control the national mind, either through the media or the government," by bringing the *shiksa* "something of Bloomsbury—a community of the faithful, observing the sacraments of literacy, benevolence, good taste and social concern."[40] While they lived together, the Roth character, in one version of the story, has an affair with his wife's daughter. In another version, he sees her as

> a replica of those over-dressed little Gentile children who used to pass our house every Sunday on their way to church, and toward whom I used to feel an emotion almost as strong as my own grandparents' aversion. Secretly, and despite myself, I came close to despising the stupid and stubborn child when she would appear in that little white church going outfit, and so too did Lydia, who was reminded by Monica's costume of the clothes in which she had had to array herself each Sunday in Skokie, before being led off to Lutheran services with her aunts Helda and Jessie.[41]

His wife's ex-husband and her daughter "were the embodiment of what my grandparents, and great-grandparents, and great-great-grandparents had loathed and feared: *shagitz* thuggery, *shiksa* wiliness."[42] Sexual revenge on the daughter could be an act of virtue for a Jew, because "Dr. Goebbels or Air Marshal Goering might have a daughter wandering out somewhere in the world, but as a fine example of the species, Lydia would do nicely" as a way of getting back at "the puritan austerity, the prudery, the blandness, the xenophobia of the women of her clan [and] the criminality of the men."[43] Lydia "lived now in a neat little apartment within earshot of the bell in the clock tower of the university whose atheists, Communists and Jews her people had loathed, and ... wrote ten pages for me every week," giving the Roth character great satisfaction.[44]

When the relationship goes sour, his Jewish relatives tell him he has himself to blame. His brother Moe faults him for sleeping with "Another fucked-up *shiksa*."[45] Moe sees his brother either as a sexual anthropologist or as gripped by a fatal obsession. "First the *lumpenproletariat*, now the aristocracy. What are you, the Malinowski of Manhattan? Enough erotic anthropology. Get rid of her, Pep. You're sticking your plug in the same socket."[46] The Roth character concludes, in

"Maureen and Susan I came in contact with two of the more virulent strains of a virus to which only a few women among us are immune."[47] After his brother tells him "a nice civilized Jewish boy with some talent and some brains" has no business sleeping with "something savage ... a little Apache"[48] (his wife is Irish and German), the Roth character concludes he "made the grotesque mistake of elevating" his wife "to the status of a human being toward whom I had a moral responsibility."[49]

The Roth character is caught between two worlds, one Jewish, the other American. According to the latter, all men are created equal. According to the former, the *goyim* are sub-human beasts. Roth married a beast; his desire to free himself from someone he mistakenly thought was human accounts for pages of violent and unpleasant rage in his books. Roth's attempt to pass from one ethnic sphere to another accounts for much of the comedy. Roth was involved in the ethnic equivalent of a sex change operation.

Ethnic reversal means that there is something intrinsically funny about the idea of a Jewish cowboy. It's the ethnic equivalent of cross-dressing. Jews weren't in America in significant numbers in the 1870s; those who were here were selling blue jeans, not herding cattle. The cowboy was never really Catholic either. How could a Catholic spend all that time in the saddle somewhere in Texas and fulfill his obligation to go to Mass on Sunday? No, the cowboy was a Protestant American. He didn't have to go to church to be pious. He could commune with God in nature, as he did regularly in the comic strip Rick O'Shay. Like a good Emersonian, he was self-reliant; nature was his church. In the mid-20th century, the cowboy became a symbol for the aspirations of the once dominant Protestant middle class, which was losing cultural ground to Catholics, Jews, and Negroes. Michael Landon, who got his start with the TV cowboy series *Bonanza*, understood this. He went on to do the *Little House on the Prairie*, a TV series which extolled American Western Protestant virtues, like self-reliance, keeping your word, hard work, etc.

Turning the cowboy into a Jew is ethnic reversal fraught with comic possibilities. Lenny Bruce did a skit on Yankele, the Jewish cowboy. Leo Kotke released an album, "Ragtime Cowboy Jew," and Kinky Friedman turned the name Bob Wills and the Texas Playboys into Kinky Friedman and the Texas Jewboys. This tradition reached a culmination of sorts in 1974 when Mel Brooks directed *Blazing Saddles*. Its "humor" puts crude language into the mouths of clergymen and women and all of the other stock characters that made the Western an American morality play. The only funny parts involve ethnic reversal; the best example is when Mel Brooks plays an Indian Chief who speaks Yiddish. "*Shvartzes*," he says upon finding a Negro family in a covered wagon. Then, in a hilarious send up of the Indian-speaking mumbo jumbo, Brooks discourses in Yiddish about what to do about Negro settlers, finally bidding them leave with "*Sey gesind*."

Compared to Philip Roth, Mel Brooks is relatively benign, but then leukemia is benign when compared to Philip Roth. Cowboy movies might have expired of their own inanition or hyperviolence in the '70s, but Brook's parody expedited the process. If Jews just ridiculed Hollywood clichés, who could fault them? Their movies would still be funny. Yet Jews like Brooks had to push the envelope beyond what the *goyim* considered decent. One taboo of the Production Code was ridiculing clergy. Brooks takes savage delight in putting filthy language into a clergyman's mouth and then having his Bible shot to pieces as he raises it in prayer. Jews like Brooks took delight in actions deeply offensive to Protestants, for whom *sola scriptura* was a pillar of faith. In post-Production Code Hollywood, the Jew could ridicule the *goyim* and their God with impunity.

As America's cultural taboos fell under the blows of Jewish ridicule, the need to ridicule and subvert intensified. With the collapse of the Hollywood production code in 1965, the attacks on manners and the absurdities of movie clichés gave way to attacks on morals, religion, and Christ. Movies, as a result, became progressively less funny. Behind the Jewish humor one could discern the dim outline of "cultural aggression"—the distillation of that ancestral grievance, the ethnically shared satisfaction of putting one over on the dumb *goy*. The more the taboos fell, the more cultural aggression became apparent; the more that became apparent, the less funny the gags became.

A good example of how Jewish humor became less funny can be gleaned from its treatment of the *Shvartze*. Ridicule of the Negro had been a staple of Jewish comedy since Al Jolson put on blackface. It is central to *Blazing Saddles*, which probably holds a record for a Hollywood film using the word "nigger." It is also integral to David Zucker's *Scary Movie 3*. By the time Zucker ridicules the *Shvartze*, however, most cultural taboos have fallen. So Zucker ridicules black funerals. "Who said this was funny?" I wondered as the corpse of a dead black woman was thrown around a funeral home. Treating a corpse with respect goes back to *Antigone*, at least in literature.

Portnoy's Complaint jumps into the fray by exposing Jewish embarrassment at their ethnocentrism. Portnoy is commissioner for Human Opportunity in New York City. He threatens his father: "if he ever uses the word nigger in my presence again, I will drive a real dagger into his fucking bigoted heart!"[50] As a teenager, Portnoy writes a radio play called *Let Freedom Ring!,* "a morality play whose two major characters are named Prejudice and Tolerance."[51] During a recitation of his play on a long ride to western New Jersey, "Tolerance," Portnoy says, "defend[s] Negroes for the way they smell."[52] Portnoy is the Jewish Messiah, who vows "to use 'the power of the pen' to liberate from injustice and exploitation, from humiliation and poverty and ignorance, the people I now think of (giving myself gooseflesh) as The People."[53] This makes Portnoy "the most moral man in all of New York, all pure motives and humane and compassionate ideals. Doesn't he know that what I do for a living is I'm good?"[54] Roth is mocking here the notion of a Jewish Messiah, or he is mocking the fact that Portnoy thinks of himself as one? Either way, it's a brilliant satire of the messianic universalism that invariably grows out of Jewish ethnocentrism. Portnoy becomes the commissioner for Human Opportunity to prove that his mother was wrong not to eat off the same plates as her *Shvartze* maid.

And yet satire has to be based on a moral sense. If the satirist sees morality as a convention every bit as arbitrary and artificial as the clichés of a cowboy movies, he will ridicule morals with just as much irreverence, and in the process of eroding the moral basis of the culture he ridicules, he will cease to be funny. The production code held the Hollywood Jews back for a while, but the Production Code expired in 1965. Since then the same corrosive solvent of ridicule has been poured onto layer after layer of culture eating its way down through the rituals of WASP culture which seemed inexplicable to European Jews, as in the Marx Brothers' *Night at the Opera*; all the way down into morals, the substratum of manners, and through that into religion. At some point during this corrosive erosion of culture, Jewish humor ceased to be funny.

James Bloom's *Gravity Fails: The Comic Jewish Shaping of Modern America* points out "American Jewish funniness is a form of cultural aggression" without any sense that the people whose culture was under attack might not find that aggression funny. Like Roth, Bloom puts morals in quotes; like Roth he seems unable to distinguish between manners and morals. Likewise, he seems incapable of understanding how the cultural aggression overwhelmed the humor. In movies like *Scary Movie 3*, humor evaporated leaving only the residue of Jewish cultural aggression behind. Firing a shotgun at a picture of Mother Teresa may be David Zucker's idea of humor, but all that remains after the long tasteless skit is the taste of cultural aggression—one more Jew making one more attack on *goyische* illusions, like thinking it is meritorious to take care of the poor in Calcutta.

Bloom correctly sees *Mad* magazine within the tradition of Jewish humor as cultural aggression, but ignores *Mad*'s ridicule of the tropes of Madison Avenue before it discovered the sexual revolution and blasphemy, whereupon it stopped being funny. Even though the Torah is a book about limits, there was something intrinsically Jewish about the inability to recognize limits—decency, propriety, all the traits Groucho Marx associated with Margaret Dumont—probably because the revolutionary Jew was at war with the Torah as an inhibiting superego to be destroyed so liberation could flourish. People who thought *Ozzie and Harriet* and the Gospel according to St. John could all be rolled up into one big ball and dismissed as *goyische* culture, which is what Roth does in *Portnoy*, wouldn't understand moral nuance or the relationship between the moral and the cultural orders.

Portnoy, in fact, links his slide into sexual depravity with the Torah. If there a distinction between the Ten Commandments and the prohibition against eating shellfish, Portnoy doesn't see it. Jewish insistence on following the law in its entirety leads Portnoy to moral relativism. If it's all irrational taboo as Freud says, then why shouldn't eating lobster lead to sexual depravity? Is Portnoy rationalizing, in the following passage, or is he giving an account of the Law that St. Paul could endorse?

> Now, maybe the lobster is what did it. That taboo so easily and simply broken, confidence may have been given to the whole slimy, suicidal Dionysian side of my nature; the lesson may have been learned that to break the law all you have to do is—just go ahead and break it! ... . [At] age fifteen, he sucks one night on a lobster's claw and within the hour his cock is out and aimed at a *shikse* on a Public Service bus. And his superior Jewish brain might as well be made of matzoh brei."[55]

The Torah is about limits, but the Revolutionary Jew doesn't respect limits because he learned from Freud and Marx that "morality" is an irrational taboo, like not eating lobster. Since the Jew learned as a child, in Portnoy's words, "it doesn't make any difference either ... how big or how small the rule is that you break, it's the breaking alone that gets His goat," all moral law is one large irrational taboo.[56] If you're going to be hanged for a dietary sheep, why not be hanged for a sexual lamb? Yet Portnoy's conscience is troubled nonetheless: "Why," he wonders, "must the least deviation from respectable conventions cause me such inner hell? When I hate those fucking conventions! When I know better than the taboos!"[57]

With reason dismissed as irrational taboo, all that is left is appetite. The superego is seen as a Nazi storm trooper; as a result, ego or reason can only choose appetite: "But then all the unconscious can do anyway, so Freud says, is want. And want! and WANT!"[58] The good Jew thus must wage war on conscience, first in himself through psychoanalysis, and then as the savior of the benighted *goyim*, especially good looking shikses. Roth redefines the Yid as id waiting to be liberated. The role of the revolutionary Jewish Messiah is to "PUT THE ID BACK IN YID! Liberate this nice Jewish boy's libido," Portnoy pleads with his psychoanalyst, "will you please? Raise the prices if you have to! I'll pay anything!"[59]

Given the tenuous Jewish understanding of the distinction between eating shellfish and committing adultery, it is not surprising that psychoanalysis has succeeded in debunking morals. So, Portnoy says, "I simply will not enter into a contract to sleep with just one woman for the rest of my days."[60] Portnoy has been liberated from marriage, the institution that might have turned him into a decent human being. He is free to be bad, "Because to be bad, Mother, that is the real struggle: to be bad—and to enjoy it! That is what makes men of us boys, Mother. But what my conscience, so-called, has done to my sexuality, my spontaneity, my courage."[61]

Convinced his vices are virtues, convinced by Reich and Freud that sexual repression is evil and "morality" is an irrational taboo, the Revolutionary Jew can transform American culture by remaking it in his distorted image. Just tell a few jokes and the idols of WASP American culture all crumble into dust. Another word for Jewish humor was "demythologizing."[62] Like Jake the Snake, the ghetto Jew from Newark, Philip Roth, according to Cooper, demythologized the world of the respectable. As Henny Youngman, whining about family and friends while eliciting laughable squeaks from the violin (the very violin that was to make of every little Jewish boy, myself included, a world-famous, urbane, poetic, dignified and revered Yehudi) demytholgized our yearnings for cultural superiority.[63]

The rise of Jewish humor meant the transformation of America into something Jewish. That transformation has been so complete that now an alternative is difficult to imagine. Is there an American humor that is not Jewish? Bloom is both fatuous and to the point when he quotes Charles Simic, "it is impossible to imagine a Christian or a fascist theory of humor."[64] By mid 20th century, "Jewish funniness," says Bloom, had triumphed over "the scenes and tropes sanctifying this New England legacy."[65] And "Alfred Kazin ratified this triumph in 1966 by dismissing earnest intellectuals and honoring such funny Jewish 'clowns and minstrels' as the 'Marx Brothers, Eddie Cantor, Al Jolson and Fanny Brice' for 'establishing the Jew in the national consciousness as a distinctly American figure … as a representative national entertainer'."[66]

Philip Roth's alter-egos are, in Bloom's words, "culture warriors" eager to "trespass on the hallowed ground of WASP dominance."[67] Roth is the successor to Groucho Marx, "standing poised to vandalize yet another monument to New England's Brahmin ascendancy,"[68] as Groucho did in *Horsefeathers* by calling himself Quincy Adams Wagstaff. The eclipse of the Irish as the nation's comedians meant what Jews thought was funny was now funny for everyone. That meant the systematic violation of taboos. It was all *goyische* idiocy anyway.

"They worship a Jew," Jake Portnoy tells his son, "do you know that, Alex? Their whole big-deal religion is based on worshipping someone who was an established Jew at that time. Now how do you like that for stupidity? How do you like that for stupidity? How do you like that for pulling the wool over the eyes of the public…. They took a Jew and turned him into some kind of God after he is already dead … I assure you, Alex, you are never going to hear such a *mishegoss* of mixed-up crap and disgusting nonsense as the Christian religion in your entire life. And that's what these big shots, so-called, believe!"[69]

What Alex Portnoy hears from his father is ethnic prejudice; what Roth writes is cultural aggression, an attack on the Resurrection, the central tenet of the faith of the majority of America's citizens. Every ethnic group has its prejudices. Jews can't be expected to believe in the Resurrection. If they did, they wouldn't be Jews, at least not in the contemporary meaning of the term. In the America that was once a republic based on ethnic pluralism, federalism and the cultural autonomy of the local community, ethnic prejudice was not a serious problem. In Imperial America, which came into its own during the period following World War II, it became a serious problem because in its imperialist phase, America was not pluralistic; one ethnic group dominated the dominant culture for its own benefit and demonized any competing ethnicities.

The existence of one dominant culture meant the prejudices of the group that controls the instruments of culture become normative. The new instruments of culture—movies, radio, TV—were largely in the hands of Jews. With the rise of media power, Jewish cultural prejudice became the norm. Moral subversion and blasphemy also became the norm. This is what the Catholic/Jewish battle over Hollywood films was about. Joe Breen, first head of the Hollywood Production code, framed the issue during the 1930s: should sexually degenerate Eastern European Jews determine the movie fare for the entire nation? Once Hollywood broke the production code in 1965, the answer became an unequivocal "Yes." "During the middle of the twentieth century," Bloom says, "a handful of Jews, who became famous by being funny, rediscovered, recovered and remade America."[70] That entailed redefining what it meant to be funny. Jewish cartoonist Jules Feiffer lamented that in 1950, "Humor was still Bob Hope," and Bloom applauds the fact that by

> importing Jewish angst, Freud, literacy, and irony into the discourse of mainstream comedy, Woody Allen, Lenny Bruce, Elaine May, Mike Nichols, and others "led comedy away form the ersatz to the authentic." This persuasive and lasting influence led the glossy monthly *Esquire* ... to pronouncing 1965 that "for good or ill, the Jewish style with its heavy reliance upon Yiddish and Yiddishisms has emerged not only as a comic style, but as the prevailing comic style." The result, according to Lee Siegel's millennial retrospect was "new life for American culture."[71]

That Jewish transformation of American humor also meant the subversion of sexual morals. Lenny Bruce and Philip Roth focusing "on genitalia as a key site of desire made the comedy of concupiscence central to Jewish funniness in the early 1960s."[72] Bloom cites the heroine in LeRoy Jones's play *Dutchman* who denounces "all those Jewish poets" whose "poems are always funny and always about sex."[73] Jones, says Bloom, "recognized in Jewish funniness a reversal of the prevailing idealistic Platonic trajectory. This overriding Western legacy maintains that, rightly regarded, fleshly desire must lead to spiritual reflection or at least to expressions of worthier aspirations than carnal appetite."[74] Like Philip Roth and Adolf Hitler, Bloom posits the Jew as quintessentially a sexual degenerate. He cites

> Daphne Merkin's reading of Jewish Eros, from the "core of the Jewish stance toward lust," its "emphasis on demystifying the erotic."[75] For all its conjugal emphasis, Merkin stresses the degree to which this stance rests on "a shrewd recognition that marital life and ... ritual" cannot "fully tame the stirrings of desire."[76]

Before long the *goyim* felt they had to imitate the Jews if they wanted to be published or performed. Jewish control of the media arose in the performing arts as early as the 1930s, when, according to Bloom,

> Cole Porter ... decided that he needed to steep his art in American popular music's ascendant Jewishness—to write "Jewish tunes" like those of Jerome Kern, Richard Rodgers and George Gershwin. In the course of consequently produc-

ing "the most enduring Jewish music" ever, Porter also heralded, in his 1934 standard, "Anything Goes," an emerging sexual frankness in entertainment and arts.[77]

In *Operation Shylock*, Philip Roth claims he got his program for cultural subversion by listening to Irving Berlin:

> The radio was playing "Easter Parade" and I thought ... this is Jewish genius on a par with the Ten Commandments.... God gave Moses the Ten Commandments, and then he gave Berlin "Easter Parade" and "White Christmas." The two holidays celebrate the divinity of Christ—the divinity that's at the very heart of the Jewish rejection of Christianity—and what does Irving Berlin brilliantly do? He de-Christs them. Easter he turns into a fashion show and Christmas into a holiday about snow ... [this] schlockified Christianity is Christianity cleansed of Jew hatred.[78]

Mad magazine continued the trend of "Jewish funniness" as "a form of cultural aggression" after World War II by regularly conflating images of George Washington and Alfred E. Newman. Actor John Goodman recalled the arrival of *Mad* in his hometown in Missouri as "the only cultural event of the month" and claimed it "formed his boyhood consciousness" by teaching him "Jewish funniness," which meant "the smart-aleck skepticism, suspicion of authority, and Yiddishisms like furghlugginer [*sic*] and portezebie [*sic*]."[79] In its campaign to ridicule "the Father of his country,"[80] *Mad* also ran variations on Larry Rivers' 1953 parody of Leutze's painting of Washington Crossing the Delaware. *Mad* became the vehicle whereby Jewish Greenwich Village Bohemia found its way into the cultural mainstream. Rivers, born Irving Grossberg in the Bronx, played the saxophone when he wasn't painting parodies. He tried to explain his version of Washington crossing the Delaware in his autobiography. He painted it to calm "paranoid fantasies" because "I was a Jew, and unless I could produce evidence to the contrary, I was a communist."[81]

His parody of Washington Crossing the Delaware was "evidence to the contrary"[82] in case he got called before the House un-American Activities Committee like "some blacklisted Hollywood Jews."[83] He had his cake and ate it too, ridiculing icons in the act of reproducing them for self-protection: "Despite my smoking of pot and my sucking of cunt and the occasional cock .... I could always point to George."[84] His guilty conscience, in other words, prompted paranoia, which he assuaged by subverting the manners and morals of the dominant culture, the superego he incorrectly assumed was the source of his guilty conscience in the first place. Alfred Kazin makes the same point in his autobiography *New York Jew* when he claims "the debunkers had destroyed Parson Weems."[85] Jules Feiffer continued the trend in *Carnal Knowledge*, which, in Bloom's words, "savaged both mid-century collegiate and courtship mores."[86] *Carnal Knowledge*, Bloom continues, "aims, in Philip Roth's phrase, to 'demythologize the respectable,'"[87] a project Roth has pursued his entire career.

When *Commentary* re-evaluated Philip Roth in 1972, the dichotomy "American vs. Jew" no longer had much meaning. There was no reason to agonize about whether being Jewish prevented *Commentary* readers from sharing the American Dream because the American Dream had become a Jewish *shtick* anyway. Milton Berle competed head to head with Bishop Fulton Sheen on prime time TV and lost. Fifty years later, Bloom says laconically, "shows like Sheen's no longer air in network prime time or even on the national cable spectrum."[88] They have been replaced by "the Shticks of numerous funny Jews, such as Seinfeld, Paul Reiser, Fran Dresher, Richard Lewis, and Jenna Elfman," not to mention the ineffable Howard Stern, whose "conquest of cable and radio, of movie theaters and bookstores, marks for better or worse the unequivocal arrival of Jewish funniness" as well as the triumph of Jewish sexual degeneracy.[89] Portnoy, the Domestic Jewish savior, obviated the problem of assimilation that plagued his father's generation of American Jews by conquering the culture, just as Albert Goldman said he would.

By the 1970s, being Jewish and being American meant one and the same thing, certainly in humor, but in other areas too. The average American had become a sexually addicted zombie, like Portnoy, content to let the offspring of ghetto Jews manage his freetime. What the Hollywood Jews were to Bill Clinton, the New York neoconservative Jews became for George W. Bush. The average American could chose Hollywood pornography or neoconservative wars in the Middle East for his nightly entertainment.

Roth was genius enough to propose the final solution to the Jewish assimilation problem in *Portnoy's Complaint*, and the Jews at *Commentary* chose to kvetch about "vindictive bleakness" and "the new class" instead of lauding him as the Einstein of his generation. Roth solved what Bloom called "the eternal Jewish conflict" namely, "maintaining their identity while participating in a wider national life" in a breathtakingly simple manner.[90] The Jew no longer had to become "an American" because America had essentially become Jewish. Portnoy, the comic Jewish Messiah, conquered America by corrupting the morals of American women. "What I'm saying doctor," Portnoy tells his psychoanalyst, "is that I don't seem to stick my dick up these girls, as much as I stick it up their backgrounds—as though through fucking I will discover America. *Conquer America*—maybe that's more like it."[91]

Yes, that's more like it. This ruthless sexual exploitation of the unsuspecting *shikses* from Irvington, New Jersey, where "there was a tree conspicuously ablaze in every parlor [and] the houses themselves are outlined with colored bulbs advertising Christianity"[92] is justified as ethnic warfare, cultural guerrilla warfare, to subvert the morals of the enemy as revenge for the *goyim*'s treatment Roth's people. In screwing the WASP patrician Portnoy calls The Pilgrim, Portnoy is taking revenge on the insurance firm that employed his father because "she could have been a Lindabury, don't you see? A daughter of my father's boss!"[93] Only in ethnic solidarity can Portnoy find the anodyne for his troubled sexual conscience, the anodyne psychoanalysis promised but could not deliver. Roth is similar to Al Goldstein, editor of *Screw*, who used Jewish ethnicity as an excuse for his pandering. "Jews," Goldstein told Luke Ford, "are into pornography because Christ sucks."[94] In other words, any transgression of the moral law can be justified as long as it can be construed as aggression against the *goyim*. "No," Portnoy says about his affair with Sally Maulsby, The Pilgrim. There was no love involved after all. It was all just ethnic aggression: "Sally Maulsby was just something a nice son once did for his dad ... there could never be any 'love' in me for The Pilgrim."[95] What Sally viewed as love was "a little vengeance on Mr. Lindabury for all those nights and Sundays Jack Portnoy spent collecting down in the colored district. A little bonus extracted from Boston & Northeastern, for all those years of service and exploitation."[96] Sexual exploitation in exchange for economic exploitation: the *quid pro quo* of the Revolutionary Jew.

Cooper cheers Roth on from the sidelines: "Seeing himself at the mercy of the *goyim*, he could approach them only obliquely through their daughters: he could 'conquer America' by debasing 'The real McCoy' or her nicknamed variants."[97] Cooper applauds Roth for "trying to achieve manhood by being bad. For a Jew of their upbringing, the second quest is harder because it is perverse. And being perverse, being a total inversion of normal expectation, it is comic," at least in the Jewish sense.[98]

The Golden Age of Jewish Humor and Cultural Subversion began in 1965 when the Jews wrested cultural control of the movies from the Catholics by releasing *The Pawnbroker*. *Portnoy's Complaint* followed four years later. Four years after that, America got Erica Jong's *Fear of Flying*, the female version of *Portnoy*, and four after that, in 1977, Woody Allen did *Annie Hall*, the real film version of Roth's book. (The visit to Annie Hall's home in Chippewa Falls is taken straight from Portnoy's visit to The Pumpkin's family in Iowa.) Shortly after the release of *Annie Hall*, *Time* eulogized Allen as an American Genius for directing *Annie Hall*, in which the schlemiel once again schtups the shiksa before the eyes of Mr. & Mrs. America, her proud parents. Woody Allen not only gets away with it, he landed on the cover of *Time* for doing it.

Jewish Humor

Chapter Thirty-One

The Jewish Take-Over of American Culture

I n 1970, when President Nixon ordered the invasion of Cambodia, setting off campus demonstrations across the country, including at Kent State, where four students were shot to death by National Guardsmen, Ron Radosh was teaching history at the City University of New York, the traditional haven for that city's Jewish revolutionaries. When the revolution came to his campus in the spring of 1970, Radosh was no longer playing the five-string banjo. He had changed his tune in just about every sense of the word, evne if he felt he was realizing the revolutionary dreams of his youth. Condemned to prove Plato right, Radosh found he needed new music for a different revolution, and so he concluded his harangue to his students by screaming "Got to Revolution/ Got to Revolution/ Pick up the cry/ Got to Revolution,"[1] which he picked up from a Jefferson Airplane song, "Volunteers." Upon hearing his revolutionary war cry, the students, Radosh says, "went wild."[2] Without any sense there might be a connection, Radosh then tells us that around the same time, "my marriage was beginning to unravel."[3]

Radosh's wife Alice was seeing a psychologist who encouraged her to get "stoned on grass and LSD" as "an advanced therapeutic technique."[4] The same therapist encouraged Radosh's wife to divorce him. Even after writing his memoir, Radosh failed to see how Jewish revolutionaries were subverted by their own ideas. Radosh supported the revolution without seeing it was self-destructive because it defined the family as an instrument of oppression. Radosh felt he and Alice probably would have stuck it out "if left to our own devices,"[5] but they were not left to their own devices because the revolution had been redefined. What Radosh calls "the Movement" was "turning towards the politics of personal relationship."[6] Instead of smashing capitalism, revolutionary Jews like Radosh and his wife, taking their cue from "the radical feminism of the early women's liberation movement," decided to "smash monogamy," and they smashed themselves and their children in the process.[7] To liberate herself from "bourgeois possessiveness,"[8] Radosh's wife carried on an affair with David Gelber, another revolutionary Jew, who would become a top-level TV producer with CBS news and then with *60 Minutes*.

Radosh "waged a desperate fight to save the marriage,"[9] he says, but given the arsenal of weapons available to a Jewish revolutionary, i.e., Marx and Freud with a heavier emphasis on Freud, the outcome was a foregone conclusion. Alice "run away with another man, poor boy," as he might have sung to the accompaniment of his five-string banjo a few years back. To cope, Radosh "took a long-awaited sabbatical to try to dig out of the wreckage of my life."[10] Radosh "spent most days severely depressed, sleeping all night and half the day, and then shut up alone watching television until I crawled into bed."[11]

In his autobiography, Dylan recounts meeting Archibald MacLeish, who told him "if anything costs you your faith or your family, then the price is too high."[12] MacLeish was right. The Left was destroyed by its fatal attraction to sexual liberation. When the Left went down in flames, it took folk music with it. Some would say it took the Jews as well. Alan Dershowitz is of that opinion, writing about the demographic collapse among American Jews in *The Vanishing American Jew*. Bob Dylan's marriage to Sara Lowndes, which produced five children, broke down a little after Radosh's for roughly the same reasons.

Both men compensated by substituting quantity for quality. Bob Dylan linked up with musicians who came to be known as "the Band," whom he lured away from Screaming Ronnie Hawkins. The Band, according to Spitz, was "one of the earliest bands to perfect the ethic of sex, drugs and rock 'n roll as an alternative life-style."[13] Dylan's music continued its downward spiral, becoming "aggressive, cynical, hard-edged, highly mannered and surrealistic."[14] The lyrics, as a result of the loud amplified music, became first incomprehensible and then inconsequential. Why should the man who revolutionized the folk song with his lyrics care about meaning "when the electricity simply picked you up and carried you into outer space for a hour or two."[15] And if the electricity didn't, drugs would. When Mick Jagger came to Dylan's apartment to pay homage, he found the revolutionary bard unconscious on the floor, offering devout homage to the god Dionysos, who had control of his music and the revolution that flowed from it.

Linking up with Danny Kalb, the Jewish Blues singer who had shared his apartment with Bob Dylan in Madison in the early '60s, Ron Radosh made up "for what I now regard as lost time with Alice," by having sex "with virtually any woman I was attracted to who crossed my path."[16] Radosh says "It was a good time to be single" because

> everyone was available, and almost no one thought twice about immediately hopping into bed on the first day. I had never thought myself particularly attractive to women, but suddenly I had a full dance card and even got a reputation as a womanizer. Some of the things I did were questionable, but in the period when smashing monogamy was the new standard of the Movement, I could always rationalize my behavior as helping to free society from bourgeois definitions of reality.[17]

Radosh still doesn't understand the consequences of his actions. "My major preoccupation, aside from socialism," Radosh says, getting to the point and also avoiding it, "became looking for new women.... I rehabilitated the sexual self-esteem that my former wife had crushed. But I wasn't especially happy."[18] During his Lothario period, Barbara Garson, author of the anti-Lyndon Johnson play, *MacBird*, called Radosh to see if he could give her "banjo lessons."[19] Within 15 minutes of arriving at her apartment, Radosh was having sex with the playwright.

The sexual revolution, in other words, had replaced the Marxist revolution, and, in doing that, it had destroyed everything that Radosh's parents had worked for. "The Marxist revolution we had hoped for was stillborn," Radosh writes, "but the sexual revolution was alive and well."[20] The sexual revolution killed the Left, just as it killed the fight for workers' rights, the antiwar movement, and the Jewish birth rate, but the Left was too intoxicated to notice. When the drug-induced intoxication wore off, their minds were so darkened by their passions that years later they still couldn't understand what had happened.

Radosh's memoir is one indication of that; Bob Dylan's is another. Radosh's memoir provides the more comprehensive picture of what happened to the revolutionary Jew in the folk music movement when the sexual revolution hit. Radosh had an extended liaison with a woman he called Judy, "an extremely pretty, outgoing and freewheeling woman, who believed in free sex anytime and anywhere" who occasionally "managed to find work in theater and film in exchange for sexual favors."[21] Judy was a true devotee of Dionysos, "a serious alcoholic, who after some days of sobriety would end up dead drunk, crazed and violent."[22] Radosh persuaded Judy to drive to Washington State, where he planned to work in an archive. Radosh described the trip as their "own version of *On the Road*,"[23] Jack Kerouac's 1957 Beatnik novel. Judy would "sometimes drink herself into a stupor and at other times insist on rounds of non-stop sex," including one session on top of Mount Rushmore.[24]

Once they arrived on the West Coast, Radosh looked up comrades from the commie folk music network only to discover they were living the same lifestyle he was. Bob Scheer, former editor of *Ramparts*, was in a radical Berkeley commune, the "Red Family," which, like Radosh, eschewed workingman's rights in favor of sexual politics and burning questions like "whether or not it was 'bourgeois' to want to close the bathroom door while using the toilet."[25]

Scheer took a fancy to Judy, and when he made a move on her in Radosh's car, Radosh kicked him out, stranding him by the side of the road. The only thing that kept Scheer's interest, other than sex, was Kim Il Sung. Scheer would enthuse for hours about "the paradise he had seen during a recent visit to North Korea" and "about the greatness of Kim Il Sung."[26] Scheer had arranged asylum in North Korea for Eldridge Cleaver, a founder of the Black Panthers on the lam from the US Government and a faction of the Panthers that wanted to eliminate him in a power struggle. Scheer was the rule not the exception. "Others in the Movement had," says Radosh, "found heaven on earth in places like Cuba and even China," so why shouldn't Scheer find paradise in Pyongyang.[27]

Once again, we have to distinguish between form and content. The form was the revolutionary Jew, blind and carnal, forever seeking heaven on earth and forever ending up disappointed. The content was the particular heaven on earth known as Moscow, Cuba, Hanoi, Nicaragua, and then later, when he got the neoconservative religion, post-Communist Poland and eastern Europe. Radosh's memoir is written in the form of a religious conversion story, except for the fact that the religion he converted to is neoconservatism, which, upon closer inspection, turns out to be just one more form of Jewish revolutionary activity and subversion. The only form that provided any political coherence to Radosh's life, which oscillated between Stalinism and Neoconservatism, was the persona of the Revolutionary Jew, determined to engage in subversive behavior even when he subverted his own marriage and family.

The revolutionary Jew was not averse to subverting his brain as well. Judy moved out of Radosh's apartment after they returned to New York, but not before encouraging him to take LSD. Chemically induced derangement was now part of lifestyle "liberation" which was, sometimes literally, killing the Left. After taking LSD, Radosh lived in "virtual terror"[28] for five days. His liberated mind noticed "monsters, snakes, devils," and "anything my imagination conjured up" would leap out of the walls and attack him, leaving him "frozen in fear, not being able to speak, walk or even move."[29] Radosh had hallucinations for weeks afterward, or at any time the residue of the LSD got metabolized from his fat cells.

After reading in *Liberation* magazine that attending political demonstrations was the best way to get laid, Radosh took a sleeping bag to a sit-in at Columbia, where, as *Liberation* had predicted, he found someone to sleep with. Allis Rosenberg was another revolutionary Jew, recently divorced from yet another revolutionary Jew, Alan Wolfe. All the revolutionary Jews, it seems, were looking for love in the wrong places. When the president of Columbia accused Radosh of criminal activity in the sit-in, Radosh became worried "that the letter could have a damaging effect on my own prospects for promotion and advancement at the City University of New York, and could easily be used against me."[30] As a result, Radosh called Alan Dershowitz, who used his well-known reputation as a legal intimidator to get Radosh off the hook, even though Radosh readily admitted, in his memoir at least, that he was guilty of all of the offenses Columbia's president laid at his feet.

Radosh's recourse to Alan Dershowitz is more than an indication of Jewish solidarity trumping political differences: it also indicated that the revolutionary Jew will turn on the movements he has created when Jews no longer control them. Without Jews like the Spingarn brothers, there would have been no NAACP, but when the Jews were no longer welcome in civil rights circles, the Jews turned on their erstwhile protégés.

In 1973, Radosh's second wife got involved in a turf battle with the feminists. Allis Rosenberg Radosh was a feminist because that was the revolutionary activity for women of her class and ethnic background in the early '70s. Allis was part of "a socialist, feminist, consciousness raising group, and was planning to obtain a Ph.D. in history at the CUNY Graduate Center" when Radosh met her.[31] She then taught in the women's studies department at Richmond College of CUNY in proletarian, i.e, ethnic, Catholic Staten Island. Richmond had already been taken over by the Left, which, in New York, meant Jews like Radosh and Rosenberg, even though "most of the students [there] were Italian Catholics far removed from any sympathy or association with the faculty teaching them."[32]

At Richmond College, however, the revolution proceeded to devour its own children. In this instance, that meant that the lesbians wrested power over tenure and promotion from the Jews, who then became counter-revolutionaries. Allis Radosh vented her anger in *The Village Voice*. "What Allis recorded in the *Voice* and what she daily came home to tell me about," Radosh says, barely keeping his indignation in check, "was almost unbelievable."[33] The women's movement had been hijacked by lesbians. Of course, the Jews had done the same thing a few years earlier, but as Breshnev and George W. Bush would claim, revolutions were supposed to be irreversible. That means that those who wrested power from others were never supposed to have it wrested from them, but it turns out that history didn't work that way. According to revolutionary principles, the fact that lesbians were the "most oppressed women," automatically catapulted them "into the vanguard of the women's movement," displacing the children of the Jewish communists who had popularized the idea of the revolutionary vanguard in the first place.[34] The revolutionary Jew was once again hoisted on his own petard. Or so it seemed. All the two incidents really meant was that the Jews would create new anti-black, anti-feminist organizations they could control under the rubric of neoconservatism. Once again the content of revolutionary activity would change, but the form—the revolutionary Jew—would remain.

By the time the revolutionary Jew got what he wanted, he no longer wanted it. The Vietnam War was a classic case. In the spring of 1975, Radosh and his new wife attended a victory celebration for the Vietcong in Central Park, where they listened to Joan Baez, "the diva of the antiwar movement," as well as "the artist who stood alongside the young Bob Dylan and epitomized the union of art and politics," and Phil Ochs, as they sang Ochs' anti-war anthem "I declare the war is over."[35] A few months later, Ochs, an alcoholic wreck, committed suicide when Bob Dylan did not include him in the Rolling Thunder revue. Radosh and his wife experienced a milder form of let down. Instead of a moment of triumph, "the end of the war," Radosh says, "produced a great void."[36] It was "an occasion for deep melancholy" because the war and the draft had been "the issue that had given meaning to our lives" and now that issue was "beginning to evaporate," and when Nixon abolished the draft, it evaporated.[37]

Radosh's melancholia is easy to understand. The end of the Vietnam War was supposed to mean the beginning of heaven on earth, as the end of capitalism was supposed to signal the same thing to his parents' generation. When the war ended, Radosh knew it didn't begin anything, certainly not heaven on earth, and so it became a reproach to the idea the revolutionary Jew had been propagating for two millennia. At moments like this, the Revolutionary Jew was haunted, for a moment, by the thought there might not be heaven on earth ever. It was a thought that recurred each time one of his gods failed. "The idea of an immediate, no-fault revolution, a fantasy of the previous decade, was no longer tenable. We would not break on through to the other side, as in the Doors' revolutionary anthem, or at least not overnight as we had hoped."[38] The Vietnam War "had been the center of everything," even for those who "thought the revolution would be cultural and had abandoned politics for dope and rock and roll."[39] But now the center of their lives was gone. "None of us admitted it," Radosh says, "but we almost all looked inside ourselves with a rising sense of panic and wondered, 'What now?'"[40] Rather than accept that heaven on earth is an illusion, the revolutionary Jew searched for it more feverishly:

> It was time when some of my old comrades went looking for love in all the wrong places—human potential movements, therapeutic ecstasies and personality cults—while others began the long march though the institutions. And I, desperately afraid that my god would fail, went looking for another party to join, communism having long since withered away for me.

October 27, 1975: The Rolling Thunder Revue

On October 27, 1975, six months after the fall of Vietnam and shortly after Rod Radosh married his second wife, three chartered buses rolled out of New York City, headed north, beginning Bob Dylan's Rolling Thunder Review, his way of compensating for the void the end of the war created in the tattered remnants of the folk song movement. It also compensated for the family he had just destroyed. Spitz claims the music "scene" destroyed Dylan's marriage. "Scene" is a code word for adultery and drugs: "The scene is what ended it. Sarah just couldn't compete with the sideshow allure of New York."[41] Spitz is more explicit when he describes the ambiance of the Rolling Thunder Revue:

> The unwritten rule in every male musician's life was that touring gave him license to go wild. It was the place where, for one or two months out of the year, he was free to get all those freaky fantasies out of his system before settling back into fidelity with the little woman and the kids. What you did on the road was your business. It was like being a member of the music masons.[42]

Sara Lowndes Dylan wouldn't file for divorce until 1977, but the Rolling Thunder Revue shows the marriage ended two years earlier. Bob Dylan compensated for the loss of his family by surrounding himself with "weirdos,"[43] people of his own background, revolutionary Jews who gave toadying approbation to his wretched excess. He missed his family nonetheless, and "as a result, he manufactured this big musical family to help fill the void."[44] The Rolling Thunder Revue may have been a *faux* family but "the spirit of it was patterned after a summer camp;"[45] indeed, the Jewish communist summer camps where many musicians learned American folk music. The Rolling Thunder Review bespoke Dylan's nostalgia for the America the Jewish cultural revolutionaries had destroyed. They were still conflicted, because the one thing the New Left refused to relinquish was sexual liberation. The Revue was to post-revolutionary America what the workers' revolutionary theater trains were to post-revolutionary Russia, an attempt at agit-prop to convince the masses that, contrary to all evidence, the revolution was still a good idea. That meant bringing sexual revolution to small towns of New England in 1975. "All those small towns whose womenfolk were struggling against the yoke of repression were sexual time bombs waiting to go off. The Rolling Thunder Revue rolled into town and—Whammo!—teenagers and young moms suddenly found themselves doing things they'd only read about in *Penthouse*. Leave it to rock musicians!"[46]

Instead of Phil Ochs, Bob Dylan chose Ramblin' Jack Elliott to accompany him. Elliott was eventually replaced by Kinky Friedman—minus the Texas Jewboys. Kinky sported menorah-embroidered silk cowboy shirts even when that parody of the singing Jewish cowboy had worn thin. The quality of Dylan's music can be deduced from his Rolling Thunder lifestyle. He put on a cowboy hat, painted his face white, and sang one song after another in the same voice without indicating when he moved from one song to another. It was in many ways a musical rendition of his sex life; the songs and the women became interchangeable and indistinguishable. The revolutionary Jew had succeeded beyond anyone's expectations. He had subverted the morals of "puritanical" America, and wrecked his own life too. Archibald MacLeish was right, "if anything costs you your faith or your family, then the price is too high."

In 1975, about the time the Rolling Thunder Revue pulled out of New York, the Bothy Band released its epoch-making album of traditional Irish music. A rhythm section propelled by Donal Lunny on the bouzouki and Michael O'Domhnaill on the acoustic guitar showed the band had been influenced by the folk revival, but the music was pure Irish ethnic, passed on the traditional intra-family way. Michael and Triona Ní Domhnaill's aunt had contributed 286 songs to the Dublin University folklore collection.

Four years later Mick Maloney arrived in Philadelphia. Under the guidance of Ken Goldstein of the University of Pennsylvania, and Dennis Clark, with whom Goldstein collaborated in the creation of the Balch Institute for Ethnic Studies, Maloney used the nearly defunct folk music network to promote traditional Irish music. An Irish music renaissance would spread for 20 years through the ruins of the old folk network. By the late '70s, popular front folk music had morphed into folk rock, which had morphed into hard rock, heavy metal, disco, and any number of minor variations promoted intensely but with diminishing returns by "the music industry." The music industry could be compared to a layer of asphalt that gradually covered large areas of fertile musical ground in the same way mall parking lots covered acres of fertile farmland. The point of the music industry was commerce and control, or commerce as a form of control, as pioneered by Jewish Businessmen like Albert Grossman, and epigoni like David Geffen. If, by the late '70s the music industry could be compared to one large metaphorical mall parking lot, then The Bothy Band's 1975 album was a hardy plant popping its first tendrils from a crack in the asphalt caused by the thaw after a long winter of ice and cold. It showed that there was stil life in the subterranean stratum of ethnic music the industry had tried to colonize and control.

1976: The Rise of Ethnic Music

Other plants soon bloomed in the cracks in the asphalt. In 1976, Jewish refugees from the defunct folk music movement formed the band Klezmorim in Berkeley. "Klezmer," musicians of the Irish revival of the 1980s said, "was God's way of keeping the Jews from taking over Irish music." When folk music morphed into Heavy Metal, the Jews turned to "Heavy Shtetl." In 1978, the Los Angeles based NAMA Orchestra released their album, Mazltov!, and Klezmer music was born. Although the term came into common parlance around 1980, the music was not new. Klezmer (based on the Hebrew kle and zmer, meaning vessels of song) was the ethnic music of the southern Jewish Pale of settlement. If New Orleans was the catch basin for Southern musical traditions and the place where they got forged into something typically American, known asJazz, Odessa played a similar role in the evolution of Klezmer, the music of the southern areas of the Pale of the Settlement. In Odessa Gypsy, Greek, and Romanian music merged into the *frehlekhs* and other manifestations of Jewish dance music eventually known as Klezmer.

Since Bob Dylan's grandmother came from Odessa, there is a certain element of irony here. When Jewish banjo pickers emerged from the rubble of the folk movement Dylan destroyed, dusting off their grandparents' 78 records, Dylan became a Christian, baptized in May 1980, and released three Christian albums that revitalized his career, allowing him to reach a new audience. Spitz, displaying the animus against Christianity one expects of Jews, claims "Dylan fans were shocked and bewildered by this newest transformation."[47] He indicates Dylan was another Jewish performer adopting an alien ethnic stage identity; his conversion was the religious version of black face. Dylan's conversion appears sincere, but whether Dylan will perdure is unclear. Life on the road destroyed his marriage, so it is unlikely that it will help him lead a life worthy of a Christian.

1977: *Time* Crowns Woody Allen an American Genius

Beginning in 1970, *Time* was in the forefront of announcing the Jewish takeover of American culture. "The United States," claimed *Time*, "is becoming more Jewish ... . Among American intellectuals the Jew has even become a culture hero."[48] *Time* quoted poet Robert Lowell: "Jewishness is the center of today's literature much as the West was in the '30s."[49] Twenty years later, *Time* repeated the theme, "Jews are news. It is an axiom of journalism. An indispensable one, too, because it is otherwise impossible to explain why the deeds and misdeeds of a dot-on-the-map Israel get an absurdly disproportionate amount of news coverage around the world."[50]

Seven years after the first article, Woody Allen released his film *Annie Hall*, and *Time* certified Allen as the quintessential Jewish comic genius. *Commentary* followed suit, if in less breathless fashion, two years laters, but not all Jews were happy at having Allen proclaimed their cultural representative. Twenty years after *Time* crowned Allen, Rabbi Samuel Dresner still expressed his reservations in an unanswered culturallly anomolous attack. The issue was: who speaks for the American Jew? If, as Dresner noted, "American Jews accept the categorization of themselves as advocates of Woody Allen," then Judaism is another word for "sexual permissiveness and even perversity," a proposition which Dresner found unacceptable.[51] According to Dresner, "The lifestyles of Jews should not determine the Jewish style of life." The former, according to Dresner, "should not be determined by the latter, even if the latter should become a majority in the Jewish community." Dresner says if American Jews become "advocates of Woody Allen," that would be "not only a betrayal of Jewish values but a betrayal of the Jewish people, for no one more than Allen has enabled so many to view the Jew, especially the religious Jew, in so corrupt a manner."[52]

Dresner thus raises the perennial issue: who defines what a Jew is? Dresner sees

> Woody Allen as the classic example of how America has become more Jewish while "American Jews are becoming less Jewish."[53] Because of his popularity and because mainline Jewish organizations leave his attacks on Jewish tradition unmentioned, Allen has become a paradigm for the majority of American Jews. To understand what that means, we must understand what Woody Allen symbolizes to most American Jews.

Woody Allen, Dresner notes, has had a "persistent fascination"[54] with incest. He has been in psychoanalysis for over 30 years; his fascination, whether expressed in his writing ("It's a whole new ball game," she said, pressing close to me. "Marrying Mom has made you my father."[55]), or through his seduction of his and Mia Farrow's adopted daughter is best explained by an analysis of Freud. Freud, too, was obsessed with incest. In his book *Moses and Monotheism*, Freud makes clear that, as in the case of the Pharaohs of Egypt, incest confers god-like status on its perpetrators. Freud also claims Moses was an Egyptian, thus de-legitimatizing the man who gave the law to Israel. David Bakan has written a book commenting on these passages; he claims Freud was a follower of the false Messiah Shabbetai Zevi whose attack on Moses was an attempt to abolish the law as Zevi did, through ritual impurity. Jews who promote sexual revolution are in this tradition: "They," Dresner says, "conjure up painful memories of the infamous seventeenth century false messiah Sabbatai Tzvi or his successor, Jacob Frank. Their coming was to mark a new age when the rule of Torah was to be superseded—'What was forbidden is now permitted'—and transgressions would become a mitzvot."[56]

"For those who seek the forbidden in Jewish guise," Dresner continues, "Sabbatianism points the way."[57] Sabbatianism gets to the heart of Judaism, a religion, says Dresner, forged in opposition to the fertility cults of the ancient Middle East. "In biblical times," Dresner continues, "Judaism waged a battle against sexual excess *not unlike the struggle now in progress*—and in those earlier times, Mosaic law was victorious. Unbridled sexuality lay at the heat of ancient pagan religion."[58] To Dresner, Jewish history is one long battle against sexual deviance. "The early biblical narratives can be read as a continuous attack on the widespread sexual deviance that challenged and often seduced the Israelites, whose failings away Scripture scrupulously records."[59] What crime was so great that it provoked God to destroy mankind, except for Noah's family, with a flood? "According to the most ancient understanding of the biblical story found in rabbinic sources, it was the violation of the natural order of sexual life."[60] "God," Dresner says, "is long-suffering of all manner of crime, save sexual immorality."[61]

Dresner is confronted with a serious dilemma, one which he cannot resolve because he lacks the theological sophistication. The Torah condemns sexual immorality. But American Jews, represented by Woody Allen, fervently support sexual deviance under the name of sexual liberation, a term the Jew Wilhelm Reich invented. Dresner tries to pin the blame on descendents of Shabbetai Zevi, like Isaac Bashevis Singer. Dresner notes Singer's early "fascination with Sabbatianism."[62] "I read whatever I could," Singer writes, "about the era of Sabbatai Zevi, in whose footsteps Jacob Frank had followed ... In these works I found everything I had been pondering, hysteria, sex, fanaticism, superstition."[63]

Not only have America's Jews become corrupted by Sabbatianism, the Sabbatian infection has become the majority position among America's Jews: the lifestyle of Jews has trumped the Jewish style of life based on the Torah.

> To cloak perversion with piety has a frightening ring, conjuring up memories of the Asherah in the temple and the antics of Jacob Frank, precisely because it blurs the distinctions between the Jewish style of life and the lifestyle of Jews, between what Judaism prescribes and what some Jews regrettably choose to do. It tends to validate the position that whatever Jews say or do can be identified as Judaism. It cripples the ability of Judaism to address the doings and sayings of Jews. How can a religion that is based four-square on marriage and the home countenance the revival of the sexual lifestyle of ancient (and modern) idolatry.[64]

It can't, but Dresner can't explain why. Dresner is more upset about Singer's popularity than about Woody Allen's. "Are Singer's writings 'true'"? he wonders.[65] "The corruption, the adultery, the demonic, the philandering, the decay, the perversion that pervade Singer's picture of Polish Jewry—is it all true? And if it is not 'true,' then why has someone not said so?"[66] The silence of American Jews indicates ambivalence, "their secret desire to repudiate the moral direction of three thousand years of Jewish history in favor of the worship of sensuality and fear of the demonic, ... finding meaning in their animal nature instead of in the power of man to transcend himself."[67] American Jews have embraced Singer's writings, "because they express what Jews secretly desire."[68] And what is that? Sexual liberation in Jewish garb, *i.e.,* Sabbatianism, which is "the one movement in Jewish history that not only broke the moral yoke of Sinai but provided a theological justification for it: 'in the transgression of the mitzvah.'"[69] Singer's public declaration of Sabbatian sympathies coupled with his popularity indicates the curtain may be going up "on a new and frightening drama in Jewish life."[70] Jewish silence on Singer "may be a sign of a sickness so severe we do not perceive its symptoms."[71] Dresner, as well as his mentor Abraham Heschel and other Yiddish writers familiar with pre-World War II Poland, consider Singers' writings one long calumny of eastern European Jews. But if that is the case, why are American Jews so interested in promoting the calumny? Because if eastern European Jewry is what Singer says, then American Jews "need feel no guilt; they can go about their way, not much different from other Americans, philandering, corrupting, and making of their faith a sham in the comforting belief that it was, after all, always like that. That's what the Jews of Eastern Europe were—philanderers, adulterers and corrupters: why should American Jews be better?"[72]

Dresner's conclusion is inescapable. If Woody Allen speaks for most American Jews, then American Jews are are no longer followers of Moses but rather followers of Shabbetai Zevi. American cultural life in the last half of the 20th century was dominated by Jewish rebellion against the Torah and adoption of the practices of Shabbetai Zevi. The overwhelming majority of American Jews, as shown by surveys Dresner cites, have defined themselves as sexual revolutionaries; because of the disproportionate role Jews play in publishing and the media, they have, in effect, established Sabbatian sexual degeneracy as the American cultural norm. According to Dresner, Judaism is about nothing "if not the centrality of virtue."[73] "How," he wonders, "can a Jew maintain any other position?"[74] He replies with understatement, "Nevertheless, some do."[75] Judaism, says Dresner, "stands as inexorably against the new paganism as it did against the old. And so should the Jew,"[76] but as the American Jew reached cultural prominence, he was also converted to Sabbatianism, "an alternate faith." So "Jewish rebellion has broken out on several levels," one being "the prominent role of Jews as advocates to sexual experimentation."[77]

Dresner again adverts to "significant elements of America's cultural elite" that "by its example, desensitizes this nation morally."[78] He thus adverts to the problem this group has created for America while their Jewishness has prohibited others from addressing the problem. He deals with the issue indirectly. "How could so many American Jewish leaders," he wonders, "have been taken in by Allen?"[79] Dresner has the cart before the horse here because those Jewish leaders have used Allen to redefine America and the American Jew in their image. They have used Allen to define the Jew as a sexually deviant cultural bolshevist. So anyone who objects to sexual deviance or Hollywood's promotion of it is as an anti-Semite. The equation is simple. Since Hollywood is run by Jews, being anti-Hollywood means being anti-Semitic. Dresner cites Richard Goldstein, writing in the *Liberal Voice*. According to Goldstein, "the Republican attack on Hollywood and the 'media elite,'" is a code for anti-Semitism, because "these are words that since the '50s connote Jewishness to people. The Republicans can't attack Jews directly, so they use codes. The notion of Woody as a kind of Jewish icon lends itself to the ideas of Jews subverting the Christian family, an idea which is very old and very dark."[80]

Dresner is again brought up short when he confronts his own ethnic group's legacy. Unable to define Jews theologically as rejectors of Christ and, therefore, revolutionaries, Dresner portrays American Jews as the people of the Old Testament. But he is brought up short because the overwhelming majority of American Jews do not accept the Torah on sexuality and have chosen instead Woody Allen or Wilhelm Reich or Alex Portnoy as their Messiah. If the Jews accepted the Torah, there would have been no culture wars in the 1960s. The devastating effect of the culture wars on America and American Jews forces Rabbi Dresner to spin one unconvincing explanation after another despite the undeniable fact that Jews played a major role in that cultural subversion of sexual morals. Since Woody Allen is a cultural icon for most Jews, most Jews have defined themselves as sexual degenerates. Dresner quotes a columnist in the *Village Voice*:

> There are two kinds of people in the world: those who think Woody Allen is the genius spokesman of our collective angst and those how think he's a filthy Jewish liberal ... elitist Communist madman. Another name for those two groups are Democrats and Republicans.[81]

Dresner is appalled at this sort of thinking, but in the end can't explain why Jews would want to define themselves as sexual revolutionaries and deviants primarily because he has been blinded by his own reading of the Torah and can't see that Jews are in rebellion against the Torah precisely because it is the word of God. American Jews declared war on the Logos at right around the time that Woody Allen won the Academy Award for *Annie Hall*.

October 1976: The Jewish takeover of American Discourse

In October 1976, Leo Pfeffer arrived in Philadelphia to give a talk entitled "Issues that Divide: the Triumph of Secular Humanism." In that talk, Pfeffer declared victory in the culture wars and announced the Jews had defeated the Catholics in their 40 years war over American culture. The terms of the Carthaginian peace imposed on the defeated American Catholics included abortion, pornography, the loss of Catholic academe, the redefinition of deviance, and the transformation of discourse. In a formal sense, *i.e.*, in reference to literary criticism, that meant war on Logos. It also meant the end of the New Criticism as everyman's democratic version of *Sola Scriptura* and its replacement with Talmudic exegesis. Catholics who began their literary careers learning the Protestant rule that every man had the right to interpret his own text, now had to be re-trained in rules of discourse according to which the Rabbi was always right.

At around the same time that Woody Allen was being celebrated as the great

American genius, Jacques Derrida and Stanley Fish changed the rules of discourse in American academic circles. Literary criticism was no longer Protestant; it was Talmudic. Those who signed up for literature classes to learn how to read a poem, now learned that there was, as Fish put it, "no text." No text meant any constitutional principle could be subverted by Talmudic reasoning by rabbis like Leo Pfeffer; and that any human right, such as the right to life, could be subverted similarly. No text meant there was no such thing as nature, as the campaign to legitimatize homosexuality showed. It also meant there was no substance or being, as Derrida's attack on "onto-theology" showed. There was a deeper grammar to this discussion, which eventuated in the campus political correctness speech codes of the 1990s. The heart of that code wasn't racial; it wasn't feminist; it wasn't homosexual; it was Jewish and expressing Jewish culture at its worst. Political correctness was the final expression of the Talmudic redefinition of American discourse which had begun in the '70s under the direction of Jewish critical theorists like Fish and Derrida.

In 1992, Fish authored an essay, "There's no such Thing as Free Speech and It's a Good Thing Too," in a book called *Debating PC*. Criticizing Benno Schmidt's view that speech should be tolerated because "freedom must be the paramount obligation of an academic community," Fish says Schmidt has "no sense of the lacerating harms that speech of certain kinds can inflict."[82] Fish therefore favored campus regulations banning "hate speech." "Speech," he says, "is never and could not be an independent value, but it is always asserted against a background of some assumed conception of the good to which it must yield in the event of conflict."[83]

The catch in this argument revolved around the conception of the good at its heart. The traditional view claimed speech was subordinated to the moral law, the good in question. The Whig Enlightenment claimed, in the case of speech, that the moral law was subject to individual freedom. This rallying cry allowed Jewish revolutionaries to take over the university. Once in power, they changed the rules. The "Good" at Duke University, where Fish taught at the time he was being proclaimed as an Apostle of Political Correctness in organs like *Newsweek*, got redefined as the will of those in power. In the absence of a "text" such as Nature, Being, Logos, the Constitution, etc., there could be no good but the will of the powerful fortified by appetite.

Two years earlier, in an article in *Newsweek* on Political Correctness entitled "Thought Police on Campus," Fish praised pluralism in a way that had already become dated, when he claimed that "Disagreement can be fun."[84] By the 1990s there was no disagreement and little fun in class. Reader Response criticism was Talmudic. There was "no text." There was no Torah; there was only Talmud, *i.e.*, opinions of literary critics who were the secular equivalent of the rabbi, always right, even when other rabbis contradicted him. Reader Response criticism, as espoused by Fish, claimed the reader did not discover meaning, he created it out of materials assembled from a text that had no real existence until he appropriated it. This idea appealed to legions of poorly educated English majors plodding through graduate schools in the mid-'70s. The fledgling critic, overburdened by texts his defective education left him unprepared to understand, leapt to avoid the labor of scholarly pursuit and rejoiced to learn scholarship was nothing but unfettered appetite applied to difficult texts. "The text means what I say it means," the dull-witted grad student chanted. "I am the hegemon of meaning," he crowed, because, Fish told him, the critic is not "the humble servant of texts." The euphoria wore off when the young literary critic discovered, like the denizens of Orwell's *Animal Farm*, that some literary critical pigs were more equal than others. *Animal Farm* was especially relevant because the same sort of transformation was taking place in literary criticism that had taken place in revolutionary France, Russia, and Germany. The passions were aroused as the instrument of revolution against the moral order, but once the revolution destroyed the old regime, there was no moral order to protect the revolutionaries from the will of their new masters.

Reader Response Criticism led to politicly correct speech codes, but the grad students of the '70s still haven't figured out why or how. Stanley Fish engaged in bait and switch. Once the maleducated, baby-boomer grad students accepted the hegemony of the reader over texts in Fish's campaign to bring down the *ancien regime*, they were informed the reader was not quite as sovereign as he had told them. Indeed, robbed of the text as the source of meaning, the "readers" had no power at all. The determiner of meaning of was not the "reader" after all, but the "interpretive community." "Fish," wrote R. V. Young, "follows here the paradigm of Jean Jacques Rousseau: an initial assertion of virtually limitless freedom (reader-response criticism) turns into total constraint, with the individual reader or interpreter figured as a blind prisoner of the collective mind."[85] Once "liberated" from coming to grips with a text, the critic had no source for his interpretations. He was dependent on the "interpretive community," the lit crit equivalent of the communist party.

Where did the interpretive community get its meanings? Fish could not answer that question, just as he could not explain how this community could change its mind. All that remained was desire, the bait that started this revolution. But the desires of the weak, disconnected from morals and a constitutive text, inevitably succumbed to the desires of the powerful. There was something "democratic" in the traditional American sense of the word, about the study of literature when the New Criticism gave everyone a chance to come up with a winning interpretation. That possibility disappeared with the disappearance of the text. When the deconstructor deconstructs all meanings and all texts, all that is left is the hegemony of his desires over everyone else's. Since there can be no appeal to an objective text with objective meaning, *e.g*, the Bible or the Constitution, the deconstructor has absolute hegemony over those who lack his power. That was the motivation behind the replacement of Shakespeare with Queer Theory and Deconstruction. Those who abolished the text were like those who abolish morals in the name of "liberation." Their ultimate goal, no matter how inchoately understood, was *libido dominandi*. The average grad student, like the average TV watcher went along with the revolution because he saw in it the validation of his own desires. What he failed to see was the simultaneous eclipse of his moral freedom. That realization usually came too late, if at all. Since the abolition of text was a fundamentally totalitarian project, it should come as no surprise that former Nazis like Paul De Man were attracted to it.

Sexual morality had to be deconstructed in the name of political power. It must have no "meaning" because if there were no meaning, no one could object when the powerful inflicted their desires on the weak. Aldous Huxley explicated the meaning of "meaninglessness" long ago in *Ends and Means*. "The philosopher," Huxley wrote,

> who finds no meaning in the world is not concerned exclusively with a problem in pure metaphysics. He is also concerned to prove that there is no valid reason why he personally should not do as he wants to do, or why his friends should not seize political power and govern in the way that they find most advantageous to themselves. The voluntary, as opposed to the intellectual, reasons for holding the doctrines of materialism, for example, may be predominantly erotic, as they were in the case of Lamettrie (see his lyrical account of the pleasures of the bed in *La Volupte* and at the end of *L'Homme Machine*), or predominantly political as they were in the case of Karl Marx.[86]

Beginning with Saul Bellow's *Mr. Sammler's Planet* in 1968, followed by *Portnoy's Complaint* one year later, then by the movies of Woody Allen, Jewish themes and ideas became mainstream American culture. At around the same time that movie-goers were lining up to see *Annie Hall*, Jewish literary critics like Stanley Fish and Jacques Derrida were changing the rules of discourse. Interpretations Professor Fish said were the privilege of "interpretive communities," meaning English departments at prestigious institutions like Johns Hopkins University, where he happened to teach. Before long any institution became ipso facto prestigious by the fact that it had hired Stanley Fish to teach there. First Duke and then the University of Illinois at Chicago became prestigious. At the same time Jacques Derrida at Yale was saying that the interpretation of texts was so difficult, that no one could do it. Readings were no longer possible; all that was possible were "misreadings."

Neither of these talmudic forms of literary criticism were compatible with American democratic ideals. According to Fish, the Torah, *i.e*, the poem or "text" as a secular surrogate for the Bible, had been swallowed by the Talmud of arcane literary theory, for which he was the chief rabbi. Anyone who disagreed was expelled from the synagogue. Jews of an earlier era were free to come up with outrageously irreverent and literarily blasphemous assertions like the claim that Huckleberry Finn and Jim were homosexuals, as Leslie Fiedler did in "Come back to the raft ag'in, Huck Honey," but the days when anyone was free to make any interpretation as long as it was based on evidence from the text were numbered. Professors who thought they had "academic freedom" were the first to learn about the new rules of discourse, but soon the lessons were taught outside of academe too. Major league pitcher John Rocker may have been earning lots of money, but it could not buy him the freedom to speak his mind.

Anyone who says something in public must take account of the rules of discourse or run the risk of punishment. By the end of the 20th century, cultural commentary was dangerous because the monuments to Jewish culture had become ubiquitous but off limits to the *goyim*. It is difficult if not impossible to comment on mainstream culture without touching some Jewish monument, yet the number of permissible interpretations was narrowing dramatically at the same time. Mass culture abounds in Jewish artifacts, but unauthorized discourse about them is prohibited.

Derrida's Deconstruction was Talmudic too. Deconstruction was an attack on Logos—synonymous with Christ—by people, in R. V. Young's phrase, "at war with the word." Derrida's Deconstruction was an attack on "real presence." What followed the revolt against Logos was a convoluted explanation of discourse that bore an uncanny resemblance to the Jewish world once the Temple was destroyed and "everything became discourse," *i.e.*, Talmudic disputation without contact with Logos:

> The surrogate does not substitute itself for anything which has somehow pre-existed it. From then on it was probably necessary to begin to think that there was no center, that the center could not be thought of in the form of a being-present, that the center had no natural locus, that it was not a fixed locus, but a function, a sort of non-locus in which an infinite number of sign-substitutions came into play. This moment was that in which language invaded the universal problematic; that in which, in the absence of center or origin, everything became discourse—provided we can agree on this word—that is to say, when everything became a system where the central signified, the original or transcendental signified, is never absolutely present outside a system of differences. The absence of the transcendental signified extends the domain and the interplay of the signification ad infinitum.[87]

Derrida's passage is an allegory, describing the destruction of the Temple, after which the Jewish people had no priesthood, no sacrifice, no Temple, no real presence, no Shekinah. After Rabbi Jochanan ben Zakkai got smuggled out of the temple and founded the rabbinic school at Javne, Judaism became a Talmudic debating society, in which "The absence of the transcendental signified extends the domain and interplay of signification ad infinitum."

As Young puts it, "Rather than a frontal assault on metaphysics, Derrida proposes subversion from within."[88] Jacques Derrida and Stanley Fish were, like Trotsky, Jewish revolutionaries. The literary critical revolution of the '70s was the mopping up operation which followed the cultural revolution of the '60s, when academe was taken over by a new group of people. Reader Response Criticism corresponded in time to the Jewish take over of American culture. The speech codes which got imposed on college campuses over the course of the 1990s which came to be known as political correctness, were in fact the practical consequences which were drawn from the Jewish takeover of discourse which occurred in America during the 1970s.

Talmudic literary Criticism and Roe v. Wade

Anyone who thinks literary criticism is at best arcane and inconsequential and at worst grist for the mills of columnists looking for the worst excesses of political correctness should read R. V. Young's *At War With the Word* carefully. This is not just a book about wretched excess in academe, although it is certanly that, the book is also about the need to maintain respect toward seminal and foundational texts because where there is no text, all politics is interpretation and all interpretation is ultimately determined by politics.

If anyone doubted literary criticism was a life and death issue, *Roe v. Wade* laid that idea to rest in 1973. In *Roe* the Supreme Court granted the average citizen hegemony over being, by arrogating to itself complete hegemony over the Constitution, the text that created the court. Desire and the will to power took precedence over the text that was supposed to rein in that power. When Attorney General Edwin Meese told the American Bar Association in 1985 that the Reagan Administration was going to appoint judges who would interpret the Constitution in light of the "original intention" of its framers, he was given an impromptu lesson in the new hermeneutics. Justice William Brennan rebuked Meese for "facile historicism."[89] The battle raged for over a year, causing columnist Joseph Sobran to opine "Liberal scholars want to apply to the Constitution a method of understanding they would flunk any undergraduate for applying to Chaucer or Milton."[90] What Sobran hadn't noticed is that the teachers he had as an undergraduate literature major were superseded by a generation which felt that the highest expression of intellectual acumen was imposing one's will on a text. "The interpretive approaches deprecated by Sobran," Young writes, "are now quite often winning moves in the race for tenure, promotion and professional standing."[91]

It should come as no surprise that reader-response criticism should arrive in the immediate aftermath of *Roe v. Wade*. The court's exaltation of the will of the mother at the expense of the child ratified the court's exaltation of its own ego at the expense of the Constitution, a text that now meant what they said it meant, like Humpty-Dumpty, irrespective of its words. The Supreme Court's *Roe* decision ratified a culture that had become in Young's words "intellectually and morally decadent in its highest and lowest reaches."[92]

1977: Jimmy Carter loses the Jewish vote.

Over the course of the '70s, America's Jews became more attached to the cause of Soviet Jewry and less enamored of a foreign policy in which détente succeeded containment. In 1974, Richard Perle, a young assistant to Senator Henry (Scoop)

Jackson, orchestrated passage of the Jackson-Vanik amendment, tying most favored nation status to the Soviet Union's willingness to let Jews emigrate. Senator Jackson's office was an early neoconservative beachhead, and Perle would later influence the Reagan administration as an assistant Secretary of Defense. In Washington, Perle became known as "the Prince of Darkness," because of his network of contacts and "his Machiavellian political tactics."[93] Perle supported deploying Pershing missiles in Europe and the missile system derogatorily referred to as Star Wars. Friedman claims Perle's "ideas and the fierce energy he exerted in advancing them, made him perhaps the central figure," In the Reagan administration, "save Reagan himself."[94]

In May 1975 US ambassador Daniel Patrick Moynihan vetoed a United Nations resolution condemning Israel and equating Zionism with racism. In a speech written by Norman Podhoretz, Moynihan said "The United States rises to declare before the General Assembly of the UN and before the world, that it does not acknowledge, it will not abide by, it will never acquiesce in this infamous act"— words that stood him in good stead with New York's Jews when he ran for the Senate as a Democrat.[95]

The Jews, however, were increasingly unhappy with the foreign policy proposed by the Democrats. In May 1977, President Jimmy Carter spoke at Notre Dame, insisting the nation must overcome its "inordinate fear of Communism."[96] The message did not resonate with the Jews trying to promote Jewish emigration from the Soviet Union. Disillusionment with the Democrats and Carter increased when Moynihan's successor at the UN, Andrew Young, resigned because of unauthorized meetings with the PLO.

By the late '70s, the Jews had begun a significant migration out of the Democratic party. The harbingers of that change had begun in the early '70s. In February 1972, *Commentary* did a political cost-benefit analysis of liberalism entitled, "Is it Good for the Jews?" In the same year, *Commentary*'s editor Norman Podhoretz and *National Review*'s editor William F. Buckley began an ecumenical dialogue, at the end of which either Podhoretz converted to conservatism or Buckley became a tool of the Neoconservatives, a convergence no matter how you looked at it. In May 1972, Robert Bartley ran a piece entitled "Irving Kristol and Friends" which gave exposure to the Jewish inspired ideology later known as "neoconservatism." After Bartley, notoriously supine when it came to Jewish interests, became editor of the *Wall Street Journal's* editorial page, Kristol became a frequent contributor. Soon William Baroody, Sr., head of the American Enterprise Institute, asked Kristol to join as a fellow. Other conservative think tanks, most notably the Heritage Foundation, followed suit and a parade of neoconservative scholars and propagandists, including Milton Friedman, Jeanne Kirkpatrick, Michael Novak, and Ben Wattenberg marched off to Washington.

One of the people joining the parade to Washington was Midge Decter. When

Ed Feulner invited her to join the Heritage Foundation, she wondered if she were being sought after to fulfill a quota as an "affirmative action baby":

> Was I perhaps there as a Jew? I very much doubted it. It must have been that I had been invited as a representative of that weird new ex-liberal breed from New York City who had somehow popped up to lend their words and publications to the conservative movement. In other words, the neocons. Indeed, when I asked Ed Feulner the question a couple of years later he said that he had "wanted to make a statement," a statement about the conservative community being, as the politicos say, a big tent.[97]

Decter concluded she had been invited to join Heritage because of "our far superior knowledge of the country's true enemies."[98] Our? Was Decter referring to Jews or neoconservatives? Eventually, the distinction would have no meaning, as David Brooks pointed out in the *Wall Street Journal* ("neo means new and con means Jew"). When the neocons arrived in Washington, those they disliked became "the country's true enemies."[99]

Over the course of the '80s, the neocons consolidated control of the conservative movement by placing their agents at the head of foundations, which in true communist fashion, funded front groups to colonize traditionalist groups and promote the neocon agenda. In 1976 Richard Nixon's former secretary of the Treasury, William E. Simon, became head of the John M. Olin Foundation. In 1978, Simon joined Irving Kristol to create the Institute for Educational Affairs "to penetrate college campuses with conservative ideas."[100] Simon was instrumental in funding conservative newspapers on college campuses, including the *Dartmouth Review*, which produced alumni like Dinesh D'Souza and John Podhoretz, who became second generation neocon polemicists.

1980: Mia Farrow meets Woody Allen

Perhaps no one symbolized Catholic ethnics getting screwed by the Jews better than Mia Farrow. Farrow was a Hollywood princess by birthright, set adrift from her Catholic moorings by the Jewish transformation of culture. After the break up of her marriage to Frank Sinatra in the '60s, she sought solace from the Maharishi in India, where she met the Beatles, Donovan, and at least one Beach Boy. Her path to spiritual enlightenment ended abruptly when the Maharishi tried to rape her in his meditation cave. What she derived from the experience was a vague sense that "Divine Being is the very substance of the universe, but that everything we experience with our senses is merely illusion."[101] As a result she began to "redefine my relationship with Christianity, Catholicism and Being."[102] Taking Thomas Jefferson as her guide, Farrow "began to discriminate between the core of [Christ's] teachings and the dogma that has been attached to it."[103] Weakened by her ignorance of the Catholic faith that was the core of her identity, Farrow was a moral accident waiting to happen. The accident began to unfold in August of

1980 when Farrow ran into the man whose "actual name was Allan Konigsberg,"[104] namely, Woody Allen.

Their romance might have been titled "Abie's Irish Rose as Directed by the Marquis de Sade." Allen behaved like a jerk from the moment they met. Allen exploded in rage because Farrow did not remember where William F. Buckley lived. Their relationship was a study in ethnic contrasts. Farrow loved children; she adopted 14. Allen hated children, except as sex objects. Farrow loved Christmas. Woody "disliked Christmas;"[105] he disrupted the family Christmas meal by running a juicer at deafening decibel levels to drown out conversation. When Farrow mentioned how beautiful the Christmas carols were at a concert, Allen responded, "Pardon me while I puke."[106] Farrow thought "Mother Teresa ... was the embodiment of everything" she "had tried to teach" her children "about true success and what one person with conviction and courage can accomplish."[107] Allen was a devotee of Sigmund Freud. As the Allen character says in *Annie Hall*, "I've been in analysis for 15 years. I'm giving it one more year. Then I'm going to Lourdes." Three years after *Annie Hall*, Lourdes came to Woody Allen instead in the person of Mia Farrow.

Mulling the role psychoanalysis played in Allen's life, Farrow concluded

> it had helped to isolate him from people and from the systems we live by, and placed him at the center of a different reality—one that exists only after he has bounced his views off his therapist. Woody lived and made his decisions while suspended in a zone constructed and controlled almost entirely by himself—a world that he used his therapists to validate. He did not acknowledge other beings except as features in his own landscape, valued according to their contribution to his own existence. He was therefore unable to empathize and felt no moral responsibility to anyone or anything.[108]

While waiting for Woody to finish a therapy session in January 1992, Farrow received a call from him that took her to the mantel in his apartment where he had placed pornographic photographs of Soon-Yi, Farrow's adopted daughter. Confronted by Farrow, Allen admitted an affair with Soon-Yi. The conversation vacillated over the range of emotions from Allen saying he was in love with Soon-Yi and wanted to marry her, to admissions of guilt, to claiming it was no big deal. "I think it was good for Soon-Yi," Allen said, "It gave her confidence."[109] Allen claimed, "I told Soon-Yi she shouldn't expect anything. I encouraged her to go ahead and sleep with other guys."[110] When Farrow confronted him by telling him "You're not supposed to fuck the kids," Allen's defenses collapsed and he admitted "I know I did a bad thing."[111]

Farrow would accuse Allen of molesting a younger adopted child of theirs but the case never went to trial, which Farrow attributes not to lack of evidence but to Allen's political clout in New York City. Her big question is "Why did I stay with Woody Allen when so much was wrong?"[112] The answer is ethnic. Farrow was weakened in her Catholic identity by the cultural revolution, the golden age of Jewish comedy, whereas Allen, the king of Jewish comedy, was strengthened in his. A dumb *shiksa* was no match for a beaky, brainy Jew holding all the cultural cards. And just what was that identity which got strengthened? A large part of it was Sigmund Freud ratifying appetite. Woody had learned from his analyst to say yes to himself every time his id said I want. The most famous line to emerge from the Farrow/Allen brawl popped up in the *Time* magazine (the same magazine which had certified him as an American genius six years before) interview. When asked if he considered his relationship with Soon-Yi a healthy, equal one, Allen answered, "Who knows?....The heart wants what it wants."[113]

So what lay at the heart of Woody's heart other than a mouth crying perpetually "I want"? After pondering the issue for a while, Farrow concluded

> deep inside Woody there was an unfathomable and uncontrollable need to destroy everything good and positive in his life, and so he tried to destroy our family. For him to have sex with one of my children, a child he had known as my daughter since she was eight years old, was not enough: he had to make me see, graphically, what he was doing. What rage did he feel against me, against women, against mothers, against sisters, against daughters, against an entire family? The pictures were a grenade he threw into our home, and no one was unharmed.[114]

If she had stuck with the sexual morality which the Catholic Church taught her as a child, Farrow would not have been harmed by Allen's sexual aggression. If she had read *Portnoy's Complaint*, Farrow would have known that Roth considered shtupping shiksas as an act of Jewish piety. What she couldn't have known is that shtupping children was also okay if "the heart wants what it wants."

Claire Bloom and the other Funny Jew, Philip Roth

The shikses weren't the only women to come away enraged and hurt by their contact with funny Jews. One year before Mia Farrow wrote her memoir about living with Woody Allen, Claire Bloom's wrote her memoir of life with the other funny Jew, Philip Roth. Would it have been consoling for Mia Farrow to learn that Funny Jew Philip Roth treated his Jewish wife as badly as he had treated the shiksa he had married three decades earlier? Like Mia Farrow, Claire Bloom ignored those who warned her about becoming involved with this funny Jew. In Rome in the late '70s, Bloom met with Gore Vidal, who warned her "Do not involve yourself with Portnoy."[115] Bloom later conceded that

> Gore turned out to be utterly correct in his advice. Philip's novels provided all one needed to know about his relationships with women, most of which had be just short of catastrophic.[116]

Bloom's book demonstrated the accuracy of Roth's claim he was not Portnoy. Roth, it turns out, was much more loathsome than Portnoy. Bloom's book was a devastating blow to Roth's claim his fiction wasn't autobiographical. Roth and Portnoy had much in common, most notably ethnic hatred of the *goyim*. Claire

Bloom cites a note he wrote to her daughter Anna when Roth bought her a bed:

> Here is the money for the whole bed. But if I ever hear that a *goy* is sleeping on the other half, I swear to you that I'll jump out of the window. And then you'll live with that for the rest of your life and you'll see how much you'll enjoy the bed. You'll hate the bed, you'll be sorry you ever saw the bed, you'll wish the bed had never been made: This is my warning to you. If you have any feeling for me at all, KEEP ALL *GOYIM* OUT OF THE BED![117]

Shortly thereafter, Roth told Bloom her daughter was not allowed to live in his house. So much for hatred of the *goyim* as the basis for ethnic solidarity. The end of their marriage coincided with the writing of Roth's *Operation Shylock*:

> He talked about it incessantly, reading passages to me that were dazzlingly incisive and entertaining. I was sure he would once again confound his critics with his superimposition of one identity upon another upon another, while delighting his admirers, who, under the spell of his masterful game, understood and appreciated this multicolored weaver of fantasy and fact. The sections recounting his Halcion-induced breakdown...and a scene devising a meeting between a "real" Philip Roth and a "fake" Philip Roth, were some of the best things he had ever achieved.[118]

Eventually the real Philip Roth met the fake Philip Roth and discovered that they were one and the same non-existent person. Deep down Roth turned out to be a shallow person. Bloom's memoir was the conclusive evidence. When John Updike wrote a mildly critical review of *Operation Shylock* in the *New Yorker*, Roth went to pieces and had to be carted off to a mental hospital, where he was given liberal doses of Prozac and lithium to "help control his rage,"[119] as Bloom puts it. But rage at what? At being celebrated far beyond what his achievements merited in the golden age of Jewish humor and cultural subversion? Ultimately, Bloom was unable to fathom either Roth's rage or his hatred—in particular, his hatred for her. Visiting Roth in the hospital, Bloom sat through a long silence as Roth sat on the edge of his hospital bed and glared at her "with absolute hatred."[120] In visiting with Roth's psychiatrist afterward, Bloom began to cry, asking "Dr. Bloch what caused Philip to hate me."[121] Bloch could given no answer. Nor could Bloom for why Roth showed "no interest in the woman he's lived with for almost 18 years" other than that "this is the life he wants. . . the life of a bitter, lonely, aging ascetic with no human ties."[122] The heart wants what it wants, I guess. Shortly after visiting Roth in the hospital, Bloom received divorce papers from Roth's lawyer, accusing her "of 'the cruel and inhuman treatment' of my husband Philip Roth."[123] It was an exact parallel to the custody papers which Mia Farrow received at around the same time from the other funny Jew, Woody Allen.

Claire Bloom should have read Roth's next book *Sabbath's Theater* before she wrote her memoir because it answers her question. Mickey Sabbath, the eponymous protagonist, is Portnoy 30 years later when funniness has evaporated leaving only the residue of cultural aggression behind. Sabbath is a puppeteer with arthritis, out of work and on hard times. In his "salad days," Sabbath ran the Indecent Theater of Manhattan, "where the atmosphere was insinuatingly anti-moral, vaguely menacing, and, at the same time, rascally fun."[124] He is a puppeteer because a puppeteer is "a lover and master of guile, artifice, and the unreal."[125] Sabbath is a "terrorist," and "a saboteur for subversion," having "the talent of a lunatic—or a simulated lunatic—to overawe and horrify ordinary people."[126] Sabbath's main talent, however, is his ability to corrupt the morals of anyone he comes in contact with, particularly dumb *shikses*. His art is most apparent in the tapes of his telephone sex with an undergrad broadcast over the university's counseling hotline as an example of his predatory sexism. "There was in these tapes," Roth writes,

> a kind of art in the way that he was able to unshackle his girls from their habit of innocence. There was a kind of art in his providing an illicit adventure not with a boy of their own age but with someone three times their age—the very repugnance that his aging body inspired in them had to make their adventure with him feel a little like a crime and thereby give free play to their budding perversity and to the confused exhilaration that comes with flirting with disgrace.... Once he passed into his fifties, the art in these tapes—the insidious art of giving license to what was already there—was the only art he had left.[127]

Sabbath uses this "art" to corrupt Drenka Balich, a big-breasted Croatian *shiksa*, who is both goddess and fetish in his diminishing sex life. Sabbath instructs Drenka in sexual degradation, for which she is eternally grateful—or eternally not grateful—because Drenka dies of cancer at the beginning of the novel. Roth elaborates the fantasy of the dirty old man beyond any possible suspension of disbelief, saying Sabbath was "the most patient of instructors."[128] He "had assisted her in becoming estranged from her orderly life and in discovering the indecency to supplement the deficiencies of her regular diet."[129] Sabbath "had sanctioned for her the force that wants more and more—a force to whose urging she was never wholly averse even before Sabbath had come along."[130] As a result, men saw "inside this woman was someone who thought like a man."[131] No wonder feminists hated Roth. Roth was almost enough to make a decent person sympathize with feminism.

Drenka should be grateful because Sabbath saved her life from "the routines of marriage that previously had almost killed" her.[132] Sabbath introduced Drenka to indecency, and for this she was supposed to be eternally grateful. "You were my teacher," Drenka writes in her diary. "My American boyfriend. You taught me everything. The songs. Shit from Shinola. To be free to fuck. To have a good time with my body. To not hate having such big tits. You did that."[133] This is the deepest expression of Roth's fantasy life, and by extension the fantasy life of the messianic funny Jew. The *goyim* are supposed to thank the Mock Messiah for corrupting them. Roth will hate the *goyim*, and the *goyim* will be grateful. The fact that Roth was praised by the culture he hated and hoped to destroy shows that his fantasy was not far removed from reality.

Drenka's policeman son has a different reaction when he reads Drenka's diary about Sabbath urinating on his mother. "You depraved my mother!"[134] he said, showing even the dumbest *goy* can figure some things out. He then takes Sabbath into custody for urinating on his mother's grave. The prospect of a trial looms (or perhaps the son will just march Sabbath off into the woods and put a bullet in his head), but a trial would necessitate reading the diary in court, exposing his mother's depravity, something that would delight Sabbath. So Sabbath is set free, feeling immortal because of what he has gotten away with—"He could not fucking die. How could he leave? How could he go?"—but, more importantly, because of his hate.[135] Sabbath can't leave; nor can he take his leave by suicide (even though he spends much of the novel entertaining this temptation) because "Everything he hated was here."[136] Sabbath is a creature whose hate increases as his ability to gratify his appetites decreases.

After Drenka's death Sabbath is left alone with his appetites, which he can fulfill with only increasing difficulty, and his hate, particularly his racial hatred, of which he is most proud. "I'm proud to say," Sabbath notes, "I still have all my marbles as far as racial hatred is concerned. Despite all my many troubles, I continue to know what matters in life: profound hatred."[137] Sabbath particularly hates the Japanese—"I'd say hating the Japanese plays a leading role in every aspect of my life"[138]—but Japanese is just another word for *goyim*. Japs, to Sabbath, are a particularly virulent strain of *goyim*.

As characters in the novel, the Japanese are virtually non-existent. *Goyim* in *Sabbath's Theater* is, as a result, another word for Catholic, particularly Catholic *shikses*, portrayed as grateful recipients of the sexual degradation they receive at the hands of Mickey Sabbath. Drenka is a Catholic Croatian. The cleaning woman in his friend's apartment is a Hispanic Catholic who performs fellatio on him while kneeling, which reminds him Catholics pray on their knees: "On her knees, crossing herself, praying—all an act to prove what?"[139] Sabbath wonders. Sexual perversion and *goyische* religion merge to indicate the perverse nature of Catholicism. Watching the Hispanic cleaning lady "dovening," was a spectacle "bringing out the Jew in him: a Catholic down on the floor. Always did."[140] It would be "interesting," Sabbath speculates, "if she prayed and blew him both at once. Happens a lot in Latin countries," at least in Philip Roth's imagination.[141]

The incident from *Sabbath's Theater* substantiates with stunning clarity the premise posited in *Portnoy's Complaint* that sexual liberation is Jewish aggression against the *goyim*. According to this Jewish fantasy, the *goyim* collaborate willingly in their sexual degradation; they are grateful for the opportunity to gratify Roth's racial hatred. When Sabbath is charged with an obscene performance outside Columbia University, he is arrested by a Jewish cop, but tried by a Catholic prosecutor, whom he refers to as "St. John's," a reference to St. John's Catholic University. When Sabbath is acquitted,

> St. John's passes by us and says, so nobody but us can hear, "and which of you gets to screw with the girl?" I said to him, "You mean, which of us Jews? We all

do. We all get to screw the girl. Even my old zaydeh gets to screw her. My rabbi gets to screw her. Everybody gets to screw her except you, St. John's. You get to go home and screw your wife. That's what you're sentenced to—screwing for life Mary Elizabeth, who worships her older sister, the nun."[142]

The attack on "St. John's" radiates ethnic hatred. Mickey Sabbath hates Catholics and, as an expression of that hatred, he tries to separate them from their sexual morals. But behind the hatred looms envy, envy at anyone who is not ruled by his own sexual desires. Mickey Sabbath is Portnoy 30 years later. In other words, Philip Roth. Sabbath is Portnoy, but Portnoy isn't funny anymore. The humor is gone; all that's left is sexual aggression and hatred.

Portnoy sees himself as a latter-day Abraham Lincoln, "the Great Emancipator,"[143] until he is brought up short by moral reality. The Great Emancipator Portnoy "wind[s] up trying to free from bondage nothing more than my own prick."[144] Portnoy, recognizing his sexual bondage, wishes vainly to be "a man once again—in control of my will, conscious of my intentions, doing as I wished, not as I must."[145] Portnoy has moments of doubt; all Sabbath has is hate. *Sabbath's Theater* is to *Portnoy's Complaint* what *Scary Movie 3* is to *Airplane*. Sabbath ranting about racial hatred corresponds with the Mother Teresa skit in *Scary Movie 3* and with its gags about Negro funerals. At some point, all of the funny Jews stop being funny, and all that is left is naked cultural aggression, naked hatred of the stupid *goyim* who pay to get ridiculed by funny Jews.

James Bloom sees hate as the "trademark"[146] of the funny Jew. Beneath singer/songwriter Randy Newman's "eclectic levity," Bloom discerns "an ability to hate that even all the drugs he took couldn't quell."[147] Hate is a trademark of the funny Jew, not because hate is funny, but because he is a Jew. Hate is a Jewish virtue.

That assertion is made not in *Mein Kampf* but in the philo-Semitic neoconservative journal *First Things*. In "The Virtue of Hate," Rabbi Meir Y. Soloveichik talks about how he rebelled against the idea that hatred was a Jewish virtue but gradually came to see the truth of the assertion. "Hate," Rabbi Soloveichik says, "can be virtuous when one is dealing with the frightfully wicked."[148]

Even granting the rabbi his premise for the sake of aruguement, we are left wondering how is this principle applied in the world of human passion? Is there a hate switch that can be turned on and off? Is there a hate beam radiating from the human soul like a laser to focus on a target without the danger of collateral damage? The rabbi's assertion doesn't answer Claire Bloom's question either. Why does Philip Roth hate his Jewish wife? Can the rabbi give us an answer to that question? Can he give us a calculus of hate which will enable us to know when it is appropriate to hate and when it is not? Or who it is appropriate to hate and who it is not? Is it legitimate to hate terrorists? The answer to that question is an unequivocal "Yes." What about suspected terrorists? What about Palestinians? What about Palestinian children playing in the immediate vicinity of suspected terrorists? Is it legitimate to hate the *goyim*? Is it legitimate to hate the *shiksa* you happen to be shtupping at the moment? Can the Rabbi who thinks that hate is a Jewish virtue explain to Philip Roth how he can keep the hate in his heart compartmentalized so that it doesn't slop over into hating his Jewish wife?

Rabbi Soloveichik, to his credit, tries to answer some of these questions. He tries with all the might of his legalistic talmudic heart to come up with a *vade mecum* on how to hate properly. "An Israeli mother," the rabbi says, "is right to raise her child to hate Saddam Hussein, but she would fail as a parent if she taught him to despise every Arab. We who hate must be wary lest we, like Goldstein, become like those we are taught to despise."[149] Soloveichik is referring to Baruch Goldstein, a Jew who "murdered 20 innocent Muslims engaged in prayer in Hebron."[150] Harvey Cox argued it was no coincidence Goldstein murdered the Jews on Purim, and Soloveichik admits "there is something to Cox's remarks. The danger inherent in hatred is that it must be very limited, directed only at the most evil and unrepentant."[151]

But does that mean the Palestinians? Or Philip Roth's wife? Who decides? Is there some Jewish pope who can infallibly adjudicate the matter? Or is each Jew free to decide whom he can hate? It's okay for Sabbath to hate the Japs, but is it okay for Roth to hate his Jewish wife? If hatred is a Jewish virtue, then Roth must be a Jewish saint, an authority to be emulated. "When hate is appropriate," the rabbi says, "then it is not only virtuous, but essential for Jewish well-being."[152] The result of the ommission of that slight detail is the ongoing bloodbath in the West Bank, where hate leads to indiscriminate revenge, which leads to more hate. With Jewish wisdom like this, it's easy to prefer the foolishness of the gospels.

Rabbi Soloveichik is right in seeing hate as a Jewish virtue. He is also right in claiming that "a theological chasm remains between the Jewish and Christian viewpoints on the matter" because "Christianity's founder acknowledged his break with Jewish tradition on this matter from the very outset: "You have hear that it was said, 'You shall love your neighbor and hate your enemy.'"[153] The rabbi is right about Christianity but wrong about the religion of the Jews, something he acknowledges inadvertently when he notes "Moses commanded us 'not to hate our brother in our hearts.'"[154] According to Soloveichik, "a man's immoral actions can serve to sever the bonds of brotherhood between himself and humanity. Regarding *a rasha*, a Hebrew term for the hopelessly wicked, the Talmud clearly states: *mitzvah lisnoso*—one is obligated to hate him."[155]

Another explanation of the discrepancy between the Talmud and Moses is possible, namely, that the Talmud is the antithesis of the teaching of Moses. The rabbi's statement that hatred is a Jewish virtue is true, but the statement is so fatuous and repugnant that only someone blinded by generations of hatred and ethnocentric prejudice could make it. Jews, as anyone who has looked at the portal of a medieval cathedral can see, are blind.

To call the rabbi fatuous, however, is not to dispute his main contention. Hatred is a Jewish virtue. The people who call themselves Jews are not interested in following Moses; in this regard they are not even Jews. They are, as St. John said, "liars." They are, again citing St. John, "the synagogue of Satan." Hate is a Jewish virtue, not because Moses taught it, but because the people who call themselves Jews are nothing more than anti-Christians who are ultimately in rebellion against the law of Moses. "The very question of how to approach our enemies," the rabbi says, "depends on whether one believes that Jesus was merely a misguided mortal, or the Son of God."[156] Precisely. Given the logic of rejection and reversal that is the essence of Talmudic Judaism, hate must be the highest Jewish virtue because love is the highest Christian virtue. In choosing to reject Christ, those who call themselves Jews reject love and Moses and everything Moses stood for.

The people who call themselves Jews remain true to the their iconographic reputation as blind by insisting on the very thing that goes against their own best interests. "Hate," the rabbi says, "allows us to keep our guard up, to protect us."[157] Soloveichik cites the "many hundreds of Jewish victims of suicide bombings" as indicating "the importance and the necessity of Jewish hate has once again been demonstrated."[158] Someone less blinded by "the virtue of hate" might have a different view of cause and effect.

"For Jews," the rabbi concludes, "God gave humanity the means for its own redemption."[159] The history of the Jews since Christ is littered with Messiahs who tried to put that idea into action, all bringing catastrophe onto the heads of the Jewish people. The difference between Alex Portnoy and Mickey Sabbath is simple but telling. Portnoy knows he is a Failed Messiah, and can laugh about it and make us laugh about it too. At the end of *Portnoy's Complaint*, Portnoy sees himself as the Messiah manqué: "I was supposed to save her life," he says of The Monkey, "and didn't."[160] The same is true of his other *shiksa*, The Pumpkin, "Someone who knew who she was. Psychologically so intense as not to be in need of salvation or redemption by me! Not in need of conversion to my glorious faith."[161] Portnoy regrets seducing and abandoning The Pumpkin:

> Christ, yes, this was one of the great *shikses*. I might have learned something spending the rest of my life with such a person. Yes, I might—if I could learn something! If I could be somehow sprung from this obsession with fellatio and fornication, from romance and fantasy, and revenge—from the settling of scores! the pursuit of dreams! from this hopeless, senseless loyalty to the long ago.... My wholesome, big-bottomed, lipstickless, barefooted *shikse*, where are you now Kay-Kay? ... The very best of the Middle West, so why did I let her go? Why did I ever let her go![162]

Roth's character "let her go" because his behavior was ruled by his disordered desires and not practical reason, another name for morality. Portnoy plays down his guilt by associating his transgression of the moral law with tearing "the tag from my mattress that says, 'Do Not Remove Under Penalty of Law'—what would they give me for that, the chair?"[163] Yes, after Jewish humor reshaped America, they would give Portnoy a chair at Harvard for his mastery in moral subversion.

From that chair, he could, as Philip Roth has, pontificate *ex cathedra* on "the ridiculous disproportion of the guilt!"[164]

James Bloom remains clueless throughout his book on Jewish humor, even to the point of proposing the funny Jew as one more Messiah manqué at the book's conclusion, just as Albert Goldman did when Portnoy appeared 30 years earlier. History repeated itself, first as tragedy and then as farce. First Karl Marx as the Jewish Messiah, then Groucho Marx as the messianic Funny Jew. "Jewish jokes," Bloom says, quoting Theodor Reik, "will spur 'the abolishment of religion.'"[165] In addition, they foster, as they fall from the mouth of the Funny Jew Messiah, "'emotional brotherhood' enfolding and giving pleasure to ever-widening 'circles of American Gentiles.' This extension of Jewishness beyond boundaries of 'blood' and faith constitutes a new quasi-tribal identity ... . Where the funny Jews' new tribalism departs from its predecessors is in repudiating blood and even faith as the basis for membership."[166]

The messianic chosen people had mutated once again. Tired of waiting for a messiah who never came the Jewish people became their own messiah in the middle of the 19th century. From that point on, it continued to mutate from the latest messianic successor of the vanguard of the proletariat, from the sexually liberated, from the neocon bobos, into the audience at the local comedy club. As proof of the efficacy of this new religion, Bloom cites the testimony of someone known as "O'Hehir," presumably Irish by the sound of his name and formerly Catholic, by the sound of his ideas. "O'Hehir" claims that Woody Allen movies are "the central factor shaping who I have become."[167] As if that weren't depressing enough, Bloom feels that the funny Jew, in this case, Woody Allen has now created a "'cult' based on a 'communal mystique.'"[168]

Jewish Discourse

Chapter Thirty-Two

The Neoconservative Era

One former liberal who claimed, to use Irving Kristol's term, that he had been "mugged by reality" was Ronald Reagan, the former governor of California who lost the Republican presidential nomination to Gerald Ford in 1976. Friedman calls Reagan "a genuine neocon,"[1] because like Podhoretz *et al* he became disillusioned when Democrats abandoned the anti-Communist crusade. "I didn't leave the Democratic Party," Reagan said, "The Democratic Party left me."[2] Faced with another four years of Jimmy ("inordinate fear of communism") Carter, the neoconservative Jews jumped off the Democratic ship they had sailed on since the New Deal and went to work for Ronald Reagan. Reagan's victory resembled the triumph of the Communists over the Whites during the Russian Civil War. Once it became clear that the Communists had won, the Jews flooded into the capital to staff the new regime.

The Reagan administration became the Jewish Camelot. *Commentary* was required reading in the White House, and a horde of neocons marched to Washington or marched from Washington's think tanks into the White House. They included Paul Wolfowitz, who worked for George Schulz at the State Department; Kenneth Adelman, who served as director of Arms Control and Disarmament Agency; William Kristol, who worked under neocon agent William Bennett at Education; Norman Podhoretz's son-in-law Elliott Abrams, who became assistant secretary of defense; and Richard Pipes, who left Harvard to become the architect for the final battle of the Cold War. About the only neocon not in Washington was Norman Podhoretz, who failed to get confirmed as head of the United States Information Agency. So many Jewish neocons received appointments that the ambivalent *New Republic* "complained 'Trotsky's orphans' were taking over the government."[3]

Authoring "Dictatorships and Double Standards" in the November 1979 *Commentary* earned Jeanne Kirkpatrick, a Democrat, a job as UN ambassador. She provided "the neocon rationale for silence ... at the behavior of those right-wing regimes that reaganistas backed in Central America." Kirkpatrick also repaid her benefactors by supporting Israel so assiduously that she was known as "the ambassador from *Commentary*."[4]

Elliott Abrams was the architect of Reagan's anti-Communist crusade in central America. After working as national chair of Campus Americans for Democratic Action, Abrams joined the staff of Henry Jackson, after Richard Perle "told him of the senator's efforts on behalf of Israel and of his strong pro-defense and anti-Soviet posture."[5] In 1977 he joined Senator Daniel Patrick Moynihan's staff. Through Moynihan he made contact with the New York neocons and married Midge Decter's daughter Rachel. Abrams wrote the memo that led to the mining of three Nicaraguan harbors. He became so embroiled in the Iran-Contra Affair that he pled guilty to two counts of withholding information from Congress. Abrams was pardoned by George H.W. Bush on his last day in office; he later served as an official in the second Bush administration, helping orchestrate the invasion of Iraq.

1981: Bernard Nathanson Testifies for the Human Life Bill

On June 18, 1981, six months after Ronald Reagan took office, Bernard Nathanson got off a short flight from New York to Washington and headed to hearings on the Human Life Bill chaired by Senator East of North Carolina. Nathanson now opposed abortion, and he intended to explain why. Nathanson's defection from proabortion ranks did not change the ethnic dimensions of the abortion struggle. His later conversion to Catholicism, in fact, confirmed the ethnic grammar of what had always been a Jewish/Catholic conflict. Between his conversion to the prolife cause and his conversion to Catholicism, Nathanson was to learn that a prolife Jew was an "invisible man."

In covering the hearings, *The New York Times* stuck to the ethnic playbook Nathanson and Lader had created. *Times* reporter Bernard Weinraub listed the academic credentials and achievements of Leon Rosenberg, a geneticist who testified for abortion on demand. Rosenberg "drew a prolonged round of applause" when he announced there was not "a single piece of scientific evidence" to determine "when life begins."[6] Dr. Irving Cushner, the Jewish gynecologist from the UCLA Medical Center, a major player in the California abortion scene, also testified for the pro-abortion side. Nathanson credits Cushner with "a peroration on abortion, love and interpersonal communication that would have done the Reverend Jim Jones credit."[7]

Nathanson testified for the prolife position along with Dr. John Willke, a Catholic physician from Cincinnati, but when the news reports appeared the following day, Nathanson's testimony wasn't even mentioned. "My name," Nathanson writes, "did not appear in the coverage. And again, my name did not appear in the *Washington Post* coverage of the hearings.... Why did the *New York Times* fail to list me as a participant?"[8] Nathanson wondered if the omission was "possibly an oversight."[9] His non-existence was strange since he "was the author of a great many of these ['60s rallying cries] (in conjunction with Friedan and Lader) that we used."[10] His changed mind should have been newsworthy in itself, except he had converted to the wrong side, and his conversion contradicted the ethnic scenario the *Times* was at great pains to preserve.

Upon reflection, the reason his name was omitted is explainable. According to the ethnic playbook, only Catholics were prolife; people who were pro-abortion had no ethnic identity. Jews, according to that playbook, were always proabortion, even though that could never be mentioned publicly. Including Nathanson's name would have ruined the ethnic scenario the *Times* was trying to maintain, according to which Jews (although it would be anti-Semitic for prolifers to bring this up) were all proabortion, whereas the anti-abortion forces were always (or only) Catholic.

The New York Times also failed to mention the video of a fetus shown at the hearings. That omission and the UPI wire service's failure to mention either Dr. Hilgers or Dr. Nathanson was tantamount to "journalistic malpractice" according to Nathanson. "Was it," Nathanson wonders,

> that the testimony of Hilgers and Nathanson was not fit to print? or was it that a reporter listening to my statement and the answers to Senator Hatch's questions, listening to Hilgers and watching that bombshell of a tape on the television, might be unexpectedly swayed to write a fair, reasoned and informative piece for the public indicating that the 1969 passwords can no longer suffice for pro-abortion arguments in 1981?[11]

Nathanson concluded that the mega-press was biased. The Lichter Rothman survey showed it was disproportionately Jewish and overwhelmingly pro-abortion. Ninety percent of the journalists questioned by Lichter and Rothman were pro-abortion. In addition, Nathanson discovered

> One in four [members of the mega-press] is Jewish. In the general population 24 in every thousand persons are Jewish, but in the mega press 230 out of every thousand are Jewish, a representation far out of proportion to their numbers in the census. This is clearly the source of the fulsome accusation from identifiably anti-Semitic sources that the media is dominated by Jews.[12]

At this point, perhaps to save himself from the accusation that he was an anti-Semite, Nathanson adds that "Lichter and Rothman are both Jewish, and so am I."[13]

Two years after Nathanson testified before Congress, on June 28, 1983, the Human Life Bill was defeated in the United States Senate by a vote of 50-49. The Senate had voted down a statement affirming that "A right to abortion is not secured by this Constitution."[14] Nathanson went on to become a celebrity among prolife groups, but in the eyes of the mainstream "mega-press,"[15] he had become a non-person. His non-existence was attributable in part at least to the fact that he had converted to the wrong side in the culture wars, but it was also attributable to the fact that, as a prolife Jew, he had no place in the manichean ethnic framework in which the abortion issue had become couched.

1981: Schmitz Hearings

Six months after Bernard Nathanson testified before Congress, state Senator John Schmitz held hearings in Los Angeles on when human life began. His hearings paralleled those in Washington. Ronald Reagan, the governor of California who signed its permissive abortion bill into law, had a change of heart and had been elected as the first president sympathetic to prolife positions since *Roe v. Wade*. To repay the Catholic ethnics who abandoned the Democratic Party to vote for him, Reagan expressed willingness to sign a bill stating human life began at conception. Schmitz was formerly the congressman representing President Nixon's San Clemente district. Schmitz had alienated Nixon, saying he had no objection to Nixon going to China as long as he didn't come back. Schmitz had alienated Jewish women's groups during hearings on breast cancer, when they objected vociferously to informed consent on breast cancer because they thought it would lead to an informed consent abortion bill. But he was taken aback by their vehemence at the abortion hearings.

Outgunned by prolife testimony, the proabortion side used street theater to divert the press from the evidence life began at conception. Jewish feminist lawyer Gloria Allred claimed that if the Human Life Bill passed, women could be prosecuted for miscarriages. She ended her testimony by claiming women would be forced to wear "chastity belts."[16] She then took an instrument of sexual torture she had purchased at an S&M shop and threw it at the Catholic Schmitz "for his wife to wear."[17]

Allred's stunt diverted the press, which did not mention the evidence that showed the fetus was a human being deserving of protection. Nor did they cover the testimony of National Council of Jewish Women spokesman Toby Egeth, who claimed "any legislation in this area [i.e., abortion] would pose a serious threat to our Constitutional right to practice our religion ... we are opposed to accidental and indiscriminate reproduction in an already overpopulated and underfed world."[18] This statement prompted Catholic prolifers to wonder "Would the NCJW prefer an exception clause to a human life amendment which would prohibit all abortions except those done on Jewish mothers in order that the NCJW could continue to practice its religion of abortion?"[19]

Annoyed the press ignored the prolife testimony in favor of Allred's attempt to infuriate Schmitz by insulting his wife and their marital relationship, Schmitz issued a press release saying "the front rows of the state auditorium were filled with a sea of hard, Jewish, and (arguably) female faces whose general countenance reassured those of us on the committee dais that had we somehow fallen from the stage we would have been devoured as so many carcasses thrown to the piranha."[20] Schmitz claimed the hearings had been subverted by "pre-organized infestations of imported lesbians and from anti-male and pro-abortion queer groups in San Francisco and other centers of decadence."[21] The press release praised hearings in other parts of the state, "held in Catholic, and therefore somewhat civilized territory."[22]

The Jews were infuriated, immediately accusing Schmitz of anti-Semitism. Julie Gertler, at the hearings as president of the National Council of Jewish Women, and presumably one of the hard, Jewish, and (arguably) female faces staring at Schmitz, "was highly offended" and her "husband was outraged" too.[23]

Schmitz's Attack of the Bulldykes press release was so frank it scared all but the hardiest prolifers. The right to life organizations folded first as the Jews orchestrated public opinion against Schmitz. Karen Bodziak, director of education for the Right to Life League of Southern California, referred to his comments as "off the wall."[24] The California Prolife Medical Association termed the language "rough" and "intemperate," but maintained it was "fair commentary" and accurate.[25] Apparently Gloria Allred in her spiky hairdo did look like a"slick butch lawyeress,"[26] the phrase Schmitz used to describe her.

One Jew came to Schmitz's defense. Dr. Kenneth Mitzner of the Los Angeles Chapter of the Jewish Life Issues Committee reported to Senator David Roberti, Chairman of the Rules Committee that "Senator Schmitz's ethnic characterization of the audience (at the LA hearing) was technically correct."[27] Catholic David Roberti, the president pro tem of the California senate who had appointed Schmitz chairman of the committee ignored Mitzner. "His comments," Roberti said of Schmitz, "are anti-Semitic and not appropriate for a senator or a chairman of a committee."[28] Roberti, a longtime abortion foe, said he planned to remove Schmitz from his posts. Schmitz claimed Roberti had caved in to pressure from pro-abortion groups and "a very heavy homosexual contingent in his district" in Hollywood and central Los Angeles.[29] "I would wear it as a badge of honor if I get stripped of my chairmanship for his issue," he said.[30] And Schmitz soon got his wish.

When Schmitz refused to apologize for calling Allred a "slick butch lawyeress," she filed a defamation suit. Schmitz paid $20,000 to settle; he also issued an apology. He was then stripped of his committee position. The facts remained eerily irrelevant. No one disputed the presence of Jewish and homosexual groups at the hearing or that they were working toward the same goal. No one disputed Jewish support for abortion. No one defended Gloria Allred's hairdo, nor did anyone define anti-Semitism, which had come to mean anything certain Jews found offensive.

In early January 1982 Los Angeles City Councilman Hal Bernson, a Jew and a promoter of abortion, orchestrated a resolution issued by the Republican party censuring Schmitz.

About the time that resolution passed, the Martin Container Corporation sent employees to repossess a 20-foot metal container from the posh Woodland Hills residence of Malvin Weissberg, who owned a pathology lab. When the workers unpacked the container, they found aborted late term fetuses. The plastic containers containing roughly 17,000 fetuses had come from Inglewood Hospital run by Dr. Morton Barke. Each container was labeled with the name of the doctor who had performed the abortion. A legal tug of war followed along predictably ethnic lines. Catholic lawmakers were outraged and wanted to arrange decent burial. The pathologist and the abortionists, who were Jewish, were defended by the press, who wanted to know how photos of the fetuses were obtained. At the behest of the Feminist Women's Health Center, Carol Sobel and Dorothy Lang of the ACLU filed for a restraining order to prevent release of the bodies.

In May 1982, Ronald Reagan wrote to Philip B. Dreisbach, Secretary of the California Pro-Life Medical Association and a pathologist who examined the bodies during a mass autopsy. "When all is said and done," Reagan wrote, "being confronted with the reality of abortion and its consequences removes all trace of doubt and hesitation."[31] Reagan said he hoped "evidence like that found in California will move those who have thus far preferred silence or inaction and encourage them to agree that something must be done. I have expressed my anticipation that Congress act expeditiously on this matter and approve a measure which will remove this evil and all its vestiges from our society."[32]

Six months after the discovery, the fetuses remained unburied, in cold storage at the LA county morgue, and the incident had been memorialized in a brochure entitled "The American Holocaust." The title was sure to antagonize pro-abortion forces by drawing attention to the irony that the Jews most likely to complain about Hitler's policies in Germany also were in the forefront of the abortion industry in California. A sidebar entitled "Who is Responsible for the American Holocaust in California?" listed names that were almost exclusively Jewish.[33]

1984: The revised Oberammergau Passion Play

When the Oberammergau passion play, purged of offensive material after 20 years of negotiations, was performed in 1984, the Jews were angrier than ever. The *New York Times* ran a piece by James Rudin, "Oberammergau Play: Still Anti-Semitic." In the play, "the Jews," says Rudin, "emerge as a corrupt, brutal people, driven by harsh and cruel law—clearly the 'bad guys' of the play."[34] Jews must redouble their efforts. Now the real concessions could begin. Rudin later claimed his column was "'the turning point, the wake-up call'"[35] for Oberammergau. "Then," Rudin says, "they felt the power of the Jews. It stunned them. It's one thing to publish in the *Journal of Ecumenical Studies*, another in the *New York Times*."[36]

The Journal of Ecumenical Studies was edited by Leonard Swidler, a Catholic theological expert whom the Jews used to undermine Catholic teaching. One wonders how Swidler felt when Rudin referred to his journal with thinly veiled contempt. By 1984, however, Swidler could not have curried Rudin's favor without the protective cover of *Nostra Aetate*, a document that, Shapiro indicates, created confusion in Oberammergau "over how to deal with a situation in which the Vatican position appears to be at odds with the very words of the Gospel."[37] Shapiro writes "at rock bottom—though few would admit it—the tension between opponents and supporters of the play was about how the founding story of Christianity was to be told and how Scripture was to be interpreted."[38]

But it was more than that as well. It was an attack on the idea of the vow as something that would be "rewarded by divine intervention,"[39] as opposed to financial calculations based on expedience, the first law of the Jewish modernity. The "villagers of Oberammergau ... remained faithful to the tradition that a vow was taken by their ancestors in 1633 ... if their lives were spared they would perform a

Passion Play in perpetuity."[40] If "the refusal to honor" a solemn vow was considered "an act of impiety," then the Jews would promote impiety, and the deracination that goes with it, by undermining the villagers' belief in the historical foundation of their vow.[41] Shapiro indicates "the identity of Oberammergau, its notion of its own past, present, and future, was closely tied to this powerful narrative. To question [the vow] was necessarily to call into doubt the exceptional nature of the village and its steadfast commitment to Passion playing."[42]

"The problem," he says, "is that the chronicle narrative—the story's only source—rests on very shaky foundations."[43] To the Jewish debunker of Christian piety, the unreliability of the play's antecedents is similar to the historical unreliability of the gospels. In fact, "The problem of the transmission of the vow story," Shapiro says, "bears an uncanny resemblance to the more controversial one raised by the Evangelists' retelling of Jesus' Passion: How accurate are versions of the past set down by writers several generations removed from the events that they describe?"[44]

The historical basis of the vow had to be destroyed because the vow validated a world the Jews find unacceptable. Shapiro cites "the Catholic Eugen Roth," who sees the vow as something that saved the villagers from modernity: "Recent years have brought such revolutionary changes to the whole globe that only a securely anchored vow, an unbroken tradition, can explain why Oberammergau remained true to itself in the midst of a disintegrating world spiritually impoverished by technical achievements and the desire for sensational distraction."[45]

Shapiro cites another writer who

uses the village as a stick to beat those who commit adultery or have stopped going to church: "In an age when many people break their vows of baptism, confirmation or marriage if they no longer feel like keeping them, it is refreshing to find a community which believes that the vow made by the ancestors is still solemnly binding on them." This may keep the pilgrims coming to see the play, but it is a myth of piety that has begun to suffocate many in Oberammergau, especially the young, when held to this impossibly high example.[46]

So we can conclude from this that Shapiro considers the Mosaic prohibition against adultery "an impossibly high example." This may explain his vehement attempts to debunk the villagers' vow. The attack on the vow is an attack on anyone who believes that a sphere of life can be reserved for something other than commercial purposes. As such, the attack on the vow becomes an attack on marriage. Those who resist the commercialization of sex are deluding themselves with "a myth of piety," which is ultimately "suffocating." The attack on the marriage vow as an "impossibly high example" becomes so vehement, one must assume that for once personal, as opposed to ethnic, motives are entering into the discussion here.

But the attack on the vow is above all else an attack on the idea of a rooted culture. The Jews clearly saw "the fantasy of Oberammergau"[47] as an affront to what they see as universal progress, which is to say the universal commercialization of every aspect of human life. Shapiro's account makes clear that the fact that Oberammergau was perceived as "inaccessible, the people neither influencing, nor being influenced by the outer world" was intolerable.[48] The idea of a "'mountain-girt' village" that was "far removed from the world...defined by progress, secularization and social revolution"[49] was clearly repugnant to Shapiro and by extension to the Jewish organizations which waged cultural warfare on Oberammergau for that reason.

Shapiro then goes into his debunking mode. "This little valley in the Bavarian mountains" is not different "from the outside world;" nor is it "strangely untouched and uncorrupted."[50] Shapiro delightedly quotes the impressions of the first tourists to arrive as a prelude to debunking them because no place on earth can escape the forces of "progress, secularization and social revolution." When Winold Reiss writes Oberammergau is "one of the few spots in all the world where faith and idealism have successfully withstood materialism and commercial greed," Shapiro responds "nothing could have been further from the truth than the idea that these were rural peasants, cut off from intercourse with the outside world by a ring of mountains."[51] The contrary impression, Shapiro says, is "a credit to the collective acting ability of the villagers ... One wonders to what extent they even began to believe it themselves."[52]

To show it is "impossible to protect the villagers from uncontrollable forces from the outside world," Shapiro attacks "the much-heralded morality of the villagers"[53] by delving into the village's illegitimacy rate. "If local records of illegitimacy rates are any indication," Shapiro says, "reports of Oberammergau's extraordinary virtue are overrated."[54] Shapiro is not the first to spread rumors to undermine their passion play. The rumors go back to 1890 when Rev. E. Hermitage Day said "some of the more malicious rumors ... were traced to disappointed Jewish financiers, who had hoped to secure a share of the profits by financing the play."[55]

Given the unrelenting Jewish attack on Oberammergau, what revisions would satisfy them? Otto Huber learned the answer when he flew to New York to meet with ADL executive director Abraham Foxman. Convinced the Bavarians had purged every remnant of anti-Semitism, Huber presented Foxman with a copy of the script and an invitation to see the play. Foxman's cold rejection took Huber aback. According to Foxman, "Everything was fine" until Huber said "his play was about love and understanding."[56] Foxman exploded. "I told him," Shapiro writes, quoting Foxman, "If you want to give me love and understanding, there are a lot of other Christian subjects. There's no absolute need to do it. Give me another play; if it's about a Crucifixion in which the Jews kill Christ, you can never clean it up enough. So don't expect an embrace."[57]

Huber was stunned. Foxman wanted Oberammergau to perform a passion play without the Crucifixion. Huber realized "the ADL wants to destroy our identity."⁵⁸ Huber then tried another approach, appealing to "Oberammergau's tradition."⁵⁹ This too got him nowhere. Foxman, recounting his version to Shapiro, told Huber "to hell with tradition if it fuels hatred and contempt that ultimately kills Jews."⁶⁰ According to Shapiro, the whole thing

> had boiled down to this: for Otto Huber, the play of Jesus' Passion really was about love and understanding. And he had somehow failed to make Abraham Foxman understand this. For Abraham Foxman, the truth was equally clear: history showed that Passion plays led people to hate and sometimes to kill Jews. He didn't need to read history books to know this either. I was informed that as a child during the war, Foxman had been torn from his family.⁶¹

The impression Shapiro gives (Foxman "didn't need history books to know this either") is that Foxman had been beaten up as a child by an enraged mob streaming out of the Passion Play in Oberammergau or somewhere else in Germany. The real story—the one that Huber should have learned before he had his meeting with Foxman—is significantly different than the one to which Shapiro alluded so cryptically. Foxman was born into a Polish Jewish family in the late 1930s. When it became apparent that the Nazis were going to overrun Poland, Foxman's biological parents gave him to a Polish Catholic woman, who understood that Foxman was now her child and that she was to raise him as her own. In later life, Foxman adverted to Polish anti-Semitism, ignoring the fact that this Polish woman risked her own life, as well as the lives of her family and neighbors by raising Foxman. As some indication that she considered Foxman her own adopted child, Foxman's Polish mother had him baptized. If, as the *Catechism of the Catholic Church* indicates, "Baptism seals the Christian with the indelible spiritual mark (character) of his belonging to Christ," then Abraham Foxman is a Catholic, "because no sin can erase this mark, even if sin prevents Baptism from bearing the fruits of salvation" (Para. 1272). If Abe Foxman is a Catholic, if, in fact, Polish Catholics risked their lives to save his, why does he hate Catholics so much? We've heard of self-hating Jews. Is Foxman a self-hating Catholic?

After the war, when Foxman was six or seven, his biological parents returned and demanded their son back. The Polish woman who had risked her life to raise Foxman as her own child refused to give him back. More important for our purposes, Foxman refused to leave the Polish woman who had raised him, the woman who was the only mother he had ever known. Foxman's biological parents went to court and prevailed. In an exercise in Jewish debunking similar to the campaign he would orchestrate against Oberammergau and Gibson's Passion Play, Foxman was told that the woman he loved as his mother was not and never had been his mother. He was also told he was not and had never been a Catholic. So, from the perspective of Foxman as a child in a Polish custody battle, the Catholic story of "love and understanding" was what Professor Shapiro might call "a myth of piety."

The Foxman story has uncanny similarities with the childhood trauma of another Jewish debunker. Sigmund Freud's Czech nanny taught him Catholic prayers and devotions and may have secretly baptized him. The nanny was removed abruptly when she was accused of theft and fired (or fired for having an affair with a member of Freud's family). Holy Mother Church's vision of love and understanding was associated in both men's minds with a mother figure who suddenly disappeared; the Catholic mother promised love but could not deliver. The vision of love the Catholic mother instilled in their minds was overruled by a harsh Jewish reality. Foxman was torn from the only mother he had ever known. Was it because the Catholic mother allowed this trauma that she must be first demonized and then punished? If Foxman's Catholic mother could not be punished, then Holy Mother Church could be punished in her stead. The pain of separation from the mother was intense and impossible to remedy. Blood and the Law triumphed over love. The only way Foxman could alleviate pain of this sort was to demonize the source of the pain, namely, his Polish mother and Holy Mother Church.

Foxman, like Freud, became a member of B'nai B'rith, the Jewish Masonic lodge, from which he waged war on the Catholic Church. Oberammergau came to symbolize the "mountain-girt" exception to a Jewish world run on commercial principles. Since Holy Mother Church and what she stands for is too good to be true, since the "mountain-girt" village couldn't protect Foxman from his rapacious Jewish parents, Abe made a virtue of necessity: he identified with what he saw as the winning side, i.e., Jewish modernity and what it stands for: blood, the law, calculation, and hate.

1984: Neocons take over the Bradley Foundation

In 1984 the Lynde and Harry Bradley Foundation received a significant infusion of cash when the Bradley family sold the firm that produced the Bradley fighting vehicle to the Rockwell Corporation. In 1985, William Simon hired Irving Kristol protégé Michael Joyce, who had succeeded Simon as head of the Olin Foundation, to head the Bradley Foundation, which had an endowment of $715 million. Joyce then used the money to fund the neocon takeover of the conservative movement. Beneficiaries included Allan Bloom, who produced *The Closing of the American Mind* with Bradley money, and William Bennett, another Kristol protégé, who was used as the neocon foil to defeat M. H. Bradford's bid to head the National Endowment for the Humanities under Ronald Reagan. Taking a cue from his mentor Irving Kristol, Joyce used the Bradley Foundation's resources to fund neocon front operations. *National Review* provided the blueprint. As Buckley had attacked the John Birch Society and Ayn Rand, the Bradley Foundation went after traditional conservativism, known by the neologism Paleoconservatism.

Friedman claims "The neocons also faced attacks from the reinvigorated Paleoconservatives."[62] The opposite was the case. The Neocons spent the early '90s on the attack, taking over one conservative institution after another. They also attacked Pat Buchanan. When Russell Kirk, a founding father of post-World War II conservatism, complained neocons often mistook Tel Aviv for the "capital of the United States," Midge Decter attacked him as an anti-Semite and worked to expel him from the movement. Kirk felt neoconservatism had more to do with Trotsky than Edmund Burke; he accused the neocons of attempting to hijack the movement.

While editing the *The Religion and Society Report* newsletter for the Paleoconservative Rockford Institute, Lutheran pastor (and soon Roman Catholic priest) Richard John Neuhaus hijacked a $250,000 Bradley Foundation grant earmarked for Rockford and used it to found the neocon organ *First Things*. According to Decter, Neuhaus then approached her to become a "fellow" at *First Things*, although "neither he nor I had any firm idea of what I would be doing as a 'fellow.'"[63] Neuhaus, however, knew what he had to do to gain neocon support. At a meeting with Rockford directors, Neuhaus told Tom Fleming, editor of Rockford's Paleocon journal *Chronicles*, "I'm going to cut you off at the knees."[64]

In December 2005, editor Dale Vree announced in the *New Oxford Review* that years before he had been approached by "a Jewish neocon with no interest in Christianity or Catholicism" who "was interested in getting us to promote Jewish neocon interests" in exchange for a significant amount of money "if we would support corporate capitalism and if we would support a militaristic US foreign policy."[65] When Vree turned the Jewish neocon down, they funded *Catholicism in Crisis* and *First Things* instead. Bradley funded *Catholicism in Crisis* (later, at the Bradley Foundation's insistence, reduced to *Crisis*), a neocon journal for Catholics, founded by Michael Novak and Ralph McInerny, to counter the influence of the American bishops. When founded in 1982, the magazine's purpose was to oppose the bishops' pastoral letter on nuclear weapons. Thus "the neocons found a way to get Catholic and Christian magazines to front for their largely Jewish neocon interests."[66] By 2003, that meant ignoring the Catholic Just War Theory and supporting instead the neocon-inspired invasion of Iraq.

Because he identified the man who tried to subvert the *New Oxford Review* as a Jew, Vree was attacked as an anti-Semite. Vree rejected the charge as well as the charge that opposition to the war was tantamount to anti-Semitism, saying that by 2005 even the Jewish magazine *The Forward* said those who claimed that the invasion of Iraq was orchestrated by Jews working in Israel's interests "can no longer be shushed or dismissed as bigots."[67]

1989: Communism Falls

Shortly after the Berlin Wall came down in November 1989, David Horowitz, a red-diaper baby and communist, converted to neoconservatism, claiming the wall's fall meant the era of "revolutionary modernity ... has finally come to a close."[68]

The revolutionary era in American foreign policy, however, was just beginning. Jews like Horowitz would promote Trotsky's politics under the name neoconservatism. The Jewish converts to neoconservatism gave uncanny substantiation to the French proverb that the more things changed, the more they remained the same. After the fall of communism, Horowitz admitted Jews had a fatal attraction to Communism and other Messianic politics, tracing it to the influence of the Lurianic Cabala. He praised the counterrevolutionary zeal of the Catholic peasants of the Vendee, but then, like the Jewish moth drawn back to the candle of Messianic politics, Horowitz became an adovocate of campus speech codes, encouraging students to inform on "liberal" professors who criticized Israel. When former president Jimmy Carter published a book in 2006 associating Israel with apartheid, Horowitz called Carter a "Jew-hater." The neocons who bragged about America's victory over communism thus showed an uncanny propensity toward communist tactics when dealing with their enemies. Richard Pipes' son Daniel, who, with Martin Kramer, ran the website Campus Watch, encouraged students to inform on their professors and "report comments or behavior that might be considered hostile to Israel."[69] The same neocons also pushed Congress to deny federal funding to professors they said displayed anti-Israel bias.

In this he was like David Frum and Richard Perle, who claimed in their book *The End of Evil* that it was every American's patriotic duty to become a government informer. The more neoconservatism spread the more it began to resemble the CHEKA. "Sometimes," Frum and Perle inform us, "the motives of those who provide the information are not very pretty."[70] But so what if "maybe they want him out of the way so that they can woo his girlfriend....information from non-saints can be just as valuable."[71] These lines would take on new and sinister meaning in the wake of the torture scandals at Abu Ghraib and Guantanamo, but all that was in the future.

Ron Radosh becomes a neocon

After railing against American imperialism for his entire life, Ron Radosh finally became a spokesman for it at the very time when it became the most serious threat to peace in the world when he too converted to neoconservatism. In the aftermath of the attack on the World Trade Center, neoconservative revolutionary Jews like Assistant Defense Secretary Paul Wolfowitz seized the initiative and began orchestrating the invasion of Afghanistan and Iraq. The uncanny similarities between the worldview of Trotsky and Irving Kristol, godfather of the neoconservative movement, have been noticed by many, but not by Ronald Radosh, who is now a proud representative of American imperialism and a recipient of state department grants to lecture the Chinese Communists about how history has left them behind. "Sponsored by the office of public diplomacy in the State Department," Radosh writes, "I stood before Chinese university students and intellectuals as a proud representative of the United States."[72] Radosh tells us that he had "a keen appreciation of the irony involved,"[73] but it is obvious that the real irony of his situation has evaded him completely. The real irony resides in the title of the last chapter of his book, "Coming Home." Radosh intends it to indicate his return to America, but it could just as easily and ironically apply to Radosh as the quintessential revolutionary Jew. It was, in other words, easy for Radosh to come home a revolutionary Jewish ideology like neoconservatism because that ideology had never gotten beyond Irving Kristol's reading of Trotsky in the first place. Neoconservatism, like the Popular Front in the '40s, folk music in the '50s, sex and dope in the '60s, and feminism in the '70s, had become the locus of revolutionary Jewish activity in the world at the beginning of the third millennium. Once the neocons hijacked America's foreign policy in the wake of 9/11 it was easy for the revolutionary Jew to come back to the home he had never left.

As Radosh moved from the Left into the neoconservative orbit, he endured the sneers of former comrades. "You really are a running dog of imperialism, aren't you?" Paul Buhle jeered at a historians' convention.[74] Buhle was right. Radosh followed neocon ideology as blindly as he had followed communist ideology. Radosh would go on to work for the USIA. He would become Olin Professor of history at Adelphi University, feeding at the trough of the Olin Foundation, a major funder of neocon subversion. Buhle, though, failed to see that Radosh the neoconservative remained a revolutionary Jew. Iraq has as much chance of becoming the next heaven on earth as any of the other meccas of failed Messianic politics.

Porn Stars and Jewish Revolutionaries

"I'm proud," Nina Hartley told the Jewish magazine *Schmate*, "of my heritage's intellectual history and its empathy with the persecuted. But I'm no Zionist. Politically, I'm left-wing. I want everyone to have a job, everyone to have food, clothing, shelter, medical care and education. Utopia might be communist but in the meantime we have to have socialism. I want everyone to have a piece."[75]

Once the majority of American Jews defined themselves as sexually deviant, pornography, along with homosexual rights, feminism, and New Age goddess worship, became a natural expression of their worldview. Because they controlled Hollywood, they could make their worldview normative for the culture. The traditional animus against majority culture combined with a decline in moral scruple led "the advocates of Woody Allen" to pornography as a form of cultural warfare. The most significant thinker in this regard was Wilhelm Reich, a Jew from Galicia who was a student of Sigmund Freud and Karl Marx who tried to marry those quintessentially revolutionary Jewish ideologies. Reich wrote the book on sexual revolution that many Jewish porn stars read. Like Nina Hartley, Richard Pacheco sees a connection between being Jewish and being a porn star. Reich is the crucial link.

"Five years before I got my first part in an adult film," Pacheco explained, "I went down to an audition for an X-rated film with my hair down to my ass, a copy of Wilhelm Reich's *Sexual Revolution* under my arm and yelling about work, love and sex, which were Reich's three principles. These things have got to be in balance or your life is going to be fucked."[76] Pacheco didn't get that job, but he didn't stop auditioning either. Nor did he stop using his Jewishness to rationalize pornographic acting. "Five years later," Pacheco says, "I auditioned for another X-rated film. That very day, I also interviewed at Hebrew Union Seminary to do rabbinical study. I made the choice that the kind of rabbi I would be, if I became one, was one that could have been performing in sex films as part of his experience."[77]

Rabbi Dresner would have felt it's a long way from the Torah to *Debbie Duz Dishes*, in which Hartley plays "a sexually insatiable Jewish housewife who enjoys sex with anyone who rings the doorbell."[78] But not Rabbi Mark Blazer of Temple Beth Ami. In 2002 Blazer invited Hartley to speak at his synagogue "about how couples can spice up their marriages and feel more comfortable with their sexuality."[79] Hartley further articulated the connection between being Jewish and being a porn star in an interview with Jewish pornographer Sheldon Ranz in 1989 in *Shmate*, in which she explains she is "Jewish culturally but not religiously."[80] Jewish is thus defined negatively. Being Jewish means being anti-Christian. "I'm generally less subservient than a typical WASP female. And I've discovered certain gender interactions are different between Jewish and non-Jewish couples."[81] Hartley was born in 1956 and grew up in Berkeley, "heavily influenced by [secular] Jewish culture. It's an intellectual town. A lot of the people who set the political agenda are Jewish."[82] Hartley sees pornography as the fulfillment of "Jewish values" because those values reflect not the Torah but the mores of secular Jews in Berkeley in the '60s. That means "there are things that you learn and ways that you think that you don't understand are more Jewish than not until you go into mainstream America and realize that other people don't think this way."[83]

Jews are different from "mainstream America," which she defines as vaguely Christian. Although Christianity and Judaism both view the Torah and the moral code it expresses as canonical, Hartley defines the Jew as someone who opposes biblical morals. She justifies pornography by adverting to revolution. Unlike their communist parents, who saw the revolution as economic, the baby boomer Jewish revolutionaries saw the issues as sexual. They took Wilhelm Reich as their guide instead of Trotsky or Lenin. As Igor Shafarevich noted, socialism always had a sexual component. It always meant communality of wives as well as communality of property. But the idea of sexual liberation has been refined, and the Jewish porn stars were aware of the refinements. Hartley "descends ideologically from the Marxist Jewish philosopher Herbert Marcuse who prophesied that a socialist utopia would free individuals to achieve sexual satisfaction. Nina descends literally from a line of radical Jews. Her grandfather (a physics professor) and her father (a radio announcer) belonged to the Communist party."[84] One of Hartley's brothers is an Orthodox Jew displeased with her vocation as porn star. They don't speak to each other. Hartley portrays him as the black sheep of the family. Ranz echoes her animus: "I don't understand how a family where the parents have a Communist background can raise a kid who grows up to be an Orthodox Jew. How did that happen?"[85] It is a classic instance of the transvaluation of values inherent in contemporary Jewish identity. Who gets to excommunicate whom?

The connection between Jews and pornography is like the connection between Jews and Bolshevism. Jews become involved in pornography for the same reason they were involved in Communism, *i.e.,* to save the world. When porn maven Luke Ford received a letter from a German Turkish girl who wanted to come to Hollywood to become a porn star, he shared it with his website readers, one of whom felt involving the girl in pornography would be an example of *"tikkun olam"* (healing the world). Whether the term is intended as ironic or not, it motivated Ford to look into the connection between Jews and pornography. It also led to criticism that Ford, who is Jewish, portrayed Jews "as dirty, parasitic merchants of smut, disease, and moral pollution—by emphasizing the high number of Jewish porn publishers throughout smut's history."[86]

Jews also used pornography for cultural warfare and moral subversion. The relationship between Jews and pornography is similar to the relationship between the communist party and the proletariat described by Marx. Just as the Jews were the vanguard of revolutionary activity in Russia, so they were in the vanguard of sexual revolution in the United States. The concept of the chosen people transformed itself into the concept of the revolutionary vanguard as the Talmud dissolved the core of Jewish identity. Messianic politics replaced waiting for the Messiah. In *The Politics of Bad Faith*, David Horowitz described how a religious paradigm, the Exodus, became a political paradigm, in other words, how the eschaton got immanentized and transformed into a Messianic political movement.

Dresner sees the same thing. In becoming, in Dresner's words, "the chief advocates of modernity,"[87] Jews dedicated themselves to Communism with messianic fervor:

> They became, for example, disciples of the new politics of communism. Some 30 percent of the early leaders of the revolution were estimated to have been Jewish. Emancipated from their ancient faith by the onslaught of modern thought, which the antiquated Judaism of the time was ill-prepared to refute, they transferred their yet unexpended messianic fervor into the new religion of Marx.[88]

When the attraction of communism waned they dedicated themselves as fervently to sexual liberation. It would be naive, or as Haberer says, "shortsighted,"[89] to claim Jews just happened to be revolutionaries just as Abe Foxman would claim Jews just happened to be in pornography. Jews were drawn to both precisely because of the hold Messianic politics acquired over them once they rejected Logos. Echoing what Dresner said, Irving Kristol expresses the Messianic, universalist vision of neoconservatism and pornography. Jewish revolutionaries, Kristol says,

> did not forsake their Jewish heritage to replace it with another form of cultural identity or ethnic belonging. What they sought can best be described as an ab-

stract and futuristic idealism of assimilation qua emancipation in a denational-
ized and secularized democratic society, ideally of universal scope. Leaving the
world of their childhood did not necessarily imply its total abandonment in one
act of irreversible forgetfulness. For many this departure under the sacred halo
of socialism was the next best solution to their own existential problems—a solution that was enormously attractive since it also held out the utopian promise of
the "genuine emancipation" of all Jews in a socialist republic of universal brotherhood devoid of national, religious, and social discrimination or even distinctions.[90]

According to Kristol, secular humanism, or liberalism, is the continuation
of revolutionary thought in America. When "emancipation unleashed within the
Jewish community latent messianic passions that pointed to a new era of fraternal
'universalism' of belief for mankind,"[91] that trajectory would not stop when communism failed; underneath communism lay the Jewish penchant for revolution,
which would find another vehicle when Communism failed. Pornography and
sexual liberation was a revolutionary vehicle for American Jews disillusioned with
the illusions of their parents. Like secular humanism, pornography was perceived
as "good for Jews," because it

> permits individual Jews a civic equality and equality of opportunity dreamed of
> by previous Jewish generations. It is natural, therefore for American Jews to be,
> not only accepting of secular-humanist doctrines, but enthusiastic exponents.
> That explains why American Jews are so vigilant about removing all the signs
> and symbols of traditional religions from "the public square," so insistent that
> religion be merely a "private affair," so determined that separation of church and
> state be interpreted to mean the separation of all institutions from any signs of a
> connection with traditional religions. The spread of secular humanism through-
> out American life has been "good for Jews," no question about it. So the more,
> the better.[92]

In her memoir, *An Old Wife's Tale*, Midge Decter noted the same phenomenon, but with a little more *Angst*. "It is no secret," she writes:

> that some significant part in the emptying of the public square had been played
> by Jewish liberals. It was understandable to me why this was so, because their
> long history had left many Jews with an atavistic fear of Christian authority—so
> the more public life could be kept strictly secular the safer they felt. But under-
> stand it or not, I believe that the religion-free public condition to which they
> have made such a vital contribution had left American society, and particularly
> American culture, vulnerable to pernicious influences.[93]

Influences like pornography? Nina Hartley's description of herself as "the
blonde Jew" porn star from "a long line of radical Jews," who "wants everyone to
have a piece—a piece of sex, a piece of the means of production, a piece of a warm
communist community" and "a piece of the promised Messianic Age—now"
doesn't seem as far-fetched as on first reading.[94] The link between the Talmud and
pornography, between Torah and its antithesis, for Jews of Nina Hartley's generation, was Bolshevism with a big assist from Wilhelm Reich.

When British journalist William Cash wrote about Jewish control of Holly-wood in the October 1994 *Spectator*, Hollywood and its academic support troops reacted with rage verging on hysteria. In the *Los Angeles Times*, Neal Gabler, au-thor of *An Empire of their Own: How Jews Created Hollywood*, attacked Cash's article as "an anti-Semitic bleat from a reactionary crackpot" that could be dis-missed "if it didn't have a respectable platform in the *Spectator* and didn't play to a pre-existing prejudice that Jews control the U.S. media."[95] Gabler attacked Cash for saying what Gabler had said in his own book! According to Cash,

> That every major studio head is Jewish today is no different from 60 years ago. "Of 85 names engaged in production, 53 are Jews," a 1936 survey noted. And the Jewish advantage holds in prestige as well as numbers. In a recent *Premiere* magazine "Special Power Issue" -ranking the 100 most powerful people in the "Industry"—the top 12 were Jewish. There were no black or British industry ex-ecutives ranked. George Steiner once famously said that to be Jewish was to be a member of a club from which you could not resign.[96]

Jewish domination of Hollywood is not limited to numbers. The numbers only approximate the extent to which Jews determine the cultural matrix of the nation's films. Cash cites an instance of the "extreme measures" non-Jews must engage in to succeed in Hollywood:

> Bill Stadiem, a former Harvard educated Wall Street lawyer who is now a screen-writer in LA, told me that he recently came across an old WASP friend in an LA restaurant who had been president of the Porcellian at Harvard—the most exclu-sive undergraduate dining-club. His friend—a would-be producer—was dressed in a black nylon tracksuit and had gold chains on his wrist; dangling around his neck was a chunky Star of David. Stadiem asked: "Why the hell are you dressed like that?" The WASP replied: "I'm trying to look Jewish."[97]

One need only think back to Jay Gatsby's attempts to pass as a WASP in F. Scott Fitzgerald's novel, *The Great Gatsby*, to see how the cultural equation changed over the course of the 20th century. As media and entertainment came to dominate the political and cultural landscape, the Jew eventually succeeded the WASP as the country's culturally dominant ethnic group, the group which set the styles for the rest of the nation.

Again, the term Jew has to be defined. "Jews in Hollywood," according to one commentator, "like most Jews in the media, academia and pornography, tend to be radical and alienated Jews, rooted neither in Judaism nor in the majority Christian culture. They tend to be rootless and politically left of center, seeking to create a rootless cosmopolitan society to reflect their own non-Judaic tradition-less values."[98] They don't cease being Jews, however, nor do they cease to act like Jews, as Cash makes clear. Cash describes then 81-year-old Lew Wasserman as at the top of Hollywood's "feudal power structure."[99] When Steven Spielberg, Da-vid Geffen, and Jeffrey Katzenberg decided to form their own production studio, they gathered at Wassenberg's estate to gain his "rabbinical blessing," after which "they spoke in 'hushed, reverential tones about the industry potentate,' and how he "spun stories about the history of Hollywood and showed them artifacts."[100] Jews, according to Cash, govern the New Establishment like rootless revolutionaries. They apply traditional Jewish prejudice against majority culture with none of the restraint imposed by the Torah's moral norms. Thus, Hollywood promulgated moral subversion during the cultural revolution of the '60s. Anyone who objected was demonized as an anti-Semite.

"Few in Hollywood (can) recall such an anti-Semitic article in a mainstream publication," wrote Bernard Weinraub, the *New York Times*' Hollywood correspondent, addressing Cash's article.[101] Hollywood concurred, filling the letters columns of local papers with horrified reactions. One letter to the editor, whose list of prominent signatories included Kevin Costner, Sidney Poitier, and Tom Cruise, worried that a new Holocaust and Spanish Inquisition was imminent.

William Cash's and Joe Breen's candor about Hollywood shows the battle over the sexualization of American culture was a battle between America's Jews and Catholics. From 1934 to 1965, Hollywood's Jews were forced to repress their "permissive, value-free attitude" in the films they made. The golden age of Hollywood was not a collaborative effort; it was Catholics saving Jews from their worst instincts. The Catholics lost, with dire consequences for the nation. The Rabbi Dresner Jew declined and the Woody Allen Jew rose as an icon for the entire culture. The Catholics lost the culture wars because they internalized Woody Allen Jewish values on sexuality, just as they adopted WASP values on birth control.

Dresner on Porn

Rabbi Dresner has a dilemma. Boston's Puritans were the first and foremost influence in America. They were Judaizers following an Old Testament Christianity, making America one of the most "Jewish" Christian nations. The Enlightenment, the intellectual matrix out of which the United States grew, abstracted Jewish morals from its religious context and made them the basis for a multi-ethnic "nation." America's Jewish roots go deep, but they also lead to Rabbi Dresner's dilemma. On the one hand, adherence to the Torah's teaching on the family can save America from moral decline. On the other, the moral decline that Dresner complains about is attributable to the cultural influence of American Jews, something he adverts to repeatedly. "Jews," he says, "have played a less than admirable role in the sexual revolution."[102] "Many liberal rabbis," he continues, "are in the forefront of the proabortion movement. In fact, surveys indicate that Jewish women are among the most likely of all groups to support 'abortion on demand'."[103] Dresner cites "a recent Gallup poll and a suppressed B'nai B'rith survey," indicating American Jews are more likely to divorce and less likely to marry than the average American; "91 percent of Jewish women agree that every woman who wants an abortion should be able to have one"; "50 percent of Jewish women signaled a high degree of affinity for feminism compared to only 16 percent among non-

Jewish women;" and, Jews favor homosexual rights more than the general population.[104] Yet, the Jewish religion says "homosexuality is a violation of the order of
creation" and the family is "divinely ordained."[105] Dresner says Jews, if they want
to participate in a family coalition, "need to put their own house in order" not only
because they have abandoned traditional values, but because they "are more likely
to live in urban areas in the forefront of social change."[106]

Part of Dresner's pathos stems from his anguish when viewing the moral decline of American Jews, which he sees as anti-Jewish, because Jews either stand for
the moral law, as introduced by Moses into human history, or they stand for nothing. Jews like Woody Allen are especially painful for Dresner because they have
become cultural icons by promoting sexual deviance and by hawking the symbols
of traditional anti-Semitism. "For the Gentile," Dresner writes, "Allen's depiction
of religious Jews as pious frauds, and worse, can only confirm ancient Christian
canards of the Jew as hypocrite, devil, despoiler of morality, and corrupter of culture."[107] Why, an anguished Dresner wonders, should American Jews rush to accept Woody Allen's categorization of them as "despoilers of morality"? Dresner
cannot answer that question. "Why Jews want to demean themselves is a question
that Hollywood 'theologians' have yet to address."[108] But the fact remains: the Jews
who dominate Hollywood and thus American culture, have defined themselves
as, in Dresner's words, "despoilers of morality and corrupters of culture."

Dresner is concerned others have noticed the same thing. He cites a letter
to the *California Lawyer* that claims "the progressive deterioration of morality
can be directly attributable to the growing predominance of Jews in our national
life."[109] Dresner is appalled, but he says the same thing. How can Rabbi Dresner
claim Jews can reform family life and morals when he's saying Jews are responsible for the moral decline in the first place? All Rabbi Dresner can say without fear
of contradiction is that anyone who takes the Torah as normative on sexual issues
will be at odds with the overwhelming majority of American Jews.

Ralph Reed Stabs Buchanan in the Back.

In 1992 Pat Buchanan ran for president against incumbent George H. W. Bush
and, like Eugene McCarthy 24 years earlier, succeeded in defeating the president
in the New Hampshire Republican primary. The real shock, however, came when
Buchanan revealed his platform. Buchanan, the former Cold Warrior and former
advisor to President Richard Nixon, shocked everyone by opposing free trade and
the deployment of American troops in Europe. Buchanan had reverted to ethnic
type by espousing labor-based Catholic politics of the old Democratic Party and
had become the conservative equivalent of a heretic. Since heretic was now a term
of honor, he was called an anti-Semite instead by the Grand Inquisitor of the Conservative movement, Bill Buckley.

In the wake of the fall of communism, the conservative alliance had nothing
to hold it together. Conservatism, as a result, proceeded to fall apart into its ethnic

components. Catholics, who awoke to the fact that their jobs had disappeared and to the fact that the neocons didn't really care about abortion, voted for Buchanan, whom the neocon Jews were portraying as a combination of Father Coughlin and Vlad the Impaler. The neocons, who had been silent on the issue of abortion, the prime political issue among conservative Catholics, finally broke their silence and said that, compared to Israel's survival, abortion was of little or no significance. The same was true, with some exceptions, of homosexuality, the other great "social issue" which motivated Catholics and Evangelicals. True to his role as conservative enforcer, Buckley attacked Buchanan as an anti-Semite in *National Review* on December 31, 1991, just as Buchanan's candidacy was picking up steam. The Republicans tried to mollify Buchanan, who gave his famous "culture wars" speech at their national convention in 1992, but the Jews in general used their influence in the media to deplore the speech, and Buchanan was not allowed to address the 1996 convention.

In the 1994 mid-term elections, the Republicans took control of both houses of Congress for the first time in two generations through the collaborative effort of Newt Gingrich and the Christian Coalition, the evangelical organization that succeded Jerry Falwell's Moral Majority. Falwell founded the Moral Majority in 1979 with significant Jewish input. Although only one Jew, Howard Philips, founder of YAF, was in on the initial planning, Falwell peddled his project to prominent Jews despite their ancestral animus to vocal Christians. Falwell included five planks in support of the state of Israel in its platform. He met with Jewish agencies "to make the Jewish community aware that we are not an anti-Semitic group and that we probably are the strongest supporter of Israel in the country."[110] "God," he said, "has blessed America because America has blessed the Jew."[111]

Mainline Jewish organizations like the ADL remained skeptical, but neoconservative Jews like Irving Kristol and the AJC's Rabbi Marc Tannenbaum reacted warmly. In 1980 Israeli premier Menachem Begin shocked liberal Jews in America by giving Falwell one of Israel's highest honors, the Jabotinsky Award. Falwell reciprocated by defending Israel's pre-emptive strike on the Osirak nuclear reactor in Iraq. The basis of this odd arrangement was Falwell's Dispensationalism, which saw the Jews as God's chosen people and the State of Israel as ordained by Scripture. Falwell's belief that the Jews were supposed to convert to Christianity during the last days was a detail passed over by the Jews in embarrassed silence in their quest for votes. That same theology led to what the Jews considered frequent gaffes, as when Falwell said the antichrist was a Jew or when he said AIDS was God's punishment for homosexuality. Jews probably greeted the demise of the Moral Majority in 1989 with a sigh of relief.

Rabbi Marc Tannenbaum claimed Falwell was awkward and inexperienced in dealing with Jews. The man who led the Christian Coalition was not. Unlike Falwell, who gave the impression that he would rather handle snakes than talk with Abe Foxman, Ralph Reed grew up in what he described as a "Jewish atmosphere."[112]

To the uninitiated, Ralph Reed appeared to be the protégé of televangelist Pat Robertson. Their theologies were politically identical with Falwell's dispensationalism. In reality, Ralph Reed was the protégé of Jack Abramoff, a Washington lobbyist later jailed for influence peddling. Reed was to the evangelicals what Buckley was to an earlier generation of Catholics. Abramoff, an orthodox Jew Friedman describes as a "conservative firebrand at Brandeis University,"[113] gave Reed his first job in Washington, hiring him as a political intern in 1981. He also invited Reed to live in his home, where he "attended services with him, and introduced Abramoff to his wife, who came from Georgia."[114] Abramoff found Reed "incredibly philo-Semitic."[115] Reed reciprocated by dealing harshly with anti-Semitism whenever it reared its head among College Republicans. In 1983, Reed succeeded Abramoff as executive director of the National College Republicans. Like Buckley before him, "Reed used his influence to prevent the more extreme elements within the conservative movement from taking over the GOP."[116] Like Buckley, Reed invariably consulted a Jewish calculus to determine which elements were "extreme."

When the ADL shot itself in the foot by attacking the Christian Right, Israel's most faithful allies in America, Ralph Reed played healer, addressing the ADL's national leadership in April 1995. Reed told the ADL "the Christian Coalition believes in a nation that is not officially Christian,"[117] so it was against school prayer—a statement which reportedly infuriated Pat Robertson. Reed told the same thing to AIPAC a month later, prompting Elliott Abrams to say Jews "need Ralph Reed."[118]

Reed showed neocons how much they needed him when he derailed Pat Buchanan's second presidential bid by throwing Christian Coalition support behind Senator Bob Dole in the 1996 South Carolina Republican primary. Buchanan's loss there took the steam out of his campaign. Deprived of one of his natural constituencies by Reed, he lacked the political clout to address the 1996 convention. Friedman credits Reed with "the modernization of Christian conservatism."[119] Given Slezkine's understanding of modernity, this means aligning Evangelical votes to Jewish interests, which is precisely how Friedman interprets Reed's role:

> Buchanan's George Wallace-like populism, his isolationism, and his attacks on neocons for their strong support of Israel outraged Jews (who saw behind the facade); his isolationism also turned off mainstream conservatives. Quietly, Reed threw the weight of the Christian Coalition behind moderate Senator Bob Dole in the crucial South Carolina primary. Buchanan's loss there dealt a fatal blow to his campaign, and Reed was widely credited with causing his defeat.[120]

When Ralph Reed left the Christian Coalition to become a lobbyist, he returned to his roots, linking up with Abramoff to play Indian tribes off against each other over gambling casinos, profiting handsomely as a double agent. In 2002, Reed, then a political consultant in Atlanta and chairman of the Georgia Republican Party, joined Rabbi Yehiel Eckstein to form "a sort of Christian AIPAC."[121] In May 2003, the ADL put an ad in the *New York Times*, in which Reed hailed the Jewish state's survival as "proof of God's sovereignty."[122]

To be fair to Bill Buckley, he once criticized the ADL for giving an award to *Playboy* publisher Hugh Hefner. Reed couldn't even muster token opposition to the ADL, prompting ADL director Foxman, whose organization had denounced Reed and his followers as hatemongers, to announce, "I am proud to have Ralph Reed as a friend and as an advocate on Israel."[123]

1997: Bishop Harry Flynn denounces Father Paul Marx

In 1997 Human Life International had scheduled its prolife conference in St. Paul, Minnesota, and Bishop Harry Flynn was invited to say the opening Mass. Instead Flynn denounced HLI president, Rev. Paul Marx, OSB, as an anti-Semite. In a statement issued by the Archdiocese of St. Paul and Minneapolis, Flynn announced he was not going to celebrate the Mass because he was "particularly troubled by some statements made by HLI founder, Father Paul Marx and some HLI literature which is divisive and harmful especially to our Jewish brothers and sisters."[124] Flynn said attributing "blame for abortion ... with one group of people ignores our shared responsibility as members of a society which treats some lives as less valuable than others."[125] Instead of saying the Mass Flynn was going to hold a prayer service with two rabbis and a representative of the notoriously pro-abortion AJC. Flynn allowed Marx and HLI to celebrate Mass at the Cathedral, but he also allowed Fight the Right, a group of militant homosexuals identified in one news report as "teenagers," who were planning to stage a "kiss-in," to engage in obscene and blasphemous acts on church property.[126]

Flynn appealed to *Nostra Aetate* to justify his actions. He could not say Mass, as he agreed to do, because

> my participation would set back the wonderful dialogue which has taken place among Christians and Jews in this Archdiocese. In the 1965 Vatican II document "Nostra Aetate," the Church states clearly that "spiritual bonds and historical links binding the Church and Judaism condemn (as opposed to the very spirit of Christianity) all forms of anti-Semitism and discrimination, which in any case the dignity of the human person alone would suffice to condemn."[127]

Flynn's reasoning was as convoluted as his syntax. He never explained how identifying Jewish participation in and advocacy for abortion constituted anti-Semitism. In February 1995 Msgr. George Higgins of the United States Catholic Conference had attacked Marx for being "divisive" and for engaging in "a flirtation with anti-Semitism."[128] But this was the first time a bishop collaborated in the attack. "In 1987," Marx wrote in his autobiography, "HLI made a careful study of involvement in the world-wide abortion movement. The undisputed conclusion of this study was that a disproportionately large number of Jews who are disloyal to Jewish teachings have led and are leading the campaign for legalized abortion. We then consulted with Orthodox Jews who confirmed these findings."[129]

By focusing on public relations rather than Jewish involvement in the abortion industry, Marx responded ineptly. In his autobiography, Marx claimed "The

Jewish people ... have a great pro-life heritage."[130] Marx repeatedly claimed "Jews who are disloyal to Jewish teaching have led and are leading the campaign for legalized abortion."[131] But he never explained what he meant by "Jewish teaching." The Torah implicitly condemns abortion, but the Talmud permits what the Torah forbids, at least with regard to a child who has not yet left (or partially left) its mother's body. In later commentary on the Talmud, the concept of "pursuer" ("*rodef*") is used to nullify the Fifth Commandment's prohibition against murder. "'*Rodef*' lowers the loophole threshold of danger to the mother to the point of non-existence, making it no bar to abortion at all."[132]

Marx added "At no time have we ever condemned the Jewish people; our targets have been only Jewish abortionists, and not because they were Jewish. The Jewish people after all have a great pro-life heritage, and as Pius XI observed, 'Spiritually we are all Semites.'"[133] The conservative Catholic press came to Marx's defense. Thomas A. Drolesky denounced Archbishop Flynn

> who sent a toady in April of 1997 to denounce the founder of Human Life International, the courageous Father Paul Marx, O.S.B., as a anti-Semite during a Mass at the Cathedral of Saint Paul. His Excellency lacked the courage to do so himself. Ah, but he has shown "compassion" for those wearing the "Rainbow Sash" at the Cathedral of Saint Paul. Monstrous liturgical abuses abound throughout the Archdiocese of Saint and Minneapolis. Nothing is done to stop these abuses.[134]

Drolesky detailed Jewish involvement in abortion, claiming "people who identify themselves as 'Jews' have led and do lead the abortion movement, not only in the United States, but all over the world."[135] Drolesky claimed "The American pro-abortion movement has always been led by those who claim to be Jewish."[136]

In the late 1960s, pro-life activists observed the abortion "rights" movement was primarily motivated and led by people who called themselves Jews. About half of all abortionists and abortion clinic owners identified themselves as Jewish, which was far out of proportion with the Jewish population, less than five percent of the United States population. Dr. Kenneth Mitzner, a California aerospace engineer who founded the pro-life League Against Neo-Hitlerism, wrote in 1973 "It is tragic but demonstrably true that most of the leaders of the pro-abortion movement are of Jewish extraction."[137] Many self-described "Jews" continue to lead the abortion movement and, most pitiable of all, "rabbis," properly cloaked in the correct trappings, proclaim abortion is not only a necessity, but a Good Thing for America.

> * All four original organizers of the most influential group of abortion pushers in the United States, the National Abortion Rights Action League (NARAL), were of Jewish birth, including now prolife Dr. Bernard Nathanson.

> * Dr. Christopher Tietze worked for the Population Institute and International Planned Parenthood Federation, and did more to promote the worldwide slaughter of innocent unborn children than any other person.

* Dr. Alan Guttmacher was president of the Planned Parenthood Federation of America for more than a decade, founded Planned Parenthood Physicians, and did more than any other doctor to promote abortion in this country. He also advocated mandatory abortion and sterilization for certain groups in the United States.

* Dr. Etienne-Emile Baulieu, inventor of the RU-486 abortion pill, was born in 1926 to a physician named Leon Blum. He changed his name in 1942.

* Stanford professor Paul Ehrlich is the "father" of the overpopulation myth. His work, *The Population Bomb*, was the spark that ignited the anti natalist movement.

* California and New York state legislators led the drive for legalized abortion in the United States. Legislators who constantly emphasized their Jewishness led the pro-abortion movement in both states; those leaders included state senators Anthony Bielenson in California and Albert Blumenthal in New York.

* Pro-abortion "Jews" dominate such anti-life groups as the American Civil Liberties Union and People for the American Way.

* Of the 41 Jewish-born members of the U.S. Senate over the last 20 years, 32 (or 80 percent) have been stridently pro-abortion.

* Numerous liberal Jewish groups openly support and advocate abortion, including the American Jewish Committee, the American Jewish Congress, the National Council of Jewish Women, Hadassah Women, the Federation of Reconstructionist Congregations, the Jewish Labor Committee, the Union of American Hebrew Congregations, B'nai B'rith Women, Naiamat USA, the National Council of Jewish Women, the National Federation of Temple Sisterhood, the New Jewish Agenda, North American Temple Youth, the United Synagogues of America, and the Womenís League for Conservative Judaism. Many of these groups were founded for the express purpose of pushing abortion.

* Betty Friedan and Gloria Steinem were both born Jewish. So was France's health minister Simone Weil, who established abortion on demand in that country despite surviving Auschwitz. At a Paris news conference, she said "We are out to destroy the family. The best way to do that is to begin by attacking its weakest member, the unborn child."

* The officially suppressed Lichter-Rothman studies revealed the following fascinating information about the "movers and shakers" of the media (both researchers, by the way, are Jewish): Leaders of the motion picture industry: 95 percent pro-abortion, 62 percent Jewish: Leaders of the television industry: 97 percent pro-abortion, 59 percent Jewish: Leaders of the news media industry: 90 percent pro-abortion, 23 percent Jewish.

* Jewish groups are in the forefront as desperate pro-abortion groups spend tens of millions of dollars in a nationwide advertising campaign to keep abortion legal. For example, the American Jewish Congress ran a ridiculous $30,000 full-

page ad in the February 28, 1989 *New York Times* entitled "Abortion and the Sacredness of Life." This statement, renamed "An open letter to those who would ban abortion," and run in the March 13- 19 issue of *Roll Call*, includes the amazing lead-in question, "Did you know that abortion can be a religious requirement? Not just permitted, but required?"[138]

"The press," Drolesky continued, "gives pro-abortion 'Jews' great play, and excuses them from actions that it would vigorously condemn pro-lifers for. Imagine what the press would do to a pro-life activist who attacked and seriously injured a Jewish abortionist with a baseball bat! Yet, when Jewish abortionist Barnett Slepian beat a pro-life activist in the head with a baseball bat and seriously injured him, the press and abortophiles whined that pro-lifers were anti-Semitic for picketing his home!"[139]

At no time do "Jewish" abortophiles become more indignant than when prolifers explain and publicize the many parallels between the original Nazi Holocaust and the one occurring in the United States right now.... Masturbation guru Sol Gordon has angrily denounced the Old/New Holocaust analogy in even more direct terms; "In our view, individuals who exhibit the least human dignity are those who compare the Holocaust, the mass murder of 6 million Jews, to abortion. There exists no comparison more immoral or depraved. It is both illogical and outrageous to suggest that the calculated murder of millions of children and adults can be equated with an individual woman's decision to terminate her pregnancy."[140] Drolesky got much of his material from Marx's *Confessions of a Pro-Life Missionary.*

In the damage control following Flynn's announcement, Marx did not appeal to the facts. Instead, he and his PR advisors Rev. Richard Welch, C.Ss.P., and Ann De Long, produced Jewish character witnesses. Rabbi Yehuda Levin, who had collaborated with Marx, appeared next to Father Marx at a press conference. Levin denounced Steven Derfler, local head of the AJC, as "unrighteous"[141] for falsely attacking Marx. Derfler's attack, though, was instructive because for once the Jews defined what they meant when they used the term "anti-Semitism." Derfler claimed Marx was an anti-Semite because he compared abortion to the Holocaust and because of "his linking of some Jews specifically to abortion."[142]

The list of Jews who worked with Marx against abortion was almost as long as the list of Jews who accused him of anti-Semitism. Judith Reisman and Rabbi Daniel Lapin testified on Marx's behalf. Bernard Nathanson, who had become a regular speaker at HLI conferences, came to Marx's defense. When asked about the accusations, Nathanson replied it was "correct"[143] to say Jews dominated the abortion industry. "For some reason Jewish doctors seem to be attracted to abortion work."[144]

Nathanson's comments came at the tail end of a campaign orchestrated by President Clinton's Attorney General Janet Reno to portray prolifers as terrorists. In 1998 the ADL joined the campaign, claiming there has been "a long-running association between anti-abortion extremists and anti-Semitism."[145] Foxman complained HLI was "inordinately preoccupied with Jews."[146] The ADL cited the murder of Jewish abortionist Dr. Barnett Slepian as an example of this conspiracy. "We are deeply concerned about the strain of anti-Semitism running through some extreme factions of the movement," ADL National Director Abe Foxman said.[147] "They make insidious claims that Jewish doctors control the practice and industry of abortion, often comparing them to Nazi war criminals."[148] Foxman also pointed out "hideous and offensive"[149] comparisons anti-abortion groups regularly make to the Holocaust. "Whatever one's position on this heartrending issue, analogizing abortion to the Nazi government's campaign to murder every Jew in the world diminishes the truth of the Holocaust and implies that ordinary women engaging in a lawful act are Nazis," said Foxman.[150] The Feminist Daily News Wire noted "Four of the five abortion providers shot by a sniper in the Upstate New York/Canadian region since 1994 were Jewish. The ADL believes that this is not a coincidence."[151] According to that news wire, "the ADL strongly believes that Jewish doctors who perform abortions are purposefully singled out by anti-abortion extremists who believe Jews are controlling the abortion industry."[152] A vain attempt to link Marx with the Nazi Eugenic movement followed. Fr. Marx got it coming and going. He was accused of being a Nazi because the Nazis claimed abortionists were Jewish; he was also accused of being an anti-Semite by associating the Holocaust with abortion.

Neither Foxman nor the news wire pointed out the fact that the ethnic demographics of the abortion industry meant that anyone who set out to shoot an abortionist was likely to shoot a Jew. Mentioning this would have lent credence to the "insidious claims" that Jews dominated the abortion industry. The Jewish promotion of abortion was at once more vicious and less explicable than the WASP promotion of birth control that preceded it. The WASP motivation was essentially ulterior. They wanted to stop the demographic surge that threatened to turn America into a Catholic country. They were tired of supporting Negroes on welfare. Jewish promotion of abortion was inexplicable on these terms. The Jews were the ascendant ethnic group in the late '60s and early '70s. Their commitment to abortion was religious, inexplicable on anything other than theological terms, something apparent in their attack on Father Marx.

To defame Marx as an anti-Semite, the feminists invoked the "blood libel."[153] According to Planned Parenthood's Karen Branan and Frederick Clarkson, HLI "resurrect[ed] that most vicious piece of historical anti-Semitism: child-killing Jews."[154] In "The Roots of Racism and the Fear of Sex in the Pro-life Movement," Poppy Dixon claimed

> During the middle ages it was common for Christians to accuse Jews of "ritual murder." Jews celebrated Passover during which they would put the blood of a slaughtered lamb on their doorpost commemorating their escape from Egypt. The Christian notion, deliberately perverted, was that Jews were required to use

the blood of Christian children to attain propitiation. Entire villages of Jews were tortured, mutilated and burned when a Christian child turned up dead or missing. And though popes, and magistrates, pleaded with local populations, and often hid Jews, the killings continued.[155]

According to Dixon:

The medical procedure of abortion has been woven into the accusation of blood libel, giving new life to this medieval lie. Pro-life advocates view abortion as women killing, or murdering, children. And it's not just women that murder children, but Jews and Asians as well.[156]

Dixon held Fr. Marx accountable for the resurrection of the blood libel because of "his anti-Semitic comments"[157] about Austrian Prime Minister Bruno Kreisky. To wit: "Until recently, the real political power in Austria was in the hands of a fanatically pro-abortion Prime Minister, Bruno Kreisky, an atheist of Jewish descent.... Although they are supremely sensitive about their own Holocaust, Austria's Jews gave me and my colleagues no help in stopping this new holocaust; on the contrary, they spoke eloquently for killing preborn babies."[158] How did Marx's denunciation of Bruno Kreisky resurrect the blood libel? The blood libel would not have entered the discussion if the Jews hadn't brought it up.

In his autobiography, *Faithful for Life*, Marx recounts meeting "a Jewish aerospace engineer,"[159] Dr. Kenneth Mitzner, who in 1970 "founded the League against Neo-Hitlerism to Fight Abortion. He also founded and led other pro-life groups."[160] After the Supreme Court's decision in 1973, Mitzner wrote it was "tragic but demonstrably true that most of the leaders of the pro-abortion movement are of Jewish extraction." In a letter to Marx in July 1987, Mitzner declared:

Jews must decide whether we condemn Hitler and his followers because mass murder is intrinsically evil or whether our quarrel is just with the choice of us as victims. If our concern is only with the killing of Jews, we have no claim on the sympathies of the rest of humanity. Some Jews ask the world to weep with us for the Jewish victims of Nazism, at the same time they promote the murder of innocent babies by abortion. Such Jews are the most contemptible of hypocrites.[161]

Shortly after *Roe v. Wade*, Mitzner wrote about Ritual Child Murder and Jewish involvement in Abortion in *Triumph*, comparing the Jewish representative responsible for California's abortion law with the priests of Moloch: "We see the frenzied face of the Molochite priest," Mitzner wrote, "eyes glowing in the firelight. Despite the beard, there is no mistaking the face. It is the face of Anthony Beilenson."[162] In Mitzner's eyes, Beilenson resembled the "Molochites" and "Hellenizers" of the Old Testament, but soon he indicts the whole tradition of revolutionary Jews, which began with the priest of Moloch

who hung the bodies of the infant victims around their murdered mothers' necks and who were finally driven out by the Maccabbees; the "black magic" Cabbalists of the Middle Ages, who frequently ate the flesh of their infant sacrifices and who did a brisk business in poisons and abortifacients; the Sabbatian sects of the

17th and 18th centuries, who sometimes covered up their own crimes by falsely accusing Orthodox Jews of ritual child murder; the Trotskyites, who won the first victory for abortion on demand in Soviet Russia in 1920; the Weimar intellectuals of the 1920s and early '30s, who taught the German people that killing "by abortion and euthanasia" was a legitimate solution to social problems, then fled Germany when Hitler defined the Jews as a social problem; and those in our country sometimes referred to as Elitists—all these and others are manifestations of the same pathological force in history. Since about the 1840s, the organizing principle has become a secular fanaticism rather than a pseudo religion, and thus direct alliance with like-hearted gentiles has become possible.[163]

Mitzner feels the accusation that some Jews engaged in ritual child murder are founded in fact:

From 1144 to 1945, almost all persecutions of the Jews were based fully or in large part on the accusation of ritual child murder. Obviously, as a charge against the Jewish people as a whole or against the mainstream of Judaism, this accusation was one of the great lies of history. Equally obviously, it frequently was based on the actual activities of some of the groups I have cited.[164]

Mitzner gives a short history of the revolutionary Jew and an explanation of how the ritual murder exposed by St. John Capistrano is linked to abortion as Jewish revolutionary activity. The lessons are counter-intuitive. On the one hand, identifying the protestors at his hearings as Jews brought the wrath of the establishment upon John Schmitz's head. On the other, it showed the Jews' sensitivity about their involvement in abortion. If Catholics and prolifers had concentrated on the facts and remained united despite the attack, the outcome might have been different.

The damaging part of the attack on Father Marx was not the testimony of the Jews, which was irrelevant and certainly predictable. The damage came from Bishop Flynn's betrayal of a fellow priest. Solidarity based on truth would have ensured a different outcome. Bringing the ethnic aspect of the abortion fight into the open would have prevented the shadow boxing that has become such a waste of time. As Bernard Nathanson said, had the ethnic card been played truthfully and consistently "permissive abortion might have been perceived as somehow anti-American."[165] If the Catholics spent less time talking about "life" in secular terms and more time portraying abortion as "the spawn of a cadre of wild-eyed Jewish radicals in New York City,"[166] more children would be alive today.

2000: Anti-Semitism is Absent from the Passion Play, but the Jews Aren't Satisfied

Ultimately it didn't matter whether the Passion Play was purged of anti-Semitism from Otto Huber's point of view. What Otto Huber learned in the expensive school of experience is that the "ADL wants to destroy our identity."[167] Dialogue, it turned out, was the best method the Jews had discovered to date to destroy rooted, ethnic Catholic identity. But that may be changing now because Shapiro tells us that "For all the ecumenical attention to a shared spiritual heritage, the play forces Jews and Christians to face the painful fact that they read differently , and that a single version of the founding story of Christianity cannot be shared."[168]

The Catholic scholars and their Jewish masters used dialogue as a pretext for destroying Catholic identity. "For many of those involved in ecumenical dialogue, Vatican II was only a start," Shapiro says.[169] "Now they are interested in seeing fresh reform."[170] But dialogue had one salutary effect. There is no split between the peasants and the Vatican II hierarchy anymore. Both groups are now singing off the same page about the Passion Play's alleged anti-Semitism. Shapiro cites one Catholic scholar who examined the script for the 2000 performance and "emphatically declared that 'there is no longer any anti-Semitism in the play.... The dangerous and all-inclusive reproach that the evil Jews had crucified Jesus is simply gone."[171]

The Jews still found "even this greatly modified version of the Daisenberger text" offensive, but "in defense of the villagers," Shapiro concedes, "the play, as written finally conforms to the doctrinal positions advocated 35 years ago by Vatican II."[172] Now that the play has been purged of anti-Semitism to the Church's satisfaction, Catholics and Jews are faced with the irreducible anti-Judaism of the gospels. "Matters now have been scraped down to barebone, to irreconcilable difference. You can hear the testiness in the voices of those who have worked so hard for the past three decades to change the play," Shapiro says.[173] He cites one Jewish source who claims "We are dealing with a genre and with a New Testament textual resource that simply has structural anti-Jewish dimensions."[174] The "priests will try to kill Jesus. The merchants will be venial [sic]. The people will be fickle and blind. That is what the New Testament gives the authors to work with."[175]

So the Jews succeeded: "after 35 years, the Oberammergau play has finally caught up with the theological position first espoused by the Catholic Church in 1965."[176] If you expect Jewish rejoicing, you will be disappointed. Shapiro writes that the alignment of village and Vatican II which the Jews sought so ardently "offered small comfort: while the village has reluctantly modified the ways in which it implicated the Jews in Jesus' death in the past few decades, the Vatican has not. Anyone who reads the Oberammergau script for the year 2000 will understand just how culpable the Church still finds the Jews and how persistent the notion that Christianity has superseded Judaism remains. In some respects, the Oberammergau play has moved ahead of the Church."[177] Shapiro finds "much irony" in this.[178] Vatican II provided the "impetus for this historical revisionism" which eviscerated the play, but it also created the alignment between the hierarchy and the peasants that destroyed Jewish "leverage."[179] Once the Vatican stopped taking people like Leonard Swidler seriously,

> Appealing to the findings of leading scholars—even Catholic ones—made little difference, since the insights of those scholars were increasingly at odds with the Vatican's official position on the role of Jews in the Passion story. *And without*

that kind of leverage there was little chance of exacting any further concession on the part of the village ... . Because Oberammergau's answer to the question, "Who killed Jesus?" was now the same one offered by the Church, Jewish organizations could no longer demand that the Church pressure Oberammergau to change its play.[180]

The Jews needed a new strategy. Discussion of doctrine had become useless so the Jews concentrated on "art." Instead of playing the hierarchy against the peasants, the Jews supported passion play director Christian Stuckl and the "reformers" who control how the play is produced and who gets what roles. The same Jews who used to insist on historical accuracy now promoted artistic freedom. Shapiro adverts to the new strategy: "The irony is that this ongoing struggle over doctrine is taking place even as the once unquestioned faith of many of the Passion players of Oberammergau—especially the young—is weakening."[181]

The Jewish strategy of "leveraging" one group of Catholics against the other hasn't changed, but the groups getting "leveraged" have. Instead of playing the hierarchy off against the villagers, the Jews are playing the "reformers" against the "conservatives." Shapiro sets the theological stage by telling readers "Christian Stueckl looks like a fallen angel."[182] Shapiro intends this as a compliment. Stueckl, says Shapiro, "comes from an old Oberammergau family. One of his ancestors is listed among those struck down by the plague in 1634."[183] He is, therefore, ideally suited for subverting the play. Stueckl had put on Shakespeare, giving it a spin Shapiro found congenial. Romeo and Juliet, for example, symbolized "the struggle between the reformers and conservatives in Oberammergau."[184] Shapiro finds it "fitting that Stueckl turned to Shakespeare's plays to satirize his village and their theatrical tastes"[185] because "theater was one of the most powerful ways of challenging conventional values."[186] This is not how Cardinal Wetter, the archbishop of Munich viewed theater. After receiving the script for the 2000 production, Wetter suggested the point of the Passion play was not merely acting but imitating Christ, "To which Stueckl replied: "I am a director of theater in Munich and Brussels. What I do is theater."[187]

What innovations does Shapiro find "dangerous and exciting?"[188] In his play about the plague, *Die Pestnot anno 1633*, traditionally performed the year before the Passion Play, playwright Leo Weismantel indicates sexual promiscuity may have had a role in bringing the plague to Oberammergau. Shapiro, from New York City and sensitive about AIDS, finds "unacceptable and offensive"[189] the suggestion of a link between sexual transgression and disease, so he cites with approval Stueckl's excision of the offending scene, eliminating "even the hint that plague had anything to do with sexual transgression."[190] So Jews approve of censorship, after all. Just as they support historical accuracy when that supports their agenda. Shapiro criticized the villagers when they added "unhistorical" elements to the Passion Play, but praised Stueckl for adding a fictional scene to *Die Pestnot anno 1633*, in which "four or five desperate young people gather around a large crucifix on stage and hurl it to the ground, saying that they have lost their faith in a God who could allow such suffering."[191]

The praise for Oberammergau's "fallen angel" is unrelenting:

Stuckl had taken what the villagers held near and dear—a play that mythologized the origins of their Passion playing—and turned it into a drama that was also about the loss of faith that many young people in Oberammergau now (as perhaps in 1634 as well) were struggling with. Once again, he had shown how willing he was to use drama to expose what Oberammergau preferred to hide.[192]

Or perhaps Stueckl was willing to use drama to promote the Jews's desired erosion of the faith that underlies the Passion Play. Stueckl played the role previously reserved for "Catholic scholars" like Leonard Swidler, in that "he had shown the villagers that their myths were not immutable."[193] Stueckl even educated his benighted grandfather, who told him: "We now realize that time doesn't stop."[194]

At a loss how to praise Stueckl further, Shapiro confers on him the highest honor in the lexicon of Jewish cultural subversion. Stueckl is "a reckless destroyer of tradition;"[195] in this, he differs from the Jews, who are not reckless. The parish priest saw through what was happening and was "furious," but Shapiro dismisses this, saying he "lost credibility with some of the younger people when he tried to stifle discussion."[196] Stueckl, though, is a wise pedagogue. When he "couldn't quite get the young disciples to understand their relationship to the High Priest, he asked them to think of Caiaphas as the Pope."[197] Shapiro concedes "once upon a time this would have been sacrilege,"[198] but not anymore.

Stueckl's behavior shows how vulnerable traditional rooted ethnic cultures are to subversion, especially when money is involved. Shapiro said repeatedly that if the people of Oberammergau had put on their play for free, the Jews would have had no "leverage" to force them to change it. Financial leverage was the only weapon the Jews had left. The Jews used it on people with theatrical ambitions, like Stueckl and set designer Stefan Hageneier, by promoting their careers. Once recognized by the outside world, their enhanced prestige in the village allowed them control of the passion play production, which they exercised with one eye on their careers. Money and professionalism subverted the passion play as effectively as they subverted sports in the United States. Since village life revolved around the play, those who controlled the play controlled village life. Village dentist Rudolf Zwink, identified by Shapiro as leader of the "conservative" faction, concedes the struggle for control of the play is over. The "reformers" have won; they have the entire production, including determining who gets what roles, firmly under their control. Rooted culture is defenseless without the faith that animates it. Once money replaced faith as the motive in putting on the play, the slide into Jewish cultural bondage was inevitable.

With collaborators like Stueckl in control of the Oberammergau passion play, the Jewish organizations withdrew the threat of boycott. Rabbi Rudin, Shapiro says, had come to trust Huber and Stueckl and understood that to blind-side them at this point would be counterproductive. The likelihood was that he would share this information with the reformers, hoping that in their desire to offer *a historically accurate play*, some or all of these suggestions might subsequently be incorporated. Although they did not know it yet for sure, there would be no Jewish-led boycott in 2000.[199]

"Instances like this," Shapiro continues, "offer the most compelling argument I know against banning or boycotting Passion plays. All censorship does is hide the problem. Theater remains one of the most powerful ways of changing the way people think, and not just audiences, but actors too."[200] Banning the passion play would prevent other people from seeing it, but by controlling it from the inside, the Jews get to turn the once pious Bavarian villagers into rootless cosmopolitans and, therefore, emissaries of *their* gospel and not the gospel of Christ.

The Jews will probably pursue both strategies simultaneously in a variation on the good cop-bad cop routine. Rabbi Klenicki still accused the villagers of anti-Semitism, something Shapiro describes as reflecting frustration or "perhaps ... the strategic maneuver of an experienced negotiator."[201] As Shapiro puts it, "In either case, they had the desired effect of extracting additional concessions."[202]

The Bavarians continued to cave. In response to Klenicki, Otto Huber made last minute changes to the 2000 performance:

> the Sanhedrin would no longer condemn Jesus to death; a speech would be added in which Gamaliel accuses Caiaphas of having failed to invite all the members of the Sanhedrin; all remaining references to the Pharisees would be deleted; and Jesus would offer a blessing in Hebrew at the Last Supper.[203]

The villagers also eliminated every reference to Jesus as the Christ, or Messiah, because the Jews found this offensive. But nothing the Bavarians did placated the Jews. The Jews were already looking beyond the 2000 performance, hoping for "continued 'collaboration and still more progress.'"[204] The ADL "was already looking toward the 2010 production. Leon Klenicki would continue to call for more changes and would criticize Oberammergau when asked about the play. But as long as Oberammergau continued on the road to reform, the ADL would continue to work for changes quietly."[205] The ADL, continued to subvert the play from within with the collaboration of Huber and Stueckl.

Also missing from the 2000 play was "its most disturbing line," the verse in Matthew in which Jews, according to Shapiro, "accept responsibility for killing Christ" by crying out "His blood be on us and on our children."[206] Even Shapiro begins to wonder why the Jews are so obsessed with this verse. Shapiro attempts to explain his own obsession. Shapiro, like many other Jews, was convinced by reading "Goldhagen's controversial thesis in *Hitler's Willing Executioners*"[207] that Germans were by nature homicidal anti-Semites suffering from their own "blood curse." Shapiro is not blind to the ironies:

> without saying it in so many words, I believed in collective German guilt, a guilt that fell not only on those who had lived through the war, but also upon their

children and their children's children. The irony is that this reflexive notion of collective guilt was precisely what I found most objectionable in the Passion play ... was not lost on me. One of the things I hoped to learn in Oberammergau was when, if ever, it would be time to bury this notion of collective guilt.[208]

The collectively guilty flee, it seems, where none pursueth. The Jews can't escape collective guilt for the death of Christ, not even when Christians absolve them. Shapiro's narrative about the attack on Oberammergau is one long proof that the repressed always returns. The Jews defeated the supine, money-grubbing Bavarian peasants in cultural battle, but it didn't matter. Matthew 27:25's omission from play doesn't matter either. The power of God's word undoes any attempt to subvert it.

So when Shapiro hears the villagers shout "*Kreuzige ihn!,*" he is overpowered by the Logos that informs the drama. The word of God, he discovers, is "contagious: at several points I had to fight the impulse to join in."[209] The Jews, despite their power and experience, failed to subvert the message of the play. "I had badly wanted the text to be better than this,"[210] Shapiro writes. "The blood curse was gone, and no death decree was issued by the Sanhedrin. Yet these omissions hardly mattered."[211] The script was still "a runaway train: all the brakes all the safeguards, all the changes made to prevent anti-Judaism from taking over, had barely slowed it down."[212] The reason is simple. The gospels are not anti-Semitic but they are anti-Jewish. There is no getting around this. Even Shapiro sees this: "It was as if the play somehow leaked this kind of thing and there was no way to seal it properly."[213]

In spite of all their worldly power, the Jews cannot suppress the truth. They murdered the Messiah who was "the way, the truth and the life," but he confounded their intention by rising from the dead. Trying to contain the truth to suppress it is like trying to seal Christ's tomb to prevent his resurrection. "There was," Shapiro reminds us despite himself, "no way to seal it properly." Even "the scaled-down version" of the Oberammergau Passion Play magnified the very thing the Jews hoped to subvert because "the anti-Jewish structure of the gospel story on which it was based was too powerful for even the best intentioned revisers to neutralize."[214]

Nostra Aetate said "neither all Jews indiscriminately at that time nor Jews today, can be charged with the crimes committed during his passion." Logically, that means that some Jews at the time of Christ were responsible for his death. Which is precisely what *Nostra Aetate* says: "the Jewish authorities *and those who followed their lead* pressed for the death of Christ." As John puts it, "the Jews were out to kill him." Does this mean the Beloved Disciple and the Blessed Mother were out to kill Christ? They were Jews, weren't they? Does this mean the Beloved Disciple and the Blessed Mother cried out "Crucify him"? No, it means that by the end of the gospel the word "Jew" is redefined as a rejecter of Christ, a definition that holds true to this day. There is no occult "blood curse" in Matt 27: 26. What the Jews expressed when they cried, "His blood be on us and our children" was rejection of Christ, which has persisted among the "Jews" to this day. That rejection was so vehement and visceral that the Jews who voiced it demanded Christ's death as its ultimate expression.

Rudin emphasizes Matt 27: 26. "That curse appears only in Matthew,"[215] he writes, playing it down. But, he then expands it into "the religious taproot for the horrific charge, that because the Jews killed Jesus, they merited eternal divine punishment for their 'crime.'"[216] Just what does Rabbi Rudin intend by putting the word "crime" in quotation marks? That Christ's death wasn't a crime? That it can't be laid at the feet of the "Jewish authorities and those who followed their lead" who "pressed for the death of Christ"? If so, Rabbi Rudin clearly doesn't accept *Nostra Aetate*. However, Rudin also refers to "the positive teachings of the Second Vatican Council in 1965,"[217] indicating he accepts it. Are people responsible for the death of an innocent man guilty of a crime? If so, why is the word in quotes? If not, why do the Jews make such a big deal about Hitler and the holocaust?

By belaboring Matt 27:26, Rudin gives the impression that an editor's blue pencil can solve the problem of the Passion Play. Mel Gibson's movie *The Passion of the Christ* was a filmed version of the Passion Play. Rudin wants to believe the real problem with Gibson's movie is the same problem that Rudin and Foxman fixed in Oberammergau. Rudin refers to Oberammergau as "the 'grandparent' of Passion Plays."[218] Matthew 27:25 was "Once an integral part of the world-famous Oberammergau Passion Play in Germany," but as a result of a 40 year campaign of cultural warfare by the ADL and the AJC, "all references to Matthew 27:25 were removed from the 2000 production and will not appear in future performances."[219]

Suddenly, the fury of the Jews over Mel Gibson's movie is understandable. They had spent 40 years wearing down the Bavarians with connivance and threats, and then Mel Gibson brought out a Passion Play on their own Hollywood turf that out-Oberammergaus Oberammergau. "It is ironic," Rudin says, grinding his teeth with understatement, "that Oberammergau, the 'grandparent' of passion plays, no longer contains the incendiary verse from Matthew, but it does appear in Gibson's version."[220] Did he mean to say "infuriating" instead of "ironic"? No sooner do the Jews get one end of the board nailed down when the other end springs up and cracks them in the head. Doubly infuriating, a Catholic beat the Jews at their own game by successfully directing, producing, and releasing a big budget film that grossed over $100 million at the box office in the first weekend after its release.

September 11, 2001 and Afghanistan

On September 11, 2001, followers of Osama bin Laden, an asset US intelligence created to fight the Soviets in Afghanistan, flew commercial airliners into the twin World Trade Center Towers and the Pentagon. The neocons took credit for the fall of communism, which they called World War III. Emboldened, they used 9/11 to embark on what Norman Podhoretz called World War IV, the conquest of the Middle East. The success of social engineering in Germany and Japan proved America could use the same techniques in the Middle East, claimed David Frum and Richard Perle in *An End to Evil: How to Win the War on Terror*. They used the plight of Islamic "women who seek emancipation from their oppression"[221] to justify aggression in the interests of Israel. "If apartheid in South Africa was our business," Frum and Perle reasoned, "it is hard to see why Saudi oppression of women is not our business."[222]

The Neoconservatives had demanded the ouster of Saddam Hussein for almost a decade before the airliners crashed into the World Trade Center. Leading the charge was Irving Kristol's son William, who started in Washington working for his father's appointee, William Bennett, and was now editor of the neocon flagship, *The Weekly Standard*. As Vice President Dan Quayle's chief of staff, Kristol orchestrated Quayle's Murphy Brown speech, which assailed TV networks for promoting illegitimacy. At Harvard, Bill Kristol became a Straussian under the influence of Professor Harvey Mansfield and learned the basics of WASP internationalism at the feet of Samuel Huntington. Bill eagerly used the mantle of victorious Cold Warrior as justification for more war. "Now that the other Cold War is over," he opined, "the real Cold War has begun."[223]

In 1993, Bill Kristol founded the Project for the Republican Future, "appointing himself," Friedman notes without irony, "guardian of the GOP."[224] In 1996, he and political scientist Robert Kagan published "Toward a Neo-Reaganite Foreign Policy" in *Foreign Affairs*, arguing for an aggressive but benevolent foreign policy for the world's only remaining superpower. Also in 1996, fellow Jewish neocons Richard Perle, David Wurmser, and Douglas Feith wrote their "Clean Break" report for Israeli Prime Minister Benjamin Netanyahu, recommending he "focus on removing Saddam Hussein from power in Iraq—an important Israeli strategic objective in its own right."[225] They also called for Israel to take steps to reorder the entire Middle East, which the United States would do as Israel's proxy.

Kristol brought out a special issue of the *Weekly Standard* in December 1997, informing the Clinton administration that "Saddam Must Go." In 1998, Kristol started the Project for a New American Century, a think tank to make the neocon agenda a reality once Republicans were at the levers of power after the 2000 elections; he also signed two open letters (along with Elliot Abrams, John Bolton, Douglas Feith, Bernard Lewis, Donald Rumsfeld, Perle, and Paul Wolfowitz) urging Clinton to remove Saddam Hussein.

Bill Kristol was part of an aggressively Jewish younger generation of neoconservatives raised to think of themselves not as outsiders but as destined to haunt the halls of power in Washington and to rule the world. David Brooks' bestseller *Bobos in Paradise* claimed Americans had become "bohemian bourgeois."[226] When a woman confronted him at a booksigning, claiming he really meant America had become Jewish, Brooks was dumbfounded because the woman was Jewish and what she said may have sounded anti-Semitic but was true. The Jews had taken over the culture not by imposing religious practices they themselves found foreign but by creating the persona of the true American. During the '50s, the real American was part of David Riesman's "lonely crowd," because Jews were on the fringe of dying WASP culture. By the first decade of the 21st century, the true American was a chest-thumping chauvinist because Jews had taken over the foreign policy establishment to promote Jewish and Israeli ends. The neoconservatives never lost touch with their revolutionary roots, perhaps because they were so immediate. "I feel no passionate attachment to Judaism, or to Zionism, or even to the Jewish people," Bill Kristol admitted; "the only magazine that entered our house was *The New Masses*."[227]

Instead of renouncing the revolutionary heritage of their fathers, the neo-conservatives redefined it. What the Comintern failed to achieve in the name of the working class, the *Weekly Standard* brought about in the name of the Jewish bohemian bourgeoisie. As before, the Jews remained in the vanguard.

It was a difficult balancing act. As soon as Jews were identified as behind any movement, the movement was condemned to die. As the neocon agenda became more identifiably Jewish, it lost supporters. Daniel Patrick Moynihan was one of the first defectors. Moynihan opposed the first Gulf War, and before his death in 2003 was showing signs of returning to his ethnic roots by expressing regret that he hadn't done more to oppose abortion. Defections from the WASP ruling class increased too as it became apparent the Jews were endangering America's national security by embroiling the country in unwinnable wars in the Middle East.

All that was in the future during the mid-'90s, when the drumbeat for America's entry into World War IV began. In 1997, Paul Wolfowitz, a Straussian from the University of Chicago, called for the overthrow of Saddam Hussein in the *Weekly Standard*. Wolfowitz, whose parents had moved from Warsaw to New York, became undersecretary of defense during the second Bush administration; he used that position to lobby for war against Iraq. Four days after the attack on the World Trade Center, Wolfowitz met with President Bush and urged him to attack Iraq before invading Afghanistan, even though there was no evidence Saddam was involved in 9/11, and there was evidence that Osama bin Laden was hiding in Afghanistan. President Bush rejected Wolfowitz's advice, but he put the invasion of Iraq in motion, asking his military advisers to develop plans.

2002: Israeli military forces take over Palestinian TV stations

At 4:30 PM on March 30, 2002, Israeli military forces took over Palestinian TV stations when they occupied Ramallah in the West Bank, immediately shutting them down. The Israeli forces then broadcast pornography over the Al-Watan TV's transmitter. Eventually, according to *The Advertiser*, an Australian newspaper, the Israelis broadcast pornography over two additional Palestinian stations, the Ammwaj and Al-Sharaq channels. A Palestinian mother of three complained about "the deliberate psychological damage caused by these broadcasts."[228] The only uncaptured Palestinian station ran a message on its screen: "Anything currently shown on Al-Watan and other local TV channels has nothing to do with Palestinian programs but is being broadcast by the Israeli occupation forces. We urge parents to take precautions."[229]

The Palestinians were outraged and bewildered. "Why in the world," one correspondent to Omanforum.com wondered, "should one do such a thing?"[230] According to the dominant culture's explanation, pornography means freedom. Were Israeli troops broadcasting pornography over captured Palestinian TV stations to spread freedom among the Palestinian people? This incident cannot be explained according to the principles of contemporary American culture. So, let's go back to the ancients.

Samson and Delilah is a good place to start. Israel was invincible militarily then too, so the Philistines decided to get the Israelite leader by other than military means. They seduced him sexually. Once Samson succumbed to Delilah's wiles, he lost his power, and Israel lost its leader. He was no longer on the field of battle, but rather, to use Milton's phrase, "eyeless in Gaza, grinding at the mill with slaves."[231]

The story of the Palestinian TV stations has a curiously Biblical ring. The Israelis turned the tables. They knew a blind opponent is no opponent. They knew, as did the ancient Greeks, that lust makes a man blind. St. Thomas Aquinas said lust "darkens the mind." Suddenly, Israel's use of pornography against the Palestinians isn't so obscure. Pornography is a weapon "Jews with an atavistic fear of Christian authority"[232] have used to weaken the dominant culture and, thereby, assure that the Jews, always a minority, are unmolested by their "Christian" neighbors. They are well-versed in the military use of pornography.

The corrosive effects of Wilhelm Reich's philosophy of control through sexual demoralization are still with us, promoted by Jews as a form of political control to weaken the power of the non-Jewish majority. The Israelis broadcast pornography over Palestinian TV stations, says one report, "to keep Palestinian youths away from joining the resistance against Israeli occupation and apartheid."[233] According to a Palestinian intelligence officer, the CIA discussed the issue with the Israelis repeatedly, but "the idea first came from the Israeli side who suggested that only these things could take Palestinian youths away from their hostile fixation on Israel."[234]

Luke Ford makes a similar point. "Why does porn attract so many non-Jewish Jews?"[235] Because "even when Jews live in a society that welcomes them instead of harassing them, many Jews hate the majority culture."[236] Pornography weakens the majority culture by moral subversion. Jews often lead in the application of new technology. That meant using high resolution photography, the VCR, and the Internet to deliver pornography just as it meant dynamite, forgery, and smuggling to bring down the Czar in Russia. English professor Jay Gertzman, whose father and uncle were arrested on obscenity charges in Philadelphia in the '50s, writes about the influence of Jews in the sex book trade in *Bookleggers and Smuthounds: The Trade In Erotica 1920-1940*: "While few Jews are radical, many radicals (and pornographers) are Jews. Writes non-Jew Ernest van den Haag in *The Jewish Mystique*, 'Out of one hundred Jews, five may be radicals, but out of ten radicals, five are likely to be Jewish.'"[237]

Like Dresner, Luke Ford feels

> Virtually all movements to change the world come from the Jews—Christianity, secular humanism, Marxism, Socialism and Communism, feminism, and the labor movement. That's part of the reason that Jews are hated. The world doesn't want to be changed. Rooted in nothing, radical Jews frequently seek to make others equally rootless by tearing down their religious, national, communal and traditional allegiances. Such Jews carry on the traditional Jewish hatred of false gods but without offering anything to replace the scorned allegiances.... Rather, the most important result of the domination of non-Jewish Jews in these fields is their war on traditional values. Porn is just one expression of this rebellion against standards, against the disciplined life of obedience to Torah that marks a Jew living Judaism.[238]

Pornography became a Jewish weapon based on Jewish fantasies of defilement. Even when Catholics are involved, it usually is on Jewish terms. According to one industry insider, "the leading male performers through the 1980s came from secular Jewish upbringings and the females from Roman Catholic day schools."[239] The standard porn scenario became a Polish Jewish fantasy, the horny Jew schtupping the Catholic Shiksa. Nina Hartley, the Jewish porn star agrees. "I have not yet met a Jewish guy who wasn't a horny rabbit,"[240] she says explaining Jewish male involvement in pornography in her 1989 interview in *Schmate*. "Plus, they get to have sex with all these beautiful blonde women ... Where else are you going to get a succession of shiksas to bed you down?"[241]

Hartley leaves out the cultural dimension. Pornography defiles Christian women, which, as Eldridge Cleaver pointed out, is a way of defiling Christianity and what it stands for.

When Luke Ford asked Al Goldstein, the publisher of *Screw*, why so many Jews were involved in pornography, Goldstein got to the theological heart of the matter. "The only reason that Jews are in pornography," Goldstein responded, "is that we think that Christ sucks. Catholicism sucks. We don't believe in authoritarianism."[242]

Goldstein's response is worth pondering. Being Jewish is Goldstein's rationalization for his unsavory business. Goldstein can hide behind centuries old Jewish antipathy to Christianity as his justification. Jews are so habituated to defining themselves as the antithesis of things Christian that they define themselves in opposition to things Judaism and Christianity hold in common, namely, the moral law and sexual prohibitions.

The conversation got progressively more theological, at least in the Goldstein mode. When Ford asked, "Do you believe in God?" Goldstein answered, "I believe in me. I'm God. Fuck God. God is your need to believe in some super being. I am the super being. I am your God, admit it. We're random. We're the flea on the ass of the dog."[243]

Luke: "What does being Jewish mean to you?"

Al: "It doesn't mean shit. It means that I'm called a kike. Rose is more of a Jew than I am. She speaks Hebrew. "[244]

Goldstein is referring to his companion, who, unlike Goldstein, was raised a religious Jew. Ford turns to Rose and asks her the same question: "What does being Jewish mean to you?"

Rose: "I feel like I am part of a worldwide spiritual community."

Al: "Jews and blacks are together. Us kikes and coons ... Like a chocolate mouse [sic]."

Luke: "What attracts you to Al?"[245]

Rose does not want to answer.

Al: "It's my big Jewish dick. My circumcision."[246]

Pornography is the latest revolutionary hope for non-neoconservative Jews who have invested their hope in the American empire. A large chunk of recent history has been shaped, in Rabbi Dresner's words, by "mesmerized Jews" who made modernity their project with a vengeance:

> Caged within ghetto bars for centuries, the Jews emerged into the freedom of Western society, where they drank in its culture, tasted its pleasure and enjoyed its power. They demanded citizenship and were so eager to be accepted by the majority that they often offered themselves, sacrificed their history, faith and way of life, their "identity," in order that the stigma of their difference might be obliterated. [247]

In fashioning modern society, where idols of politics, culture, and impulse are worshipped, Jews have played a major role in part because in the world's largest Jewish community of Eastern Europe, the Middle Ages did not gradually give way to the influences of Enlightenment science and reason. For most of East European Jewry, the Middle Ages extended into the 19th century and beyond. Many grandparents of today's American Jews emerged overnight, it seemed, from benighted, poverty-stricken villages, little touched by the secular culture, into the bright lights of modernity with its abundance of new knowledge and undreamt-of opportunity. Jews, mesmerized by what they saw and read and heard, were among the chief advocates of modernity.[248]

Stephen Steinlight, in a study on immigration for the AJC, indicates Jewish political power, following hard on the heels of disastrous Jewish demographics, is on the wane. Perhaps this explains the desperation of Goldhagen's attack on Pius XII, or the neocon desperation in attacking Iraq or the outpouring of Jewish sympathy for pornography on the Internet.

2002: Bush Pressures Sharon

Even as late as 2002, Bush wasn't fully on board with neocon plans to wage World War IV. Thinking America could diffuse Muslim animus, Bush chose the dangerous course that rendered his father a one-term president. He pressured Ariel Sharon to halt Israel's expansion in the occupied territories. Bush "had enormous potential leverage at his disposal,"[249] but he didn't reckon with the Israel Lobby, which had grown stronger since it thwarted his father's reelection. Sharon pulled out all stops, accusing Bush of trying "to appease the Arabs at our expense," warning Israel "will not be Czechoslovakia."[250] Bush was reportedly furious at Sharon likening him to Neville Chamberlain, but he was no match for the Israel Lobby. On April 4, 2002, George Bush ordered Sharon to "halt the incursions and begin withdrawal."[251] Two days later, he reiterated, adding he meant "withdrawal without delay."[252]

The Israel Lobby attacked the weakest link, Secretary of State Colin Powell, sent by the president to bring the Israelis to Bush's approach. Robert Kagan and William Kristol attacked Powell in the *Weekly Standard* as having "virtually obliterated the distinction between terrorists and those who fight terrorists."[253] Faced with an Israeli lobby-orchestrated revolt in Congress and among his Dispensationalist evangelical supporters, Bush backed down. On April 11, Ari Fleischer, Bush's Jewish press secretary, claimed Bush felt Sharon was "a man of peace."[254] Bush reiterated that claim when Secretary of State Powell returned from his failed mission. Bush also claimed Sharon had agreed to his call for a full and immediate withdrawal, but this was not true.

As if to show who really ran America's foreign policy, the House of Representatives appropriated $200 million so Israel could better "fight terrorism." The WASP establishment was appalled. In October 2004, Brent Scowcroft, one of its last vocal representatives, claimed Sharon had Bush "wrapped around his little finger."[255] The academic arm of the WASP establishment was equally gloomy in assessing Bush's craven capitulation to the Israelis and their neoconservative front men in America, claiming in a controversial report

> Sharon and the [Israel] Lobby took on the President of the United States and triumphed. Hemi Shalev, a journalist for the Israel newspaper *Ma'ariv*, reported that Sharon's aides "could not hide their satisfaction in view of Powell's failure. Sharon saw the white in President Bush's eyes, they bragged, and the President blinked first." But it was the pro-Israel forces in the United States, not Sharon or Israel, that played the key role in defeating Bush. In caving in to Ariel Sharon and the Israel Lobby, Bush "revers[ed] the stated policy of every President since Lyndon Johnson by "endors[ing] unilateral Israeli annexations of the Occupied Territories."[256]

2003: America invades Iraq

In March 2003 the Israel Lobby pushed America into war with Iraq. Colin Powell, the last representative of WASP restraint in the Bush Administration, was humiliated when neocons sent him to testify before the UN with documents he knew were dubious at best and outright fabrications at worst. According to Robert Woodward of the *Washington Post*, Powell "was appalled at what he considered overreaching and hyperbole. Libby was drawing on the worst conclusions from fragments and silky threads."[257]

Powell went along, conceding by his actions that the Lobby had become all-powerful. Having faced Bush down over the settlements in occupied territory, the Likudniks in Israel and the United States put on a media campaign that all but ordered Bush to do their bidding and invade Iraq. In September 2002, Israeli Foreign Minister Shimon Peres announced, "the campaign against Saddam Hussein is a must."[258] Shortly after, the *Wall Street Journal* ran a piece entitled "The Case for Toppling Saddam," in which Benjamin Netanyahu declared, "Today nothing less than dismantling this regime will do."[259] Netanyahu added "I believe I speak for the overwhelming majority of Israelis in supporting a pre-emptive strike against Saddam's regime."[260] Authors Walt and Mearsheimer claim "it would be wrong to blame the war in Iraq on 'Jewish influence,'" but they concede the supporters of the war were overwhelmingly Jewish: "Within the United States, the main driving force behind the Iraq war was a small band of neoconservatives, many with close ties to Israel's Likud Party," and they then quote the Jewish press to the same effect:

> According to the *Forward*, "As President Bush attempted to sell the ... war in Iraq, America's most important Jewish organizations rallied as one to his defense. In statement after statement [Jewish] community leaders stressed the need to rid the world of Saddam and his weapons of mass destruction." It added that "concern for Israel's safety rightfully factored into the deliberations of the main Jewish groups."[261]

The media drumbeat continued throughout fall 2002 and into early 2003, culminating in an attack on "Unpatriotic Conservatives" by David Frum in the March 19, 2003 *National Review*. A key component of the publicity campaign leading to the war was manipulation of intelligence information by the Office of Special Plans, run by Abram Shulsky, Wolfowitz's protégé, who created false intelligence with assistance from pro-Israel think tanks. Retired Air Force Colonel Karen Kwiatkowski has written about high ranking Israeli military men, bustling past their security escorts, making a beeline for Shulsky's Pentagon office.

These salvoes began an unrelenting public relations campaign to win support for invading Iraq. Manipulation of intelligence to make Saddam look like an imminent threat was key to this campaign. Walt and Mearsheimer cite Barry Jacobs of the AJC, who acknowledges

> the belief that Israel and the neoconservatives conspired to get the United States into a war in Iraq was "pervasive" in the US intelligence community. Yet few would say so publicly, and most that did ... were condemned for raising the issue. Michael Kinsley put the point well in late 2002, when he wrote that "the lack of public discussion about the role of Israel ... is the proverbial elephant in the

room: Everybody sees it, no one mentions it." The reason for his reluctance, he observed, was fear of being labeled an anti-Semite. Even so, there is little doubt that Israel and the lobby were key factors in shaping the decision for war. Without the Lobby's efforts, the United States would have been far less likely to have gone to war in March 2003.[262]

The American invasion of Iraq in March 2003 initially appeared successful because of staged media events that included an American tank—off camera, of course—pulling down a statue of Saddam Hussein to the cheers of a few Iraqi spectators. The scene was deliberately reminiscent of the statues of Lenin that came down in the aftermath of the fall of Communism. The premature victory celebrations culminated when Bush landed a fighter jet on an aircraft carrier, whose conning tower was adorned with the banner "Mission Accomplished."

When an enraged mob strung up the corpses of mutilated Americans in Falluja in the spring of 2004, it was clear the mission was far from accomplished. President Bush barely had time to get out of his flight suit before the neocons sensed something had gone wrong. In late spring, 2003, neocons Frum and Perle published *An End to Evil* "as a means of trying to summon Americans back to the mood of determination and resolution of 9/11."[263] They could "feel the will to win ebbing in Washington."[264] They added that their foes had "been proven wrong when they predicted the US would sink into a forlorn quagmire in Iraq,"[265] but they were trying to convince themselves. Even the uniformly upbeat Murray Friedman ended his book on neoconservative Jewish intellectuals by conceding "The invasion of Iraq may well be the disaster that critics of the war have charged."[266] The mission bogged down in a quagmire that made Vietnam seem like a picnic by comparison. But anyone who held the neoconservatives responsible for the debacle was denounced as an anti-Semite.

2006: Walt and Mearsheimer

That is precisely what happened when a report by Professors John J. Mearsheimer of the Department of Political Science at the University of Chicago and Stephen M. Walt of the John F. Kennedy School of Government at Harvard began circulating on the internet. In the initial euphoria after the fall of communism, neoconservatives had numerous allies among the WASP foreign policy establishment. Francis Fukuyama gushed that the neocons had brought about the "end of history." Once the Iraq war began to sour, Fukuyama, spokesman for the severely diminished WASP elite, had second thoughts. They distanced themselves from the debacle in Iraq. The Walt/Mearsheimer study was commissioned by the *Atlantic Monthly*, which got cold feet and refused to publish it. Instead it appeared in the *London Review of Books*. Walt and Mearsheimer predicted what would happen once their article was published:

anyone who says that there is an Israel Lobby runs the risk of being charged with anti-Semitism, even though the Israeli media themselves refer to America's "Jewish Lobby." In effect, the Lobby boasts of its own power and then attacks anyone who calls attention to it. This tactic is very effective because anti-Semitism is loathsome and no responsible person wants to be accused of it.[267]

The lobby that did not exist then proceded to attack professors Walt and Mearsheimer. It exerted influence to get articles attacking Walt and Mearsheimer in virtually every major outlet of the mainstream print media, just as Abe Foxman predicted it would. "There is no Israel 'Lobby'" screamed the *New York Daily News*, one of its main organs. That was the *Daily News's* title to a David Gergen piece that orginally appeared in *U.S. News and World Report*, published by Mort Zuckerman, another member of the press section of the Israeli Lobby. Gergen's rebuttal was typical, even if more groveling than most. Gergen claimed their charges were "wildly at variance with what I have personally witnessed in the Oval Office over the years."[268] In one of the most disingenuous line in a disingenuous article, Gergen wrote:

Over the course of four tours in the White House, I never once saw a decision in the oval office to tilt US foreign policy in favor of Israel at the expense of America's interest. Other than Richard Nixon—who occasionally had terrible things to say about Jews, despite the number on his team—I can't remember any president even talking about an Israeli lobby. Perhaps I have forgotten.[269]

Perhaps the lobby that does not exist told Gergen to forget what he knew.

"Yes, It's Anti-Semitic,"[270] screamed Eliot Cohen in the *Washington Post*, fulfilling the authors' prediction. Like many independent-minded pundits who barked when the lobby that does not exist yanked their chains, Cohen smeared Walt and Mearsheimer by linking them to White Supremacist David Duke. But, as Walt and Mearsheimer noted, when it comes to the Israel Lobby, the ordinary rules of journalism did not apply.

The remnant of the deeply chagrined WASP establishment now views its erstwhile Jewish allies as the domestic version of Osama bin Laden. Neoconservatism, like the Civil Rights movement of the '60s and the Whig/Masonic subversion of France in the 18th century, was a black operation which got out of control. What would John J. McCloy and the originators of anti-Catholic psy ops under the aegis of ADA liberalism say to spiritual descendants like Francis Fukuyama and Brent Scowcroft? That the Jesuits who wrote for *Civiltà Cattolica* in the 1890s were right? That any nation that rebelled against God's order would end up being ruled by Jews?

Probably not.

Epilogue

The Conversion of the Revolutionary Jew

On June 15, 2006, the General Convention of the Episcopal Church in the United States passed a resolution condemning the Gospels as "anti-Jewish" documents. Since the conclusion which the Episcopalians drew from their recognition of that fact was that the Scriptures should be censored, especially their liturgical use, by removing anything a Jew might find offensive, many Episcopalians concluded that this was the final apostasy in a long slide which began at the Lambeth Conference of 1930 when that church approved the use of contraceptives. Whether it is or it isn't is beyond our purview here. No matter what conclusions the Episcopalians draw from the fact, the statement that the Gospels are anti-Jewish is, beyond a shadow of doubt, true. The only real question is why it took the Episcopalians four hundred years to wake up to this fact or why they didn't draw what seems to be the more logical conclusion, namely, that if Episcopalians want to be faithful to the example of Jesus Christ, they must be anti-Jewish as well.

The Episcopalians did not say that the Scriptures were anti-Semitic. If they had said that, the statement would have been false. Anti-Semitism is a relatively recent word. It was popularized in 1870 by a German named Wilhelm Marr. It refers to race, and claims that Jews are hateful because of certain ineradicable biological characteristics. That idea led to Hitler, but the defeat of Hitler led to a redefinition of the word. Anti-Semitism now has an entirely different meaning. An anti-Semite used to be someone who didn't like Jews. Now it is usually someone whom Jews don't like. No Christian can in good conscience be an anti-Semite, but every Christian, insofar as he is a Christian, must be anti-Jewish. In contemporary parlance the two terms are practically synonymous but their meanings are very different, and the distinction is deliberately obscured for political purposes.

On October 16, 2004 President Bush signed into law the Global Anti-Semitism Review Act, which establishes a special department within the U.S. State Department to monitor global anti-Semitism, reporting annually to Congress. As one of the major steps in the implementation of that law, Secretary of State Condaleeza Rice swore in Gregg Rickman as head of the State Department's office of global anti-Semitism on May 22, 2006. Rickman had ties with both Jewish organizations and congress. He was staff director for former Sen. Peter Fitzgerald (R-Ill.), and chairman of the Republican Jewish Coalition. But his main qualification for the job was the role he played in conjunction with Senator Alfonse D'Amato (R-NY) in shaking down $2 billion from the Swiss banks during the late '90s. "Gregg Rickman, working with Sen. D'Amato, is almost single-handedly the one who uncovered the corruption and the immorality of the Swiss banks," according to William Daroff, vice president for public policy of the United Jewish Communities, the umbrella body of North American Jewish Federations, and director of its Washington office. Journalist Ron Kampeas added "That kind of doggedness will serve him well in his new capacity, according to representatives of groups that liaise between Washington and small, vulnerable Jewish communities overseas."[1]

Mr. Rickman will not have to define anti-Semitism. His state department office has already in effect done that for him. In its "Report on Global Anti-Semitism," the U.S. State Department does not define the term but proceeds to list a dazzling array of beliefs or actions that count as Anti-Semitic. In many cases the belief referred to is merely one that certain Jewish organizations don't like.[2]

In spite of 40 years of Jewish exaggeration and *chutzpah*, certain facts remain. The Church is not and cannot possibly be anti-Semitic, because the term refers primarily to race and racial hatred. The Church cannot promote racial hatred of any group, certainly not of the Jews because its founder was a member of that racial group. However, the Gospel of St. John makes clear that there is a deep and abiding Christian opposition to the Jews who rejected Christ. This "*Judenfeindlichkeit*," if we use Brumlik's word, is part of the essence of Catholicism. The Church opposes "Jews" because they have defined themselves as rejecters of Christ. The Church is anti-Jewish, but unlike the Jews, who, according to Rabbi Soloveichik in *First Things*,[3] can believe that hatred is a virtue, Christians are told to love their enemies. The "Jews," by which St. John means the Jews who rejected Christ, became by that fact Christians' enemies, but all Jews had been transformed by the coming of Christ. They had to accept him as the Messiah or reject him. Those Jews who accepted Christ as the Messiah became known as Christians. Those Jews who rejected him became known as "Jews."

II

In fall 2003, Mahathir Mohammed, prime minister of Malaysia, announced, "The Jews rule the world by proxy. They get others to fight and die for them."[4] Mahathir was immediately denounced as an anti-Semite and accused of "an absolute invitation for more hate crimes and terrorism against Jews,"[5] although he said no such thing and many Jews agreed with him. Henry Makow felt Mahathir's speech "opposed terrorism." Another Jew, Elias Davidsson, a native of Jerusalem, feels Jews do rule the world by proxy. He explains:

> As a Jew myself (but opposed to Zionism) I need no encouragement from Malaysian PM Mahathir Mohammed to observe what should be obvious to the blatant eye: Namely that Jews effectively rule US foreign policy and thus determine to a great extent the conduct of most countries.... So it is with the proposition that Jews control the world. Surely they do not control every single action; surely it does not mean that every Jew participates in the "control." But for all practical purposes the proposition holds.

What distinguishes a Jew like Davidsson from a Jew like, say, Stanley Fish, is not ethnicity, nor even politics, but their divergent forms of literary criticism. Davidsson believes in the objectivity of statements. He holds the Malaysian Prime Minister to what he actually said and so finds nothing anti-Semitic in it. "Mahathir," Davidsson says,

> has neither asked to discriminate against Jews, let alone to kill Jews. It is shameful to equate him to the Hitlerites. He urges Muslims to fight Jews by adopting modern methods, technology and educate themselves, in other words to surpass Jews in excellence. What's wrong with that? By this he is doing service to the Muslims (over 1 billion people) and to humanity. Jews must know their place and content themselves with influence derived from their small number. Jews must learn some humility....[6]

The "Jews", if by that term we mean the cabal that rules as the Sanhedrin, the Kahal, the politburo, the ADL, or other major Jewish organizations, has centuries of experience dealing with Jews like Makow and Davidsson. The *modus operandi* of Jewish leaders working over Jews who disagree with them goes back to the time of Christ, when, according to the Gospel of St. John, the parents of the man born blind refused to speak "out of fear of the Jews, who had already agreed to expel from the synagogue anyone who should acknowledge Jesus as the Christ." Any Jew who chooses Logos (in any form) over Talmud will feel the ire of organized Jewry. Spinoza[7] felt it in Amsterdam in the 17th century; in our day Norman Finkelstein has felt it. Since it sounds preposterous to call Jews who disagree with other Jews anti-Semites, the modern Kahal has created a new term. They are called "self-hating Jews" as they are expelled from the modern synagogue of acceptable speech.

The Kahal was the autonomous legal system which the Jews established in Poland to take care of their own legal affairs. The spirit which informed that legal body was the Talmud. According to the Jewish Encyclopedia, the Talmud is "the supreme authority in religion... for the majority of [Jews]."[8] The Catholic Church has never disputed the centrality of the Talmud to Jewish life. However, in addition to that the Church has always seen the Talmud as a "systematic deformation of the Bible" in which "The pride of race with the idea of universal domination is therein exalted to the height of folly... the Ten Commandments are not of obligation in their regard.... With regard to the Goyim (non-Jews) everything is allowed: robbery, fraud, perjury, murder...."[9] Whenever its contents were made known, Christians have condemned the Talmud as incompatible with any rational social order. Jewish converts to Catholicism from the time of Nicholas Donin onward have condemned the Talmud as well. Numerous popes have condemned the Talmud because it was a direct assault on both the divinity of Christ and the moral law as handed down by Moses. According to the ex-Rabbi Drach, "the Talmud expressly forbids a Jew to save a non-Jew from death or to restore to him his lost possessions, etc, or to take pity on him."[10]

The Talmud was created to keep Jews in bondage to Jewish leaders by prohibiting all contact with Logos, whether that is understood as the person of Christ or the Truth or reasoning based on true principles and logic. Taught to deceive by the Talmud, Jews end up deceiving themselves and playing into the hands of the leaders who manipulate them for their own ends.

The Talmud has also led to revolution. You also don't have to be religious to be talmudic. Karl Marx was an atheist, but according to Bernard Lazare, he was also "a clear and lucid Talmudist," and, therefore, "full of that old Hebrew materialism which ever dreams of a paradise on earth and always rejects the far-distant and problematical hope of a garden of Eden after death."[11] Marx, despite his early writings, was the quintessential Talmudist and the quintessential Jewish revolutionary, and as such he proposed one of the most influential false Messiahs in Jewish history: world communism. Baruch Levy, one of Marx's correspondents, proposed another equally potent false Messiah, namely, the Jewish Race. According to Levy,

> "the Jewish people taken collectively shall be its own Messias.... In this new or-ganization of humanity , the sons of Israel now scattered over the whole surface of the globe... shall everywhere become the ruling element without opposition.... The governments of the nations forming the Universal or World -Republic shall all thus pass, without any effort, into Jewish hands thanks to the victory of the proletariat.... Thus shall the promise of the Talmud be fulfilled, that, when the Messianic epoch shall have arrived, the Jews will control the wealth of all the nations of the earth."[12]

So, there was some basis for what Mahathir said, as well as ample evidence— the creation of the state of Israel, for instance—that world Jewry had advanced to-wards a position of inordinate power in the world since Levy wrote to Karl Marx. The Jews could not shake themselves loose from the notion they were God's cho-sen people, not even after they stopped believing in God. By rejecting Christ, they condemned themselves to worship one false Messiah after another—most recently Communism and Zionism. In *La Question du Messie*, the Lemann brothers, both of whom converted from Judaism to Catholicism and became priests, compared present day Jews to the Israelites at the foot of Mount Sinai: "having grown weary of waiting for the return of Moses ... they feasted and danced around the golden calf."[13] Rejecting the supernatural Messiah who died on the cross, the Jews con-demned themselves to repeat the cycle of enthusiasm leading to disillusionment throughout their history. Their illusions found fulfillment in and lent themselves to the creation of the Jewish state. On January 6, 1948, the chief rabbi of Palestine announced "Eventually it [Israel] will lead to the inauguration of the true union of the nations, through which will be fulfilled the eternal message to mankind of our immortal prophets."[14] In Jewish messianism, fantasies of racial superiority alternate with contradictory fantasies of universal brotherhood. "The great ideal of Judaism," *The Jewish World* announced in February 1883, "is that ... the whole world shall be imbued with Jewish teaching and that in a Universal Brotherhood of Nations—a greater Judaism in fact—all the separate races and religions shall disappear."[15]

The Jews were condemned to seek heaven on earth through false Messiahs from the moment they chose Barabbas over Christ. When the Jews refused to be "heralds of a supernatural kingdom"[16] they condemned themselves to the endless task of imposing a vision of a naturalistic heaven on earth, "and they have put all their intense energy and tenacity into the struggle for the organization of the future Messianic Age."[17] Whenever a nation turns from the Supernatural Messiah, as during the French and Russian revolutions, that nation "will be pulled into the direction of subjection to the Natural Messias"[18] and, in effect, ruled by Jews.

Does that mean that every Jew is a bad person? No, it does not. Jewish leadership controls the "Synagogue of Satan," which in turn controls the ethnic group into which Jews are born. No one has control over the circumstances of his birth. That is why anti-Semitism, if by that term we mean hatred of the Jews because of immutable and ineradicable racial characteristics, is wrong. Over the course of their lives, Jews come to understand that theirs is an ethnic group unlike any other. In spite of the propaganda of racial superiority which the Talmud seeks to inculcate in them, many Jews come to understand that a peculiarly malignant spirit has taken up its home at the heart of their ethnos. Once they become aware of the magnitude of that evil, Jews are faced with a choice. Depending on the disposition of the heart, which only God can judge, they either dedicate themselves to that evil or they reject it—completely as in the case of St. Paul, Nicholas Donin, Joseph Pfefferkorn and other Jews too numerous to mention—or inchoately, as in the case of the Jews of conscience who refuse to go along with something which they know is morally wrong, be that abortion or the eviction of Palestinians from their ancestral lands.

The purpose of the Talmud is to prevent defections from the "Synagogue of Satan." Behavior based on the Talmud leads to resentment on the part of non-Jews. Jewish leaders promote that behavior knowing it will cause reactions because "Pogroms in which the rank and file of the Jewish nation suffer serve the useful purpose of keeping them in absolute dependence on their leaders."[19] The Trotskys promote the revolution and the Braunsteins suffer. Jewish leaders promote pogroms, such as the Gomeler Pogrom of 1905 or when Mossad agents deliberately killed Iraqi Jews[20] to spread panic, because pogroms promote fear, which is how the Kahal keeps ordinary Jews in line.

Alice Ollstein, a Jewish high school student from Santa Monica, CA, noticed this at the American Israel Public Affairs Committee Conference in Washington, DC, in 2006. She went as an enthusiastic Zionist but returned "feeling manipulated, disturbed and disgusted with a great deal of what I witnessed there."[21] She witnessed non-stop fear mongering. The "first thing" she noticed was "the carefully manufactured atmosphere of fear and urgency." The hall where the plenary sessions were held was always filled with dramatic classical music, red lighting and gigantic signs reading "Now Is The Time." That, combined with the montages of terrorism footage projected onto six giant screens, whipped the audience into a "Save Israel" fervor that most found inspiring... the audience seemed eager to agree to anything that would protect Israel—even war.... Each speaker played upon the audience's deepest fears.[22]

Neoconservatives in charge of the fear-mongering, in particular, John Podhoretz, son of Norman and a columnist for *The New York Post*, "got to have the first word and the last word on almost every question."[23] Ollstein found the comparisons AIPAC drew between Iranian President Mahmoud Ahmadinejad and Hitler particularly manipulative:

To the tune of more dramatic classical music, the six enormous screens flashed back and forth between Hitler giving anti-Jew speeches and Ahmadinejad giving anti-Israel speeches. The famous post-Holocaust mantra "Never Again" popped up several times. Everything was geared toward persuading the audience that another Holocaust is evident ... unless we get them first.[24]

Alice Ollstein resented "being forced to think" the Prime Minister of Iran was "pure evil through clever sound bites and colorful images." She felt manipulated by what Professors Walt and Mearsheimer have characterized as the main agent of the Israel Lobby in America. She is not the only Jew who feels this way. Zionism now finds itself in a state of wretched excess that signals a reaction is about to set in. Jewish disillusionment with the god that failed known as Communism came to be known as neoconservatism. The Jewish reaction to Zionism can be seen in the proliferation of "proud, self-hating Jews."

In response to a Danish magazine's anti-Muslim cartoons in March 2006, a group of Israelis organized an anti-Semitic cartoon contest. Gilad Atzmon, who described the contest on his web site, finds it natural: "a few Jews who happen to be ethically motivated and talented enough to express themselves would raise their voices"[25] to protest a black operation designed to get European countries so annoyed at the Muslim reaction to the cartoons that they would support a nuclear attack on Iran's nuclear facilities. Atzmon claims "the morally deteriorated conduct of the Jewish state and its supportive Jewish lobbies around the world" has engendered "a celebration of what I tend to define as 'proud Jewish self-hatred.'"[26]

Atzmon is only half joking. The heart of this parody is the slowly spreading disillusionment with Zionism among Israelis. As Israel rules the world through proxies like AIPAC, the Jews they claim to speak for are undergoing deep disillusionment. Atzmon, an Israeli musician and former Israeli soldier, who has nominated himself as spokesman for the proud, self-hating Jew, believes "it is the proud SHJs that will bring Israeli Zionism and even global Zionism down."[27] Born an Israeli, Atzmon had been subjected to Zionist propaganda for his entire life. One day he didn't believe it anymore:

The very program that worked so well and still works at large in the instance of my former fellow countrymen failed in my case. Not only had I stopped loving myself, I somehow failed to hate the Goyim. This is when I realized for the first time that actually there was no anti-Semitism around. Somehow, when I stopped loving myself, I also started to suspect the entire official Jewish historical narrative, both the Zionist one as well as the biblical one. How to say it, it didn't take long before I started to question the official Zionist Holocaust tale."[28]

Belief in Zionism, like belief in Communism, was an all or nothing proposition. Once the first doubt took root, the entire edifice was doomed to collapse. The first thing Atzmon doubted was the dogma "Jew-hating is an irrational act of madness or some backward Christian tendency."[29] Unlike Ruth Wisse, who articulated a dogma of contemporary Judaism, "anti-Semitism is not directed against the behavior of Jews but against the existence of Jews,"[30] Atzmon entertained "the possibility that anti-Jewish feelings may come as a response or even retaliation to Jewish acts":

The more I learned about the subject, the more I realized that anti-Jewish feelings are often intentionally generated and orchestrated by Jews themselves. This was when I became conscious that self-loving Jews love to be hated, and more than that, they need it. Indeed, Zionism is maintained by anti-Semitism. Without anti-Semitism there is no need for a Jewish State and without the Holocaust there wouldn't even be a Jewish State.[31]

Jewish organizations like AIPAC and the ADL, he says, "are all remarkably good in generating hatred against Jews,"[32] which generates fear that keeps the average Jew in bondage. During his soliloquy, Atzmon concludes that as a proud, self-hating Jew he hates neither Jews nor Judaism, which he defines in ethnic terms. His quarrel is with what he calls "Jewishness," because

Jewishness is what is left for the Jews once religious context is stripped away. Jewishness is what many Jews interpret as their identity. It is a wide set of characteristics that many self-identifying Jews recognize as a form of unique belonging. Jewishness is a broad concept that serves as the distinguishing quality that many Jews identify with. In fact, it is the Jewishness that stands at the core of the Jewish racial orientation. Jewishness is the supremacist tendency that draws its force from a materialist secularized misinterpretation of the Judaic code. It is Jewishness rather than Judaism that fuels Zionism with murderous zeal. It is Jewishness that stands in the core of Jewish nationalism. It is Jewishness which bonded the Bundists and their followers amongst the various Jews sans frontiers, it is Jewishness that unites the settlers in the West Bank. Jewishness is exactly what the self-loving Jews love in themselves.[33]

What Atzmon calls Jewishness is what Nicholas Donin and Joseph Pfefferkorn and the Fathers Lemann called the Talmud, *i.e.,* the racist, messianic ideology that drives Jewish revolutionary activity. As we have seen, many Jews have awakened to realize some dark evil force has colonized their ethnic group for centuries. That evil is the Talmud, the constitution for the synagogue of Satan, the cabal that has ruled Jews through fear for 2000 years. Atzmon isn't alone in feeling disillusionment. Yuri Slezkine says "The Zionist revolution is over":

> The original ethos of youthful athleticism, belligerence and single mindedness is carried on by tired elite of old generals. Half a century after its founding, Israel bears a distant family resemblance to the Soviet Union half a century after the October Revolution. The last representatives of the first Sabra generation are still in power, but their days are numbered.[34]

The rhetoric of racial superiority is hopelessly outdated, even when surrounded by the window-dressing of holocaust victimhood. Holocaust culture postponed the final reckoning, but by the beginning of the 21st century "The rhetoric of ethnic homogeneity and ethnic deportations, tabooed elsewhere in the west, is a routine element of Israeli political life."[35] The realization arrives half-way through Steven Spielberg's film *Munich*, when the Jewish toy maker turned bomb maker tells Avner Kauffman, "Jews don't do wrong because our enemies do wrong ... We're supposed to be righteous."

It is unclear whether the proud, self-hating Jew can leverage disillusionment with Zionism to escape the dialectic of Jewish history with its cycle of enthusiasm followed by disillusionment followed by new enthusiasm. That would require understanding what Atzmon calls "Jewishness." Jewishness is not another version of ethnicity like Irishness or Polishness. It is an ideology, the Talmudic deformation of Logos that has helped to cause so much suffering for the past 2000 years.

The Catholic Church has always condemned anti-Semitism because hatred of the Jewish race is wrong in and of itself. Beyond that, anti-Semitism is an inappropriate response to what Atzmon calls "Jewishness." Anti-Semitism is a competing form of "Jewishness." Anti-Semitism cannot deal with "Jewishness," because a Jew is not someone who can be defined as having Abraham's DNA in his cells. Most Jews aren't even Semites. The Jew insofar as he appropriates "Jewishness" is primarily a theological construct. He is a rejecter of Christ. The Talmud, as we have said, was created to keep the Jewish people in bondage to a leadership that has existed under various manifestations throughout history—the Sanhedrin, the Kahal, the Politburo, the ADL and AIPAC. Each has proposed a false messiah as the antidote and alternative to the true Messiah, and each has led to violent reaction or equally violent disappointment. Sixty years ago, the Communist empire spread across the earth, and yet the Jews who had supported Stalin faithfully experienced widespread disillusionment with Communism. The same thing is happening now to Zionism, at the very moment when the Israel Lobby has reached the pinnacle of worldly power.

If this is the case, what are the options at the present time? In one of his more cryptic moments, Atzmon claims that "Salvation is the Masada of the Proud, Self-Hating Jew." Atzmon is referring to the mass suicide which followed the 70 AD insurrection against Rome which eventuated in the destruction of the Temple. The

21st century version of Masada would be much more dramatic because today's despairing Zionists have nuclear weapons, a fact which lends new urgency to dissuading the Jews from taking the whole world with them when they go through one of their inevitable periods of disillusionment.

The other option is conversion, the option which has always been there since the beginning. This means conversion to Logos in all of its forms, from philosophical realism and the tenets of onto-theology to acceptance of Jesus Christ as the one and only Messiah. It also means an equally firm rejection of all forms of Talmudic deception, including sexual liberation, racism, Messianic politics, and deconstruction.

The Catholic Church has urged conversion of the Jews throughout its history, but it now seems incapable of assisting in that conversion because it has been lamed by an interpretation of *Nostra Aetate* that contradicts the Gospels. One ritual of post-*Nostra Aetate* ecumenism entails having a church dignitary stand up at an ecumenical gathering—after the Jews have denounced the Church as the font of anti-Semitism and the cause of Hitler's genocide—to announce that the Jews do not need Christ as their savior. In May 2001, at a meeting of the international Catholic-Jewish Liaison Committee, Walter Cardinal Kasper, the Vatican official in charge of relations with the Jews, tried to quell Jewish discomfort over the Congregation for the Doctrine of the Faith's *Dominus Iesus* by claiming "God's grace, which is the grace of Jesus Christ according to our faith, is available to all. Therefore the Church believes that Judaism, i.e., the faithful response of the Jewish people to God's irrevocable covenant is salvific *for them*, because God is faithful to his promises."[36]

In placating the Jews, Kasper contradicted the Gospels and 2000 years of Church teaching; he also contradicted *Dominus Iesus*, which claimed:

> There is only one salvific economy of the one and triune God realized in the mystery of the incarnation, death and resurrection of the Son of God, actualized with the cooperation of the Holy Spirit and extended in its salvific value to all humanity and to the entire universe. "No one, therefore, can enter into communion with God except through Christ by the working of the Holy Spirit."[37]

Kasper also contradicted Pope John Paul II's 1990 encyclical *Redemptoris Missio*, which claimed:

> Christ is the one Savior of all, the only one able to reveal God and lead to God. In reply to the Jewish religious authorities who question the apostles about healing the lame man, Peter says: "By the name of Jesus Christ of Nazareth, whom you crucified, whom God raised from the dead, by him this man is standing before you well ... And there is salvation in no one else, for there is no other name under heaven given among men by which we must be saved." ... salvation can only come from Jesus Christ.[38]

Trying to extricate himself from the theological briar patch into which he had just thrown himself, Kasper claimed in a speech at Boston College that Jews could be saved if they "follow their own conscience and believe in God's promises as they understand them in their religious tradition, they are in line with God's plan, which *for us* comes to historical completion in Jesus Christ."[39]

In saying "for us," Kasper implied there were two ways of salvation, a contradiction of the Gospels and *Dominus Iesus,* which holds that all those saved, including non-Christian, are saved through Christ and the Church. Kasper, however, was not alone. In August 2002, the US Bishops' Committee for Ecumenical and Interreligious Affairs, along with the US National Council of Synagogues, issued "Reflections on Covenant and Mission," which claimed: "A deepening Catholic appreciation of the eternal covenant between God and the Jewish people, together with a recognition of a divinely given mission to the Jews to witness to God's faithful love, lead to the conclusion that campaigns that target Jews for conversion to Christianity are no longer theologically acceptable in the Catholic Church."[40]

Once the heretical nature of these statements became apparent, Cardinal Keeler tried to control the damage, saying that "Reflections on Covenant and Mission" did not constitute a formal position of the US bishops, but rather "the state of thought among participants in the dialogue between Catholics and Jews."[41] The paper was never promulgated as an official document of the bishops' conference.

But its existence indicates *Nostra Aetate* had caused a deep crisis in the Church. To participate in ecumenical dialogue with Jews, Catholic "experts" had to make heretical statements. They had to deny fundamental tenets of Catholic theology. The Church suddenly could not articulate a coherent position because denial of the Gospel had become the *conditio sine qua non* of dialogue with the Jews.

This problem went all the way to the top. Viewing Pope John Paul II's relations with the Jews, an ultramontane American Catholic commentator concluded "Even Pope John Paul II ... could occasionally create the impression that the Church was perhaps now prepared to cut a few corners in the interests of better relations"[42] with the Jews. In the "Declaration on the Relation of the Church with Judaism," delivered to a Jewish group in Mainz, Germany, in 1980, "John Paul II," says the same commentator, "actually made the remark that the old covenant with the Jews had in fact 'never been revoked by God.'"[43]

The statement was theologically defensible because God never revoked the covenants with Noah or Abraham, but it suggested the "new and everlasting covenant" Christ established did not apply to the Jews.

Pope John Paul II's gestures were even worse. His prayer at the Wailing Wall was theatrical but ambiguous. Jews pray there for restoration of the Temple. No pope would ever contemplate doing such a wicked thing, but Jewish artists memorialized his gesture and the ambiguity it embodied to justify their call for a ban on "proselytism." No wonder Roy Schoeman is confused. Schoeman is a Jewish convert to Catholicism who speculates about the end times. Schoeman, in his book, apparently looks forward to restoration of the Temple without understanding that it would be tantamount to the abomination of desolation of which Revelations speaks.[44]

The idea of the Jews converting at the pinnacle of their worldly power is implausible except from a theological perspective, but since the Jew is an essentially theological construct, that is precisely how we should view the issue. The synagogue of Satan is the antithesis of the Church. So, if Christians, following St. Paul, can say, "when I am weak, then I am strong," (2 Corinthians 12.10) the synagogue of Satan would have to say the opposite, namely, "when I am strong, then I am weak." That corresponds uncannily to the phenomenon of the "proud, self-hating Jew" we have been discussing.

The final collapse of Jewish resistance to Logos will take place when they have reached the pinnacle of worldly power. At no time in the past 2000 years have Jews had more power than now. The Jews possess Jerusalem and, according to reports, plan to rebuild the temple, lending credence to the belief the stage is set for that last great battle over who will rule the Jewish soul. Fr. Augustin Lemann, a Jewish convert, feels the conversion of the Jewish people is certain, based on the testimony of many Church Fathers. "There is a well-known tradition cherished by the faithful," says St. Augustine, "that in the last days before the Judgment, the great and admirable Prophet Elias is to explain the law to the Jews and to lead them to the acceptance of the True Messias Our Christ."[45] "These carnal Israelites," he says, "who today refuse to believe in Jesus Christ, will one day believe in Him ... Osee foretells their conversion in the following terms: 'The children of Israel shall sit many days without king and without prince and without sacrifice, and without altar and without ephod and without theraphim."[46] "Who is there," Denis Fahey interjects, "who does not see in this a portrait of the present state of the Jewish people."[47]

Augustine is not alone in his belief that, near the culmination of human history, the Jews will convert. St. Thomas Aquinas says, "as by the fall of the Jews, the Gentiles who had been enemies were reconciled, so after the conversion of the Jews near the end of the world, there will be a general resurrection by which men will rise from the dead to immortal life."[48] According to Father Lemann,

> The prophet Elias then shall return upon the earth to bring back the Jews to the Savior. Our Lord Himself has clearly affirmed it (Matt: XVII, II).... The fathers are the patriarchs and all the pious ancestors of the Jewish people, the sons represent the degenerate race of the time of Our Lord Jesus Christ and of the succeeding centuries. It is however only some time before the second coming of Our Lord Jesus Christ, before the dreadful day of the Divine Judgment dawns that our Savior will send the prophet Elias to the Jews to convert them and to save them from chastisement.[49]

St. Paul claims this conversion will take place at the end of time, until then the Jews will "fill up their sins always: for the wrath of God is come upon them to the end."[50] St. Jerome also believes the Jews will convert at the end of the world when they "find themselves in dazzling light, as if Our Lord were returning to them from Egypt."[51] According to Suarez, "The conversion of the Jews will take place at the approach of the Last Judgment and at the height of the persecution which Antichrist will inflict on the Church."[52] The Jews will, by all accounts, express hostility to Christ until the moment of conversion. The conversion will be dramatic and in the last times Christians will resemble Jews "because of our sins, in fact they will be worse."[53] Origen supports the contention of Yuri Slezkine that modernity is Jewish. St. John Chrysostom claims "God will recall the Jews a second time,"[54] when Christians have abandoned the faith. Jews will become Christians when Christians have become Jews.

The Antichrist will then appear, and, according to Suarez, he will be a Jew who will find "his chief support among the Jews."[55] He will "restore the city of their ancestors and its temple in which they have always taken a special pride" because if he did not, he could not "get himself accepted as the Messias by the Jews who dream of earthly glory for Jerusalem and imagine that that city will become the capital of the future Messianic kingdom."[56] If Suarez were catapulted into the future to contemplate the state of Israel in 2008, he might conclude the end times are at hand. If he read Atzmon's website, he might conclude that the conversion of the Jews is at hand too. The unprecedented strength of the Jews coupled with the unprecedented weakness of the Church allows apocalyptic explanations; in fact, it demands them.

At the end of history, the antichrist will be stronger than ever before, and the Church will be weaker than ever before. Then the messianic kingdom of heaven on earth, the kingdom of maximal wealth and power for the Jews, will be at hand; all the synagogue of Satan has sought for centuries will seem within its grasp. The Jews then will have a choice; according to Christian tradition, many will choose Christ. Why is easy to explain. Rabbi Dresner does so in his book on the plight of the American family which is really a tract on the plight of American Jews, who:

> in their search for passion and pleasure and power, have lost themselves in the kingdom of Caesar. Is it not ironic that the descendants of those who wrote the Psalms and offered prayer to the world became, according to all accountings, the least worshipful.... The chosen people seemed to flatten into normality, becoming what the prophets had warned against: "like the nations." ... Many postmodern Jews have discovered a puzzling truth. No license has replaced the Law; no symphony, the Psalms, no chandelier, the Sabbath candles; no opera, Yom Kippur; no country club, the synagogue; no mansion, the home; no Jaguar, a child; no mistress, a wife; no banquet, the Passover seder; no towering metropolis, Jerusalem; no impulse, the joy of doing a mitzvah; no man, God.[57]

At the heart of Rabbi Dresner's panegyric, we uncover the psychological mechanism that will lead to the Jews' conversion. When they are strong, they are weak. Alan Dershowitz said something similar about Jewish demographics in America in *The Vanishing American Jew*. The more wealth and power the Jews accumulate, the weaker they become because wealth deprives the Jew of his perhaps most perduring illusion, *i.e.*, Tevye would be happy "if I were a rich man." Tevye's grandchildren are far richer than he could have imagined, but as a result, many have become "proud, self-hating Jews," and their number is growing. Money is the least important issue. As Rabbi Dresner indicates darkly, "Jews have tried all things." After having "exhausted modernity," Jews now "seek the recovery of the sacred."

Rabbi Dresner did not understand that the sacred cannot be recovered by performing outmoded rites. The Jews cannot find the sacred among the dead, only among the living. The Church can save the world from a nuclear Masada only if it reasserts its traditional position, "*Sicut Iudeis non.*" No one may harm Jews or disturb their worship, but Christians also have a duty to prevent Jewish subversion of faith and morals. The Church should condemn anti-Semitism, "hatred of the Jews as a race," but should not allow the Jews to define the term, because the Jews, in Denis Fahey's words, will use "the word to designate any form of opposition to themselves"[58] or the cultural subversion in which they may be engaged. According to the Jewish definition, "anyone who opposes Jewish pretensions is more or less mentally deranged."[59]

The Church has never been anti-Semitic. Traditional Catholic teaching has always involved a delicate balancing:

> On the one hand, the Church has spoken for the Jews to protect their persons and their worship against unjust attacks .... On the other hand, the Church has spoken against the Jews, when they wanted to impose their yoke on the faithful and provoke apostasy. She has always striven to protect the faithful from contamination by them. As experience in past centuries showed, if the Jews succeeded in attaining to high offices of State they would abuse their powers to the detriment of Catholics, the church always strove to prevent Catholics from coming under their yoke. They were forbidden to proselytize and were not allowed to have Christians as slaves or servants.[60]

At the darkest hour of Nazi persecution during the '30s, Pope Pius XI defended the Jews, proclaiming "anti-Semitism is inadmissible. We are spiritually Semites."[61] Less well known is the rest of what he said. After affirming it was "impossible for Christians to be Anti-Semites," Pope Pius XI went on to say "we acknowledge that everyone has the right to defend himself, in other words to take the necessary precautions for his protection against everything that threatens his legitimate interests."[62]

In his gloss on Pius XI's speech, Denis Fahey reiterates what the Church has always proclaimed:

> On the one hand, the Sovereign Pontiffs strive to protect the Jews from physical violence and to secure respect for their family life and their worship, as the life and worship of human persons. On the other hand, they aim unceasingly at protecting Christians from the contamination of Jewish Naturalism and try to prevent Jews from obtaining control over Christians. The existence of the second needs to be strongly stressed because to some extent it has been lost sight of in recent times. Catholics need to be made familiar, not only with the repeated Papal condemnations of the Talmud, but with the measures taken by the Sovereign Pontiffs to preserve society from the inroads of Jewish naturalism. Otherwise

they will be exposed to the risk of speaking of Pope St. Pius V and Pope Benedict XIV, for example, as Anti-Semites.[63]

Opposition to Jewish ambition is not anti-Semitism, even if Jews portray it that way. The Christian must oppose anti-Semitism, defined as hatred of the Jewish race, but he must also oppose the Jewish agenda of opposition to Logos. The Catholic must oppose the agenda of the revolutionary Jew, not least when he has adopted, however sincerely, the tropes of conservatism to disguise his aims.

St. Pope Pius X felt the end times had arrived in 1903, and in a sense he was right. By the time the dust settled after World War I, Europe's remaining Catholic empires had been toppled and the Jewish communist antichrist was on the throne of Russia's Christian Czar. Perhaps Pius X had a vision of the future when he wrote in October 1903 that:

> Whosoever weighs these things has certainly reason to fear that such perversion of mind may herald the evils announced for the end of time and as it were, the beginning of those calamities and that the son of perdition of whom the Apostle speaks may have already made his appearance here below. So great are the fury and hatred with which religion is everywhere assailed, that it seems to be a determined effort to destroy every vestige of the relation between God and man. On the other hand—and this is, according to the same Apostle, the special characteristic of Antichrist—with frightful presumption man is attempting to usurp the place of his Creator and is lifting himself above all that is called God.... is dedicating the visible world to himself as a temple, in which he has the pretension to receive the adoration of his fellow men. 'So that he sitteth in the temple of God showing himself as if he were God.'"[64]

There have been "many Antichrists"[65] throughout history, and the Jews, according to Father Lemann, have welcomed them all: "Down the centuries, the Jews have welcomed all the enemies of Jesus Christ and his Church and have constituted themselves their auxiliaries. In the Great Sanhedrin, held at Paris in 1807, they applied the Biblical titles, exclusively reserved to the Messias to Napoleon, though Napoleon was not of Jewish blood. They even welcomed the principles of the French Revolution as the Messias: 'The Messias came for us on Feb. 28, 1790, with the Declaration of the Rights of Man.'"[66]

Inspired by Pius X's statement, Msgr. Robert Hugh Benson wrote *Lord of the World*, a novel that appeared in 1907 and was set roughly 100 years in the future, *i.e.*, in 2007. In the novel a weakened English pope confronts an antichrist with the iconic name of Julian Felsenburgh on the plains of Megiddo. In June 2006 Pope Benedict XVI announced he was going to Megiddo in 2007. Megiddo is another word for Armageddon. The apocalyptic aura of his visit was overshadowed by the apocalyptic nature of the age. George Bush, like Julian the Apostate, was locked in an unwinnable war and threatening to extend it eastward by dropping nuclear weapons on Iran. The conversion of the Jews did not seem imminent. The Jews had never been more powerful; the Church, the antagonist of the synagogue of Satan for 2000 years, had never been weaker. But appearances can deceive. Benedict

XVI, the author of *Dominus Iesus*, had said, even before becoming pope, that he looked forward to the conversion of the Jews. Reversal was in the air.

The Jewish Revolutionary Spirit

Endnotes to Introduction

1 All quotes in this section are taken from Faith, Reason and the University—Memories and Reflections, talk given by Pope Benedict XVI at the University of Regensburg 12th September 2006 (accessible at http://www.vatican.va/holy_father/benedict_xvi/speeches/2006/september/documents/hf_ben-xvi_spe_20060912_university-regensburg_en.html).

2 See Justin Raimondo, Rotten in Denmark 8th February 2006 http://www.antiwar.com/justin/?articleid=8512 and In Defense of Pope Benedict 18th September 2006 http://www.antiwar.com/justin/?articleid=9709 .

3 Hilaire Belloc, *The Jews*, p. 148-9 (Omni Publications [3rd ed.] 1983).

4 On this matter see Norman G. Finkelstein, *Beyond Chutzpah: On the Misuse of Anti-Semitism and the Abuse of History* (University of California Press 2005), and Alexander Cockburn & Jeffrey St Clair (eds.), *The Politics of Anti-Semitism*, (AK Press 2003).

5 St John Chrysostom quoted in *The New Testament with Commentary by Father Haydock* p. 1494, (Catholic Treasures 2000). Paul makes it clear that only "some" of the Jews, out of the nation of Jews, were cut off for unbelief. The word "some" distinguishes those in Israel who were unfaithful from those who remained faithful (Romans 11.4). Robert Sungenis, *Not By Faith Alone* p. 279 f68 (Queenship 1996). The Jewish people is "not absolutely and without remedy cast off for ever; but in part only [many thousands of them having been at first converted] and for a time: which fall of theirs God has been pleased to turn to the good of the Gentiles". See Challoner, quoted in *The New Testament with Commentary by Father Haydock*, p. 1494.

While race is not directly relevant to individual salvation, it still plays a role in defining the Jewish people referred to above. Jews, being of the race of Abraham, can be ingrafted back into their "own olive-tree" by converting to Christ—the fulfillment of the promises of Abraham. But those that reject Christ still constitute a people that will perdure. If any person persists in his unbelief he cannot be saved—assuming what may well be lacking, full knowledge and consent in so doing. Yet Christ, who in Christian belief is God Himself, offers all people His Love unceasingly. St Paul explains of the Jewish people, that insofar as they reject Christ, "a hardening has come upon part of Israel, until the full number of the Gentiles come in, and so all Israel should be saved, as it is written..." (Romans 11.25-26).

He further adds "As regards the gospel, they are enemies of God, for your sake: but as regards election they are beloved for the sake of the forefathers. For the gifts and calling of God are irrevocable" (Romans 11. 28-29).

The "gifts and calling" of God refers to the spiritual blessing God wants to give Israel—i.e., the salvation promised to Abraham, Isaac, Jacob and Moses (see Genesis 12.3 and Galatians 3.8). It is for this reason that Paul reminds us at Romans 2.28-29 that "he is not a real Jew who is one outwardly, nor is true circumcision something external and physical. He is a Jew that is one inwardly, and real circumcision is a matter of the heart, spiritual and not literal. His praise is not from men but from God." In other words, those Jews who are not hardened, but who make up a "remnant chosen by grace" (Romans 11. 5) are those that receive the call willingly and turn to Christ. But God's call to the fulfillment of the Abrahamic promises is always there for the Jewish people. And that people will be with us till the Second Coming, when, Christians believe, they will, as a distinct people, play a significant role during the End Times.

In thinking about the fulfillment of the Abrahamic covenant we need to remember that it is still active and has been made part of the New Covenant in Christ—i.e., it is a covenant of grace (Galatians 3:27-29; Romans 4:13-17; Hebrews 10:16-18) [See CASB Apologetics Study Bible The Gospel According to Matthew p. 218, Queenship 2003]. But references to the Old Covenant in Scripture mean not the Abrahamic covenant but the Mosaic covenant of the Law (2 Corinthians 3:7, 14). The Mosaic Law had purely moral precepts, expressed in the Decalogue, which mostly coincide with the commandments of the natural moral law accessible to all. Insofar as the Decalogue embodies the natural moral law, Christ makes clear that concerning the Law and the Prophets he has come "not to abolish them but to fulfill them." (Matthew 5.17) i.e.,—raise them to a higher plane.

The ceremonial precepts of the Mosaic Law no longer have force and have been formally repealed [See e.g. Romans 7. 1-4. Aquinas further holds that to observe them *as binding* is mortally sinful (Summa Theologiae Ia 2ae, q. 103 art.4, ad 1).]. In any case, it is not obedience to the Law alone that saves. St Paul comments: "...before faith came, we were confined under the law, kept under restraint until faith should be revealed. So that the law was our custodian until Christ came, that we might be justified by faith. But now that faith has come, we are no longer under a custodian; for in Christ Jesus you are all sons of God, through faith. For as many of you as were baptized into Christ have put on Christ. There is neither Jew nor Greek, there is neither slave nor free, there is neither male nor female; for you are all one in Christ Jesus. And if you are Christ's, then you are Abraham's offspring, heirs according to promise." (Galatians 3.23-29).

The Old Mosaic Covenant of Works of the Law could not of itself save and was, St Paul says, but the shadow of things to come (Colossians 2.17). Such a law, while a special gift to the Jews, was imperfect in form (consisting mainly of prohibitions) as well as in the manner of fulfillment. "It did not possess the power of justifying those to whom it was given, nor was it intended for this purpose." An aim of the Law was "to remind the Israelites of their sinfulness and to inspire them with a desire for Christ, who was to fulfill and perfect the law." [Quoted in *Handbook of Moral Theology*, p. 139 Vol.1. (1925) 3rd Edition, B.Herder Book Co.]

St Paul reminds us that "Do we then overthrow the law by this faith? By no means! On the contrary, we uphold the law."(Romans 3.31). Yet it is not the law of the Mosaic covenant that can ultimately justify—(i.e., bring about salvation of itself), even though principles of it are maintained.

So it is this covenant that many religious Jews refer back to, often through the lens of the later Talmud. The Christian believes such a Covenant has now been set aside once and for all and that the Jewish people is clinging to (and partly defined by) a Covenant that has not only been removed, but whose preparatory purpose has been fulfilled in Christ, founder of the Church—the New Israel.

6 As this is only a rough outline of a definition I leave to one side difficulties in classifying e.g. Jewish heretics, children acquired by adoption or more recently gamete donation etc. It should also be noted that "converts' are regarded in certain branches of Judaism as having an inferior position to cradle Jews (see Kevin MacDonald, *A People That Shall Dwell Alone: Judaism as a Group Evolutionary Strategy* Ch.4 and references therein. (Praeger 1994).

7 Jacob Neusner, "Defining Judaism," p. 5 collected in *The Blackwell Companion to Judaism*, ed. Jacob Neusner & Alan J. Avery-Peck (Blackwell Publishing 2003).

8 Ibid. p. 6.

9 Roy Schoeman, *Salvation is from the Jews: The Role of Judaism in Salvation History from Abraham to the Second Coming*, p. 360 (Ignatius 2003).

10 Instructive is the case of the Jewish convert and Carmelite monk Oswald Rufeisen (subsequently known as Brother Daniel) who appealed for Israeli citizenship under the Law of Return on the grounds of his ethnicity. His appeal was rejected by the Israeli government on the grounds of his conversion to Catholicism (decision upheld on appeal by the Supreme Court). Finally the decision at (Rufeisen v Minister of the Interior, (1962) 16 PD 2428) was that any Jew converting to another religion would lose their preferential access to Israeli citizenship. Nevertheless, as Neusner suggests, conversion to Christianity is problematic in a way that moves toward other religions are not. (N.B. Orthodox Jewish religious teaching holds that once a Jew always a Jew—but nevertheless holds that conversion to Christianity is especially egregious).

11 It is noteworthy that the charge of idolatry made against Christ and Christians by certain rabbis contrasts strongly with the comparatively mild denunciations of Muslims in Jewish discourse. According to the controversial Israel Shahak, "Although the stock epithet given to Muhammad is 'madman' ('*meshugga*'), this was not nearly as offensive as it may sound now, and in any case pales before the abusive terms applied to Jesus", *Jewish History, Jewish Religion: The Weight of Three Thousand Years*, p. 98, (Pluto Press 2002).

12 Peter Schaefer, *Jesus in the Talmud* (Princeton University Press 2007). The same can be said of the later *Toledot Yeshu* (though of course this work does not occupy the place in

udaism that the Talmud does). Schaefer also notes that, "The Babylonian Jews in the Sasanian Empire, living in a non-Christian and even progressively anti-Christian environment, could easily take up, and continue, the discourse of their brethren in Asia Minor; and it seems as if they were no less timid in their response to the New Testament's message..." (p. 129) In other words, amongst Babylonian Jews at least, there was no Christian persecution immediately preceding the writing of the attacks on Christ in the Talmud.

The

3 See Schoeman p. 124-132.

4 *Catechism of the Catholic Church*, 598 (Geoffrey Chapman 1994).

5 This is an important point to make. Jews, as Belloc noticed, have sometimes benefited from revolutionary movements, but often suffered. (Belloc p. 53) Some have sympathised with such movements; some have opposed them. But such statements are concerned with a given political order. What we are concerned with is the undeniable fact the Jew is by definition, a rejecter of Christ and therefore, insofar as he is a rejecter of Christ he is, in some sense, a rejecter of the true order of the world. As Father Denis Fahey put it: "It is absurd and confusing to speak of that opposition as a plot or a conspiracy, for not only is it clear to us but the Jews proclaim it openly. We must always bear in mind that the world is one, and that it is only through acceptance of Our Lord Jesus Christ as the True Messias that we can live our lives as the objective order of the world demands." (Father Denis Fahey, *The Kingship of Christ and The Conversion of the Jewish Nation*, p. 57 (The Christian Book Club of America 1993).

6 John Henry Newman, *The Arians of the Fourth Century*, p. 13-15 (WIPF & Stock Publishers 1996).

7 Ibid. p. 16.

8 Louis Israel Newman, *Jewish Influence on Christian Reform Movements* (New York: Columbia University Press, 1925).

9 Kevin MacDonald, *Culture of Critique*, p.v-vi. 1stBooks 2002). Writers like Walter Lacquer (*The Changing Face of Anti-Semitism: From Ancient Times to the Present Day* (Oxford: Oxford University Press, 2006) have said that many leaders of e.g. the radical left in the West "especially...the Trotskyites and similar groups..." were "non-Jewish Jews" (p. 181). MacDonald's definition however accommodates such people because 1) they remain Jews insofar as they have not converted, especially to Christianity (see Neusner) and 2) they can be said to be leaders of a Jewish movement if they fulfill the

second criterion that MacDonald proposes. Moreover, as Albert S. Lindemann points out (*Esau's Tears: Modern Anti-Semitism and the Rise of the Jews* (Cambridge: Cambridge University Press, 2000), Jewish ethnic background played an important role in divisions between differing communist factions (p. 452). The same author also notes that even "non-Jews" like Lenin could be considered "jewified" on account of their praise of things Jewish and seemingly inconsistent acceptance of the legitimacy of Jewish nationalism (p. 433).

20 It should be noted that despite whatever elements of the natural moral law remain in religious Judaism, the defining rejection of Logos must, to a greater or lesser extent, undermine adherence to natural law—a law the very point of which is to lead to the Higher Logos. It should further be noted that the 10 Commandments are alleged by some to occupy no special place in observance within the 613 *mitzvot* of Rabbinic Judaism and that any overemphasis on them/ daily recitation is allegedly condemned in the Talmud, tractate Berachot 12a. The extent to which the Decalogue is regarded by Jews as concerned with natural moral truths is also disputed. Moreover, the Jewish understanding of Old Testament texts is markedly different from the Christian. As Guenter Stemberger points out, referring to tractate Abot (an addition to the Mishnah): "Moses received not just the "Torah," that is the Pentateuch, but Torah as such, i.e., not limited to its written expression, from Sinai, and handed it on in an unbroken succession to Joshua, the elders, and so on until the Rabbinic masters of the second century. What is written in the Mishnah and has no evident basis in the Bible is therefore nevertheless part of the Torah revealed to Moses on Sinai...In a second stage, this oral Torah has to be united with the written Torah"— ultimately the oral and written Torah are essentially the same revelation. Stemberger, as if to emphasise the difference from Christianity adds, "In a period in which Judaism had to share the text of the written Torah with Christianity, which had taken it (in the form of the Septuagint) as part of its Jewish heritage, the oral Torah became the essential mark of the true people of God, distinguishing them from all those who knew only the written Torah.", Guenter

Stemberger, *The Formation of Rabbinic Judaism* p. 88 collected in *The Blackwell Companion to Judaism*, ed. Jacob Neusner & Alan J. Avery-Peck (Blackwell Publishing 2003). Attempts have been made to suggest that Natural Law is a constant element in Jewish thought (David Novak, *Natural Law in Judaism*, Cambridge University Press 1998). Such a position is at odds with the view of the vast majority of Jewish scholars, and it is hard to see how a Natural Law ethics is to be found in e.g. the Mishna and the Babylonian Talmud (as opposed to the Old Testament—which, however, is interpreted through latter texts). Michael A. Hoffmann II notes that there are "numerous examples of Old Testament denigration and nullification in the Talmudic and post-Talmudic texts...The Talmud , at tractate 49b, relates how the execution of the prophet Isaiah was a justifiable penalty for his having said of the Israelite people that they had unclean lips (Isaiah 6.5). This is what the oral tradition of the Pharisees and their rabbinic heirs, taught about the prophet Isaiah, that he was killed and that he got what he deserved for having offended the Israelites by daring to say they had unclean lips. Christ knew the oral traditions of the Pharisees and this may be what he was referring to when he stated in Matthew 23.31 "you are witnesses against yourselves" concerning the murder of the prophets." (Johann Andres Eisenmenger, *The Traditions of the Jews*, edited by J.P Stehelin, Introduction by Michael A. Hoffmann II p. 80-81 (Independent History & Research 2006)). Official Catholic teaching is clear on the relationship between Christ, the Natural Law and rejection of Christ. Pope Pius XI in the Encyclical *Mit Brennender Sorge* (14/03/1937) wrote: "No faith in God can for long survive pure and unalloyed without the support of faith in Christ. "No one knoweth who the Son is, but the Father: and who the Father is, but the Son and all to whom the Son will reveal Him" (*Luke* 10. 22). "Now this is eternal life: That they may know thee, the only true God, and Jesus Christ whom thou has sent" (*John* 17. 3). Nobody, therefore, can say: "I believe in God, and that is enough religion for me," for the Savior's words brook no evasion: "Whosoever denieth the Son, the same hath not the Father. He that confesseth the

Son hath the Father also" (1 John 2. 23)... It is on faith in God, preserved pure and stainless, that man's morality is based. All efforts to remove from under morality and the moral order the granite foundation of faith...lead[s]...to moral degradation. (14,29). Even more striking in the context of this discussion is Pope Leo XIIIs statement in *Tametsi Futura Prospicientibus* (01/11/1900): "When Jesus Christ is absent, human reason fails, being bereft of its chief protection and light, and the very end is lost sight of, for which, under God's providence, human society has been built up. This end is the obtaining by the members of society of natural good through the aid of civil unity, though always in harmony with the perfect and eternal good which is above nature" (8).

It is important to understand the relationship between Higher and Lower logos. The Higher Logos (Christ) is understood as part of the supernatural order. To understand Jesus as the Second Person of the Trinity requires the special supernatural gift of faith; it doesn't just follow logically by a process of human reasoning, from discerning the natural moral law (logos) inscribed in the hearts of all men (Romans 1-2). So likewise, going in reverse order, rejecting Christ by resisting the theological virtue of faith offered by the Holy Spirit does not of itself mean, in theory or practice, rejecting the "lower logos" of natural law.

However, as M. A. Krapiec, O.P. following St. Thomas Aquinas, says "to become aware of the existence of the law of nature is nothing other than to become aware of one's own ratinality, proportional to the nature of contingent being. This means that the human being, existing contingently, is a being "through participation in the Absolute. By participating in the Absolute, he or she particpates, at the same time, in its rationality and also in Eternal Law.... An inferior being participates in a superior being, and particularly, contigent beings participate in the Absolute, by the fact that they are: a) caused by the Absolute (that is God is the efficient cause), b) The Absolute is for them a model, that is, the ultimate exemplary cause, c) The Absolute is for them at the same time the final cause.... If, therefore, we affirm that natural law is the participation in Eternal Law, this means that the human being's naturally oriented inclinations come from the Absolute, in the sense of triple causality of external causes described above" (*Person and Natural Law*, Peter Lang, 1993, p. 199).

Given the above, we can say that to knowingly reject the revealed Higher Logos can never be an act in accordance with the Natural Law (lower Logos). We might say that such an act is pragmatically contradictory. However, to knowingly reject Higher Logos is also to create a certain instability in one's ability to discern the lower logos, even though the lower logos can be known naturally. For access to the lower logos is partly reliant on the contingent nature of the human subject. And to admit this contingency is to begin to admit the existence of an Absolute Who, Christians believe, has revealed Himself in the Second Person of the Trinity as the Higher Logos. Rejectionism in the sense applied in this volume to Jews (though not to any specific individuals) will inevitably affect appreciation of the Natural Law.

21 Modras 346-7.

22 Daniel Jonah Goldhagen, *A Moral Reckoning: the Role of the Catholic Church in the Holocaust and its Unfulfilled Duty of Repair*, p. 37 (Vintage 2003).

23 Yona Metzger, Yesterday, Today and Tomorrow, *America*, October 24th 2005.

24 Shahak p. 92-93. He also claims that Jewish prayers asking that Christians "may perish instantly" have a long history and have in recent times regained popularity in certain Jewish congregations close to the Gush Emunim. Nor can they be said to have originated as a result of Christian persecution, for they were allegedly recited while Christians were still a persecuted minority.

The Scripture passages that form the basis of the prayer are full of references to veils, blindness etc. St Paul strikingly states that "Since we have such a hope, we are very bold, not like Moses who put a veil over his face so that the Israelites might not see the end of the fading splendour. But their minds were hardened; for to this day, when they read the old covenant, that same veil remains unlifted, because only through Christ is it taken away. Yes, to this day whenever Moses is read a veil lies over their minds; but when a man turns to the Lord the veil is lifted" (2 Corinthians 3.12-16).

Before these words were written Christ had spoken of the blindness of Israel: "'You shall indeed hear but never understand, and you shall indeed see but never perceive'" (Matthew 13.14-16).

The pope's recent intervention on the issue of the Good Friday prayer has apparently led to Walter Cardinal Kasper now rejecting dual covenant theology. See Thomas Pink,http://www.ratzingerfanclub.com/blog/2008/04/

kaspers-attack-on-dual-covenant.html

Endnotes to Chapter One

The synagogue of Satan

Heinrich Graetz, *The History of the Jews* Philadelphia: The Jewish Publication Society of America, 1894), Vol. II, p. 67.

Graetz, Vol. II, p. 142.

The Book of Daniel, The St. Joseph Edition of the New American Bible

Leibel Resnick, *The Mystery of Bar Kokhba: An Historical and Theological Investigation of the Last King of the Jews* (Northvale, NJ: Jason Aronson, Inc. 1996), p. 4.

Ibid.

David Herman, "Flaunt it, baby!" *The Guardian*, June 12, 2003. Howard Jacobson, "Up, up and oy vey," *The Times*, March , 2005.

7 Graetz, Vol. II, p. 142.

8 Klaus Wengst, "Die Darstellung "der Juden" im *Johannes-Evangelium als Reflex Juedish-Judenchristlicher Kontroverse in Teufelskinder oder Heilsbringer: Die Juden im Johannes-Evangelium* (Frankfurt am Main: Haag & Herchen Verlag, 1990) (all translations are mine), p. 22.

9 Wengst, p. 22.

10 Philip S. Kaufman, OSB, *The Beloved Disciple: Witness against Anti-Semitism* (Collegeville, Minnesota: The Liturgical Press 1991), p. 56

11 Micha Brumlik, "Johannes, das Judenfeindliche Evangelium," in *Teufelskinder*

oder Heilsbringer, (all translations are mine), p. 2.

12 Brumlik, p. 7.

13 Brumlik, p. 9.

14 Ibid.

15 Ibid.

16 Gerald Caron, *Qui son les "Juifs" de l'evangile de Jean?* (Montreal: Bellarmin, 1997), p. 18 (all translations mine).

17 Caron, p. 23.

18 Brumlik, p. 9. In this chapter the Jews that reject Christ will be referred to as "Jews" whereas those who are ethnically Jews and do not reject Christ will be referred to as Jews. This will only be done in this chapter for it recounts a transitional period in the history of the Jews. In later chapters the convention will be dropped.

19 Brumlik, p. 2.

20 Kaufman, p. 56.

21 Kaufman, p. 61.

22 Ibid.

23 Brumlik, p. 10.

24 Brumlik, p. 11.

25 Brumlik, p. 19.

26 Brumlik, p. 20.

27 Ibid. (My emphasis).

28 Caron, p. 264.

29 Caron, p. 30.

30 Caron, p. 265.

31 Caron, p. 266.

32 Caron, p. 268.

33 Caron, p. 269.

34 Caron, p. 275.

35 Caron, p. 277.

36 Reinhold Leistner, *Antijudaismus im Johannesvangelium? Darstellung des Problems in der neueren Auslegungsgeschicte und Untersuchung der Leidensgeschichte* (Bern und Frankfurt/M: Herbert Lang, 1974), p. 35 (all translations are mine). Christ's words at Matthew 23:2-3 are concerned with the holiness of the chair of Moses and the need to obey what was not contrary to the law of Moses (but to ignore the corruptions of that law that the Scribes and Pharisees had introduced).

37 Wengst, p. 30.

38 Caron, p. 236.

39 Austin Flannnery, OP, editor, *Vatican Council II: The Conciliar and Post-Conciliar Documents* (Collegeville, MN: The Liturgical Press, 1980), p. 741.

40 Caron, p. 282.

41 Caron, p. 251.

42 Graetz, Vol, II, p. 164.

43 Resnick, p. 147.

44 Graetz, Vol. II, p. 166.

45 Brumlik, p. 12.

46 Kevin McDonald, "Zionism and the Internal Dynamics of Judaism," *Occidental Quarterly,* Vol 3, No. 3.

47 Ibid.

48 Ibid.

49 Graetz, Vol. II, p. 6.

50 Graetz, Vol. II, p. 256.

51 Graetz, Vol. II, p. 258.

52 Ibid.

53 Graetz, Vol. II, p. 259.

54 Graetz, Vol. II, p. 284.

55 Graetz, Vol. II, p. 291.

56 Graetz, Vol. II, p. 292.

57 Graetz, Vol. II, p. 306.

58 Graetz, Vol. II, p. 308.

59 Graetz, Vol, II, p. 337.

60 Graetz, Vol. II, p. 338.

61 Graetz, Vol. II, p. 335.

62 Graetz, Vol. II, p. 327 (my emphasis).

63 Graetz, Vol. II, p. 340.

64 Graetz, Vol. II, p. 396.

65 Ibid.

66 Ibid.

67 Graetz, Vol. II, p. 409.

68 Resnick, p. 149.

69 Ibid.

70 Graetz, Vol. II, p. 409.

71 Resnick, p. 159.

72 Resnick, p. 153.

73 Graetz, Vol. II, p. 410.

74 Resnick, p. 6.

75 Graetz, Vol. II, p. 412.

76 Graetz, Vol. II, p. 410.

77 Resnick, p. 27.

78 Resnick, p. 137.

79 Resnick, p. 137-38.

80 Ibid.

81 Graetz, Vol. II, p. 418.

82 Graetz, Vol. II, p. 419.

83 Graetz, Vol. II, p. 422.

84 Ibid.

85 Graetz, Vol. II, p. 423.

86 Ibid.

87 Ibid.

88 Graetz, Vol. II, p. 424.

89 Graetz, Vol. II, p. 568-9.

90 Graetz, Vol. II, p. 425.

91 Graetz, Vol. II, p. 424.

92 Graetz, Vol. II, p. 431.

93 Ibid.

94 Graetz, Vol. II, p. 559.

95 Graetz, Vol. II, p. 564.

96 Ibid.

Endnotes to Chapter Two

Julian the Apostate and the Doomed Temple

1 Giuseppe Ricciotti, *Julian the Apostate*, trans. M. Joseph Costelloe, S.J. (Milwaukee: The Bruce Publishing Co., 1960), p. 6.

2 Ricciotti, p. 7.

3 Ibid.

4 Ricciotti, p. 42.

5 Ricciotti, p. 12.

6 Ricciotti, p. 27.

7 Ibid.

8 Ricciotti, p. 33.

9 Ricciott, p. 35.

10 Ibid.

11 Ricciotti, p. 36.

12 Ibid.

13 Ricciotti, p. 39.

14 Ricciotti, p. 38.

15 Ricciotti, p. 39.

16 Ricciotti, p. 41.

17 Ricciotti, p. 121.

18 Ricciotti, p. 126.

19 Ricciotti, p. 140.

20 Ricciotti, p. 141.

21 Ibid.

22 Ricciotti, p. 44.

23 Ricciotti, p. 135.

24 Ricciotti, p. 143.

25 Ricciotti, p. 157.

26 Ibid.

27 Ricciotti, p. 168.

28 Ricciotti, p. 169.

29 Ricciotti, p. 47.

30 Ricciotti, p. 48.

31 Ibid.

32 Ricciotti, p. 187.

33 Ricciotti, p. 220.

34 Ricciotti, p. 179

35 Ibid.

36 Ibid.

37 Ricciotti, p. 182.

38 Ricciotti, p. 184

39 Ricciotti, p. 194

40 Ricciotti, p. 198.

41 Ibid.

42 Ibid.

43 Ricciotti, p. 195.

44 Ricciotti, p. 197.

45 Ricciotti, p. 200. Paul Johnson, in his best-selling philo-Semitic *A History of the Jews* (Perennial Library 1988), completely ignores both the dry persecution of Christians and, incredibly, the alliance between

Julian and the Jews with regard to rebuilding the Temple.

46 Ricciotti, p. 202.

47 Ricciotti, p. 207.

48 Ricciotti, p. 45.

49 Robert Wilde, *The Treatment of the Jews in the Greek Christian Writers of the First Three Centuries* (Washington, DC: the Catholic University of America Press, 1949), p. 87.

50 Wilde, p. 84.

51 Wilde, p. 102.

52 Wilde, p. 103.

53 Wilde, p. 103.

54 Wilde, p. 107

55 Ibid.

56 Wilde, p. 108.

57 Wilde, p. 107 (my emphasis).

58 Ibid.

59 Wilde, p. 112.

60 Wilde, p. 107.

61 Wilde, p. 127.

62 Wilde, p. 141.

63 Wilde, p. 143.

64 Wilde, p. 144-5.

65 Wilde, p. 145.

66 Wilde finds "references in early patristic literature" which "offer evidence that the Jews had a hand in the persecution of Christians" in: Justin in the *Dialogue with Trypho*: 10; 16; 17:3; 49:9; 108: 110: 117; 122; 131:2; 133, as well as in the *Apologia*, I:31; in Irenaeus, *Adv. Haereses*: 4:21, 3; 4:28, 3; in Tertullian, *Scorpiace*: 10 (PL 2:143) *synagogas Judaeorum fontes persecutionem, Ad Nationes* 1:14 *quod enim aliud genus seminariuim est infamia, Apologet. 7 Tot hostes ejus quot extanei, et quidem proprii ex aemulatione Judaei*; in Hippolytus, *In Dan* 1:21; in Origen, *Contra Celsum*: 6: 27; in Cyprian, *Epistolae*: 59:2; in Eusebius, *HE* 5:16; and in Epiphanius, *Haereses*: 29:9. Wilde, p. 145.

67 Wilde, p. 188.

68 Wilde, p. 146.

69 Wilde, p. 188.

70 Wilde, p. 191.

71 Wilde, p. 127.

72 Ibid.

73 Wilde, p. 199.

74 Ibid.

75 Wilde, p. 212.

76 Wilde, p. 230.

77 Wilde, p. 209.

78 Wilde, p. 231.

79 Ibid.

80 Ibid.

81 Wilde, p. 232.

82 Ibid.

83 Ibid.

84 Ibid.

85 Wilde, p. 153.

86 Ibid.

87 Wilde, p. 154.

88 Wilde, p. 160.

89 Wilde, p. 165.

90 Ibid.

91 Ibid.

92 Ibid.

93 Wilde, p. 164.

94 Ibid.

95 Wilde, p. 149.

96 Ibid.

97 Ibid.

98 Wilde, p. 104.

99 Wilde, p. 200. In talking of alliances it is worth recounting an incident in Jerusalem often forgotten. In 614 AD after the capture of Jerusalem by the Persian army under King Chosroes the Jews allied with them to slaughter Christians. According to the eminent Jewish historian Salomon Munk, the Persian army was accompanied by 26,000 Jews, who upon reaching the Holy City, "took revenge upon the Christians for the cruel persecutions and many humiliations they had suffered over the centuries. It is claimed that 90,000 Christians perished." According to Graetz "...the Jews relentlessly destroyed the Christian sanctuaries. All the churches and monasteries were burnt down, and the Jews undoubtedly had a greater share in this deed than did the Persians." According to Elliott Horowitz, in *Reckless Rites: Purim and the Legacy of Jewish Violence* (Princeton University Press 2006, p. 232-233 for quotes above) there has been much histori-

cal stonewalling (which he documents) of this event in the twentieth century. As he notes "[E]ven-handed assessments of the reciprocal role of violence in Jewish-Christian relations were to become increasingly rare in post-Holocaust Jewish historiography, both in the land of Israel and in the Diaspora" (p. 235).

Horowitz further points out the skewed history that some twentieth (in contrast to nineteenth) century Jewish historians of this period recount. He notes that Salo Baron "did mention the late sixth-century expulsion of the Jews from Antioch, but he laced his account with subtle doses of lachrymosity.... Baron referred rather one-sidedly to the "humiliating punishment meted out to their entire community for the transgression of a single coreligionist," but buried deep in a Baronian-length footnote the information that the said co-religionist "had at one time insulted the image of the Virgin Mary," and gave no hint as to the precise nature of the insult. Baron thus allowed (or constructed) his narrative to suggest that that the local Byzantine-Christian authorities simply had it in for Antioch's Jews. Moreover, by thus presenting the 592-593 expulsion as cruelly arbitrary, he was able to put a rather positive spin on the "sanguinary riot" (not "bloody massacre"!) which the Jews of Antioch "staged" in 610, during which they "killed the patriarch." According to Baron, this was part of the "score" the Jews had "to settle" with the local authorities for their earlier expulsion—a score which could look quite different to anyone who knew the "humiliating punishment" had been assigned the Jews after one of their co-religionists had allegedly urinated on an image of the venerated Virgin in 610 [a]ccording to [Graetz] the Jews "fell upon their Christian neighbours...and retaliated for the injuries which they had suffered; they killed all that fell into their hands, and threw their bodies into the fire, as the Christians had done to them a century before. The Patriarch Anastasius, an object of special hate, was shamefully abused by them, and his body dragged through the streets before he was put to death...." Horowitz later notes, "[T]he tendency of Jewish historiography, both academic and popular, to ignore the slaughter of Jerusalem's Christians in 614 and/or

the Jewish role therein only strengthened after the city came under exclusive Jewish rule as a consequence of the Six Day War" (p.238-243).

Paul Johnson in *A History of the Jews* writes of the 614 massacre: "in 611 when the Persians broke into Palestine, taking Jerusalem three years later after a twenty-day siege. The Jews were accused of assisting them. But if, as the Christians alleged, the Persians had given, in return, a promise to restore the city to the Jews, they certainly did not keep their word." (p. 166). This passage, ignoring a welter of firsthand accounts and subsequent scholarly work completely glides over the enormities that the Jews were involved in, thereby proving Horowitz's point. Horowitz, in talking of the subject of Jewish violence generally recalls, with wry irony, Jean Paul Satre's description of the Jews as "the mildest of men, passionately hostile to violence. That obstinate sweetness which they conserve in the midst of the most atrocious persecution, that sense of justice and of reason which they put up as their sole defense against a hostile, brutal, and unjust society, is perhaps the best part of the message they bring to us and the true mark of their greatness" (p. 187 quoting *Anti-Semite and Jew*).

100 St. John Chrysostom, *Discourses against Judaizing Christians*, trans. Paul W. Harkins (Washington, DC: The Catholic University of America Press, 1979), p. xxix.

101 Graetz, Vol. II, p. 597.

102 Graetz, Vol. II, p. 596.

103 Stanley L. Jaki, *To Rebuild or Not to Try?* (Royal Oak, MI: Real View Books, 1999), p. 16

104 Jaki, p. 19.

105 Ricciotti, p. 224.

106 Ricciotti, p. 223.

107 Ricciotti, p. 224.

108 Chrysostom, p. 137.

109 Ibid.

110 Chrysostom, p. 138.

111 Chrysostom, p. x.

112 Chrysostom, p. xxi.

113 Chrysostom, p. xxiv.

114 Jaki, p. 5.

115 Chrysostom, p. 139.

116 Ricciotti, p. 225.

117 Jaki, p. 6.

118 Ibid.

119 Chrysostom, p. 139.

120 Ibid.

121 Jaki, p. 12.

122 Ibid.

123 Ibid.

124 Ibid.

125 Jaki, p. 13.

126 Ibid.

127 Jaki, p. 15.

128 Jaki, p. 8.

129 Ricciotti, p. 225.

130 Ibid.

131 Jaki, p. 20.

132 Ibid.

133 Chrysostom, p. 139.

134 Chrysostom, p. 139-40.

135 Ricciotti, p. 226.

136 Ricciotti, p. 225.

137 Graetz, Vol. II, p. 600.

138 Ibid.

139 Ibid.

140 Ricciotti, p. 225.

141 Ibid.

142 Graetz, Vol. II, p. 601.

143 Ibid.

144 Ricciotti, p. 259.

145 Christopher Walter, *The Warrior Saints in Byzantine Art and Tradition* (Aldershot: Ashgate, 2003), p. 105.

146 Graetz, Vol II, p. 602.

147 Chrysostom, p. 138.

148 Chrysostom, p. 140.

149 Ibid.

150 Chrysostom, p. 136.

151 Chrysostom, p. xxiv.

152 Chrysostom, p. xxii

153 Chrysostom, p. xxxviii. Augustine's view of the Jews is summarized thus by historian Thomas F. Madden: "It was St. Augustine who laid the second foundation of the medieval Church's attitude toward the Jews. Writing in the late fourth and early fifth centuries, Augustine rejected the claims of some Christians that the Jews were the servants of the devil. At the core of Augustine's philosophy on the Jews were the words of Psalm 59: "Slay them not, lest my people forget: scatter them by thy power; and bring them down, O Lord our shield." The Jews, Augustine wrote, were clearly wrong. The course of history had shown that their faith and rituals had been supplanted. But they served as a constant reminder of the antiquity of the Christian faith and the glorious gift of salvation that Christ had poured out on the Gentiles. Clinging to their scriptures, the Jews were a witness for the veracity of the Old Testament and its prophecies of Christ's coming. Augustine insisted that Jews should be treated with respect because they belonged to God, who would bring them one day to the fullness of salvation." (The Church and the Jews in the Middle Ages, *Crisis Magazine*, January 2003).

154 Ibid.

155 Ibid.

156 Chrysostom, p. 4.

157 Ibid.

158 Ibid.

159 Chrysostom, p. 7.

160 Ibid.

161 Chrysostom, p. 8.

162 Ibid.

163 Chrysostom, p. 9.

164 Ibid.

165 Chrysostom, p. 13.

166 Chrysostom, p. 15.

167 Chrysostom, p. xxxix.

168 Chrysostom, p. 18.

169 Chrysostom, p. xxxix.

170 Chrysostom, p. 92.

171 Chrysostom, p. 171.

172 Ibid.

173 Chrysostom, p. 172.

174 Chrysostom, p. 175.

175 Chrysostom, p. 19. Paul Johnson, in his aforementioned *A History of the Jews*, says of Chrysostom, whom he mentions once: "John Chrysostom (354-407) delivered eight 'Sermons Against the Jews' at Anti-

och, and these became the pattern for anti-Jewish tirades, making the fullest possible use (and misuse) of key passages in the gospels of St Matthew and St John. Thus a specifically Christian anti-Semitism, presenting the Jews as murderers of Christ, was grafted onto the seething mass of pagan smears and rumours, and Jewish communities were now at risk in every Christian city" (p.165). Typically Johnson provides no evidence for Chrysostom's "misuse" of Scripture.

176 Chrysostom, p. 20.

177 Chrysostom, p. 21.

178 Chrysostom, p. 23.

179 Chrysostom, p. 11.

180 Ibid.

181 Ibid.

182 Chrysostom, p. 14-5

183 Chrysostom, p. 25.

184 Ibid.

185 Chrysostom, p. 154

186 Chrysostom, p. 169.

187 Chrysostom, p. 6.

188 Ibid.

189 Chrysostom, pp. 66-7.

190 Chrysostom, p. 206.

191 Ibid.

192 Chrysostom, p. 207.

193 Ibid.

194 Chrysostom, p. 217.

195 Chrysostom, p. xlvii.

196 Chrysostom, p. 68.

197 Ibid.

198 Chrysostom, p. 221.

199 Edward A. Synan, *The Popes and the Jews in the Middle Ages* (New York: The Macmillan Company, 1965), p. 30.

200 Synan, p. 19.

201 Ibid.

202 Synan, p. 22.

203 Synan, p. 25.

204 Synan, p. 28.

205 Synan, p. 28.

206 Synan, p. 27.

207 Ibid.

208 Synan, p. 40.

209 Ibid.

210 Synan, p. 42.

211 Ibid.

212 Synan, p. 44.

213 Synan, p. 37.

214 Ibid.

215 Synan, p. 38.

216 Ibid.

217 Synan, p. 49.

218 Synan, p. 50.

219 Synan, p. 49.

220 Synan, p. 44.

221 Ibid.

222 Synan, p. 46.

223 Ibid.

224 Synan, p. 47.

225 Synan, p. 46.

226 Ibid.

227 Synan, p. 36.

228 Graetz, Vol. II, p. 611.

229 Graetz, Vol. II, p. 609.

230 Graetz, Vol. II, p. 634.

231 Ibid.

232 Graetz, Vol. II, p. 635.

233 Ibid.

234 William Thomas Walsh, *Philip II* (New York: Sheed and Ward, 1937), p. 241.

235 Ibid.

236 Graetz, Vol. IV, p. 423.

237 Walsh, p. 242.

Endnotes to Chapter Three

Rome Discovers the Talmud

1 Leonard B. Glick, *Abraham's Heirs: Jews and Christians in Medieval Europe* (Syracuse: Syracuse University Press, 1999), p. 92.

2 Heinrich Pesch, *Lehrbuch der Nationaloekonomie/Teaching Guide to Economics* (Lewiston, NY: The Edwin Mellen Press, 2002).

3 Glick, p. 93.

4 Norman Cohn, *The Pursuit of the Millennium: Revolutionary messianism in medieval and Reformation Europe and its bearing on modern totalitarian movements* (New York: Harper & Row, 1961), p. 60.

5 Cohn, p. 61.

6 Cohn, p. 6.

7 Cohn, p. xiii.

8 Cohn, p. 6.

9 Ibid.

10 Cohn, p. xiii.

11 Cohn, p. 1.

12 Cohn, p. 2.

13 Ibid.

14 Cohn, p. 4.

15 Ibid (my emphasis).

16 Cohn, p. 22.

17 Cohn, p. 12.

18 Lea Dasberg, *Untersuchungen ueber die Entwertung des Judenstatus im 11. Jahrhundert* (Paris: Mouton & Co, 1965) Etudes Juives IX, (Translations mine), p. 183.

19 Dasberg, p. 174.

20 Cohn, p. 74.

21 Cohn, p. 96.

22 Cohn, p. 137.

23 B. H. Liddell, *Strategy* (New York: Praeger, 1967), p. 380.

24 Synan, p. 70.

25 William Thomas Walsh, *Characters of the Inquisition* (New York: P. J. Kenedy & Sons, 1940), p. 76. In talking of the barbarities of the First Crusade, Kevin MacDonald refers to the historian R. Chazan's *European Jewry and the First Crusade* and notes that "the intensity of Jewish commitment in the face of hostility of the Crusaders and burghers in 1096 may have provoked disgust and horror among the Christians as well as contributed to their belief that the Jews had a great deal of animosity toward Christianity... Jews readily accepted death and even slaughtered each other rather than accept conversion to Christianity.... Chazan comments that "Jewish rejection of Christianity [as witnessed by this behavior] is seen as a sentiment which, by its intensity, leads to the shattering of normal moral and ethical constraints. One might easily hypothesize a connection between the 1096 reality of Jewish parents willing to take the lives of their own children rather than submit to conversion and the subsequent image of Jews capable of taking the lives of Christian youngsters out of implacable hostility to the Christian faith." *Separation and its Discontents: Toward an Evolutionary Theory of Anti-Semitism*, (1stBooks, 2003) p. 146.

26 Glick, p. 98.

27 Norman F. Cantor, *The Sacred Chain: The History of the Jews* (New York: HarperCollinsPublishers, 1994), p. 169.

28 Walsh, p. 76. Probably the world's most eminent historian of the crusades, Jonathan Riley-Smith, has in books such as *What Were the Crusades?* convincingly argued that the main motivation for the Crusades (or at least part of it) was spiritual rather than material, territorial or a thirst for blood.

29 Glick, p. 163.

30 Ibid.

31 Ibid. For Jewish attitudes to the charging of interest to Gentiles see Shahak (2002) p. 95-96.

32 Glick, p. 235.

33 Ibid.

34 Glick, p. 156.

35 Glick, p. 117.

36 Glick, p. 115.

Endnotes

37 Ibid.

38 Glick, p. 235.

39 Glick, p. 119.

40 Jeremy Cohen, *The Friars and the Jews: The Evolution of Medieval Anti-Judaism* (Ithaca and London: Cornell University Press, 1982), p. 47.

41 Walsh, p. 75.

42 Glick, p. 105.

43 Ibid.

44 Glick, p. 109.

45 Glick, p. 102.

46 Glick, p. 103.

47 Cohn, p. 99.

48 Cohn, p. 101.

49 Cohn, p. 116.

50 Synan, p. 77

51 Synan, p. 75

52 Glick, p. 122.

53 Ibid.

54 Ibid.

55 Cantor, p. 169.

56 Ibid.

57 Glick, p. 122.

58 Synan, p. 77.

59 Ibid.

60 Synan, p. 78.

61 Synan, p. 75.

62 Ibid.

63 Synan, p. 81.

64 Ibid.

65 Synan, p. 82.

66 Synan, p. 98.

67 Glick, p. 120 (my emphasis).

68 Ibid.

69 Cantor, p. 169 (my emphasis).

70 Ibid.

71 Cohn, p. 66.

72 Cantor, p. 173.

73 Cantor, p. 169.

74 Ibid.

75 Glick, p. 184.

76 Glick, p. 185.

77 Cohen, p. 28.

78 Cohen, p. 44.

79 Walsh, p. 53

80 Walsh, p. 60.

81 Walsh, p. 61.

82 Walsh, p. 70.

83 Cohen, p. 48.

84 Louis Israel Newman, *Jewish Influence on Christian Reform Movements* (New York: AMS Press, Inc., 1966), p. 311.

85 Newman, p. 312.

86 Ibid.

87 Ibid.

88 Walsh, p. 70.

89 Ibid.

90 Ibid.

91 Ibid.

92 Walsh, p. 46.

93 Cantor, p. 196.

94 Walsh, p. 70.

95 Newman, p. 1.

96 Ibid.

97 Newman, p. 13.

98 Ibid.

99 Glick, p. 184.

100 Ibid. To say that Jews were not citizens did not give anyone the right to harm them. In *Dignitatis Humanae* (12) unjust behavior on the part of Church authorities in the past is recognized. But this is not to say that the basic principle of *Sicut Iudeis non* was not and is not defensible.

101 Synan, p. 95.

102 Ibid.

103 Ibid.

104 Ibid.

105 Synan, p. 88.

106 Ibid.

107 Synan, p. 89

108 Ibid.

109 Ibid.

110 Synan, p. 90.

111 Synan, p. 91.

112 Synan, p. 231.

113 Graetz, Vol. III, p. 501.

114 Synan, p. 231.

115 Ibid.

116 Synan, p. 232.

117 Synan, p. 223.

118 Synan, p. 226.

119 Synan, p. 227.

120 Ibid.

121 Graetz, Vol. III, p. 501 (my emphasis).

122 Walsh, p. 28.

123 Ibid.

124 Cantor, p. 177.

125 Ibid.

126 Ibid.

127 Cantor, p. 178.

128 Ibid.

129 Ibid.

130 Ibid.

131 Ibid.

132 Ibid.

133 Glick p. 187.

134 Ibid.

135 Ibid.

136 Glick, p. 188

137 Ibid.

138 Cantor, p. 179 (my emphasis).

139 Cantor, p. 176.

140 Ibid.

141 Cohen, p. 177.

142 Glick, p. 241.

143 Cantor, p. 169.

144 Ibid.

145 Cohen, p. 86.

146 Cohen, p. 87.

147 Cohen, p. 88.

148 Cohen, p. 87.

149 Cohen, p. 58.

150 Cohen, p. 60

151 Cohen, p. 60. Schaefer (2007) notes that the Babylonian Talmud blasphemes Christ in the context of passages that explain the destruction of the Temple in terms of a punishment for Talmudic rigidity in the face of danger. The narrative is intended to bypass any suggestion of another cause for its destruction. The emperor Titus is punished, according to texts, by being burnt and scattered forever. The punishment fits the crime of burning the Temple. For Jesus, sitting in excrement in Gehinnom is punishment for the crime, according to Schaefer, of heresy (including idolatry and blasphemy). Jesus' words at Matthew 15:17-20 (and Mark 7:18-23) dismiss Pharisaic purity rules, effectively stating that "food is not impure but human intention and actions are impure." For Schaefer, "[T]he rabbinic counter-narrative about Jesus' punishment would then invert his attack on the Pharisaic purity laws by having him sit in excrement and teaching him (and his followers) the lesson: you believe that only what comes out of the mouth defiles, well, you will sit forever in your own excrement and will finally understand that also what goes into the mouth and comes

of the stomach defiles" p. 83-91. Schaefer also makes the fascinating point that the passage may also be an allusion to the dispute at John 6:48-59 concerning how to understand the idea of eating Jesus' flesh. Schaefer says the Talmud here, "argues Jesus is dead and remains dead and eating his flesh won't lead to life...the initiator of this bizarre heresy [of the eucharist] is appropriately punished by sitting in what his followers excrete, after allegedly having eaten him: excrement!" p. 93.

152 Ibid.

153 Cohen, p. 260.

154 Cohen, p. 109.

155 Cohen, p. 242.

156 Ibid.

157 Glick, p. 195.

158 Glick, p. 196.

159 Cohen, p. 242.

160 Cohen, p. 243.

161 Ibid.

162 Cohen, p. 244.

163 Ibid.

164 Cohen, p. 261.

165 Cohen, p. 262.

166 Cohen, p. 257.

167 Cohen, p. 66.

168 Ibid.

169 Glick, p. 196.

170 Cohen, p. 67.

171 Ibid.

172 Cohen, p. 68.

173 Ibid.

174 Ibid.

175 Cohen, p. 67.

176 Glick, p. 198.

177 Glick, p. 199. Johnson (1988) says of the encounter between Donin and Yehiel that "the 1240 confrontation was not...'a debate'...adding that the rabbi...was in effect the witness for the defense, and the 'debate' consisted of his interrogation" (p. 217-218). Shahak (2002) says "a powerful attack, well based in many points, against talmudic Judaism developed in Europe from the 13th century." Shahak refers to "serious disputations held before the best European universities of the time and on the whole conducted as fairly as possible under medieval circumstances" (p. 21). He further adds in an accompanying footnote (p. 105) that Jews were treated more favorably than Christian heretics in debate.

178 Glick, p. 200.

179 Cohen, p. 71.

180 Cantor, p. 181.

181 Cantor, p. 180.

182 Cohen, p. 64.

183 Synan, p. 110.

184 Glick, p. 201.

185 Glick, p. 202.

186 Cohen, p. 80.

187 Cohen, p. 83.

188 Ibid.

189 Cohen, p. 97.

190 Cohen, p. 98.

191 Ibid.

192 Cohen, p. 108.

193 Cohen, p. 106.

194 Ibid.

195 Cohen, p. 107.

196 Ibid.

197 Synan, p. 122 (my emphasis).

198 Cohen, p. 127.

199 Ibid.

200 Cohen, p. 146.

201 Cohen, p. 168.

202 Cohen, p. 232.

203 Cohen, p. 189.

204 Cohen, p. 234.

205 Cohen, p. 48.

206 Cohen, p. 49.

207 Glick, p. 260.

208 Glick, p. 261.

209 Ibid.

210 Cohen, p. 168.

211 Cohen, p. 179.

212 Cohen, p. 185.

213 Glick, p. 240.

214 Ibid.

215 Cohen, p. 193.

216 Cantor, p. 179.

217 Cantor, p. 195.

218 Synan, p. 133 (my emphasis).

219 Glick, p. 269.

220 Ibid.

221 Synan, p. 134.

222 Ibid.

223 Cantor, p. 193.

224 Ibid.

225 Ibid.

226 Ibid.

227 Cantor, p. 187.

228 Glick, p. 109.

229 *Fellowship of Catholic Scholars Quarterly*, Vol. 29, #2, Summer 2006, p. 19 (my emphasis).

Endnotes to Chapter Four

False Conversion and the Inquisition

1 William Thomas Walsh, *Characters of the Inquisition* (New York: P. J. Kenedy & Sons,1940), p. 142.

2 Synan, p. 52.

3 Ibid.

4 Ibid.

5 Walsh, p. 141.

6 Ibid.

7 Lea Dasberg, *Untersuchungen ueber die Entwertung des Judenstatus im 11. Jahrhundert* (Paris: Mouton & Co, 1965), p. 179. (Translations mine).

8 Henry Charles Lea, *A History of the Inquisition of Spain* (New York: The Macmillan Company, 1908), p. 87.

9 Lea, p. 96.

10 Walsh, p. 142.

11 Ibid.

12 Lea, pp. 97-8.

13 Lea, p. 98.

14 Walsh, p. 142.

15 Walsh, p. 144.

16 Lea, p. 103.

17 Lea, p. 104.

18 Lea, p. 105.

19 Ibid.

20 Lea, p. 108.

21 Baer, p. 110.

22 Yitshak Baer, *A History of the Jews in Christian Spain* (Philadelphia: The Jewish Publication Society of America, 1966), p. 109.

23 Synan, p. 56

24 Synan, p. 57.

25 Kamen, p. 10.

26 Synan, p. 57.

27 Ibid.

28 Kamen, p. 70.

29 Synan, p. 56.

30 Synan, p. 54.

31 Baer, p. 254.

32 Walsh, p. 144.

33 Lea, p. 112.

34 Henri Gheon, *St. Vincent Ferrer* (New York: Sheed and Ward, 1939), p. 118.

35 Gheon, p. 120. Paul Johnson, while admitting that Ferrer deplored the rioting writes: "The riots showed clearly that the Jews posed a 'problem' to society to which a 'solution' must be found. Hence Ferrer and his clerical colleagues were responsible for a series of anti-Jewish policies approved by Spanish favoured antipope Benedict XIII, and for the selection as King of Aragon of Ferdinand I, who began to implement them. The war against the Jews was taken out the hands of the mob and made the official business of church and government. (*A History of the Jews* p. 222, Perennial Library, 1988). Johnson does not explain why Ferrer was wrong to look for a solution to the generally recognized Jewish problem.

36 Gheon, p. 112.

37 Ibid.

38 Lea, p. 113.

39 Ibid.

40 Walsh, p. 120.

41 Baer, p. 141.

42 Walsh, p. 121.

43 Baer, p. 143.

44 Ibid.

45 Baer, p. 148.

46 Ibid.

47 Lea, p. 119.

48 Baer, p. 163.

49 Baer, p. 164.

50 Baer, p. 172.

51 Baer, p. 178.

52 Baer, p. 179.

53 Ibid.

54 Baer, p. 190.

55 Baer, p. 201.

56 Ibid.

57 Baer, p. 174.

58 Baer, p. 225.

59 Ibid.

60 Baer, p. 226.

61 Ibid.

62 Ibid.

63 Ibid.

64 Baer, p. 228.

65 Baer, p. 229.

66 Baer, p. 205.

67 Baer, p. 255.

68 Baer, p. 259.

69 Baer, p. 210.

70 Ibid.

71 Baer, p. 213.

72 Baer, p. 218.

73 Ibid.

74 Ibid.

75 Baer, p. 224.

76 Kamen, p. 10.

Endnotes to Chapter Five

The Revolution Arrives in Europe

1 Maria Tischler, "Boehmishe Judengemeinde 1348-1519," *in Die Juden in den boehmischen Laender* (Muenchen/Wien: R. Oldenbourg Verlag, 1983), p. 4. (All translations mine.)

2 cf. Peter Hilsch, "Die Juden in Boehmen und Maehren im Mittelalter und die ersten Privilegian," in *Die Juden in den boehmischen Laender* (Muenchen/Wien: R. Oldenbourg Verlag, 1983), p. 15.

3 Howard Kaminsky, *A History of the Hussite Revolution* (Berkeley and Los Angeles: University of California Press, 1967), p. 145.

4 Kaminsky, p. 34.

5 Kaminsky, p. 54.

6 Ibid.

7 Kaminsky, p. 55.

8 Ibid.

9 Kaminsky, p. 48.

10 Kaminsky, p. 49.

11 Kaminsky, p. 48.

12 Kaminsky, p. 70.

13 Thomas A. Fudge, *The Crusade against the Heretics in Bohemia, 1418-1437* (Burlington, VT: Ashgate, 2002), p. 72 (my emphasis).

14 Kamninsky, p. 88.

Endnotes

15 Graetz, Vol. IV, p. 222.

16 Ibid. (my emphasis).

17 Norman Cohn, *The Pursuit of the Millennium: Revolutionary messianism in medieval and Reformation Europe and its bearing on modern totalitarian movements* (New York: Harper & Row, 1961), p. 14.

18 Frederick G. Heymann, *John Zizka and the Hussite Revolution* (New York: Russell and Russell, 1955), p. 42.

19 Ibid.

20 Ibid.

21 Heymann, p. 49.

22 Kaminsky, p. 19.

23 Fudge, p. 78.

24 Heymann, p. 55.

25 Kaminsky, p. 88.

26 Heymann, p. 102.

27 Ibid.

28 Ibid.

29 Fudge, p. 87.

30 Ibid.

31 Louis Israel Newman, *Jewish Influence on Christian Reform Movements* (New York: AMS Press, Inc., 1966), p. 437.

32 Ibid.

33 Newman, p. 435.

34 Ibid.

35 Newman, p. 436.

36 Ibid.

37 Newman, p. 435.

38 Ibid.

39 Newman, p. 445.

40 Ibid.

41 Newman, p. 446.

42 Ruth Gladstein, "Eschatological Trends in Bohemian Jewry during the Hussite Period," in *Prophecy and Millenarianism : Essays in Honour of Marjorie Reeves*, edited by Ann Williams (Burnt Hill: Longmans, 1980), p. 246

43 Ibid.

44 Heymann, p. 12.

45 Kaminsky, p. 109.

46 Graetz, Vol. IV, p. 219.

47 Graetz, Vol. IV, p. 220.

48 Fudge, p. 92.

49 Fudge, p. 254.

50 Fudge, p. 188.

51 Norman Cohn, p. 230.

52 Ibid.

53 Newman, p. 449.

54 Newman, p. 448.

55 Newman, p. 449. It is interesting to note here certain parallels with Jewish revival movements in the pre-Christian Greco-Roman world and how they considered themselves true heirs of the covenant. Jewish theologian Dan Cohn-Sherbok describes them thus: "The Samaritans...regarded themselves as inheritors of the original promise made to Israel. Situated on Mount Gerizim, they rigorously followed Pentateuchal law, rejecting the interpretations of Scripture expounded by official Judaism...they viewed Moses as the sole prophet of Israel who would return as a messianic figure...The Nazaraioi practised an ascetic way of life. Abstaining from meat as well as Temple sacrifice, they kept the Sabbath, circumcision and other Jewish practices. The Essenes...in opposition to the Temple cult in Jerusalem...adopted eschatological doctrines concerning Davidic and Aaronic Messiahs...Critical of official Judaism, they envisaged the present as an era of darkness presided over by the powers of Belial. The Pharisees...desired to attain perfection by separating from their co-religionists so as to strictly observe Jewish law...they strove to lead the nation back to true Torah Judaism. According to Pharisaic doctrine, they were the true inheritors of the ancient Israel and the promise of messianic fulfilment." *The Crucified Jew: Twenty Centuries of Christian Anti-Semitism* (Wm B. Eerdmans Publishing Co. 1997) p. 6-7.

56 Ibid.

57 Kaminsky, p. 283.

58 Kaminsky, p. 284.

59 Kaminsky, p. 289.

60 Kaminsky, p. 291.

61 Kaminsky, p. 292.

62 Kaminsky, p. 294n (all translations mine).

63 Ibid.

64 *"Legis Christi zelator praecipuus,"*

65 Fudge, p. 95.

66 Kaminsky, p. 295.

67 Heymann, p. 66.

68 Heymann, p. 67.

69 Heymann, p. 69.

70 Ibid.

71 Fudge, p. 254.

72 Fudge, p. 261.

73 Fudge, p. 259.

74 Fudge, p. 267.

75 Kaminsky, p. 311.

76 Kaminsky, p. 337.

77 Kaminsky, p. 338.

78 Kaminsky, p. 341.

79 Hannah Arendt, *On Revolution* (New York: The Viking Press, 1963),

80 Kaminsky, p. 341.

81 Kaminsky, p. 339.

82 Kaminsky, p. 315.

83 Kaminsky, p. 319 (my emphasis).

84 Ibid.

85 Ibid.

86 Ibid.

87 Ibid.

88 Ibid.

89 Kaminsky, p. 321 (my emphasis).

90 Kaminsky, p. 322.

91 Ibid.

92 Fudge, p. 148.

93 Kaminsky, p. 338.

94 Heymann, p. 93.

95 Heymann. p. 100.

96 Josef Macek, *The Hussite Movement in Bohemia* (Prague: Orbis, 1958), p. 36.

97 Ibid.

98 Macek, p. 39.

99 Ibid.

100 Kaminsky, p. 336.

101 Macek, p. 37.

102 "Sie sprechen ez sull auch kain fegfiure seyn, dann wann der mensch hy in armut sey, daz sull sin fegfiure sein."

103 Kaminsky, p. 340.

104 Kaminsky, p. 345.

105 Ibid.

106 Kaminsky, p. 347.

107 Kaminsky, p. 348.

108 Ibid.

109 Kaminsky, p. 350n.

110 Kaminsky, p. 351.

111 Kaminsky, p. 353.

112 Kaminsky, p. 355.

113 Gladstein, p. 245.

114 Ibid.

115 Ibid.

116 Newman, p. 451.

117 Newman, p. 453.

118 Graetz, Vol. IV, p. 222.

119 Graetz, Vol. IV, p. 224.

120 Ibid.

121 Graetz, Vol. IV, p. 225.

122 Gladstein, p. 243

123 Gladstein, p. 245.

124 Gladstein, p. 246.

125 Ibid.

126 Ibid.

127 Gladstein, p. 247.

128 Ibid.

129 Gladstein, p. 250.

130 Ibid.

131 Heymann, p. 122.

132 Heymann, p. 129.

133 Heyman, p. 136.

134 Heymann, p. 139.

135 Fudge, p. 143

136 Fudge, p. 146.

137 Heymann, p. 145.

138 Heymann, p. 168.

139 Heymann, p. 170.

140 Kaminsky, p. 385.

141 Kaminsky, p. 388.

142 Kaminsky, p. 400.

143 Heymann, p. 156

144 Ibid.

145 Kaminsky, p. 412.

146 Heymann, p. 261.

147 Kaminsky, p. 430.

148 Heymann, p. 261.

149 Ibid.

150 Ibid. A truly Christian view of sexual liberation as social control can be found in the writing of St Paul. "As you know," St. Paul writes in his first letter to the Corinthians (6:16), "a man who goes with a prostitute is one body with her, since the two,

as it is said, become one flesh. But anyone who is joined to the Lord is one spirit with him." Paul goes on to warn the Christians in Corinth against fornication because "all the other sins are committed outside the body; but to fornicate is to sin against your own body." Paul seems to be saying here that a transcendent union is created each time a man engages in sexual intercourse. When that union takes place within marriage, it bonds a man to his wife and creates a family. When it takes place outside of marriage, the sexual agent is bound to something inferior as his sexual partner. He is bound to the object of his lust, and now the same sexual force that created union in the family creates bondage. It took the evil genius of the Marquis de Sade and the Enlightenment to understand the political implications of Paul's warning that "all the other sins are committed outside the body." Sexual passion is an especially effective form of social control because it is so internalized by the fornicator that he feels that in defending his passions he is defending his very self. The government, then, that incites and protects the gratification of these passions will gain a hold over its citizens in a way more deep-seated than any other.

151 Kaminsky, p. 481.

152 Kaminsky, p. 490.

153 Heymann, p. 295.

154 Heymann, p. 347.

155 Kaminsky, p. 347.

156 Fudge, p. 153.

157 Ibid.

158 Fudge, p. 154.

159 Ibid.

160 Fudge, p. 159.

161 Heymann, p. 158.

162 Ibid.

163 Ibid.

164 Ibid.

165 Heymann, p. 166.

166 Fudge, p. 114.

167 Fudge, p. 115, n161.

168 Ibid.

169 Heymann, p. 390.

170 Heymann, p. 401.

171 Fudge, p. 107.

172 Heymann, p. 444.

173 Ibid.

174 Fudge, p. 115.

175 Fudge, p. 120.

176 Heymann, p. 477.

177 Ibid.

178 Heymann, p. 479

179 Cohn, p. 235.

180 Cohn, p. 241.

181 Heinrich Graetz, *Volkstuemliche Geschichte der Juden* (Leipzig: Verlag von Oskar Leiner, no date)Vol III, p. 58. (All translations are mine.)

182 Johannes Hofer, *Johannes von Capestrano: Ein Leben im Kampf um die Reform der Kirche* (Innsbruck-Wien-Muenchen: Tyrolia Verlag, 1936), p. 487.

183 Graetz, op. cit., p. 59.

184 Graetz, op. cit., p. 81.

185 Hofer, p. 493.

186 Hofer, p. 276. In the original German edition of his biography of Capistrano, Hofer cites Browe, who says "it is hard for us to comprehend today how often during the Middle Ages churches were broken into and hosts stolen."

187 Rev. John Hofer, *St. John Capistran, Reformer*, transl by Rev. Patrick Cummins, OSB (St. Louis: Herder, 1947), p. 276.

188 Hofer, *St. John Capistran*, p. 278.

189 Hofer, *St. John Capistran*, p. 275.

190 Hofer, *St. John Capistran*, p. 276.

191 Ibid.

192 Ibid.

193 Hofer, *St. John Capistran*, p. 279.

194 Ibid.

195 Hofer, p. 498. (cf. n234, in the German edition.)

196 Hofer, *St. John Capistran*, p. 279. For detailed scholarly Jewish studies recounting actual cases of Host desecration by Jews, as well as accounts of Jewish attacks on Christian symbols such as the crucifix (transgressions committed in the full knowledge that their consequence would be death) and the malicious labelling of Christians as Amalek and Christendom as the realm of Esau or Edom, see Elliott Horowitz, *Reckless Rites: Purim and the Legacy of Jewish Violence* (Princeton 2006) and Israel Jacob Yuval, *Two Nations in your Womb: Perceptions of Jews and Christians in Late Antiquity and the Middle*

Ages (University of California 2006). Both books also deal with and bravely point out the existence of the Jewish ritual blood sacrifices of (Jewish) children, a topic seldom dealt with. In a less scholarly and more controversial manner Jewish convert Israel Shamir has written on these subjects as well as hypothesized regarding the ritual sacrifice of Christian children by Ashkenazi Jews. His writings are available at www.israelshamir.net and the site includes a link to the English translation of the highly controversial and withdrawn book of Dr Ariel Toaff (professor of the Jewish University of Bar Ilan) *Passovers of Blood: The Jews of Europe and Ritual Murders.* For an account of a deliberate misrepresentation of "blood libel" cases designed to exaggerate later German anti-Semitism see Norman G. Finkelstein and Ruth Bettina Birn *A Nation on Trial: The Goldhagen*

Thesis and Historical Truth, (Owl Books 1998) p. 21.

197 Ibid.

198 Ibid.

199 Hofer, *St. John Capistran*, p. 280.

200 Graetz, op. cit. p. 62.

201 Ibid.

202 Hofer, *St. John Capistran*, p. 280.

203 Ibid.

204 Ibid.

205 Hofer, *St. John Capistran*, p. 281.

206 Ibid.

207 Ibid.

208 Ibid.

209 Ibid.

210 Hofer, *St. John Capistran*, p. 284.

Endnotes to Chapter Six

The Converso Problem

1 Henry Charles Lea, *A History of the Inquisiton of Spain* (New York: The Macmillan Company, 1908), p. 110.

2 Yitshak Baer, *A History of the Jews in Christian Spain* (Philadelphia: The Jewish Publication Society of America, 1966), p. 231.

3 Ibid.

4 Henry Kamen, *The Spanish Inquistion: A Historical Revision* (New Haven: Yale University Press, 1998), p. 29.

5 Ibid.

6 Norman F. Cantor, *The Sacred Chain: The History of the Jews* (New York: HarperCollins Publishers, 1994), p. 189.

7 Ibid.

8 Cecil Roth, *A Life of Menasseh Ben Israel: Rabbi, Printer, and Diplomat* (Philadelphia: The Jewish Publication Society of America, 1934), p. 6 (my emphasis).

9 B. Netanyahu, *The Origins of the Inquisition in Fifteenth Century Spain* (New York: Random House, 1995), p. xii.

10 Ibid.

11 Ibid.

12 Ibid.

13 Netanyahu, p. xix.

14 Netanyahu, p. 45.

15 Ibid.

16 Ibid.

17 Netanyahu, p. 44.

18 Netanyahu, p. 47.

19 Netanyahu, p. 46.

20 Ibid.

21 William Thomas Walsh, *Characters of the Inquisition* (New York: P. J. Kenedy & Sons), p. 216.

22 Baer, p. 250.

23 Baer, p. 251.

24 Baer, p. 255.

25 Walsh, *Characters*, p. 145.

26 Baer, p. 369.

27 Baer, p. 273.

28 Baer, p. 274.

29 Lea, p. 121.

30 Baer, p. 277.

31 Ibid.

32 Walsh, *Characters*, p. 146.

33 Lea, p. 126.

34 Baer, p. 280.

35 Ibid.

36 Baer, p. 281.

37 Ibid.

38 Ibid.

39 Ibid.

40 Walsh, *Characters*, p. 144.

41 Baer, p. 283.

42 Baer, p. 289.

43 Ibid.

44 Baer, p. 294.

45 Baer, p. 299.

46 Baer, p. 304.

47 Lea, p. 188

48 Lea, p. 151.

49 Ibid.

50 Lea, p. 152.

51 Lea, p. 155.

52 Walsh, *Characters*, p. 151.

53 Walsh, *Characters*, p. 148.

54 Walsh, *Characters*, p. 151.

55 Lea, p. 160.

56 Kamen, p. 37.

57 Baer, p. 424.

58 Kamen, p. 37.

59 Kamen, p. 38.

60 Kamen, p. 40.

61 Kamen, p. 41.

62 Lea, p. 162.

63 Ibid.

64 Walsh, *Characters*, p. 153.

65 Walsh, *Characters*, p. 70.

66 Walsh, *Characters*, p. 14.

67 Walsh, *Characters*, p. 71.

68 Ibid.

69 Walsh, *Characters*, p. 72.

70 Walsh, Characters, p. 22.

71 Lea, p. 131.

72 Kamen, p. 60.

73 Baer, p. 327.

74 Ibid.

75 Baer, p. 329.

76 Baer, p. 331.

77 Baer, p. 333.

78 Baer, p. 336.

79 Ibid.

80 Baer, p. 337.

81 Baer, p. 338.

82 Baer, p. 339.

83 Baer, p. 344.

84 Baer, p. 367.

85 Lea, p. 253.

86 Kamen, p. 55.

87 Baer, p. 368.

88 Baer, p. 369.

89 Baer, p. 330.

90 William Thomas Walsh, *Philip II* (New York: Sheed and Ward, 1937), p. 252.

91 Ibid.

92 Baer, p. 434.

93 Kamen, p. 24.

94 Baer, p. 440.

Endnotes to Chapter Seven

Reuchlin v. Pfefferkorn

1 Hans-Martin Kirn, *Das Bild vom Juden im Deutschland des fruehen 16. Jahrhunderts: dargestellt and den Schriften Johannes Pfefferkorns* (Tuebigen: J.C.B. Mohr (Paul Siebeck) 1989), p. 221. (All translations are mine.)

2 Ibid.

3 Erika Rummel, *The Case against Johann Reuchlin: Religious and Social Controversy in 16th Century Germany* (Toronto: University of Toronto Press, 2002), p. 3.

4 Ibid.

5 Graetz, Vol. IV, p. 423.

6 Graetz, Vol. IV, p. 424.

7 Graetz, Vol. IV, p. 425.

8 Graetz, Vol. IV, p. 424.

9 Kirn, p. 183.

10 Ludwig Geiger, *Johann Reuchlin: Sein Leben und Seine Werke* (Nieuwkoop: B. de Graaf, 1964), p. 210. ('Translations mine.)

11 Rummel, p. 8.

12 Rummel, p. 53. For more detail on such curses see Schaefer, Yuval and Horowitz.

13 Rummel, p. 54.

14 Rummel, p. 55.

15 Ibid.

16 Ibid.

17 Ibid.

18 Ibid.

19 Rummel, p. 54.

20 Rummel, p. 8.

21 Ibid.

22 Rummel, p. 60.

23 Ibid.

24 Ibid.

25 Ibid. In other words the 'Jewish' spirit, through a perverse understanding of the Torah, helps to create or assist heresies in their rebellion against the meaning of the New Covenant's fulfillment of the Old. For any understanding of the Old without an infallibly guaranteed understanding of the New after the foundation of the latter will naturally be liable to corruption.

26 Rummel, p. 61.

27 Graetz, Vol. IV, p. 429.

28 Rummel, p. 128.

29 Rummel, p. 129.

30 Ibid.

31 Rummel, p. 130.

32 Ibid.

33 Ibid.

34 Ibid.

35 Rummel, p. 131.

36 Rummel, p. 10.

37 Graetz, Vol. IV, p. 441.

38 Charles Zika, *Reuchlin und die Okkulte Tradition der Renaissance* (Sigmarigen: Jan Throbecke Verlag, 1998), p. 166. (Translations mine.)

39 C.S. Lewis, *The Abolition of Man* (New York: Macmillan, 1947), p. 87-8.

40 Zika, p. 46.

41 Zika, p. 48.

42 Zika, p. 43.

43 Rummell, p. 7.

44 Rummel, p. 16.

45 Ibid.

46 Graetz, Vol. IV, p. 433.

47 Ibid.

48 Rummel, p. 88.

49 Ibid.

50 Ibid.

51 Graetz, Vol. IV, p. 442.

52 Ibid.

53 Rummel, p. 92.

54 Geiger, p. 228.

55 Ludwig Geiger, *Johann Reuchlin: Sein Leben und Seine Werke* (Nieuwkoop: B. de Graaf, 1964), p. 230. (Translations mine.)

56 Rummel, p. 87.

57 Rummel, p. 92.

58 Rummel, p. 93.

59 Rummel, p. 94.

60 Ibid.

61 Ibid.

62 Rummel, p. 96.

63 Rummel, p. 11.

64 Ibid.

65 Ibid.

66 Ibid.

67 Ibid.

68 Ibid.

69 Graetz, Vol. IV, p. 426.

70 Graetz, Vol. IV, p. 436.

71 Kirn, p. 183.

72 Rummel, p. 132.

73 Ibid.

74 Ibid.

75 Ibid.

76 Rummel, p. 133.

77 Rummel, p. 12.

78 Ibid.

79 Geiger, p. 238.

80 Geriger, p. 251.

81 Geiger, p. 252.

82 Graetz, Vol. IV, p. 448.

83 Ibid.

84 Geiger, p. 240.

85 Rummel, p. 134.

86 Geiger, p. 270.

87 Rummel, p. vii.

88 Ibid.

89 Rummel, p. 99.

90 Rummel, p. 100.

91 Ibid.

92 Rummel, p. 13.

93 Ibid.

94 Rummel, p. 138.

95 Graetz, Vol, IV, p. 446.

96 Geiger, p. 342.

97 Ibid.

98 Rummel, p. 144.

99 Ibid.

100 Ibid.

101 Rummel, p. 102.

102 Rummel, p. xii.

103 Geiger, p. 297.

104 Geiger, p. 297.

105 Graetz, Vol, IV, p. 452.

106 Graetz, Vol, IV, p. 454.

107 Ibid. (my emphasis).

108 Ibid.

109 Kirn, p. 172.

110 Rummel, p. ix.

111 Rummel, p. 110.

112 Ibid.

113 Ibid.

114 Rummel, p. 116.

115 Rummel, p. 117.

116 Graetz, Vol. IV, p. 456.

117 Ibid.

118 Ibid.

119 Graetz, Vol. IV, pp. 457-8.

120 Graetz, Vol. IV, p. 461.

121 Graetz, Vol. IV, p. 467.

122 Ibid.

123 Graetz, Vol. IV, p. 466.

124 Rummel, p. 137.

125 Ibid.

126 Rummel, p. 138.

127 Graetz, Vol. IV, p. 435.

128 Geiger, p. 162.

129 Rummel, p. 31.

130 Zika, p. 17.

131 Geiger, p. 169.

132 Ibid.

133 Ibid.

134 Geiger, p. 176.

135 Ibid. (my emphasis).

136 Rummel, p. 148.

137 Ibid.

138 Rummel, p. 149.

139 Kirn, p. 184.

140 Zika, p. 104.

141 Zika, p. 108.

142 Ibid.

143 Rummel, p. 22.

144 Rummel, p. 139.

145 Zika, p. 74.

146 Zika, p. 168.

147 Kirn, p. 138.

148 Graetz, Vol IV, p. 469.

149 Kirn, p. 174.

150 Rummel, p. 160.

151 Graetz, Vol. IV, p. 468.

152 Kirn, p. 175, n. 222.

153 Zika, p. 190.

154 Pike, p. 625.

155 Albert Pike, *Morals and Dogma* (XXVII Knight of the Sun, or Prince Adept, p. 744).

156 Pike, p. 745

Endnotes to Chapter Eight

Thomas Muentzer and the Peasant Revolt

1 M. Luthers *Werke* Weimarer Ausgabe Bd. 15, p. 214. (All translations mine.)

2 Ibid.

3 Hans-Juergen Goertz, *Thomas Muentzer: Apocalyptic Mystic and Revolutionary* (Edinburgh: T&T Clark, 1993), p. 48.

4 Ibid.

5 Goertz, p. 50.

6 Ibid.

7 Ibid.

8 Klaus Ebert, *Thomas Muentzer: Von Eigensinn und Widerspruch* (Frankfurt am Main: Athenaeum, 1987), p. 76. (Translations mine.)

9 Ebert, p. 79.

10 Ibid.

11 Ebert, p. 60.

12 Ebert, p. 78.

13 Ebert, p. 78.

14 Ebert, p. 79.

15 Fudge, p. 131.

16 Ibid.

17 Fudge, p. 259.

18 Macek, p. 72.

19 Macek, p. 101.

20 Cohn, p. 241.

21 Goertz, p. 53.

22 Goertz, p. 54.

23 Ebert, p. 87.

24 Goertz, p. 61.

25 Goertz, p. 60.

26 Goertz, p. 64.

27 Ebert, p. 85.

28 Ibid.

29 Ibid.

30 Goertz, p. 69.

31 Goertz, p. 72.

32 Ibid.

33 Fudge, p. 131.

34 *Revelation and Revolution: Basic Writings of Thomas Muentzer,* trans. and ed. by Michael G. Baylor (Bethlehem: Lehigh University Press, 1993), p. 18.

35 Ibid.

36 Baylor, p. 55.

37 Baylor, p. 57n

38 Baylor, p. 17.

39 Baylor, p. 18.

40 Ibid.

41 Baylor, p. 18.

42 Ebert, p. 233.

43 Ebert, p. 234.

44 Baylor, p. 18.

45 Rummel, p. 24.

46 Rummel, p. 26.

47 Graetz, Vol. IV, p. 470.

48 Graetz, Vol. IV, p. 469.

49 Walsh, Philip II, p. 245.

50 Graetz, Vol. IV, p. 471.

51 Walsh, Philip II, p. 248.

52 Walsh, Philip II, p. 259.

53 Walsh, Philip II, p. 258.

54 Walsh, Philip II, p. 249

55 Ibid.

56 Walsh, Philip II, p. 248. While Jews hold to the Talmud, which distorts the Old Testament, the Christian heretics distorted the Old Testament by rejecting the guarantor of the interpretation of the Old Testament by the New. In doing so, they perverted both Testaments, ignoring St. Augustine's dictum, "The New Testament lies hidden in the Old; the Old is made explicit in the New." It is in their essential rejection of this dictum and selective and unreliable partial acceptance of Scripture that both Jews and the Christian heretics share a crucial similarity.

57 Graetz, Vol. IV, p. 423.

58 Graetz, Vol. IV, p. 471.

59 Graetz, Vol. IV, p. 470.

60 Graetz, Vol. IV, p. 471.

61 Walsh, Philip II, p. 248.

62 Ibid.

63 Walsh, Philip II, p. 249.

64 Hartmann Grisar, S.J., *Luther* (Freiburg im Breisgau: Herdersche Verlagshandlung), vol. II, p. 442.

65 Goertz, p. 90.

66 Baylor, p. 155.

67 Ibid.

68 Baylor, p. 156.

69 Ebert, p. 102.

70 Baylor, p. 161.

71 Baylor, p. 22.

72 Ebert, p. 122.

73 Goertz, p. 105.

74 Baylor, p. 62.

75 Baylor, p. 23.

76 Baylor, p. 157.

77 Baylor, p. 16.

78 Baylor, p. 37.

79 Ebert, p. 111.

80 Goertz, p. 8.

81 Goertz, p. 105.

82 Ibid.

83 Goertz, p. 108.

84 Ibid.

85 Baylor, p. 163.

86 Baylor, p. 167.

87 Baylor, p. 80.

88 Baylor, p. 81.

89 Rummel, p. 28.

90 Rummel, p. 34.

91 Rummel, p. 35.

92 Ibid.

93 Rummel, p. 34.

94 Ibid.

95 Ibid.

96 Ebert, p. 130.

97 Ebert, p. 223.

98 Ebert, p. 126.

99 Ibid.

100 Ebert,p 128.

101 Ibid.

102 Goertz, p. 115.

103 Baylor, p. 168.

104 Baylor, p. 169.

105 Ibid.

106 Ibid.

107 Baylor, p. 37.

108 Ibid.

109 Luther, WA 15, p. 219.

110 Luther, WA 15, p. 220.

111 Ibid

112 Baylor, p. 143.

113 Ibid.

114 Baylor, p. 144.

115 Ibid.

116 Baylor, p. 147.

117 Ibid.

118 Baylor, p. 151.

119 Baylor, p. 152.

120 Ibid.

121 Baylor, p. 174.

122 Baylor, p. 148.

123 Ibid.

124 Ibid.

125 Ibid.

126 Baylor, p. 110.

127 Baylor, p. 105.

128 Baylor, p. 107.

129 Ibid.

130 Ibid.

131 Baylor, p. 114.

132 Cohn, p. 252.

133 Cohn, p. 253.

134 Ibid.

135 Baylor, p. 111.

136 Ibid.

137 Baylor, p. 113.

138 Baylor, p. 111.

139 Baylor, p. 112.

140 Ibid.

141 Baylor, p. 113.

142 Ibid.

143 Ibid.

144 Ibid.

145 Ibid.

146 Ibid.

147 Ibid.

148 Ebert, p. 141.

149 Baylor, p. 42.

150 Baylor, p. 171.

151 Baylor, p. 176.

152 Baylor, p. 177.

153 Baylor, p. 178.

154 Baylor, p. 180.

155 Baylor, p. 181.

156 Baylor, p. 178.

157 Goertz, p. 139.

158 Ibid.

159 Goertz, p. 133.

160 Ibid.

161 Ibid.

162 Baylor, p. 188.

163 Baylor, pp. 188-9.

164 Ibid.

165 Ibid.

166 Luther, WA 15, p. 238.

167 Goertz, p. 174.

168 Goertz, p. 217.

169 Newman, p. 454.

170 Newman, p. 501.

171 Ibid.

172 Ibid.

173 Newman, p. 454.

174 Newman, p. 471.

175 Newman, p. 499.

176 Newman, p. 498.

177 Newman, p. 455.

178 M. Luthers *Werke*, Weimarer Ausgabe Bd. 18, "Wider die rauebersichen und mo-erderischen rotten der Bauern," p. 344.

179 Goertz, p. 176.

180 Baylor, p. 191.

181 Baylor, pp. 191-2.

182 Cohn, p. 266.

183 Baylor, p. 191.

184 Baylor, p. 192.

185 Goertz, p. 177.

186 Goertz, p. 81.

187 Baylor, p. 194.

188 Ibid.

189 Baylor, p. 196.

190 Ibid.

191 Goertz, p. 180.

192 Goertz, p. 182.

193 Ebert, p. 126.

194 Ibid.

195 Goertz, p. 189.

196 Ebert, p. 226.

197 Baylor, p. 202.

198 Goertz, p. 50.

199 Goertz, p. xvi.

200 Ibid.

201 Ebert, p. 245.

Endnotes to Chapter Nine

The Anabaptist Rebellion

1 Herman von Kerssenbroick, *Geschichte der Wiedertaeufer zu Muenster in Westphalen* 1771, p. 102. (All translations mine.)

2 Sigrun Haude, *In the Shadow of "Savage Wolves": Anabaptist Muenster and the German Reformation during the 1530s* (Boston Leiden Cologne: Humanities Press, Inc. 2000), p. 24.

3 Haude, p. 26.

4 Cohn, p. 280.

5 Ibid.

6 Cohn, p. 281.

7 Anthony Arthur, *The Tailor-King: The Rise and Fall of the Anabaptist Kingdom of Muenster* (New York: St.Martin's Press 1999), p. 7.

8 Arthur, p. 8.

9 Kerssenbroik, p. 176.

10 Kerssenbroik, p. 177.

11 Kerssenbroik, p. 179.

12 Kerssenbroik, p. 181.

13 Kerssenbroik, p. 183

14 Kerssenbroik, p. 184.

15 Arthur, p. 16.

16 Ibid.

17 Kerssenbroik, p. 185.

18 Ibid.

19 Arthur, p. 16.

20 Kerssenbroik, pp. 185-6.

21 Arthur, p. 19.

22 Arthur, p. 113.

23 Arthur, pp. 15-16.

24 Arthur, p. 175.

25 Haude, p. 21.

26 Ibid.

27 Arthur, p. 14. According to David Klinghoffer, "The heritage of Protestantism has been a mixed one for Jews...Luther prepared the way for the planting of new ideas, which eventuated in the first hints of religious tolerance in the eighteenth century, in whose last decades Jews were being freed from the ghettoes...This new freedom was no boon to Judaism. On the contrary, it resulted in Jewish defections to Christianity, or Christianized forms of Judaism... Whereas in medieval Europe there was one form of Christianity you could accept or reject, Protestantism created countless new variations on the theme of Jesus as Messiah." *Why the Jews Rejected Jesus* (Three Leaves Press 2006) p. 184-185, my emphasis.

28 Ibid.

29 Haude, p. 21.

30 Arthur, p. 28.

31 Arthur, p. 61.

32 Ibid.

33 Arthur, p. 41.

34 Ibid.

35 Ibid.

36 Arthur, p. 42.

37 Arthur, p. 33.

38 Cohn, p. 290.

39 Kersenbroik, p. 11.

40 Kerssenbroik, p. 12.

41 Kerssenbroik, p. 18.

42 Arthur, p. 66.

43 Arthur, p. 72.

44 Ibid.

45 Kerssenbroik, p. 546.

46 Ibid.

47 Kerssenbroik, p. 547.

48 Kerssenbroik, p. 27.

49 Haude, p. 14.

50 Arthur, p. 96.

51 Haude, p. 34.

52 Arthur, p. 94.

53 Cohn, p. 293.

54 Arthur, p. 101.

55 Arthur, p. 103.

56 Ibid.

57 Haude, p. 14.

58 Arthur, p. 109.

59 Cohn, p. 300.

60 Arthur, p. 110.

61 Ibid.

62 Haude, p. 15.

63 Cohn, p. 298.

64 Kerssenbroik, p. 132.

65 Ibid.

66 Kerssenbroik, p. 137.

67 Arthur, p. 113.

68 Arthur, p. 114.

69 Arthur, p. 115.

70 Ibid.

71 Arthur, p. 116.

72 Arthur, p. 121.

73 Kerssenbroik, p. 115.

74 Kerssenbroik, p. 116. The force of the association between the "Tailor King" and the subordination of the entire German empire can be seen from the historian Michael Burleigh's following vignette from the Third Reich: "in July 1934, Victor Klemperer...discussed with his wife Eva a speech by Hitler booming from an outdoor loudspeaker. Klemperer noted, 'the voice of a fanatical preacher. Eva says: Jan van Leyden. I say Rienzi'...Eva Klemperer was not alone in drawing comparisons between Hitler and Anabaptist sectarians of the sixteenth century. The same comparison occurred to...Friedrich Reck-Malleczewen...who in 1937 penned a portrait of Hitler only thinly disguised as the Anabaptist leader Jan Bockelson, responsible for a reign of terror in sixteenth-century Muenster. The book was subtitled History of Mass Lunacy." *The Third Reich: A New History* (Pan Books 2000) p.4-5.

75 Arthur, p. 138.

76 Arthur, p. 142.

77 Cohn, p. 304.

78 Kerssenbroik, p. 158.

79 Kerssenbroik, p. 159.

80 Kerssenbroik, p. 162

81 Arthur, p. 146.

82 Kerssenbroik, p. 177.

83 Ibid.

84 Ibid.

85 Haude, p. 26.

86 Arthur, p. 165.

87 Arthur, p. 168.

88 Arthur, p. 170.

89 Arthur, p. 173.

90 Ibid.

91 Ibid.

92 Ibid.

93 Arthur, p. 176.

94 Arthur, p. 184.

95 Haude, p. 37.

96 Haude, p. 41.

97 Haude, p. 27.

98 Arthur, p. 188.

99 Ibid.

100 Ibid.

101 Haude, p. 85.

102 Haude, p. 25.

103 Haude, p. 137.

104 Cohn, p. 309.

105 Cohn, p. 315.

106 Ibid.

Endnotes to Chapter Ten

ohn Dee, Magic and the Transformation of England

1 William Thomas Walsh, *Philip II* (New York: Sheed and Ward, 1937), p. 40.

2 Walsh, p. 142.

3 Walsh, p. 38.

4 Ibid.

5 Walsh, p. 39.

6 Barbara W. Tuchman, *Bible and Sword* (New York: New York University Press, 1956), p. 54.

7 Ibid.

8 Tuchman, p. 52.

9 Ibid.

10 Jacques Maritain, *Three Reformers: Luther, Descartes, Rousseau* (New York: Charles Scribner's Sons, 1937), p. 142.

11 Tuchman, p. 79.

12 Tuchman, p. 80.

13 Tuchman, p. 82.

14 Ibid.

15 Tuchman, p. 54

16 Walsh, p. 171.

17 Hilaire Belloc, *The Servile State* (Indianapolis: Liberty Fund, 1977), p. 92.

18 Belloc, p. 93.

19 Belloc, p. 95.

20 ibid.

21 Belloc, p. 96.

22 Walsh, p. 155.

23 Benjamin Woolley, *The Queen's Conjurer: The Science and Magic of Dr. John Dee, Adviser to Queen Elizabeth I* (New York: Henry Holt and Company, 2001), p. 34.

24 Woolley, p. 35.

25 Woolley, p. 17.

26 Woolley, p. 45.

27 Ibid.

28 Ibid.

29 Frances A. Yates, *The Occult Philosophy in the Elizabethan Age* (London: Routledge & Kegan Paul, 1979), p. 1.

30 Woolley, p. 50.

31 Woolley, p. 22.

32 Woolley, p. 55.

33 Ibid.

34 Woolley, p. 56.

35 Steven Nadler, *Spinoza: A Life* (Cambridge: Cambridge University Press, 1999), p. 5.

36 William Thomas Walsh, *Characters of the Inquisition* (New York: P. J. Kenedy & Sons), p. 179.

37 Ibid.

38 Ibid.

39 Henry Kamen, *The Spanish Inquistion: A Historical Revision* (New Haven: Yale University Press, 1998), p. 31.

40 Walsh, *Characters*, p. 216.

41 Walsh, *Philip II*, p. 104.

42 Ibid.

43 Walsh, *Philip II*, p. 562.

44 Walsh, *Philip II*, p. 411.

45 Walsh, *Philip II*, p. 91.

46 Walsh, *Philip II*, p. 95.

47 Ibid.

48 Walsh, *Philip II*, p. 91. Walsh's harsh judgment is not shared by many historians. A more recent assesment of Charles V says, "In his tenacious purusit of internal Church reform and his defence of Christnedom in its entirety, Charles was actually more Catholic than the popes of his time .... He had shown clearly how seriously he took his role as protector of the Church and Christianity, and how much he was prepared to sacrifice for it.... For Charles, the choice of leading his military operations himself seems to have been dictated by his awesome sense of duty, his missionary instincts and his innate feeling of honour. For these he sacrificed his personal comfort, for his physical ailments caused him much pain on all his moves, and in all his encampments" Wim Blockmans, *Emperor Charles V, 1500-1558* (Hodder Arnold 2001), p. 140.

Contra Walsh, others argue that Charles's advice to his son Philip not to restore confiscated lands to the Church was probably wise in the circumstances. Moreover, others argue that Phiip was never in a position to decide matters of this kind.

49 Marvin O'Connell, *Thomas Stapleton and the Counter Reformation* (New Haven and London: Yale University Press, 1964), p. 10.

50 Marvin R. O'Connell, *The Counter*

Reformation 1559-1610 (New York: Harper Torchbooks, 1974), p. 102.

51 Ibid.

52 Louis Israel Newman, *Jewish Influence on Christian Reform Movements* (New York: AMS Press, Inc., 1966), p. 602.

53 Walsh, *Philip II*, p. 248.

54 Ibid.

55 Walsh, *Philip II*, pp. 244-5.

56 Walsh, *Philip II*, p. 248.

57 Walsh, *Philip II*, p. 249.

58 Ibid.

59 Newman, p. 511.

60 Newman, p. 514.

61 Newman, p. 515.

62 Ibid.

63 Newman, p. 518.

64 Ibid.

65 Newman, p. 572.

66 Newman, p. 579.

67 Newman, p. 515.

68 Newman, p. 591.

69 O'Connell, *Counterreformation*, p. 125.

70 O'Connell, *Counterreformation*, p. 132.

71 O'Connell, *Counterreformation*, p. 134.

72 Thomas Francis Knox, *The First and Second Diaries of the English College, Douay* (London: David Nutt, 1888), p. xvii.

73 Ibid.

74 Knox, p. xviii.

75 Knox, p. xvii.

76 Walsh, *Characters*, p. 219.

77 O'Connell, *Counterreformation*, p. 76.

78 O'Connell, *Counterreformation*, p. 72.

79 Walsh, *Philip II*, p. 279.

80 Walsh, *Philip II*, p. 302.

81 Woolley, p. 62.

82 Ibid.

83 Walsh, *Philip II*, p. 196.

84 Ibid.

85 Frances A. Yates, *The Occult Philosophy in the Elizabethan Age* (London: Routledge & Kegan Paul, 1979), p. 3.

86 Yates, p. 76.

87 Yates, p. 82.

88 Yates, p. 95.

89 Yates, p. 82.

90 Ibid.

91 Christopher Marlowe, *Tamburlaine, Doctor Faustus, The Jew of Malta, Edward II* (Oxford: Clarendon Press, Oxford Drama Library, 1995), p. 141.

92 Marlowe, p. 143.

93 Woolley, p. 63.

94 Walsh, *Philip II*, p. 303.

95 Walsh, *Philip II*, p. 241.

96 Walsh, *Philip II*, p. 310. The Parker quote is from Piers Paul Read, *The Templars* (The Phoenix Press 2001) p. 303.

97 Walsh, *Philip II*, p. 242.

98 Marvin O'Connell, *Thomas Stapleton and the Counter Reformation* (New Haven and London: Yale University Press, 1964), p. 23.

99 O'Connell, *Stapleton*, p. 28.

100 O'Connell, *Stapleton*, p. 30.

101 Knox, p. xix.

102 Knox, p. xxiii.

103 Ibid.

104 Ibid.

105 Knox, p. xxv.

106 O'Connell, *Stapleton*, p. 28.

107 O'Connell, *Stapleton*, p. 29.

108 Woolley, p. 63.

109 Ibid.

110 Ibid.

111 Woolley, p. 65.

112 Woolley, p. 70.

113 Woolley, p. 69.

114 Woolley, p. 66.

115 Woolley, p. 73.

116 Ibid.

117 Walsh, *Philip II*, p. 353.

118 Walsh, *Philip II*, p. 93.

119 Graetz, Vol. IV, p. 595.

120 Graetz, Vol. IV, p. 594.

121 Ibid.

122 Walsh, *Characters*, p. 217.

123 Yates, p. 88.

124 Woolley, p. 75.

125 Woolley, p. 142.

126 Woolley, p. 78.

127 Woolley, p. 85.

128 Walsh, *Philip II*, p. 374.

129 O'Connell, *Stapleton*, p. 31.

130 Ibid.

131 O'Connell, *Stapleton*, p. 32.

132 Ibid.

133 Ibid.

134 Ibid.

135 O'Connell, *Stapleton*, p. 33.

136 Ibid.

137 O'Connell, *Stapleton*, p. 32.

138 O'Connell, *Stapleton*, p. 33.

139 Ibid.

140 O'Connell, *Counterreformation*, p. 235

141 Walsh, *Philip II*, p. 410.

142 Walsh, *Philip II*, p. 419.

143 Walsh, *Philip II*, p. 248.

144 Walsh, *Characters*, p. 263.

145 Walsh, *Philip II*, p. 320.

146 Walsh, *Philip II*, p. 469.

147 O'Connell, *Counterreformation*, p. 151.

148 O'Connell, *Counterreformation*, p. 150.

149 O'Connell, *Counterreformation*, p. 167.

150 Knox, p. xxxv.

151 Ibid.

152 Knox, p. xxxvi.

153 O'Connell, *Counterreformation*, p. 241.

154 Woolley, p. 117.

155 Francis Bacon, *The Advancement of Learning and New Atlantis* (Oxford: Clarendon Press, 1974), p. 234.

156 Ibid.

157 Bacon, p. 235.

158 John Dee, *The Limits of the British Empire*, ed. Ken Macmillan (Westport, CT: Praeger, 2004), p. 17.

159 Ibid.

160 Knox, p. l.

161 Ibid.

162 Ibid.

163 Knox, p. li.

164 Knox, p. xlix.

165 Ibid.

166 Knox, p. lxi.

167 Knox, p. xlix.

168 Charles Nicholl, *The Reckoning: the Murder of Christopher Marlowe* (Chicago: University of Chicago Press, 1992), p. 97.

169 Knox, p. lxix.

170 Knox, p. lxxvii.

171 Nicholl, p. 123.

172 Nicholl, p. 124.

173 Ibid.

174 Ibid.

175 Nicholl, p. 131.

176 Woolley, p. 129.

177 Ibid.

178 Woolley, p. 148.

179 Woolley, p. 149.

180 Woolley, p. 150.

181 Ibid.

182 Woolley, p. 147.

183 Ibid.

184 Ibid.

185 Woolley, p. 162.

186 Woolley, p. 163.

187 Woolley, p. 167.

188 Woolley, p. 141.

189 Ibid.

190 Ibid.

191 Walsh, *Philip II*, p. 608.

192 Woolley, p. 189.

193 Woolley, p .205.

194 John Bossy, *Giordano Bruno and the Embassy Affair* (New Haven: Yale University Press, 1991), pp. 100-1.

195 Bossy, p. 101.

196 Ibid.

197 Bossy, p. 99.

198 Bossy, p. 19.

199 Woolley, p. 210.

200 Woolley, p. 214.

201 Ibid.

202 Woolley,p. 221.

203 R. J. W. Evans, *Rudolf II and His World: A Study in Intellectual History 1576-1612* (Oxford: The Clarendon Press, 1973), p. 196.

204 Ibid.

205 Nicholl, p. 248.

206 Nicholl, p. 259.

207 Nicholl, p. 248.

208 Ibid.

209 Evans, p. 226.

210 Evans, p. 160.

211 Evans, p. 240.

212 Evans, p. 241.

213 Evans, p. 35.

214 Evans, p. 36. (All translations mine.)

215 Yates, p. 88.

216 Ibid.

217 Evans, p .36.

218 Woolley, p. 233.

219 Woolley, p. 228.

220 Evans, p. 225.

221 Evans, p. 224 (my emphasis).

222 Woolley, p. 236.

223 Nicholl, p. 102.

224 Nicholl, p. 103.

225 Walsh, *Philip II,* p. 635.

226 Ibid.

227 Ibid.

228 Walsh, *Philip II*, p. 636.

229 Walsh, *Philip II*, p. 637.

230 Ibid.

231 Ibid.

232 Nicholl, p. 104.

233 Nicholl, p. 100.

234 Ibid.

235 Nicholl, p. 101.

236 Nicholl, p. 113.

237 Nicholl, p. 114.

238 Nicholl, p. 162.

239 Ibid.

240 Ibid.

241 Nicholl, p. 164.

242 Woolley, p. 239.

243 Woolley, p. 240.

244 Woolley, p. 244.

245 Ibid.

246 Woolley, p. 245.

247 Woolley, p. 255.

248 Woolley, p. 259.

249 Ibid.

250 Woolley, p. 260.

251 Woolley, p. 261.

252 Woolley, p. 262.

253 Yates, p. 107.

254 Ibid.

255 Ibid.

256 Yates, p. 116.

257 Yates, p. 160.

258 Ibid.

259 Yates, p. 161.

260 Yates, p. 160.

261 Ibid.

262 Woolley, p. 262.

263 Woolley, p. 263.

264 Ibid.

265 Ibid.

266 Woolley, p. 264.

267 Ibid.

268 Ibid.

269 Woolley, p. 267.

270 Nicholl, p. 98.

271 Nicholl, p. 92.

272 Nicholl, p. 232.

273 Nicholl, p. 93.

274 Nicholl, p. 96.

275 Nicholl, p. 95.

276 Nicholl, p. 207.

277 Marlowe, p. 139.

278 Ibid.

279 Marlowe, p. 141.

280 Marlowe, p. 143.

281 Ibid.

282 Marlowe, p. 141.

283 Ibid.

284 Ibid.

285 Marlowe, p. 142n.

286 Marlowe, p. 143.

287 Marlowe, p. 145.

288 Marlowe, p. 147.

289 Ibid.

290 Marlowe, p. 180.

291 Marlowe, p. 151.

292 Nicholl, p. 213.

293 Nicholl, p. 215.

294 Yates, p. 120.

295 Ibid.

296 Ibid.

297 Ibid.

298 Yates, p. 121.

299 Ibid.

300 Yates, p. 122.

301 Evans, p. 226.

302 Ibid.

303 Nicholl, p. 220.

304 Yates, p. 104.

305 Yates, p. 106.

306 Yates, p. 77.

307 Ibid.

308 Marlowe, p. 255.

309 Marlowe, p. 256.

310 Ibid.

311 Ibid.

312 Marlowe, p. 278.

313 Ibid.

314 Yates, p. 124.

315 Ibid.

316 Yates, p. 125.

317 Marlowe, p. 316.

318 Marlowe, p. 320.

319 Marlowe, p. 321.

320 Yates, p. 133.

321 Ibid.

322 Yates, p. 77.

323 Yates, p. 155.

324 Yates, p. 156.

325 Ibid.

326 Yates, p. 157.

327 Yates, p. 163.

328 Yates, p. 167.

329 Yates, p. 113.

330 Yates, p. 114.

331 Nicholl, p. 323.

332 Nicholl, p. 285.

333 Nicholl, p. 41.

334 Nicholl, p. 286.

335 Nicholl, p. 288.

336 Nicholl, p. 46.

337 Ibid.

338 Nicholl, p. 43.

339 Nicholl, p. 44.

340 Nicholl, p. 290.

341 Nicholl, p. 40.

342 Nicholl, p. 55.

343 Ibid.

344 Nicholl, p. 56.

345 Nicholl, p. 20.

Endnotes to Chapter Eleven

Menasseh ben Israel and the Failed Apocalypse

1 Steven Nadler, *Spinoza: A Life* (Cambridge: Cambridge University Press, 1999), p. 21.

2 Nadler, p. 15.

3 Cecil Roth, *A Life of Menasseh Ben Israel: Rabbi, Printer, and Diplomat* (Philadelphia: The Jewish Publication Society of America, 1934), p. 38.

4 Roth, p. 45.

5 Roth, p. 47.

6 Ibid.

7 Ibid.

8 Ibid.

9 Roth, p. 16.

10 Graetz, Vol. V, p. 49.

11 Graetz, Vol. V, p. 91.

12 Roth, p. 39.

13 Graetz, Vol. V, p. 6.

14 David S. Katz, *Philosemitism and the Readmission of the Jews to England 1603-1655* (Oxford: Clarendon Press, 1982), p. 158.

15 Christopher Hill, *Society and Puritanism in Pre-Revolutionary England* (New York: Schocken Books, 1964), p. 22.

16 Hill, p. 24.

17 Barbara W. Tuchman, *Bible and Sword* (New York: New York University Press, 1956), p. 83.

18 Ibid.

19 Katz, p. 159.

20 Katz, p. 21.

21 Ibid.

22 Katz, p. 23.

23 Ibid.

24 Ibid.

25 Katz, p. 24.

Endnotes

26 Ibid.

27 Ibid.

28 Ibid.

29 Ibid.

30 Katz, p. 26.

31 Katz, p. 28.

32 Ibid.

33 Ibid.

34 Katz, p. 130.

35 Katz, p. 29.

36 Tuchman, p. 87.

37 Ibid.

38 Katz, p. 31.

39 William Laud, *The Works of the Most Reverend Father in God, William Laud, D.D., sometime Lord Archbishop of Canterbury*, Vol. I, Sermons (Oxford: John Henry Parker, 1848), p. 17.

40 Laud, p. 18.

41 Ibid.

42 Laud, p. 19.

43 Ibid.

44 Laud, p. 20.

45 Tuchman, p. 83.

46 Katz, p. 40.

47 Hill, p. 180.

48 Louis Israel Newman, *Jewish Influence on Christian Reform Movements* (New York: AMS Press, Inc., 1966), p. 22.

49 Newman, p. 95.

50 Newman, p. 96.

51 Ibid.

52 Menasseh Ben Israel, *The Hope of Israel*, The English Translation by Moses Wall, 1652, ed. Henry Mechoulan and Gerard Nahon (New York: Oxford University Press, 1987), p. 11.

53 Ibid.

54 Roth, p. 14.

55 Catechism of the Catholic Church (Liguori, MO: Liguori Publications, 1994), 1272.

56 Norman Cohn, *The Pursuit of the Millennium: Revolutionary messianism in medieval and Reformation Europe and its bearing on modern totalitarian movements* (New York: Harper & Row, 1961), p. 27.

57 Cohn, p. 28.

58 Cohn, p. 30.

59 Cohn, p. 1.

60 Roth, p. 53.

61 Roth, p. 59.

62 Peter Gaunt, *Oliver Cromwell* (London: Blackwell Publishers, 1996), p. 31.

63 Gaunt, p. 35.

64 P. G. Rogers, *The Fifth Monarchy Men* (London: Oxford University Press, 1966), p. 12.

65 Ibid.

66 Rogers, p. 149.

67 Ibid.

68 Frances A. Yates, *The Occult Philosophy in the Elizabethan Age* (London: Routledge & Kegan Paul, 1979), p. 177.

69 Yates, *Occult*, p. 179.

70 Yates, *Occult*, p. 181.

71 Edward Phillips, *The Life of Milton in John Milton Complete Poems and Major Prose*, ed. Merritt Y. Hughes (Indianapolis: Bobbs-Merrill Company, Inc., 1957), p. 1031.

72 Ibid.

73 Ibid.

74 Ibid.

75 Ibid.

76 Hughes, p. 1032.

77 Hughes, p. 1031.

78 Hughes, p. 1040.

79 Hughes, p. 712.

80 Hughes, p. 1040.

81 Hughes, p. 700.

82 Hughes, p. 1040.

83 Hughes, p. 700.

84 Hughes, p. 703.

85 Hughes, p. 704.

86 Ibid. (my emphasis).

87 Hughes, p. 712.

88 Ibid.

89 Hughes, p. 1032.

90 Hughes, p. 1040.

91 Hughes, p. 1032.

92 Hughes, p. 701.

93 Ibid. (my emphasis).

94 St. Augustine, *City of God*, (New York: Doubleday, 1958), p. 234.

95 Graetz, Vol. V, p. 26.

96 Graetz, Vol. V, p. 27.

97 Graetz, Vol. V, p. 7.

98 Graetz, Vol. V, p. 6.

99 Kant, *Werke* Bd. vii, p. 205-6.

100 Graetz, Vol. V, p. 5.

101 Ibid.

102 Iwo Cyprian Pogonowski, *Jews in Poland: A Documentary History The Rise of Jews as a Nation from Congressus Judaicus in Poland to the Knesset in Israel* (New York: Hippocrene Books, Inc.1993), p. 66.

103 Pogonowski, p. 65.

104 Ibid.

105 Pogonowski, p. 68.

106 Ibid.

107 Ibid.

108 Graetz, Vol V, p. 2.

109 Pogonowski, p. 67.

110 Walsh, *Philip II*, p. 532.

111 Walsh, *Philip II*, p. 527.

112 Walsh, *Philip II*, p. 532.

113 Ibid.

114 Ibid.

115 Ibid.

116 Walsh, *Philip II*, p. 533.

117 Ibid.

118 Iwo Cyprian Pogonowski, *Poland: An Illustrated History* (New York: Hippocrene Books, Inc. 2000), p. 93.

119 Walsh, *Characters*, p. 142.

120 Ibid.

121 Graetz, Vol, V, p. 7.

122 Ibid.

123 Graetz, Vol, V, p. 10.

124 Pogonowski, *Jews*, p. 23.

125 Gerschom Scholem, *Sabbatai Sevi: The Mystical Messiah 1626-1676* (Princeton: Princeton University Press, 1973), p. 2.

126 Scholem, p. 60.

127 Helen Litton, *Oliver Cromwell: An Illustrated History* (Dublin: Wolfhound Press, 2000), p. 28.

128 Gaunt, p. 104.

129 Gaunt, p. 105.

130 Graetz, Vol, V, p. 6.

131 Ibid.

132 Graetz, Vol, V, p. 27.

133 Ibid.

134 Cohn, p. 322.

135 Cohn , p. 323.

136 Ibid.

137 Cohn, p. 326.

138 Cohn, p. 334.

139 Cohn, p. 337.

140 Cohn, p. 340.

141 Cohn, p. 358.

142 Cohn, p. 359.

143 Cohn, p. 360.

144 Ibid.

145 Litton, p. 45.

146 Litton, p. 17.

147 Litton, p. 36.

148 Gaunt, p. 115.

149 Gaunt, p. 116.

150 Litton, p. 50.

151 Litton, p. 55.

152 Gaunt, p. 117.

153 Litton, p. 59.

154 Litton, p. 63.

155 Gaurt, p. 129.

156 Litton, p. 77.

157 Graetz, Vol. V, p. 119.

158 Graetz, Vol. V, p. 120.

159 Scholem, p. 45.

160 Scholem, p. 46. See also Paul Johnson, *A History of the Jews* (Perennial Library 1988) p. 260-262.

161 Scholem, p. 47.

162 Scholem, p. 52. There are however a minority of Jews who still believe that the redemptive task remains with the Messiah. See Yakov M. Rabkin, *A Threat From Within: A History of Jewish Opposition to Zionism* (Zed Books 2006).

163 David Horowitz, *The Politics of Bad Faith: The Radical Assault on America's Future* (New York: The Free Press, 1998), p. 130.

164 Scholem, p. 75.

165 Scholem p. 64.

166 Ibid.

167 Horowitz, p. 131.

168 Ibid.

169 Ibid. (my emphasis).

170 Scholem, p. 67.

171 Scholem, p. 9.

172 Scholem, p. 113.

Endnotes

173 Ibid.

174 Ibid.

175 Scholem, p. 139.

176 Graetz, Vol. V, p. 118.

177 Scholem, p. 166.

178 Scholem p. 139.

179 Katz, p. 177.

180 Katz, p. 178.

181 Ibid.

182 Katz, p. 184.

183 Katz, p. 111.

184 Katz, p. 119.

185 *Menasseh ben Israel and his World*, edited by Yosef Kaplan, Henry Mechoulan, and Righard H. Popkin (Leiden: E. J. Brill, 1989), p. 67.

186 Katz, p. 152. Also in John Dury, "An Appendix," in Edward Winslow, *The Glorious Progress*, p. 93.

187 Ibid.

188 Menasseh, p. 70.

189 Ibid.

190 Menasseh, p. 224.

191 Ibid.

192 Menasseh, p. 225.

193 Menasseh, p. 257.

194 Menasseh, p. 238.

195 Katz, p. 8.

196 Menasseh, p. 92.

197 Katz, p. 190.

198 Katz, p. 196.

199 Rogers, p. 42.

200 Rogers, p. 57.

201 Gaunt, p. 99.

202 Roth, p. 214.

203 Katz, p. 120.

204 Ibid.

205 Katz, p. 125.

206 Menasseh, p. 231.

207 Ibid.

208 Katz, p. 99.

209 Graetz, Vol. V, p. 36.

210 Roth, p. 232.

211 Roth, p. 236.

212 Roth, p. 238.

213 Katz, p. 222.

214 Katz, p. 220. For scholarly discussions of these cases and others see Israel Jacob Yuval, *Two Nations in Your Womb: Perceptions of Jews and Christians in Late Antiquity and the Middle Ages* (University of California Press 2006) and Elliott Horowitz, *Reckless Rites: Purim and the Legacy of Jewish Violence* (Princeton University Press 2006).

215 Katz, p. 221.

216 Ibid.

217 Katz, p. 222.

218 Ibid.

219 Katz, p. 223.

220 Katz, p. 4.

221 Katz, p. 212.

222 Katz, p. 240.

223 Katz, p. 216.

224 Katz, p. 219.

225 Katz, p. 204.

226 Ibid.

227 Roth, p. 256.

228 Katz, p. 227.

229 Ibid.

230 Roth, p. 256.

231 Tuchman, p. 93.

232 Katz, p. 232.

233 Roth, p. 271.

234 Katz, p. 234.

235 Rogers, p. 101.

236 Rogers, p. 105.

237 Scholem, p. 190.

238 Scholem, p. 192.

239 Scholem, p. 196.

240 Ibid.

241 Scholem, p. 122.

242 Graetz, Vol. V, p. 130.

243 Graetz, Vol. V, p. 135.

244 Ibid.

245 Graetz, Vol. V, p. 134. According to Johnson, the difference between Zevi and previous sixteenth-century Messiahs was that his candidature was conceived and presented not only against a background of Orthodox learning, which both he and his impresario possessed, but also in specific terms of Lurianic science with which the whole of Jewry was now familiar. *A History*

of the Jews (Perennial Library 1988).

246 Graetz, Vol. V, p. 135.

247 Graetz, Vol. V, pp. 134-5.

248 Graetz, Vol. V, p. 136.

249 Scholem, p. 520.

250 Scholem, p. 533.

251 Graetz, Vol. V, p. 139 (my emphasis).

252 Scholem, p. 556.

253 Scholem, p. 549.

254 Graetz, Vol. V, p. 137.

255 Scholem, p. 272.

256 Ibid.

257 Scholem, p. 273.

258 Ibid.

259 Scholem, p. 274.

260 Scholem, p. 281.

261 Scholem, p. 286.

262 Scholem, p. 399.

263 Scholem, p. 398. In the light of the Messianic upsurge Johnson notes that "Responding to Nathan's call to penance ... Jews prayed, fasted and took constant ritual baths. They lay down naked in the snow. They scourged themselves" *A History of the Jews* (Perennial Library, 1988), p. 271.

264 Scholem, p. 387.

265 Scholem, p. 388.

266 Scholem, p. 404.

267 Scholem, p. 602.

268 Scholem, p. 579.

269 Scholem, p. 624.

270 Ibid.

271 Scholem, p. 661.

272 Scholem, p. 666.

273 Scholem, p. 672.

274 Scholem, p. 674.

275 Scholem, p. 680.

276 Ibid.

277 Scholem, p. 684.

278 Graetz, Vol. V, p. 155.

279 Scholem, p. 754.

280 Ibid.

281 Scholem, p. 758.

282 Graetz, Vol. V, p. 158.

283 Scholem, p. 824.

284 Scholem, p. 823.

285 Scholem, p. 825.

286 Scholem, p. 823.

287 Scholem, p. 824.

288 Ibid.

289 Graetz, p. Vol. V, p. 162.

290 Scholem, p. 665

291 Scholem, p. 823.

292 Scholem, p. 867.

293 Graetz, Vol. V, p. 5.

294 Scholem, p. 799.

295 Scholem, p. 80s.

296 Ibid.

297 Ibid.

298 Scholem, p. 802.

299 Scholem, p. 693.

300 Scholem, p. 798.

301 as Bernard Levy said in a letter to Karl Marx.

302 Scholem, p. 692.

303 Scholem, p. 693.

304 Ibid.

305 Scholem, p. 793.

306 Ibid.

307 Ibid.

308 Ibid.

309 Scholem, p. 694. Nathan explained Zevi's apology by arguing that, far from being a betrayal, it was in fact the beginning of a new mission to release the Lurianic sparks which were distributed among the gentiles and in particular Islam. While the Jews were restoring the sparks scattered among themselves, the Messiah had the far more difficult task of gathering in the sparks in the alien world. Only he could do it and it meant descending into the realm of evil. Paul Johnson, *A History of the Jews* (Perennial Library 1988) p.272.

310 Scholem, p. 739.

311 Scholem, p. 764.

312 Scholem, p. 770.

313 Scholem, p. 774.

314 Scholem, p 890.

315 Chaim Potok, *Wanderings: Chaim Potok's History of the Jews* (New York: Alfred A. Knopf, 1978), p. 344.

Endnotes to Chapter Twelve

The Rise of Freemasonry

1 Frances A. Yates, *The Rosicrucian Enlightenment* (London and Boston: Routledge & Kegan Paul, 1972), p. 38.

2 Ibid.

3 Yates, *Rosicrcucian*, p. 188.

4 Yates, *Rosicrcucian*, p. 126.

5 Yates, *Rosicrcucian*, p. 127.

6 Ibid.

7 Yates, *Rosicrcucian*, p. 128.

8 Alfred Dodd, *Francis Bacon's Personal Life Story* (London: Rider & Company, 1986, first published in 1910), p. 138.

9 Ibid.

10 Dodd, p. 140.

11 Ibid.

12 Dodd, p. 141.

13 Dodd, p. 158.

14 Yates, *Rosicrucian*, p. 129.

15 Ibid.

16 Francis Bacon, *The Advancement of Learning and New Atlantis* (Oxford: Clarendon Press, 1974), p. 225.

17 Ibid.

18 Ibid.

19 Bacon, p. 229.

20 Ibid.

21 Bacon, p. 230.

22 Ibid.

23 Bacon, p. 235.

24 Bacon, p. 234.

25 Ibid.

26 Bacon, p. 235.

27 Bacon, p. 239.

28 Bacon, p. 241.

29 Bacon, pp. 244-5.

30 Bacon, p. 245.

31 Bacon, p. 245.

32 Walsh, *Philip II*, p. 319.

33 Ibid.

34 Walsh, *Philip II*, p. 320.

35 Walsh, *Characters*, p. 238.

36 Ibid.

37 Walsh, *Characters*, p. 297.

38 Walsh, *Characters*, p. 298.

39 Ibid.

40 Yates, *Rosicrucian*, p. 40.

41 Ibid.

42 Yates, *Rosicrucian*, p. 20.

43 Yates, *Rosicrucian*, p. 21.

44 Yates, *Rosicrucian*, p. 104.

45 Yates, *Rosicrucian*, p. 119.

46 Ibid.

47 Marsha Keith Schuchard, *Restoring the Temple of Vision: Cabalistic Freemasonry and Stuart Culture* (Leiden, Boston, Koeln: Brill, 2002), p. 528.

48 Ibid.

49 Schuchard, p. 529.

50 Schuchard, p. 552.

51 Ibid.

52 Schuchard, p. 559.

53 Schuchard, p. 552.

54 Ibid.

55 Schuchard, p. 555.

56 Schuchard, p. 558.

57 Schuchard, p. 547.

58 Ibid.

59 Ibid.

60 Ibid.

61 Schuchard, p. 537.

62 Schuchard, p. 541.

63 Schuchard, p. 535.

64 Schuchard, p. 537.

65 Katz, *Philosemitism*, p. 219.

66 Schuchard, p. 538.

67 Ibid.

68 Schuchard, p. 539.

69 Schuchard, p. 540.

70 Ibid.

71 Schuchard, p. 541.

72 Ibid.

73 Walsh, *Philip II*, p. 309.

74 Schuchard, p. 546.

75 Schuchard, p. 579.

76 Schuchard, p. 583.

77 Schuchard, p. 589.

78 Schuchard, p. 590.

79 Schuchard, p. 591.

80 Cecil Roth, *A History of the Jews in England* (Oxford: The Clarendon Press, 1949), p. 176.

81 Schuchard, p. 592.

82 Yates, *Rosicrucian*, p. 227.

83 Schuchard, p. 568.

84 Schuchard, p. 596.

85 Schuchard, p. 597.

86 Ibid.

87 Christopher Dawson, *The Gods of Revolution* (London: Sidgwick & Jackson, 1972), p. 16.

88 Schuchard, pp. 612-3.

89 Schuchard, p. 615.

90 Ibid.

91 Schuchard, p. 652.

92 Ibid.

93 Ibid.

94 Schuchard, p. 617.

95 Schuchard, p. 619.

96 Schuchard, p. 616.

97 Schuchard, p. 619.

98 Schuchard, p. 699.

99 Schuchard, p. 700.

100 Schuchard, p. 732.

101 Dawson, p. 16.

102 Roth, *History*, p. 104.

103 Ibid.

104 Ibid.

105 Roth, *History*, p. 200.

106 Schuchard, p. 773.

107 Schuchard, p. 770.

108 Ibid.

109 Ibid.

110 Dawson, p. 16.

111 Ibid.

112 Dawson, p. 20.

113 Margaret C. Jacob, *The Radical Enlightenment: Pantheists, Freemasons, and Republicans* (London: George Allen & Unwin, 1981), p. 83.

114 Dawson, p. 22.

115 Jacob, *Radical*, p. 249.

116 Jacob, *Radical*, p. 153.

117 Jacob, *Radical*, p. 50.

118 Jacob, *Radical*, p. 61.

119 Jacob, *Radical*, p. 62.

120 Jacob, *Radical*, p. 145.

121 Ibid.

122 Jacob, *Radical*, p. 225.

123 Jacob, *Radical*, p. 203.

124 Jacob, *Radical*, p. 145.

125 Ibid.

126 Jacob, *Radical*, p. 168,

127 Marquis de Sade, *Justine, Philsophy in the Bedroom, and other writings*, compiled and translated by Richard Seaver & Austryn Wainhouse (New York: Grove Press, 1965), p. 605.

128 Jacob, *Radical*, p. 169.

129 Jacob, *Radical*, p. 247.

130 Jacob, *Radical*, p. 168.

131 Jacob, *Radical*, p. 223.

132 Jacob, *Radical*, p. 226.

133 Jacob, *Radical*, p. 227.

134 Ibid.

135 Jacob, *Radical*, p. 160.

136 Ibid.

137 Jacob, *Radical*, p. 227.

138 Jacob, *Radical*, p. 230.

139 William J. Whalen, *Christianity and Freemasonry* (Milwaukee: The Bruce Publishing Company, 1958), p. 16.

140 Jacob, *Radical*, p. 99.

141 Ibid.

142 Ibid.

143 Margaret C. Jacob, *Living the Enlightenment: Freemasonry and Politics in 18th Century Europe* (New York: Oxford University Press, 1991), p. 66.

144 Ibid.

145 Jacob, *Living*, p. 67.

146 Jacob, *Radical*, p. 55.

147 Jacob, *Radical*, p. 130.

148 Schuchard, p. 785.

149 Schuchard, p. 786.

150 Ibid.

151 Jacob, *Radical*, p. 124.

152 Whalen, p. 75

153 Whalen, p. 76.

154 Whalen, p. 16.

Endnotes

155 Whalen, p. 17.

156 Ibid.

157 Jacob, *Living*, p. 68.

158 Jacob, *Radical*, p. 131.

159 Ibid.

160 Jacob, *Radical*, p. 132.

161 Jacob, *Radical*, p. 162.

162 Jacob, *Living*, p. 49.

163 Jacob, *Radical*, p. 129.

164 Jacob, *Radical*, p. 130.

165 Jacob, *Living*, p. 37.

166 Jacob, *Living*, p. 6.

167 Jacob, *Radical*, p 102.

168 Ibid.

169 Francis J. Crowley, "Voltaire a Spy for Walpole?" *French Studies*, Vol 18, 1964, pp. 359

170 Ibid.

171 Dawson, p. 26.

172 Jacob, *Radical*, p 104.

173 Crowley, p. 356.

174 Jacob, *Radical*, p. 230.

175 Dawson, p. 27.

176 A. Barruel, *Memoirs Illustrating the History of Jacobinism*, with an introduction by Stanley L. Jaki (Fraser, MI: Real View Books, 1995), p. 166.

177 Barruel, p. 162.

178 Barruel, p. 197.

179 Jacob, *Living*, p. 90.

180 Ibid.

181 Jacob, *Living*, p. 73.

182 Jacob, *Living*, p. 75.

183 Jacob, *Radical*, p. 111.

184 Jacob, *Radical*, p. 162.

185 Jacob, *Living*, p. 115.

186 Jacob, *Living*, p. 147.

187 Jacob Katz, *Jews and Freemasons in Europe 1723-1939* (Cambridge, MA: Harvard University Press, 1970), p. 2.

188 Katz, p. 13.

189 Jacob, *Living*, p. 115.

190 Katz, p. 14.

191 Ibid.

192 Ibid.

193 Ibid.

194 Pope Leo XIII, *Humanum Genus* (Rockford, IL: Tan Books and Publishers, Inc., 1978), p. 16.

195 *Humanum Genus*, p. 12.

196 Jacob, *Living*, p. 23.

197 Jacob, *Living*, p. 24.

198 Ibid.

199 Jacob, *Living*, p. 70.

200 Jacob, *Living*, p. 7.

201 Jacob, *Living*, p. 93.

202 Jacob, *Radical*, p. 217.

203 Jacob, Living, p. 23.

204 Jacob, Radical, p. 235.

205 B. H. Liddell, *Strategy* (New York: Praeger, 1967), p. 380.

206 Ibid.

207 Ibid.

208 Jacob, *Living*, p. 113.

209 Barruel, p. 229.

210 Barruel, p. 230.

211 Jacob, *Living*, p. 57.

212 Jacob, *Living*, p. 72.

214 Dawson, p. 47.

215 Jacob, *Living*, p. 172.

216 Jacob, *Living*, p. 10.

217 Ibid.

218 Ibid.

219 Ibid.

220 Dawson, p. 58.

221 Ibid.

222 Dawson, p. 72.

223 Dawson, p. 73.

224 Dawson, p. 59.

225 James H. Billington, *Fire in the Minds of Men: Origins of the Revolutionary Faith* (New York: Basic Books, 1980), p. 26).

226 Francois Furet, *The French Revolution: 1770-1814* (Oxford: Blackwell Publishers, 1988), p. 62.

227 Billington, p. 32.

228 Billington, p. 29.

229 Ibid.

230 Billington, p. 31.

231 Ibid.

232 Billington, p. 32.

233 Billington, p. 30.

234 Billington, p. 27.

235 Billington, p. 28.

236 Nesta H. Webster, *The French Revolution: A Study in Democracy* (London: Constable and Company, Ltd., 1920), p. 27.

237 Ibid.

238 Webster, p. 28.

239 Webster, p. 27.

240 Webster, p. 30.

241 Webster, p. 28.

242 Ibid.

243 Webster, p. 29.

244 Ibid.

245 Webster, p. 27.

246 Webster, p. 28.

247 Webster, p. 29.

248 Ibid.

249 Webster, p. 30.

250 Webster, p. 32.

251 Ibid.

252 Webster, p. 34.

253 Jacob. *Living*, p. 175.

254 Ibid.

255 Jacob, Living, p. 202.

256 Billington, p. 29.

257 Ibid.

258 Billington, p. 31.

259 Jacob, *Living*, p. 203.

260 Ibid.

261 Jacob, *Living*, p. 213.

262 Ibid.

263 Jacob, *Living*, p. 173.

264 Jacob, *Living*, p. 175.

265 Jacob, *Living*, p. 178.

266 Michel Riquet, *Augustin De Barruel: Un Jesuite face aux Jacobins francs-macons 1741-1820* (Paris: Beauchesne, 1989), p. 11. (All translations mine.)

267 Barruel, p. xiv.

268 Riquet, p. 75.

269 Barruel, p. xii.

270 Riquet, p. 73

271 Riquet, p. 72.

272 Riquet, p. 81.

273 Barruel, p. xiii.

274 Barruel, p. xix.

275 Barruel, p. xxii.

276 Riquet, p. 115.

277 Ibid.

278 Barruel, p. 299; see also Riquet, p. 89.

279 Barruel, p. 299; see also Riquet, p. 89.

280 Barruel, p. 299.

281 Riquet, p. 90.

282 Riquet, p. 91.

283 Riquet, p. 100.

284 Jacob, *Living*, p. 11.

285 Jacob. *Living*, p. 18.

286 Jacob, *Living*, p. 11.

287 Ibid.

288 Barruel, p. 74.

289 Ibid.

290 Ibid.

291 Barruel, p. 112.

292 Barruel, p. 114.

293 Barruel, p. 244.

294 Barruel, p. 220.

295 Barruel, p. 820.

296 Barruel, p. 19.

297 Jacob, *Radical*, p. 113.

298 Jacob, *Radical*, p. 114.

299 Barruel, p. 22.

300 Barruel, p. 27.

301 Barruel, p. 28.

302 Barruel, p. 313.

303 Ibid.

304 Barruel, p. 314.

305 Ibid.

306 Ibid.

307 Barruel, p. 315.

308 Barruel, p. 317.

309 Barreul, p. 318.

310 Ibid.

311 Ibid.

312 Ibid.

313 Ibid.

314 Barruel, p. 320.

315 Ibid.

316 Barruel, p. 327.

317 Ibid.

318 Barruel, p. 339.

319 Vicomte Leon de Poncins, *The Secret*

Powers behind Revolution: Freemasonry and Judaism (Rancho Palos Verdes, CA: GSG & Associates, 1996, reprint of 1929 edition), p. 101.

320 Poncins, p. 102.

321 Paul Johnson, *A History of the Jews* (New York: Harper and Row, 1987), p. 320.

322 Dawson, p. 90.

323 Ibid.

324 Franz Kobler, *Napoleon and the Jews* (New York: Schocken Books, 1976), p. 17.

325 Kobler, p. 18.

326 Kobler, p. 45.

327 Kobler, p. 51.

328 Kobler, p. 57.

329 Kobler, p. 60.

330 Kobler, p. 62.

331 Kobler, p. 59.

332 Kobler, p. 64.

333 Ibid.

334 Ibid.

335 Ibid.

336 Kobler, p. 68.

337 Kobler, p. 72.

338 Kobler, p. 76.

339 Kobler, p. 56.

340 Kobler, p. 81.

341 Kobler, p. 82.

342 Kobler, p. 85.

343 Kobler, p. 100.

344 Kobler, p. 97.

345 Kobler, p. 143.

346 Ibid.

347 Kobler, p. 152.

348 Kobler, p. 153.

349 Kobler, p. 174.

350 Kobler, p. 175.

351 Kobler, p. 162.

352 Riquet, p. 133.

353 Ibid.

354 Ibid.

355 "*tout la bassesse et tous les vices du judaisme,*"

356 Riquet, p. 134.

357 Daniel Pipes, *Conspiracy* (New York, The Free Press, 1997), p. 75.

358 Ibid.

359 Dawson, p. 134.

360 Dawson, p. 136.

361 Ibid.

362 Kobler, p. 166.

363 Kobler, p. 185.

364 Kobler, p. 183.

365 Kobler, p. 184.

366 Kobler, p. 202.

367 Kobler, p. 208.

Endnotes to Chapter Thirteen

The Revolution of 1848

1 Gotthold Ephraim Lessing, *Werke und Briefe in 12 Baenden*, Band 9 Werke 1778-1780 (Frankfurt am Main: Deutscher Klassiker Verlag, 1993), p. 557: "Kaum war der Vater tot, so koemmt ein jeder/ Mit seinem Ring, und jeder will der Fuerst/ Des Hauses sein. Man untersucht, man zankt/ Man klagt. Umsonst; der recht Ring war nicht/ Erweislich." It is worth noting of Lessing the following: "In 1749 the young Protestant dramatist Gotthold Lessing put on a one-act play, *Die Juden*, which for the first time in European literature presented a Jew as a refined, rational human being. It was a gesture of tolerance, warmly reciprocated by Lessing's exact contemporary, a Dessau Jew called Moses Mendelssohn (1729-86)." Paul Johnson, *A History of the Jews* (Perennial Library 1988), p. 299-300..

2 Lessing, p. 559.

O so seid ihr alle drei/ Betrogenen Betrueger! Eure Ringe/ Sind alle drei nicht echt. Der echte Ring/ Vermutlich ging verloren. Den Verlust/ Zu bergen, zu ersetzen, liess der Vater/ Die drei fuer eine machen. (*Nathan der Weise*, III, 7).

3 Ibid. Mein Rat ist aber der: ihr nehmt/ Die Sache voellig wie sie liegt. Hat von/ Euch jeder seinen Ring von seinem Vater:/ So glaube jeder sich seinen Ring/ Den echten.—Moeglich; dass der Vater nun/ Die Tyrannei des Einen Rings nicht laenger/ In seinem Hause dulden wollen!

4 Amos Elon, *The Pity of It All: A History of Jews in Germany 1743-1933* (New York: Metropolitan Books, 2002), p. 62.

5 Elon, p. 63.

6 Barbara W. Tuchman, *Bible and Sword* (NewYork: New York University Press, 1956), p. 145.

7 Elon, p. 58.

8 Elon, p. 56. David Klinghoffer, an Orthodox Jew, says of Mendelssohn that he, "sought to evade the confrontation with Christianity. He valued tolerance more than truth." *Why the Jews Rejected Jesus* (Three Leaves Press 2006) p.219-220.

9 Ibid.

10 Nora Levine, *The Jews in the Soviet Union since 1917* (New York: New York University Press,), p. 49.

11 Elon, p. 76.

12 Elon, p. 70.

13 Elon, p. 69.

14 Elon, p. 4.

15 Elon, p. 74.

16 Elon, p. 80.

17 Elon, p. 107.

18 Chaim Potok, *Wanderiings* (New York: Alfred A. Knopf, 1978), p. 375.

19 Elon, p. 97.

20 Ibid.

21 Alexander Solschenizyn, *Zweihundert Jahre Zusammen* (Muenchen: Herbig, 2002), p. 46. All translations from *Zweihundert Jahre Zusammen*, the German edition of *Dvesti let Vmeste*, are my own. I have not included the German in the notes because it is itself a translation from the Russian.

22 Solschenizyn, p. 47.

23 Solschenizyn, p. 39.

24 Solschenizyn, p. 47ff.

25 Solschenizyn, p. 49.

26 Solschenizyn, p. 50.

27 Solschenizyn, p. 52.

28 Solschenizyn, p. 53.

29 Solschenizyn, p. 56.

30 Solschenizyn, p. 63.

31 Solschenizyn, p. 64.

32 Solschenizyn, p. 66.

33 Solschenizyn, p. 69.

34 Solschenizyn, p. 74.

35 Solschenizyn, p. 114.

36 Solschenizyn, p. 79.

37 Solschenizyn, p. 77. Yuri Slezkine, in reflecting on these kinds of issues in modern day Russia observes, "According to the Polls, Russian Jews who think of themselves as Jewish or binational are more "achievement-oriented" than Russian Jews who think of themselves as Russians. Or, perhaps, more to the point, the Russian Jews who specialize in dangerous and (according to most Russians) morally suspect occupations are naturally keener on preserving their strangeness (Jewishness)...the Mon people of Thailand were divided into rich farmers and river traders. The farmers thought of themselves as Thai and were unsure of their Mon ancestry; the traders thought of themselves as Mon and felt strongly about not being of Thai descent. The main question for the future of Jews in Russia is not whether Jews will become farmers (as some tsars and Communists had hoped). In the age of universal Mercurianism (the Jewish Age), the main question is whether the Russians will learn how to become Jews." *The Jewish Century* (Princeton University Press 2004) p. 362-3.

38 Solschenizyn, p. 70.

39 Ibid.

40 Solschenizyn, p. 35. For a limited survey on the prejudices and the punishments of the Kahal over a lengthy period see; Israel Shahak and Norton Mezvinsky, *Jewish Fundamentalism in Israel*, 2nd ed. (Pluto Press 2004).

41 Solschenizyn, p. 113.

42 Solschenizyn, p. 96.

43 Erich Haberer, *Jews and Revolution in Nineteenth-century Russia* (Cambridge: Cambridge University Press, 1995), p. 6.

44 Ibid.

45 Haberer, p. 5.

46 Haberer, p .13.

47 Haberer, p. 8.

48 Haberer, p. 20.

49 Elon, p. 138.

50 Elon, p. 183.

51 Elon, p. 184. According to Marx biographer Francis Wheen, Heine "Shortly before his death in 1856 he wrote his last will

and testament begging forgiveness from God if he had ever written anything 'immoral'..." *Karl Marx* (Fourth Estate 2000) p. 65.

52 Elon, p. 185.

53 Elon, p. 130.

54 Elon, p. 131.

55 Ibid.

56 Elon, p. 82.

57 Elon, p. 131.

58 Elon, p. 141.

59 Elon, p. 144.

60 Ibid.

61 Elon, p. 146.

62 Paul Johnson, *A History of the Jews* (New York: Harper & Row, 1987), p. 344.

63 Johnson, p. 345.

64 Elon, p. 147.

65 Heinrich Heine, Wikipedia.

66 Elon, p. 148.

67 Elon, p. 144.

68 Jonathan Frankel, "The Communist Rabbi: Moses Hess," *Commentary* (Vol. 41, #6) June 1966, p 81.

69 Karl Marx, "On the Jewish Question," in *The Marx-Engels Reader*, ed. Robert C. Tucker (New York: W. W. Norton & Company, 1978), p. 47.

70 Marx, p. 48.

71 Ibid.

72 Ibid.

73 Ibid.

74 Marx, p. 49.

75 Ibid.

76 Ibid.

77 Marx, p. 52.

78 Marx, p. 50.

79 Marx, p. 52.

80 Marx, p. 51.

81 Ibid.

82 Elon, p. 150.

83 Elon, p. 151.

84 Elon, p. 153.

85 Ibid.

86 Ibid.

87 Elon, p. 157.

88 Ibid.

89 Ibid.

90 Elon, p. 161.

91 Elon, p. 163.

92 Ibid.

93 Elon, p. 164.

94 Frankel, p. 80.

95 Frankel, p. 81.

96 Moses Hess, *Rom und Jerusalem: Die Letzte Nationalitaetenfrage* (Tel Aviv: Hozaah Ivrith, Co. Ltd., 1935), p. 5. All translations are mine.

97 Ibid.

98 Hess, p. 6.

99 Hess, p. 21.

100 Tuchman, p. 115.

101 Hess, p. 12.

102 Hess, p. 13.

103 Ibid.

104 Hess, p. 15.

105 Hess, p. 22.

106 Hess, pp. 24, 26.

107 Hess, p. 26.

108 Ibid.

109 Hess, p. 29.

110 Hess, p. 41.

111 Hess, p. 42.

112 Ibid.

113 Hess, p. 49.

114 Hess, p. 66.

115 Ibid.

116 Hess, p. 84.

117 Hess, p. 89.

118 Hess, p. 97.

119 Hess, p. 102.

120 Hess, p. 103.

121 Hess, p. 110.

122 Hess, p. 112.

123 Hess, p. 125.

124 Hess, p. 126.

125 Hess, p. 130.

126 Hess, p. 129.

127 Hess, p. 130.

128 Ibid.

129 Ibid.

130 Hess, p. 132.

131 Hess, pp. 140-1.

Endnotes to Chapter Fourteen

Otillie Assing and the American Civil War

1 Amos Elon, *The Pity of It All: A History of Jews in Germany 1743-1933* (New York: Metropolitan Books, 2002), p. 136.

2 Eugene D. Genovese, *From Rebellion to Revolution: African Slave Revolts in the Making of the Modern World* (Baton Rouge, LA: Louisiana State University Press, 1979), p. 4.

3 Genovese, p. 104.

4 Ibid.

5 Genovese, pp. 93-4.

6 Genovese, p. 96.

7 Genovese, p. 96.

8 Ibid.

9 Genovese, p. 90.

10 Genovese, p. 97.

11 Genovese, p. 45.

12 Genovese, p. 49.

13 Genovese, (p. 128).

14 Genovese, p. 124.

15 Genovese, p. 104.

16 (Genovese, p. xix).

17 (Genovese, p. 27).

18 Otto Scott, *The Secret Six: John Brown and the Abolitionist Movement* (Murphy, CA: Uncommon Books, 1979), p. 88.

19 Ibid.

20 Scott,

21 Genovese, p. 116.

22 Genovese, p. 81.

23 Scott, p. 113.

24 Scott, p. 89.

25 Scott, p. 74.

26 Scott, p. 75.

27 Scott, p. 73.

28 Ibid.

29 Scott, p. 74.

30 Scott, p. 78.

31 Scott, p. 146.

32 Scott, p. 161.

33 Maria Diedrich, *Love Across Color Lines: Ottilie Assing and Frederick Douglass* (New York: Hill and Wang, 1999), p. 28.

34 Diedrich, p. xxii.

35 Diedrich, p. 7.

36 Diedrich, p. 8.

37 Deidrich, p. 10.

38 Deidrich, p. 29.

39 Ibid.

40 Ibid.

41 Diedrich, p. 54.

42 Diedrich, p. 70.

43 Diedrich, p. 68.

44 Ibid.

45 Diedrich, p. 11.

46 Diedrich, p. 33.

47 Diedrich, p. 35.

48 Diedrich, p. 26.

49 Diedrich, p. 13.

50 Diedrich, p. 26.

51 Diedrich, p. 65.

52 Diedrich, p. 77.

53 Diedrich, p. 81.

54 Diedrich, p. 43.

55 Diedrich, p. 82.

56 Diedrich, p. 84.

57 Diedrich, p. 83.

58 Diedrich, p. 84.

59 Ibid.

60 Diedrich, p. 179.

61 Diedrich, p. 178.

62 Diedrich, p. 177.

63 Diedrich, p. 172.

64 Diedrich, p. 179.

65 Ibid.

66 Diedrich, p. 182.

67 Diedrich, p. 183.

68 Scott, p. 182.

69 Scott, p. 184.

70 Scott, p. 176.

71 Ibid.

72 Scott, pp. 176-77.

73 Richard M. Weaver, *The Southern Tradition at Bay: A History of Postbellum Thought* (New Rochelle, NY: Arlington House, 1968), p. 391.

74 Weaver, p. 389.

75 Scott, p. 354.

76 Scott, p. 178.

77 Scott, p. 163.

78 Ibid.

79 Scott, p. 164.

80 Scott, p. 185.

81 Scott, p. 56.

82 Scott, p. 55.

83 Scott, p. 56.

84 Ibid.

85 Scott, p. 220.
86 Oswald Garrison Villard, *John Brown, 1800-1859: A Biography 50 years After* (New York: Alfred A. Knopf, 1943), p. vi.
87 Villard, p. viii.
88 Villard, p. 1.
89 Scott, p. 202.
90 Scott, p. 263.
91 Scott, p. 202.
92 Scott, p. 217.
93 Scott, p. 229.
94 Ibid.
95 Scott, p. 243.
96 Scott, p. 249.
97 Scott, p. 261.
98 Diedrich, p. 117.
99 Diedrich, p. 120.
100 Diedrich, p. 256.
101 Ibid.
102 Ibid.
103 Diedrich, p. 141.
104 Diedrich, p. 143.
105 Diedrich, p. 230.
106 Diedrich, p. 227.
107 Diedrich, p. 228.
108 Ibid.
109 Ibid.
110 Ibid.
111 Diedrich, p. 229.
112 Ibid
113 Diedrich, p. 211.
114 Diedrich, p. 213.
115 Ibid.
116 Diedrich, p. 214.
117 Diedrich, p. 215.
118 Scott, p. 284.
119 Diedrich, p. 215.
120 Scott, p. 287.
121 Scott, p. 288.
122 Villard, p. 433.
123 Villard, p. 427.
124 Villard, p. 538-9.
125 Scott, p. 236.
126 Scott, p. 235.
127 Scott, p. 299.
128 Villard, p. 563.
129 Ibid.
130 Villard, p. 539.
131 Villard, p. 545.
132 Scott, p. 309.
133 Ibid.
134 Ibid.

135 Villard, p. 475.
136 Villard, p. 529.
137 Villard, p. 476.
138 Villard, p. 517.
139 Villard, p. 566.
140 Villard, p. 567
141 Villard, p. 581.
142 Villard, p. 531.
143 Diedrich, p. 219.
144 Scott, p. 301.
145 Diedrich, p. 219.
146 Diedrich, p. 220.
147 Diedrich, p. 221.
148 Ibid.
149 Ibid.
150 Ibid.
151 Diedrich, p. 222.
152 Ibid.
153 Ibid.
154 Diedrich, p. 240.
155 Diedrich, p. 236.
156 Diedrich, p. 268.
157 Diedrich, p. 286).
158 Ibid.
159 Diedrich, p. 242.
160 Diedrich, p. 248.
161 Diedrich, p. 260.
162 Diedrich, p. 268.
163 Ibid.
164 Diedrich, p. 267.
165 Diedrich, p. 292.
166 Ibid.
167 Diedrich, p. 293.
168 Ibid.
169 Ibid.
170 Weaver, p. 345.
171 Weaver, p. 347.
172 Weaver, p. 350.
173 Weaver, p. 359.
174 Weaver, p. 348.
175 Diedrich, p. 187).
176 Ibid.
177 Diedrich, p. 368.
178 Diedrich, p. 367.
179 Murray Friedman with the assistance of Peter Binzen, *What Went Wrong? The Creation and Collapse of the Black-Jewish Alliance* (New York: The Free Press, 1995), p. 35.
180 Friedman, p. 43.
181 Ibid.
182 Ibid.
183 Friedman, p. 44.

Endnotes to Chapter Fifteen

From Emancipation to Assassination

1 Haberer, p. 13.

2 Haberer, p. 12.

3 Ibid.

4 Solschenizyn, p. 133.

5 Levine, p. 3.

6 Solschenizyn, p. 133.

7 Solschenizyn, p. 153.

8 Solschenizyn, p. 155.

9 Haberer, p. 13.

10 Haberer, p. 14.

11 Ibid.

12 Solschenizyn, p. 137.

13 Ibid.

14 Solschenizyn, p. 139.

15 Solschenizyn, p. 140.

16 Haberer, p. 11.

17 Ibid.

18 Ibid.

19 Haberer, p. 10.

20 Jacques Derrida, "Stucture, Sign, and play in the Discourse of the Human Sciences," in *The Stucturalist Controversy: The Languages of Criticism and the Sciences of Man*, ed. Richard Macksey (Baltimore: Johns Hopkins University Press, 1972) p. 249.

21

22 Solschenizyn, p. 213.

23 Solschenizyn, p. 214.

24 Haberer, p. 16.

25 Haberer, p. 25.

26 Solschenizyn, p. 210.

27 Solschenizyn, p. 206.

28 Solschenizyn, p. 208.

29 Haberer, p. 74.

30 Ibid.

31 Haberer, p. 75.

32 Haberer, p. 76.

33 Haberer, p. 57.

34 Haberer, p. 68.

35 Ibid.

36 Haberer, p. 92.

37 Haberer, p. 95.

38 Haberer, p. 107.

39 Haberer, p. 111.

40 Levin, p. 10.

41 Haberer, pp 155-6.

42 Haberer, p. 174.

43 Haberer, p. 151.

44 Haberer, p. XIII.

45 Haberer, p. 188.

46 Haberer, p. 200-1.

47 Haberer, p. 119.

48 Haberer, p. 122.

49 Haberer, p. 124.

50 Ibid.

51 Haberer, p. 125.

52 Solzhenizyn, p. 211.

53

54 Haberer, p. 151. Albert Lindemann notes that "The rise of the Jews and the parallel, seemingly contradictory pauperization of large numbers of them, had major implications in the Russian Empire, culminating after the turn of the century in a Jewish counteroffensive, inside and outside Russia, against the oppressive rule of the tsars....The overall rate of Jewish population growth for Jews in Russia in the sixty year period from 1820 to 1880 was about 150 per cent, whereas the non-Jewish population increased only 87 percent....Anti-Semitism in Russia...was hardly a hatred without palpable or understandable cause; it had something quite directly to do with a fear that Jews threatened vital Russian interests and values. And this fear, although it connected with exaggerated, even preposterous fantasies about Jews, was related to real factors....For many Russians, their country's Jewish population appeared as a rapidly growing and increasingly hostile body, actively if secretly collaborating with those enemies....Traditional Jews were objectionable enough to [Slavophile] Russian nationalists, but at least Jews of that sort were politically passive...But as hundreds of thousands of Jews began to abandon

their traditional ways and embrace western ideologies, they appeared even more menacing—and were ever more menacing." *Esau's Tears: Modern Anti-Semitism and the Rise of the Jews* (Cambridge University Press 2006) p. 280-281.

55 Haberer, p. 201.

56 Ibid.

57 Haberer, p. 202.

58

59 Haberer, p. 203.

60 Ibid.

61 Solzhenizyn, p. 220.

62 Haberer, p. 263.

63 Haberer, p. 191.

64 Haberer, p. 202.

65 Tuchman, p. 149.

66 Potok, p. 376.

67 Solzhenizyn, p. 181.

68 Ibid.

69 Solzhenizyn, p. 188.

70 Ibid.

71 Solzhenizyn, p. 191.

72 Solzhenizyn, p. 195.

73 Ibid

74 Solzhenizyn, p. 196.

75 Haberer, p. 203.

76 Haberer, p. 217.

77 Haberer, p. 223.

78 Ibid.

79 Haberer, p. 225.

80 Haberer, p. 211.

81 Haberer, p. 253.

82 Haberer, p. 202.

83 Haberer, p. 203.

84 Haberer, p. 187.

85 Haberer, p. 204.

86 Ibid.

87 Haberer, p. 188.

88 Ibid.

89 Haberer, p. 199.

90 Haberer, p. 200.

91 Haberer, p. 201.

92 Haberer, p. 13.

93 Solschenizyn, p. 266.

94 Solschenizyn, p. 271.

95 Haberer, p. 253.

96 Haberer, p. 254.

97 Haberer, p. 253.

98 Haberer, p. 239.

99 Haberer, p. 243.

100 Haberer, p. 244.

101 Haberer, p. 245.

102 Haberer, p. 248.

103 Haberer, p. 254.

104 Ibid.

104 Ibid.

106 Haberer, p. 267.

107 Solschenizyn, p. 281.

108 Solschenizyn, p. 283.

109 Ibid.

110 Haberer, p. 268.

111 The account of the pogrom at Kishinyov is taken from Solschenizyn, p. 311ff.

112 Solschenizyn, p. 320.

113 Solschenizyn, p. 321.

114 Solschenizyn, p. 327.

115 Solschenizyn, p. 321.

116 "On the Jewish Question in Europe," *Civiltà Cattolica,* Vol. VII, Facicule 961, 23 October 1890, p. 16.

117 The account of the pogrom at Gomel is taken from Solschenizyn, p. 330ff.

118 Solschenizyn, p. 331.

119 Ibid.

120 Ibid.

121 Solschenizyn, p. 332.

122 Solschenizyn, p. 438.

123 Solschenizyn, p. 441.

124 Solschenizyn, p. 334.

125 Solschenizyn, p. 335.

126 *Civiltà*, p. 23.

127 *Civiltà*, p. 33.

128 *Civiltà*, p. 32.

129 Ibid.

130 *Civiltà*, p. 8.

131 Ibid.

132 Ibid.

133 Solschenizyn, p. 245-6.

134 *Civiltà*, p. 8.

135 *Civiltà*, p. 16.

136 *Civiltà*, p. 22.

137 Elon, p. 275.

138 *Civiltà*, p. 32

139 Solschenizyn, p. 307.

140 Solschenizyn, p. 306.

141 Solschenizyn, p. 305.

142 *Civiltà*, p. 18.

143 *Civiltà*, p. 21.

144 Ibid.

145 *Civiltà*, p. 22.

146 Ibid.

147 Ibid.

148 *Civiltà*, p. 26.

149 Solschenizyn, p. 338.

150 Solschenizyn, p. 285.

151 Solschenizyn, pp. 289-90.

152 Solschenizyn, p. 293.

153 Solschenizyn, pp. 293-4.

154 Solschenizyn, p. 229.

155 Solschenizyn, p. 228.

156 Elon, p. 271.

157 Ibid.

158 Ibid

159 Solschenizyn, p. 273.

160 Solschenizyn, p. 261.

161 Solschenizyn, p. 340.

162 Solschenizyn, p. 350.

163 Solschenizyn, p. 352

164 Solschenizyn, p. 230.

165 Solschenizyn, p. 233.

166 Solschenizyn, p. 234.

167 Solschenizyn, p. 237.

168 Solschenizyn, p. 401.

169 Solschenizyn, p. 388.

170 Solschenizyn, p. 393.

171 Solschenizyn, p. 403.

172 Solschenizyn, p. 404.

173 Solschenizyn, p. 455.

174 Solschenizyn, p. 417.

175 Solschenizyn, p. 420.

176 Solschenizyn, p. 423.

177 Solschenizyn, p. 430.

178 Solschenizyn, p. 432.

179 Solschenizyn, p. 433.

Endnotes to Chapter Sixteen

From Redemption to the NAACP

1 Harold Cruse, *The Crisis of the Negro Intellectual* (New York: William Morrow & Company, 1967), p. 477.

2 Weaver, p. 307.

3 Thomas Dixon, Jr., *The Clansman: An Historical Romance of the Ku Klux Klan* (Ridgewood, NJ: The Gregg Press, 1905/1967), p. 45.

4 Ibid.

5 Dixon, p. 46.

6 Dixon, p. 46-7.

7 Dixon, p. 8.

8 Dixon, p. 9

9 Dixon, p. 40.

10 Dixon, p. 42.

11 Dixon, p. 116.

12 Dixon, p. 84.

13 Dixon, p. 98.

14 Dixon, p. 137.

15 Dixon, p. 153.

16 Dixon, p. 182.

17 Dixon, p. 294.

18 Dixon, p. 183.

19 Dixon, p. 186.

20 Weaver, p. 306.

21 Dixon, p. 216.

22 Dixon, p. 277.

23 Dixon, p. 262.

24 Dixon, p. 335.

25 Dixon, p. 341.

26 Dixon,, p. 326.

27 Dixon , p. 341.

28 Dixon, p. 374.

29 Dixon, p. 57.

30 Dixon, p. 79.

31 Dixon, p. 101.

32 Dixon, p. 108.

33 Dixon, p. 371.

34 Dixon, p. 291.

35 Dixon, p. 94.

36 Weaver, p. 307.

37 Friedman, p. 50.

38 Michael J. Pfeifer, *Rough Justice: Lynching and American Society 1874-1947* (Urbana and Chicago: University of Illinois Press, 2004), p. 2.

39 Pfeifer, p. 3.

40 Pfeifer, p. 13.

41 Pfeifer, p. 14.

42 Pfeifer, p. 22.

44 Friedman, p. 46.
45 Charles Flint Kellogg, *NAACP: A History of the National Association for the Advancement of Colored People* (Baltimore: Johns Hopkins Press, 1967), p. 10.
46 *Blacks and Jews on the Couch: Psychoanalytic Reflections on Black-Jewish Conflict*, ed. Alan Heimreich and Paul Marcus (Westport, CT: Praeger, 1998), p. 17.
47 Friedman, p. 7, Cruse, p. 59.
48 Friedman, p. 47.
49 Ross, p. 29.
50 Ibid.
51 Ross, p. 30.
52 Ross, p. 66.
53 Friedman, p. 52.
54 Freidman, p. 53.
55 Ibid.
56 Friedman, (p. 58).

57 William B. Gatewood, "Booker T. Washington and the Ulrich Affair," *Journal of Negro History*, Vol. 55, No. 1. (January 1970), pp. 29-44, p. 29.
58 Gatewood, p. 30.
59 Ibid.
60 Gatewood, p. 39.
61 C. Vann Woodward, *Tom Watson: Agrarian Rebel* (New York: Rinehart & Company, Inc., 1955), p. 426.
62 Gatewood, p. 41.
63 Friedman, p. 56.
64 Ross, p. 52.
65 Ross, pp. 58-9.
66 Edmund David Cronon, *Black Moses: The Story of Marcus Garvey and the Universal Negro Improvement Association* (Madison: The University of Wisconsin Press, 1955), p. 130.

Endnotes to Chapter Seventeen

The Trial of Leo Frank

1 Cruse, p. 478.

2 Steve Oney, *And the Dead Shall Rise: The Murder of Mary Phagan and the Lynching of Leo Frank* (New York: Pantheon, 2003), p. 323.

3 Oney, p. 316.

4 Oney, p. 323.

5 Ibid.

6 Oney, p. 325.

7 Ibid.

8 Oney, p. 328.

9 Oney, p. 242.

10 Oney, p. 331.

11 Ibid.

12 Oney, p. 366.

13 Oney, p. 335.

14 Oney, p. 336.

15 Ibid.

16 Oney, p. 453.

17 Oney, p. 99.

18 Oney, p. 184.

19 Ibid.

20 Ibid.

21 Oney, p. 186.

22 Oney, p. 346.

23 Ibid.

24 Ibid.

25 Oney, p. 347.

26 Ibid.

27 Oney, p. 348.

28 Ibid.

29 Ibid.

30 Oney, p. 356.

31 Oney, p. 357.

32 Oney, p. 362.

33 Ibid.

34 Oney, p. 366.

35 Ibid.

36 Cruse, p. 123.

37 Oney, p. 375.

38 Ibid.

39 Oney, p. 377.

40 Oney, p. 378.

41 Oney, p. 8.

42 Oney, p. 384.

43 Ibid.

44 Oney, p. 394.

45 Oney, p. 395.

46 Ibid.

47 Oney, p. 393.

48 Ibid.

49 Oney, p. 397.

50 Oney, p. 398.

51 Oney, p. 402.

52 Oney, p. 403.

53 Oney, p. 398.

54 Oney, p. 404.

55 Ibid.

56 Oney, p. 405.

57 Oney, p. 410.

58 Oney, p. 487.

59 Oney, p. 419.

60 Ibid.

61 Oney, p. 420.

62 Ibid.

63 Oney, p. 446.

64 Oney, p. 447.

65 Oney, p. 453.

66 Ibid.

67 Oney, p. 456.

68 Ibid.

69 Oney, p. 462.

70 Oney, p. 452.

71 Oney, p. 457.

72 Oney, p. 462.

73 Ibid.

74 Ibid.

75 Ibid.

76 Oney, p. 467.

77 Oney, p. 468.

78 Oney, p. 467.

79 Oney, p. 468.

80 Oney, p. 449.

81 Oney, p. 477.

82 Oney, p. 479.

83 Oney, p. 480.

84 Ibid

85 Ibid.

86 Oney, p. 485.

87 Oney, p. 493.

88 Oney, p. 495.

89 Oney, p. 504.

90 Oney, p. 200.

91 Oney, p. 506.

92 Ibid.

93 Ibid.

94 Ibid.

95 Oney, p. 508.

96 Ibid.

97 Oney, p. 512.

98 Oney, p. 558.

99 Oney, p. 574.

100 Oney, p. 575.

101 Oney, p. 574.

102 Oney, p. 578.

103 Oney, p. 580.

104 Oney, p. 584.

105 Oney, p. 589.

106 Oney, p. 590.

107 Oney, p. 591.

108 Ibid.

109 Oney, p. 592.

110 Ibid.

111 Oney, p. 593.

112 Ibid.

113 Oney, p. 599.

114 Ibid.

115 Oney, p. 604.

116 Oney, p. 606.

117 Mary Phagan, *The Murder of Little Mary Phagan* (Far Hills, New Jersey: New Horizon Press, 1987), p. 236.

118 Friedman, p. 63.

119 Friedman, p. 65.

120 Friedman, p. 67.

121 Friedman, p. 71.

Endnotes to Chapter Eighteen

Bolshevism Heads West

1 Solschenizyn, p. 479.

2 Solschenizyn, p. 486.

3 Solschenizyn, p. 487.

4 Salo Baron, *The Russian Jew: Under Tsars and Soviets* (New York: Macmillan, 1976) p. 192.

5 Solschenizyn, p. 488.

6 Solschenizyn, p. 491.

7 Solschenizyn, p. 472.

8 Solschenizyn, p. 477.

9 Solschenizyn, p. 473.

10 Elon, p. 308.

11 Elon, p. 316.

12 Elon, p. 311.

13 Ibid.

14 Elon, p. 312.

15 Alexander Solschenizyn, *Zweihundert Jahre Zusammen: Die Juden in der Sowjetunion,* hereafter cited as Vol. II (Muenchen: Herbig, 2004), p. 54.

16 Solschenitsyn, Vol. II, p. 60.

17 Solschenitsyn, Vol. II, p. 62.

18 Solschenitsyn, Vol. II, p. 66.

19 Solschenitsyn, Vol. II, p. 36.

20 Solschenitsyn, Vol. II, p. 246.

21 Also cited in Solschenitsyn, Vol. II, p. 39.

22 Nora Levin, *The Jews in the Soviet Union since 1917, Volume I The Paradox of Survival* (New York: New York University Press), p. 49.

23 Levin, p. 10.

24 Solschenitsyn, Vol. II, p. 125.

25 Solschenitsyn, Vol. II, p. 126.

26 Baron, p. 202.

27 Baron, p. 203.

28 Ibid.

29 Solschenitsyn, Vol. II, p. 93.

30 Solschenitsyn, Vol. II, p. 92.

31 Solschenitsyn, Vol. II, p. 96.

32 Solschenitsyn, Vol. II, p. 83.

33 Solschenitsyn, Vol. II, p. 84.

34 Ibid.

35 Solschenitsyn, Vol. II, p. 82.

36 Ibid.

37 Solschenitsyn, Vol. II, p. 98.

38 Solschenitsyn, Vol. II, p. 109.

39 Solschenitsyn, Vol. II, p. 110.

40 Solschenitsyn, Vol. II, p. 123.

41 Amos Elon, *The Pity of It All: A History of Jews in Germany 1743-1933* (New York: Metropolitan Books, 2002), p. 344.

42 Elon, p. 346.

43 Ibid.

44 Ibid.

45 Elon, p. 343.

46 Elon, p. 359.

47 Elon, p. 350.

48 Elon, p. 347.

49 Elon, p. 353.

50 Ronald J. Rychlak, *Hitler, the War and the Pope* (Huntington, IN: Our Sunday Visitor Press, 2000), p. 14.

51 Daniel Jonah Goldhagen, "Pius XII, the Catholic Church, and the Holocaust: What Would Jesus Have Done?" *The New Republic,* January 21, 2002, p. 24.

52 Ibid.

53 Ibid.

54 Ibid.

55 Ibid.

56 Ibid.

57 Ibid.

58 Donn de Grand Pre, *Barbarians Inside the Gates: The Black Book of Bolshevism* (San Pedro, CA: GSG & Associates, 2000), p. 62.

59 Goldhagen, p. 22.

60 Daniel Jonah Goldhagen, *Hitler's Willing Executioners: Ordinary Germans and the* Holocaust (New York: Alfred A. Knopf, 1996) and Daniel Jonah Goldhagen, *A Moral Reckoning: the Role of the Catholic Church in the Holocaust and its Unfulfilled Duty of Repair* (New York: Alfred A. Knopf, 2002).

61 Goldhagen, p. 24.

62 Norman Finkelstein and Ruth Birn, *A Nation on Trial: The Goldhagen Thesis and Historical Truth* (New York: Metropolitan Books, 1998), p. 95.

63 Finkelstein and Birn, p. 80.

64 Charles Krauthammer, "Antisemitism thriving in Europe," *South Bend Tribune,* April 30, 2002, A7.

65 Winston S. Churchill, "Zionism versus Bolshevism: A Struggle for the Soul of the Jewish People," *Illustrated Sunday Herald,* February 8, 1920, p. 5.

66 Grand Pre, p. 61.

67 Baron, p. 202.

68 Ibid.

69 Baron, p. 203.

70 Ibid.

71 Grand Pre, p. 61.

72 Vicomte Leon de Poncins, *The Secret Powers Behind Revolution* (Rancho Palos Verdos, CA: GSG Associates, no date), p. 122.

73 Johannes Rogalla von Bieberstein, *"Juedischer Bolschewismus": Mythos und Realitaet* (Schnellroda: Edition Antaios, 2003), p. 65 (all translations mine).

74 Bieberstein, p. 63.

75 Bieberstein, p. 182.

76 Bieberstein, p. 65.

77 Grand Pre, p. 61.

78 Grand Pre, p. 59.

79 Levin, p. 73.

80 Finkelstein and Birn, p. 133.

81 Nathan Glazer and Daniel Patrick Moynihan, *Beyond the Melting Pot: The Negroes, Puerto Ricans, Jews, Italians and Irish of New York City* (Cambridge, MA: The MIT Press, 1963), p. 268.

82 Grand Pre, p. 62.

83 Ibid.

84 Ibid.

85 Levin, p. 2.

86 Levin, p. 4.

87 Levin, p. 10.

88 Ibid.

89 Erich Haberer, *Jews and Revolution in Nineteenth-century Russia* (Cambridge: Cambridge University Press, 1995), p. 150.

90

91 Elon, p. 364.

92 Elon, p. 374.

93 Ibid.

94 Bieberstein, p. 270. For Hitler himself the ideological view of race and biology was fundamental to his thinking. In a speech Hitler claimed, "For the National Socialist Movement is not a cult movement; rather it is a *volkisch* and political philosophy which grew out of considerations of an exclusively racist nature. This philosophy does not advocate mystic cults, but rather aims to cultivate and lead a Volk determined by its blood." In commenting on these passages Michael Burleigh notes "the modern overemphasis upon Nazi biologistic politics is misleading, for it takes the scientists' self-estimation at face value...simply ignoring such revealing concepts as 'the racial soul' is actively misleading" *The Third Reich* (Pan Books 2001) p. 253-254. Such ideologies differ radically and in every way from Christian legislation aiming, however misguidedly, to curb the excesses seemingly encouraged by the Talmud, encouragement that was documented by the scholar Johann Andreas Eisenmenger in Germany in the 17th century.

95 Bieberstein, p. 271. Lindemann observes, with regard to Jews and Bolshevism: "determining the exact number of Jews in the leading ranks of the party is nearly impossible, in large part because of the difficulties of deciding who was Jewish. Simple numbers or percentages fail to address the key issues of visibility and qualitative importance; Jews as prominent party leaders were undoubtedly much more numerous than in the rank-and-file." Lindemann notes, of the party's central committee, the "assertiveness and often dazzling verbal skills of Jewish Bolsheviks, their energy, and their strength of conviction." He goes on to say "it seems beyond serious debate that in the first twenty years of the Bolshevik Party the top ten to twenty leaders included close to a majority of Jews. Of the seven "major figures" listed in *The Makers of the Russian Revolution*, four are of Jewish origin, and of the fifty-odd others included in the list, Jews constitute approximately a third, Jews and non-Russians close to a majority." *Esau's Tears: Modern Anti-Semitism and the Rise of the Jews* (Cambridge University Press 2006) p. 429-430. For some percentages of Jewish involvement in various Bolshevik Committees and the Cheka see Yuri Slezkine, *The Jewish Century* (Princeton University Press 2006) p. 176-177.

96 Bieberstein, p. 245. One person who understood exactly what a Jew was and what the Christian's duty was to such a one was Edith Stein. In her final testament, written in 1939, she says: "I joyfully accept in advance the death God has appointed for me, in perfect submission to his most holy will. May the Lord accept my life and death to the honor and glory of his name, for the needs of his holy Church...for the Jewish people, that the Lord may be received by his own and his Kingdom come in glory...." Roy Schoeman, Stein's fellow convert, reflects on what St. Edith Stein must have thought about the Holocaust and concludes: "she saw in it an aspect of expiatory suffering, expiating the Jews' rejection of Christ. She saw in it a redemptive value for the redemption of the whole world. She saw a specific link between her sacrifice and the special grace needed to bring about the conversion of the Jews." Roy Schoeman, *Salvation is from the Jews: The Role of Judaism in Salvation History from Abraham to the Second Coming* (Ignatius 2003) p. 162 and p.165.

97 Bieberstein, p. 273.

98 Ibid.

99 Bieberstein, p. 196.

100 Bieberstein, p. 271.

101 Bieberstein, p. 281.

102 Bieberstein, p. 219.

103 Elon, p. 366.

104 Elon, p. 402.

105 Ibid.

106 Bieberstein, p. 239.

107 Bieberstein, p. 227.

108 Philip Roth, *The Plot Against America* (Boston: Houghton, Mifflin, 2004), p. 176.

109 Bieberstein, p. 245.

110 Bieberstein, p. 7.

111 Bieberstein, p. 258. Wiesel has shown a propensity to blaspheme God on occasion (see Roy Schoeman, *Salvation is from the Jews: The Role of Judaism in Salvation History from Abraham to the Second Coming* (Ignatius 2003) p. 152-159 and make dubious claims about his past (see David O'Connell, "Elie Wiesel and the Catholics," *Culture Wars*, November 2004) as well as making morally dubious statements about the behavior of the Israeli government (see Norman G. Finkelstein and Ruth Bettina Birn, *A Nation on Trial: The Goldhagen Thesis and Historical Truth* (Owl Book 1998) p. 91-92.

112 Bieberstein, p. 264.

113 Bieberstein, p. 265.

114 Ibid.

115 Bieberstein, p. 226.

116 Ibid.

117 Ibid.

118 Bieberstein, p. 12.

119 Ibid.

120 Bieberstein, pp. 12-3.

121 Bieberstein, p. 17.

122 Bieberstein, p. 232.

123 Bieberstein, p. 235.

124 Bieberstein, p. 104.

125 Bieberstein, p. 236.

126 Bieberstein, p. 259

127 Bieberstein, p. 77.

128 Bieberstein, p. 265.

129 Bieberstein, p. 227.

130 Bieberstein, p. 260.

131 Bieberstein, p. 24.

132 Bieberstein, p. 183.

133 Bieberstein, p. 185.

134 Bieberstein, p. 178.

135 Bieberstein, p. 242.

136 Bieberstien, p. 244.

137 Bieberstein, p. 87. Jewish writer David Klinghoffer says of Buber that he "saw the special essence of the Jewish soul as having pre-existed Sinai...by its nature it sees God at once...also by nature the Jewish soul feels the worlds, in a remarkably visceral way, as unredeemed....Taken together these "foci of the Jewish soul" tend to rule out an acceptance of Jesus as Messiah. The first precludes belief in the Incarnation...a concept that violates what the Jew knows about the transcendent and yet immediately present God. The second precludes the Christian opinion that the Messiah has already come to redeem the world....Because of the two-fold essence of the Jewish soul, in the presence of Jesus worship, with rare exceptions, "secular" and "religious" Jews alike feel the same reaction, the same refusal, the same instinctive turning away. In a word: No." David Klinghoffer, *Why the Jews Rejected Jesus* (Three Leaves Press 2006) p. 216-217.

138 Bieberstein, p. 231.

139 Ronald Modras, *The Catholic Church and Antisemitism: Poland 1933-1939* (Chur: Harwood, 1994), pp. 346-7.

140 Bieberstein, p. 269. Michael Burleigh notes of Graf von Galen that he was "a Jesuit-educated aristocratic reactionary whose opposition to Nazi neo-paganism was implacable, beginning with his early hostility to Rosenberg and ending with his principled denunciations of wartime euthanasia, stances not incompatible with rabid anti-Bolshevism or support for his country at war." *The Third Reich* (Pan Books 2001) p. 292.

141 Bieberstein, p. 132.

142 Bieberstein, p. 141.

143 Bieberstein, p. 237.

144 Bieberstein, p. 236.

145 Bieberstein, p. 266.

146 Bieberstein, p. 280.

147 Bieberstein, p. 277.

148 Solschenizyn, p. 231.

149 David Horowitz, *The Politics of Bad Faith* (New York: The Free Press, 1998), p. 119.

150 Horowitz, p. 119.

151 Horowitz, p. 140.

Endnotes to Chapter Nineteen

Marcus Garvey

1 Edmund David Cronon, *Black Moses: The Story of Marcus Garvey and the Universal Negro Improvement Association* (Madison: The University of Wisconsin Press, 1955), p. 16.

2 David Levering Lewis, *W. E. B. Du Bois: The Fight for Equality and the American Century 1919-1963* (New York: Henry Holt and company, 2000), p. 53.

3 Ibid.

4 Lewis, p. 54.

5 Lewis, p. 51.

6 Ibid.

7 Ibid.

8 Cronon, p. 130.

9 Harold Cruse, *Plural but Equal: A Critical Study of Blacks and Minorities and America's Plural Society* (New York: William Morrow, 1987), p. 152.

10 Cruse, *Plural*, p. 153.

11 Cruse, *Plural*, p. 152.

12 Cruse, *Plural*, p. 160.

13 Friedman, p. 123.

14 Friedman, p. 124.

15 Friedman, p. 123.

16 Friedman, p. 125.

17 Ibid.

18 Friedman, p. 126.

19 Friedman, p. 128.

20 Friedman, p. 127.

21 Cronon, p. 23.

22 Friedman, pp. 84-85.

23 Friedman, p. 85.

24 Friedman, p. 76.

25 Yuri Slezkine, *The Jewish Century* (Princeton: Princeton University Press, 2004), p. 1.

26 Cruse, *Plural*, p. 135.

27 Cruse, *Plural*, p. 136.

28 Ibid.

29 Cruse, *Plural*, p. 137

30 Cruse, *Plural*, p. 138.

31 Friedman, p. 115.

32 Charles Flint Kellogg, *NAACP: A History of the National Association for the Advancement of Colored People* (Baltimore: Johns Hopkins Press, 1967), p. 239.

33 Lewis, p. 4.

34 Ibid.

35 Ibid.

36 Ibid.

37 Lewis, p. 5.

38 Kellogg, p. 239.

39 Ibid.

40 Kellogg, p. 240.

41 Ibid.

42 Ibid.

43 Kellogg, p. 286.

44 Ibid.

45 Ibid.

46 Ibid.

47 Kellogg, p. 287.

48 Ibid.

49 Kellogg, p. 288.

50 Kellogg, p. 289.

51 Ibid.

52 Cronon, p. 47.

53 (Lewis, p. 62).

54 Lewis, p. 63.

55 Lewis, p. 500.

56 Lewis, p. 66.

57 Lewis, p. 65-66.

58 Lewis, p. 66.

59 Lewis, p. 62.

60 Ibid.

61 Lewis, p. 66.

62 Lewis, p. 84.

63 *Blacks and Jews on the Couch: Psychoanalytic Reflections on Black-Jewish Conflict*, ed. Alan Heimreich and Paul Marcus (Westport, CT: Praeger, 1998), p. 18.

64 Ibid.

65 Friedman, p. 78.

66 Ibid.

67 Ibid.

68 Lewis, p. 69.

69 Lewis, p. 71.

70 Lewis, p. 341.

71 Ibid.

72 Lewis, p. 98.

73 Lewis, p. 77.

74 Cronon, p.99

75 Lewis, p. 80.

76 Ibid.

77 Lewis, p. 79.

78 Ibid.

79 Cronon, p. 101.

80 Ibid.

81 Ibid.

82 Cronon, p. 111.

83 Friedman, p. 78.

84 Friedman, p. 79.

85 Lewis, p. 113.

86 Cronon, p. 115.

87 Cronon, p. 118.
88 Cronon, p. 119.
89 Lewis, p. 83.
90 Lewis, p. 149.
91 Ibid.
92 Ibid.

93 Cronon, p. 130.
94 Lewis, p. 150.
95 Cruse, *Plural*, p. 153.
96 Cronon, p. 145.
97 Cronon, p. 152.

Endnotes to Chapter Twenty

The Scottsboro Boys

1 Lewis, p. 10.
2 Friedman, p. 152.
3 Cruse, *Plural*, p. 80.
4 Dan T. Carter, *Scottsboro: A Tragedy of the American South* (Baton Rouge, LA: Louisiana State University Press, 1969), p. 52.
5 Cruse, *Crisis*, p. 54.
6 Ibid.
7 Cruse, *Crisis*, p. 57).
8 Ibid.
9 Cruse, *Crisis*, p. 130.
10 Ibid.
11 Cruse, *Crisis*, p. 51.
12 Cruse, *Crisis*, p. 147.
13 Cruse, *Crisis*, p. 148.
14 Cruse, *Crisis*, p. 149.
15 Cruse, *Crisis*, p. 163.
16 Carter, p. 72.
17 Carter, p. 84.
18 Carter, p. 86.
19 Ibid.
20 Carter, p. 87.
21 Ibid.
22 Ibid.
23 Carter, p. 22.
24 Files Crenshaw, Jr. and Kenneth A. Miller, *Scottsboro: The Firebrand of Communism* (Montgomery, Alabama: The Brown Printing Company, 1936), p. 60.
25 Ibid.
26 Carter, p. 105.
27 Douglas O. Linder, "The Trials of the Scottsboro Boys," www.law.umkc.edu/faculty/projects/FTrials/scottsboro/scottsb.htm
28 Carter, p. 148.
29 Carter, p. 64
30 Cruse, p. 147.
31 Carter, p. 121.
32 Carter, p. 122.
33 Carter, p. 123.
34 Crenshaw, p. 58.
35 Crenshaw, p. 62.
36 Carter, p. 131.
37 Carter, p. 126.

38 Carter, p. 127.
39 Carter, p. 153.
40 Crenshaw, p. 61.
41 Crenshaw, p. 62.
42 Carter, p. 132.
43 Crenshaw, p. 122.
44 Crenshaw, p. 123.
45 Carter, p. 136.
46 Carter, p. 106.
47 Carter, p. 109.
48 Carter, p. 110.
49 Carter, p. 119.
50 Carter, p. 147.
51 Carter, p. 121.
52 Carter, p. 152.
53 Carter, p. 156.
54 Carter, p. 158.
55 Carter, p. 160.
56 Carter, p. 163.
57 Carter, p. 169.
58 Carter, p. 276.
59 Carter, p. 277.
60 Ibid.
61 Carter, p. 278.
62 Crenshaw, p. 260.
63 Ibid.
64 Carter, p. 102.
65 Carter, p. 209.
66 Carter, p. 78.
67 Ibid.
68 Carter, p. 70.
69 Ibid.
70 Ibid.
71 Carter, p. 80.
72 Carter, p. 81.
73 Carter, p. 83.
74 Carter, p. 210.
75 Ibid.
76 Carter, p. 202.
77 Carter, p. 225.
78 Carter, p. 231.
79 Carter, p. 186.
80 Carter, p. 187.
81 Ibid.
82 Carter, p. 232.
83 Ibid.

84 Carter, p. 234.
85 Ibid.
86 Carter, p. 239.
87 Carter, p. 240.
88 Ibid.
89 Carter, p. 242.
90 Carter, p. 244.
91 Ibid.
92 Carter, p. 245.
93 Ibid.
94 Ibid.
95 Carter, p. 246.
96 Carter, p. 247.
97 Carter, p. 250.
98 Carter, p. 256.
99 Ibid.
100 Ibid.
101 Carter, p. 267.
102 Carter, p. 271.
103 Carter, p. 272.
104 Carter, p. 309.
105 Crenshaw, p. 251.
106 Carter, p. 310.
107 Carter, p. 311.
108 Carter, p. 312.
109 Carter, p. 318.
110 Carter, p. 312.
111 Ibid.
112 Carter, p. 253.
113 Linder, op cit.
114 Ibid.
115 Carter, p. 385.
116 Ibid.
117 Linder, op cit.
118 Cruse, *Crisis*, p. 169).
119 Haywood Patterson and Earl Conrad, *Scottsboro Boy* (Garden City, NY: Doubleday & Co., Inc., 1950), p. 57.
120 Ibid.
121 Patterson/Conrad, p. 18).
122 Patterson/Conrad, p. 66.
123 Ibid.

124 Patterson/Conrad, p. 58.
125 Ibid.
126 Patterson/Conrad, p. 112.
127 Carter, p. 452.
128 Ibid.
129 Ibid.
130 Crenshaw, p. 12.
131 Crenshaw, p. 248.
132 Carter, p. 460.
133 Crenshaw, p. 292.
134 Crenshaw, p. 294.
135 Crenshaw, p. 286.
136 Ibid.
137 Friedman, p. 72.
138 Ibid.
139 Carter, p. 251.
140 Cruse, Crisis, p. 125.
141 Lewis, p. 399.
142 Friedman, p. 94.
143 Irving Louis Horowitz, *Daydreams and Nightmares: Reflections on a Harlem Childhood* (Jackson and London: University Press of Mississippi, 1990), p. 87.
144 Horowitz, p. 20.
145 Ibid.
146 Horowitz, pp. 3-4.
147 Horowitz, p. 4.
148 Horowitz, p. 63.
149 Horowitz, p. 78.
150 Horowitz, p. 5.
151 Horowitz, p. 86.
152 Horowitz, p. 88.
153 Horowitz, p. 87.
154 Cruse, *Plural*, p. 148.
155 Cruse, *Plural*, p. 150.
156 Ibid.
157 Cruse, *Crisis*, p. 496.
158 Ibid.
159 Ibid.

Endnotes to Chapter Twenty-one

Revolutionary Music in the 1930s

1 Richard A. Reuss with Joanne C. Reuss, *American Folk Music and Left-Wing Politics, 1927-1957* (Lanham, MD: The Scarecrow Press, 2000), p. 34.

2 Ralph Vaughan Williams, *National Music and other Essays*, second edition (Oxford, New York: Oxford University Press, 1987), p. 62.

3 Reuss and Reuss, p. 26.

4 Reuss and Reuss, p. 67.

5 Reuss and Reuss, p. 26.

6 Reuss and Reuss, p. 40.

Endnotes

7 Ibid.

8 Reuss and Reuss, p. 35.

9 Reuss and Reuss, p. 41.

10 Ibid.

11 Ibid.

12 Reuss and Reuss, p. 42.

13 Ibid.

14 Reuss and Reuss, p. 43.

15 Reuss and Reuss, p. 45.

16 Ibid.

17 Reuss and Reuss, p. 44.

18 Reuss and Reuss, p. 50.

19 Reuss and Reuss, p. 46.

20 Reuss and Reuss, p. 48.

21 Ibid.

22 Reuss and Reuss, p. 47.

23 Ibid.

24 Reuss and Reuss, p. 46.

25 Reuss and Reuss, p. 49.

26 Reuss and Reuss, p. 48.

27 Reuss and Reuss, p. 49.

28 Reuss and Reuss, p. 52.

29 Reuss and Reuss, p. 53.

30 Reuss and Reuss, p. 82.

31 Reuss and Reuss, p. 83.

32 Reuss and Reuss, p. 42.

33 Reuss and Reuss, p. 74.

34 Ibid.

35 Reuss and Reuss, p. 75.

36 Reuss and Reuss, p. 122.

37 Reuss and Reuss, p. 60.

38 Ibid.

39 Reuss and Reuss, p. 69.

40 Reuss and Reuss, p. 19.

41 Reuss and Reuss, p. 124.

42 Reuss and Reuss, p. 125.

43 Reuss and Reuss, p. 76.

44 David King Dunaway, *How Can I Keep from Singing: Pete Seeger* (New York, New York: McGraw Hill Book Co., 1981), p. 41.

45 Dunaway, p. 194. Dunaway, p. 195.

46 Reuss and Reuss, p. 110.

47 Barbara Kirshenblatt-Gimblett, in *Judaism: A Quarterly Journal of Jewish Life and Thought*; Issue No. 185. Vol. 47, no. 1 (Winter 1998), pp. 49-78.

48 Thomas J. Herron, "When is a Church Burning not a Hate Crime?: Jewish Lightning Hits Father Coughlin's Shrine," *Culture Wars* (November 2002), p. 26.

49 Ibid.

50 Herron,

51 Philip Roth, *The Plot Against America* (Boston: Houghton, Mifflin, 2004), p. 264.

52 Roth, *Plot*, p. 228.

53 Roth, *Plot*, p. 264.

54 Roth, *Plot*, p. 265.

55 Ibid.

56 Roth, *Plot*, p. 266.

57 Herron, p. 25.

58 Rogalla von Bieberstein, p. 14.

59 Reuss and Reuss, p. 150.

60 Ibid.

61 Reuss and Reuss, p. 151.

62 Reuss and Reuss, p. 154.

63 Ronald Radosh, *Commies: A Journey Through the Old Left, the New Left and the Leftover Left* (San Francisco: Encounter Books, 2001), p. 36.

64 Ibid.

65 Reuss and Reuss, p. 160.

66 Ibid.

67 Ibid.

68 Ibid.

69 Reuss and Reuss, p. 138.

70 Reuss and Reuss, p. 161.

71 Reuss and Reuss, p. 139.

72 Reuss and Reuss, p. 11.

73 Reuss and Reuss, p. 128 (my emphasis).

74 Shlomo Shafir, *Ambiguous Relations: The American Jewish Community and Germany since 1945* (Detroit: Wayne State University Press, 1999), p. 41.

75 Ibid.

76 Shafir, p. 38.

77 Shafir, p. 42.

78 Shafir, p. 63.

79 Ibid.

80 Ibid.

81 Rev. Denis Fahey, CSSp, *The Kingship of Christ and the Conversion of the Jewish Nation* (Palmdale, CA: Christian Book Club of America, 1993), p. 138.

82 Fahey, p. 140.

83 Ibid.

84 Shafir, p. 47.

85 Shafir, p. 45.

86 James Shapiro, *Oberammergau: The Troubling Story of the World's Most Famous Passion Play* (New York: Pantheon Books, 2000), p. 183.

87 Ibid.

88 Reuss and Reuss, p. 180.

89 Reuss and Reuss, p. 181.

90 Radosh, p. 122.

91 Reuss and Reuss, p. 209.

92 Ibid.

93 Mark Slobin, ed.,*American Klezmer: Its Roots and Offshoots* (Berkeley: University of California Press, 2002), p. 17.

94 Slobin, p. 18.

95 Slobin, p. 19.

96 Ibid.

97 Shafir, p. 37.

98 Shafir, p. 67.

99 Shafir, p. 88.

100 Heinze, p. 98.

101 E. Michael Jones, *The Slaughter of Cities: Urban Renewal as Ethnic Cleansing* (South Bend, St. Augustine's Press, 2004).

102 Norman G. Finkelstein, *The Holocaust Industry: Reflections on the Exploitation of Jewish Suffering* (New York, Verso, 2000), p. 15.

103 Murray Friedman, *The Neoconservative Revolution: Jewish Intellectuals and the Shaping of Public Policy* (Cambridge: Cambridge University Press, 2005), p. 19.

104 Heinze, p. 162.

105 Heinze, p. 273.

106 Friedman, p. 20.

107 Ibid.

108 Friedman, p. 18.

109 Ibid.

110 Elliott Abrams, "Judaism or Jewishness," *First Things* (June/July 1997), p. 19.

111 Ibid.

112 Abrams, p. 21.

113 Abrams, p. 22.

114 Ibid.

115 Friedman, p. 23.

116 Friedman, p. 25.

117 Friedman, p. 23.

118 Friedman, p. 24.

119 Friedman, p. 25.

120 Ibid.

121 Ibid.

122 Leo Pfeffer, "The 'Catholic' Catholic Problem," *Commonweal* (August 1975), p. 302-305.

123 Ibid.

124 Ibid.

125 Ibid.

126 Reuss and Reuss, p. 251.

127 Reuss and Reuss, p. 253.

128 Slezkine, p. 315.

129 Ibid.

130 Finkelstein, p. 14.

131 Ibid.

132 Finkelstein, p. 15.

133 Slezkine, p. 313.

134 Friedman, p. 65.

135 E. Michael Jones, "Manipulating Catholic Support for the War: The Black Operation Known as Conservatism," in *Neoconned Again: Hypocricsy, Lawlessness, and the Rape of Iraq* (Vienna, VA: I H S Press, 2005), p. 175.

136 Friedman, p. 76.

137 Friedman, p. 28.

138 Friedman, p. 77.

139 Radosh, p. 48.

140 Radosh, p. 46.

141 Ibid.

142 Radosh, p. 48.

143 Ibid.

144 Ibid.

145 Radosh, p. 152.

146 Radosh, p. 162.

147 Radosh, p. 26.

148 Radosh, p. 25.

149 Radosh, p. 39.

150 Radosh, p. 33.

151 Radosh, p. 35.

152 Kirshenblatt-Gimblett, op. cit.

153 Kirshenblatt-Gimblett, op. cit.

154 Radosh, p. 49.

155 Ibid.

156 Radosh, p. 54.

157 Radosh, p. 53.

158 Ibid.

159 Radosh, p. 54.

160 Radosh, p. 58.

161 Radosh, p. 59.

162 Bob Spitz, *Dylan: A Biography* (New York: McGraw-Hill Publishing Company, 1989), p. 101.

163 Radosh, p. 62.

164 Radosh, p. 63.

165 Radosh, p. 62.

166 Ibid.

167 Ibid.

168 Ibid.

169 Ibid.

170 Radosh, p.48.

171 Ibid.

172 Ibid.

173 Radosh, p. 152.

174 Radosh, p. 162.

175 Radosh, p. 26.

176 Radosh, p. 25.

177 Radosh, p. 39.

178 Radosh, p. 33.

179 Radosh, p. 35.

180 Kirschenblatt-Gimblet, op. cit.

181 Ibid.

182 Radosh, p. 49.

183 Ibid.

184 Radosh, p. 54.

185 Radosh, p. 53.

186 Ibid.

187 Radosh, p. 54.

188 Radosh, p. 58.

189 Radosh, p. 59.

190 Bob Spitz, Dylan: A Biography (New York: McGraw-Hill, 1989), p. 101

191 Radosh, p. 62.

192 Radosh, p. 63.

193 Radosh, p. 62.

194 Ibid.

195 Ibid.

196 Ibid.

Endnotes to Chapter Twenty-two

Lorraine Hansberry

1 Truman K. Gibson, Jr., "We Belong in Washington Park," *Chicago History*, Fall 2006 (Vol. 34, No. 3), p. 35.

2 Ibid.

3 Gibson, p. 36.

4 Gibson, p. 29.

5 Edward Kantowicz, *The Archdiocese of Chicago: A Journey of Faith* (Booklink) p. 13.

6 Kantowicz, p. 18.

7 Ibid.

8 Kantowicz, p. 24.

9 Kantowicz, pp. 24-25.

10 Kantowicz, p. 31.

11 Friedman, p. 107.

12 Ibid.

13 Friedman, p. 131.

14 Friedman, p. 136.

15 Friedman, p. 137.

16 Ibid.

17 Friedman, p. 134.

18 Friedman, p. 138.

19 cf. My discussion of Paul Blanshard in *The Slaughter of Cities* (South Bend: St. Augustine's Press, 2004).

20 Friedman, p. 139.

21 Friedman, p. 141.

22 Ibid.

23 Gibson, p. 43.

24 Anne Cheney, *Lorraine Hansberry* (Boston: Twayne, 1984), intro.

25 Cheney, p. 2.

26 Cheney, p. 3.

27 Cheney, p. 18.

28 Cheney, intro.

29 Friedman, p. 122.

30 Jerry Watts, ed., *Harold Cruse's The Crisis of the Negro Intellectual Reconsidered* (New

York: Routledge, 2004), p. 19.

31 Watts, p. 21.

32 Cruse, *Crisis*, p. 18.

33 Friedman, p. 120.

34 Friedman, p. 122.

35 Friedman, p. 121.

36 Friedman, p. 127.

37 Friedman, p. 148.

38 Friedman, pp. 150-1.

39 Friedman, p. 151.

40 Friedman, p. 152.

41 Friedman, p. 279.

42 Ibid.

43 Ibid.

44 Friedman, p. 280.

45 Friedman, p. 181.

46 Friedman, p. 290.

47 Ibid.

48 Friedman, p. 289.

49 Friedman, p. 280.

50 Ibid.

51 John Steinbeck, *Travels with Charley in Search of America* (New York: Penguin, 2002), p. 193.

52 Steinbeck, p. 205.

53 Friedman, p. 162.

54 Friedman, p. 121.

55 Friedman, p. 162.

56 Friedman, p. 163.

57 Ibid.

58 Friedman, p. 172.

59 Friedman, p. 174.

60 Friedman, p. 178.

61 Friedman, p. 181.

62 Friedman, p. 183.

63 Friedman, p. 188.

64 Friedman, p. 191.

65 Friedman, p. 193

66 Friedman, p. 185.

67 Friedman, p. 196.

68 Ibid.

69 Ibid.

Endnotes to Chapter Twenty-three

The Birth of Conservatism

1 Friedman, p. 46.

2 Jones, "Black Operation," p. 175.

3 Ibid.

4 Ibid.

5 Ibid.

6 Ibid.

7 Friedman, p. 81.

8 Friedman, p. 83.

9 Friedman, p. 84.

10 Friedman, p. 85.

11 Friedman, p. 90.

12 Friedman, p. 92.

13 Ibid.

14 Friedman, p. 95.

15 Ibid.

16 Friedman, p. 87.

17 Friedman, p. 88.

18 Ibid.

19 Friedman, p. 89.

20 Ibid.

21 Ibid.

22 Ibid.

23 Friedman, p. 98.

24 Aiyana Elliot, director, *The Ballad of Ramblin Jack*, Plantain Films, Winstar video, 2001.

25 Ibid.

26 Radosh, p. 15.

27 Ibid.

28 Radosh, p. 18.

29 Radosh, p. 19.

30 Ibid.

31 Radosh, p. 41.

32 Ibid.

33 Ibid.

34 Ibid.

35 Ibid.

36 Radosh, p. 15.

37 Ibid.

38 Ibid.

Endnotes

39 Ibid.

40 Radosh, p. 17.

41 Ibid.

42 Radosh, p. 65.

43 Ibid.

44 Ibid.

45 Mike DelVecchia, "A.K.A. Gene Shay," www.phildelphiawriters.com:80.

46 Ibid.

47 Ibid.

48 Ibid.

49 Ibid.

50 Ibid.

51 Bob Dylan, *Chronicles* (New York: Simon & Schuster, 2004), p. 7.

52 Ibid.

53 Ibid.

54 Spitz, p. 396.

55 Ibid.

56 Dylan, p. 55.

57 Ibid.

58 Dylan, p. 92.

59 Dylan, p. 18.

60 Ibid.

61 Dylan, p. 19.

62 Spitz, p. 311.

63 Spitz, p. 153.

64 Dylan, p. 20.

65 Ibid.

66 Spitz, p. 538.

67 Ibid.

68 Dylan, p. 37.

69 Ibid.

70 Ibid.

71 Dylan, p. 55 (my emphasis).

72 Dylan, p. 83.

73 Ibid.

74 Ibid.

75 Dylan, p. 83-4.

76 Ibid.

77 Dylan, p. 52.

78 Spitz, p. 166.

79 Spitz, p. 167.

80 Ibid.

81 Spitz, p. 169.

82 The Ballad of Ramblin Jack. winstar.com, synopsis.

83 Ibid.

84 Ibid.

85 Ibid.

86 Spitz, p. 125.

87 Radosh, p. 69.

88 Radosh, p. 76.

89 Ibid.

90 Radosh, p. 77.

91 Ibid.

92 Ibid.

93 Ibid.

94 Dylan, p. 22.
Ibid.

95 *60 Minutes* interview, Bob Dylan.

96 Spitz, p. 117.

97 Spitz, p. 176.

98 Ibid.

99 Spitz, p. 177.

100 Ibid.

101 Ibid.

102 Spitz, p. 178.

103 Ibid.

104 Dylan, p. 76.

105 David Walsh, "A Conversation with Dave Van Ronk," World Socialist Web Site, wsws.org, May 7, 1998

106 Ibid.

107 Spitz, p. 178.

108 Ibid.

109 Ibid.

110 Spitz, p. 180.

111 Ibid.

112 Spitz, p. 140.

113 Spitz, p. 180.

114 Spitz, p. 182.

115 Spitz, p. 225.

116 Ibid.

117 Spitz, p. 228.

118 Spitz, p. 227.

119 Martin Scorcese, *No Direction Home.* PBS Documentary.

120 Ibid.

121 Spitz, p. 189.

122 Ibid.

123 Spitz, p. 190.

124 Spitz, p. 192.

125 Spitz, p. 194.

126 Digital Tradition Mirror, "Folk Sing-

er's Blues"

127 Spitz, p. 132.

128 Spitz, p. 136.

129 Ibid.

Endnotes to Chapter Twenty-four

The Second Vatican Council Begins

1 Vicomte Leon de Poncins, *Judaism and the Vatican: An Attempt at Spiritual Subversion* (London: Britons' Publishing Company, 1967), p. 12.

2 Joseph Roddy, "How the Jews Changed Catholic Thinking," *Look* magazine (Volume 30 No.2), January 25, 1966.

3 Poncins, p. 12.

4 Roddy.

5 Ibid.

6 Ibid.

7 Poncins, p. 13.

8 Roddy.

9 Poncins, p. 11.

10 Ibid.

11 Robert Blair Kaiser, *Clerical Error: A True Story* (New York: Continuum, 2002), p. 86.

12 Kaiser, p. 191.

13 Kaiser, p. 86.

14 *Preparatory Reports Second Vatican Council*, trans. Aram Berard, S.J. (Philadelphia: The Westminster Press, 1965), p. 51.

15 Ibid.

16 Ibid.

17 Berard, p. 52.

18 Berard, p. 153.

19 Berard, p. 154.

20 Berard, p. 155.

21 Heinze, p. 242.

22 Heinze, p. 243.

23 Heinze, p. 242.

24 Ibid.

25 Kaiser, p. 200.

26 Ibid.

27 Ibid.

28 Ibid.

29 Ibid.

30 Ibid.

31 Kaiser, p. 112.

32 Kaiser, p. 101.

33 Kaiser, p. 102.

34 Ibid.

35 Roddy.

36 Ibid.

37 Ibid.

38 Ibid.

39 Ibid.

40 Ibid.

41 Ibid.

42 Ibid.

43 Ibid.

44 Roddy.

45 Kaiser, p. 125.

46 Kaiser, p. 189.

47 Kaiser, p. 140.

48 Ibid.

49 Ibid.

50 Kaiser, p. 181.

51 Kaiser, p. 190.

52 Ibid.

53 Kaiser, p. 191.

54 Ibid.

55 Kaiser, p. 213.

56 Ibid.

57 Kaiser, p. 214.

58 Kaiser, p. 229.

59 Kaiser, p. 230.

60 Kaiser, p. 260.

61 Kaiser, p. 205.

62 Kaiser, p. 149.

63 Ibid.

64 cf. E. Michael Jones, *John Cardinal Krol and the Cultural Revolution*, p. 257.

65 Kaiser, p. 240.

66 Ibid.

67 Michael Serafian, *The Pilgrim* (New York: Farrar, Straus, and Company, 1964), p. 51.

68 Serafian, p. 52.

69 Roddy.

Folk Music Meets the Civil Rights Movement

1 Radosh, p. 76.

2 Ibid.

3 Radosh, p. 80.

4 Ibid.

5 Radosh, p. 83.

6 Spitz, p. 238.

7 Ibid.

8 Reuss and Reuss, p. 10.

9 Reuss and Reuss, p. 1.

10 Reuss and Reuss, p. 2.

11 Ibid.

12 Reuss and Reuss, p. 3.

13 Ibid.

14 Reuss and Reuss, p. 4.

15 Ibid.

16 Reuss and Reuss, p. 6.

17 Spitz, p. 233.

The Sign in Sidney Brustein's Window

1 Friedman, p. 204.

2 Friedman, p. 205.

3 Cruse, *Crisis*, p. 480.

4 Friedman, p. 216.

5 Robert Nemiroff, *To be Young, Gifted and Black: Lorraine Hansberry in her own Words*, adapted by Robert Nemiroff (Englewood Cliffs, NJ: Prentice-Hall, Inc., 1969), p. 198.

6 Nemiroff, p. 201.

7 Ibid.

8 Friedman, p. 113.

9 Cruse, *Crisis*, p. 488.

10 Friedman, p. 113.

11 Cruse, *Crisis*, p. 488.

12 Cruse, *Crisis*, p. 489.

13 Cruse, *Crisis*, p. 102.

14 Cruse, *Crisis*, p. 484.

15 Cheney, p. 24.

16 Ibid.

17 Lorraine Hansberry, *The Sign in Sidney Brustein's Window*, Robert Nemiroff, editor (New York: Random House, 1987), p. 211.

18 Hansberry, *Brustein*, p. 320.

19 Hansberry, *Brustein*, p. 289.

20 Cheney, p. 52.

21 Cheney, p. 54.

22 Cheney, p. 62.

23 Hansberry, *Brustein*, p. 266.

24 Cheney, p. 61.

25 Cheney, p. 63.

26 John W. Donahue, "Bench Marks," *America*, 140.2 (20 Jan 1979), p. 144.

27 Cheney, p. 24.

28 Nemiroff, p. 185.

29 Nemiroff, p. 186.

30 Ibid.

31 Cheney, p. 31.

32 Richard M Leeson, *Lorraine Hansberry: A Research and Production Sourcebook* (Westport, CT: Greenwood Press, 1997), p. 8.

33 Cheney, p. 32.

34 Hansberry, *Brustein*, p. 162.

35 Hansberry, *Brustein*, p. 187.

36 Hansberry, *Brustein*, p. 190.

37 Hansberry, *Brustein*, p. 284.

38 Leeson, p. 83.

39 Friedman, p. 214.

40 Watts, p. 4.

41 Watts, p. 125.

42 Watts, p. 133.

43 Cheney, p. 32.

44 Kantowicz, p. 56.

45 Kantowicz, p. 62.

46 Kantowicz, p. 56.

47 David J. Garrow, *Bearing the Cross: Martin Luther King, Jr. and the Southern Christian Leadership Conference* (New York: William Morrow and Company, Inc., 1986), p. 500.

48 John McGreevy, *Parish Boundaries*, p. 197.

49 Stephen B. Oates, *Let the Trumpet Sound: The Life of Martin Luther King, Jr.* (New York: Harper and Row, 1982), p. 388.

50 Garrow, p. 493.

51 Friedman, p. 239.

52 Friedman, p. 241.

53 Ibid.

54 Friedman, p. 249.

55 Friedman, p. 253.

Endnotes to Chapter Twenty-seven

The Third Session of the Council Begins

1 Poncins, p. 10.

2 Poncins, p. 133.

3 Ibid.

4 Ibid.

5 Ibid.

6 Ibid.

7 Poncins, p. 143.

8 Ibid.

9 Poncins, p. 138.

10 Poncins, p. 139.

11 Ibid.

12 Ibid.

13 Poncins, p. 137.

14 Roddy.

15 Ibid.

16 Ibid.

17 Ibid.

18 Ibid.

19 Ibid.

20 Ibid.

21 Ibid.

22 Ibid.

23 Slezkine, p. 1.

24 Friedman, p. 12.

25 Friedman, p. 13.

26 Friedman, p. 17.

27 Friedman, p. 204.

28 Slezkine, p. 325.

29 Friedman, p. 16.

30 Friedman, p. 16.

31 Ibid.

32 Heinze, p. 323.

33 Ibid.

34 Ibid.

35 Slezkine, p. 319.

36 Slezkine, p. 2.

37 Heinze, p. 6.

38 Heinze, p. 13.

39 Ibid.

40 Heinze, p. 14.

41 Heinze, p. 111.

42 Heinze, p. 108.

43 Heinze, p. 109.

44 Heinze, p. 112-13.

45 Heinze, p. 281.

46 Heinze, p. 283.

47 Heinze, p. 284.

48 cf. E. Michael Jones, *Libido Dominandi: Sexual Liberation and Political Control*, p. 464ff

49 Ibid.

50 Heinze, p. 312.

51 Ibid.

52 Heinze, p. 315.

53 Heinze, p. 296.

54 Heinze, p. 298.

55 Spitz, p. 304.

56 Ibid.

57 Ibid.

58 Spitz, p. 308.

59 Ibid. (my emphasis).

60 Ibid.

61 Spitz, p. 309.

62 Spitz, p. 310.

63 Ibid.

64 Spitz, p. 313 (my emphasis).

65 Walsh, Van Ronk interview, wsws. org.

66 Ibid.

67 Ibid.

68 Dunaway, p. 266.

69 Dunaway, p. 257.

70 Ibid.

71 Poncins, p. 152.

72 Poncins, p. 134.

73 Poncins, p. 154.

74 Ibid. In truth it was people like Poncins who showed the greatest respect for Jewish tradition precisely because he saw it as his own. Joseph Cardinal Ratzinger, who has reflected much on Jewish questions wrote of the fulfillment of the old promises: "On the one hand Jesus broadened the Law, wanted to open it up, not as a liberal reformer, not out of lesser loyalty to the Law, but in strictest obedience to its fulfillment, out of his being one with the Father in whom alone the Law and promise are one and in whom Israel could become blessing and salvation to the nations. On the other hand, Israel "had to" see here something much more serious than a violation of this or that commandment, namely the injuring of basic obedience, of the actual core of its revelation and faith: hear O Israel, your God is one God....The universalizing of the Torah by Jesus...is not the extraction of some universal moral prescriptions from the living whole of God's revelation. It preserves the unity of cult snf ethos. The ethos remains grounded and anchored in the cult, in the worship of God, in such a way that the entire cult is bound together in the Cross, indeed, for the first time has become fully real.... on the Cross Jesus opens up and fulfills the wholeness of the Law and gives it thus to the pagans, who can now accept it as their own in this its wholeness, thereby becoming children of Abraham." *Many Religions—One Covenant* (Ignatius 1999) p. 39-42.

75 Poncins, p. 31.

76 Ibid.

77 Poncins, p. 18.

78 Poncins, p. 18-9.

79 Yona Metzger, "Yesterday, Today and Tomorrow," *America*, October 24, 2005), p. 13-4

80 Poncins, p. 28.

81 Poncins, p. 54.

82 Poncins, p. 55.

83 Poncins, p. 59.

84 Poncins, p. 11.

85 Poncins, p. 140.

86 Ibid.

87 Poncins, p. 141.

88 Poncins, p. 78.

89 Poncins, p. 78-9.

90 Poncins, p. 102.

91 Ibid.

92 Poncins, pp. 104, 106.

93 Poncins, p. 35.

94 Ibid.

95 Ibid.

96 Ibid.

97 Poncins, p. 36.

98 Ibid.

99 Ibid.

100 Poncins, p. 37.

101 Poncins, p. 120.

102 Ibid.

103 Poncins, p. 34.

104 Poncins, p. 33.

105 Poncins, p. 154.

106 Roddy.

107 Ibid.

108 Ibid.

109 Ibid.

110 Ibid.

111 Ibid.

112 *Vatican Council II*, Austin Flannery, O.P., editor (Collegeville: Liturgical Press, 1980), p. 741. On this crucial question Joseph Cardinal Ratzinger reflects that, "For the believing Christian who sees in the Cross, not a historical accident, but a real theological occurrence, these statements [CCC 598] are not mere edifying commonplaces in terms of which one must refer to the historical realities. Rather these affirmations penetrate into the core of the matter. This core consists in the drama of human sin and divine love; human sins leads to God's love for man assuming the figure of the

Cross. Thus on the one had, sin is responsible for the Cross, but on the other, the Cross is the overcoming of sin through God's more powerful love...Jesus' blood raises no calls for retaliation but calls all to reconciliation. It has itself become, as the Letter to the Hebrews shows, a permanent Day of Atonement to God". *Many Religions—One Covenant* (Ignatius 1999) p. 44-45. While Ratzinger focuses on the theological meaning and the Catechism's words at 598 David Klinghoffer discusses historical question of Jewish rejection of Christ in the gospels. While only using the term rejection in scare quote he revealingly says: "To be precise, among those who knew him, rather than outright denial, it was more a turning away, a questioning of the authenticity or even the importance of the personas he adopted." *Why the Jews Rejected Jesus* (Three Leaves Press 2006) p. 48.

113 Poncins, p. 147.

114 Poncins, p. 147-8.

115 Poncins, p. 148.

116 Poncins, p. 145.

117 Roddy.

118 Ibid.

119 Ibid.

120 Ibid.

121 Ibid.

122 AS III, VIII, p. 640, his translation

123 AS III, VIII, p. 648, his translation.

124 Brian Harrison, O.S., "Letters to the Editor," *Culture Wars*.

125 *Origins*, (December 19, 2002, Vol. 32, No. 28), p. 464 (my emphasis).

126 Roddy.

127 *Vatican Council II*, p. 741.

128 Poncins, p. 149.

129 Poncins, p. 149-50.

130 Poncins, p. 150.

131 Ibid.

132 Shapiro, p. 12.

133 Shapiro, p. 74.

134 David O' Connell, personal communication.

135 Shapiro, p. 74.

136 Ibid.

137 Shapiro, p. 46.

138 Shapiro, p. 12.

139 Shapiro, p. 14.

140 Shapiro, p. 80.

141 Shapiro, p. 96.

142 Shapiro, p. 95.

143 Shapiro, p. 96.

144 Shapiro, p. 89.

145 Shapiro, p. 90.

146 Ibid.

147 Ibid.

148 Ibid.

149 Shapiro, p. 91.

150 Ibid.

152 Ibid. (my emphasis).

153 Shapiro, p. 92 (my emphasis).

154 Ibid.

155 Ibid.

156 Jones, *Libido*, p. 462.

157 Friedman, p. 107.

158 Friedman, p. 115.

159 Friedman, p. 127.

160 p. 353. For authoritative accounts of how the 1967 Six Day War was basically a war of Israeli aggression see Zeev Maoz, *Defending the Holy Land: A Critical Analysis of Israel's Security and Foreign Policy* (University of Michigan 2006), and Tom Segev, *1967: Israel, the War, and the Year that Transformed the Middle East* (Metropolitan Books 2007).

161 Friedman, p. 124.

162 See also lukeford.com

Endnotes to Chapter Twenty-eight

Jews and Abortion

Endnotes

1 Bernard N. Nathanson, MD with Richard N. Ostling, *Aborting America* (Toronto: Life Cycle Books, 1979), p. 35.

2 Nathanson, *Aborting*, p. 1.

3 Ibid.

4 Nathanson, *Aborting*, p. 5.

5 Ibid.

6 Ibid.

7 Nathanson, *Aborting*, p. 13.

8 Nathanson, *Aborting*, p. 14.

9 Nathanson, *Aborting*, p. 23.

10 Ibid.

11 Nathanson, *Aborting* ,p. 28.

12 Nathanson, *Aborting*, p. 31.

13 Ibid.

14 Nathanson, *Aborting*, p. 60.

15 Bernard Nathanson, MD, *The Abortion Papers: Inisde the Abortion Mentality* (New York: Frederick Fell Publishers, Inc., 1983), p. 192. Protestant minister and NARAL executive Committee Member, Jesse Lyons of the Riverside Church, assembled clerical abortion promoters, including representatives from: the National Council of Churches, YMCA, Women's Division of the United Presbyterian Church; Union of American Hebrew Congregations, Lutheran Church in America; Women's Division of the United Methodist Church; United Church of Christ; United Methodist church; United Presbyterian Church in the USA; Clergy Consultation Service; American Jewish Congress; American Friends Service committee; American Ethical Union, and American Baptist Convention. Interested but unable to attend: Churchwomen United; Episcopal Churchmen of the USA; Unitarian Universalist Association; Women's Federation Episcopal Church; B'nai Brith, and the American Humanist Association. Ibid.

16 David Horowitz, *The Politics of Bad Faith: The Radical Assault on America's Future*, (New York: The Free Press, 1998),p. 74.

17 Nathanson, *Aborting*, p. 33.

18 Ibid.

19 Nathanson, *Aborting*, p. 51.

20 Ibid.

21 Nathanson, *Aborting*, p. 52.

22 Ibid.

23 Nathanson, *Aborting*, p. 33.

24 Nathanson, *Aborting*, p. 61.

25 Nathanson, *Papers*, p. 187.

26 Nathanson, *Papers*, p. 200.

27 Ibid.

28 Ibid.

29 Nathanson, *Papers*, p. 180.

30 Nathanson, *Papers*, p. 181.

31 Nathanson, *Papers*, p. 185.

32 Nathanson, *Papers*, p. 186.

33 Ibid.

34 Nathanson, *Papers*, p. 186, 188.

35 Nathanson, *Papers*, p. 189.

36 Ibid.

37 Nathanson, *Papers*, p. 190.

38 Ibid.

39 Ibid.

40 Nathanson, *Papers*, p. 191.

41 Nathanson, *Papers*, p. 192.

42 Nathanson, *Papers*, p. 200.

43 Nathanson, *Papers*, p. 201.

44 Ibid.

45 cf. E. Michael Jones, *Slaughter of Cities*.

46 Nathanson, *Papers*, p. 213.

Endnotes to Chapter Twenty-nine

The Black Panthers

1 David Horowitz, *Radical Son: A Journey through Our Times* (New York: The Free Press, 1997), p. 221.
2 Horowitz, *Radical*, p. 161.
3 Horowitz, *Radical*, p. 162.
4 Hugh Pearson, *The Shadow of the Panther: Huey Newton and the Price of Black Power in America* (Reading, MA: Addison-Wesley Publishing Company, 1994), p. 110.
5 Horowitz, *Radical*, p. 275.
6 Horowitz, *Radical*, p. 227.
7 Friedman, p. 239.
8 Pearson, p. 53.
9 Pearson, p. 125.
10 Horowitz, *Radical*, p. 164.
11 Horowitz, *Radical*, p. 111.
12 Ibid.
13 Horowitz, *Radical*, p. 117.
14 Horowitz, *Radical*, p. 108.
15 Ibid.
16 Horowitz, *Radical*, p. 275.
17 Horowitz, *Radical*, p. 254.
18 Ibid.
19 Ibid.
20 Ibid.
21 David Horowitz, *The Politics of Bad Faith: The Radical Assault on America's Future* (New York: The Free Press, 1998), p. 118.
22 Horowitz, *Bad Faith*, p. 119.
23 Horowitz, *Bad Faith*, p. 128.
24 Horowitz, *Bad Faith*, p. 131.
25 Ibid.
26 Ibid.
27 Horowitz, *Bad Faith*, p. 119.
28 Horowitz, *Bad Faith*, p. 125.
29 Horowitz, *Radical*, p. 254.
30 Horowitz, *Radical*, p. 279.
31 Horowitz, *Radical*, p. 40.
32 Ibid.
33 Horowitz, *Radical*, p. 41.
34 Horowitz, *Radical*, p. 44.
35 Horowitz, *Radical*, p. 18.
36 Horowitz, *Radical*, p. 30.
37 Horowitz, *Radical*, p. 27.
38 Horowitz, *Radical*, p. 32.
39 Irving Louis Horowitz, *Daydreams and Nightmares: Reflections on a Harlem Childhood* (Jackson and London: University Press of Mississippi, 1990), p. 63.
40 I. L. Horowitz, p. 65.
41 Ibid.
42 I. L. Horowitz, p. 71.
43 I. L. Horowitz, p. 67.
44 I. L. Horowitz, p. 78.
45 I. L. Horowitz, p. 77.
46 Horowitz, *Radical*, p. 39.
47 Horowitz, *Radical*, p. 40.
48 Horowitz, *Radical*, p. 43.
49 Ibid.
50 Horowitz, *Radical*, p. 44.
51 Horowitz, *Radical*, p. 43.
52 Horowitz, *Radical*, p. 44.
53 Horowitz, *Radical*, p. 102.
54 Horowitz, *Radical*, p. 103.
55 Ibid.
56 Ronald Radosh, *Commies: A Journey Through the Old Left, the New Left and the Leftover Left* (San Francisco: Encounter Books, 2001), p. 108.
57 Horowitz, *Radical*, p. 103.
58 Horowitz, *Radical*, p. 276.
59 Horowitz, p. 161.
60 Pearson, p. 104.
61 Pearson, p. 106.
62 Ibid.
63 Dan T. Carter, *Scottsboro: A Tragedy of the American South* (Baton Rouge, LA: Louisiana State University Press, 1969), p. 250.
64 Pearson, p. 107.
65 Tom Wolfe, *Radical Chic & Mau-Mauing the Flak Catchers* (New York: Farrar, Straus, and Giroux, 1970), p. 126.
66 Horowitz, *Radical*, p. 168.
67 Ibid.
68 Horowitz, *Radical*, p. 163.
69 Horowitz, *Radical*, p. 102.
70 Horowitz, *Radical*, p. 162.
71 Ibid.
72 Ibid.
73 Horowitz, *Radical*, p. 164.
74 Ibid.
75 Pearson, p. 147.
76 Pearson, p. 150.
77 Pearson, p. 152.
78 Ibid.
79 Ibid.
80 Pearson, p. 156.
81 Wolfe, p. 6.
82 Ibid.
83 Horowitz, *Radical*, p. 170.
84 Pearson, p. 215.
85 David Horowitz, *Hating Whitey and other Progressive Causes* (Dallas, TX: Spence Publishing Company, 1999), p. 126.
86 Horowitz, *Whitey*, p. 137.
87 Horowitz, *Whitey*, p. 133.
88 Pearson, p. 339.
89 Ibid.
90 Ibid.
91 Ibid.

92 Pearson, p. 225.

93 Ibid.

94 Pearson, p. 247.

95 Horowitz, *Whitey*, p. 98.

96 Ibid.

97 Ibid.

98 Ibid.

99 Horowitz, *Whitey*, p. 104.

100 Horowitz, *Whitey*, p. 99.

101 Horowitz, *Radical*, p. 235.

102 Horowitz, *Radical*, p. 173.

103 Horowitz, *Radical*, p. 174.

104 Horowitz, *Whitey*, p. 120.—"Other than making love to a Sister, downing a pig is the greatest feeling in the world. Have you ever seen a pig shot with a .45 automatic, Sister Elaine?...Well, it's a magnificent sight"—

105 Ibid.

106 Horowitz, *Whitey*, p. 120.

107 Horowitz, *Radical*, p. 269.

108 Pearson, p. 294.

109 Pearson, p. 308.

110 Pearson, p. 314.

111 Horowitz. *Radical*, p. 309.

112 Horowitz,,*Radical*, p. 310.

113 Horowitz, *Radical*, p. 309.

114 Ibid.

115 Horowitz, *Radical*, p. 347.

116 Horowitz, *Radical*, p. 276.

Endnotes to Chapter Thirty

The Jewish Messiah Arrives Again

1 James D. Bloom, *Gravity Fails: The Comic Jewish Shaping of Modern America* (Westport, CT: Praeger, 2003), p. 24.

2 Alan Cooper, *Philip Roth and the Jews* (Albany: State University of New York Press, 1996), p. 106.

3 Philip Roth, *Portnoy's Complaint* (New York: Vintage, 1994), p. 3.

4 Ibid.

5 Roth, *Portnoy*, p. 152.

6 Ibid.

7 Ibid.

8 Ibid.

9 Roth, *Portnoy*, p. 152-53 (my emphasis).

10 Ibid.

11 Cooper, p. 110.

12 Cooper, p. 111.

13 Cooper, p. 116.

14 Eldridge Cleaver, *Soul on Ice*.

15 Ibid.

16 Cleaver.

17 Roth, *Portnoy*, p. 209.

18 Ibid.

19 Cooper, p. 109.

20 Ibid.

21 Ibid.

22 James Bloom, p. xii.

23 Roth, *Portnoy*, p. 233.

24 Irving Howe, Philip Roth Reconsidered, *Commentary*, (December 1972), p. 74.

25 Howe, p. 76.

26 Ibid.

27 Ibid.

28 Ibid.

29 Norman Podhoretz, "Laureate of the New Class", *Commentary*, (December 1972), p. 4.

30 Ibid.

31 Ibid.

32 Cooper, p. 5.

33 Roth, *Portnoy*, p. 150.

34 Cooper, p. 168.

35 Cooper, p. 169.

36 Cooper, p. 110 (my emphasis).

37 Cooper, p. 10.

38 Cooper, p. 12.

39 Philip Roth, *My Life as a Man* (New York: Holt, Rinehart and Winston, 1970), p. 34.

40 Roth, *Man*, p. 58.

41 Roth, *Man*, p. 70.

42 Roth, *Man*, p. 94.

43 Ibid.

44 Roth, *Man*, p. 70.

45 Roth, *Man*, p. 161.

46 Ibid.

47 Roth, *Man*, p. 172.

48 Roth, *Man*, p. 190.

49 Roth, *Man*, p. 245.

50 Roth, *Portnoy*, p. 75.

51 Roth, *Portnoy*, p. 170.

52 Ibid.

53 Roth, *Portnoy*, p. 171.

54 Roth, *Portnoy*, p. 174.

55 Roth, *Portnoy*, p. 79.

56 Roth, *Portnoy*, p. 80.

57 Roth, *Portnoy*, p. 124.

58 Roth, *Portnoy*, p. 103.

59 Roth, *Portnoy*, p. 124.

60 Roth, *Portnoy*, p. 104.

61 Roth, *Portnoy*, p. 124.

62 Cooper, p. 104.

63 Cooper, p. 100.

64 Bloom, p. 119.

65 Bloom, p. 15.

66 Ibid.

67 Bloom, p. 16.

68 Ibid.

69 Roth, *Portnoy*, p. 40.

70 Bloom, p. 1.

71 Ibid.

72 Bloom, p. 65.

73 Bloom, p. 66.

74 Ibid.

75 Ibid.

76 Ibid.

77 Bloom, p. 67.

78 Bloom, p. 23-4.

79 Bloom, p. 48.

80 Ibid.

81 Bloom, p. 27.

82 Ibid.

83 Bloom, p. 28.

84 Ibid.

85 Ibid.

86 Bloom, p. 34.

87 Bloom, p. 35.

88 Bloom, p. 137.

89 Ibid.

90 Bloom, p.

91 Roth, *Portnoy*, p. 235 (my emphasis).

92 Roth, *Portnoy*, p. 144.

93 Roth, *Portnoy*, p. 237.

94 The material on Al Goldstein was taken from Luke Ford's website, lukeford.com, before it was bought out by the pornography industry and turned into a pro-porn organ. Luke Ford switched to lukeford.net.

95 Roth, *Portnoy*, p. 240.

96 Roth, *Portnoy*, p. 241.

97 Cooper, p. 104.

98 Ibid.

Endnotes to Chapter Thirty-One

The Jewish Takeover of American Culture

1 Radosh, p. 95.

2 Ibid.

3 Radosh, p. 103.

4 Ibid.

5 Ibid.

6 Ibid.

7 Ibid.

8 Ibid.

9 Radosh, p. 105.

10 Ibid.

11 Ibid. The weapon that is Marxism is seen by certain thinkers as a specifically Jewish ideology. Yuri Slezkine records that, "Socialism, according to [Nikolai] Berdiaev, is a form of 'Jewish religious chiliasm, which faces the future with a passionate demand for, and anticipation of, the realization of the millenial Kingdom of God on earth and the coming of Judgement Day, when evil is finally vanquished by good, and injustice and suffering in human life cease once for all.'" Slezkine carries on, "Add to this the fact that Jewish liberty and immortality are collective, not individual, and that this collective redemption is to occur in this world, as a result of both daily struggle and predestination, and you have Marxism." Berdi-

aev says of Marxism, "Karl Marx, who was a typical Jew, solved, at history's eleventh hour, the old biblical theme: in the sweat of thy brow shalt thou eat bread....The teaching of Marx appears to break with the Jewish religious tradition and rebel against all things sacred. In fact, what it does is transfer the messianic idea associated with the Jews as God's chosen people to a class, the proletariat." Yuri Slezkine, *The Jewish Century* (Princeton University Press 2004) p. 91-92. See also the discussions on Judaism and leftist ideologies in Kevin MacDonald, *The Culture of Critique: An Evolutionary Analysis of Jewish Involvement in Twentieth-Century Intellectual and Political Movements* (1st Books 2002).

12 Dylan, p. 112.

13 Spitz, p. 318.

14 Spitz, p. 330.

15 Spitz, p. 355.

16 Radosh, p. 106.

17 Ibid.

18 Radosh, p. 111.

19 Radosh, p. 112.

20 Ibid.

21 Radosh, p. 106.

22 Ibid.

23 Radosh, p. 107.

24 Ibid.

25 Ibid.

26 Radosh, p. 108.

27 Radosh, p. 109.

28 Radosh, p. 110.

29 Ibid.

30 Radosh, p. 115.

31 Radosh, p. 116. Dershowitz has not exactly joined Radosh on his journey toward neo-conservatism. Instead, he has attempted to play upon his "civil liberties" background to attract the liberal-left while justifying state-sanctioned torture, Israeli atrocities, and defaming anyone daring to criticise Israeli government policies. In recent times, and with an eye on his audience, Dershowitz has gone as far as to re-write history and falsely claim that he opposed the 2003 Iraq war before it was launched. For more on this see Norman G. Finkelstein, *Beyond Chutzpah: On the Misuse of Anti-Semitism and the Abuse of History* (Verso Books 2005); Tim

Wilkinson *Dershowitz and the Iraq War* http://www.counterpunch.org/wilkinson01312007.html and Tim Wilkinson *Alan Dershowitz's Sinister Scheme* http://www.counterpunch.org/wilkinson09142006.html

Dershowitz is also a leading practitioner of an old technique of dealing with those who dare to critique Israel (and/or Jewish lobby groups) practised in the 1950s when "the American Jewish Committee developed a strategy it called "dynamic silence" to combat the activities of Gerald L. K. Smith. Working together, officials of the American Jewish Committee, the American Jewish Congress and the ADL would approach the publishers of major newspapers and owners of radio stations in cities where Smith had scheduled appearances to ask that Smith be given no coverage whatsoever. If newspapers and radio stations failed to cooperate on a voluntary basis, Jewish organizations were usually able to secure their compliance by threatening boycotts by Jewish advertisers. This strategy of dynamic silence was extremely effective in suppressing Smith and other right-wing anti-Semites." Benjamin Ginsberg, *The Fatal Embrace: Jews and the State* (Chicago: University of Chicago Press, 1993) p. 124.

32 Radosh, p. 117.

33 Ibid.

34 Ibid.

35 Radosh, p. 131.

36 Ibid.

37 Radosh, p. 121.

38 Radosh, p. 133.

39 Radosh, p. 131.

40 Ibid.

41 Spitz, p. 450.

42 Spitz, p. 482.

43 Spitz, p. 509.

44 Spitz, p. 481.

45 Ibid.

46 Spitz, p. 483.

47 Spitz, p. 531.

48 Samuel H. Dresner, *Can Families Survive in Pagan America?* (Lafayette, LA: Huntington House, 1995), p. 275.

49 Ibid.

50 Ibid.

51 Dresner, *Families*, p. 222.

52 Dresner, *Families*, p. 223.

53 Dresner, *Families*, p. 297.

54 Dresner, *Families*, p. 207.

55 Dresner, *Families*, p. 202.

56 Dresner, *Families*, p. 160.

57 Dresner, *Families*, p. 161.

58 Dresner, *Families*, p. 66 (my emphasis).

59 Dresner, *Families*, p. 82.

60 Dresner, *Families*, p. 83.

61 Dresner, *Families*, p. 85.

62 Dresner, *Families*, p. 160.

63 Dresner, *Families*, p. 184.

64 Dresner, *Families*, p. 155.

65 Dresner, *Families*, p. 177.

66 Ibid.

67 Dresner, *Families*, p. 191.

68 Ibid.

69 Dresner, *Families*, p. 184.

70 Ibid.

71 Dresner, *Families*, p. 195.

72 Ibid.

73 Dresner, *Families*, p. 210.

74 Ibid.

75 Ibid.

76 Dresner, *Families*, p. 214. The reflections of Joseph Cardinal Ratzinger help us to see the position which Rabbi Dresner is in. Ratzinger reveals, "First of all must we remember that the fundamentally "new" covenant—the covenant with Abraham—has a universalist orientation and looks toward many sons who will be given to Abraham. Paul was absolutely right: the covenant with Abraham unites in itself both elements, namely, the intention of universality and the free gift. To that extent, right from the beginning, the promise of Abraham guarantees salvation history's inner continuity from the Patriarchs of Israel down to Christ and to the Church of Jews and Gentiles. With regard to the Sinai covenant, we must again draw a distinction. It is strictly limited to the people of Israel; it gives this nation a legal and cultic order...that as such cannot simply be extended to all nations. Since this juridical order is constitutive of the Sinai covenant, the law's "if" is part of its essence. To that extent it is conditional, that is, temporal...the Law is not only a burden imposed on believers....As seen by Old Testament believers, the Law itself is the concrete form of grace. For to know God's will is a grace.....the Messiah, the Christ, does not make man lawless, does not deprive him of justice. Rather it is characteristic of the Messiah—he who is "greater than Moses"—that he brings the definitive interpretation of the Torah, in which the Torah is itself renewed, because now its true essence appears in all its purity and its character as grace becomes undistorted reality.....The Torah of the Messiah is the Messiah, Jesus, himself....To imitate him, to follow him in discipleship, is therefore to keep the Torah, which has been fulfilled in him once and for all. Thus the Sinai covenant is superseded. But once what was provisional in it has been swept away, we see what is truly definitive in it." *Many Religions—One Covenant* (Ignatius 1999) p. 68-71. The Talmud, however, appears to specifically disallow the idea that the Messiah is Jesus himself. "In responding to Chrstian argument, any believing Jew would naturally turn to the oral traditions. The rabbis who instructed and ministered in the period immediately after the editing of the Mishnah, the *amoraim*, picked up the thread of messianic teachings that started with the Bible. In the Talmud, especially the eleventh chapter of its tractate *Sanhedrin*, we find their voluminous rendering of the tradition about events that will accompany the appearance of the Messiah" David Klinghoffer, *Why the Jews Rejected Jesus* (Three Leaves Press 2006) p. 139.

77 Dresner, *Families*, p. 193.

78 Dresner, *Families*, p. 217.

79 Dresner, *Families*, p. 219.

80 Dresner, *Families*, p. 221.

81 Ibid.

82 Paul Berman, ed. *Debating PC* (New York: Dell, 1992) p. 233.

83 Ibid.

84 *Newsweek*, "Taking Offense" (December 24, 1990), p. 48.

85 R. V. Young, *At War with the Word*, (Wilmington, DE: ISI Books, 1999), p. 133.

86 Aldous Huxley, *Ends and Means: An Inquiry into the Nature of Ideals and into the Methods Employed in their Realization* (New York & London: Harper & Brothers Publishers, 1937), p. 315-16.

87 Young, p. 62-3.

88 Young, p. 63.

Endnotes

89 Young, p. 116.

90 Young, p. 117.

91 Young, p. 118.

92 Young, p. 119.

93 Friedman, p. 157.

94 Friedmna, p. 160.

95 Friedman, p. 149.

96 Friedman, p. 145. Following the Mossad orchestrated deposing of Andrew Young (see below in main text), and in the face of further Israeli provocation the following presidential outburst is recorded by Andrew and Leslie Cockburn: ""If I get back in," said President Carter in the spring of 1980, "I'm going to fuck the Jews."" The same authors report that; "Israeli hostility to Carter went back to the early days of his administration, when he had given indications thar he might actually be serious about pressuring Israel to make concessins to the Palestinians living under its occupation, and had even made reference to a Palestinian 'homeland'." During the early 1980's the power-balance betwen Washington and the Israeli lobby was already reaching extraordinary levels; "In *The Real Anti-Semitism in America*, Nathan Perlmutter, the national director of the ADL, asserted that....[c]ontemporary anti-Semitism....lay in the actions of "peacemakers of Vietnam vintage..." and "nowadays is getting a bad name and peace too favourable a press" from a left that is "snipng at American defense budgets." As the Cockburns put it: "If the leader of a respectable and powerful lobbying organisation lobbying for Israel could equate a lack of support for the Pentagon's budget with anti-Semitism, the US defense lobby had found itself a loyal ally indeed." *Dangerous Liaison: The Inside Story of the US-Israeli Covert Relationship* (The Bodley Head 1992) p. 313-314; p. 189-190.

97 Midge Decter, *An Old Wife's Tale: My Seven Decades in Love and War* (New York: HarperCollins Publishers, 2001), p. 153-4.

98 Ibid.

99 Ibid.

100 Friedman, p. 132.

101 Mia Farrow, *What Falls Away: A Memoir* (New York: Doubleday, 1997), p. 134.

102 Ibid.

103 Farrow, p. 135.

104 Farrow, p. 193.

105 Farrow, p. 272.

106 Ibid.

107 Farrow, p. 266.

108 Farrow, p. 288.

109 Farrow, p. 274.

110 Ibid.

111 Ibid.

112 Farrow, p. 259.

113 Farrow, p. 306.

114 Farrow, p. 283.

115 Claire Bloom, *Leaving a Doll's House* (Boston: Little, Brown and Company, 1996), p. 239.

116 Ibid.

117 Claire Bloom, p. 165.

118 Claire Bloom, p. 191.

119 Claire Bloom, p. 204.

120 Claire Bloom, p. 211.

121 Claire Bloom, p. 204.

122 Claire Bloom, p. 213.

123 Claire Bloom, p. 220.

124 Philip Roth, *Sabbath's Theater* (New York: Houghton Mifflin Company, 1995), p. 97.

125 Roth, *Sabbath*, p. 147.

126 Roth, *Sabbath*, p. 151.

127 Roth, *Sabbath*, p. 213-14.

128 Roth, *Sabbath*, p. 9.

129 Ibid.

130 Ibid.

131 Ibid.

132 Ibid.

133 Roth, *Sabbath*, p. 428.

134 Roth, *Sabbath*, p. 446.

135 Roth, *Sabbath*, p. 451.

136 Ibid.

137 Roth, *Sabbath*, p. 325.

138 Roth, *Sabbath*, p. 326.

139 Roth, *Sabbath*, p. 171.

140 Roth, *Sabbath*, p. 172.

141 Roth, *Sabbath*, p. 177.

142 Roth, *Sabbath*, p. 323.

143 Roth, *Portnoy*, p. 251.

144 Ibid.

145 Roth *Portnoy*, p. 252.

146 James Bloom, p. 36.

147 Ibid.

148 Rabbi Meir Y. Soloveichik, "The Virtue of Hate," *First Things* (January 2003, pp. 41-46)

149 Ibid.

150 Ibid.

151 Ibid.

152 Ibid.

153 Ibid.

154 Ibid.

155 Ibid.

156 Ibid.

157 Ibid.

158 Ibid.

159 Ibid.

160 Roth, *Portnoy*, p. 250.

161 Roth, *Portnoy*, p. 251.

162 Roth, *Portnoy*, pp. 217, 219.

163 Roth, *Portnoy*, p. 273.

164 Ibid.

165 James Bloom, p. 158.

166 Ibid.

167 James Bloom, p. 160.

168 Ibid.

Endnotes to Chapter Thirty-Two

The Neoconservate Era

1 Friedman, p. 151.

2 Ibid.

3 Friedman, p. 153. Defining neoconservatism is not a straightforward matter. Kevin MacDonald characteizes it as a Jewish movmenent: "Neoconservatism is better described in general as a complex interlocking professional and family network centered around Jewish publicists and organizers flexibly deployed to recruit the sympathies of Jews and non-Jews in the service of Israel." For MacDonald the neoconservatives are a semicovert branch of the wider Israel Lobby. *Understanding Jewish Influence: A Study in Ethnic Activism* (Washington: Summit, 2004), p. 66-7.

Journalist Melanie Phillips, an English religious Jew, says: "If the neocons aren't really conservative, they differ even more strikingly from their Christian co-counter-revolutionaries. For the neocon view of the world is a demonstrably Jewish view. Christians see man as a fallen being, inherently sinful. The neocons have the Jewish view that mankind has a capacity for both good and ill. Christians believe humanity is redeemed through Christ on the cross: the neocon approach is founded on the belief that individuals have to redeem themselves. Christians believe in transforming humanity through a series of mystical beliefs and events. Neocons believe in taking the world as it is, but encouraging the good and discouraging the bad. It is this impulse to *tikkun olam*... that gives the neocons the optimism that so distresses old-style paleoconservatives....[T]he neocon belief that good can prevail over evil... that lay be hind the wars against Afghanistan and Iraq." "The Politics of Progress: The Left, the Right and the Jews," Talk at the Limmud Conference, 28 December 2004. Phillips supports the use of nuclear weapons, is highly ambiguous over the use of torture, and is, in practice, highly opposed to traditional just war theory.

4 Friedman, p. 154.

5 Friedman, p. 168. Elliott Abrams is on record as saying Jews living outside Israel should "stand apart from the nation in which they live," quoted in Jonathan Cook, *Israel and the Clash of Civilisations: Iraq, Iran, and the Plan to Remake the Middle East* (Pluto Press, 2008), p. 24

6 Nathanson, *Papers*, p. 8.

7 Nathanson, *Papers*, p. 25.

8 Ibid.

9 Ibid.

10 Nathanson, *Papers*, p. 39.

11 Nathanson, *Papers*, p. 46.

12 Nathanson, *Papers*, p. 103.

13 Ibid.

14 Nathanson, *Papers*, p. 211.

15 Nathanson, *Papers*, p. 107.

16 Senate Constitutional Amendments Com-

mittee Hearing, December 16, 1981, Los Angeles

17 Ibid.

18 "Successful Hearings on the Human Life Amendment to the California Constitiution" California Pro Life Medical Association News (vol. 3 #1).

19 Ibid.

20 *Los Angeles Times,* "Sen Schmitz Lashes Out, Catches Flak," 12/23/81

21 Ibid.

22 *Los Angeles Times,* "Senate Action Against Schmitz to be Proposed," 12/24/81

23 Ibid.

24 Ibid.

25 California Pro Life Medical Association News (vol. 3 #1).

26 Senate Constituional Amendments Committee Hearing.

27 California Pro Life Medical Association News (vol. 3 #1)

28 "Senate Action Against Schmitz to be Proposed"

29 Ibid.

30 Ibid.

31 Letter to Philip B. Dreisbach, MD

32 Ibid.

33 Including Anthony Beilenson, author of the 1967 Abortion Act; Howard Berman, the abortion advocacy leader who represented Beverly Hills; Henry Waxman, Hollywood's pro-abortion Congressman; Gloria Bloom Allred, the feminist attorney who threw the "chastity belt" at John Schmitz; Norman Lear, the TV producer who financed abortion groups and would produce the '70s sitcom attack on Catholic ethnics, "All in the Family;" Carol Sobel and Dorothy Lang of the California ACLU; Julia Gertler, LA president of the National Council of Jewish Women; Joseph Marmet, a Beverly Hills abortionist charged with 32 counts of Medi-Cal fraud; Morton Barke, owner of the Inglewood Hospital where the dumpster fetuses were aborted; Merle Goldberg, a fugitive for performing illegal abortions; Harvey Karman, inventor of the Karman canula, responsible for the deaths of numerous women; Mel Levine, representative from Beverly Hills; and Irvin Cushner, a UCLA professor who would travel the country telling lawmakers no one knew when life began.

34 Shapiro, p. 36.

35 Ibid.

36 Ibid.

37 Shapiro, p. 83.

38 Shapiro, p. 39.

39 Shapiro, p. 104.

40 Shapiro, p. 11-2.

41 Ibid.

42 Ibid.

43 Ibid.

44 Shapiro, p. 105.

45 Shapiro, p. 109.

46 Ibid.

47 Shapiro, p. 115.

48 Ibid.

49 Ibid.

50 Shapiro, p. 120.

51 Shapiro, p. 120-21.

52 Ibid.

53 Shapiro, p. 124.

54 Ibid.

55 Shapiro, p. 128.

56 Shapiro, p. 33.

57 Ibid.

58 Ibid.

59 Ibid.

60 Ibid.

61 Ibid. The details of Foxman's upbringing (related in the text to follow) were gleaned from a personal communication with Iwo Cyprian Pogonowski.

62 Friedman, p. 134.

63 Decter, p. 177.

64 Personal Communication from Tom Fleming.

65 Dale Vree, *New Oxford Review* (December, 2005)

66 Ibid.

67 Ibid.

68 Horowitz, p. 139.

69 campuswatch.com.

70 David Frum, Richard Perle, *An End to Evil: How to Win the War on Terror* (New York: Random House, 2003), p. 78.

71 Frum and Perle, p. 79.

72 Radosh, p. 205.

73 Ibid.

74 Radosh, p. 167.

75 Pornqueens.xxx-posed.com/ninahart-ley.

76 lukeford.com.

77 Ibid. See also Nathan Abrams, "Triple-exxxthnics: Jews in the American Porn Industry," *The Jewish Quarterly*, Winter 2004 (Number 196).

78 Pornqueens.

79.CNN.com/2002/SHOWBIZ/News/2/14/showbuzz#5.

80 Pornqueens.

81 Ibid.

82 Ibid.

83 Ibid.

84 Ibid.

85 Ibid.

86 lukeford.com.

87 Dresner, *Families*, p. 324.

88 Dresner, *Families*, p. 325.

89 Erich Haberer, *Jews and Revolution in Nineteenth-century Russia* (Cambridge: Cambridge University Press, 1995), p. 150.

90 Irving Kristol, *Neoconservatism: The Autobiography of an Idea* (New York: The Free Press, 1995),

91 Kristol, p. 448.

92 Kristol, p. 449.

93 Decter, p. 179.

94 Pornqueens

95 lukeford.com

96 Ibid.

97 Ibid.

98 Ibid.

99 Ibid.

100 Ibid.

101 Ibid.

102 Dresner, *Families*, p. 155.

103 Dresner, *Families*, p. 39.

104 Dresner, *Families*, p. 78.

105 Dresner, *Families*, pp. 79, 81.

106 Dresner, *Families*, p. 77.

107 Dresner, *Families*, p. 238.

108 Ibid.

109 Dresner, *Families*, p. 222.

110 Friedman, p. 207.

111 Ibid.

112 Friedman, p. 212.

113 Ibid.

114 Friedman, p. 213.

115 Ibid.

116 Friedman, p. 214.

117 Friedman, p. 219.

118 Friedman, p. 220.

119 Ibid.

120 Friedman, p. 214.

121 Friedman, p. 221.

122 Ibid.

123 Ibid.

124 Statement by Archbishop Harry Flynn regarding Human Life International, issued by Archdiocese of St. Paul and Minneapolis, April 2, 1997.

125 Ibid.

126 "Human Life International on defensive in controversy," Clark Morphew, *St. Paul Pioneer Press*, 4/15/97, B3.

127 Statement by Flynn.

128 Rev. Paul Marx, OSB, *Faithful for Life: The Autobiography of Father Paul Marx, OSB* (Front Royal, VA: Human Life International, 1997), p. 288.

129 Paul Marx, p. 284.

130 Ibid.

131 Ibid.

132 Personal Communication, Edgar Suter, MD.

Jewish historian Andrew Heinze notes, of the Orthodox Jewish position on abortion: "Orthodox rabbinic opinion on abortion ranges from strict to lenient, depending on the circumstances." *Jews and the American Soul: Human Nature in the Twentieth Century* (Princeton 2004) p. 408 f4.

David M. Feldman, in his authoritative *Marital Relations, Birth Control and Abortion in Jewish Law* (Schocken Books 1974) analyzes an array of divergent Orthodox opinions on abortion from the relatively stringent (though far more permissive than Catholic teaching would allow) to the very permissive. Feldman notes of therapeutic abortion, "to save her [the mother's] life up to the moment of birth, or to save her life even after the moment of birth when death to both is the alternative—is mandated by the Mishnah....The more timely "abortion" in the earlier stages, is very likely not even contemplated in the Mishnaic law." Of the rabbinic attitude to abortion Feldman notes: "it can best be described as bifurcating into two directions, both of which will presuppose that the foetus is not a person; yet one approach builds *down* and the other builds *up*" p. 284. In discussing both stringent and lax positions Feldman notes a constant principle in these debates: "[T]he principle that a mother's pain "comes first," however, is the most pervasive of all factors in the consideration of the abortion question. It produces the *following fundamental generalization*: if a possibility or probability exists that a child may be born defective and the mother would seek an abortion on grounds of pity for the child whose life will be less than normal, the Rabbi would decline permission....If, however, an abortion for the same potentially deformed child were sought on the grounds that the possibility is causing severe *anguish to the mother*, permission would be granted" p. 291-292. This is, according to Feldman, a valid statement of the Orthodox Jewish attitude (though individual rabbis may vary). That the Orthodox Jewish position (or range of positions) is deeply unreliable in terms of a consistent defence of young human life cannot be doubted.

133 Paul Marx, p. 284.

134 http://www.christorchaos.com.

135 Ibid.

136 Ibid.

137 Paul Marx, p. 287.

138 christorchaos.com.

139 Ibid.

140 Ibid.

141 "Human Life International officials reject charges that organization is anti-Semitic," Nolan Zavoral, *Minneapolis Star Tribune*, 4/15/97, p. B2

142 Ibid.

143 Paul Marx, p. 288.

144 Ibid.

145 Feminist Daily News Wire, November 3, 1998.

146 Ibid.

147 Ibid.

148 Ibid.

149 Ibid.

150 Ibid.

151 Ibid.

152 Ibid.

153 Poppy Dixon, "The Roots of Racism and the Fear of Sex in the Pro-life Movement," www.postfun.com/pfp/features/98/oct/bloodlibel.html.

154 Ibid.

155 Ibid.

156 Ibid.

157 Ibid.

158 Ibid.

159 Paul Marx, p. 287.

160 Ibid.

161 Ibid.

162 Dr. Kenneth M. Mitzner, "The Abortion Culture," *Triumph*, March 1973 (vol. 8, #3), p. 22.

163 Ibid.

164 Ibid.

165 Nathanson, *Papers*, p. 189.

166 Ibid.

167 Shapiro, p. 33.

168 Shapiro, p. 99.

169 Ibid.

170 Ibid.

171 Shapiro, p. 21.

172 Shapiro, p. 99.

173 Ibid.

174 Shapiro, p. 214.

175 Ibid.

176 Shapiro, p. 215.

177 Ibid.

178 Ibid.

179 Ibid.

180 Shapiro, pp. 216, 215 (my emphasis).

181 Shapiro, p. 100.

182 Shapiro, p. 187.

183 Ibid.

184 Shapiro, p. 192.

185 Shapiro, p. 193.

186 Ibid.

187 Shapiro, p. 190.

188 Shapiro, p. 193.

189 Shapiro, p. 196.

190 Ibid.

191 Ibid.

192 Ibid.

193 Shapiro, p. 197.

194 Ibid.

195 Ibid.

196 Shapiro, p. 196.

197 Shapiro, p. 200.

198 Ibid.

199 Shapiro, p. 216 (my emphasis).

200 Shapiro, p. 220.

201 Shapiro, p. 212.

202 Ibid.

203 Ibid.

204 Shapiro, p. 213.

205 Ibid.

206 Shapiro, p. 21.

207 Shapiro, p. 28.

208 Shapiro, p. 141.

209 Shapiro, p. 217.

210 Shapiro, p. 218.

211 Ibid.

212 Ibid.

213 Ibid.

214 Shapiro, p. 219.

215 A. James Rudin, "A Jewish View of Gibson's Passion," Religious News Service, 2004.

216 Ibid.

217 Ibid.

218 Ibid.

219 Ibid.

220 Ibid.

221 Frum and Perle, p. 174.

222 Frum and Perle, p. 179.

223 Friedman, p. 185.

224 Friedman, p. 228.

225 John J. Mearsheimer and Stephen M. Walt, "The Israel Lobby and U.S. Foreign Policy," *London Review of Books,* Vol. 28, No. 6 (March 23, 2006) or online at www.lrb.co.uk, p. 34.

226 Friedman, p. 230.

227 Ibid.

228 omanforum.com.

229 Ibid.

230 Ibid.

231 Merritt Y. Hughes, ed., *John Milton: Complete Poems and Prose* (Indianpolis: Bobbs-Merrill, 1957), p. 552.

232 Omanforum.com

233 omanforum.com.

234 Ibid.

235 lukeford.com.

236 lukeford.com.

237 lukeford.com

238 lukeford.com.

239 lukeford.com

240 Pornqueens.

241 Ibid.

242 lukeford.com.

243 Ibid.

244 Ibid.

245 Ibid.

246 Ibid.

247 Dresner, *Families*, p. 234.

248 Dresner, *Families*, p. 324.

249 Walt and Mearsheimer, p. 26.

250 Walt and Mearsheimer, p. 27.

251 Walt and Mearsheimer, p. 28.

252 Ibid.

253 Ibid.

254 Ibid.

255 Walt and Mearsheimer, p. 29.

256 Ibid.

257 Walt and Mearsheimer, p. 33.

258 Walt and Mearsheimer, p. 31.

259 Ibid.

260 Ibid.

261 Ibid.

262 Walt and Mearsheimer, p. 34.

263 Frum and Perle.

264 Frum and Perle, p. 5.

265 Frum and Perle, p. 11.

266 Friedman, p. 240.

267 Walt and Mearsheimer, p. 24.

268 David Gergen, "There is no Israel 'Lobby'," *New York Daily News*, (April 3, 2006), p. 68.

269 Ibid.

270 Eliot A. Cohen, *Washington Post*, (April 4, 2006).

The Conversion of the Revolutionary Jew

1 Appointment of monitor adds teeth to the fight against anti-Semitism, Jewish Telegraph Agency, 05/18/2006. In *The Holocaust Industry: Reflections on the Exploitation of Jewish Suffering 2nd Edition* (Verso 2003) Norman Finkelstein notes that Rickman wrote of the Swiss, whom he was helping to "shakedown" by inflating claims for Holocaust reparation, "Down deep, perhaps deeper than they thought, a latent arrogance about themselves and against others existed in their very makeup. Try as they did they could not hide their upbringing." To which Finkelstein adds: "Many of these slurs are remarkably like the slurs cast against Jews by Anti-Semites" (p. 93-94).

2 The Report on Global Anti-Semitism is available at http://www.state.gov/g/drl/rls/40258.htm

3 Meir Y. Soloveichik, "The Virtue of Hate," *First Things*, February 2003.

4 Views on Jews by Malaysian PM: His Own Words, *New York Times*, October 21, 2003.

5 Rabbi Abraham Cooper (Simon Wiesenthal Center L.A), "Mahathir Attack on Jews Condemned," CNN.com/World, October 17 2003.

6 In Support Of Malaysian PM's Comments On Jews, Elias Davidsson , www.israelshamir.net.

7 While Spinoza certainly saw through some of the worst aspects of Jewish Talmudic thought, we do not hereby mean to assert that his "rationalism" led neatly towards any deep appreciation of Logos. The point here is that rejection of Talmud is enough for excommunication especially if guided by even a minimal appreciation of reason.

8 Jewish Encyclopedia available online: http://www.jewishencyclopedia.com/view.jsp?artid=32&letter=T. See also Denis Fahey, CSSp, The Kingship of Christ and the Conversion of the Jewish Nation (Palmdale, CA: Christian Book Club of America, 1993), p. 89.

9 Fahey, p. 86.

10 Fahey, p. 89.

11 Fahey, p. 98-99.

12 Fahey, p. 100.

13 Fahey, p. 97.

14 Ibid.

15 Fahey, p. 98.

16 Fahey, p. 49.

17 Ibid.

18 Ibid.

19 Fahey, p. 56.

20 Naeim Giladi, *Ben-Gurion's Scandals: How the Haganah and the Mossad Eliminated Jews*, (Dandelion Books 2003).

21 http://www.jewishjournal.com/home/preview.php?id=15634

22 Ibid.

23 Ibid.

24 Ibid.

25 http://www.giladatzmon.com

26 Ibid.

27 Ibid.

28 Ibid.

29 Ibid.

30 George F. Will, 'Final Solution' Phase 2, *Washington Post*, 02/05/2007.

31 http://www.giladatzmon.com

32 Ibid.

33 Ibid.

34 Yuri Slezkine, *The Jewish Century* (Princeton: Princeton University Press, 2004), p. 367.

35 Slezkine, p. 364.

36 K.D. Whitehead, "Book Review Essay, Ecumenism and Interreligous Dialogue: unitatis Redintegratio, Nostra Aetate," *Fellowship of Catholic Scholars Quarterly*, Summer 2006, p. 15 (emphasis added).

37 Ibid.

38 Whitehead, p. 18.

39 Whitehead, p. 19 (my emphasis).

40 Ibid.

41 Ibid.

42 Whitehead, p. 17.

43 Whitehead, p. 18.

44 Schoeman, 314-315. Schoeman has subsequently denied that this is his view, but does appear to be the view expressed in his book.

45 Fahey, p. 101.

46 Ibid.

47 Fahey, p. 102. John Henry Newman, in a passage very much in line with the thesis of this book also expressed beautifully the fate of the Jews in the light of Christ: "It was their belief that His protection was unchangeable, and that their Law would last for ever;—it was their consolation to be taught by an uninterrupted tradition, that it could not die, except by changing into a new self, more wonderful than it was before;—it was their faithful expectation that a promised King was coming, the Messiah, who would extend the sway of Israel over all people;—it was a condition of their covenant, that, as a reward to Abraham, their first father, the day at length should dawn when the gates of their narrow land should open, and they should pour out for the conquest and occupation of the whole earth;—and, I repeat, when the day came, they did go forth, and they did spread into all lands, but as hopeless exiles, as eternal wanderers.

Are we to say that this failure is a proof that, after all, there was nothing providential in their history? For myself, I do not see how a second portent obliterates a first; and, in truth, their own testimony and their own sacred books carry us on towards a better solution of the difficulty. I have said they were in God's favour under a covenant,—perhaps they did not fulfil the conditions of it. This indeed seems to be their own account of the matter, though it is not clear what their breach of engagement was. And that in some way they did sin, whatever their sin was, is corroborated by the well-known chapter in the Book of Deuteronomy, which so strikingly anticipates the nature of their punishment. That passage, translated into Greek as many as 350 years before the siege of Jerusalem by Titus, has on it the marks of a wonderful prophecy; but I am not now referring to it as such, but merely as an indication that the disappointment, which actually overtook them at the Christian era, was not necessarily out of keeping with the original divine purpose, or again with the old promise made to them, and their confident expectation of its fulfilment. Their national ruin, which came instead of aggrandizement, is described in that book, in spite of all promises, with an emphasis and minuteness which prove that it was contemplated long before, at least as a possible issue of the fortunes of Israel. Among other inflictions which should befall the guilty people, it was told them that they should fall down before their enemies, and should be scattered throughout all the kingdoms of the earth; that they never should have quiet in those nations, or have rest for the sole of their foot; that they were to have a fearful heart and languishing eyes, and a soul consumed with heaviness; that they were to suffer wrong, and to be crushed at all times, and to be astonished at the terror of their lot; that their sons and daughters were to be given to another people, and they were to look and to sicken all the day, and their life was ever to hang in doubt before them, and fear to haunt them day and night; that they should be a proverb and a by-word of all people among whom they were brought; and that curses were to come on them, and to be signs and wonders on them and their seed for ever. Such are some portions, and not the most terrible, of this extended anathema; and its partial accomplishment at an earlier date of their history was a warning to them, when the destined time drew near, that, however great the promises made to them might be, those promises were dependent on the terms of the covenant which stood between them and their Maker, and that, as they had turned to curses at that former time, so they might turn to curses again.

This grand drama, so impressed with the characters of supernatural agency, concerns us here only in its bearing upon the evidence for the divine origin of Christianity; and it is at this point that Christianity comes upon the historical scene. It is a notorious fact that it issued from the Jewish land and people; and had it no other than this historical connexion with Judaism, it would have some share in the prestige of its original home. But it claims to be far more than this; it professes to be the actual completion of the Mosaic Law, the promised means of deliverance and triumph to the nation, which that nation itself, as I have said, has since considered to be, on account of some sin or other, withheld or forfeited. It professes to be, not the casual, but the legitimate offspring, heir, and successor of the Mosaic covenant, or rather to be Judaism itself, developed and transformed. Of course it has to prove its claim, as well as to prefer it; but if it succeeds in doing so, then all those tokens of the Divine Presence, which distinguish the Jewish history, at once belong to it, and are a portion of its credentials.... The prophecies announced that the Messiah was to come at a definite time and place, Christians point to Him as coming then and there, as announced; they are not met by any counter claim or rival claimant on the part of the Jews, only by their assertion that He did not come at all, though up to the event they had said He was then and there coming. Further, Christianity clears up the mystery which hangs over Judaism, accounting fully for the punishment of the people, by specifying their sin, their heinous sin. If, instead of hailing their own Messiah, they crucified Him, then the strange scourge which has pursued them after the deed, and the energetic wording of the curse before it, are explained by the very strangeness of their guilt;—or rather, their sin is their punishment; for in rejecting their Divine King, they ipso facto lost the living principle and tie of their nationality. Moreover, we see what led them into error; they thought a triumph and an empire were to be given to them at once, which were given indeed eventually, but by the slow and gradual growth of many centuries and a long warfare" (*An Essay in Aid of A Grammar of Assent*, p. 434-438, (Longmans, Green and Co. 1903).

48 Fahey, p. 105. Cardinal Schoenborn recently reflected that "By welcoming the

Gospel, the Jews are witnesses of God's fidelity to his promise, while the Gentiles are witnesses of the universality of his mercy. These two appeals in the Church reflect the twofold way of the same salvation in Christ, one for Jews and one for Gentiles. Thus the same Jesus Christ is simultaneously "a light for revelation to the Gentiles, and for glory you people Israel" (Luke 2:32, "Judaism's way to salvation," *The Tablet*, 29 March 2008).

49 Fahey, p. 106.
50 Fahey, p. 107.
51 Fahey, p. 108.
52 Ibid.
53 Fahey, p. 110.
54 Ibid.
55 Fahey, p. 188.The Church, however, does not take a definitive position either for or against the belief that the Antichrist will be a Jew.
56 Ibid.
57 Samuel Dresner, *Can Families Survive in Pagan America?* (Lafayette, LA: Huntington House, 1995), p. 329-30.
58 Fahey, p. 78.
59 Ibid.
60 Fahey, p. 80.
61 Fahey, p. 82.
62 Ibid.
63 Fahey, p. 83.
64 Fahey, p. 177 quoting II Thess, II, 4.
65 I John II, 18.
66 Fahey, p. 187.

Index

Symbols

A

Index

Index

Index

Index

Marx Brothers 980, 982
Marxism 103, 176, 468, 469, 523
Marx, Karl 51, 95, 103, 231, 328,
    443, 469, 483, 494, 559, 560,
    1114
Marx, Rabbi David 713, 718
Marx, Rev. Paul 1040
Mary, Queen of England 327–335
Mary Queen of Scots 388
Masada 43, 52, 55, 176, 260, 1070,
    1071, 1075
Maskilic Jews 566, 578, 647
mask of Catholicism 207, 269, 341,
    362, 410
Maslow, Abraham 922
Masonic Lodge 474, 486, 503
Masons 231, 255, 350, 484, 486,
    492, 493, 496-8, 509, 512,
    514, 515, 520, 522, 523, 525,
    526, 529, 531, 536, 538, 541,
    542, 545, 548
Mason, Senator 633
Mass 70, 82, 159, 160, 164, 166, 167,
    184, 208, 277, 283, 296, 297,
    298, 304, 317, 344, 345, 348,
    361, 364, 373, 385, 394, 454
Massachusetts Bay Colony 479
mass movements 171
Matej of Janov 164
materialism 176, 483, 495, 503, 511
Mather, Increase 459
Matthys, Jan 298, 301, 302, 303,
    305, 306, 307, 308
Mattuck, Maxwell 781
Maurach, Reinhard 757
Mauriac, Francois 891
Maximillian I 228, 230, 254
Maximillian II 358
Maximus of Ephesus 58, 59, 62, 64
May, Elaine 983
Mayern, Sir Theodore 420
Mayer, Sione 679
May Laws of 1882 670
Mayne, Cuthbert 364, 370
Mazarek, Tomas 538
Mazzini 622, 626, 681
McCarthy, Eugene 1037
McCarthy, Joe 777, 839, 840, 853,
    1037
McCloy, John J. 830, 831, 832, 1061
McDonald, Kevin 42, 1084
McDowell, Bishop William G. 797,
    805
McInerny, Ralph 1029
McKay, Claude 765, 771, 787, 788,
    855
McKissick, Floyd 961
Mead, Margaret 763, 834
Mearsheimer, John J. 1059, 1060,
    1061, 1068, 1156
medieval Christians 100
medieval Judaism 130, 444

medieval warfare 157, 174, 175, 182,
    192
Meese, Edwin 1005
Megiddo 164, 1076
Mehemed IV 462
Melanchthon 257, 263, 264, 269, 270,
    273, 295, 296, 298, 299, 340
Mel Gibson 31
Melville, Herman 616
Memmi 927
Menahem 43, 44
Menasseh ben Israel 47, 351, 369,
    409-11, 413, 416, 418, 419, 438,
    446, 447, 454, 458, 484, 487, 554,
    1110, 1113
Mendelssohn, Felix 582
Mendelssohnian Enlightenment 580,
    648, 653
Mendelssohn, Moses 47, 555, 563-8,
    571, 577, 578, 583, 609, 611, 647,
    653, 666, 669, 738, 749
Mendes 357, 358, 404
Mendez, Alvaro 386
Mendez, Bishop 892
mendicant orders 108, 117
Mennonites 310, 323
Mensheviks 733, 747, 756
Menshikov, M. 687
Mercator 367
Mercurio, Giovanni 232
Mercurius, St. 78
mercy 45, 170, 280, 286, 310, 395, 424
mercy of God 105
Merkin, Daphne 983
Merkulov, M. M. 652
Mersenne, Fr. Martin 349, 482, 483,
    493
meshumadim 206, 214, 215
Messiah 564, 566, 570, 573-5, 581, 592,
    593, 654, 755, 918, 928, 931, 953,
    967, 971, 972, 973, 975, 979, 981,
    985, 997, 1000, 1011, 1015, 1016,
    1033, 1050, 1051, 1147
Messianic Era 51, 52
messianic politics 29, 43, 45-9, 51, 53,
    64-9, 71-3, 80, 89, 94, 96, 97, 99,
    103, 107, 142, 143, 151, 153, 156,
    157, 162, 165, 171, 173, 174, 182,
    185, 193, 231, 295, 300, 310, 319,
    324, 341, 348, 351, 368, 380, 404,
    417-18, 425, 435, 437, 443, 444,
    448, 456, 457, 458, 460, 463,
    464, 468, 469, 478-9, 487, 530,
    552, 553, 554, 555, 556, 606, 653,
    658, 685, 737, 746, 753, 756, 813,
    861, 924, 953, 967, 1030, 1031,
    1033, 1071
messianism 44, 573, 748, 754, 929, 953
Metternich, Klemens von 556, 583,
    590, 677
Metzger, Yona 927
Meyer, Albert Cardinal 913

1183

Index